TRANSACTIONS

OF THE

AMERICAN SOCIETY

OF

CIVIL ENGINEERS

(INSTITUTED 1852)

CENTENNIAL TRANSACTIONS

VOLUME CT

1953

Edited by Sydney Wilmot, M. ASCE, Publications Consultant,
for the Secretary, under the direction of the Committee on Publications.

NEW YORK
PUBLISHED BY THE SOCIETY

1953

FOREWORD

A century, in itself, is a long time, and when it happens to coincide with the life of a great profession, it takes on added significance. It deserves recognition and it warrants celebration. This is precisely what prompted the great gathering in Chicago, Ill., in September, 1952, to commemorate the hundredth anniversary of the founding of the American Society of Civil Engineers. In fact the entire year of 1952 was one long gala occasion in American civil engineering circles.

Many members and friends participated—tens of thousands of them came to Chicago and were vocal in their praise of the program. Whether they enjoyed the papers in person or whether they only wished they might have, they desired the written engineering record, and this need the Society is attempting to meet in its several publications. Perhaps the largest group of subjects were those of a historical or review flavor, having a centennial type of text and context. Such are included in this *Centennial Transactions,* Volume CT of the long and notable series.

In viewpoint, the volume incorporates many a backward look, frequent evaluation of present accomplishments and trends, and here and there a peep into the future. Choice of material for inclusion was not simple; omission of many fine papers was unavoidable. The criteria for acceptance were: A civil engineering topic of importance; an over-all picture, up to a hundred years in coverage; and a generalized nontechnical approach—in short, what has appropriately been termed "centennial significance." Not only the Chicago convention, but other ASCE meetings and sources contributed, as noted in the contents pages.

Time, in a way, is the essence of a centennial and this one was no exception. True, in selecting these papers from many hundreds available, the preeminently current or local topics had to be passed by. On the other hand, most papers of primarily centennial character embodied the time element, either expressly or by inference. Since this practice differs from the usual *Transactions* custom, it deserves emphasis. In general the viewpoint is that of the centennial year, and words such as "now" or "past decade" refer to the year 1952. Likewise, the "century" most often meant is that of 1852–1952.

As to organization or framework of the volume, the sequence of subjects goes from the general to the particular—in the order of profession-wide history, engineering education, and the technical fields, alphabetically. The latter generally relate to the Society's Technical Divisions which sponsored many of the programs; where possible, the sections are arranged similarly—over-all subjects first, then particular treatments.

Necessarily, topical classification cannot be too rigid. For example, some waterways and irrigation papers could fit equally in the construction section; some construction papers might qualify just as well for transportation. The general criterion for assignment was to give preference to the group that sponsored the paper. In any particular instance, the Subject Index will resolve the question. This applies also to details of treatment, as a result of overlapping of subject matter by independent authors, writing about allied items of historic import. However, the duplication is slight, and has been permitted in the interest of basic coverage of each topic—the Subject Index gathering together all similar references.

Much of the volume is history and much history, in effect, is biography. Men cannot be separated from their accomplishments. At the same time some reasonable limit of personal references had to be set, even at the expense of inconsistency. The general solution has been to confine credit as far as possible to outstanding older engineers, now deceased. In some minds this may raise specific questions of regrettable omissions, but at least it should avoid the charge of seeming discrimination against numberless eminent authorities now alive.

Decision to issue Volume CT as an added *Transactions* involved practical publication complications. It would have imposed intolerable loads on the regular Headquarters force, so the wise conclusion was reached, to have it handled by a separate, temporary staff. Fortunately, specially qualified former Society employees were available. The time element, to accelerate all schedules and bring out the book at the earliest possible date, even before the regular 1953 issue, Volume 118, was another hurdle.

In contents, accuracy, and style, the *Centennial Transactions* will not betray any hint of its rapid evolution, from an idea to a finished product in the mails, fully indexed, in a matter of 8 months. Such speed is not to be approved or recommended. It merely throws light on the wonderful efficiency and cooperation—of authors, editors, and printers. Collectively they are responsible for the fine output, and individually they have the profession's generous thanks for the excellent result.

The *Centennial Transactions* should be a reference of increasing value for many years. It is the Society's large permanent contribution to the centennial concept—dedicated to the accomplishments, the ideals, and the potentialities of the great civil engineering profession.

SYDNEY WILMOT, M. ASCE
Publications Consultant

CONTENTS

(Alphabetical Indexes Begin on Page 1273)

VII. SANITARY ENGINEERING

XIII. ALLIED INTERESTS

AMERICAN SOCIETY OF CIVIL ENGINEERS

Founded November 5, 1852

TRANSACTIONS

Paper No. 2575

CIVIL ENGINEERING THROUGH THE AGES

By Charles J. Merdinger[1]

Synopsis

The history of civil engineering is best visualized by tracing the engineer him-self—his works and his traditions, his influence on his environment, culminating in the mighty accomplishments of the twentieth century. Always he has sought to build, specializing in works of static form. The ancients contributed considerably —Egypt with mathematics, Greece with philosophy and theory, and Rome with vast structures not duplicated for many centuries. In medieval times the Church contributed cathedrals. In the Renaissance, Leonardo da Vinci, Galileo Galilei, and Isaac Newton were notable forerunners of modern civil engineers. In the nineteenth century, professional societies emerged in many lands and with them, technical schools. In England and the United States advances in theory and practice were achieved in all major fields, such as bridges, buildings, cities, and sanitation. This trend has continued in the present century, spurred on by the impact of the automobile and airplane. Thus the civil engineer has trans-formed the physical world and, with it, human history.

Introduction

Engineers are so concerned in the present with making plans for the future that they rarely, if ever, look into the past. Historians, however, have done a great deal of looking into the past in such fields as philosophy, politics, economics, art, law, medicine, and social customs. Strangely enough these historians have generally overlooked the field of engineering; it is stranger still, when one con-siders that the history of engineering is the most interesting history of all, for it is the story of the advance of civilization itself. Where does the fault lie, that people are still ignorant of the trials and triumphs of this great profession? Surely it rests in part with the historians, but just as surely it rests with the engineers themselves, who have stood silent so long, expecting contruction works to tell the story completely.

With this Centennial of Engineering a step forward is being taken, to tell the world the engineer's story of progress during the past 100 years. However

---

[1] Commander (CEC), U. S. Navy, Public Works Officer, Adak, Alaska.

1

admirable this step may be, it must not halt here. Engineers must see to it that the history of engineering through the ages takes its place with the histories of other great professions. They must, therefore, encourage not only technical research—for which they are already famous—but also historical research in the engineering profession. This research must be a continual living thing, reaching back to antiquity yet stretching out to tomorrow. Its importance demands that it be served by scholars of the first rank. Here, then, is a challenge to universities

FIG. 1.—JOHN SMEATON (1724–1792) FIRST MAN ON RECORD TO CALL HIMSELF A "CIVIL" ENGINEER

and to the engineers outside the academic world—to preserve in writing the landmarks of the engineer's noble calling.

Although much remains to be learned about the history of engineering, something is known of its highlights. It is recognized, for instance, that civil engineering is looked on as the parent of all other forms of engineering, and it is in the civil field, therefore, that any proper historical approach to the profession must be made.

The Function of the Engineer.—The first man on record to call himself a civil engineer was the eighteenth century Englishman, John Smeaton (Fig. 1). Although "civil engineer" was a new title at this time, the simple designation "engineer" had already had a long history. Derived from the Latin *ingenium*, which means natural capacity or invention, the word "engine" probably sired the title "Engineer," for the early engineer was largely concerned with the making and operating of engines of war such as catapults, battering rams, and the like. It naturally fell to his lot to devise defenses against these weapons as well, so history shows him branching out into the building of fortifications and other works to resist or aid siege. The classic example of the works of the engineer in ancient times was described by Plutarch in his "Life of Marcellus":

"When the Romans attacked them [the Syracusans] both by sea and land, they were struck dumb with terror, imagining that they could not possibly resist such numerous forces, and so furious an assault. But Archimedes soon began to play his engines, and they shot against the land-forces all sorts of missive weapons and stones of an enormous size with so incredible a noise and rapidity, that nothing could stand before them; overturning and crushing whatever came their way, and spreading terrible disorder throughout the ranks. On the side toward the sea were erected vast machines, thrusting forth on a sudden over the walls huge beams with the necessary tackle, which striking with a prodigious force on the enemy's galleys sunk them at once; while other ships, hoisted up at the prows by iron claws or hooks like the beaks of cranes, and set upright on the stern, were plunged to the bottom of the sea; and others again by ropes and grapples were drawn toward the shore, and after being whirled about, and dashed against the rocks that projected below the walls, were broken to pieces and the crews perished. * * * At last the Romans were so terrified, that if they saw but a rope or a stick put over the walls, they cried out 'Archimedes was levelling some machine at them'; and turned their backs and fled."

In time the engineer's job came to include all types of construction, such as roads and bridges, needed to facilitate the movements of an army. In every case his primary task was to contrive or to build something, and that function has continued to this day. The very root of the word, *ingenium,* indicates the engineer's mission in society; it is to do, to act, or to make. The aim of the scientist is to know, but the aim of the engineer is to do—by applying science to his work. This application of science has resulted in a more efficient utilization of materials and has given rise to the oft-quoted definition of engineering as "the art of doing well with one dollar which any bungler can do with two after a fashion."

Civil Engineering Defined.—It was John Smeaton, the first "civil" engineer, who sought to distinguish his civilian construction work from that of the military engineer. Just what constituted civil engineering remained a rather indefinite concept until the profession was defined in the charter granted in 1828 to the Institution of Civil Engineers at London, England, as:

" * * * the art of directing the great sources of power in nature for the use and convenience of man, as the means of production and of traffic in states, both for external and internal trade, as applied in the construction of roads, bridges, aqueducts, canals, river navigation and docks for internal intercourse and exchange, and in the construction of ports, harbours, moles, breakwaters and lighthouses, and in the art of navigation by artificial power for the purposes of commerce, and in the construction and application of machinery, and in the drainage of cities and towns."

Gradually the term "civil" engineer became restricted to those who were engaged chiefly with works of a static nature such as roads and tunnels, whereas those concerned primarily with the operation of moving machinery adopted the designation "mechanical" engineer. In time, various other specialties came to be recognized, and new branches such as "chemical" and "electrical" engineering were born.

A century after the granting of the 1828 charter, civil engineering had become only one of the many branches of the engineering profession and had changed somewhat in the fields it covered. Engineering had come to be defined as "the professional and systematic application of science to the efficient utilization of natural resources to produce wealth." The subfields of civil engineering—officially adopted in 1929 by the California State Board of Engineering Examiners—included the following:

" * * * highways, bridges, water supply, inland waterways, harbors, drainage, irrigation, water power, flood control, municipal improvements, railroads, tunnels, airports, airways, purification of water, sewage, refuse disposal, foundations, framed and homogeneous structures, buildings, city and regional planning, valuation and appraisals, and surveying (other than land surveying)."

Engineers in All Civilizations.—In other ages and in other civilizations the engineer was known by other names—as a sage, architect, philosopher, or wise man—but his function was essentially that of his modern counterpart. Regardless of what he called himself or what other duties he performed, the object of this paper is briefly to trace the engineer and his works from earliest times to the present.

In a sense, the story of engineering is a story of mankind, for no less than law and government has technology been a mark of the civilized world. Arnold J. Toynbee in "A Study of History" recognizes twenty-one "civilizations" in the history of the world, most of them related as parent or offspring to one or more of the others: Namely, the Andean, Babylonic, Central American (Mexic and Yucatec), Egyptiac, Far Eastern-Japanese Offshoot, Far Eastern-Main Body, Hellenic, Hindu, Hittite, Indic, Islamic (Arabic and Iranic), Mayan, Minoan, Orthodox Christian-Main Body, Orthodox Christian-Russian Offshoot, Sinic, Sumeric, Syriac, and Western. He further counts as "abortive civilizations" the Far Eastern Christian, the Far Western Christian, and the Scandinavian societies. His "arrested civilizations" include the Eskimos, the Nomads, the Osmanlis, the Polynesians, and the Spartans.

Archeological and historical evidence thus far is too meager to warrant dwelling at length on the progress of civil engineering in most of these societies. Their effect on the main stream of engineering thought appears to be negligible. Little time, therefore, will be devoted to the history of civil engineering elsewhere than in the Hellenic and Western World, for the main task of this paper is to trace the traditions of the profession which have culminated in the civil engineering of the twentieth century.

ENGINEERING OF THE ANCIENTS

It is generally accepted that, in some parts of the world by 4000 B.C., man had learned the use of fire, the working of flint, and the manufacture of baskets, boats, clothing, houses, pottery, and weapons. It is also probable that nowhere had he advanced much beyond that stage. During the next millennium, however, a gradual increase was made in social organization and technical achievement along the banks of the Nile in Egypt. To the semilegendary founder of the First Dynasty, Menes (circa 3200 B.C.), are attributed the first large-scale hydraulic, drainage, and irrigation works.

A brilliant period of activity followed in the 500 years from 3000 to 2500 B.C., an era which witnessed among other things the erection of the pyramids. A crude form of surveying developed, and elementary mathematics came to be used. The earliest known work on mathematics is a papyrus copied about 1550 B.C., but it describes operations which might date to the Old Kingdom (2980–2475 B.C.). Of particular interest to engineers is the fact that its author Ahmes used a decimal notation but no zero. For the next 3,000 years civilization in Egypt showed alternate decline and revival, but no appreciable advance was made in the art of civil engineering.

The outstanding engineering feature of the Middle Empire appears to have been the construction of rock-cut tombs, whereas huge masonry temples marked the contribution of the great Theban kingdom which arose about 1700 B.C. Surveying, hydraulic works, and building construction then made up the bulk of early Egyptian engineering, but it is doubtful whether these had any direct effect on the works of succeeding or contemporary civilizations. The most significant thing about Egyptian engineering is the fact that here, for the first time, is evidence of man building to a plan instead of haphazardly, and using mathematics to insure the results desired. This contribution is slight when compared with the works of modern civil engineering, but gigantic when compared to the works of primitive man.

Early civilizations also sprang up in Asia in the valleys of the Indus and of the Tigris and Euphrates, but today's small knowledge of them makes it difficult to evaluate their contributions to the development of engineering. Even in the case of the Minoan civilization in the Aegean, the task is still difficult. Recent finds by archeologists have revealed that these people—who probably flourished between 2000 and 1000 B.C.—had water supply and disposal systems. They were skilled in the use of large masonry blocks, which they placed in walls, buildings, and roads. From this point on, the trail grows hazy once more, not to be picked up again until the time of the Hellenic Greeks.

Theoretical Concepts Dominant in Greek Civilization.—Greek engineering drew its inspiration from the philosophers who began to flourish during the seventh and sixth centuries B.C. in the Greek colonies of Asia Minor. First of the schools of importance as far as engineering is concerned was that established at the commercial city of Miletus. Here the names of Thales (circa 640–546 B.C.), Anaximander (circa 611–547 B.C.), and Anaximenes (flourished before 494 B.C.) stand out as originals in the field of scientific speculation. Thales, who is probably best remembered for having stated that everything is derived from water, is reputed to have traveled to Egypt where he learned mathematics. Although very little direct acquisition of knowledge can be traced to this source, it is probable that the information and ideas which Thales and those who followed him obtained from alien lands aroused their interest in technical matters.

However, the importance of the Milesian school rests not so much on what it achieved, but on what it attempted. The Greek mind was brought into contact with Babylonia and Egypt, and the vigor of the questions asked by these early philosophers inspired subsequent investigators. Despite the early exchange of ideas in many fields, however, there is little evidence that Greek architecture— apart from the mathematics connected with it—derived from Egypt or from any other earlier civilization. The shaping of Greek thought continued in many "schools" subsequent to that of the Milesians, but the important point to be gathered is that groups of men sat down to think in a rational manner about technical and other matters. From thought came science, and following on the heels of science came engineering.

The Greek philosophers are usually remembered as being interested in knowledge for its own sake, abhorring any dealings with practical things. They considered mathematics a study of eternal things—ideas—and thus as much superior to "applied mathematics" as heaven is to earth. Nevertheless, the philosophers are counted among the early engineers. Witness the case of Archimedes of Syracuse (287–212 B.C.) who reputedly declined to describe on paper his "practical" works because he considered such a course undignified, but who proved his willingness and ability to translate theory into practice at the defense of Syracuse, previously recounted. Archimedes' greatest contribution to engineering lay not in his engines of war, however, but rather in the theoretical foundations he gave to hydrostatics and mechanics.

Also theoretical was the other great Greek contribution to engineering—the laying of the foundations of geometry. About 650 B.C. geometry consisted of a few rules of thumb, but by the time of Pythagoras (circa 582–500 B.C.) it was becoming a theoretical science. It reached maturity with Euclid, whose "Elements" (circa 300 B.C.) literally translated remained the one standard textbook on the subject until the latter part of the nineteenth century. Euclid, who had a Platonian contempt for practical utility, probably never dreamed that some 2,000 years later his theories would provide a basis for much of the practical work of the engineer.

The summing up and perfecting of geometry came during the Alexandrine period—a period which also saw great strides made in astronomy. Science at Alexandria, Egypt, a commercial city, tended to be more practical than it was in Greece itself, and names like Ctesibius and Hero immediately recall thoughts of mechanics and machines. Alexandria, which had been founded in 332 B.C., succeeded Athens as the philosophical center of the world, retaining this leadership from 300 B.C. to 300 A.D. However, the beginnings of scientific engineering which started there did not fully develop, and after about 200 A.D. contributions from this source became purely scholarly. A slow decline set in, and this seat of Greek learning finally died when the Arabs overran Egypt in 642 A.D. Greek science, however, did continue in a fossilized state at Byzantium, until the Turks sacked the city in the fifteenth century.

Despite the eminent names connected with engineering, it can scarcely be stated that as a group the Greeks were great engineers. They built few roads, bridges, tunnels, or canals. They made no great contributions in the fields of water supply, irrigation, or harbor works. The mountainous character of their country undoubtedly contributed in a large measure to their relatively low output. Small city states tended to remain in isolation, for extensive roads over the mountains would have been expensive affairs. For the most part, nature endowed Greece with a coast line of natural harbors, making extensive artificial harbor works unnecessary. Mountain streams or springs were generally close to the city states they served, and thus elaborate water supply systems were likewise unnecessary. Because of the rugged terrain, it was difficult to unite the country politically and economically, and without this unity great public works were impossible.

Engineering is an economic as well as a scientific achievement; to know how to accomplish a task is not enough, someone has to provide the money. In the case of the Greek city states, few were interested in contributing large sums to projects which did not directly concern their own city. What commercial intercourse there was could be carried on more economically by a few sea-going ships than by a vast network of roads with their necessary bridges and tunnels. There is no doubt that the Greeks had the ability to construct great works where they felt that the result (usually more esthetic than "practical") justified the cost. Evidence of this may still be seen in the remains of the Grecian temples which have won the praise of architectural critics throughout the centuries (Fig. 2). It was chiefly in this field of building construction that a Greek engineering tradition was passed on to the Roman world. Greek mathematics and astronomy, in the main, by-passed the Romans and were passed to Western Europe via the Arabs and Byzantine Greeks.

Summing up, then, the main Greek contribution to civil engineering was theoretical rather than practical, for the Greeks developed mathematics and geometry which later became so important in engineering. This emphasis of theoretical over practical was due in part to the attitude of the philosophers who led Greek thought; it was due in greater measure to the country's geography—or to be more precise, its topography—which in turn shaped its political and economic life. The construction of vast public works, consistent with the technology of the times, could not be justified from an administrative or commercial standpoint, and so such structures were never brought into being.

Romans Develop Practical Civil Engineering.—With the emergence of Rome in Italy as the dominant power in the world, civil engineering reached a peak it did not again achieve until the nineteenth century. The Romans are not remembered, as are the Greeks, for their creative intellectual powers, but they made a name as efficient organizers—soldiers, lawgivers, and engineers. Founded in the eighth century before the Christian era, Rome slowly grew in strength and influence until it dominated, in the time of Hadrian (second century A.D.), practically the whole world bounded by the Mediterranean, the North Sea, the Atlantic, and the Caspian Sea.

Many factors acted to hold this vast empire together, not the least of which were the Roman laws, the Roman legions, and the Roman roads. Road building on a large scale was begun in the latter part of the fourth century B.C., and it continued over the greater part of five centuries as the power of the state grew. The construction of these roads was such that their remains furnished the inspiration for a revival of road building in seventeenth century France, and even today evidences of the old roads are still to be found.

The permanence and solidity which were manifested in the roads were characteristics which extended throughout all Roman engineering endeavors. Aque-

ducts, bridges, tunnels, canals, and all forms of hydraulic works fell within the
scope of the Roman engineers during the time of the republic and, later, under
the emperors. In the first century A.D. the City of Rome had a public water sup-

FIG. 2.—RUINS OF ERECHTHEUM AT ATHENS, GREECE, EXAMPLE OF GRACE AND BEAUTY IN
GRECIAN BUILDINGS

ply system which furnished a per capita quantity equal to that of many modern
European cities. The existing exposed aqueducts (Fig. 3) in various parts of
what was once the Roman Empire still excite wonder among people used to all the
technical advances of modern civilization.

Similarly many fine masonry bridges still stand, having weathered the onslaughts of nature for nearly 2,000 years. Masonry theatres, temples, baths, and triumphal arches also remain—mute testimony that the Romans extended their constructive genius to every phase of their public and private life. The

FIG. 3.—ROMAN AQUEDUCT PONT DU GARD (CIRCA 19 B.C.) NEAR NÎMES, FRANCE, WHICH TOWERS TO A HEIGHT OF APPROXIMATELY 160 FT AND EXTENDS ALONG ITS TOP FOR A DISTANCE OF 885 FT, ITS LARGEST ARCH HAVING A SPAN OF 80 FT 5 IN.

Italian coast is notoriously poor in natural harbors, but here again the Romans proved themselves equal to the challenge and produced the artificial harbors necessary to maintain a fleet which regarded the Mediterranean as *Mare Nostrum*.

In their construction practice the Romans inherited the semicircular arch from the Etruscans and borrowed the post and lintel from the Greeks. According to the architect Vitruvius (first century B.C.) the Romans saw much that they liked in Greek construction methods and use of materials, and the Greek influence is readily seen in many of the large Roman buildings, from both the architectural and constructional viewpoint. Entirely Roman in essence, however, was their fine natural cement which gave a monolithic character to much of their "concrete" and which was not duplicated in quality until the nineteenth century. Apart from this, the Romans used the same materials which had been used by their predecessors—namely, wood, stone, and brick.

Vitruvius and Frontinus, two main Roman authorities on engineering, leave the impression that Roman engineering was a highly developed rule-of-thumb "craftsman's" engineering rather than the more scientific art of today. Unfortunately no engineering computations have survived to indicate how much of their work was guided by something that might be called science. The Roman structures themselves show definite evidence of the use of mathematics and geometry in layout and construction. Closer inspection reveals that they were overdesigned —by modern standards at least—a further indication that they were derived more from rule-of-thumb methods than from basic scientific principles. However, the modern engineer might slyly observe that they simply used a larger "safety factor" in those days.

Most of the public works were supervised and built by the state, slave and soldier labor being used extensively. The ultimate economy of that type of construction is open to question, but at the time it probably seemed an inexpensive method. This policy certainly encouraged a heavy type of construction which would have been too expensive for private enterprise. In their initial constructive efforts the Romans were not hindered by topography as were the Greeks before them. Having built up their organizations on relatively easy terrain, the Romans were able to move to more arduous tasks gradually and in time to tackle the most difficult of problems. Thus, with native topography and then organization in their favor, the Romans were able to rise to the later topographical challenges which had kept the Greeks from ever getting started.

The Romans were also challenged by new conditions, easy enough to master, which evoked further response from them. A case in point is the lack of natural harbors in Italy and the skill acquired by the Roman engineers in waterfront construction. Strong government and technological excellence went hand in hand; they were mutually helpful. As the boundaries of the empire were pushed outward, for example, the roads followed; and they, in turn, made efficient administration of the newly won territories possible. After a period of consolidation the Romans were able to extend their boundaries once more.

Engineering then, as Rome was on the ascendency, was alternately an effect and cause of strong government. When the government began to break down, however, technology could not save it. The engineers did not at first lose their skill and know-how, they simply lost the funds to maintain the works they had built. Not only were they unable to advance their techniques; they were unable —through lack of practice—to retain all that was best in their profession. Along with the other hallmarks of an advanced civilization, the art of civil engineering slowly died among the crumbling ruins of the Roman Empire in the fifth century.

The Dark Ages, the Middle Ages, and the Renaissance

Knowledge Kept Alive by Arabs.—With the fall of the Hellenic and Roman civilizations, knowledge reached a low ebb in the Western World, but it was not snuffed out altogether. A culture of mixed Greek, Roman, and Jewish origin survived at Byzantium and in the countries which stretched from Syria to the Persian Gulf. During the early part of the seventh century Mohammed (circa 570–632) and his followers united Arabia and subjugated Persia, Syria, Iraq, and Egypt along with the northern coast of Africa, Armenia, and Asia Minor. Mu'awiya, first of the dynasty of the Ommiads, became sole ruler of Islam in 661 on the death of the Caliph Ali, Mohammed's cousin and son-in-law, and in his capital at Damascus the learning which had been preserved by the Nestorian Christians and other conquered groups slowly rose to the surface.

A further and greater impetus to learning was given by the Abbassides who replaced the Ommiads in 750. The capital was then moved to Baghdad which shared the distinction with Alexandria and Andalusia in Spain of being the greatest centers of learning in the Arab world. From the latter part of the eighth century until the twelfth, the Arabian schools made important contributions in the fields of mathematics, astronomy, physics, and medicine. Generally speaking, these contributions were not in the nature of new discoveries but were rather the collection and preservation of the knowledge of previous civilizations. Isolated instances of civil engineering appear in the Moslem world of this period but, apart from studies akin to surveying, they seem to bear little relation to subsequent development in this field.

Finally the great period of Arabic learning was brought to an end by a fanatic Islamic priesthood in the twelfth century. The importance of the Arabic civilization rests in the fact that it served as the "funnel" into which the knowledge of Greece, the Near East, and, to some extent, India and even China passed. Here it was absorbed and passed on to the Western World of the Middle Ages.

The Church, The Center of Learning.—The withdrawal of the Roman legions from Western Europe not only marked the end of a stable political organization in that area, but also ushered in an age of ignorance, which lasted for centuries. Only in the Church did a strong organization survive, and it was the Church also which kept a flicker of learning alive in a continent dominated by semibarbaric Germanic tribes.

Probably the last to show the true spirit of ancient philosophy was the noble Roman Christian Boethius (circa 420–524) who wrote compendiums and commentaries on Plato and Aristotle. His works, together with those of Cassiodorus (490–580) and Isidore of Seville (circa 560–636), formed an important link between the classicists and the medievalists.

Public works came to a complete halt as old Roman roads, bridges, and aqueducts slowly fell into decay. Only under Charlemagne (742–814) was any concerted attempt made to revive the art of civil engineering, but it withered away soon after his death. What scholarship there was devoted itself more to mystical philosophies and to religion than to practical mechanical arts. Nevertheless, it was the medieval monastery which led the way to a revival in engineering. In the twelfth century pious monks in Italy, France, and England began taking up the task of building bridges and other works modeled after Roman remains. Monastery water supply and drainage systems also began to appear about this time, as did the great Gothic cathedrals which still excite admiration.

Master craftsmen, guided more by experience and tradition than by scientific

FIG. 4.—MEDIEVAL IRRIGATION (FROM GEORGIUS AGRICOLA'S "DE RE METALLICA" (1556))

calculations, were the architects and engineers of these great works. The later Middle Ages were also marked by the construction of irrigation (Fig. 4) and drainage canals in both Holland and Italy, and for generations Dutch and Italian engineers were regarded as supreme in all types of hydraulic work. In time the ecclesiastics passed their knowledge and skills to the laity in the great period of enlightenment which followed.

Classical Learning Returns to Europe.—Here and there, Europe was prepared for the new learning which percolated in from the Arabic world. By the latter half of the twelfth century the schools made up of collections of students and masters began to take their modern form of universities at places such as Bologna and Salerno, Italy; Paris, France; and Oxford, England. To be sure, the nature of the subjects studied bore little relation to engineering—except possibly in the field of mathematics—but the questions asked represented a new interest in learning. Even mathematics was of little use to the engineer of the time; its value to the enginering profession was not to be realized until a later age. An increasing desire for secular knowledge led to the translation of many old works from Greek to the Latin. Often, of course, the texts suffered in translation which might, for example, go from Greek to Syriac, Syriac to Arabic, Arabic to Spanish, and Spanish to Latin. The effect of this new knowledge was to stimulate further thought and discussion.

Mystical Neo-Platonism, which had come to represent ancient philosophy, gave way to the more rational and more scientific outlook of Aristotle, and Aristotle's science and Christian doctrine were combined by St. Thomas Aquinas (1225–1274) in the system which came to be known as Scholasticism. The whole of the Thomist philosophy was founded and built up on reason, and sought to explain God and natural phenomena in this light. Friar Roger Bacon (circa 1214–1294) urged that reason alone was not sufficient and that observation and experiment were needed in the interpretation of nature. In addition to experiment, Bacon valued the use of mathematics, but he was three centuries ahead of his time in this respect and gathered no great following among the medievalists.

The Renaissance, An Era of "Ideas."—Throughout the medieval period the laity bowed to the ecclesiastics in most matters, for the established religion was thought to have the ability to decide—on the authority of Scripture and tradition—not only questions of theology and morality but even some matters of scientific interest as well. In the fourteenth century, however, the Papacy and a rich Mediterranean trade brought forth a monied and leisure class in Italy which began to look beyond the confines of its narrow mental prison. Interest in the classical world was intensified, partly because the Roman remains were everywhere in evidence to excite curiosity, partly because further commercial interests brought people together in towns, and partly because Italian traders formed a contact with the older civilizations of the past.

Greek scholars, fleeing before the Turkish horde which sacked Constantinople in 1453, gave a fresh impetus to the study of Greek in the West, and the perfection of the art of printing at about this time helped to diffuse the new knowledge. Thus, during the fifteenth century the cult of the classics became almost a passion among the ruling and merchant classes. The influential merchants soon perceived, however, that the answers to all "practical" questions could not be found in the works of the ancients, the Arabs, or the scholastics. Once more a fresh approach to knowledge was clearly in order.

Except in the field of architecture and building construction, the Renaissance was more a time of ideas than of action in so far as it affected the engineering profession. Most of the construction of the period was that done by military engineers in the employ of some duke or prince. Fortifications and artillery, the main interests of the engineer in the early Middle Ages, still occupied the bulk of the engineer's time.

In some cases, however, the engineer was more than just a constructor of fortifications; he was—for want of a more descriptive term—a "Renaissance man," a man who knew practically everything there was to know in his day. Such was Leonardo da Vinci (1452–1519), architect, biologist, engineer, painter, philosopher, and sculptor, who lived successively in the Italian courts of Florence, Milan, and Rome, and died in France, a friend and servant of Francis I. He rejected reliance on authority in favor of seeing for himself, and he was among the first to urge that scientific work must start by experiment and end with conclusions. He is particularly remembered among engineers for his contributions to hydraulics, especially in the field of canal and lock construction. However, he left no published writings (although his "Notes" were subsequently put in book form), and so his influence on the progress of engineering was probably small.

Mathematics and astronomy went forward with the times. Fifteenth and sixteenth century astronomers George Purbach, Regiomontanus, Nicholas Copernicus, and Tycho Brahe all made significant contributions which were felt in navigation and subsequently in surveying (Fig. 5) and cartography. Geometry from the Greeks was firmly established; and algebra, introduced by the Arabs, was gradually taking hold. These two subjects also entered engineering via surveying but were not generally employed elsewhere in the profession until the nineteenth century. Pioneering work in statics was begun in the latter part of the sixteenth century by the Dutchman Simon Stevin, and important studies on the magnet were made by William Gilbert of Colchester, England, during the same period.

Experimental Science in the Seventeenth Century.—Until about 1600 accumulation of knowledge was gradual, with little attempt to systematize it, and very little effort to adapt it to practical use. The seventeenth century not only witnessed a continuation of the harvesting of facts, but also saw the rise of experimental science. Francis Bacon, Lord Verulam (1561–1626), recognized the value of extensive experimentation, but he found difficulty in selecting the right experiments to indicate the answers to his questions. His main contribution lies in the fact that he reversed the view of Archimedes—who felt that practical devices should remain unrecorded—by setting up as a lofty object the making of scientific devices for man's practical use.

Throughout the seventeenth century men continued to lay solid foundations for sciences which would soon blossom forth in terms of practical application. Probably the man who contributed most in starting science on its triumphant course was the Italian, Galileo Galilei (1564–1642), who, in his work on dynamics and statics, combined observation and induction with mathematical deduction tested by experiment, and thus ushered in the true method of physical research. The century was marked by the contributions of some of the brightest names in science—namely, William Gilbert, Johannes Kepler, Robert Hooke, Evangelista Torricelli, Blaise Pascal, Robert Boyle, Christian Huygens, and Sir Isaac Newton. Newton (1642–1727) exerted the widest and most profound influence. His "Philosophiae Naturalis Principia Mathematica," published in 1687, has been considered by many the greatest book in the history of science. His concepts of force, momentum, and acceleration provided an excellent starting ground for the engineers

Admit B *my ſtation where I place mine Inſtrument* A *the marke whoſe altitude I deſire a-boue the leuell of mine eye, though I may not by reaſon of ſundry impediments approch nigh vnto it, nor ſee the baſe. Firſt I meaſure the Hypothenuſall line* A B, *by the precepts tofore giuen, which I ſuppoſe* 500 *pace, then perceiuing through the ſightes of my Semicircle the marke* A, *I finde* 10 *partes in my Scale of Altitudes, intercepted with the Perpendicular line, the ſquare thereof ioyned to* 14400 *produceth* 14500 *my Diuiſoure. Then doe I multiplye the Square of* 500 *in* 100, *the Square of the partes cut in the Scale, ſo haue I* 25000000, *which diuided by* 34500, *the Diuiſor, before reſerued, your Quotient Quadrate roote will bee very nigh* 41 *pace* 31 *Inches, and this is the true difference or vnequalitie of leuell betweene the marke* A, *and the Centre of your Semicircle* B, *ſo that if a Well be ſoonke of ſuch deapth that the bottome thereof were lower than* A 41 *pace* 31 *Inches, as I admit the line* A C, *then may you certainly affirme, that* C *the bottome of that Well is leuell with* B, *and yet may you not thereby, inferre that from a Fountaine head, lying of equall heigth with* B, *you may naturally deriue water to* C, *for the leuell of waters is circulare, as I haue before in the Booke declared: And heere I thinke it not amiſſe to giue you a precept how to finde the diuerſitie of theſe leuelles, whereby yee may exactly reſolue ſundrie queſtions pertaining to Water woorkes, wherein diuers haue greatly erred, obſeruing not this difference.*

FIG. 5.—MEDIEVAL SURVEYOR (FROM FIRST BOOK IN ENGLISH ON SURVEYING, "A GEOMETRICAL PRACTICE, NAMED PANTOMETRIA" BY THOMAS DIGGES (1571))

who began to translate theory into practice in the latter part of the eighteenth century.

Among the chief advances of the seventeenth century were the formation and growth of scientific societies. The first such society to be formed was the "Accademia Secretorum Naturae" at Naples in 1560, and it was followed by two other

Italian groups, the Accademia dei Lincei (1603) and the Accademia del Cimento (1657) of Florence. The next body of importance to be formed was the Royal Society which was given a charter at London by Charles II in 1662, and 4 years later Louis XIV gave official recognition to the Académie des Sciences at Paris. Lagging somewhat behind was the Berlin Academy which did not receive its charter until 1700.

In the early years those societies gave scant consideration to civil engineering; but, toward the latter part of the eighteenth century, the relation of engineering to science came to be more and more recognized by the societies, especially in England. Also of great importance during the seventeenth century were the various inventions which made the measurement of length and time exceedingly more accurate than had even been possible before. This advance was, in turn, reflected in improved surveying and better maps.

The Rise of the Engineers—the Eighteenth Century

France.—Although the seventeenth century is looked on chiefly as a period of scientific speculation, it also marks the early beginnings of modern civil engineering in France. It was during this century that the old Roman roads were unearthed, a discovery which had far-reaching effects in the development of the road in France. Even more important was the rise of the barge canal, encouraged by the ministers Maximilien de Béthune, Duc de Sully, Armand Duplessis, Duc de Richelieu, and Jean Baptiste Colbert. Again it was a strong government seeking to increase its strength with public works which pushed the lines of transportation rapidly across the country. As the seventeenth century drew to a close, it was evident that the foundations were in the making for what subsequently proved to be the great engineering tradition of the French.

Recognition of the need for trained civil engineers was signalized in France by the opening in 1760 of the first engineering school in the world, the École des Ponts et Chaussées. The school was the outgrowth of earlier institutions which dated back to the founding of the Corps des Ponts et Chaussées at Paris in 1716. Here for the first time a systematic attempt was made to derive empirical data from past construction work in order to build future structures more efficiently. Essentially, of course, engineers had always built in this manner, but heretofore the empirical information was stored in men's heads, and little effort was made to arrange it scientifically. Thus, the habit of experimenting, thinking, and drawing conclusions as practiced by the seventeenth century philosophers and scientists began to bear fruit in the practical world.

The Corps concentrated its efforts mainly on masonry bridges and permanent roads. Before the century was out the French bridges were unexcelled anywhere in the world and the French roads had reached their highest peak of development since the time of the Romans. The eighteenth century in France also saw a continuation of the work of the brilliant French mathematicians, who laid much of the theoretical groundwork in mechanics and hydraulics. Edme Mariotte and James Bernoulli of the seventeenth century were ably followed by Daniel Bernoulli, M. Parent, C. A. Coulomb, and Girard of the eighteenth.

England.—Across the channel in England a new class of engineers also began to emerge in the eighteenth century, but they differed somewhat from their theoretically trained French counterparts. For the most part, the early English engineers were blacksmiths, wheelwrights, masons, and the like—definitely "practical" men and largely self-educated in the field of scientific principles. Generally speaking, these men progressed empirically, and scientific principles followed rather than led their inventions. In a few cases, of course, they were men of science in addition to being men of "practical" outlook. Most noteworthy in this class were Smeaton and James Watt, who proceeded from scientific principles to practical achievement and vice versa.

The most important of the practical inventions of the century was the steam engine, first put in a usable form for pumping water by Savery in 1698 and shortly thereafter improved by Thomas Newcomen. Its early use was confined almost exclusively to the pumping out of mines, but when Watt made it into a machine of reasonable efficiency in the last quarter of the century a whole new world of power was opened. Up to this time the English textile industry had found its rate of spinning hampered for want of a more efficient prime mover than the water wheel. Merchants and traders were in the position of being able to sell their products more rapidly than they could be manufactured, for Great Britain's command of the seas had brought her immense overseas markets which clamored for English manufactured goods.

With the introduction of Watt's engine the old "mills" were soon converted to steam, and new factories sprang up in places formerly bypassed because of their lack of quickly moving streams. The total effect was to increase production and to accelerate the movement of workers from their individual spinning wheels at home to those at the factory. The whole thing was like a snowball rolling downhill. Factory sites became towns and towns grew into cities, a factor which brought new calls on the engineer.

The rise of industrialism brought up a new difficulty—transportation was hopelessly inadequate. The problem was solved initially by the introduction of canals. Englishmen had long been accustomed to using their navigable rivers for trade, so it was not an entirely novel idea that they should resort to canals to move both raw materials and the newly manufactured goods. When it was found that a canal could be a commercially sound investment, the rising industrial class proved full of ready backers, and from about 1760 to 1830 the canal reigned supreme in the transportation field in Great Britain.

Topography and climate proved favorable for this type of construction, and most of the early civil engineers received their initial instruction in canal building. The very nature of the work not only gave them a good background in cutting canals and in erecting waterfront structures, but also stimulated the construction of bridges, aqueducts, and tunnels. Such training was designed to stand the profession in good stead as increasing demands were placed on it in the nineteenth century.

The demand for better transportation was also reflected in the emergence of the turnpike roads. Like the canals they were the product of private enterprise, but unlike the canals they received little praise during the eighteenth century. Indeed, most of them deserved all the verbal abuse they got. Little attempt was made on the part of turnpike trusts to secure the services of competent engineers to direct the construction of these roads, and the results showed it. No real progress was made until the early nineteenth century when John McAdam introduced the relatively inexpensive broken stone road. His method rapidly found favor in Great Britain and soon became popular all over the world.

Summary of Progress During the Century.—Although the eighteenth century looks rather barren of scientific achievement when compared with the century that preceded (and the one that followed), engineering did advance. In France and in England—the main centers of engineering activity in this period—the scientific men faded somewhat into the background but the practical men came to the fore.

Not only did a class of "civil" engineers as distinct from "military" engineers arise but, even in the army, the duties of engineers became more sharply defined. The Corps de Génie, founded in 1690 by Sébastien le Prestre, Marquis de Vauban, merged with the artillery in 1755 for a time but it soon confined its functions to engineering as it is now known. After the rebellion of 1715 the artillery and engineers of Britain were separated by royal warrant (1716), but they remained for a time loosely joined together under the Board of Ordnance. In the United States artillerists and engineers were grouped together in 1794 and were separated in 1802 when the Corps of Engineers was organized at the United States Military Academy at West Point, N. Y. Military and civilian engineers alike turned their attention toward roads, bridges, and harbor works during this period with a vigor unknown since classical times. Impressive as these beginnings were, they were but the first trickle of what was to become a flood of technology in the nineteenth century.

Modern Civil Engineering

The point at which civil engineering entered the "modern" stage is, of course, an arbitrary one, for no clear-cut line can be drawn separating the old from the new. Perhaps the best course is to observe when civil engineers themselves decided that their calling was noble enough to warrant recognition as a profession. This decision was represented, in the main, by the formation of the professional societies which came into being in many countries throughout the course of the nineteenth century. First of these was Great Britain's Institution of Civil Engineers, established in 1818 and incorporated in 1828. Prominent among those which followed the British lead were the Maatschappi ter Bevordering der Bouwkunst (1843) of Holland, the Association des Ingèn (1847) of Belgium, the Société des Ingénieurs Civils (1848) of France, the American Society of Civil Engineers (1852) of the United States, the Verein Deutscher Ingenieure (1847) of Germany and Austria-Hungary, and the Societe degli Ingeneri (1868–1870) of Italy.

Technical Schools.—The same period saw the rise of the technical school—the engineering college—which was to play such a large part in fusing the artisan and the scientist into a new product, the modern engineer. In Europe the instruction was largely carried out under government bureaus as in the case of the École des Ponts et Chaussées, or under professional engineers as in the case of the "Mechanics Institute," founded in 1823 by George Birkbeck at Glasgow and London.

In the United States the task fell largely to army officers, professional educators, and educational scientists. Civil engineering was, of course, included in the curriculum of the United States Military Academy. Then, in 1819, Capt. Alden

Partridge, a former commandant at West Point, started the American Literary, Scientific and Military Academy at Norwich, Vt. This academy, which became Norwich University in 1834, gave a prominent place to civil engineering in its cultural and military program, and some of its early graduates played an important part in the establishment of the American Society of Civil Engineers.

The first truly civilian technical school in the United States was the one founded at Bowdoin College in Brunswick, Me., by Benjamin Hale in 1822, but it lasted only 10 years. In 1824, Stephen Van Rensselaer founded a school at Troy, N. Y., for teaching "the sons and daughters of farmers and mechanics" the application of science to "agriculture, domestic economy, the arts and manufactures." General engineering soon entered the curriculum, followed by civil engineering in 1829. Rensselaer Polytechnic Institute along with the United States Military Academy then furnished most of the native scientifically trained engineers in the country until the middle of the century.

Thomas Telford, Engineer.—Encouraged by their government, French engineers of the eighteenth century had reached a peak of achievement in their profession unrivaled by that of any other nation. A combination of factors which included British sea power, the invention of the spinning jenny, and the invention of the steam engine acted to develop engineers in Great Britain rapidly during this time so that, as the nineteenth century dawned, the superiority held by the French passed to the British.

The history of the early years of modern civil engineering—as here defined—is, therefore, largely a history of the accomplishments in Great Britain. It starts with Telford (1757–1834), first president of the Institution of Civil Engineers. Like most of the engineers of the day, his formal education was slight, and he began work at an early age as a mason's apprentice. Through native intelligence and diligent self-education Telford raised himself to a position where he was regarded as the most eminent civil engineer of his time. His influence was felt in every part of Great Britain and in many continental countries as well, for he designed and supervised the construction of numerous roads, bridges, buildings, canals, tunnels, drainage systems, and harbors. In fact, he engaged in every type of construction known to the civil engineer of the time with the exception of railroads, and he was well past his prime when they began to emerge. His name survives in a type of road construction and his statue stands in Westminster Abbey, but his memory is even better served by a living organization which points with pride to him at its first head. No man was more eminently qualified than he to lead civil enginering in its first official footsteps from the realm of a skilled trade to the full dignity of a respected profession.

The Emergence of the Railroad.—In Telford's declining years the steam engine, which was rapidly bringing about a revolution in industry, extended its influence to the transportation field. Horse-drawn railways had long been known in mining circles (Fig. 6), but the introduction of the steam locomotive suggested to men of vision the practicability of a transportation service never before dreamed of, and George Stephenson's "Rocket" showed in the Rainhill Trials of 1829 that the steam locomotive was now ready to take its place in the commercial world. The opening of the Liverpool and Manchester Railway in the following year signaled the beginning of the railway age.

The same factors which had acted to popularize canals almost a century before—climate, topography, wealth, technical ability, and commercial incentive

FIG. 6.—MEDIEVAL MINING AND THE EARLY RAILROAD (FROM GEORGIUS AGRICOLA'S "DE RE METALLICA" (1556))

—again came into play. Canals had been satisfactory in their time, but the flood of goods which began to move in the early nineteenth century practically overwhelmed them. Lack of centralized control in the early building period had resulted in canals of varying size being linked together.

This lack of uniform scale meant naturally that a maximum efficiency in barge size and loading could seldom be achieved. Although it was only one of many factors which played a part in sounding the death knell of the canals as railroads gradually overtook and all but eliminated them, probably its greatest importance lay in the fact that it served as a valuable lesson to the builders of the railroads when the problem of one or many gages had to be faced. The outcome, of course, was the adoption of a standard gage on English main lines—a gage which was subsequently adopted on a majority of main lines throughout the world.

Not only did the railroad change the face of the countryside; it materially affected the progress of civil engineering as well. The art of tunneling advanced once more, as it had during the canal boom. Drilling and blasting techniques were improved, and the tunnel shield appeared. Engineers began to burrow under rivers and under cities already built to permit their trains to reach ever-increasing markets. With the development of the subaqueous tunnel came the use of compressed air and a knowledge of how to use it safely. This knowledge was, in turn, incorporated in foundation work, especially in the case of bridge piers. Here more knowledge and experience were accumulated and returned again to the tunnel men.

Railroads Influence Bridge Design.—Increasing train loads also brought about a change in the design of bridge superstructures. Hitherto masonry arch bridges had stood for centuries, capable of withstanding the normal punishment of man and nature. They continued in use in the early days of the railroad, but it soon became apparent that masonry construction would reach its economic limit long before that condition was reached by the track, locomotive, or other rolling stock. Clearly some new material or some new principle of design, or both, were needed in the railway bridge.

With iron boilers for the locomotives and iron rails for the tracks, it was only a matter of time before iron bridges would take their place alongside the other pieces of iron equipment on the railroads. The manufacture of cast iron and wrought iron had been slowly improving throughout the eighteenth century, and demand increased with the years. Despite this improvement, a combination of quality and quantity was lacking until the latter half of the nineteenth century when Bessemer and Siemens-Martin steels came on the market. Some iron railroad bridges were constructed during the first half of the century but they were for the most part, modest pioneering efforts, noted for neither their structural nor their esthetic qualities.

Of special significance was the development of the bridge in the United States at this time. Vast quantities of timber readily at hand made timber framed structures only natural, with the result that a new structural type, the truss, was popularized and perfected. Slowly iron began to replace timber in the truss until at last (1845) the all-iron-truss railroad bridge was a reality. The challenge provoked by the railroad had been answered by the production of a bridge which combined both a new material and a new principle of design.

Water Supply and Sewage Disposal Problems Arise.—Tunnel and bridge construction were but two of the many sections of civil engineering tremendously influenced by cast iron and the steam engine early in the nineteenth century. The increase in trade and industrialization brought an increase in towns and an increase of populations, thus rendering obsolete the older systems of water supply designed for relatively small numbers. A solution to the pumping problem was found by the introduction of the steam engine, but this in turn raised the question of where to get a suitable pipe which could contain the high heads produced by the new machine. Cast iron, which had made the steam pump possible, once more proved the answer.

No sooner had the method of supplying an adequate amount of water to a large community been established, however, than a further problem—that of a pure supply—arose. Initially, before the germ theory of disease came to be generally accepted, water treatment was designed simply to improve clarity, taste, and odor. The first full-scale filtration of a municipal supply, like other significant advances in the civil engineering of the period, was carried out in Great Britain in 1829.

As had been the case before, however, solution of one problem merely brought others to the fore. Supplying and clarifying the water represented only half the job; getting rid of it after it had been used was the other. Haphazard drainage systems had seemed sufficient when towns were small and when "privy-middens" could be used almost exclusively for waste without undue annoyance, but the rapid expansion of the towns in England in the nineteenth century was accompanied by intolerable sanitary conditions, which could not be overlooked by social reformers, doctors, or engineers. The 1844 Report of the Commission on the Health of Towns shocked the nation into activity, and resulted in the gradual adoption of the water-carriage system of sewage disposal.

In most cases the raw sewage was simply carried to the nearest stream or body of water and dumped. Here again a new problem was created, for the pollution of rivers and streams was accelerated as a result, and potable water supplies were threatened. This called for renewed efforts in the field of water treatment and a newer approach to the sewage disposal problem in the latter half of the century.

Most solutions to previous problems coming under the scope of the engineer had been discovered by the further application and extension of engineering principles, but the water supply and sewage disposal questions were found to have other roots in the fields of medicine, chemistry, and bacteriology. Many of the same factors that had been responsible for the advancement of engineering techniques acted on these fields, and now all were joined on a common ground. The contributions of Louis Pasteur, Robert Koch, and others in showing how diseases could be transmitted threw a new light on the whole matter and led to an increased appreciation of the necessity for adequate and safe supply and disposal systems.

Experiments on water treatment and sewage disposal proceeded side by side, with the result that an advance in one field became an advance in the other. The latter part of the century witnessed extensive trials with chemicals and with various types of filters, and by the end of the century the basic problem of providing proper sanitary facilities for large populations had been solved.

Progress in Waterfront Construction.—A great part of England's expanding prosperity during the nineteenth century was due to her supremacy of the seas. In the final analysis, a fleet—if it is to remain powerful—must have excellent shore facilities to service it. Thus the civil engineer was identified with yet another phase of material progress, for he was called on to erect harbors and docks and all manner of waterfront works to service this ever-growing fleet of merchantmen. The introduction of steam in place of sail gradually brought about the construction of larger vessels, which, in turn, meant greater improvement to waterfront structures.

Experience gained in this type of work, combined with that obtained from drainage, irrigation, water supply, and sewerage construction, brought forth the same sort of interchange of ideas with mutual benefits resulting as had been the case in so many other phases of engineering progress. With his increased hydraulic skill the civil engineer was ready to take on the job of building the large ship canal—as exemplified by that at Suez, Egypt (1869)—when increased trade and the steamship made such a venture worthwhile.

Industrialization, But No City Planning.—Thus far this account has considered primarily the rise of modern—nineteenth century—civil engineering in Great Britain, but the story is roughly the same in other countries. The Industrial Revolution took place in England first, so it was natural that the early developments in civil engineering should also have their home there. Countries whose industrialization closely followed that of Great Britain found themselves with problems very similar to those of the English and their methods of solution and their mistakes generally followed the English pattern.

Those countries whose industrialization lagged behind Great Britain's a great deal did not make—or have to make—the same mistakes, but were able to profit by the experience of those who preceded them. Particularly was this true in the case of town planning. Some cities in the eastern United States show the same lack of planning for future growth that is exhibited in many of the early industrial cities of Great Britain—both having begun to grow about the same time— but most of the cities in the western United States, which developed at a later date, exhibit some thought in their layout. Although town planning is older than Vitruvius, it seems to have been generally overlooked by most engineers, except those of France in the heyday of nineteenth century construction, and not until the twentieth century was widespread attention devoted to the subject.

New Building Materials Introduced.—Until the nineteenth century the civil engineer was limited in his choice of building materials to stone, brick, or timber— the same materials that had been in use for centuries. By this time he had brought their use close to the economic and esthetic limits, with the result that further progress would be dependent on the introduction of new materials. New materials appeared in the form of portland cement concrete and steel.

Portland cement was introduced in Great Britain in 1825, but decades passed before concrete reached a popular stage. Steel, on the other hand, was adapted to almost every conceivable use soon after Henry Bessemer announced the discovery of his converter in 1856. Its effect was felt in every branch of construction. Longer bridges, taller buildings, greater floating drydocks, heavier trains, and stronger construction equipment—all were made possible now that great quantities of steel could be produced economically. Adding iron or steel bars to concrete to obtain reinforced concrete also began in the latter half of the century, but not until the twentieth century did this material gain the confidence of most builders.

Scientific Training Made Available to All.—A quick glance at the growth of civil engineering in the nineteenth century reveals certain obvious factors which affected it, such as the inventions of new machines and the introduction of new materials, but closer scrutiny will show an equally important—although more subtle—factor, the influence of thought and education. As previously noted, the growth of thought culminated in the brilliant scientific discoveries of the seventeenth century. Eighteenth century thinkers turned their questions more to politics and economics and discoursed at length on the dignities and rights of man. This thought pattern carried over into the nineteenth century in the form of practical Christian societies devoted to the principle of raising the standards of living of the underprivileged.

In heeding the demands of these groups, society called on the engineer to use his ingenuity and skill to bring about material improvements for this purpose. Thus, the engineering profession was affected directly by the wave of humanitarianism (and commercialism) which began to sweep over the Western World at this time. Indirectly the profession was affected even more. One result of the reform was the establishment of a greater number of regular educational institutions than had ever been known before. Education was no longer for the rich and privileged alone; it was rapidly coming to be regarded as a birthright of the common man. Accordingly, more people took an active interest in the ever-increasing fields of knowledge opening up on all sides.

Slowly, isolated scientific bits of knowledge come to be fitted together and re-examined in relation to the whole of the physical world. Mathematics moved rapidly from the realm of abstract theory to that of practical application, and the study of the strength of materials increased in importance proportionally. Almost imperceptibly theory and engineering practice were drawn closer and closer together, until finally the two were inseparable. The uniting of the two was pointed out by Maquorn Rankine in "The Harmony Between Theory and Practice in the Science of Enginering," an address he delivered on being appointed to the Chair of Engineering at Glasgow University in Glasgow, Scotland, in 1855. In place of the theorist of the seventeenth century and the "practical" man of the eighteenth century stood a new figure of the nineteenth century—the engineer, scientifically trained to accomplish practical ends.

Modern Engineering Based on Scientific Principles.—The question arises as to just when the engineer ceased to work by rule of thumb and was able to predict and plan his results by the use of scientific laws and mathematical reasoning. Strictly speaking, rule of thumb has not yet disappeared from engineering, as every engineer knows. The designer who adds on that safety factor and the construction superintendent who adds a little more water to the concrete mix merely affirms that engineering has not yet completely passed to the realm of science but, rather, still remains something of an art. Nevertheless, no modern engineer will build a work of any appreciable size without a set of plans which are derived from scientific laws and mathematical reasoning. It must be decided then when the emphasis in engineering design shifted from calculations based on rule of thumb to those based on truly scientific principles.

Actually, the time when this shift became significant did not coincide with the beginning—as here defined—of modern civil engineering. Previously the beginning of modern civil engineering has been associated with the name of Telford and with the incorporation of Great Britain's Institution of Civil Engineers in 1828— the time when civil engineering came to be formally recognzed as a profession both by its members and by the outside world. At that time engineering still had most of its roots of design in "practical" rather than in scientific principles.

By the middle of the nineteenth century, however, the shift to the scientific emphasis in design had become apparent. Two works, one American and the other French, stand out above the rest in ushering in this new era. Squire Whipple's (Hon. M. ASCE) first treatise on stresses in trusses (1847) and M. de Sazilly's analysis of dam design (1853) mark the beginning of truly rational and scientific design in civil engineering. From then on, design passed out of the hands of the "practical" men into the hands of those with scientific training, and progress in the profession leaped forward at an astounding pace during the latter half of the nineteenth century.

New Demands Made by Automobiles and Airplanes.—Notable as were the engineering accomplishments and changes in the nineteenth century, they were but a prelude to the wonders which were to be wrought in the twentieth. Concrete and steel construction climbed from initial clumsy and halting efforts to a maturity characterized by economy and beauty. The growing tempo of city life demanded more and better services in transportation, puol.. health, and commercial and private structures. Larger flood-control projects, bigger dams, and more complex powerhouses were the civil engineer's contribution as electricity became more a part of everyday life.

Emergence of the automobile, however, provoked the biggest response of all from civil engineering. Its introduction was to the twentieth century what the railroad had been to the nineteenth and the canal to the eighteenth. The old system of road making was out; new materials and new techniques were needed to cope with this latest vehicle to take the road. Not only roads were affected, but bridge and tunnel design came in for radical revision. New designs for lighter loads meant further experimenting with hitherto unsatisfactory or undiscovered materials.

The influence of the automobile and the road on the lives of ordinary citizens has been tremendous. Like the railroad, subway, and tramcar, it has enabled people to live at some distance from their work and yet commute comfortably each day. As a result, cities have gradually spread out as successive waves of fugitives from the factories have settled down in relatively uncongested residential suburban areas. Fresh farm produce, brought long distances from the country, has become normal fare for the average city dweller, and few think it extraordinary to travel miles for a simple day's outing. Obviously a profound change has been brought about in a half a century in the lives and habits of the people served by such transportation.

Small wonder that air age enthusiasts predict sweeping changes in the world of the future! Here again the civil engineer is primarily concerned, for his is the responsibility for designing and building the runways and airports. Clearly the profession has continued to move with the times, for in every age the civil engineer has been involved wherever any carrier has touched solid ground.

Facilitating every type of transport, be it on or in the land, sea, or air, has always been one of the primary functions of civil engineering throughout its long history. The influence of transport in shaping the political and economic world has been, of course, so great as almost to defy description. Without roads or harbors or airports and the appropriate carriers to use them, civilization—as known by the Western World—would soon vanish. The movement of raw materials to the factories would be cut off, industry would stop, trade would die, city populations would starve, governments would fall, anarchy would reign. True, nations would lose their ability to wage war on one another, but then nations as such would soon cease to exist. The clock would be turned back 6,000 years as man returned to the primitive state.

Perhaps this picture is somewhat overdrawn, but it does serve to dramatize the contribution of the civil engineer in the shaping of the modern world. In a similar vein the fate of cities may well be imagined were they deprived of the water supply and sewerage systems which have made their safe growth possible— and who will deny the advantages to mankind derived from the drainage and irrigation of countless acres of formerly worthless land?

Environment As a Factor in Engineering Progress.—Briefly then, this paper recounts the influence of the civil engineer on his environment; but there is a further point to be considered—the influence of the environment on the civil engineer. In every case of outstanding engineering achievement the same factors have been in evidence. First of all, topography has been favorable in initial instances—tough enough to evoke a response, but gentle enough to be overcome. Aided by their increased confidence and guided by their past experience, engineers from a country with such topography have been able to go into areas of increasing topographical difficulty and master conditions which would have been insurmountable had they attempted to lay the foundations of their skill there. Climate has had a similar effect. Practically all engineering knowledge has originated with people from temperate climates who have been neither all but overwhelmed by arctic blasts nor enervated by tropic heat.

Another decisive factor has been wealth, both in the form of workable materials and in the form of financial backing. The first depends on nature, but the second may stem from government or private enterprise. Regardless of the source of the financial backing, however, government must be regarded as another factor, for only under relatively stable political organizations has true engineering progress been made. Commercial benefits have provided much of the incentive in engineering, but a great measure of credit must also be given to those men of public spirit who have, with no thought of financial gain, labored to make this a better world in which to live.

The combination of all these factors has encouraged engineering development where the seed of rational thought has been firmly planted. From thought has come knowledge, and from knowledge, power—power of man over his environment. In the final analysis, the effect of the engineer on his environment and the effect of the environment on the engineer cannot be separated. One has continually acted and reacted on the other until cause and effect are hopelessly intermingled. One fact emerges clear, however—the engineer has played a leading role not only in changing the face of the earth but in shaping the destiny of nations and of men as well.

BIBLIOGRAPHY

"A History of the Institution of Mechanical Engineers," by R. H. Parsons, The Institution of Mech. Engrs., London, 1947.

"A Short History of Ancient Peoples," by R. Souttar, Hodder & Stoughton, London, 1904.

"A Short History of Mediaeval Peoples," by R. Souttar, Hodder & Stoughton, London, 1907.

"A Short History of Science," by F. Sherwood Taylor, Wm. Heinemann, Ltd., London, 1939.

"A Shorter History of Science," by W. C. Dampier, Cambridge Univ. Press, London, 1945.

"A Study of History," by Arnold J. Toynbee, abridged by D. C. Somervell, Oxford Univ. Press, London, 1949.

"Civil Engineer," *Encyclopædia Britannica*, 14th Ed., London, 1937.

"Economic Geography," by C. C. Colby and A. Foster, Ginn & Co., New New York, N. Y., 1944.

"Economic Theory of Railway Location," by A. M. Wellington, John Wiley & Sons, Inc., New York, N. Y., 1886.

"Encyclopaedia of Islam," by M. Th. Houtsma, T. W. Arnold, R. Basset, and R. Hartmann, Luzac & Co., London, 1913.

"History of Western Philosophy," by B. Russell, George Allen & Unwin, Ltd., London, 1947.

"Human Understanding and Its World," by K. W. Monsarrat, Hodder & Stoughton, Ltd., London, 1937.

"Lives of the Engineers," by S. Smiles, John Murray, London, 1904.

"Science Past and Present," by F. Sherwood Taylor, Wm. Heinemann, Ltd., London, 1945.

"The Century of Science," by F. Sherwood Taylor, The Scientific Book Club, London, 1943.

"The Earth and the State," by D. Whittlesey, Henry Holt & Co., New York, N. Y., 1944.

"The Engineering Profession," by T. J. Hoover and J. C. Fish, Stanford Univ. Press, Stanford University, Calif., 1941.

"The Quest for Power," by H. P. Vowles and M. W. Vowles, Chapman & Hall, Ltd., London, 1931.

"The Study of the History of Science," by G. Sarton, Harvard Univ. Press, Cambridge, Mass., 1936.

AMERICAN SOCIETY OF CIVIL ENGINEERS

Founded November 5, 1852

TRANSACTIONS

Paper No. 2576

A HUNDRED YEARS OF AMERICAN CIVIL ENGINEERING, 1852–1952

By J. K. Finch,[1] M. ASCE

Synopsis

Commemorating the one hundredth anniversary of the American Society of Civil Engineers (ASCE), this paper is a record of the events that give the birthday its special significance. The writer divides his subject historically into two parts—the half preceding, and the half succeeding, the turn of the twentieth century. Each part traces the growth of specialties in civil engineering—railways, bridges, foundations, highways, water supply, sanitation, irrigation, power, public works, transportation, construction, tunnels, and dams. Throughout the narration are many fascinating and factual references to the personalities that have made the profession and the ASCE great.

Introduction

The century of progress celebrated by the ASCE in 1952 may also be regarded as marking the fiftieth century in the history of the engineering profession. As known today, civil engineering is but the modern version of an ancient practical art, the art of construction, which is as old as civilized life itself. From its beginnings in Egypt and Mesopotamia at least three thousand years before Christ, the traditions and practices of the ancient master builder have been handed down, carried forward, and added to as an essential service in the evolution of western civilization and the democratic way of life.

One would expect, therefore, that American engineering would owe much to importations from abroad. It is commonly assumed, in fact, that the first engineers in the United States were of foreign—notably military—origin and that Americans simply appropriated—ready-made—engineering ideas and methods from earlier European workers.

No engineering technique is ever lost. Engineers are constantly working over, revising, improving, and adding to past practices and methods. Man has built roads, canals, and bridges for centuries. Americans imported many devices from

---

[1] Cons. Engr., New York, N. Y.; Dean Emeritus of the School of Eng. and Renwick Prof., Civ. Eng. Emeritus, Columbia Univ., New York, N. Y.

Europe, but American engineering owes relatively little to European techniques and practices. It has grown and developed from pioneer beginnings in a peculiarly American manner to meet peculiarly American needs, wants, and ideas. In part such independent growth has been due to the fact that Americans have been too busy with their own problems to follow with care progress abroad. To a major degree it has been due to the totally different economic and social life that has conditioned American development in comparison with the older civilizations of Europe.

American engineering had its beginnings about 50 or 60 years before the founding of the ASCE in 1852. As early as 1838 a British visitor, David Stevenson, sensed some of these fundamental differences that have characterized engineering development in the United States:

> "The zeal with which the Americans undertake, and the rapidity with which they carry out every enterprise, which has the enlargement of their trade for its object, cannot fail to strike all who visit the United States as a characteristic of the nation. English and American engineers are guided by the same principles in designing their works, but the different nature of the materials employed in their construction, and the climate and circumstances of the two countries naturally produce a considerable dissimilarity in the practice of civil engineers in England and America. At first view one is struck with the temporary and apparently unfinished state of many of the American works and is very apt, before inquiry into the subject, to impute to want of ability, what turns out, on investigation, to be a judicious and ingenious arrangement to suit the circumstances of a new country, of which the climate is severe—a country where stone is scarce and wood is plentiful and where manual labor is very expensive. It is vain to look to the American works for the finish which characterizes those of France, or the stability for which those of Britain are famed."[2]

The "plentiful material" was timber; in fact, the major problem in the construction of early American canals and railways was that of removing the forests, trees, and stumps that encumbered the routes. In his "American Notes" of 1842, Charles Dickens describes the monotony of travel on these lines through a lane cut in virgin wilderness. Timber was not only plentiful but also well adapted to inexpensive, relatively temporary construction in a country with meager financial resources and where the uncertainty of future requirements did not justify a more permanent form of building. As a result, America built in timber rather than in the more solid, permanent, and costly stone which was characteristic of British and Continental practice. There were few great American stone buildings and bridges comparable to those abroad; but, as a result of their preoccupation with framed construction, American engineers initiated the modern era of the truss bridge.

Similarly, as Stevenson wrote, skilled labor was "very expensive" even in 1838. This fact exercised an especially strong influence in the premachine days during which Stevenson lived, but it continued to dictate the character of later American design and production even as it does today. Its manifestations are manifold. It has been the predominating factor in the rise of American power tools, labor-saving machines, and mass production. It has encouraged standardization and

---

[2] "Sketch of the Civil Engineering of North America," by David Stevenson, Weale, London, England, 1838.

has led to the modern development of automatic and semi-automatic equipment. In bridge design, it resulted in efforts to minimize the time and cost of construction through the development of plans in which field operations were reduced to a minimum. The typical American pin-connected truss was thus born of these same basic conditions.

The character and scope of economic needs also strongly color (if, indeed, they do not dictate) the type of work to which engineers devote their efforts. In the United States, the nineteenth century was preeminently a time in which the dominating problem was transportation, and in this sphere the railroad soon became "king." Great Britain's railroad problem was solved almost completely by 1840, that is, in 10 or 15 years. By this date there were more miles of track in the United States than in Great Britain, but the maximum rate of building was not reached until the decade from 1880 to 1890 when more than 70,000 miles were put down; and the maximum railroad mileage in the United States (more than 250,000 miles—enough to circle the globe ten times) was not attained until 1920.

The tremendous, unparalleled, and unequaled industrial growth of the United States has been a twentieth century phenomenon. To be sure, the nineteenth century had begun with tallow candles and ended with electricity; it came in on horseback and went out in the automobile; it began with the stagecoach and closed with the airplane; it started with an uncertain postal service and ended with the telephone; it ushered in Eli Whitney's interchangeable manufacture; it saw Yankee ingenuity devise "The American System"; and it witnessed the development of modern power-driven tools and equipment—all these surely marked great advances in American industry and in engineering services—but, by 1900, American manufacturing was still localized in some fourteen North Atlantic and North Central states. Agriculture still remained the greatest industry, and the maximum employment in agriculture was not reached until 1910.

This change in the basic character of American economic life has led to the statement that, whereas it was the civil engineer who dominated the engineering of the nineteenth century, it has been the electrical, mechanical, and chemical— the industrial—engineers who have led professional advance in the twentieth century. This comparison seems strange when it is recalled that the past 50 years have witnessed the greatest construction period the world has ever known. However, there has also been a basic change in civil engineering interest. By 1900 the major railroads had been built; but a new transportation problem—that of the motorcar—was emerging as railway building interest declined. Mechanical and power advances likewise gave rise to a new era of construction. The decade about 1900 was marked by the last of the hand methods, by the rise of power equipment, and by the replacement of cut stone and brick in heavy construction by mass-produced concrete. Motor transportation also ushered in a new era of bridge and tunnel construction that has led to notable advances in design and new span-length records. In short, modern advances in sister professions have not eclipsed corresponding advances in civil engineering. On the contrary, they have greatly strengthened the power of the civil engineer; they have added to his problems and the scope of his services.

Certainly one of the fundamental changes has been in the engineer's clients. The railroads were built privately whereas the highways are public—primarily state—works. Similarly, great modern records in dam construction—an area in which Americans made no notable advances in the nineteenth century—have resulted from the needs of municipalities and the great reclamation, flood control, and other works of the Federal Government. In fact, the scope of modern civil engineering is so great today that only as public works—only through governmental resources—has it been possible to finance these record-making undertakings.

The story of a century of civil engineering progress, therefore, may be divided into two periods—the 50 years before and the 50 years since the turn of the century in 1900.

The writer is conscious that in attempting to write about the trends of an entire century, he has omitted mention of many great engineers and engineering works. He is also aware that no single engineer can write with assurance on each of the many branches of the profession. He hopes, however, that he has noted the major advances in the evolution of American civil engineering.

PART I. THE NINETEENTH CENTURY

THE FIRST AMERICAN ENGINEERS

American engineering, as already noted, had its beginning, perhaps, 50 or 60 years before the ASCE was founded. There were a few French engineers who served with the American forces during the Revolution, but the first indigenous American engineers were a group of highly-skilled and able engineer-builders, generally known as "the early American bridge builders." They were the product of pioneer American life, skilled craftsmen, especially in timber construction, who went about the newly-created states, building timber bridges to meet local needs. One must turn back to the Middle Ages to find their parallel in the itinerant craftsmen who traveled through western Europe building bridges and

FIG. 1.—"PERMANENT BRIDGE" AT PHILADELPHIA, PA., BUILT BY TIMOTHY PALMER IN 1805

cathedrals. Like their ancestors, these American pioneers developed an intuitive structural sense, a "feeling for structure," to an almost uncanny degree. All one needs to do is to study the design for the Permanent Bridge[3] (Fig. 1) at Philadelphia, Pa., built by "the ingenious Timothy Palmer" of Newburyport, Mass., in 1805, to realize that here was a man who, knowing nothing of structural analysis and stresses, nevertheless, possessed a clear understanding of the action of a trussed arch. William H. Burr, M. ASCE, has paid a well-deserved tribute to the long-range effects of their labors:

> "The names of Palmer, Burr and Wernwag were connected with an era of admirable engineering works, but with bridge analysis practically unknown, and the simplest and crudest materials at their disposal, their resources were largely constituted of an intuitive engineering judgment of high quality and remarkable force in the execution of their works never excelled in American

---

[3] "A History of the Development of Wooden Bridges," by Robert Fletcher and J. P. Snow, *Transactions*, ASCE, Vol. 99, 1934, p. 326.

Engineering. The works they constructed form a series of precedents which have made themselves felt in the entire development of American bridge building."[4]

THE TRUSS BUILDERS

The immediate descendants of this early band may be grouped as "the truss builders." Many of the earlier bridges were combination structures—a timber rib or ribs integrated with a truss, often of the lattice type. One may regard such a structure as a reversed form of the suspension cable and the stiffening truss, but one may also argue that the designer did not have sufficient faith in the truss alone as a supporting structure; he added to it the age-old and faithful arch. At any rate it was as the result of the labor of Ithiel Town (1784–1844), William Howe (1803–1852), the two Pratts, Thomas W. (1812–1875), M. ASCE, and his father Caleb, and their associates, that the truss emerged as a distinct, independent, and self-sufficient bridge form.   ·

However, it cannot be claimed that these men invented the truss. Some form of roof truss was undoubtedly used in the Greek temples of ancient times. Andrea Palladio, the Renaissance architect, had a very clear conception of truss action, and timber truss bridges had been built abroad for centuries; but it remained for an age in which the main structural material was timber and thus centered in frame construction, to start the truss bridge on a career of widespread use and continuous development that still goes forward today.

THE BIRTH OF THE TRANSPORTATION ERA

These early works were not parts of transportation routes but were built to meet local highway needs. The main impetus to the further development of American engineering came as a result of the movement of the American people westward—a migration and flow from the coastal colonies to the west which was not to end until the Pacific coast had been reached and the continent conquered. An outstanding and pioneer work of this second era was the Erie Canal (Fig. 2).[5]

The construction of the Erie Canal (1817–1825) was only one of at least three major bids made by the coast states to bring to the growing ports of Baltimore, Md., Philadelphia, and New York, N. Y., the economic advantages of trade with the newly awakening Ohio area. In this venture New York possessed topographic advantages which proved to be determining. The long stretch of 363 miles through the Mohawk Valley posed no such problems of rise and fall as those encountered by her southern competitors. The Erie was a vital factor in creating the Empire State and making New York the leading port of the nation.

Baltimore soon decided that the Chesapeake and Ohio Canal had a very slight chance of surmounting the Cumberland Gap. It never did. That city turned to the Baltimore and Ohio Railroad, which, begun on July 4, 1828, did not reach the Ohio River until 1853. On the other hand, Philadelphia, through a remarkable combination of canals and canalized rivers plus the famous Allegheny Portage Railroad, finally surmounted the Appalachian barrier and reached Pittsburgh,

[4] "Ancient and Modern Engineering and the Isthmian Canal," by William H. Burr, John Wiley & Sons, Inc., New York, N. Y., 1902, p. 77.
[5] "Memoir on the Completion of the New York Canals," by Cadwallader D. Colden, New York, N. Y., 1825.

Pa., in 1834. It was a relatively short-lived triumph, however, for 20 years later, the Pennsylvania Railroad took over.

The Erie Canal has been referred to as "the first American Engineering School," and the Baltimore and Ohio as "the first Railroad University." Among the pioneer builders who designed and directed these constructions were the chief engineers of the Erie Canal, Benjamin Wright (1770–1842) and James Geddes (1763–1838), products of frontier life in the Mohawk Valley, local surveyors, lawyers, and judges. Both had passed on before the ASCE was born. The chief engineer of the Baltimore and Ohio was Jonathan Knight (1787–1858), a Quaker surveyor, and his assistant was Lt.-Col. Stephen H. Long (1784–1864).

Among these great pioneer American works another Erie project deserves attention—"The Lion of Railways" as it was called. This great work—passing

FIG. 2.—LOCK, LOCK-KEEPER'S CABIN, AND CANALBOAT, ON THE ERIE CANAL (1817–1825)

through the southern tier counties of New York, 463 miles of forests—is usually recalled as the financial plaything of Daniel Drew, Jay Gould, and James Fisk. Actually begun in 1832, the Erie Railroad involved some of the most outstanding railroad construction of its day (Fig. 3) and was finally completed in 1851. A major group of American engineers played a part in the venture. Among others, William Wierman Wright, M. ASCE, was active in the early days, as were Horatio Allen and Julius W. Adams, Past-Presidents and Hon. Members, ASCE; and it was James P. Kirkwood, Past-President ASCE—later to pioneer in filtration work—who completed the famous Starrucca Viaduct (Fig. 4), at Lanesboro, Pa.

This was one of the few great American stone masonry structures in an age when timber was the usual material. Costing $320,000, it was said to have been the most expensive railroad structure of its day; it was designed and built by Kirkwood, after three earlier contractors had failed. An even later generation—George S. Morison (1842–1903), Past-President ASCE, and others—created new records on this notable line.

FIG. 3.—CASCADE ARCH ON THE ERIE RAILROAD

FIG. 4.—THE STARRUCCA VIADUCT AT LANESBORO, PA., 1848

Happily, the ASCE also claims as a member the man who probably was the outstanding American professional engineer of the mid-nineteenth century, John Bloomfield Jervis (1795–1885), Hon. M. ASCE, who began his career on the Erie Canal in 1817 (Fig. 5). He closed it 50 years later with the rehabilitation of the Pittsburgh, Fort Wayne, and Chicago Railway. What a remarkable career it was! He engineered the Delaware and Hudson Canal, incline and railroad; he built the first railroads in New York State, the Mohawk and Hudson and the Schenectady and Saratoga in 1830–1833; and he planned the enlargement of the Erie Canal and its Chenango extension. For New York City he put through the first Croton water supply, the first notable American gravity supply (1836–1842) with the famous High Bridge and the distributing reservoir, long a New York landmark located at the present site of the Public Library on Fifth Avenue and Forty-Second Street. Jervis was consulted on the Cochituate supply for Boston, Mass., and on the Hudson River Railroad. He toured Europe and stood with Robert Stephenson at the Straits of Menai in Wales when the remarkable tubes of the Menai Bridge were put in place. He worked on the Michigan Southern and Northern Indiana Railway in 1850–1851 and on the Chicago and Rock Island Railroad, and he pulled the Pittsburgh, Fort Wayne, and Chicago Railroad out of bankruptcy to a 10% dividend in a little more than 2 years.[6]

Canals, water supplies, and railroads thus enter the story. The Canal Era involved some most outstanding projects, and certainly the Delaware and Hudson Canal which Jervis directed was one of the most daring and courageous undertakings ever attempted under private sponsorship in the United States. The incline on this line, over the mountain from Honesdale, Pa., to Carbondale, Pa., was in the immediate charge of John H. McAlpine, whose son, William J., Hon. M. ASCE, was third President of the Society.

For the short haul from the foot of the incline to the canal Jervis sent young Allen to Great Britain to buy a locomotive. In 1829 Allen operated the "Stourbridge Lion"[7] on the Delaware and Hudson tracks, the first full-size locomotive to be used in the United States. Among the treasures of the Engineering Societies Library in New York City is a portfolio of drawings of some of Jervis' works which are of special interest in reflecting the practice of the day. In sharp contrast to the thousands of fully detailed dimensional plans covering a modern engineering work, these plans are mere general outline sketches. They recall an era when the details of a lock gate, for example, were left to the builder-craftsman with the brief requirement that the gate be fully, securely, and properly fitted, framed, and bolted.

In the water supply area it should be noted that Philadelphia was the pioneer American city. The famous Center Square pumping plant was built in 1801 under the direction of Benjamin Henry Latrobe, Sr. (1764–1820). This plant occupied the site of the present City Hall; its steam pumping engine was one of the earliest used in the United States. It soon proved inadequate, however; in fact, the urban water supply problem has been a continuous one from those early days to the present time. Thus, in 1819–1822, largely as the conception of Frederic Graff (1775–1847), the Fairmount Works at the falls of the Schuylkill

---

[6] "A Memoir of American Engineering," by John B. Jervis, *Transactions*, ASCE, Vol. VI, 1877, p. 39.

[7] "A Century of Progress in Civil Engineering," by J. K. Finch, *Civil Engineering*, September, 1952, p. 36.

River above the city were built. Louis Wernwag previously had built his record span 340-ft timber-trussed arch at this famous site in 1812. Graff's design was also a pumped supply driven by water wheels; but it was especially notable because cast-iron water mains were used here for the first time in the United States, instead of the older bored-log pipes.

FIG. 5.—JOHN BLOOMFIELD JERVIS, 1795–1885

Although Jervis' work was quite varied, the railroad soon came to dominate the picture. Following the pioneer federal construction of the Cumberland Road, the highway problem had been turned over to the states, and they in turn left it to local authorities. As a result, American roads were in about the same condition a century later when the call to rescue the farmer from the mud, plus the bicycle craze and the introduction of the motorcar, ushered in the modern High-way Era. The Canal Era likewise soon passed. Canals were not only slow and dependent on "open weather" but also limited by topographic and hydrological conditions.

The nineteenth century was predominantly a transportation century and in this field the railroad soon became supreme. The major American engineering triumphs of this era are primarily in railroad location and railroad bridges. This was the heyday of the civil engineer and the railroad was his outstanding concern. Indeed, even in the mechanical engineering of the day one looks to transportation for the outstanding developments—that is, to the locomotive, the steamboat, and the steamship. The Industrial Power Age was still to come.

THE AMERICAN RAILROAD BRIDGES

The timber bridge was generally a composite structure. Wrought iron was used not only for fastenings but also for some tension members. The Howe truss was particularly adapted to such construction. With the introduction of the all-metal bridge, the Pratt form, with outward sloping diagonals, proved more economical; it reduced the length of compression members to a minimum. Truss invention, therefore, did not stop with Town's design; the Pratt, Bollman, Fink, Whipple, Post, Long, and other new forms were added.

Another most important step leading to more economical design was the de-velopment of a rational method of truss analysis by Squire Whipple (1804–1888), Hon. M. ASCE, a farmer boy who, after graduation from college and earlier rail-road experience, published a pamphlet in 1847 on the stress analysis of the truss.

Another truss analyst was Herman Haupt (1817–1905) the resourceful bridge builder of the Civil War period of whom Abraham Lincoln remarked:

> "Gentlemen, I have witnessed the most remarkable structure that human eyes have ever rested upon. That man Haupt has built a bridge across Potomac Creek, about 400 feet long and 80 feet high, in nine days with common soldiers, over which loaded trains are running every hour, and, upon my word, there is nothing in it but bean poles and cornstacks."[8]

Haupt was also the first chief of the Hoosac Tunnel in Massachusetts, and an oil pipeline pioneer.

It now became possible to compute stresses, for assumed loads and proportion members accordingly. A modern era of bridge analysis and design was inaugurated.

The first metal bridges, however, also involved a combination of materials. In 1841 Whipple patented a bowstring truss with a cast-iron upper chord and wrought diagonals, and lower tie—a type which still survives on some of the older country roads. Albert Fink (1827–1897), Past-President ASCE, one of the German immigrants of 1848, invented his famous truss when he was working with Benjamin H. Latrobe, Jr. (1807–1878), who had succeeded Knight on the Baltimore and Ohio Railroad. His first bridge was that over the Monongahela at Fairmont, Va. (later W. Va.), built in 1852 with three 205-ft spans. It was the longest iron railroad bridge of its day. Although a through bridge, it was similar to the "suspension truss" introduced by Wendell Bollman (1814–1884).

---

[8] "A Century of Progress in Civil Engineering," by J. K. Finch, *Civil Engineering*, September, 1952, p. 38.

The chords and posts were of cast iron, the tension rods of wrought iron. Although the Fink truss has survived in the roof truss form, it has disappeared as a bridge structure, and the use of cast iron in bridges was even shorter lived. There were some startling failures, and it was but a few years before the all-wrought-iron bridge appeared.

Certainly one of the leading figures in the evolution of the American truss bridge was Jacob Hayes Linville (1825–1906), M. ASCE. A farmer boy and college graduate, Linville followed Haupt in 1863 as bridge engineer of the Pennsylvania Railroad. He wrote:

> "I went to Altoona with a young wife, with everything new to me. The bridges of the line were nearly all a wreck; I knew nothing of bridges and had at my disposal nothing but Haupt's old book, all wrong. Orders came in to build new iron bridges and I had to hustle, with many sleepless nights and days spent over old patterns and new plans involving many changes and improvements in the plans of the original cast iron chord, arch, and posts of the old Pratt type."

FIG. 6.—RAILROAD TRUSS BRIDGE BY JACOB H. LINVILLE, M. ASCE, 1872–1876

Actually the fault did not lie entirely with Haupt. Traffic was increasing rapidly, locomotive loads constantly growing, and older structures becoming obsolete. The pressure of increasing demands and sleepless nights became chronic with the railroad bridge engineers of the post-Civil War years when railroad building was expanding at an ever-increasing rate.

Linville had built the Arsenal Bridge over the Schuylkill River for the Pennsylvania Railroad in 1861 which established some of the standards he was to develop later. The old, brittle, and dangerous cast-iron posts were abandoned for compression members built up of wrought-iron plates and shapes, and the eyebar tension member appeared for practically the first time. In 1863 John W. Murphy introduced an all-wrought-iron truss, and a completely new era in American bridge building began.

Linville's first record-breaking span was that over the Ohio River at Steubenville, Ohio, in 1863–1864. Fink regained the lead in 1868–1870 with his Louisville, Ky., truss also over the Ohio (two spans, 360 ft and 390 ft); but then turned to the analysis of railroad operating costs, while Linville came back in 1872 with his Newport, Ky., and Cincinnati, Ohio, span of 420 ft to regain the record (Fig. 6). The standards that Linville developed, however, were far more important than his record truss spans. Modern steel shapes and built-up columns were originated in this wrought-iron era. Then in 1873 Louis G. F. Bouscaren (1840–1904), M. ASCE, was the first to use a series of concentrated loads simulating locomotive loadings in bridge design. Even earlier, in 1864, Andrew Carnegie had incorporated the Keystone Bridge Company, and Linville had become its consulting engineer. Between 1870 and 1875 the railroads abandoned their earlier design practice and began to buy bridges designed by these bridge companies under standard specifications. Bridge building became a problem of not only competitive bids but also competitive designs.

In this era also the typical American pin-connected truss became the dominating form of design. Theodore Cooper, M. ASCE, published his classic paper, "American Railroad Bridges," in which he estimated that 7,000 railroad trusses longer than 100 ft had been built in the United States by 1889—all of the pin-connected type.[9]

All this American preoccupation with built-up columns, eyebars, and pin-connected trusses, and with speed and ease of erection left British engineers not only cold but also skeptical. In the first place British construction took a different form. Great Britain had always been a shipbuilding nation and her metal bridges appear to have reflected this skill with, and interest in, shipbuilding techniques, in curved plates, and solidly riveted joints. An interesting paper, entitled "American Iron Bridges," discusses this controversy between the designers in the two countries.[10]

The famous Royal Albert Bridge over the Tamar River at Saltash in Cornwall, England (built by Isambard K. Brunel in 1859) was a two-span bowstring type in which the upper chord was a single huge tubular member $12\frac{1}{4}$ ft by 17 ft in cross section. Robert Stephenson's equally famous railroad bridge over the Menai Straits was a great box girder, so huge, in fact, that the train passed through the tube itself. Even as late as 1883–1890, when Sir John Fowler and Sir Benjamin Baker, Hon. M. ASCE, built one of the wonders of the modern world—the great Firth of Forth cantilever, in Scotland, with its two 1,710-ft spans—the huge compression members were laboriously built up in place, plate by plate in tubular form, still reflecting a ship or boiler type of construction (Fig. 7).[11]

The rectangular built-up column, of course, is still in use today; but time has demonstrated the wisdom of the British contention that pin-connected bridges are "loose jointed" and subject to excessive vibrations. They forced trains almost invariably to reduce speed, and the twentieth century has witnessed a change in American design to the fully-riveted joint. In their day, however, pin-connected joints made for rapid erection. Witness, for example, the replacement of the famous old timber trestle on the Erie, the Portage Viaduct (which was destroyed by fire in 1875), by Morison with a new iron structure in the unbelievably brief period of 6 weeks.

THE CANTILEVER BRIDGE

In basic principle the cantilever is undoubtedly very ancient but as a modern form of bridge it is less than a century old. Two of the world's greatest

---

[9] "American Railroad Bridges," by Theodore Cooper, *Transactions*, ASCE, Vol. XXI, 1889, p. 1.
[10] "American Iron Bridges," by Zerah Colburn, *Proceedings*, Inst. C. E., Vol. 22, 1862, p. 540.
[11] "The Forth Bridge in its Various Stages of Construction," by Philip Phillips, R. Grant and Son, Edinburgh, Scotland, 1885.

spans, the Firth of Forth (Fig. 7) and the Quebec, over the St. Lawrence in Canada, are cantilevers and have only been exceeded by modern highway suspension bridges, designed for lighter loads. Nevertheless, it is probably safe to state that the cantilever principle has had importance as a construction procedure equal to its importance as a bridge form.

One of the most obvious changes in American bridge construction during the past 50 or 60 years becomes evident when one compares earlier with more recent erection procedures. Arches and trusses are not self-suporting until completed and must, thus, be supported by falsework during erection. For example, when

FIG. 7.—FIRTH OF FORTH CANTILEVER BRIDGE, IN SCOTLAND, 1883–1890

the Washington arch over the Harlem River in New York City was built in 1888, a perfect forest of timber was used to support the girder ribs. Similarly, Morison's famous Cairo (Ill.) Bridge over the Ohio River involved two truss spans of 518.5 ft which had to be supported by falsework with the floor more than 100 ft above river level.

However, a remarkable record was made in the erection of this bridge. Upon completion of the falsework the first truss was erected in 6 days. The great timber bents and bracing were then taken down, the supporting piles were pulled from the river bed, driven again to support the reerected falsework for the second span, and 33 days later the second span was completed. Such great timber structures are no longer seen. Trusses are erected by cantilevering out to two or three supporting bents and great arches like the Hell Gate Bridge, in New York City, are erected using temporary backstays to permit cantilevering. Thus, although the cantilever bridge came into use primarily to carry railroads over long spans and deep water streams, where supporting falsework could not be used, the cantilever principle has revolutionized bridge construction.

Certainly one of the pioneers in the adoption of the cantilever bridge and cantilevered construction was Charles Shaler Smith (1836–1886), M. ASCE. In 1876 he built a bridge over the Kentucky River, at Dixville, Ky., but his most notable cantilever was erected for the Canadian Pacific Railroad over the St. Lawrence River at Lachine, Que., Canada. With side spans of 269 ft and two main spans of 408 ft it prefigured many of the modern highway structures. It was especially significant in that it was a continuous bridge, a single structure over five piers, and in its erection the foregoing modern methods were employed quite fully.

Not until the twentieth century were the advantages of continuity fully recognized. The advent of reinforced concrete has usually been credited for this important development which more probably originated, at least in the United States, as an evolution in cantilever construction. Continuous design seems to have been a natural outcome of cantilever evolution; and, in many spans of this type, the cantilever principle is so blended with the continuity element that only an expert can distinguish the structural functions. This combination plan characterized the famous Memphis (Tenn.) cantilever over the Mississippi River built by Morison, in 1892. Unfortunately it was an unsymmetrical structure—an anchor arm of 225 ft, two main cantilever arms with suspended span covering the channel in a 790-ft leap, and then two extraordinary 621-ft trusses built continuously over the common pier.

Incidentally, Morison's career is undoubtedly one of the most unusual in the annals of engineering. He was graduated from law school in 1863, practiced law with a famous firm in New York, disliked thoroughly the equivocal requirements of legal practice, turned to bridge work in 1867, and built ten bridges over the Missouri River, one over the Ohio River, and five over the Mississippi River—from law practice to a top-ranking bridge expert without any formal instruction. His first engineering work was with Octave Chanute (1832–1910), Past-President ASCE, who, turning in later life from railroad work to aviation, was probably the most important American pioneer in aerodynamics. Chanute was a supporter of the Wright brothers, Orville and Wilbur, who paid him high tribute.

The most prevalent type of cantilever bridge is probably better represented by such works as the bridge over the gorge of the Niagara River built under Charles Conrad Schneider (1843–1916), Past-President ASCE, in 1883. It marked another American erection record. Built in 33 weeks, it provided the familiar cantilever arms supporting a suspended span between them for a total of 470 ft. The Poughkeepsie (N. Y.) cantilever over the Hudson River, built about the same time (1889) of similar form, was particularly notable for its deep foundations built in timber caissons by the open-dredging process, and was one of the outstanding earlier examples of this type of construction.

Although John A. Roebling (1806–1869), M. ASCE, had built his famous double-deck suspension span at Niagara Falls, N. Y., in 1855, as a combined railroad and highway structure, it became evident that the relatively flexible character of suspensions did not suit them to the ever-increasing locomotive and train loads that were coming into use. Notable suspensions were built, of course, but the cantilever best met railroad needs and it largely dominated the long-span field until the beginning of the Highway Era with its lighter loads and even longer span requirements. It has been remarked, in fact, that most of the greater railroad spans were built before 1900 and that the task of the railroad bridge engineer then became that of replacing these earlier, often wrought-iron, structures with heavier steel constructions. Like all generalizations this requires qualification. Many notable cantilevers for both railroad and highway use have been built since 1900.

ARCHED BRIDGES

The stone arch bridge never achieved an important place in American practice. Henry G. Tyrell[12] estimated that, in 1885, there were less than sixty such arches in the world with spans longer than 120 ft and of these, twenty-seven were in France, thirteen in Italy, ten in Great Britain, two in Spain, two in Austria, and only one in the United States—The Cabin John (220-ft span) on the Washington (D. C.) aqueduct built by Gen. Montgomery Meigs, M. ASCE, in 1864. However, a brief revival of interest in the stone arch developed when William Brown, M. ASCE, then chief engineer, began about 1888 to replace some of the old bridges of the Pennsylvania Railroad with stone or concrete arches of solid-filled spandrel constructions. The spans were short, and permanence and full-speed operation were the objectives.

At the turn of the century the stone arch, of course, gave way to concrete; but, as in the case of its stone ancestor, American engineers did not lead in the development of concrete. Modern American concrete bridges have almost invariably been inspired by earlier European designs. In the evolution of steel arches, however, American engineers have long been active leaders.

Ead's famous arch over the Mississippi River at St. Louis, Mo., built in 1874 is generally regarded as the granddaddy of American metal arches. It was equally notable as a pioneer foundation and an erection undertaking and as one of the first American bridges in which steel was used, replacing in part (the ribs) the usual wrought iron. The story of this great bridge has been beautifully recorded by C. M. Woodward.[13] James Buchanan Eads (1820–1887), M. ASCE, not only put through this great work but also pioneered later in building the Mississippi jetties which cleared the South Pass and opened New Orleans, La., to sea-going shipping. Although of frail health, he was one of the most dynamic, forceful, bold, and determined personalities the civil engineering profession has ever produced. He gathered around him younger men of outstanding engineering abilities, among others Cooper, and it is said that these associates were largely responsible for the details of the projects he fathered and promoted.

The St. Louis arch involved three record arch spans, two 502 ft long, with a center leap of 520 ft. Of the two piers and two abutments, three were carried down to rock by the pneumatic process, the two easterly ones at depths of 115 ft and 136

[12] "History of Bridge Engineering," by Henry G. Tyrell, Chicago, Ill., 1911.
[13] "A History of the St. Louis Bridge," by C. M. Woodward, G. I. Jones & Co., St. Louis, Mo., 1881.

ft below high water. It was a record-breaking task, one that has since been equaled but never exceeded. However, in reading the story of the 600 "submarines," who labored below the river slowly excavating beneath the caissons, one notes that, in spite of the best medical advice of the day, almost every rule was broken. There were one hundred and nineteen cases of "the bends" (caisson disease) and fourteen deaths.

The arches themselves were unique. They were formed of iron tubes, each tube section, 12 ft in length, built up of six staves of chrome steel from $1\frac{7}{8}$ in. to $2\frac{1}{8}$ in. thick. The remainder of the structure was wrought iron. In erection, backstays were used to permit cantilevering out from the abutments, while a heavy skewback with cables supported the simultaneous erections outward from each pier. Eads' masterpiece, begun in 1868, was opened on July 4, 1874.

Among the later notable American arches was the Washington Bridge over the Harlem River in New York City, built by William R. Hutton, M. ASCE, in 1886–1889, with two, two-hinged girder ribs of 510 ft each. In 1896 L. L. Buck, M. ASCE, completed his arch over the much bridged Niagara Gorge, a spandrel-braced structure of a type widely used in later work, replacing Roebling's pioneer suspension with a 550-ft span. Then in 1898 the so-called Niagara-Clifton arch was built just below the Falls with a record span of 840 ft. It was the third bridge at this site, the original 1,260-ft suspension of 1868 having been blown down in 1889 and then rebuilt. Today a fourth span—Rainbow Arch[14]—occupies this site. The record-span American arches, however, were to come after the turn of the twentieth century.

SUSPENSION BRIDGES

The basic idea of suspension spans not only is very ancient but also has turned up among primitive people the world over. Apparently its more effective development waited on the provision of suitable and reasonably permanent material for cables. When wrought iron was produced in reasonably large quantities (that is, as a construction material) in the late eighteenth century, the modern suspension bridge was born.

It seems clear that it was James Finley (1762–1828) of Fayette County, Pennsylvania, who was the first to bring this type of structure forward (Fig. 8). He wrote:

> "In the year 1801, I erected the first bridge of this construction on the turnpike between Uniontown and Greensburg, Pa., in a contract * * * to build a bridge of 70 ft span, $12\frac{1}{2}$ ft wide, and warranted it for 50 years [all but flooring] for the consideration of $600. Nothing further of the kind was attempted for six years. The exclusive right was secured by patent in 1808."

In Fig. 8, the reproduction of an old print, is shown the construction advocated by Finley. The substantial railing, built up with continuous chords of wood plank, constituted a very effective stiffening truss, which later developed into an important and fundamental detail of suspension bridge design. By 1810 some six Finley bridges had been erected in the United States. The British suspension pioneer was Capt. Sir Samuel Brown (1776–1852) who patented a chain suspension in 1817.

---

[14] "Rainbow Arch Bridge Over Niagara Gorge: A Symposium," *Transactions*, ASCE, Vol. 110, 1945, p. 1.

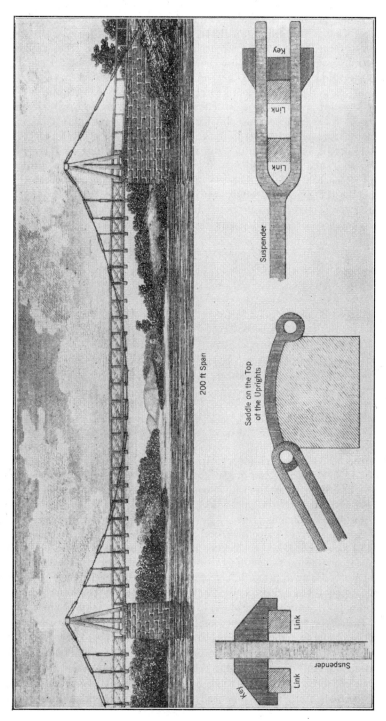

Fig. 8.—The Chain Bridge, by James Finley

The cables of these early works were formed of wrought-iron chain using long links. Thomas Telford (1757–1834), pioneer British road and bridge builder, in the record-breaking (579-ft) Menai suspension bridge of 1826, used cables composed of groups of wrought-iron bars each of which was welded end to end to form a continuous cable. The next improvement was French in origin. Louis J. Vicat (1786–1861) in his Argental Bridge of 1830 developed both the wire cable and the so-called spinning process of erection, and the modern wire suspension was born. A Swiss engineer, Joseph Chally, established a record (810 ft) in 1834 at Fribourg, Switzerland; but, in 1851, the American wire cable pioneer, Col. Charles Ellet, Jr., built a span of 1,010 ft over the Ohio River at Wheeling, Va. (later W. Va.), and the United States has since held the records for great spans (Fig. 9). This bridge failed because of a twisting undulatory motion of the Tacoma (Wash.) type, in a windstorm in 1854.

Among the American pioneers Roebling, who had built some smaller suspensions, notably those used to carry the wooden troughs of canals over valleys,

FIG. 9.—THE SUSPENSION SPAN AT WHEELING, VA. (LATER W. VA.), BY COL. CHARLES ELLET, JR.

became the leader in suspension construction with his bridge over the Niagara Gorge in 1855. This was one of the great earlier triumphs of American bridge building. Crossing the gorge with a span of 825 ft, this "double-deck" work supported a railroad on the upper deck and highway traffic on the lower deck of the substantial stiffening truss.

The early history of suspension bridges is notable for the many failures that occurred, but Roebling was sufficiently farsighted and appreciative of the basic problems of suspension bridge design to escape the disasters that overtook other early workers. Finley appears to have conceived the suspension as a combination structure—that is, as a light truss supported by hangers from the cables. No wind action ever disturbed any of his bridges. His plan was not followed by Sir Samuel Brown, or by Telford, Ellet, or the other early builders, however. Their bridges were simply light suspended timber platforms possessing little if any longitudinal stiffness. The loads for which they provided were relatively light, and a stiffening truss for distributing these loads was unimportant. Its function in preventing distortion due to wind, however, seems to have been ignored or not appreciated. As a result practically all their bridges either failed or were badly damaged through exactly the same type of wind undulations that were, years later, to wreck the Tacoma Narrows Bridge. One of Brown's bridges lasted only 6 months. Telford's bridge exhibited the same undulations within a month after completion, performed again in 1836, and, in 1839, the platform roadways were badly damaged. As stated, Ellet's Wheeling bridge (Fig. 9) was almost completely wrecked in 1854, and there were other notable failures, including that of a remarkable 1,260-ft span at Niagara just below the Falls, built by Samuel Keefer, M. ASCE, in 1869—14 years after Roebling's famous work farther down the Gorge.

Roebling, however, faced the problem of heavier loads, for he advocated and

FIG. 10.—SUSPENSION BRIDGE ACROSS NIAGARA GORGE, BY JOHN A. ROEBLING, M. ASCE, 1855

built suspension bridges for railroad service, and also seems to have been particularly concerned with the dangers of oscillations caused by wind. The two decks of his Niagara span were supported on the top and bottom chords of a substantial timber truss. In addition, guy cables (Fig. 10) extended down to the side of the gorge providing "hold-down' ties against any possible wind action. When his Brooklyn Bridge in New York City was built in 1883 four trusses were used to support and distribute the interurban train loads; and, although clearance requirements did not permit tie-down cables, he used the diagonal stays from the towers, "storm cables" as he called them (Fig. 11), which are a notable characteristic of this famous structure.

Although the suspension bridge proved too flexible for ever-increasing locomotive loads (Roebling's Niagara Bridge being replaced with an arch in 1899), it

---

was developed for interurban use and thus became a combination structure, a suspended truss. Then, with the modern demand for longer spans for relatively light highway loads, a new era of suspension bridge building was inaugurated. The stiffening truss became less important as a load-distributing element, the platform type of design again appeared, and the Tacoma failure of 1940 repeated the earlier experiences of Brown, Telford, Ellet, and their followers. The rise and decline of the stiffening truss thus brought modern engineers face to face with an aerodynamic problem which had not been solved at the time it first appeared a century ago.

FIG. 11.—BROOKLYN BRIDGE AND THE SKY LINE OF LOWER MANHATTAN IN NEW YORK, N. Y.

STEEL AND FOUNDATIONS

Steel was used at St. Louis, and steel rails had been rolled and used as early as 1865; but not until 1879 was the first American all-steel bridge erected. The United States had lagged behind Great Britain in the production of iron and did not pass her until after 1890. Andrew Carnegie, Henry C. Frick, and others initiated the American steel industry about the time of the Panic of 1873. This led, in 1901, to the formation of the first $1,000,000,000 corporation in the United States—the United States Steel Company—and a real Steel Era began.

The first American bridge venture in this new metal was on the Chicago, Alton, and St. Louis Railroad over the Missouri River at Glasgow, Mo., about 100 miles east of Kansas City, Mo. There were five truss spans of about 314 ft each. The chief engineer was Gen. William Sooy Smith (1830–1916), M. ASCE, who insisted in his not being confused with his son and rival, Charles Sooysmith, M. ASCE.

In addition to this "first," the General also pioneered in the introduction of the pneumatic process in the United States.

The history of foundation methods is one of the most fascinating and important in the annals of engineering. The best the great French bridge engineers of the eighteenth century could do was to reach a depth of perhaps 10 ft or 12 ft below water level, limited as they were to open cofferdams and hand and water-driven pumps. In 1805 Palmer had established a record of 41 ft in sinking the west pier of his Permanent Bridge at Philadelphia. The modern record was that reached with an open-steel sheet-pile cofferdam at the west pier of the George Washington Bridge over the Hudson River (New York City) in 1930—with a depth of rock varying from 60 ft to 80 ft below water level.

For greater depths the so-called open-dredging method, such as was used at Poughkeepsie and especially for the Hawkesbury Bridge in Australia, was employed. The invention of the pneumatic process by an eccentric and colorful British admiral, Thomas Cochrane, Earl of Dundonald, in 1830, opened a new era in foundation engineering. In Great Britain, Sir William Cubitt used compressed air in his Rochester Bridge in 1851, and in 1859 the younger Brunel (Isambard K.) used the process in closing out the bottoms of the cofferdams for his Saltash Bridge. In the Kiel Railroad Bridge in Germany (during the same period) some improvements were made in the process, and French engineers added to this specialized technique. Nevertheless Sooy Smith deserves to be numbered among these pioneers, for he began a bridge at Savannah, Ga., over the Savannah River on the Charlestown and Savannah Railroad in 1859 using "pneumatic piles" of a type previously proposed by Alexander Holstrom.[15] Therefore, the method was well developed when Eads adopted it at St. Louis; but he proposed to use it—and did so—for previously unheard-of depths.

In later years the rise of the American "skyscraper" was to owe much to the pneumatic process permitting adequate foundations under tall buildings; but in still more recent years other methods have been adopted wherever possible to avoid the high cost of pneumatic work occasioned by the extreme precautions now enforced to protect the worker from caisson disease.

THE ERA OF RAILROAD STRATEGY

The bridge development outlined in this paper was almost entirely stimulated and made possible by railroad expansion. The story of the growth of American railroads, therefore, is a major part of nineteenth century engineering. The first phase of railroad history in the United States is largely characterized by the building of isolated local lines between existing centers of traffic. In the second phase many of these lines were joined together to form major lines or systems. The New York Central System, for example, was formed by the consolidation of the Hudson River Railroad with several unconnected links in the Mohawk Valley to reach from New York to Buffalo, N. Y. Then the Lake Shore and Michigan Southern Railroad was added, and Chicago, Ill., became the western terminal.

In this second consolidation phase there were not only inevitable clashes for the control of this or that route but competitive efforts to break into the terri-

---

[15] "Pneumatic Foundations," by William Sooy Smith, *Transactions*, ASCE, Vol. II, 1873, p. 411.

tory of other lines—such as the struggle between the "Central" and the "Pennsylvania." Beginning over the control of the West Shore Railroad by the Pennsylvania Railroad, this struggle resulted in the "Central" entering Pennsylvania Railroad territory by building the structures which, in the past few years, have finally found use as part of the Pennsylvania Turnpike. Similarly, the battle which Gould waged to secure an entrance into Pittsburgh was typical of the latter stage of this era of eastern railroad strategy; but the center of interest was turning west.

Some long lines had been almost entirely completed as a unit—such as the Pennsylvania and the Erie railroads—and, by the time of the Civil War, when a new horizon had opened in the far west, both northern and southern interests struggled to secure the mid-continent connection of a projected Pacific railroad.

The outcome of the war ended the controversy; but, when President Lincoln was called upon to settle the question of the eastern terminus of the Pacific railroad he decided on Omaha, Nebr.—miles ahead of the eastern roads which were building west—and the first to reach this frontier town was destined to join up this first Pacific route.

William Barclay Parsons (1859–1932), Hon. M. ASCE, wrote a stirring statement[16] regarding the building of the Union and Central Pacific railroads, which, meeting at Promontory, Utah, at the north of Great Salt Lake in 1869, first opened the continent by rail:

> "Although in the building of these lines there was not a single piece of spectacular or outstanding designing, and nothing worthy of describing in text books on engineering, except the discovery of the most favorable pass crossing the Rocky Mountains, nevertheless, in their entirety they stand unsurpassed in the art of construction. Here was a railway projected before the Civil War began and completed soon after it was ended, extending westward from a sparse agricultural settlement on the Missouri River to the mining camps of the Pacific Coast. The intervening 1,500 miles were almost a *Terra incognita* * * * . To do the planning, to gather the materials, and to carry such an enterprise to successful completion demanded an extraordinary combination of vision, executive ability, technical skill, unflagging enthusiasm, and indomitable courage, and the result was not merely the laying out of a railway but the making of an empire. What calling can point to a single act of comparable achievement?"

In the East, the railroad problem became largely one of economical and effective operation of consolidated lines; but the Union Pacific opened a new era of romantic railroad building in the West, which did not end until after the turn of the twentieth century and in which many outstanding engineers of the period participated.

Fink, the truss inventor, was one of the first to undertake the study of operating economics. His careful analysis of the operating expenses of the Louisville and Nashville Railroad was published in 1873–1874 under the title, "The Cost of Railroad Transportation." However, it is Arthur M. Wellington (1847–1895), M. ASCE, who usually comes to mind in this connection, for his earlier studies

---

[16] "Engineering and Economics," by William Barclay Parsons, address at inaugural meeting of Columbia Univ. Student Chapter, ASCE, November 3, 1927, pp. 7–8.

(1877–1887) were finally expanded into a huge volume, "The Economics of Railroad Location," which many older engineers recall as a formidable text of student days.

Wellington pointed out that, whereas, the ill-designed bridge fell down and the bunglers' bungling was thus revealed and evident to everyone, the weaknesses of a poorly planned railroad—its sins of location, bad grades, and other factors affecting operating costs and income—are so hidden that it fails through "* * * a gentle but unceasing ooze from every pore which attracts no attention." He also phrased that famous definition of the engineer as "* * * a man who can do that well with one dollar which any bungler can do with two after a fashion." The creation of the Interstate Commerce Commission (ICC) in 1887 (in the public interest of fair play and the elimination of rate discrimination) put an end, not to the principles that Wellington so forcefully championed, but to the premises on which his applications of these principles in railroad work were based. His operating analyses were adopted by the ICC, but the railroads were caught between the millstones of government regulation and union domination. Although they are still the arteries through which the economic lifeblood of the nation flows, they face a situation today that is completely different from that of "the Era of Railroad Strategy."

In the western field one, among the many names that should be noted, is that of John F. Stevens (1853–1943), Past-President and Hon. M. ASCE. Edward H. Harriman had undertaken a courageous and farsighted task in improving the operating qualities of the Southern Pacific Railroad by changes in grade and alinement, in anticipation of securing greater traffic revenue thereby. However, he then sought control of the Union Pacific and, when attacked by James J. Hill, F. ASCE, carried the battle into Hill's camp—the Northern Pacific. The famous Northern Pacific "corner" on the New York Stock Exchange in 1901 finally led to a compromise.

Stevens was chief locating engineer for Hill in these romantic days when opposing forces used tactics approaching open warfare. It was Stevens who discovered Marias Pass where the Northern Pacific crosses the Rocky Mountain divide and where his statue stands today. Later he was to put the Panama Canal on its way to completion and, as President Theodore Roosevelt put it, "* * * get the dirt flying * * *"; but he was first of all a railroad man, a true leader of men, who, through sheer determination and force of character, accomplished the seemingly impossible.

William Van Horne (1843–1915), another similar forceful personality—a product of the same school—followed Sir Sandford Fleming (1827–1915), M. ASCE, "The Father of Canadian Engineers," in putting through the Canadian Pacific, the "Canadian Railroad University" as it has been called. This triumph brought Van Horne honorary knighthood.

This romantic era of railroad expansion and building has passed; the great railroads of the United States have been built; but the generation that built them produced some of the greatest American engineers, if not indeed the greatest in the history of the profession. They were leaders of men in the full sense of the title.

WATER SUPPLY AND SANITATION

Some notable earlier water supplies have been mentioned—Philadelphia, New York, and Boston—but the United States lagged badly in this field. Perhaps a preoccupation with railroads led the nation to neglect its urban problems. As late as 1840 four out of five American workers, it is true, were still on the farms of the country, but cities and towns were growing rapidly. By 1900 three out of five people were engaged in other, presumably urban, pursuits. However, whereas there were some seventeen American cities that had at least some type of water supply in 1800, in 70 years this had grown only to 243. Then in the decade between 1870–1880 there was a sudden spurt. The number doubled only to redouble in the next 5 years and again in the next 5 years, so that, by 1896, there were 3,196 city supplies.

This rapid growth in the closing years of the nineteenth century has been half-jestingly attributed to the activities of pump salesmen. There is probably an element of truth in the story. Many American cities and towns were supplied from streams or wells, and thus the supply required pumping. Many of these works originated as private ventures. About 1870 Birdsell Holly of Lockport, N. Y., a builder of pumping engines, began a canvass of towns that had no supplies and inaugurated a plan of organizing pumping companies. By 1880 some 51% of American supplies were privately owned and by 1890 this had increased to 57%. In fact even some of the larger cities, like San Francisco, Calif., were supplied by such private companies until well into the twentieth century.

In one respect at least (quantity), these American supplies far surpassed European practice. There was no American experience on which to base consumption estimates when the original Croton supply for New York City was projected. A liberal European, British unit of 22 gal per capita per day was assumed. Not only did it prove to be inadequate, but population growth soon made it necessary to force the Croton aqueduct to operate in part as a pressure conduit. Alfred W. Craven (1810–1879), Past-President ASCE (in whose office ASCE was formed), had the unenviable task, as chief engineer of the Croton Aqueduct, of trying to meet these increasing demands from 1849 to 1868. In fact, not until the late 1880's was a new aqueduct put in service, and not until 1907 had the possibilities of the Croton watershed been exhausted with the construction of the storage of the "New" Croton or Quaker Bridge Dam.

This new Croton aqueduct was a bold and epoch-marking venture. Older practice had favored cut-and-cover construction following a winding grade contour, a plan that dates from the aqueducts of ancient Rome. The New Croton, on the other hand, was practically a straight 32-mile grade tunnel. It came to ground level only where it crossed depressions. Many men, familiar as earlier members of the Metropolitan Section, ASCE, were connected with this Croton development—Isaac Newton, M. ASCE, E. S. Chesbrough (1813–1886), Past-President ASCE, Benjamin S. Church, Adams (1812–1899), and others.

Similar problems of seeking ever-greater supplies to meet mounting needs in a nation where the slogan was that water should be as free as air, perplexed the people of other cities in increasing numbers—Boston (in 1873–1879 and again in 1895–1904), Baltimore, Rochester, N. Y., and many others. Cities on the Great Lakes turned to supplies pumped from these inexhaustible sources; others, like

St. Louis drew on river supplies. In far away Australia the Coolgardie, a famous pipeline of 1898–1903, deserves mention for it predated the Colorado River–Los Angeles (California) supply of a later day. It was 351 miles long, and the water was raised 1,290 ft by eight pumping stations.

It was about 1863 that a railroad engineer, Kirkwood (1807–1877), was literally forced to give up his railroad career and undertake the solution of the water supply problem of Brooklyn, N. Y. In 1865 he was called to Cincinnati and the next year to St. Louis. Here the Mississippi provided an abundant but turbid supply, and filtration was obviously needed to remove suspended matter. (There is an amusing story attributed to Mark Twain to the effect that one can distinguish a Mississippi Valley dweller from an Easterner by merely giving him a glass of turbid water. The Easterner allows it to settle. The Mississippian stirs it up "to get the full value" before drinking it.) Kirkwood was sent to Europe to study the plants that had been built there; and, as a result, he published a report in 1869 that became an American classic.[17] It describes seven British, six French, three German, and two Italian works. Another pioneer undertaking of this period was the establishment of the Lawrence Experiment Station by the State Board of Health of Massachusetts in 1887.

Robert Koch, discover of the cholera bacillus in 1883, had turned his attention to water-borne diseases; but the spread of typhoid was still not fully understood as late as 1900—or, at least, public opinion had not been sufficiently aroused to remedy unsanitary conditions. Towns pumped their supplies from streams polluted by the sewage of towns higher up. Lake cities not only drew their supplies from the lake but discharged their sewage into this convenient catch-all. With the turn of the century typhoid epidemics became common occurrences and attention turned from the use of filtration to remove solids to its development as a bacteria-removing device.

In 1900 Allen Hazen (1869–1930), M. ASCE, published his treatise on "The Filtration of Public Water-Supplies," and a number of larger cities turned to the construction of extensive filtration plants of high bacterial efficiency. Then about the time of World War I, the fact that bacteria could be killed by the injection of a few parts per million of chlorine into the water was discovered. Today almost all American supplies are so treated and the art of filtration seems to have been abandoned, even in some cases where its original purpose—the physical improvement of the supply—seems desirable. It was estimated in 1925 that in about one third of cities with 2,500 and more people the supply was filtered while in two thirds of the cities it was simply disinfected.

The battle to secure adequate sewage facilities in cities was likewise fought against public apathy and indifference. Even Paris, France, more or less adequately supplied with storm drains, relied largely on cesspools for sewage until 1880. Undoubtedly the cholera epidemics—Paris in 1832 and London, England, in 1832, 1849, and 1854—were a potent force in attracting adequate attention to this problem of preventing the pollution of the subsoil of cities. The pioneers in this movement in Europe were M. F. E. Belgrand in Paris, and William Haywood and Sir Joseph W. Bazalgette in London, the latter owing much to the support

---

[17] "Report on the Filtration of River Waters for the Supply of Cities As Practiced in Europe," by J. P. Kirkwood, D. Van Nostrand Co., New York, N. Y., 1869.

of a pioneer of public health, Sir Robert Rawlinson. Another British engineer, William Lindley, who has been called the "Father of Municipal Engineering," had worked even earlier in Germany at Hamburg in the 1860's and 1870's.

In this awakening to one of the major problems of urban life American engineers played a parallel part. It has been stated that "The first application of engineering skill to the design of sewers * * * was in 1857" when Adams prepared plans for Brooklyn. He struggled with this problem while Kirkwood was busy with the water supply. Chesbrough worked at Boston but is generally regarded as the father of Chicago's water supply and sewage system. Joel H. Shedd (1834–1915), M. ASCE, who worked at Providence, R. I., was another founder of American sanitary engineering.

In general the Americans followed European practice providing for storm flow and sewage in one "combined system"; but, as the century came to a close, the battle between the advocates of a separate system and the supporters of the combined system occupied the center of the sanitary stage. That colorful figure, Col. George E. Waring (1833–1898), whose force of "white wings" swept the streets of New York City, was a staunch supporter of the separate system. The major argument was largely economic—separate sewers could be smaller and cost less—and would appeal to cleanliness, thus leaving the problem of storm drains for later solution. Since both had to be provided ultimately, this earlier bitter battle, apparently, has long been forgotten.

In construction, concrete came into use as early as 1885 and modern standards of sewer design were quite fully developed by the end of the century. On the other hand, disposal in these earlier days was generally regarded merely as a matter of dilution in a nearby watercourse. With the turn of the century it was becoming clearer that there were limits to this practice and the sewage treatment problem began to receive some attention.

IRRIGATION

Although relatively little has been written about American irrigation until the movement that resulted in the establishment of the Bureau of Reclamation of the United States Department of the Interior (USBR), in 1902, the great bulk of American works had been constructed before this time by private companies, especially by cooperative and district organizations.

It has been claimed that "the classic land of modern irrigation" is the great plain of the Po River in northern Italy. Works here go back as early as the twelfth century. One of the major Italian undertakings of the nineteenth century was the Canal de Cavour (1862–1869); but the greatest of all irrigation works were those of British colonial engineers in India and, later, in Egypt. Sir Arthur T. Cotton proposed the earliest of these modern works and, among many others, Col. Sir Proby T. Cautley should also be noted. The projects that brought millions of India's acres into cultivation began in the 1830's with the earlier delta works, reached a new level in the 1860's with the great valley systems, and have been continued down to the present day. In boldness of conception and scope, they had no parallel until the USBR began its great construction program of the twentieth century.

Irrigation projects in the United States in the nineteenth century can claim no such honors as these great British undertakings in India and Egypt; yet, from a few thousand acres irrigated in 1850 there was an increase to about 1,000,-000 acres by 1880 and to 9,000,000 acres by 1900. In spite of this significant increase, with very few exceptions the undertakings were unspectacular, and few indeed were ever recorded in technical literature. They were not government sponsored but rather resulted from the efforts of small groups, almost invariably very limited in funds and unable to undertake costly and expensive construction. However, by 1902, when the USBR was organized, practically all the more easily constructed and less costly projects had been developed.

Certainly the Mormons were one of the pioneer groups to undertake irrigation when they settled in the Salt Lake area of Utah in 1847. Between 1870 and 1880 several cooperative colonization projects, notably that of the Greeleyites in northern Colorado, were quite successful. In 1880 a young Canadian engineer, George Chaffey (1848–1928) initiated a similar undertaking at Etiwanda and Ontario near Los Angeles, then a Mexican town of perhaps 12,000 population. In 1886 Chaffey and his brother went to Australia but the colonies they started were taken from them, and George Chaffey returned to his greatest work, the Imperial Valley Project in Southern California. He was misunderstood and bitterly attacked later by President Theodore Roosevelt while the risky ventures of later workers in 1905 led to the famous disaster which diverted the Colorado River into the Salton Sink (below sea level) and, until the Southern Pacific Railway came to the rescue, threatened to submerge most of the valley. The career of a notable irrigation pioneer was thus frustrated.

It seems clear that few irrigation projects have been successful unless they have been cooperative ventures springing from the needs of established settlers or unless some plan of colonization has been part of the project. The settlement of new land is a gradual process, returns come slowly, and seldom do pioneers have the initial resources to carry heavy irrigation costs. In the earlier western ventures temporary types of low-cost construction were used—timber headworks, drops, and flumes—so as not to burden growing and relatively feeble undertakings unduly. The writer recalls brush dams, for example, which washed out annually but which could be rebuilt in a few days with farm labor at little cost, whereas the interest on a permanent structure not only would be many times greater but would have to be met in "hard money." At best, irrigation projects were risky ventures. Many failed, many were burdened with unreasonable interest charges; yet, through individual effort, partnerships, cooperative associations, irrigation districts, and commercial organizations nearly 90% of American irrigation works have been built.

The later projects left for redevelopment by the USBR have been far more extensive and costly. The construction has been of a permanent type and settlement has been open to the public, with the result that these works—notable and record breaking as they may have been—almost without exception, have usually failed to return even moderate interest charges on the large investments involved.

A Notable Half Century

In summarizing these first 50 or more years of a century of American civil engineering two major characteristics are evident. In the first place, there was the dominant position which "railroading" had played in directing engineering interests, coupled with the monopoly position the railroads occupied in the transportation field. The young man entering the civil engineering profession in these earlier years almost invariably began as a railroad man. It is difficult, in fact, to name a single outstanding civil engineer before the turn of the century who had not had at least some railroad experience. Similarly, for many—probably the majority —of communities the railroad was the only means of communication with the outside world. Many Americans lived and died without ever having traveled but a few miles from their birthplace. It was indeed an era not only when the railroad was king but when it was the sole effective means of transportation.

However, it was also an era of individual initiative and of local community cooperation. The dominating men in the demand for engineering services almost invariably comprised small groups of private investors or promoters bent on exploiting the resources of a continent of unparalleled natural resources and golden opportunity. It was an age in which the needs of an urban community life were met, often reluctantly, by purely local, cooperative effort. Town or city dwellers were forced to cooperate to meet pressing commuity needs. Neither the state nor the Federal Government played any important part in fathering the public works of the nineteenth century.

The changes which the next half century were to witness in American life and in American civil engineering (Part II) were to be little short of revolutionary.

PART II. THE PAST FIFTY YEARS

An Engineering Age

The past half century in the United States has been characterized by a spread and integration of engineering products and methods throughout American life from the city to the farm and from the home to the factory. There have been created a completely new economy and new culture. On the one hand, the discoveries and, especially, the methods of modern science have greatly added to, strengthened, and extended the scope and power of engineering practice. An ancient art has been transformed in many of its technical procedures from a purely empirical, qualitative practice into a far more certain and exact quantitative science. Both bigger and better engineering works have been made possible. However, above all, Americans have come to rely on engineering in its new and widened scope for the basic essentials that make modern life possible. The western world has become dependent as never before in human history on continued scientific and engineering progress for its very existence.

In attempting to trace this remarkable change, engineers are apt to focus attention on the outstanding developments and effect of the sister engineering professions—on the notable advances in power and mechanical engineering; on the rise of electrical engineering; and on the contributions of the mining and metallurgical and of the newly born chemical engineers. It has been only in the past half century that the possibilities of an age of mechanical power have been more fully realized.[18] As late as 1903 Morison, whose bridge building triumphs have been noted in Part I, published a masterly essay, under the title "The New Epoch," in which he outlined some then unrealized engineering potentialities, especially of what he referred to as "the manufacture of power."

After more than a century of the steam engine, manufactured power was providing in 1900 on an average but two silent slaves to relieve the men, women, and children of the country of part of the physical burdens of life. In the past half century this has increased more than fiftyfold while the average modern industrial worker has at his command the labors of more than 100 mechanical or electrical men. The gasoline engine and, in industry, the electrical utilization of power have increased man's productive power many times and have revolutionized life not only in the factory but in the farm and in the home.

Similarly, metallurgical and, especially, chemical advances—the latter stemming from the discovery during World War I that the United States was dependent on Germany for many of the essential chemicals of modern life—have brought new products and new materials undreamed of 50 years ago.

Nevertheless all this notable progress in these other engineering branches has by no means eclipsed the advances which have taken place in civil engineering itself. In fact, they have created new opportunities for service and added greatly to the power of the civil engineer. It was a mechanical invention, the steam locomotive, for example, which, little more than a century ago, created the railroad era and provided the American civil engineer with his major employment throughout the nineteenth century. Another mechanical invention, the motorcar, 50 years ago ushered in the Highway Era, the problems of which today constitute a major area of civil engineering practice. Similarly improved materials—steel and cement, for example—have made possible new structural triumphs

---

[18] "The New Epoch," by George S. Morison, Houghton, Mifflin & Co., Boston and New York, 1903.

whereas the mechanization of construction equipment has made possible projects of a scale far beyond the dreams of earlier workers.

However, there have also been other, fundamental changes in this past half century that have vitally affected civil engineering practice, notably in the character of the civil engineer's clients.

On the one hand, continued urban development has resulted in ever-increasing need for municipal public works—water supplies, better provisions for sanitation, rapid transit, bridges, tunnels, and highways. On the other hand, the Highway Era has forced the states, long relatively inactive, engineeringly speaking, to take up the burden of highway planning and building. At the same time, beginning with the turn of the century, the Federal Government, which had long confined its construction activities to the domain of interstate and foreign commerce—rivers, harbors, and waterways—embarked not only on such national ventures as the Panama Canal but on the reclamation of public lands by irrigation and on a host of flood-control and other projects far beyond the financial capacity of the private enterprise of earlier days to undertake. In short, civil engineering, from a practice largely concentrated in private undertakings and municipal improvements, has been expanded not only to state but to national service.

Thus, the United States of today is vastly different from that of 1900. It is a country which all branches of the engineering profession have been instrumental in creating and which relies to a vital degree on engineering services and continued engineering progress for its existence and future development.[19]

Paralleling these changes in the material life, broadening as the potentialities of this Engineering Age have been more fully understood, a radical change has occurred in the public viewpoint and attitude toward the role of engineering and engineered industry in modern life. The era when a few forceful men—Carnegies or Rockefellers—were free to exploit natural resources and technological advances in their own interests has given way to the impersonal modern business or industrial corporation, to the conservation of resources in a wider public interest, and to engineering brought to the service of all people. There has, in short, been a complete change in the economic and social thinking and environment which conditions engineering activities.[20]

Before considering a few of the notable civil engineering works of the twentieth century, therefore, some of these more general changes and advances should be discussed—improved techniques in design, changes in materials, and construction methods, the demands of the Highway Era—which have affected the engineering profession as a whole.

SCIENCE VERSUS EMPIRICISM

It seems desirable to begin with a note on a change in engineering techniques which, although it began shortly before the ASCE was founded a century ago, has been especially characteristic of technical progress in all branches of engineering in the past half century. In fact, to the scientific mind and, to a lesser

---

[19] "Engineering and Western Civilization," by J. K. Finch, McGraw-Hill Book Co., Inc., New York, N. Y., 1951.
[20] "The Big Change, America Transforms Itself," by Frederick L. Allen, Harper & Bros., New York, N. Y., 1952.

degree to many engineering teachers, the so-called "wedding" of science and engineering which took place about 100 years ago not only has marked an outstanding change in engineering practice but has created modern engineering. Indeed, in the popular mind engineering has come to be regarded as merely an application of science, an applied science. Actually, although it is true that some discoveries of natural science have led to almost immediate inventions in engineering, it has been through scientific contributions to the rationalization of engineering techniques that science has played its most important role in modern engineering development.

Thus, few of the structures which the engineer employs today have been the result of scientific discovery. Engineers knew and used the beam, the arch, and the truss for centuries before modern science was born. The steam engine, the steamboat, and the locomotive all preceded the advent of the modern theory of heat—in fact, the search for a better understanding of these devices was a major incentive to scientific progress. Similarly, today, the science of aerodynamics followed the Wrights' invention of the airplane. However, without exception all these as well as a host of other products, processes, and methods have been vastly improved—a better result achieved at less cost—through the application of the scientific method in their study, analysis, and design.

Every practical art contains the germs of a practical science. In its earlier days engineering design was based solely on an intuitive "feeling for structure," a structural judgment ripened through apprenticeship and actual experience in construction. More exact understandings slowly replaced some of this earlier empiricism. French workers of the late eighteenth and early nineteenth centuries gave special attention to the development of more fully rationalized and more fully quantitative techniques, as opposed to purely qualitative ones. British engineers in the years just before the founding of the ASCE did much to give these studies a more practical, useful form—to bridge the gap between theory and practice. Nevertheless, it is difficult for the modern engineer to realize that even simple beams were selected solely on a basis of judgment and experience until some 10 or 12 years before ASCE was born. Indeed it was Whipple who in 1847 wrote, as has been noted, the first textbook on the analysis of trusses.

However, American engineers made relatively few contributions in the earlier years of this movement. The first and most obvious result of such more exact knowledge is a saving in materials—each part of a bridge, for example, can be proportioned to its load and overdesign is avoided. Such savings are seldom possible except at a greater expenditure of labor in fabrication and construction. With material plentiful and relatively cheap but with skilled labor very costly, such refinements in design were overshadowed in the United States by the requirements of rapid and easy construction.

On the other hand, these conditions were reversed in Europe; and, furthermore, the general attitude in foreign lands favored a high degree of finish. As a result, European engineers turned to the more refined type of analysis and design whereas American engineers emphasized, as has been remarked, the simple, easily built plan.

Thus, although American engineering schools were almost invariably founded on a "scientific" basis, even as late as 1900 American structural texts dealt only with the analysis of "simple" beams and "simple" structures. Indeed the majority of nineteenth century American engineers were not engineering school graduates—they had, it was said, earned their degrees in the hard school of apprenticeship and practice.

In this connection it is interesting to recall the reaction of a noted American engineering author to the more highly mathematical and quantitative techniques which had been developed in Europe. Writing in 1871, John C. Trautwine stated in the preface to his famous "Civil Engineering Pocketbook":

> "The writer does not include Rankine, Mosely, and Weisbach, because, although their books are the productions of master-minds, and exhibit a profundity of knowledge beyond the reach of ordinary men * * * they are but little more than striking instances of how completely the most simple facts may be buried out of sight under heaps of mathematical rubbish."

It is difficult to put one's finger on any single factor which has led to the changed viewpoint of the present day. The movement toward the rationalization of earlier empirical understandings is not confined to engineering alone; it is a characteristic of the modern age. Increasing the size of structures to a point where uncertain factors can no longer be ignored or provided for by generous overdesign has unquestionably forced more exact structural analysis. However, probably the increasing complexity of modern design brought about by the use of continuous and statically indeterminate structural forms has been a major influence.

As early as 1892 Morison, noting the economy of continuity, had adopted continuous construction in his famous Memphis cantilever. C. R. Grimm, M. ASCE, in the Kinzua (Bradford, Pa.) Viaduct on the Erie in 1900 anticipated the vierendeel type of bracing. Thus, although American engineers have not led the world in developing the theory of statically indeterminate and continuous structures, the use of such forms has come about as a natural evolution in American practice. Also, the development of reinforced-concrete construction was a major contributing factor. Built-in-place continuity was a natural form for concrete; and it was also essential for economy in competition with other materials.

The coming of the airplane, a flying structure in which reduction in weight added another premium to material economy, soon posed new problems of the statically indeterminate type. In 1917 Gustav Lindenthal (1850–1935), Hon. M. ASCE, built his record-breaking continuous truss for the Chesapeake and Ohio Railroad over the Ohio River at Sciotoville, Ohio, which not only was 1,550 ft long, continuous over a center pier, but provided, by design and in erection, for the reduction of secondary stresses. Lindenthal, it should be noted, was of Austrian birth and had been educated in Europe. The further development of this new era has in fact owed much to imported talent.

Then following World War I a pioneer motor parkway was built and, for the first time in centuries, a completely new form of structure was introduced. The rigid frame was adopted on the Bronx River Parkway in New York in 1922. It has proved so economical that it has become the standard type for many crossings of moderate spans such as those occurring in highway work and railroad grade separations. Although German mechanicians had developed the theory of such frames, particularly as applied to building construction, the engineering birth of rigid frames in the United States thus came as the result of a search for the most economical structure to meet a special need.

By 1926 *Engineering News-Record* remarked editorially:

> "In recent years structural practice has turned unmistakably toward fuller use of the continuous form of structure. One phase of this departure from precedent is represented in the adaptation of continuous construction to concrete bridges in Westchester County, with results so impressive in increased efficiency and esthetic range as to forecast an important influence on future short-span practice."

Engineers are likely to forget that the external work done on a frame (and thus the work it must absorb in the stressing and deformation of its parts) is measured by one-half the product of the load and the distance through which it moves when placed on the structure—in other words, the deflection under load. Continuous structures deflect far less than the simple forms. Thus if continuity can be attained at an added cost which does not exceed these material savings, it obviously results in over-all economy. On the one hand, material costs have been rising in the United States; on the other hand, the mechanization of construction, apparently, has restrained, in part at least, a proportional rise in the labor costs of construction. Saving of materials has become of greater importance in determining the over-all economy of a design.

In regard to the advances in suspension bridge and arch design, it was largely due to the work of Leon S. Moisseiff, M. ASCE, that the older approximate analysis (which made the Williamsburg suspension in New York such a clumsy structure) was replaced by the deflection theory in the far more graceful Manhattan Bridge design of 1909—the first really scientifically designed suspension bridge.

European workers have contributed much to arch analysis. The Austrian Society of Engineers and Architects conducted a comprehensive series of arch tests beginning in 1890 which encouraged the development of the modern elastic theory. The fact that two-hinged, and even three-hinged, arches were long popular may be attributed, at least in part, to the simpler analysis such construction made possible. The earlier concrete arches in the United States were of the stone voussoir type but, in more recent years, engineers have turned to some of the more slender, daring European types. Greater technical understanding has led to new designs.

The nineteenth century witnessed not only these advances in the structural field but also important developments in the mechanics of fluids and soils. Before World War I, hydraulics was still in the "coefficient" stage, with large-scale experiments essential to results applicable in practice. Even Clemens Herschel, Past-President and Hon. M. ASCE, inventor of the venturi meter and one of the nation's pioneer hydraulic engineers, saw little hope of better understanding through a more highly mathematical and scientific attack in this field. The European work of Edwin Reynolds and others, however, led to more inclusive understandings of fluid behavior, and the generalizations of dimensional and dynamic similarity have given a new viewpoint and new vision in the entire field of fluid mechanics. In the area of hydraulic structures to be noted later, the contribution of American engineers to basic knowledge and understanding has been far more fundamental.

The latest area of empiricism to be attacked has been the difficult field of soil mechanics. About 1925 study began on the involved problem of relating and evaluating the many variables that determine soil behavior. In the engineering schools of the United States, during the 1930's, the study of soil mechanics replaced the older, almost purely descriptive, courses dealing with foundations and earth structures. Today (1952), remarkably accurate forecasts can be made of settlement and soil behavior.

Finally, since about 1940, new concepts of the factor of safety in structures have been brought forward. The limitations of the older "common theory" of flexure have received increasing attention. A more exact modern elastic theory is also being taught in many American schools, and increasingly applied. Past practice has held to the criterion of the elastic limit in design. Today—largely as a result of the structural problems posed by the airplane—engineers are turning to the study of phenomena beyond the elastic limit—buckling, plasticity, and creep. The "ignorance" element in the older factors of safety is being narrowed through the fuller understanding resulting from this effort to find a rational approach to, and evaluation of, these phenomena. Engineering science "marches on."

It is always dangerous to attempt predictions, but there are still quite wide differences in practice between the United States and Europe. Will that gap tend to close in the future?

The foreign engineer is deeply impressed with the size and speed of American work, but he feels that American engineers have been probably the most conservative engineers the world has ever known. One will seek in vain, in the United States, for examples of the daringly thin-shell reinforced-concrete construction which one finds on the Continent. This difference results from not only the struggle to balance labor and material costs, but also varying needs and demands. American engineers have emphasized steel for buildings as well as for bridges. In the past few years, however, they have been finding that, in some cases, the thin-shell reinforced-concrete type of structure has advantages. Many of the extreme European designs will not be adopted, but it seems safe to predict that, in the future, there will be a much wider use of varied structural forms than in the past. They not only will be predicated on changing needs and economics but, to a major degree, will be the children of the newer and more complete technical understandings of the twentieth century.

MATERIALS

In earlier centuries engineers were limited in construction to timber and stone, to lime, and pozzolanic cement, and to a minimum amount of metal for tools and fastenings. The nineteenth century was the beginning of a true "Age of Metal." The transitions from timber and wrought iron, to wrought and cast iron, to all-wrought iron, to steel and wrought iron, and, finally, to all-steel in bridge construction have been noted. With the turn of the century American bridge engineers were busily engaged in replacing earlier wrought-iron bridges with stronger steel structures designed for heavier locomotive and train loadings.

Although earlier progress in wrought-iron days had developed the standard rolled shapes and such typically American forms as the "eyebar" and "built-up" column, the larger structures which the new era required raised problems of the mechanics of such members which were not fully resolved. In fact, it was the inadequacy of the cross bracing, or latticing, on one of the heavy compression members of the lower chord of the anchor end of the Quebec Bridge which led to the collapse of this great work in 1907. The first advances of the new century in steel construction may be said, therefore, to have occurred in the testing of full-size steel members. The ASCE *Transactions* reflected these developments.

Improved steel-mill rolling methods also began to affect output and design early in the present century. By 1907 steel I-beams 24 in. deep, weighing 115 lb per ft, were being rolled. The introduction of vertical rolls made possible the "wide-flanged" beam and the H-section weighing as much as 420 lb per ft, replacing in a single section many compression members that would have been built up in earlier days. Similarly, the modern 36-in. WF-beams have replaced former plate-girder constructions.

Although the twentieth century is an age of alloy steels, this type of metal has had but limited use in construction. Only in the largest structures do the savings in dead load plus a tonnage sufficiently great to warrant special manufacture justify the higher cost of such metals. Nickel steel was used in the Queensborough cantilever at New York City in 1909; both nickel and silicon steel appeared in the Metropolis (Ill.) truss of 1917; and silicon was used in the Bayonne (N. J.), George Washington, and some other great bridges. The usual "structural grade" carbon steel, however, is still standard. Although it has been used in a few bridge structures, aluminum must still be regarded as an experimental construction material.

Interesting as these changes in the metal field are, they are completely overshadowed by the rise of concrete and reinforced-concrete construction. It seems almost unbelievable that, prior to 1900, portland cement was so costly that stone was used for bulk as well as finish masonry, primarily to conserve mortar. Natural cement (apparently first introduced on the Erie Canal about 1820 by Wright's assistant, Canvass White) was the standard binder for bulk concrete. Indeed, the Croton Dam (1895–1907) marks both one of the last uses of stone masonry and natural cement and the first use of portland cement in a great American structure. During these years the infant American portland cement industry, born of the patent of S. Taylor in 1871, grew some tenfold and then twentyfold, so that, by 1922, the United States was producing more than 100,000,000 bbl per yr.

The basic factor in this change, of course, was mass production. The small number of men who could be employed on stone masonry limited output, and, as labor costs have risen, stone masonry has become a mere costly veneer which, under special conditions, is applied to a few concrete structures largely for esthetic reasons.

So rapid was this eclipse of stone—and to a lesser degree brick—by concrete that Ira O. Baker,[21] M. ASCE, in his famous text, "A Treatise on Masonry Con-

---

[21] "A Treatise on Masonry Construction," by Ira O. Baker, John Wiley & Sons, Inc., New York, N. Y., 9th Ed., 1899.

struction," observed in 1899 that a complete revision was necessary in a book which, published only 10 years earlier, was almost exclusively devoted to stone and brick.

A major step forward in American concrete practice dates from the Joint Committee Report of 1912, which established nomenclature and basic formulas. Arthur N. Talbot, Past-President and Hon. M. ASCE, of the University of Illinois, at Urbana, was responsible for much of the pioneer testing and study on which this important report was based. The direct results of the introduction of concrete and reinforced concrete in the replacement of stone, brick, timber, and even steel construction, however, were only part of its total effect on civil engineering practice. It also produced notable changes in structural forms and influenced basic trends in the technique of design.

CONSTRUCTION

Progress in engineering is not measured by refinements in design—by what might be—but by what has actually been done—by completed works. In short, all the techniques and understandings of engineering have no point or purpose other than improved production or construction. Advances in the construction industry, therefore, are an essential; they constitute the fundamental evidence in the measurement of engineering progress.

Both the architectural and the civil engineering professions are involved in the construction industry, but it is the latter which is identified with what is known as heavy construction. It is true that this industry is composed of a large number of highly competitive smaller organizations, but in the past half century it has been subject to the same forces and influences that have affected all American industries. The trend has thus been toward the organization of larger and more resourceful companies, toward ever-greater mechanization of methods, and toward the engineering planning and conduct of construction operations. The old days of the rough and ready contractor bossing a group of husky laborers have given way to fully planned construction, using the most powerful machines modern engineering can provide. Some of the best engineering minds today find that construction offers a challenge to constructive thinking and intelligent action, as well as rewards of accomplishment, that no other activity affords.

Many forms of construction equipment date far back in history. Hand-operated hoists—the major tools of the stone masonry era—earlier forms of water pumps, and even the tup type of pile driver operated by some dozen or more men, go back to the Roman period. Indeed even the modern dipper dredge, manpowered by a treadmill, was used in the eighteenth century in Holland and France. Almost all the hand tools—hammers, chisels, picks, and shovels—were known and used in the even more remote past.

About the time ASCE was founded, however, the new power of steam began to be applied to the operation of construction equipment. It was the British engineer, James Naysmith, inventor of the steam forging hammer, who, in 1845, applied the same principle in the steam pile driver, first used at the naval dockyards at Devonport, Great Britain. The steam shovel seems to have been an

American invention going back to the patent of 1839 (Fig. 12) granted to William S. Otis. It did not come into wide use, however, until after the Civil War—in short, the steam shovel waited for the great era of railroad building to become standard equipment. The largest shovels today, however, are used in open-pit mining.

Earth excavation has also added to its equipment the bulldozer as well as earlier scraper and drag types of excavators. The Panama Canal (1902–1914), with its 270,000,000 cu yd of excavation, a steam shovel job, is still a record, but new tools have so facilitated the moving of earth in more usual construction that

FIG. 12.—EXCAVATOR PATENTED BY WILLIAM S. OTIS, 1839

cuts and fills are made today on modern highways that would have been regarded as "heavy" (even in railroad work) in the earlier 1900's.

In the rock field the major developments came during the Civil War era. The use of gunpowder in excavation had grown slowly. Wedging, chiseling, and fire-setting methods had persisted well into the seventeenth century. Then, in 1829, an American, Moses Shaw, used electric ignition, thus increasing the safety of blasting with gunpowder. By 1857 the blasting machine was in use. In 1867, 10 years later, Alfred B. Nobel of Sweden, invented a safe and effective way in which to use nitroglycerine in the form of dynamite. It was first tried in the United States in the Hoosac Tunnel in 1866 and, about the same time, came into use in American mining practice.

The rock drill has had a varied history. J. J. Couch of Philadelphia patented[22]

[22] "Tunneling, Explosive Compounds, and Rock Drills," by Henry Sturgis Drinker, John Wiley & Sons, Inc., New York, N. Y., 1878.

(Fig. 13) a percussion steam rock drill in 1849, and Joseph W. Fowle of Boston brought out the first direct action drill in 1851. In the United States the Burleigh drill, designed by Charles Burleigh of the Putnam Machine Company in 1866, was the first to come into general use—again on the Hoosac Tunnel (1856–1876). Abroad the Italian Sommeiler "unlocked the stone portals of Mont Cenis [Switzerland]" with his compressed air drill of 1861.

French engineers had developed some continuous earth excavating equipment, largely of the ladder and bucket type, in connection with the construction of the Suez Canal, completed in 1869; but, as in so many other cases, the change in American practice came with the turn of the century. A now almost forgotten task, the Chicago Drainage Canal (1892–1900) has been called the "American

FIG. 13.—ROCK DRILLING MACHINE, INVENTED BY J. J. COUCH, 1849

School of Excavating Machinery." Special equipment, mainly for transporting material from the canal prism to the spoil banks, was designed for this work.

To one who recalls the construction of the first New York City subway (1900–1904) the changes of the past 50 years are especially vivid. This was one of the last great American pick-and-shovel jobs. The uptown sections were excavated in open cut with temporary wood bridges carrying cross traffic over "Parsons' Ditch" as it was called. In the side streets small hand-fired steam boilers supplied the drills and derrick hoists, while pick-and-shovel men loaded spoil into buckets, and horse-drawn carts carried it away. In the next few years, with the extension of the subway to lower New York City, the modern method of planking over the streets and excavating under this apron came into use.

In the technique of placing material, many of the most striking changes are best illustrated by developments in the construction of earth and masonry dams. The Fort Peck Dam on the Missouri River in Montana (1935–1940) involved the placing of some 120,000,000 cu yd of fill. It was an hydraulic job. The Grand Coulee Dam on the Columbia River in the State of Washington has required the placing of more than 100,000,000 cu yd of concrete in a single structure—more than double the remarkable total for the Panama Canal some 30 years earlier. Speed of production has been equally outstanding. At the Kensico Dam (1910–1916) in southern New York State 3,572 cu yd of concrete placed in one 8-hour day and 84,450 cu yd in 1 month were recorded (Fig. 14). On the Grand Coulee 20,684 cu yd were deposited in 24 hours and more than 400,000 cu yd in 1 month. All these records have been made possible through the coordinated planning of plant and the fullest possible use of mechanization in heavy construction. Similar developments have taken place in other areas.

FIG. 14.—KENSICO DAM IN SOUTHERN NEW YORK STATE, UNDER CONSTRUCTION, 1913

In the building of steel bridges one notes the absence of the tremendous forests of timber falsework which were formerly used to support such work during construction. The trend toward the cantilevering method of erection or the use of a few temporary supporting bents had been noted in earlier nineteenth century work. It set the pattern of modern erection. In suspension bridge building, however, modern cable spinning methods have made it possible to handle some sixteen wires in a single pass and thus greatly increase the speed of this difficult operation.

With these developments, increased technical knowledge has been basic in making bigger and better structures possible; but there have been some works in which progress is to be measured almost entirely by improvements in construction alone. In subaqueous tunneling, for example, design has been standardized, and improved construction methods have been a determining factor. This observation will hold true for many foundation and underpinning operations.

Thus, although the mechanical concrete mixer dates back at least to 1871, only since 1900 has the basic change from hand-placed stone masonry to mass produced concrete vividly affected the placing of materials. This change has been paralleled in these same 50 years by a mechanization of construction which has fully kept pace with the general mechanization of American industry.

FOUNDATIONS

It has been estimated that, on an average, half the cost of a bridge goes underground—is involved in providing the invisible substructure which supports the visible superstructure. In many cases of masonry dam construction even this is too modest an estimate.

The history of foundations is a fascinating story of the engineer's effort to secure substructures of sufficient depth to avoid undermining by scour and to reach a level having adequate bearing power for the superstructure. Unquestionably many more early bridges failed and were destroyed by undermining of their foundation than through defects in superstructure. In relatively few cases has nature provided conditions which make it possible to follow the Biblical advice and build on rock. Bridges are often needed over alluvial streams where rock is at an unreachable depth.

Vitruvius described the Roman plan of diverting the flow of a stream to one side during low-water conditions by means of a temporary earth embankment—unwatering the site, driving piles when necessary, and then building up the piers above water level before reversing the diversion and repeating the operation in the other half of the channel. French engineers of the eighteenth century developed not only the cofferdam process but also a method of cutting piles underwater and the use of the caisson. Apparently, however, even with their best efforts it was seldom possible to unwater foundations deeper than 10 ft or 12 ft below water level. It was general practice to make provision against undermining by piling stones around the bridge piers. This foundation difficulty was undoubtedly a factor in the emphasis the French placed on increasing the waterway under stone arch bridges by using elliptical or flat segmental spans.

In 1805, at Philadelphia, Palmer created a record in open caisson work when he reached 41 ft below high tide in building his Permanent Bridge over the Schuylkill River. The most recent record using a modern steel sheet-pile cofferdam and modern pumping equipment, was the 60 ft to 80 ft reached in the 89-ft by 98-ft foundation of the west tower of the George Washington Bridge, in 1930. The development of adequate power-driven pumping equipment has been a vital factor in foundation progress, but another basic innovation in foundation work has been primarily of British origin.

In 1830 one of the most colorful and romantic personalities in British naval history, Lord Cochrane, patented the pneumatic process, using air pressure within to balance the water pressure from without. After earlier British use this method was introduced in the United States by such pioneers as Eads, Sooy Smith, and others. Daniel E. Moran, M. ASCE, later developed the material lock, and compressed air became one of the advances which ushered in the Skyscraper Era in the early 1900's.

There are limits to human endurance, however, as regards the air pressure under which man can work. Eads' record at St. Louis (in 1874), of more than 120 ft, requiring more than 50 lb per sq in. above atmospheric pressure, has never been exceeded. Furthermore, strict labor laws have properly limited working conditions under air pressure and this method has become extremely costly. There have been some ingenious additions to the process such as using air only to excavate and close off the lower part of a caisson after a critical depth has been reached, but engineers have turned to other methods for deeper foundations and have sought alternate forms of construction to avoid or minimize the use of the pneumatic method.

Two of the most extensive pneumatic caisson works ever undertaken were those in lower New York City connected with the Hudson Terminal Building on Church Street and the Federal Reserve Bank on Liberty Street. In both cases it was necessary to provide for deep lower floors below the ground-water level. In 1900 Alfred Noble, Past-President ASCE, used a wall of caissons completely enclosing the lower level of the Mutual Life Building. In the Hudson Terminal Building (1906–1907), however, fifty-one pneumatic caissons, sealed on a rock bed from 70 ft to 110 ft below curb, completely enclosed, "bottle-tight," the train platforms and the still lower power substation which is 77 ft below the street and 58 ft below water level. Similarly, the caisson-cofferdam of the Federal Reserve Building attracted widespread attention in 1921–1922. Its "cellar" is 85 ft deep and five stories below street level; it covers an entire block. The material was essentially a quicksand, and the rock surface was very irregular. As a result, many of the caissons had to be underpinned to seal them to the rock. The consultants stated later:

> "No such operation had ever before been attempted, and it is certain that it will never be attempted again if it can be avoided. Even with the utmost precautions and with the most careful balancing of air pressures the risks involved were tremendous."

Nevertheless, in the Barclay-Vesey building of the New York Telephone Company on West Street (New York City), a similar construction provided five floors below street level (70.5 ft) and 3,125,000 cu ft of useful space, which is no minor consideration in an area of the city where land has sold as high as $700 per sq ft.

In the bridge field a modification of the old French *caisse*, or caisson, has become, perhaps, the most spectacular of modern methods for the building of deep bridge foundations. The caissons of the Hawkesbury Bridge in Australia, built by the open-dredging process, constituted a record for some years—185 ft below water level in water 59 ft deep. The Poughkeepsie cantilever, built about the same time (1889) and reaching 134 ft below water level witnessed the first use of this method in the United States. Numerous other applications can be cited, and one of the most accurate examples of this kind of work was on the ventilating shafts of the Holland Tunnel (New York City). However, the problem of guiding a caisson (built as a floating structure in a dockyard) to the site, and then maintaining it in a vertical position as it is sunk becomes ever more difficult as the depth of water in which it is to be used increases.

In building the piers of the Suisun Bay railroad cantilever (1930) near San Francisco, a unique plan of creating "sand islands" was used. These were enclosed in steel sheet piling and formed a firm setting for the caissons, which were sunk by open dredging.

At Carquinez Straits (California) in 1927 there was 90 ft of water with only 40 ft to 45 ft of mud and soil overlying rock, while strong tidal currents (as much as 7 ft per sec) made the problem of positioning and holding the caissons very difficult. The task was accomplished successfully. The greatest of modern works, however, was the founding of the central, common anchorage pier of the double suspension spans of the Bay Bridge at San Francisco in 1935. Here the world's largest caisson, 92 ft by 197 ft, was sunk in more than 100 ft of water in the swift tidal currents of the bay to a depth greater than 200 ft below low tide. The problem of guiding this huge floating box into position and of maintaining verticality as it was sunk led to the adoption of a unique design. The usual interior dredging cells (fifty-five in this case) formed by partitions within the caisson were capped with steel domes. Used to create buoyancy by means of pneumatic pressure and coupled with a sequence of dredging in other cells, the device and plan proved effective in sinking this great caisson to its final predetermined position.

Before 1900, foundation problems centered in railroad bridges, but there was an interval, before the Highway Era, in which building foundations occupied the principal attention of foundation experts. Various special methods were developed, in addition to the pneumatic procedure, and the deepest foundations in the world are those of the Cleveland Union Terminal Building in Ohio, 250 ft below curb level, and built by the so-called Chicago-well method of open excavation.

The recent trend, however, has been toward the use of piles or a modified type of concrete pile construction. The invention and development of both precast concrete piles and those built in place inside a previously driven steel shell, constituted one of the innovations of the "Age of Concrete." The latter method immediately suggests the possibility of sinking a nest of steel pipes to rock, or other suitable bearing material, excavating by water jet and air, filling them with concrete, and thus providing a cluster of concrete columns, with lateral support from the surrounding earth. Depths greater than 100 ft have been reached, and many building foundations have been constructed which, in earlier years, would have required pneumatic work.

A notable example of this type of foundation work, and of speed in building, was the Bank of the Manhattan Company Building on Wall Street (New York City) erected in 1929. The site was occupied by an old building some sixteen stories high, but in less than one year (from May 16, 1929, to March 31, 1930) a new, record-breaking skyscraper 930 ft high (equivalent to about seventy stories) had been erected and tenants were moving in. As the older building was being demolished, sectional pipe foundations, 44 in. in diameter, were jacked down beneath it by a special underpinning process. By the time this demolition was finished, the foundations were sufficiently completed to permit the erection of the steel for the new building; and, as the new structure went up, they were finally and fully constructed.

Thus, the past 50 years have certainly added to the records of engineering advances in foundation construction and have established methods and techniques that promise to endure for many years to come.

THE TRANSPORTATION PROBLEM

If the engineers of the nineteenth century could have foreseen the development of the twentieth century, it is quite clear that the American transportation system would have been quite different from that on which engineers have had to build in the past 50 years. The railroad dominated the earlier years to the almost complete exclusion of any other form of transportation. Highways were neglected; rivers and canals were regarded as too slow and uncertain. Pipelines for oil were bitterly opposed whereas other competitive forms (notably motor trucks and airplanes) were to enter the transportation field at a later date. During the present century the nation has been in a period of transportation changes in which the dominating position of the railroads has been in process of adjustment to what will undoubtedly continue to become a more fully coordinated system in which each of the various forms of transportation will find its own peculiar and most economically favorable use.

During the past 50 years the emphasis in railroad work has changed from new building and construction to problems of operation and operational improvement. Ground between the controls of the ICC (now the dictator of railroad life) and the increasing demands of labor, American railroads seek to maintain their position as the main transportation arteries of economic life and to improve their competitive position and service. The railroad problem no longer centers in civil engineering. It is primarily an operational and financial headache.

On the other hand, many engineers, as well as the public, fail to realize the notable operating improvements which this century has brought in railroad transportation. After a remarkable performance in World War I, United States railroads were returned to private operation facing major problems of neglected maintenance and run-down rolling stock; but improvements in roadbed and maintenance, in cars and locomotives, in operating speeds, and in train loads have been continuous. Larger steel cars have replaced the old wooden box cars, and the modern steel vestibule passenger coach has created a new era in passenger comfort. The tractive power of the better freight locomotives (in 1900, about 25,000 lb) by 1933 had been raised (including the booster which actuates the wheels under the cab) to more than 100,000 lb. Fuel consumption was reduced 50% or more and train speeds increased twofold to threefold.

Later moves toward electrification, however, failed to develop after pioneering by the New York Central and New Haven lines in 1907. The notable freight installations on the Norfolk and Western Railroad in 1915, the Great Northern Railroad in 1927, and also on the Chicago, Milwaukee and St. Paul Railroad—now seem to have been special projects. The modern motive power is the diesel locomotive, first introduced for switching service about 1930. In fact it has been only through constant operating improvements that American railroads have survived the heavy burdens that the twentieth century has placed on them.

Back in the era of Calvin Coolidge, the President stated, but did not resolve, another basic transportation question. He remarked:

> "Our whole century-old policy of developing navigable streams at tremendous cost is either a piece of inconceivable and colossal folly, or else we as a people have been inexcusably remiss in taking advantage of our opportunities."

Ardent advocates can still be found on both sides of this question. In 1929 Herbert Hoover, Hon. M. ASCE, then President of the United States, opened the Ohio River canalization from Cairo, Ill., to Pittsburgh. Since then the Upper Mississippi River has been similarly canalized and navigation is considered to constitute one of the basic economic justifications for the works of the Tennessee Valley Authority. In more recent years other elements—flood control, power development, and irrigation—have been brought into the picture until these multiple-purpose projects seem to defy any reasonable economic analysis.

These works are in the hands of the Corps of Engineers, the USBR, and special authorities. Although few engineers may fully approve their economic justification, the constructions to which they have led are among the most outstanding and spectacular that this country has produced. One will hunt in vain elsewhere in civil engineering practice for the special forms of dam construction which are peculiar to river canalization while the dams of the USBR and the Tennessee Valley Authority are among the most outstanding and beautiful structures of modern American concrete design.

Nevertheless, although the railroads pay a tax bill of about $1,000,000 per day, these arteries of water-borne traffic are taxfree and generally tollfree. Similarly, until the imposition of the gasoline tax in the later 1920's transportation on American highways carried little of the cost burden of providing the routes on which it was carried. In addition to their other problems, the railroads have thus faced publically subsidized competition from waterways and highways.

The harbor duties of the Corps of Engineers also constitute a special field of civil engineering practice which, to a major degree, is limited to the Corps. Maintenance is a continuing problem and harbor works are constantly under way, but recent years have witnessed no major new construction. The problem has become one of constant dredging, repair, and improvement. Similarly, in marine work such as drydocks, the Civil Engineer Corps of the United States Navy is the outstanding performer. Such great installations as those at Brooklyn, Philadelphia, Portsmouth, N. H., and other naval stations, constitute the outstanding marine constructions in the United States.

A famous civil engineer of the Civil War period (Haupt) engineered one of the first great pipelines that brought oil from the Pennsylvania fields to the Atlantic seaboard. World War II created the "Big Inch" line (22 in. in diameter) extending 1,254 miles from Longview, Tex., to Phoenixville, Pa. Today pipes have taken over from the railroads, and 95% of all crude oil requirements are met by the pipeline. In the past few years, natural gas lines have been built which will exceed in length even these tubular methods of oil transportation.

With the turn of the century the airplane has also entered the transportation field. Its civil engineering implications have been twofold. Its use has required the planning and construction of many great airfields; and, being essentially a flying structure, its design has posed new problems and stimulated new developments in the field of structural analysis and design.

The outstanding single transportation achievement of the twentieth century, however, has been the Panama Canal, "the greatest of geographical surgical operations." At least four men deserve the major credit for carrying through to completion this great task to which the United States fell heir following the earlier failure of the French company of Ferdinand de Lesseps. The Union Pacific Railroad had been built by private enterprise, encouraged to accept the great risks involved by generous grants of public lands. The financial and other hazards of Panama were recognized as constituting a national challenge. Under the dynamic leadership of President Theodore Roosevelt the political problems of the Canal Zone were solved and the United States embarked on the first of its great modern national engineering ventures. It was Dr. William C. Gorgas of the Army Medical Corps who stamped out "yellow jack" on the Isthmus and made construction possible. It was John F. Stevens, Hon. M. and Past-President ASCE, the builder of western railroads, who organized construction, "made the dirt fly," and it was Col. G. W. Goethals, M. ASCE, who completed the work of lock and dam building, a specialty in which Stevens felt he lacked first-hand experience (Fig. 15). Rising 85 ft from the Atlantic to the level of Gatun Lake, passing through the mountain backbone which connects two continents in the famous Culebra Cut, the canal, notable primarily for the magnitude of the operations involved, is 50 miles in length from sea to sea. As a single venture the Panama Canal will long remain an outstanding monument of engineering achievement. On the other hand, the far less spectacular challenge of the modern Highway Era has exercised a far more widespread and important influence on civil engineering practice and professional development.

As previously noted, the highways of the United States had remained, with few exceptions, unimproved local dirt roads throughout the nineteenth century. The bicycle craze of the 1890's added some emphasis to the better road slogan, "get the farmer out of the mud," but it was the advent of the automobile that created the modern highway era. Two major problems immediately arose: How to build roads and how to finance their construction.

As late as 1902 Baker, in his pioneer text,[23] "A Treatise on Roads and Pavements," noted:

> "It is frequently claimed that the public would be benefited by placing the care of the roads in the hands of engineers, but there is no evidence that any considerable number of engineers comprehend either the principles of road making necessary for the improvement of our country roads, or the economic limitations and political difficulties of the problem."

In a few cases certain states early recognized the implications of this new transportation era that was in the making. New Jersey, for example, began to supplement limited local resources with state aid in 1891. However, the federal Bureau of Public Roads, established under the Department of Agriculture in 1893, soon became the leader in forwarding the highway movement. Originally educational in character, it assumed new importance in 1916 when federal aid was added to state and local resources in meeting the problem of construction costs. Such federal aid was made contingent on the organization, within each state, of an adequate highway department. Few states had such departments but they were quickly formed; and, today, their needs, in both staff and consulting services, constitute a major source of engineering employment.

---

[23] "A Treatise on Roads and Pavements," by Ira O. Baker, John Wiley & Sons, Inc., New York, N. Y., 1903.

FIG. 15.—THE GATUN LOCKS IN THE PANAMA CANAL, 1912

Thus, although the great era of railroad building had reached its crest before 1900 it was succeeded by a highway era, the problems of which are still urgent. Finances were a critical problem in earlier days. Even as late as 1921 funds for highway building were being sought through increased local taxes, and federal and state aid. Then, in 1923, the gasoline tax was discovered and, by 1926, all but four states were using this new source of revenue both for highway and other needs. Finally, with the rediscovery of the toll road, a new era of even greater highway building has emerged.[24]

In the middle years of the modern Highway Era there was also a movement toward the relief of traffic bottlenecks by the construction of major bridges as privately-owned toll structures. Here again public interest intervened and the public authority type of sponsorship stepped in. The Port of New York Authority, created by joint action of the states of New York and New Jersey, has been responsible for such notable works connecting the two states as the George Washington and Bayonne bridges, and the Lincoln Tunnel. The Triborough Bridge Authority has built other great bridges and tunnels, and these are only two of many similar state-created public authorities spread across the country.

Although highway planning and building have thus replaced the railroad interests of the nineteenth century as a major civil engineering activity, American engineers have been taken to task for not exercising a longer range vision in building to meet the needs of this new means of transportation. In very few cases indeed have funds been made available to permit more than an effort to keep up with current needs. Furthermore there has been a totally unpredictable growth in the use of motor vehicles and, thus, in the demand for ever greater facilities. One recalls with a smile the statement of Woodrow Wilson made in 1906:

> "Nothing has spread socialistic feeling in this country more than the use of the automobile. To the countryman they are a picture of arrogance and wealth with all its independence and carelessness."

Here was a mastermind who could not foresee the day when there would be a motor vehicle for every three people in the United States, when working men as well as those of "arrogance and wealth" would be users of this new transportation device.

Earlier road surfacing using water-bound macadam and gravel soon proved inadequate for automobiles, and the concrete type of surfacing, using portland cement or bituminous binder, came into use before World War I. The problem centered on the passenger car which comprised more than 90% of highway traffic. Having found a lasting surfacing, attention turned (when World War I was over) to the battle between speed and safety. In 1924 the Bronx River Parkway between New York City and White Plains, N. Y., was opened, providing for crossings by bridges, thus giving an uninterrupted route, with a speed limit of 35 miles per hr then regarded as phenomenal. Its sharp curves are in marked contrast to the straight alinement of the Merritt Parkway in Connecticut (1936) with a speed limit of 55 miles per hr. However, a new era of highway

---

[24] "Revenue Bonds Build 118-Mile Expressway," by Enoch R. Needles, *Civil Engineering*, January, 1952, p. 31.

building has now begun. These passenger car routes (trucking being prohibited) have been built in areas of high passenger traffic—notably as highway arteries to great cities. Similarly major truck line "throughways," joining cities of high commercial trucking traffic, are now being planned.

In the Era of Railroad Strategy there was a battle between the Pennsylvania and the New York Central railroads. It was compromised when the latter actually undertook the construction of a line westward through Pennsylvania. It was the old roadbed and tunnels of this abandoned railroad venture that became part of the Pennsylvania Turnpike in 1940. New Jersey has completed a new throughway

FIG. 16.—AIR VIEW OF PART OF THE NEW JERSEY TURNPIKE

in the same general pattern (Fig. 16); New York's throughway is under construction (1952); and Connecticut, Ohio, Colorado, Oklahoma, and other states are following suit.

A relatively new consideration enters in the design of trucking routes. Passenger cars have no difficulty with grades, but grades vitally affect trucking costs. The new alinements thus seek to keep grades to approximately 3%. Speeds are set as high as 60 miles per hr, and these new arteries are being built on alinement standards that approximate—in many cases exceed—the railroad alinement standards of a half century ago. Their costs are even greater. Few railroads cost as much as $1,000,000 per mile and more, which is not unusual in "throughway" construction in the highly industrialized and developed urban areas which these new highways are designed to serve.

The modern highway problem is not limited to the provision of adequate routes for highway traffic. The problem of providing space for the parking of cars in all cities, great and small, and of leaving space for truck deliveries, is ever more pressing and, unlike that of highway building, is yet unsolved. New highways may be financed by bond issues supported by tolls, but it is clear that parking meters do not solve parking congestion—there simply is not room on city streets for the cars that daily flood into urban areas—and, apparently, "the end is not yet."

TUNNELS AND SUBWAYS

Tunnels.—Modern methods of both land and subaqueous tunnel construction were quite well developed in the nineteenth century, but there have been recent changes in purpose which have vitally affected the scope and extent of such undertakings.

The great land tunnels of Europe have been primarily the Alpine railroad bores. The Mont Cenis Tunnel (1857–1871), 8.25 miles long, was a pioneer work. The St. Gotthard Tunnel, 9.26 miles long, followed (1872–1882). The Arlberg Tunnel, 6.2 miles long, was built next (1880–1883); and finally the famous Simplon Tunnel, 12.4 miles long, still the record bore with no intermediate shafts, was constructed (1895–1906).

The Simplon Tunnel undoubtedly inspired one of the major developments of the present century—the pioneer tunnel or heading method. It was built as a two-bore, twin-tunnel work primarily because of rock problems, and the difficulties that a single large bore would have involved. However, this fact made it possible to run one smaller heading ahead of the full-section operation in the other—thus not only making this first bore into a service line for the full excavation of its twin but providing, by cross cuts, for attack on the adjoining full section from more than one heading. So successful and valuable did this plan prove to be that the so-called pioneer heading (in some cases a side tunnel built solely to serve and expedite the main tunnel operation as in the Moffat Tunnel, 1923 to 1927) became almost standard practice where no intermediate shafts were used.

The construction of the Rogers Pass Tunnel on the Canadian Pacific Railroad (1913–1916) marked the first development of this plan. It was named after Maj. Rogers, "right-hand man" of the American railroad engineer, Van Horne, who completed the Canadian Pacific Railroad through to the west coast. It has since been renamed the Connaught Tunnel.[25] The Moffat Tunnel, although projected in earlier days, was not built until 1923 to 1927. The parallel, pioneer tunnel in this case has later become a water conduit. The Cascade Tunnel (1925–1928) which carries the Great Northern Railroad through the Coast Range, is the longest railroad tunnel in the western hemisphere—7.8 miles. Both the pioneer heading method and an intermediate shaft were used on this work, which set a speed record of 1,157 ft of heading in 1 month.

Highway work has succeeded railroad work, but land tunnels for highways are infrequent. The modern tunnel records have been made in aqueduct building for urban water supplies.

---

[25] "Construction Methods for Rogers Pass Tunnel," by A. C. Dennis, *Transactions*, ASCE, Vol. LXXXI, 1917, p. 448.

The new Croton Aqueduct for New York City, built in the 1880's, abandoned the cut-and-cover design and was almost entirely a tunnel work. In the Catskill supply (Fig. 17) of 1905–1917 both forms of construction were used; but the newer West Catskill Project involves about 85 miles of tunnel. In both length and difficulty, however, the Colorado River-Los Angeles Aqueduct, which involved more than 100 miles of difficult tunnel excavation, overshadows other American projects.

Although many land tunnels have been completed by shear persistence and determination in the face of discouraging obstacles (notably the inflow of water and heavy rock pressures), two earlier subaqueous British works illustrate the dogged determination of the tunnel builder in overcoming such dangers and obstacles. It required 13 years to conquer the estuary of the Severn near Bristol (1873–1886); and the tunnel built under the Mersey River between Liverpool and Birkenhead, during the same period, was a similar but somewhat less difficult work, constructed "in the clear" (with no air pressure or shield), in heavy water-bearing rock.

British engineers also perfected the shield-and-air process and demonstrated it in the United States. In fact there is no tale of danger and determination in tunnel work which outranks that of the Thames Tunnel (1825–1843), in London constructed by Sir Marc I. Brunel, which was the first great subaqueous work with one of the largest cross sections ($22\frac{1}{4}$ ft high and $37\frac{1}{2}$ ft wide) ever built. No air was used (the work being flooded out twice), but a crude sectional shield was employed. Great Britain also pioneered in subway building and in the London Underground of 1886 the shield-and-air method was used extensively.

The first American experience with this highly specialized type of work began with the Hudson and Manhattan Tubes in lower New York City as early as 1879; but a fatal blowout in 1880 trapped some twenty "sandhogs" in an inrush of water and a long delay followed. Then, in 1889 a firm of British contractors, Pearson and Sons, "took over," and the ASCE membership came to know Charles M. Jacobs, M. ASCE, and J. Vipond Davies, M. ASCE, who made their later careers in the United States. Sir Benjamin Baker and the British tunnel pioneer, James H. Greathead, were consultants, but not until 1905 was this work completed. It included the remarkable caisson and foundation of the Hudson Terminal Building previously noted.

In the meantime, in 1903, one of the most comprehensive, imaginative, and daring plans ever conceived by the engineer was undertaken by the Pennsylvania Railroad. Plans were made to bring its passenger trains into New York City and eliminate the delays and uncertainties of ferry service. Back of the Lower Palisades on the east edge of the "New Jersey Meadows" the line went underground, passed under the Hudson River in two 23-ft tubes, entered the great terminal station at Thirty-Fourth Street in Manhattan, continued across the city to pass under the East River, and finally emerged in Long Island City. Many ASCE members served on this work under the inspiring leadership of Noble as chief engineer.[26,27]

The first subaqueous New York City tunnel to be completed was the East River Gas Tunnel (1892 to 1894) on which Jacobs was chief engineer and Davies

[26] *Transactions,* ASCE, Vol. LXVIII, September, 1910.
[27] *Ibid.,* Vol. LXIX, October, 1910.

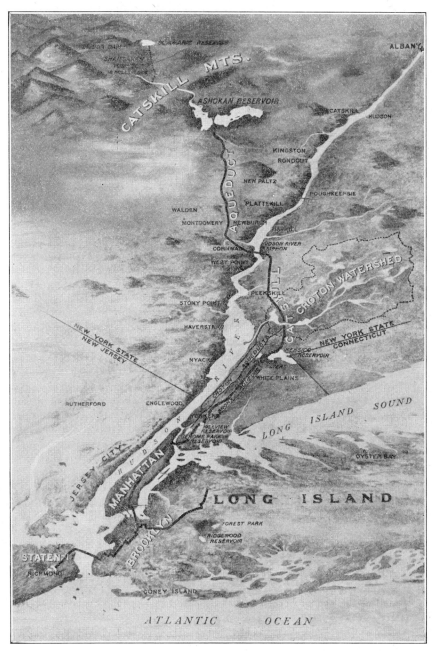

FIG. 17.—THE CATSKILL WATER SUPPLY FOR THE CITY OF NEW YORK, N. Y.

his assistant. In the now almost forgotten Astoria Gas Tunnel (1911 to 1915) Mr. Davies also carried through a notable rockwork in the face of difficulties with soft and water-bearing material.

The Holland Tunnel between New York City and Jersey City, N. J., the first vehicular tunnel reflecting the modern highway era, was constructed from 1921 to 1927. It posed some difficult problems of matching tunnel operation with openings left in the caissons sunk for the foundations of the ventilating towers, but the technique of subaqueous shield-and-air work was by this time fully developed and the tunnel workers were backed up in their air and other needs by modern plant and equipment. In fact New York has become the most tunneled city of the world, and such works are accomplished so quickly and quietly today that they are scarcely noted in the press. The most recent New York tunnels, the Brooklyn-Battery and the Queens-Midtown, are both notable vehicular constructions.

In the meantime another method of subaqueous tunnel construction had been developed. A unique procedure had been followed in the tunnel under the Harlem River in the extension of the first New York subway to the Bronx. A trench dredged in the river bottom was enclosed by sheet piling on the sides and covered over, and then the tunnel was built under air pressure in this covered passageway. However, in the Detroit (Mich.) River Tunnel (1906–1910) what were essentially steel tunnel forms were sunk in a trench in the river bottom. Tremie concrete was deposited in these forms to complete the tubes which could then be unwatered. This was a twin-tube railroad tunnel; but in constructing the Oakland (Calif.) estuary tube (1925–1928), a vehicular tunnel of large diameter (32 ft), what amounted to a subaqueous pipe-laying technique was followed. The tube of reinforced concrete was built in sections in drydock, and bulkheaded to provide buoyancy. The sections were then sunk in place, the joints being formed by tremie concrete collars.

In the Detroit-Windsor (Ont., Canada) Vehicular Tunnel, begun in 1928 as the Oakland work was being completed, the earlier plan used in the railroad tunnel at this site was followed. This subaqueous method is particularly adapted to situations where the tunnel passes under a river at not too great a depth while the "shield-and-air" procedure still remains the standard practice under usual conditions.

Subways.—In the subway field Great Britain can also claim priority. The first London "underground" came in the period from 1860 to 1863, a steam-operated line built in London clay. Subway construction in the United States was initiated in Boston where, in 1895–1898, trolley tracks were removed from the surface to a pioneer subway construction. The first New York subway of 1900–1904, however, was the first great American project in this field.

A plan to increase speed of transportation in New York City by subway construction, inspired by the London work, had been agitated as early as 1864; but even in 1900 the idea of an underground railroad in New York was regarded as visionary. Parsons later recalled:

"I was 35 years of age when I became Chief Engineer of the Rapid Transit Commission. When I look back now, I am glad I was not older. I doubt if I could now undertake or would undertake such a work under similar conditions. But I had the enthusiasm of youth and inexperience. If I had fully realized what was ahead of me, I do not think I would have attempted the work. As it was, I was treated as a visonary. Some of my friends spoke pityingly of my wasting my time on what they considered a dream. They said I could go ahead making plans, but never could build a practical, underground railroad. This skepticism was so prevalent it handicapped the work."

The excavation methods in this last great pick-and-shovel job have been noted. One of the major problems was that of relocating or rebuilding the maze of water, sewer, gas, and other pipelines for which no adequate plans were available and which ran under all the streets. Perhaps the greatest tribute to the skill and foresight of this young engineer rests, however, in the fact that, after half a century of subway construction, the basic form he adopted—steel bents of columns and beams with concrete jack arches between—still remains a standard form of construction.

The effect of subway building on traffic growth is illustrated by the fact that, whereas in 1864 the twelve horse-car lines of New York were estimated as carrying about 61,000,000 passengers who took about 87 rides per year (the population then being 700,000), in 1917 there were more than 1,000,000,000 passengers annually in Manhattan and the Bronx alone and every citizen averaged about a trip a day.

Contract No. 1 of the New York Subway included the 18.5 miles of four-track and two-track line from City Hall to Kingsbridge and Bronx Park. There were some rock tunnel sections, but the major part of the construction was in open cut. Contract No. 2, on which new methods first appeared, was from City Hall south, with a tunnel under the East River to Brooklyn.

Subway building in New York has since become a more or less continuous process. One of the most difficult of the later projects was the Nassau Street loop, begun in 1928, to connect the Brooklyn and Manhattan Transit tracks with the Montague Street Tunnel to Brooklyn and permit "loop" operation. A tremendous problem of underpinning adjoining buildings in this narrow canyon of the lower city added to the difficulties.

Abroad, London has reinforced her "inner circle" with outside lines, and the famous Metropolitan of Paris has likewise been extended. Chicago and Philadelphia have followed New York and much publicity has been given to the palatial Russian venture. Cost versus needs and demands are the determining factors. It seems safe to state, however, that the topography of Manhattan—a long island with the main business area concentrated at one end—presents a transportation problem that even continuous subway building seems unable to solve satisfactorily.

BRIDGES

At least two major factors have influenced bridge design in the twentieth century—the Highway Era and the rapid growth in the use of concrete.

The coming of the automobile and the rise of highway traffic created a new demand for bridge construction on a scale far beyond anything demanded by the railroads in their greatest days. In the first place, the financial aspects of the problem have changed. While railroad passenger traffic (never a primary source of income) has steadily declined, motor vehicle use has continued to mount in volume. The economic justification of great structures has been increasing, and funds to build them have been available. Also, highway loads are far lighter than railroad loadings, and records for long-span bridges have been broken—especially for the suspension bridges and light arches, which are not suited to heavier railroad loads. In these fields, older span records have been doubled or more than doubled in the past 25 years. However, the record spans of the more rigid, heavier truss types—simple, continuous, and cantilever—still remain with the railroads.

At the turn of the century, the great Quebec railroad cantilever was the most notable engineering work under construction. The disastrous failure of this bridge in 1907 was a severe blow to American and Canadian engineering prestige. The cause of the failure was quickly diagnosed. A major compression member of unprecedented size had been inadequately latticed to maintain the relative position of its parts. It was also mishandled in transit, and it buckled under load. Unfortunately, as was remarked at the time:

> "In construction work there is often the pressure for lower cost. It requires courage of a high order on the part of the engineer to resist it. Engineers are sometimes under the authority of laymen with whom financial considerations may seem more important than safety." *Theodore Cooper*

One of ASCE's most respected and honored members, then considered the dean of American bridge engineers, hoped to crown a long and honorable career with the completion of a record-breaking venture, and never recovered from the shock of the Quebec failure. Needless to say, special testing machines were developed; tests of compression members were made on a far larger scale than had hitherto been possible; and efforts to rationalize the design of such members were redoubled.

The Canadian Government took charge of the Quebec Bridge project, and a new design was completed in 1917. Special credit should be given to the courage of the two Canadian bridge companies which, with steel from the United States, reassured the public as to the integrity of the engineering profession. They were required not only "to assume full responsibility for the designs, plans and specifications" but to guarantee by a deposit of more than a million dollars "the satisfactory erection and completion of the bridge." This they did in spite of another partial failure, the collapse of the 640-ft suspended span (in itself a record-breaking truss) when it was being lifted into position between the two great 580-ft cantilever arms.

Later cantilever spans have not equaled the Quebec Bridge in length, but the type has been widely used in the Highway Era. During the 1920's, before the quasi-public authority form of financing became dominant, several privately financed highway toll structures were erected. Among these were such notable cantilever bridges as the Carquinez Straits Bridge of 1927, with two 1,100-ft spans. In 1930, the Longview cantilever over the Columbia River, between Washington and Oregon (having a main span 1,200 ft long) was opened, and the Port of New York Authority completed two smaller spans (750 ft each) in New York. In the 1930's the Montreal-South Shore (Quebec, Canada) span of 1,097 ft and the Cooper River bridge of 1,050 ft at Charleston, S. C., were among the works that carried forward the history of the cantilever.

The steel arch, representing a type of structure that has occupied an important place in the history of American bridges, also reached a new stage of development with the completion of the Hell Gate arch over the East River at New York in 1912–1917. Lindenthal was chief engineer in charge of this project. The basic form followed at Hell Gate was used earlier in the beautiful Bonn and Dusseldorf bridges over the Rhine in Germany, designed by R. Krohn in 1898, with spans of 614 ft and 595 ft. The Hell Gate arch, however, not only had a record span (1,017 ft) but also is a four-track structure designed for very heavy railroad loadings. Boldly built by cantilevering out from each shore, the halves of this great work were lowered by jacks to join at the center of the span.

However, two similar great arches of the early 1930's have surpassed the Hell Gate span record by almost two thirds. The New York Port Authority completed the Bayonne arch, a 1,652-ft highway span; and, in Sydney, Australia, a heavier structure (carrying rapid transit and electric cars in addition to highway traffic) is but 2 ft less in span.

Several notable arches of the spandrel-braced form, following the first Niagara Gorge arch, have also been built. Among these is the spectacular Lee's Ferry Bridge over the Colorado River in Arizona—not of record span (616 ft) but built far from railroads and almost 500 ft above the river level. One of the most interesting developments in this field has been in the use of arch-cantilever and tied-arch forms. At times it becomes extremely difficult for the nonexpert to classify some of these modern structures. Nevertheless, the trend has been toward more graceful forms, and the tied arch, in particular, represents the ultimate in this modern movement toward an apparent simplicity of form and a "streamlined" effect.

The record for length of truss spans has remained with the railroads. The earlier record of 519 ft established by Linville in 1876 (Fig. 6), however, was not greatly exceeded until 1917. These earlier works had paralled chords, but Burr introduced the broken upper chord, or camel-back truss with his 550-ft span at Cincinnati, in 1888. This form has become standard. In 1917, C. H. Cartlidge, M. ASCE, of the Chicago, Burlington and Quincy Railroad, with Ralph Modjeski, M. ASCE, as consultant, built the longest simple truss span on record—the Metropolis Bridge over the Ohio River between Illinois and Kentucky, with a main span of 720 ft and four other spans exceeding 555 ft. Silicon steel was used in this work for the first time in the United States; and nickel steel, for the tension members—permitting unit stresses of 30,000 lb per sq in. and 35,000 lb per sq in., respectively. Like most American bridges, it is a high truss rather than the relatively shallow and heavier type that is more usual abroad. The Castleton Bridge over the Hudson River on the New York Central Railroad below Albany, N. Y., with spans of 400 ft and 600 ft, is another example of modern simple truss design. The Suisun Bay Bridge of the Southern Pacific with seven spans of 531 ft each is still another notable truss structure.

However, Lindenthal broke even the Metropolis Bridge record by tying two 750-ft trusses together in the Sciotoville Bridge on the Chesapeake and Ohio Northern Railroad over the Ohio River, also completed in 1917. This continuous truss design was remarkable in several ways. It brought to the fore ideas that had been developing for many years in American practice.[28] It seemed to nullify

---

[28] "The Continuous Truss Bridge Over the Ohio River at Sciotoville, Ohio, of the Chesapeake and Ohio Northern Railroad," by Gustav Lindenthal, *Transactions*, ASCE, Vol. LXXXV, 1922, p. 910.

the opinion of some engineers that, when difficult foundation conditions prevailed, some settlement of piers was inevitable and such settlement would vitally affect the stresses in continuous structures. It would, perhaps, be reasonable to argue that increasing confidence in the knowledge of foundation and soil mechanics has thus been a factor in the increase in continuous forms of construction.

Lindenthal's great bridge also carried to an unprecedented extent the practice of erecting such structures so as to avoid or minimize the effect of secondary stresses. The trend toward the use of cantilever erection is well exemplified in this work. At this time, the old huge gantry crane that straddled the entire truss, gave way to the "creeper traveler" (running on the upper chord with portable cranes at the floor level) that characterizes modern practice.

However, the twentieth century has been preeminently the Century of the Suspension Bridge. As it began, the Williamsburg span of 1,600 ft (4 ft longer than the Brooklyn Bridge, shown in Fig. 11) was being completed in New York City (1903). It was a record span but it is undoubtedly less graceful than many other suspension bridges, with its tremendously heavy stiffening truss supported in the end spans on towers. This span length was more than doubled 30 years later in the sharply contrasting lightweight and daring George Washington span of 3,500 ft over the Hudson River. The present record span—the 4,200 ft of the Golden Gate Bridge at San Francisco raised this record to 2.6 times the length of the Brooklyn Bridge.

It is fascinating to follow these increases in span in these more than 30 years. The great growth has come in the past 15 years. It was 20 years before the Williamsburg Bridge record was broken by the Bear Mountain (in New York State) span of 1,632 ft, a private toll venture built in 1924. Then came the Phila-delphia-Camden (N. J.) Bridge of 1,750 ft over the Delaware River in 1926. The Detroit River span of 1929 finally exceeded the length of the Firth of Forth cantilever and again gave span-length laurels to the suspension type. Other notable, if not record-breaking spans, have followed in rapid succession.

There was a bit of excitement in 1927, caused by the discovery that specially heat-treated wire, which was expected to permit higher unit cable stresses, was too brittle to meet essential manipulations in spinning. It was quickly discovered and quickly corrected. Nevertheless, in 1940, one of the most spectacular (and almost unbelievable) failures occurred that has ever marred professional practice. The Tacoma Narrows Bridge, an extremely light highway structure, developed a peculiar undulating, twisting motion as the result of a relatively moderate cross wind (said to have been but 40 miles per hr), and the entire floor system was completely wrecked and fell to the water below. Actually, history was repeating itself, but under conditions that seemed to make its earlier teachings of little importance.

In the earlier nineteenth century, when suspension bridges were first built, they were usually constructed for relatively light highway or pedestrian loads. Thus, their floors were usually suspended platforms hung from the cables. However, when Roebling built the Niagara Gorge suspension (Fig. 10) for railroad as well as highway use, a stiffening truss was essential to provide sufficient distribution under the heavier railroad loads to reduce local deflection to reasonable amounts. Although such inherently flexible structures proved unsuitable for railroad use, many suspensions, such as those over the East River at New York, were used for trolleys and heavier interurban trains. Thus, the suspension bridge actually became a combination structure; it was essentially a suspended truss. Interest centered on the mechanics of design, and the Manhattan Bridge of 1909 in New York City may be regarded as the first combination suspension bridge to be scientifically designed (by the deflection theory).

The increase in light highway needs caused the truss to decrease in importance as a load-distributing element. In such modern structures as the George Washington Bridge, the Golden Gate Bridge, and some other recent bridges, it has almost completely disappeared. At Tacoma Narrows, it was replaced by very light, ribbon-like girders on each side of the roadway. In short, designers had returned to the earlier type of suspended platform bridge.

Many of these earlier platform structures had been badly wrecked by wind— an action that was prevented by the stiffening truss and a problem of earlier days that had been forgotten. Because the new bridges had concrete floors, far heavier than the older timber platforms, wind action did not seem possible; but the failure of the Tacoma Narrows Bridge exactly paralleled such fatal earlier behavior as that encountered in Ellet's famous Wheeling suspension in 1854, in two early works at Niagara Gorge, and in several British bridges, including the great Menai span.

It became apparent that several other recent bridges were subject to the same aerodynamic action that had wrecked "Galloping Gertie," as the Tacoma Narrows Bridge was called. Various forms of snubbing cables or increases in the depth of stiffening trusses have been used to correct this situation. However, the answer probably will be that such dynamic action can be avoided by special provisions in the design of the floors for such bridges.

The movable bridge is a type of structure that recalls the drawbridge of the medieval castle and which the Dutch, faced with the problem of many canal crossings, pioneered. Some American swing spans were built in the nineteenth century, such as the timber Rock Island (Ill.) Bridge that provided Abraham Lincoln with a law case. The first bridge over the Chicago River, built in 1856, probably was also the first all-iron swing span and was an early example of the rim-bearing type. The swing type has appeared best suited to the heavier railroad loads. The Highway Era has emphasized the use of the bascule and lift forms.

Chicago has long been a center in this development. In 1893, William Scherzer, M. ASCE, developed the rolling lift; and, in 1905, Joseph B. Strauss introduced a bascule form that has had wide use. Spans of this type are limited in length to slightly more than 200 ft, but they provide a full, clear channel, unencumbered by any center pier. For longer spans, the vertical lift bridge has been used, a railroad span of 365 ft having been built over the Ohio River at Cincinnati, in 1922. The Manhattan lift bridge on the Triborough Bridge connection in New York City is an example of a modern highway bridge of this type.

Any type of movable bridge[29] results in an interruption of traffic. Therefore, with modern large-volume, high-speed highway traffic, the use of such bridges is avoided wherever possible. This is done by using a fixed high-level span to provide

---

[29] "Movable Bridges," by Otis E. Hovey, John Wiley & Sons, Inc., New York, N. Y., 1926.

the channel clearance required by the Corps of Engineers, which controls all structures crossing over or under navigable waters.

Although there has been wide use of reinforced concrete in the United States, the introduction of new forms of construction and their use in structures of record span was primarily of European origin. The development of a high-strength cement marked the first step in this story. As early as 1796, James Parker had patented a product that was intermediate between natural and portland cement, but Joseph Aspdin is usually credited with the invention of the latter product in 1824. The great French pioneer, Vicat, began to study cements in 1812; and, in 1824, he introduced concrete in his highway work to an extent never before attempted in modern construction.

A French gardener, Monier, using the European cement, received a patent for a reinforced-concrete, wire mesh, or frame construction in 1867; and in the same year, associated with F. Coignet, exhibited beams, pipes, etc., at the Paris Exposition. The idea was quickly taken up in the United States. Ernest L. Ransome, Affiliate, ASCE, began working with this combination of material in 1874, and 10 years later patented the first deformed reinforcing bar. The period from 1890 to 1905 was the era of the "systems" of concrete reinforcement. However, theories of design were being evolved. The famous Joint Committee of Engineering Societies, appointed in 1903–1904, reported in 1908. Its final report of 1912 established design standards, and the use of reinforced concrete became general.

In the bridge building field, the concrete arch began, after 1900, to replace stone arch construction. The latter type of work was costly, and never reached the stage of development in the United States that it did abroad. The first great American concrete arch bridge was the beautiful Walnut Lane Bridge over Wissahickon Creek at Philadelphia (1907–1908). It was essentially a ring-stone, voussoir arch built of plain concrete with a main span of 233 ft.

Like other concrete arches, it followed a form of design that had been developed first in the Luxemburg stone arch built by M. Séjourné, Inspector General of Ponts et Chaussées, in 1903. The great central arch of Séjourné's bridge was a 275.5-ft span; but, instead of the usual solid voussoir barrel, it was composed of two huge stone ribs. Furthermore, it prefigured modern open-spandrel concrete arch design in that the floor was not carried on spandrel walls but on arches supported by these ribs. The Luxemburg Bridge was undoubtedly a daring feat in stone, and it is notable chiefly because it established a new form of design that was especially adapted to reinforced-concrete construction.

The first great concrete arch was the Grünwald Bridge of 1904. However, the rib plan was not followed, a thin solid arch barrel being used. The open-spandrel idea here first appeared in a truly modern form, the floor being supported by spandrel columns. In 1905 *Engineering News-Record* commented:

> "The small thickness of the arch ring, the lightness of the whole construction, should be particularly noted as they define results which have barely been reached with stone."

Engineers were thus still thinking of this new material as a substitute for stone. American practice reflected this attitude. Designers clung to rather massive design and appeared somewhat hesitant in adopting the reinforced-concrete arch ring, capable of taking bending as well as compressive stresses. European engineers went forward with the development of the elastic theory, basic to such design, and daringly experimented with this really new type of structure. The Austrian Society of Engineers and Architects had carried out a series of arch tests beginning in 1890; and, as command of the mechanics of the problem developed, new forms began to appear.

In the earlier arches, the floor was of a simple beam type that spanned between the spandrel column supports. The arch ring was the main working ele-

FIG. 18.—CORTRIGHT CREEK CONCRETE ARCH BRIDGE, RANDLE-YAKIMA HIGHWAY IN WASHINGTON

ment. However, it became clear that the floor could be designed to act as a load distributing system, relieving the arch ring of much of the bending stress and permitting it to become a relatively slender compression ring. It would be difficult to trace this evolution in detail, but the Swiss certainly built some of the most slender and daring of this modern type of reinforced-concrete arch. The Langwies Bridge on a Swiss electric line—completed in 1915 with a span of 315 ft—was a notable early example of this "spidery" type of construction. In the United States, west coast highway engineers have pioneered in the use of this very daring and graceful form (Fig. 18).

The United States has, therefore, a large number of concrete bridges, including the great Tunkhannock (Pa.) Viaduct (1912–1915) on the Delaware, Lackawanna and Western Railroad, thousands of beam-and-slab bridges, hundreds of arches, and probably an almost equal number of rigid-frame structures. However, the general trend has been toward conservative, established design, and the use of steel for longer spans. Cellular forms of construction, like that introduced in the Pont del Resorgimento over the Tiber River in Rome by Hennebique in 1911, or the daring long-span structures and other construction by the great modern French concrete expert, E. Freyssinet (such as the novel 430-ft arch over the Seine River at St. Pierre-du-Vauvray, France, in 1924, the great Plougastel span of 612 ft at Brest, France, or the remarkable hangars at Orly Field, Paris)—these and other European innovations, especially in building construction, have as yet found little or no place in American practice. Perhaps some of this development may find application in the United States in the years immediately ahead.

DAMS

Hydraulic works immediately bring up dams. The greatest dams in the world have been built in the United States, and American engineers have adopted new types and new understandings in the design of such structures. Two major influences have sponsored this development. Until the USBR commenced its program of great dam construction in the west, major works in the United States were built to the requirements of eastern urban water supplies, chiefly those of New York City and Boston. At the turn of the century, attention centered especially on the New Croton which took 15 years to build. Begun in 1892, it was not completed until 1907. It was in many respects a transition structure as well as the highest dam in the world of its day—297 ft above its foundations. The story of the gravity dam goes back several centuries in engineering history. New Croton Dam was not a new form, but it was of record size and a type of structure with which American engineers had had relatively little experience.

Apparently, the forerunner of the modern masonry gravity dam was constructed first in Spain, during the sixteenth century. Later examples were built in France; but, as Edward Wegmann, M. ASCE, observed, prior to the publication of de Sazilly's "profile" of 1853, all these structures were of extravagant cross section and indicated a complete lack of rational theory regarding the design of masonry dams. De Sazilly's brief paper in the *Annales des ponts et chaussées* opened a new era in dam construction, but the outstanding contributors to the further development of masonry dams were British colonial engineers.

In India, the Murtha Canals Project (1869–1879), one of Great Britain's pioneer works in the development of modern irrigation, involved masonry dams of unprecedented size. Colonel Fife and his associates built the Poona Dam (107 ft high) and the Bhatgarh Dam (127 ft high and a mile long). Between 1886 and 1891 W. Clark built the Tansa Dam for the water supply of Bombay, 1.67 miles long with a maximum height of 118 ft. A shorter structure, the Periyar Dam (1887–1897), reached the height of 173 ft.

During the period when the Croton Dam was under construction, British colonial engineers also created the great storage basin on the Upper Nile River by the construction of the Assuan Dam. Begun in 1898, it was completed in 1902, and has since been twice increased in height. However, the Croton Dam was nearly 100 ft higher than earlier works, and the engineers of this work, lacking the experience gained at Assuan, successfully met a notable challenge.

New Croton Dam was the last great American dam of cut-stone masonry. It was both the last in the United States in which natural cement was used and the first in which American portland cement was employed, and it served to stir eastern interest in another type of dam that had been evolving primarily in the West. It was proposed to use an earth dam with a masonry core wall for the southern end of this work; and, although it was finally built of masonry section throughout, the comments of the consultants of 1901 have special interest in view of later American earth-dam developments. They agreed that, for heights of up to nearly 70 ft, an earth embankment that had a solid foundation and was made of well-selected earth, was as durable and safe as masonry.

The construction of the Kensico Dam (built as an emergency storage reservoir for the new Catskill Aqueduct) ushered in a completely new era in dam construction. The dam was begun in 1910 and completed in 1917. The placing of stone masonry was largely by hand labor, and the speed of construction was limited by the number of workers who could be used. At the Kensico Dam a "cyclopean concrete" was substituted, and dam construction became a mass production job. Masonry construction was mechanized. Work trains brought in buckets of concrete and the cyclopean masses of rock, and electrically operated derricks hoisted and dumped them into the forms. A "skin" of stone masonry was later applied, primarily for esthetic purposes.

The earliest dams of the USBR, such as the Roosevelt Dam (completed in 1911) in Arizona and Pathfinder Dam in Wyoming (1905–1910) were, like New Croton Dam, stone masonry structures. However, concrete was used in the great Arrowrock Dam on the Boise River in Idaho (348.5 ft high) although it was not the cyclopean type employed at the Kensico Dam. The Arrowrock Dam (1911–1916) marked the first use of "spouted" cobble concrete, a construction method that was widely used for many years. Fig. 19 shows this dam during its construction. However, it finally became clear that the excessive amount of water necessary for spouted concrete resulted in a segregated mixture with a large percentage of voids. This produced a porous product. The Aluminum Company of America was one of the first to turn from this wet mix to a far drier and less porous concrete in its Calderwood (Tennessee) and Chute à Caron (Quebec, Canada) dams, built about 1930. This concrete required the use of special, bottom-dump buckets that permitted placing a "dry" concrete without dropping it, thus avoiding segregation. At the same time, the USBR constructed the Diablo Dam in Washington. It was 425 ft high. A similar dry mix was used, but it was placed by an ingenious belt conveyer that was hung from a derrick boom with a short tube of the tremie type (known as an "elephant trunk") at the end.

While these changes in the basic material were under way, a new type of dam construction was also developing. As early as 1883, the Bear Valley Dam in California, a small stone structure 65 ft high had been built as an arch with a vertical axis. In the narrow canyons of the West, such arch dams of relatively thin section, carrying the water pressure to the side walls rather than to the base as in the gravity form, found frequent use in the new Era of Dam Construction that was beginning. The Pathfinder Dam in the deep canyon of the North Platte River and the Shoshone (Buffalo Bill) Dam (1905–1910) in Wyoming (both built by the USBR) took this form, the latter being a record-breaking structure 328 ft high but only 200 ft long at the crest. Other notable arch dam construction projects followed these earlier works. The Pacoima (Reagan) Dam (1928) in California, built for Los Angeles flood control, set a new record of 385 ft; the Diablo Dam (1930) in Washington raised this record to 425 ft; and the Owyhee Dam (1930) in Oregon, which was 405 ft in maximum section, had a deep cutoff trench 520 ft below its crest.

These dams were designed as arches, but the Lake Cheesman Dam (1904) in Colorado, although of full-gravity section, was built on a curved plan "for

FIG. 19.—CONSTRUCTION OF ARROWROCK DAM, ON THE BOISE RIVER IN IDAHO

additional stability." The arch-gravity type thus came into being. The Roosevelt Dam of the USBR on the Salt River Project, 280 ft high, followed this plan, as did the Arrowrock Dam (Fig. 19). However, it soon became evident that, unless precautions were taken to fill the contraction joints that were used in all these concrete structures, arch action could not take place until deflection under gravity action had brought the structure together as an arch. Indeed, the arch form might weaken the dam from the gravity-action standpoint. By 1928, the USBR had published a method for analyzing such structures by the "trial-load" method, and for determining how much of the load is carried by arch action and how much by gravity action. Thus dams like Owyhee, noted previously as being of the arch type, are actually thin gravity sections, some three quarters of the load being carried by the arch while one quarter is taken by gravity action.

The record dam of the present day, the Boulder Canyon or Hoover Dam (1931–1936), on the Colorado River in Arizona-Nevada, which is 730 ft high, is of this arch-gravity type. Special methods were provided for cooling the concrete and subsequently grouting the contraction joints.

These great modern dams involve large volumes of concrete. The Kensico Dam required some 900,000 cu yd, Wilson Dam at Muscle Shoals, Ala., exceeded this with 1,250,000 cu yd, Hoover Dam raised the record to more than 3,000,000 cu yd, and Grand Coulee Dam on the Columbia River in Washington required 10,000,000 cu yd of concrete. Modern plant and equipment made it possible to place more than 400,000 cu yd in 1 month at Grand Coulee.

Earth dams of remarkable height and size have also been built. They are undoubtedly the oldest form of dam but, as noted in describing the Croton Dam construction, earlier eastern practice in the United States regarded them as best suited to relatively low constructions—less than 100 ft in height. There had been a number of failures and the eastern viewpoint was naturally conservative. On the other hand, western builders who did not work in such highly settled areas and who faced the need to use local materials at remote and inaccessible sites, turned to earth construction. Furthermore, although eastern practice usually required a masonry core wall and depositing and compacting of the earth fill in layers, western engineers used the hydraulic method, a development from hydraulic mining practice.

The attention of eastern engineers was directed to these new ventures by a paper by James D. Schuyler,[30] M. ASCE. However, between 1918 and 1924 a great step forward occurred when this type of dam was adopted for the retaining reservoirs of the Miami Conservancy District flood-control project in Ohio. Careful tests were made and techniques were developed that made the advantages of earth dam construction clear.

The first great record-breaking dam of this type was the 216-ft-high Davis Bridge Dam in Vermont, completed in 1923. The Tieton Dam of the USBR on the Yakima Project in Washington raised this record to 232 ft in 1925. Then the Wanaque Dam, a water supply dam in northern New Jersey, again stirred eastern interest and was followed by the Cobble Mountain Dam for the water supply of Springfield, Mass., which established a new record of 245 ft in 1930. The Saluda Dam in South Carolina held the volume record of approximately 11,000,000 cu yd until the Fort Peck Dam construction (1935–1940) in Montana, with more than 120,000,000 cu yd, completely dwarfed all earlier records.

The rock-fill dam is another western type, also adopted to use local materials. The Morena Dam of 1914 in California long held the record for this type. It was 267 ft high. In 1925, the Dix River Dam for the water supply of Danville, Ky., set a new record of 275 ft. However, in 1931, the Salt Springs Dam for the Pacific Gas and Electric Company in California raised the record to 330 ft.

Space will not permit mention of other special types of dams—the slab-and-buttress reinforced-concrete dam, multiple arch dams, multiple dome dams, movable dams, and other forms—which have been adopted under special conditions and in which similar records for size and height have been established. The United States undoubtedly made a great contribution in this field, but one of the most interesting developments in dam buildings is of British origin. British colonial

---

[30] "Recent Practice in Hydraulic-Fill Dam Construction," by James D. Schuyler, *Transactions*, ASCE, Vol. LVIII, June, 1907, p. 196.

engineers not only pioneered in gravity dam construction, but evolved a special form of dam which, for low heights, could be built on a porous foundation. The barrages, or diversion dams, such as those on the Nile, must be built in porous alluvial deposits of great depth. The ingenious plan of blanketing the river bottom with an impermeable apron and erecting the barrier on this apron does not provide a completely watertight structure, but it permits the design of a stable dam that will serve its purpose.

WATER SUPPLY AND SEWAGE DISPOSAL

Two major problems have perplexed the water supply engineer in the twentieth century. Not only urban growth, but increasing per capita use of water, has made the search for and development of new or additional sources of supply a continuing problem. In earlier years, there were usually available adequate supplies of water from uncontaminated sources, but the disposal of sewage by dilution in streams has led to the contamination of these sources. The problem has thus become twofold—one of quantity and one of purity.

In the first phase, local sources of supply (springs and wells) became polluted as urban centers became more densely populated and the number of cesspools increased. The change to pumped river and lake supplies thus at first led to an improvement in public health. Almost invariably, such water supplies came first and there were few sewers to pollute these sources of supply. In fact, it has always been far easier to secure public support for a water supply than for either the construction or proper maintenance of sewers and sewage disposal plants. Many earlier sewage works suffered from this attitude and it is still a major problem in the progress of sewage disposal.

By the 1890's it was becoming clear that the building or extension of sewers that discharged their effluent into the nearest watercourses was making the extensive use of raw river water or lake water dangerous. There were many cases of typhoid epidemics, and the problem of arousing public opinion and support for improvement became less difficult. The situation was, however, complicated by the fact that many water supplies were company owned, and great expenditures for new or improved water supplies were not financially warranted. An old era was passing, and the twentieth century has witnessed the purchase of most of the larger privately-owned water supplies by the municipalities served. Very few larger cities are still supplied with water by private companies.

In an effort toward improvement, three steps were clearly possible. Those fortunately located cities that could turn to still relatively unpolluted sources did so. This usually meant going "back country" to sparsely settled areas and developing gravity supplies. Among the recent outstanding great works of this type have been those for New York City, Boston, Los Angeles, San Francisco, and some other large centers. Such projects are usually very costly, and only a wealthy community can afford them.

New York City exhausted the possibilities of the Croton watershed and, between 1905 and 1914, built the Schoharie and Ashokan dams. To bring this water to the city, a 75-mile aqueduct and a system for distribution to the city mains by deep tunnel were built at a cost of $220,000,000. It was the greatest work of its kind ever done. In sharp contrast, Los Angeles, a city that had grown from a Mexican town in a few years, built a 233-mile canal and pipeline and tunnel from Owens Valley. This was a far longer but much less costly undertaking. It included some constructions that would have been regarded as risky if not dangerous in the East.

In both these cases the intervening years have led to new demands. New York City is now completing an additional West Catskill supply, and Los Angeles has built a new supply some 400 miles from the Colorado River. The latter is unique in its series of pumping plants and powerhouses that overcome and utilize some of the large ascents and descents on the line. It has also involved some of the most difficult tunneling of modern times.

Boston has also been forced to draw on the drainage basin of the Connecticut River in the Ware and Swift valleys to supplement the earlier supplies of the metropolitan area. San Francisco, long served by private companies, completed the first step in a vast water supply project with the Bay Crossing Aqueduct of 1926. However, not until 1934 did flow from the Hetch Hetchy Reservoir reach the city through a remarkable 155-mile pipeline.

Chicago, which secures its water supply from Lake Michigan, temporarily solved its sewage problem by the simple expedient of the Chicago Drainage Canal of 1900, which discharges into the Mississippi River drainage basin. However, this unusual solution of the problem of keeping a city from polluting its own supply has led to the requirement that Chicago build proper works to treat its sewage. In fact, many cities are forced to utilize more or less polluted supplies and to treat the water before distributing it.

It seems difficult to realize that not until the 1880's did Koch and others make clear the role of bacteria in the spread of disease. In about 1890, a report of the pioneer Massachusetts Board of Health called attention to the biological processes through which sewage may be purified. However, this difficult and costly solution of the problem was avoided in practice and the removal of dangerous bacteria was accomplished by filtration, a technique hitherto employed solely to reduce turbidity and color. As previously noted, Hazen's notable book, "The Filtration of Public Water-Supplies," appeared in 1900. It emphasized "bacterial efficiency" and coagulation and described the design of both the slow sand, gravity and the rapid, mechanical, pressure forms of filters. Many cities embarked on the construction of extensive filter plants, and there was much discussion of the process. Details of design and construction occupied many pages of the technical press. Little Falls, N. J., in 1902, established a pioneer rapid filtration plant. However, larger cities usually installed the gravity type.

The period around 1910 witnessed the search for a chemical method of destroying harmful bacteria in water without destroying its potability and safety for human use. Hypochloride of lime was used in 1908, ozonation followed in 1910, then liquid chlorine was used successfully at Fort Myer, Va. The problem seemed to be solved, and this process is now almost universally followed and is used by nearly every city in the United States. Nevertheless, this solution is not completely satisfactory as many supplies provide hard water. Softening is a costly process and few cities charge water rates that permit its use. In many other cases, objectionable quantities of chlorine are used and little attention is paid to color or turbidity.

The general American attitude that water should be as free as air has also led to excessive consumption and waste of water. Many large cities use as much as 150 gal per capita per day and more; and, even in smaller towns, consumption is seldom less than half this quantity—far in excess of European standards. These excesses and the increased costs of additional supplies caused a strong movement in the 1920's toward basing water rates on metering rather than charging the usual flat rates. However, many cities continued to follow the older practice, and a water supply problem of ever-increasing difficulty has remained.

In no field does the modern city face a greater problem than in that of sewage disposal. The pollution of streams and lakes has reached such a condition that greater attention to this admittedly difficult and costly task of disposing of human wastes can no longer be forgotten or ignored. In this field, the past 50 years have been largely spent in study, research, and experiment.

The disposal of raw sewage by dilution would undoubtedly have continued unabated if state health boards had not intervened. The problem is usually that of removing the small solids content and turning into watercourses not a bacterially pure effluent, but one of sufficient stability so that it will not be objectionable.

Of course, irrigation has been used in the past. As made clear by the Massachusetts studies earlier noted, the problem is basically biological. The early cesspool became with the turn of the century a septic tank in which anaerobic bacteria digested the solids and a liquid effluent could be disposed of in subsoil beds. The next step was the improvement of this device in the two-story tank of the German Imhoff or Emscher type. Later, as knowledge of these processes developed, the activated sludge technique came into use—for the first time in Texas in 1916. Various mechanical and other procedures for handling sludge have since been devised.

In the meantime, methods of giving aerobic bacteria a chance to operate and thus produce a more stable liquid effluent were being evolved. The first intermittent filters were built at Medford, Mass., in 1887. In 1901 the first trickling filter was installed at Madison, Wis. The largest plants of recent years have been those at New York and Chicago. In 1939, the latter began the operation of the world's largest activated sludge plant at its Southwest Station. In the same year, step aeration was incorporated into the Tallman's Island activated sludge plant in New York, and the operation of New York's Jamaica plant was switched to a modified aeration process in 1943.

This field of civil engineering practice is highly specialized. A few highlights of a vast American problem have been noted here, but no mention has been made of changes and improvement in the many details of mechanical equipment and construction which have taken place. Unquestionably, however, this problem of the satisfactory treatment of sewage before disposal into streams and lakes is still far from solution. A federal stream pollution law was finally enacted in 1948 after 50 years of agitation. This long neglected problem will, thus, apparently receive greater attention in the future. However, this, at least, may be said: Although the medical profession claims the lion's share of credit for the remarkable improvements in public health in the past half century, no small share of this credit should go to American sanitary engineers who have, in spite of public apathy and indifference, provided the water supplies and sanitary facilities that are basic to such improvement.

FUTURE INCREASED SPECIALIZATION

What have been the effects of the remarkable civil engineering advance and development of the twentieth century? Had it been possible to look ahead 100 years ago when the ASCE was founded—or even 50 years ago when this new era of unparalleled construction opened—engineers could undoubtedly have avoided some reconstruction and, perhaps, some failures. In fact, civil engineers, in forecasting future needs, probably venture longer predictions—for example, in the case of great urban water supplies—than any other group of engineers. However, in regard to possible trends and developments in the scope and character of professional practice in the future, many uncertain and extraneous influences make more than an attempt at projected hindsight impossible.

It thus seems certain that man's search to find a rational basis for action (which, reflected in the scientific approach to the problems of design, has so greatly extended the scope and power of engineering activity) will continue at an ever-increasing pace. Scientific, engineering, and industrial research directed toward greater understanding and greater control of material surroundings is the keynote of the modern search for progress and power.

This, in turn, must inevitably lead—as it already has led in medicine—to greater specialization in engineering. One of the first changes will probably be a finer distinction between the designer and the production or construction type of engineer. This trend is already under way. The all-around structural engineer of the past, who was both a capable designer and an able and practical builder represents a rapidly passing type.

The day when men such as Kirkwood could turn from railroad to sanitary engineering has also passed. With organized specialization and increasing complexity of techniques, the distinction between the professional engineer and the technical assistant is also becoming stronger. In the future, there will be few indeed who, lacking specialized education, will rise from the ranks to professional leadership as has been done in the past.

The grave dangers involved in these trends cannot be denied. A complete divorce between design and construction would be fatal, for design is but a means to intelligent and economical construction. Similarly, overemphasis of science and specialization in educational programs may lead to the development of a narrow engineering mind, incapable of seeing all the many factors to be considered in the planning of any great engineering work.

Also, the construction industry itself rapidly is becoming an increasingly engineered activity. The planning of the construction plant is a major problem in engineering design, and the scheduling of operations and the direction of forces are major managerial problems. Eventually it will be found that much of the new construction technique can be taught more quickly and effectively by the formal processes of the classroom than solely through apprenticeship as it so largely is today.

It once seemed that the independent consulting engineer was about to disappear. Cities were inclined to have their own engineering forces, states tended to fully take over all highway problems, and the Federal Government showed a similar attitude in the matter of engineering. In the conduct of normal, routine operations and extensions this pattern will undoubtedly be followed. However, it is uneconomical (and perhaps impossible) for any organization to maintain specialists in all branches of a profession that is becoming ever more specialized. Furthermore, it is wasteful to build up a special staff to undertake new work that is temporary in character or only occurs at infrequent intervals. Therefore, there will probably be an increase in specialized consulting offices in the future.

What changes may be expected in engineering equipment and construction methods, and what continuing or new demands for civil engineering services may be forthcoming? With constantly increasing labor costs, it appears that mechanization in construction must increase although it already seems that the ultimate in this field has been achieved. Unlike the consumer-goods industries, the capital-goods work of the civil engineer usually requires the production of but one unit. Every construction job—because the work is built in place to meet special conditions—involves a new product. Perhaps there will be far more prefabrication in the future in connection with many minor civil engineering structures or parts.

Nevertheless, demand finally will determine the extent of future activities in civil engineering. Growing and expanding economic requirements constitute the main determining factors. The needs and wants of thousands of towns and cities are the backbone of sanitary practice. The existing problems of highway traffic are still far from solution and furnish the major problems of structural offices. The great works of the Federal Government may be spectacular and record breaking but they do not "keep the wheels turning" in civil engineering. A strong and healthy economy and a widespread material well-being continue to be the greatest assurances of a perpetual demand for types of civil engineering services that will challenge the best efforts of engineers and stimulate continued professional development in the years to come.

AMERICAN SOCIETY OF CIVIL ENGINEERS

Founded November 5, 1852

TRANSACTIONS

Paper No. 2577

AN ENGINEERING CENTURY IN CALIFORNIA

ADDRESS AT THE ANNUAL CONVENTION, SAN FRANCISCO, CALIF., MARCH 4, 1953

By Walter L. Huber,[1] President, ASCE

Synopsis

Engineering development in California parallels that of the Society—both are a century old. Only the first 75 years of activity are described, leaving the past quarter century to current observation and general familiarity. As illustrated by many vivid examples and personalities, water was ever the prime consideration, for first mining, then irrigation, and finally power. Meanwhile large population increases caused crises in domestic supplies, solved by major aqueducts from distant sources. Spectacular accomplishments in transportation, particularly in railroading over the Sierras, are also a prideful part of California history. Throughout, the names of great engineers, responsible for the mighty works, shed luster on the century-old state, the profession, and the ASCE.

As the Society enters its second century of existence, it may be well to review the progress of engineering in California during the past 100 years. The life of this community as one of the forty-eight states of the Union is nearly coincident with that of the ASCE. Certainly there could be no more appropriate time or place for this review than by a California President at a Society meeting in San Francisco. Attention will be largely confined to the first 75 years of the century; the developments of the past 25 years are better known, and their omission will avoid the possible embarrassments incidental to discussing contemporaries.

First Water Demands.—Hydraulic engineering has loomed large in California during all its historical existence. Spanish settlement preceded the American occupation by more than three quarters of a century. San Francisco was founded in 1776—the year of the Declaration of American Independence. Spanish and Mexican occupation of California brought what may be called its pastoral period. It was the period of cattle raising on a large scale—the period of the Spanish ranchos, with limited commerce and practically no manufacturing or industries. The principal engineering works were those developed by the Missions for irriga-

---

[1] Partner, Huber and Knapik, San Francisco, Calif.

97

tion. These were in many instances quite extensive and well designed for the immediate needs of the lands to be served.

Discovery of gold at about the beginning of the American occupation changed the California mode of living, but not the California need for water. Then began a development of a remote area which challenged the ingenuity of engineers. Indeed, the problems presented for solution engendered originality and self-reliance in men whose records and achievements have been lost in many instances. Only the outstanding ones can now be remembered. After all, fame is fickle.

An Engineer Correspondent.—One of the first names to be mentioned in connection with the American occupation is that of Lt. George H. Derby of the Topographical Engineers, a predecessor organization to the Corps of Engineers, United States Department of the Army. He was an engineer of ability and a wit of great ingenuity. Perhaps his fame comes more from his "extracurricular" activities than from his engineering studies and reports, although these latter are exceptional. His official tasks, while he was assigned to duty in California, were very evidently not sufficient to keep him fully occupied. His brilliant writings as a newspaper correspondent, first at San Francisco as John Squibob and later at San Diego as John Phoenix, are covered in nontechnical writings and will not be further discussed here.[2,3] They show a resourceful wit which is unfortunately lacking in some serious engineers.

Occasionally flashes of these qualities, also, appear in his official reports. For instance, in his Sacramento Valley report of 1849, after commenting on the probability of comfortable subsistence and shelter for troops at a proposed military post, he stated:

> "I can conceive of no advantages to be derived from establishing a post in that vicinity. There would be no inhabitants to protect, and nothing in fact to protect them from."

As evidence of his engineering skill, it is of interest to note that in 1952 an adequate channel for turning the San Diego River through Mission Bay was completed substantially in accord with the recommendations which Lieutenant Derby made 100 years before.

Hydraulics in Gold Mining.—The attention of Americans arriving in the rush, following John Marshall's discovery of gold in 1848, naturally turned to the mines. From the first, water was an important, if not a determining, factor in mining operations. The newcomers soon learned that the smaller California streams dried up in the long, arid summers and that then water for even one-man placer operations was not available. They also learned the advantages of joining in community ventures to construct canals to convey water from the live streams for sluicing operations, to say nothing of culinary purposes. Here necessity again proved to be the mother of invention and brought forth the very extensive system of canals which were built in a comparatively short time.

To this day the design and construction of these canals are feats to excite admiration. The engineers who planned and built them were often pioneering beyond precedent. With the development of hydraulic mining, whereby whole

---

[2] "The Topographical Reports of Lieutenant George H. Derby with Introduction and Notes by Francis P. Farquhar," *Special Publication No. 6*, California Historical Soc., San Francisco, Calif., 1933.
[3] "John Phoenix, Esq.," by George R. Stewart, Henry Holt & Co., New York, N. Y., 1937.

hillsides were sluiced down by hydraulic jets (Fig. 1), further gigantic problems were imposed on these early engineers. Self-reliance was their dominant characteristic. They met the challenge. By 1867 there were 5,328 miles of main canals with probably 800 miles more of branch ditches.[4]

Unfortunately, records of the accomplishments of these early engineers are now all too incomplete. They were too busy to leave adequate historical data.

FIG. 1.—EARLY MINING IN CALIFORNIA—EXCAVATING AND TRANSPORTING MATERIAL BY A
BATTERY OF HYDRAULIC MONITORS

Some names do shine through this obscurity, like that of J. Ross Browne (Fig. 2), engineer and statesman, who, aside from his engineering activities, was the official reporter of the California Constitutional Convention of 1850. Also, the investigations of hydraulic flow in pipes under high head by Hamilton Smith, Jr., M. ASCE, were probably the first of their kind. These hydraulic experiments in California have carried his name through subsequent engineering literature.

Inventive Pioneers.—Most of these men were both mining and hydraulic en-

---

[4] "Geologic Guide Book Along Highway 49," *Bulletin No. 141,* California Div. of Mines, San Francisco, Calif., September, 1948.

gineers, but as experts in hydraulic mining they were concerned with problems of water storage and the application of water under high heads by means of long pipelines which exceeded all precedents. In handling these problems, the early California mining engineers were unexcelled anywhere; their services were widely sought in South Africa, South America, Australia, Canada, Siberia, and many other localities. A few of those whose names should be recorded are: Augustus J. Bowie, M. ASCE, Browne, Alexis Janin, A. H. Brigham, Gardner F. Williams, Hennen Gennings, and Cleveland Perkins.

The invention and improvement of required equipment kept pace with field development. Lester A. Pelton, master mechanic at one of the mines, is reported

FIG. 2.—J. ROSS BROWNE, WHO DID MUCH FOR CALIFORNIA BEYOND, AS WELL AS, IN ENGINEERING

to have been watching the operation of a so-called "hurdy-gurdy" wheel used to develop power by hydraulic means. He noted that, when the stream of water was diverted to the side of the buckets by misalinement, the efficiency was at least not greatly reduced and was probably increased. This observation led to his experiments and the development of the type of water wheel which still bears his name and which has revolutionized the production of hydroelectric power by high-head plants.

In his studies Pelton was assisted by Browne. Further experiments leading to improvements of Pelton wheels were made by Frederick G. Hesse of the University of California at Berkeley. Byron Jackson pioneered in the development of needed pumping equipment, and his name has been carried on by the company which he founded.

Hydraulic mining on streams tributary to the Sacramento River was stopped in the early 1880's through court action because it was fouling the streams with mining detritus. Silt was carried far down to even the main river channels, where it threatened both navigation and the agricultural values of the rich farm lands which had been developed by this time. Hydraulic engineering then turned to fields other than mining, more particularly to irrigation and municipal water supplies. These will be discussed later, but in the meantime great strides were being made in another field, that of railroad building.

FIG. 3.—ORIGINAL RIGHT OF WAY AND WOOD-BURNING EQUIPMENT, CENTRAL PACIFIC RAILWAY

Feats in Railroading.—The greatest of all California's pioneer railroad builders was Theodore Dehone Judah, M. ASCE. After some experience in railroad building in New York State he came to California in 1854 at the request of Col. Charles L. Wilson to become chief engineer of the Sacramento Valley Railroad Company, then recently formed to build a line out of Sacramento, but wholly within the Sacramento Valley. Work began under Judah's direction in 1855. Although his efforts were greatly hindered by financial problems, the road was completed by September 9, 1856, to Folsom (some 25 miles); and a celebration commemorating the sixth anniversary of California's admission to the Union included an excursion on the first passenger train west of the Rocky Mountains.

Rolling equipment, including wood-burning locomotives (Fig. 3), had largely been brought from the eastern seaboard by sea and river transportation. This first excursion train was pulled by the locomotive "Nevada." Gilbert H. Kneiss describes an interesting nonscheduled stop:

> "Everyone jumped down and flocked to the poor 'Nevada,' disgraced on so grand an occasion. John Robinson [General Superintendent of the Railroad] was up in the cab with the engine crew, and all three knelt before the open fire door—not praying, though some of the words were very similar. A flue had burned through, water was pouring onto the grates, and what had been the fire was a soggy mass of charred cordwood. The 'Nevada' was through for the day.
>
> "Fortunately, the train was only a couple of miles short of Saulsbury's Inn and Stage Station. Robinson sprinted up the ties, coattails flying, while the passengers followed more leisurely. At the Inn the barkeeper told them the superintendent had commandeered a horse and galloped off for Folsom and a hot locomotive. He also mentioned that he could provide refreshments 'vinous and liquorish in character' to shorten the delay. It was a more exhilarated party by the time the 'Sacramento's' whistle screamed that Robinson was back."[5]

Judah's experience with this pioneer railroad only enlarged his dream of a transcontinental railway. His time was divided between California and Washington, D. C., in efforts to promote this dream. At Sacramento he interested a number of citizens, among them Leland Stanford, Collis P. Huntington, F. ASCE, Mark Hopkins, and Charles Crocker—the men who were to carry out the project. On June 28, 1861, the Central Pacific Railroad was incorporated. The history of the organization, location, and construction of the Central Pacific Railway eastward from Sacramento to its junction with the Union Pacific Railroad at Promontory, Utah, on May 10, 1869, to complete the first transcontinental railroad, is a long and very interesting one—too long, in fact, for inclusion in this paper, particularly since it is so well told by John D. Galloway,[6] Hon. M. ASCE, in his "The First Transcontinental Railroad."[7] In this book Galloway, commenting upon the work of Judah, who died on November 2, 1863, before construction of the railroad was even nearing completion, states:

> "For over seventy years since the completion of the railroad on the lines projected by Judah, the traffic of Central California and the West has been carried over the Central Pacific. In spite of the fact that eight other transcontinental railroads have been built, the central route retains its preeminence. The railroad was built on the route selected by Judah, and that is his monument. None better could be devised for any man."

Other Transportation Successes.—After the completion of the Central Pacific, railroad building continued apace in California. The Southern Pacific Railroad Company was formed, and the Central and Southern Pacific were merged. S. S. Montague had succeeded Judah as chief engineer of the Central Pacific, and the road was completed under his engineering guidance. Later the combined system was to have able engineering direction by other Members of the ASCE, notably William Hood and W. H. Kirkbride.

---

[5] "Bonanza Railroads," by Gilbert H. Kneiss, Stanford Univ. Press, Stanford University, Calif., 1941, p. 16.
[6] "Theodore Dehone Judah—Railroad Pioneer," by John D. Galloway, *Civil Engineering*, Pt. I, October, 1941, p. 586; and Pt. II, November, 1941, p. 648.
[7] "The First Transcontinental Railroad," by John Debo Galloway, Simmons-Boardman, New York, N. Y., 1950.

In Judah's honor a splendid memorial (Fig. 4) stands on the grounds of the railroad station at Sacramento, in order, according to the inscription on its base:

"That the West may remember Theodore Dehone Judah, pioneer, civil engineer and tireless advocate of a great transcontinental railroad—America's

FIG. 4.—MONUMENT TO THEODORE DEHONE JUDAH, M. ASCE, IN SACRAMENTO, DEDICATED AT ASCE MEETING, APRIL, 1930; UNVEILED, FEBRUARY, 1931

first—this monument was erected by the men and women of the Southern Pacific Company * * *."

The site and stone block were dedicated by the Society at its Spring Meeting, April 26, 1930, with Kirkbride, who had promoted the project, as main speaker.

Construction of railroads in Southern California and in the San Joaquin Valley, later to be merged in the Santa Fe System, was another phase of the rapid development. William B. Storey, M. ASCE, a native San Franciscan, was chief engineer of the Valley Railroad constructed in the San Joaquin Valley (1895-1898). When this was merged with the Santa Fe, he went on to be chief engineer and later president of that railroad.

Another problem of transportation, this one localized, was posed by the steepness of San Francisco hills; the resourcefulness of pioneer engineers produced the cable car as a solution. The first cable car used anywhere ran on Clay Street in San Francisco about 1873. Propulsion was secured by a "grip," which clamped on an endless traveling cable. Credit for the design and construction of this type of transportation was largely due to Andrew S. Hallidie. Its use spread to all parts of the world. In recent times it has been supplanted by more modern systems, except on routes with the steepest inclines such as, for instance, some of the San Francisco streets.

Turning to Irrigation.—Although much of the attention of the early Californians was centered on the mines, it did not take long for many of them to learn that "All * * * that glitters is not gold." Indeed, many of them were better suited by experience and temperament to farming than to mining. They soon turned in great numbers to the rich unoccupied agricultural lands. For a time the crops of the Central Valley were largely grains and such other crops as could be grown without irrigation. This method, termed dry farming, was dictated by the long, rainless summer season. Irrigation was known to the early Spanish settlers and was practiced on a moderate scale; but development of large-scale irrigation projects awaited the resourcefulness of American engineers. Another challenge was met.

During the first years of American occupancy settlers built small ditches leading water from the nearby streams to the fertile lands of the coastal plain of Southern California. However, it was soon realized that direct diversion from streams was impracticable unless there were supplemental storage facilities since the streams largely dried up or disappeared in the summer season, when water for growing crops was most needed. For this reason Bear Valley, Hemet, Sweetwater, and Cuyamaca reservoirs were constructed or begun in the 1880's.

One of the pioneers of irrigation engineering in California was P. J. Flynn, M. ASCE, who had been an irrigation official in India for the British Government. His book on irrigation canals and irrigation works, published in 1892, is still an interesting volume. James Dix Schuyler, M. ASCE, left as his monuments some of the principal irrigation structures of Southern California, including Sweetwater and Hemet dams. Others who might be mentioned were H. N. Savage and J. M. Howells, Members, ASCE. Howells contended with the difficult problems of both construction and operation of the system of the San Diego Flume Company (Fig. 5) through a period of financial depression and deficient water supply.

Water for the Central Valley.—While irrigation development was proceeding in Southern California, it was not being neglected in the remainder of the state, particularly in the great Central Valley. The major storage reservoirs now functioning for irrigation and related developments have generally been constructed since 1900. To describe or even to list all the structures by which more than 6,000,000 acres of California lands are now irrigated is beyond the scope of this

FIG. 5.—COCHES TRESTLE OF SAN DIEGO FLUME COMPANY, ONE OF SEVERAL IMPORTANT WOODEN
STRUCTURES OF THIS WATER PROJECT, COMPLETED ABOUT 1889

brief review. Most of this development has been financed and constructed, and is being operated, by irrigation or other districts authorized by California law.

The engineers who planned and directed this work were leaders in their field. Walter James was one of the first. Luther Wagoner, Arthur L. Adams, C. E. Grunsky, Edwin Duryea, I. Tielman, F. C. Herrmann and Harry L. Haehl (all Members of the ASCE except Tielman) made important contributions, to mention only those in the first three quarters of the century under consideration. During the final quarter federal agencies have entered the field of water resource development in California. Both the Corps of Engineers and the Bureau of Reclamation, United States Department of the Interior, have planned comprehensive projects, some of which are under construction.

Demands for City Water.—Another field which has occupied the attention of some of the greatest hydraulic engineers is that of municipal water supply. A. W. von Schmidt, who came to California in 1849, brought the Spring Valley Water Company's first supply to San Francisco. His was a versatile career, and he soon went on to other fields: The first survey of the oblique boundary between California and Nevada; the survey of the Mount Diablo Base Line of the Public Lands Surveys, across the High Sierra; demolition of Blossom Rock, a menace to navigation in San Francisco Bay; construction of the first drydock at Hunters Point; and so on.

The planning and construction of the Spring Valley Water Company system was largely the work of Hermann Schussler, M. ASCE, who came to California in the early 1860's and literally grew up with the organization. Although this was his greatest interest, he found time for other exercise of his talents, notably bringing water to Virginia City in neighboring Nevada. There, in 1872, he built a pipeline under a then unprecedented head and it is still in service. This development was made in cooperation with William R. Eckart, M. ASCE. Completion of the system of the Spring Valley Water Company to the stage where it was acquired by the City of San Francisco was directed by Herrmann and by George A. M. Elliott, M. ASCE, the company's final general manager and chief engineer.

Long before its acquisition of the Spring Valley System, the City of San Francisco had planned and constructed at least all the initial stages of its Hetch Hetchy Project, bringing water from the Sierra Nevada, 150 miles distant. The original filings for this project were made under the supervision of Marsden Manson, M. ASCE; but the design and construction were accomplished under the direction of M. M. O'Shaughnessy, M. ASCE, who was city engineer of San Francisco from 1912 to 1932 and who was probably its greatest builder of municipal works.

Other Distant Municipal Supplies.—From 1878 until his death in 1935 William Mulholland, M. ASCE, was connected with the Los Angeles water system, and after 1886 he was in full charge. Thus, his service began before the city had reached anything approaching metropolitan status. He early realized that an adequate water supply was perhaps a determining factor in assuring the city's growth. His was the vision that led to the construction of the Owens Valley Aqueduct to bring water from the eastern side of the Sierra Nevada more than 200 miles distant. In this development he was ably assisted by J. B. Lippincott, Hon.

M. ASCE, and many other capable engineers. This project has recently been extended to bring water more than 300 miles from Mono Basin sources.

Even this development did not provide for the region's phenomenal growth, as Mulholland was the first to appreciate. Supplemental supplies for Los Angeles and many other Southern California cities, including San Diego, are now derived from the distant Colorado River through the great Metropolitan Aqueduct. The first chief engineer on this work was F. E. Weymouth, Hon. M. ASCE.

After the local sources of municipal water supply along the east side of San Francisco Bay had proved inadequate, the interested cities joined in a municipal utility district and brought water from the Mokelumne River some 100 miles away in the Sierra Nevada. This development was accomplished under the direction of A. P. Davis, Past-President, ASCE, formerly chief engineer and director of the Bureau of Reclamation. The discussion of the problems of other smaller cities of California in securing their water supplies could greatly expand this recital.

Early Power for Southern California.—Hydroelectric development and long-distance electric power transmission have been great factors in the growth of California. When and where electric power was actually first developed by water power is a disputed point. There are several instances of electric lighting in Northern California mining regions by water-driven power devices as early as the 1880's, but transmission was still an obstacle to be overcome.

In his book "P. G. and E. of California,"[8] Charles M. Coleman states that:

"* * * there is evidence that a small direct-current generator installed at Highgrove near Colton in Southern California was placed in operation in June, 1887, to supply San Bernardino, eight miles away. The plant was placed on the ditch system of the Riverside Water Company."

The first real installation in California for the transmission of hydroelectric power is generally conceded to be that of the San Antonio Light and Power Company, which built a plant on San Antonio Creek.

This development was due to the vision and persistence of Cyrus G. Baldwin, president of Pomona College at Claremont. He had many difficulties with eastern manufacturers of electrical equipment, but finally triumphed. The plant was of 150-hp capacity. Transmission was at 10,000 v, single phase. The line to Pomona was 13¾ miles in length, and this was very soon extended to San Bernardino with an over-all measurement of 28¾ miles. Service began in 1892.

In 1893 the 700-kw Mill Creek No. 1 plant, now part of the system of the Southern California Edison Company, commenced operation with an 11,000-v, three-phase transmission line to Redlands, some 7½ miles distant. This was the first three-phase power put to use. H. H. Sinclair had an important part in this development.

Hydroelectric Development for Sacramento Valley.—In 1895 the Folsom plant of a predecessor organization of the Pacific Gas and Electric Company began transmitting power from Folsom to Sacramento (22 miles) at 11,000 v. Other hydroelectric plants of the present Pacific Gas and Electric Company system

---

[8] "P. G. and E. of California," by Charles M. Coleman, McGraw-Hill Book Co., Inc., New York, N. Y., 1952, p. 103.

followed in rapid succession; but the next great precedent-breaking step was the transmission of electric power from the Colgate plant (Fig. 6) to Oakland, a distance of 142 miles, at 60,000 v, in 1901. This line also included the record-breaking cable span of 4,427 ft across the Straits of Carquinez, designed and built under Galloway's direction.

The story of the development of the great hydroelectric system which covers Northern California is too long for inclusion in this paper; but fortunately it is preserved in Coleman's very interesting and complete book.[8] It is perhaps in order to mention the names of some of the engineers who helped in the pioneer

FIG. 6.—ORIGINAL COLGATE POWER PLANT OF BAY COUNTIES POWER COMPANY, ON THE NORTH FORK OF THE YUBA RIVER, BUILT ABOUT 1900—NOW RECONSTRUCTED AND A PART OF THE SYSTEM OF PACIFIC GAS AND ELECTRIC COMPANY

development as, for instance, Eckart; Galloway; A. M. Hunt, M. ASCE; F. G. Baum; James H. Wise, A. M. ASCE; D. H. Duncanson; and Howells. There were many others. To expand the list to the present day would make it resemble a section of "Who's Who in Engineering."

In Other California Areas.—Development in Central and Southern California kept pace with that of Northern California. Power from Big Creek, a tributary of the San Joaquin River, was transmitted to Los Angeles in 1913 over the first 150-kv transmission lines by the Pacific Light and Power Company, a predecessor of the Southern California Edison Company. Subsequently these lines were raised for greater ground clearance and beginning in 1923 were the first to use 220,000-v transmission.

Much of history and romance is reflected in the development of the Pacific Light and Power Company system, including construction of long tunnels and a large multiple arch dam. The Big Creek-San Joaquin Project uses the same water through successive drops totaling almost 6,000 ft, obtaining about 4,500 kw-hr per acre-foot of water. The hydroelectric system of the City of Los Angeles began with the Owens Valley Aqueduct plants, and its early story is closely related to that of the aqueduct.

Power for Eastern Slopes.—On the eastern side of the Sierra Nevada the system of the California Electric Power Company has been constructed in the face of many physical obstacles imposed by remoteness and by deserts and very high mountains. It derives its water supply from mountain slopes reaching to elevations of nearly 14,000 ft, covered in part by living glaciers. Through five plants on its Bishop Creek system, it utilizes a drop of approximately 4,000 ft. Its Silver Lake plant on Rush Creek has a static head exceeding 1,900 ft.

Some of the problems of constructing long transmission lines have themselves been feats. The demand for power for mines in the Tonopah region brought about the company's original development many years ago. To reach this market required transmission lines from Bishop Creek more than 100 miles distant and over the White Mountains. The most favorable route reached elevations exceeding 10,000 ft. Horses were used in the construction—and it cost 85¢ per day to water a horse. Much of the California Electric Power Company's development bears the imprint of Charles O. Poole, M. ASCE, an engineer of great ability and resourcefulness. Poole plant on Leevining Creek was named for him.

State and Government Activities.—Any discussion of the development of the water resources of California must include mention of the important investigations made by the state. William Hammond Hall, M. ASCE, was the first state engineer of California. Serving in this capacity from 1878 to 1889, he directed surveys and investigations covering hydrological and physical conditions which were included in reports that are still valuable.

After his time the office of state engineer lapsed until it was recreated in 1907; but serious work along hydraulic lines was not resumed until 1912, when W. F. McClure, M. ASCE, was appointed state engineer. Under his direction and by mandate of the legislature there were initiated studies which have been carried on by his successors to afford the most complete inventory and planning of water resources accomplished by any state. From these studies have grown plans for the Central Valley Project and other major developments.

The work of the Corps of Engineers has been important. In addition to Lieutenant Derby, already mentioned, others whose part in the early work should be mentioned are Gen. B. S. Alexander; Col. George H. Mendell, M. ASCE; Col. W. H. Heuer, M. ASCE; and Gen. William W. Harts, M. ASCE, the first President of the San Francisco Section, ASCE. H. H. Wadsworth, M. ASCE, long a valued member of the civilian staff, had much to do with developing the system of levees and by-passes, which alleviate flood conditions in the Sacramento Valley. The work of the Corps has been expanded beyond the dreams of the early pioneers and has been continued by a long line of worthy successors.

No account of engineering in California would be complete without special mention of George Davidson, Hon. M. ASCE. His service with the United

States Coast and Geodetic Survey covered a period of 60 years. He arrived soon after the American occupation and was stationed in San Francisco for much of his long life. It was he who was responsible to a great degree for the fine harbor charts and coast charts and for the publication of the "Pacific Coast Pilot." Some of his reminiscences were interesting. He told his confrere, Otto von Geldern,

Fig. 7.—John Debo Galloway, 1869–1943, Hon. M. ASCE, Consulting Engineer and Historian, Who "Had a Part in Practically Every Major Engineering Project in Northern California During a Period of Forty Years"

M. ASCE, that, when he was in charge of his scientific parties, his pay as a young Coast Survey officer was $75 a month, whereas the more valuable member of the party, the cook, received $150 a month.

Problems of Earthquakes and Bridges.—The San Francisco fire and earthquake of 1906 imposed a task for local structural engineers, but it also afforded them a great opportunity to build a modern city better adapted to resist the forces of convulsive nature. In spite of the demands of commercial interests, the improved standards for building construction then set have remained. To be sure, some later earthy activities, as at Santa Barbara and Long Beach, and more recently in Kern County, have served as valuable reminders that the standard should not be lowered. Among the engineers who had an important part in the rebuilding of San Francisco following the disaster of 1906 were Galloway; Maurice C. Couchot, M. ASCE; John B. Leonard, M. ASCE; and C. H. Snyder, M. ASCE. A Society committee under Galloway (Fig. 7) made an exhaustive study of "Effects of Earthquakes on Engineering Structures," especially referring to the 1923 Japanese disaster, and produced a monumental report now on file in the Engineering Societies Library in New York, N. Y.

Although two examples of engineering achievement fall in the past quarter century, perhaps they should be mentioned in passing. The great San Francisco-Oakland Bay Bridge, one of the world's greatest, was built under the direction of Charles H. Purcell, Hon. M. ASCE, to connect San Francisco with the cities on the easterly shore of San Francisco Bay. At about the same time the Golden Gate Bridge was built under the direction of Joseph B. Strauss to connect San Francisco with the north coast counties. Its suspension span of 4,200 ft is the longest in the world.

Looking Backward and Forward.—The century of engineering just past in California has been filled with interest and even romance. It is hoped that historians will some day do it justice. The field is vast indeed. The completion of a century does not represent a break in the endless march of time and of events such as those here enumerated. The larger story will never be completed.

Centuries are merely milestones to measure arbitrarily certain periods of time which men may have chosen to consider. This concept may well lead to wonderment as to what is in store in the century now beginning. Engineers are accustomed to making studies leading to predictions of conditions or developments in the future, but to visualize the enormousness of those which will affect the next century is beyond the power of any man now living. Certainly the engineer will do his part and will cope with each situation as it arises, as he has always done. Who could say more?

AMERICAN   SOCIETY   OF   CIVIL   ENGINEERS

Founded November 5, 1852

TRANSACTIONS

Paper No. 2578

THE ENGINEERING PROFESSION IN EVOLUTION

By J. K. Finch,[1] M. ASCE

Synopsis

The role of the professional engineering society is twofold. On the one hand, it aims to enlarge technical knowledge and strengthen professional practice through the sharing of technical understandings and ideas and the exchange of practical experiences. On the other, it seeks to strengthen and extend those high standards of professional conduct and service which have characterized engineering from its earliest beginnings some fifty centuries ago. Although, through evolution and additions to its ranks, the profession today comprises some half dozen or more major branches of specialized interest and, in many cases, of diverse origins, these ancient and fundamental concepts and standards, these basic aims and ideals of professional practice which are common to all of them, give a unity of purpose and conduct which holds together these different groups in one professional family.

The evolution of civil engineering, the oldest branch, and its growth in professional stature through some fifty centuries of service is outlined in this paper. Particular reference is made to the origin of standards of professional conduct and practice and the role of the professional societies in strengthening and extending the contributions of the engineer in the service of modern civilization.

At some remote period in the past, man's early ancestors, blundering out of the jungle or abandoning a nomadic way of life, began to live in permanent settlements and to shape their environment to their needs rather than to rely solely on the precarious first-hand gifts of nature. With this act what is known as civilization was born. With the advent of civilized life the specialist in community works and construction—the man today called an engineer—came into being.

"Civilization," states Gilbert Murray, the noted British student and interpreter of Greek life and thought,

" * * * is the process whereby a human society in search, as Aristotle puts it, of 'a good life for man,' gradually overcomes the obstacles, material

---

[1] Cons. Engr., New York, N. Y.; Dean Emeritus of the School of Eng. and Renwick Prof. of Civ. Eng. Emeritus, Columbia Univ., New York, N. Y.

and other, that stand in its way and makes man increasingly master of his environment."

In the valley of the Nile in Egypt and that of the Tigris-Euphrates in Mesopotamia are found the earliest records of a settled, agricultural way of life and the first examples of the engineer's skill in overcoming the material obstacles to a more abundant and certain life.

In Ancient Egypt.—It is said that historians had expected to find in the fertile valley of the Nile remains which would reveal a gradual evolution from a neolithic culture to civilized life. On the contrary, this change appears to have taken place almost overnight. The transition from the earliest cut-stone masonry to the greatest mass of cut stone man has ever put together, the Great Pyramid, took but 150 years—a mere tick of the clock of time. In this same period—between 3000 and 2500 B. C.—a purely agricultural life was supplemented with an interchange of manufactures; the first Industrial Revolution took place. The rapidity of development in the Pyramid Age in ancient Egypt, the Golden Age of her long history, has no parallel in human records until modern times.

Throughout this period the master builder—architect, engineer, and administrator—occupied the highest position he has ever attained. He was a noble of the court, a trusted adviser of the King, "top brass" in the material and economic phases of what rapidly became a highly organized and stabilized way of life.

Listen to the statement of a member of the famous partnership of obelisk experts, Senmut and Ieni, of about 1550 B. C. Ieni recalls in his tomb inscription his various titles: "Pasha, Count, Chief of all the Works in Karnak, Controller of the Double-houses of Silver and Gold, Sealer of all contracts," and so forth. He then enumerates some of his major engagements, the great copper doors he erected, the obelisks, and other works. However, it is clear that he was not held back by any modern sense of modesty for he concludes:

"I became great beyond words: I will tell you about it, ye people: listen and do the good that I did—just like me. I continued powerful in peace and met with no misfortune: my years were spent in gladness. I was neither traitor nor sneak, and I did no wrong whatever. I was foreman of the foremen and did not fail. * * * I never hesitated, but always obeyed superior orders. * * * and I never blasphemed sacred things."

As Reginald Englebach, an expert on ancient Egyptian construction, remarks in his fascinating study, "The Problem of the Obelisks": "If he could work with Oriental labor for some 30 or 40 years without blaspheming it was not the least of the accomplishments of this ancient master builder."

A somewhat similar situation seems to have prevailed in the Mesopotamian area equally early, the master builder occupying a top position in the life of his day. However, this civilization involved many ups and downs, with military developments, perhaps, the outstanding characteristics.

Historic Greek Practice.—Nevertheless, if these and several minor civilizations are passed over and ancient Greek life, a culture which has given so many guiding ideas in art, literature, and philosophy, is considered, a sharp contrast is found in the master builder's position in the life of his day. The picture of Greek life has unquestionably been distorted by the enthusiasms of Greek scholars who seem to feel that the world has retrogressed since the ages of Homer and Herodotus, of Plato and Socrates, of Phidias and Euripides, of Athens and Sparta. A bit of common sense makes it clear that poet and historian, philosopher, sculptor and dramatist could not have done the practical work of the world without which life cannot exist. Slaves and traders, miners and diggers of tunnels, master builders and technicians made possible a civilization which one is inclined to visualize as composed only of artists, poets, and philosophers.

On the one hand, there was a supremacy of mind over matter in the lives and thoughts of the small group of citizens who comprised the Greek state. Manual labor was regarded as demeaning. Plato felt that even those who were interested in geometry—that is, the science of land measurement—had vulgarized mathematics. Archimedes, popularly acclaimed for his mechanical inventions, apologized for them, claiming they were carried out merely for his diversion and amusement. It was an attitude toward life which was to hold back material progress for centuries and of which the shreds still remain.

However, in the Greek *architekton* the modern engineer immediately recognizes a fellow worker who followed the same basic principles and held the same viewpoints as are followed today. This high priest of the technicians was not simply an architect, although the word is the origin of the present title. He was a master builder, architect, civil and mechanical engineer, miner, and, on occasion, a military engineer. He was the originator of surveying methods and construction principles still used today. He had a keen eye for economic considerations, seeking to accomplish his ends with a minimum use of labor and material. His Egyptian forebear had been satisfied with rules of thumb and possessed an extraordinary ability in organizing labor. In the Greek *architekton* may be recognized the first true engineering mind.

Roman Accomplishments and Ideals.—Greece gave way to Rome; and, with the advent of the Roman *architectus*, the emphasis again changes. Here was the practical man, the builder rather than the thinker, the greatest public works engineer of ancient times who spread all over the ancient world material standards of urban life not again equaled, after the fall of Rome, for more than a thousand years. The contributions of the Romans do not rest on advances in engineering science and theory but primarily on the art of construction.

Vitruvius, about 15 B. C., advocated the middle way but left no doubt as to his position. "Knowledge is the child of practice and theory," he wrote; and he warned:

> "It follows, therefore, that master builders who have aimed at acquiring manual skill without scholarship have never been able to reach a position of authority to correspond to their pains, while those who relied only on theories and scholarship were obviously hunting the shadow not the substance."

In Vitruvius also is found an early, if not the first, statement of a professional principle which is still regarded as a fundamental ideal in professional engineering life. Of the engineer he wrote:

> "Let him not be grasping nor have his mind preoccupied with the ideas of receiving perquisites, but let him with dignity keep up his position by cherishing a good reputation. No work can rightly be done without honesty and incorruptibility."

Likewise no one can read that remarkable later book on the water supply of Rome from the pen of Frontinus, Commissioner of Water Supply in the reform administration of the Emperor Nerva about 100 A. D., without gaining a healthy respect for the care and thoroughness, the attention to detail, the insistence on first-hand knowledge, and the high purpose, "the honesty and incorruptibility," of this able Roman engineer-administrator. A page from this ancient record is shown in Fig. 1.

As in the case of ancient Egypt, the Roman engineering forces were highly organized. There were experts in land and construction surveying; there were levelers; there were construction inspectors and quantity surveyors, masonry superintendents, and tunnel experts. However, engineering in those days was a practical art, still unencumbered with mathematical complexities and the intricacies of structural mechanics. These workers were the technicians of the art. The real engineers, those on whose shoulders initiative and decision rested, were the top government officials of the day—such as the Consul Appius Claudius and later emperors like Trajan and Hadrian.

A number of letters between the Emperor Trajan and Pliny, his governor in Asia Minor, have been preserved. They emphasize this fact. Here is one brief exchange on a water supply problem, in which Pliny wrote to the Emperor:

"The citizens of Nicomedia, Sir, have expended three millions three hundred and twenty nine sesterces [about $117,000] in building an aqueduct; but, not being able to finish it, the works are entirely falling to ruin. They made a second attempt in another place, where they laid out two millions. But this likewise is discontinued; so that after having been at an immense charge to no purpose, they must still be at further expense, in order to be accommodated with water. I have examined a fine spring from whence the water may be conveyed over arches (as was attempted in their first design) in such a manner that the higher as well as level and low parts of the city may be supplied. There are still remaining a very few of the old arches; and the square stones, however, employed in the former building may be used in turning the new arches.

"I am of the opinion part should be raised with brick, as it will be the easier and cheaper material. But that this work may not meet with the same ill-success as the former, it will be necessary to send here an inspector of aqueducts or a master builder skilled in the construction of this kind of waterworks. And I will venture to say, from the beauty and usefulness of the design, it will be a construction well worthy the splendor of your times."

To this Trajan replied:

"Care must be taken to supply the city of Nicomedia with water, and that business, I am well persuaded, you will perform with all the diligence you ought. But really it is no less incumbent upon you to examine by whose misconduct it has happened that such large sums have been thrown away upon this, lest they apply the money to private purposes, and the aqueduct in question, like the preceding, should be begun, and afterwards left unfinished. You will let me know the result of your inquiry."

With the collapse of the Western Roman Empire in the fifth century the culture of the past was temporarily lost to western man—with one notable exception. Modern life was born in the Dark and Middle Ages amid material remains

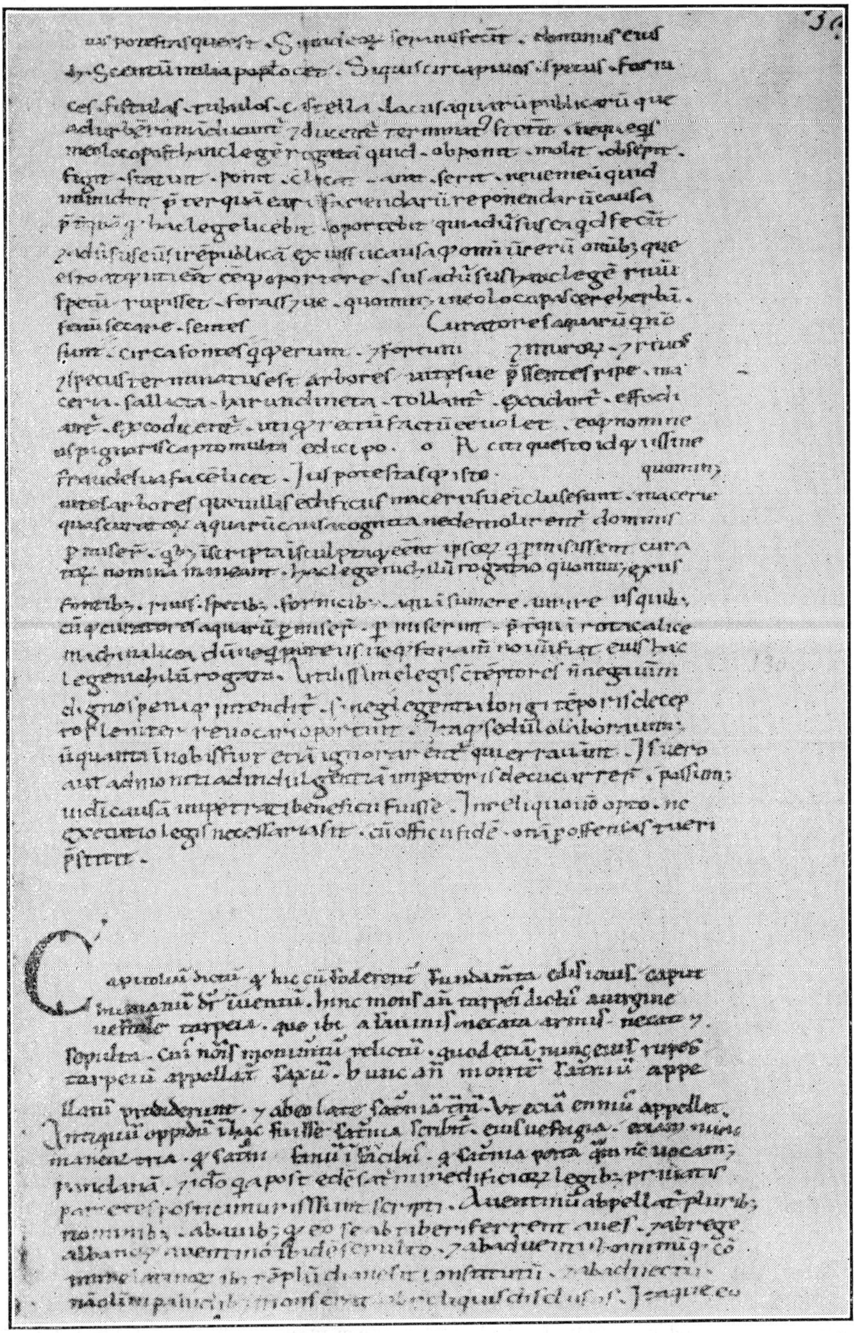

FIG. 1.—THE MONTE CASSINO MANUSCRIPT OF FRONTINUS' "WATER SUPPLY OF ROME"; A PAGE FROM THE EARLIEST KNOWN COPY, ORIGINALLY WRITTEN ABOUT 97 A. D.; AFTER CLEMENS HERSCHEL, PAST-PRESIDENT AND HON. M. ASCE

—the roads, aqueducts, and bridges of Roman times—among these mute reminders of what had been and what again could be.

The "Engineer" Evolves.—The Middle Ages mark one of the most fascinating periods in engineering history. Then the word engine and the title engineer first appeared.

A Roman historian, Tertullian, writing about 200 A. D. of a battle between the Carthaginians and the Romans, noted the dismay of the former when the Romans brought up a new and extraordinary *ingenium,* a battering ram. As a matter of fact the Assyrians had used this device centuries earlier, but the new name stuck. Battering rams, ballista, catapults, and similar machines became known as "engines" of war. It was about a thousand years, however, before the man who planned, made, and operated these engines became known as an "ingeniator," that is, an engineer.

The advent of gunpowder in the thirteenth and fourteenth centuries was a major factor leading to the introduction of new techniques which ultimately resulted in a break in the ranks of the old master builder. Even as late as the eighteenth century men were to be found practicing as what now would be called architects, as military engineers, and as civil engineeers. However, fortress and cathedral building and military operations, of course, dominated the earlier scene.

One of the most interesting and oldest engineering documents of the pre-printing era which has survided is the notebook of one of the itinerant craftsmen of these days. Dating from about 1230 A. D. it reflects an age when craftsmanship predominated. Across these seven centuries or more comes the message contained in this little leather-covered engineer's notebook:

> "Wilars de Honecort salutes you, and implores all who labor at the different kinds of work contained in this book to pray for his soul, and to hold him in remembrance. For in this book may be found good help to the knowledge of the great powers of masonry and of devices in carpentry. It also shows the powers of the art of delineation, the outlines being regulated and taught in accordance with geometry."

Epic of Leonardo.—Unfortunately, in spite of this professed interest in delineation, de Honecort would get an "F" in drafting in any modern engineering school. Several centuries later, however, Leonardo da Vinci produced some remarkable sketches of engineering speculations, visionary machines, and devices. Leonardo also wrote a letter applying for a job which, although it could not be recommended as a model to be followed by the young engineer today, reveals both the fact that civil and military engineering, as well as architecture, were still practiced by one man and that Leonardo, like de Honecort, was still a free-lance worker seeking employment under this or that military leader or political despot, or, occasionally, working for some budding municipal government.

Leonardo's letter, seeking a position with Ludovico Sforza, who later became Duke of Milan, is too long to quote in full. He began:

> "Having, My Most Illustrious Lord, seen and now sufficiently considered the proofs of those who consider themselves masters and designers of instru-

ments of war and that the design and operation of said instruments is not different from those in common use, I will endeavor without injury to anyone to make myself understood by your Excellency, making known my own secrets and offering thereafter at your pleasure, to put into effect all those things which for brevity are in part noted below—and many more, according to the exigencies of the different cases."

He then proceeds to tell of these secrets which vary from military bridges to water supplies, from siege operations to sculpture in marble and bronze, from stone throwers and cannon to a covered wagon which clearly anticipates the tank of World War I, and closes: "may it please your Excellency, to whom as humbly as I possibly can, I commend myself."

Evidently Leonardo moved from post to post. One recalls that he died in France, whither he had gone in the train of Francis I.

French Ascendency.—In fact, leadership in engineering passed from Italy to France in the later sixteenth century. Here engineers of diverse origins were undertaking civil works and again building and defining basic professional attitudes and ideas that had been lost since Roman times.

Thus, Pierre-Paul Riquet, the tax collector who, in 1680, with a very practical turn of mind, projected and built the Canal du Midi across France just north of the Pyrenees, in writing to the famous French finance minister, Jean-Baptiste Colbert, stated:

"My enterprise is the dearest of my offspring; I look chiefly to the glory of it, and to your satisfaction, not my profit, for though I wish to leave the honor to my children, I have no ambition to leave them great wealth. * * * My object is not to enrich myself, but to accomplish a useful work, and prove the soundness of my design, which most people have hitherto regarded as impossible."

Here may be seen the urge of the creative instinct, the overwhelming desire to see the child of one's imagination take form and function. Riquet put his fortune in this work and, fortunately, it proved in later years a most successful and profitable venture.

There have, in fact, been great engineers who have denied that they have been motivated primarily by either such creative obsessions or humanitarian motives. They would, at least, agree, however, with Francis, Lord Bacon's statement:

"I hold every man a debtor to his profession; from the which as men of course do seek to receive countenance and profit, so ought they of duty to endeavor themselves by way of amends to be a help and ornament thereunto."

Riquet, however, put "my enterprise" on an even higher level.

Another leader of this group of great French pioneers of modern engineering was the famous military engineer and fortress builder of the Age of Louis XIV, Sébastien le Prestre, Marquis de Vauban. François Marie Arouet de Voltaire, not noted for his compliments, hailed Vauban (Fig. 2) as "first of engineers and first of citizens." In fact, Louis de Rouvroy, Duc de Saint-Simon, coined the title "citizen" to apply it to this famous French patriot.

Pioneers in France.—From a professional engineering standpoint Vauban deserves equal fame. As already noted, engineers were a completely unorganized group. Vauban had himself first been loosely attached as a military engineering

FIG. 2.—SÉBASTIEN LE PRESTRE, MARQUIS DE VAUBAN, 1633–1706 ;
FROM PORTRAIT IN WAR OFFICE IN PARIS, FRANCE

consultant to Louis II de Bourbon, Prince de Condé, much as Leonardo had served Cesare Borgia and others. In 1672 he proposed that a special arm of the French Army be created, the engineers. This led ultimately to the creation of the Corps du génie. Thus, the military engineers were given a unity and a sense of professional standing, and they began to work together in a common cause for fuller understanding, greater technical competence, and improved service. Leonardo's "secrets" were part of his own stock in trade. The way was opened by Vauban to a wider sharing of technical developments and to professional growth and progress.

In 1716, under its first chief engineer, Jacques Gabriel, III (Fig. 3), a similar association took place in the civil engineering domain; the famous French highways corps, the Corps des ponts et chaussées was created. Some 30 years later, in 1747, a school was set up to train men for service in this corps—the equally famous École des ponts et chaussées, which still carries on in Paris.

FIG. 3.—JACQUES GABRIEL, III, 1666–1742, FIRST CHIEF ENGINEER OF THE
CORPS DES PONTS ET CHAUSSÉES

Through a curious combination of circumstances, medical schools were part of the earliest university organizations. Actually, there was little in common between the interests of such schools and the ideals of letters and learning which the university title connotes. Both American medical and law schools long remained essentially proprietary schools having few if any recognized admission standards until early in the twentieth century when preliminary study in the liberal arts became essential to admission. In sharp contrast, admission to engineering schools has always been exacting, and the standards for the Ecole des ponts et chaussées were no exception.

Whereas the distinction between the military engineer and what would now be termed the civil engineer seems to have continued to develop in eighteenth century France, a strong tie still remained between the latter and the architects. Bernard Forest de Bélidor, writing about 1740 on hydraulic works, titled his four interesting volumes "Architecture hydraulique." Jean-Rodolphe Perronet, first director of the Ecole, engineer of the famous Pont de la Concorde in Paris, and deserving the title of "Dean of French Bridge Builders," took pride in his membership in the Institute of Architects. Engineering was still, like architecture, an empirical art and was still limited largely to structures, an area in which both the architect and the engineer had long served.

The Influence of John Smeaton.—On the other hand, British practice turned both to mechanical and industrial and to civil works which had little relationship to the traditional field of the architect. Smeaton, about 1750, referred to his profession as that of the civil engineer to distinguish it, it is said, from military engineering. Apparently there had never been in Great Britain any liaison between architecture and engineering such as that which so long prevailed in France. The two professions continued to draw farther and farther apart as the engineer turned to such unarchitectural pursuits as machines and transportation and, especially, as the growing interest in a more scientific, rationalized approach in engineering design led to the rise of a new technique which the architect declined to follow.

Smeaton undoubtedly also did more to bring to engineering professional standing and public recognition in Great Britain than had any other of the famous earlier British engineers. Many of these "giants of the early days"— Thomas Telford, John Rennie, George Stephenson, and others—although they rest in Westminster Abbey in London, began life as humble workers, millwrights, or masons. In sharp contrast Smeaton came of an established family and received an excellent education. He was a member of the Royal Society and had been taken to task by some of his fellows for following such a "navvy," that is, laborer's calling, as engineering. The ancient Greek belittlement of all interest in man's material welfare was still, it may be noted, a factor in the British attitude toward the engineering profession. Smeaton's accomplishments made it clear that the engineering profession provided a challenge not only to men of action but to the best brains the nation could produce.

It was Smeaton also who initiated an idea which led to the organization of the first British society of engineers. As Samuel Smiles put it:

"During the time spent by Mr. Smeaton in town, he was accustomed to meet once a week on Friday evenings, in a sort of club, a few friends of the same calling—canal makers, bridge-builders, and others of the class then beginning to be known by the generic term of Engineers. The place of meeting was the Queen's Head Tavern in Holborn; and after they had come together a few times, the members declared themselves a Society, and kept a register of membership,—free social conversation on matters relating to their business being the object of their meetings. Some personal differences, however, occurring * * * Mr. Smeaton withdrew from the club which came to an end in 1792."

Engineering Societies Emerge.—Exactly why the Smeatonian Society broke up is not revealed; but, apparently, Smeaton while open to conviction, was a man of rather positive views. At any rate this club or society was revived the year after his death under the sponsorship of William Jessup, Rennie, and others. By 1818 an association of younger engineers had also been formed for their mutual improvement; and, in 1820, Thomas Telford (Fig. 4), then at the height of his remarkable career, was asked to become the first president of the group which was incorporated 8 years later as the Institution of Civil Engineers.

FIG. 4.—THOMAS TELFORD, 1757–1834, FIRST PRESIDENT OF THE INSTITUTION OF CIVIL ENGINEERS OF GREAT BRITAIN; BUILDER OF CANALS AND BRIDGES

In 1847 the Institution of Mechanical Engineers was founded with George Stephenson of locomotive and railroad fame, as its first president. In 1852, 5 years later, the American Society of Civil Engineers, first national association of engineers on this continent, came into being, with James Laurie as its first president (Fig. 5).

Almost invariably these societies or institutions have had as their primary purpose the same desire for mutual improvement that inspired earlier groupings of engineers. The great bulk of engineering practice is based on precedent, and the engineering society thus offers an opportunity for the exchange of views and ideas springing from the varied experience of its members. To this has been added in ever-increasing amounts the more theoretical type of paper which seeks to rationalize experience and to extend knowledge into new areas.

The major function of the engineering society has, therefore, been that of developing improved professional understanding through association—in order that the engineer might more fully and effectively serve mankind in his search for the good life.

Engineering societies have done far more than this, however. Through standards of admission and the adoption of codes of ethics and practice they have aided in protecting the public from the charlatan and the incompetent.

FIG. 5.—JAMES LAURIE, 1811–1875, FIRST PRESIDENT OF ASCE, 1852; CONTINUED IN OFFICE UNTIL ITS REORGANIZATION IN 1867

Improved practice and standards, and continued engineering progress, are essential to both the American way of life and to the more widespread material well-being of all people. Professional development and improvement not only are professionally desirable but serve a great national, social, and economic need of modern life.

A Preachment.—An outstanding mathematician and understanding philosopher once remarked: "While the ideals of individual engineers may be worthy or unworthy the ideal of engineering is great and mighty."

Unable to find in a long study any rascals among the engineers who have achieved reputation and position in the profession, the writer would question the first part of this statement. He would agree also with Bacon that engineering is but one way in which man may earn his daily bread; and who can say whether idealism or the desire for life is the more compelling motive? However, the profession does justify the terms "great and mighty." It is, together with the art of healing, one of the great instruments of the humane tradition, of man's search for the good life for all men. As former President Herbert Hoover, Hon. M. ASCE, once observed: "It is the purpose of engineering to increase the standards of life and living for all the people."

Engineers are the instruments of material advance in man's struggle toward a better life. They are essential builders of what has been slightingly referred to as the creation of a mass culture. Consciously or unconsciously their labors make not for the elevation of the few but for the equality of the many. They believe, as western civilization believes, that all men, women, and children in this world are entitled to a fair share and opportunity to enjoy the rewards of life. They seek to provide for all those material satisfactions on which the higher life of the soul and spirit are built. In short, engineers serve mankind.

On the other hand, the way of life they have created falls into one great and pressing danger. As that able Spanish thinker, José Ortega y Gasset noted, the ascendency of the masses is very apt to result, through the intolerance and shortsightedness of the masses, in their neglect of the fact that their commanding position and power springs not from the labors of average men but from those few to whom God has seen fit to give special gifts. Among these few are the engineers, special agents in man's redemption of man. It is not only to strengthen professional understanding and increase professional power in the service of man but also to preserve, to recognize, and to encourage the development of the rare and outstanding gifts of professional capacity on which such service rests, that the professional engineering society exists.

AMERICAN SOCIETY OF CIVIL ENGINEERS

Founded November 5, 1852

TRANSACTIONS

Paper No. 2579

FUTURE POSSIBILITIES IN CIVIL ENGINEERING

By John B. Wilbur,[1] M. ASCE

Synopsis

The influences acting on the future of civil engineering are discussed in this paper. The present era is a time of transition. Rationalism is replacing empiricism, and civil engineering is becoming a dynamic branch of applied science The various factors to be considered by the major branches of the profession in the future are outlined. Fresh opportunities, presented by the development of materials and methods, will occupy the future. New areas of service will open, requiring the skill and knowledge of well-trained civil engineers. The paper also discusses trends which have developed.

Introduction

Civil engineers may well take pride in their profession. They can look to the past with an immense degree of satisfaction, deeply conscious of their heritage—not only of the vast reservoirs of knowledge that have been bequeathed to them, but of the high ideals of public service that have guided their predecessors as, under their stewardship, civil engineering has become the foundation of modern civilization. It is only necessary to consider the modern city—its dependence on highways, railways, airports, water supply systems, sewage disposal systems, hydroelectric power, skyscrapers, and other construction involving structural design—to realize that this statement is not overdrawn. Without these things, cities as they are known today could not exist.

Present Development

Nevertheless this homage to the past does not imply that civil engineering today is in a staid or quiescent state; quite the contrary, it is in the midst of a fundamental evolution. This is a period of transition when empiricism is being set aside for rationalism, when civil engineering is rapidly emerging as a dynamic

---

[1] Head, Dept. of Civ. and San. Eng., Massachusetts Inst. of Tech., Cambridge, Mass.

branch of applied science, heavily dependent on basic science itself and on a wide range of research programs, many of which are now under way.

Within recent years this change has been very evident. There has been, for example, the effect of the science of soil mechanics on the more empirical art of foundation engineering, and the impact of fluid mechanics on hydraulic engineering. Still another instance is the recognition of the degree to which progress in sanitary engineering depends on an understanding of basic chemical and biological processes. The manner in which the present era will be evaluated by the civil engineer of tomorrow is to some degree a matter of speculation. However, it seems likely that the engineer of the future will view it as a period most typified by this transition from empiricism to rationalism, a time when the profession made rapid strides under the impact of basic science and research.

FUTURE PROSPECTS

If it is difficult to anticipate tomorrow's evaluation of today's activities, it is even more hazardous to attempt to look into the future of the profession and speculate as to what lies ahead in civil engineering. However, the uncertainties involved are scarcely sufficient to discourage the attempt. Since there are few projects of a civil engineering nature that do not require an estimate of future conditions, the realization that coming events may prove some expectations incorrect does not excuse the engineer from looking ahead as best he can. Actually, the hazard involved is related more closely to the details of such speculation than to the basic trends.

Transportation.—In looking to the future of transportation engineering, for example, there is ample room for uncertainty as to whether thinking should be in terms of interplanetary transportation or of such mundane things as rocket ships and conveyor belts. From this auspicious beginning, the conservatism of the civil engineer comes to the fore. He decides that it is safer and perhaps more meaningful if speculation is confined to things whose future pattern has at least begun to emerge.

To illustrate, it appears likely that the spheres of operation for the different modes of transportation will become more clearly defined. Thus the long-distance hauling of heavy solids, with the accent on speed, will undoubtedly be dominated by railroads on land and by ships at sea, whereas the long haul of fluids, especially on land, will be accomplished by pipelines. For the long-distance transportation of passengers and of lighter goods, air travel promises to take the lead, whether over land or sea. For shorter hauls, however, whether of heavy goods, light goods, or passengers, the motor vehicle will probably predominate, with two important exceptions—namely, the transportation of passengers by rapid-transit systems in congested areas and the movement of heavy solids by conveyor belts along lines of exceptionally high volume traffic.

This clarification of function, together with new technological developments, will lead to transportation that is faster, safer, more comfortable, and, most important of all, less expensive. Such transportation will contribute effectively to raising the standard of living, not only because it will reduce the cost of distributing goods, but because better transportation, together with better systems of communication, will make it practicable to coordinate business and industrial activities at locations that are some distance from each other. Thus momentum will be added to the current trend toward decentralization of cities, with the result that more people can live, work, and play in areas that are less congested. Behind all this, the civil engineer will play the important role of providing the basic ground facilities for all types of transportation, a service so vital that it touches every sphere of human endeavor.

Hydraulics.—Similarly, in considering the future of hydraulic engineering, it is easy to let the imagination run rampant and envisage startling innovations. However, this is scarcely necessary in bringing into focus tomorrow's crucial role for this branch of the profession. It need only be remembered that, with a growing population, it will become more and more necessary to grow food under diverse conditions of climate, and that water is the key to this problem. Hydraulic engineers, benefiting greatly by advances in aeronautics, oceanography, and meteorology, will so increase their skills that water, one of the most basic natural resources, will be conserved in the true sense; that is, it will be used more wisely in serving the needs of mankind. This will be accomplished in such a manner that topsoil, the thin upper crust of earth on which the food supply of the earth also depends, will be conserved and used, rather than swept into the sea by erosion and floods.

More extensive development of water power, and perhaps growth in the importance of wind power, will also influence the conservation of natural resources, especially in connection with conservation of nonrenewable fuels. It appears probable that nuclear power, although it will be available in some locations as a by-product of other operations, is not destined to compete in an important way with power from conventional sources in the forseeable future. Its greatest use will be for special applications, often of a military character, in which cost is a secondary consideration.

Sanitary Engineering.—Major advances in sanitary engineering, achieved as a result of basic research in biology and chemistry, will create new methods of water and sewage treatment that will be both more rapid and more economical than those in use today. The automatic radio tracer apparatus (Fig. 1) has proved valuable in basic sanitary research. Speed of treatment will be especially important, since this factor will make possible much smaller treatment plants that, being less expensive to build, will become economically available to almost every city and town for both water and sewage. Such treatment methods will be equally important in the field of industrial wastes, since factories and mills will be more willing to attack this problem voluntarily, and the necessity of resorting to legislative pressure will be reduced.

In this connection, the reclamation of by-products from industrial wastes, often producing returns that exceed the cost of treating the wastes, will be a noteworthy factor. The sanitary engineer will without doubt become a key man in the battle to conserve natural resources—not only by helping to use water more effectively and reclaiming for re-use part of the content of refuse, sewage, and industrial wastes, but by cleaning up lakes and streams, thus making possible larger crops of fish and wildlife, as well as greatly improved recreational facilities.

Structures.—Structural and foundation engineering will keep pace with the demands of construction, both within and beyond the scope of the civil engineering field. Better methods of analysis and design, ingenious new structural layouts, better use of existing materials, and almost complete mechanization of fabrication and erection, all will play their part in reducing construction costs. Decreased cost, of course, is of utmost importance, since more structures can be built with available funds. However, perhaps the most spectacular advances in structural engineering will result from the introduction of new, and often synthesized, construction materials, once again demonstrating the vital role of basic research in civil engineering progress. Chemical treatment so as to change the physical

FIG. 1.—AUTOMATIC RADIO TRACER APPARATUS

properties of soil is an example of a development that could, conceivably, have far-reaching consequences.

Perhaps, in the future, it will not be necessary to adapt structural design to soil conditions as they exist at a given site. It may be possible to obtain the soil properties needed for a desired type of construction by proper methods of chemical treatment, a more positive approach to the art and science of foundation engineering. Studies now under way at the Massachusetts Institute of Technology in Cambridge have developed methods of stabilizing soil by the addition of calcium acrylate (Fig. 2). However, the addition of chemicals is not necessarily limited to soil as a construction material. Possibly the properties of concrete can be modified in an exciting manner—changed, for example, so that much higher tensile stresses and strains can be resisted.

Summary.—As the writer looks to the future, he would like to think that the fear of atomic warfare will no longer be a major consideration. Although other factors will be of utmost importance if this happy condition is to be brought about, the contribution of the civil engineer should not be minimized. Hydraulic engineers will do much to increase the power and food supply of the world. Sanitary engineers will play an important part in improving the environment in which people live. Transportation engineers will help distribute the goods of the world. At the same time, structural and foundation engineers, as the servants of the other three, will do their share by building the structures that make

FIG. 2.—APPARATUS FOR SOIL STABILIZATION

progress possible. All these activities will contribute directly to a higher standard of living throughout the world, and thus help remove one of the major causes of war.

INFLUENCES ON THE FUTURE

Social Considerations.—There are certain common denominators in the foregoing speculations that deserve special mention, and the first of these is the increasing degree to which social considerations will underlie the planning of civil engineering projects in the future. The conservation of natural resources, the protection of people against man-made perils as well as the perils of nature, the betterment of the environment in which they live—these are examples of social objectives toward which civil engineers will direct increasing attention. This does not mean that there are not now engineers who are socially minded, but rather that, in future, civil engineers will have to think more and more in terms of the broad social implications of the projects they build. Inevitably they will have to balance intangible as well as tangible factors in attempting to arrive at solutions that are best "on the whole." Also, they will need to recognize that the rigorous procedure of analysis, important as it is, has limitations and must

FIG. 3.—MODEL TEST OF TWO-HINGED TRUSS

sometimes be supplemented with the less formal and partly intuitive procedure of synthesis.

Dependence on Basic Sciences.—A second common denominator lies in the increasing importance of the basic sciences and fundamental research. The model test of a two-hinged truss (Fig. 3) is typical of the work now under way. The current transition from empiricism to rationalism promises not only to continue, but to be emphasized in the future. The importance of this trend, measured in terms of its effect on the civil engineer's ability to render more effective service.

has already been strongly suggested. However, there are further implications of tremendous importance to the future of civil engineering, since a profession flourishes in a creative environment.

One of the first realizations that comes to the civil engineer who seeks better ways of doing things in his profession is that the other fields of science and engineering have much to offer in the way of new ideas and new tools. For example, aerodynamics has stimulated hydraulics, colloidal chemistry is helping soil mechanics, and the development of electronics is an aid to instrumentation in civil engineering research. Unless an engineer is involved in creative endeavor, he tends to follow the beaten path and this—in spite of the fact that his grave responsibilities are such that he cannot "make haste rapidly"—prevents him from profiting fully from advancements in other areas.

The world of science is moving at a rapid pace. Herein lies not only the opportunity but the obligation of the civil engineer. It is impossible to state just what advances will be made in the future, but these advances will surely come. It is known, too, that if there is a firm foundation in fundamentals it is much easier to recognize the potential value of each advance to civil engineering, and to profit thereby.

New Opportunities.—Moreover, the birth of each new branch or phase of engineering will create new opportunities for the civil engineer. In the past, for example, aeronautical engineering made the airport necessary. Mechanical engineering, through the motor vehicle, led to the development of traffic specialties. Chemical engineering has created many stream-pollution problems.

Again, it is difficult to state just what new branches of engineering will create new opportunities for civil engineers in the future. A current example is the development of nuclear engineering with its attendant problems of structural design and waste disposal, but this is just one example that points the way toward things to come. Whatever the new developments may be, they are potentially fraught with opportunities for the civil engineer, but he must be armed with a fundamental approach to his profession if he, rather than others, is to gain the satisfaction that comes from entering new fields of service.

However, if the new areas of service that are created by other professions are of interest, even greater opportunities exist in contributing as a full partner to some of the great advances of science and engineering that the future holds in store. Examination of some of the outstanding achievements of science and engineering during recent years—and again the spectacular development of nuclear energy might be cited as an example—leads to the conclusion that teamwork between the various specialties not only in science and engineering, but in industry as well, has been the dominant characteristic. A wide, frontal attack has been involved, in which the rather artificial barriers of strict professional lines have been minimized, or even dissolved. Through coordination of activities, each group has contributed its best toward the solution of a problem that was too complex for any one group to handle by itself.

It should be observed, however, that if groups are to work together effectively, there must be a common ground on which all can meet. Empirical procedures, necessary as they may be in some instances, do not constitute an ideal base for collaboration. The reduction of procedures to basic elements—to basic science, which serves as a common denominator for all the fields of scientific and engineering endeavor—is far more likely to permit the kind of collaboration that promises to typify the future. This is true regardless of what field of engineering may be under consideration.

Thus research, while helping the civil engineer in his constant effort to serve mankind in his own professional area, serves a still greater purpose. It reduces his work to the common denominator of basic science and enables him to work more effectively as a teammate with his fellow engineers and scientists.

Trends in Civil Engineering

Earlier in this paper it was suggested that tomorrow's civil engineer would view the present era as a period of transition from empiricism to rationalism, a time when the profession made rapid strides under the impact of basic science and research. Now it is further suggested that, as an attempt is made to appraise the future of civil engineering, the most important possible observation is that the trend now under way will flower. Tomorrow's civil engineer, imbued with an appreciation of research and well grounded in the basic sciences, will operate in a larger sphere that brings him into continued and intimate contact with the other branches of science and engineering and will thereby open even wider the doors of opportunity for service to mankind.

It is true, of course, that not all civil engineers of the future will be direct participants in creative work. Those who put into practice the new methods that will be developed will always play a most essential role. However, it will be those who find better ways of doing things who will blaze the path into the future, and it is on them that attention should be centered. It seems quite likely that future effort in the professional education of civil engineers will be especially focused on these potential leaders. Such a conclusion does not exclude from great importance the sound training of many men for the competent execution of vital tasks that must be carried out with utmost care and skill, but simply recognizes the special contribution to the profession and to society that will come from those who have been endowed with the spark of creative ability.

Transportation, water control, and suitable environment, for all of which the civil engineer provides structures and basic ground facilities, underlie every theater of human activity. Essential today, they will be needed even more vitally as civilization becomes more complex. The keys to the future of civil engineering are threefold:

1. A growing awareness of social values, leading to sounder planning.
2. An increasing emphasis on fundamental research, leading to better design.
3. The wiser management of men and equipment, leading to improved methods of construction.

Of these three keys, research is the most important, for only by extending the boundaries of knowledge can a profession maintain its stature, and forge its way to the new frontiers that always lie ahead.

AMERICAN SOCIETY OF CIVIL ENGINEERS
Founded November 5, 1852
TRANSACTIONS

Paper No. 2580

BACKGROUNDS OF ENGINEERING EDUCATION

By Frederic T. Mavis,[1] M. ASCE

Synopsis

The art of engineering is as old as civilization itself, and remnants of structures still stand as monuments to ancient master builders. Related science was focused on geometry, statics, hydraulics, and construction. Ideas on "engineering" education that were written 2,000 years ago have been restated again and again by engineering educators in different words.

The Romans were the greatest builders of antiquity, and they reached their peak of accomplishment about the first century A. D. After Rome fell, near the end of the fifth century, western Europe regressed for 1,000 years into "ages" which were not wholly "dark." Even then men were thinking and learning and building and looking forward. A revival of cultural progress was ushered in by the invention of printing in the fifteenth century. A reawakening of art and learning, beginning in Italy, soon spread beyond the Alps.

Before the eighteenth century, training for engineering was by apprenticeship. Schools for engineers grew out of the need for more well-trained men than this system could provide. The French led in the development of engineering education, and other Europeans soon followed. The first school of applied science in any English-speaking country was established in the United States in 1802. By 1852, formal engineering education had taken firm root, and leadership was gradually transferred from continental schools to this country, which has been the scene of real progress during the past 100 years. Highlights of this evolution, with special reference to industrial and economic development, show the great advances achieved.

Introduction

Engineering in its broadest terms is the art of directing the great sources of power in nature for the use and convenience of man. It is an art as old as civilization itself, because men have always had to wrestle with the power of nature.

Men must obey nature's unwritten law. They may yield to it passively, or by their ingenuity and enterprise bend it to their own convenience and use.

[1] Prof. and Head, Civ. Eng. Dept., Carnegie Inst. of Tech., Pittsburgh, Pa.

Nature does not change her course because men argue—however eloquently—that things should not be as they are; nor is she impressed by strong muscles and bluster. Nevertheless, all around there is evidence that fierce nature can be transformed into a useful servant or a household pet by those who will learn her ways, and plan ingenious means to work in harmony with her.

The story of man's learning and planning to adapt power in nature to his use and convenience is primary; the story of his teaching is secondary. Learning and teaching go together, and a few diligent students will soon reflect the strength of their teachers; but what can a teacher do among "students" who will not learn?

HISTORY

If engineering arts are as old as civilization, engineering education cannot lag far behind. It is necessary to fall back on legend and history to support this viewpoint.

The Mosaic Legend.—Probably no other legend is more deeply rooted in mankind's mores than the legend of the creation and the fall of man—the legend of Adam and Eve, of Cain and Abel—and there has been much speculation about where Cain got his wife. The First Book of Moses is often tiresome with genealogy and "begats," but it merits thoughtful reading in the present study of engineering and education.

When Cain was banished, he found his wife in the land of Nod and raised his family there. (What engineering teacher does not get his eight o'clock classes from the same place and keep them there much of the time he is lecturing?) According to this legend, Cain built a city which he named after his first son, Enoch. Today, the job of planning cities—of building them, of supplying them with water and with facilities to remove wastes, of providing ways that men and goods can be transported efficiently in and between cities, and often of managing municipal enterprise itself—is the work of a civil engineer.

Whether Cain was the first woman-born civilized man is not important; but the legend that he constructed the first engineering works of civilized man by building a city is interesting. The Mosaic legend is not in conflict with the first premise of this study—namely, that, whatever it may have been called, civil engineering is coeval with civilization. Furthermore, all other branches of engineering as they are known today—except "strict" military engineering—have grown from the main stem of civil engineering within the past 100 years.

If the line of "begats" is followed, it will be seen that the sixth lineal descendant of Adam in the Cainite line is Lamech, son of Methusael, who introduced polygamy by marrying Adah and Zillah. Between them he had three sons who fathered a good bit of civilized enterprise themselves. According to the Mosaic legend,

" * * * Jabal: he was the father of such as dwell in tents, and of such as have cattle" (Genesis, Chapter 4, Verse 20).
" * * * Jubal: he was the father of all such as handle the harp and organ" (Genesis, Chapter 4, Verse 21).
" * * * Tubal-cain, an instructer of every artificer in brass and iron: * * *" (Genesis, Chapter 4, Verse 22).

In the "begats" in the Sethite line, there is found another Lamech, who was a son of "old man" Methuselah and the father of Noah. Noah may have been the world's first flood forecaster and shipping magnate! The Mosaic legend continues

> "And Noah began to be an husbandman, and he planted a vineyard: * * *" (Genesis, Chapter 9, Verse 20).

and suggests that he was the first man to become drunk by consuming too much of the wine that was produced on his lands. (Wine in those days was a commodity much like money is today!)

Thus it is recorded in the Mosaic legend that commerce, music, and instruction in the mechanic arts had their beginnings in the seventh generation of descendants of Adam by the "wicked" Cain, and that flood forecasting, shipping, and intoxication were introduced at about the same time by a descendant of the "good" Seth.

Progress of Ancient Engineering.—The span of years between Tubal-cain, "instructer of every artificer in brass and iron," and the engineering teacher of today is uncertain—but certainly it is long. Meanwhile, civilized man practiced irrigation and a crude art of surveying from earliest times, and he must have understood much more of the world about him than men today are likely to give him credit for.

It is not necessary to discuss the structures, monuments, and hydraulic works of the Egyptians and Babylonians; the architecture of the Greeks; the roads, bridges, buildings, aqueducts, baths, and water laws of the Romans; or the specifications and contracting procedures of antiquity. There will likewise be no speculation about the knowledge of ancient engineers on such subjects as: Rollers, levers, pulleys, and inclined planes; the theory of arches, and the practice of building them to be useful and beautiful for more than 2,000 years; the science of mechanics, and its application to arts of peace and war; geometry and astronomy; logic, and the mind tracks of induction and deduction; law to govern rulers and those they ruled; rhetoric and the art of persuasion; music and art and sculpture; and the education and training of youth.

Nevertheless, all these bear significantly on the advancement of civilization—and with it, engineering and engineering education. Who today can expect to have his works live 2,000 years from now? However, that is exactly what is happening to the works of Archimedes in mechanics; of Euclid in geometry; of Vitruvius in building construction and engineering education; and of Frontinus in water supply and law.

Vitruvius' Ideas for Today.—In the province of ideas it is not always easy to distinguish "old" from "new." Compare ideas about the education of an engineer today with Vitruvius' ideas about the education of an *architectus* 2,000 years ago. (Incidentally, the *architectus* of Vitruvius' time is the common ancestor of today's engineer and architect. In dealing with the history of engineering education, it is fair to translate the Latin *architectus* into "engineer" and grant that "architect" would be an equally appropriate translation.)

After describing clearly the interplay of craftsmanship and technology in the work performed by the engineer, Vitruvius suggested how the engineer should be trained. He wrote, in effect, that engineers:

> " * * * who without culture aim at manual skill cannot gain a prestige corresponding to their labours, while those who trust to theory and literature obviously follow a shadow and not reality. But those who have mastered both [skill and culture], like men equipped in full armour, soon acquire influence and attain their purpose."

The engineering student, he added, must have both a natural gift and also readiness to learn. For neither talent without instruction nor instruction without talent can produce the perfect master. The engineer should be a man of letters, a skilful draftsman, a mathematician, and a diligent student of philosophy. He also should be familiar with historical studies, acquainted with music, not ignorant of medicine, learned in the opinions of lawyers, versed in astronomy and astronomical calculations, and so forth.

To those who would wonder that anyone could master so many subjects, Vitruvius said that all these studies:

> " * * * are related to one another and have points of contact. * * * For a general education is put together like one body from its members. So those who from tender years are trained in various studies recognize the same characters in all the arts and see the intercommunication of all disciplines, and by that circumstance more easily acquire general information."

What more need be said of continued learning?

Vitruvius stressed the importance of being

> " * * * fair-minded, loyal, and what is more important, without avarice; for no work can be truly done without good faith and clean hands. Let [the engineer] not be greedy nor have his mind busied with acquiring gifts; but let him with seriousness guard his dignity by keeping a good name."

What more need be said of ethics?

He would be smug who would assume that ideas on engineering education today are far ahead of ideas the Romans had 2,000 years ago. He would be a little less than stupid to ignore other parallels between great peoples who lived and worked at opposite ends of the twenty centuries of the Christian era.

The Romans reached front rank among civilized peoples about the first century A. D., and the end of their decline is usually marked by the burning of Rome near the end of the fifth century. The decline was a gradual process involving "bread and circuses"—more "bread" following more "circuses" in a dizzy spiral. The people were unable or unwilling to see the inevitable dangers of political programs that gave away "benefits" and took away personal rights and self-respect—and people and politicians coasted to destruction. The fall of Rome was brought about more by the fiddling of Nero and his predecessors than by the actual burning of the City of Rome!

ADVANCEMENT IN MEDIEVAL TIMES

Western Europe fell apart after Rome lost its leadership, and 1,000 years passed before a widespread revival of culture was ushered in by the invention of printing in the fifteenth century. However, this period was not wholly dark.

The monks made great efforts to keep civilization alive. One mendicant order, Brothers of the Bridge, built and maintained roads, bridges, and wayside shelters. "Ingeniators" or master builders were in great demand to build private homes for the nobles and to make and operate engines of war.

The name "engineer" came into being to designate ingenious men who did engineering work. The very mention of such names as Roger Bacon, John of Salisbury, and Pierre Abelard suggests that science and education were not dead in the twelfth century either. Great changes took place since the destructive action of the Crusades was counteracted by the knowledge that followed the Crusaders back out of the East. Gunpowder had been invented and

FIG. 1.—HYDRAULIC LABORATORY INSTRUCTION IN THE 1760's: INSTRUCTOR (LEFT FOREGROUND) RECORDING; STUDENTS MEASURING VELOCITY WITH PENDULUM METER, PITOT TUBE, AND PADDLE WHEEL AND LEVELING WITH U-TUBE AND ROD (BACKGROUND)—FROM TITLE PAGE, "SPERIMENTI IDRAULICI," BY FRANCESCO DOMENICO MICHELOTTI, TORINO, 1767

its use in war sounded death to the medieval castle. One common soldier with firearms was more than a match for many nobles in heavy armor!

A great revival of art and learning started in Italy, and soon spread beyond the Alps. The mariner's compass was invented—and with it came new courage to explore more unknown worlds. A science of mechanics was firmly grounded— and with it came new courage to explore more of the world's unknowns. Indeed, when Galileo Galilei was born in 1564 (about 50 years after Leonardo da Vinci's death), the world was more than half medieval; and, when he died in 1642 (the year Isaac Newton was born), the world was more than half modern.

Good books were being printed and widely disseminated; part of the title page of an early engineering work published in Italy, although at a later date, is reproduced in Fig. 1. The minds of men were as great as they have been in any age—

and, once men were free to think, they thought great thoughts that brought some of the greatest advances in all time. At the end of the medieval period the old art of casting bells and cannon was reborn as the art of making machinery and metal cylinders. The modern world was being born—and among the engineers and scientists who helped with the delivery are such men as Nicholas Copernicus, da Vinci, Simon Stevinus, Galileo, Christian Huygens, Newton, Blaise Pascal, and Sébastien le Prestre, Marquis de Vauban.

PROGRESS IN MODERN TIMES

Before the eighteenth century, training for engineering was by apprenticeship. If the right masters and apprentices can be brought together, there is no better method; but the system is not geared to handle large numbers of students. Schools for engineers grew out of the need for more well-trained men than the apprentice system could provide. The French led in the development of engineering as an art-science in schools of higher learning, and other Europeans and Americans soon followed their lead.

Jean-Rodolphe Perronet (Fig. 2), engineer to Louis XV of France, was given the job of building a system of national highways. Realizing the importance of good technical training, he transformed his staff into a school of men working together in 1747, and this school was legalized and officially named the École des Ponts et Chaussées in 1775. Because of this, Perronet is sometimes called the father of engineering education.

Great economic and political changes were taking place in France and America in the late eighteenth century. Equally great changes were taking place in engineering, manufacturing, transportation, commerce, and agriculture. The spinning jenny and the steam engine were invented and later the cotton gin. The industrial age had begun. A new shingle appeared in the professional world: John Smeaton, "civil engineer"—and a new adjective was coined to distinguish one branch of the engineering profession from another. Two famous technical schools were founded in the latter part of the eighteenth century: The Bergakademie at Freiberg in Saxony in 1766 and the École Polytechnique at Paris, France, in 1794. Even so, engineers in England were trained by apprenticeship for many years.

American state universities came into being with the laying of the cornerstone of the University of North Carolina at Chapel Hill in 1793. The first student was Hinton James, who became a civil engineer. He entered the University early in 1795, was graduated in 1798, and left in a "record book" the titles of original and "exceptionally meritorious" compositions that he presented on Saturdays. Little is known of subjects he was "taught" as a student; but the titles of his original compositions show that he "learned" science, business, and economic geography— sound preparation for the civil engineer of his day. Later he became assistant to Chief Engineer (Robert) Fulton on navigation developments, and superintendent of work for improving the Cape Fear River, in North Carolina.

In the United States, where so many men have entered state universities, it is interesting to note that the "first" was to graduate and become a good civil engineer!

In the early 1800's power was applied to transportation, and all industry in Europe and America advanced rapidly. More technical schools were needed to train men who could lead and guide mechanized industry. In 1802 the United States Military Academy was established at West Point, N. Y.—modeled after the École Polytechnique. Gen. Sylvanus Thayer was one of its first superintendents

Fig. 2.—Jean-Rodolphe Perronet (1708–1794), First Director of the École Des Ponts et Chaussées; Greatest of French Bridge Engineers in the Era of Stone Arches

(Fig. 3). It was the first school of applied science in any English-speaking country. Other schools taught engineering: Polytechnic Institute of Vienna, Austria, 1815; Norwich University, Northfield, Vt., 1819; Royal Polytechnic of Berlin, Prussia, 1821; Rensselaer Polytechnic Institute, Troy, N. Y., 1824; University College, London, England, 1840; Union College, Schenectady, N. Y., 1845; and Harvard University, Cambridge, Mass., 1847.

Formal engineering education now had taken firm root—even if it was highly mathematical and dealt largely with theory. Leadership was being transferred from continental schools to the United States. It was in this country that real progress became evident in formal engineering education during the next 100 years beginning in 1852.

AMERICAN ADVANCES, 1852–1859

In 1851 the first international exhibit was held in London, England. Industrial products from many countries were displayed and there was increased interest in

FIG. 3.—BREVET BRIG.-GEN. SYLVANUS THAYER (1785–1872), EARLY SUPERINTENDENT OF UNITED STATES MILITARY ACADEMY, WEST POINT, N. Y., AND FOUNDER, JUST BEFORE HIS DEATH, OF WHAT IS NOW THAYER SCHOOL OF ENGINEERING AT DARTMOUTH COLLEGE, HANOVER, N. H.

technology. The American Society of Civil Engineers was founded in 1852, and engineering education went forward rapidly. After Yale University at New Haven, Conn., added engineering to its program of study in 1852 and the University of Michigan at Ann Arbor included it in 1853, there were eight schools of engineering in the United States—and all of them are active today.

At Rensselaer, B. F. Greene studied methods and programs of engineering education in Europe and reorganized his own work. In 1855 he published as his director's report, "The True Idea of a Polytechnic Institute"—a classic that merits study today. It is natural, he wrote, to question the utility of such studies as rhetoric and philosophy to technical men when the time spent in formal engineering education is so short. Nevertheless, there should be balancing elements in a course necessarily so materialistic. No studies, he reasoned, are more suitable than rhetoric and philosophy for developing the mind, and they should be given a prominent place in the educational program of every polytechnic institution. Rensselaer was thus firmly established as a technical university and was influential in shaping engineering education in the United States.

Programs Evolved, 1860–1899

In 1862—during the War Between the States—the First Morrill Act granted land for colleges of agriculture and mechanic arts. The number of publicly supported schools grew, and each one that received land grants included engineering in its program. Many private schools followed this lead. After the close of the Franco-Prussian War in 1871, there was increased activity in science and technology in Europe, and this trend was reflected in the United States. The number of engineering schools had increased to seventy by 1872.

In a paper on "The Education of Civil Engineers," T. C. Clarke, Past-President, ASCE, told members of ASCE in 1874 that the educational program should stress learning general principles in the schools and acquiring technical knowledge in practice. This was a highly controversial issue among engineers in the 1870's. A. L. Holley, M. ASCE, argued the other side in a paper on "The Inadequate Union of Engineering and Science," read before the February, 1876, meeting of the American Institute of Mining Engineers (AIME) (founded in 1871). Engineering schools were laying too much emphasis on abstract principles, he argued; and he advised putting the actual practice first and the theoretical study later. Debate was brief but sharp, and the issue was referred to a committee to continue the discussion at a joint meeting of ASCE and AIME at the Centennial Exposition at Philadelphia, Pa., in June, 1876.

Twenty-five engineers, prominent in education and practice, took part in this two-day discussion. The consensus was that education to prepare real engineers must be broad—stressing essential underlying principles and a considerable range of so-called cultural studies. Practical training was also necessary early in the professional life of the engineer.

The Exposition of 1876 in Philadelphia was the first in the United States, and it stimulated widespread interest in science and engineering. It is not surprising, then, that the number of schools which taught engineering increased to eighty-five by 1880.

The Second Morrill Act of 1890 provided further support for colleges of agriculture and mechanic arts. When the Columbian Exposition was held in Chicago, Ill., in 1893, engineering was taught in more than one hundred schools, and interest in engineering was still growing.

The Society for the Promotion of Engineering Education (SPEE) was organized under the chairmanship of Ira O. Baker, M. ASCE (Fig. 4), professor of civil engineering at the University of Illinois in Urbana, as Section E of the World's Engineering Congress. Papers at that meeting were presented by men inspired—indeed it is a humbling experience to reread Volume One of "Engineering Education," dated 1893.

BASIC STUDIES, 1900–1919

In 1907, the SPEE invited the "Founder Societies" in engineering and the American Chemical Society to appoint delegates to a joint meeting to report on the appropriate scope of engineering education and on the degree of cooperation and unity that might be advantageously arranged between engineering schools.

FIG. 4.—IRA OSBORN BAKER (1853–1925), M. ASCE, PROFESSOR AT THE UNIVERSITY OF ILLINOIS IN URBANA; CHAIRMAN OF SPECIAL ENGINEERING CONGRESS IN CHICAGO, ILL., 1893, WHICH FOUNDED THE SOCIETY FOR THE PROMOTION OF ENGINEERING EDUCATION

The Carnegie Foundation for the Advancement of Teaching and the General Education Board were invited to appoint delegates the next year. The members of national technical societies, asked to express their opinions of the essential characteristics of an engineer, rated them in the following order of importance:

1. Character, integrity, resourcefulness, initiative.
2. Judgment, common sense, scientific attitude, perspective.
3. Efficiency, thoroughness, accuracy, industry.
4. Understanding of men, executive ability.
5. Knowledge of fundamentals.
6. Technique of practice and business.

In 1917, C. R. Mann reported that the division of time in the one hundred and twenty-five schools studied was 20% to the humanities, 30% to mathematics and basic science, and roughly 50% to technical work.

By 1918, Mann's investigation was completed. His final report, "A Study of Engineering Education," was published by the Carnegie Foundation for the Advancement of Teaching.

INVESTIGATIONS, 1920–1939

In 1922, the Council of SPEE proposed that another investigation be made of the objects of engineering education and the adequateness of the curriculum. Carnegie Corporation funds, and others, were granted. W. E. Wickenden was named director of the investigation with H. P. Hammond, M. ASCE, as associate director in charge of relations with engineering colleges. Many organizations and faculty committees helped in securing data and submitting reports.

The two-volume "Report of the Investigation of Engineering Education, 1923–1929" reached four main conclusions:

1. An undergraduate course should be a coordinated program of three stems of subject matter: Science, engineering methods, and social relations. The last year should be focused on the student's major subject.

2. The three stems of engineering education should be unified into one branch with unity of administration.

3. An undergraduate course should be 4 years long.

4. A graduate should continue his development either by formal graduate study in a school or by individual study after he enters practice.

This report guided engineering education through the postwar years of the 1920's and the depression of the 1930's. When he was president of SPEE in 1933, Wickenden stated that during the 10 years of the investigation engineers had acquired an envied position among college teachers. A sense of unrest and uncertainty had given way to a sense of assurance. These were the happy fruits of the SPEE's wise policy of promoting a program of stimulation, rather than one of standardization.

Engineering, however, which had given birth to many industries, was itself feeling the pains of growth and social pressure during the 1930's. Engineering education had to examine itself again in its social and economic surroundings of the early 1940's. Charles F. Scott may well have set the stage for a new appraisal when he wrote:

> "What are the causes leading to new trends? * * * Our environment—the world about us—is changing. The science which engineers apply is expanding. * * * Development of engineering education depends upon the willingness and ability for adaptation to changing environment. * * * Is it to be * * * education via the scientific, engineering route, or specific engineering via the educational ladder?"

WAR INFLUENCES, 1940–1952

An SPEE Committee on Aims and Scope of Engineering Curricula under Hammond published a report in 1940. The committee stated that the flexible 4-

year undergraduate curriculum, followed by graduate work, would meet needs better than a longer undergraduate curriculum; that the undergraduate curricula should be made broader and more fundamental through increased emphasis on basic sciences and humanistic and social studies; that there were advantages in the parallel development of the scientific-technical and the humanistic-social sequences of the engineering curricula; and that the integrated program which extends throughout the entire undergraduate period should therefore be preserved.

Soon after this report was published, the United States was a participant in World War II, and every engineer—student, teacher, and practitioner—was buffeted by crises, hullabaloo, and an avalanche of directives. Engineering educators were bedeviled by changing winds. What lay ahead? What might be the pattern of engineering education after the war? Robert E. Doherty, then president of Carnegie Institute of Technology at Pittsburgh, Pa., and president of SPEE, appointed a committee on engineering education after the war, and again Hammond was selected as chairman.

The committee, reporting in 1944, found that the specific purposes are essentially those recommended in the 1940 report on Aims and Scope of Engineering Curricula. It advised that the humanistic-social stem should require a minimum of 20% of the student's time and noted that, unless instruction included the elements of practice (Fig. 5), it would be in science rather than in engineering. Events had shown one major extension to be needed: A more positive indoctrination in civic and professional responsibilities.

WHAT LIES AHEAD

From legendary times until today, no men essential to human progress have kept in better step with the vicissitudes of civilized progress than have engineers and their teachers. At the close of World War II colleges found their enrolments decimated—and a few years later their burdens were increased more than tenfold. Nevertheless, engineers not only have survived this torrent of change but have periodically taken their bearings in the enlightenment that history and mastery of their profession gives them—and they have projected into the uncertain future plans which have been realistic enough to make engineering a little better, and standards of living a little higher, through periods of prosperity, depression, and war.

In learning to deal with the forces of nature—to keep in step with her and to apply her laws to the material and economic welfare of all mankind—the engineer learns to deal realistically with things as they are; and he does not waste too many tears about things that might have been. Today's engineering heritage is in large measure the realism and strength and courage that one must acquire if one is to work in the vanguard of inevitable change. In dealing with the caprice of mother nature the engineer has been pretty successful; in dealing with the cussedness of human nature he has limitless challenges and opportunities.

Who can tell what changes lie ahead? Engineers may study the "laws of politics" in days to come, and harness the overgrown giant of governing machinery which has become master of the United States rather than her servant. Would engineers bungle that job more than politicians have? Time only can

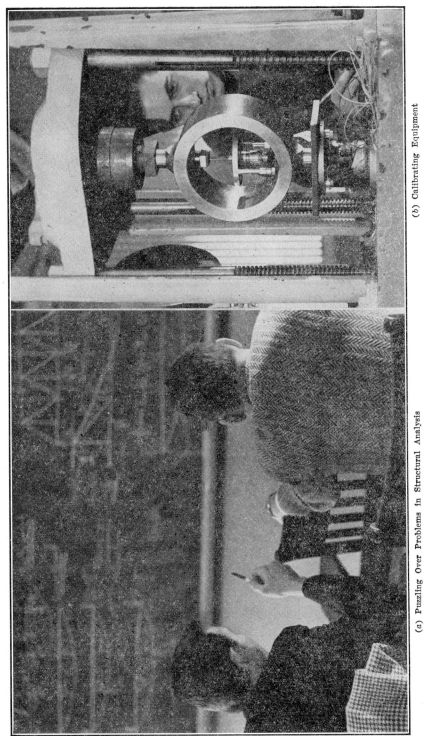

(a) Puzzling Over Problems in Structural Analysis

(b) Calibrating Equipment

Fig. 5.—Civil Engineering Students, 1953 Model, Working on Practical Projects

answer that. Just one rhetorical question emerges in conclusion: Could politicians have done as well in bending the forces of nature to man's convenience and use as engineers have? The job of harnessing politics for the use and convenience of man is yet to be accomplished—and it had better be begun now!

BIBLIOGRAPHY

"The Wisdom of Confucius," by Lin Yutang, The Modern Library, New York, N. Y., 1938.

"Vitruvius on Architecture," edited and translated by Frank Granger, Harvard Univ. Press, Cambridge, Mass., 1945.

"Frontinus and the Water Supply of Rome," by Clemens Herschel, Longmans, Green & Co., New York, N. Y., 1913.

"The Notebooks of Leonardo da Vinci," by Edward McCurdy, Garden City Pub. Co., New York, N. Y., 1941–1942.

"The Works of Francis Bacon," by Basil Montagu, Carey & Hart, Philadelphia, Pa., 1842.

"The History of the Inductive Sciences," by William Whewell, John W. Parker, London, 1847.

"The History of Magic and Experimental Sciences," by Lynn Thorndike, The Macmillan Co., New York, N. Y., 1923.

"Aims of Education and Other Essays," by A. N. Whitehead, Williams & Norgate, Ltd., 1932.

"Conflict of Studies and Other Essays," by Isaac Todhunter, The Macmillan Co., New York, N. Y., 1873.

"Too Much College," by Stephen Leacock, Dodd, Mead & Co., New York, N. Y., 1940.

"Engineers and Ivory Towers," by Hardy Cross and Robert Goodpasture, McGraw-Hill Book Co., Inc., New York, N. Y., 1952.

AMERICAN SOCIETY OF CIVIL ENGINEERS

Founded November 5, 1852

TRANSACTIONS

Paper No. 2581

ACHIEVEMENTS IN ENGINEERING EDUCATION

By Thorndike Saville,[1] M. ASCE

Synopsis

Engineering education has grown tremendously in stature and importance during the past century. This paper reviews the development of engineering schools, their faculties and curricula, and the forces affecting their progress. Evening programs, graduate study, research, and other factors that have posed problems during the past 100 years are discussed. The relationship between engineering education and the professional societies is described, with emphasis on the formation of various intersociety groups.

Introduction

The achievements in engineering education during the past century are contemporaneous with, and an inextricable part of, the achievements in the geographical expansion, industrialization, and urbanization of the United States during this same period. It is a far cry from the simple single curriculum in the physical sciences, mathematics, drafting, surveying, and the practical arts of construction available in the half-dozen institutions professing to give "engineering" 100 years ago to the 20 major curricula now accredited in one or more of 148 engineering colleges in the United States. The 3-year civil engineering curriculum (such as it was) in 1852 has not only proliferated into many specialized 4-year undergraduate curricula, but has expanded into substantial postgraduate study and research in many fields.

Faculties have changed from a few scientists and practical men of good will, concerned with the problems of transportation and the mechanical arts, to highly trained specialists versed in the theory and practice of a profession that has come of age. In 1852 there were probably no more than twenty-five or thirty scientists or professionally trained people in the engineering schools. Today there are about 7,500.

Undergraduate enrolment increased from perhaps 250 in 1852 to 1,400 in 1870 and to a maximum, in accredited engineering colleges, of about 109,000 in 1940. Enrolment in these colleges decreased during World War II, then in-

---

1 Dean, Coll. of Eng., New York Univ., New York, N. Y.

creased to a peak of about 230,000 in 1947 and has now (1951–1952) declined to about 128,000.

Recipients of the first (bachelor's or equivalent) degree in engineering increased from about 25 in 1852 to more than 48,000 in 1950. Declining enrolments since then have resulted in fewer graduates. From about 30,000 graduates in 1952, it is estimated a minimum of some 18,000 graduates will be reached in 1956 with a moderate increase thereafter. During the past century the total number of engineers in the United States has increased from a few hundred in 1852 to 7,000 in 1880 and to more than 400,000 in 1952. The accelerated demand for engineers is well illustrated by the experience of five major industries (manufacturing, mining, construction, transportation, and public utilities) in which the number of engineers per 100,000 workers has increased from 150 in 1880 to 1,500 in 1950.[2]

Engineering colleges have increased from 6 in 1852 to 17 in 1870, 85 in 1880, 126 in 1918, and 148 in 1952. The final total refers to colleges having one or more curricula accredited by Engineers' Council for Professional Development (ECPD).

Facilities have improved from the rented quarters used for many years by Rensselaer Polytechnic Institute in Troy, N. Y., to the respectable laboratories and classrooms of most of the accredited engineering colleges, and to the awe-inspiring and elaborate structures of a few of the great private and publicly supported institutions of today.

This quick review of certain quantitative achievements in engineering education during the past century presents no conception of the qualitative improvements that have taken place or of the concern of the engineering societies and of engineering educators with changes brought about by the ever-enlarging applications of science to industrial and agricultural pursuits and to the health and convenience of the people. This responsibility belongs to the engineer, and the success with which he meets it is dependent in large measure on the scope and adequacy of his education. It is the purpose of this paper to describe briefly the major changes that have taken place over the past century, particularly during the past 50 years.

CURRICULA IN THE FIRST 50 YEARS

Prior to 1870 the chief aim of engineering curricula was to train civil engineers to meet the problems of an era of rapid geographical expansion and growth in urban population. The instruction was largely confined to mathematics (algebra, geometry, trigonometry, and calculus); a year each of physics, chemistry, astronomy, geology, history, and a foreign language; 2 years of surveying; 2 years of English; and courses in the practical applications of "machines," "constructions," "hydraulic works," "earthwork and masonry," and, in some cases, mining and metallurgy.

The rapid growth of industrialization following the Civil War brought about a demand for more varied, rigorous, and comprehensive education for engineers. This stimulated the establishment of many new engineering colleges and engineering departments in existing institutions. Between 1870 and 1890 the number

---

[2] "Employment Outlook for Engineers," *Bulletin No. 968*, Bureau of Labor Statistics, Washington, D. C., 1949.

of institutions offering formal programs in engineering had increased from 17 to 110. The Morrill Acts of the 1860's provided a powerful stimulus to the establishment of the land-grant colleges, in which instruction in the "mechanics arts" rapidly evolved into engineering curricula. A number of schools of mining engineering developed between 1864 and 1880. Mechanical engineering began to emerge as an important separate curriculum in the 1880's; and electrical engineering, in the following decade. Chemical engineering was offered by two or three colleges in 1900.

The period from 1870 to 1900 was one of transition. The major curricula in civil, mining, mechanical, electrical, and chemical engineering developed in the order named from empirical and so-called "practical" instruction based on didactic teaching in the classroom to what became, for the ensuing 50 years, the conventional engineering curriculum—namely, 4 undergraduate years, the first 2 devoted largely to basic studies in the natural and mathematical sciences and the last 2 increasingly occupied with specialized courses pertaining to the particular professional discipline being pursued. A notable innovation, peculiar to American engineering education, was[3] "the great development in laboratory methods of teaching, a field where American leadership has been especially marked." Another contribution peculiar to engineering education in the United States is the emphasis placed on the economic and management phases of engineering, particularly in the formation of separate curricula in industrial engineering.

CURRICULA IN THE PAST 50 YEARS

The period from 1900 to 1950 was not marked by any profound changes in either the philosophy or the practice of undergraduate education, except for the inauguration of the "cooperative plan" and the development of formal degree programs given in the evening in a number of the larger metropolitan centers. Both are described in other sections of this paper.

Curriculum Trends.—During these past 50 years there has been a rather marked trend toward more rigorous treatment of the professional courses given in the last 2 years of the undergraduate curriculum. Scientific discoveries and advances in scientific knowledge have necessarily been reflected in their applications to engineering. To understand and to apply this new knowledge has in turn required more extensive study in mathematics and the physical sciences. A trend toward more such study in the undergraduate curriculum has been discernible but not marked during the past 50 years.

Increased emphasis has been given to the social-humanistic studies, but these must remain circumscribed as long as the present type of rigid undergraduate curriculum persists.

The proper and feasible balance between fundamental science, professional subjects, and the "art of engineering" has been a perennial subject of controversy. A description of the situation presented by Robert Fletcher, M. ASCE, of the

---

[3] "A Comparative Study of Engineering Education in the United States and Europe," by W. E. Wickenden, *Bulletin No. 16,* SPEE, 1929.

Thayer School of Engineering (Dartmouth College, Hanover, N. H.), in a paper before the International Engineering Congress in 1905 is applicable today:

> "Extreme views are held. Some would have the college programs cover an all-around training in fundamental subjects only, grounding the students in the basal principles of mathematics, mechanics and physical science, and those which determine engineering practice in general, giving due time also to broader culture, but giving only unavoidable attention to details. Others, arguing that this is above all things an age of specialists, would have the student begin to differentiate his studies with reference to some specialty even in the secondary school. Others claim the more common arrangement is necessary and sufficient, that which devotes two or three years of a four years course to the more general underlying subjects, and the final two years or one to study and practice in the special direction. Others argue that the specialty is the life work and should be begun last, and that the schoolwork therein is better done in a fifth or post graduate year."

The slight tendency toward more rigorous upper-class subjects and toward more fundamental science in the lower-class subjects has been paralleled by a marked trend toward an increase in the number of separate undergraduate curricula both recognized and proposed. The 5 or 6 basic undergraduate curricula bearing the names of the great "founder" engineering societies began to have "splinters" break off after 1900, as did the societies themselves. Just as separate organizations were formed for highway, railway, sanitary, radio, refrigeration, safety, power, automotive, ceramic, and other specialists, so newly designated curricula have proliferated in the engineering colleges, in many cases with similar designations. Today 20 such curricula are accredited by ECPD, and proposals for more have been submitted. This subject is discussed further under the heading, "Accreditation."

The Cooperative Plan.—Reference has been made to a notable experiment in engineering education that has had both a rise and a fall during the past half century. The "Cooperative Plan of Engineering Education" was inaugurated at the University of Cincinnati (Cincinnati, Ohio) in 1906 by Herman Schneider, A. M. ASCE. The plan is defined[4] as:

> "* * * an integration of class room work and practical industrial experience in an organized program under which students alternate periods of attendance at college with periods of employment in industry, business, or government."

This plan had considerable vogue between 1910 and 1930, but as late as 1949 only 6 of the 148 accredited engineering colleges require it for all their undergraduate students; 12 others utilize the plan for some of their students, either on an elective basis or for a particular curriculum or group; and 11 accredited engineering colleges adopted the plan, and subsequently abandoned it. The plan is regarded as distinctly successful by most of the 18 accredited institutions utilizing it for all or part of their students. It has obvious advantages of the "learning while doing" character. Its success depends on continuous and rather expensive

---

[4] "A Survey of Cooperative Engineering Education," *Bulletin No. 15,* U. S. Office of Education, Washington, D. C., 1949.

supervision by the educational institution of the kind of practical work in which the students are engaged and the coordination of such work with the curriculum content at a given time. The failure of the majority of accredited engineering colleges to adopt or to continue the cooperative plan is believed to be due to a variety of difficulties, of which added length of time to receive a degree, greater cost, difficulty of suitable employment in depression periods, and objections of labor unions are among the more important. The increased availability of engineering curricula given in the evening in larger metropolitan centers (discussed subsequently) has provided a less expensive and in part a more realistic substitute for the formal cooperative plan.

Evening Degree Programs.—In the early 1920's 4 institutions in New York City, N. Y., one in Washington, D. C. and one in Pittsburgh, Pa., began to offer formal engineering curricula in the evening for which degree credit was given. The ECPD accrediting committee had some misgivings as to the adequacy and equivalency of these programs as compared to the usual 4-year full-time day program. However, after study and the reports of special subcommittees, 4 such curricula were accredited in 1936, 3 in New York and 1 in Pittsburgh. By 1951 ECPD had accredited evening programs in only 6 institutions—3 in New York, 1 in Newark, N. J., 1 in Pittsburgh, and 1 in Cleveland, Ohio. However, many of the engineering colleges accredited for full-time day curricula are offering unaccredited evening programs of substantial size. The 6 institutions having accredited evening programs reported approximately 6,500 students in 1951, out of a total of 13,400 evening students in all the accredited institutions. There were 3,500 evening students enrolled in evening degree programs in 1924.

The evening programs are primarily designed for those financially unable to pursue a 4-year full-time day program. Such students are employed during the daytime, frequently in subprofessional occupations analogous to those utilized under the cooperative plan. To a degree, therefore, evening programs represent a modification of that plan. The evening programs require a minimum of 6 years, and customarily $6\frac{1}{2}$ to 8 years before the first degree is obtained. These programs, when carefully and conscientiously administered, are proving in all respects the equal of the full-time day programs. There are tendencies that have to be watched to be certain that course content, student performance, and quality of instruction are maintained on a satisfactory basis. In some institutions an undue number of students may be enrolled in evening programs who are not primarily interested in obtaining a degree, but are more concerned in the vocational utility of a single course or a few courses.

On the whole, carefully formulated and well-administered evening engineering curricula are fulfilling a definite public need for students unable to finance a full-time day program, and the graduates constitute an important supplement toward helping meet the demand for more engineers. The programs have been successful in the few metropolitan centers where they have been operated for many years, and there is a real need for the development of additional accredited evening curricula in a good many other areas, particularly where manufacturing industries can supply a sufficient volume of students.

Faculty

Obviously, the quality of instruction in engineering is dependent largely on the caliber of the faculty charged with imparting it. Just as instruction and curricula content have tended to become more rigorous and more specialized, so has the faculty tended to become more learned and more competent in special areas of science and technology. The early engineering teachers were scientists or practical men who looked to Europe, and particularly to France, for the engineering and scientific texts and treatises that formed the basis for most formal teaching. Since 1880, and particularly during the past 50 years, an entire literature of engineering education has become established in the United States, which for careful preparation, scope of coverage, theoretical and practical content, and excellence of format has no equal in the world. This literature has increasingly reflected the growing stature of engineering faculties.

Another index of the accomplishments of the staffs may be measured by the great increase in the percentage of the total number of teachers who hold advanced degrees. From the rather sparse and unsatisfactory statistical data that exist, it is probable that during the past 50 years the percentage of faculty members engaged in teaching engineering subjects who hold an advanced degree has increased from perhaps 25% in 1900 to about 45% in 1920, to 60% in 1940, and to at least 75% in 1950. Some concern has been expressed lest too great emphasis be placed on advanced degrees, particularly the doctorate, as a prerequisite for faculty advancement or appointment to the higher grades. However, since the employers of engineering graduates evidence an increasing desire for a greater proportion with a postgraduate degree, and pay an attractive differential for them, it is essential that the instructors be qualified to prepare such graduates.

A considerable percentage of professional members of faculties is engaged for a part of the year either in actual practice of engineering or in research in one of its specialties, or both. The great increase in the number of the faculty engaged in research is mentioned elsewhere, and most engineering colleges today encourage both outside practice and research in moderation. Moreover, there is a constant infiltration of engineers from industry and government into the faculties, a procedure that has much to commend it, but that is increasingly difficult under current conditions of higher salaries in practice. Some attention is being given to exchange arrangements with industry, whereby engineers in industry and in engineering college faculties will be given concurrent leaves of absence for a year to fill each other's places. Arrangements of this sort, if widely adopted, may do much to broaden engineering teaching and be equally beneficial to the cooperating employer.

The character of the man, the composite of his personality, his professional achievements, his concern about students and about engineering, and his philosophy of life—all are important elements in selecting a teacher. The securing of the right kind of teachers has always been a major problem in engineering education, and it remains so today.

Graduate Study

Before 1890 there were only 6 institutions that conferred advanced degrees in engineering. Only 3 earned doctorates had been conferred at the end of 1896.

Not until the second decade of the twentieth century was any substantial number of graduate students enrolled or were many postgraduate degrees conferred. Since then, the accelerated impact of science on engineering and technology has created an ever-increasing need for engineering graduates who have been educated in specialties beyond the extent possible in a 4-year undergraduate program. By 1921 some 40 engineering colleges were offering graduate work, 368 graduate students were enrolled, and 178 postgraduate degrees were awarded. However, some of these degrees were awarded by institutes of technology and in such fields as chemistry, biology, or geology. The first differentiating statistics appear in 1934, when graduate registration totaled about 2,800 and the postgraduate degrees awarded numbered nearly 1,200.

Prior to the outbreak of World War II, graduate registration in 1939–1940 had increased to 4,582 enrolled for the master's degree (1,318 degrees awarded) and 624 for the doctor's degree (108 degrees awarded). The phenomenal developments in the applications of science that took place during the war years created a marked increase in the demand for engineers with postgraduate education. The engineering colleges were quick to respond, too quick on the part of some institutions not adequately equipped in faculty or facilities. Enrolment in 1951–1952 was 16,452 (5,134 degrees awarded) for the master's degree and 2,875 for the doctor's degree (586 degrees awarded). It is interesting to note that with a declining enrolment in undergraduate curricula for each year since 1947, there has each year been an increase in graduate students.

An interesting comparison may be drawn between evening work on the undergraduate and graduate levels. About 10% of the total number of undergraduate students is enrolled in evening programs, whereas 10,000 (52%) of the 19,300 graduate students are enrolled in programs or courses given in the evening. At least 23 institutions have enrolments of more than 100 graduate students in evening courses. Nearly all these are in industrial centers. The magnitude of these evening graduate programs is an indication of the extent to which engineering colleges have met the demand by employed engineers for further education. The evening courses are in some instances given in cooperation with industry (as in the Westinghouse program), and in many instances the employer subsidizes all or part of the cost of the employee's education. Also many students who did not exhaust their veterans' benefits are using this means of acquiring a postgraduate education while employed.

RESEARCH

Research as performed in engineering colleges may be broadly defined in two categories: (*a*) That undertaken by faculty members and graduate students to advance knowledge and supported by institutional resources or by grants from foundations, and (*b*) that sponsored by government agencies or private industry. Prior to World War II the major research activities of the privately endowed institutions were predominately in class (*a*), and class (*b*) sponsored research was performed chiefly in the land-grant colleges through their engineering experiment stations.

Before 1940, research was recognized as contributing significantly to education in attracting scientifically minded men to the faculties, as stimulating to instruction, and as being necessary in postgraduate education. However, nearly every report of groups investigating engineering education from time to time deplored the meagerness of research activities at all except a few of the larger or more enlightened institutions. Beginning about 1940 in a few institutions peculiarly adapted for research in special applications of science to the war effort, the support of research by Federal Government agencies has reached large proportions and is distributed among a good many engineering colleges. Nearly all are seeking more.

The contributions of the engineering colleges toward applying science to new developments and processes have been tremendous during the past decade. A great service has been rendered the nation, and many institutions, faculty members, and students have benefited in various ways. No longer may it be stated that engineering colleges are not sufficiently alert to research. Nevertheless, the availability of such great amounts of federal funds for sponsored research has brought problems to the colleges, problems of some magnitude and not yet resolved. Among them are dangers from the preoccupation of some faculty with research projects to the detriment of good teaching; the assignment of good teachers to research projects for all or a significant part of their time; and the restriction of federally supported research programs to those of interest to a given agency, to the detriment of the prosecution of more basic or fundamental research on which faculty members might prefer to be engaged.

From the foregoing discussion, the question will at once be asked: What has industry done to encourage research in the engineering colleges, one of whose major functions is to supply industry with well-educated personnel? Unfortunately, and somewhat illogically the answer is: An insignificant amount when measured by its reliance upon engineering education for its present existence and for its future performance. Industrialists have been frank, and often indiscriminating, if not ignorant, critics of engineering education. They have been prompt to support measures to insure their continued supply of engineering graduates (as within the present framework of the Engineering Manpower Commission), but they have conjured up every conceivable argument and legal device to excuse them from any considerable support of the educational institutions on whose graduates their future is based. To research, which might be supposed to represent an area of support that would offer a quid pro quo, their contributions on the whole have been relatively small in amount and not administered according to any broad policy. To be sure, some industries have made fairly substantial grants for research, usually in some developmental field of direct interest to them, but the support of basic research in engineering has been extremely meager considering the vast industrial interests involved. The support of graduate fellowships by industry has been somewhat better, and a real achievement has taken place during the past few years with the establishment of a number of quite generous fellowships by a few large industries with no strings attached. Doubtless the situation is not entirely the fault of industry, and there is need for engineering education to do more to convince industry that its support of research is warranted on a much larger scale than has been experienced heretofore.

Out of the present situation there will undoubtedly emerge more rational and yet adequate policies and procedures that will enable the engineering colleges to give research its proper place in a broad program for engineering education, which it is their chief concern to formulate and continuously to improve.

AUXILIARY EDUCATIONAL SERVICES

The major obligation of engineering education is to develop graduates who are competent to practice and to lead in the profession. However, from time to time engineering educators are called on in the interest of the public welfare or safety to render educational services auxiliary to professional education. For many years engineering colleges, particularly those supported by public funds, have operated courses of relatively short duration for the training of subprofessional personnel. The "short schools" for water-works operators, highway personnel, power plant operators, and the like have rendered and continue to render a distinct public service.

> "During the first World War the engineering colleges of the country were responsible for a major portion of the vocational training programs of the U. S. Army, which was almost entirely concerned with the training of mechanics, and gave practically no attention to training on the engineering level."[5]

Except in relatively circumscribed areas, continued production of professional engineering personnel was not regarded as an essential element in winning the war, and the engineering colleges were thus allocated a program of subprofessional character, which they performed with versatility and enthusiasm.

Perhaps the greatest contribution of engineering colleges as a group to the prosecution of World War II was the Engineering, Science, and Management War Training Program under the auspices of the United States Office of Education:

> "More than 1.5 million men and women received special training during the period October 9, 1940 to June 30, 1945 in short intensive college level courses designed to prepare for technical and scientific work in war industries. * * * The Federal Government expended nearly 60 million dollars to cover the actual costs incurred."[5]

This program was conceived, organized, administered, and operated by the engineering colleges of the United States.

One sentence will suffice to describe the Army Specialized Training Program (ASTP) during the latter part of World War II. The ASTP was conceived by the War Department, a fantastic substitute for collegiate education dreamed up by the military and "professional educators" (not engineering) and designed primarily to produce badly needed engineers for the armed services with some specialists in linguistics and other areas, in an abbreviated curriculum. It was a dismal failure from the standpoint of engineering education in which the engineering colleges participated reluctantly both as a national duty and as a substantial alternative to educational oblivion.

---

[5] "Engineering Science and Management War Training," *Bulletin No. 9*, U. S. Office of Education, Washington, D. C., 1946.

Certainly one of the great achievements of engineering education in the United States has been its freedom from any dogmatism that its obligations were fixed toward any narrow professional objective. It has continuously demonstrated an adaptability to serve as national needs or military dicta required in times of emergency, and to guide and help in many areas auxiliary to its major purpose in times of peace.

Relation to the Engineering Societies

It may be stated unequivocally that engineering education enjoys a relationship to the engineering societies unique in the annals of professional education. No other profession has any organization of its educational members comparable to the American Society for Engineering Education (ASEE), no other profession has an association of professional societies devoted to educational and related activities comparable to ECPD. It is not surprising therefore that engineering education, in the truly professional sense, has developed rapidly since 1893 when the predecessor of the ASEE was established, and that the impact of the profession itself on the education of its practitioners stems from the establishment of ECPD in 1932. No system of professional education could remain static or complacent when subjected to the constant scrutiny of the committees and divisions of its own members, supplemented by continuing appraisals and criticisms from a group representing the major professional societies and the licensing boards of the several states.

The Society for the Promotion of Engineering Education (SPEE) was organized at the Congress of Engineers held in connection with the great World Columbian Exposition in Chicago, Ill., in 1893. Engineering education was Division E of the Congress. Ira O. Baker, M. ASCE, of the University of Illinois at Urbana was chairman, and C. Frank Allen, M. ASCE, of the Massachusetts Institute of Technology at Cambridge was secretary. Allen, in rendering his secretarial report, stated "that a society had been organized by the members of the Division for the promotion of engineering education." Thus one may say that the ASCE in a sense fathered the SPEE. Weight is lent to this conclusion by the fact that two of the first three and fourteen of the first twenty-five presidents of SPEE were members of the ASCE.

The SPEE began with 70 members, and now (1952) has more than 7,000. It early started studies of various facets of engineering education, and initiated in 1907 a practice followed from time to time ever since—a request for the professional engineering societies to collaborate in its major investigations. In that year it invited the civil, mining, mechanical, electrical, and chemical engineering societies to join it in forming a Joint Committee on Engineering Education, to explore all the aspects of the subject. The member societies of this committee now constitute (with the National Council of State Boards of Engineering Examiners and the Engineering Institute of Canada) the ECPD. The committee was organized, and the ASCE (in 1908) made an appropriation for its operation, the first recorded grant from an engineering society for an investigation of engineering education. However, the committee still lacked adequate funds for its investigation. In 1916, the chairman of the committee, Desmond FitzGerald, Past-President and Hon. M. ASCE, reported that "after we [ASCE] had spent all our spare cash in carrying on the work of this Committee, we naturally turned our eyes to the Carnegie Foundation."[6] The Carnegie Foundation undertook the task, and in 1918 issued a report by C. R. Mann entitled "A Study of Engineering Education." This report was the first of a number of significant studies and investigations into the general field of engineering education sponsored jointly in one way or another by the SPEE (or its successor) and the professional engineering societies.

The SPEE was reorganized in 1946 to provide for more effective administration and better recognition of the several elements in engineering education—the individual teacher, the work of committees and divisions, the geographical sections, administration, and research. The name was changed to the American Society for Engineering Education (ASEE). This society has individual membership and also associate membership for organizations with a major interest in engineering, such as industries, research institutes, and the like. It has always had as active members, many who were prominent in practice, such as presidents, chief engineers, and personnel managers of industry. This has provided important stimuli for many activities, and has introduced the important element of considering practical and present needs into its many achievements. The ASEE has active divisions constantly concerned with improvements in instruction in the several curricula and the major supporting sciences and nontechnical subjects. It has various special committees that have from time to time issued notable reports which have had a profound influence on engineering education. The best known, most exhaustive, and most influential of these reports was the "Investigation of Engineering Education," a monumental study extending over 10 years (1923–1934) financed by the Carnegie Foundation, the engineering societies, and certain industries. It still forms the platform from which later studies have taken off.

The ASEE is an extraordinary phenomenon in professional education. There is nothing approaching it as related to the other professions. Its achievements and the constant preoccupation of hundreds of its members with major facets of engineering education are too little appreciated by the profession which it serves. Its annual meetings, attended by upward of 1,000 of its members, discuss reports of committees and papers dealing with new educational ideas and procedures. An enumeration of the names of a few of its divisions and committees is illustrative of its concern with current problems. In addition to the divisions dealing with all major curricula and supporting courses, there are divisions of relations with industry, graduate studies, technical institutes, and so on. Its major committees include selection and guidance, research, atomic energy education, young engineering teachers, and improvement of teaching. Its Manpower Committee was the progenitor of the Manpower Commission of Engineers Joint Council. Reference will be made later to a new Committee on Evaluation of Engineering Education.

The ASEE publications have a world-wide distribution, and are regarded as authoritative sources of historical background, current practice, and statistical data. They have had a substantial influence on engineering education in this and other countries.

---

[6] *Proceedings*, SPEE, Vol. XXIV, 1916, p. 46.

ENGINEERS' COUNCIL FOR PROFESSIONAL DEVELOPMENT

As the engineering profession became larger in numbers, as an increasing proportion of its members were college graduates (from perhaps 25% in 1852 to 85% in 1952), as the engineering societies grew in numbers and influence, a professional consciousness developed, which in 1932 produced a need for the ECPD. The six societies that participated in the Joint Committee on Engineering Education in 1907 (ASCE, American Institute of Mining and Metallurgical Engineers, American Society of Mechanical Engineers, American Institute of Electrical Engineers, American Institute of Chemical Engineers, and ASEE) initiated steps to form the Council and invited the Engineering Institute of Canada and the National Council of State Boards of Engineering Examiners to participate.

The ECPD is a conference body commissioned:

> "* * * to promote efforts * * * toward higher professional standards of education and practice, greater solidarity of the profession, and greater effectiveness in dealing with technical, social, and economic problems."[7]

It will be noted that engineering education was regarded as of prime importance, and it has continued to be one of the major concerns of ECPD. This concern has been implemented by the activities of two standing committees over the past 20 years, those on education and on guidance. The Committee on Education (originally the Committee on Engineering Schools) has dealt with accreditation of engineering curricula; the Committee on Guidance (formerly student selection and guidance), with information on engineering as a career supplied to secondary school students and with the determination of aptitudes for engineering study in development of testing procedures. More recently a new and important committee has been established, that on adequacy and standards of engineering education.

ACCREDITATION

Engineering Colleges.—By 1932, more than 135 institutions of higher education were offering degree curricula in engineering. It had become obvious that marked differences occurred in educational standards, the strength and breadth of curricula, the qualifications of faculties, and the adequacy of facilities. Some process of determining the composite of these criteria as a basis for recognition of the graduate as acceptable for membership in the professional societies and for admission to state license examinations was obviously needed. The growth of state licensing laws was beginning to develop the danger that separate accrediting procedures would be set up in each state, with resulting differences in standards and practices and general confusion.

Hence ECPD created the Committee on Engineering Schools (later the Committee on Education) to represent the entire profession and the state licensing boards. This was a formidable and delicate task. Hence a distinguished committee was appointed under the chairmanship of Karl Compton of the Massachusetts Institute of Technology and members representing the participating societies of ECPD. The committee spent 4 years in making its initial studies, and

---

[7] "ECPD—A Challenge," ECPD, New York, N. Y., 1947.

published the first general list of accredited curricula in 1937. Of 626 curricula inspected in 129 institutions visited, 374 were accredited for a limited time and 71 accredited provisionally in 107 institutions. Action was deferred on 8, and 173 were not accredited. The committee has continued its activities; and, as of 1951, 680 curricula were accredited fully or provisionally in 148 institutions.

There is not space to describe in detail all the policies and procedures affecting accreditation, but the operations of the committee represent some major achievements in engineering education. Therefore, since the accrediting process has profound implications on the progress of engineering, and since the rapid increase in attainments required by the engineer and the enlarging diversity of his employment have raised anew some old problems and have created new challenges, a brief résumé of the basic principles heretofore applied to the accrediting process is in order:

1. Only specific curricula, not institutions, are accredited.

2. Inspection with a view toward accreditation is made only on the invitation of an institution.

3. The purpose of accreditation is to identify those institutions that offer professional curricula in engineering worthy of recognition as such, and shall apply only to curricula leading to degrees.

4. Only undergraduate curricula have thus far been accredited.

5. Accreditation is based on both qualitative and quantitative criteria, but no "standards" have been formulated or applied. Accreditation is also based largely on the over-all judgment of a qualified inspection committee, which applies general criteria listed in each annual report of ECPD.

The original intention of ECPD was to recognize for accreditation only the 6 major curricula; but, as mentioned previously, the proliferation of engineering societies was paralleled by a proliferation of engineering curricula. Pressures from the engineering colleges and from segments of the profession itself forced the Committee on Education to recognize additional curricula. The first list of accredited curricula (for the New England and Middle Atlantic states only) published in 1936 expressed the principle that:

> "ECPD will recognize the six major curricula (chemical, civil, electrical, mechanical, metallurgical and mining engineering) represented in its own organization, *and such other curricula* as are warranted by the educational and industrial conditions pertaining to them."

This left the door wide open and, in the very first list referred to previously in this paper, 14 curricula were recognized, 13 of which (the largest at any institution) were offered at the Massachusetts Institute of Technology.

Since then proliferation has continued to be resisted by ensuing ECPD committees, but it has been a losing battle. The latest (1951) ECPD report lists 20 different accredited curricula. Applications are pending from various engineering colleges for recognition of some 15 new curricula, ranging from coal mining engineering to fire protection engineering. All that is needed is a curriculum in combustion engineering and there will be a trinity of engineering specialists, one of which will procure the fuel (coal mining), the next will burn it (combustion engineering), and the third will put out the fire (fire protection engineering).

Technical Institutes.—The provision of appropriate education for those who serve the engineering profession in subprofessional capacities, as engineering aids, technicians, and the like, has long been a subject of discussion. ASEE reports 20 years ago called attention to the importance of such education, and urged the recognition of technical institutes for their necessary and avowed purposes, lest many more be tempted to follow the example of the few, and metamorphose themselves into weak engineering schools. In recognition of the importance of technical institutes in the general scheme of technical education, a Division of Technical Institutes was established in ASEE after World War II. In 1945 ECPD undertook to extend the accrediting process to technical institutes that offered 2-year terminal post-high school programs.

A subcommittee of the Committee on Education of ECPD administers the accreditation of technical institutes, 23 of which are now (1951) accredited. The accreditation process is based to a degree on the criteria described previously for engineering colleges, with due allowance for the different type of curricula and objectives. Technical institutes have come of age. The guidance provided them and the recognition accorded them represent an important achievement by engineering during the past decade.

GUIDANCE

The selection of qualified students for admission to engineering colleges has been a matter of study and experiment ever since the Mann report of 1918 called attention to the promising tests developed by Thorndike and by Thurstone. Subsequently the ECPD has collaborated with ASEE and many engineering colleges in the development and application of various testing programs. The most ambitious was the Measurement and Guidance Project in Engineering Education operated from 1943 to 1948. Substantial financial support was furnished by the Carnegie Foundation. The project was absorbed into the Educational Testing Service when it was created in 1948 to merge a number of testing programs. Many engineering colleges have used numerous testing devices in attempts to select better their entering students, and to predict their subsequent performance in engineering. Nearly all have been modified, and experimentation continues. This facet of engineering education contains many unresolved and debatable problems.

ADEQUACY AND STANDARDS

From time to time as engineering expanded as a profession, as it felt the impact of new scientific knowledge, as its graduates were catapulted into fields in which applied science or other professional disciplines required both the specialized knowledge and the skill of the engineer, recurring controversies have arisen as to: (1) The content of the engineering curriculum, (2) its objectives, and (3) its length. Another such period of inquiry and decisions is again present. ECPD recognized this by the creation, in 1950, of a Committee on Adequacy and Standards. Its first report, published in 1951, called attention to the wide variation in the quality of engineering curricula, even though they met the minimum standards imposed by the accrediting procedure. It pointed out the need for more adequate knowledge of the fundamental sciences, the different methods in use for relating this knowledge to engineering education, and the basic premise that:

> "Differentiating characteristic of the engineering function is the ability to utilize the sciences for the creative process of design and development of useful apparatus, structures, or other works * * *."

The committee suggested a reappraisal of engineering education, which is now under way.

Conclusion

The foregoing account of some of the major achievements in engineering education during the past century has perforce omitted many significant developments, experiments, and related topics. It should be clear that progress in engineering education has been substantial, and that the achievements are significant and numerous. However, it is equally obvious that serious problems are still ahead, of which curriculum content, proliferation of curricula, length of the undergraduate curriculum, postgraduate education, and selection and guidance are among the more important. The ASEE and ECPD have recognized the challenge, and there was established by ASEE in June, 1952, a Coordinating Committee on the Evaluation of Engineering Education, to work jointly with the ECPD Committee on Adequacy and Standards of Engineering Education. The results of the joint inquiry will undoubtedly mark an important milestone in the future of professional education in engineering.

The continued alertness of engineering educators and the engineering societies in meeting the ever-expanding requirements of sound and adequate education for the engineering profession has produced substantial achievements. Nevertheless, this very alertness and the lack of complacency that have happily characterized these groups, especially during the past half century, have created an awareness that the time is at hand for some serious soul searching to insure equal achievements for the future. There is a ferment at work that has had as its first product the initiation of the evaluation process just mentioned.

The real measure of the accomplishments in education is the contribution of its product to the profession of engineering. The recognition accorded that profession; the almost fantastic progress in industrial development and production conceived and managed by engineers; the great structures designed and built by them for the comfort, convenience, and health of the people; the increased number of great public and private enterprises directed by engineers—all have been contemporary with the improvements in engineering education. Indeed, achievements in engineering education, resulting in an ever-more-competent profession, have in no small measure been responsible for the economic and social progress of the United States. Engineering is a peculiar profession. It ranges over a broader and far more diverse spectrum of future employment than any other profession. Thus, the professional education of its future members is an unusually complex and difficult matter.

The important conclusions from any objective appraisal of engineering education over the past century indicate that its achievements have been real and significant: The changing requirements of the profession have been anticipated and met; those engaged in engineering education have been alert to needs required by circumstance and science; and, finally, as in any forward moving profession, problems of change and adjustment are clamoring for solution in the new period of transition ahead. These will be solved by the collaboration of all elements of the profession as other problems have been resolved in the past.

AMERICAN SOCIETY OF CIVIL ENGINEERS
Founded November 5, 1852
TRANSACTIONS

Paper No. 2582

PROSPECTS AND PROGRAMS—ENGINEERING EDUCATION

By S. C. Hollister,[1] M. ASCE

Synopsis

The principal influences affecting the present status of engineering education are discussed in this paper. Major trends in population, economy, and industry have a definite relation to the type of curricula offered in the engineering schools. The writer briefly presents the problems faced by today's engineer—depletion of natural resources, unstable economy, increasing population, and others—and the effect of these problems on education is evaluated. Several possible avenues of solution are explored, and ways of utilizing available engineering talent to the fullest degree are suggested.

Introduction

The past 80 years have witnessed a change in the United States from an essentially agrarian nation to one of industrial power. The development has resulted chiefly from the introduction and utilization of technology. This basic change has had a profound effect on the country's international position and on its potentiality for moral and spiritual, as well as economic, leadership.

During the past 50 years the population of the United States has doubled. Production, however, has increased to $4\frac{3}{4}$ times what it was at the turn of the twentieth century. This increase has come about largely because the nation has been able to develop and apply, at the hand of the worker, about $4\frac{1}{2}$ times as much energy as was available in 1900.

Not only has the engineer made possible this increase in production; he has profoundly influenced transportation and communication as well. The world has shrunk in size in terms of the movement of goods and people. Every part of the world now may listen to every other part so that all may know the doings of any people as they occur.

Some of the earlier steps in industrial development could be achieved with little more than native ingenuity. However, engineering education, once introduced, became increasingly effective, until now it is a necessity, for both the maintenance and the advancement of the technological system.

---

[1] Dean, Coll. of Eng., Cornell Univ., Ithaca, N. Y.

Since preparation by way of education always precedes accomplishment, it follows that the planning of engineering education requires an estimation of the future and its needs. The groundwork for 25 years hence is being laid today. A look ahead, therefore, into the world of a quarter of century from now should furnish some guiding principles on which the future trends of engineering education should rest.

The Engineer's Problem

It is the engineer's lot to be called into situations in which there are serious problems. There are many of these confronting this country, solutions of which will have to be found in the relatively near future. Such problems tax the ingenuity and capacity of the engineering profession.

Economic.—A whole group arises from economic sources. The United States has always plunged into full use of its natural resources with very little thought of what might occur after the sources have been exhausted, and they have been depleted at a terrific rate. It has been stated that when these resources are gone others will surely be found to take their place. How replacements were to be found was left largely to Yankee ingenuity and technical know-how. In many spots the time has now come when the know-how to meet some of these basic deficiencies must be developed.

Depleted Resources.—From one source it is learned that for every barrel of petroleum taken out of the ground two more barrels of petroleum have been discovered. Thus it has been concluded that there is an inexhaustible supply of petroleum. All that needs be done is to develop new methods of detecting the petroleum that is not at present known about, and new methods of producing and refining petroleum that is known about but that is in such form that at least a considerable part cannot readily be extracted by available means at a reasonable economic cost. Although it has been stated that there is an inexhaustible supply of petroleum in the United States, during the past decade, the nation has changed from an exporting to an importing country as far as this particular material is concerned. During that decade the same corner was also turned with lumber; and, in the prior decade, with zinc and copper. The United States is about to become a large importer of high-grade iron ore. Of course, tin, nickel, natural rubber, chromium, and most manganese have to come from other countries, along with lesser quantities of economically strategic materials.

Population Growth.—It is expected that population in the next 25 years will increase by 20%. This growth will affect what is needed to maintain the basic economy at a reasonable level. In addition, continuing commitments abroad, where in many places rising populations menace the economic balance, must be cared for.

In agriculture it is expected that the yield per acre by 1975 will have to be increased more than 40%. Some of this added yield will be achieved through further engineering developments and some through new conceptions, new discoveries, and new controls in plant science. The result in production, however, is that the number of people fed per farm worker must be increased in 25 years by 40%.

Water Control.—It is no news to people in many parts of the United States that one of the critical materials now in short supply is water—water for irrigation, water for industrial uses, water for drinking purposes, and water for navigation. Although the nation has an enormous supply of water, it frequently is in the wrong place or occurs in the wrong season. Immense problems lie ahead in meeting the situation so that there may be redistribution, reclamation of used water, and conversion of sea water into a potable supply. However, any new process must be economical or it will be of no avail.

Timber Resources.—Another problem that faces the country is the development of a sound policy and practice respecting timber resources. This subject has been actively discussed for at least 50 years, but the problem is still to be solved, and the engineer faces the need for further development in the economical use of wood products, or for an adequate substitute for a fair amount of the present supply.

Coal.—There appears to be a very large supply of coal. One of the problems, however, is not whether there is an ample quantity of coal of good quality, but how it may be wrested from its present natural site and supplied at points where it can be used effectively. Possible conversion in the natural site to another form, such as gas, which may be removed and transported more easily than the original solid coal, is one possibility that has been studied to some extent. The amount of coal needed 25 years from now may conceivably be 100% in excess of the present production. It must be recalled that one means of covering the shortage of petroleum is by the synthetic manufacture of petroleum products from coal. It must also be recalled that petroleum is a raw product from which many chemicals are developed—a process that is being rapidly accelerated. This use is in addition to that of petroleum as fuel, and may eventually form a major part of the demand on coal, if the raw source is transferred to that material.

Natural Gas.—Another natural resource that is being consumed at a terrific rate is natural gas. Its consumption has increased threefold in the past 15 years. Like petroleum, this fuel is being used extensively in its crude form. The day may not be far distant when the need for special products made from distillation will become critical. At such time there may be cause to regret the inefficient use of the material in its crude form, and its depletion to the point at which the supply is below the required need in more effective form.

Electricity.—To a constantly increasing degree, electrical energy is being utilized to multiply the effectiveness of a man-hour of work. Most electrical energy is available through thermal power. Although some hydroelectric power may still be developed in the future, it will not form even one quarter of the total source of electrical energy that will be needed in another 25 years. In other words, the major expansion of the future will be through the development of further thermal power with its consequent demand on coal, natural gas, and petroleum.

POSSIBLE SOLUTIONS

Whether in the field of materials or in the field of fuels, the ultimate goal is constantly to work toward the harnessing or utilization of supplies or materials or energy that are well nigh inexhaustible. For example, many products that are now wasted might conceivably be converted into useful substances. Solar energy, which is available in parts of the United States in abundance around the calendar, might some day be the source of power that now requires the consumption of priceless natural resources. The constant struggle toward this ultimate goal eventually will set more and more men free throughout the world. The more general the occurrence of the base source of materials or power the more free will mankind become.

Financial Readjustment.—Thus far this paper has discussed largely the consequences of the need of expanding the economy because of an expanded population. There are other factors that place great burdens on the engineering profession. Consider for a moment a continuing international situation that necessitates heavy taxes. The tax burden, it is generally agreed, is about as high as it can well be short of all-out war. Stated in another way, each man has just about reached the saturation point of his buying power. If wages and prices go up together, of course buying power is not increased, except during the transition stage. The nation cannot afford always to be in that transition stage. The problem therefore is what can be done to give people greater services for the same amount of money.

Design Simplification.—There are a great many things that need redesign in the interest of saving money. As an example, it is extremely difficult today for a young man, regardless of the field in which he is working, to acquire a home and a young family at the same time. The cost of present-day construction is forcing more and more people to undertake building their homes with their own hands. This is one answer to the labor organizations that undertake to place artificial barriers in the way of necessities by actually demanding pay for no work. The economy in the past has supported a certain amount of boondoggling, but there is a limit to what people will stand, after which checks and balances are developed by the consumer.

Cost Reduction.—However, housing is only one form of commodity, the cost of which is too high. Other appliances must be considerably simplified and reduced in cost, thus providing an opportunity for the purchase of still others that now cannot be afforded. For example, automobiles are too highly priced. An inexpensive car, one that will furnish transportation with comfort but not luxury, is urgently needed. Cheaper radios, television sets, refrigerators, air conditioners, washing machines, and the like should also be developed. In time these improvements may come, but they are necessary now.

The American people have learned to do many things the expensive way. The nation will have to learn to keep essential things simpler. This calls for the highest form of skill in design of which the engineer may be capable. The present tendency is to add gadgets on top of gadgets, to the point where sheer accumulation is burdensome. People need to learn how to live more simply, and engineers need to learn how to design more simply, so that more commodities will be available.

In no part of the present economy is it more essential that simplification be practiced than in the conduct of war. In a continuing emergency there is no place for the old theories of war that held that costs of materiel were no object so long as the war was won. At present, it is absolutely necessary that resources be saved and that the United States still be in the position to win a war. In fact, unless resources are conserved, the nation may fall, either in war or in peace.

New Products.—There is still another area in which the American economy suggests much work for the engineer. With continually increasing mechanization, more wealth is created with fewer actual man-hours of labor. Obviously this condition would bring about unemployment if it were not for the fact that new products may be made with the labor saved in the first operation. The result, heretofore, has been a continually expanding industrial organization. Whether this process can go on ad infinitum has not yet been ascertained in the world. Whether the system can be applied to countries that have a greater population per unit of area than that of the United States likewise has not been determined. The engineer is being called on to work out these theories, both at home and abroad, especially in countries with less fortunate living conditions than those in the United States.

ENGINEERING EDUCATION

Without considering the pressures on the economy resulting from the need of other nations for American support, or from the need of continued military preparedness, it is already clear that engineering problems are piling up for the profession at a rate far greater than the rate of population increase. In fact, the problems are appearing at a constantly increasing rate, and there is no end in sight.

The writer has already reported that the point has now been reached in the development of engineers where no percentage increase of engineers in terms of the total population may be expected. Thus, the percentage of engineers in the total population is leveling off, whereas the really tough problems accumulating before the profession are piling up at a rate far greater than the rate of population growth. This is another way of illustrating the point that engineering services to the community at large are increasing per engineer available for such service.

Role of Engineering Education.—What effect has all this on engineering education? It may well be asked just what is now being put into the hands and heads of students that will really be effective in dealing with the kind of problems that are likely to arise in the future. How has the scientific and technical preparation which students must master been strengthened?

It is very clear that no sharp line can be drawn between the various techniques that will be in use 25 years or 50 years from now; but it is certain that the principles on which these technical developments will be based are principles that are now available in the basic sciences. The problem, then, is to strengthen the basic science content of the curricula. The importance of this conclusion is emphasized when it is recalled that the problems awaiting solution are tougher than the problems that have been answered, and require a more fundamental approach.

Engineering Aides.—Another approach to the total problem of engineering manpower is the realization that, with the requirement of increased effectiveness for each engineer, there must be a readjustment to reinforce the work of each engineer. Thus, there should be a supply of capable engineering aides. The training of these technical aides in itself must be advanced beyond past practice. This suggests the possibility of modifying the educational system to provide for the development of the professional engineer at a higher level than heretofore, and also to develop technical aides at a higher level of training than is at present customary. It may well be that the pattern of professional schools in the future will involve a more extended program than is now available, supported by 4-year curricula that will be calculated to develop subprofessional personnel. It is conceivable that all these programs would be collegiate degree-granting ones, but of different duration and resulting in different degrees. The writer is not at this point discussing graduate study as such, but is dealing with the education of the great majority of engineers who will go out to practice the profession.

CONCLUSION

It is obvious that the engineering profession is looking toward a period in which the function of the engineer will be increasingly important in economic and political affairs, as well as in technical progress. In planning the education of engineers no reduction should be permitted in the little time that is now being spent in broadening the professional engineer's background of knowledge. On the contrary, it is essential that such courses be extended to provide a richer education than is presently possible.

In all the foregoing, it is evident that there is a great need for expansion of creative activities. Recently a leading industrialist argued that the natural resources of the United States were inexhaustible. He cited cases in which there was a present knowledge of large deposits and the hope that many more deposits could be added to these if better methods of exploration, discovery, extraction, and processing were developed. If these improvements were possible, then natural resources would truly be inexhaustible. Apparently he did not readily recognize that the inexhaustibility that he was depending on was largely the inexhaustible ingenuity of engineers.

It is this inexhaustibility of engineering resource that concerns those who are interested in engineering education. As educators, these men must address themselves more assiduously to the task of developing the student's imaginative, creative ability to a higher level than has been achieved in the past. In fact, many teaching methods have not been aimed at this objective.

It should not be interpreted that imagination can be placed, by teaching processes, in the head of someone who has no imaginative power. The writer firmly believes, however, that imaginative, creative ability may be enhanced by teaching methods. In the world today, and in the engineering profession, creative talent is the most urgently needed and the most highly prized attribute.

Whether engineering educators accomplish the goal of service to the profession in the form here suggested is not important. What is important, however, is that they address themselves vigorously to the task of appraisal of the situation, and then arrive at an adequate, equitable, and effective program.

AMERICAN SOCIETY OF CIVIL ENGINEERS

Founded November 5, 1852

TRANSACTIONS

Paper No. 2583

LOOKING AHEAD IN ENGINEERING EDUCATION

By L. M. K. Boelter[1]

Synopsis

The role of the prophet is precarious. Based on the expansion of knowledge in the physical sciences, and the life sciences, supported by a study of the engineering profession and engineering education of today, an extrapolation will be hazarded in this paper. A guide line is established by the extent to which the prognostications of engineering education of the last generation have been realized. Again, early engineering education is examined to discover whether old ideas can be resuscitated and utilized.

Looking ahead in engineering education is indeed a precarious undertaking. It is assumed that there is a temporal region of experience from which a rational extrapolation may be made. To this end heavy reliance is here placed on the historical data presented in the reports of the American Society for Engineering Education (1).[2] Evidence of lag in effectuating ideas of engineering leaders and of cyclic repetition (probably of a period equal to a generation) as well as failure to apply the experimental method to pedagogical procedures and to curricular changes may be found in the literature, including college catalogs.

Again, the earlier lack of acceptance of engineering in the universities of the United States as well as in Germany (2) has left vestigial scars and other effects manifested in the academic organizational structures and attitudes. The establishment of institutes of technology and land-grant colleges has had a salutary effect on the position of engineering in the higher educational structure of the United States.

Definitions

Before undertaking a review of developments, trends, and prospects in engineering education, it is advisable to consider the implications of a few terms that are widely used:

---

[1] Dean, Coll. of Eng., Univ. of California, Los Angeles, Calif.
[2] Numerals in parentheses, thus: (1), refer to corresponding items in the Bibliography at the end of the paper.

1. Engineering As an Art.—In the application of ideal systems of the world-in-being, many force fields are effective which are unknown, cannot be analyzed, or, it may well prove, offer such problems that analysis is too expensive. The knowledge of the professional engineer, based on scientific training but amplified by practical experience, fills the gap between the results of analysis and the behavior of the actual system (Fig. 1). Often he does not employ mathematics beyond arithmetic as a language, his modes of expression being his native tongue and graphics (drawing); and his discipline is formal logic. He senses the magni-

FIG. 1.—NETWORK ANALYZER, UTILIZED TO SOLVE HYDRAULIC PIPELINE AND ELECTRICAL TRANSMISSION LINE PROBLEMS; ALSO FOR ENGINE MANIFOLD AND TORSIONAL VIBRATION PROBLEMS

tudes of variables which can be neither formulated nor evaluated by the scientist. Extrapolation from system to system with reasonable assurance of acceptable results with the details unknown is indeed hazardous; the exercise of this procedure accounts for the stature of the professional engineer. Briefly, he deals with a mass of unformulated knowledge.

2. Training.—Training is the acquisition of knowledge and skills which are to be utilized in the solution of a particular problem or to be directed toward a particular end.

3. Education.—Education is the acquisition of knowledge and skills which are to be utilized to solve general problems or a range of problems such as are faced throughout a "full" life.

BACKGROUNDS

The first engineering works rest in antiquity. Products of engineering and architecture can scarcely be separated at the beginning of history. The great accomplishments of the ancients need not be recounted here, except to observe that the progenitor of the modern professional engineer was not always required to conserve national resources or to practice economy. On the other hand, he had much less power available with which to perform the assigned tasks. The early engineer expended a goodly amount of energy developing engines of war.

Transmission of knowledge in ancient times was either through shrewd observations of the existing engineering works or through the master-pupil relationship, although certain records were maintained also. The first American engineering curricula (1) may be characterized as applied science containing a liberal core of social-humanistic studies. Shop courses were introduced fairly early and remained in one form or another in many curricula for at least two generations. Engineering laboratory instruction was also begun fairly early in the period of the germination of engineering instruction—in approximately 1870.

Throughout the succeeding years a gap grew between the sciences—physics and chemistry particularly—and their application to the engineering courses and to the profession. Engineering could no longer be characterized as applied science; rather, it emerged as a science in its own right and in addition great stress was laid upon the art of engineering. However, the bases on which engineering instruction were built did not change with the change in philosophy and content of the physical sciences. Thus a gap of approximately one generation developed between knowledge as added to the sciences and its application in industry. This gap was reduced to several years during World War II. Parenthetically, developments in the physical sciences have, however, resulted in the creation of new engineering curricula. This gap between the formulated and experimental knowledge of the physical sciences and the content of engineering courses and the application to the design of engineering systems cannot again be allowed to develop.

Segments of the physical sciences may be neglected in science departments. These areas must be assumed by engineering, but their assumption must not prevent the transmission of new knowledge of the physical sciences into engineering.

ENGINEERING CURRICULAR SUPPORTS

The 4-year professional undergraduate curriculum is still considered to be standard and has proved satisfactory although certain colleges of engineering maintain 5-year curricula. However, five supports for the curriculum can be developed so that the 4-year curriculum will remain a "unique segment" of engineering education. These supporting elements will be briefly discussed:

1. Considerable opinion exists to the effect that at least 2 years can be subtracted from the precollege school experience (3) of a student who has the intellectual capacity for college work and who also possesses the necessary physical stamina. In other words, the material now presented can be compressed into a lesser time, or the equivalent of 2 years of appropriate work may be added between the kindergarten and high school graduation. Canadian and European experience will aid in pointing the way.

The subject material to be introduced in the 2 years saved will receive careful attention. The University of Chicago at Chicago, Ill., in its University College has studied intimately the recasting of knowledge (4), the emphasis on particular modes of reasoning, and desirable methods of instruction (5).

2. The work-study program (often formalized and called the cooperative program) deserves much more thoughtful attention and support. With a slight change in the college calendar and scheduling of all required courses each term, students may be given the opportunity of industrial employment on a technical level commensurate with their maturity, training, and education. Briefly, an industrial (or governmental) organization would set aside one job in which two, three, or four students will serve seriatim each year depending on the college calendar. The undergraduate professional curriculum demands the support of this program for survival.

3. The engineering profession should encourage and develop an internship program to begin directly after the award of the baccalaureate. Certain industrial organizations have made great strides in postgraduate study for their employees (6); but the profession has not yet effectively and formally recognized a post-bachelor's program for the training and education of a professional engineer. It is significant that the engineering societies require for membership a certain number of years "in responsible charge," and some state laws require that engineers-in-training serve under registered professional engineers.

The college of engineering, the employer, and the engineer-in-training (or junior engineer) acting in concert would, in the following tentatively presented plan, arrange an individual program consisting of part or all of these components:

    (a) On-the-job employee instruction by supervisors;
    (b) On-the-job self-study;
    (c) On-the-job courses;
    (d) Off-the-job courses, social-humanistic and technical; and
    (e) Off-the-job self-study.

The program will be designed to aid the engineer-in-training to achieve professional status, to insure more effective performance of the job assignments during the training program, and to fill such gaps in general knowledge and specific applications as will allow the most effective discharge of his duties as a citizen.

An examination, with or without a dissertation based on the total training and educational experience of the candidate for the previously selected period (say, 4 to 5 years), will climax this internship program. The initiation of the program at an early date is imperative to the future well-being and strength of the profession.

4. The postgraduate education of the engineer-in-training and that of the professional engineer should receive attention through an intensified adult education program, under an engineering extension system. Technical courses to (a) broaden the engineer and (b) specialize his experience, and general courses to (c) give depth and meaning to his contributions to society, will be available. Correspondence courses planned to meet specific needs will be more generally obtainable. Techniques will be designed to aid the engineer who is located in out-of-the-way places, both domestic and foreign. Publications of the engineering societies will be utilized to increase the pertinence of the postgraduate educational experience.

5. Finally, a dynamic graduate program leading to either a science or an engineering degree is in a virile stage of growth. Graduate work in engineering assumed a master-pupil relationship in its early days, with emphasis on the original individual investigation. Accompanying its growth will come a recognition that a change in the method of instruction is necessary. Courses are now replacing seminars and instructors are undertaking the direction of many research proj-

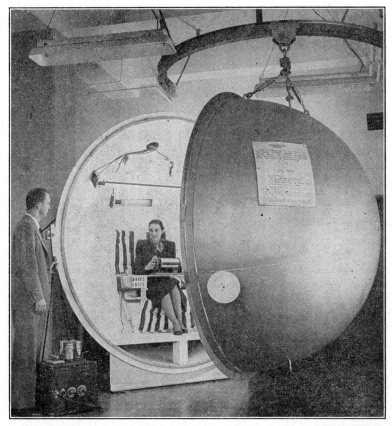

FIG. 2.—INTEGRATING SPHERE, UTILIZED TO MEASURE LUMINOUS FLUX, AND TO STUDY FUNDAMENTAL PROBLEMS OF SEEING

ects—the result in many instances has been that graduate work either has become an image of undergraduate instruction or has retained the master-pupil relationship on a larger scale. In both cases, the effectiveness of the instructional methods must be examined.

Graduate students may wish to obtain a foundation which will allow them to practice the engineering of tomorrow, in which a knowledge of the modern concepts in the physical and life sciences is essential (Fig. 2). Others may wish to broaden their base in engineering, whereas still others may wish to specialize in a branch or a phase of engineering. Combinations of the three objectives, although resulting in dilution, are also a possibility.

As graduate work in engineering becomes an accepted part of the training and education of the professional engineer, the present dichotomy will be resolved through the development of two paths toward advanced degrees. Along one path leading to the degrees of Master of Science and Doctor of Philosophy (or their equivalent) the discipline of research, with special accent on the techniques of analysis, will be emphasized, with the subjects chosen either to decrease the gap between the physical and life sciences and engineering, or to broaden the student's background in engineering. In summary, this graduate experience may be designated as existing in the area of engineering science.

The other stem, clearly a professional one, leading to the degrees of Master of Engineering and Doctor of Engineering will be developed around the discipline of design, with emphasis on the techniques of synthesis of engineering systems with the objectives of either broadening or deepening the student's background in engineering. This graduate experience may be designated as existing in the field of engineering as an art, strongly supported by engineering science.

In both paths (the word curriculum being avoided in designating graduate work), the methodology of engineering will be employed, and a greater emphasis will be placed on the social-humanistic content of the graduate experience. Other professional groups, for instance, a medical group at one university, are now administering these two graduate programs seriatim with the professional sequence coming first.

Graduate programs designed for full-time professional employees have been in existence for many years and are now quite common (6). Examples of earlier programs are: General Electric Company and Union College at Schenectady, N. Y.; and Westinghouse Electric Corporation and the University of Pittsburgh at Pittsburgh, Pa. However, Purdue University at Lafayette, Ind., has established a unified program for the Master of Science degree which will serve as a guide for off-campus work (as also have Ohio State University at Columbus, University of Maryland at College Park, and University of California at Berkeley), as well as for a study of the unified curriculum concept (7).

ENGINEERING AS A PROFESSION

More practicing engineers are now concerned with the content, significance, and responsibility of the profession (8) than were in the past; however, there were some activity and concern early in the twentieth century (9). Two events have contributed to this favorable climate. First, the present shortage of engineers has caused the professional engineer to resurvey the position of the profession locally and nationally as he presents the facts to school counselors and to prospective engineering students. Organizations like Engineers' Council for Professional Development, American Society of Engineering Education, and Engineers Joint Council, as well as local engineering groups, have done excellent work.

Again, the registration procedure in many states requires the appraisal of the professional experience of the candidate, and the examination which is set is designed to evaluate the professional capabilities of the candidate. These forces require concentrated attention to the question of the status of the profession. Thus the ethical, esthetic, cultural, economic, and technical content of engineering is evolving, and the methodology implicit in the practice of the profession is slowly emerging.

Increased professional consciousness will reflect itself in the curricula. With time there will be greater emphasis on engineering instead of on a specialty or a branch. This changed attitude is, and will be, revealed in the philosophy of engineering instruction. The greater appreciation of the unity of knowledge (10) will influence both the profession and the curricula. For instance, systems analysis (or systems engineering or operations analysis) will become an essential part of the climactic segment of the curriculum. Less attention will be paid to individual courses—their number will be reduced (11a); but more attention will be given to the thoroughness and content of individual courses in regard to their articulation with other courses. The academic experiences of the student will be planned and executed as a part of an activity beginning in the eighth (or ninth) grade, extending to achievement of professional status some 15 years later.

TECHNICAL INSTITUTES

In the organization of an engineering department in industry, a variety of talents and training is needed. The profession will in the future vigorously support the development of training programs for those groups which form a part of the organization of the profession. Other professional groups have done this and are taking leadership in assuming responsibility for the training of contributing groups.

If properly organized, the leadership of the engineering department in an industrial unit should reside in a professional engineer. A fraction of the group will be professional engineers; another segment will be composed of engineers-in-training; and still another segment will consist of those who have completed a 2-year program (technical institute type) or its equivalent (1a). Some years ago many 4-year engineering students withdrew during the first 2 or 3 years of a college curriculum. Was this abbreviated experience the optimum desirable for the semiprofessional? Is there not a better way of training these young men?

Technical institute types of programs have been introduced in many sections of the United States to answer this question—for instance, by Pennsylvania State College at State College, Purdue University, in the junior colleges of California, in New York State, and in private, including proprietary, schools. Broadly speaking, the courses in these programs should not rest on study of formal physics, chemistry, and mathematics beyond high school. Physical systems are described verbally and numerically. Numerical methods of analysis are used. Students learn about particular systems. Physical and chemical principles are taught and illustrated in connection with the system or apparatus under consideration. Arithmetic methods are introduced as needed. Verbal description and analysis replace symbolic description and analysis, the former augmented through pictorial means (drawings and sketches). Activities ancillary to engineering, such as timekeeping and scheduling, as related to the system or apparatus or job, are taught in terms of the system under consideration.

Pre-engineering courses do not suffice for this program. Imaginative guidance is needed and can be contributed by professional engineers, educators, and teachers.

A 4-year program including the equivalent of 2 years of general education (humanities, economics, accounting, language, literature, and history) and 2 years of technical institute work, closely integrated, will fulfil a need for a man with a college training who will work with and assist the professional engineer. Alternatively a 4-year program including general education courses and certain science and applied science courses (partly equivalent to, but not identical with, engineering science courses) deserves consideration as a training regime for others who will work with and aid the professional engineer or who intend to enter engineering curricula for further study.

FLOW OF INFORMATION

As an educational center the engineering college is a component in a flow circuit. Knowledge flows outward through the undergraduate student, the graduate student, faculty consultation, faculty texts, and technical publications. Channels like the newspaper, house organ, radio, and television have not been exploited adequately. However, within the next generation the professional engineer will utilize more effectively these latter media of communication.

On the other hand, the return flow path from industry and the field to the engineering school has not been established as a conscious effort. Catalogs, advertisements, house organs, and sectioned and working models, often available to the faculty and student, serve as a partial return path.

Thus it will be proposed that a function of industry is to utilize knowledge, which process will generate further knowledge. In sum, the function of utilization results in the generation and diffusion and differentiation of knowledge. This information must flow back to the college where it should be formulated, integrated, and generalized. Still further fragmentation of knowledge by the engineering college will be considered indefensible (10)(11b). This is a research task, appealing to the imaginative instructor, which the engineering school will accept in parallel with the projects now in being (12).

Relative to the documenting of engineering works, the product is the final record of an engineering design. Buildings, bridges, television sets, gas turbines—all are the living examples of the application of engineering methodology for the satisfaction of the needs of man. However, the idea on being reduced to practice has also been committed to paper through drawings, designs, and specifications. An account of these engineering works may reach engineering publications and textbooks in part and very late. The time lag between discoveries and their general use can and will be reduced by increasing the breadth and effectiveness of repositories of engineering knowledge and the assumption by the engineering college of a new role in the return path in the flow circuit.

INDUSTRIAL FUNCTIONS

Industrial functions (13) of importance to the engineer, often cited, are design, research, development, production, construction, sales, service, and maintenance.

However, these functions have not yet been carefully defined. For instance, what are the disciplines of the design function? Does a universal design methodology exist? The attention of professional engineers and of teachers should be directed

Fig. 3.—Electron Microscope, Utilized to Study the Structure of Metals and of Air Pollutants

to the problem of establishing the meaning of the design function and to develop its methodology.

Again the existing experimental data will be sifted and further data will be gathered (Fig. 3) in order that the production (14) and construction functions (and others) may be placed upon an analytical basis. Herein lies one of the greatest challenges to engineering educators.

THE CURRICULUM

In this "outlook" little has been mentioned about the undergraduate curriculum. Some of its elements are presented in references (15) (16) (17) (18) (19a) (20). Considerable thought has resulted in a tentative formulation of the content of the engineering curriculum, of engineering methodology, and of the disciplines underlying engineering (18). A place has been found in modern curricula for the presentation of analytical plus experimental modes of solution and for the science as well as for the art of engineering.

A clarion call for the return of certain social-humanistic studies to the engineering curriculum (21) and their recognition as a stem paralleling the technical stem has refocused attention on the trend toward specialization—in this case the exclusion of nontechnical engineering courses—which appears to be part and parcel of the "natural" evolution of curricula in modern American colleges.

The effects of specialization and fragmentation, which are natural results of scholarship devoted to the rational extension of knowledge, on courses, curricula, and instructor attitudes, have been examined recently. The conclusion was reached that both general education and the discipline of synthesis (building or assembling in contrast with analysis) suffer in present curricular arrangements and teaching methods (22).

The social-humanistic content of the engineering curriculum will find its expression as an integral part of the totality of student development, rather than in separate compartments or courses. The integrating of engineering—discovering the disciplines of the several branches and establishing those disciplines which are common to engineering—will also automatically include the requisite elements of knowledge referred to as the social-humanistic (23). One of the great unifying forces of engineering education will prove to be a rational inclusive treatment of the properties of materials; their reasonable use is the cornerstone of engineering practice. On the other hand, that segment of the student's education designed to equip him to meet the social and intellectual requirements of society (above and beyond his professional competence) will serve as another unifying force.

GENERAL EDUCATION

Goals of a total education have been listed (24) as: (a) To arouse interest, (b) to develop skills, (c) to convey knowledge, (d) to emphasize the importance of understanding and appreciation, (e) to establish attitudes and ideals, and (f) to cultivate habits. The part of total education (consisting of the effect of the environment on man and his reaction) which may be considered as general education has been defined (2a) as:

> "* * * the study of certain essential areas of knowledge together with the acquisition of certain basic skills which should be required of all students. These requirements should meet the needs of all human beings both as partici-

pating members of the community and as individuals who must undergo basic life experiences, irrespective of their future vocation."

That part of total education and general education which is now included in each 4-year engineering curriculum will need to be established explicitly. Total and general education goals should be formulated. The social-humanistic content of the curriculum will thus acquire more meaning and greater significance. The way is being illuminated by several colleges in the United States, such as, for example, the Carnegie Institute of Technology in Pittsburgh, Pa. (15). The Engineers' Council for Professional Development has progressed in this area and will continue its excellent work in cooperation with professional education groups.

TEACHING

Methods of instruction and teaching techniques (19)(25) are receiving much attention, especially through the support of the American Society for Engineering Education. The introduction of the summer school for engineering teachers (1b) was a great step forward but a return to the conception of breadth, rather than attention to detail, will characterize future activities of this type. The new vehicles of communication (recordings, films, radio, and television) will each be tried and tested by engineering teachers during the coming years. The application of the experimental results obtained through a study of the several methods and techniques will represent a milestone in pedagogy.

SUMMARY

In summary, the curriculum will be based on principles of transfer of knowledge and of skills; on the inculcation of a consciously formulated methodology, utilizing examples for incentive, continuity, and temporal pertinence; and on illustrations of natural (physical and life) phenomena, but with primary emphasis on the phenomena themselves and their analytic formulation. Throughout the engineering educational process the complete growth of the student will be facilitated with his teacher as central (25). He will be encouraged to "know himself," to know others (and society), and to be a living example of the interrelationship between the physical and human worlds. For him there cannot exist two stems (technical and social-humanistic) but rather a synthesis not only of the knowledge of the physical world but of knowledge itself (11c). In particular, he will be given the opportunity to express himself orally (in addition to the present emphasis on written expression) and to give vent to creativeness—in other words, to "be himself." The student will feel that he is responding to an exciting stimulating experience which has great human implications and effects.

This "outlook," it is hoped, contains both bases for action and stimuli for discussion. For only from free unprejudiced discussion will the truth emerge. Each engineering school must find its own solution of the engineering student-faculty-industry relationship within a generally understood and agreed-on framework.

BIBLIOGRAPHY

(1) "Report of the Investigation of Engineering Education 1923–1929," by W. E. Wickenden, *Engineering Education*, S.P.E.E., Pittsburgh, Pa. (*a*) Vol. II, p. 11. (*b*) Vol. II.

(2) "The Abuse of Learning," by Frederic Lilge, The MacMillan Co., New York, N. Y., 1948. (*a*) p. 311.

(3) "The American Educational System," by John D. Russell, Riverside Press, Cambridge, Mass., 1940, pp. 221–222.

(4) "The Sciences Programs in the College of the University of Chicago," by M. C. Coulter, Z. L. Smith, and J. J. Schwab, reprinted from "Science in General Education," edited by E. J. McGrath, Wm. C. Brown Co., Dubuque, Iowa, 1948.

(5) "Teaching by Discussion in the College Program, A Report," by J. Axelrod, B. S. Bloom, B. E. Ginsburg, W. O'Meara, and J. C. Williams, Jr., The College, Univ. of Chicago, Chicago, Ill., January, 1949.

(6) "Cooperative Engineering Education at Graduate Level from the Viewpoint of Industry," by L. M. Lindville and K. B. McEachron, Jr., *Journal of Engineering Education*, May, 1950, pp. 475–479.

(7) "Graduate Engineering Program of the U. S. Naval Ordnance Plant," by W. E. Howland and G. A. Hawkins, Purdue Univ., Lafayette, Ind., 1951.

(8) "The Nature of Engineering," by M. P. O'Brien, *Journal of Engineering Education*, November, 1950, pp. 133–141.

(9) "Addresses to Engineering Students," by John A. L. Waddell and John L. Harrington, Waddell & Harrington, Kansas City, Mo., 1911.

(10) "Impure Science," by Phillip Wylie, *Bulletin of the Atomic Scientists*, August, 1951, pp. 196–200.

(11) "The Aims of Education," by A. N. Whitehead, Mentor Books, New York, N. Y., 1949. (*a*) p. 14. (*b*) p. 37. (*c*) p. 58.

(12) "Engineering Research," by L. M. K. Boelter, *Mechanical Engineering*, December, 1948, p. 978.

(13) "Whither Engineering?" by A. A. Potter, *ibid.*, January, 1934, p. 3.

(14) "Engineering in the Fabrication Industries," by L. M. K. Boelter, *Proceedings*, 4th Annual Industrial Eng. Inst., Univ. of California, Los Angeles and Berkeley, Calif., 1952, p. 22.

(15) "The Development of Professional Education," by R. E. Doherty, Carnegie Press, Pittsburgh, Pa., 1950.

(16) "Differentiating Characteristics of an Engineering Curriculum," by S. C. Hollister, *Journal of Engineering Education*, January, 1950, pp. 291–294.

(17) "Horizons in Engineering Education," by Thorndike Saville, *ibid.*, March, 1949, pp. 344–354.

(18) "The Design of an Undergraduate Engineering Curriculum," by L. M. K. Boelter, Chemical Eng. Div., A.S.E.E., Northwestern Univ., Evanston, Ill., 1951.

(19) "A Discussion of Engineering Teaching," by L. M. K. Boelter, *Agricultural Engineering*, November, 1947, pp. 512–516. (*a*) Appendix VI.

(20) "Specific Objectives of Electrical Engineering Curricula," by Eric Walker, *Electrical Engineering*, June, 1952, pp. 514–518.

(21) "Report on Humanistic-Social Studies in Engineering Education," *Journal of Engineering Education*, January, 1946, pp. 338–351.

(22) "The Social Implications of Scientific Progress," Mid-Century Convocation of the Mass. Inst. Tech., John Wiley & Sons, Inc., New York, N. Y., and the M.I.T. Press, Cambridge, Mass., 1950, Chapter VII, pp. 300–352.

(23) "The College and the Community," Harper & Bros., New York, N. Y., 1952, Chapter VI, pp. 67–75.

(24) "General Education in the Land-Grant Institutions," by Edmund E. Day, *Journal of Engineering Education*, March, 1952, pp. 331–336.

(25) "Teacher in America," by Jacques Barzun, Little, Brown & Co., Boston, Mass., 1946, Chapters 7 and 14.

(26) "Experiences with Junior College Transfers in Engineering," by Harold P. Rodes, *Journal of Engineering Education*, January, 1950, p. 322.

AMERICAN SOCIETY OF CIVIL ENGINEERS

Founded November 5, 1852

TRANSACTIONS

Paper No. 2584

ENGINEERS' CONTRIBUTION IN DEVELOPING AMERICAN CITIES

By Harold M. Lewis,[1] M. ASCE

Synopsis

Members of the engineering professions, particularly civil engineers, have contributed much to city development. Although there is a great deal to admire in American cities, in some respects—particularly in regard to overcrowding and congestion—they tend to get out of hand. In these phases of urban growth, the engineer must do his part to find means of controlling the "monsters" that he has helped to create.

Introduction

Definition of Terms.—It may be helpful to define the principal terms in this paper. The word "engineer" is a much overworked title, and has been used in some cases by mechanics, tradesmen, and others who have no right to do so. This title belongs only to the professional engineer, one who has been educated in one of the engineering colleges or universities and is qualified, after a period of training in professional practice, to obtain a professional license in some form of engineering. Occasionally a self-educated man, without attending college, has through exceptional application to his work reached the same objective.

There is a glamor to engineering, as the engineer is thought of as one who creates structures and accomplishes what seemed to be the impossible. He works with his brains, is a master of formulas, and is also adept with the pencil on the drawing board. He can fashion things with tools and knows how to direct the labors of a large construction gang. Generally, he is a modest individual, content to find happiness in his profession and his friends.

By the "development of cities" is meant the building of places in which men congregate to work or to live. These places include those suburban areas that act as dormitories or satellites of metropolitan centers. They include all municipalities, large or small—cities, towns, and villages.

The city may contain huge factories and towering business centers; outlying shopping centers with low buildings and acres of parking space; recreation areas;

---

[1] Cons. Engr. and City Planner, New York, N. Y.

residence districts of apartments, modest homes, or palatial estates; airports, other terminals, and elaborate port improvements.

EARLY CITY PLANS AND PLANNERS

The plans of ancient and medieval cities were frequently influenced by the need of defense against attack. In other cases they were designed primarily to give eminence to groups of public buildings. The walled cities of France are an example of the former and have no counterpart in the United States where the

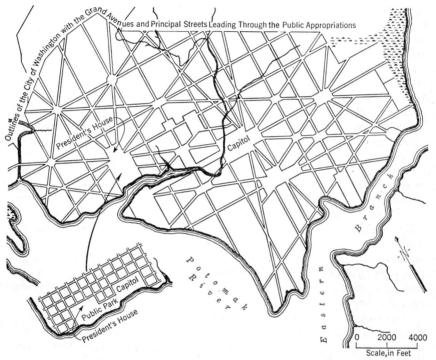

FIG. 1.—ORIGINAL PLAN FOR WASHINGTON, D. C., AS DRAWN UP BY MAJ. PIERRE CHARLES L'ENFANT, WITH SKETCH PLAN BY THOMAS JEFFERSON SUPERIMPOSED

early stockades against Indian attack have left no final imprint on city plans and where the early forts, such as those that guarded the entrances to the harbor of New York, N. Y., are now merely historical landmarks. Early Roman and Greek cities, the Hittite cities of Asia Minor, and the Mayan cities of Central America— all provide examples of the second type of plans. Also the plans of many capital cities, notably the national capital at Washington, D. C. (Fig. 1), have been strongly influenced by the desire to provide predominating sites for public buildings.

In medieval times there are examples of the combination of architect, engineer, and artist in a single man—for instance, Leonardo da Vinci (1452–1519). Most people think of him as the artist who painted the famous "Mona Lisa" and the fresco of "The Last Supper"; but when he obtained employment with the Duke of Milan it was as a military engineer who was prepared to undertake the design and construction of buildings and weapons for defense. Later da Vinci became chief engineer for Cesare Borgia. He was an inventor and research scientist. He developed a spring-driven mechanical car and made sketches for an airplane, a triple-barreled gun, two-level highways, and other contrivances not in common use until centuries after his death.

In the case of the early American cities, the primary responsibility for initial plans often rested with laymen. The basic plan of Philadelphia, Pa., was drawn up by William Penn, a statesman, in 1682. The City of Washington was, however, designed in 1791 by Maj. Pierre Charles L'Enfant, a French Army engineer. The plan of early Detroit, Mich., is the Governor's and Judges' Plan of 1807; Governor William Hull directed the work and the judges acted as a land board. The first large-scale plan of New York City was prepared by a commission of three prominent citizens appointed by the state legislature in 1807—Gouverneur Morris, lawyer and statesman, Simeon De Witt, surveyor-general of New York State, and John Rutherford, a lawyer, who later, in 1816, was appointed as commissioner to study a canal between the Delaware and Raritan rivers. All these men must have employed engineering talent in the actual surveys and preparation of plans.

As cities grew and urban problems became more complicated, the practice by a municipality of referring these problems to committees of boards of aldermen or city councils for investigation and recommendation proved inadequate. Such a group might have thought it necessary to employ a party of surveyors, or even one or two men who were recognized engineers. It is now the custom to rely on a well-qualified engineering staff in a city large enough to justify such a staff, or, in smaller cities, to call on one of the consulting organizations of technically trained men acknowledged as experts in their particular line. Thus municipal legislators have come to distinquish between political and engineering decisions and are quite content to delegate the responsibility for the latter, in both design and construction, to engineers.

The civil engineer and surveyor, even in the days of the American colonies, was a respected individual. He was and still is a kind of pioneer in the establishment of any new city, as he is the first man on the ground. It is his duty to make the first topographic surveys; and his work will influence, if it will not control, the lines of transportation and the adequacy of terminal facilities in the future city. The way in which he lays down the lines and grades of streets and the arrangement of blocks will, if he exercises vision and imagination, result in a community that can develop efficiently. If he lacks these qualities, someone else may later have to plan expensive projects to correct defects in the initial layout.

INFLUENCE OF ENGINEERING DEVELOPMENTS

Nature has done much to determine the sites of cities, but they have also been influenced by the works of man. The amazing growth of American cities has resulted from a series of engineering projects and inventions.

Canals.—The inland waterways represent the first development of this kind. One of the earliest studied in the United States was a waterway connecting the

Potomac and Ohio rivers, a charter for which was granted in 1784. However, construction of the canal was not started until 1828. In the meantime, the Erie Canal across New York State was built between 1817 and 1825, the first survey being under the direction of Simeon De Witt, already mentioned as having participated in the early planning of New York City. This canal did much to establish the supremacy of the Port of New York as a gateway to the Great Lakes and the upper reaches of the Mississippi Valley. Engineers were the prime movers in these and later waterway projects, many of which were laid out and built under the direction of the Corps of Engineers of the United States Army.

Railroads.—The railroad systems that were built in the United States in the decades between 1830 and 1870 were made possible by the invention of the steam engine by James Watt, a Scotch inventor, and its application to the locomotive, by George Stephenson, an English engineer. Spanning the continent, the railroads were responsible for the growth of large cities, at their terminals and at the main centers in the railroad network, such as Chicago, Ill., and St. Louis, Mo.

When engineers developed electric power as a possible substitute for steam power, the suburban electric railroads initiated the first big decentralization movement in metropolitan areas. Here the civil engineer and the electrical engineer combined forces.

Electric power was also used extensively in local transit systems, first for trolleys; then, in the 1880's, for elevated railroads in Boston, Mass., New York, and Chicago; and finally, in the twentieth century, in cities of several million population, for the modern rapid transit subway. In this case, civil, electrical, and mechanical engineers have all made contributions. The high-speed local transit systems have made possible tremendous urban concentrations; and at the same time they have enlarged the radius of urban growth around these centers.

Communications.—The inventions of the telegraph and telephone made possible the centralization of large business and maufacturing concerns in a single office from which they can, in a few seconds, contact employees and business associates around the world and arrange contracts or other agreements. Without these engineering aids, cities, particularly their business centers, could never have grown to their present size. Incidentally, modern methods of communication have greatly reduced the amount of travel that would otherwise be necessary in the conduct of business.

Miscellaneous.—The steel frame building, a product of the structural engineer, is another engineering development that has permitted cities to build upward as well as outward, and has aided other trends toward centralization.

The motor vehicle, which has now been perfected to such a point that the whole population of the United States could be put on wheels at one time, has a reverse influence and has provided a powerful incentive toward decentralization in metropolitan districts. It has brought within commuting reach of metropolitan centers practically all areas within a radius of 30 miles to 40 miles, instead of only radial bands along the lines of the railroads. All the interstices between these lines have been made accessible for development. The motor truck has enabled industry to locate along main highways as well as along railroads and waterways and, in bringing within reach relatively inexpensive land, has encouraged the use of low buildings with ample open spaces around them.

All this intensive expansion would again have been impossible without the development by civil engineers of modern sanitation facilities. These have involved bringing from long distances abundant supplies of pure water and the purification of nearby supplies. It has also been dependent on methods of sewage purification in order to avoid a serious threat to health.

THE MODERN AMERICAN CITY

As a result of all these engineering accomplishments, the modern American city has become a very complex organism, normally growing but also subject to decay and sometimes death. It has assumed definite characteristics that can be described briefly.

The larger cities have at their center groups of towering buildings that are called skyscrapers (Fig. 2). Some of these structures house offices; and others,

FIG. 2.—MODERN SKYSCRAPERS IN NEW YORK, N. Y.

of generally lesser height, are residential apartments. In some cases one finds a combination of uses with penthouses perched on the tops of downtown office buildings. Some people have suggested the development of vertical cities, in which stores, offices, and dwellings would be piled one on top of another within the same structure, and one might live, work, and play in the same building, using the elevator rather than the motor vehicle or subway for local transportation.

Automobiles are found everywhere—in cities large and small there are passenger cars, trucks, and buses. Frequently the streets are choked with them, and movement is reduced to a mere trickle. On the modern expressway, however, they may be seen moving along at 50 or more miles an hour. Even here they may be backed up for miles as the week-end vacationer struggles homeward on a Sunday evening. Throughout the cities shiny plumbing is found—toilets, bathtubs, showers, kitchen sinks, and electric washers. No other country can boast anywhere near the same amount of these facilities, to all of which the engineer has contributed in design and construction. For the most part, city dwellers discharge their wastes into sewers that in many cases are routed to and through elaborate treatment plants.

Where cities have expanded across waterways, bridges and, more recently,

FIG. 3.—BRIDGES ACROSS MILWAUKEE RIVER, MILWAUKEE, WIS.

FIG. 4.—MAJOR RIVER CROSSING NEAR NEW YORK, N. Y.

vehicular tunnels, have become one of their most distinctive and best publicized features (Fig. 3). Here the engineer and architect have collaborated; but, as bridge spans have increased, the bridges have become more predominantly engineering structures. New York, Chicago, San Francisco, Calif., Pittsburgh, Pa., and Boston illustrate such cities (Fig. 4).

Within the last decade distinctive features of American cities, most evident as one views them from the air, are the large new residential neighborhoods that have been developed as single operations, replacing the original individual home building that was previously the general practice (Fig. 5). Many of these new neighborhoods have within them their own shopping districts surrounded by acres of parking space.

However, do not be misled—all is not rosy in the urban areas. Far too many overcrowded tenements still remain—many of which do not have modern plumbing accessories, but are supplied only with a common cold-water line to serve a

FIG. 5.—APARTMENT DEVELOPMENT IN NEW YORK, N. Y.

group of families. The 1950 census classified about one out of every ten dwelling units in New York City as either dilapidated or without a private bath. Where old residential buildings have been permitted to reach a state of disrepair, becoming a menace to health and safety, slum districts have been created. These may be only part of the blighted urban areas, which may also include dilapidated business and industrial structures. The blighted areas have become economic liabilities, rather than assets, to the municipalities in which they are located—breeding places of disease and juvenile delinquency.

Automobiles parked in the streets and trucks unloading at the curb have, in many cases, made local highways almost useless for the purposes for which they were created—that is, movement of vehicles and access to abutting property. Modern transit lines with all their mechanical efficiency are jammed with passengers during the morning and evening rush hours; in some cases creating conditions that have become almost unbearable.

As this picture of urban growth and the engineer's contribution to it is reviewed, it might well be wondered whether the engineer has not inadvertently caused congestion, for which he must now find a cure. Evidently there is ground for the opinion expressed at the beginning of this paper that in some cases engineering inventions have created "monsters" that engineers must now find means of controlling.

HANDICAPS OF EARLY CITY ENGINEERS

American cities grew so fast in their early stages that the city engineer was constantly faced with immediate problems and had little time to dream about the future. Most of the decisions affecting the physical plan of the city were made by politicians, who, in some cases, may have wished to do favors for some of their constituents and, in order to do so, overrode the recommendations of the engineer.

However, in many cases the blame for shortsighted planning rested with the engineers. Too many of them were narrow minded, content to follow rather than to lead. They did not have the broad training in related sciences with which the present engineering graduate is equipped.

THE MUNICIPAL ENGINEER

As cities grew, there came into being full-time local engineering staffs devoting themselves to the technical problems of planning, constructing, and operating the various public facilities and utilities under municipal ownership. These men are the "municipal" engineers, generally including and operating under the direction of a city engineer, or a borough or a village engineer, who, in some cases, is officially designated as the head of a Public Works Department. They are primarily civil engineers, although they may work with mechanical engineers, electrical engineers, or chemical engineers who design and operate structures and equipment related to these special fields.

The responsibilities of this group, and particularly of the city engineer or other official who heads the technical staff, have been increasing by leaps and bounds. In a municipality that has reached a population of several hundred thousand or more, the city engineer is now expected to be a jack-of-all-trades.

Formerly he was concerned primarily with the improvement of streets and roads, which required knowledge of various types of pavement, the design and construction of sewers and drainage systems, and the supply and distribution of adequate water. Today he must also be familiar with the various methods of sewage treatment and disposal, with procedures for purifying water supply, and with the collection and disposal of refuse, garbage, and other wastes, involving a knowledge of the relative advantages of incineration, land fill, or other special treatment. He is concerned with the lighting of streets and public buildings, and possibly also with the design and operation of municipal plants to produce and distribute electric current or other sources of power. He may be responsible for the construction and maintenance of local transit facilities, and must be well versed in traffic control, building codes, and zoning ordinances. Some of these many physical facilities may be designed, under contract, by consulting engineering firms; but even in such cases the municipal engineer's advice is needed to assure that the projects are well suited to the city's needs and can be economically operated.

Although New York City, with its about 8,000,000 residents is an unusual case, the writer believes the responsibilities of municipal engineers in that city may provide interesting examples of the points just mentioned.

New York has no official with the title of city engineer. Instead there was created in 1902, shortly after the present Greater New York was incorporated, the position of chief engineer to the then Board of Estimate and Apportionment, now the Board of Estimate, which is the upper legislative body of the city. The Board has charge, among other things, of all appropriations for physical improvements. Before any such project can be considered by the Board, no matter in what agency it originates—a city-wide department or the office of one of the five borough presidents—it is referred to the chief engineer for report. He makes a detailed investigation and may recommend alterations and then submits his written report to the Board. Very rarely is the recommendation of the chief engineer even questioned by the members of the Board of Estimate. Their primary concern is when and how to finance a project, and they are quite content to leave the technical details to the judgment of the chief engineer.

This confidence exists very largely because such officials have not been political appointments, but have been selected purely on merit. Several years after the initial appointment the office was placed under municipal civil service so that political changes could not interfere with the operation of the office. All other engineering staffs within the city are now also under civil service. The original chief engineer of the Board of Estimate and Apportionment—the writer's father, Nelson P. Lewis, M. ASCE—served through several administrations from 1902 until his retirement from the city service in 1923. The esprit de corps among the various engineers in New York City service is promoted and encouraged by the Municipal Engineers of the City of New York—a society established in 1903 that had four hundred and forty members at the close of 1951.

CONTRIBUTIONS OF BRANCHES OF THE ENGINEERING PROFESSION

Special contributions of different branches of the engineering profession to the development of American cities may be briefly summarized as follows:

The mechanical engineer is responsible for many types of equipment forming essential parts of various public works. He has, metaphorically, contributed the wheels that make the machinery turn—largely to him goes the credit for the automobile.

The electrical engineer has contributed to the supply of power and light and communication by cable, by wire, and through the air by radio. He has perfected the mechanism for translating power into high-speed transportation.

The chemical engineer has developed the manufacturing processes from which the modern structural materials, including both alloys and plastics, have evolved. Through the refining of petroleum products many new materials have been found.

The mining and metallurgical engineer has developed natural resources to produce light and strong materials that are being used increasingly in modern structures.

The civil engineer, however, has dealt most with the solution of general city-wide problems, and his imprint is more clearly defined than the imprints of other engineers on city plans and structures, above and below the ground.

Although it has been pointed out that many city planning problems are essentially engineering ones, it is not intended to deprecate in any way the importance and need of men in the other professions, notably the architects and landscape architects, in formulating city plans. Close cooperation with economists, social workers, the legal profession, and other groups is also important. In large cities particularly, the preparation of a city plan requires the collaboration of men from all these backgrounds.

The following branches of municipal engineering are closely related to city planning: Highway design and construction; traffic control and the design and construction of parking facilities; sanitary engineering; communications—interurban and local; surveying and mapping, including aerial surveys; structural engineering, including bridges; and general construction, including structures and foundations.

The City Planning Profession

The formulation of a separate profession of city planning may be said to have started with the founding in 1917 of the American City Planning Institute, now the American Institute of Planners. At that time there was no special training in city planning in colleges and universities and the Institute's membership was drawn from all the foregoing groups and included several civil engineers. Of the nineteen individuals who have served as president of the Institute, six have been members of the ASCE.

In 1924 the City Planning Division of the ASCE was established, its first two chairmen being Nelson P. Lewis and Edwin A. Fisher, Hon. M. ASCE, long the City Engineer of Rochester, N. Y. Although this Division contains a substantial number of city planners, it also includes many other civil engineers who are in public service, in general consulting work, in education, with industrial concerns, with public utility companies, and in other activities. Its varied membership shows the increasing interest of civil engineers in urban problems as related to city planning.

In many cases city engineers are serving directly on city planning commissions and thus making dual contributions to the development of their cities. In other cases, engineers have made important contributions to elements of a city plan, for example, on the Bronx River Parkway Commission and the Westchester County Park Commission. These two commissions, through first the Bronx River Parkway north of New York City and later through adjacent Westchester's magnificent system of county-wide parkways, laid the foundation for the modern parkway, now an important feature of urban and suburban planning.

URBAN REDEVELOPMENT

Much city planning in the United States is some form of replanning and many cities are now interested in such urban redevelopment as may be carried out under the United States Housing Act of 1949. Actually, reconstruction under this legislation is just getting under way.

The contribution of this act was that it set up procedures and made available federal funds by which blighted urban areas might be acquired, cleared, and redeveloped with the Federal Government meeting two thirds of any loss that would result in the resale of these properties, the municipality putting up the other third. In each case a blighted area must now be predominantly residential or its proposed new use must be predominantly for residence. The redevelopment must, in every case, conform to a comprehensive plan for the future growth of the city.

In addition to the general city planning opportunity that such work presents and in which engineers may participate, there are other distinct engineering problems involved. In practically all cases these blighted areas are now supplied with utilities—streets, sewers, water mains, and gas lines. The replanning should make the most economic use of these, and their redesign is a task of the engineer. There must also be a careful determination of what would be the most suitable land use—whether for residence, industry, or business, or a combination of these. Although this is essentially a city planning problem, the engineer can certainly contribute to the finding of the best answer.

BROADENING OF ENGINEERING VIEWPOINT AND OPPORTUNITIES

Nowadays engineering graduates are receiving a broadened training, particularly through the inclusion of such subjects as economics, the formulation of reports, public speaking, and appreciation of the arts. Technological developments during World War II gave a tremendous impetus to interest in, and appreciation of, what the engineer can do.

The professional engineer must be well versed in theories and their application. However, he is much more than a mere technician. He is well equipped to assume leadership in the formulation of broad policies and in a study of why and where a project should be located as well as of how it should be designed. Many engineering firms are now prepared to render comprehensive service in formulating, designing, and operating large-scale projects, whether these are part of city development, or whether they are located in the wide open spaces.

SUMMARY

The opportunities for engineers and particularly civil engineers in urban development may be summed up as follows:

(1) In city planning offices, where they may be supervisory personnel as director of planning or planning engineer and where the younger men may be important staff members cooperating with other specialists.

(2) In the offices of city engineers and departments of public works, where they directly serve the legislative body.

(3) In administrative positions, for municipal government or management. More and more engineers are holding such positions as managers of cities, towns, and villages where the manager form of municipal government has been established.

(4) As members of municipal planning boards, serving generally as unpaid officials.

(5) As members on advisory committees, where their special knowledge can be of great benefit.

(6) In civic affairs, where they should take a more active part in those local community organizations without whose active support sound city planning and sound legislation cannot be assured.

In brief, the engineer is already contributing, but can increase his contribution to urban development—as a city servant, a city official, and a leading citizen.

AMERICAN SOCIETY OF CIVIL ENGINEERS

Founded November 5, 1852

TRANSACTIONS

Paper No. 2585

TODAY'S ENGINEER AND TOMORROW'S METROPOLITAN PROBLEMS

By L. P. Cookingham [1]

Synopsis

The trend toward urbanization is continuing at a fast pace in the United States. However, the growth of large metropolitan areas creates problems for the central city as well as for the suburbs that depend on it. This paper lists and discusses these problems from the standpoint of the central city. Several solutions are offered, and examples are given of successful experiments in urban cooperation.

Introduction

Engineers in general are busy, harried, modern-day individuals. Collectively they can probably match any other profession for ulcers, heart ailments, and nervous indigestion—all indications of the overburdened and the conscientious. For this reason, they are not always able to take time out to consider the impact of their activities on the millions of their fellow men. In reflection, however, it should be realized that the plans of today are the seeds of tomorrow's fruit. The pertinent question is whether that fruit will be bitter or sweet. This question is going to be answered, in large part, by the engineering profession.

Problems Created by Urbanization

Trends of Urbanization.—Since the writer is most familiar with urbanization from the standpoint of the central city within the metropolitan area, this paper will discuss the subject from that viewpoint. The following list gives some of the facts on the subject of urbanization:

(1) The United States today has an urban economy.

(2) The trend toward urbanization is continuing at an unslackened pace.

(3) The suburbs of metropolitan areas are growing much faster than are the central cities of these metropolitan areas.

---

[1] City Mgr., Kansas City, Mo.

194

(4) The industrial decentralization, which began in the 1920's, is manifest in the migration from older metropolitan areas to newer metropolitan areas.

However, within this whole pattern of urbanization are two incongruous factors. On one hand, there is the economic compulsion toward centralization in urban or metropolitan areas; and, on the other hand, there is the individual passion for decentralization as evidenced by the common ambition to achieve the status of a gentleman farmer.

From 1940 to 1950 the one hundred and sixty-eight standard metropolitan areas of the United States Census Bureau registered more than 80% of the nation's population increase, indicating the pressure for economic centralization. However, the individual urge for space and the better life of the suburbanite is indicated by the fact that more than half of that population increase was in the suburbs rather than in the central cities.

This trend is most dramatically illustrated by the twelve largest metropolitan areas, in which about 72% of a population increase of better than 6,500,000 people in the past decade occurred in the suburbs, not in the central cities. The trend prevails to a lesser extent in the smaller metropolitan areas. Kansas City, Mo., and Cincinnati, Ohio, experienced a central city growth only 10% less than the growth in their suburban areas.

Urbanization Creates Problems for Metropolitan Areas.—The trend toward urbanization creates many problems both for the central city and for the suburban community. These problems emanate from loss of tax revenue, loss of upper-income and middle-income residents, and loss of business to the central city. Other considerations are a higher incidence of blighted properties along with an increased demand for many municipal services.

The suburb has problems too, such as its economic dependency on the central city and a rising demand for municipal services. Therefore, it may be seen that both the central city and the suburb are handed many problems as a result of urbanization. These are vital because of the importance of the urban economy, and because the urban population constitutes better than 60% of the nation's total census. It is necessary to take a close look at these problems in order that they may be fully understood.

Loss of Revenue.—Probably the most distressing and most immediate problem from the standpoint of the central city is the loss of revenue resulting from the migration of upper-income and middle-income residents and of businesses and industry to the suburbs. American cities today are the hardest pressed governmental units financially, and this loss of revenue has only complicated an already complex problem.

Recently a large automobile company constructed a multimillion dollar assembly plant just outside Kansas City's corporate limits. Kansas City is glad to have the additional 10,000 jobs for its residents, but it has already been necessary to widen access roads to the new plant at considerable expense to the resident taxpayer without any part of the cost being paid by the industry, which is outside the taxing jurisdiction of the city.

A more complete picture of a decreasing tax base is furnished by St. Louis, Mo. In 1939 the suburbs surrounding St. Louis received 31% of the area's retail trade, but in 1948 this had increased to 37% and is still going higher.

It has been more than 10 years since a retail building or an office building more than one-story high has been built in downtown St. Louis. Nevertheless, most residents of the suburbs earn their living in St. Louis, expect the best in municipal services while there, and quite often rely on the city to furnish the cultural and recreational facilities that the suburbanites enjoy along with the residents and taxpayers of the central city.

Kansas City, too, is a central city. According to the best available estimates, more than 10% of the total number of persons employed within the city commute to work daily to earn their livelihood (Fig. 1). Although these people pay little or no taxes to Kansas City, they use the city parks on Sunday, congest the streets, visit the municipal auditorium, and expect fire, police, and health protection,

FIG. 1.—STREAM OF CARS THROUGH OUTER RESIDENTIAL AREAS, MORNING AND EVENING,
EVIDENCE OF EXTENSIVE COMMUTING FROM OUTSIDE CITY LIMITS

and all other services while they are in the city. When their day's work is done, they leave the central city and all its problems and responsibilities to the taxpayers who remain residents of the central city and, as such, cannot escape these responsibilities.

This situation is not peculiar to Kansas City or St. Louis. On the contrary, it is typical, to a greater or lesser extent, of every metropolitan central city in the United States. Its cumulative effect is a decline of tax revenues and a demand for increased municipal services, the cost of which must be made up by the taxpayer remaining in the central city.

Demand for Increased Services.—Many of the new services being rendered or considered by municipalities result from demands created by the suburbs that have sprung up about them. For example, in Kansas City the traffic volume has increased more than 60% since 1946. Of course, not all this increase is caused by suburban residents, but the morning and afternoon rush-hour glut of suburban residents has required drastic measures to move traffic in and out of the downtown area each day. Trafficways, freeways, expressways, and off-street parking are being demanded and are expected.

Consequently, a plan that should take care of all freeway and expressway needs for the foreseeable future has been developed. The work embraced in this plan for freeways and expressways, at today's construction prices, will cost $128,000,000—much of which must come from the taxpayers of the central city, although the facilities will be used daily by the suburbanites who enter the city going to and from their work (Fig. 2).

Fig. 2.—Aerial View Depicting Southwest Trafficway, Aiding Ever-Increasing Traffic Volume in Kansas City, Mo.

However, increased traffic volumes are not answered by freeways and expressways alone. Once quick access to the downtown area is provided, adequate storage space for automobiles coming to the central business area becomes a necessity. Not so long ago off-street parking was a desirable convenience; now it is a necessity.

Even though a city provides access and storage areas for the constant increase in the number of privately-owned automobiles, it is still not out of the woods, for on the other side of the picture, problems of local transit emerge. Certainly the provision of easy access to, and convenient storage in, the downtown area for automobiles is doing nothing to assist the passenger-hungry public transit companies, which are forced to ignore the economic laws of supply and demand if they are to exist.

This is only the beginning! As the upper-income and middle-income groups move to the suburbs, the lower-income groups that remain in the city desire more and better recreational facilities. If these facilities are made good enough, the suburbanites will come back to the central city at night or during other leisure time for recreation. Thus, park facilities, playgrounds, community recreation centers, and athletic fields must be expanded and multiplied (Fig. 3).

As the metropolitan area expands, the central city is looked to for water service, sewer outlets, fire protection, police protection, and ofttimes other services. The extension of municipal services by the central city to the surrounding suburbs is a particularly vexing problem. Some central cities have been able to force consolidation by high charges for services to suburbs, with the lure of lower costs

Fig. 3.—Feeding Time at Seal Pool, Kansas City, Mo.; by Car Count, About 40% of Those Using City Recreational Facilities, from Out of Town

after consolidation. Other central cities, hampered by restrictive laws and covenants, are forced to subsidize surrounding dormitory towns. Chicago, Ill., for example, must sell its water to suburbs at no more than it charges its own residents.

Competition Between Central City and Suburb

Competition is the very essence of American life. It is one of the cornerstones of the greatness of the United States, but competition can reach a point of no return, and that is just what is happening to the central city and the suburb.

Competition for business and industry between the two has, in some cases, become "cutthroat" with a very small minority the only beneficiaries. The duplication of municipal services, the tax subsidies, and the multiplicity of special quasi-governmental districts are staggering and costly beyond imagination. Competition for housing and industrial developments is not unusual.

Usually the area without such accepted protective devices as zoning ordinances, building codes, and fire codes competes unfairly with the central city, which realizes the importance of such controls. The result of this competition for the central city is loss of business and industry, inadequate housing which is usually followed by slums and blighted areas, and, of course, higher costs with a shrinking tax base.

According to the Census Bureau, the average city of 100,000 population or more will have about 20% substandard living units. In some cases the total will run as high as 49% or as low as 10%. In either extreme, it is too high. Recent studies have shown that these areas, on the average, will contribute only 6% of the

Fig. 4.—Although Out of City, Typical Suburban Community, with Impending Tax Increases for Sewers, Paved Streets, Fire, and Police Service

tax revenue but will be the cause of about 45% of expenditures for services. This type of competition is not healthy.

Problems from Standpoint of Suburbs

On the other side of the scale, the suburbs also merit consideration. What kind of problems do they have? The writer is not so familiar with this phase as perhaps he should be, but there are some points that should be briefly mentioned.

It must be remembered that the suburb is populated, by and large, with the rugged individualist—that person who has fled the cares and responsibilities of city life for the freedom and quiet of suburban life. However, he was indoctrinated amid the full roar of city life, and therein lies the beginning of many of the suburb's problems. For although this person wants the freedom and individuality of rural living, he is accustomed to, and still demands, many of the conveniences of the city (Fig. 4).

He wants water, fire protection, at least a minimum of traffic control, schools, parks, sewers, some type of surface on the streets if not paving, and finally, after becoming established, he decides he needs the protection of zoning and, perhaps, even planning. However, he wants all these services at the typical suburban tax rate—an obvious impossibility.

Consider, also, the degree to which most suburbs are dependent on the central city. Often the central city must provide whatever health and medical facilities are to be available. Probably most of the suburbanites earn their living in the central city. For example, a quarter of the people working in San Francisco, Calif., live outside the city; and Dallas, Tex., provides jobs for possibly as many as 75% of the adults residing in surrounding communities.

Indeed, the suburb more often than not is economically dependent on the central city. This is not always the case, for there are outlying areas in close proximity to central cities that offer jobs for residents of the mother city. Nevertheless, the entire suburban area is dependent on the central city. Without it, there would be no suburbs.

The basic problem for the suburb is the clash between human desires for country living on the one hand and for city conveniences on the other hand. A perfect example of what this can lead to is furnished by the Township of Mission, which is just over the Kansas state line from Kansas City. Thousands of people have migrated from Kansas City to Mission in the past few years to escape from big city burdens and responsibilities and to participate in suburban living.

However, their demands and, in fact, their needs for city services have resulted in the incorporation of several municipalities in Mission Township; and those very people who left Kansas City to get away from it all will have to move on to more distant points or assume the responsibilities that are inevitable when suburban communities become of age.

SOLUTIONS

These are some of the problems: Loss of revenue; loss of upper-income and middle-income residents; cutthroat competition for business, industry, and housing; increased demand for municipal services; and economic dependency of suburbs on central cities.

What are the solutions? What can be done to relieve these conditions? The problems can be alleviated and solved if the American people, their leaders, and their public officials have the courage and foresight to tackle the job.

However, these problems will demand bold, sweeping actions that only the bravest will dare to instigate. There is no single answer. The solution will differ from area to area and in varying circumstances. Nevertheless, all answers should be predicated on a sincere desire to make every community a better place in which to live.

No other profession can contribute more to this better life than the engineering profession. The research, the planning, the design, and the execution of all work and services for the modern city will be performed by the engineer. The extent of his vision and his knowledge of human needs will determine the type of communities in the generations ahead.

Planning.—One of the best ways to assure future generations of the best in urban living is to engage in sound, enlightened planning. Only in this way can there be any hope of controlling future developments.

A central city should take the leadership in establishing an over-all metropolitan planning agency. Basic precepts must be agreed on and the development of the entire area considered and studied as a whole rather than as an area splintered by fictional and arbitrary boundaries imposed by law. There are several examples of this type of operation—the Citizens Regional Planning Council of Greater Kansas City, Greater Dallas Planning Council, Future Springfield (Ill.) Incorporated, and the San Francisco Bay Area Council—to mention a few.

Engineers can help to spread this idea, and should assume leadership in their respective communities in every effort to provide a better city, whether it be only the central city or the entire metropolitan area. The facts to be considered by the lay boards should be assembled, analyzed, and presented by a technically trained staff whose broad concept of the community's needs can be translated into action through community leadership. Members of the engineering profession who are willing to devote some time to civic affairs should be well represented on such boards, because their knowledge and appreciation of these problems are exceeded by those of the members of no other profession.

Planning, as an end in itself, is not enough. Any such agency must have both formal and informal agreements for cooperation and must be supported by zoning and land-use ordinances that will give effect to the planning. In addition, the metropolitan planning agency must have the cooperation of all member jurisdictions to make the program effective.

Annexation.—Cities that are not surrounded by other incorporated areas have turned to annexation. Annexation is not a complete solution in itself, but certainly is a major step forward. In 1950, more than 380 cities of better than 5,000 population completed land acquisitions. Kansas City, itself, adopted an area of almost 20 sq miles; and other annexations which will add an additional 50 sq miles to the area of the city are still pending.

An annexation program must be preceded by intensive study and sound planning. There should be sufficient advantages both to the central city and to the annexed territory to justify the step. In the case of growing cities, annexation is justified if only from the standpoint of planning and controlling periphery areas.

The capital improvement program is one of the engineer's major contributions to the development of the central city and to its annexation policy. In formulating a capital program, streets, sewers, and bridges should not be emphasized to the exclusion of playgrounds, parks, and the preservation of an area's natural beauty. If these points are remembered, the people of the United States will have better and more desirable cities in the future.

Creation of Authorities.—What of the city that is unable to annex? It may be that state laws governing the situation are too restrictive, or perhaps the central city is already surrounded and being slowly strangled by suburban incorporated areas. Such municipalities are the hardest hit by urbanization. They have no ready solution and thus far have discovered no satisfactory way to protect themselves from the outward migration of business, industry, and people.

They are faced with a slow economic death. Some of the most important metropolitan areas in the United States fall within this category. St. Louis and Chicago are two examples.

One solution has been the creation of metropolitan authorities for specific purposes. Examples of such arrangements are the New York (N. Y.) Port Authority in the field of transportation, the Chicago Sanitary District in the field of health, and the Hartford (Conn.) Water Authority in the utility field.

There are circumstances that justify authorities, particularly where a state boundary must be straddled. However, authorities tend to be unresponsive to the taxpayer, a step removed from the citizen control that is so essential in local government. Nevertheless, the authority should not be overlooked as part of the over-all solution. It can make its contribution.

Functional Consolidation.—Another partial answer to urbanization is functional consolidation, which is a watered-down type of authority. Under this plan, the incorporated governments of an area voluntarily agree to merge their facilities for certain functions. An example of the need for this type of action is Cook County, Illinois, with one hundred different police departments. There are many successful examples of functional consolidation, such as the city and county hospital systems of Dallas, with each governmental unit contributing half of the costs of maintenance and operation.

Assistance from the Federal Government.—Inasmuch as the United States has an urban economy, the problems of urbanization are of nation-wide concern. Two of the problems which have been mentioned earlier (blighted properties and ever-increasing traffic volumes) have been recognized by the Federal Government; and laws have been passed that are intended to assist in solving them. Such laws are the Highway Act of 1944, under which the construction of many metropolitan freeways and expressways will be financially aided, and the Housing Act of 1949, which embodies provisions pertaining to urban redevelopment.

These two pieces of legislation offer valuable assistance to cities attempting to keep pace with the changing economy and social structure of the United States. Thus, the Highway Act, under present taxing structure, makes it possible for a city to construct a comprehensive network of expressways and freeways by paying only a part of the cost of these multimillion dollar projects, the balance of the cost being shared by the state and the Federal Government.

On the other hand, the Housing Act puts the Federal Government and local governments in partnership with private enterprise for the purpose of redeveloping city properties that have become submarginal in use and tax deficient in practice. Under this law, a slum area may become an off-street parking area, a light industrial area, a residential area, or even a park or recreational facility.

These two federal acts appear to provide a very welcome degree of flexibility with which the central city can meet the challenge of the suburbs, by making the close-in sections of the central city as desirable as any part of the whole metropolitan area. Otherwise, the cost of redeveloping slums and of constructing needed city highways would be prohibitive, unless a drastic revision and reallotment of taxing powers were accomplished.

Urban redevelopment offers a new hope for the hard core of the older central cities. Here is an opportunity to clear the undesirable blight that is prevalent in most American cities, and to replace it with developments that will be just as desirable as any in the suburbs and still have locational advantages not

Before

After

FIG. 5.—VIEWS OF TRANSFORMATION IN DOWNTOWN KANSAS CITY, MO., FROM DECREPIT, BLIGHTED AREA TO BEAUTIFUL, NONCOMMUTING APARTMENTS; EFFECTIVE ARGUMENT FOR URBAN REDEVELOPMENT

possible in the more remote areas. If central cities are to continue, urban redevelopment will reestablish good living and new opportunities in areas which only a few years ago were considered hopeless (Fig. 5).

Physical Consolidation.—Several types of solutions and partial solutions to the problems raised by the trend toward urbanization have been suggested: Annexation, creation of authorities, functional consolidation, and area-wide planning. However, an obvious solution has not been mentioned nor have many cities and metropolitan areas considered it. This is the process of consolidation! The logical consolidation of governmental units into one agency—physical and functional consolidation—will, if properly handled, do away with tremendous waste, duplication, and paralyzing confusion.

What justification is there for arbitrarily dividing one area into small and puny satellites? There is very little justification in most cases and the cost of such a division is an unnecessary burden to the taxpayer. When will the people of the nation finally realize this fact, and be willing to do something about it?

There must be laws providing for consolidation which are just as forward looking as the best annexation laws. In proposing such consolidation laws as may be desirable, consideration should be given to the establishment of standards that justify or compel consolidation. These standards should be centered about a determination of whether or not the suburb could survive without subsidy from the central city. Also reasonableness in opposing consolidation should be stressed. In this way, sense will emerge out of the hodgepodge of governmental agencies presently operating in many metropolitan areas which in reality are socially and economically contiguous.

Conclusion

No single one of the remedies mentioned previously will solve the problems of the metropolitan area. They are far too complex for simple solution. However, combinations of the proposed solutions will help the situation immeasurably. The central cities must furnish the leadership and inspiration in this battle for metropolitan area existence. Those central cities already surrounded will have to use planning and consolidation. Other central cities, not surrounded, should resort to planning and annexation. Perhaps some consolidation will also be needed in the latter case.

Those metropolitan areas divided by state boundaries may have to resort to the establishment of authorities, functional consolidation, and a basis of taxation which will be broad enough to insure that all who use the central city's facilities share in their cost. The so-called earnings tax, now utilized by dozens of American cities, appears to be the best basis of taxation yet devised to accomplish this objective.

A determination should be made of what cities have to offer business, industry, and home environment. If the wrong commodity has been emphasized, now is the time to change. New York, realizing it could no longer hold sway as a heavy manufacturing center, built itself up as a transportation and financial center. Other metropolitan areas must face these problems also. They must realize that they are in a competitive market for business, industry, and people; and, to secure them, cities must offer desirable facilities to these potential customers.

One consideration that has not been sufficiently covered is finance. In fact, it could well serve as the subject for another paper and is a most important part of the problem. Shall financial aid come from federally collected and locally shared tax monies? Shall the cities resort to their own taxing powers? Are these powers sufficient? Some cities have instituted earnings taxes. Others have turned to city sales taxes. Still others receive substantial help from their state governments. Whatever the plan, an economically sound and equitable tax system is essential to a final solution.

The problems presented in this paper essentially concern human beings. Expressways, redevelopment projects, off-street parking facilities, recreation and park developments, sanitation and health facilities, and all other requirements for urban living are designed to fulfil the requirements of the human beings who look to the engineer for the better city of the future. The engineering profession should be as well represented on public bodies as is the legal profession. Were it not for the engineer who is willing to forego some of the greater rewards of his profession to engage in civil service, the cities of the United States would be less desirable than they are today.

AMERICAN SOCIETY OF CIVIL ENGINEERS

Founded November 5, 1852

TRANSACTIONS

Paper No. 2586

AMERICA'S COSTLIEST BEDROOMS: THE SUBURBS

By Richard G. Baumhoff[1]

Synopsis

America's suburbs are called "bedroom" towns, and by and large they have proved to be serious problems for the central city. This paper discusses the basic principles behind the growing suburban trend. The pattern of development is traced, and the effect of decentralization on the city and on the suburb is evaluated. Several suggestions are offered as to a working arrangement between the main city and its dependent suburbs.

Introduction

Americans move from the city to the suburbs because the city is outmoded. The city no longer meets their needs and desires. The city, not very important in colonial days, was beginning to evolve toward its modern character about the middle of the nineteenth century—that is, about at the start of the 100 years of professional progress begun by the ASCE in 1852. Engineers and engineering had a lot to do with the creation of the modern city, and it is fitting that they should scrutinize the result—and ponder what to do with this Gargantua, if not indeed this Frankenstein, in the next 100 years.

The electrical engineer created the life-giving current of the city. The mechanical engineer developed its marvelous factories. The civil engineer has his imprint everywhere in the city. The hydraulic engineer brought in the water, and the sanitary engineer installed that prime essential to the existence of any city, the sewer. The chemical engineer has cast a magic spell. The automotive engineer is the hero or the villain of urbanism, depending on the point of view. Fortunately, at last, the planning engineer has come into his own, and perhaps his work can preserve and enhance the metropolitan city of the twentieth century.

Decentralization

The effect of the exodus to the suburbs is alarming. This flow away from the old central city of the nineteenth century began as a drift in the first quarter of

---

[1] Administrative Staff, *St. Louis Post-Dispatch*, St. Louis, Mo.

the twentieth century and by the second quarter became a tide. Perhaps now, in the early stage of the third quarter, this exodus is at its peak, but there may be a veritable flood yet to come. Good engineering, and good civics, must have a great deal to do with the answer.

Suburban Growth.—It is altogether likely that the twenty-first century will see a new kind of city and a new conception of urbanism. More than a quarter of the nation's people now live in the twelve largest metropolitan districts, and the bulk of the entire population resides in distinctive metropolitan areas. The new cities, or at least the struggling start of them, sprawl over rough circles of 5-mile, 10-mile, 15-mile, or even 50-mile or 60-mile radii. The greatest growth of population in the past 12 years, or longer, has been in the suburban belts surrounding the central cities, rather than in the old central cities.

Indeed, the 1950 census disclosed seven metropolitan districts whose population in the outer ring of suburbs and satellite cities either is greater than the population of the central cities or is approaching that condition. The following data will demonstrate this fact:

Metropolis	Population of central city	Population of balance of district
Los Angeles, Calif	1,970,000	2,397,000
Boston, Mass.	801,000	1,568,000
Pittsburgh, Pa.	676,000	1,536,000
San Francisco-Oakland, Calif	1,159,000	1,081,000
St. Louis, Mo	856,000	824,000
Washington, D. C.	802,000	661,000
Buffalo, N. Y.	580,000	509,000

People moved to the suburbs because the old cities were dirty, smoky, and noisy; because the urban centers were poorly planned for modern living and modern transportation; because they were poorly governed and badly financed; and because all too often their public schools were poor and ridden with selfish politics. These conditions were true of all larger cities and many of the medium-sized ones, with a few limited exceptions in place or period.

Washington (D.C.), as planned by Pierre Charles L'Enfant, remains picturesque but very largely unsuitable for a kind of urbanism he did not envision. The Centennial of Engineering was held in Chicago, Ill.—a city that is perhaps the prime example of why people move out to the suburbs if they can. St. Louis, unfortunately, has had some compelling reasons for decentralization, more physical than political in nature.

Historically, the suburban trend antedates the automobile, but it was the motorcar that hastened and expedited the exodus from the city. Without the passenger automobile and the motor truck, metropolitan cities surely would collapse. In the early days it was the well-to-do and the middle-class white-collar groups that left the tightly established central cities and populated the new suburbs pin-pointed on the periphery. They went where they could have fresh air, flowers, vegetables, and safety and health for their children, and all the pleasure of a leisurely semirural life.

That picture is changed now. All classes of people live in the suburbs: The well-to-do and the very wealthy; the white-collar man and woman and the factory hand; and the professional man and the artisan. Many cities are even developing

—perhaps without fully realizing it—some ill-flowering suburban slums of the underprivileged classes.

TRENDS IN ST. LOUIS

The Central City.—St. Louis can serve as an average example of the changed city. The central city, where the bulk of the population formerly dwelt, is nearly two centuries old. The central city is heavily built up, mostly in antiquated gridirons that fail to match at the edges, and very little desirable land is still vacant. Unlike many cities, St. Louis has done a remarkable job of smoke elimination, but only within its own political confines. Other notable physical and civic steps have been taken toward remaking the city. However, not enough has been done, and in many respects the old city has been content to forego improvement.

Examples of Decentralization.—Now, as the data previously cited have indicated, virtually half of the people who really are St. Louisans actually dwell in three neighboring counties in Missouri and three in Illinois. Such suburbanites, for example, daily drive 25 miles or more from their picture-window cottages on the Ozark ridges of Jefferson County to a new factory and airport district spreading over a once-lovely valley near the Missouri River. These St. Louisans rarely get closer than 6 miles to the artificial or political boundary of the old city.

A small but lively advertising agency was founded in a downtown St. Louis office building only 17 years ago. Later it shifted to a midtown location. Recently it moved to a modern, low building in a largely residential neighborhood in University City, 2 miles west of the St. Louis city limits. As stated on the Sunday real estate page, the new quarters were obtained:

> "* * * after a check revealed that agency personnel could save three traveling hours per person each week in going to and from work, and account executives and other officials would save additional hours in making client contacts."

Furthermore, the new offices have parking space, whereas the midtown site was in an area in which parking was a near-impossibility. University City, incidentally, now is the fifth largest municipality in Missouri but is purely a "bedroom suburb."

The Brown Shoe Company, one of the old firms in a leading St. Louis industry, has moved its general offices to a handsome new building in Clayton, 3 miles beyond St. Louis (Fig. 1). The great Monsanto Chemical Company has contemplated establishing important offices in open country, adjoining some of the finest suburban residential developments, 6 miles west of St. Louis. National records and publications centers for the United States Army are being built in Overland, 3 miles beyond the city. New industries locate mainly in the outer belt. There is a concentration of heavy industry, part of the backbone of metropolitan St. Louis, in the Illinois bottoms, across the Mississippi from the central city.

More or less the same phenomenon may be observed all over the United States, as activities formerly considered an integral part of the city proper have spilled over to the suburban belt.

FACTORS INFLUENCING THE SUBURBAN TREND

Air Nuisances.—Not many cities have taken effective steps, such as those of St. Louis and Pittsburgh, toward smoke abatement. A newer menace, yet to be dealt with in many cities, arises from industrial fumes, as demonstrated alarmingly several years ago in the outskirts of Pittsburgh. Most urban Americans have become all too well accustomed to the cacophony of daily life—horns, shrieking brakes, bells, whistles, locomotives, blaring radios, television sets, and all the undertones of city noise. Thornton Wilder, writing recently in *The Atlantic Monthly,* quoted an old saying that the eternal silence of infinite space

FIG. 1.—AERIAL VIEW OF CLAYTON, MO.

fills one with fright—and, as a play on that observation, that the intermittent racket of the little neighborhood reassures people.

Nevertheless, such reassurance has its limitations. The noise of urban life grates on the nerves. Whether people realize it or not, the relief from this discord has been one of the attractions of the suburbs. What city can point to any effective measures aimed at silencing the bedlam?

Crowding.—The narrow city lot in its monotonous pattern of rectangles, and the narrow streets usually part of that pattern, have had a lot to do with the shift to the suburbs. They created an old-fashioned, uninspired, and uninspiring city of stores and offices crowded together; one of houses, flats, and apartment buildings so close that they lacked light, air, and privacy; and one of encroaching industry, and of motley, ill-assorted uses. Urban development was traceable in large measure to the physical limitations of such transportation as first the horsecar and later the streetcar, which appears to be following the horsecar as a

vanishing vehicle of mass transportation. This city pattern resulted in an artificially built-up valuation of city land.

Obsolescence.—Perhaps some of the dwelling houses and commercial structures erected in the United States during the latter third of the nineteenth century and the ensuing queerly complacent years before World War I were too well
built. They have lasted too long. There is nothing wrong with the idea of building for long life, but the trouble with many of the old structures in the city is
that they simply were not designed for today's needs. Their plumbing, windows,
entrances, vertical and horizontal communications, the paradoxical stuffiness under their tall ceilings, and many other things are against them.

Thus the typical American "downtown" area finds itself with outmoded office
buildings, stores, and lofts that have been more or less modernized inside and out
in a makeshift patchwork. Here, air conditioning and new elevators are installed; there, a "contemporary" glass or stone façade is laid on for the height
of a story or two, whereas the gewgaws and doodads of the gay nineties remain
on view above.

There is also a broad belt of slums and blight around the downtown area,
where old mansions have become rooming houses under the "trickle down"
theory of fulfilling urban housing needs, and tenements have spread cancerously
to fill the unsavory "dilapidated" column of the housing census.

Small wonder, then, that people go to the more livable, colorful, attractive
dwellings of altogether new design, in pleasant surroundings. These new homes
are dotting what not long ago were the farms and wooded hillsides of the outskirts of the old cities.

Industrial and Commercial Needs.—Meanwhile, the trend has developed
rapidly and strongly toward shifting stores, factories, and business offices of all
kinds from the central city to the suburbs. The modern factory requires a big
site, with plenty of open space, that it either cannot find or cannot afford in the
old city. Business establishments have begun to discover that it is vastly more
convenient for clerks as well as executives to work in the suburbs, where they live,
and avoid travel into the crowded central area. As the movement grows, it is
bound to make such a shifting of business more and more logical, as the people
in contact with business concerns themselves move toward the periphery. An outlying site for a business office or a factory also offers certain advantages of contact for motor trucks and for those who travel by airplane and automobile, while
losing none of the advantage of a railroad siding for freight.

The movement of stores, both large and small—the department store, the
smart specialty shop, and the general service concern—to the suburbs has become universal. There are even instances of at least some smaller shops moving
outright rather than merely opening branches of their downtown places. The
newest and seemingly smartest type of such commercial suburbanitis is the big,
integrated shopping center, with competing department stores and specialty
shops, with service establishments and professional men's offices—and with ample,
convenient, and usually free parking space. With such developments, why should
the buyer go downtown from his suburban home if he can avoid it? Why would
not people move to the suburbs when living thus is made so much more pleasant
and convenient?

When this decentralization of shopping was getting started, there was considerable fear that it meant the doom of the big main stores in the city. By now there seems to be considerable evidence, particularly in the comments and actions of some of the big merchants themselves, that there is still money to be made downtown as well as in the suburbs. Certainly some of the canniest merchants in the larger cities are going ahead with ambitious branches of their downtown stores and continuing to do business at the same old stand, too. Evidently it is a matter of merchandising technique, involving just what and how to sell in each kind of store.

Robert Moses, the remarkable planner—and doer—of New York, N. Y., had some interesting comments on this subject in a recent question-and-answer interview.[2] The discussion was as follows:

"Q. Isn't retailing spreading out all over the suburbs as population spreads, and doesn't that bring up a problem of revamping the whole retail area?

"A. I don't think so. I know many department store executives. Many have established prosperous branch stores in the suburbs. But what's the matter with their trade at their old main stores? It looks pretty good to me. They are always threatening to move out when a hike in the sales tax is under discussion but they never go.

"Q. They are not losing volume to those branches?

"A. I don't see how they could do much more at the old stores. People are almost trampled to death now at peak loads. Of course, the new suburban branches get trade generated by new housing. But I don't think that anything has gone very sour with any of the big downtown stores that are well run. Look at theaters. There are red-barn theaters all over the suburbs and even in the back country, but people still want to go to Broadway shows.

"Q. So the branch stores really represent expansion?

"A. That's right. After all, there are lots of people in the suburbs who don't want to drive all the way into town. They buy locally and ought to."

Changing Atmosphere.—Most old cities, it must be conceded, still have some pleasant neighborhoods, retaining good characteristics. These areas are either the rather limited sections recently developed or districts with good deed restrictions, private streets, and kindred preservative factors. However, such special cases usually are hard pressed by blight at their fringes and by the encroachments of traffic, noise, and commerce.

Real Estate Values.—A compelling reason for the shift to the suburbs was, and in many places still is, the availability of land at a much cheaper price than in the old cities. True, the suburban land is usually undeveloped; but even after grading and installation of streets, sewers, and utilities, it often is cheaper than city land. Furthermore, it is vacant; the developer does not have to pay for, and remove, antiquated buildings.

Coupled with this situation has been the tendency, at least in the recent past, to place unrealistically low assessments for taxation on the suburban land. In addition, heretofore, the level of suburban tax rates has been markedly lower than in the city. Many suburban homes have been located in areas having

---

[2] *U. S. News and World Report,* August 8, 1952, p. 28.

no municipal government, or in perhaps only rudimentary towns, so that they were free of municipal taxation. On top of the foregoing factors was the general tendency in the suburbs to have no zoning, no building codes, no subdivision regulation, or to have only weak and poorly enforced rules in those fields. Now the suburbs are beginning to impose such restrictions.

Nevertheless, people get light, air, space, safety, and room for their children, their pets, and their outdoor activities, and, perhaps most of all, a vague, comfortable feeling of independence in the suburbs.

Administrative Corruption.—The old central cities had vicious political machines, graft, and poor government all too often. The suburbs, in their early days and even in the 1930's, had something of the atmosphere of the vaunted New England town. Their administrators then were civic-minded volunteers. Suburbanites felt they counted for something at the town hall but held a blind, although not always erroneous, fear of dominance at the central city hall. As the suburbs grew, their own government, of course, became more complex and called for hired administrators. This hired help could not be paid too well, if taxes were to be kept down to the old friendly level, and thus the troubles of public administration multiplied. However, many a suburban resident continues today to cherish an ostrichlike feeling of political independence and superiority—even if he can no longer name his alderman or his representatives in the state legislature.

Ease of Communication.—The automobile naturally has played a tremendous part in opening up the suburbs and at the same time in causing the congestion that makes the central city less inviting. It is easier to park in the suburbs, although they, too, have developed motor congestion. Clear avenues and highways in which to utilize the tempting power of the automobile are closer at hand in the suburbs. The suburban home has its own garage or carport, in contrast to the elusive curb space sought nightly by many a city dweller.

THE PATTERN OF SUBURBAN DEVELOPMENT

Imposing the far-flung suburban belts around the old central cities has created the new metropolitan city that has transformed the face of the nation. The United States has become more and more an urban community. This transformation is visible everywhere—around New York City in three states, around St. Louis in two states, on the benchlands of the great plains at Billings, Mont., and in the sprawling urban empire of Los Angeles.

Varied Growth.—Not many years ago, suburban development was most apparent in the familiar ribbon pattern along the main railroads and highways and the suburban transit lines. Now it is being consolidated. The varicolored roofs of the pleasant-looking little cracker box houses and the odd shapes of the misnamed ranch houses are scattered among the woods, in the ravines, and on the old cornfields. There is both much that is good and much that is bad in this new development, and some of the mistakes of the old cities are being repeated in the suburbs.

This paper is not intended to be an argument either in favor of the suburbs or in favor of at least partial desertion of the old cities. That is not the point.

The writer likes the suburbs, the old cities, and the new metropolitan cities. A fascinating condition confronts the nation, not a theory. The problem is to make sure that the new metropolitan city is workable, livable, and attractive, from core to periphery. In the solution of that problem lies a great challenge for the best engineering minds, to a very considerable extent. The political scientist, the public administrator, the lawmaker, and, notably, John Q. Citizen must join in the endeavor.

What people are beginning to realize is that the suburbs cannot be made part of the city and still be kept aloof and semirural. Suburban land values have inflated. Tax assessments and tax rates have soared in the suburbs, just as in the

FIG. 2.—TYPICAL SUBURBAN APARTMENT DEVELOPMENT NEAR ST. LOUIS, MO.

old cities, as new and improved services were demanded by the growing public while prices skyrocketed. New municipalities and other new taxing bodies have sprung up.

Essential Services.—American suburbs are commonly called "bedroom" towns, and these have become, by and large, the costliest bedrooms in the nation (Fig. 2). The costs of providing transportation; water, sewers, and streets; fire, police, and health protection; recreation; and many other facilities for these ballooned supercities have gotten out of hand. Services simply cannot be provided for a metropolis of, say, 15-mile radius, proportionately as cheaply and efficiently as for one of 5-mile radius. Incidentally, these radii may be taken as around average, respectively, for the typical new metropolitan city and the old core.

Traffic Problems.—Mass transportation for the overgrown metropolitan cities presents what seems at the moment an almost insurmountable problem. Automobile competition makes the outlying transit service unattractive to private operators and poses a need of heavy subsidy in public operation. Traffic congestion has spread far into the suburbs. Rush-hour traffic tangles at main suburban intersections are common now, whereas they were almost unknown prior to the end of World War II.

FATE OF THE OLD CITIES

The United States needs central cities. They are essential in the economic scheme, for they still must furnish the bulk of the wealth for public services, for commercial and industrial advancement, and for philanthropy. They are the natural centers for recreation, art and other forms of culture, dissemination of information, and many other amenities that make life worth living. Without them, there would be no suburbs. The neon signs of the suburban drive-in will never wholly replace the bright lights of downtown. If the cities are not preserved, the effects on the life and welfare of the nation would be so far-reaching as to stagger the imagination. The Lewis Mumford school of decentralization seems to overlook the natural tendency and need of like interests to be close together and for varying interests to have convenient interchange.

Robert Moses, as shown in the previously mentioned interview, does not think that the old cities are doomed. He foresees the possibility that Congress and the states may abandon the important field of low-rent public housing, but believes that the remaking of the old cities will continue with private enterprise participating actively in the publicly aided slum-clearance movement. He thinks that cities well located with respect to various economic factors will continue to grow, and that much depends on the spirit and determination of a city's people; as he stated in an interview:

> "When it comes to expense you have to worry more about decentralization than about the cost of rebuilding central slums. What is the matter with Los Angeles? It's too decentralized. There isn't any central shopping section. There aren't enough highly developed central places where you can collect large rents and taxes. There are just little centers all over and every city service, down to the policeman on his beat, has to cover an enormous area. That sort of city is the most expensive to operate."

Incorporation of Suburbs in the Central City.—William Zeckendorf, the forceful New York real estate man, who has moved all about the United States in course of his operations, declares: "Satellite towns, which are the products of decentralization, are parasites." He has a solution for this condition, which he stated as follows:[3]

> "Every satellite town saps off the buying power, the taxing power, and the vital factors that make for a cohesive, comprehensive, healthy city. This is just as though the United States suddenly lost the taxing power of California and New York through their setting up independent operation, but continued with the central bureaucracy and cost of maintenance of the Army and Navy,

---

[3] "Cities Versus Suburbs—a Struggle for Survival," by William Zeckendorf, *The Atlantic Monthly,* July, 1952, p. 24.

and so on. It wouldn't take very long for the U. S. to go broke on such a basis, and as long as this sort of thing can be done by the satellite towns around the mother city, we are jeopardizing the entire fiscal and political future of our great municipalities. What I conceive as the answer would consist of a change in the basic law, providing that municipalities have the right of unilateral incorporation or of involuntary incorporation of the communities that live on them at the periphery. The satellite communities should be forced into the large city and taxed to make them a contributing part of the whole community. The test as to whether a community is an independent community is simple and obvious, and if it fails to meet the test, then it should be incorporated into the large city. Otherwise, the township should retain its independence. This test should be: 'Can this community survive financially, socially and economically without the benefits from the large city?' Take employment, for example. Does the bulk of employment or earning power and other benefits come from the mother city or is the town a self-reliant, independent community? If the former is the case, which it happens to be in 90 per cent of the satellite towns in the immediate vicinity of large cities, then the city should have the right to incorporate the town. The net results would be beneficial."

Zeckendorf's idea is arresting, and there are strong practical arguments for it. However, one foresees the possibility that the exact test suggested might not stand up, with the continuing outward shifting of business and industry, which may tend to make more and more satellite towns seemingly self-reliant. At least the publication of his proposal emphasizes the growing attention that is being given to the problem of modern urbanism.

Cooperative Agreements.—The well-established Port of New York Authority, which deals with many phases of transportation of vital importance to the nation's number one metropolitan district, is a striking example of one approach to solving the needs of the cities. Another and basically similar device is the Bi-State Development Agency at St. Louis, but it has been hamstrung by political fears and suspicions and has not so far achieved extensive improvements. Neither of these enterprises has sufficient powers and latitude to cover the whole field of metropolitan needs. However, these and other such agencies could be given such powers.

A fine basic legal precedent for this type of undertaking is found in a simple clause of Missouri's 1945 Constitution. The background is this: The City of St. Louis withdrew from St. Louis County in 1876 and since has operated independently as a city and quasi-county within its rigidly fixed boundaries. The Constitution made provisions for various types of merger of the two areas, but the suburban county would not join the city and the proud city would not return to the county. Thus, when the Constitution was last revised an additional power was added, as follows:

"The people of the city of St. Louis and the people of the county of St. Louis shall have power * * * to establish a metropolitan district or districts for the functional administration of services common to the area included therein."

This simple language opens the way to sensible unified administration of almost any urban service—police, fire, hospitals, health, transportation, highways, traffic regulation, parks and playgrounds, sewers, water, and so on. Only recently has there been any active move to take advantage of the provision. First, petitions were put in circulation to start the machinery for a metropolitan sewer district, and later there were petitions to form a metropolitan transit district. (Both sets of petitions were successful, and by 1953 two boards of freeholders were set up to work out both plans.)

The constitutional provision requires separate petitions by a relatively small number of voters of city and county. On certification of the sufficiency of signatures, administrative and judicial officials are required to name a board of freeholders to draft a plan for the particular functions. The city and the county each have nine members of this board and a nineteenth is selected by the governor from out-state Missouri, to avoid a deadlock. The plan drafted for whatever functional administration is proposed would be submitted to city and county voters at separate, coincidental special elections. It would become effective on approval by a simple majority of these voting in each area. Apparently the board of freeholders would have great freedom in laying down a full charter for the agency concerned.

Agencies set up by this method apparently would have taxing power and provision for capital funds for their specific needs. However, one serious objection to this plan is that it would not solve the demand for better over-all financial support of the metropolitan community. This difficulty might be at least partly overcome if the metropolitan agency so established were given sufficiently broad functions. Of course, in that event such an agency would resemble a large-scale municipal government in many ways.

General Views.—Apart from the foregoing specific suggestions for action, here are some of the things the metropolitan cities need, in general:

1. Genuine public and official acceptance of planning—and of action to fulfil the plans. Planning here is used in the broad sense of capital and operating finance, with economic and sociological implications, as well as in the physical sense. It is not used in the questionable sense of a political philosophy.

2. Sounder financing. It is difficult to visualize any type of public revenue not based heavily on the value of land and its improvements; but there is a need for a broad and fair and workable system of other taxes to keep the cities going. Restrictions on sources of taxation open to the great cities should be lifted to some extent. If the earnings tax or the income tax is to spread far among cities, surely it needs much refining from the present examples in operation. Sound and properly flexible methods of property assessment are badly needed in numerous communities. Many cities would benefit from eliminating outmoded statutory and constitutional restrictions on issuance of bonds for public improvements, and from putting the revenue bond on firmer footing. However, the metropolis should not be allowed to go unrestrained in tapping the people's pocketbooks, and a realistic modernization in the interest of economy and efficiency should be adopted.

3. Less restraint on local self-government by the states. Cities remain today legally the creatures of the states and politically at the mercy of legislators and state officials elected from rural areas, who lack adequate realization of the problems of the modern city.

4. Recapture of the leaders in civic and political affairs who have been lost to the suburbs.

5. An end to jurisdictional conflicts that cross city limits, county lines, state borders, and the boundaries of all kinds of special districts.

In short, a replanning, remaking, and rethinking for American cities is needed. The shift to the suburbs is here to stay. The nation should proceed to develop a fine and strong metropolitan city to meet modern requirements. Even though the writer might like to share the dream of some political scientists for some sort of latter-day city-state, a literal fulfilment scarcely seems likely. Engineers, who made and perfected the telephone, the automobile, radar, and television, ought to be able to point the way to the new American metropolis in their second century of progress.

AMERICAN SOCIETY OF CIVIL ENGINEERS

Founded November 5, 1852

TRANSACTIONS

Paper No. 2587

WHAT CONSTRUCTION MEANS TO AMERICA

By Willard T. Chevalier,[1] M. ASCE

Synopsis

The United States standard of living has moved upward on steps fashioned by construction. This paper tells that inspiring story and stresses the essentiality of construction to the maintenance of an expanding economy. In addition, the continued need for economic freedom and incentive in advancing the engineering arts and the construction processes is emphasized.

To answer adequately the question—"What does construction mean to America?"—construction must be viewed in its three quite distinct aspects: The first and most obvious is revealed in its product, the vast diversity of works and structures that it contributes to American life. The second is its position as an industry in its own right, an aggregation of men, equipment, tools, and all the necessary operating paraphernalia assembled in effective organizations under competent management. The third is its force as a dynamic factor in the national economy, exerting influence on the cycle that affects and reflects the economic well-being of the nation as a whole.

What construction means to America, then, is the combined effect of all these. Obviously, it is possible to present here only a hilltop view of this vast operation known as "construction," and briefly to appraise its significance in the national scene.

The Product of Construction

Construction, considered in the first of its three aspects, has been defined as the process by which man adapts his physical environment to his needs. Probably the United States is the preeminent example of this process in its most intensive form. Within the short span of four or five generations, half a continent has been transformed from a wilderness into a nation of 160,000,000 people. Moreover, during this period, these people have created an environment within which they can enjoy a living standard unparalleled in history. In this country, less than 7%

---

[1] Exec. Vice-Pres., McGraw-Hill Pub. Co., Inc., New York, N. Y.

of the population of the world, living on 6% of the land area, produces nearly 50% of the world's income.

At this point, it should be emphasized that a material standard of living is in question. This is not to be confused with those intellectual and spiritual standards, which may or may not accompany a high material standard of living. It is a capital mistake to assume, as often happens, that an abundance of material wealth will insure a high standard of human happiness or intellectual progress. However, that concept is outside the scope of this discussion, and is mentioned here only to make clear that construction is primarily a servant of material progress.

All the fixed physical plant and facilities that make possible high living standards are the products of construction. The log cabins built by the pioneers, the wells they dug, and the trails they hewed out of the forests were its first fruits. Over a century and a half, these primitive facilities have been so increased in variety, in size, and in cost that they now include all the amazing fixed plant of American industry, commerce, and community life. They are embodied in dwellings and business buildings, mines and factories, far-flung highway and railroad networks, dams, airports, tunnels, sanitary installations, and irrigation and flood-control works.

The Rise of the Specialist.—This constant growth in the diversity and size of structures has of necessity developed specialists in their design, construction, and operation. These men have long since taken over the tasks once performed by the pioneers, each of whom provided his own necessities. One compelling reason for specialization was the unceasing extension of scientific frontiers in the United States. Out of this came the development of new materials, techniques, equipment, structures, and other facilities required to render an ever higher degree of service and satisfaction.

Coupled with this scientific progress was the insatiable drive of the class-free American to have more and to enjoy more of the world's goods, his adventurous willingness to try new products and methods, and his open-minded reception of the salesmen who pursued him in behalf of those producers and merchants who offered him something new or something better. Above all, there beckoned always the geographical frontiers of a new nation, moving steadily westward as each successive surge revealed new challenges, new opportunities, and new wealth for those who dared to face and grasp them. Pioneers among these technical specialists were the civil engineer, the architect, and the mining engineer. As requirements increased and mechanical power became available, more specialized help was provided by mechanical and electrical engineers. After them, came the chemical engineer, the automotive engineer, and a host of other even more highly specialized technicians.

The civil engineer and the architect design the fixed facilities that compose the nation's physical plant; the mechanical and electrical engineers animate them for usefulness; the mining and chemical engineers provide the materials required for the entire process. It is the peculiar function of construction to realize the designs of the engineers—that is, to assemble the labor, materials, equipment, and the specialized skills and management needed to convert those designs into the fixed structures and facilities seen on every hand.

Community Services.—As one measure of the task performed by the construction industry in building the United States of today, it will help to take a quick look at some of the essential services it provides to make community living possible and to make Americans more productive and efficient.

Water Supply.—In 1850, a century ago, there were only about 100 water works in the United States. In 1885, there were about 1,000; in 1895, about 3,000; and in 1924, about 9,000. In 1952, there were perhaps 12,000.

Less important, however, than the number of the nation's plants, is the improved quality of the water supplied to its communities (Fig. 1). When filtration was introduced early in the twentieth century in Philadelphia, Pa., the num-

FIG. 1.—PRETTY BOY DAM ON THE GUNPOWDER RIVER, BY WHICH BALTIMORE, MD., SECURES AN UPLAND SOURCE OF PURE WATER SUPPLY

ber of typhoid cases dropped within less than 5 years from more than 600 to less than 100 per 100,000; and within the next 20 years, to practically none. Typhoid deaths traceable to water supplies are practically unheard of in the United States today. Other water-borne diseases also are rapidly disappearing.

As the cities outgrew their nearby water sources, it became necessary for them to seek farther and farther afield to find adequate supplies of pure water. New York, N. Y., draws Delaware River water through the world's longest tunnel, 85 miles in length. Los Angeles, Calif., taps the Colorado River 400 miles away. Denver, Colo., brings its water from the other (west) side of the Continental Divide.

Sewage Disposal.—The increasing consumption of water by cities and towns made necessary corresponding improvement of their facilities for sewage disposal. In the early days, most raw sewage was dumped in the nearby streams; but these eventually were needed to supply pure water for other communities. In 1886 the establishment of the Lawrence (Mass.) Experiment Station marked the beginning of advanced sewage disposal practice in the United States. Today, although there is still room for more improvement, modern sanitation has made city living safer and more healthful than that in many rural communities (Fig. 2).

Transportation.—Scarcely less vital is the matter of transportation. Residents of the modern city must be able to get to their work and home again, and their food and other supplies must be conveyed to convenient points for wholesale and retail distribution. In the early stages of urban development, the horse-drawn conveyance gave way to the electric streetcar. Later, the streetcar, with its tracks

Fig. 2.—Sewage Treatment Works at Boise, Idaho, 1950, an Example of Improved Sanitation

built into the pavements, was replaced by the bus. In some of the larger communities, speedy long-distance transportation was forced overhead or underground on rapid transit railroads; and, as the individual motorcar achieved all but universal acceptance, it became necessary to build expressways through and around cities (Fig. 3). The first of these appeared in St. Louis, Mo., in 1936.

As efficient transportation is necessary to the functioning of each single community, it was essential to provide transportation for freight as well as passengers between communities and to every region of an expanding country. The first expression of this need was through turnpikes and Conestoga wagons, then through canals. The latter half of the nineteenth century was the great era of railroad building which first connected the inland regions with the eastern seaboard, and then tied together the Atlantic and the Pacific regions into one nation. Next, the motorcar brought the roads, and better roads fostered the expanding use of more motorcars. By the time the railroads had finished their building, they had spread

FIG. 3.—HOLLYWOOD FREEWAY, LOS ANGELES, CALIF., COMPLETED IN 1951, A HIGH-COST, HIGH-CAPACITY CITY FACILITY

a network of some 224,000 miles of line across the country. Today, this is supplemented by 3,000,000 miles of highways—some of them six-lane and eight-lane freeways, that frequently cost $1,000,000 a mile to construct, and sometimes as much as $5,000,000.

Reclamation and Flood Control.—As the railroads and the highways opened up new land, there arose a greater demand for reclaiming large areas from desert and marsh. In 1902, a national reclamation act was passed, which inaugurated a half century of dam and reservoir building to impound the waters needed by the new land. All the projects required their quotas of canal and pumping plant construction (Fig. 4).

As the early settlements, first located in the river valleys, were developed into

Fig. 4.—Contra Costa Irrigation Canal, Important Unit of the Central Valley Project in California

great cities and fertile farm lands, the problem of flood control raised its head. Man-made facilities had encroached on the flood plains, and flood damage became a substantial item in the national economy. Levees were built to confine the streams. More frequently than not, they failed to curb the peak floods. This in turn made it desirable to build dams to hold back some of the flood flow.

As reclamation and flood-control dams harnessed more and more streams, the possibilities of using impounded waters to generate electric power were widely preached (Fig. 5). Soon this factor became as important in river control as flood prevention or irrigation.

CONSTRUCTION AS AN INDUSTRY

All these services and facilities—and many more—were the products of construction. They either created new wealth or conserved wealth already in being.

Thus, the United States, dependent on construction to provide the physical facilities essential to its growth, nourished a construction industry of unprecedented skill and capacity.

Next construction must be considered in its second aspect: What are the dimensions of the industry which performs this vital function of providing and keeping up to date the physical plant that contributes so much to material and economic progress?

As of 1951, the three largest industries in the United States were: (1) Metalworking in all its branches, (2) manufactured foods and beverages, and (3) construction. The total output of the national economy in 1951 was $329,000,000,000, and construction accounted for $40,500,000,000, or 12.3%. Of this 12.3%, 9.4% was for new construction and 2.9% for maintenance and repair.

Construction, then, is a vast enterprise in itself. It is a large share of the na-

Fig. 5.—Wheeler Dam of the Tennessee Valley Authority in Northern Alabama—a Great Structure That Provides Power As Well As River Control

tional effort devoted consistently to the expansion and improvement of the fixed plant and facilities required by industry, commerce, and community life.

The established contractors and speculative builders of the United States include some 245,000 private businesses, ranging from very small to very large. From their nature, construction operations must be performed at the site of the project. No substantial part of the total ever can be concentrated under one roof or in one city. Thus the construction industry is and must remain a dispersed industry, a stronghold of competitive effort and of individual free enterprise. Of these 245,000 firms, some 7,000 go in for the large projects of heavy construction. About 38,000 erect buildings either as contractors or as speculators, or owner-builders, for sale or rent. The remaining 200,000 are special-trades contractors or subcontractors for specialized segments of the construction process.

Employed in the construction industry are more than 3,000,000 workers, nearly 5½% of all American labor. As a gage of the capital invested in the industry, the value of construction equipment alone aggregates more than $4,000,000,000.

Contrary to the impression held by many uninformed people, the construction industry is not a happy hunting ground for fly-by-night operators. Any industry that must operate on a job-to-job basis, that is highly competitive, that must frequently get its jobs by open bidding, and that is composed of a large number of small specialized units will, from its nature, be subject to a greater turnover than a more stable, fixed industry such as manufacturing.

Nevertheless, some of the largest contracting firms in the United States have been in business for many years. One of the largest has been in operation almost a century and a quarter. Many, from small beginnings, have grown into great operations. One of these companies in its first year, 1912, handled $75,000 worth of work. In 1951, its fortieth year, the same company completed work valued at $312,000,000, of which $82,000,000 was in foreign countries.

However, many of the very large construction projects today have outgrown in size and financial risk the capacity of the single construction company. In reply to this challenge, the industry has devised a flexible system of joint ventures whereby several companies pool their technical brains, their capital, and their equipment to bid on a particular job and carry it through to completion. The Grand Coulee Dam on the Columbia River in Washington, the greatest concrete dam in the world, is an example of such a project, involving the cooperation of ten companies from six states—each company a large operator in its own right.

It is estimated that the construction industry employs in its regular plant more than 2,000,000 pieces of heavy equipment. For example, it uses in the United States alone something like 900,000 trucks, 245,000 tractors, 130,000 pumps, 120,000 concrete mixers, 78,000 motor graders, 47,000 heavy-duty power shovels and cranes, and 42,000 air compressors. In addition, of course, the industry buys, handles, and installs each year more than 200,000,000 bbl of cement, nearly 3,000,000 tons of fabricated structural steel, brick in the billions of units, and lumber in the billions of board-feet.

At this time, known projects, proposed for future construction, top $65,300,000,000, exclusive of housing and smaller local projects. This total represents only a quarter of the estimated need for public and private heavy construction during the next few years. Obviously, construction, as an industry, is one of the largest and most essential.

CONSTRUCTION AND THE NATIONAL ECONOMY

Finally, construction should be viewed as a factor in the national economy. It is an axiom of American business that large construction volume and mounting prosperity go hand in hand. Which of the two is the cause and which the effect is a subject of perennial debate. There are good arguments on both sides.

From the short-term standpoint, it is certain that the demands and the psychology of a swelling boom tend to bring out new construction projects. To that degree, the construction volume is the result of the boom. However, over a long term, it is equally certain that the consistent development of new products, coupled with rising efficiency and productivity in industry, creates the additional purchasing power that makes for higher standards of living and business activity. Furthermore, as is well known, construction plays an essential role in this modernization of productive processes.

An Expanding Economy.—Most Americans understand pretty well that the consistent maintenance and elevation of high living standards must result from an expanding economy. However, it is not so clear just what that term means and just what creates an expanding economy.

Many conditions may account for the continuing infusion of new wealth that makes for an expanding economy. In the sixteenth century, Europe enjoyed an expanding economy based on the discovery of new lands and new wealth in the western hemisphere and elsewhere in the formerly unknown world. In the nineteenth century the United States had an expanding economy based on the opening of the West with its new lands and new wealth, together with the stimulation of wealth production by the invention of mechanical power.

In the twentieth century, the United States is still—or, perhaps, again—in an expanding economy; but this one is not based on the discovery of new natural wealth. To be sure, there still are some geographical areas to be exploited and there still is room for more intensive cultivation of the known areas. Nevertheless, the present expanding economy is based for the most part on technology—that is, the findings of scientists as translated by engineers and industries into new forms of wealth and greater capacity to produce.

Importance of Construction.—As noted in this quick review of construction in the development of the United States, it is in large measure through construction that scientific progress has been put to work. The builder who provides so many of the works and facilities makes possible an increase in output and more production from every hour's work.

New construction accounts for almost half of all private investment. Gross private domestic investment, not counting inventories, is estimated at $48,200,-000,000 for 1951. Of this amount, 48.3% was spent for new construction and the rest for machinery and other producers' durable equipment.

This process is never ending as long as technology continues to spark and fuel an expanding economy; for the purpose and the effect of technical progress is to make obsolete the standards and methods of yesterday. New discoveries engender new products and services and thus more efficient and more productive machines and other facilities. This constant replacement of the outmoded by what is newer and better is the outward and visible sign of the expanding economy; and construction is one of its major prophets.

A few years ago, a European visitor was crossing one of the highest passes of the Continental Divide in the Rockies. The highway was under improvement; it was being widened and surfaced, and its grades were being eased to facilitate the increasing traffic. The visitor commented, "Only a very rich country could be doing this." To which the writer replied, "Perhaps, but only a country that does this can be rich." Thus the construction activity of the nation is at most a cause and at least a measure of the nation's standard of living.

It is impossible to estimate the effect of construction on the over-all productivity of the American economy; but it is clear that continued expansion of industry depends on the maintenance and expansion of power, transportation, and the other facilities provided by the construction industry. In addition, the health and happiness—the incentives—of the work force are closely bound up with the existence of an adequate and expanding supply of good homes, schools, hospitals, highways, and community facilities.

It must be remembered, however, that the short-term impact of construction when it is stepped up as the result of a boom tends to create an instability in the economic cycle that is the most vulnerable feature of the American economy. Obviously, expenditures for new construction are subject to much greater swings than are those experienced by most other segments of the economy. Between 1929 and 1933, the physical volume of new construction dropped 68% whereas the gross national product (in constant dollars) fell only 28%. During the recovery period from 1933 to 1937, the gross national product rose by 43% whereas new construction shot up by 104%. During the prosperous 1920's, new construction was about 11% of the gross national product; during the 1930's, it dropped to 6%. In passing, it is worthwhile to note that, as of the 1950's, the new construction share of business activity has been in the bracket of 8% to 9%.

Moreover, as construction constitutes more than 12% of the gross national product and as its workers represent more than 5% of those gainfully employed, such swings exert a heavy influence on the national economy as a whole. The effect is even more widespread than these data indicate. For every five workers directly employed in construction, another six workers in the industries that supply materials and equipment are severely affected by its fluctuations. Thus, about 10% to 11% of the labor force are dependent in some degree on construction for jobs. These extreme swings are not inevitable. The construction industry and the Federal Government now have the means, between them, to cut the ups and downs substantially.

Government can help primarily in two ways:

1. It can concentrate its own major construction programs as much as possible in periods when other construction activity is lowest.

2. It can use its system of mortgage guarantees and its control of the interest rate and the supply of credit to help stabilize home building.

Industry can do its part in promoting stability by keeping construction costs down and by continually searching for new ways to make a better product.

Need for Building Construction.—One way to smooth out home building is to broaden the market by developing a replacement market; and lower costs are likely to be the key. Much of the present housing is inadequate, but it often is not replaced, simply because the home-building industry cannot provide better housing at a cost people are willing to pay. Prices and rents for existing dwellings will probably be lower in the future as more vacancies appear, and builders will have to cut costs if they want to compete with older dwellings.

The housing industry and the people who make its materials have developed many new techniques to bring costs down: Prefabrication of sections, or even of entire houses; cheaper, more standard building materials; and increased utilization of machinery. More needs to be done in these directions, and more progress must be made in eliminating restrictive union practices and obsolete building codes that now curb the use of superior methods.

Determined application of cost-reducing techniques could also develop a larger replacement market for industrial and commercial buildings. Manufacturers can often improve their productive efficiency by moving into a well-designed new building—for example, a Cleveland (Ohio) die and machinery company was able to save about 5% on total manufacturing costs as the result of moving into a new plant. Retail stores also can improve sales and save on overhead in a modern structure. However, companies will not be interested in moving into new buildings unless their cost is reasonable in relation to the savings they make possible—hence the need for lowering costs.

WHAT OF THE FUTURE

The facts, however, outweigh the problems. Higher standards of living depend on an expanding economy. Construction has been a dynamic force in assuring such an expansion. How can it continue to play an equally vital role in the future?

Fig. 6.—Paducah, Ky., Protected from Ravages of Ohio River by an Extensive Flood Wall

For most of the past century, its nourishment was drawn from an urge to exploit the ever-widening geographic frontiers. New cities required new water supplies and sewage plants. The railroad and the highway reached out into virgin territory. New land needed the quickening waters of reclamation projects, and growing settlements demanded protection from floods (Fig. 6) and sought new sources of power. Today, the original installation of the United States is well in hand. The day of providing new facilities in open, uninhabited territory is about over. Where does construction go from here?

To a considerable degree, it must work back over the same area to rebuild to ever higher standards. Even more important, it must provide the new facilities demanded by a people who are seeking better living conditions, who are intent on achieving a higher degree of national security in a disturbed world, and who command the ever-increasing productivity that is necessary to realize those objectives.

In the domain of home building alone, it is safe to say that no more than a few hundred thousand persons have the home of their dreams. A hundred million others will not be satisfied until they are housed in a manner more in keeping with twentieth century standards. These new homes (Fig. 7) must be built and equipped with all the power-using gadgets designed to make living easy and efficient. To supplement these, new power-generating facilities must be built and factories must be constructed in which to manufacture the products that an advancing science constantly promises to the people.

The modernization of existing facilities and the construction of new ones point to as big a job in the partly built United States of 1952 as that which was done

FIG. 7.—A NEW, SELF-CONTAINED COMMUNITY OF SINGLE FAMILY HOMES—LEVITTOWN, LONG ISLAND, N. Y., WITHIN COMMUTING DISTANCE OF NEW YORK CITY

to provide the bare necessities during the pioneer period of the nineteenth century. At that time, the extending geographic frontiers offered an opportunity for the construction industry to grow as it built the physical plant of a new nation. However, the new frontiers of technology are no less challenging, and the opportunity is at hand to rebuild that plant to meet the aspirations of a people who never have been willing to accept for tomorrow the living standards of today.

The basis of this hope for the future of the country, as well as of construction, is implicit in the character of the American economic system with its distinctive reliance on freedom for the individual. As has been indicated, construction genius has played an important part in building the United States to its present high level of productivity. Other factors also have helped: National resources, human labor, funds for investment, and powerful incentives. None of these was new in the history of the world; they all had played their parts in the development of other nations in other eras. In the case of the United States, the new factor was individual and personal opportunity—equal opportunity for every individual to shape his own destiny, and to rise as high as he could through his own intelligence, skill, and willingness to work. On such equality of opportunity the American enterprise system has been founded.

Just as the amazing physical expansion of the country during the past century derived in large measure from this atmosphere of individual freedom, it is certain that a continued expansion, now arising from scientific and technological progress, will find its chief motive power in that same freedom of mind and spirit. It is the duty of every American to safeguard this wellspring of national genius.

AMERICAN SOCIETY OF CIVIL ENGINEERS

Founded November 5, 1852

TRANSACTIONS

Paper No. 2588

THE CONTRACT METHOD FOR AMERICAN CONSTRUCTION

By H. E. Foreman [1]

Synopsis

The construction industry, through cooperation between engineers and contractors, has made many material contributions toward the welfare of the United States. Construction activity is traced from the earliest days of history to the present. Special emphasis is placed on the role of the industry in the development of the United States. The paper gives statistics that show the size and importance of construction today.

The construction industry, through cooperation between engineers and contractors, has made many material contributions toward the welfare of the United States. Construction activity is traced from the earliest days of history to the present. Special emphasis is placed on the role of the industry in the development of the United States. The paper gives statistics that show the size and importance of construction today.

Introduction

Civil engineers and general contractors are members of the construction team that has done so much to make the United States a leading nation of the world.

In recent years there has been a steady increase in the proportion of men in executive and ownership positions in general contracting firms who are civil engineers. This indicates that, since the business of construction is constantly becoming more complex, a sound engineering training is essential, and also that there is constant improvement in the quality of construction men.

Certainly it is significant that the Construction Division of ASCE has grown from its original membership of 1,615 when it was established in 1926, to more than 12,300 at present, making it the Society's largest Technical Division. This is perhaps appropriate because construction now has become the largest single industry in the nation. ASCE records show that approximately 40% of the membership of its Construction Division are owners, executives, or managers of contracting companies.

This paper will attempt to trace the development of the construction industry and the contract method in the United States. The subject is so vast that little more than a brief introduction to it can be given here. There is a wealth of material, but much of it is uncoordinated. Apparently those who have been engaged in the construction industry, not only in the United States but also

---

[1] Managing Director, Assoc. General Contractors of America, Inc., Washington, D.C.

throughout the world in all ages, have been so busy doing their job that they have not taken the time to record their activities for future generations.

The purpose of this paper is to mention briefly a few highlights that illustrate significant points about the construction industry and the vital part it has played in the development of the nation.

Construction Through the Ages

Early History.—The history of the human race is in large part the story of man's struggle against his environment. In that struggle the basic needs of men and women have been food, clothing, and shelter. Of these, the most durable is shelter. As far back in history as archeologists have been able to find traces of human life, they have also found evidence of construction. Presumably one of the first wants of man was shelter for himself and his family.

As soon as civilizations began to develop, there arose the need for structures and facilities for the production of goods, trade and commerce (Fig. 1), transportation, education, religion, the development of natural resources, public buildings, safeguards to health, life, and property, and the many other types of facilities that modern civilization has found necessary or desirable.

Ancient Greece.—Little is known about the construction industry in early times, when the wonders of the ancient world were built. However, in the time of ancient Greece, when many structures were built which are still famous today, law and custom prescribed relationships between the contractors and the government that are strikingly similar in principle to the contractual relationships prevailing today.

The contractors were required to work continuously, to hire sufficient numbers of qualified workmen, and to guarantee quality of performance. There were penalties for delays or failure to complete the work. Payments were made in instalments as columns or pediments rose to completion. The precedent was established that a percentage of the contract price be retained until the project was completed.

Roman Civilization.—During the days when Imperial Rome ruled a great part of the world, construction companies much as they are known today came into being. Their Greek predecessors worked independently in small groups; but the Roman contractors formed large companies to undertake the huge construction projects of the time. They came to realize the complexity and the risks involved. They believed that by incorporating many talents under a single management the risks could be minimized and better controlled. The Romans who undertook whole projects were awarded their contracts under a bidding system similar to that in existence today.

Medieval Period.—After the fall of Rome the construction industry as such seems to have generally faded from view. Construction of a durable nature that was continued during medieval times seems to have been carried on mainly by the churches, whose efforts were concentrated on the building of cathedrals, abbeys, and works of that nature.

In Egypt, where it has been estimated that there were barracks for 4,000 workmen to prepare the stone for the great pyramids, and in Mesopotamia where there were vast irrigation projects, much of the actual construction work was done by slaves, who were often prisoners of war. This custom seemed to prevail also in Greece and Rome, although some of the more skilled workers were free men. The designers, who were also responsible for the execution of the work, were men in high positions at court.

FIG. 1.—ILLUSTRATIVE OF MODERN TREND IN COMMERCIAL BUILDING; LEVER BUILDING IN NEW YORK, N. Y., WITH GREEN GLASS AND STAINLESS STEEL EXTERIOR AND OPEN ARCADED STREET FLOOR

What little is known about the contractors of medieval England points to their having risen out of the ranks of the free masons. Training was later specialized to develop two types of masons: One skilled in the actual stonework and the other in the planning and designing of buildings. The former apparently was the forerunner of the modern contractor; the latter, of the modern architect.

Rules for the mason's craft were drawn up in London in 1356. One of the most interesting rules is one that provided for a guarantee of ability and responsibility. As described by Martin S. Briggs:[2]

> "Anyone undertaking a contract was to come before the good man for whom he was going to work, with four or six experienced masons who should swear that he was capable of doing the job, and that if he failed they would themselves complete the work on the same terms."

In early England, the builder was the master mason who fulfilled the three functions of designer, builder, and master of the works. In the latter capacity he supervised the operations to make certain that they were done properly and that the workmen were paid according to their ability.

DEVELOPMENT OF THE CONSTRUCTION INDUSTRY

Although the construction industry as developed in this country is unique—just as the nation itself is unique—its principal traditions came from England. The early methods, materials, contract forms, and practices of the industry came primarily from England and from the other European countries from which the settlers emigrated.

Early American Construction.—Written contracts were in use in the early days. Sumner C. Powel has reported [3] that the first full contract recorded in the town book of Sudbury, Mass., in 1642, provided in part as follows:

> "* * * the said Ambrose doth promise to build a sufficient cart bridge over the river three foote above highwater and twelve feet wide from the one side of the river to the other, provided that the towne doth fell & cross cutt the tymber and saw all the plank and carry it to place and when it is ready framed, the town doth promise to help him to raise it."

In another contract in Sudbury, dated February 17, 1642:[3]

> "It is agreed between the townemen of the towne on the [one part] * * * and John Rutter on the other part that the said John * * * for his parte shall fell, saw, hew a frame house for a meeting house thirty foote long, twenty foote wide, eight foote between joynte, three foote between studde, two cross dorments in the house, six clear story windowes with four lyghts a peece and foure with three lyghts a peece and to ententise between the studde which frame is to be ready to raise the fourth week in May next.
> "And the towne for their parte do covenant to draw all tymber to place and to help rayse the house being framed and allsoe to pay to the said John Rutter for the said house six pound, that is to say three pound to be paid in corne at three shillings a bushell or in money in and upon the twenty-seventh day of this present month and the other three pounds to be payd in money, corne or cattle, the corne and cattle to be prized by two men of the town, one to be chosen by the towne and the other to be chosen by John Rutter, and to be paid at the time that the frame shall be by the said John Rutter finished."

The American construction industry did not get its real start until after the Revolution. England had used the American Colonies primarily as a source of

---

[2] "A Short History of the Building Crafts," by Martin S. Briggs, Oxford Univ. Press, Oxford, England, 1925, p. 25.
[3] *Journal*, Soc. of Architectural Historians, March, 1952, p. 8.

raw materials for its factories. Much of what was built during colonial days was done by the British or under their direction. Not until the United States became independent did the nation set out by its own efforts to become self-sufficient.

After the American Revolution there was the immediate need for structures to house manufacturing processes so that goods formerly supplied by Great Britain could be produced at home. The *American Peoples Encyclopedia* reports that:[4]

> "The history of construction in the United States reflects in an exaggerated form the forces of industrialism which combined to cause fundamental changes in building, and to constitute the activity as an 'industry' in its own right throughout the Western civilization."

As a result of the need for large industrial buildings, the amateur designer and the anonymous builder yielded to the professional architect and workman, and building design changed to meet new needs. Techniques and methods still followed earlier procedures; but the needs of factories for large rooms, for floors and walls of great strength to support heavy machinery, for illumination, temperature control, and ease of mobility for materials and personnel demanded more than could be supplied by previous structural theories and customary erection techniques. These demands led to the development of new techniques.

A decisive point in the history of American construction was the elevation of the mechanic to the rank of engineer, with a professional status distinct from that of the architect. The Encyclopedia adds:[4]

> "The engineer's dedication to technology assured the rapid development of new methods and new processes to which subsidiary industries could contribute an increasing share."

Some of the construction work done during the first half of the nineteenth century gives an indication of how the industry developed, and how important it was to the opening up and development of the nation. For more than 200 years after the early settlements were made in Virginia and New England, the rivers were the principal highways. Colonial America expanded along those waterways, first up the rivers flowing into the Atlantic and then down those flowing to the Great Lakes and the Mississippi.

However, under the pressure of continued and rapid expansion these natural means of transportation and communication ceased to be adequate, and it became essential to provide access to large parts of the country that were distant from the coast line and the principal waterways. Canals were built to furnish a route for settlers to go west and to make possible their livelihood after they got there. During the early decades of the nineteenth century, civilization spread rapidly along the rivers and into the wilderness through a spreading network of canals.

Canals.—The first canal construction undertaken in this country was on the Dismal Swamp Canal in Virginia. It was started in 1787 and is still the oldest canal in use in the United States. The first canal to be completed in this country was built at South Hadley, Mass., from 1792 to 1796. It was financed privately

---

[4] *American Peoples Encyclopedia*, Spencer Press, 1953, Vol. 6, p. 155.

with funds raised partly by public lottery which, in England and the United States, seems to have been a popular method for raising funds.

The first major canal was the Erie Canal, opened to traffic from the Hudson River to Buffalo, N. Y., in 1825. This canal paid its own expenses and all those of New York State for many years, and millions of its surplus earnings were later used to develop the state's early railroad lines. The canal was one of the principal reasons for the growth and development of the City of New York, N. Y., as a major port.

Early canals in the United States were built by private stock companies because the authority of the Federal Government to construct such structures as canals and highways was a bitterly contested political issue. The contract method of construction was used. Contracts were usually for short stretches, enabling many contractors to work on one canal. At one time there were 6,000 bids for contracts to be awarded on 110 sections of the Ohio canals, varying in length from 2,000 ft to 14 miles, depending on the number of locks or other structures per section. This work attracted not only local bidders, but those who had worked in other states.

Despite floods, malaria, labor shortages, and a lack of trained engineers, contractors built more than 4,500 miles of canals in the United States from 1800 to 1850 at a cost of more than $200,000,000. Ohio alone had a canal system almost 1,000 miles in length.

By joining the inland areas with the Atlantic, the canals launched the development of the Middle West. The economic benefits were incalculable. Examples such as the following from Ohio are typical: From 1820 to 1840 the population increased from 581,000 to more than 1,500,000. Property value increased from $59,000,000 in 1825 to $440,000,000 in 1850. Also, the price of flour increased from $3 to $6 per bbl between 1826 and 1835, and the price of wheat trebled between 1820 and 1832.

Highways.—The need for a comprehensive system of adequate highways was foreseen more than 100 years before it approached a semblance of reality. There has been a complete cycle in the relation of the Federal Government to highway construction during the nation's history. First the Federal Government participated directly in the work. Then it retired and turned the work over to the states. They in turn left it to counties or other local authorities until New Jersey reversed the trend in 1891 by state aid. The current federal-aid system was established in 1916.

The importance attached to early roads is evidenced by the Act of 1802, which admitted Ohio to the Union. This contained a provision setting aside 5% of the net proceeds from the sale of public land in that state for the construction of public roads leading from the navigable waters emptying into the Atlantic to Ohio's border and through the state.

One of the first roads built by the Federal Government was financed by funds resulting from the sale of public lands in Ohio, which amounted to more than $600,000 by 1806. In that year Congress appropriated $30,000 of that sum and authorized President Thomas Jefferson to appoint a commission of three "discreet and disinterested citizens" to lay out a road running westward from Cumberland, Md. This was the beginning of the famous Cumberland Road, now

United States route 40, which had been strongly advocated in 1785 by George Washington, who as a colonel in the British Army in 1754 had widened the trail at Wills Creek, near Cumberland, to allow passage of his artillery.

On May 8, 1811, Henry·McKinley, a Maryland contractor, signed a contract with Albert Gallatin, Secretary of the Treasury, for the first section of that road starting in Cumberland and "ending at a place on said road two miles and two hundred and forty-six perches distant." A perch was 16.5 ft, or the equivalent of a rod in length. For that he bid and was to be paid $21.25 for each perch.

The contract contained essentially the same features as present-day contracts. It was publicly advertised and awarded to the lowest bidder; a completion date was established with a penalty for nonfulfilment; provision was made to assure payment to subcontractors and suppliers; and a schedule of partial payments to the contractor was set up.

On or near the Cumberland Road two important events in road building occurred: The first macadam surfacing in the United States was laid on an 11-mile stretch between Boonsboro and Hagerstown, Md., in 1823, and the first cast-iron bridge was built in Brownsville, Pa., in 1839, both by contractors. Construction of the Cumberland Road was supervised by the Corps of Engineers.

Railroads.—Another great factor in opening and developing the nation during the early 1800's was the railroads. Valuable as the canals were, there arose pressing needs for additional methods of transporting goods from the Middle West to the East across the mountains.

The first railroad to be chartered and built in the United States was the Baltimore and Ohio, the first stone of which was laid on July 14, 1828. Construction was begun on the section between Baltimore, Md., and Wheeling, Va. (later W. Va.), which had been surveyed by the United States Topographical Engineers, now the Corps of Engineers.

The value of the contract method of construction was apparent to the founders of the railroad. On July 14, 1828, notice was publicly given that between August 1 and 11 proposals would be received for the grading and bridge construction on the first twenty-six sections from Baltimore to Ellicott's flour mill, a distance of 12 miles. Contractors were at work on all sections by October 1. The value of using contractors is indicated by the second annual report of the president, who stated in part:

> "The directors are not aware that any prejudicial consequences resulted from the short notice which preceded the first letting, or that greater competition would, at that time, have caused any material change in the contract prices which, although they are believed sufficient in every case to insure the contractors against loss, are not thought to be generally higher than has usually been paid under similar circumstances.
>
> "So great, however, are the increased facilities now experienced from the improvements which have been introduced by the contractors on several sections by means of temporary railways for the removal of earth, that a great reduction of cost will accrue to the contractors. The profitable results of these improvements will be felt in subsequent contracts."

This prediction proved true, prices being lower on the next lettings. The ingenuity of contractors reduced the cost of the entire line.

Building Construction.—After the Civil War (Fig. 2), the new industrialism expanded throughout the country with lightning rapidity. The great fire in Chicago, Ill., in 1871 accented the need for fireproof construction. The availability of steel in the middle 1880's revolutionized building construction because the steel framework could support the weight of the building, and walls no longer had to be so heavy or so thick. In the 1870's portland cement was introduced, and with it came a great influence on design and construction in nearly all fields.

FIG. 2.—PONTOON BRIDGE BEING CONSTRUCTED IN 1864 BY ARMY ENGINEERS DURING THE CIVIL WAR AT BELLE PLAIN LANDING, VIRGINIA; FOR COMPARISON WITH SUBSEQUENT METHODS

In Chicago in 1885 the first building with a steel skeleton was built, revolutionizing building construction. This structure was the Home Insurance Building on the northeast corner of South La Salle and West Adams streets. Heated arguments which developed in later years as to the validity of this claim were settled in 1931 when the building was torn down. Three committees of engineers and architects investigated and agreed that it was in fact the first building to utilize skeleton construction as the basic principle of its design.

Construction Machinery.—One of the greatest contributions the United States has made to construction is the development and use of machinery. Although the first steam shovel was built in 1837, the greatest progress in machinery was in the latter part of the nineteenth century, and in the twentieth century. Horse-drawn scoops were used as early as 1805, but the development of powerful scrapers did not come until the twentieth century.

The fresno scraper, the horse-drawn forerunner of the bulldozer, was patented in 1882. Although steam tractors were used in agriculture as early as 1890, not until 1903 was the first crawler tractor manufactured. The use of low-pressure heavy-duty tires for construction equipment did not come into use until the 1930's, after the contractors on the Bay Bridge in San Francisco, Calif., had used airplane tires on some of their equipment.

When the past 100 years in construction are reviewed, one cannot help but be impressed by the tremendous changes and the tremendous strides that have been made during that period. Although there were marvelous construction projects in the past—such as the Pyramid of Cheops, which took 30 years to build (and has, incidentally, half the volume of Boulder Dam on the Colorado River in Arizona-Nevada, which was built in 5 years); the 4,000-mile Inca high-way, which rises to heights of 15,000 ft; the Chinese Wall; and hundreds of others—they are particularly remarkable for having been built almost entirely by hand. Most American construction 100 years ago was by hand, and aside from some use of cast iron or wrought iron, little change or improvement had been made over the methods of the past.

Today, such challenges as the unprecedented dams, irrigation, flood-control, and power projects of the West are taken in its stride by the construction industry (Fig. 3). It is worthy of note that in just one phase of the industry, the building of highways, construction contracts awarded by state highway departments throughout the country in one year, 1951, were for a total of 54,650 miles.

THE EARLY CONTRACTOR

There is evidence that shortly after the settlement of some of the earliest American colonies it was the practice to have construction performed by contractors with written contracts. When buildings were primarily of wood, or brick and stone, the contractor generally was the master mason or master carpenter.

However, when structures became more complex; when steel, concrete, and other new materials came into use; when plumbing, heating, lighting, and, later, elevators were incorporated in buildings; and when new machinery was introduced—it was no longer possible to have all the work under the direction of the mason or the carpenter.

When the construction industry was undergoing its period of fast growth and change after the Civil War, there were apparently also growing pains in its organization. It became necessary to develop some kind of organization that could combine and coordinate the various skills required for the new features of building.

Although more research needs to be done on this turning point in the history of the construction industry, it appears that somewhere during the middle 1880's the general contractor, as he and his organization are known today, first became recognizable.

(a) World's Largest Dam, with Spectacular Overflow

(b) Greatest Pumping Effort—Two of Twelve 12-Ft Pipes, Raising Water 280 Ft

FIG. 3.—RECORDS BROKEN ON ONE PROJECT, AT GRAND COULEE DAM ON THE COLUMBIA RIVER IN WASHINGTON

Before the bona-fide general contracting firms were organized to take complete and undivided responsibility for the execution of a project, it appears that occasionally the architect or engineer who designed the project also coordinated the work of the various individual contractors and supervised their operations. Sometimes this function apparently was fulfilled by the owner, or a representative of the owner, such as the Corps of Engineers in the case of government construction.

Early contracts were much the same as contracts now, calling for guaranteed quality; penalties for delays or failure to complete the work; assurance that suppliers, subcontractors, and labor would be paid; and periodic payments with a percentage retained for payment on completion and acceptance. Most public works contracts seem to have been awarded after competitive bidding, as is the custom today, and they were at firm prices or so much per unit.

In private work, there appears to have been some use of contracts on the basis of cost plus 10%, but that type of contract has been almost entirely replaced by the cost-plus-a-fixed-fee contract. There is considerable evidence that, in earlier days, work privately financed was often undertaken and completed without formal contract, and that much of it proceeded on the basis of a verbal understanding or of letters.

Construction Industry Today

Volume.—A good way of making evident the development that has taken place in the construction industry in the United States is to glance at its present activities. During 1951 it was the largest single industry in the country. The volume of new construction put in place was more than $31,000,000,000, according to the revised estimates of the departments of Commerce and Labor. In addition, approximately $9,000,000,000 worth of maintenance and repair operations was performed in 1951 to bring the total volume of construction activity to $40,000,000,000. This exceeded the total value of agricultural production, which normally has been the greatest industry in the nation. Nearly one dollar in every eight created in end products and services in the United States in 1951 was a construction dollar.

Employment.—Throughout 1951 an average of 2,250,000 men were employed each month by general contractors and subcontractors at the sites of construction projects. For each man working at the site, from two to four other jobs were created elsewhere in the production or transportation of materials and in the performance of services for the industry.

Finance.—Of this construction, more than $21,000,000,000 was privately financed, and more than $9,000,000,000 was invested in public funds. Of the private funds invested, almost $11,000,000,000 went into residential construction; more than $5,000,000,000 into nonresidential building for industrial, commercial, religious, educational, health, and other institutional purposes; and more than $3,000,000,000 into public utilities.

Of the public funds, more than $3,000,000,000 was invested for educational and other public institutions; approximately $2,500,000,000, for highways (Fig.

4); almost $1,000,000,000, for conservation and development of resources; and more than $1,000,000,000, for military construction.

During the first 6 months of 1952, another record of nearly $15,000,000,000 in new construction was established. The impetus for a large volume of construction in 1952 came from military, industrial, and public utility construction.

These data on construction activity are too big for ready comprehension; but they do clearly indicate that the construction industry is performing a tremendous amount of work for the nation and all its communities.

FIG. 4.—CLOSING A HIGHWAY TOLL STRUCTURE ALMOST 7 MILES LONG—RAISING A 400-TON SUSPENDED TRUSS, WHICH COMPLETES 33,000-TON JOB, THIRD LARGEST IN THE UNITED STATES, OVER CHESAPEAKE BAY NEAR ANNAPOLIS, MD.

CONTRIBUTIONS OF THE CONSTRUCTION INDUSTRY

Construction now is not only a huge industry, but its work is fundamental to the growth and development of the nation and its communities, and it plays a part in practically every aspect of civilized life.

A slogan used by the Associated General Contractors (AGC)— "America progresses through construction"—is believed to be true. Also, the role of the construction man, like that of the engineer, seems to be little understood by the general public.

One of the reasons the United States has become a great nation is that there have been not only the genius, the foresight, and the courage to develop new industries and better ways of exploiting resources but also a progressive and ever-developing construction industry that could fulfil the nation's needs for physical facilities—an industry that has striven to retain its flexibility.

Essentially it must be broadly dispersed in all its phases to meet local needs promptly. Through joint ventures the construction industry has learned to put its units together in any combination necessary to do the job. It must be present in all its phases at all times in every community if the full function of the industry is to be performed.

Although there are no accurate statistics on the volume of construction in the early days of the nation, a brief reading of history will indicate what a tremendous role in the country's growth has been played by the construction industry in building for many purposes: Industrial, conservation and development, transportation, commercial, residential, community, governmental, health, educational and institutional, national defense, civil defense, and disasters. The industry has also kept pace in providing facilities for recent developments in such fields as aviation, electronics, and atomic energy. These are some of the reasons why all those men and women who are a part of the construction industry in one capacity or another can and do take pride in their accomplishments.

New construction is probably the most spectacular function of the construction industry, but the industry has many other jobs. The physical facilities of the United States, which were built by the industry, also need to be maintained, repaired, and remodeled from time to time to fit new conditions, and the industry must do these things also if it is to be most useful. Nearly a quarter of the industry's work is for this purpose.

When disasters strike,—such as earthquakes, tornadoes, explosions, floods, and heavy snows—the damage must be repaired, and water, light, gas, and other facilities must be restored to operation. This is another task of the construction industry. On occasions such as the explosion at Texas City, Tex., the tremendous snows in the Great Plains states, the floods in the Kansas City, Mo., area, and other emergencies, contractors and others in the industry have mobilized immediately in cooperation with civic authorities and started their workmen and their machines to work clearing debris and repairing damage. Some time later they took the time to consider what should be the proper compensation.

The AGC has cooperated with the Federal Civil Defense Administration and has submitted a comprehensive plan on how the facilities of the industry can best be mobilized in the event of an emergency, and many other organizations in the industry have done likewise.

In 1947, the Army initiated its Affiliation Program, by which reserve units in which each man is specially fitted for his military assignment by his civilian work, are recruited and trained for call to active duty when necessary. The AGC was asked to cooperate with the Corps of Engineers in sponsoring and recruiting reserve construction units. So far seventy-six units have been sponsored and twenty-one have been called to active duty. Two have been engaged in Korea, where they have performed the outstanding engineering feats of that campaign. Many engineers, architects, and others in the industry have joined these units. There are also two units in the European Theater.

These activities of the construction industry serve to emphasize why the industry is so fundamental to the welfare of the nation and its communities.

CONSTRUCTION FOR NATIONAL DEFENSE

Construction is as important to the national defense as it is to the peacetime development and progress of the nation. During World War II the construction industry completed work valued at more than $49,000,000,000. This work constituted, at that time, the world's greatest single construction program, and it represented an expenditure of approximately $400 for each man, woman, and child in the United States. The war was actually won by fighting men, but they had to be supported by the products and services of American industry. One of those industries was construction.

Camps virtually as complete as cities had to be set up before men could be trained and sent overseas. Factories had to be constructed before airplanes, tanks, guns, munitions, and other weapons of war could be produced in quantities sufficient to overwhelm the enemy. Yards had to be built before a bridge of ships and a seven-ocean navy could be launched. Bases had to be constructed before attacks could be directed at the enemy.

It was necessary that this work be completed before many other parts of the war program could be undertaken. Because of this, construction was the first major industry to attain large-scale defense and war production. By the time of Pearl Harbor it was converted 75% to war work, and at one time more men were mobilized on construction work for the Army than were in the Army itself.

Had construction failed in any part, other phases of the war effort would have been hampered, perhaps disastrously. However, there were no bottlenecks in construction; the work was completed at unprecedented speed. The speed cost money, but by helping to hasten the end of the war it saved lives.

As members of the armed services, construction men, with their methods and machinery, helped to develop the capacity for building airfields, docks, railroads, and pipelines (Fig. 5), and for moving millions of tons of supplies at speeds never before attained in military operation. The nation's capacity to construct both at home and in combat areas was such that the wartime Chief of Army Engineers was able to report:

> "By the war's end it was evident that American construction capacity was the one factor of American strength which our enemies most consistently underestimated. It was the one element of our strength for which they had no basis for comparison. They had seen nothing like it."

Should there be another war and the United States be subjected to bombings or other catastrophes, the construction industry will be immediately available to clear debris and restore essential facilities to use in minimum time. There is no way in which such work can be done except by the construction industry.

SUMMARY

The construction industry, throughout the history of the United States, has had, still has, and always will have a tremendously important part in the development, growth, and progress of the nation and its communities, and will serve as a medium through which investments can be made in facilities that serve people. It has kept pace with, and helped in the development of, practically all other industries, and is able to make use of their discoveries to build constantly better facilities with greater speed and efficiency.

Labor has also kept pace with the development of new materials, new and greater designs. Workmen have had to be continually trained in new techniques while preserving their ancient skills. This has been done under a comprehensive program. American workmen have fully measured up to the challenge.

FIG. 5.—PIPELINE CONSTRUCTION: BOTH CIVILIAN AND MILITARY NEEDS MET BY REMARKABLY SPEEDY CONSTRUCTION; TRACTORS WITH SIDE BOOMS HANDLING LONG SECTION OF LARGE PIPE NEAR BASSFIELD, MISS., IN 1949

The industry is huge in size, and produces an amazing variety of products under every conceivable circumstance, yet its methods and internal organization have developed often with growing pains, until they are of such flexibility that the industry can execute any structural need of the people any place in the world.

By experimentation through the years, and now by cooperation between such organizations as the ASCE, American Institute of Architects, AGC, and many others, there has developed a type of joint, cooperative relationship within the construction industry that best fits its purpose, and that permits fair and equitable treatment of all those who are connected with construction operations.

General contractors, who represent the logical development in the industry to fulfil the need for organizations to take complete responsibility for the construction of projects and to correlate all the skills, materials, and machinery required, look forward to an even greater century in partnership with engineers. The engineer's qualities of skill, imagination, and courage have been complemented by the initiative of contractor in devising new methods, and together a team is formed that today continues its advance toward an ever-expanding vision of a greater United States of America.

AMERICAN SOCIETY OF CIVIL ENGINEERS

Founded November 5, 1852

TRANSACTIONS

Paper No. 2589

LOWERING CONCRETE COSTS BY IMPROVED TECHNIQUES

By John R. Hardin,[1] M. ASCE

Synopsis

Concrete construction has benefited greatly from improved designing, advancing technology, and field techniques. In the office, methods evolved to combat cracking in large dams have succeeded, yielding truly monolithic masses. In the laboratory, improvements have been devised and perfected, especially in air entrainment, aggregate selection, and special cements. On the job, numerous refinements are appearing: In more consistent fine aggregates for the newer concretes; in automatic mixer production, for economy and control; in more efficient handling plant, especially cableways and trestles; and in advanced mechanical equipment, such as vibrators. Thus better products and longer life spell greater economies, as illustrated mainly by the bigger projects. However, smaller jobs also have gained, particularly in improved equipment, largely for transporting and placing concrete.

Typical definitions of economy include the ideas of thrift, saving, husbandry or wise management, and providence—exercising forethought. Obviously, then, economies in concrete construction should be considered from two angles—economies that result, first, in reductions in original cost, and, second, in longer life and lowered maintenance because of superior initial quality. Conceivably, the latter objective may result in a somewhat higher first cost than could otherwise be realized by omitting certain advances in technique. However, wise management and the exercise of forethought—desiderata just mentioned—dictate that minimizing first cost should not be the only goal, if a high level of quality with long life and low maintenance cost in the finished structure is to be achieved.

It is sometimes necessary to draw a fine line when attempting to attain a satisfactory balance between first cost and quality. Nevertheless, it is for this balance that the engineer strives in his attempt to realize the greatest ultimate economies in concrete construction today.

Remarkable progress has been made since the 1920's toward more economical concrete work. Economies in first cost, which in many instances can be closely

---

[1] Brig. Gen., U. S. Army; Asst. Chf. of Engrs., Office of Chf. of Engrs., Corps of Engrs., Washington, D. C.

estimated in dollars and cents, have been realized as a result of improved techniques in design, construction, and concrete technology. Probably more important, however, are the economies resulting from longer life and lower maintenance cost; these techniques have served to produce structures with much longer useful lives and at much lower costs. Such advances were particularly notable during the 1940's, and further improvements are being made today.

IMPROVEMENTS IN DESIGN

One of the outstanding economies in the construction of large gravity-type concrete dams has resulted from an improvement in design. As recently as 10 years ago, it was considered next to impossible to construct a gravity dam more than 250 ft high without objectionable vertical cracking parallel to the axis. Such cracks tend to divide the structure into parts that preclude the normal monolithic action assumed in the design. Undesirable and possibly dangerous cracking had occurred in dams lower than 250 ft. Cracks were caused by the large and nonuniform changes in volume resulting from temperature variations due to heat generated by the cement as it sets and the subsequent cooling of the concrete.

To Eliminate Cracks.—As a remedy, designers attempted to solve this aggravating problem by the incorporation of "designed cracks" into the structure—forming one or more longitudinal joints, depending on the over-all size, to divide the monoliths into two or more parts. With this design it was necessary to provide artificial cooling of the parts of each monolith to the "final" or "stable" temperature. Then, by grouting the joints, the parts were made into one monolith, insuring unified gravity action.

For cooling, extensive pipe systems had to be embedded in the concrete during construction as also did a large grout-pipe system with grout stops. The work of forming the joints, installing and operating the cooling systems, and placing the grout pipes and grouting the joints is expensive. Also, because each item is complicated and time consuming, limitations are imposed on the scheduling and execution of all the other construction operations.

Creating Actual Monoliths.—Even this advanced practice has since been superseded. Now, by virtue of new and proved techniques, it is no longer necessary to use longitudinal joints in large gravity dams. Instead the blocks or "monoliths" are constructed as true monoliths from the upstream to the downstream faces, without intervening joints. The volume changes accompanying temperature variations are controlled within safe limits by a combination of methods. These include refrigeration of the materials to reduce the placing temperature of the concrete; selection of cement having favorable heat-generating characteristics; use of very low cement factors for the interior concrete; and regulation of the construction program to avoid situations conducive to cracking.

Concrete-placing temperatures in very large concrete dams are kept below 50° F; cement factors as low as 2¼ bags per cu yd are regularly used; and either moderate-heat or low-heat cement is specified. The extremely low cement factors have been made possible by the use of entrained air in the concrete, and by proper and uniformly controlled aggregate grading. On two large Corps of

Engineers dams, each more than 400 ft high, elimination of the longitudinal joints and the associated items of cooling and grouting has resulted in saving at least $2,000,000.

These new techniques have successfully removed the danger of cracking (Fig. 1); in fact, even minor cracking has been virtually eliminated. At the

FIG. 1.—CONSTRUCTION OF PINE FLAT DAM ON THE KINGS RIVER IN CALIFORNIA, HAVING TRULY MONOLITHIC BLOCKS, WITHOUT INTERVENING JOINTS; FINISHED STRUCTURE 440 FT HIGH, WITH 2,400,000 CU YD OF CONCRETE

same time, important improvements in quality have resulted, with expected increases in useful life and lower maintenance cost.

DIVIDENDS FROM CONCRETE TECHNOLOGY

Important and appreciable economies in concrete construction have been realized in recent years through advancements in concrete technology. One of the most important is the development of techniques for air entrainment; even a small volume of air in concrete results in marked increase in both its plastic and its hardened properties. Improvements in plastic properties, particularly placeability with a reduced water requirement, coupled with greater cohesiveness of the mix and reduced segregation, have made it possible to save large quantities of cement, to reduce placing costs, and to improve surface quality and appearance. The extremely low cement factors now being used in the interior of large mass concrete dams are only possible by utilizing entrained air.

Benefits of Air Entrainment.—From experience on the two dams previously mentioned, it is estimated that an average of ½ bag of cement per cubic yard of concrete has been saved by air entrainment, or nearly 500,000 bbl. Similar savings in cement have been made on numerous other Corps of Engineers projects since entrained air was adopted for all Corps work about 6 years ago. In that period an estimated 2,500,000 bbl of cement has been saved by this practice.

Entrained air vastly improves the quality of the hardened concrete, making its resistance to weathering and attack by agressive agents many times greater than that of non-air-entrained concrete. Development and application have been so rapid it has not yet been possible to fully estimate the resulting great improvement in quality. It is believed safe to conclude, however, that all other factors being equal, air-entrained concrete will increase the useful life of structures many years and reduce maintenance and repairs very appreciably. Its use for 6 years on Corps of Engineers work alone should result in economies totaling several millions of dollars due to increased useful life and reduced maintenance.

Better Aggregates.—Another important improvement in concrete technology has been the development of new techniques for evaluating the quality of materials. The greatest strides have been made in evaluating the quality of aggregates. For many years arbitrary limits on certain "pseudo" properties such as abrasion loss, sulfate loss, and deleterious substances were relied on to select aggregates. A paradox resulted in that aggregates of good quality were sometimes rejected, and vice versa. Also, because of the uncertainties involved, contractors were justifiably prone to add large contingencies to their bids. Several years ago the Corps of Engineers adopted a procedure which has proved entirely satisfactory and has resulted in large economies—that is, selection and identification of the best economically available aggregates for a project in advance of advertising the work.

New laboratory techniques, including accelerated freezing and thawing, petrographic examination, and tests for alkali-aggregate reactivity, have been devised for determining the relative quality of aggregates. Reliance is no longer placed on the use of arbitrary limits on pseudo properties. Investigations are started in the early planning stage, are carried to conclusion during the design stage, and culminate in the selection of one or more sources which are named in the contract specifications. The work includes an extensive reconnaissance to locate potential sources, a complete laboratory evaluation to assure that the aggregate is of satisfactory quality, and a thorough prospecting of the acceptable sources to establish that ample quantities are available. Also, processing tests are conducted on material from undeveloped sources to determine whether the material can be successfully processed, and to establish the necessary procedures.

All information bearing on costs is made available to bidders. As a result, the doubts regarding aggregates that have plagued contractors and engineers alike in years past are largely eliminated, and contingencies to cover uncertainties are removed from the bidding. Aside from the fact that this is considered to be a sound engineering approach to the problem, the cost of all these investigations is only a small fraction of the contingencies which a contractor might otherwise be forced to include in his bid. Hence, substantial economies are being realized.

Substitute Cementing Materials.—Improvement in the evaluation of aggregates is only one part of the program by which laboratory investigations are effecting economies in concrete construction. In the past, the laboratory has been too often thought of as the place of confinement for the so-called abstract thinker. It and its technicians are now assuming their rightful place in the realm of concrete technology, design, and construction. Economies in both first cost and improved quality are being realized from laboratory investigations.

One of the more important aspects has been the development of special cements and pozzolanic materials for use with portland cement. The objectives are to lower costs, improve the plastic properties of the fresh concrete, reduce temperature changes and the accompanying volume changes, and better the elastic and related properties of the hardened concrete. Among the special cements, two—slag and natural—have been successfully used in several Corps projects in which approximately 6,000,000 cu yd of concrete were placed. An appreciable reduction in cost was realized as well as other improvements. Although pozzolanic materials have not been used extensively in Corps of Engineers work, laboratory investigations now under way, and the experience of others, indicate that large savings in first cost and improvements in concrete characteristics are possible through the use of such materials as "fly ash," treated shales, and natural pozzolans.

Before such materials can be adopted, they must be proved in the laboratory. The use of laboratories in the past has resulted in many savings in first cost; however, the greatest economies realized are in the quality of concrete construction. The most prominent and far reaching of these so far has been the discovery and application of air entrainment.

Advanced Techniques of Construction

The construction industry has demonstrated remarkable ingenuity in developing new plants to realize advancements made in concrete technology. Invariably when new and more strict requirements have been added in the specifications, there has been a negative reaction on the part of the "practical" construction man. His reaction is usually that he "can meet these requirements but it will increase the cost." In some instances this has been true, but it must be realized that the engineer has weighed this increased first cost against longer life and reduced maintenance cost in the finished structure. In many instances, however, requirements which in the beginning appeared to be destined to increase the first cost of the concrete have, in the long run, resulted in marked dollar economies, as well as in vast improvements in quality.

New Limitations, Fine Aggregate.—Specifications for grading and uniformity of fine aggregate have been tightened up in recent years, particularly for large mass concrete dams. Since the advent of air entrainment, specification limits on grading have been set to insure a "sand" somewhat finer than that for non-air-entrained concrete. In terms of fineness modulus, a sand in the range of 2.40 to 2.50 is now used as compared to one in the range of 2.70 to 2.90 for non-air-entrained concrete. The amount of extreme fines—minus No. 100—which is now desired and required, is less, however, than was normally used in non-air-entrained concrete.

In the matter of uniformity, the requirements are such that limitations in grading, expressed in terms of variation in fineness modulus, are very strict. These requirements are essential if the greatest benefits are to be derived from the use of entrained air. Without strict control of grading and uniformity for fine aggregate, it would not be possible even with air entrainment to consistently produce the extremely low cement-factor concrete which is essential to close control of volume change in large mass concrete dams.

Processing for Uniformity and Sizing.—To meet the specifications for grading and uniformity, a more careful approach has been necessary to the design of aggregate processing and handling plants (Fig. 2). In the last 4 or 5 years con-

Fig. 2.—Coarse Aggregate Screening Plant and Storage Bunkers, Detroit Dam in the Willamette Basin in Oregon

tractors have designed, constructed, and operated successfully aggregate plants in which a high degree of flexibility and high rates of production have been the outstanding features. When the strict grading and uniformity requirements of the Corps of Engineers were first put into the specifications, contractors were prone to insist that the cost of aggregates would be excessively high. As experience has been gained, however, two important points have been demonstrated.

1. To produce a uniform aggregate, the rate of production must be uniform. As a result, new plants have been designed to operate at high uniform rates with a minimum of dependence on manual control. High rates of production have resulted in maximum utilization of equipment with a minimum of labor cost. Although difficult to estimate, real economies have resulted as reflected in recent trends in bid prices.

2. Carefully selected equipment reduces wastes in the processing of fine aggregate. In the case of natural sand, new techniques are successfully producing sand with minimum waste. In several cases, the hydraulic sizer is being utilized, which can separate natural sand into as many as eight fractions. An excess in any size fraction can be stored for later use, providing against a deficiency in case of change in grading of the raw material—wide variations being normal in natural aggregate deposits. Without the hydraulic sizer, it is necessary to waste large quantities of poorly graded material; or to use costly excess quantities of cement, an intolerable handicap on large dams, where very lean interior mass concrete is an essential part of volume-change control.

FIG. 3.—ROD MILL FOR MANUFACTURING SAND, ON THE DETROIT PROJECT IN THE WILLAMETTE BASIN IN OREGON

Finer Grinding.—In natural deposits where excesses in the coarse fractions are predominant, another technique is being successfully applied. Grinding equipment—generally a rod mill (Fig. 3)—is used in conjunction with the hydraulic sizer. The excess coarse material is ground in the rod mill and added to the sand to supply fines, in which most sands are usually deficient. The same trends are evident in plants for the production of stone sand. Hydraulic sizers are being utilized, and the newest and most modern plants also use the rod mill as the principal grinding equipment. Many of the recent plants have installed the "center periphery discharge" type of rod mill which, on the basis of experience, has a lower waste factor than the "overflow" type.

The question of whether first cost of fine aggregate that meets the stricter requirements has increased or decreased may still be debatable; however, there is ample logic and growing evidence that the over-all cost has decreased. In any event the advantage of the minimum practical cement factor as a principal means of controlling volume change is ample justification for the rigid requirements, as is the better quality of the structures.

Automatic Concrete Production.—Batching and mixing plants have also been improved in the past 20 years with resulting economies. The most notable improvements—in accuracy, dependability, speed, and efficiency—have been in large central mix plants such as are used wherever volume production is essential.

Fig. 4.—Modern Concrete Production at Pine Flat Dam on the Kings River in California, Showing Mixing Plant, Cooling Plant, Final Aggregate Screening Tower, and Long Aggregate Conveyor

For many years the view was held that batching and mixing of concrete could never be classed as a "manufacturing" process because of the lack of accuracy and efficiency. This view was justified on the basis of operation 25 years ago when volumetric batching was in general use and cement was delivered, stored, handled, and batched in bags.

Mixing plants of that era could be identified by the ever-present cloud of white dust which resulted from the breaking of cement bags. Removing cement from storage, transporting it to the mixing plant, stacking it into "batch size" piles, and "busting" bags for a typical large mixing plant required a large labor crew. Modern plants (Fig. 4) of the "automatic" or "fully automatic" type are capable of continuous high rates of production and accuracy in batching which is equivalent to that of some manufacturing processes. By comparison plants

15 years ago, which were classified as "semi-automatic," required three men besides maintenance personnel. Two of these were "batcher" men and the third was the mixer dump man.

In modern "automatic" or "fully automatic" plants, one man does the work, and production rates average vastly higher. All other operations related to batching and mixing, including reclaiming and delivery of aggregates to the mixing plant; and unloading, storage, and delivery of bulk cement are also accomplished more efficiently and with greatly reduced manpower. These improvements have brought important and sizable economies in production and have resulted in better structures.

Two Types of Plant.—Plant and methods for transporting and placing have also progressed in the past 25 years with consequent economies. As in the cases of production, batching, and mixing, many of the important improvements have been in plants for large volume work. Two types in general use 25 years ago were the "tower and chute" and the "guy derrick." The tower-and-chute type of plant had one major fault—concrete mixes had to be designed to fit its characteristics rather than the requirements of the structure. In attempting to minimize the disastrous segregation that resulted from excessive handling, concrete technicians designed oversanded mixes which required excessive cement. The high resulting cost of the concrete and the poor quality of the finished structures led to the abandonment of this type of plant.

The guy derrick plant was a forerunner in many respects of the trestle-type plant of today. Concrete was usually discharged into a bottom-dump bucket directly from the mixer, transferred to a pickup point on bucket cars, and lifted into the forms by derrick. This plant embodied the basic principle of "least handling is best handling," and in the respect no fault could be found with it. Its basic deficiencies were lack of mobility and lack of speed. Setting and resetting "guy derricks" were expensive and time consuming, and the coverage of each individual derrick was very limited.

At Wilson Dam on the Tennessee River in Alabama 30 years ago, a plant was used which resembled in many respects the present trestle plant. Terry cranes, similar in design and operation to the revolver cranes of today, were operated on track supported on piers which formed part of the dam. Concrete was delivered to the cranes in bottom-dump buckets on service trains. Basically the characteristics of this plant were satisfactory, but it could not compare in efficiency or speed with present-day trestle plants.

Cableways for Distribution.—Two types of concrete transporting and placing plants, with variations to suit job conditions, have come into general use. In the cableway-type plant (Fig. 5), concrete is transported to the cableway "hook" from the mixing plant in bottom-dump buckets on flat cars or by "transfer car" to a bottom-dump bucket on the cableway hook for delivery to the forms. This type of plant has been very successful for many years; however, improvements have been made in its design recently which have greatly increased speed and economy.

By comparison, one of two large cableways operating alone on a large project during the period from 1935 to 1938 achieved a maximum sustained average rate of production of about 140 cu yd per hr with a 6-cu yd bucket. This rate was achieved with the second cableway idle. With both operating, the total rate was limited by the mixing-plant capacity, which was about 180 cu yd per hr. On a large Corps of Engineers project now under way in California, a single "high-speed" cableway using an 8-cu yd bucket has achieved a sustained average rate of production in excess of 270 cu yd per hr.

Advantages in Trestle Plant.—The trestle-type plant of today (Fig. 6) is extremely flexible; and, because several placing rigs can be utilized on a single trestle, greater total rates of production can usually be achieved than with cableways under comparable circumstances. Generally, however, site conditions rather

FIG. 5.—VIEW ALONG AXIS OF DETROIT DAM IN THE WILLAMETTE BASIN IN OREGON, DURING CONSTRUCTION; FROM LEFT, AGGREGATE PLANT, CABLEWAY HEAD TOWERS, AGGREGATE AND COOLING PLANT, CEMENT STORAGE, AND MIXING PLANT

than production rate will decide the choice of plant. Whereas the cableway is more adaptable to the canyon-type site, the trestle is better suited to wide rivers and low abutments.

Concrete for this plant is delivered in bottom-dump buckets on flat cars from the mixing plant to either revolver cranes or hammer-head cranes for delivery to the forms. Economies have largely been made by ingenious use of equipment. On most projects utilizing this type of plant in recent years, the bucket trains have required two men for operation—one dinkey operator and one bucket hooker. On one recently completed project, controls for operation of the dinkey were mounted on the bucket car, and one man performed both jobs.

Better Equipment.—Improvements in the design of bottom-dump buckets, for transporting very dry, low cement-factor, interior mass concrete for large dams, have also been made in the past few years. The new buckets have made it possible to place such concrete efficiently. Their design is based largely on an investigation carried out by the Corps of Engineers in 1946 and 1947, involving design, construction, and field trials. Several manufacturers have designed buckets based on these tests.

One of the features of the new type bucket (Fig. 7) is the "controllable dump," which has largely eliminated the great objection to the cableway as a concrete-placing unit. The discharge of the "controllable-dump" bucket is regulated either by opposing air cylinders or by a double-acting air cyclinder. With free discharge buckets, cableway "bounce" during dumping resulted in very objectionable segre-

FIG. 6.—MODERN TRESTLE-TYPE PLANT, ILLUSTRATED BY BULL SHOALS DAM ON THE WHITE RIVER IN ARKANSAS-MISSOURI, UTILIZING HAMMER-HEAD AND REVOLVING CRANES

gation of dry, low cement-factor cobble concrete. The controllable-dump bucket allows rapid discharge without segregation. Appreciable economies and improvements in quality have resulted.

Probably the most important development in equipment for concrete placing is the mechanical vibrator. In the opinion of many engineers, this improvement is second in importance only to air entrainment. The large placing crews with hip boots and spades, a familiar sight 30 or 40 years ago, standing ankle deep in "wet" concrete (Fig. 8), have given way to small crews equipped with powerful heavy-duty internal vibrators. Placing rates, expressed as cubic yards per man-hour or man-day have been increased many times since the internal vibrator was introduced. Even more important, it has made possible the use of larger maximum-size aggregate and the placing of very dry concrete. Both these features have resulted in great economies in cement as well as in improvements in quality.

Smaller Projects Benefit.—Developments in transporting and placing equipment have generally related to high-rate, large-scale production. Equally important improvements have been made in equipment for smaller jobs. One of the most significant of these is the positive displacement pump for transporting concrete by pipeline, which has contributed materially to economies in placing relatively small quantities of concrete distributed over a large area. This operation, which requires a minimum of manpower, has largely revolutionized certain types of building construction.

Fig. 7.—Placing Dry, Low Cement-Factor Concrete in Pine Flat Dam on the Kings River in California, with New-Type, 8-Yd Bucket, Having Regulated Discharge to Eliminate Cableway Bounce

The familiar picture of a few years back was a maze of confusion—large placing crews spading and spreading the concrete, equally large crews constantly rearranging "duck boards," and scores of "Georgia buggies" moving to and from the mixer. Now there is the ultimate in orderliness. With a fraction of the manpower, the concrete is pumped to its final position through a pipe which is highly maneuverable. Reductions in first cost as well as a remarkable improvement in quality of concrete have resulted. By virtue of a rare mechanical temperament, the pump will not successfully deliver an improperly designed mix, or concrete that varies in consistency over a wide range, or concrete that is segregated. It therefore serves faithfully as a first-rate inspector.

Paving Economies.—Important economies in construction of concrete pavements have resulted from progress in construction plant equipment and procedures. Efficient machine methods for compacting and trimming the subgrade have largely replaced the hand methods of past years. Heavier side forms, and auxiliary equipment for handling and setting forms, have conserved manpower and improved quality. Mixing plants have increased in size and efficiency until, with the largest new mixers, rates of production have been almost doubled over those of 10 to 15 years ago. Plants now in use can produce in excess of 100 cu yd per hr for long sustained periods.

Fig. 8.—Concreting at Wilson Dam on the Tennessee River in Alabama, in 1922, with Chute from Track Hoppers; Concrete Car Above Conveying Typical Wet Concrete of that Day

Mechanical spreaders and mechanical floats have replaced hand methods with improved efficiency and quality. Recent designs have reduced expansion joints and increased the load-carrying capacity of pavements. Air entrainment has also resulted in marked economies and better quality. Surface scaling due to de-icing, nonskid treatments, and weathering has been largely eliminated by the use of entrained air, with the result that pavement life has been lengthened and maintenance materially reduced.

Success Through Cooperation.—Many important economies have thus been made in recent years through improved techniques in concrete construction in spite of a friendly feud between the engineer on the one hand and the construction man on the other. Invariably, when the engineer adds new and more strict requirements in the specifications, the construction man accuses him of being an intolerable theorist who never gives cost proper consideration. Just as invariably, the engineer replies that the construction man has no appreciation of those engineering features that are necessary to assure quality in the finished structure, and that he can put only one value on a structure—first cost. Also, just as invariably, the two work together while appearing to be the bitterest of enemies, and the inevitable result has been and will continue to be better techniques in design and in construction which both decrease first cost and add quality, to the benefit of all concerned.

AMERICAN SOCIETY OF CIVIL ENGINEERS

Founded November 5, 1852

TRANSACTIONS

Paper No. 2590

MANAGEMENT-LABOR RELATIONS IN CONSTRUCTION

By Lester C. Rogers,[1] M. ASCE

Synopsis

Close relationships between management and labor are esssential in the construction industry because great reliance must of necessity be placed on the individual craftsmen and supervisors for sound, quick decisions under widely varying conditions.

Over the past century, partially to offset the power of large employers, labor
has organized into unions that are now instruments of great bargaining and political power. Much of this growth and strength came through the encouragement
of the "New Deal" government of the last two decades.

With the rapid development of the unions came, as might be expected, some
misuse of power and lack of discipline. Probably the most serious problem in
the construction industry has been that of jurisdictional disputes between various
craft unions. Public opinion became aroused to such an extent over these problems that Congress was able to pass the Taft-Hartley Act in 1947. The Act attempts to protect and preserve collective bargaining by restoring to the employer some of his reasonable rights lost under the Wagner Act, and tries to
prevent jurisdictional disputes and secondary boycotts.

Under this law management and labor combined to form a Joint Board for the
Settlement of Jurisdictional Disputes on which labor is represented by the Building Trades Department of the American Federation of Labor and management by
individual members of the Associated General Contractors of America, and by
the organization of various types of specialty contractors. Although there is
much room for improvement, the Joint Board has done much to lessen the losses
of time and consequent losses of money to owners, contractors, and wage earners
alike in jurisdictional disputes. Both management and labor recognize the serious-
ness of this particular problem and are endeavoring to work toward a better
rapport in this and other management-labor problems in the construction industry.

More than a century ago, when the writer's father's grandfather started the
construction of the first lighthouse for the budding lake port 80 miles north of

---

[1] Pres., Bates and Rogers Constr. Corp., Chicago, Ill.

Chicago, Ill., now the thriving City of Milwaukee, Wis., that hyphenated term "labor-management relations" had never been thought of, much less heard, in the sparsely settled and booming area of the Northwest Territory.

Doubtless Great-grandfather Jake simply picked out a few of his neighbors whom he knew were skilled with the saw and square, the stonecutter's tools, or the No. 2 shovel, made a deal with them, and all went to work to build a lighthouse. "Jurisdictional disputes," another unheard-of phrase and unknown problem, were settled before they arose by great-grandfather's assignment of the tasks each man was to do.

Good Labor Relations Essential

Close and sound relationships between management and labor in the construction industry have always been essential. Construction, except in a very few limited areas, is not in any way a line-production or factory process where the artisan performs exactly the same task day after day after day. Therefore in this field, whether in a small concern or a large one, reliance must be placed at all times on the ability of the individual craftsman and the foreman to make quick decisions with good judgment in all sorts of constantly developing emergencies ranging from minor matters to crucial dangers.

The crane operator swinging large loads in a wind (Fig. 1), the steel gang setting and fastening the framework of bridge or building high above the ground, the sandhogs burrowing away below the surface in water and muck held back only by the pressure of compressed air and the know-how of the men, the tractor operator "dozing" a trail along the edge of the cliff, the carpenter throwing in bracing when rain-softened earth loses it stability—all these men together, and each of them separately, have in their own hands in large measure the ability to make a success or a failure of that particular contract. Thus mutual respect, good relations, and above all, intelligent understanding between management and labor in construction are of the greatest importance.

In the early years of the history of the United States the relation of manager to labor was in large degree that of a supposedly benevolent despot with a paternalistic interest in his workmen which covered both his trade and his morals. The carpenter apprentice was bound out in his middle teens for a 5-year period to learn from his master "the art, trade, or mystery of house carpentry." While he was absorbing the "mysteries" of his trade, the young man was prevented by the terms of his indenture from playing cards, dice, or any other "unlawful" game. Ale houses, taverns, and gaming places were not to be frequented; nor was the apprentice to marry during the period of his indenture. To quote,

> "Nor shall he commit any acts of vice or immorality which are forbidden by the Laws of the Commonwealth; but in all things, and at all times, he shall carry and behave himself towards his said Master, and all others, as a good and faithful Apprentice ought to do."

In return for this exemplary conduct, the master contracted to teach the apprentice as long as he could learn, and to provide him with suitable clothing, board and lodging, two washings per day, 3 months of schooling in the evenings of the winter months, and a set of carpenter tools when he completed his indenture. However, the men who had risked so much to come to the shores of this new continent were independent souls who believed in the inherent worth and dignity of

Fig. 1.—Crane Operation, a Key Factor in Successful Construction As Indicated in Laying 72-In. Concrete Pipe on Savannah River Project for Atomic Energy Commission

the individual and who wanted freedom from domination, whether paternalistic or tyrannical.

Early Efforts to Organize

Faint stirrings of opposition to the authority of the contractor appeared in attempts of the master carpenters in Philadelphia, Pa., to organize for the purpose of fixing wages and enforcing a closed shop, even before the Declaration of Independence was written. In 1802, the carpenters of Savannah, Ga., petitioned the legislature to incorporate them into a union so that they would have "equal level and recognized social footing with others."

A few decades later, as the nation grew, men of great courage and skill were pioneering with the same spirit of independence in the development of an industrial establishment which was to make the United States unique among the nations of the world. These giants of industry and finance believed completely in free enterprise and their own individual freedom to follow whatever course of action in their judgment would bring financial success. The only "social security" they wanted was that which came by the sweat of their brow, the hardness of their nerve, and the skill of their hands and brains.

In their drive for success, many of them were ruthless in their tactics with the public, with their competitors, and, most important, with their own labor. Decency, fair dealing, and human rights were frequently brushed aside in the mistaken idea that men who worked with their hands were made of clay inferior to that of the manager. Many an owner believed that the great financial risks he took could legitimately be passed on to, and squeezed out of labor, for, after all, had he not developed the jobs which the men held?

The changing atmosphere of this young country from that of agriculture to that of urban industrialism brought about a more complicated and, of necessity, a more highly organized society. The limitations of urban life brought problems in unemployment. The craftsman, out of a job, could not go back to working his few acres or find a place on his neighbor's farm as he could in the smaller agricultural communities. He was forced to rely on his own meager savings, or on charity probably grudgingly given. His pride was injured and his sense of justice aggrieved.

Belief in a man's individual freedom and constitutional rights was not the sole property of owners and of management. With these many developments and changes in the social and economic structure of the nation, champions of the working man arose to challenge the industrial might and to claim rights for labor.

Thus, even while great-grandfather and his neighbors were setting the masonry for the lighthouse in the free country atmosphere around the little lake village of Milwaukee, the pressures of city life and the effects of the early stages of the industrial revolution were starting a pattern in the seacoast cities such as Boston, Mass., New York, N. Y., and Philadelphia, that would in time cover most of the United States.

The large construction labor unions, as now known, came into being largely in the last quarter of the nineteenth century, and followed the English pattern of organization by craft. In 1881 they banded together to form the American Federation of Labor. A year later Samuel Gompers was elected president of this Federation. No more useful mental exercise and philosophical study, and no more practical wisdom could be recommended to the leaders of labor today than that they study carefully and often the tenets of the labor union policy of Samuel Gompers, especially with reference to labor's position in the political arena.

The growth of the unions was a slow and painful one for many years, fraught with violence, lawlessness, and bloodshed. Fearless and reckless men on both sides spurred on the battle, each group firm in the belief that its rights and its freedoms were being jeopardized and usurped.

Labor Under New Deal

The mushroom development of the unions occurred, of course, with the depression and the advent of the New Deal with its drive for voting power and its unscrupulous and dangerous pitting of class against class. Although the New Deal worked most closely with the leftish mass unions, the pace set by these mass unions and the pressures developed thereby in the rank and file of all workers forced the leaders of the more conservative crafts unions to fall in line if they would not lose their leadership to more radical factions.

Furthermore, under the New Deal, the Federal Government became the chief buyer of construction through direct contracts by its various agencies and through subsidies to the states. Since the New Deal was determined to advance unionism, the Federal Government stipulated in its contracts and subsidies that the wage regulations and job requirements should be the union wages and union regulations of the areas. The pendulum of power had now swung far in the opposite direction from the days of the 1890's.

Some contractors do not employ union labor, but the great bulk of those who work in and around the large centers of population and those who handle large public works contracts at first were forced to, and now in many cases do, use union labor preponderantly.

Every major economic and social trend, such as the growth in strength and numbers of union organization, has both good features and bad features. Mainly in the early days, the growth of the unions tended to improve the standard of living of the working population. To many contractors the existence of a pool of craftsmen, assembled and available through union offices in the larger cities, has been a decided advantage. Furthermore, although there always have been and always will be, many irritations and dissatisfactions in dealing with and working through union organizations, it probably can be said that these same irritations and union demands for high wages have had some tendency to make construction management more efficient and more resourceful in an effort to keep costs within a competitive range in the face of high labor rates and expensive working rules.

JURISDICTIONAL DISPUTES

On the other hand, there are serious defects in the situation. There is no need to outline the unfortunate aspects of the alleged domination of the individual and his output in some areas, or to point out the economic waste resulting from feather-bedding rules of which some trades are accused. The fact that each international union is a collection of autonomous locals often makes it difficult for the international to maintain discipline in all locations.

By far the worst problem which has arisen to plague the owner, the contractor, and the unions as well is that of jurisdictional disputes. These result from technological developments, the introduction of new materials, new methods, and new machinery, and similarity of job types, combined with the not unnatural struggle by union officials and their unions to seize every class of work which, by any stretch of the imagination, they can argue should be handled by their particular craft. For example, untold thousands of dollars were lost 30 years ago by workers, contractors, and owners over the question of whether sheet-metal workers, iron workers, or carpenters should place the then new metal trim and corner beads which were being substituted for wood.

The recent use of steel mesh in walls as a backing for plaster, and in floors as a support and reinforcement for concrete, brings the lathers and the iron workers into conflict. What shall govern—the nature of the material, or the use to which it is put?

Carpenters and laborers long fought over the right to strip forms on concrete work (Fig. 2). The struggle between the electrical workers and the iron workers for the erection of steel transmission towers over many miles of new power line construction has been a bitter one.

These disputes, because of the size and power of the various international unions which are involved, become a battle of giants which not only consume the time and the capital of the owner and the contractor but take many pay checks from the pockets of the craftsmen, who can least spare the money. Also, with the growth of the C.I.O. (Congress of Industrial Organizations) unions containing

Fig. 2.—Concrete Work, Long a Major Element of Conflict, As to What Craft Should Handle Forms; Intricate Saucer Foundation at Syracuse, N. Y., Here Shown, to Support 225-Ft Spherical Steel Laboratory, for Nuclear Submarine Power Tests

construction maintenance crews ready to perform without interunion disputes, these jurisdictional battles are endangering the very future of the craft unions.

The actual jurisdictional rights of the nineteen international unions in the construction field are the result of the initial grant by the American Federation of Labor itself, made when each union joined the Federation, plus various interpretations which have been agreed on from time to time by two or more unions as questions arose. These rights are held sacred by the individual unions.

In the years gone by, the settlement of jurisdictional disputes was considered by the unions to be entirely within their own purview. All efforts by contractors or owners to take part in jurisdictional settlements were refused, except in three localities. The Building and Construction Trades Department of the American Federation of Labor attempted to work out settlements on its own through a national board, which it had established, and later by "spot decisions," or one-job decisions, by the president of the Building and Construction Trades Department.

However, the American Federation of Labor is organized so that each international union is a sovereign power, and in forming the Building and Construction Trades Department within the Federation, the nineteen international unions involved granted to the Department only certain limited authority. This same situation holds true with the over-all authority of the American Federation of Labor itself.

Therefore, the necessary power to enforce jurisdictional decisions which had been or might have been made simply did not exist. For this reason, and because of the constant interplay of the great forces of internal politics among the unions, decisions were delayed and sidestepped with great frequency. The matter seemed almost impossible of solution.

It has frequently been proposed that the easy solution of this unsatisfactory condition is to turn to the noncraft, C.I.O. type of organization, but this involves the probable loss of valuable features of the existing status. For example, there is a pride of craftsmanship developed in the apprentice training and from experience through the years. It may be argued that such pride no longer motivates the craftsman, but unbiased examination will show that it does exist, that it is worthwhile, and that it should be encouraged and developed rather than discarded. As has already been pointed out, reliance on the craftsman in construction—on his skill, experience, and integrity—is a fundamental necessity.

In the past, in only three cities—Boston, New York, and Chicago—have the international unions recognized local settlements of jurisdictional disputes by local boards composed of union and contractor representatives, as binding on the local and international unions. The local boards in these cities have handled the problem with great skill for many years and have never conflicted with the previous national decisions which had been made.

The great swing of the pendulum from the side of the giants of industry at the end of the nineteenth century to the side of the giants of labor unions within the past two decades brought with it the same opportunities and the same tendencies for abuse of power. The American citizen, though, still can and does rebel against undue concentration or misuse of power in any segment of society.

In an attempt to control the situation, in 1947, Congress passed the Labor Management Relations Act, usually known as the Taft-Hartley Act. This law defined unfair labor practices in such a way that it became a necessity for labor and advisable for management to join together in at attempt to solve the problem of jurisdictional disputes.

The law made it an unfair labor practice in a jurisdictional dispute involving a contractor and two unions for any two of the parties to the dispute to decide the assignment of the work in question. Such action in effect would coerce the third member into either doing the work or not doing it, and such coercion is illegal. To assign work legally, prior agreement is necessary between all parties that each and all would be bound by any decision mutually decided on.

JOINT BOARD IS HELPFUL

Thus the industry and the unions, it might be said, by a process of artificial insemination conceived and, after 2 years of severe and protracted labor pains, brought forth the National Joint Board for Settlement of Jurisdictional Disputes. The Joint Board is composed of representatives of construction employers and labor working under an impartial chairman chosen by the two groups. Although the Joint Board has no legal authority in itself, the National Labor Relations Board recognizes the special competence of the Joint Board in settling jurisdictional matters and would doubtless confirm its decisions in the great majority of cases, were an aggrieved disputant to carry the case to the top board.

The bible of the Joint Board is the so-called "Green Book" which contains: (1) A complete copy of the agreement between all three groups which established the Joint Board—namely, the Building and Construction Trades Department, the Associated General Contractors of America, and the participating Specialty Contractors Employers' Association; (2) a copy of the procedural regulations governing its operation; and (3) a copy of all prior written agreements between unions on various jurisdictional cases.

Because of the terms of the Taft-Hartley law, all participants using the services of the Joint Board must sign stipulations agreeing to accept and be bound by the Board's decisions. These stipulations were signed for the unions by the president of the Building and Construction Trades Department, with the intent of binding its nineteen constituent unions. Since the various specialty contractors have traditionally worked on a union basis, their Employers' Association representatives signed for their entire membership.

In the case of the general contractors represented by the Associated General Contractors, the situation is different. The agreement establishing the Board specifically binds only those contractors employing members of the unions affiliated with the Building and Construction Trades Department. Therefore, because the labor practices of general contractors range all the way from completely open-shop operators to completely unionized operators, each individual general contractor who comes within the requirements of the agreement must sign his own individual stipulation.

When a dispute arises, with all factions signed up, the general contractor is given the authority to assign the disputed work to the men who are entitled to it under decisions and agreements in the "Green Book" or, in their absence, according to the usual practice in that particular area. The contractor and the unions must continue to work on this basis while the case is being presented to the Joint Board. When a decision has been made by the Board itself, or by the parties under pressure from the Joint Board, the work is then assigned in accordance with the decision.

If all contractors and unions with jurisdictional disputes would follow through on all phases of this carefully formulated and agreed-on plan, the plague of lost time from jurisdictional disputes would be at an end. Of course, such perfection is to be hoped for, but is seldom achieved. In some instances contractors have failed to assign work in accordance with the correct area practice. In other cases contractors have closed down their work through a mistaken idea of their duty or because of bad feeling. In many cases one union or both unions have walked off the job, sometimes deliberately and sometimes because of lack of control of the local by the international.

Although there have been many defections of this sort, most of them have been minor in the loss of time involved, and they can be overcome to a large degree by better education of both parties as to their rights and duties, and by greater integrity and discipline on the part of the signatories with regard to the moral and practical value of their written word.

There has been one instance of a serious defection from the signed agreement. One group of specialty contractors and the union which these contractors employ gave notice of their intention to withdraw from the plan because of a decision unfavorable to this union. This is one of the nineteen unions supposedly bound by the stipulation signed by the president of the Building and Construction Trades Department. It is self-evident that every decision by the Joint Board must militate against one or more of the parties involved. There must be sufficient moral integrity in the parties to accept adverse decisions when they come if the plan is to succeed.

A withdrawal from the signed pledge, such as has been described, poses many complications and endangers the rights of construction employers and unions who are faithful to their agreement. Architects and engineers, as well as owners, can take action to prevent similar defections by means to be suggested later.

The Joint Board actually has been very effective in reducing the lost time and attendant costs of jurisdictional disputes. It has handled, in the 4 years of its life, some fifteen hundred cases involving work stoppages and many times that number where no stoppage of work was involved. The Board has processed these cases largely through encouraging settlements mutually developed by the parties without resort to expensive legal procedures, except in a very minor number of instances. Perhaps one of its major contributions has been the development of a sound and workable method for the orderly settlement of jurisdictional disputes—one of the fundamental needs in the construction industry. It also has been instrumental in bringing about final settlement and agreement on a national scale of several of the most difficult and long-standing disputes between certain trades.

Disputes Can Be Cut Down

Owners and, more important, their advisers the architects and engineers, can assist in the excellent work of the Board and can aid those unions and contractors who are honestly and earnestly endeavoring to reduce the cost and incidence of jurisdictional disputes.

Most jurisdictional problems arise in highly specialized fields of work, especially in building construction (Fig. 3). When the architect or engineer draws his specifications for the specialty phases of his project, such as the heating, plumbing, or electrical work, he, in effect, sets the pattern under which the subcontractors will attempt to work.

It is not to be expected that the consulting engineer can be aware of all the changes, agreements, and customs with regard to union jurisdictions in the many geographical areas into which his design work takes him. However, if he were to consult with local trade association representatives or experienced contractors in the region before he published his specifications, he might well avoid inadvertent invitations to jurisdictional trouble.

Then, as a very significant step, it is suggested that architects and engineers, in drawing contracts and specifications, include a clause in their contracts, requiring each and every general contractor and each and every subcontractor to sign an agreement to come under the Joint Board for Settlement of Jurisdictional Disputes and to be bound by its findings. This would benefit owners by greatly reducing the likelihood of costly jurisdictional delays. At the same time this requirement would protect both contractors and unions who are seriously trying to make the plan work. It is to be hoped that such a clause might become standard practice in building contracts.

FIG. 3.—ERECTION OF BUILDINGS, A SOURCE OF JURISDICTIONAL DISPUTE AND A CHANCE FOR COOPERATIVE SOLUTION; STRUCTURAL STEEL WORK FOR NEW PLANT, AMERICAN STEEL AND WIRE COMPANY, WAUKEGAN, ILL.

These suggestions are not partisan in any sense of the word but, as a matter of fact, serve the best interests of everyone—the owners, the architects, the engineers, construction management, and the labor unions alike. The Washington, D. C., staff of the Associated General Contractors, the chapter secretaries, or any contractor will be happy to furnish all possible necessary and pertinent data in connection with this suggested advance in which engineers, architects, and contractors can cooperate.

Responsible union leaders recognize the value of good contractor-union relationships in promoting steady work, and they recognize the serious threat of jurisdictional strikes to their unions and to the construction industry. As a recent example, the nineteen general presidents of the international unions affiliated with the Building Trades Department passed a resolution banning picket lines in the case of jurisdictional disputes. This is a definite step forward in preventing work stoppage.

Slowly but with increasing certainty, the unions are coming to realize the responsibility and the dangers inherent in having practically a monopoly of the labor supply. Although their paths seem at times to diverge considerably, there is no question but that the ultimate aims of both the contractors and the top craft-union leadership in the building trades coincide in a mutual desire for a stable, profitable construction industry.

There are hopeful and constructive signs. Both labor and management are constantly working toward more reasonable understanding. The United States needs to be rid of control boards which stimulate wage and price increases instead of stabilizing them. The construction industry needs to be rid of governmental and political interference in the guise of so-called "emergencies." Then, once again, full responsibility can be placed on the unions to put their own houses in order. Contractors and the unions will be free to bargain together without government interference, and increasing good can result.

Union leaders should recognize that living standards are only raised, in the last analysis, by increased production; also they should recognize the inherent dangers to their own cause in a labor government and the need for, and the value to, labor of maintaining a strong, competitive free enterprise.

Construction management and engineers in public bodies and industrial organizations need to be realistic in their assessment of the place of the unions in present society and to realize the forces which frequently coerce union leadership to make decisions and take actions which seem to be against the public interest.

That phase of human relationships which involves the contacts and the contracts between management and labor will always be an intriguing, baffling, and most important problem for the responsible top leaders in labor, engineering, and construction. It is an ever-present problem for which there can be no permanent solution. If approached with integrity, good will, and a desire for real understanding, it is a rewarding and profitable study and will doubtless reappear as a subject for the agenda of the second Centennial of Engineering.

AMERICAN SOCIETY OF CIVIL ENGINEERS
Founded November 5, 1852
TRANSACTIONS

Paper No. 2591

THE MECHANIZATION OF CONSTRUCTION WORK

By Francis Donaldson[1]

Synopsis

Man's conquest of his physical world has depended on intelligent methods and improvements, on development of tools and materials for construction, and particularly on productive application of power—first, hand power, then animal power, then steam, and finally electricity and internal combustion engines. Through this growing mechanization he has accomplished wonders. Although his works do not yet rival some of the early exploits—pyramids and obelisks—or anywhere near equal the Great Wall of China in total immensity, still today's civil engineer is making remarkable records in terms of yield for unit effort expended. Modern examples of machines in earth excavation and transport, in all kinds of rock excavation, in sinking foundations, and in building with steel and concrete, show phenomenal results. The present challenge is therefore in the moral realm—to make civilization not bigger, but better.

Someone has defined engineering as "the art of doing with one dollar what any darned fool can do with two." This definition is true as far as it goes, but it covers only one of the two phases of engineering, the second being to do things that no fool, no matter how well supplied with dollars or man-hours, can do at all.

Nowadays the two phases have blended so that it may be difficult to recognize the distinction between them, but the distinction is there nevertheless. The first phase began before history, starting with the invention of the first tool—probably a hammer. It has continued and still continues to develop with the improvement of tools and the invention of new ones. The second phase began ages later, when man learned how to utilize mechanical power, for then he became able to concentrate power, to furnish large quantities or large continuous flows of energy to a small delivery point, and thus to perform physical feats theretofore impossible. Now of course the blending of the phases, the application of mechanical power to all kinds of tools, has become one of the most important tasks of the engineer.

[1] Vice-Pres., Mason & Hanger, New York, N. Y.

272

A few examples will clarify these ideas. For the first phase, comparisons between ancient and modern construction jobs may be drawn; and, for the second, accomplishments which have only recently become possible may be listed.

First Phase—Ancient

Earthwork and Masonry.—To start, it is necessary to go back some six or seven thousand years to ancient Babylonia. The Mesopotamian irrigation systems, by which the waters of the Tigris and Euphrates were spread over millions of acres of desert sands, must have involved quantities of excavation and fill, comparable to those of the largest modern schemes; the Great Pyramid of Egypt, containing 3,000,000 cu yd of masonry, the biggest individual block in the world until the construction of the Grand Coulee Dam across the Columbia River in Washington, was built about 2700 B. C.; the Great Wall of China, still by far the world's greatest connected masonry structure, containing approximately 300,000,000 cu yd—thirty Grand Coulee dams—was constructed more than a century before Christ.

These projects were all built with primitive tools, long before even the word "mechanization" was thought of. However, they were built, and it would be interesting to compare the required man-hours per cubic yard with those required for similar work today.

The cost records of the Mesopotamians, like King Ozymandias himself, are long since covered by the desert sands, but records of similar projects performed by primitive methods in India in modern times will give some idea of the labor involved. On canal excavation in earth, a well-organized gang consists of a shoveler who loads baskets containing about ⅜ cu ft each, a lifter who raises the baskets to the heads of the bearers, and for a moderate haul—say, 300 ft—three bearers who carry and dump the baskets. This gang should move about ½ cu yd per hr at a labor cost of 10 man-hours per cu yd. By comparison, one man on a modern 12-cu yd carryall scraper will handle 120 cu yd per hr at a labor cost, if maintenance labor is included, of approximately 1/60 man-hour per cu yd—a 120 to 1 improvement.

The construction of both the Great Pyramid and the Great Wall of China involved quarrying and masonry work rather than excavation. Herodotus stated that to build the pyramid required the labors of 100,000 men for 20 years, but John A. Miller, M. ASCE, believes that this maximum labor force worked only during the flood period of the Nile, or about 3 months per yr. Making this assumption and allowing further for periods of building up and tapering off the forces, the labor cost comes to 400 man-hours per cu yd. A similar interpretation of the data reported for the Great Wall indicates a cost of about 150 man-hours per cu yd. It is to be expected that a 480-ft pyramid would cost much more per unit of volume than a 30-ft wall; but, to make another comparison, the labor cost of the 10,500,000 cu yd of concrete in Grand Coulee Dam was about 2 man-hours per cu yd or perhaps 3 man-hours per cu yd if the manufacturing cost of purchased cement is included.

Quarrying.—Vast quantities of stone were quarried by the ancients for their magnificent masonry structures. Until fire setting was invented by the Romans, quarrying was the only known method of excavating rock. The old artisans, quarrymen, riggers, and masons became extraordinarily skilful in the production, transportation, and setting of stone building blocks. They used freely monoliths of sizes and weight which, even with modern machinery, engineers would not attempt to handle today. Three wall stones in the Acropolis of Baalbek weigh 800 tons apiece; the numerous Egyptian obelisks weigh from 200 to 400 tons each.

Monoliths.—For quarrying and shaping stones, the Egyptians used bronze core drills and also saws that cut by abrasion with sand fed to their edges; but how they moved and set these monoliths is not certain. It is thought that they constructed temporary inclined planes of earth or rubble and dragged the blocks on sleds or rollers up the planes and into position. To pull a 400-ton obelisk in this way up a 10% grade must have required a tug-of-war team of about 2,000 men.

Centuries later the Romans moved several large obelisks as well as many smaller ones from Egypt to Rome. By this time they must have learned to use the block and tackle and to apply animal power, but at any rate the Romans reerected the obelisks and made no fuss about it.

Some 1,500 years later, at the behest of the Pope, an engineer named Domenico Fontana lowered, transported, and reerected one of these obelisks. His feat was considered a milepost in engineering construction; and engineers came from all over Europe to watch the operation. His method was to construct around the column a timber scaffold strong enough to carry a number of large fall blocks; to lead their fall lines to horse-driven capstans; and, by simultaneous operation, to raise and lower the 330-ton column onto a cradle. After dragging the cradle on rollers to its new location the scaffold was reconstructed and the lifting operation repeated. Forty capstans, eighty horses, and four hundred men were required.

Probably the biggest job of this kind in history was the quarrying, transportation, and erection, by the Fontana method, of the Alexander Column in St. Petersburg, later Leningrad, U.S.S.R. This monument, which still stands in the Palace Square, consists of a base 24 ft square and 6 ft high, a 20-ft pedestal, and a shaft 13 ft in diameter and $98\frac{1}{2}$ ft high—all of granite, surmounted by a bronze capital and a bronze statue. The stones were quarried in Finland and brought by barge on the River Neva to a point near the site. The base weighs 300 tons and the shaft 1,100 tons. This work, done in 1834, before mechanical power had been applied to construction, was an extraordinary feat, yet it apparently never created a ripple of interest. How many of the engineers of today have ever heard of it?

Rock Excavation.—As understood today, rock excavation was unknown to the ancients, for it depends on the use of explosives. The application of gunpowder to the breaking of rock was really the beginning of the second phase of engineering. Subaqueous excavation of earth or rock was also impossible for the ancients, but they understood the construction of cofferdams and the lifting of water by man, animal, and wind power. One of the earliest tunnels on record was thus built under the River Euphrates.

Mining and Tunneling.—The art of mining, including shaft sinking and tunneling in rock and dry earth, was well advanced long before the time of Christ. Earth was dug and rock chiseled out by hand, at least until the Romans began the fire setting technique. It was not amusing to work in a tunnel in those days: To build a wood fire against the face; to wait until the surface rock becomes red hot; to fight one's way in through the fumes and throw cold water on it; and then to muck the spalled fragments. In comparison, today's silicosis would be a pleasure. Muck was hoisted by man or animal power, or carried up ladders on human backs.

In spite of all these difficulties the Romans built some notable tunnels, the greatest of which was holed through in the first century A.D. to drain Lake Fucino. It has been stated that this tunnel had a section 19 ft high and 9 ft wide, that it was more than 3 miles long, that it was driven from twenty-two shafts or slopes, some nearly 400 ft deep, and that, reportedly 30,000 men were employed for 11 years to build it. It is obvious that even by working four shifts a day it would be impossible to employ 7,500 men on each shift in forty or forty-five headings of this size; so it is likely that the report should be interpreted as meaning that 30,000 different persons worked on the job in 11 years. The labor turnover must have been high and the casualties terrible.

If all shafts and headings were worked simultaneously with as many men as possible and if an employment curve is rationalized, the progress works out to an average daily advance of 3 in. per heading per day, at a labor cost of 300 manhours per cu yd. Compare this with a daily progress on the 25-mile Downsville Tunnel of the New York City (N. Y.) water supply of more than 40 ft a day, and a labor cost on modern hydro tunnels in Scandinavia of 1 man-hour per cu yd to $1\frac{1}{4}$ man-hours per cu yd.

Pumping.—Throughout the ages the handling of water has been one of the most important tasks of the engineer. For this purpose various sources of power other than animal muscles have had their first application—wind, flowing water, and eventually steam. Here again the concentration of power inaugurated by the steam engine opened new possibilities.

Allied with handling water is the finding of it. The evolution from wells dug by hand to drilled wells was slow; the real development of the art of drilling waited on mechanical power.

Second Phase—Mechanization

By comparison some examples may be cited of things the ancients could not have done, some of which may be included in the second phase of engineering:

1. Structures depending on steel in large quantities and in many different shapes—

  (a) Skyscrapers,
  (b) High towers,
  (c) Deep cofferdams, and
  (d) Great bridges.

2. Construction made possible by a concentration of power through the use of steam and internal combustion engines, electricity, compressed air, and hydraulic pumps in various combinations—

  (a) Deep mine shafts and deep mining,
  (b) Deep dredging in harbors and seas,
  (c) Excavation in wet ground requiring predrainage,
  (d) Compressed air caissons and subaqueous tunnels,
  (e) River diversions, and
  (f) Deep drilling.

3. Rapid transportation made possible by concentrated power—
   (a) Railways,
   (b) Automobiles,
   (c) Boats and ships, and
   (d) Greatest of all, human flight.

As mentioned previously, the phases blend. At Grand Coulee Dam the earth and rock excavation could have been performed, the sand and gravel dug, and the concrete mixed and placed by hand, given enough workers and enough time; but no Pharaoh, however powerful and however ruthless, could have diverted the Columbia River between floods. Neither could he have commuted to work in the

FIG. 1.—OLD METHODS OFTEN ECONOMICAL FOR A NEW JOB—MANUAL EARTH EXCAVATION, WITH HAND SHOVEL AND BASKET, ON THE LERMA CANAL, MEXICO, IN 1943, WHICH COST ONLY 7¢ A YARD IN AMERICAN MONEY

morning as do millions throughout the world, including many Egyptians, no doubt. Also, he could not have traveled from Cairo, Egypt, to Chicago, Ill., in 30 hours.

This review of history naturally leads to the idea of the mechanization of construction work. In some detail machinery and mechanical power will be discussed in their application to the branches of the art already mentioned.

Earth Excavation—Equipment for Loading and Transport

Early Tools.—Perhaps the first tool was not a hammer after all, but a crude shovel with which some cave man leveled his sleeping place. The shovel improved with the discovery and application of metals (Fig. 1); the hammer developed into a pick; and, after the wheel was invented, the wicker basket turned into a wheelbarrow and the barrow into wagons and carts drawn by animals ranging from dogs to elephants. Someone combined the ideas of shovel and sled and created the horse-drawn drag scraper, a device that has moved a lot of dirt cheaply in its day. Then, for longer hauls, wheels were added and wheeled scrapers and fresnos came into being. In the flatlands American railways were largely built with these tools.

In thorough cut, in hard earth, and in rock, the picked or broken material had to be shoveled by hand. The best vehicle for this purpose proved to be the two-wheeled tip cart drawn by a single horse or mule. Such a cart can be backed into the cut or to the shoveler and its body is easily loaded through the open back end; but its capacity is small and, except for short hauls, a wagon drawn by two or more horses is a cheaper means of transport. Such wagons are hard to load by hand but have been designed to dump automatically.

Fig. 2.—Elevating Grader, Propelled by Caterpillars, Which Loads About 1,200 Cu Yd of
Fine Sandy Clay Loam per Hour

To meet this problem in soft ground the elevating grader was devised. This consists of a wheeled scraper with a scoop designed so as to discharge its load continuously onto an elevating belt discharging in turn into a transverse loading belt. Drawn by several teams of horses, the grader will deliver a steady stream of dirt to a wagon traveling beside it; and it can move dirt fast—40 to 50 cu yd per hr. The development of the tractor made possible an increase in capacity to 100 to 150 cu yd per hr, loading trucks instead of wagons. Now one company makes a grader which, propelled by two 20-ton tractors, has a capacity of 1,000 to 1,500 cu yd per hr (Fig. 2).

The Power Shovel.—Of course the real revolution in dirt moving began with the steam shovel, invented in 1835 but which really came into use in the 1880's. The first practical model was equipped with a boom which swung like a gate (Fig. 3); then came a boom pivoted beneath and swung from the top of a fixed A-frame —the total swing was thus limited to about 180°. For many years this design was followed. These machines were considered too heavy to put on road wheels and so were mounted on railroad trucks and operated on tracks. Although awkward, they could load any kind of material into any type of car or wagon and were employed in building most of the later railroads in hilly country, in the excavation of the great Culebra (later Gaillard) Cut of the Panama Canal, and in literally thousands of other projects, great and small.

The railroad shovel had several grave disadvantages—namely, the difficulty and cost of supplying the boiler with fuel and suitable water as well as the cost of frequent boiler repairs; the limited range of action due to the fixed A-frame; and, most of all, the cost of grading for, and building track ahead of, the shovel as it advanced. The application, between 1905 and 1925, of two old inventions made possible a different type of shovel which obviated these troubles: The

FIG. 3.—OTIS STEAM SHOVEL, BUILT IN 1837, THE PROGENITOR OF A FAMOUS LINE OF EXCAVATING MACHINES, WITH A CAPACITY OF 1½ CU YD

development of gasoline and diesel engines eliminated the boiler entirely; the crawler or caterpillar track not only did away with track laying but permitted the construction of a base wide and stable enough to support a completely revolving shovel.

The growth in size and capacity of the power shovel has been astounding. From the original model with a 1½-cu yd dipper, it has progressed through the 5-cu yd railroad shovels used at Panama to the 8-cu yd and 10-cu yd giants used today on large excavation projects (Fig. 4) and to the super giants for coal stripping—one of the latest has a 36-cu yd bucket and motors totaling 900 hp, and it weighs nearly 1,500 tons. Power has changed from a locomotive boiler and engine with 8-in. by 12-in. cylinders through gasoline to diesel engines. The larger shovels are electrically operated. Operating controls have changed from throttle valves and levers to pushbuttons actuating a variety of complicated electrical and mechanical devices. The operating cycle has been reduced from more than 1 min to 20 sec to 25 sec; the actual output per hour has been increased from about 150 cu yd to more than 1,000 cu yd.

Draglines.—The rotating shovel made possible a similar development of the

Fig. 4.—A Giant of These Days—Diesel-Electric Shovel with 10-Cu Yd Dipper—Used on Fort Randall Dam on the Missouri River in South Dakota

Fig. 5.—One of Largest Walking Draglines, with a 30-Cu Yd Bucket, Stripping Overburden at Open-Pit Coal Mine, Danville, Ill.

dragline bucket, since a long boom could be substituted for the shovel boom and dipper stick. The original 1-cu yd boiler-plate bucket constructed in Illinois in 1905 has grown to a 30-cu yd monster (Fig. 5), operated on a 200-ft boom. The boom and its machinery rotate like a shovel, and the base itself walks instead of traveling on caterpillars. The dragline has become standard for levee work and similar soft ground excavation in the midwest and south.

Another useful modification of the rotating shovel is the back-hoe boom, which permits the machine to dig a trench behind itself. These booms are now available in sizes up to 1½ cu yd.

Grab Buckets.—The grab bucket, especially the clamshell type developed by Leonardo da Vinci, has evolved into many forms—digging buckets with teeth for trench and cofferdam excavation; rehandling buckets for sand, gravel, and iron ore; and rock grapples. The orange-peel type, however, has remained substantially unchanged. Standard sizes now range from ½ cu yd to 7½ cu yd for clam-

Fig. 6.—Combined Traction—Self-Loading Scraper with Giant Pneumatic Tires; Power by Caterpillar Diesel

shells and from ⅔ cu ft to 3 cu yd for orange peels—the tiny size is used for hand digging in underpinning cylinders. Again the rotating shovel, with a crane boom, is the customary equipment in construction work.

Caterpillars.—The caterpillar track applied to the tractor began a second revolution in earth moving methods. This crawler tractor has become a symbol of power and determination; it will go and pull or push anything anywhere. It draws huge trucks and wagons and self-loading wheeled scrapers (Fig. 6) and, equipped with a bulldozer blade or other attachment, digs cellars, strips topsoil, or overturns forests. The 130-hp, 18-ton tractor has become standard equipment, for it will handle four-wheel scrapers of up to 23-cu yd capacity. This scraper or "pan," with a pusher tractor to help load it (Fig. 7), will move 100 cu yd of earth per hr on a 1,000-ft haul—quite a contrast to the days of the horse.

The crawler-tread tractor is a relatively slow-moving vehicle; hence for long hauls its supremacy is being lost to rubber-tired tractors and self-propelled scrapers. This change has been made possible by the development, largely for airplanes, of huge pneumatic tires. The tractor or scraper is simply provided with enough big tires to carry the load even on soft ground, but it can nevertheless attain high speed on a good road. A modern scraper of this type has four wheels under the tractor end, with tires of 12 in. by 24 in. and 24 in. by 25 in., and two wheels under the rear end with 27-in. by 33-in. tires. It has two 190-hp motors, a hauling capacity of 24 cu yd, and a speed of 30 miles per hr.

Transportation.—Scrapers excepted, digging equipment requires some method of taking the dirt away—tip carts and horse-drawn wagons have been mentioned. The old-time wagon-box body was soon replaced by a body with removable sides and loose slats in the bottom, and then by a body with bottom-dumping doors. When the rotary shovel superseded the railroad shovel and the gasoline or diesel

Fig. 7.—Modern Scrapers Loaded by Aid of Caterpillar Pushers Excavating Cut for Railroad in Brazil, 1949

engine took the place of animal power, wagon bodies reverted to the box type but were pivoted at the rear and provided with an end gate hinged at the top, as well as with a mechanical or hydraulic hoist to tip the body and to load up to a dumping angle. Trucks of this type are now universal and are manufactured in sizes ranging up to a capacity of 34 tons with 400-hp diesel motors.

Railroad-type steam shovels were largely served by railroad equipment. For many years 4-cu yd side-dump cars drawn by steam dinkey locomotives running on a 36-in. gage track were standard equipment; hundreds of dinkeys and thousands of cars were all over the United States. Now they have joined the dodo and are seen no more.

For long hauls and on very big jobs like the Panama Canal, 12-cu yd to 30-cu yd standard-gage dump cars were used. These cars, modernized and dumping by compressed air, are still to be found on certain railroads and in open-pit mining operations.

Today even this equipment has been largely replaced by trucks and by tremendous bottom-dump wagons. In design these are much like the big scrapers already described, with capacities up to 25 cu yd and with engines up to 380 hp.

Conveyors.—Under favorable conditions belt conveyors have been used advantageously for transportation of material. Their cost for actual hauling is very low; but they require special loaders and stackers, and do not take kindly to boulders. At Grand Coulee Dam the main conveyor for excavation had a 60-in. belt, was 1 mile long with a lift of 400 ft, and handled 2,000 cu yd per hr.

Miscellaneous Excavating Equipment.—This review has generally followed American development where digging is a bite at a time. European engineers tended toward continuous digging with chain-and-bucket excavators, and many of this type with large capacities have been employed on canal work. American engineers have used this principle mostly for underwater digging, and for trench-

FIG. 8.—HYDRAULIC DREDGE *New Jersey,* WITH A 30-IN. SUCTION AND 5,000 HP

ing machines. On large pipelines trenching machines are used that will handle 350 cu yd per hr and are capable of digging ½ mile of trench for a 30-in. pipe in an 8-hour shift.

Hydraulic Excavation.—When high-pressure water is available, or water and cheap power, hydraulic excavation is sometimes economical. A water jet directed against the cut with a big nozzle or monitor will both dig and transport dirt downhill. This practice for a long time was standard in placer mining, and the method is now used for trimming slopes on the Panama Canal.

Dredges.—For subaqueous excavation, types of dredges have been developed which correspond to the machines used in the dry—dipper dredges like power shovels for hard digging; clamshells for sand and silt; ladder dredges with bucket chains for sand, gravel, and gold; and hopper dredges and hydraulic dredges for excavating and transporting material that can be pumped through a pipe (Fig. 8). Dippers range in capacity from 10 cu yd to 16 cu yd; and clamshells, to 18 cu yd. The usual gold dredge with 8-cu ft buckets on the ladder has a capacity of about 250 cu yd per hr, but several 16-cu ft monsters have been built. The hydraulic dredge is provided with a centrifugal pump, a cutterhead which breaks and feeds material to the pump's suction pipe, and a discharge pipe usually carried in part on pontoons. A big dredge may have a 30-in. discharge line, capable of handling more than 20,000 cu yd of material per day to a distance of 2 miles, and will require 3,000 hp at the pump and 600 hp at the cutter. Similar pumps are sometimes used in the construction of earth dams. The pump sucks from a "hog box" into which excavated material is dumped.

Compaction of Earth.—Watertight earthen embankments were first obtained by compacting the earth with human feet. Then animals were employed, goats, sheep, and, in India, elephants. Eventually rollers of different types were de-

Fig. 9.—Modern Earth Dam Compacted with Sheepsfoot Rollers—Each Diesel Caterpillar Pulling Four Rollers, with a Total Weight of 40 Tons

veloped. It was found, however, that smooth rollers, no matter how heavy, compacted only the surface of the fill, so "sheeps' feet" were added. A modern sheepsfoot roller weighing 15 tons will compact an area 10 ft wide and will exert a pressure of 640 lb per sq in. on the "foot," some 6 in. beneath the surface of the fill. Such rollers are pulled by caterpillar tractors back and forth over the fill (Fig. 9), previously dumped and spread in 7-in. layers by bulldozers, until the desired degree of compaction is attained. About fourteen passes are required for the cores of earth fill dams.

Where a dam is built by the hydraulic method, the discharge pipes are arranged so as to dump the material on the casings of the dam, the water being allowed to flow to a pond maintained along the axis of the dam and then being pumped out after the solids have settled. This operation grades the material from coarse in the casings to fine in the middle.

Rock Excavation

Power shovels and similar machinery, with trucks and wagons, will load and transport rock once it has been broken. Improvements in the breaking process have followed a separate development. Excavation as opposed to quarrying really began when gunpowder was used in German mines in the seventeenth century, and the art took a big jump forward with the invention of dynamite in 1870. Although blasting methods have of course been improved, the real problem since then has been concerned with drilling holes.

Drilling.—Percussion drilling in rock must have followed closely after the invention of steel. A man pounding a drill with a hand hammer became the symbol of rockwork. Then drill teams were organized with one man to hold and turn the drill, and with one, two, or even three men to pound it with sledge hammers. The use of the sledge became an art; and workmen were proud of their ability to strike hard and accurately down, sidewise, or even up. For down holes a churn drill was sometimes used, a heavy bar raised and dropped by four men standing around it. Even as recently as 50 years ago a large part of the rock broken in the United States was drilled by hand.

With plenty of labor available it was possible to do work in the open quickly by using enough drillers; but, in tunnels, where the area of the working face is limited, rapid progress demanded faster drilling. It was therefore natural that the first mechanical rock drills were developed for two long tunnels, the Hoosac Tunnel in Massachusetts after 1856 and the Mont Cenis Tunnel under the Alps. The European engineers struggled with hydraulic drills or borers, but the American engineers started with compressed air as a source of power. Today it is practically the only source.

Development of the air drill was rapid, and several strong firms were soon actively competing for business. The early models were all piston drills which imitated the action of the churn drill; for down holes water was poured in and the reciprocating drill steel pumped or splashed the cuttings out of the hole most inefficiently. Then, about 1908, hollow drill steel became available, and J. G. Leyner in Colorado was able to make practical a drill which he had invented some 10 years before. This hammer drill washed out the cutting by feeding both water and compressed air to the cutting edge through the hole in the steel. The resulting increase in efficiency soon forced the big drill companies to buy Leyner's patent rights, and the piston drill was no more.

Piston drills had to be rigidly mounted, hence tripods and various types of bars were developed to carry them. In the open they could be, and often were, operated by steam. Hammer drills for down holes in the open are made in sizes that are hand held and require no mountings; for larger sizes the wagon mounting is standard. The guide frame, at first vertical, is now pivoted so that holes may be drilled at any angle.

For deep holes of large diameter in quarries or similar work the churn or well drill is still used. Such drills are now mounted on caterpillar tracks and are powered by diesel engines. The core drill or diamond drill is of course required for exploration.

The development of hard steel for drill bits was unable to keep pace with that of the machine drill; in hard rock half the machine's efficiency was lost by wear and breakage of the cutting edge, so that the handling and sharpening of bits became a major task. In the United States detachable bits were devised which can be changed at the drill and sharpened by grinding. German metallurgists made more durable cutting edges by brazing strips of tungsten carbide to the drill rods.

The development of this type of cutting edge, interrupted in Germany by World War II, was taken over by Sweden. In Sweden, mining and tunneling operations are far ahead of those in the United States in this respect. The increase in drill efficiency is remarkable. In hard granite the best steel bit will be blunted after drilling 1 ft or 2 ft, whereas a carbide bit will cut from 250 ft to 300 ft in the same rock. Carbide bits may be sharpened by grinding with a diamond wheel. The Swedes continue to attach the carbide strip directly to the drill rod, believing that when the bit is worn out the rod is partly crystallized and that it should be discarded. American practice is to use detachable bits with carbide edges. The Swedes also stick to a chisel bit as contrasted with the American cross bit.

In quartzitic rock, drilling, even wet drilling, fills the air with minute particles of silica. These in concentrations of more than 10,000,000 per cu ft may cause silicosis in the lungs of the driller. Good ventilation is therefore essential. For locations where this is not available an oversize vacuum cleaner is built, with its suction hose terminating in a ring around the drill steel at the collar of the hole.

For the soft midwestern shales the coal saw has been modified to saw a 6-in. kerf, 8 ft deep, at the desired boundary of the excavation (Fig. 10), thus making line drilling unnecessary and eliminating overbreak.

Explosives.—Since the invention of dynamite, progress in the art of breaking rock has consisted in the development of explosives producing less unpleasant fumes, such as nitrogelatine with wood pulp as an absorbent, and of flameless powder or other forms designed to meet specific conditions, and in the control of individual explosions. At first all shots were fired with a fuse, cut to lengths that produced nearly simultaneous or successive firings as desired. Then came the electric detonator, enabling a group of holes to be fired at the same instant. This was safer, but required successive loadings and connections for several rounds of holes. Finally the delayed-action exploder was developed, permitting as many as twelve rounds to be fired in succession by a single electrical impulse.

Quarrying.—Such drilling and blasting equipment has been applied to quarrying; and, in quarries producing stone for crushing, its use with big power shovels and trucks has lessened the labor cost tremendously. The quarrying of building stone, however, remains a laborious operation.

Two additional devices have been worked out to lessen labor cost, both harking back to the Egyptians but both power operated—a calyx drill and a wire saw. These cut by abrasion as of old but are now complementary. Two holes are drilled big enough to contain the sheaves around which the wire operates; and, as the sheaves are gradually lowered, the wire cuts a narrow vertical kerf between them.

Shafts in Rock.—Shaft sinking must have been one of the earliest forms of mining activity but it was the last to be mechanized. For centuries broken rock was carried up ladders on human backs; then winches were invented, driven by

manpower, horsepower, water power, and finally steam and electricity. Methods
of drilling and blasting progressed; but, until recently, shafts were mucked by
hand into tip buckets. As a matter of fact the fastest sinking progress ever attained, nearly 450 ft in a month, in South Africa, depended on hand mucking.

Now in the United States clamshell buckets are used to load large shaft
buckets. In one scheme a bucket provided with an independent pneumatic closing
mechanism is hoisted, by an independent engine in or on top of the shaft, only
high enough to dump into the bucket, and is guided and operated by a foreman

FIG. 10.—COAL SAW WHICH CUTS CYLINDRICAL KERF, WORKING FINE SHALE ROCK FROM GANTRY—
FOR PENSTOCK TUNNELS TO POWERHOUSE, FORT RANDALL DAM ON MISSOURI RIVER IN SOUTH DAKOTA

and four muckers on the shaft bottom. Another mucker consists of a clamshell
bucket operated by a traveling crane, its rails being supported by a structural
frame suspended by four cables leading to winch drums at the top of the shaft.

Water handling in shafts has always presented a great problem, and a wide
variety of methods have been used. In brief, the art has progressed from bailing
to pumping of all sorts and from pumping to grouting water-bearing fissures and
thus avoiding the issue.

Shafts in Earth.—At first shafts in earth were sunk by digging and timbering.
Methods of forepoling and sheet piling were devised centuries ago. The difficulty
and danger of such methods really forced shaft sinkers to mechanize, as soon as
mechanical power became available.

The first departure from the early method of shaft construction was the use of hollow caissons which sink of their own weight when the material inside is removed. Brickwork soon replaced weighted timber for building caissons and then concrete replaced brick. The grab bucket permits excavation in the wet until the cutting edge reaches rock or hard ground.

In 1830 Thomas Cochrane, Earl of Dundonald, conceived the idea of closing the top of the caisson and pushing the water away from the cutting edge with compressed air pumped through the bulkhead. This of course required an air lock in the bulkhead to pass men and materials. His bold idea was a success and made it possible to sink and seal caissons in difficult wet ground much more safely.

Generally speaking, shaft caissons will not sink much beyond 100 ft, since the outside skin friction increases until movement stops and cave-ins occur. Since very deep overburden exists in certain European mining districts, other means of sinking had to be attempted. One method was to construct within the first caisson a second, built of cast-iron segments, which was sunk with hydraulic jacks bearing against a ledge attached to the first caisson. Sometimes even a third caisson was required and depths of 400 ft were reached successfully. At several sites the interior cast-iron drum collapsed and the shafts were lost.

To reach still greater depths in Europe, the freezing method was developed. In this process a ring of cased holes approximately 3 ft apart is drilled around the shaft location, interior pipes are inserted, and chilled brine is circulated within the casings for several months, until a huge column of frozen ground is created. The shaft is then sunk through the frozen ground and lined in the open. Scores of difficult jobs have been done successfully in this way, and depths attained far beyond the reach of caissons.

Up to now, American engineers and contractors have been backward in using this idea, and the only job done in this country comparable to those in Europe was the recent sinking of a potash shaft in New Mexico. This shaft penetrated 350 ft of wet rock with unconsolidated layers of sand and silt, and required the drilling by rotary drills of twenty-eight 360-ft holes located on a 31-ft circle around the shaft.

Also developed in Europe to a much greater extent than in this country is the cementation of rock fissures by drilling deep holes and grouting them in advance of excavation. American engineers attempt this, but usually do it less thoroughly.

Tunnels in Rock.—The demand for speed in driving rock tunnels created the pneumatic drill and progress in the art depended for several decades on its development. Piston drills and the heavy columns and arms upon which they were mounted were poor tools for drilling horizontal holes, and hand-mucking gangs could load all the muck they produced. With the rapid improvement of the Leyner drill and the introduction of drill carriages and the full-face method of drilling, mucking became the retarding factor and a demand arose for machines to do it.

In bores as large as railroad tunnels or larger, railroad-type shovels, equipped with short booms and dipper sticks and operated by compressed air, were used even in the heading-and-bench days to load dump cars behind the bench. Today electric rotary-tunnel shovels do the same kind of job; and, when the haul is not too long, diesel-powered trucks often take the place of cars. In small tunnels, shovel loading is not feasible, and beginning about 1915 flip-over bucket loaders came on the market. In general, this type digs by moving bodily against the muck pile; the bucket then casts its load onto a belt which discharges into the car or truck. The 100-hp electric Conway loader (Fig. 11) now has a capacity of 100 cu yd per hr in good digging and will operate in a 12½-ft circular bore. For smaller tunnels the Eimco type loader, whose bucket discharges directly into a car behind, is a popular and satisfactory machine.

FIG. 11.—CONWAY LOADER FOR MUCKING LARGE TUNNEL, FORT RANDALL PROJECT ON THE MISSOURI RIVER IN SOUTH DAKOTA

Greater speed and better safety standards brought forth many other mechanical improvements, of which these few can be mentioned:
(1) Automatic drill feed;
(2) Carriage with drills mounted on booms which permit almost instantaneous setup and movement;
(3) Cherry-picker, or transfer platform, to reduce switching time for cars behind the loader;
(4) Storage-battery locomotives with quick-change batteries;
(5) Cars with roller bearings; and
(6) Powerful blowers, discharging up to 10,000 cu ft of free air per minute through 5 miles of pipe.

Most of these ideas originated in the United States, and this country holds all records for speed in driving rock tunnels. However, although most American tunnel men are skeptical, the Scandinavians do drive tunnels more economically. Today in Norway and Sweden, tunnels in good rock with a cross section of 250 sq ft or more are being driven for a total labor cost of $1\frac{1}{4}$ man-hours per cu yd. The engineers and managers seek economy rather than speed, and favor short headings. The workers cooperate, in that a member of the tunnel workers' branch of the construction union is willing to do, and does do, any kind of job in a tunnel, and the question of jurisdiction does not arise. In 1948 at Vinstra in Norway a long hydro tunnel with a cross section of 325 sq ft was driven from a number of headings, with crews of four men per heading per shift, at a rate of slightly more than 10 ft per heading per day of three 8-hour shifts. At each heading the four men drilled, blasted, and mucked an average of 40 cu yd of solid rock, and in addition laid track, extended pipe and wires, and operated the dinkey to the dump. All drilling was done with jackhammers on jack legs.

Tunnels in Earth.—As in shaft sinking, ingenious methods of timber support for tunnels in earth were devised centuries ago; but where the ground was so wet that inflowing water carried material with it no timbering was adequate. To overcome this difficulty the English engineer Sir Marc Brunel devised the tunnel shield in 1818, and in 1825 began using it to drive a tunnel beneath the Thames. After 17 years of effort and many disasters he finally completed the tunnel. A quarter of a century later another Englishman, James H. Greathead, improved the shield and applied the pneumatic process successfully in driving a second tunnel under the same river.

Today shield tunneling with compressed air is commonplace; and in New York, N. Y., alone there are some thirty-eight subway, railroad, or vehicular tubes beneath the Hudson and East rivers, each tube about a mile long. Greathead's shield has traveled a long way from the Thames.

The plant required for one of these tunnels, especially a vehicular bore, is most impressive. From 7,000 to 20,000 cu ft of free air must be allowed for each heading. For the four headings on the Manhattan side of the Fulton Street Tunnel 28,000 cu ft of compressor capacity was provided, driven by 3,000 electrical horsepower. The jacks used in the shields have 10-in. plungers and work under pressures sometimes reaching 6,000 lb per sq in. Since eighteen are required for a subway shield and thirty for a vehicular, the hydraulic pump and accumulators must be large.

Subaqueous tunnels are lined with bolted segments, usually of cast iron. Each segment weighs from 1,700 lb to 3,000 lb, so an hydraulic erector pivoted on the center line of the shield is used to install them. Hydraulic and pneumatic bolt tighteners do the heavy work of bolting the segments together.

Usually muck taken in through the shield pockets is moved to the shaft in cars. At the Sumner Tunnel under Boston (Mass.) harbor, the excavated clay was transported from the heading to the disposal bins by belt conveyors in the tunnel and by a scraper conveyor up the shaft. An ingenious double-barreled lock with gates and air valves that opened and closed automatically was used most successfully to carry the stream of muck through the air bulkhead.

Foundations

Deep foundations are essentially modern. The ancients had to rely on the ground as they found it, and bad guesses as to underlying material damaged or wrecked innumerable great edifices. With mechanical power came the ability to penetrate, to reach a firm stratum—either by boring for explorations, by deep pile driving, or by shaft sinking methods for support. Foundation failures have become relatively rare.

FIG. 12.—TWO RIGS FOR DRIVING BATTER PILES, AT ALAMEDA AIR BASE, OAKLAND, CALIF.; LARGER HAVING 96-FT LOADS AND WEIGHING 85 TONS

Pile Driving.—Piles were driven in ancient days by hand power and later, after the invention of leads, by tripped drop hammers raised by winches. Penetration and supporting power remained low until the steam hammer was adapted to pile driving. Then it became possible to drive practically any wooden pile that could be obtained and depths of 80 ft to 100 ft were reached frequently.

Large leads were developed to handle a heavy hammer and long piles (Fig. 12), their bed frames moving forward and backward on greased rollers, and sliding sidewise. Now leads are usually carried on a rotating frame, similar to that of a power shovel, and mounted on wheels or caterpillar treads. For water work they are carried on a scow.

Two types of hammers are in use, the Vulcan, a long-stroke single-acting machine in which the steam only lifts, the hammer falling of its own weight, and the McKiernan-Terry or double-acting type. The former is generally used on large wooden piles, the latter on steel piles and sheet piling.

Construction Records.—Unlike other branches of construction work, progress in pile driving has not improved much since the steam hammer was perfected, although man-hours per pile have been reduced. For wood piles the record was made in 1918 at Hog Island in the Delaware River below Philadelphia, Pa., when one crew drove two hundred and twenty 65-ft piles an aggregate length of 14,300 ft, in 9 hours.

Other types of piles developed in the last three or four decades are: The H-beam pile; the blown-out pipe pile; the drilled-in caisson, combining drilling and driving; various concrete piles; and, most important of all, the interlocking steel sheet pile, which makes possible open excavation to much greater depths than before. One of the box cofferdams for the George Washington Bridge across the Hudson River between New York and New Jersey was 85 ft below the water surface at the deepest point.

In addition to cofferdams of various types, caissons, open and pneumatic, are particularly suitable for bridge pier foundations. The limit of compressed air work remains at a little more than 100 ft below the water surface, but many open caissons in suitable material—silt or soft clay—have been dredged to much greater depths. One of the Tacoma (Washington) Bridge caissons went down to −225 ft.

Building Construction

Considering actual structures, the moderns excel the ancients in the use of only two materials—structural steel and concrete. Structural steel, of course, is a product of mechanized factories and did not exist previously. In the uses of concrete, its design and control, and in the speed at which it is produced and placed, today's engineers have gone far beyond the wildest dreams of the builders of old.

Steel.—Erection methods have changed little since structural shapes became available—guy derricks for buildings and various kinds of travelers for bridges. The use of air hammers for driving rivets has become universal. Autogenous welding by gas or electricity is overcoming its early faults and is being used more and more in steel fabrication of all kinds. The big advance has really been in the production of more useful sections, which the Gray mill, invented in England and brought to the United States in 1904, made possible. Nowadays 36-in. rolled girder beams weighing 300 lb per ft and H-columns with a cross section of 125 sq in. are in common use.

Concrete.—The increasing use of concrete has necessitated the development of so many appliances that space permits only a brief list:

   a. Rock crushing and screening plants with capacities up to 1,000 tons per hr. A big primary breaker has jaws with a 5-ft. 6-in. by 7-ft 0-in. opening and weighs 280 tons.

b. Automatically controlled conveyors for handling all materials in the plant and thence to the batcher plant.

c. Pneumatic equipment for unloading bulk cement from cars, storing it in silos, and delivering it to the batcher.

d. Automatic weighing and recording batchers which control the ingredients of each batch of concrete within 2%.

e. Improved mixers—stationary, with tilting conical drums for central plants, up to the 6-cu yd size; truck mounted, for delivering concrete over wide areas, water being added and mixing carried on en route; caterpillar mounted, with tandem drums for rapid paving; and others for special purposes.

f. Devices for handling concrete to the form—caterpillar cranes; long-boom whirler cranes on tracks; giant cantilever cranes; cableways; Rex pumps; and pneumatic blowers.

g. Pneumatic and electric vibrators for compacting concrete.

h. Refrigerating equipment and freezing plants for chilling aggregates and mix water. Someone said that every yard of concrete now placed in a major dam has to have a college education.

Incidentally the Grand Coulee Dam still has the record for fast pouring and is likely to keep it for some years to come. In October, 1939, 530,475 cu yd were placed.

Summary

Certain phases in the history of construction work have been recounted, together with the development of their mechanization. It has been shown how animal power was replaced by steam and steam by internal combustion engines and electric motors; how the invention of new equipment has tremendously increased the efficiency of all tools both new and old; and how machines for handling large quantities of materials themselves grow bigger and bigger. However, what may not have been emphasized is that the rate of improvement and development of things mechanical has increased in recent years. Progress today is on the fast rising part of the logistic curve.

In short, modern engineering is acquiring the ability really to rebuild the earth and the question arises: "How do we want it rebuilt in order to make it a better place to live?" Certainly restoring wasted soil, conserving forests, purifying waters, and eliminating dreadful slums are all on the right path. However, if all this effort merely covers urban areas with skyscrapers and factories and the countryside with transmission towers and concrete superhighways; if it only converts all the rivers into chains of lakes by building more and greater dams; then, no matter what the noble purpose, the gain is indeed of doubtful value. It is high time for engineers in general and construction men in particular to ask themselves: "Where are we going?"

AMERICAN SOCIETY OF CIVIL ENGINEERS

Founded November 5, 1852

TRANSACTIONS

Paper No. 2592

WORLD'S BEST HIGHWAYS THROUGH MODERN EQUIPMENT

By A. N. Carter,[1] A. M. ASCE

Synopsis

Modern equipment has had a tremendous effect on the development of the excellent highway system now found in the United States. The influence of mechanization on highway building has been profound as indicated by tracing the evolution of various types of equipment. An important role has been played by professional and governmental groups in fostering better highways.

Further improvements in economy are feasible, in such matters as designs and standards, equipment and materials, mechanization, and building programs—indeed, in all facets of a large integrated industry. Engineering and construction together can meet the challenge.

Introduction

Need for Mechanization.—Development and skilful use of modern construction equipment have permitted the United States to build by economical methods the world's best system of highways. The extensive use of the automobile by Americans in their daily lives and the great area of this country have created the tremendous demand for improved roads.

This need has been met by much pioneer work in planning, designing, and constructing highways. No small part of this pioneer effort has been devoted to the development of more satisfactory construction machinery and the more effective use of this equipment. The continuous upward spiral of wages and the continuous increase in highway engineering standards and specifications have demanded increased mechanization. As a result of these several factors, highway contractors in the United States are now using equipment and methods that are attracting world-wide attention.

The Effect of Mechanization.—Only through mechanization could such outstanding accomplishments as the world record for the continuous placing of concrete have been accomplished. This record was made when 26,700 cu yd of

---

[1] Mgr., Highway Div., Associated Gen. Contractors of America, Inc., Washington, D. C.

concrete for the seal of the east anchor pier of the new Delaware Memorial Bridge, across the Delaware River between New Jersey and Delaware, was placed in 7.4 days. Another outstanding record was the construction in 1950, by one paving crew, of 4,700 lin ft of 11-ft-wide concrete pavement in 1 day, and the construction by a number of contractors of the 118-mile, $255,000,000 New Jersey Turnpike in 2 years. The New Jersey Turnpike included 52,000,000 cu yd of earthwork, more than two hundred and sixty structures (of which five were major bridges), and 7,000,000 sq yd of pavement.

Because these accomplishments have resulted from the many recent advances in highway construction equipment, it is appropriate to review the evolution of such equipment and its influence on road-building methods. The development of today's economical construction procedures cannot be credited to any one group; rather it is the result of the combined efforts and cooperation of the engineering profession, public officials, the manufacturing industry, equipment distributors, producers of materials, labor, and the contracting profession.

This joint effort has paid big dividends, and without it the cost of highways would be prohibitive. The ingenuity and cooperation of all segments of the highway industry have been necessary to provide the tremendous mileage of American highways with the limited funds that have been available.

ROAD CONSTRUCTION EQUIPMENT

Rollers.—The changes in road construction equipment in the past 50 years have been revolutionary. The pages of history reveal the following highlights: One of the first machines built especially for highway construction was the roller, which was designed to aid in compaction. Some rolling equipment may have been used in constructing the Roman roads, but the first major practical application of rolling equipment appears to have been made by French engineers in 1829. The first application in England was recorded soon after this date.

In 1865 a steam roller was designed and built by Gellerat and Company of Paris, France. The steam-powered three-wheeled roller, much similar to that in Fig. 1, was first manufactured in the United States in the 1880's by the Harrisburg Foundry and Machine Company, Harrisburg, Pa. Tandem rollers were developed about the same time. In 1908 the Kelly-Springfield Company, Springfield, Ohio, designed and built the first gasoline-powered tandem roller produced in the United States. Today one takes for granted the excellent American-made rollers, which feature four speeds forward and four in reverse, high-speed transmissions, low-pressure hydraulic steering systems, all-welded steel frames, and high-speed heavy-duty engines, either gasoline or diesel.

Earth Movers.—A United States patent on a self-loading cart was issued as early as 1850, and United States patents were granted for wheeled scrapers in 1884. The earliest type of carrying scraper (Fig. 2) did not appear until after 1900. About 1924 the self-propelled scraper was placed in service. A United States patent for a road grader was issued to A. Kimball as early as 1855. In 1863 another was issued to C. W. Pisgah of Ohio.

What may have been the first factory-produced American blade grader was constructed in 1879 by the Western Wheeled Scraper Company, Fairfield, Iowa.

FIG. 1.—EARLY STEAM ROLLER ON ROAD JOB NEAR GENEVA, N. Y.

FIG. 2.—CARRYING SCRAPER (1930)

A curved blade was suspended beneath a conventional wagon box and large hand levers were employed to raise and lower the blade.

A steel-frame, reversible-blade grader (Fig. 3) was manufactured in 1888 by the F. C. Austin Company, Chicago, Ill. However, not until 1922 or perhaps shortly before, were rubber tires used on graders, and in 1924 the self-powered grader appeared. In 1927 the first dual-drive power grader was produced at Harvey, Ill. Roughly 10 years later, the all-wheel drive and the all-wheel-steer power grader were introduced.

One of the first bulldozer blade attachments in this country was used at about the turn of the century on a project of Foley Brothers, pioneer railroad builders. This firm attached an improvised bulldozer blade to a steam-traction engine. In

Fig. 3.—Horse-Drawn Blade Grader

1915 the Western Wheeled Scraper Company was manufacturing what was perhaps the first factory-built bulldozer. It was operated with the power from two horses or mules.

More than 100 years ago the first power shovel was built, a crude rig powered by steam (Fig. 4 being a later model), in tremendous contrast to today's shovels, which include a crawler-mounted unit handling a 50-cu yd bucket.

The earliest American self-laying track-type tractors appeared soon after 1900. One of the first was constructed at Stockton, Calif., about 1905. That machine moved in a manner suggesting a crawling caterpillar; hence the name "caterpillar" tractor, which was registered as a trademark and has become world famous.

Improvements.—The twentieth century was well advanced before the appearance of what has been termed modern equipment. However, then things began to happen fast and American equipment was revolutionized. In the 1920's horsepower and mule power were replaced by the gasoline engine.

In the early 1930's construction costs were further reduced by substituting diesel power for gasoline. In the late 1930's costs were lowered still more by the use of rubber tires, the development of rigs of greater speed, improvements in ease and safety of operation, and the production of units of greater capacity.

EQUIPMENT DEVELOPMENT

Standardization.—As more types of equipment were developed and placed in service, standardization became a problem. The Associated General Contractors of America, Inc. (AGC), in cooperation with other groups, has worked hard on

FIG. 4.—STEAM SHOVEL AND BOTTOM-DUMP WAGONS ON ROAD JOB (1914)

this job. Much of the early work was aimed at standardization of concrete mixers. The first standards officially sponsored by the AGC were published in 1924. Before that time, the determination of size was left to the manufacturer. It is recorded that there were some twenty different sizes of building mixers and ten different sizes of paving mixers. The cost of producing such a diverse line is obvious, and the promotional efforts of the manufacturer were often more confusing than instructive. Since then there have been twenty revisions of these standards. The spacing of sizes is so designed that one size takes up where another leaves off, and there are no needless intermediate sizes. The manufacturer must guarantee a certain minimum capacity under standard rating conditions.

Similar standardization has since been applied to numerous other types of contractor's equipment, such as self-priming centrifugal pumps, shovels, cranes, truck mixers, agitator trucks, and air compressors.

Improvements Still Needed.—Despite the many important improvements made in construction equipment in recent years, contractors are seeking additional progress. Advancements they would like to see include: More flexible equipment; more refinements on equipment; higher speed in machines; equipment that is easier on the operator; units that can produce for longer periods without shutdowns for repair or maintenance, other than routine work; machines of lighter weight; units requiring fewer operators, in view of the high wages paid today's skilled and unskilled workers on highway construction; greater ease in maintenance and repair of equipment; and greater standardization of repair parts and of the actual equipment itself.

Cooperation Leads to Progress.—Mechanization, combined with the resourcefulness of engineers, equipment manufacturers, and contractors, and their zeal to complete each project more quickly and at reduced costs have resulted in development of the world's greatest highway system. The highway engineering profession is to be congratulated on the spirit with which it has tried new materials, improved designs, and introduced scientific methods. Great credit also is due the contracting industry. A few decades ago construction methods were crude and simple, and the premium for good management was not too high.

Construction Costs

With today's huge investment in equipment, the high wage rates for all crafts, and high standards of performance set by the engineers in charge, contracting management demands top-caliber superintendents and project managers. Without such people the contractor is soon out of business. The low cost of highway construction over the years proves that both engineers and contractors have met the challenge successfully.

Influence of Equipment.—When engineers of the Bureau of Public Roads, United States Department of Commerce, were asked to comment on the influence of the use of equipment on highway construction costs, as revealed by the Bureau's index for excavation, they reported as follows:

"Since the Bureau's index was started we have made a continuous study of the contractors' cost as determined by wage rates and the price of equipment and materials, plus other factors. Over the years there has been a continued rise in labor rates, in the price of equipment and materials, and in the contractors' overhead. If these increases had not been offset by the development and skillful use of modern construction equipment, road excavation costs today would be about three times as great as they actually are."

This analysis is borne out by the price trend for common excavation. The Bureau of Public Roads (BPR) index, started in 1922, is based on the average of all federal-aid projects awarded by all the state highway departments. The base period for the BPR index is the 5-year period from 1925 through 1929. The composite mile is assumed to require 17,491 cu yd of excavation, 3,726 cu yd of paving, 16,000 lb of structural steel, and 68 cu yd of structural concrete.

The BPR index shows that in the 18-year period from 1922 to 1940 common excavation costs were reduced continuously, as shown by Fig. 5. In the early 1940's construction prices had to rise as a result of the impact of World War II, greatly increased wage rates, higher prices for materials, shortage of equipment, and decreased efficiency of labor. However, the national average for common excavation for the calendar year 1951 is lower than that for 1923, the second year of the BPR index. The index figure for the calendar year 1923 was 133.3, and that for the calendar year 1951 was 111.3, or 15.2% lower.

FIG. 5.—VARIATION OF EXCAVATION AND LABOR COSTS

The continued decrease in the cost of common excavation was obtained despite the continued increase of refinements in specifications and engineering designs.

In contrast to the reduction of the cost of common excavation, wage rates on road work climbed continuously during the same years. Table 1 which was supplied by the BPR, gives the average hourly wage rates for unskilled labor on all federal-aid projects. The national average, which was $0.38 for 1923, in 1951 had skyrocketed to $1.27, an increase of 243%. Moreover, today skilled labor is

TABLE 1.—AVERAGE WAGE RATES PER HOUR ON FEDERAL-AID HIGHWAYS

Calendar year	Hourly rate	Calendar year	Hourly rate	Calendar year	Hourly rate
FOR SKILLED LABOR [a]		FOR UNSKILLED LABOR		FOR UNSKILLED LABOR	
1947	$1.68	1929	$0.39	1941	$0.48
1948	1.82	1930	0.39	1942	0.58
1949	1.98	1931	0.36	1943	0.71
1950	2.03	1932	0.32	1944	0.74
1951	2.25	1933	0.38	1945	0.78
FOR UNSKILLED LABOR		1934	0.42	1946	0.83
1922	$0.32	1935	0.41	1947	0.91
1923	0.38	1936	0.40	1948	1.02
1924	0.39	1937	0.40	1949	1.13
1925	0.38	1938	0.40	1950	1.19
1926	0.38	1939	0.42	1951	1.27
1927	0.39	1940	0.46		
1928	0.40				

[a] Data available for 5 years only.

used on many operations on which unskilled labor was employed in the past. The variation in the highway excavation index as compared with the average unskilled wage rate also is shown in Fig. 5.

Unfortunately, data regarding wage rates for skilled workers are available for only 5 years. The rates for these years, as taken from BPR records, are included in Table 1. The table shows that, whereas the skilled-labor rate rose 28% during this period, unskilled rates jumped almost 40%.

Future Construction.—Today, America's highways are woefully inadequate. The country's road construction needs are placed at between $40,000,000,000 and

$60,000,000,000. Indications are that the American highway user is willing to invest more for highway improvements, as proved by the fact that additional financing for road construction at the state level has been secured in more than thirty states since 1945. The outlook for an increased road program is bright, but close cooperation of all groups interested in road construction will be required if the job is to be accomplished effectively.

ROLE OF THE ASSOCIATIONS

Highway contractors in the United States, by working through their state organizations and the national office of AGC, are continually striving to develop more economical construction procedures and practices (Fig. 6). Much of this

FIG. 6.—MODERN ELEVATING GRADER AND POWER WAGONS

work is being accomplished through cooperative committees set up jointly with other organizations.

For example, much of the work of the Joint Committee of the ASCE and the AGC pertains to highway construction. The ASCE representatives include a nationally known highway consulting engineer. The AGC members include two highway contractors, both of whom have served as national presidents of AGC, plus two members from firms that do extensive highway work.

The work of the ASCE-AGC Joint Cooperative Committee has included projects aimed at securing:

(1) Higher salaries for engineers, particularly those employed by state highway departments and other highway agencies.

(2) Better training for student engineers through improved courses dealing with construction and summer employment by contractors on construction projects.

(3) Improved specifications and planning for all types of construction, including highway work.

(4) Allotment by defense agencies of sufficient supplies for construction programs of major importance to the national economy and to national defense, particularly highway transportation.

The AGC also works closely with highway engineers throughout the United States to secure more economical construction practices and methods. This program is spearheaded by the Joint Cooperative Committee organized in 1921 between the American Association of State Highway Officials and AGC. Some projects of this group are similar to those arranged with the ASCE, but in addition include continued work to secure more satisfactory public relations programs in connection with highway operations. Also, considerable work has been done to obtain more uniformity in state regulations regarding the transportation from job to job of large road-building machines. When increased uniformity is obtained, benefits to the contractor will follow; and he in turn will be able to submit lower bids, and the state departments to secure more economical prices.

Contractors are cooperating with highway departments on a program to obtain constitutional amendments to protect highway user funds for highway improvements. Such amendments are still needed in twenty-five states.

The AGC works closely with the Bureau of Public Roads and the Highway Research Board in an attempt to develop better and more satisfactory construction procedures and practices.

Joint cooperative committees between the AGC and both the Associated Equipment Distributors (AED) and the Construction Industry Manufacturers Association (CIMA) have been in operation for a few years. Cooperation with AED and CIMA is aimed at securing improved equipment for all types of construction operations and in making most effective use of that now available. Much has been done to standardize procedures for purchase and distribution of replacement parts, to fix the rated capacities of different equipment, and to pass along to manufacturers the suggestions of contractors on how the design of various machines might be improved. In the work of all the joint cooperative committees, the aim has been to get the maximum benefit from every construction dollar.

Investment in Equipment.—The highway contractor's investment in construction equipment is large. Thomas H. MacDonald, Hon. M. ASCE, then Commissioner of the Bureau of Public Roads, not long ago stated in a public address that studies by his staff showed that generally the contractor's investment in equipment on a road job was about 90% of the amount of the contract. In other words, on a $100,000 job he might be using $90,000 worth of equipment.

Because of the contractor's large investment in equipment, a few suggestions are listed as to steps that might be taken by highway engineers and officials to permit contractors to operate more effectively and thereby submit lower bids to awarding agencies:

1. Permit the contractor free use of new types of equipment.

2. Be sure land is available and the job ready for the contractor to move in and start work when bids are opened.

3. Use local construction materials as much as possible. (This will also reduce the cost of materials.)

4. Prepare designs that will permit maximum use of the splendid construction equipment now available.

5. Cut hand labor to a minimum.

6. Award programs in contracts of various sizes.

7. Work for greater standardization of design so as to obtain savings, for example, through the use of the same type of bridge forms in neighboring states.

8. Use specifications without revision for as long a period as feasible and practicable; that is, do not change the general specifications each year, and when they are revised obtain the contractor's suggestions by contacting his state organization.

9. Make the specifications of neighboring states as uniform as possible. Contractors see no need for one state to specify that all batches of concrete be mixed for at least 2 min and for a nearby state to specify a 1-min minimum mixing period.

10. Utilize to the fullest extent each year's construction season so as to permit maximum use of the contractor's equipment and personnel, and thereby get better prices.

11. Endeavor to set up a balanced construction program. For example, if a highway department schedules a large volume of black-top work for one year and none the next, it will be difficult for the construction industry to keep in step, and higher prices will result.

12. Pay the contractor promptly for completed work and reduce to a minimum the retained percentage on partial payments; the financial responsibilities of the contractor are extensive.

CONCLUSION

A tremendous challenge lies ahead in meeting the highway needs of the United States. It is the belief of the AGC that the civil engineering profession and the construction industry, through cooperative effort, will meet that challenge in a commendable manner and thereby make the United States a stronger nation and a better country in which to live.

AMERICAN SOCIETY OF CIVIL ENGINEERS

Founded November 5, 1852

TRANSACTIONS

Paper No. 2593

SPEEDY AND ECONOMICAL CONSTRUCTION THROUGH MECHANIZATION

By Harold W. Richardson,[1] M. ASCE

Synopsis

The American construction industry has a challenging background—the notable edifices and large projects of antiquity, colonial days, and the national expansion period. Earth moving, being a major factor, has advanced by leaps and bounds, with steam power and now with gasoline and diesel engines spelling out the steps. Crawler treads and rubber tires were only slightly lesser factors. World War II showed that the industry could meet the crisis and acquit itself with glory. All these accomplishments were largely based on efficient and dependable mechanical devices, products of native ingenuity. With such potentiality the future of American construction, despite new hazards, is assured.

Back in the dim dawn of history, 100,000 Egyptian slaves toiled and struggled for 30 years to place 3,000,000 cu yd of masonry in the Great Pyramid of Cheops on the banks of the Nile. Today, about 1,500 American construction workers place that same amount of masonry in Hungry Horse Dam on the South Fork of the Flathead River in Montana in less than 30 working months—and they do not have to toil or struggle, either. That achievement represents the triumph of mechanization of the construction industry.

Nevertheless, had the Pyramid of Cheops been built at the start of the ASCE Centennial period in 1852, the construction operations would have differed but little from those of ages ago. To be sure, mules and oxen might have replaced slave labor for hauling, but the principal power applied to construction would still have been the muscles of man.

Construction Marvels of Old.—Before the mechanized marvel of modern construction is gloated about, it is fitting to pay tribute to the builders of old. With only a superficial knowledge of the principles of the wheel, lever, and pulley, those ancient stalwarts built such wonders, in addition to the Pyramids, as the Great Wall of China, the vast irrigation works of the Tigris, Euphrates, and Nile

---

[1] Editor, *Construction Methods and Equipment,* New York, N. Y.

valleys, the Hanging Gardens of Babylon, the Roman aqueducts and the Roman roads, the Colosseum at Rome (Fig. 1), and the Grecian palaces—all projects to make engineers mighty proud, had they been built today.

Since the day when man crawled out of natural caves and built his first abode of poles and animal skins, construction has been the mark of civilization. As civilizations rose, prospered, and fell through the ages, their construction glories rose and died with them. The ancient splendors of China, Egypt, Araby, Greece, Rome, and Mexico were based on construction achievement as were the medieval splendor

FIG. 1.—HISTORIC STRUCTURE, BUILT FOR PERMANENCE—RUINS OF THE COLOSSEUM IN ROME, WHICH WAS ARRANGED TO SEAT 107,000 SPECTATORS

of France and Germany and even the start of American civilization, especially during the first century of the republic's life. Also, the construction wonders that took place during the nineteenth century cannot be overlooked—the canals, bridges, roads, and railroads that pushed the United States through the wilderness.

Engineers of this modern mechanized construction world look back on all this with awe and admiration, not knowing how the pioneers built so boldly and so well with what they had to work with. Those who now take powerful construction juggernauts and mechanized tools all as a matter of course, can but wonder how their forebears built so well with human brawn, supplemented only in part by animal power.

Pioneering Steam Shovels.—William Smith Otis might be called the father of mechanized construction, for when a youth only 20 years old in 1836 he applied for a patent on the first steam excavator, forerunner of the modern power shovel. Young Otis really started something, for the construction equipment industry has now grown to produce machines, tools, and parts valued in 1951 at nearly $1,500,-000,000. This vast array of mechanical might permitted some 3,000,000 American construction workers to build $31,000,000,000 worth of projects in that year alone.

However, this spectacular advance in construction mechanization followed no smooth, even path. It moved slowly at first—not until 40 years after the first Otis patent was a successful steam shovel placed on the market. Then for the rest of the nineteenth century and through the early years of the twentieth century, steam dominated as construction power, reaching its zenith with the building of the Panama Canal.

The first steam shovels, and their companion cranes and draglines, were rail mounted. Then they slowly took to steel wheels, which gave way eventually to part crawler and then to full crawler tracks. The first full-revolving shovel was produced by Thew in 1895.

Steam and Animal Power.—Meanwhile, the steam hoist was developed, resulting in the efficient stiffleg derrick that built so many bridges and other structures in the near past. Another most important application of steam was to the rock drill, way back in 1849. The tractor, which occupies a dominant position today in construction power, was first brought out as a steam rig on wheels by Holt in 1885, followed by Best in 1894. By 1905 Holt had put the tractor, still steam powered, on present-day crawlers.

Curiously enough, it was during the steam power era in American construction that animal power came into greatest use, aided by such tools as the slip, Fresno and wheel scrapers, the dump cart and wagon, and that most economical of all earth-moving machines, the elevating grader. Sweating men, horses, and mules built the far-flung American railroad system. The 2,221-mile Union Pacific-Central Pacific transcontinental line was built in less than 4 years. In 1887 Winston Brothers Company, still one of the great construction firms in the United States, pushed the Great Northern westward from Minot, N. Dak., into Montana, grading 500 miles in 5 months with 3,300 teams and 8,000 men. In the same year 643 miles of track were laid in 7½ months with 225 teams and 650 men.

Steam never did entirely supplant animal power—it took gas and diesel engines to do that—but steam did supplement horses and mules by loading their dump wagons. Steam equipment simply did not have the mobility offered by animals, and mobility has ever been a prime factor in mechanized construction. The nearest steam ever came to ousting horse and mule hides was in building big embankments with steam-loaded, steam-drawn rail dump cars working from trestles.

Gasoline Takes Precedence.—During the first quarter of the twentieth century mechanical power gained momentum in construction, sparked by the advent of the gasoline engine. Holt and Best applied gas power to crawler tractors in 1908 and 1913, respectively. Thew brought out the first electric shovel in 1903, and gas shovels began to appear 10 to 15 years later. Mack produced the first gas-powered dump truck in 1905 (Fig. 2). During the first two decades gasoline engines also were installed—slowly to be sure—in mixers, pavers, pumps, and compressors.

World War I gave further impetus to construction equipment and set the stage for significant developments during the 1920's. The first truck crane was built for the United States Army in 1918. Purchase of surplus dump trucks from the army by contractors after the war sounded the death knell of team and railroad haul in construction.

During the 1920's steam gave way to gasoline engines as the prime power in

FIG. 2.—MACK DUMP TRUCK, VINTAGE OF 1913

construction equipment. Three other events in this decade were also most significant: The application of the bulldozer to crawler tractors in 1923; the formation of the Caterpillar Tractor Company in 1925 by merging the old Best and Holt companies which brought the crawler tractor into the prominence it still occupies today as a leading construction machine; and again in 1923 the introduction of the power-controlled scraper by LeTourneau, a name that looms large in equipment development in the past quarter century.

New Trends in Equipment.—Despite the economic depression, equipment progress continued through the 1930's, the most important advances being the wide application of rubber tires to construction machinery, giving it speed and mobility, and the adoption of diesel engines as major power units (Fig. 3). One or two shovel manufacturers had installed diesel engines in their products in 1928 and 1929, but the first diesel caterpillar tractor in 1931 really paved the way for diesel power in construction.

In 1933 LeTourneau set the pattern that still prevails today by adding a

Fig. 3.—Rubber Tires and Diesel Engines for Earth Moving—Caterpillar Scrapers and Diesel Tractors Tackling Heavy Earthwork at Berry Field Extension, Nashville, Tenn., 1952

Fig. 4.—Loaded 15½-Cu Yd Euclid Single-Engine Scraper (Left) "Push-Loading" Twin-Powered Scraper, for Charlotte, N. C., Airport

front apron to his carrying scraper, already on pneumatic tires, thus making it a true carryall instead of a glorified drag scraper. In 1938 that company pioneered again with the first two-wheel tractor unit for scraper and wagon haul. Meantime, Euclid was developing its four-wheel tractor and bottom-dump wagon units (Fig. 4) and was, along with other manufacturers, perfecting large and larger end-dump trucks. The first double-drum 34-E paver was introduced in 1938, revolutionizing concrete road-building procedure.

During the first half of the 1940's construction equipment came into glory: First, in the rapid and unprecedented construction of camps, air bases, harbor facilities, and war plants; second, in military combat units. Literally, bulldozers came first on many a battle front, followed closely by cranes, shovels, dump trucks, and road machinery. Construction, mechanized right to the front lines, became part of military strategy. The astounding achievements of the Seabees and the Army Engineers testify to that fact; and behind the lines Americans built faster than ever before to enable industry to supply the sinews of war. Mechanized construction helped speed the victory.

Since World War II further equipment development has been phenomenal, until today construction is close to being fully mechanized. Almost every construction operation, with the exception of a few building trade procedures, now is served by powered tools and machines—from small hand tools and wheelbarrows to gigantic shovels and earth movers.

Old machines have been improved and modernized, and a host of new equipment is appearing. The trend is ever toward faster, easier, and more efficient— and thus more economical—operation; toward increasing dependability, mobility, length of life, and ease of service and maintenance.

An Industry Come of Age.—What does all this mean to American civilization and economy? It means that the construction equipment industry has put into the hands of the constructors of the nation a combined mechanical might never before achieved in the building history of the world. However, all this mighty power would be useless if it were not for the ability, ingenuity, resourcefulness, experience, and know-how of the American contractor and construction organizations. They have developed skilled operators to run the machines and get efficient service out of them. They have the uncanny ability to apply the available equipment and tools to best advantage. They, with this array of mechanical aids, are developing ever faster, better, and cheaper ways in which to build. They have created an exciting, bold, and useful industry—modern construction—to serve mankind better.

Modern construction has taken the backbreaking toil out of manual labor. It has substituted manual skill for sweat. It has given construction workers mechanical aids so that they might better use their talents for greater and more economical production. Lastly, it has kept cost down to within the ability of the owners, both public and private, to buy construction services.

Today the construction industry fears not man, nature, or the devil. It stands ready to serve to any extent and at any place, to meet any challenge, to build anything anywhere. Current operations, all fresh in mind, prove this: The 118-mile Jersey Turnpike completed in less than 2 years; the mammoth flood-control, power, and irrigation projects now under way; the vast atomic energy plants; the defense plants; industrial expansion work; pipelines (Fig. 5); military establishments; and so on. The list is endless, but still awesome. Furthermore, modern construction is just as fast and efficient in building the everyday, smaller projects: Roads, schools, housing, buildings, utilities, recreational facilities, and water and sewerage plants. The same speed, efficiency, and quality of performance are characteristic of all jobs from smallest to largest.

Prospects and Patents.—What of the future? Just more of the same. Even better machines and tools will be available in greater variety. More speed in construction and more efficiency are certain. Some day the few remaining hand operations, such as plastering, bricklaying, and plumbing, will be mechanized—giving employment to more men in these trades than ever before.

Fig. 5.—Mechanized Pipeline Construction near Limon, Colo., Part of 10,000-Ft Daily Progress; Boom on Caterpillar Tractor Handling Six 40-Ft Joints of 20-In. Gas Line

Nevertheless, because of their very nature, construction procedures will never equal manufacturing assembly-line operations. The manufacturer sets up a permanent plant, assembles his raw materials, makes, and then distributes his products. The constructor sets up a temporary plant, assembles his raw materials, and then fabricates the product in place. No structure he ever builds is exactly the same as any he ever has built or ever will build again. Even though the designs may be identical, which seldom is the case, weather, ground, water, personnel, and other conditions are bound to vary. Furthermore, the constructor must create a new production organization and a new plant for every project, plan it out in advance, use it, and then break it up and disperse it.

However, even in these temporary plants the equipment industry has given the constructor some production processes that are mighty close to continuous assembly-line operations. The gigantic aggregate processing and concrete plants on the big dams are good examples, with their pushbutton controls, automatic proportioning, and graphical recording of results. Continuous earth moving is

FIG. 6.—ATHEY FORCE-FEED LOADER PICKING UP AND CRUSHING SCARIFIED MATERIAL FROM OLD ROAD FOR NEW SURFACING

approached by the Euclid loader that scoops up the earth and tosses it into passing power wagons with scarcely a break. Bituminous and concrete highway paving operations (Fig. 6) are also close to continuous processes.

Certainly, the United States can look forward with confidence to the fact that the construction industry will ever serve her well, in peace or in war. It will continue efficiently and swiftly to create physical projects for the betterment of mankind, for an ever-increasing standard of living, and a better way of life.

AMERICAN SOCIETY OF CIVIL ENGINEERS

Founded November 5, 1852

TRANSACTIONS

Paper No. 2594

IRRIGATION IN THE UNITED STATES

By George D. Clyde,[1] M. ASCE

Synopsis

Irrigation—the act of applying water artificially to soil to provide moisture for plant growth—has been practiced since the beginning of recorded history. Great civilizations of antiquity were supported by irrigation agriculture. The Indians were practicing irrigation when the Spaniards came to the Americas. Irrigation agriculture as a major industry in the United States began with the Mormon Colony in Salt Lake Valley, Utah (1847) and the Union Colony at Greeley, Colo. (1870). Early development was most rapid in Utah, Colorado, California, and Idaho. Prior to 1900, practically all work was done by private enterprise and private capital, during which time about 7,000,000 acres were irrigated. From 1900 to 1952, an additional 12,000,000 acres were brought under irrigation by private enterprise and nearly 6,000,000 acres were provided with a full or a supplemental water supply by the Bureau of Reclamation, United States Department of the Interior. During the past decade, supplemental irrigation in humid and subhumid areas has grown rapidly.

An additional 15,000,000 acres may be brought under irrigation with the full development of the available water supplies. Irrigation efficiencies can and should be greatly increased. Research in soil, water, and plant relations is essential if maximum returns, on a permanent and profitable basis, are to be obtained from the soil and water resources of this nation.

Water and Agriculture

Water Is Life.—Without water there can be no life. The progress and development of mankind have been governed by the location and accessibility of life-giving water. Just as the seas, covering almost three fourths of the earth's surface, govern and regulate the earth's climate, so also does the cycle of precipitation and runoff determine the course of man's habitation and civilization. The relentless return of water from the sky to the land and back to the ocean has formed its own paths near which the earth's people have settled. When these paths cross

---

[1] Chf., Div. of Irrig. Eng. and Water Conservation, Soil Conservation Service, U. S. Dept. of Agriculture, Logan, Utah.

regions receiving little water from the skies, they become the threads to which all life clings.

It is striking to note the fact that the most prosperous nations of antiquity rose and flourished along the rivers of arid regions. Surmounting their agricultural problems, these countries became most advanced in the arts and sciences and in cultural pursuits. Small wonder that some rivers are worshiped as holy, in the arid lands which they support.

Basic Concepts of Irrigation.—Since the beginning of time, the principal source of food for man and animal has been plants. Plants also furnished fiber for clothing and, often, shelter. Plant life is dependent on a proper climatic environment and the presence of three major elements—soil, water, and air. If any of these three is missing, regardless of the climate, ordinary agricultural plant life cannot exist.

Distribution of the land areas of the earth in relation to precipitation are given in Table 1 (1).[2] More than half of the earth's surface is arid or semiarid;

TABLE 1.—LAND AREAS OF THE EARTH IN RELATION TO PRECIPITATION

Climatic classification	Annual precipitation, in inches	Percentage of land area
Arid	Less than 10	25
Semiarid	10–20	30
Subhumid	20–40	20
Humid	40–60	11
Humid—wet	60–80	9
Very wet	More than 80	5
Total		100

and three fourths, subhumid or drier. Thus, adequate moisture for firm crop production is assured on only about 25% of the earth's surface. Furthermore, the cereals, corn, and small grains except rice, which form the bulk of man's diet, do not grow well under humid or very wet conditions.

Water is the limiting factor in the major food-producing areas of the world. Droughts have been the principal cause of the world's major famines. Not long after man discovered that he could sow seeds and produce crops he also learned that, if he planted along streams, he could divert and apply the life-giving water to the soil if precipitation failed to occur. As a result, the early major civilizations were developed in arid or semiarid regions where irrigation agriculture supplied the food and fiber needs of the people.

Nature provided for irrigation by making the soil a water-and-air storage reservoir as well as the source of plant food and the anchorage for plant roots. Under conditions of adequate rainfall, the soil storage reservoir is filled from precipitation. In those areas where natural moisture is deficient, irrigation is practiced to fill up the soil storage. The plants, through their root systems, empty the soil moisture reservoirs. Irrigation water is applied to refill them.

In the arid and semiarid areas nearly all the moisture needs of crops are met by irrigation. In humid and subhumid areas, the major moisture needs are supplied by rain and only a relatively small part need be supplied by irrigation. Both full irrigation and supplemental irrigation firm up agricultural production.

---

[2] Numerals in parentheses, thus: (1), refer to corresponding items in the Bibliography at the end of the paper.

ANCIENT IRRIGATION

Irrigation has no recorded beginning. The practice extends back to the earliest historical records. In the arid regions where the first great recorded civilizations flourished, the application of water to the fields was so natural and necessary that little was written of it. The Book of Genesis, Chapter 2, paragraph 10, records: "And a river went out of Eden to water the garden * * *." Again II Kings, Chapter 3, paragraphs 16 and 17, states:

"And he said, Thus saith the Lord, 'Make this valley full of ditches.' "
"For thus saith the Lord, 'Ye shall not see wind, neither shall ye see rain; yet that valley shall be filled with water, that ye may drink, both ye, and your cattle, and your beasts.' "

Paintings and sculptures of early Egypt often show peasants bailing up water at least as early as 2000 B.C. (2). Irrigation was practiced in Egypt more than 4,000 years ago.

One of the oldest canals in the world is the Bohr Yusef in Upper Egypt, dating from Biblical times when Egypt was known as "the granary of the world." Tradition states that this canal was constructed by the Patriarch Joseph (Yusef) in the days of his captivity (3). When the famine came, Joseph's brothers who had sold him came to him for grain—grain grown on the irrigated lands of the Valley of the Nile.

In Asia Minor.—The Tigris and the Euphrates rivers, watering what some historians consider the "cradle of civilization," were partly regulated by the Babylonians to provide water for irrigation and flood control. The ancient city of Babylon was protected from floods by a system of cement brick embankments on both banks of the Euphrates; and to supplement these structures and to store water for irrigation a large reservoir 42 miles in circumference and 35 ft deep was constructed.

The sixth king of the First Dynasty of Babylon (4), whose reign ended about 2250 B.C., had an elaborate code of laws dealing with water. These laws decreed that men and beasts had the first right to the use of water, households were second, irrigation third, and navigation fourth. Penalties for wasting water were specific. The water code of King Hammurabi (4), 1950 B.C., provided:

"If a man open his canal for irrigation and neglect it and the water carry away the adjacent field, he shall measure out grain on the basis of the adjacent field."

From the beginning of the dynastic period in Iraq (about 3000 B.C.) throughout the 1,000 years that followed, countless dedicatory tablets, clay record cones, and commercial records have been recovered on many of which the construction of canals to irrigate the land is mentioned (5). The King of Hogash built the canal of Eden in about 2900 B.C.

In 1000 A.D., there were more than 3,000 miles of canals around Baghdad, one single canal being nearly 300 miles long. In 1258 (6), the country was destroyed by Hulagu. Dams failed, canals were cut, administrative organizations were broken up, and maintenance of canals, structures and lands was neglected. Repeated invasions made restoration of physical control of users impossible. Their water supplies cut off, crop failure followed and the civilizations perished.

There is evidence that irrigation was practiced in the Western Hemisphere (Peru) before the beginning of the Christian era. Here the ruins of one conduit 125 miles long for conveying water from the mountains to Lima, the capital of Peru, still remain (7).

The Spread of Irrigation

Eastern Hemisphere.—Irrigation spread from China, India, and the Euphrates, Tigris, and Nile River valleys to Carthage and Phoenicia and thence to Greece and Italy (2). The practice of irrigation was carried across the Mediterranean to Spain by the Moors, who left some remarkable masonry dams dating back to about 100 A.D. During the height of the Roman colonization, impressive structures for conveying and storing water were built throughout the Roman Empire including France, Germany, and the British Isles. One of the most efficient systems of irrigation ever to be built is found in the Piedmont and Lombardy regions of Italy. The irrigation and drainage systems are effective, and the water is apportioned and regulated by decrees passed down from local rulers.

Western Hemisphere.—The practice of irrigation and the basic laws governing water rights were carried to the western hemisphere by the Spaniards, but there they found irrigation agriculture was already established. Hernán Cortes, an early Spanish explorer, found the natives of Mexico irrigating their fields from wide ditches dug from the streams to the fields. In Peru, evidences of well-developed systems of irrigation were found in stone aqueducts. Irrigation and fertilization of the soil were known and used by the Indians at the time of the Spanish invasion (7).

Inca Garcelaso de la Vege (1500–1559) reports:

> "Where land was irrigated, the water was distributed 'by measure, so that there might not be any quarrels and rancor among the Indians over its division,' each owner was granted a set number of hours for irrigation according to his needs without preference. A rigorous punishment was meted out to those who failed to irrigate their fields."

Early Irrigation in the United States

Wheat and rice were the germs of civilization in Europe and Asia, respectively. Corn and maize were the crops which enabled the natives to settle down to a sedentary living in the Americas. Archeologists (8) have proved that the natives in the Americas had practiced agriculture many centuries before the white man arrived and that this agriculture was based on irrigation.

Indian Agriculture.—The Indians who lived along the banks of the desert rivers had corn in their possession, and it is believed that they practiced flood irrigation along the bottom lands of the Gila River in Arizona and New Mexico. It is but a short step from the flooding of the bottom lands to the construction of canals to convey the water to the higher benchlands. Such construction probably took place about 700 A.D.

These desert farmers were known as "Hohakam." For some unknown reason, they disappeared, and later the lands they occupied were settled by the Pima Indians. In 1694 when Father Kino (Eusebia Francisco) first visited Gila River Valley, the Pima tribe lived in several villages, each with its own irrigation ditch and local organization. The total population at the time American trappers first appeared among them was about 4,000, divided into 800 or 900 families, each farming about 10 acres. They inhabited about a dozen villages. This was the irrigation agriculture of the United States when the Spaniards came.

Spanish Colonization.—In 1598 (9), Juan de Onate, with an army of 700 soldiers and 130 families, constructed a pueblo at the confluence of the Rio Chama with the Rio Grande in New Mexico. Although the Indians were practicing irrigation, the colonizers with the assistance of 1,500 Indians dug canals on a comprehensive scale, to divert water from mountain streams and the Rio Grande itself for irrigation purposes (10).

The earliest irrigation ditches in Texas were built by the Spaniards and Indians along the Rio Grande below El Paso, Tex., during the seventeenth century (11). In 1755 a colony of Spaniards established a community north of the Rio Grande in Texas and in 2 years had dug six canals. By 1840 several Mexican families had settled in the Arkansas River Valley in Colorado near La Junta. These people engaged in farming and practiced irrigation principally by flooding from the adjoining stream.

Beginning in 1769, under the leadership of Father Junipero Serra, the Spaniards established in San Diego, Calif., the first of a string of missions in what is now the State of California extending to Sonoma beyond the San Francisco Bay. Their primary purpose was to introduce Christianity to the Indians. They had to produce their own food and clothing. The padres were quick to apply their knowledge of irrigation and to divert water to irrigate vegetable gardens, fruit orchards, and small grain fields. Military forces soon followed, and these had to be provisioned from the land. Little agricultural expansion took place, however, prior to the discovery of gold in California. An early rock dam built at the San Diego Mission (Fig. 1) is now more than 150 years old.

Frontier Expansion.—By 1800 the migration westward in the United States reached the Mississippi River. East of the Mississippi the climate is humid, and irrigation was considered unnecessary. The desire for growth and new lands led to the Louisiana Purchase in 1803, and Meriwether Lewis and William Clark were commissioned to explore this territory and find a route to the Pacific Ocean. Trappers, hunters, miners, and adventurers began to move westward across the great plains over the Rocky Mountains and to the Pacific Coast. Trading posts were established.

Colonists, farmers looking for land, moved westward behind the trappers. They found a changed climate; vegetation was different and sparse. Grazing was good and small grains would grow, but other crops needed more water than was available from precipitation. Few stopped en route to establish farms. Many pushed on over the Oregon Trail to western Oregon and Washington where precipitation was generally adequate for crop production.

Others followed the Santa Fe Trail to the Rio Grande Valley in Texas and New Mexico where the Mexicans were practicing crude irrigation along the river bottoms. No attempt was made, however, to establish an agricultural commonwealth in these areas. Irrigation was practiced only to produce the minimum food supplies needed by the trappers, miners, and frontiersmen. Up to about 1825 the total acreage irrigated by the Spaniards, Mexicans, and Indians in the territory now occupied by the western United States probably did not exceed 30,000 acres.

The Mormons As Pioneer Farmers.—Only one group of Anglo-Saxon colonists prior to 1850—the Mormons—sought to establish an agricultural commonwealth in an arid region. They were seeking to worship as they chose, without interference from the people who persecuted them for their beliefs. Their leaders were familiar with the reports from the trappers and explorers, and knew that the land was arid. However, they had no other purpose than developing a commonwealth

FIG. 1.—OLD MISSION DAM NEAR SAN DIEGO, CALIF., 150 YEARS OLD AND STILL IN USE

supported from the products of the soil. The Mormons expected to irrigate, and they took with them seeds and the necessary tools. Quoting from Orson Pratt's diary:

"July 23, 1847. Encamped near the bank of a beautiful creek of pure cold water * * *. In about two hours after our arrival, we began to plow, and the same afternoon built a dam to irrigate the soil.

"July 24, 1847. This afternoon we commenced planting potatoes after which we turned the water upon them and gave the ground quite a soaking."

From this humble beginning, irrigation agriculture as a way of life and a source of food and fiber has spread over the arid and semiarid states and supplemental irrigation in the humid and subhumid areas has spread throughout the nation. Although organized irrigation is now practiced in all the western states, the beginning and rate of development varied widely in the different states.

MODERN IRRIGATION

Early development of irrigation planning and practice varied in different regions according to experience and local needs. There was little government advice and only limited interregional exchange of ideas. Experiences of the seventeen western states to date are therefore the best index of the material progress attained.

Utah.—Utah was the first state to establish irrigation agriculture as a major industry. The Mormons encountered the problem of aridity and discovered that its successful solution was the price of existence. They knew little of the art of irrigation, but they did know that moisture in the soil was essential to plant growth. They arrived in Salt Lake Valley in late July, 1847, when the need for planting was urgent, since their slender stock of provisions would not long protect them from starvation. It was this emergency which produced the first community irrigation canal built by Anglo-Saxons in the United States (12).

The beginning of irrigation in Utah was different from that in other states. Here agriculture was from the first the principal industry, whereas in many other areas, almost up to 1900, irrigation was incidental to mining and stock raising. Because of the paramount importance of irrigation, new laws and customs relating to water use had to be established (13). Nevada and California borrowed their early water laws and customs from the miners. Utah made hers firsthand and declared public ownership of natural resources, including water, to be one of the foundation principles of the state.

From the first, irrigation in Utah was a cooperative undertaking (14). When it was decided to establish a new settlement and the site was selected, the church authorities appointed leaders with experience in colonization and selected a sufficiently large body of colonists to construct irrigation canals and to provide protection from Indians. This group moved as a body to the site, which was usually near the mountains and adjacent to a stream from which the water supply was obtained. An area about a mile square was reserved for a town site. This area was divided into 10-acre blocks, each of which was subdivided into eight lots. A lot was large enough for the family residence, garden, orchard, barn, and outbuildings. Irrigation water was provided. The lands immediately adjoining the town and subject to irrigation were divided into 5-acre and 10-acre plots. Beyond these small plots were the larger irrigated farms of 20 to 40 acres. Each family was assigned a lot, a small plot, and a large plot of ground. Land speculation was not permitted.

Irrigation canals were projected and dug. Diversion dams and head gates were built. There were few surveyors; often the course of the canal was located and the grade fixed by sighting over a pan filled with water. Diversion dams consisted of brush and rock (Fig. 2).

There were no contractors to build the irrigation works. The people with limited equipment had to build the canals and necessary structures themselves. Many sections of these early canals were dug through solid rock with hammers, wedges, bars, and picks as the only tools—that meant cooperation. Each man dug his own share of the canal as fixed by the area of his land to be irrigated.

By 1850 there were 926 improved farms in Utah, covering a total area of 16,333 acres; and, by 1860, 3,636 farms with a total area of 77,219 acres. After

18 years (1865), nearly 150,000 acres were under irrigation, 1,000 miles of canal had been dug, and nearly 65,000 people were living in fair comfort on the reclaimed land (15).

This rapid and systematic growth of irrigation in Utah, on a basis of community units, was made possible by the great influx of converts to the Mormon faith and by their industry and their willingness to follow the leadership of the church in building an irrigation agriculture in the face of untold hardships. It was far different from the garden irrigation that had been practiced at the missions and by the Indians and trappers along the stream channels in the past.

FIG. 2.—BRUSH AND ROCK DAM; WEBER-DAVIS CANAL NEAR OGDEN, UTAH, BUILT ABOUT 1860

California.—In the meantime, irrigation was becoming established in other parts of the West. In California John A. Sutter settled in the Sacramento Valley, and by 1844 had established a fort and was irrigating some land around it. This, however, was strictly an individual undertaking and resembled the developments around the early Spanish missions. Considerable irrigation was being practiced at that time in the vicinity of Los Angeles by the Spanish soldiers.

During the period from 1850 to 1870, settlers in southern California built small ditches from the streams of the coastal plain near Los Angeles. In the Sierra Nevada foothills water was acquired from mining ditches, irrigation being accelerated by the demand for food brought on by the expansion in population that accompanied and followed the Gold Rush. Some storage reservoirs were constructed in southern California in the early 1880's, but the major storage developments in central California were made subsequent to 1900 (16).

By 1875 water had been diverted from the Kings River for the irrigation of lands along its banks. Frank Dacy, an early California irrigation farmer, wrote (17):

> "In 1875 a small irrigation ditch from the King's River made the soil produce beyond all expectation. As a result, all government lands were taken by settlers. In 1880 we brought in the Fowler Switch Canal, 40 feet on the bottom, 60 feet on the top, 5 feet deep and 20 miles long. Land bought at the government price of $1.25 per acre now sells for from $15 to $50 per acre depending on the soil and the location. Fruits are grown in large quantities; sweet potatoes, yams and watermelons grow prolifically. Raisin and wine grapes cannot be surpassed."

About the same time some land was being irrigated with water from the Kern River and several artesian wells had been dug for stock watering.

The railroads came in 1886 and agriculture boomed. In 1887 California passed its first Irrigation District Act, which, as amended, granted authority to irrigation and similar districts to finance, construct, and operate irrigation works. This marked the beginning of a period of rapid expansion, through the activities of individuals, cooperatives, water utilities, and the Bureau of Reclamation, from 1,000,000 irrigated acres in 1889 to approximately 6,619,000 acres in 1950 (18).

Colorado.—In 1852 the population of Colorado consisted of transient trappers, Mexicans, and Indians along the Rio Grande, Arkansas, and Platte rivers where the irrigation of gardens and small grain fields had been practiced for many years. The first priority to use water in Colorado recognized by the courts was dated April 10, 1852, at San Luis on the Rio Grande (9). Between 1852 and 1870 many small tracts of land were irrigated along the Rio Grande, the Arkansas, and South Platte rivers by individuals, partnerships, or small groups.

In 1869 (17), Horace Greeley organized the Union Colony, which established the second agricultural empire in the United States to be based on irrigation. This colony settled on the Cache La Poudre River at what is now Greely, in 1870. The colonists first dug a large canal for conveying water from the river to the surrounding tablelands, then known as the "Great American Desert." It was a community effort. Large blocks of land totaling more than 30,000 acres were brought under irrigation. The farms varied in size from 80 to 160 acres.

Irrigation development was rapid on the South Platte River during the period from 1870 to 1890. At the same time irrigation was being established on the Arkansas at Fountain, and on the headwaters of the Colorado River. The period was one of wild speculation—irrigation companies were organized, and canals were built out of proportion to the acreage irrigated. The principal causes of the failure which resulted were overexpansion, inadequate water supplies, and poorly constructed works.

About 1890 irrigation development became more stable. Attention was given to improved works and storage to firm up the late season water supplies. Return flow was captured for irrigation use and the principle of water exchanges established, to take advantage of storage reservoirs on the lower reaches of the stream. Colorado set a pattern of irrigation practice and established the principles that the ownership and control of water rested in the state and that management of canals should be local and by those immediately interested—the water users (19).

Colorado was a pioneer in transmountain diversions, involving conveyance from the west slope of the Rocky Mountains, where waters of the Colorado were plentiful, through tunnels to the east slope where supplies were inadequate. The largest of these transmountain diversions is the Colorado-Big Thompson Project now (1952) nearing completion.

Nevada.—Irrigation was first practiced on a small scale in Nevada in 1850 around the first permanent settlement, in Carson Valley. By 1858 the cattle industry had become established, and it was necessary to supplement the natural forage with hay. The settlers found that, by irrigating the natural meadows, considerable forage could be harvested to carry the stock over the winter.

The discovery of the Comstock Lode at Virginia City caused a mining boom, and the rapidly increasing population had to be fed. Diversified farming under irrigation was established to produce food for the miners. The principal irrigated area, however, remained in natural irrigated pasture. Railroad transportation and the passage of the Reclamation Act (1902) gave further impetus to irrigation development and diversified farming.

Arizona.—In the 1860's the Mormons settled along the Gila and Salt rivers. They cleared land, dug ditches, and dammed unruly streams. Most of the streams in Arizona are very erratic, varying from small flow to enormous floods. The water supply at low flow was inadequate for the land in cultivation, and the flows in excess of the immediate needs or canal capacities were lost, because of the lack of storage facilities. Often the floods washed out the diversion dams.

Man's struggle with these southwestern streams is one of the outstanding episodes of all pioneering in the United States. The early settlers had little knowledge of hydraulics and no equipment with which to combat the treacherous streams. The history of irrigation along the Gila, the Salt, and the Little Colorado rivers tells of heartaches and courage. The settlers built their own canals and diversion dams, but the remains of abandoned homes and fields bear mute testimony that the settlers unaided could not, in many cases, cope with floods of the magnitude encountered (20). Since the completion of the Roosevelt Storage Dam and the Granite Reef Diversion Dam on the Salt River in 1910, irrigation in Arizona developed rapidly, utilizing both surface and underground water supplies.

Idaho.—The first permanent settlement in Idaho was established by thirteen Mormon families in 1860 at Franklin. An irrigation agriculture was established, and 4 miles of canal were built to deliver water to farms. Boise Valley was settled in 1830 (17). Soon many types of grass, grains, fruits, and vegetables were grown. By 1866, one canal 14 miles long was diverting water out of the Payette River, and another 20 miles long was under construction. Irrigation developed rapidly along the Snake river; and, by 1890, 217,000 acres were being irrigated.

The passage of the Carey Act in 1894 gave great impetus to irrigation in Idaho. Under the act, 629,000 acres were added to Idaho's irrigated area. Much of the area had an inadequate water supply. The Reclamation Act in 1902 gave further impetus to irrigation and made possible the construction of storage reservoirs to provide full water supplies to new projects and supplemental supplies to old projects. Raw sagebrush land (Fig. 3) became very productive when cleared and irrigated.

Oregon.—Irrigation was first practiced in Oregon in the 1860's following the gold rush in the Grande Valley. During the next 40 years development was limited to areas along river bottoms for the production of grass and hay on the cattle ranches. With the passage of the Reclamation Act and the construction of the Umatilla, Vale, Klamath, and Owyhee projects, irrigation expanded rapidly.

Wyoming.—The first ditches built in Wyoming were along the Oregon Trail in the vicinity of the military posts. The oldest of which there is any record was built in 1857, and several others were constructed in the early 1860's (13).

Most of the arable area is at relatively high elevation and was originally covered with grass. As a result, the cattle industry started early, and grass and forage still occupy the greater part of the irrigated land. Irrigation as practiced

FIG. 3.—TYPICAL RAW LAND BEFORE CLEARING SAGEBRUSH AND PREPARING FOR IRRIGATION

on these cattle ranches consisted largely of wild flooding to inundate the meadow-lands, but some garden crops and cereals were produced for home consumption.

After the Civil War, settlement began in earnest, principally by cattlemen who located on every spring, creek, or water hole, but not until about 1900 was serious attention directed to diverting water from the larger streams for extensive irrigation development. In 1900 Buffalo Bill (W. F. Cody) and George Beck diverted water from the Shoshone River to irrigate 15,000 acres of land near Cody. Since the passage of the Reclamation Act, the Shoshone, Riverton, and Kendrick projects have been built; and, except for the irrigation of mountain meadows, these projects supply water to most of the irrigated land in Wyoming.

Washington.—The western 40% of the state is humid, whereas the eastern part is arid. The water supply available to the arid area is scanty except that from the Columbia River, which is difficult to divert. The first irrigation in Washington was instituted by Marcus Whitman, who established a mission at Walla Walla in 1841. Only a small area of garden and orchard was originally included, but by 1846 considerable acreage was being irrigated to furnish food for the mission. Irrigation development was slow up to 1907 when the federal reclamation projects in the Yakima Valley, totaling 200,000 acres, began to come into production. The Columbia Basin Project, now under construction, will add about 1,000,000 acres to Washington's presently irrigated acreage.

Texas.—In succession to the early work by the Spaniards and Indians along the Rio Grande in the seventeenth century, irrigation agriculture was reestablished by Anglo-Americans at Balmorhea in 1853. However, not until after the Civil War did irrigation development really start. During the period from 1860 to 1889, irrigation was established at El Paso on the Rio Grande and at Fort Stockton, Del Rio, Uvalde, San Saba, and San Angelo, all in west Texas. Rice irrigation began in 1895.

In 1889 the first irrigation project in the Lower Rio Grande Valley was established when water was pumped from the river to irrigate 500 acres of land. After the coming of the railroad to the Lower Valley in 1904, development was rapid. In 1910 citrus growing was established, and in 1926 the first cotton was planted. Up to 1951 more than 650,000 acres in the Lower Rio Grande Valley had been planted to citrus fruit, cotton, vegetables, irrigated pastures, and general farm crops.

Irrigation was introduced in the High Plains in 1891 when 10 acres were supplied from windmills on the Morrison farm in Hale County. By 1914 approximately 140 wells were in operation. Development was slow, and in 1934 there were only about 300 irrigation wells in the area. The drought of the 1930's increased interest in irrigation, and by 1940 there were 3,200 irrigation wells. The number increased to 4,300 in 1946, and it is estimated that there were 17,000 irrigation pump wells on the High Plains in 1950 furnishing water for more than 2,000,000 acres.

Nebraska.—The climate of Nebraska varies from arid in the west to subhumid in the east. Early farmers gambled on the rain and irrigation developed slowly. John Burke dug a small ditch to water corn and vegetables near Fort Pearson on the Platte River in 1866. A few other ditches diverted water out of the Platte and Republican rivers during the period from 1866 to 1890, but it took the drought of 1890–1894 to establish irrigation agriculture in Nebraska. In 1889 a state law was passed establishing the doctrine of appropriation as the basis of irrigation water rights thereafter acquired.

Several years of adequate rainfall followed the drought of 1890–1894, and the construction of irrigation projects lagged. Many ditches were not used, and some were abandoned. Many companies went broke. Following the passage of the Reclamation Act in 1902, irrigation agriculture again surged forward. The North Platte and Mirage Flat projects have been completed, and several new projects are under construction as a part of the Missouri Basin Multiple Use Plan.

Kansas.—Like Nebraska, Kansas is partly subhumid and partly arid. Little irrigation was practiced there prior to 1890, although a few irrigation companies were organized in the late 1870's and early 1880's. Most of these either went out of business or delayed construction during the relatively wet years of the late 1880's. The drought of 1890–1894 revived interest in irrigation and many areas were developed. Subsequent to the drought, wet years again occurred and irrigation lapsed into an unimportant activity. Following the passage of the Reclamation Act, a reclamation project was constructed at Garden City. This, too, had difficulty surviving, as a result of alternate wet and dry years.

By 1922, about 50,000 acres were irrigated in Kansas, largely in the Arkansas River Valley between Garden City and the Colorado-Kansas state line, by direct diversion from the Arkansas River. Some ground water was pumped for irrigation purposes. The limited irrigation expansion in Kansas between 1920 and 1950 resulted largely from the development of ground-water supplies and a small amount of surface storage. Reclamation projects now under construction (1952) in the Republican River Valley will add greatly to the irrigated areas in Kansas.

New Mexico.—The old irrigation projects, called "community acequias," in New Mexico were originally built by the Indians, but most of those now in use are of Spanish-American origin. Important exceptions are in San Juan County, where the majority of the community ditches were started in the 1870's and 1880's by settlers from other states. In 1910 there were 480 community ditches (acequias) in New Mexico. Much of the irrigated land is still in the typical Mexican farm— long narrow strips stretching from the river to the foothills. The farms are small. The ditches are short, diverting directly from the stream, and are usually owned in common by the farmers, who elect one of their members to distribute the water. Maintenance and repairs are handled by labor assessments against the users. The ancient water rights of these community acequias have been jealously guarded in present New Mexico law.

Modern irrigation in New Mexico began with the construction of the Carlsbad and Rio Grande (1906) reclamation projects. Since that time additional reclamation projects, Tucumcari, Fort Sumner, Middle Rio Grande, and Vermejo, have been built or are under construction, increasing the total irrigated area to about 690,000 acres in 1950.

Montana.—Irrigation in Montana was first practiced by the Jesuits during the 1840's to supply food for the St. Mary's Mission in the Bitterroot Valley. Irrigation agriculture as a business started with the gold rush and the establishment of mining camps which had to be supplied with food.

The first irrigation ditches in the Gallatin Valley diverted water out of the East Gallatin River in 1864, but the era of ditch construction by mutual companies and corporations did not begin until the early 1880's. During the next 10 years, the development of irrigation was rapid. By 1890 most of the easy diversions and short canals had been built. Neither capital nor equipment was available to build the larger diversions and long canals needed to reach the lands distant from the rivers.

In 1894 the Federal Government passed the Carey Act to aid irrigation development. Many projects were started, but few were finished. With the passage of the Reclamation Act in 1902, new irrigation projects were started—Lower Yellowstone in 1904, Huntley in 1905, and Milk and Sun rivers in 1906. Since that time several additional reclamation projects have been built.

In 1907 the state sought to aid development and passed the Irrigation District Law. In 1934 the State Legislature created the Water Conservation Board which has since constructed many small irrigation projects.

Montana passed its first irrigation law in 1865 authorizing the construction of irrigation ditches. The appropriation doctrine was recognized in legislation enacted in 1872 and in following years. In 1921 the Montana Supreme Court ruled that the riparian doctrine was unsuited to conditions in the state and that it never had prevailed there since the enactment of the statutes in 1865.

South Dakota, North Dakota, and Oklahoma.—The first irrigation in South Dakota was along the streams emerging from the Black Hills shortly after the area was opened for settlement. By 1906, 29,000 acres were reported under irrigation by simple gravity diversions in the Cheyenne Basin. In 1910 the Bureau of Reclamation delivered water to the Belle Fourche Project, bringing about 36,000 acres under irrigation. Since that time, the Angostura and Rapid Valley projects have been built, making the total irrigated area in South Dakota in 1950 84,000 acres.

In 1936 there were only about 10,000 acres of irrigated land in North Dakota. The drought of 1934 gave impetus to irrigation and the Lewis and Clark and the Buford-Trenton projects were constructed, covering about 15,000 acres. In 1951 the Heart Butte Project, with 13,000 acres, was completed.

Oklahoma is in the marginal rainfall belt. Irrigation has never been a major problem. Approximately 4,000 acres of land are being irrigated along river bottoms. The Altus Project, built by the Bureau of Reclamation, supplies the only real irrigation in the state. It provides water for between 30,000 and 40,000 acres.

Irrigation in the West is big business. Table 2 shows the irrigated acreage and related data as reported by the 1950 United States Census of Irrigation (21). Nearly 26,000,000 acres are being irrigated, and a total of nearly $2,000,000,000 has been invested in irrigation works in nineteen western states; the remaining irrigation potential there is from 15,000,000 to 20,000,000 acres.

Irrigation in Humid Areas.—Humid and subhumid areas in the United States are generally considered to include all the land lying east of the 98th meridian plus the coastal areas of northern California, Oregon, and Washington. These areas, however, are subject to short periods of drought during which moisture in soil storage is not sufficient to supply the plant needs. The total seasonal precipitation may be ample for the production of many crops, but its distribution is such that moisture deficiencies occur during the growing season which reduce the yields and lower the quality of the product. The precipitation pattern of the humid and subhumid areas in the United States shows frequent periods of 15-day duration or more, with less than 1 in. of precipitation. Large areas are also subject to major droughts such as occurred in 1890, 1894, 1899, 1934, and 1952.

Successful irrigation agriculture in the arid areas suggested a method of combating these droughts, and irrigation to supplement precipitation soon spread over the subhumid and humid areas. Little irrigation was practiced in the humid regions of the United States prior to 1900, largely because of the difficulty of surface-water diversions, uneven topography, and the early pumps, pipelines, and sprinkler systems. The prices of farm crops did not justify the extra costs of irrigation.

Development of irrigation in the humid and subhumid areas continued slowly until about 1920, when improved farm prices and availability of pumping and sprinkler equipment increased interest in supplemental irrigation, particularly in New Jersey, New York, Florida, Arkansas, and Louisiana. By 1940 a total of 298,000 acres was being given supplemental irrigation. Other factors that gave further impetus were: The drought of the 1930's; high farm prices resulting from World War II; improved transportation, processing, and marketing facilities;

TABLE 2.—IRRIGATED ACREAGE AND RELATED IRRIGATION DATA FOR 1950, BY STATES, FROM THE "UNITED STATES IRRIGATION CENSUS"

States	Irrigated area[a,b]	No. of storage dams	Reservoir capacity[c]	No. of diversion dams	Length of canals and ditches[d]	Length of pipe lines and siphons[d]	No. of pumped wells	Area irrigated from ground water	Area irrigated by sprinkler[b]	Total diversions[c]	Average farm delivery[e]	Capital investment in works and water rights[f]
Arizona	979	237	3,626	552	4,800	316	4,361	524	4.0	3,750	3.7	137.6
Arkansas	419	86	40	108	683	19	3,662	367	1.6	.....	1.5	14.2
California	6,599	1,507	8,712	4,708	21,183	10,088	72,117	556	181.8	24,400	2.9	640.5
Colorado	2,944	1,105	2,021	7,709	18,729	251	4,988	245	8.2	10,800	2.6	163.3
Idaho	2,168	313	5,125	5,121	15,159	487	888	39	10.0	22,226	5.1	130.0
Kansas	141	42	26	127	542	13	1,343	92	3.1	100	1.6	5.9
Louisiana	598	58	31	319	3,477	61	3,365	256	1.0	571	2.0	21.5
Montana	1,809	577	1,599	8,139	15,499	110	142	1	15.5	5,650	3.1	81.8
Nebraska	887	96	134	488	4,613	88	7,127	339	8.3	3,880	1.8	56.5
Nevada	723	176	687	4,065	3,388	123	254	3	1.4	1,578	2.4	20.2
New Mexico	691	448	3,186	1,286	5,763	168	3,846	262	1.8	2,178	2.8	61.1
North Dakota	36	6	1	15	193	7		15	0.3	289	2.4	2.9
Oklahoma	44	27	149	20	354	19	160	9	2.1	27	...	18.1
Oregon	1,338	470	2,369	6,231	8,405	572	2,770	34	98.8	5,227	3.4	74.4
South Dakota	84	94	205	281	964	8	27	1	0.4	183	1.6	6.6
Texas	3,151	508	1,403	438	10,092	1,168	15,070	1,860	41.5	4,523	2.3	144.4
Utah	1,167	474	2,424	3,080	9,621	300	1,925	27	1.7	5,410	2.9	56.5
Washington	618	205	6,437	1,861	4,984	1,514	2,098	34	67.8	5,278	4.3	178.3
Wyoming	1,475	415	4,371	5,228	9,822	56	248	9	0.6	8,479	2.5	60.0
Total	25,871	6,844	42,546	49,766	138,271	15,307	122,425	4,673	449.9	104,549	2.7[g]	1,868.3

a As reported by Irrigation Enterprises. b In 1,000 acres. c In 1,000 acre-ft. d In miles. e In acre-feet per acre. f In million dollars. g Average.

better irrigation equipment, particularly portable sprinklers; and greater availability of electricity in rural areas.

In the decade from 1940 to 1950, the area of irrigated lands in the humid parts of the United States increased from less than 300,000 to more than 500,000 acres. These data do not include the ricelands of Louisiana, Arkansas, and East Texas where some 1,600,000 acres were being irrigated in 1950 (22).

The role irrigation will play in humid areas is not clear, but the land under irrigation is sure to increase. At present irrigation is supported by high farm prices, which more than offset the increased costs. The water supply in many areas is questionable because during periods of drought the small streams are dry and ground-water supplies are limited. Legal rights to use the water for irrigation are cloudy because no principles governing such use have been established. Irrigation from a vast network of farm ponds offers much promise. The total potential irrigated area in the twenty-nine eastern states has been estimated as about 3,000,000 acres.

Development by Types of Irrigation Enterprise

A number and a variety of efforts have been made to accomplish needed irrigation. These are related historically and overlap in time of operation. However, they can be understood most clearly by consideration of each type of enterprise separately. Comparative coverage and finances are shown in Fig. 4, whereas development and accomplishments will be described individually.

Cooperative.—During the first stage of irrigation development, when the people settled along the river and creek bottoms, the problems of diversion and conveyance were not difficult. The homesteader built an individual ditch bringing water from the stream to his land. He grubbed the sagebrush, diverted water, and put his land under cultivation. The arrangement may have been a partnership where two families joined their effort and diverted water on their land; or it may have been one of those pioneer enterprises in which the farmers themselves, by their own labor and always with limited capital, in a spirit of cooperation set about to dig ditches and bring water to dry land.

With the passing years came more settlers, and the rivers and creek bottoms with easy diversions and short canals were no longer sufficient. Better lands were found on the benches often distant from the sources of water. The construction of diversion dams on unruly streams and canals from the rivers to the benchland over rough topography, often through solid rock, and with little or no equipment is the saga of irrigation. Every irrigated section furnishes an illustration of such development, showing the pioneer spirit and optimism of those who visualized farms and homes far removed from the streams. Early projects were constructed by the water users cooperatively, and such capital as was needed for the larger works and longer canals was private capital—there was no government aid.

Water rights early became a problem. Irrigation is a consumptive use and as such was contrary to the riparian doctrine, which governed in the humid areas. A new rule of law became necessary, recognizing that first in time is first in right. This rule, called the doctrine of appropriation, was law in many states, whereas others continued to recognize the riparian doctrine modified to permit use for irrigation. Early legislation covered the acquisition of water rights and in many

cases specified that notice of intent to divert water at a given point must be given
and that the water so diverted had to be put to beneficial use.

An early method of posting notice was taken from mining practices. A note
stating that so much water would be diverted and used to irrigate a certain area
of land was written and nailed to a tree, or put in a can nailed to a tree, at the
point of diversion. The statutes provided that copies of the notices must be filed
in the appropriate county records. Legislation was passed in most states providing for the organization of unincorporated associations and mutual companies.

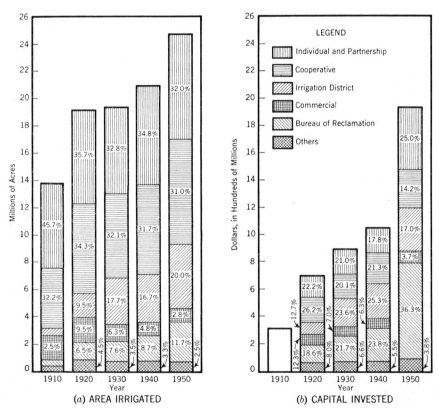

FIG. 4.—IRRIGATION DEVELOPMENT IN THE UNITED STATES, BY TYPE OF ENTERPRISE; SEVENTEEN
WESTERN STATES

These pioneer enterprises flourished up to about 1880 when most of the more
easily developed projects were built. The two outstanding examples of cooperative
enterprise in this period were the Mormon Colony in Utah, where 160,000 acres
were put under irrigation prior to 1880, and the Union Colony in Colorado where
in 12 years, beginning in 1870, 150,000 acres were put under irrigation (23).

Outside of Utah and Colorado, most of the early irrigation work was done by
individuals and partnerships on a limited scale, particularly in the more remote
areas and where ground water was the source of water supply. The more difficult
diversions and larger areas required cooperative effort such as characteriized
irrigation development in Utah and Colorado.

The mutual or cooperative irrigation company—a private association of irrigation farmers, organized for the purpose of providing irrigation water, at cost, primarily for the use of the members only (24)—was the most frequent type. Being a private organization, membership was voluntary. In some parts of the West, particularly in southern California, these organizations are known as mutual water companies. Each state has a general corporation law, which is well adapted to mutual irrigation enterprises and under which most such incorporations take place.

Irrigation Districts.—The natural flow of western streams does not coincide with the demand for moisture by the crops. These streams are snow fed; the high-water flow is in early spring when the snow melts and the flow decreases as the growing season advances. On the other hand, the demand for water for irrigation increases as the growing season advances. Therefore, irrigation on any one stream was limited by the low-water flow.

By 1880 most of the streams were developed to the limit of the low-water flow and land areas immediately adjoining the stream. There was plenty of water, but it had to be stored in reservoirs until needed; and there was plenty of land; but long canals were required to reach it. Many large streams such as the Columbia, Snake, Owyhee, Yakima, Colorado, and Bear rivers required costly diversion dams to divert the water and long expensive canals to get the water out of the canyons to the land. Individuals, partnerships, and mutual companies were unable to finance such construction because they had no security to offer for outside capital.

A public or quasi-public type of organization was needed in order to force all beneficiaries of a development to participate in the cost and to provide a means of financing such developments. Irrigation districts met these basic requirements. An irrigation district is a public corporation—organized under general state laws for the purpose of providing a water supply for the irrigation of lands within its boundaries; empowered to issue bonds; having the power of taxation; and deriving its revenue chiefly from assessments levied upon the land (24). Lands of an objecting minority may be included and assessed if they will be benefited by the district improvements.

The Wright Act of California (1887) was the first of this type (24). This act, as revised, is the present California District Law. Each of the seventeen western states now has a general irrigation district law patterned after the California law under which irrigation districts may be organized, financed, and operated. The irrigation district type of organization, either the standard or the special form, has been widely used for the rehabilitation of old and the construction of new projects.

Commercial.—The prosperity which followed the development of the pioneer irrigation enterprises was so marked that capital soon became interested. The picture of unlimited land, so unproductive that it could be secured for practically nothing, being made highly productive through the application of water, brought visions of easy money to many financial institutions. Capitalistic enterprises followed the pioneer development.

The first great boom in irrigation construction occurred in the late 1880's and early 1890's. Large areas of land were brought under irrigation through the promotion of commercial irrigation companies. Many of these enterprises were organized in conjunction with land-selling schemes, the promoters expecting to derive their profits chiefly from the sale of land. Other companies were organized to sell water or water rights to owners of land.

It was quickly discovered that many dangers and difficulties attend an irrigation enterprise that is not principally fostered, supported, and managed by the water users themselves. Sometimes years elapsed between the time the project was completed and the time when crops returned a profit. Interest charges during this interval became prohibitive. In other cases the landowners refused to buy the water. Speculation and inadequate water supplies caused other companies to fail. It was soon demonstrated that commercial irrigation enterprises were not, as a rule, profitable.

Carey Act Projects.—In spite of the interest in commercial companies in the early 1890's, the development of irrigation was lagging because of the difficulty of financing the large and expensive projects. The boom in construction which began about 1885 was followed by a long period of depression during which little construction took place. Meanwhile, people were moving westward in search of new homes and farms. It was admitted that irrigation was a necessity and highly beneficial to the country, yet work lagged. There were tremendous areas of agricultural land susceptible to irrigation and valuable only if irrigated, but under existing laws their development was beyond the reach of private capital.

To meet this situation in part, Congress in 1894 passed the Carey Act, hoping to overcome the difficulties tending to slow irrigation progress. This act authorized the Secretary of the Interior, on application of an arid state, to withdraw from public entry any land susceptible to irrigation from a common source, on condition that the state would provide for its irrigation. Each individual state was required to file maps showing the water source and the proposed method of supplying water to the land. The provisions of the Carey Act were adopted by all the western states except the semiarid plain states.

Idaho and Wyoming were especially active in developing Carey Act projects. The largest and most successful project is located near Twin Falls, Idaho. By 1916 the total area patented to states (25), was 761,455 acres. Of this, more than 500,000 acres were in Idaho; and 152,000 acres, in Wyoming. Small acreages in Carey Act projects have been completed in Colorado, Montana, Utah, Oregon, and Wyoming; but, except for the Twin Falls Project in Idaho, Carey Act projects have not been successful, largely because of financial difficulties, failure to tie the land to the water, and problems of water supply.

Irrigation Development Lags.—Individual, partnership, and cooperative effort had brought under irrigation the more accessible and easily developed areas. Private capital, through commercial enterprises and the sale of irrigation district bonds, stimulated development during the late 1880's, but it was insufficient to meet the demand for more farms. To encourage the development and reclamation of the arid lands, Congress had already passed the Desert Land Act in 1875 and the Carey Act in 1894. Neither of these solved the problem of the construction of the bigger and more extensive works necessary to supply water for the thirsty lands distant from the streams and to provide necessary storage to eliminate late season water shortages.

By 1890 more than 3,500,000 acres of land were being irrigated. This acreage was more than doubled (7,263,813 acres) (26) during the next 10 years as a result of irrigation districts, commercial enterprises, and Carey Act projects. All developments up to this time had been made with private capital and were restricted to easy diversions, short canals, and limited storage.

Fundamental principles of water rights had been established in the respective states by 1900. The states were recognized as having title to the waters within their boundaries; whereas the title to the land came from the Federal Government. A few states, notably Colorado and Wyoming, had set up methods of establishing water rights, but it remained for the courts to settle water controversies between users. Most of the claims for water were excessive, and wasteful use of water was the rule.

In 1901 President Theodore Roosevelt, in his first message to Congress, urged the adoption of some policy by the Federal Government for the reclamation of arid lands on an extensive scale. He stated:

> "In the arid region it is water, not land, which measures production. The western half of the United States would sustain a population greater than that of our whole country today if the waters that now run to waste were saved and used for irrigation."

The experience of 50 years has verified this statement.

The Reclamation Act.—The resulting legislation was born of necessity. Westward migration had been going on at an ever-increasing rate for more than 50 years. The Pacific Ocean prevented further westward movement, and the population pressures kept building up. In most states, agriculture followed mining and livestock and was dependent on irrigation. Easily developed water supplies had been exhausted, and the necessary monetary capital for storage, diversion works, and long canals was not available. The Federal Government was the only agency with control over the public lands in the western states and with adequate finance to construct the necessary irrigation works.

Popular demand for more farm opportunities in the West and the national economic situation led to the enactment on June 17, 1902, of the Reclamation Act (32 Statute 388), which gave to the Secretary of the Interior authority to make examinations and surveys for, and to locate and construct, irrigation works for the purpose of supplying water to the arid lands. This law embodied a new concept of cooperation between the people and their government in the construction of water-resource facilities of a size and an importance never before attempted. The act originally covered sixteen states (Arizona, California, Colorado, Idaho, Kansas, Montana, Nebraska, Nevada, New Mexico, North Dakota, Oklahoma, Oregon, South Dakota, Utah, Washington, and Wyoming). Later Texas and the Territory of Alaska were added.

The original purpose of the Reclamation Act was to provide water for irrigation of public lands. It soon developed that many areas already under irrigation needed supplemental water. On February 21, 1911, the Reclamation Act was amended (36 Statute 925) to permit the Bureau of Reclamation to supply supplemental water for privately-owned projects.

In 1939 the act was further amended (53 Statute 1187) to provide for flexibility in fixing annual repayment rates, to amend contracts for old projects in distress, and to allocate costs to irrigation, power, municipal water supply, and other miscellaneous purposes. Project costs allocable to irrigation, but beyond the water user's ability to pay, may be assigned to be covered by the return on revenues from power, municipal, or other uses. The amended act also made allocations to flood control and navigation nonreimbursable. The act of August 14, 1946 (60 Statute 1080), provided that costs allocated to preservation and propagation of fish and wildlife were also to be nonreimbursable. Irrigation under the Reclamation Act thus became a part of a multiple-use basin-wide development.

Growth Under the Reclamation Act.—The original act required that at least one reclamation project be built in each of the sixteen reclamation states and that the funds required for the construction of these projects would be derived from the sale of public lands and coal, oil, timber, and mineral resources. The first reclamation project was established on the Salt River in Arizona, and construction began in 1903. Since then, the Bureau of Reclamation has built ninety-five dams with a combined storage of 83,000,000 acre-ft, thirty-five power plants with a total capacity of 43,000,000 kw, 16,000 miles of irrigation canals, and 3,000 miles of transmission lines. The Bureau has supplied 5,500,000 acres of land with a full or supplementary water supply and has provided enough water and power for 9,000,000 persons (27).

Few irrigation projects involving heavy construction or complicated engineering structures had been built prior to the passage of the Reclamation Act. The history of reclamation is a history of engineering progress. The Bureau of Reclamation in its 50 years of existence has virtually created the science of irrigation engineering as it relates to the development of water resources, hydraulic structures including concrete and earth dams, canals, pipelines, control structures, pumping plants, surface and underground distribution systems, and power plants. Its Engineering Laboratory at Denver, Colo., is the nerve center of design and testing. Its staff of technicians, its backlog of knowledge of engineering and construction, and its physical facilities are mobilized for mass attack on the complex problems of water-resource development. Its published literature is a world source of technical information.

The Bureau has constructed the world's highest dam (Hoover) on the Colorado River in Arizona-Nevada, the world's largest (Grand Coulee) on the Columbia River in Washington, and probably the world's most complicated irrigation project (the Central Valley in California). It has dug tunnels through the Continental Divide to make the waters of the Pacific drainage area irrigate lands draining into the Atlantic.

These great structures are only the highlights. The real contribution lies in the 2,900,000 acres of new lands brought into production through irrigation and the 2,600,000 acres which were supplied with supplemental water so that they could support maximum production, in the more than 125,000 prosperous new homes reclaimed from desert and sagebrush lands, and in the support these irrigated areas give to business and to the state and the national economy. Crops worth $7,800,000,000 have been produced on projects provided with a full or supplementary water supply by the Bureau of Reclamation. For 6 consecutive years, 1945 to 1951, the annual gross crop value has exceeded $500,000,000 (28).

Based on census records (21) and annual reports (29) of the Bureau of Reclamation, Fig. 5 shows the growth, cost, and crop value of lands irrigated on reclamation projects. Irrigation in the United States has been developed predominantly by private enterprise (individuals and partnerships, and cooperatives and irrigation districts). The development of irrigation by type of enterprise from census data is shown in Fig. 4(a).

Up to 1920, the largest investment in irrigation works was by individuals,

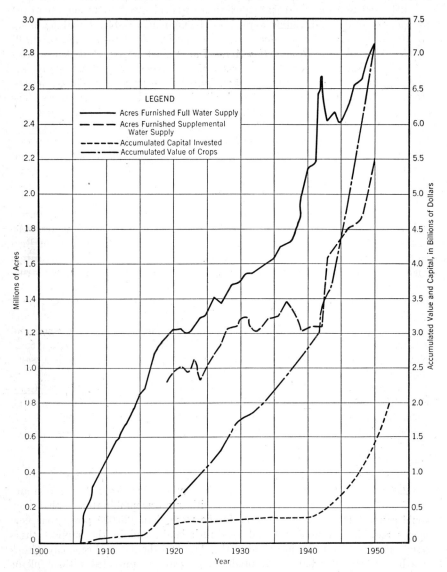

FIG. 5.—GROWTH OF RECLAMATION PROJECTS IN THE UNITED STATES

partners, and cooperative enterprises. From then on, the investment in irrigation districts and reclamation projects increased rapidly, and by 1950 the capital invested in irrigation districts and reclamation projects exceeded the total investment in all other types of enterprise, according to census records (Fig. 4(b)).

During the 50 years from 1852 to 1902, approximately 7,000,000 acres of land were put under irrigation by individuals, partners, cooperatives and commercial enterprises with local labor and limited private capital. The period from 1902 to 1952, sparked by the passage of the Reclamation Act, saw the construction of difficult, complicated, and expensive projects and the introduction of the concept of basin-wide developments for, in addition to irrigation, municipal water supplies, power and industrial uses, public health, fish and wildlife protection, recreation, navigation, and flood control. During this period while the Bureau of Reclamation with federal funds was supplying either full or supplemental water supplies to approximately 6,000,000 acres of land, a total of 12,000,000 acres of land was brought under irrigation with private capital largely through the expansion of areas already irrigated by companies or districts, the organization of new companies or districts, and the use of ground water by individuals or small groups. These private developments since 1902 have not been as spectacular as the federal projects, but they have increased and stabilized irrigation agriculture in the West.

Development of Irrigation Structures

Over the years there has been a wide change in materials used and in the size of structures built for irrigation. The most dramatic progress is in the methods of construction. Manpower, mules, and horses have been replaced by powerful machines capable of literally moving mountains—jobs which the mind of man could not conceive 100 years ago.

Dams.—The first diversion dams built were similar to those which had been used for centuries by the Indians and early Spanish-American people of the Southwest. Construction materials for these small structures were obtained at or near the site, utilizing brush, rocks, logs, and soil. If a farmer wished water from a creek, it was common practice to load up the wagon with barnyard manure and dump his load in front of some logs and brush previously placed across the creek. If this dam washed out, back to the barnyard he would go for material for a new dam.

Frequently rock material was available near a dam site, labor was cheap, and only a limited amount of cement and other materials needed to be hauled to the site. During this phase of development, some very fine arch-type masonry dams were constructed. They still stand (Fig. 1) and are admired for their architecture.

The next step was to the construction of concrete dams (Fig. 6). During this era, Hoover Dam, Grand Coulee Dam, and many others of large size were built and became monuments to the ingenuity of designing and construction engineers.

The most recent step is the construction of large earth-fill dams. A dam built of earth requires many times as much material as one constructed of concrete. Until machinery was developed for rapidly and economically moving and placing earth materials, few large earth dams were built. Now, large trucks, carryalls, or continuous belts rapidly move a steady stream of soil from the borrow pits to the dam site, and a mountain "grows" across the river to create a storage reservoir.

Canals and Ditches.—Construction of canals and ditches has followed a pattern somewhat similar to that of dams. The first ditches were built by hand or by plowing a furrow. If the ditch proved to be too small, it was plowed deeper. As more land was cleared and planted, small horse-drawn scrapers were used to enlarge the ditch, which might now be called a canal. Further enlargement or construction of new canals utilizes ditchers, power shovels, draglines, and other heavy earth-moving equipment.

When the first ditches or canals were constructed (Fig. 7), little thought was given to any kind of lining. There were usually adequate supplies of water in the streams; and, if the canal leaked badly, it might be enlarged to take care of the seepage and still deliver the desired amount of water to the farms; or occasionally silt would be dumped into the canal at the upper end, mixed with the water, and allowed to deposit throughout the leaking section. This period was followed by the expensive and time-consuming job of hand shaping the

FIG. 6.—MODERN CONCRETE DIVERSION DAM IN NEW MEXICO

canal section, forming it with lumber, and hand mixing and placing a concrete lining (Fig. 8). Today, machines are used for all this work. Automatic machines may move ahead, shaping the section and placing the lining. Also, other materials, such as asphalt, glass fabric, and clay are being developed for canal linings.

Structures for Canals and Ditches.—When irrigation first began in the West, head gates and control structures were extremely crude, and measuring devices were unknown. Head gates have changed from brush, sod, and wood construction to concrete poured in place, precast concrete, and metal gates (Fig. 9).

The first erosion-control structures placed in the ditches were probably of brush. Old wagon wheels and similar junk were frequently thrown into the ditch where erosion was taking place. Then came the simple concrete drops and the improved overflow and drop-inlet structures. Finally, in many areas, water has been completely controlled by being placed in underground pipes for distribution to and on the farms.

Furrow-Control Structures.—The first method of controlling water to furrows consisted of a shovelful of soil, a piece of sod, a few rocks, or a handful of grass.

FIG. 7.—TYPICAL UNLINED IRRIGATION CANAL IN ARIZONA

FIG. 8.—LINING A CANAL THE HARD WAY, AT BOISE, IDAHO, IN THE 1920'S

With such controls, close regulation of furrow streams was practically impossible. Some furrows would have little water in them. Others would overflow, and large quantities of soil would be washed from the fields. Now spiles or siphons (Fig. 10) of plastic, rubber, or metal and gated flumes and pipes (Fig. 11) are in common use for controlling the flow of water to the individual furrow.

Sprinkler Systems.—Sprinkler irrigation developed slowly, because of high costs, inefficient equipment, and low farm prices. Since 1940, the installation of sprinkler systems has been very rapid in many sections of the country, because of the improved financial condition of the farmers, better pump and sprinkler equipment, and the recognized need for controlled water application. Sprinkler systems are used almost universally where supplemental irrigation is practiced in humid and subhumid areas and in arid areas where rough topography or sandy soil makes surface applications impractical.

PRESENT STATUS OF IRRIGATION

That one-half acre put under irrigation on July 23, 1847, in Salt Lake Valley has in the short space of 105 years grown to nearly 25,000,000 acres (Fig. 12). Irrigation agriculture has become a basic industry supporting a new empire in the seventeen western states, and supplemental irrigation has spread across the humid and subhumid areas of the East and South. The simple brush, rock, and earth dams have been followed by such massive structures as the Hoover, Shasta (on the Sacramento River in California), and Grand Coulee dams. Storage reservoirs, control structures, wells, pumping plants, and more than 125,000 miles of canals and laterals constructed at a cost of more than $2,000,000,000 guarantee water for growing crops when and in the quantities needed.

Efficiency.—Americans have been notoriously wasteful in the use of their natural resources. Water is no exception. After 100 years of experience the over-all irrigation efficiency is less than 30%. Nearly one-half the water diverted from streams is lost in conveyance, and half of that delivered to the farm is lost before the water gets to the plant root.

Permanency of an Irrigation Agriculture.—Great civilizations supported by an irrigation agriculture have failed. The failure may be traced to the destruction of the source of water supply by invasion, erosion, or siltation. It may have been due to misuse of the soil or excessive water applications that caused waterlogging, salinity, or the accumulation of alkali. Whatever the cause of past failures, it is now established that irrigation agriculture based on a full knowledge of the interrelationship between the soil, water, and plants and a management practice which will use and conserve these basic resources is both permanent and profitable.

Research.—During the first 50 years of irrigation experience, little attention was paid to soil, water, or the crop. Only staple food and forage crops were grown. Beginning about 1900, it was recognized that soils varied widely and responded to different treatment; that it was possible to apply too much water; and that new crops, tillage practices, and application of fertilizers were needed. The United States Department of Agriculture and state agricultural experiment stations were established. Irrigation research began about 1900, but it soon became evident that research alone would not make irrigation agriculture permanent.

Three programs are necessary to a full and complete use on a permanent basis

Fig. 9.—Example of Concrete Diversion Weir and Head-Gate Control Structure

Fig. 10.—Use of Siphons for Controlling Flow Into Furrows

of the water, soil, and plant resources. Research by the Department of Agriculture and the state experiment stations has made great progress in establishing the basic soil, water, and plant relationships. The extension services, both federal and state, have conducted effective educational programs relating to irrigation agriculture; and the action agencies, including the Soil Conservation Service, the Bureau of Reclamation, and the Indian Service, have adapted the results of research and education to farm practices. Teamwork in research, education, and action has established irrigation agriculture as both permanent and profitable.

FIG. 11.—CONTROLLING FLOW INTO FURROWS WITH GATED PIPE

Continued teamwork in research, education, and action will guarantee full and efficient use of presently developed resources and the ultimate full development and efficient use of the undeveloped soil, water, and plant resources of the United States.

FUTURE IRRIGATION DEVELOPMENTS

The first 100 years of irrigation agriculture in the United States saw the development of nearly 25,000,000 acres of land supplied with water from surface and ground sources. About one half of this area suffers a water shortage every year. Ground-water supplies in such major areas as the San Joaquin Valley in California, the Salt River Valley in Arizona, and the High Plains of Texas are being exhausted faster than they are being replenished. Water applications in many areas are excessive, causing waterlogging, salinity, and loss of soil fertility. Conveyance losses are high, and farm irrigation efficiencies are low.

Increased Irrigation Efficiencies.—Rehabilitation of existing irrigation systems and improving methods of water application will greatly increase the

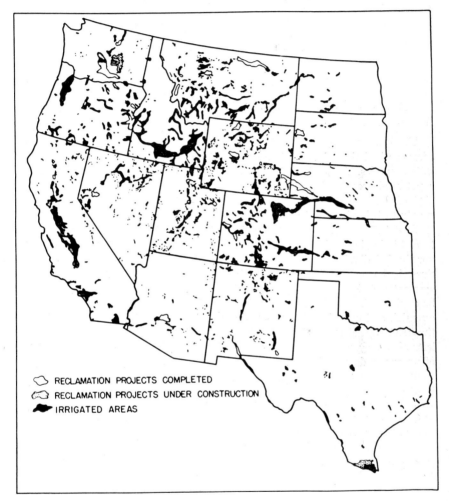

RECLAMATION PROJECTS COMPLETED
RECLAMATION PROJECTS UNDER CONSTRUCTION
IRRIGATED AREAS

FIG. 12.—MAP OF IRRIGATED AREAS IN THE SEVENTEEN WESTERN STATES, 1952

efficiency of water use (30). The present over-all efficiency of water use is less than 30%. By lining canals and laterals and improving distribution schedules, conveyance losses can be materially reduced. The irrigation efficiency on most farms is less than 50%. By adopting improved methods of water application and irrigating according to the needs of the crop, this can be increased to 70% or 80%. It is not unreasonable to expect an over-all efficiency of 50%. If this low efficiency were generally reached, it would practically double the present available water supplies.

By extending the use of both surface and ground storage, the water saved by increasing the irrigation efficiency would be available to reduce seasonal water shortages and to provide full supply for the undeveloped areas within existing projects. It is estimated that as such as 25,000,000 acre-ft of water annually could be made available by increasing the over-all irrigation efficiency from 25% to 50%.

Development of New Areas.—There are large areas of undeveloped arable land in the western states. Water is the limiting factor. It is estimated that about 400,000,000 acre-ft of water is the annual runoff from western streams. Of this, probably not more than 100,000,000 acre-ft are now being used to irrigate 25,000,000 acres of land. The Bureau of Reclamation (31) estimates that, with present technical knowledge and facilities, about 135,000,000 acre-ft of water annually is susceptible to development.

The Bureau also estimates that in the seventeen western states about 40,000,000 acres can be irrigated to produce crops with the presently developed or potential water supplies. Approximately 25,000,000 acres are now being irrigated, leaving a potential area for future development of 15,000,000 acres. In addition, about 40% of the presently irrigated area must be provided with a supplemental water supply to bring it to full production.

Sound Water Management Practices.—The most important aspect of the future of irrigation agriculture is neither the increased efficiency in the use of water nor the full development of the presently undeveloped land and water resources through the construction of huge basin-wide multiple-use projeects. Water management practices that will insure a high level of production in perpetuity must be established. Solution of soil erosion, siltation, and surface storage problems is essential, and more intelligent and widespread use of underground water storage through artificial recharging of the underground aquifer is necessary. The problems of conveyance to reduce seepage and waterlogging and to increase efficiency of water use demand immediate attention.

Problems relating to water application are numerous and complex. They involve getting water into the soil, storing water in the soil, and removing the excess waters from the soil. The kind of soil, surface and subsurface, the quality of water, and the tillage practices all influence the optimum water management practice. It is an established fact that some soils deteriorate under irrigation, that waterlogging, salinity, and alkali will destroy the ability of land to produce. Consumptive use and irrigation water requirements must be established for different crops under different climatic and site conditions.

The necessity of perpetuating agriculture in arid regions confronts the statesman, the scientist, and the engineer. The way to meet it is clear. The development of the sciences and their application to irrigation agriculture must be continued. A liberal allotment of funds, intelligence, and physical energy must be made to studies of water supply and its physical control, consumptive use and irrigation water requirements; methods of water application; and drainage and reclamation of saline and alkali soils—to the end that a maximum use on a permanent and profitable basis may be made of the nation's soil and water resources.

The progress of irrigation in 100 years has been beyond the engineer's wildest dreams. The problems today are as important as those which faced the pioneers 100 years ago and much more complicated; but today the engineer has 100 years of experience, more knowledge, better techniques, and equipment with which to solve them.

In closing, the following is quoted from A. F. Doremus, M. ASCE, former Utah State Engineer:

"Born of necessity and despised as menial, irrigation has grown to be king of the rapidly developing West, and by virtue of its power to bless and benefit mankind, it has compelled the respect and admiration of all. Its promise is potent, its progress sure."

BIBLIOGRAPHY

(1) "Irrigated Soils," by D. W. Thorne and Howard B. Peterson, The Blakiston Co., Philadelphia, Pa., 1949.

(2) *Encyclopædia Britannica*, 1948 Ed.

(3) "The Irrigation Works of India," by Robert B. Buckley, Spon & Chamberlain, New York, N. Y., 1905.

(4) "Ancient Water Codes," by Charles E. Stone, Columbia Basin Comm., Seattle, Wash. (unpublished).

(5) "Irrigation and Land Use in Ancient Mesopotamia," by J. W. Gruber, *Agricultural History Magazine*, April, 1948.

(6) "Ancient Mesopotamia and the Irrigation Systems That Made it a Fertile Territory," by A. Selwyn Brown, *Scientific American Supplement*, May 13, 1916.

(7) "Latin-American Civilization," by Baily W. Diffie, Stackpole & Heck, Harrisburg, Pa., 1945.

(8) "Fifteen Hundred Years of Irrigation History," by Old S. Helseth, *Reclamation Era*, December, 1947, p. 251.

(9) "Early Irrigation in the Western States," by George Thomas, Univ. of Utah Press, Salt Lake City, Utah, 1948.

(10) "Arizona and New Mexico," by H. H. Bancroft, A. L. Bancroft & Co., San Francisco, Calif., 1882–1890, p. 132.

(11) "Early Irrigation in Texas," by E. P. Arneson, *Southwestern Historical Quarterly*, Vol. 25, Austin, Tex., October, 1921, p. 121.

(12) "The Conquest of Arid America," by W. E. Smythe, The Macmillan Co., New York, N. Y., 1905.

(13) "Irrigation Institutions," by Elwood Mead, The Macmillan Co., New York, N. Y., 1903.

(14) "The Development of Institutions Under Irrigation," by George Thomas, The Macmillan Co., New York, N. Y., 1920.

(15) "A Century of Irrigation," by J. A. Widtsoe, *Reclamation Era*, May, 1947, p. 99.

(16) "Water Resources of California," *Bulletin No. 1,* Sacramento, Calif., 1951.

(17) "Irrigation in the United States," by R. J. Henton, *Progress Report*, U.S.D.A., Washington, D. C., 1890.

(18) "Reclamation As a Federal Investment," by F. D. Helm, *Reclamation Era*, March, 1935, p. 63.

(19) "History of Agriculture in Colorado," by A. T. Steinel, Colorado State Agricultural Coll., Fort Collins, Colo., 1926.

(20) "Mormon Settlement in Arizona," by J. H. McClintock, Manufacturing Stationers, Inc., Phoenix, Ariz., 1921, pp. 213–214.

(21) "United States Irrigation Census," U. S. Dept. of Commerce, Bureau of the Census, Washington, D. C., 1950.

(22) "First Committee Report on Supplemental Irrigation in the United States," U.S.D.A., Washington, D. C., January, 1952 (unpublished).

(23) "Colorado an Agricultural State," by W. E. Pabor, in "History of Agriculture in Colorado," Colorado Agricultural and Mechanical Coll., Fort Collins, Colo., 1926, p. 202.

(24) "Selected Problems in the Law of Water Rights in the West," by W. A. Hutchins, *Miscellaneous Publication No. 418*, U.S.D.A., Washington, D. C., 1942.

(25) "Elements of Western Water Law," by A. E. Chandler, Technical Pub. Co., San Francisco, Calif., 1913.

(26) "United States Agricultural Census," Bureau of the Census, U. S. Dept. of Commerce, Washington, D. C., 1899.

(27) "Forty-Nine Years of Progress," *Irrigation Engineering and Maintenance*, U.S.B.R., July, 1951, p. 21.

(28) "Reclamation Anniversary Facts," U.S.B.R., Denver, Colo., 1952.

(29) "Annual Reports," U.S.B.R., Denver, Colo.

(30) "History of Irrigation in Utah," by O. W. Israelsen, *Civil Engineering*, October, 1938, p. 672.

(31) "The Reclamation Program," U.S.B.R., Denver, Colo., June, 1948.

(32) "Crop Summaries," U.S.B.R., Denver, Colo.

AMERICAN SOCIETY OF CIVIL ENGINEERS

Founded November 5, 1852

TRANSACTIONS

Paper No. 2595

UNITED STATES WATER LAW

By S. T. Harding,[1] M. ASCE

Synopsis

The development of water law in the United States is reviewed, and its present status is appraised, in this paper. In general, greater progress has been made in the definition of principles and their applications to the determination of water rights for surface streams than for ground waters. This is the result of the earlier utilization of surface streams and their less involved conditions of supply and use. Similar advances in ground water have been retarded by more complex conditions of occurrence and greater difficulties in the measurement and control of use. Greater use of ground water, particularly in areas now overdrawn, is forcing attention to the resultant problems. Several western states are now seeking to improve conditions through various methods of control.

Problems relating to the use of water can and should be solved without major modifications in the present basic concepts of water law. Future changes should amplify and refine present fundamental principles. Such changes will represent regulation under the police power rather than the taking of rights recognized under present established principles.

The Centennial of Engineering covers the period during which the present water law in the United States has been developed. Title to the use of water becomes important only when the demand exceeds the available supply. A century ago there were many uses of water, but the amount of use had not resulted in such deficiencies that complete definition of the basis of title to use was required.

In the humid eastern states the early settlers, coming principally from England and finding conditions generally similar to those in the area from which they came, naturally transplanted the English common law of waters to their new homes. This law, which gave riparian rights on surface streams and complete title to underlying ground waters to the landowner, met such needs as arose in the settlement of these humid areas.

Water had been used for irrigation for what was then a relatively long time in some southwestern areas in the United States under practices brought in

---

[1] Cons. Engr., Berkeley, Calif.

by the Spaniards. Not until extensive use of water for mining began in the western states just about 100 years ago did the need arise for the development of a system of title to the water in surface streams which was adapted to the arid conditions in the western states. The customs developed by the early western miners became the principles of the system of appropriation rights now so thoroughly established in the arid areas of the United States.

Over the past 100 years each of these two basic principles of water law has been subjected to the modifications needed to meet the requirements of a country progressing from pioneering conditions to a stable economy. Further changes are occurring and will continue to be necessary to keep water law abreast of expanding development.

Under the federal system of government there is no national system of water law. Each state may adopt the one which it considers best. With the wide diversity in climatic conditions in the different states this is a major advantage in securing systems of water law suited to local conditions. The general system of riparian rights has been found to be well adapted to humid areas. Similarly the appropriation doctrine has been found to be preferable for conditions in arid areas. However, it is difficult to select and apply an appropriate system of title in the semi-arid states. In some states variations have been used within the state in order to meet more nearly the climatic conditions of the different parts.

Water law is a technical subject having many finely-drawn distinctions. This paper will not attempt to examine the more technical features, but rather will present a general survey of present practices with a discussion of the development and changes which may occur in the future.

No excuse is needed when an engineer undertakes to discuss a legal subject such as water law. The greater part of the procedure involving rights to the use of water relates to factual matters. The administration of water law is mainly under the direction of engineers, who require a knowledge of the controlling legal principles although their work is concerned mainly with the application of such principles to the widely varying physical conditions of water supply. Engineers in this field should be and are qualified to discuss the general policies of water law.

The physical conditions under which surface and underground waters are produced differ so materially that separate systems of title are needed. The flow in surface streams must be used as it occurs or it will be lost. The water may be conserved by diversion of direct flow or by storage, but the actual surface flow leaving the stream system is lost. Ground water is itself a form of storage and permits much more flexibility in the time and rate of its use. Surface waters are accessible for measurement and can be divided readily among legitimate consumers. Ground waters are difficult to administer quantitatively as measurement generally has to be made by some form of indirect determination. The development of water law can be discussed more conveniently by treating these two classes of water supply separately.

SURFACE WATERS

As previously mentioned, the older of the two systems of title to the use of water prevalent in the United States is known as the riparian rights doctrine, which was transplanted from England. In England water was needed for domestic and stock use and the generation of power at mill sites. Thus there was developed a recognition of advantage of position in securing water, and the riparian owners along the stream were given the rights to its flow. Between different riparian owners, rights were generally relative, each being entitled to a reasonable share of the available supply. This system is generally well adapted to the humid eastern states where consumption is usually less than the available supply. Also, each riparian owner may develop the power within the section of the stream under his riparian ownership.

The appropriation system is the outgrowth of early mining practices in the West, which at that time was open public land without laws for acquirement by the miners. Thus the miners made their own rules for both land and water titles. Among the miners, priority of possession, continuation of operation, and limitation on the area which could be acquired were the basic rules of title to mineral claims. These rules were matched in the title to the use of water for the mining claims by priority of appropriation, diligence in construction and use, and the restriction of the amount withdrawn to reasonable needs. Although there were similar practices in other areas, the development of this system among the miners was largely spontaneous and original. These principles remain today as the main basis for the appropriation system of water rights.

For arid areas the appropriation system has demonstrated its adaptability to the conditions. Priority of right to the one first in time would be capable of abuse if the prior right were not limited by the requirement of diligence in completing actual use and if the extent of the right were not in turn limited to the amounts needed under reasonable standards of beneficial use.

The appropriation system is now established as the exclusive system in the more arid western states. In the three Pacific coast states, early recognition of riparian rights has been overcome by restrictions on their application, so that in Oregon and Washington nearly all rights are now practically on an appropriation basis. California went further in recognizing riparian rights and took longer to work out a basis for their limitation. In California reasonable use is still recognized for riparian lands on a riparian-right basis but the former unreasonable advantage of riparian lands over nonriparian areas is no longer in effect. In the semi-arid states of the Great Plains, conflicts between the riparian and appropriation systems have not been extensive. Large projects based on storage are proceeding without essential distinction between riparian and nonriparian lands.

Acquirement of New Rights.—Under the riparian system, water rights are inherent in the land, and no separate procedure is required to secure rights to the use of water. Under the appropriation system, title to the use of water is obtained under a procedure which is separate from the acquirement of title to the land on which the water is to be used.

The procedure for the acquisition of appropriation rights has developed over the past 100 years from a simple declaration of intention to a state-supervised form of application, permit, and license. This change is the natural result of the need for a more definite, readily available, and up-to-date record of the status of rights during their period of acquirement. The early users were only required to post a notice of intention at their proposed point of diversion and to record a copy of the notice with the county.

No further steps were necessary to record which notices had been followed by actual construction, and there was no limit on the amount of water which could be claimed. At present nearly all western states require that an application to appropriate water be made to some state agency. The degree of discretionary control over the granting of such applications differs widely among the individual states. In Colorado the application is still only a declaration of intention with control by the state limited to the content and form of the application. In several other states, the state agency has varying degrees of authority to reject applications. Grounds for rejection may be inadequacy in the application itself, absence of unappropriated water in the source sought to be appropriated, lack of financial resources to carry out the project, or such a generality as not being in the public interest.

The western states have generally been averse to granting extensive discretionary powers to administrative officials to reject applications for appropriating the waters of the state. This policy in the early years was the result of fear that favoritism might be used and monopolies in water rights created. Some states still provide in their constitutions that the right to appropriate water shall not be denied. In such states, regulation is limited to requirements regarding the form and content of applications to appropriate.

As water supplies have been more fully used, support has developed for state guidance in apportioning the remaining unappropriated water so that it not only may be used beneficially but also may best serve the needs of the state. This policy has resulted in preferences between different classes of use and methods whereby the state could itself appropriate the remaining unused waters for state-selected and state-controlled projects.

In regard to preferments, domestic use, which now includes stock watering, is always rated first. Municipal use receives the same priority as domestic use although municipal use includes industrial uses. Second preference is generally given to irrigation in the western states. Power and mining usually rank third.

Such preferences apply only to unappropriated water. When title has once become vested, a preferred use has no authority to take water from an inferior use except by proper condemnation procedure. When applications to appropriate the same water supply may be pending at the same time, preferences between classes of use can be utilized to select the applicant to receive the permit.

State withdrawal of unappropriated water or direct appropriation by the state is authorized in some states. Withdrawal can be used to withhold acquirement until plans offering the greatest public benefit can be worked out. Also, by direct appropriation the state can retain control of unappropriated water until a project considered to be best adapted for the maximum benefit can be planned and undertaken. Such state appropriations do not require state construction, as priority can be waived for projects meeting the state's program.

Determination of Existing Rights.—No western state adopted methods of acquirement of water rights through state procedure until after many rights had become vested through use. To secure a definition of all rights on any stream, some form of quiet title or adjudication procedure is required.

Early adjudications of water rights in the United States were left entirely to court action between the contending claimants. Whereas suits to quiet title to land are a recognized and useful procedure, title to the use of water does not lend itself to a similar action by individual claimants. Titles belonging to all water users on a stream are interrelated, and all claimants need to be brought into a single action if the results are to be effective. Thus, court procedures were established in which all claimants could be made parties in a single adjudication with the decision binding on all. The cumbersomeness of such factual determinations, when conducted under the restrictive rules of court practice, led, in turn, to the establishment of administrative forms of adjudication by state agencies having semijudicial powers. In the latter case the administrative agency was authorized to secure its own record of facts by its own field investigations rather than being limited to the evidence presented by the contending parties. The administrative agency method reduces the conflict of testimony on factual items as the measurements of such an agency are generally accepted by the claimants. This procedure has been found to shorten the time and reduce the cost of adjudications. It is now in effect in some form in nearly all the western states.

As determination by administrative or semijudicial state agencies touches closely the functions of the courts, conflicts in jurisdiction have to be avoided. Different procedures are used in various states. In Wyoming the decisions of the administrative agency are final unless appealed to the courts. In Oregon, the administrative decision is always reported to the court and becomes final only when approved by the court. These differences affect procedures rather than results. Several states have found it preferable to follow the Oregon procedure in order to avoid the constitutional questions that might be raised if the full powers of a lower court were given to the administrative office.

It is essential that when all the existing rights have been defined on a stream some procedure be available whereby later rights can be defined without involving adjudicated rights. This result is secured when application to a state agency is required, the processing of which includes granting a permit to proceed and issuing a license on completion of construction and use. The license then becomes the equivalent of a supplemental decree to the new right, which has a priority based on its time of initiation.

Administration of Water Rights.—It is not enough to define the extent of the individual rights to the use of water from any stream. It is also necessary to provide procedure for the administration of the stream to assure that the owners of the rights receive the supply to which they are entitled at the time and in the amount of their needs.

The appropriation system lends itself to the definition and administration of water rights more readily than the riparian system. An essential element in the administration of any system of title to the use of water is the definition of each right so that the administrating agency is only required to administer and not to determine a changing status of the rights themselves. Individual riparian rights, being relative, change quantitatively with changes in the available water supply. Appropriation rights are separate individually and are served in the order of priority. In arid areas recognizing riparian rights, difficulties in administration have resulted in limitations on riparian use which represent an approach to placing the riparian users on an appropriation system.

On a stream having many users, where the supply at times may be insufficient for all needs, administration of daily diversions is essential for orderly use. The administrators are usually called water masters or water commissioners. They work under the direction of the court making the adjudication, where the court method is in force. They work as state employees where the administrative method has been followed. However, a court may use state employees as its water commissioners. As a water master does not have judicial powers and cannot define water rights, a definition of rights is required before a water master can function. The costs of administration are usually assessed against water users, with state participation in some states.

Interstate Streams.—In the United States, each state has jurisdiction over the waters within its boundaries but no direct jurisdiction within any other state. State boundaries were not determined by drainage areas, and there are many interstate streams. Obviously an upper state cannot be allowed to use its waters without regard to the rights of lower states. To meet such conditions the federal courts are available to determine conflicts in use between the states. Federal court adjudication has been found, like state court adjudication, to be time consuming and expensive with the resulting decision based on a technical application of legal principles that is not always most advantageous to the states involved. Federal courts have generally adopted the principle of equitable apportionment of the available supply between the states, leaving the detailed division of the share of any state among the users in that state to the state concerned.

A more direct procedure was needed for interstate streams as well as for streams within the states. This was found in the so-called interstate compacts. The federal constitution provides that states may enter into compacts covering matters of joint interest. These compacts are subject to approval by Congress before they become effective. An interstate compact is, in effect, a treaty between the states. Interstate water compacts have been held to be binding and limiting on individual rights within a state.

The compact method has largely replaced federal court adjudication for interstate streams. This statement applies to the apportioning of water on interstate streams in arid areas and to eastern streams where the subject of the compact may be either pollution or other forms of stream use.

Both adjudication in federal courts and interstate compacts seem preferable to their alternative, which is complete federal control of interstate streams. Although no system of dividing an inadequate water supply among claimants to its use can be expected to work to the entire satisfaction of all concerned, the advantages of retaining local control in the states are considered to outweigh greatly any claimed benefits from a single federal jurisdiction over all streams. It is incumbent on the supporters of continued state control to insure effective operation if the establishment of federal control is to be prevented.

Present Conditions and Future Needs.—On nearly all western streams, the extent of use has reached the point where the supply is less than the demand at least during parts of the year. This condition requires, and has resulted in, some form of definition of existing rights so that the streams can be administered and each right can secure the use to which it is entitled. Such adjudications and administration of appropriation rights have become well established and stabilized in the states where need for them has arisen. Further changes can be expected to be related to improvement in details rather than in fundamental principles.

There are now many streams in the western states for which rights have been defined and service is effectively administered. These include the Snake River in Idaho and the South Platte River in Colorado where extensive storage facilities have been constructed with the resulting commingling of natural flow and storage releases in the river channels.

In surface waters, as use continues to approach the total supply, projects for water development will continue to depend on regulation of the variable stream flows by storage. Closer administration will be required to meet the problems of determining the waters available for storage and of commingling the released stored water with the natural flow. Since return flow will continue to increase, a more complete definition of the character of rights to its use will be necessary for the many conditions under which it may occur. Transfers of water from the drainage area of origin to more valuable locations are becoming more frequent. The definition of what preference, if any, is to be given to the areas of origin in securing the use of the remaining unappropriated waters, is an active issue in some states.

How can these problems be solved? Surface waters are now being administered efficiently where conditions of use require effective supervision. As the need arises on additional streams, the same problems can be met by the application of present practices. No basic changes appear to be called for in the fundamental principles of the appropriation system or in the general administrative methods now being applied. Further definition and application of the basic principles to the increasingly complex conditions of use will continue to be needed and can be readily provided.

At present several western states fail to recognize the importance of adequate administration of the water rights on their streams. Often the head of the state agency in charge of administration of water rights, usually an engineer, is not given continuation of tenure and compensation commensurate with the value of his work to the state and the responsibilities of his position. Improvements in these conditions are needed if the states are to meet their responsibilities in water matters.

GROUND WATER

The development of the systems of title to the use of ground water has paralleled that for surface supplies since both have resulted from customs in areas of earlier use. In the case of ground waters the early courts had difficulty visualizing the nature of the supply for which they were attempting to establish rights.

In England ground waters were regarded as a part of the property of the surface landowners similar to the soil or underlying rock. Under strict English common law there could be no injury to others by the use of ground water because any use was within the right of the overlying owner to the property under his land. This rule was transplanted to the eastern states.

With the increased use of ground water, conflicts necessarily arose. The courts were reluctant to depart from the certain and easily applied English rule into any new field where decisions would be required on factual matters then poorly understood. Just a little more than 100 years ago an eastern court (Roath versus Driscoll, 20 Connecticut 533, 1850) stated, in discussing ground water:

> "It rises to great heights and moves collaterally, by influences beyond our apprehension. These influences are so secret, changeable and uncontrollable, we cannot subject them to the regulations of law, nor build upon them a system of rules, as has been done with streams upon the surface."

In spite of the difficulties involved, the cases where inequity occurred from the application of the English rule gradually forced the courts to modify this rule. Variations include the adoption of the rule of malice under which an overlying owner may not take ground water from his land merely because of malice toward his neighbor. Also, excessive taking for commercial sale which injured others has been restricted in some states. These were merely the first steps that led to legal recognition that ground water moved underground and that extensive taking affected the supply on adjacent lands. Eventually the courts in several eastern states adopted the so-called American rule under which overlying owners have varying degrees of correlative rights in the common ground-water supply.

Extensive use of ground water in California beginning about 1900 resulted in the need for a definition of the principles applicable to the title to its use. A system of correlative rights was adopted under which development has proceeded at a rapid rate. The experience in California, and in other states with extensively developed ground-water supplies, has furnished a background on which the merits of the different systems of title to ground water can be tested.

In California all persons owning land over a ground-water supply have equal rights in securing an equitable part of the available supply. Except for conditions where adverse use may have ripened into a prescriptive right, priority among overlying owners is not recognized. If the ground-water supply exceeds the reasonable needs of the overlying owners, the surplus may be taken for non-overlying use. For distant takers, priority governs relative rights.

This system has been in use for nearly 50 years in California with some amplification of its details but without change in its fundamental basis. A recent decision (City of Pasadena versus City of Alhambra, 207 P 2d 17) recognized what has been termed mutual prescription for both overlying owners and distant takers, under which the available supply in an overdrawn basin was prorated among all established users of both types. The general effect of this decision will depend on the extent to which its principles may be applied in other areas and under other conditions.

Other western states have found it necessary to define the basis of title to the ground water in their areas. New Mexico has adopted a system of limitation on draft from artesian basins where the state engineer finds the safe yield is being fully used. Idaho follows a system of appropriation for all ground waters as well as for surface streams. Arizona has very recently reconsidered the basis of title applicable to ground-water use (Bristor versus Cheatham, 240 P 2d 185, decision of January 12, 1952—rehearing granted later).

Although the legal principles relating to surface and ground waters are different in many states, physically these two types of water supply may be closely related. The law of surface waters is applied to subterranean streams where they can be identified. The former rule that a subterranean stream must have definable bed and banks has been broadened to include the subflow of a stream where withdrawal from the subflow increases the percolation from the stream. Some streams receive their flow as influent seepage from the adjacent ground water. In other cases the ground water has its source in the effluent flow from the streams. Thus it is difficult to adjudicate equitably between the users of these two types of water supply. Adjustments in such cases can be made more readily if the same basic principles are used for both surface and ground waters.

There are few extended ground-water areas in the arid states in which the naturally available ground-water supply is sufficient to meet the demands of the ultimate consumption of its service area. Unless the outcome is to be left to economic competition, with less efficient plants dropping out as pumping lifts increase, workable methods of defining rights and controlling use will have to be found and applied.

The general situation regarding the regulation of ground waters is similar to that for surface streams except that it is more difficult to determine and regulate the available supply. On surface streams the number of users is generally limited, and the available supply is accessible for measurement. When the draft on a surface stream exhausts the supply, the result is evident. For ground water there may be several thousand individual users drawing on a supply where overdraft may become known only by its effects after it has occurred for some time. Ground-water users generally obtain their supply from within their own land areas and are accustomed to regarding withdrawals as matters of their own choice. Both the physical and the human problems in regulating ground-water use are much more complex than those for surface streams.

The principles relating to the rights to the use of ground water in California have been adequately defined yet recognized overdrafts are occurring without any attempts to apply these principles through judicial procedure. Ground water has a relatively high value, and a continuation of overdraft without seeking to secure limitations on ground-water use must represent some failure in the effectiveness of the principles or in the procedure for their enforcement.

This situation exists because of the difficulty in defining the conditions to which the principles of law can be applied rather than because of any lack of definiteness or reasonableness in the principles themselves. To secure judicial relief it is necessary to define the area of overlying land, the extent of its existing supply, the present extent of use, and the reasonable needs of the existing users. The burden of the proof of these items is so great, the resulting cost of ground-water litigation so high, and the outcome so uncertain that, except in a few instances, the users in California areas have preferred to let economic competition take the place of general adjudication. Overdraft, if continued, results in increased lifts with the less economic uses being forced to give way and to abandon their operation. This situation occurred in some areas during the 1930's but has been offset in recent years by the increased prices received for irrigated crops. In time, the forced reduction in draft will reduce the use to the average replenishment, but the process leaves all surviving users subject to the pumping lift at which such abandonment occurred. Limitation of draft at the beginning of development to the average replenishment would have caused the same result in the amount of permanent use with the advantage of maintaining a much lower pumping lift.

The preceding comments apply particularly to areas of ground-water draft in the San Joaquin Valley. Here the areas supplied from the different sources of replenishment are indefinite and overlapping. It is difficult to prove that draft in one part will produce a definable effect in another part of the area. Relief has been sought by importing additional water supplies. In fact, the Central Valley Project had ground-water replenishment for its main incentive. Relief will, in turn, be a temporary solution unless further increases in use are regulated in some form. The consumptive needs of the areas available for irrigation exceed both local supplies and the importation from the present Central Valley Project.

There has been extended litigation in California over ground water, but this has been mainly between individuals or small groups and there have been no general adjudications of entire ground-water areas. In Southern California one such judicial decision has been made and another one is under way. In both these instances the areas in question have ascertainable boundaries.

Probable Trend in Ground-Water Regulation.—The increased knowledge of ground-water hydrology and the increased efficiency of pumping equipment are resulting in a rapid increase in the use of ground water wherever it is available in the western states. This trend is forcing and will continue to force the adoption of methods for the regulation of ground-water use.

In spite of the administrative complexities involved, public interest will insist on some means by which short-lived developments based on excessive overdraft can be avoided. It will be to the best interests of both the ground-water consumers and the public in the different western states if the solutions to these problems are worked out within the background of existing legal principles and with full consideration of the views and interests of the present users. The solutions reached do not need to be uniform in the different states any more than the policy for surface streams needs to be uniform.

How Much Can Established Systems of Water Law Be Changed?

Water rights are real property, and a system of title to the use of water when once adopted may not be changed if the change results in the taking of existing property rights without due process of law. Due process of law means taking for a public use and payment for the value of the property taken.

Because of the relatively large values created by the use of water in arid areas, it is impracticable to make radical changes in a system of title to the use of water once it has been confirmed in any area to such an extent that compensation must be paid to established rights. Values will have become fixed by the time development has proceeded far enough to demonstrate the need for change. No reversals in the system of water law requiring compensation have been made in any state after any given system has once become legally recognized.

The foregoing conditions do not mean, however, that principles of water law, when once adopted, become so rigid that modifications may not be made as need for change develops. All property is subject to reasonable regulation. Restrictions can be placed on the use of private property if necessary to prevent injury to others. Such restrictions come within the scope of what is termed the "exercise of the police power." The police power is not limited to the field of water law. Building and zoning ordinances in cities are well-recognized examples of the exercise of the police power.

Restrictions in the Public Interest.—Use of property may be restricted without compensation even if the usefulness of the property so restricted is reduced, provided the actions are in the public interest and are required for the benefit of the public. The changes now being made in water laws mainly come within the scope of regulation of existing rights in the public interest. They are subject to determination by the courts as to whether or not the proposed regulation is non-discriminatory and a reasonable exercise of the police power. In some instances the courts have modified the basis of title used in early development where it was held that the early basis had not been established to the extent that its change constituted a taking of property.

California furnishes an example of two methods of amending the earlier systems to meet later needs. When experience showed that the legislatively adopted system of riparian rights was blocking the effective use of surface waters, a constitutional amendment was passed in 1928 making all uses of water subject to reasonableness. Under the interpretation of this amendment by the courts, riparian owners are now protected in their established riparian titles but use under such titles must be reasonable in relation to methods and amounts. This decision is an example of modifying an established system of title to the use of water by a police-power regulation on its applications.

Ground-water use in California also furnishes an example of a change from an early practice to a different basis of title where the early practice had not become fully established. Early California cases involving ground water were not extensive and did not concern matters of widespread effect. When use of ground water did become extensive about 1900, it was realized that a different rule from that used in early cases was required if equitable results were to be secured and full development of the ground water was to be obtained. The courts recognized this condition and in a thoroughly argued and carefully considered case (Katz versus Walkinshaw, 141 California 116) held that previous cases had not fixed a system of title to ground water in California. The court then proceeded to consider and to adopt the system which it found would best meet the needs of the state.

For some matters in the field of water law, determination of the basis of use has been so incomplete that the courts can now find support for material changes without encountering constitutional prohibitions against the taking of property without due process of law. In certain western states the use of ground water has not reached the point where controversies have resulted in a full definition of the nature of title to its use. In such instances the courts may still be free to approve the adoption by statute or constitutional amendment of the system now considered to be adapted to the needs of such states. Utah, which in 1935 changed from a form of correlative rights to an appropriation system for percolating ground water, is an example in this field.

WATER RIGHTS FOR FEDERAL PROJECTS

Water law in the western states developed on the basis of local construction of local projects. Local forms of public organizations, such as irrigation districts, provided for the construction and management of water projects. There was practically no direct undertaking of water resources development by the Federal Government until the passage of the Reclamation Act in 1902. To date there has been only limited direct construction of state water projects by any of the western states.

The entry of the Federal Government into the water field as a proprietor of new projects introduced many new problems. It was recognized that it was necessary for federal projects to comply with the same conditions for the acquirement and use of water that applied to other owners. Section 8 of the original Reclamation Act required the government to follow state procedure to obtain water rights for its irrigation projects. This principle has been continuously in effect.

The Federal Government has always exercised control over navigable streams under the commerce clause of the federal constitution. To avoid conflict between the use of water to sustain navigation and its use for consumptive purposes, such as irrigation, the 1944 Flood Control Act made navigation in states lying wholly or in part west of the 98th meridian subordinate to the use of water for beneficial consumptive purposes.

It would appear that these provisions would be adequate to require federal water projects to conform with the system of water law in each state. Even on the earlier federal projects, some difficulties arose as federal agencies could, and in nearly all cases did, conduct litigation regarding federal projects in the federal courts.

Over the years, as federal programs covering water projects have been expanded, federal agencies, restive under their obligation to follow state laws, have sought to establish freedom from restraints. Various theories have been developed for this purpose. In several cases, although admitting that the Federal Government must recognize existing rights, federal agencies have contended that the Federal Government still had the right to withdraw unappropriated water from further nonfederal acquirement on a basis similar to that under which public lands may be withdrawn from further entry. This claim should have been fully answered by its rejection by the United States Supreme Court in Nebraska versus Wyoming (325 United States 589).

Government Asserts Authority.—More recently the Federal Government has asserted its "paramount authority" over all waters and has recently filed suit to establish such authority on a California stream in a proceeding known locally as the Fallbrook case. To date this controversy has been the subject of extensive outcry in the public press and has not reached the courts.

Another development in recent years has been the so-called "valley authority" program for the completely integrated use of all water within a stream basin, as illustrated by the Tennessee Valley Authority. Advocates of controlled development and planned economy have been active in seeking the creation of similar authorities in several western drainage areas. To date advocates of the existing system of private development, supplemented by federal aid on those projects beyond the scope of local resources, have succeeded in preventing the radical changes that would occur if the Federal Government were to dominate water development and use in the arid states. Water plays a vital part in the economy of these areas.

Supplanting present policies and laws by the directives of a federal agency would be the equivalent of replacing the present system of local government in the water field and practically eliminating local control. As the halfway point in the development of western water resources has been reached or passed, those having present rights to the use of water are deeply concerned over the way such rights might be affected by the establishment of a completely new and independent federal system. The preservation of recognized rights is as important to the arid states as are projects to develop remaining unappropriated water supplies.

Strength of State Administration of Water Laws.—Efforts to transfer the control of all waters to some federal agency are a natural outgrowth of the entry of the Federal Government into the construction of projects to develop water resources. Although state control of water use would be essential even if the Federal Government had remained an impartial party in water use, such state control has become even more necessary now that the Federal Government has acquired a major proprietary self-interest through its investment in federally constructed projects.

A major element in the strength of state administration of water laws has been the absence of any extensive self-interest on the part of the states in individual projects. Should any state undertake extensive construction of water projects, it would materially decrease its usefulness as the administrator of use of water by nonstate projects. The Federal Government is now so deeply involved in water development in the western states that it cannot act as an impartial judge between its projects and those of local origin.

The creation of valley authorities in western basins is being actively resisted by nearly all states and by local water interests within the basins. It is noticeable that nearly all promotion of such authorities has come from federal sources, either directly or indirectly. The decision as to whether or not such a radical change as that represented by a change from local control to federal authorities should be made is too important to be adopted on the basis of the self-interest of those desirous of becoming the administrating employees of the federal agencies.

National Water Policy.—Closely allied to the principles of title to the use of water are the public policies relating to its use. Present federal policies relating to water are generally recognized as confused and in some cases contradictory. The need for reconsideration and revision of national water policies has led to the recent report on this subject by the President's Water Resources Policy Commission.

During the period this commission was preparing its report, the Engineers Joint Council prepared and issued a report setting forth its views in this field.

There is a greater need for a redefinition of federal water policies than there is for revision and changes in water laws. It is hoped that progress in other matters now requiring the attention of Congress will soon permit it to give constructive consideration to this urgent subject.

Needs in Field of Water Law.—There is a growing need for more complete definition of rights to water under the many variable conditions of its use. This need is the natural result of greater use of water resources. More exactness is essential both in the principles and in their applications.

Any problems can and should be solved without major modifications in the present basic concepts of water law. Future changes should amplify and refine rather than fundamentally revise. Relatively speaking, such advances are more necessary for ground-water supplies than for surface streams.

No system of water law can be completely equitable in all its applications. In this, water law is no different from the other branches of the law of property. Perfect systems of law cannot be devised by human beings who themselves are not perfect in their aims and activities. In spite of these conditions the United States now has a generally good and workable body of water law well adapted to the needs to which it is applied. None of its possible defects furnishes justification for radical changes or departure from the established state and federal relationship in this field.

After 45 years of experience in the field of water-rights procedure in most of the western states, the writer is thoroughly convinced that present practices are well adapted to the arid areas. Under these practices progress may appear at times to be slow. This is the result of the caution with which proposals for change are considered. Experienced water users in the western states have become skeptical about the gains that it is claimed can be secured from radical changes in present basic principles of title to the use of water or programs for restricting present practices of local control. The field of water law in the western states is not static, and healthy progress is being made in meeting changed conditions as they arise.

AMERICAN SOCIETY OF CIVIL ENGINEERS

Founded November 5, 1852

TRANSACTIONS

Paper No. 2596

PLANNING AN IRRIGATION PROJECT TODAY

By J. W. Dixon,[1] M. ASCE

Synopsis

The ultimate purpose of an irrigation project, whether it is public or private, is to benefit the farmer, the businessman, the industrialist, the consumer, and finally the nation. Such projects have important and recognizable effects on the economy and social fiber of the areas where they are located, whether in the United States, or elsewhere. Six tenths of 1% of the world's land area is irrigated, and feeds 25% of the world population. With world population growing at 70,000 people a day, and with less land under cultivation than there was 15 years ago, irrigation becomes more significant. To meet community and regional needs, most projects serve more purposes than one, such as irrigation, flood control, hydroelectric power, municipal and industrial water supply, navigation, public health, fish and wildlife, recreation, and drainage. Participation of local interests in the planning, operation, and repayment of project costs contributes to project success. Throughout the world, leadership is needed within each country so that its particular needs can best be met according to its own devices and yardsticks. In the future, irrigation will probably be as firmly rooted in the eastern states as in the western ones. Increased supplies and better distribution of water, by salt-water conversion and artificial precipitation are intriguing prospects, since, for each four persons who sit down to dinner in 1950, there will be five to sit down in 1975.

A Challenge to the Engineer

Any proposal for the development of natural resources which is to be considered seriously must be appraised not only in its own light, but also in terms of how well it fits into, and becomes a part of, the best development for the whole area in which it is to be located.

Planning an irrigation project in the United States today should be based on an understanding of where this country and also where the world is heading in the matter of irrigation and related activities. The most constructive approach must start with the engineer himself, the man who is responsible for preparing the project plans, for he must always keep in mind that the ultimate purpose of

[1] Director of Project Planning, Bureau of Reclamation, U. S. Dept. of the Interior, Washington, D. C.

the irrigation project is to benefit not only the farmer on the ground, but the businessman who buys and sells his products, the industrialist whose operations depend on the project, and, finally, the consumer. The engineer who plans projects must have these thoughts so clearly embedded in his mind that they are automatically built into his project.

This professional responsibility and opportunity is being recognized more and more widely. Carleton S. Proctor, Past-President ASCE, stated at the Annual Dinner Meeting of the District of Columbia Section, ASCE, in Washington, D. C., on February 19, 1952:

> "The engineer's pride may shrink as the lesson becomes clear that all of the principles upon which this great progress has been built, and all that we and our profession have stood for, are today being challenged. * * * In perfecting labor-saving devices, mechanizations for rapidly increasing living standards, the facilities for mass entertainment and travel, we [engineers] have largely ignored our responsibilities for the social impacts, for the economic repercussions, and the cultural implementations of our work."

In a similar vein, Alberto Lleras, Secretary-General of the Organization of American States (Pan American Union) referred at the same meeting to

> " * * * the tremendous disparity between this Republic [the United States], and the twenty others [nations] of the hemisphere, in wealth, power, productivity, living standards and technical progress."

He also stated that:

> " * * * there probably could never exist a greater force, a political and economic power more homogeneous and invincible than that of three or four hundred million Americans all with a standard of living on a par with that enjoyed today by one-half of the people of the hemisphere."

As stated in a recent *Engineering Societies News Letter,*

> "The engineering profession is certain of its future technologically, but society is by no means certain of its future politically. The next few years will undoubtedly see the engineering profession placing less stress on its technical abilities, and turning more and more toward a concerted program of techno-political activities."

These facts are being recognized to a greater and greater extent in the nerve centers of the profession. A practical challenge faces the engineer—if he has done only a technician's job, he will have failed as a truly professional practitioner (Fig. 1).

This, then, is the challenge to the engineer. He must recognize that a resource development, such as an irrigation project, is not just something to build for the benefit of the immediately present landholders; it is a permanent economic asset; it affects the social fiber not only of the project area, but also of the surrounding region, and inevitably becomes an increment in this larger world situation.

To Bring the Picture Into Focus.—Technologically, the United States has been sound and aggressive in its irrigation development. In techno-political activities, however, it has much to learn, but it must go forward with a full realization of the place of irrigation in the economic structure of the country and of the world.

The Bureau of Reclamation (United States Department of the Interior) has a peculiar responsibility, for it desires, and quite naturally, to devote its attention to the development of the United States. However, in doing so the Bureau has

Fig. 1.—The Columbia River, an Economic Challenge to Engineers: Survey of Kettle Falls, Now Disappeared Under Backwater from Grand Coulee Dam in Washington, Which Gave Data for Best Total Development of Nation's Foremost Power Stream

also taken into account the effect of its actions in other areas. The responsibility has double significance: It has a direct effect simply by its existence; and it has become important because of the role the United States has assumed in giving technical assistance to irrigation developments throughout the world.

Varied Conditions.—In this country, there are wide extremes in climate. Many parts of the West are arid deserts. The middle tier of states vacillate from semi-

TABLE 1.—IRRIGATED FARM LAND IN THE UNITED STATES AND SEVERAL TERRITORIES

(Data from Preliminary 1950 Census; Series IR50–1 and Series AC50–1)

States	Census of Irrigated Lands 1939 (acres)	Census of Irrigated Lands 1949 (acres)	Ratio, 1949 to 1939
SEVENTEEN WESTERN STATES			
Arizona	653,263	979,014	1.5
California	5,069,568	6,618,595	1.3
Colorado	3,220,685	2,940,502	0.9
Idaho	2,277,857	2,168,323	0.9
Kansas	99,980	140,992	1.4
Montana	1,711,409	1,809,908	1.1
Nebraska	610,379	887,505	1.5
Nevada	739,863	722,896	0.9
New Mexico	554,039	691,429	1.2
North Dakota	21,615	35,759	1.7
Oklahoma	4,160	44,189	10.6
Oregon	1,049,176	1,338,226	1.3
South Dakota	60,198	84,356	1.4
Texas	1,045,224	3,148,115	3.0
Utah	1,176,116	1,166,659	0.9
Washington	615,013	617,362	1.0
Wyoming	1,486,498	1,475,069	0.9
Total	20,395,043	24,868,899	1.2
OTHER STATES			
Alabama	281	367	1.3
Arkansas	161,601	418,644	2.6
Connecticut	520	8,088	15.6
Delaware	7	404	57.7
Florida	132,362	362,909	2.7
Georgia	158	21	0.1
Illinois	307	1,510	4.9
Indiana	685	5,384	7.9
Iowa	2,258	1,386	0.6
Kentucky	205	485	2.4
Louisiana	447,095	598,056	1.3
Maine	143	2,398	16.8
Maryland	67	697	10.4
Massachusetts	2,049	18,507	9.0
Michigan	2,960	13,901	4.7
Minnesota	2,968	4,235	1.4
Mississippi	94	5,086	54.1
Missouri	960	2,089	2.2
New Hampshire	25	622	24.9
New Jersey	7,956	28,117	3.5
New York	5,948	19,248	3.2
North Carolina	246	2,083	8.5
Ohio	4,536	5,810	1.3
Pennsylvania	3,356	7,251	2.2
Rhode Island	109	1,631	15.0
South Carolina	411	6,408	15.6
Tennessee	311	1,012	3.3
Vermont	..	303	..
Virginia	687	2,817	4.1
West Virginia	270	40	0.2
Wisconsin	2,345	9,781	4.2
Total	780,920	1,529,290	2.0
FORTY-EIGHT STATES			
Total	21,175,963	26,398,189	1.2
OTHER UNITED STATES POSSESSIONS			
District of Columbia	..	13	..
Hawaiian Islands	132,661	118,846	0.9
Virgin Islands	..	13	..

arid to semihumid, changing alternately in irregular cyclical swings. The East generally is humid, but even in the East the annual crop loss from drought periods is amazing. Irrigation is essential to economic activity in large sections of the West. In the East, it is being practiced at an increasingly rapid rate, because it pays. Thus, in the United States, people have the opportunity to work with, and to see, many types of irrigation developments, under widely varying conditions. The distribution of irrigation practice throughout the United States, as determined during the last two censuses, is shown in Table 1.

Still the United States is no different in the way it has approached the irrigation problem from most countries throughout the world. It is true that this

Fig. 2.—Scofield Dam and Reservoir, a Single-Purpose Project, Which Is Rock-Faced, Earth-Fill Structure, 125 Ft High, Providing 13,000 Acre-Ft of Supplemental Irrigation for 16,000 Acres near Price, Utah

country has mechanized construction to a high degree, but it started, as most countries did, with single-purpose irrigation projects (Fig. 2). That type was the most readily conceived and the cheapest to build. The projects were usually relatively small, and they came easily within the mental grasp of everyone concerned.

Power, Too.—Then about 1909 the United States began developing hydroelectric power in connection with irrigation dams, and using the power not only for the operation of the irrigation works on the projects, but also for general consumption in the area. Gradually, as the number and size of projects were enlarged, the power systems were tied together to form larger and more effective transmission systems. That process is still going on.

During the same period, and as experience and comprehension of how to utilize opportunities grew, storage capacity to control the floods began to be incorporated in reservoirs. This multiple-purpose function is now important and will become increasingly so, as more and more of the base flows of the streams are put to beneficial uses and as, finally, flood flows are all that remain for further irrigation development and for additional municipal and industrial water supplies.

Multiple-Purpose Idea.—It would be impossible to fix a definite date on which the multiple-purpose concept was born, or to establish when it matured into recognized use. It would be fair to state that it was introduced about 30 years ago, and existed in relatively unused solitude for another 10 years. However, multiple-purpose projects are now thoroughly accepted, and an engineer would be considered remiss if he did not consider all possible uses, in connection with the planning of any irrigation project.

The objective of the multiple-purpose project is simply to create the greatest total amount of benefits at minimum total cost, and with a minimum number of conflicts among the services it is to perform. Each purpose, together with the resultant economic benefits and costs, is considered in the light of other possible present or future uses of water, and the ultimate result is a project that most nearly reaches full economic development of the potential resources at hand. Through such analyses, it is possible to resolve many conflicts among the various uses of water, and to achieve a well-balanced total project.

Conserving Resources.—Planning for a major irrigation project cannot be disassociated from planning for development of other natural and economic resources, including consideration of the opportunities that may be created for commerce and industry (Fig. 3).

When this fact is fully assimilated on a world-wide basis, and when the real need for food throughout the world becomes something that the whole world is working on and not just talking about, the reclamation engineer will be, in truth, a tool for world peace. Already the Bureau of Reclamation is very conscious of this situation for at present technical men are giving assistance in more than twenty other nations under the Technical Cooperation Administration and Mutual Security Administration programs, or otherwise working in cooperation with the State Department.

A nation will not prove to be economically strong for any great length of time unless it safeguards and develops its basic water resources. Historians have known this, and archeologists have proved it in exposing the abandoned fields and the masterpieces of vanished civilizations in north Africa. Americans have learned their lesson there, and in some of their own lands that have been despoiled. The past 150 years have also demonstrated the fruits of an expanding economy, by creating new wealth in the forms of food, clothing, the products of industry, and the stability which comes from economic well-being. Well-planned irrigation projects, and programs to conserve and save the soil and prevent floods, are some of the ways that this result is being brought about—ways by which to avoid the spade of the archeologist in the United States.

Basic Data and Purposes.—It must not be presumed, however, that a sound water, and topographical and climatological data, together with information it is always necessary first to have adequate basic data, such as stream-flow records, precipitation records, determinations of the quantity and quality of water, and topographical and climatological data, together with information on minerals and related physical resources, and many other factors. Those are the foundations on which irrigation and related development programs must be predicated.

Fig. 3.—Buffalo Bill Dam on the Shoshone Project near Cody, Wyo., Spectacular Tourist Site —a Multiple-Purpose Structure, 325 Ft High, with 456,600 Acre-Ft of Storage, Providing 100,000 Acres of Irrigation and 10,600 Kw of Power

There is no simple rule that can define which purposes are capable of being served, or should be served, in any given project, until all the analyses are made. They will vary from project to project, in terms of both the need for those services in the project area, and the capability of the project to render the desired service.

Objectives to Be Considered

Nine purposes are most common: Irrigation, flood control, hydroelectric power, municipal and industrial water supplies, navigation, public health, fish and wildlife, recreation, and drainage. It can be said without contradiction that they are as applicable in most other parts of the world as they are in the United States. If these nine purposes are evaluated correctly, and are competently provided for, other values will also develop in consequence.

Irrigation.—Irrigation has been practiced throughout world history, but its degree of success, and the methods used, vary tremendously. Many countries recognize irrigation as essential to survival. It was not necessary to national survival in the United States 200 years ago, but today it is an essential part of the economy, and will become increasingly so.

The United States passed the date line when its exportation of foodstuffs exceeded its importation 30 years ago. There is no more land under cultivation today than in 1920. Nevertheless, 45,000,000 more people are being fed—and on a higher standard of living.

Agriculture Versus Population.—Many factors have helped make this production possible, and a few of them are sufficiently outstanding to bear mentioning. One reason, of course, is the tremendous increase in irrigated land—and it is exceedingly high-production land (Fig. 4). Another reason is that the use of synthetic fibers, such as rayon and nylon, has released land from cotton growing, which has become available for raising food. Also, the use of fertilizers has increased, and the quality of seed and of farming practices has improved. Perhaps one of the most surprising reasons, though, is that through the rapid growth in the use of automobiles, tractors, and trucks the number of horses has been so reduced that 60,000,000 acres of land, formerly used to grow hay and fodder, have now been converted to the production of food for humans.

The place of irrigation throughout the world has even more vital significance. The land that is irrigated represents only about six tenths of 1% of the world's land area, yet that small irrigated acreage supports about 25% of the world's entire population.

Each year the world population increases by 20,000,000 people. If that amount is brought down to size for easy mental grasp, the result is that each day the world has to feed 70,000 more people than it did the preceding day.

Notwithstanding this fact, the land under cultivation in the world stopped expanding many years ago. During the decade from 1940 to 1950, there was a 3% decrease in the cultivated areas of the world. In short, and despite the war, the world population increased by 200,000,000 people between 1940 and 1950, without any corresponding increase in the area of cultivated land to feed it. Sir John Orr, who was the first President of the United Nations Food and Agriculture Organization, said: "In the race between population and food, population is winning."

The consequence is alarming, for nearly half the people on earth do not have enough to eat from the day they are born until the day they die. Then, too, they die early, for their life span is only about two thirds of that in the United States.

To maintain present standards of living and at the same time to be realistic, plans in the United States contemplate an increase in population of at least 40,000,000 people within the next 25 years. Obviously, this country must provide for at least its own part of this increasing world population.

World Conditions.—A fairly recent survey made by the Bureau of Reclamation concerning the status of irrigation throughout the world disclosed that

FIG. 4.—HIGH PRODUCTION BY IRRIGATION: FIELD OF PINTO BEANS SHOWN BEING CULTIVATED, 15 MILES NORTH OF RIVERTON, WYO.

India, Pakistan, and China have the largest number of acres under irrigation, from 30,000,000 to at least 50,000,000 acres in each country. The United States is fourth with 26,000,000 acres; and there are many other countries that have substantial irrigated areas such as Egypt, Mexico, Chile, Argentina, Brazil, Java, Italy, France, Japan, Iraq, and the Soviet Union.

Probably nowhere in the world, however, is it more apparent that food is essential for economic and physical survival than in the southern Asiatic countries. That is a great area of new governments and an awakening people. Its leaders are fully aware of the needs, and they are doing their utmost to meet those needs, but it is an uphill fight. Surprisingly, those same areas of wide-spread poverty and concentrated wealth also hold to a large degree the secret of their own relief, because they are blessed with rich, but undeveloped natural resources. Such unbalance is understandable, but no less undesirable.

Conditions in the United States have tended to get out of balance at times, but usually in the opposite direction from that in south Asia. The problem here is one of allowing engineering progress occasionally to get ahead of the ecology and the developmental policy which the Federal Government, or some of its groups of leading citizens, have supported. Neither state of unbalance is good, but at least it can be said that the American variety of unbalance keeps the nation fed, clothed, and occupied.

Financing Practices.—During that same survey of irrigation throughout the world, another most interesting discovery was made. It dealt with the national policies of the several countries for financing irrigation projects. Most countries assist the development of irrigation projects in one degree or another. Nations which have had irrigation as a standard practice over the longest periods of time are the ones that provide the greatest degree of federal participation. Those nations have found that to do so is sound financial policy, not only because economic and social benefits result, but because the federal governments are repaid many times over in one way or another.

For example, in Thailand, formerly Siam, it appears that the government pays 100% of the costs of the irrigation works and recoups its investment from the excise taxes. The reverse of that financial practice generally applies in countries which are younger in terms of irrigation as a national undertaking. Here in the United States, for example, the irrigator is required to repay directly all or a substantial part of the irrigation costs. As a minimum he is required to repay all that he can afford to repay.

Nevertheless, this is still the national policy in spite of the fact that examination of fifteen federal reclamation projects, collectively costing $285,000,000, shows that the Federal Government, to date, has collected some $525,000,000 in individual income taxes from those same areas—and that income will continue. In addition, other federal taxes such as corporation income taxes and excise taxes have produced, in those same areas, an additional $250,000,000. Hence, it may be noted that, by making an investment of $285,000,000, the Federal Government has collected, mainly from the immediate beneficiaries, $775,000,000, not counting the direct repayments of project costs by the water and power users.

The economic effect of creating this new weath is not just local—it is national. The social effect is equally real, with firmly rooted and prosperous towns and satisfied hard-working citizens. The economic impact of the federal reclamation program in the United States can be measured by the fact that the value of the crops produced annually, crops that would not otherwise exist, is more than $500,000,000.

Economy in Land Use.—National policies may be the result of popular demand, which is the case in the United States; or they may be born of necessity as is the case in Egypt, which is solely dependent on irrigation for its agricultural existence. The 13,500,000 people in Egypt are supported by only

5,400,000 acres of land, about one acre for every three persons. Compare this with the United States standard which at present is more than two cultivated acres for each person. In other words, here about seven times as much land is devoted to the support of one person as in Egypt. The general living standard in Egypt, of course, cannot be compared with that in this country, but the comparison illustrates what can be done with a limited land area. Three quarters of the entire population of Egypt is engaged in work related to agriculture. With improved irrigation techniques, and the construction program which is now under way or contemplated, there is certain to be an uplift in living standards.

The actual achievements on the Salt River Valley Project in Arizona, as shown in Fig. 5, specifically illustrate the economic results of a federal reclamation project in the United States. Construction of the project began in 1903.

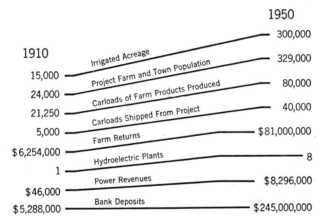

FIG. 5.—GROWTH OF AN IRRIGATION PROJECT ; EXPERIENCE OF MARICOPA COUNTY, SALT RIVER VALLEY, ARIZONA, 1910 TO 1950

Before development by irrigation, the Salt River Valley was essentially an arid desert wasteland, suitable at best, and only in small parts, for grazing lands. Initially it was partly developed by private capital, and then was further developed on a repayable basis with technical and financial assistance by the Federal Government. It now contributes materially to the national economy as well as to the livelihood and production of that large community. Included in the Salt River Project is the City of Phoenix, largest in Arizona, with a population of 105,442 in 1950. Phoenix and the surrounding urban, suburban, and farm tracts is an area of high cultural and economic development.

Flood Control.—The precious resource called water can also be an enemy if it is allowed to go unleashed (Fig. 6). The control of floods has been practiced for centuries in one form or another, but systematic flood-control plans are not universal, and have only been under way in the United States on any broad scale for a few decades..

In arid areas, such as in the Central Valley of California, combined irrigation and flood-control reservoirs are standard practice. They capture the floodwaters and hold them in storage for release, later, to serve irrigation. In arid areas where seasonal floods also occur, therefore, flood control may be considered to be a normal use of most multiple-purpose projects. The regular practice of capturing water for irrigation purposes results in flood-control benefits.

Hydroelectric Power.—Hydroelectric power is another, and an important, means of developing water resources. Generated as it is by falling water, it derives energy from a renewable resource and conserves irreplaceable sources such as coal, oil, or gas. In the United States it is the "paying partner" for the irrigation developments. Although single-purpose hydroelectric power

Fig. 6.—Havoc Created by the 1948 Summer Flood on the Columbia River; an Industrial Plant near Portland, Ore.

plants can be, and are constructed, the federal projects in the United States are developed more often and most economically in combination with storage reservoirs constructed also to provide water for irrigation purposes (Fig. 3), or for the improvement of navigation, or for the control of floods, or for a combination of uses. Even so, except regionally, federal power has not been carried to the lengths practiced in Switzerland, Norway, Sweden, and Japan where hydroelectric plants have been the major influence in bringing mechanization to industry.

When power is generated at a federal irrigation project, some of it, of course, is used on the project itself, and the surplus is sold commercially at wholesale. Power from such projects and from navigation and flood-control projects has had a major contributing influence on the extractive industries in such areas as the Pacific Northwest for the operation of mines and for timber operations; and large blocks of energy have been provided for basic industries, such as the conversion of bauxite into aluminum.

Some day atomic energy may become a source of commercial and domestic energy. However, authorities on that subject admit that they are unable to foresee such a prospect at this time.

Municipal and Industrial Water Supplies.—One of the most vital requirements for water is to meet the domestic needs of cities and villages, and of the industry usually found there.

An adequate supply for city purposes 30 years ago was considered to be 50 gal of water a day per person, but that amount is no longer sufficient. Per capita use is increasing, and is now from two to three times the former requirement in many, if not most, cities, largely because industrial uses have increased by almost 40% in the past 10 years.

It is encouraging that an ever-increasing number of public and private officials are beginning to recognize that careful study needs to be made of the available water supply before an industry is located in any particular area. By the same token, they are beginning to realize that the character of the industry must be examined carefully, for different industries require different amounts and different qualities of water in their processes. To sharpen this point:

(*a*) The manufacture of a ton of rayon yarn, depending on the process, requires from 250,000 gal of water to 400,000 gal of water;

(*b*) The manufacture of a ton of roofing felt requires from 7,000 gal of water to 14,000 gal of water; and

(*c*) The manufacture of a ton of steel requires several tons of water.

Navigation.—Many multiple-purpose reservoirs built essentially for irrigation under the reclamation laws, such as the great Shasta Dam on the Sacramento River in California, contribute to the improvement of navigation (Fig. 7). That same dam stores irrigation water for one of the greatest projects in the world, generates large amounts of power, and, by its releases of stored water, repulses the invasion of salt water from the sea into the rich delta area at times when the natural stream flows are low. Whenever multiple-purpose projects are to be built, the need for improvement of navigation should be ascertained; and, if such improvement is economically justified, provision should be made to render this service.

Public Health.—By the same token, in the planning of irrigation reservoirs, provision of storage for municipal and industrial water supplies should be made. Furthermore, under certain circumstances, stored waters may be released to dilute polluted waters further downstream. Also, occasionally, opportunity is found to control or eliminate that internationally renowned malaria carrier, called the mosquito. In some projects the reverse is true, and particular care must be exercised in developing the reservoir operation plans so that the reservoir does not contribute to the reproduction of mosquitos.

Fish and Wildlife.—Water, fish, and wildlife are usually good friends (Fig. 8). It would be shortsighted if the planning of an irrigation project failed to take into account the favorable as well as the adverse effects which a proposed project may have on these valuable resources. As in the case of public health, the plan of reservoir operation must be carefully worked out if the greatest possible benefits are to be attained.

Recreation.—Recreation is a product of every irrigation project where reservoirs are involved. Experience has more than demonstrated that the reservoir will be used for recreational purposes. In consequence, this fact must be taken into account at the outset to assure inclusion of practical facilities in the plans at the time they are being prepared.

Drainage.—Although the practice of reclaiming lands by drainage can be carried on independently, it is almost always a necessary part of a plan for an

FIG. 7.—THE CENTRAL VALLEY PROJECT IN CALIFORNIA, EVENTUALLY TO PROVIDE 150 MILES OF NAVIGATION UP THE SACRAMENTO RIVER ; VIEW SHOWING GRAIN BARGES DOCKED AT SACRAMENTO

irrigation project (Fig. 9). The placing of irrigation water on the lands in some areas causes leaching of basic salts from the soils, and these waters must be drained off. In other areas, the character of the soil, or the topography, or both, necessitate drainage works.

MULTIPLE-PURPOSE AND BASIN-WIDE PLANS

There are other and less common purposes that can be served in connection with the development of an irrigation project; but the foregoing nine illustrate the desirability of considering multiple-purpose uses of the projects whenever circumstances indicate practicability and economic justification. When the multiple-purpose concept becomes a clear and workable tool of the engineer, it automatically takes him two steps further.

The first step is the recognition of the relationship of all projects within a given river basin, each to the others. This result is inevitable, and thus was born the basin-wide concept with each single-purpose and each multiple-purpose project in a river basin integrated so as to give the best over-all result. As the water resources of any given river basin become more and more fully utilized, it is essential to approach the planning job on a basin-wide basis, for the new

FIG. 8.—CANADIAN HONKER GEESE OVER TULE LAKE SUMP, WILDLIFE REFUGE IN CALIFORNIA, WHERE THE BIRDS HAVE NESTING GROUNDS AND MAY BE SEEN THE YEAR AROUND

projects must complement and not interfere with the existing developments; and, at the same time, the new projects must not forestall full ultimate development.

The next inevitable step is the interbasin or regional plan. Through the exportation of water from one river basin to another, those basins that have a surplus can contribute to those that have a deficiency. The flow of electric energy through systems of transmission lines is by no means controlled by watershed boundaries; nor are mineral deposits, timber growths, or the lines of commerce. Thus, the regional characteristics of interbasin plans are inherent, but it takes imagination and care, during the period of plan preparation, if the engineer is to recognize all the intrinsic possibilities.

In the development of the irrigation program in the United States engineers are already working on that basis, and indeed some projects are substantially completed. The Colorado-Big Thompson Project in Colorado, through its integrated assemblage of storage reservoirs, pumping plants, water conveyance systems, and power generation structures, takes water from the western slope of the Rocky Mountains through a 13-mile-long tunnel to the cultivated lands on the eastern slope. This project, straddling as it does the Continental Divide, must be taken fully into account in the plans for the development of the Colorado River Basin on the west and of the Platte River Basin on the east.

Fig. 9.—A Deep Drain, Imperial Irrigation District in California, Typical of 1,500 Miles of Ditches, 6 Ft to 12 Ft Deep, Which Prevent Land from Becoming Waterlogged

Plans for similar projects such as the Fryingpan-Arkansas Project in Colorado, are substantially completed. Preliminary study, on a reconnaissance basis, has been given to a much larger extension of the same principle—the United Western Project, which, if undertaken, could at least double the horizon of the economic limit for total irrigation in the West. It must be obvious that the economic, social, legal, political, and interregional problems connected with any such undertaking will be at least as difficult to work out as the engineering complications.

INTERNATIONAL PLANS

The responsibility for the development of water resources and for the improvement of the economic and cultural development of the nations of the world rests not only with each country for itself, but among the countries. Leadership is essential within each country so that its particular needs can best be met according to its own devices and yardsticks.

Particular leadership is also needed among the nations, for solutions of controversies and the preparation of plans to utilize, for the benefit of all concerned such international streams as the Danube, Nile, Rio Grande, St. Lawrence, Columbia, and Indus. The countries of Afghanistan and Iran are now holding conferences looking toward the settlement by amicable means of the problem of the Helmand River. India and Pakistan are working diligently and constructively, through the good offices of the International Bank for Reconstruction and Development, to resolve certain highly complicated situations which resulted from the creation of the new country of Pakistan. The fruits of sound international agreements are real and wholesome, and here again they may involve, or have a direct bearing on, the peace of the world.

An example of the forthright and productive effort of this character is the Falcon Dam in Texas which the United States and Mexico have under construction on the Rio Grande. It is the first international dam of any such proportions in the world, and other dams are to follow. Each country will share the water and power to be developed, floods will be reduced, and each country will have an improved irrigation development from the floodwaters which would otherwise waste to the sea.

In 1949, the United Nations took a forward step on the international scene and conducted the "Scientific Conference on Conservation and Utilization of Resources." Through such media, and through such groups as the Economic and Social Council of the United Nations, international leadership and understanding might be stimulated, for almost every conservation program includes activities for the use and control of water. Similarly, through such distinguished and continuing commissions as the International Joint Commission between the United States and Canada, and the International Boundary and Water Commission between the United States and Mexico, it will be possible to work out mutually satisfactory plans or solutions for specific proposals.

The composition of a plan, its purposes, and the peoples which it serves dictate many of the controlling principles on which it must be predicated. There are, nevertheless, other controlling principles—namely, those laid down as basic policy within each nation as a guide.

Principles of Federal Development in the United States

One fact that must always be kept in mind in a federal irrigation or multiple-purpose project in the United States is that it is a public, rather than a private, service. As its initial goal it must be useful to the man on the ground.

Joint Participation.—The initial federal Reclamation Law of 1902 embodied what were in those days startling new concepts of cooperation between the people and their government in the construction, operation, and maintenance of irrigation projects. It created the principle of repayment by the beneficiaries. This, in turn, quite naturally caused the potential beneficiaries to want to study the proposed projects with the engineers as the investigations unfolded. Such procedure cannot be commended too highly for, by the time the plan is adopted, everyone knows just what it is, why it is the way it is, what type of development may be expected to result, and who is expected to repay what costs.

Directors of an irrigation district sometimes employ competent outside consulting engineers to review the Bureau's plans—a valuable double check. Furthermore, as the directors are concerned about the future of the district, they want to be able independently to certify that they are obtaining the best possible plan—the one that will give them what they want, and at a cost that they can afford—before they sign a recordable contract in behalf of all the irrigators on the project to repay the assigned share of the project costs.

In addition, and as a result of succeeding laws, Executive Orders, and interagency agreements which have been adopted primarily in the past 15 years, the Bureau also cooperates with many other federal agencies, including the several in its own Department of the Interior, such as the Geological Survey, the Bureau of Mines, the Fish and Wildlife Service, the National Park Service, the Bureau of Land Management, the Bonneville Power Administration, and the Southwest Power Administration. There are also other cooperating agencies not in the Department of the Interior, such as the "Civil Functions" part of the Corps of Engineers, the Federal Power Commission, the Department of Agriculture, the Federal Security Agency, and the Department of Commerce. Furthermore the Bureau has always extensively cooperated with the governors of the states or their designated representatives, and state agencies.

Federal and Local Interests.—Many, if not all, of those groups review the plans both during the course of their preparation, and also when they are in final form. Admittedly, this galaxy of participation and review complicates the procedure, but in principle the effort results in products that represent the best possible plan of development. Certainly, as a minimum benefit, all affected interests have full opportunity to express their views and to make suggestions which can then be taken into account in any practical modification of the plan.

The Federal Government policy is that the local irrigation district officials not only participate in the planning of the jobs and in the repayment of the project costs, but also, as soon as they are capable of undertaking it, take over the operation and maintenance of the irrigation works. It is also the federal policy to adopt such steps as are practicable to avoid speculation in lands that are to be put under irrigation, and to spread the project benefits among the public.

It is fast becoming recognized in the United States that an undeveloped renewable or stable resource, such as water or land, is not a resource in the bank. It is a resource being wasted.

In connection with the disposition of hydroelectric power, it is the policy to transmit and dispose of power and energy in such a manner as to encourage the most widespread use thereof at the lowest possible rates to consumers, consistent with sound business principles.

Land Limitation.—The Federal Government also encourages, as a matter of both law and policy in connection with irrigation projects, the development of family-sized farms (Fig. 10), presently limited to a maximum of 160 acres per owner. This is a point on which Americans have heard a great deal of argument. The land limitation feature is admittedly arduous to administer, and there are vocal groups who insist on its retention, and others who suggest its repeal. Improvements might be made; however, it is of interest that every nation that has clung to the feudal landholding system experienced one of three results: (1) Final collapse as population pressures mature; (2) a shift over to popular landowner-ship patterns; or (3) a dormant economy, with a small but wealthy ruling class, and a large relatively uneducated working class.

One other important aspect of the federal policy with regard to the irrigation developments is that water rights for all projects are secured in accordance with the laws of the states in which the projects are located. This procedure is correct for the rights and privileges of every state with regard to development of its natural resources are recognized.

Benefits.—A book could be written on the benefits from irrigation and multi-ple-purpose projects. In fact, there are parts of many books already written on

Fig. 10.—The Family-Sized Farm (Here Producing Sugar Beets) on the Sunnyside Project near Yakima, Wash., Illustrating the Primary Benefits of Irrigation and Electric Power—Security and Good Living

that subject. Generally, benefits fall in two categories, direct (Fig. 10) and indirect (Fig. 5), and there are many in each category.

There is general agreement within the United States on the kinds of direct benefits, and how to measure them, but spirited discussion ensues on how to measure the indirect benefits. Everyone agrees that the indirect benefits exist, but not many seem to agree on how to evaluate them. For the sake of brevity, only the most ordinary types of benefits in each group are listed in Table 2.

Quite aside from specific benefits resulting from an individual project, there are two other types which are regional or national in character. They are: (1) The opportunity to create a balanced economic development within a region—and a balanced economy is conducive to a healthy free enterprise; and (2) competi-tion. As former Assistant Commissioner of Reclamation, W. R. Nelson, M. ASCE, has stated:

"The benefits of reclamation are shared in one form or another by merchants, transportation systems, manufacturers, laborers and practically all business people throughout the Nation."

Take a project in Idaho as an example. In 1949 approximately 40% of the volume and 72% of the value of all railroad shipments of freight into the project area were from the thirty-seven states east of the Rocky Mountains.

Assuming that the federal policy for irrigation developments, as adopted by representative government, will continue—and it has a very live program today—

TABLE 2.—SUMMARY OF BENEFITS FROM IRRIGATION AND MULTIPLE-PURPOSE PROJECTS, BOTH DIRECT AND INDIRECT

Purpose	Direct benefits	Indirect benefits

Irrigation	1. Increase in family living.
	2. Increase in cash income.
	3. Accumulation of equity.
		1. Increased net income of:
		   a. Local and nonlocal handling, processing, and marketing of farm products.
		   b. Enterprises supplying goods and services to farmers.
		2. Increased land value of local residential property.
		3. Settlement opportunities.
		4. Employment opportunities.
		5. Investment opportunities.
		6. Community facilities and services.
		7. Stabilization of local and regional economy.

Power	Gross power revenue adjusted for gains or losses at downstream plants.	1. Share of returns to distributors of project power. 2. Saving to consumers from lower power rates. 3. Benefit attributable to power in final production of goods and services.
Domestic, municipal and industrial water supply	Measured by alternate cost, or water revenues.	Usually described but not measured.
Flood control	1. Reduced damage to land and other property. 2. Reduced damage to agricultural crops. 3. Reduced interruption of business, industry, and commerce. 4. Higher grade use of land formerly flooded.	
Navigation	1. Savings to shippers compared to alternate cost. 2. Savings in time and operating cost from improvement of existing waterway. 3. Recreational value for small boat traffic. 4. In some cases, stimulation of business activity.	
Pollution abatement	Alleviation of bacterial concentration, nuisance conditions, low oxygen content, and toxic and waste concentration.	
Fish and wildlife conservation	1. Increased value of annual yields for fishing and hunting. 2. Gross market value of commercial fish and fur.	
Salinity control	Value of damage prevented, increased use, and maintenance costs avoided.	
Sedimentation control	Value of damage prevented, reduction in costs, increased value of service provided, and value of extended life of facilities.	
Recreation	Judgment evaluations.	

some of the procedures and approaches that are taken in the planning of an irrigation project or a multiple-purpose project may well be discussed.

PROCEDURES—AND THE WHYS

The planning of an irrigation project is a progressive operation that has grown out of experience.

Four Reports.—The first form of investigation is the "reconnaissance report." It is based on the use of information and data already available from any reasonably reliable source, together with a field examination by experts, supplemented by a minimum amount of original work. Its purpose is to ascertain the desirability of continuing the investigation on a more refined basis. The report represents a sieving process. If the reconnaissance report indicates that a feasible and desirable project of the character contemplated may result from further studies, the recommendation, of course, is to continue. However, if the report indicates the unlikelihood that the project will be found desirable and feasible, that is the end of it.

The next step is the "project report." Its purpose is to ascertain facts with a sufficient degree of exactitude to permit the Commissioner of Reclamation and the Secretary of the Interior to make a positive recommendation for or against the project. The report covers the size and character of the project; the type of lands to be served and their whereabouts; the cost of the project; the other services to be rendered by the project, such as flood control, navigation, the generation of hydroelectric power, or any others; the allocations of cost to each of the services; the manner and extent of repayment for each service; the benefits and costs; and all other germane facts. The investigations which underlie the project report are carried to a degree of finality that will assure the proper decision on the merit and effects of the proposal, but they do not go as a rule into final designs. Project reports are used primarily in connection with the authorization of projects.

The next step is the "definite plan report." Exactly as its title indicates, it is a refinement of the project report and serves as a basis for the preparation of the actual design drawings. It is made after the project is authorized and before construction is begun. This administrative document for use by the Department serves to control the execution of the plan unless the plan is modified by official approval from the Commissioner for good and sufficient reasons.

In addition to these three reports, there is a fourth, or "basin plan report." It assembles and relates reconnaissance and project reports for a given river basin and correlates them into an over-all basin plan. Not all the projects described in the basin report need to be investigated with the same degree of exactitude. Since a report on a basin plan may contain data on more than a hundred potential projects, it would be unwise to hold up the initiation of development until all potential projects had been equally investigated. Also, since a basin report covers many projects, it would take decades before the last one on the list would be ready for initiation; and in all likelihood the economic conditions would have changed and modification in many details of the plan would be desirable in any event. These changes can be accommodated most easily, and most cheaply, during the formative period of a plan for a particular project rather than during the final stages.

In consequence, when the basin report is to be used as a basis for authorization, it may contain data on fifty or one hundred or more individual project proposals; but it will recommend for authorization, as an initial stage of development, only three or five individual projects, and those projects will have been investigated and reported on separately, each by an accompanying regular project report. The essential purpose is therefore to relate the specific project proposals to the conditions and requirements of the basin, and to set up an over-all, but intentionally fluid, pattern for ultimate basin-wide development.

Interstate Compact Apportionment.—No discussion of the planning of an irrigation project would be complete without mentioning briefly the interstate compact procedure. An interstate compact is an agreement between two or more states on a formula or other schedule for allocating among the states the waters of an interstate stream.

Such compacts are not new. They date back to the year 1785, and strangely enough, are based on a negative provision in the United States Constitution which provides that except by the approval of Congress no states shall enter into compacts among themselves for any purpose. In order to enter into an interstate agreement of this character the states must therefore obtain the approval of Congress.

During recent years the procedure has been used much more extensively than in the early days of the nation, and furthermore has been improved by the appointment in each case of a United States Commissioner, by the President, generally with the approval of the states concerned. The United States Commissioner represents the interests of the nation as a whole, serves as chairman and arbiter, and makes his report to the President and Congress as a basis for congressional approval of the finally negotiated compact. After a compact is negotiated, and affirmatively acted on by the legislatures of the states, favorable congressional action formalizes the compact and puts it into full effect of law on a permanent basis, unless it is amended by subsequent legislation.

Compacts have not been limited to the resolution of interstate water apportionment problems, but have been used also for agreements concerning the regulation of navigation and of fishing, the exercise of jurisdiction over waters of streams that serve as state boundaries, and the pollution of streams. However, nearly all the compacts from the 1920's to date have been concerned directly with the problem of apportioning among the states the use of waters from interstate streams.

An apportionment of water among the states could be accomplished by semiarbitrary division without detailed study of the needs or opportunities to utilize the water within the several states. The most successful compacts, however, are developed after painstaking studies of all possible and probable uses of water within each state. These studies are usually made by whatever technical services are available from within the states, supplemented by extensive engineering and legal assistance from the federal agencies. All the data are furnished to the members of the Compact Commission so that each may develop a complete understanding and evaluation of the situation.

Assuming, as is usually the case, that there will be a greater need for water than there will be water to meet the need, the Commission then, by processes that are usually different in every case, attempts to arrive at an equitable division among the states.

Basin Plan Apportionment.—An interesting by-product of this procedure is the fact that by the time the Commission has come to its conclusion, it has also, in large measure, agreed on the most important elements in the multiple-purpose river basin plan for the area involved. This leads naturally to a brief discussion of the alternative procedure of using the basin plan itself as a means of accomplishing an apportionment of stream flows.

By its very nature, a basin plan shows those projects which are proposed for early authorization and construction, together with those which may come into the program at a later date. If the basin plan is understood and accepted by the states, the elements of an equitable apportionment of water automatically result, and many of the purposes of the compact have been accomplished.

It is debatable whether this procedure has greater advantages than the compact procedure, and there are arguments on both sides. The basin plan procedure remains more flexible than a legislatively adopted compact, and has the advantage that mutually accepted revisions can be made from time to time during the course of development of the plan without the costly and time-consuming procedures of negotiating a new compact and securing the approval of both the state legislatures and Congress. This very advantage, however, is sufficient to alarm some proponents of the compact procedure, for they may feel apprehensive that a neighboring state might be successful in securing approval of a modification of a basin plan to its own advantage, and thereby injure the position of the other states.

Comparative Events.—Each procedure has its own advantages and each is being used. The great Missouri Basin Project is successfully utilizing the basin plan approach through the coordinating influences of the Missouri Basin Inter-Agency Committee which enjoys active federal agency and state participation. The Colorado River Basin plans are based on the compact procedure. The Columbia River Basin has been using the basin plan procedure until just recently when a law was enacted permitting the development of a compact.

The ingredients for the success of either procedure are: A willingness to negotiate, the desire to develop a workable solution, statesmanship, patience, understanding, and the financial and technical resources to carry through, once started.

It should be observed that a close relationship exists between these requirements, and the requirements for successful international treaties involving either international streams or boundary waters. The major difference between interstate compact procedures within the United States, and procedures for resolution of international problems is that, when the problem is within the United States alone, additional tools are at hand for the resolution of the difficulty if negotiations fail—tools such as Congress or the courts. These additional tools are not usually available on international water problems. Therefore, for international problems, the first four requirements for a successful negotiation are most important, to wit: A willingness to negotiate, the desire to develop a workable solution, statesmanship, and patience.

Technical Elements in Common.—This is neither the time nor the place to discuss carefully the scores of highly technical problems that are involved in planning an irrigation project in the United States today. Certain elements, however, are found in all irrigation projects regardless of their character or size:

(1) There must be land.

(2) The land must be of suitable character for continued irrigation practice.

(3) There must be water.

(4) The water must be available in the proper quantity and quality, and at the time when needed, whether it comes from a flowing stream, underground sources, or from reservoir storage.

(5) There must be diversion works, and supply works such as canals, siphons, and other conduits to carry the water from its source to the area where it is used.

(6) Regulating works must be available to control the time and rate of delivery.

(7) There must be distribution works to get the water out onto the land where it is to be used, whether by ditches or through sprays.

Fig. 11.—Engineer Trainee from a Foreign Land Studying Triaxial Shear Test for Soils at Engineering Research Center of Bureau of Reclamation at Denver, Colo.

When large projects are involved and great rivers are to be utilized, the works are large, complex, and costly. The complexities increase when additional purposes such as flood control, or the generation and transmission of hydroelectric power, are introduced. The plan for each project, large or small, must be tailor-made. More tailors, and generally more skilled tailors, are required for large projects, and a great deal more cutting and fitting is required before the final plan is ready for adoption.

Research and Training.—Continuing hydrologic studies, operation studies, and operation records should be kept for best results, and a program of basic research and engineering training is highly desirable. A great project is big business and, as such, warrants continuous improvement of the services it renders.

The Bureau of Reclamation is proud to feel it has one of the finest research centers in the world, and the improved techniques that have been developed through its operation have saved their costs many times over in the program of the Bureau. In addition, the information has been made available to the entire world for use on public and private, and large and small, projects alike.

Likewise the Bureau has made its techniques available publicly, through its training program (Fig. 11). In the first 8 months of fiscal year 1952, the Bureau has accepted fifty-seven engineers in training—from Australia, Burma, Pakistan, India, Thailand, Iraq, Israel, Italy, Turkey, Southern Rhodesia, Great Britain, and Venezuela. This policy has brought together representatives from each of the five continents of the world, and, interestingly, representatives of bordering countries who are disputing each other's rights over the waters of international streams. In addition to these trainees, scores of observers come to spend from a week to several months studying the Bureau projects and the Bureau systems.

However, none of the costs involved in these training programs is financed as a part of the Bureau of Reclamation domestic program. It is done without cost to the water or power users of the United States, through a number of different sources of funds, often with the government of the trainee's country participating directly.

Data for Planning.—For the purpose of this paper, it will suffice to list two major categories of technical considerations to be taken into account during the planning of an irrigation project. In the following section, items under group *A* are essentially limited to engineering considerations, whereas those in group *B* cover the economic aspects of project formulation and economic justification. Obviously, the two are intertwined during the many steps of investigation and plan preparation, but they have been separated here for simplified consideration.

Just as land and water are essential ingredients for any irrigation project, engineering and economic considerations are necessary in determining the answers to the three basic questions: (1) What type of project is best suited to the circumstances; (2) will it pay; and (3) should its construction be recommended?

A. Items To Be Considered in Planning a Multiple-Purpose Project

1. Project Area:
   a. Physical geography—
      (1) Location
      (2) Physical features
      (3) Climate
   b. Settlement—
      (1) History
      (2) Population
   c. Industrial development—
      (1) Local industry
      (2) Transportation
      (3) Land uses
      (4) Irrigation
      (5) Other water uses
      (6) Undeveloped resources

    d. Economic conditions—
- (1) General
- (2) Relief problems
- (3) Community needs
- (4) National needs

    e. Investigations and reports—
- (1) Previous investigations
- (2) History
- (3) Scope

2. Water Supply:
    a. Water resources
    b. Quality of water
    c. Consumptive use or depletions
    d. Diversion requirements
    e. Return flow
    f. Evaporation
    g. Special uses
    h. Water rights
    i. Development of project rights
    j. Operation studies
    k. Shortages

3. Designs and Estimates:
    a. Geology—
- (1) Explorations
- (2) Construction materials

    b. Design and construction problems—
- (1) Accessibility
- (2) Rights of way and relocations
- (3) Materials
- (4) Design flood
- (5) Construction period
- (6) Special problems
- (7) Diversion during construction

4. Cost Estimates:
    a. Investigation and construction
    b. Repairs
    c. Operation and maintenance

5. Alternate Plans:
    a. Comparison of plans
    b. Alternate or supplementary
    c. Relative merits
    d. Evaluation

6. Irrigation:
    a. Project lands—
- (1) Soils
- (2) Topography
- (3) Drainage
- (4) Salinity and alkalinity
- (5) Land classification

    b. Present agricultural development—
- (1) Crops
- (2) Livestock
- (3) Farms and farmers

        (4) Finances
        (5) Economic outlook
    c. Anticipated agricultural economy—
        (1) Adaptability
        (2) Crops
        (3) Livestock
        (4) Farm improvements
        (5) Settlement
        (6) Benefits
    d. Repayment and administration—
        (1) Repayment ability
        (2) Organization
        (3) Development period

7. Power:
    a. Present development
    b. Power market
    c. Potential development and alternative sources
    d. Interties
    e. Revenue

8. Flood Control:
    a. Historical floods
    b. Potential floods
    c. Regulation
    d. Benefits

9. Silt and Debris Control:
    a. Problems
    b. Data
    c. Damage
    d. Control
    e. Benefits

10. Drainage:
    a. Special
    b. Plans
    c. Benefits

11. Municipal and Domestic Water Supply:
    a. Present use
    b. Population trends
    c. Industrial development potentials
    d. Water requirements
    e. Water treatment
    f. Plans
    g. Benefits
    h. Alternative sources of supply

12. Fish and Wildlife Conservation:
    a. Existing developments
    b. Special problems
    c. Plans
    d. Benefits

13. Recreation:
    a. Population tributary
    b. Existing facilities
    c. Needs
    d. Development
    e. Benefits

14. Stream Pollution Abatement:
    a. Present conditions
    b. Problems
    c. Treatment
    d. Plans
    e. Benefits

15. Navigation and Transportation:
    a. Existing conditions
    b. Need
    c. Water requirements
    d. Plans
    e. Benefits

16. Over-All Benefits and Allocation of Costs:
    a. Effect on surrounding area
    b. Regional and national benefits
    c. Allocation of costs
    d. Ratio of costs and benefits
    e. Pros and cons of project development

B. Economic Aspects of Project Formulation

1. Establishment of Need for the Project:
    a. Need for intensification or stabilization of agricultural economy by providing new or supplemental irrigation
    b. Present and future demand for electric power
    c. Present and future demand for municipal and industrial water
    d. Protection from maximum probable flood
    e. Solution of sediment, salinity, pollution, and drainage problems
    f. Need for conservation and development of recreation and fish and wildlife resources
    g. Effect, favorable or unfavorable, on existing developed lands, power, or transportation facilities

2. Resources Available for Meeting Needs:
    a. Water supply
    b. Lands suitable for irrigation
    c. Dam and reservoir sites
    d. Geology and minerals

3. Selection of Type of Project:
    a. Elimination of less effective sites by map study
    b. Elimination of other alternative reservoir sites by reconnaissance estimates of cost per unit of storage
    c. Detailed analysis of a few sites, considering—
      (1) Various potential uses
      (2) Various ways of accomplishing each purpose
    d. Selection of optimum combination of purposes and extent to which each purpose is developed
    e. Evaluation of tentative plan—
      (1) Engineering feasibility
      (2) Economic feasibility (repayment)
      (3) Economic justification (benefits and costs)
      (4) Superiority to alternative plans

4. Economic Analysis of Irrigation:
   - a. Selection of irrigable area—
     - (1) Determination of mapping specifications—
       - (a) Experience in comparable developed areas
       - (b) Economics of production in area—productive capacity, cost of production, and costs of land development
       - (c) Expression of economics of production in physical mapping criteria (soils, topography, and drainage)
     - (2) Land classification (soil, topography, and drainage)
     - (3) Selection of land to be irrigated—
       - (a) Character of land and water supply
       - (b) Engineering plan
       - (c) Economic justification and feasibility of adding specific tracts
   - b. Present and future agricultural economy—
     - (1) Size and type of farms
     - (2) Production by land classes
     - (3) Income based on expected prices
     - (4) Area-wide summary of farm budgets
   - c. Evaluation of irrigation—
     - (1) Extent of development that will maximize net benefits
     - (2) Repayment potential—
       - (a) Development period up to 10 years
       - (b) Repayment period, normally 40 years
     - (3) Local attitudes and repayment organization

5. Economic Analysis of Hydroelectric Power:
   - a. Present development and market analysis
   - b. Potential generation from head and minimum firm flow
   - c. Optimum size plant based on cost per unit of power and competitive power rates
   - d. Financial feasibility based on revenue versus cost of production
   - e. Optimum transmission and interties
   - f. Estimate of benefits
   - g. Economic justification, ratio of benefits to costs

6. Economic Analysis of Municipal and Industrial Water Supply:
   - a. Present development and market analysis
   - b. Determination of most economical additional supply
   - c. Analysis of benefits, costs, and repayment
   - d. Competition with irrigation for a limited water supply

7. Economic Analysis of Flood Control:
   - a. Degree of protection afforded by various control plans
   - b. Selection of optimum plan with regard to justifiable investment based on benefits

8. Sediment, Salinity, Pollution, and Drainage Problems:
   - a. Determination of most economical plan
   - b. Estimate of benefits

9. Fish, Wildlife, and Recreation:
   - a. Existing conditions and special problems
   - b. Optimum development in combination with other purposes
   - c. Special damage prevention measures
   - d. Estimate of benefits

10. Navigation, Transportation, and National Defense
11. Designs and Cost Estimates for Multiple-Purpose Project
12. Evaluation of Multiple-Purpose Plan:
    a. Economic effect on surrounding area
    b. Allocation of costs
    c. Regional and national benefits, positive and negative
    d. Ratio of benefits to costs
    e. Project pay-out study
    f. Pros and cons of project development

WHAT OF THE FUTURE?

It is easier to be an historian than a prophet. Nevertheless, a few conclusions may be drawn on the direction in which the United States is heading.

1. Although its significance is not yet generally recognized, the practice of irrigation is already nation-wide in scope. The amount of land under irrigation in the East is much less than in the West, but percentagewise, irrigation is expanding faster in the East than in the West. It will continue to do so for many years at least. The East is already beginning to experience some of the growing pains that originally caused so much difficulty in the West when one project usurped the water supply of another. It is to be hoped that the East will recognize this, in time to take such steps as are necessary to develop its plans on a sound, economic, and coordinated basis.

2. Population growth in the United States is such as to require expansion in the practice of irrigation. The country needs more land and more production, and increased irrigation will be one of the essential means of meeting that need.

3. Although small individual, and even large single-purpose projects will be developed, and although they are very important to their localities and collectively to the nation, the over-all development during the next 30 years will give increasing emphasis to basin plans, with some type of basin or regional project cost accounting.

4. The drive toward one uniform national water policy, as compared to the present array of differing policies among the several agencies, will go foward; and improvement, if not full realization of that goal, will be achieved. The transition is most apt to be gradual, but the growing executive, congressional, and public understanding of the present situation will bring about some healthy improvements.

5. It is reasonable to look forward with something better than hope to the day when it will be both practical and economical to convert salt water into fresh water in bulk quantities. Systematic research on this has been started, and laboratory tests give reasonable hope that within the next decade or two, it may be an accepted practice. The economic impact of this conversion would be tremendous.

6. Another of the scientific family of developments is artificial precipitation. To start an argument in almost any engineering office, it is merely necessary to state that artificial precipitation either is, or is not, practicable. More research on this subject is needed to know which answer, if either, is correct. Although some excellent scientific work has been done, it is regrettable that this research,

unlike that on the conversion of salt water to fresh water, has not been approached on a broad and coordinated scale. Only a steady progress of basic scientific research may in the end pay off; but the consequence of a proved and successful technique for artificial precipitation on the planning of irrigation projects could be almost unlimited.

Neither the United States, nor most of the nations in the world, can await the proved success of such new prospects as these to fill the "fifth plate." It must be realized that for every four people who sit down for dinner in 1950, there will be five in 1975. It must be recognized also that the number of acres of cultivated land to supply the food for each individual is decreasing and that more efficient and better production methods must be found within the United States, if present standards of diet are to be maintained. The same condition exists throughout many parts of the world, and in some countries the situation may become so severe that the question will be one of survival.

To quote the Hon. Isadore Lubin, United States Representative to the Economic and Social Council of the United Nations:

"A Nation which is divided in purpose may again reunite. A nation which has lost its liberty may again attain it. But a nation which squanders its resources can rarely recover them. And a nation which fails to develop its resources can never grow intrinsically strong."

Therefore, in the hands of the engineers and their colleagues who have a responsibility for the planning of irrigation projects, there is a tool—making better use of all related resources to assist in fostering sound economic prosperity. It is well within reason that their efforts may contribute to the peace of the world.

AMERICAN SOCIETY OF CIVIL ENGINEERS

Founded November 5, 1852

TRANSACTIONS

Paper No. 2597

FORWARD STEPS IN IRRIGATION ENGINEERING

By L. N. McClellan,[1] M. ASCE

Synopsis

Irrigation in the United States has greatly expanded during the 50 years that the Bureau of Reclamation, United States Department of the Interior, has been active—5,000,000 acres are now served by government construction. At the same time growing needs have been met by refinements of designing practice, exemplified by advances in high dams, through trial-load analysis, temperature and crack control, and model testing. Although not so spectacular, methods used in earth-dam construction have also progressed, and mechanical equipment has been perfected. In all 20,000 miles of canals have been built. Studies have also improved operating and maintenance procedures for the vast system. Construction innovations have been introduced, through mechanized equipment and large-scale contracting—for concrete work, earth moving, and canal lining. Power development and pumping plants are now functional parts of the great irrigation enterprise.

Irrigation "practice" is as old as civilization itself. Early civilizations in arid areas depended on irrigation and flourished where canals brought water from nearby streams to sustain plant life and assure crop yields. Irrigation "engineering," on the other hand, is of comparatively recent origin. Its progress has been marked by rapid advancement, particularly during the past 100 years when the settlement and development of the western states were made possible through irrigation enterprise.

Since the enactment of the Reclamation Act 50 years ago, on June 17, 1902, the construction of irrigation works by the Federal Government has brought water to more than 5,000,000 acres of western land. This acreage is exceeded five times by private irrigation developments in the United States and many times over by irrigated areas in other countries. However, its development has been a potent influence on the welfare and stability of a large section of the West.

From an engineering standpoint, the accomplishments of the Bureau of Reclamation in the design and construction of irrigation works—and in the develop-

---

[1] Chf. Engr., Bureau of Reclamation, U. S. Dept. of the Interior, Denver, Colo.

ment of associated hydroelectric power—have contributed a substantial volume and diversity of experience to irrigation practice. They have also assisted in the evolution of reclamation policy and economic principles.

DESIGN PROGRESS

The ever-increasing demand for irrigation has been a vital force in the advancement of irrigation engineering. The need for closer conservation has impelled successive progress in design as demands on scant western water supplies have become stronger. Changes in the basic concepts of irrigation projects fostered new engineering designs. The evolution of the relatively simple irrigation project into the multiple-purpose development and, more recently, the coordinated development of river basins have presented new challenges in the design phase of irrigation engineering.

Rapid construction progress during the first 5 years of reclamation activity was made possible by the adaptation of construction equipment and skills developed during the era of large-scale railroad construction from 1880 to 1900. To a considerable extent, improvements in design during this period and later years accompanied the development of construction equipment, particularly excavating machinery.

The early formative period encouraged many modifications in design as work progressed. As later irrigation projects embraced structures of increasing size and complexity, flexibility of design methods and reliance on empirical procedures gave way to more thorough study of site and materials and to more complete designs before the start of construction.

Design of Concrete Dams.—Early irrigation undertakings in the West depended for the most part on the use of unregulated stream flows brought to the land by ditches headed at small diversion dams. These unregulated flows, however, were not sufficient for irrigation needs, and dams of increased height and volume were required to store and regulate water.

A basic contribution to the design of dams has been the improvement of hydrologic techniques in forecasting stream runoff, which have enabled the designer to provide economical spillways of capacity adequate to pass reservoir overflows from floods with safety. The adoption of the unit hydrograph in 1932, and subsequent refinements in computing and analyzing runoff from rainfall and snow melt, have aided greatly in planning and designing dams and reservoirs.

Experience in the development of early concrete and masonry dams, such as Buffalo Bill (on the Shoshone River in Wyoming), Roosevelt (on the Salt River in Arizona), Pathfinder (on the North Platte River in Wyoming), Arrowrock (on the Boise River in Idaho), and Elephant Butte (on the Rio Grande in New Mexico), led the way to the design of dams with heights and volumes previously considered impossible to attain. Advances followed in the design of multiple-arch dams, reinforced-concrete slab and buttress dams, and other special types of concrete dams.

The principle of trial-load analysis, which was evolved during the 1920's for the first time took into account the interaction of horizontal beam or arch action with vertical cantilever action in the structure to determine the economic safety factor. Its first important application was in the design of Hoover Dam (on the Colorado River in Arizona-Nevada).

New procedures were worked out to control the temperature of the concrete placed in Hoover Dam. The potentially high temperature developed in the mass concrete of the 726-ft-high dam was counteracted by the use of low-heat cements and by an embedded pipe cooling system, through which river water and refrigerated water were circulated to remove the excess heat resulting from cement hydration. To localize shrinkage and to minimize random cracking, it was built in vertical blocks separated by contraction joints, which were grouted to make the structure a monolith after temperatures became stable. The same procedure was adopted for later massive dams.

With the establishment of the Bureau's engineering laboratories in the early 1930's, hydraulic models were used extensively to confirm designs for spillways

FIG. 1.—EXAMPLE OF LARGE EARTH DAM, ONE OF TWELVE RECLAMATION DAMS COMPLETED ON THE MISSOURI RIVER BASIN PROJECT; ENDERS DAM ON FRENCHMAN CREEK IN NEBRASKA

and outlet works for dams. Experience demonstrated that hydraulic models provided a reliable means of ascertaining and alleviating undesirable conditions such as subatmospheric pressures on water-passage surfaces and the choking of shaft spillways.

During the 1930's, procedures were developed for grouting dam foundations to improve their watertightness and stability and to reduce uplift pressures under concrete dams. Grouting techniques were improved by more accurate determination of spacing, location, and depth of drill holes, and by close control of grout mixtures and pressures for varying conditions.

Earth Structures.—Much progress has been made in the design and construction of earth dams (Fig. 1). Many of the early earth dams were designed with little attempt at analysis of structural behavior. They were built with only elementary selection of materials and control of moisture and compaction. However, the experience derived from their construction, and advances in soil mechanics, led to the adoption of definite design principles and construction control.

Compacted earth-fill dams have been accepted for wide use, and they are now economically designed with the same assurances of safety and permanence as are other types. In the transition of earth-dam design since about 1925, important advances have been made in basic soil mechanics and in design techniques. Methods of analyzing the stability of earth embankments were developed. Data obtained from settlement and internal-pressure measurements, conducted at most major earth dams since 1935, and the criteria evolved for moisture control, ma-

Fig. 2.—General View of Davis Dam, Forebay, Power Plant, and Spillway; a Main Structure on the Colorado River in Arizona-Nevada, Next Below Hoover Dam, Reregulating Flow for Power, Irrigation, and Delivery to Mexico

terial selection, and embankment placement have contributed substantially to the advancement of earth-dam design and construction. A recent structure of this type is Davis Dam (Fig. 2) on the Colorado River in Arizona-Nevada.

Mechanical Adjuncts.—Design of hydraulic equipment to control the release of water has paralleled progress in dam design. Problems of deterioration of valves and gates by cavitation and corrosion have been lessened through better hydraulic and mechanical design and the development of more resistant materials. The increasing demand for larger gates and valves to operate under higher heads has led to progressive improvement in operating gates, emergency gates, and regulating valves.

Butterfly valves or sliding leaf gates have been developed for emergency closure of penstocks and outlet pipes. To adapt the sliding leaf gate to the higher heads, ring followers and wheels were added to withstand the high thrust and reduce the friction. Gates of this type have been designed for 120-in. conduits and for heads of more than 600 ft.

One of the earliest regulating valves was of the cylinder type. Higher heads required improved designs which were represented first by a needle-type valve. Several major changes resulted in the interior differential needle valve, followed by the tube valve, and finally by the present hollow-jet valve. Sizes have been built up to 108 in. in diameter and for heads in excess of 460 ft.

Efficient Canals.—Since 1902, approximately 20,000 miles of canals and more than 200,000 related irrigation structures on reclamation projects have been de-

FIG. 3.—FRIANT DAM, SOUTHERN STRUCTURE OF THE CENTRAL VALLEY PROJECT IN CALIFORNIA, SHOWING BEGINNING OF FRIANT-KERN CANAL, LARGE IRRIGATION ARTERY, 155 MILES LONG, WITH 5,000-CU FT PER SEC CAPACITY

signed and constructed. The canals, lined and unlined, range in capacity from a few cubic feet per second up to 16,000 cu ft per sec.

The design of large canals (Fig. 3) and of smaller conveyance and distribution structures has been directed toward one basic objective—to deliver water in adequate quantity from the source of supply to the point of use efficiently and at minimum cost. Over the past 50 years, refinements in hydraulic theory and soil mechanics techniques, the development of canal linings, and improvements in construction equipment and controls have aided in reaching this engineering goal. The methods developed for underdrainage of linings and stabilization of canal banks, and improvements in weed control and other maintenance procedures, have also made possible greater efficiency and economies in water distribution.

Prior to the start of reclamation construction in the West, little consideration was given to the establishment of canal standards. An initial undertaking was the development of hydraulic and earthwork standards for trapezoidal canal sections. These early compilations were progressively improved, and are now widely accepted as standards in the design of hydraulic channels.

Lining Methods.—In the years that followed, emphasis was given to lowering costs of canal construction and to improving canal alinements, particularly those of main supply arteries. This endeavor was given further impetus by initiation of a lower-cost canal lining program in 1946. Research and investigation of materials and methods in field, laboratory, and design offices have reduced the costs of lining many canals. Concrete linings and pneumatically-placed mortar linings have been improved A far-reaching development is the elimination of steel reinforcement in concrete canal linings except under certain conditions—thus making possible a saving of 10% to 15% in the total cost of the linings.

Fig. 4.—Installing a Buried Asphalt Membrane on the Casper Canal of the Kendrick Project in Wyoming; Thin Layer of Sprayed Asphalt, Shown Dark, Being Covered with Protective Earth Layer by Dragline

Two general types of asphaltic canal linings have been developed and are being used successfully—buried asphalt membrane (Fig. 4) and asphaltic concrete. The newly-developed buried membrane consists of a thin layer of asphalt sprayed in place at high temperature and covered with a protective layer of earth materials.

Earth linings have proved economical. The heavy-type compacted earth lining is particularly effective as a low-cost lining for medium-size and large-size canals. This lining, about 3 ft thick (Fig. 5), is inexpensive to place where suitable materials are available, requires little protection from erosion, and is about as impervious as concrete lining.

Other Developments.—Improvements in the design and manufacture of concrete pipe have made possible its wider use for distribution systems and canal structures. The early pipe, cast in small sizes by hand-tamping mortar into forms, has been replaced by mass-produced concrete pipe with diameters up to 9 ft, and in special cases up to 15 ft. Operation of reinforced-concrete pipe under progressively higher heads accompanied the introduction of metal joints and later of rubber-gasket joints.

In addition to these important design advances, the past 50 years have been characterized by progress in the design of diversion dams, large wasteways, detention dikes, high-head pipelines, and appurtenant canal features such as checks, drops, and turnouts. Inverted siphons constructed of concrete pipe or cast-in-place concrete have largely replaced the timber-trestled flumes of early designs.

FIG. 5.—CONSTRUCTION OF FRIANT-KERN CANAL IN CALIFORNIA, USING HEAVY TYPE OF COMPACTED EARTH LINING, HANDLED BY TRACTOR AND SCRAPER

Automatic controls for checks and wasteways and devices for measuring flows in large canals have been found useful in the operation of modern irrigation systems.

ECONOMIES IN UPKEEP

Dams, reservoirs, and distribution systems on reclamation projects must be properly operated and maintained if the investment in irrigation and related work and the welfare and interests of the citizens on reclamation projects are to be protected. During early reclamation activity little consideration was given to the proper techniques of water application and land management. In later years more attention was given to the requirements of the crops and to the water-holding capacity of the soil, and still greater attention was directed toward decreasing losses of both water and soil on the farm.

There has been a significant trend in recent years toward mechanization of irrigation project operation. Two-way radio communication systems have been installed, and maintenance personnel can communicate directly with the operating office. Through remote-control systems, operators at central locations can control the operation of gates or other works many miles away by electrical circuits. Automatic equipment in pumping plants has made possible the unattended operation of such facilities.

Through research in the chemical laboratories, new economical methods have been developed to control aquatic weeds. Aromatic solvents such as cheap coal-tar naphtha have been found to be more effective in killing aquatic weeds than previous expensive hand or mechanical methods.

In the early years of reclamation development, inadequate consideration was given to surface and subsurface drainage. The importance of preventing the destruction of valuable land by waterlogging, salts, and alkalies was not recognized.

To maintain the productivity of irrigated lands, investigations were begun in 1911 to determine the elevation of ground waters, and the construction of necessary drainage facilities was undertaken. Through increased knowledge in recent years of the physical and chemical characteristics of soils and of the factors affecting ground-water movement, it has been possible to construct efficient drains, wells, and other drainage relief devices as integral parts of irrigation projects. After projects are constructed, the productive capacity of the land is maintained through continuing drainage studies and activities.

Progress in Construction

During the past 50 years, a tremendous advance in construction art has taken place. Great improvements were made in internal-combustion engines and self-propelled machinery. In particular, the development of equipment for the excavation, conveyance, and placement of materials was outstanding. New and improved machines, because of their greater capacity, durability, and speed of performance, made possible the accomplishment of work on a scope and a volume that otherwise might have been economically infeasible. On reclamation projects the magnitude of the work undertaken closely paralleled the development of equipment and the allied improvements in construction plants and methods. Progress in construction through the development of new equipment and methods is strikingly demonstrated by comparison of early methods with modern practices.

Canals.—At the time reclamation construction in the West began, the horse-drawn drag scraper—slip or fresno—was the principal implement used in the excavation of canals, although steam shovels were used as early as 1903 on canal construction on the Newlands Project in Nevada. The moving of excavated materials, until about 1910, was done principally by horse-drawn wheeled scrapers and one-yard wagons.

By 1915, the transition from horsepower to gasoline power was well under way, and by 1920 the gasoline engine and the steam engine had been so developed for heavy construction purposes that they had almost entirely replaced the horse and mule. About 1930, draglines of large capacity were developed. Some of these machines, rated at 18-cu yd capacity were used in 1934 for construction of the 80-mile All-American Canal in California.

The development of internal-combustion engines and electric power had a similar effect on concrete canal lining and on excavation. The first canal lining machine was used on the Umatilla Project in Oregon in 1914. This machine, like the others that followed later on other projects, traveled on rails at the top of each canal bank, finishing the concrete lining over the entire canal perimeter as it moved along the canal. In recent years, these large machines have lined canals of more than 100-ft width on the Columbia Basin (Washington) and Central Valley (California) projects.

Concrete Dams.—Advances in construction of concrete dams, particularly in the past 25 years, have been made possible by greatly improved techniques of concrete manufacture and methods of transportation and placement. Beginning with the construction of Hoover Dam in 1931, accurate batching and mixing plants have been used to assure automatically predetermined proportions of aggregate, cement, and water, and consistent uniformity of mix.

At Grand Coulee Dam, on the Columbia Basin Project, which contains 10,585,000 cu yd of concrete, the aggregate processing plant had a rated capacity of 3,000 tons per hr to 4,000 tons per hr and was designed to wash, screen, and store separately four sizes of gravel and three sizes of sand. Concrete was delivered to the dam at the average rate of 1 cu yd every 5 sec. At one time, the rate of placement of concrete reached 20,600 cu yd during a 24-hour period.

Despite the short season at Hungry Horse Dam on the South Fork of the Flathead River in Montana (Fig. 6) more than 2,000,000 cu yd of the 3,000,000-cu yd structure were placed in 17 working months. In August, 1951, alone, more than 227,000 cu yd of concrete were placed in the dam.

Earth Dams.—Since 1925, embankment control for rolled earth dams involving close supervision of excavation, placing, and compaction of the materials has become a recognized procedure.

Earth moving and placing equipment, including large elevating graders, tractor-drawn scrapers holding 30 or more cubic yards of material, fast-moving bottom-dump wagons of equally large capacity, and sheepsfoot rollers have made possible great advances in earth-dam construction. Comparison of the rates of progress in building the Belle Fourche Dam (1906–1910) on the Belle Fourche Project in South Dakota and the construction of Bonny Dam (1948–1951) on the Missouri River Basin Project in Colorado is interesting. In the working season of 1909 at the Belle Fourche Dam, 529,000 cu yd were placed in the dam in about 7 months. At Bonny Dam, which was completed a year and a half ahead of schedule, more than 1,000,000 cu yd were placed during the maximum month of November, 1949.

ADMINISTRATION OF RECLAMATION CONSTRUCTION

The Reclamation Act of 1902 gave the Secretary of the Interior authority to let contracts for constructing principal works on reclamation projects. Difficulties were encountered early in contract work because many contractors were inexperienced in such undertakings and were unprepared to assume the financial responsibility required to complete government contracts.

Because of these difficulties and ensuing problems in obtaining suitable labor during the period of great expansion of construction in the West, beginning about 1905, contracts became increasingly difficult to fulfil. For these reasons, from 1911 to 1923 reclamation construction was for the most part by government forces.

However, from 1923 to the present time, most Bureau of Reclamation work has been carried out by contract. This period, during which increased expansion of reclamation activities took place, was paralleled by an equally important growth in the skills and abilities of the contractors participating. Modern contracting organizations generally are well equipped and organized—technically, financially, and administratively.

The success of reclamation undertakings may be credited in large part to the ingenuity, capacity, and resourcefulness of the contracting industry. In recent years, the contractual relationships between the Bureau and contractors have been

FIG. 6.—HUNGRY HORSE DAM ON THE SOUTH FORK OF THE FLATHEAD RIVER IN MONTANA, COMPLETED IN OCTOBER, 1952, AFTER SETTING CONCRETING RECORDS BY LATEST CONSTRUCTION TECHNIQUES ; AND OBTAINING ECONOMY SAVINGS BY USE OF FLY ASH AS AN ADMIXTURE

strengthened by periodic conferences and mutual study of problems. This cooperation has been reflected in reduction of construction costs and improved quality of performance.

ROLE OF HYDROELECTRIC POWER

The first reclamation projects were constructed for a single purpose—to provide irrigation. However, early in the experience of the Bureau, power became an important adjunct to irrigation. The first hydroelectric power installation on a reclamation project was a small temporary plant on the Salt River Valley Project in Arizona, built in 1906 to supply electric power for the construction of Roosevelt Dam.

Passage of the Boulder Canyon Project Act in 1928 signified a marked advance in the concept of water conservation and in the importance of hydroelectric power development for reclamation projects. This act embodied for the first time the concept of multiple-purpose development of water resources. The Boulder Canyon Project comprises Hoover Dam and Power Plant, Imperial Dam and Desilting Works, and the All-American Canal system. Sale of the power generated will repay 90% of the cost of the project, with interest.

The Reclamation Project Act of 1939 increased the maximum period of power leases from 10 to 40 years, and authorized rates that would recover not only the costs allocated to power but also an appropriate share of the construction costs allocated to irrigation where such costs were in excess of the water users' ability to pay.

Progress in Pumping for Irrigation

Early pumping plants were built on several reclamation projects, among them the Huntley Project in Montana and the Minidoka Project in Idaho. These plants pumped water to lands too high to be served by the gravity systems.

As the possibilities of pumping methods in certain areas became increasingly apparent, and were enhanced by the development of hydroelectric power, additional pumping plants were constructed and placed in operation. Heights of pumping lifts increased with the improvement of pump efficiency, and the feasibility of pumping for irrigation likewise increased.

In the summer of 1951, a new era in pumping for irrigation began. Three of the world's largest pumping plants were placed in initial operation. Largest of these is the Grand Coulee Pumping Plant on the Columbia Basin Project. This plant will house twelve pumping units, each capable of delivering 1,350 cu ft per sec of water at a rated head of 310 ft. Each pump is driven by an electric motor of 65,000 hp. Four of the pumping units are completed and were utilized during the irrigation season of 1952 to pump water for delivery to 66,000 acres of land—the first irrigation block of the huge project.

The second largest pumping installation is the Tracy Pumping Plant on the Central Valley Project. The plant is the prime mover in the transfer of surplus water from the Sacramento River to lands in the San Joaquin Valley. The installation consists of six units, each rated at a capacity of 767 cu ft per sec at a head of 197 ft.

Another recently constructed plant is the Granby Pumping Plant on the Colorado-Big Thompson Project in Colorado. This pumping plant lifts water to the western portal of the Adams Tunnel, which carries it from the western slope of the Rocky Mountains through the Continental Divide to the eastern slope. The plant houses three pumps, each rated at a capacity of 200 cu ft per sec at the maximum pumping head of 186 ft.

Problems Still to Be Met

Irrigation engineering in the future faces challenging problems. Water for new irrigation projects must be transported greater distances, which will bring new problems of storage, pumping, and conveyance. The exchange of water through multiple-basin exportation systems may be necessary before full utilization of western water resources can be realized. Other complex and diversified problems in the development of domestic water supplies, flood control, and control of silt will be imposed on future reclamation undertakings. The experience gained in irrigation engineering during the past 50 years will be of immeasurable value in the development of the more difficult and complex irrigation projects of the future.

AMERICAN SOCIETY OF CIVIL ENGINEERS

Founded November 5, 1852

TRANSACTIONS

Paper No. 2598

PARALLEL IRRIGATION DEVELOPMENT— UNITED STATES AND AUSTRALIA

By Lewis R. East,[1] M. ASCE

Synopsis

There is a remarkable parallelism between irrigation progress in the State of Victoria, Australia, and the western part of the United States. This paper traces the background of the development and the steps taken by the State of Victoria to capitalize on American talent and know-how.

Major milestones in water utilization—in both legislation and construction— are briefly reviewed. The particular success of the irrigation fields surrounding the River Murray is described, as are the engineering works behind this outstanding project.

Introduction

The history of irrigation in the State of Victoria has been interlinked with that of the United States in a truly unusual way over a long period.

Early Inquiries in the United States.—What may well be the first comprehensive description of the irrigable area of the United States was compiled in 1885 from previously unpublished records of the United States Agricultural Bureau. This work was done expressly for a minister of the Government of Victoria, Alfred Deakin, who had come to the United States to gain a knowledge of irrigation. The information was gathered by Col. Richard J. Hinton and was transmitted to Deakin by E. A. Carmen, Acting Commissioner of Agriculture, in a letter dated April 7, 1885.

Deakin's own report, published as *Parliamentary Papers* after his return to Victoria in 1885, contained a wealth of information in regard to every aspect of irrigation as practiced at that time and as observed by Deakin himself. The report was accompanied by detailed descriptions and drawings of many works inspected by the engineer—J. D. Derry—who went to the United States with Deakin. At that time this report probably provided the best, if not the only, comprehensive reference then available on irrigation in the western United States.

Deakin called special attention to the question of water rights, and to the legal

---

[1] Chairman, State Rivers and Water Supply Comm., Melbourne, Victoria, Australia.

difficulties that had so greatly handicapped and retarded the full utilization of American water resources. He compared the water laws of the various states, and stressed the marked advantage enjoyed by the State of Colorado whose constitution embodied the provision that "All streams within its boundaries were declared to be public property." California, on the contrary, he stated, was under a cloud of litigation and the value of the property in irrigation lands and works threatened in that state was estimated at $200,000,000.

He emphasized the similarity between Australia and the United States:

> "California is like Victoria—a new country, settled by the pick of the Anglo-Saxon race, attracted in the first instance by gold discoveries, and remaining after that excitement passed away to build up a new nation under the freest Institutions and most favourable conditions of life. California is almost exactly the same age as our Colony, and, in soil also, the two countries are not unlike. California, with the same population as Victoria, has twice our area."

He concluded that: " * * * the parallel between Southern Australia and the Western States of America was as complete as such parallels could be." He then remarked that Australia should naturally look to those states to learn successful irrigation methods. Dissimilarities as well were pointed out by Deakin, and it is of interest today to quote his statement in 1885:

> "There are not only likenesses but unlikenesses * * * and among them one of the chief is the attitude of the State towards every form of enterprise including * * * water supply. State Governments in America never have done anything in the way of undertaking or assisting in the construction of irrigation works. They are not expected to undertake them, and there does not appear any likelihood of their ever having any proprietary connection with them. The Central Government maintains, if possible, an attitude of even greater indifference."

Deakin continued:

> "All the irrigation works of Western America, with certain minor exceptions, have been constructed and maintained wholly and solely by private persons. Not only has the Government spent nothing upon them, but it has known nothing of them. In Colorado the State Engineer has issued one report. In California the State Engineer has issued one report. In no other State or territory is there either report or register of water rights. These two reports * * * are the only official papers published by any State bearing upon irrigation."

That was the situation in 1885. What Deakin saw in the United States convinced him of the need for reservoirs to hold surplus flows for time of need. He also realized the necessity of accurate water measurement to provide for the greatest economy in use. Deakin mentioned that, as a matter of fact, there were at that time no drainage works worthy of the name in the United States. He noted that irrigation made small holdings under intense culture profitable. In addition, he recognized that, where water was attached to the land and rights were indisputable, the tendency was to cut up the land into small farms, and was impressed by the success of small settlements in Utah.

He concluded his investigations by reporting that he

" * * * could discover no irremovable obstacle to the achievement in Victoria in proportion to its irrigable area by means of irrigation of all that had been achieved in the Western States of America."

However, from his point of view, American experience gave no answer to the question of whether the state should accept responsibility for the construction of headworks for irrigation.

Deakin later visited Egypt, India, and Italy, and prepared reports on irrigation in those countries.

Victoria's Irrigation Act—1886

As a direct result of the recommendations of a Royal Commission, of which Deakin was chairman, the Victorian State Parliament passed a comprehensive irrigation act in 1886 that went a long way toward nationalizing the water resources of Victoria and that made possible the remarkable development of water supply and irrigation that has since taken place.

Deakin stated in Parliament:

" * * * Our plans for irrigation will not be worth the paper they are printed on unless we are absolutely sure that they cannot be interfered with by the existence of any such thing as riparian rights."

His irrigation act of 1886 marked a new era in the history of water supply legislation. This revolutionary act vested in the Crown the right to the use of water in any stream, lake, or swamp; provided that no riparian rights could be established in the future that might prevent the use of water for irrigation; authorized the construction of national headworks by the state; and enabled directly elected trusts to carry out their local schemes with money advanced by the government.

It was proposed that, as irrigation trusts were constituted, the more important regulation and storage developments should be undertaken by the State. The first national work authorized was commenced in 1887.

Chaffey Brothers

While in the United States in 1885, Deakin met George and W. B. Chaffey—two young Canadian brothers who had established successful irrigation settlements at Etiwanda and Ontario in California, and elsewhere. Deakin was more impressed by Ontario than by anything else he saw in North America, and, at his invitation, George Chaffey and later his brother came to Australia to investigate the possibilities of similar enterprises in Victoria.

The result was spectacular. The Chaffeys saw in a remote, arid, and desolate corner of Victoria, bordered by the River Murray, the possibility of a great irrigation settlement. To their ability and enterprise in planning high-lift pumping plants, in laying out the settlements, and in inducing settlers to go to places hundreds of miles from the railway and from the sea, Australia owes a number of thriving irrigation settlements now totaling 100,000 acres of vineyards and citrus groves along several hundreds of miles of the River Murray. Their genius in transforming a wilderness into a wonderland is widely acknowledged today.

The Chaffey brothers began work in 1887; and, although they themselves did not reap the reward they deserved, their enterprise ushered in a new era in Victorian irrigation. The Mildura and the Renmark schemes, started by them in 1887, were among the earliest in the world involving high-lift pumping on a large scale.

George Chaffey later went back to the United States and played a most prominent part in the development of the Imperial Valley in California—for many years the largest irrigation venture in the world. The experience that he obtained in Mildura—a region that is rainless for months at a time, with shade

FIG. 1.—IRRIGATION VINEYARDS, MILDURA, VICTORIA, AUSTRALIA

temperatures rising well over 100° for many days in succession—showed him that white people could work and thrive under conditions of intense dry heat (Fig. 1).

Thus, the United States owes incalculable benefits to the strange set of circumstances that not only brought George Chaffey to Australia, but sent him back to the United States equipped and acclimatized for the conquest of the Colorado Desert, in which it had long been believed people could not live and work.

LATER DEVELOPMENTS

Local Irrigation Trusts.—By 1899 there were nearly ninety irrigation and water works trusts in operation in Victoria (Fig. 2). However, engineering progress had been much faster than that of the landowners; and, when an attempt was made to collect the necessary revenue to meet interest on the cost of works, the whole system of local management broke down. In that year (1899) a relief act was passed, writing off three quarters of the money owed by the trusts to the government.

The reasons for the failure of these schemes, which had been constructed and administered by locally elected irrigation trusts were: First and foremost, insufficient conservation of water and abundance of channels without enough water to fill them when it was most needed; second, divided control of the sources of supply; third, ignorance of irrigation; and, fourth, the inability of local management to face the financial position, and its consequent unwillingness to impose charges that would compel the proper utilization of the water by the irrigators.

Further Legislation.—Although the 1886 act prevented the establishment of

Fig. 2.—Goulburn Weir—First Australian Diversion Dam

any riparian rights "after" the passage of the act, it did not define the "existing" riparian rights. No legislative action, however, was taken in regard to either this problem or the trusts until 1905.

By the water act of that year, the common law principles relating to riparian rights were fundamentally modified and the respective rights of the Crown and private persons were clearly defined. A vital provision was that, where any stream or lake forms the boundary or part of the boundary of an allotment of land, the bed and banks thereof shall be deemed to have remained the property of the Crown and not to have passed with the land so alienated.

Since 1905 riparian rights in Victoria have been clearly defined by statute, and there has been absolutely no litigation in regard to riparian rights or water rights of any kind.

State Rivers and Water Supply Commission.—The 1905 water act abolished the irrigation trusts and provided for a new form of corporate body—the State

Rivers and Water Supply Commission—to undertake the whole task of water conservation and distribution through the state. It was one of the earliest organizations of its kind to be entrusted with the development of the water resources of a very large region.

Realizing that sound irrigation and water supply development must always be based on the availability of water supplies when they are required, and that this availability could be assured from Victoria's intermittently flowing streams only by the storage of winter flows for use in summer, the Commission from its inception followed a most progressive policy of water conservation.

Elwood Mead.—An appointment that had far-reaching consequences was made in 1907 when Elwood Mead (at that time Chief of the Irrigation Investigations Bureau in the United States Department of Agriculture), M. ASCE, was invited by the Victorian Government to accept office as chairman of the State Rivers and Water Supply Commission. Mead held that post for 8 years before returning to the United States, and the contribution he made to Victorian irrigation development was very great indeed.

A policy that he introduced, which has proved outstandingly successful, was one of closer settlement of irrigated lands, and of compulsory charges for the water provided for irrigation whether used or not. Mead indicated that small holdings and closer settlement were the surest method of assuring the success of an irrigation development and that a compulsory charge for water, apportioned as water rights, was the most potent influence to make men learn how to use the available water properly. This system compelled those owning lands in irrigation areas to make use of their advantages, or to sell to those who would, and thus put an end to landholding practices, which left vast tracts undeveloped for speculative purposes. Mead also insisted that the irrigation authority should have control of the acquisition and subdivision of land in the irrigation area because of the intimate connection of this work with the construction of water supply projects.

He brought some Americans to Victoria and also arranged for several young Victorians to go to the United States to study irrigation at the University of California in Berkeley. Mead—who later became Commissioner of the Bureau of Reclamation, United States Department of the Interior—was undoubtedly an historic figure in Australia, in that all later irrigation development in Victoria has been based on the principles that he introduced.

River Murray Commission.—As chairman of the State Rivers and Water Supply Commission, Mead was associated with an event of the greatest importance in the history of water conservation in Australia. In 1914, just before he returned to the United States, an agreement was concluded among the states of New South Wales, Victoria, and South Australia and the Commonwealth of Australia for harnessing the waters of the River Murray (Fig. 3). This great river has a catchment area of more than 400,000 sq miles. It has been navigated by steamers as far as 1,370 miles from its mouth. One of its tributaries is 1,760 miles long, and another is more than 1,000 miles long.

The River Murray Agreement, which was ratified by the four parliaments concerned in 1915, provided for the construction of two large reservoirs and many weirs and locks along more than 1,000 miles of river, for the allocation of the

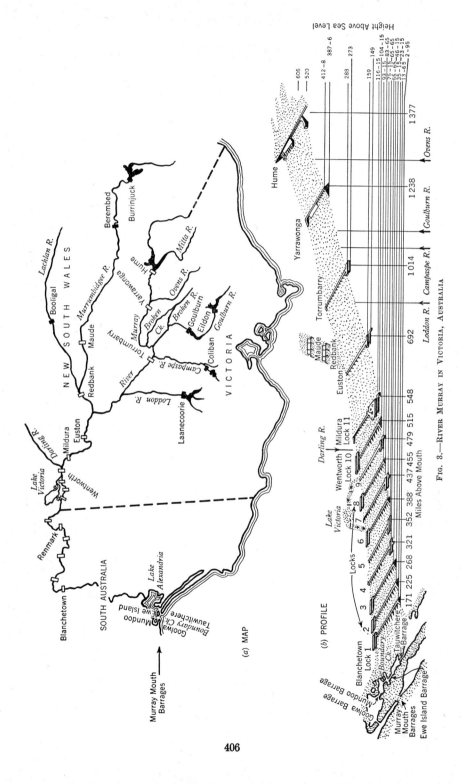

Fig. 3.—River Murray in Victoria, Australia

water between the three states concerned, and for the appointment of a River Murray Commission to give effect to the agreement.

The River Murray Commission, however, is not a constructing authority itself, its responsibility being limited to arranging for the construction of the works by existing state authorities, which design, build, and maintain them subject to the approval and direction of the River Murray Commission (Fig. 4). The Agree-

(a) HUME DAM

(b) TAUWITCHERE BARRAGE

FIG. 4.—MAJOR STRUCTURES ON RIVER MURRAY IN VICTORIA, AUSTRALIA

ment was later modified to provide for certain additional works, including particularly interesting barrages, totaling about 4 miles in length, across the mouth of the River Murray to prevent salt water from entering the Murray Mouth Lakes and the lower river during periods of low flow. These barrages, as well as two large reservoirs and sixteen weirs, have been constructed, and have been outstandingly successful. Many of the weirs (Figs. 5 and 6) were built to a design recommended by an American engineer, E. N. Johnston, M. ASCE, of the Corps of Engineers, United States Army.

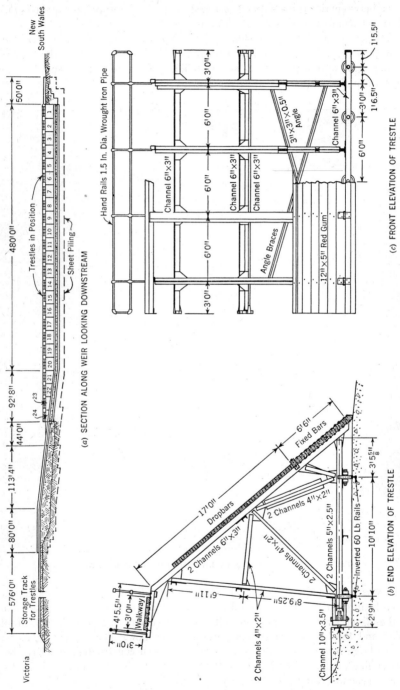

(a) SECTION ALONG WEIR LOOKING DOWNSTREAM

(b) END ELEVATION OF TRESTLE

(c) FRONT ELEVATION OF TRESTLE

FIG. 5.—MILDURA WEIR, IN VICTORIA, AUSTRALIA

FIG. 6.—MILDURA WEIR, VICTORIA, AUSTRALIA, WITH TRESTLE UNIT WITHDRAWN FROM RIVER MURRAY

Two other weirs however were built to a novel design evolved by a Victorian engineer, John Stewart Dethridge. These structures consist of a number of movable steel trestles on wheels running on a concrete and steel track across the bed of the river (Fig. 5). The weirs have been in successful operation for 25 years and have required very little maintenance.

FIG. 7.—ERECTION OF POWERHOUSE OUTLET—EILDON DAM ON THE GOULBURN RIVER IN VICTORIA, AUSTRALIA

SUMMARY

Irrigation development in Victoria for nearly three quarters of a century has been remarkably and intimately associated with irrigation development in the western states of the United States. Step by step Australia has been guided by the example of the United States.

Australia's water law embodies the best features of similar American legislation, and possibly goes further. Engineering practice, both in design and construction, closely follows American standards. Agricultural developments are also keeping pace.

Information given by Americans to Deakin in 1885 guided him in the preparation of basic legislation dealing with water law. The example set by the Chaffeys at Mildura showed the possibilities of high-lift pumping in the preparation of arid lands for intense culture. The closer settlement and fiscal policies of Mead provided what was required to make irrigation the success it is today.

Some of the present leaders in Australia's irrigated agriculture received their early training at the University of California. Weirs have been patterned on structures proved in American streams. Australia has been encouraged to proceed from large dams to very large dams by that great leader in American dam design, J. L. Savage, Hon. M. ASCE, and at the present time the Utah Construction Company is demonstrating how an American contractor goes about building such a structure (Fig. 7). Both in the United States and overseas, Americans have freely given of their knowledge to all who have sought information.

AMERICAN SOCIETY OF CIVIL ENGINEERS
Founded November 5, 1852

TRANSACTIONS

Paper No. 2599

STRUCTURES FOR IRRIGATION DIVERSION AND DISTRIBUTION

By J. Ernest Hill,[1] A. M. ASCE

Synopsis

Since the beginning of national reclamation in the United States there have been 50 years of growth, as illustrated by the construction of works for diverting and distributing large volumes of water. Concrete weirs or overflow dams involve problems similar to those on major structures, but on a smaller scale. Economy in building large canals has followed the development of costly plant for continuous operation in excavating, compacting earth, trimming slopes, and placing concrete lining. To a lesser extent, asphalt and cement mortar linings are also used to prevent seepage losses. Special structures of concrete, in the form of large siphons or conduits, are sometimes needed, with economy derived especially from movable metal forms. Throughout, designers, construction engineeers, and contractors have worked in harmony to produce maximum results at minimum cost.

During the past 50 years, according to the Bureau of Reclamation, United States Department of the Interior, it and its predecessor, the Reclamation Service, have supplied water to more than 6,000,000 acres of irrigable lands in the seventeen western states. On sixty-two operating projects, there are ninety-six dams, four hundred ninety-five pumping plants, and thirty-nine power plants. Water is carried to the land in 20,000 miles of canals and laterals, together with 200,000 irrigation structures. Approximately 4,333,333 kw of hydroelectric power are being generated from its power plants. These reclamation land and water developments comprise a capital investment of approximately $2,000,000,000.00, with new projects adding about $500,000,000.00. It is readily apparent that reclamation projects have contributed a great deal to the construction volume of the West, and indirectly to the industrial business of the East.

The multipurpose projects of recent times have involved major construction. After 15 years of building activity, the Central Valley Project in California was placed in operation in 1951. It is understood that the Colorado-Big Thompson Project in Colorado, under construction since 1939, should be completed in about

1954. The Columbia Basin Project in Washington, started in September, 1933, received its first water for crops in 1952. The construction of laterals and sublaterals to complete the project will extend over a period of some 10 years in the future. The Missouri River Basin Project authorized by the Flood Control Act of 1944 is under construction by the Bureau of Reclamation and the Corps of Engineers of the United States Army. This project includes the ultimate irrigation of more than 6,000,000 acres with several large dams in Nebraska, Montana, Wyoming, and North Dakota. Canal systems are being constructed as dams are completed. The whole development will require more than one hundred dams, forty power plants, and thousands of miles of canals. The sizes of canals and distribution structures will compare with those previously built on the larger projects.

Diversion Structures

Diversion of water from a stream or river into an irrigation canal is usually accomplished by constructing a dam or a weir which will raise the stream water surface sufficiently to provide the required flow. These structures are usually of the overflow type or open channels with gates. They generally have a broad apron foundation with cutoff walls of steel sheet piling or of reinforced concrete at the upstream and downstream ends. The base of the dam is a heavy reinforced-concrete slab resting on the native material of the stream bed.

Additional support may be given to the base by piling, as is the case with Leasburg Dam on the Rio Grande in New Mexico. The overflow section may be a small solid concrete dam with shaped crest or it may be a gravel-ballasted hollow concrete shell as at the Imperial Dam near Yuma, Ariz., on the Colorado River. The Roza Dam on the Yakima River in Washington is a gravity section structure with an overflow spillway and roller gates for controlling the elevation of the water surface. This dam is founded on solid rock.

Physical Elements.—The construction problems on diversion dams are very much the same as those on any other dams that form a complete barricade across a stream. The unwatering of the foundation and the diversion of the water must be complete, but on a smaller scale than for large storage dams. As on all reclamation work, the planning of the construction operations and the methods to be employed are the responsibility of the contractor. Because of the small scope of work, it is generally not economically feasible to assemble the construction plant and equipment that would minimize to the greatest extent all elements of risk. However, the specifications may be prepared so that the elements of nature are defined as clearly as is consistently possible—such elements as: Climate, stream runoff, materials in the dam foundation, and topography of the area.

Information on the weather, which is readily available from numerous weather observation stations, is necessary for determining the working seasons for the different types of construction and for evaluating the protection that must be provided during the work and for the parts completed. Data on stream runoff may not be available for as long a period as those on weather conditions, but they are generally available for the period that the project has been under study. The value of stream runoff data cannot be overemphasized for planning stream diversion and foundation unwatering operations.

Essential Data.—The specifications should include complete information on the locations and logs of test pits and drill holes. If the structure and excavation limits for the structure are outlined on the topographic map showing the location of drill holes and test pits, the critical areas for foundation conditions will become more apparent, and this will greatly help the contractor in evaluating the work. A careful analysis of the material drilled through and of the possible underground formations, made at the time the drilling operation is in progress, will aid greatly in avoiding misclassification of materials and of foundation structure. If these errors are found only after work is in progress, they prove very costly.

A topographic map of the job area will aid the contractor in reviewing and analyzing the information given on logs of drill holes. Such a map will be of value in laying out construction operations and in determining quantities of excavation to be done. This map should also show the man-made improvements which must be removed, protected, and replaced.

CANAL CONSTRUCTION

Canals and distribution systems include main canals, branch canals, and laterals, and such waste canals as may be needed to carry undelivered water into natural channels or drainages; conveyance structures such as chutes, drops, transitions, inverted siphons, tunnels, flumes, aqueducts, closed conduits, and crossings at railways, highways, and streams; regulating works consisting of checks, turnouts, and gate structures; protective structures including automatic or siphonic spillways, tributary flood overchutes, settling basins, and sand traps; and miscellaneous structures consisting of drainage inlets, culverts, bridges, and other incidental construction.

Most canals have a trapezoidal cross section with side slopes consistent with the natural angle of repose of the material in which the canal is constructed. A semicircular section, the most efficient section, has been used in the lower Rio Grande Valley of Texas, where the type of soil is favorable to its use. As the canals are designed to carry water for the largest acreage possible, they are usually located along the higher edges, or perhaps center ridges, of the irrigable land. Thus, they are generally in a sidehill cut or a thorough cut, except for crossings of natural drainage.

Embankment and Core Bank.—The construction of canals starts with the clearing and grubbing, if necessary, of sagebrush and other vegetation from the excavation and embankment areas. The embankment section for unlined canals consists of a core bank—from 6 ft to 10 ft wide at the top, with side slopes of $1\frac{1}{2}$ to 1, and so located that one side forms the inside (water side) slope of the canal or serves as a core within the embankment—and an overlay section on the outer side of the embankment, to reinforce the core bank. It is general practice for concrete-lined canals, and for unlined canals where the water surface will be more than 4 ft above the original ground, to construct the core bank as compacted embankment to the same top dimensions and side slopes as the core bank.

After the clearing and grubbing operation, the embankment and core-bank areas are bond plowed for a depth of 6 in. and the compacted areas are consolidated with a sheepsfoot roller (Fig. 1). They are constructed of materials obtained from the canal prism or borrow areas, and generally with tractor and scraper units. The sheepsfoot roller is used for compaction with the water applied by sprinkler trucks, by hose and sprinklers from pipelines, by irrigation of the borrow pits, or by a combination of these. Where the canal is to be lined with concrete, a great deal of water will also be required for trimming the canal for the concrete lining and for the concrete. A quick coupling pipeline for the full length of the job has proved to be the cheapest and most dependable method of handling the water.

It may be of interest to note how the first core-bank section came into use on canal work. J. A. Terteling and Sons, Incorporated, on one of their early contracts with the Bureau of Reclamation in southern Idaho, placed the topsoil from a gravel and cobblestone material on the water side of the embankment to stop

FIG. 1.—MATERIAL FOR EMBANKMENT (LEFT) OBTAINED FROM CANAL PRISM BY SCRAPER AT RIGHT, AND COMPACTED BY SHEEPSFOOT ROLLERS

the cobblestone from rolling back into the canal. This procedure did not offer any particular problem as the excavation was being made with a dragline. The Bureau of Reclamation engineers at once recognized this as a good practice from the standpoint of sealing the gravel embankment and soon thereafter introduced the construction of core banks into their specifications.

Machines Used for Excavation.—A problem for contractors in constructing core-bank and compacted embankment sections is that the size of scraper units giving the lowest over-all cost is too large for the narrow top width of the required section. This results in a large overrun of the caterpillar-and-scraper excavation, which is the most expensive element of the average cost used in bidding on the canal excavation work.

The larger part of canal excavation is made with draglines casting the material as an overlay to raise and reinforce the core banks and compacted embankment sections or as waste in the thorough cuts. Generally, the excavation quantities will be greatly in excess of embankment quantities. The draglines used vary from the smallest to the largest sizes of crawler machines and to the large walking-type machines. The contractor, of course, selects the size that will give the most economical operation for the canal and job. The tops of the embankments built with draglines may be graded with bulldozers to provide surface drainage or a road for canal maintenance operation.

Excavation of laterals and sublaterals follows along the same pattern of operations as on the main canals. However, to minimize the number and size of borrow pits, which may become stagnant pools from the drainage of irrigated lands, the excess excavation from cuts is used for building embankments. On these jobs the engineers have staked out the work so that the first construction operation involved excavating the cut sections down to the canal berm and placing this material in the embankment section up to about the berm level. At this point the canal has the appearance of a road grade. The excavation of the canal prism then becomes the second operation. The larger lateral prism sections are excavated with draglines. On the smaller laterals and sublaterals a back-hoe type of shovel may be used. However, the tractor-drawn vee-plow ditcher mounted on wheels, with hydraulic controls for regulating the depth of cut, has proved highly satisfactory and very economical. The Chattin ditcher developed by a farmer in Idaho for maintenance of unlined laterals and farm ditches has also been used successfully by contractors.

It has been estimated that one third of all the water diverted from western streams for irrigation is lost in transit to the farm land. The seepage losses in canals and laterals are considered to account for almost 25% of the total water diverted, or for about 75% of the total loss. These losses have been minimized by lining the canals with concrete, asphaltic concrete, asphalt membrane, "shotcrete," earth, and variations of these.

Trimming and Compacting.—The early canals and the large canals which require lining today are lined with concrete, from 2 in. to $4\frac{1}{2}$ in. in thickness. A lined canal is constructed in three steps: The rough excavation of the canal itself as discussed previously; the trimming of the canal section to the subgrade dimensions and to the lines and grades for the canal; and the placing of the lining material. In the early days the subgrade for the lining was trimmed by hand and the fine grading was done from ribbons set to grade parallel with the slope and at right angles to the canal. The ribbons were spaced to agree with the concrete panel width desired, and limited to the maximum width that could be rodded and finished by hand labor. Concrete was placed in alternate panels.

On the larger canals specially designed equipment has been built to do the trimming of the subgrade (Fig. 2). Most of these machines are similar in design and principle of operation. They consist of a steel truss in the shape of the canal cross section mounted at each corner on carriages which travel on steel rails laid along the canal banks. Two lines of bucket excavators mounted on chains travel from the center line of the canal up the side slope and deposit the excavated materials on a system of belt conveyors which in turn dump it onto the canal bank. These machines also have their own power for travel on the rails, with a separate power unit for each end of the machine to facilitate travel on radial lines on curves.

Grade for the depth of cut is maintained by jacks at each corner of the machine, operated either manually or by electrical controls with a pointer traveling along a taut piano wire set on steel stakes on the canal banks. This type of machine will trim up to 1,000 ft of complete canal section in one day. The disadvantage of this machine is that it is very expensive to build and also to modify for different sizes of canal. As the great weight of these machines requires 90-lb to 110-lb rails, the canals should be designed with 8-ft to 10-ft berm widths on top of the canal bank for sufficient crosstie length and working room.

On jobs where only a short length of a large canal is to be lined, machines for trimming one slope at a time have been built. One of the latest such machines,

Fig. 2.—Sequence of Canal Lining Operations: Fine Grading of Subgrade by Trimmer at Far Left; Batched Aggregates for Concrete Lining Supplied by Large Trucks in Foreground and Mixed by Pavers on Canal Berm in Middle; Large Equipment in Canal Section Being Lining and Finishing Machines; Curing Jumbo, Nearest, Which Facilitates Final Treatment of Lining

used on the Columbia Basin Project, consisted of a line of bucket excavators mounted on a truss spanning one slope and supported at each end by a carriage traveling on rails on top of the canal bank and the canal bottom near the toe of the side slope. This machine proved very efficient and could be easily modified for different sizes of canal.

Trimming machines for small canals have some form of a simple truss conforming to the shape of the canal and generally have fixed blades with the top end leading, so that the material is drawn to the bottom of the canal. Barber-Greene-type bucket elevators pick up the excavated material and deposit it on a belt conveyor which dumps onto the canal bank. The earlier machines for large canals were built on this order.

The required construction procedure for concrete-lined canals in rock is overexcavation so that no point of rock extends closer than 3 in. to the underside of the canal lining. This overexcavated area is then backfilled with a free draining material such as pit-run sand and gravel, with no rock larger than that which will pass a 3-in. screen. This material is placed in 6-in. layers, parallel to the slope on the sides, sprinkled, and consolidated by rolling. On large canals the grid roller, handled by a crawler crane either on the canal invert or on the canal bank, has been used with good results. A large pneumatic compactor supported from and traveling along a specially designed boom on a crawler crane has also been used successfully (Fig. 3). The compactor will consolidate a 6-in. layer in two passes.

Fig. 3.—Compaction of Side Slopes by Means of an Air-Operated Tamper; Crawler Cranes in Tandem Providing the Two Passes Needed to Consolidate a 6-In. Layer

Canal Lining by Machine.—To work with continuous trimmers, continuous slip-form concrete canal lining machines have been designed. They also consist of a truss conforming to the shape of the canal and are mounted to travel on the same rails as the trimmers. The truss supports: (1) Continuous tube vibrators which ride through the concrete, (2) a steel plate slip form set to the finished canal dimensions, and (3) follower floats with spring-applied pressure for giving a smooth finish to the concrete. Grade is controlled in the same manner and by the same piano wire as for the trimmer. This machine is also self-propelled.

A finishing jumbo, a much lighter machine, travels along right behind the liner. Cement finishers ride this machine to cut the contraction joints and to put the final touches on the finishing of the concrete surface. The concrete curing jumbo follows behind the finishing jumbo; it is also a canal-prism-shaped truss spanning the canal and traveling under its own power. The mastic for the contraction joints and the curing compound are carried on this machine and applied from it. These several machines are shown in operation in Fig. 2, whereas Fig. 4 is an over-all view of a similar large project.

Because of relaxing tolerances on alinement and grade in recent years, several new types of concrete lining equipment have been designed. One which has proved successful on small canals is a slip form of the same shape as the canal, supported directly on top of the concrete being placed and on skid shoes on top of the canal banks. This machine is tractor drawn.

FIG. 4.—GENERAL SCENE WHICH SHOWS LINING OF A LARGE CANAL IN CURVED ALINEMENT, WITH MASSIVE MACHINES FOR TRIMMING, PLACING CONCRETE, FINISHING, AND CURING; WITH STRETCH OF FINISHED LINING IN FOREGROUND

A simple and fairly inexpensive lining arrangement for short reaches, and one that can be readily modified for different sizes of canal, is shown in Fig. 5. Trimming has been completed and reinforcement placed. Batches of concrete are mixed in a paver and placed by a crawler crane, both operating from the bottom of the canal. Trussed structures, moving on top and bottom rails at proper grade, carry slip forms that insure an accurate surface for the freshly placed concrete. The cement finishers' jumbo, with which the surfacing is done, the contraction joints cut, and the curing compound applied, is part of the inclined framework.

The rate at which lining can be placed by any of the machines is determined largely by the speed of mixing the concrete and of supplying it to the form. Of course, the trimming operations must be geared to stay well ahead of the lining operations. Most canal jobs have a central concrete aggregate batch plant where the aggregates and portland cement are batched and dumped into compartmented trucks for transportation to a paver or pavers located on the canal banks alongside the lining machine (Fig. 2). The pavers dump the mixed concrete into hoppers mounted over belt conveyors which deposit the mixture into a central hopper on the lining machine. Electric-motor-powered carts mounted on rails

FIG. 5.—LINING ONE SIDE OF A CANAL IN ROCK, USING CRAWLER CRANE TO HANDLE CONCRETE AND INCLINED TRUSSES, SPANNING FROM RAILS AT BOTTOM AND TOP, TO PLACE AND FINISH THE CEMENT WORK

distribute the concrete into smaller hoppers and elephant trunks at fixed locations along the full canal width of the lining machine.

Asphalt and Other Lining.—In its program to lower the cost of canal linings, the Bureau of Reclamation has used other materials than portland cement concrete, such as the hot-mix type of asphaltic concrete. In this construction a central hot-plant mix of sand, gravel, and asphaltic cement is dumped into a slip form of which the forward part rides on the subgrade and the form itself rides on the asphaltic concrete being placed. The mixture is compacted or consolidated by adding sandbags to the trailing hot plate of the slip form. In one design the slope hot plates were formed as tubes with oil burners at the bottom end. Asphalt cement of 60 to 70 penetration was used on the early projects, but 50 to 60 penetration material has been used on later jobs. The lining is generally placed about 2 in.

thick. The subgrade for asphaltic concrete can be trimmed with comparatively simple equipment as relatively wide tolerances in the dimensions can be permitted.

Another type of low-cost canal lining which has been used in recent years is buried asphalt membrane. This lining is a thin coating, about $\frac{1}{4}$ in. to $\frac{3}{8}$ in. thick, of catalytically blown asphalt, sprayed on a prepared subgrade at a temperature of about 375° F. To protect the asphalt from heat, air, radiation caused by the sun, and such mechanical injury, as by hoofs of animals, an earth and gravel covering is placed on this lining. The construction procedure then is: (a) To overexcavate the canal prism for the depth of protection to be placed on the lining, which ranges from 10 in. to 18 in. and requires no regular trimming operation as such; (b) to drag the subgrade, removing loose materials and providing a relatively smooth surface; (c) to consolidate the sides and bottom of the canal by rolling; (d) to sprinkle the subgrade; and (e) to apply the asphalt with hand-carried distributor spray bars fed by a standard asphalt distributor traveling on the canal bank.

Asphalt is applied in two passes on the canal sides and in one in the bottom at a minimum rate of $1\frac{1}{4}$ gal per sq yd for the full lining thickness. The last operation consists of placing the earth cover over the membrane lining with drag-line, motor patrol, or angle dozer. The writer's observation on construction has been that the cover material should be placed as soon as possible. In this manner, sagging of the lining on the side slopes will not occur, and the wind will be prevented from eroding the sand from under the lining at the top of the slope and eventually from blowing the lining against the opposite side of the canal very much like a blanket. The asphalt does provide a tough flexible lining which perhaps needs subgrade priming to provide penetration and bond to avoid sagging on slopes. Other asphalt membrane linings have also been used.

Still another type of low-cost lining is "shotcrete." This term designates a portland cement mortar that is forced by air pressure through a nozzle onto the earth surface of the canal. The subgrade must be firm but need be only reasonably smooth. On one job the bottom of the lateral was overexcavated sufficiently to take the excess material from the sides, which were hand trimmed. The 1-cu ft cement gun was served by a $1\frac{1}{2}$-in. hose and nozzles, a 315-cu ft per min compressor, and an 11-S mixer—all mounted on a 10-ton low-bed trailer which was towed along the canal. As the desired thickness, $1\frac{1}{2}$ in. to 2 in. has to be built by successive passes, which are time consuming and expensive, and as the proportion of portland cement used is greater, the costs on this type of lining will not compete with those for the asphalt linings. However, this lining can be used favorably for repair of concrete-lined canals.

SIPHONS AND CONDUITS

Of conveyance structures for distribution systems probably siphons with their transitions provide the most interesting construction. They carry canal flows under highways, railways, streams, and across long and deep valleys. Small-capacity siphons are constructed of reinforced-concrete pipe, lined concrete pressure pipe, and even steel pipe. Larger siphons, which must carry great volumes of water at a comparatively low head, are essentially reinforced-concrete pipes cast in place and constructed in sections 25 ft long. At locations of large hydraulic head the siphon may be a steel pipe or may be lined with steel, as is the case in the Soap Lake Siphon on the Columbia Basin Project. The joint between the 25-ft sections is made watertight with either a flat rubber seal or a wrought-iron water stop (Fig. 6).

Preparations for Concreting.—Construction of a concrete siphon includes the excavation and trimming of the subgrade, the placing of reinforcing steel, the setting and moving of the steel forms, the pouring and curing of concrete, and the placing of backfill. After the rough excavation has been made, the subgrade is trimmed accurately to the neat concrete lines and, in sandy loose material, is

FIG. 6.—END VIEW OF COMPLETED BAND OF CONCRETE SIPHON, SHOWING WROUGHT-IRON WATER STOP, AS USED BETWEEN 25-FT SECTIONS

covered with a skin coat of portland cement grout to prevent raveling. To support the reinforcing steel, which is placed ahead of the forms, small pockets are dug out of the subgrade in two lines at about the third points in the bottom width, and are filled with concrete into which are inserted short steel stubs. A heavier reinforcing bar or small angle is then welded to the stubs in the longitudinal direction, to serve as the support for the cages of the double reinforcing steel.

After the steel has been placed for a section or several sections, a set of inside steel forms is put in position (Fig. 7). In one type the inside form is supported on a double-beam system placed under the crown of the form section and spanning the length of two sections. The beam in turn is provided with post supports at the end and near the midpoint.

Movable Forms.—This arrangement permits the form to be moved with rollers riding on the beam and the beam in turn to be moved, riding on suspension rolls on the form, which is in the position of the previously placed concrete. In another type, two sets of inside forms are used. Each set is made so that it can telescope

FIG. 7.—SIPHON CONSTRUCTION FROM WORKING END: OUTSIDE AND INSIDE FORMS IN PLACE AND FINE GRADING FOR NEXT 25-FT SECTION IN PROGRESS

and can pass through the set that is in place and supporting the concrete. These forms are supported and travel on rails set above the invert, the rails being held by the same system of concrete anchors and stubs as the reinforcing steel previously mentioned.

Outside forms for both types of inside forms are made to ride on rails set about 2 ft beyond the finish line of the outer concrete surface. The outside form framework may be designed to act as a gantry in moving the forms and in supporting a deck structure for concrete placing; or a separate outside gantry may be provided. The adjustments for setting the forms in correct position are made with a combination of hydraulic jacks and screw jacks. The bulkhead forms are of steel, and are also in sections of such size that they can be readily handled by two men.

In order to place the concrete in the invert with less difficulty, the inside form is left open at the bottom for 30° each side of center; and the concrete in this area is hand finished. The top 60° of the outside form is also left open to expedite placing concrete (Fig. 7). In most forms the concrete for the invert and the sides is placed with elephant trunks through openings at three different levels in the outside form. The concrete is generally vibrated internally. Once the crews are organized for this work, the construction of siphons with these traveling forms becomes a very efficient and economical operation.

Large Twin Conduit.—The contractors for the canal feeding water from the pumping plant to the equalizing reservoir of the Grand Coulee Project on the Columbia River had a very interesting problem in the construction of the 25-ft-diameter twin reinforced-concrete conduits, which are generally referred to as the cut-and-cover section and which were constructed in the same manner as siphons. This feeder canal traverses through earth, shale, granite, and basalt in its length of 1¾ miles. The nature of the earth materials is such that slides result whenever a cut is made at the toe of a slope. The Federal Government had started excavation of the feeder canal with its own forces in 1946 and had to stop in 1947 when the materials in a heavy cut near the center of the job continued to slide and threatened to release the whole hill into the canal excavation.

Design of the open canal was then changed to the twin-barrel conduit, and the work was included in the contract for the North Dam and the completion of the Feeder Canal. The design of the cut-and-cover section was adopted so that the hill above could be supported by a heavy backfill over the structure. The specifications provided that the twin conduit was to be constructed from the upstream end to the critical slide area and then from the downstream end, to meet at the critical area, which was about 300 ft long.

Work went along well until the construction from the downstream end had advanced to the point where it was necessary to excavate the critical area. Until that time the placing of backfill over the structure had to follow the excavation by a distance not to exceed 200 ft. As excavation advanced into the slide area, movement of the hill was again detected. It was apparent that support for the hill above had to be provided if the work was to be successful. The contractor proposed to the Bureau of Reclamation a plan of operation as follows: Load the area to be excavated with additional material to provide sufficient weight as the length of the cut was reduced; and advance the backfill operations to within 75 ft of the excavation. This proved to be very sound engineering thinking, and the work was completed without further trouble.

Varied Problems.—The construction of other conveyance and regulatory structures involves very much the same general difficulties as occur on any reinforced-concrete construction. Transitions and siphonic spillways, however, provide problems of formwork which tax the ingenuity of engineers and carpenters (Fig. 8).

Multitudinous and varied problems are presented to contractors in the construction of irrigation diversion dams and irrigation distribution systems, which in practice cover every type of work. There are dams, which may be concrete

Fig. 8.—Open Warped Transition in Concrete, from Square Section of Large Siphon Outlet to Trapezoidal Canal Section Which Taxed the Ingenuity of the Engineer, the Carpenter, and the Reinforcement Layer

or earth fill; there are pumping plants and power drops; there are canals, siphons, tunnels, transitions, drops, and chutes; there are checks, turnouts, diversion structures, and wasteways; and there are bridges for highways, railroads, and pipelines. Incidental to all these, and sometimes a part of the contracts, is the construction of highways, railroads, streets, water systems, sewer systems, and buildings for offices, shops, and warehouses. In spite of this wide field of activity, the

Bureau of Reclamation has done a tremendous and wonderful job. It is only fair to note that these results were achieved in large measure from the close cooperation and harmony that have existed between the contractors and the engineers.

How Costs May Be Lowered

However, engineers and contractors cannot be satisfied that they have done their best on irrigation construction until the costs have been brought down to the lowest level. The farmer, who must repay the costs of construction, is the only one competent to judge whether the costs are low enough, consistent with the use of the land. Obviously the cost of irrigation of land suitable for row crops can be higher than for land on which a cover crop, as alfalfa, will be grown.

Organization Important.—Since the end of World War II, when irrigation work was again resumed with renewed vigor, it appears that costs have been increased more than those for other types of general construction. Whatever the explanation, much benefit can be derived by analyzing elements of design and construction which can bring these costs down.

The contractors for their part must train construction personnel in the knowhow of maximum efficiency in the use of labor and equipment. They must devise more and better equipment for doing the work. Examples of what has been done are the continuous trimming machine, the canal lining slip form, and the collapsible steel forms for siphons. They should set up organizations which will perform this type of work and become familiar with the problems peculiar to it.

Designs for Saving.—However, the engineers who plan and design the work, who prepare the job requirements for the specifications, and who supervise and inspect construction, truly hold the key to the greatest economies. Canal and lateral structures are standardized for type and uniformity of construction except for dimensions. Design engineers can well afford to review the basic elements of cost in arriving at a decision on establishing sizes of similar structures. It is known that on average irrigation work today's cost of portland cement, sand and gravel, and reinforcing steel will be from $16.00 to $19.00 per cu yd of concrete. The batching, mixing, and hauling will add from $1.50 to $4.00. Thus, the costs directly chargeable to a cubic yard of concrete will vary roughly from $17.50 to $23.00, a minor part of the concrete costs for the bulk of the irrigation concrete work.

Costs of building forms for the average structures, however, will amount to approximately $18.00 to $45.00 per cu yd, depending on the number of uses that may be obtained. Thus the design of structures should take into consideration the dimensions of form areas and the total form area, instead of the volume of concrete—that is, it will very often be cheaper to use a little more concrete than to build complete new sets of forms for a similar structure of slightly different dimensions. Structures which definitely can be considered for uniformity of size include division boxes, county and farm bridges, drainage culverts, weirs, pipe inlets, and turnouts.

Improving Specifications.—Construction engineers can help by constantly reviewing inspection requirements for consistency with natural conditions on the job, by recognizing physical limitations of contractors' equipment, and by specifying the use of standard commercial materials wherever possible. The engineers can also do a great deal to lower costs by recognizing the effect of increased laboratory study on the preparation of construction specifications. In the years since World War II, there has been much more laboratory study of construction materials and design. These studies, of course, are performed under man-controlled conditions with the object of getting optimum results. They have had a definite effect on the requirements given in the specifications for the performance of the actual construction. Often it appears that the refinements are beyond what might be considered consistent for the use and the expected life of the structure.

It is possible that in the not-too-distant future the requirements for processing aggregates and for designing mixes for concrete used in irrigation distribution structures will be reviewed with the object of lowering costs. Some such discussion has already taken place in engineering journals about concrete construction in general. By and large, every effort should be made to use nature's materials on the job with the minimum amount of processing and refining consistent with the use of the structure.

Specification engineers will be able to help in lowering costs by establishing bid price items which will clearly define the work to be done. Quite often those items which cannot be clearly defined as to conditions and quantity of work are set up under a lump sum pay item, or are made an incidental part of a unit price item. Thus, in bidding the contractors must use a "crystal ball" to guess as to possible costs and then add a percentage for contingencies to make the guess good. In short, if the specifications are prepared so that the owner will assume the risk, the prices for the work in this highly competitive field will be the lowest possible.

AMERICAN SOCIETY OF CIVIL ENGINEERS
Founded November 5, 1852
TRANSACTIONS

Paper No. 2600

ECONOMY DICTATES RECLAMATION DESIGN

By L. N. McClellan,[1] M. ASCE

Synopsis

Reclamation design, in its evolution through service experience, coupled with analysis and tests, has always given full consideration to costs. Economy has been realized by permissible uniformity of design, especially for smaller structures, by standardized concrete forms and reinforcing, by adjustments to take advantage of available materials, by justifiable increased allowable stresses, and by adaptations to large-scale construction operations. Design, however, did not stand alone in the advance of construction economy, but was powerfully aided by better tools and machinery, and by the construction industry's remarkable progress in capacity and skill. Refinement of specifications and contract practice supplemented these developments. The combined effect is to produce lower cost reclamation works, with more service value and permanence.

In greater degree than most other types of construction, reclamation construction is controlled by dictates of economy. The basic law requires that its beneficiaries, chiefly the irrigators under reclamation works, repay the cost of these works; and, as the irrigators have only a limited margin of profit from their farming operations, the repayment obligation imposes an onerous burden. From the earliest days of the Bureau of Reclamation (United States Department of the Interior), its engineers have therefore given intensive study to designing for minimum cost. Many examples of outstanding design and construction economy will be found in the works of even the years immediately following the inauguration of reclamation in 1902. Recent years have added to the pressure for construction economy by steadily mounting price and cost levels and by the changing nature of reclamation tasks.

Modern reclamation construction has to deal with much larger and more complex developments than those of past decades. The available sites and other controlling conditions are less favorable, and today each new project calls for extended comparative studies to find what layout, type of design, and details will

---

[1] Chf. Engr., Bureau of Reclamation, U. S. Dept. of the Interior, Denver, Colo.

involve the lowest cost consistent with efficient service. Thus the Bureau is compelled to give close attention to designing for economical construction.

It is conceded that the requirements of quality and economy are closely related, and that the increasing use of site and material exploration, structural analysis, and physical investigation tends naturally toward lower cost as well as more efficient service. Engineering design by its very nature aims at economy as well as adequate service. Reclamation therefore cannot claim that its striving for economy is unique. Nevertheless, it is believed that, since the Bureau has been forced to consider costs with unusual care, others engaged in extensive hydraulic construction may find help from its experience.

General Design Procedures

The cost of a structure comprising a number of elements is increased if the several elements differ in form, size, and details or if the manual or machine procedure involved must be varied. Conversely, economy is favored by uniformity of design and adaptation to a minimum number of craft processes. In applying this well-known truth, the Bureau has made increasing use of standard designs, both for works built in place and for manufactured machinery and equipment. In contrast to early practice in reclamation construction, which favored individual design of each structure or plant to fit the particular conditions of the case, design standardization is now recognized as an important aid to economy.

Uniform Designs.—Hundreds of standard design sheets developed over the years but utilized only to a limited extent are being drawn into regular service, after bringing them up to date if necessary, in the light of operating experience and other changed conditions. Such structures as canal turnouts, trashracks, roadways, and radial gates are especially adaptable to standardization (Fig. 1). Large gates and valves are among the exceptions; also power and pumping plants obviously must be fitted to the particular conditions of the individual case and therefore require special design.

The value of uniformity has been recognized by modifying designs of concrete structures to reduce form costs. Unnecessary diversity has been reduced by drawing up a limited list of standard reinforcement shapes for normal design. At the same time many details of reinforcing steel were simplified, as by reducing the extent of the use of hooks and the length of laps at splices. Adoption of the new high-bond reinforcing bars contributed to making these economies possible.

Materials Adapted to Use.—When defense needs limited the supply of certain materials, it became necessary to adapt designs to the use of readily available materials and sizes. Substitutes for many critical materials had to be utilized. Supply limitations in some cases affected construction economy by threatening to delay the completion of urgently needed works, such as power plants, and here it was necessary at times to expedite construction by paying overtime, by diverting materials from one job to another, and by other expedients. Although such expediting added to immediate costs, it saved money in other ways. A power plant was enabled to earn earlier power revenues, which paid many times over for the extra cost incurred in quicker completion.

Simultaneously with design modification of the kinds indicated, material improvement in concrete design with resulting construction economy was realized through increasing knowledge of cement properties and concrete production, including the selection and grading of aggregates. The improvement of quality which accompanied the cost reduction was supplemented by better knowledge of material properties and stress analysis, thus paving the way for the adoption of increased working stresses. Concrete working stresses in dams and other struc-

Fig. 1.—Scene on Coachella Branch, All-American Canal in California, Indicating Use of Standardized Designs Such As the Check, at Right, and the Automatic Radial Gate Structure, at Left

tures have been raised to 1,000 lb per sq in. and 1,350 lb per sq in., respectively, with corresponding gains in economy (Fig. 2), whereas steel stresses have been increased to 24,000 lb per sq in.

Construction Needs Considered.—Paralleling the advancement of design, construction requirements have been modified to provide economy consistent with satisfactory service results. A particularly significant modification was the establishment of dimensional tolerances for concrete construction. In addition, a carefully defined schedule of finishes for each specific element or surface of a structure had an important influence in reducing construction costs by eliminating needlessly expensive finishes.

The adaptation of designs to economical use of construction machinery received much thought. Canal dimensions were studied to determine those best suited to efficient use of canal excavating and lining machinery. Uniform wall-panel sizes and column dimensions in buildings were specified where applicable. Designs for concrete structures in all cases were developed with a view to the simplification and maximum reuse of forms.

IMPROVEMENTS IN DAM DESIGNING

The specialized problems of designing large concrete dams have presented an opportunity for many construction economies in recent years. Thus, as a result

FIG. 2.—CONSTRUCTION ECONOMY TO BE EFFECTED ON PROPOSED YELLOWTAIL DAM ON THE MISSOURI RIVER BASIN PROJECT IN MONTANA, BY USING NEW COMPRESSIVE DESIGN STRESS OF 1,000 LB PER SQ IN., SAVING HUNDREDS OF THOUSANDS OF CUBIC YARDS OF CONCRETE

of experience with stress analysis of concrete arch and curved gravity dams by the trial-load method, it has been found that in many cases the cross section and mass can be reduced materially. Accumulated stress observations on large dams, including Hoover (on the Colorado River in Arizona-Nevada), Grand Coulee (on the Columbia River in Washington), and Shasta (on the Sacramento River in California), support this conclusion, as the observed stresses agree closely with the results of the trial-load stress calculations. The volume of concrete in several recently designed arch dams has been reduced by an amount approaching 15%—an economy that will amount to millions of dollars when these designs are put under construction.

Concrete Quality.—Economy of another sort is being obtained at the Hungry Horse (on the South Fork of the Flathead River in Montana) and Canyon Ferry (on the Missouri River in Montana) dams through the use of a lean concrete in the interior (2 cu ft of cement per cu yd), under a surface layer of richer concrete. At the same time both dams make use of pozzolanic admixture and air entrainment, for the combined purposes of improving the workability of the concrete mixture, assisting in saving cement, and controlling destructive chemical effects.

Although developed more than 20 years ago, the block and slice construction of concrete dams continues to improve, with gain to both structural quality and economy, as does the associated practice of cooling the concrete after placement and subsequently integrating it into a monolithic structure by grouting the contraction joints.

Construction of Earth Dams.—Development of earth dams has been no less active. Evolution of the Bureau of Reclamation practice of zoned earth-dam construction has led to progressive refinements, a great increase in the usefulness of earth dams, and a continuous gain in economy of construction. The basic practice of utilizing the local soil materials to fullest extent, including the required excavation, is a fundamental source of construction economy. Although initial site exploration usually gives complete information on the kind and quantity of local materials, the zoning of the dam is modified during construction whenever required to fit the materials actually found, for maximum economy.

Study of hydrostatic and flow conditions in earth dams and their foundations has also made it possible to realize construction economies. Use of pore-pressure measurement has assisted in detecting drainage deficiencies and increasing the stability of the embankment. In certain cases, where underflow conditions justified, it became possible to reduce the scope of foundation cutoffs. By controlling embankment compaction to realize the design conditions in full, the security and permanence of even very high earth dams can now be assured at reasonable cost.

Earthwork Practice.—Improved knowledge of foundations under earth dams also makes it possible to economize by selective grouting instead of complete foundation grouting. Developments of this kind, assisted by full utilization of laboratory soil tests, a thorough system of field test control, and constant reliance on soil mechanics, have led to steady reduction in the construction costs of reclamation earth dams. The proportioning of spillways to assure safety against overtopping in floods has also furnished opportunities to economize by restricting the service spillway to floods of moderate size and providing an emergency, or in effect a fuseplug, spillway to pass high flood volumes. This type of construction is of course permissible only where the geologic conditions and the topography make it compatible with permanent safety.

In considering earth-dam construction, it is important to keep in mind the profound influence of modern construction machinery and practices on costs. Excavating machines, transporting equipment, and compaction rollers not only give assurance of obtaining virtually perfect embankment construction under a wide range of physical conditions but have demonstrated that the work can be accomplished at a speed and economy that heretofore seemed wholly beyond attainable limits. Without the assistance of the improved construction art, the designer's efforts would have had decidedly more limited effect.

Canals, Power and Pumping Plants

In other fields also, extensive progress in construction economy has been realized by reclamation designers. Improved canal design has contributed to economy in many directions. Standard canal specifications, the proportioning of canal widths, and arrangement of structures so that construction equipment can operate to best advantage have been prominent factors in saving unnecessary expense in construction. Within the past 2 years, omission of reinforcement in the concrete lining, except at those special locations where reinforcement is indispensable, has become another large factor in economy. Designs have been simplified for construction by eliminating warped transition structures in the majority of cases.

A leading subject for economy in recent years has been canal lining. Increasing recognition of the injurious effect of seepage from canals has led to the development of special instruments to test soils along canal lines, as an aid in forecasting the need for lining. Extensive study has been given to designing and trying out in practice various new types of lining, lower in cost than the thick reinforced concretes formerly used. With the development of linings of asphaltic membrane and asphaltic concrete, compacted earth, and silted earth, the over-all costs of both main canals and laterals have been significantly reduced. Much still remains to be done in this field, but first cost is now and will continue to be a controlling guide in developments.

Among special conveyance structures, high-head siphons have been studied extensively for possible cost reductions. Reinforced-concrete cylinder pipe—that is, reinforced-concrete precast or monolithic pipe lined with a thin steel water-retaining shell—has been used on a large scale. Its most notable development is the great Soap Lake Siphon of the Columbia Basin project in Washington, a built-in-place cylinder pipe structure 22 ft to 25 ft in diameter and about 2 miles long, operating under hydrostatic heads as high as 225 ft. As compared with steel pipe, the alternative type of construction, this siphon saved $2,700,000 in first cost and will save large additional sums annually in reduced maintenance.

Perhaps more study has been given to designing for economy in the field of power and pumping plants than in any other department of reclamation design. Every plant in recent years has undergone intensive study of varied alternatives of layout, frame design, walls, and roof, to arrive at the lowest cost of construction. As materials were found to be available, the adopted designs aiming at minimum cost provided for a reinforced-concrete frame and walls; a riveted steel or welded steel frame with walls of concrete, brick, or fabricated panels; and a roof of concrete, timber, or precast panels (Fig. 3). In numerous cases the advisability of an underground plant has been studied from the standpoint of economy as well as that of security.

Economy Is Secured

Parallel with advances in design, several other factors have contributed progressively to reduction of reclamation construction costs. Improvement in construction skill and equipment, already mentioned, must be recognized as a leading factor. Development of better materials through the constant efforts of industry

(a) Simple Architectural Treatment, According to Functional Use, at Tracy Plant on the Central Valley Project in California

(b) Structural Steel Frames Found to Yield Savings at Wellton-Mohawk Plant No. 2, on the Gila Project in Arizona

FIG. 3.—EXAMPLES OF CONSTRUCTION OF PUMPING PLANTS FOR ECONOMY

in cooperation with Bureau engineers and testing experts is another important element of economy. The increasing use of tests and laboratory research must also be credited with large contributions in reducing reclamation costs. Although this subject is too broad for detailed coverage here, special mention should be made of the wide use of hydraulic model study and of such special arts as chemical and petrographic analysis in aiding the evolution of highly efficient designs at minimum cost, and in developing materials capable of serving reclamation operations more satisfactorily (Fig. 4).

Better Specifications.—Finally, the development of modern specification and contract practice calls for recognition as a factor in lowering construction costs.

FIG. 4.—TECHNIQUES OF DESIGN AND CONSTRUCTION ARE PROVED IN TESTING LABORATORY; RESEARCH ENGINEERS MEASURE STRESS DISTRIBUTION ON LOADED 25-FT REINFORCED-CONCRETE BEAM AT BUREAU OF RECLAMATION LABORATORIES IN DENVER, COLO.

Development of standard specifications was one of the earlier steps toward cost reduction. However, specification improvement has gone on continuously and extensively for a number of years, reducing the contractor's risks and thereby the cost of his operations. Unnecessarily severe requirements imposed by past design practice have largely been eliminated, and closer cooperative relations between designer and contractor have been established.

A few specific items illustrate specification improvements that contribute to cost reduction. It has been made regular practice to define the sources of materials in detail. Where several contractors are required to work simultaneously, the scope of their respective responsibilities is carefully defined, with a view to eliminating confusion, overlaps, and omissions. More thorough information on the construction site and subsoil, based on extended advance exploration, furnishes better definition of the contract requirements.

More Equitable Contracts.—The contractor's risk has been reduced by dividing major schedule items that are subject to possible increase or decrease of quantities into a basic quantity and a possible added quantity, so that by covering his distributive costs under the first item he will be secure against loss in case of reduction and yet can do any added work at the lowest possible price. On some large jobs, provision has been made to pay the contractor for the major items of his fixed plant.

Contracts have been subdivided to permit greater competition and to limit the effect of delays. Progressive payment for river-control operations has been specified in a number of cases. Excavation classification has been simplified where feasible, and overhaul requirements have been placed on the basis of mile-yards in lieu of the old-time station-yards. Finally, under the current material-control conditions, full priority information is included in specifications wherever necessary. By these and similar means, the cost of construction both to the contractor and to the Bureau has been reduced, work has been speeded, and cooperative relations have been maintained, all in the interests of ultimate economy.

Progress in economies during the past decade, which is especially notable, must be credited in large part to the unprecedented volume and complexity of reclamation construction. Combined with the pressure of rising price levels, this factor proved a compelling motive for cost reduction.

It is not possible, unfortunately, to report how much the cost of reclamation construction has been reduced by the design and auxiliary efforts outlined previously. However, a few items are known in terms of dollars. The Delta-Mendota Canal in California, built without the originally contemplated reinforcement, showed a saving of nearly $3,000,000. Hungry Horse and Canyon Ferry dams, by virtue of reduced cement proportions, saved more than $5,000,000. The bold reinforced-concrete conduit design of Soap Lake Siphon cost $2,700,000 less than the best alternative structure. However, these single economies are only incidental.

The over-all effect of many years of designing for construction economy is composed of the progressive reduction of contract bids and payments, and these are not amenable to comparison because of the varying nature of the work and the local conditions. It is safe to state, however, that tens of millions of dollars have been saved in the cost of reclamation construction, and that future reclamation will profit by additional millions of savings annually, secured through continued attention to costs and by coordinating the objectives of the designer with those of the construction engineer.

AMERICAN SOCIETY OF CIVIL ENGINEERS

Founded November 5, 1852

TRANSACTIONS

Paper No. 2601

DIVERSION STRUCTURES AND DISTRIBUTION SYSTEMS FOR IRRIGATION

By W. H. Nalder,[1] M. ASCE

Synopsis

Although simple diversions were the rule in early irrigation systems, the same general principles govern later, more elaborate developments. Experience has indicated the needs, and advances in science have dictated the solutions. As a result, provision has been made for fish migration, disposition of heavy bed load, and proper control of extra water or waste. Modern improvements and practice are described, with examples cited to illustrate engineering trends as applied not only to diversons but also to canals and pipe systems—covering a wide range of problems due to the variety of conditions met and limitations imposed in the western states.

Historical Background

The origin of modern irrigation in the United States was almost coincident with the founding of the ASCE in 1852. The vast migration during the middle of the nineteenth century to the arid regions of western United States, inspired by the gold discoveries in California, the opening of the Oregon Territory, and the Mormon settlement in Utah, soon established the necessity for the fruits of agriculture. It also became evident that successful crop production was impractical without some supplemental water supply in addition to the sparse rainfall over most of this area.

The growth of ancient civilizations in Egypt, Arabia, Persia, and other countries of the Middle East and Far East paralleled closely the irrigation developments in these countries. There are canal systems in China that have been in continuous operation for 2,000 years. In South America, Mexico, and the southwestern part of the United States the natives are known to have irrigated their crops as early as the seventh century.

Credit for the first modern irrigation in the United States can be given to the Mormons, who arrived in the Salt Lake Valley, Utah, in 1847. By 1860

---

[1] Retired; formerly Chf. Designing Engr., Design and Constr. Div., Bureau of Reclamation, Denver, Colo.

437

developments in various other western states were recorded. However, the total acreage of land under irrigation did not increase greatly for the next 30 years. Starting in 1890 the expansion was very marked, as a result of the rapid settlement of the entire western part of the United States.

Development of Irrigation Engineering

Early irrigation projects in this country depended on temporary diversions and small canals or ditches leading to small plots of land close to the streams. Such works, usually consisting of a rock weir in the stream bed and open ditches leading directly to the farm land, were constructed for the most part without engineering assistance. As the need for more irrigated land heightened and the areas to be served extended farther from the source of water supply, bigger and more extensive projects became necessary. As larger and longer conveyance channels were required, new problems in controlling the diversion and distribution of the water appeared, and irrigation engineering practices and principles were developed to meet the requirements.

As early as 1870 the shortage of water was recognized in many western states, and laws were enacted to establish proper controls over the storage, diversion, and distribution of available water supplies. The rapid growth of irrigated agriculture soon brought the engineering profession into all the various phases of water supply, project planning, design and construction of the canals and structures, and operation and maintenance of the entire irrigation system.

Diversion Structures in General

Design of a modern diversion structure embraces many complex problems. It usually includes detailed study of the hydraulic characteristics of the river as well as of the diversion plan and may entail complicated problems of design for structures to be built on unstable foundations. A few examples and illustrations will be given subsequently in this paper.

The diversion structure generally consists of an overflow weir or an open, gated channel for raising and holding the water at the required diversion elevation; a canal headworks for controlling the diverted water; a sluiceway in front of the headworks to keep the channel free of silt deposits; and generally some arrangement for removing silt and sands from the water entering the canal. The exact location of a diversion structure is usually dictated by certain factors other than selection of ideal foundation conditions.

Water delivery elevations or location of the conduit leading away from the structure may place the diversion structure on unfavorable material. Such foundation sites necessitate detailed study of the existing materials, selection of the proper type of structure, and exacting structural design. Conditions may favor a solid concrete overflow weir on a rock foundation, or they may require a lightweight, hollow concrete shell with long upstream and downstream aprons to be supported on a sandy, unstable foundation. Piling may be required to assure stability in the structure. Unstable foundations require extensive articulation of the concrete to care for differential settlement. This articulation is made watertight by installing rubber water stops in all joints below high water surface.

Treatment of Suspended Matter.—The existence of suspended silt or gravel bed load in a river from which irrigation water is to be diverted into the distribution system is a major problem to the designer. The bed load can be excluded by setting the headworks gate sills above river elevation, but eventually even a moderate bed load would deposit and build up to the gate sill elevation. Thus, it is necessary to design a sluiceway that will be effective in removing any deposition of bed-load material in front of the headworks gates.

The most effective plan is to provide an open channel through the dam immediately adjacent to the headworks, which is gated for periodic operation as the removal of sediment is required. When the sluiceway gates are open, any deposits of sand or silt in front of the head gates are sluiced downstream in the river. Other devices such as Dufour or vortex tube sand traps have been used, and have advantages where continuous sluicing is required or when the diverted water is taken out at an elevation lower than river-bed level.

Some of the larger rivers, such as the Colorado, carry such a great suspended silt load that it becomes necessary to devise means of preventing the silt from entering the distribution systems fed from those rivers. Excessive amounts of silt in the diverted water would create objectionable deposits in the canal system and reduce the carrying capacity or, if carried onto the land, could have a detrimental effect on crop production. For these reasons an effective desilting works is one of the most important features in diversion structures on heavily silt-laden rivers. The simplest of desilting works is a settling basin—generally an enlarged canal section below the headworks which reduces the water velocity to a point where the silt load will settle out and can then be sluiced out of the basin back into the river.

A more complicated and interesting desilting works was designed for the All-American Canal System, immediately downstream from Imperial Dam on the Lower Colorado River in California (Fig. 1). This structure was designed to remove 70,000 tons of sediment per day from 12,000 cu ft per sec of diverted water. Here the water is diverted into six settling basins where the velocity is reduced to 0.2 ft per sec, allowing the sediment to settle to the bottom. In the desilting basins seventy-two electrically-powered, slowly rotating scrapers, 125 ft in diameter, gradually work the deposited sediment to sludge pipe outlets at the center of the scrapers. The sediment is then sluiced back to the river through these sludge pipes. The diverted water thus relieved of much of its suspended sediment passes from the basins over skimming weirs to the All-American Canal.

Experience in the practical application of the basic principles of the transportation of sediment in liquids has improved design practices and procedures in handling this problem.

Provision for Fish.—The protection of fish in some rivers introduces additional design considerations in water diversion. The incorporation of fish ladders in the Roza Diversion Dam, on the Yakima River in Washington (Fig. 2), and in the Easton Diversion Dam on the same river, shown in greater detail in Fig. 3, is a novel solution for passing fish over these dams. A succession of baffle walls closely spaced in a rather steep chute from the top of the dam to the downstream water forms a series of pools, the water flowing through shallow drops between pools. The fish can jump these low drops from pool to pool and thus travel past the dam in either direction. Rotating drum screens were placed in front of the headworks at Roza Diversion Dam to prevent the fish from entering the Yakima Ridge Canal. The drum screens were made to rotate in order to pass floating debris over them and to prevent clogging the screens.

Other installations have used electric fish screens, consisting of several electrodes extending into the water immediately in front of the headworks. These electrodes carry a low voltage current which shocks the fish within a certain range and thus turns them away from the canal headworks.

Other examples of typical diversion dams may be cited as follows: Grand Valley Diversion Dam on the Colorado River near Grand Junction, Colo., which

FIG. 1.—AERIAL VIEW OF IMPERIAL DAM, IN CALIFORNIA—ALL-AMERICAN CANAL DESILTING BASINS AND HEADWORKS AT LEFT; AND GILA PROJECT HEADWORKS AT RIGHT

uses the roller crest gate extensively (see Fig. 4); Dunlap Diversion Dam on the Niobrara River in Nebraska, a smaller project (Fig. 5); and Nimbus Diversion Dam and Power Plant (Fig. 6) under construction (1952) on the American River in California. (The canal headworks for Nimbus Dam, not shown in Fig. 6, will be built near the left end of the dam. The power plant will serve as an afterbay plant for the larger Folsom Dam and Power Plant under construction jointly by Corps of Engineers, United States Department of the Army, and the Bureau of Reclamation.)

CANALS AND DISTRIBUTION SYSTEMS

In the pioneer days of modern irrigation engineering the canals rarely extended more than a few miles from the diversion structures to the farm deliveries. As these smaller projects were completed, and suitable, additional lands were

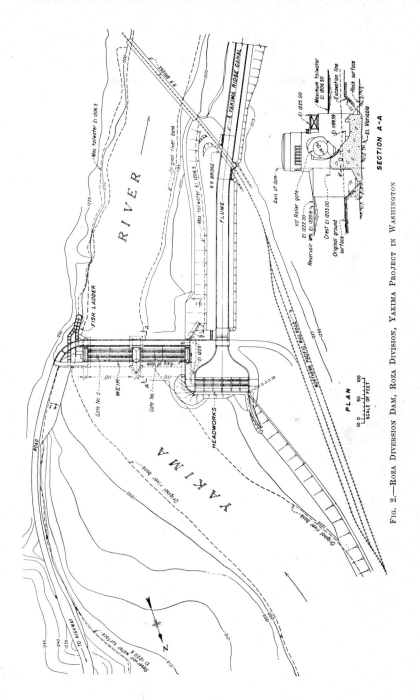

FIG. 2.—ROZA DIVERSION DAM, ROZA DIVISION, YAKIMA PROJECT IN WASHINGTON

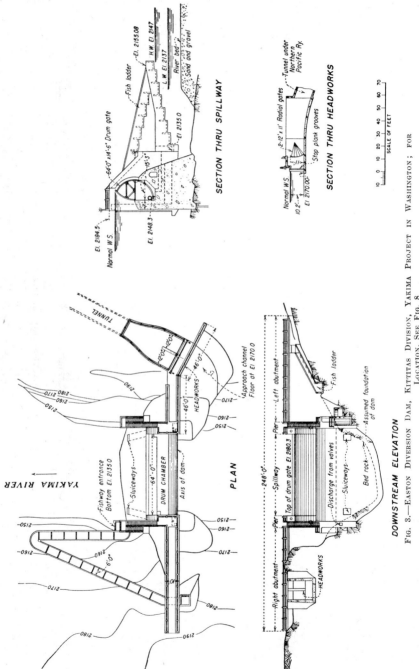

FIG. 3.—EASTON DIVERSION DAM, KITTITAS DIVISION, YAKIMA PROJECT IN WASHINGTON; FOR LOCATION, SEE FIG. 8

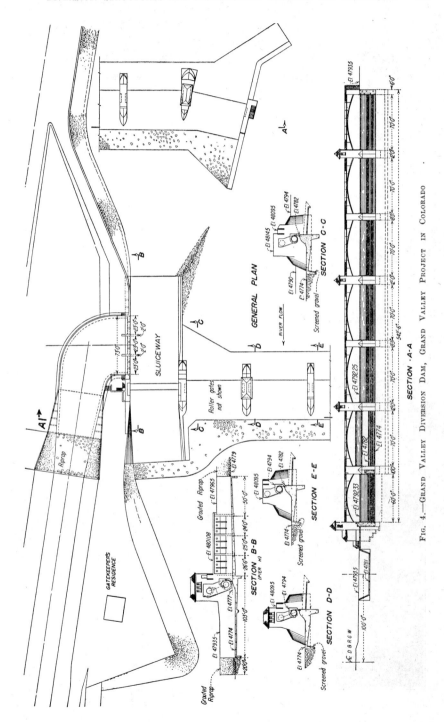

Fig. 4.—Grand Valley Diversion Dam, Grand Valley Project in Colorado

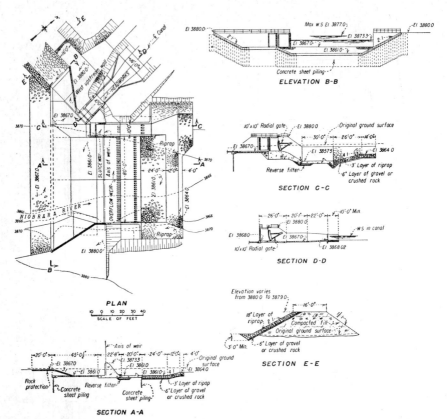

FIG. 5.—DUNLAP DIVERSION DAM, NIOBRARA RIVER, MIRAGE FLATS PROJECT IN NEBRASKA

FIG. 6.—DRAWING OF NIMBUS DIVERSION DAM AND POWER PLANT, CENTRAL VALLEY PROJECT IN CALIFORNIA

found farther away from the rivers, the problem of carrying the irrigation water over longer distances from the river bottoms brought the engineer into the field of irrigation to plan and design proper canals and structures to convey the water from the source of supply to the point of use. The increased length of modern canals and their far-flung distributaries which deliver the water to numerous farm turnouts have multiplied design problems.

Some of the larger and longer canals of recent construction are the 15,000-cu ft per sec All-American Canal, 80 miles long, and its 2,500-cu ft per sec Coachella Branch, 145 miles long, in Southern California (Fig. 7); the 5,000-cu ft per sec Friant-Kern Canal, 153 miles long, and 4,600-cu ft per sec Delta-Mendota Canal, 120 miles long, in the Central Valley of California; and the 4,500-cu ft per sec East Low Canal, 130 miles long, and the 5,100-cu ft per sec West Canal, 88 miles long, in the Columbia Basin in Washington. These tremendous undertakings have produced some remarkable engineering experiences and advancements.

The terms "canals" and "distribution systems" include a great variety of channels, conduits, and structures, such as main canals, branch canals, laterals, wasteway channels, and the many and varied structures required to operate the system. Main canals are usually open channels, either unlined or lined, as are all the canals just named; but they may be closed conduits or aqueducts if rough terrain or other factors make the location of a free-flow open channel uneconomical or infeasible.

To give a more representative example of the layout of canals and distribution systems, Fig. 8 shows a skeleton map of a typical smaller development, the Kittitas project, which serves highly developed land surrounding Ellensburg, Wash. Water is diverted from the Yakima River at the Easton Diversion Dam (Fig. 3), and carried in an open main canal through rough sidehill terrain involving many special structures to the dividing point between the South Branch and the larger North Branch canals.

Near its head, the latter crosses the Yakima River in what is perhaps the most notable structure on the project. The river at this point is in a deep, narrow rock gorge, and the canal crosses it by an inverted siphon built in tunnel and carried sufficiently below the surface to support the calculated hydrostatic pressure. Inasmuch as this support proved inadequate, Bureau engineers learned much from the experience as to what can and cannot be safely done. The many small laterals leading from the main branch canals with their multitude of structures illustrate a typical distribution system.

Importance of Hydraulic Losses.—The design of open canals necessitates the application of hydraulic principles in laying out an efficient canal cross section to carry the required quantity of water on the grade or slope established in the field —taking into account all the head losses through the various structures in the canal. The fundamental principles involved in the flow factors of open channels have been fairly well known for a great many years and application of such factors as slope of canal, cross-sectional area, hydraulic radius, and roughness has been the basis for the design of an open canal. For many years engineers have had a rough idea of maximum and minimum allowable velocities for water running in certain soil materials and of the techniques necessary to prevent scour at high velocity and deposition of sediment at low velocities. The Lacey and Kennedy

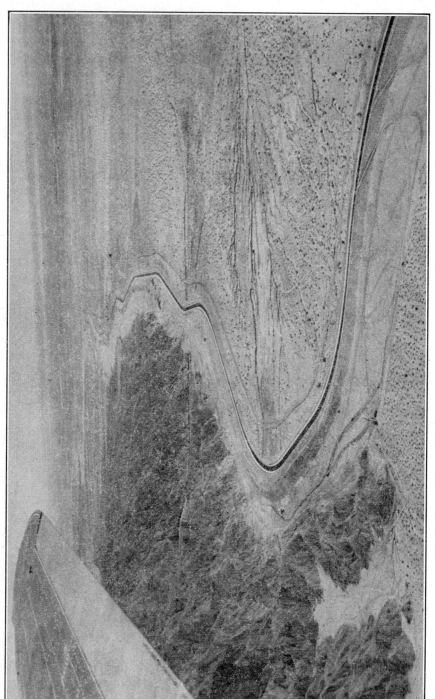

FIG. 7.—AERIAL VIEW OF COACHELLA CANAL, ALL-AMERICAN CANAL SYSTEM IN CALIFORNIA

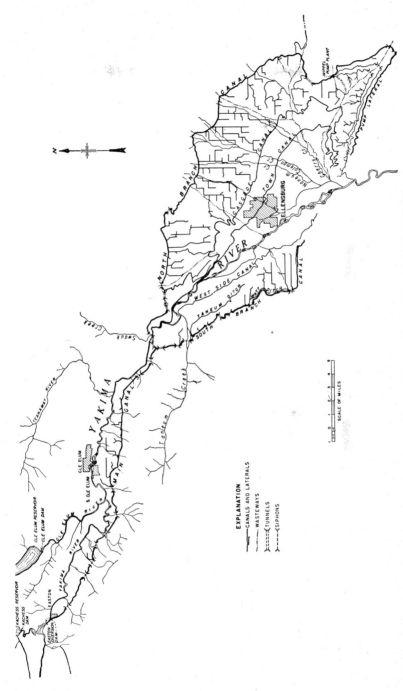

Fig. 8.—Map of Kittitas Division, Yakima Project in Washington

formulas for nonsilting, nonscouring velocities have been used as guides in designing open channels.

Inasmuch as most Bureau of Reclamation canals are designed to carry relatively clear water, the problem is mainly one of scour, and considerable study has been made of the principles of stable channel design as they relate to the scour aspect. Investigations have been concerned with study and correlation of the various factors of the theory of tractive forces in establishing maximum allowable, nonscouring velocities in open channels. An attempt is being made to establish a series of tentative values of limiting tractive forces which may be used to improve canal design methods and to eliminate, as far as possible, the uncertainties involved in existing procedures.

With the increasing scarcity of water, the importance of water losses from the canal through percolation becomes of great concern. Soil analysis is necessary and, unless the material is found to be reasonably impervious, some type of lining must be provided to prevent those losses. However, the matter of cost, more than ever in these times of high prices, is second only to engineering sufficiency in the mind of the designing engineer. Costs must be considered not only for construction but also for anticipated annual operation and maintenance expense. Studies in recent years have brought out much information on the reduction of the cost of suitable canal linings. Concrete lining was, for many years, used almost exclusively. It is still used under certain conditions, and is considered the most permanent and reliable lining material. However, the Bureau of Reclamation has been actively investigating other materials for the last $5\frac{1}{2}$ years in its lower cost canal lining program. "Shotcrete," asphaltic concrete, buried asphalt membrane, compacted earth, bentonite, soil cement, and combinations such as asphalt membrane with "shotcrete" cover have been investigated and used with varying degrees of success.

Closed conduits are designed to convey the water where topographical or other conditions eliminate the practicable use of open channels, or where scarcity or value of water necessitates the reduction of conveyance losses to the practical minimum.

Controlled Wastage.—Wasteway channels are nearly always open channels leading away from the main canals to natural drainage channels. They are located at strategic points, to provide an escape channel for waters in the canal system in excess of its normal carrying capacity. These waters may enter the canals from flood runoff or may be diverted water in excess of the quantity being taken out for irrigation. The entire canal capacity may be diverted through these wasteways in the event of an obstruction or break in the canal. The wasteways are primarily protective structures to provide a means for the orderly removal of excess waters from the canals—to prevent overtopping the canal banks and damaging the canals and property below them.

Artificial wasteway channels are usually lined, inasmuch as they are, in most cases, laid out on a rather steep grade. The design does not end with the consideration of the artificial channel; the natural drainage channel into which the water is directed is examined carefully to determine its carrying capacity and the possibilities of detrimental erosion resulting from the superimposed waste water. Here again, the theory of tractive forces is playing an important role in the deliberations of the design engineer.

Accessory Structures.—The modern irrigation system requires a great number and variety of structures to carry the water properly, to control it, and to protect the system from failures. Canal structures may be divided into three classes according to their functions: Conveying, regulating, and protective. The conveyance structures are lined canals, chutes, drops, culverts under railroads and highways, flumes, inverted siphons, tunnels, and closed conduits; the regulating structures are checks, orifice structures, Parshall flumes, turnouts, and weir structures; and the protective structures are culverts under the canal for side drainage, overchutes, spillways, drainage inlets, and wasteways. The design of all these structures involves various phases of hydraulic, structural, mechanical, and electrical engineering.

Technical knowledge and practical experience both have their places in these problems. In many cases model studies of proposed structures in the research laboratory provide added data on physical behavior and operating efficiency, and are of inestimable value to the designer. Materials engineers have been of great assistance in improving the character and performance of construction materials going into canal structures.

Very few new basic design principles have been introduced in recent years, but numerous advances have been made in the application of long-known formulas and in the extensive use of model studies to augment design procedures. Notable among these is the knowledge gained in controlling the hydraulic jump. Proper design of drops and chutes and particularly the size and shape of the stilling pools can now assure control of the hydraulic jump and turbulence of the water leaving such a structure. Another forward step in design which should show gratifying results in the years ahead is the comparatively recent introduction of prestressed reinforced-concrete members in construction. Doubtless, the application of this new type of concrete construction will improve designs in many fields of engineering.

The large concrete structures required in modern canals have presented new problems to the designer in many ways. Not the least of these, and one which has been successfully resolved, is the need for relief from temperature and settlement cracking, which cannot be disregarded in huge structures. Temperature stresses induced in these thin slab structures over a wide temperature range surpass the structural stresses.

In many cases, unstable foundation materials under such large base slabs make differential settlement of the structure a definite possibility. The solution lies, it is believed, in articulating the structures at the proper points to control the inevitable movements and resulting secondary stresses due to these causes. Articulation of the structure and sealing the joints with rubber water stops against leakage into the foundation material have been successfully used on Bureau structures for the past 15 years.

Pipes for Distribution.—One of the latest problems and one which is currently in the later stages of solution is the design of extensive precast concrete pipe, for low and moderate head distribution systems. The Coachella Valley Distribution System in Southern California and the Friant-Kern Canal Distribution System in the Central Valley of California have provided much valuable knowledge in the design of such works. Two outstanding problems which have confronted the designer in this connection are the suppression of surges in long, low-head pipes and the design of a satisfactory flexible joint for precast concrete pipe.

The Coachella system was constructed with pipe stands at certain intervals and with overflow baffles in them to maintain a constant low head on the line. In certain long reaches of pipe where the pipe stands occurred at regular intervals, the water would start surging in each length of pipe between stands, and the surge was amplified as it progressed from one reach to the next. In its worst stage water would overflow the stand on the swing one way and completely dry up the stand on the opposite swing.

Through a mathematical analysis of the flow characteristics of this regular harmonic motion, the natural period of surge and the amplification factor for any reach of pipe can be computed. This makes it possible to predetermine whether a surge might occur in the pipe lateral, and the magnitude of the surge. Thus, later pipe distribution lines were designed to preclude any arrangement of pipe reaches and pipe stands that would amplify a water surge to unmanageable proportions.

Of the many problems encountered in designing these concrete pipe distribution systems, the development of a flexible, watertight joint has been one of the most interesting. Rubber-gasketed joints appeared to offer the greatest advantages and possibilities, and several adaptations of this type have been devised. The use of rubber gaskets in pipe joints certainly is not new, but recent developments have produced less costly joint assemblies while retaining the advantages of the flexibility of a compressed rubber-gasket joint.

In General.—Although thus far only big jobs have been discussed, it should be emphasized that much of the engineering work going into the proper design of an irrigation system involves channels and structures of small capacity and seemingly minor importance. Each farm turnout and measuring weir has its purpose and all must be carefully coordinated in the over-all plan so that water can be delivered to the remotest tract of land with the same efficiency as in carrying water to the turnout.

It is important, also, to acknowledge the fine cooperation received from the construction contractors in working out design problems and especially in obtaining information on possible alternative methods of construction that would improve engineering designs. Contractors' comments on construction problems as they relate to design procedures are always welcome, and their replies to many special inquiries are always prompt and most helpful.

AMERICAN SOCIETY OF CIVIL ENGINEERS
Founded November 5, 1852
TRANSACTIONS

Paper No. 2602

WATER POWER OVER A CENTURY

By W. F. Uhl,[1] M. ASCE

Synopsis

Early water-power projects in the United States were mostly in New England, where the product could be used by mills on the site. About 1850 came a new development or extension—a number of factories began to use a larger source of power, locally and cooperatively. Still there was no convenient method of transmitting the energy, so steam power—a new giant—almost preempted the field. The next or last phase began around 1900, with the introduction of electrical transmission. Today this serves both water and thermal power; it has permitted the hydro plant to attain a major stage of development. Central stations have become the key of the industry, with government units of growing importance.

About 100 years ago and again about 50 years ago, there were two fairly distinct breaks in the development and the use of water power. They represent approximately the second and third phases of the over-all development and cover the period of particular interest at this time—the centennial years. However, for the sake of continuity it may be of interest to review briefly the first phase of water-power development.

This earlier phase was much longer. It goes back to ancient times and extends into the history of the United States, comprising in all a period of more than 200 years (from about 1650 to 1850). It includes the first uses of water power for driving the small industries of American pioneers, ancestors of the present 150,000,000 people in the United States.

One of the earliest water-power developments was constructed by Israel Stoughton in 1634 at the Lower Falls of the Neponset River between Milton and Dorchester, Mass. Here power was used to drive a gristmill, a sawmill, and a powder mill. In recent years a hydroelectric plant has been built at the same site. Thus, the site has been in constant use for water power for more than 300 years. Another early practical application of water power in this country was in a tidal plant built on Mill Creek near Boston, Mass., in 1631.

The gristmill was a most important community industry in the early days,

---

[1] Pres. and Cons. Engr., Chas. T. Main, Inc., Boston, Mass.

and as a result many towns grew up around the mill dams. Since the amount of power required by sawmills and gristmills was small, the plants usually consisted of low dams on small streams, operating water wheels of the pitchback, overshot and undershot, or breast wheel (Fig. 1)[2] types.

Transmission Limitations Govern.—Of particular centennial significance is the second phase of water-power development, starting about 100 years ago with the introduction of the then generally adopted factory system in industry. Such industries required greater amounts of power than had been previously used, and the result was larger water-power developments.

About 1850 the old overshot and breast water wheels were being largely supplanted by turbines developed by James B. Francis, Past-President and Hon. M. ASCE, and Uriah A. Boyden. These turbines were more readily adaptable both in physical form and in output for use with the increased requirements. Here again necessity was the mother of invention.

FIG. 1.—ONE OF SEVERAL CAST-IRON BREAST WHEELS, 16 FT IN DIAMETER, INSTALLED IN PRESCOTT MILLS, LOWELL, MASS., IN 1844

Demands of the new factory system were frequently met by water-power developments built on a cooperative basis on the larger rivers and led to a new type of planned industrial city. The pattern of these developments was set by the practical impossibility of transmitting power, except for short distances, from the water wheel to the driven pulley by ropes, belts, gears, and shafting. Therefore the energy-producing medium, water, had to be brought by a canal or a system of canals to the point where the power was to be used.

In a typical development a company purchased land and water rights, and built a dam and canal system. The canals were laid out to permit the construction of industrial plants between water levels, usually with differences of elevation of about 15 ft between adjacent canals, or between the canal above and the river below. Frequently the same company laid out the entire town including streets, parks, and other facilities. The water-power company sold land and water rights to power-using industries.

First of the large-scale developments of cities planned around water power

[2] "The American Mixed-Flow Turbine and Its Setting," by Arthur T. Safford and Edward Pierce Hamilton, *Transactions*, ASCE, Vol. LXXXV, 1922, p. 1237.

was at Lowell, Mass. The navigation canal of the Proprietors of the Locks and Canals on the Merrimack River, founded in 1792, was utilized, together with the existing dam. The first mill on this canal, that of the Merrimac Company, was established in 1822.

Other similar developments on the Merrimack River were made at Manchester, N. H., and Lawrence, Mass. At Manchester the Amoskeag Manufacturing Company in 1831 purchased land and developed water power for two small cotton

Fig. 2.—Municipally-Owned Power Development on Savannah River, Built by City of Augusta, Ga., in 1847 and Used As Late As 1875

mills. By 1845 the dam and most of the present canal system, and many of the mills which later formed the Amoskeag Manufacturing Company, were built. At Lawrence the development was made by the Essex Company incorporated in 1845, and the canal system as it now exists was laid out and largely built by 1870.

Elsewhere in New England and in such other places as Cohoes, N. Y., Richmond, Va., Appleton, Wis., Augusta, Ga. (Fig. 2), and Minneapolis, Minn., similar projects were organized. These resulted in the development of many of the industrial centers of that era.

Development of water power at Holyoke, Mass., on the Connecticut River in 1848, involved the construction of a dam of unprecedented size, and the canal system comprising three levels was the largest built up to that time.

Nearly all water-power development prior to 1850 was carried out east of the Mississippi River, and as late as 1880 only about 5% of the then 1,352,500 hp of water-power development existed west of the Mississippi River.

Competition from Steam.—After about 1860 development of water power lagged for two principal reasons. One was the scarcity of suitable sites within the limitations of mechanical power transmission; and the other, the then rapidly improving economy of steam-power production.

Late in the eighteenth century early forms of the steam engine were developed in Europe, but their use was largely confined to pumping water. Within a period of 50 years the steam engine had been perfected to the extent that it became a dependable, although expensive, source of power. The development of a practical steam engine led to the establishment of industries in places where water power was not available in the quantities needed. The first of these plants were the Naumkeag Steam Cotton Mills of Salem, Mass., founded in 1845, and the Wamsutta Mills of New Bedford, Mass., built in 1846.

TABLE 1.—COMPARATIVE AMOUNTS OF STEAM AND WATER POWER IN USE, 1850–1900

Year	Horsepower of water power	Horsepower of steam power	PERCENTAGE OF TOTAL	
			Water	Steam
1850	662,000	488,000	57.5	42.5
1860	930,000	820,000	53.0	47.0
1870	1,205,000	1,491,000	44.5	55.5
1880	1,352,500	2,710,000	33.5	66.5
1890	1,521,500	5,904,000	20.5	79.5
1900	1,860,000	12,503,000	13.0	87.0

In 1848 the steam engine was further improved by the invention of the Corliss valve, resulting in the adoption of this type of engine in many plants either as a sole source of power or as a supplement to water power.

The effects of improved economy of steam-power production can best be realized from a comparison of the relative amounts of water and steam power in use during the period from 1850 to 1900 (Table 1). This includes power for manufacturing, in mines and quarries, for irrigation and drainage, in electric central stations, and for electric railroads.

It will be noted that the increase in use of water power from 1870 to 1880 was only about 147,000 hp, or 12%. In the same time the capacity of steam-power plants installed for manufacturing and all other purposes for which water power was used increased about 1,219,000 hp, or 82%. Previous to 1880 very little water power was used for other than manufacturing purposes and in mines and quarries.

About 12,000 hp was so used in mines and quarries in 1850. By 1890 water power used for these purposes reached a maximum of 250,000 hp. By 1900 the use of water power in mines and quarries was somewhat less than 100,000 hp, having been largely displaced by steam power. By this time a substantial amount of water power was used for irrigation and drainage and for electric generation in central and railway stations.

Electricity Enters the Picture.—The beginning of the third phase of water-power development in this country occurred about 50 years ago. It coincides largely with the development of the art of alternating-current electric generation and its long-distance transmission. In September, 1882, the world's first hydro-electric station was placed in operation at Appleton. The earliest application of the transmission of power using step-up and step-down transformers was made at Great Barrington, Mass., on March 16, 1886.

These were small-scale experimental works, and large-scale hydroelectric development did not take place until 1895, when the first important Niagara Falls (N.Y.) plant was put into commercial operation. History records the fact that,

FIG. 3.—HYDRO DEVELOPMENT AT NIAGARA FALLS, N. Y., IN 1882, CAPABLE OF SUPPLYING 4,000 HP

when the extensive development of water power at Niagara Falls (Fig. 3) began to be seriously considered about 1890, it was thought that the best method to transmit the power to factories at relatively short distances from the Falls would be by compressed air.

The extensive revival of water-power activities which started about 1900 could not have taken place without the concurrent development of the art of transmission and distribution of electric energy, since most of the water power naturally adaptable for economical development was located at points somewhat remote from the market for power.

Long-distance electric transmission of energy in the United States dates from

1893, when the polyphase system was first used for carrying a current of high
voltage from the plant of the San Antonio Light and Power Company, at Pomona,
Calif., to San Bernardino, Calif., a distance of 19 miles. The transmission voltage
was 10,000. By 1900 transmission of electric current at 40,000 v had been accomplished. By 1909 this was successfully increased to 110,000 v and to 220,000 v
by 1923.

It was the chemical and central-station industries which revived the development of water power about 1900. Between 1900 and 1910 water-power capacity
increased by more than 2,000,000 hp or about 115%.

The development of hydroelectric power at Niagara Falls marked the beginning of the electric furnace art, together with the discovery and adaptation of
many substances that are now essential basic materials in American industry.
Aluminum, calcium carbide, and many of what are now common commodities
were only laboratory curiosities prior to the development and use of Niagara
power.

The first customer of the Niagara Falls Power Company was the Pittsburgh
Reduction Company, for manufacturing aluminum. Next came the Carborundum
Company. These were shortly followed by many others making products now
considered indispensable—such as ferro-alloys, sodium, silicon, magnesium, potassium, phosphorous compounds, and graphite—also some employed in the fixation
of atmospheric nitrogen. For a period of about 30 years following the Niagara
development, the aluminum, pulp and paper, and some other chemical industries
built their plants where large-scale low-cost water power was available within
electric transmission distance.

Rivalry with Central Stations.—The electric central-station industry which
today produces the major part of the power used for industrial and domestic
purposes may be considered to have started with the construction of Thomas A.
Edison's famous Pearl Street Station in New York City, N. Y., which began operations September 4, 1882. It expanded rapidly, once the advantage of electric
generation and transmission and distribution of power was recognized.

Although steam power increased in production more rapidly than water power
after 1860, its cost was comparatively high. As late as 1900, it required from 3 lb
to 5 lb of coal to produce 1 hp-hr. This fact and the successful electric transmission stimulated the development of water power.

Indeed, the electric furnace and the art of electrical generation and transmission of power stimulated the development of water power to such an extent that
it increased from 1,860,000 hp in 1900 to 14,000,000 hp in 1930. In 1900 only
13% of the total power capacity was water power. By 1930 water-power capacity
had increased to about 20% of the total for industrial and domestic use. During
the following 20 years, from 1930 to 1950, the capacity of water-power plants
almost doubled but, because of attendant growth of other sources, increased to
only about 23% of the total power capacity, water and thermal, by 1950 (Table 2).

Very little water power was developed by industry after 1930, and only about
2,000,000 kw of such power has been developed by privately-owned utilities since
that date. By comparison, more than 7,000,000 kw of publicly-owned water-power
capacity has been developed in the same period.

It is interesting to note, as shown in Table 3, that the use of electric power generated in central stations increased more rapidly after 1910 than the power generated by industries for their own use, and that the latter reached a peak about 1920.

Future Potential.—No accurate data are available regarding the amount of water power that remains undeveloped in this country. Information issued from time to time is often quite misleading. Confusion arises from terms sometimes used in estimating the amount of undeveloped water power, such as:

1. Economically feasible;
2. Technically possible;
3. Engineeringly feasible; and
4. Within the range of possible economic feasibility.

TABLE 2.—WATER AND THERMAL POWER CAPACITY IN THE UNITED STATES, 1900–1950

Year	Horsepower of water power	Horsepower of thermal power	PERCENTAGE OF TOTAL	
			Water	Thermal
1900	1,860,000	12,503,000	13.0	87.0
1910	4,100,000	25,860,000	13.7	86.3
1920	7,800,000	38,000,000	17.0	83.0
1930	14,000,000	55,300,000	20.2	79.8
1940	17,250,000	60,250,000	21.4	78.6
1950	26,300,000	90,500,000	22.7	77.3

TABLE 3.—AMERICAN POWER PRODUCTION IN CENTRAL STATIONS AND INDUSTRIAL PLANTS, 1900–1950

Year	Total water and thermal horsepower	Total central-station horsepower	Total industrial-plant horsepower	Total industrial-plant kilowatts
1900..........	14,363,000	2,800,000	11,563,000	8,100,000
1910..........	29,960,000	8,400,000	21,560,000	15,200,000
1920..........	45,800,000	18,300,000	27,500,000	20,000,000
1930..........	69,300,000	46,500,000	22,800,000	16,200,000
1940..........	77,500,000	56,500,000	21,000,000	14,900,000
1950..........	116,800,000	97,000,000	19,800,000	14,000,000

Estimates of potential water power should state the amount available 100% of the time and for other percentages of time.

Obviously all power available for less than 100% of the time is marginal power and less valuable for most industrial purposes. Such marginal power can be utilized to advantage where it can be fitted into an interconnected power system having a proportionately large amount of fuel-burning steam or other thermal power plants. Marginal power output from hydroelectric plants may cost more than the incremental fuel costs of thermal power plants. If so, the over-all cost of power may well increase rather than decrease as a result of utilizing water power.

Estimates of undeveloped water power in the United States vary all the way from 50,000,000 hp to 100,000,000 hp; 50,000,000 hp is assumed to be available about 50% of the time and about 35,000,000 hp, 90% of the time.

Adequate field surveys of many of the streams on which undeveloped water power is assumed to exist are not available. In some cases the records of stream flow do not cover a sufficient length of time to permit reliable conclusions to be reached. At many sites the factors which determine the proper size of installation are unknown and can only be derived by further and more exhaustive studies.

Records of rainfall and stream flow cover a limited period. However, a study of such records as are available indicates that with time new minimum and maximum rainfall periods and consequent stream flows are experienced. Thus droughts and floods seem to become more severe. Actually, they probably are no more so than those that occurred in past centuries. As yet reliable records cover relatively short periods. Only a few rainfall records exceed 100 years and most stream-flow records cover less than a 50-year period.

There is now about 26,000,000 hp of installed water-power capacity. How much of this is dependable capacity, and for how much of the time it is dependable, is difficult to determine.

Quite accurate records of water-power capacity and output are available for public utility, municipal, and government-owned plants, covering the recent past. In 1950 the water-power capacity of these plants totaled about 17,675,000 kw (about 25,000,000 hp), and their output amounted to about 96,000,000,000 kw-hr. This was about 29% of the total electric-power generation by public and private utility plants in that year.

In 1920 hydroelectric generation by utilities was about 40% of the total, the other 60% being generated by thermal power plants.

In 1950, industrial establishments producing electric energy for their own use accounted for only about 1,000,000 kw of water-power capacity and about 5,000,000,000 kw-hr of water-power generation.

Thermal Sources As Adjuncts.—Availability of electric power is becoming increasingly dependent on thermal generation. It is of interest that the Tennessee Valley Authority, which started out as a water-power project, now has 3,144,050 kw of steam-plant capacity, which either is in service or is planned to be in operation by 1954. By that time its installed water-power capacity is planned to amount to 2,656,900 kw, or nearly 500,000 kw less than its steam-power capacity.

In 1920, the Federal Government generated less than one half of 1% of the central-station water power produced in this country. By 1950, it generated about 40% of the central-station water power. By including cooperatives, power districts, and state projects, these data become somewhat less than 1% in 1920 and 43% in 1950. (Notable plants on the Columbia River, built by the Corps of Engineers and the Bureau of Reclamation, are shown in Figs. 4 and 5.) Adding municipal electric utilities, the total becomes 4.5% of all water power generated by government-owned plants in 1920 and 47.3% in 1950.

The government-owned or publicly-owned water-power plant capacity amounted to about 5.2% in 1920 and 45.4% of the total central-station water-power plant capacity developed in this country in 1950.

The *Electrical World News Issue* of March 3, 1952, published data (Table 4) which show to what extent the Federal Government has entered the field of water-power development and control under management of the Interior Department.

FIG. 4.—POWERHOUSE OF BONNEVILLE DAM, NEAREST TO TIDEWATER OF A NUMBER OF PROJECTS ON
THE COLUMBIA RIVER; BUILT BY THE CORPS OF ENGINEERS FROM 1933 TO 1937,
WITH A CAPACITY OF MORE THAN 500,000 KW

FIG. 5.—GRAND COULEE DAM IN WASHINGTON, CONSTRUCTED BY THE BUREAU OF RECLAMATION AND
COMPLETED IN 1942, WHICH IS LARGEST OF ALL SUCH STRUCTURES TO DATE, AND
ALSO UPPERMOST ON THE MAIN STEM OF THE COLUMBIA RIVER IN THE
UNITED STATES—TOTAL CAPACITY, 3,000,000 HP

Basis of Information.—This compilation of historical data concerning water-power use and resources in the United States during the past century is based on a large mass of information from many sources, some of which is necessarily approximate, including the writer's personal experience during the last half of this period.

TABLE 4.—PUBLIC WATER-POWER DEVELOPMENTS UNDER INTERIOR
DEPARTMENT CONTROL, 1952

Agency	Present	Ultimate	No. of plants
(a) OPERATING PLANTS, CAPACITY IN KILOWATTS			
Bureau of Reclamation...............	2,124,700	2,550,700	24
Bonneville Power Administration........	2,496,400	2,496,400	2
Southeastern Power Administration.......	335,600	569,600	4
Southwestern Power Administration......	158,600	342,100	3
Bureau of Indian Affairs..............	10,320	10,320	2
Bureau of Mines[a]	22,500	22,500	1
National Park Service[b].................	520	520	2
National Park Service.................	2,355	2,355	3
Total operating plants............	5,150,995	5,994,495	41
(b) PLANTS UNDER CONSTRUCTION			
Bureau of Reclamation...............	1,197,550	1,679,250	13
Bonneville Power Administration........	3,559,600	3,863,600	10
Southeastern Power Administration......	738,000	750,000	7
Southwestern Power Administration......	344,000	526,500	5
Total under construction...........	5,839,150	6,819,350	35
(c) AUTHORIZED PLANTS NOT YET UNDER CONSTRUCTION			
Bureau of Reclamation	1,183,900	1,499,400	28
Bonneville Power Administration........	4,074,000	4,445,000	10
Southeastern Power Administration.....	1,125,210	1,543,210	20
Southwestern Power Administration....	831,100	1,163,635	19
Total authorized	7,214,210	8,651,245	77
Operating	5,150,995	5,994,495	41
Under construction	5,839,150	6,819,350	35
Grand total of 1, 2, and 3.........	18,204,355	21,465,090	153

[a] Steam plants. [b] Internal combustion plants.

It would be too burdensome to credit all sources of information in detail. Much material published by various government and private agencies is available but the most useful and reliable information on developed water power, especially covering the earlier part of the 100-year period, is available from the United States Census Reports. A special water-power Census Report was prepared for 1880 from Part I of which Figs. 2 and 3 are taken. This classic should be studied by all those interested in the history of water power in the United States.

AMERICAN SOCIETY OF CIVIL ENGINEERS
Founded November 5, 1852
TRANSACTIONS

Paper No. 2603

SUPPLY OF WATER POWER IN THE UNITED STATES

By F. M. Gunby,[1] M. ASCE

Synopsis

In olden times, the simple water wheel, served by its nearby dam and canal, was purely of local value. Introduction of the turbine increased efficiency but not the range of service. Next came steam generation, expanding the over-all power picture, to the detriment of water power, 'relatively. A new phase began with electricity, by making large hydro generating units feasible and in particular by greatly extending the area of distribution. Tabulations and graphs with country-wide coverage, supplementing the economic findings, show the tremendous strides that have since been made in hydroelectric power production. However, economic limitations have now appeared, since western generating and eastern load centers do not coincide and since many regions are fast approaching depletion of unused hydroelectric possibilities. Meanwhile engineering, by better designs and practices, is partly meeting the increased needs by greater effectiveness.

Sources of Water Power

Water power, the oldest form of mechanical energy used by man, is of interest both from a historic and from an economic standpoint. It is so intimately mixed with the whole field of energy that considerable reserve is needed in treating it.

For present purposes water power may be considered as the energy available from falling water. The amount of power at a given site depends on the amount of fall or the head, and on the amount of water flowing. The latter is usually variable, thus making the amount of power variable, and thereby presenting many problems.

A typical water-power development is found on a stream where nature has produced favorable conditions—that is, where a dam can reasonably be built to create, or aid in creating, a head and preferably a large pond. Other accessories are added, including intake gates with water passages, sometimes consisting of long penstocks, to conduct the water to the hydraulic turbines in a powerhouse;

---

[1] Assoc., Chas. T. Main, Inc., Boston, Mass.

a turbine unit with its control apparatus and also an electric generator and its controls; and a tailrace to take the water back to the stream after it has passed through the turbine and given up its power. The electric energy must then be carried to the place of ultimate use—maybe a kitchen or a factory—possibly many miles away from the powerhouse.

Ideally, nature should provide a large stream of steady flow and a narrow gorge in which to build a dam on good rock foundations—a site just upstream from a high waterfall, and just downstream from a large valley which can be flooded without damaging home, farms, towns, roads, railroads, and other facilities. These favorable conditions should exist near a big city requiring all the power produced, thus minimizing the transmission charges. Under such perfect circumstances, it can be expected that the cost of the delivered water power, including not only the operating costs for labor, supplies, and maintenance, but also the fixed charges for interest, depreciation and obsolescence, taxes, and insurance will be low. The result would be what is popularly called cheap water power—which is nowadays almost impossible to obtain.

Early Water-Power Developments

Use of water power in the United States started in early colonial days for grinding grain, sawing wood, and similar simple needs. As the manufacturing plant came into being, water power, then about the only source of energy, was expanded and its production and transmission were improved. The availability and use of water power gave New England and nearby territory one of the principal tools that enabled that section to become a great manufacturing center.

Early water wheels—principally the undershot, overshot, and breast types— were largely built of wood. They were suitable for only low heads, and small amounts of power according to modern standards. Probably the best of them reached 80% efficiency.

Turbine Replaces Water Wheel.—The period starting about 1830 saw the beginnings of the development of the modern hydraulic turbine. Early examples were the outward-flow Fourneyron and Boyden wheels, which have now disappeared, and the Francis wheel, by which name the reaction turbine of today is designated. The list of pioneers includes many men who have contributed greatly to the field of water-power development. From these beginnings, the turbine has progressed to the modern hydroelectric units of today with sizes in the 100,000-kw range and heads up to about 900 ft for Francis turbines, with the impulse turbine being used for higher heads.

The early water-power companies with their dams and canals could have been the forerunners of the present-day electric utilities. The difference is that water power rather than electricity was transmitted and sold. They too had complaints that rates were too high. The first of these companies was the Proprietors of the Locks and Canals in Lowell, Mass., in 1822; and later there were others as far west as Minnesota and as far south as Georgia.

Steam As a Supplementary Source.—In 1850, 662,000 hp of water was developed in the United States, and the steam engine was making itself felt. From then on with the advent of larger factories, better mechanical transmission methods, better water wheels, and better steam engines and boilers, the amount of power increased rapidly. This increase brought to the fore one of the inherent weaknesses of nearly all water power—the fact that, since only a part of the installed capacity is firm power available all the time, requirements beyond this firm power must be supplied from some other source for the remainder of the time.

Prior to about 1900 the steam engine was the only practical means of supplying this necessary supplemental power. As time went on and as factories grew larger and steam engines became more efficient, steam power became more and more important and water power was no longer absolutely essential. Factories were built without any water power at all.

This improvement in steam power posed the question at times whether a particular water-power project was worth developing or, if the wheels or other parts had worn out, whether it was worth redeveloping. In other words, was the water power valuable? Sometimes the answer was yes and sometimes no. Many of the old small developments which were vital at the beginning of their use have now been abandoned.

Water Power in Today's Power Supply

The nearly simultaneous advent of electricity and of the public utility industry opened a new wide field for power just before the turn of the twentieth century. Electricity made it possible to develop many water-power sites not previously feasible and it also made the use of large units possible.

It is advisable to consider the country-wide power supply and to visualize the place of water power. Most of the United States is becoming well interconnected with tranmission lines so that much energy can be transferred between water and fuel generation, between utility companies, and with government-controlled plants. This condition makes for a high over-all efficiency.

Water power is variable in amount by its very nature. The interconnection with other sources of power helps to reduce the adverse effects of this variability.

The earlier water-power sites were near their markets and were generally located where natural conditions were favorable. The best locations have already been developed so that those remaining are less favored in these respects. At present, natural conditions are usually such that more work has to be done by man than on former sites, and the transmissions are longer so that the whole cost of development and therefore of fixed charges is higher per unit of power.

Total Electric Power Load in 1950

Federal Power Commission (FPC) reports show that the electric industry had installed in 1950 about 69,000,000 kw of generating capacity, of which 17,500,000 kw was hydro and the remainder used fuel power. In addition, industrial and railway stationary plants had for their own use more than 14,000,000 kw, of which about 1,000,000 kw was hydro power. The United States then had a grand total of about 83,000,000 kw, of which 18,500,000 kw was hydro power.

During 1950 the electric utility industry produced 330,000,000,000 kw-hr of which about 95,000,000,000 kw-hr, or 29%, was hydro power. The industrial and

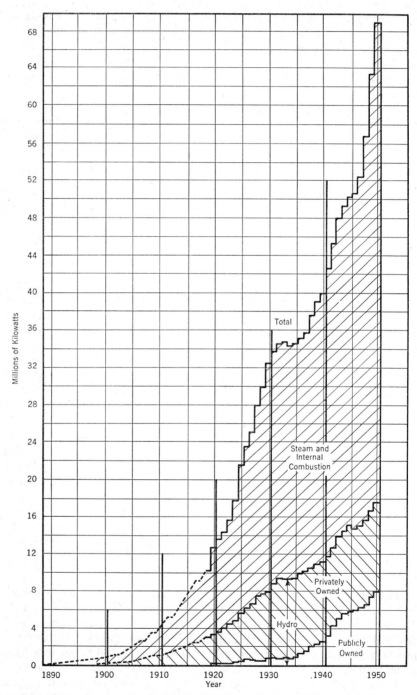

FIG. 1.—INSTALLED CAPACITY OF ELECTRIC UTILITY GENERATING PLANTS IN THE
UNITED STATES, 1889–1950

railway stationary plants added about 55,000,000,000 kw-hr of fuel-generated energy and 5,000,000,000 of hydro, making a grand total of about 390,000,000,000 kw-hr for that year. Hydro power produced 26% of this total. Also, in 1950, privately-owned utility plants had 80% of the total installed capacity and produced 81% of the total energy. The balance was from publicly-owned plants.

These long-term developments are indicated in Figs. 1 and 2. They show the effect of the prosperity of the 1920's; the economic depression of the 1930's; the war expansion; and the boom of today. Breakdown by geographical areas,

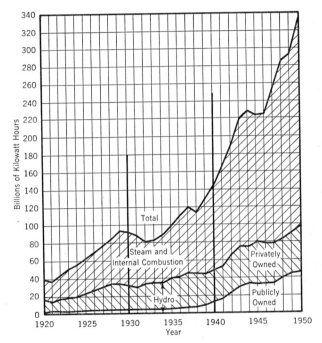

FIG. 2.—PRODUCTION OF ELECTRIC ENERGY BY ELECTRIC UTILITIES IN THE UNITED STATES

showing recent power production and increases since 1940, is given in Table 1. Total production more than doubled in the 10 years from 1940 to 1950.

A graphic comparison by areas appears in Fig. 3. Scales are the same for the nine graphs so the eye gives comparable pictures of the relative amount of power used, and of the importance of hydro sources.

WATER-POWER AND FUEL-POWER EXPANSION

Between 1920 and 1950, the total electric production of the utilities increased from 39,000,000,000 kw-hr to 330,000,000,000 kw-hr, or $8\frac{1}{2}$ times the 1920 total (Fig. 2). During the same period the hydro production expanded six times; and fuel-generated production, ten times.

The increase in installed capacity was at a much slower rate than that of the kilowatt-hours produced. This is doubtless accounted for by an improved load

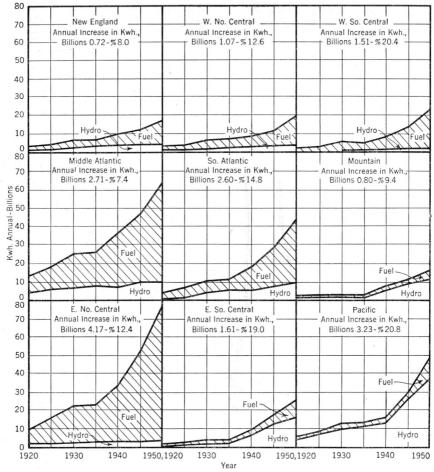

FIG. 3.—SUPPLY OF POWER IN THE UNITED STATES; PRODUCTION OF HYDRO POWER; AND TOTAL KILOWATT-HOURS BY GEOGRAPHIC AREAS (FROM FEDERAL POWER COMMISSION REPORTS)

TABLE 1.—TOTAL ELECTRIC ENERGY BY FUEL AND WATER POWER IN 1950 AND ANNUAL INCREASE BY GEOGRAPHICAL AREAS

Geographic area	Installed capacity (in million kw)	Production in 1950 (in billion kw-hr)	AVERAGE ANNUAL PRODUCTION INCREASE 1940 TO 1950	
			(In billion kw-hr)	%
New England	4.05	16.2	0.72	8.0
Middle Atlantic	13.22	63.4	2.71	7.4
East North Central ...	16.08	75.3	4.17	12.4
West North Central ...	5.02	19.2	1.07	12.6
South Atlantic	8.86	43.6	2.60	14.8
East South Central ...	4.46	24.6	1.61	19.0
West South Central ...	4.72	22.5	1.51	20.4
Mountain	3.44	16.5	0.80	9.4
Pacific	9.05	47.8	3.23	20.8
Totals	68.90	329.1	18.42	12.7

factor and more effective use of capacity. The annual plant factor for all utilities increased from 35.3% to 56.9% during this period whereas the hydro plant factor increased from 48.4% to 63.8%. During the same period the privately-owned utility plants increased their production from water power 3.4 times, while the publicly-owned plants increased it 45 times.

In 1920 the privately-owned utility hydro plants had 3,500,000 kw of capacity installed, and this had increased by 1950 to 9,700,000 kw, or 2.8 times. In the same period the publicly-owned hydro capacity increased from about 200,000 kw to 8,000,000 kw, or 40 times the 1920 amount.

POTENTIAL OR UNDEVELOPED WATER POWER

Data for the amount of potential water power are of course less exact. There are also controversies as to how near an approach to the maximum theoretical amount of potential power can ever be made in reason and as to how long it will be before conditions might change so that developments which are unattractive now might become worthwhile.

The Federal Government is the only known source of data on water power for the country as a whole. In 1920, the FPC came into being:

> "* * * to provide for the improvement of Navigation, the development of water power, and the use of the lands of the United States in relation thereto. * * *"

It has taken over the work of reporting statistically on the amount of water power in the country, both developed and potential. Much of the information herein is from FPC reports.

Government Data.—Reports have been made from time to time, as to the amount of water power available. The first of these, antedating the FPC work, were by the United States Geological Survey (USGS). A summary, in Table 2, shows the total of developed and potential water power. The language in the various reports describing what is meant by potential water power is well guarded, as it needs to be for a subject having so many variables. For simplicity, in this paper such language is omitted.

Great variations in data and rapid increases in recent years indicate uncertainty as to what the available potential water power is. Caution, therefore, is indicated. The records for rainfall, stream flow, and such features cover only a relatively short period and leave a large element of doubt about the amount of flow. In many cases the field data on construction conditions and knowledge as to damages and flowage rights are incomplete, and there are bound to be many unknowns at the time estimates of the amount of potential water power are made.

In its 1950 Annual Report the FPC gives the estimated potential water power for the United States as about 88,000,000 kw for the capacity to be installed—about double that in 1921. The expected average annual production is listed as 391,000,000,000 kw-hr, which compares with 275,000,000,000 kw-hr in 1935—the earliest estimate (Fig. 4). Of interest are the great rise in estimated capacity since 1935 and the fact that production of energy is predicted to increase at a much slower rate than is "installed capacity," as indicated by the flatter slope of the energy curve.

Basis of Appraisal.—To plan hydro developments successfully and economically, whether a single plant or one of a series of adjacent plants, requires rather complete data as to: Load factor, the shape of the load curve to be served, the other sources of power for serving it, the stream flow and its variations, the effect of pondage, and many other elements. The mere production of energy is rarely the only requirement.

As an example, one large plant under construction, designed to meet an initial load condition with an installation of 160,000 kw and an annual output

TABLE 2.—TOTAL WATER POWER IN THE UNITED STATES, BOTH DEVELOPED AND POTENTIAL, AS REPORTED BY VARIOUS SOURCES

Date of report	Source of report or data	TOTAL WATER POWER	
		Capacity[a]	Production[b]
1880	United States Department of the Interior (east of Mississippi River only)	9.1	...
1908	USGS[c] (Secretary of the Interior thought available development might be between 56,000,000 kw and 112,000,000 kw).....................	53.6	...
1921	USGS,[c] based on flow available 50% of the time plus the 6,900,000 kw already developed	47.1	...
1924	FPC,[d] based on flow 50% of the time and only on feasible sites with an available market	46.0	...
1935	FPC,[d] based on "installed capacity" for potential power and on the 9,000,000 kw in existing plants	61.6	314.0
1947	FPC,[d] based on potential plus installed power	92.1	....
1948	FPC,[d] based on potential plus installed power	92.8	476.5
1949	FPC,[d] based on potential power plus 16,600,000 kw in existing plants	90	470.0
1950	FPC,[d] based on potential power plus 16,500,000 kw in existing plants	104.6	478.1

[a] Capacity, in millions of kilowatts.   [b] Production, in billions of kilowatt-hours.
[c] United States Geological Survey.   [d] Federal Power Commission.

of 700,000,000 kw-hr, was planned for an ultimate installation with an increase of 75% in capacity and a corresponding increase in annual kilowatt-hour output of only 4%. During the work, the ultimate capacity is being installed, so presumably the load curve and the load factor to be served must have radically changed in the interim.

It is helpful in getting a more useful picture of the water-power situation to break down the data into geographic areas. There has to be a usable relation between a source of water power, which is always immovable, and its market, much of which also cannot be moved. There are engineering and financial limits to the distances which may separate them.

Physical Difficulties in Transmission.—The greatest distance over which large blocks of power are now being transmitted is less than 300 miles and only a few lines approach this. There is no probability of transmitting any large fraction of the water power available, say, in the Rocky Mountains to displace fuel-generated power in the Middle West or in the East. The effect on delivered cost of power from long transmission is also a deterrent.

This situation is illustrated by Fig. 5, which indicates the great degree of interconnection which exists in the eastern part of the country and along the Pacific Coast and the comparatively few interconnections in the great area between.

If it is assumed that the existence of transmission lines and interconnections may be taken as an over-all indication of the general market for power, this map shows rather impressively the lack of these facilities in those areas, Mountain and parts of the Pacific, that contain most of the potential water power. The small graphic scale of Fig. 5 shows what the 300 miles of the present maximum transmission distance looks like, and the impossibility of transmitting power from the Mountain area to the great market around Lake Erie—or east of the Mississippi.

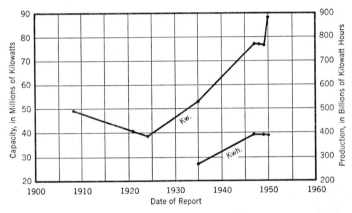

Fig. 4.—Potential (Undeveloped) Water Power in United States As Reported by Various Sources

As shown in Table 3, about 53,000,000 kw, or 60% of the potential capacity proposed as of 1950, is in the Mountain and Pacific areas; and about 262,000,-000,000 kw-hr, or 67%, of the potential energy is in the same two areas. The South Atlantic area ranks third and the Middle Atlantic and West North Central areas are tied for fourth place in undeveloped water power. The 1921 USGS Report showed about the same preponderance of water power in these two western areas.

Future Increase.—In Col. 4, Table 3, the annual increase is taken as the average during the 10-year period ending in 1950. It will be noted that in only three areas would the potential water power supply the increase for 20 years or more.

If kilowatt-hours were the only feature to consider, the results shown in Table 3 would be conclusive. However, in estimates, particularly for water power, the vital requirements for firm power, load factor, and economics must be included. The effect would be to change the number of years shown in Col. 4, and the variations might be large. If the water power did not fit economically into the load and other conditions to be met, the result could be serious.

Fuels must provide the bulk of the energy for the United States as a whole,

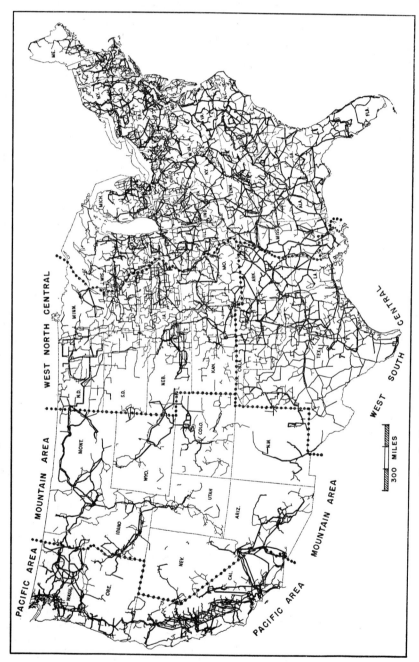

FIG. 5.—PRINCIPAL INTERCONNECTED ELECTRIC TRANSMISSION LINES

and for most of the geographic areas. Of course, much fuel also must be burned in those areas favored by the water-power situation.

WATER POWER ECONOMICALLY AVAILABLE

The development of the power industry has been based on the principles that the power must be needed; that it will be available where and when wanted; and that its cost must be as low as conditions permit. The industry offers one of the best examples of mass production. Through his work in power development, the engineer has made wonderful contributions to the public good. It is one of the few fields in which the unit price to the consumer has trended downward rather than upward over the years.

TABLE 3.—POTENTIAL WATER POWER IN THE UNITED STATES

(From the Federal Power Commission Report for 1950)

Geographic area (1)	Installed generating capacity, in millions of kilowatts (2)	Average annual generation, in billions of kilowatt-hours (3)	No. of years potential water power would supply necessary increase in kilowatt-hours [a] (4)
New England	3.25	10.2	14.3
Middle Atlantic	6.50	25.1	9.3
East North Central	2.39	11.3	2.7
West North Central	5.81	25.2	23.5
South Atlantic	8.18	26.0	10
East South Central	4.79	20.2	12.5
West South Central	3.59	10.4	6.9
Mountain	23.43	100.4	125
Pacific	30.14	162.3	50.2
Totals	88.08	391.1	21.2

[a] The requirements as to firm power, and so forth, are not reflected by Col. 4.

In this accomplishment the engineer has used his skill not only in continually developing technical improvements but in aiding in applying sound economic principles to the financial problems involved. He must continue this practice.

Common Basis for Comparison.—For many years it has been an accepted principle that the value of a service may be measured by comparing the cost of that service with the cost of getting the same service by some other method. This principle applies to water power.

In determining if a given water-power development should be made, the cost of its output delivered at the market should be compared with the cost of fuel-generated power delivered at the same market. The cost for both sources of power must include all elements of operating and fixed charges.

The rates for the fixed charges of interest, depreciation, taxes, and insurance should be measured by the going market conditions which reflect what citizens would do acting as investors rather than as involuntary contributors through taxes. The 55,000,000 kw of privately-owned utilities plus the 14,000,000 kw of industrial and similar generating plants have been built by investors, whereas the 13,700,000 kw of publicly-owned capacity have been built largely by taxes in one form or another.

As an example of results from surveys of the same area made by groups with different points of view, the case of the New England area may be taken. Here a survey was made by the New England Council and an opportunity arose to compare its results with those expected by the FPC.

Illustrated by New England Case.—In its 25 years of work the New England Council has earned a respected place in the region. It is a private body and acts under the auspices of the New England governors. In 1948 it appointed a Power Survey Committee to collect and analyze factual data on the power situation in New England, with water power included as a part of the study. When the report was completed, one of the New England Senators secured from the Federal Power Commission its data on the amount of potential water power in New England.

The following is a summary of the reports covering the territory:

Report	Kw
1. The Council's report was based on normal and usual practice for water-power development in New England and on flows available 20% of the time. It included some dual-purpose projects by the Army Corps of Engineers but not the Passamaquoddy tidal project (between Maine and New Brunswick, Canada) or the international boundary streams. It omitted some questionable water power that the Council stated might be developed. It showed potential water power available 20% of the time from thirty-seven projects totaling.....................................	500,000
2. The FPC in a staff memorandum for the same thirty-seven projects showed potential water power (but without stating how much of the time it would be available) totaling about..............	1,000,000
3. The FPC staff memorandum—also for New England as a whole including multipurpose developments but omitting Passamaquoddy and international boundary streams and covering the same thirty-seven projects, plus seventeen more, all of which were considered to be: (a) Technically possible, (b) engineeringly feasible, and (c) within the range of possible economic feasibility—showed potential water power totaling about......	2,000,000

The seventeen additional projects mentioned in report 3 are probably among those the Council felt were "questionable," as noted in report 1.

The Council commented that the additional 500,000 kw included by the FPC for the thirty-seven projects in report 2 is purely marginal capacity; that this marginal power output may well cost more than the fuel cost at steam plants; and that, when this is so, the overdevelopment of water resources will most certainly increase the cost of power rather than reduce it. It may also be pointed out that with enough money at hand any project is: (a) Technically possible, and (b) engineeringly feasible. The Council report was predicated on all private financing; the FPC stated that its data were all based on public financing. This comparison of reports covering the same territory is recited so that any engineer may put his own value on it.

In appraisal, it should be remembered that much of New England is highly industrialized and thickly settled, and land is rather intensively used for farms, homes, business, and recreation. Naturally, much of the early settlement and development was in the valleys and later around the water-power sites. As a result, locations which long ago could have been developed or redeveloped to advantage are now so hemmed in that the destruction of values resulting from redevelopment would be greater than the water power is worth. These conditions hamper, or even preclude, utilizing water-power sites which might be attractive in a less highly developed area.

Cost Trends

Costs of output for water power are composed of the same elements as for fuel power. Water power is usually not immune to fuel costs because fuel has to be used to supplement water, but the effect of fuel cost is not so great as when all power is fuel generated. As a point of interest, the Tennessee Valley Authority, which started with all water power, will have in 1954 about 500,000 kw more steam capacity than hydro capacity.

The total cost of power is made up of operating costs and fixed charges. Operating costs for labor, fuel, supplies, repairs, and maintenance are usually greater for fuel-using plants than for water-power plants. On the other hand, fixed charges such as interest, depreciation, taxes, and insurance are nearly always higher on water-power projects and form a large part of the total expense. Now that the favorable hydro sites have been developed, those remaining will have higher construction and transmission costs and therefore higher fixed charges. The effect can only be higher over-all production costs for future hydro power.

When the over-all cost of production of hydro power is higher than the over-all cost of production of fuel-generated power, which is frequently true, the expression "cheap water power" cannot apply.

Improvement in Technology

Progress in hydroelectric technology has kept pace with that in other fields. The results from the efficiency standpoint have been less spectacular, principally because reasonably high efficiencies were obtained years ago. No new cycles seem possible.

Some of the early water wheels reached an efficiency of 80% or more. The highest the writer has seen quoted today is $94\frac{1}{2}\%$ for a 100,000-hp unit in Canada. Room for improvement is not great.

Better Designing.—During the past several decades the design for reaction turbines has moved from the multirunner units for comparatively low heads to the modern vertical single-runner turbine mounted directly under its generator, with the moving parts suspended from a thrust bearing. Probably no other factor contributed so materially to the advance to the modern large-size vertical turbine as the advent of the Kingsbury type of thrust bearing.

In the same period great improvements have been made on water passages to and from the turbines, and increased knowledge has been gained from cavitation research. Also stainless steel has been developed as protection against cavitation. As a result, both Francis-type and propeller-type turbines have increased speeds, with consequent economies.

Limitation on the size of Francis-type turbines has been fixed principally by the maximum diameter of runner that can be shipped in a single piece. Larger diameters have been built with split runners but only for moderate heads.

Development of the propeller-type turbine has increased the speed at which units can operate under moderate heads with resulting economy. The adjustable-blade Kaplan unit has made it possible to adapt the propeller unit to wide variations in flow and head conditions without sacrificing efficiency. Recent trends in installation of such units at heads of more than 100 ft have increased their adaptability.

Similar progress has been made with impulse turbines. Increased capacity of these units has resulted from development of multinozzle vertical-shaft installations.

Advances in Engineering Practice.—The present top for individual generator size is about 120,000 kva. Prediction of size limits would essentially have to be based on improvement in turbine practice resulting in higher speeds. Thus, generator outputs would be increased without exceeding present rotor weights, which are fast approaching the economic limits of structures and handling methods.

Generators for the larger units usually have direct-connected stabilized exciters and a closed ventilating system consisting of an air housing and surface air coolers. There have been a few outdoor and semi-outdoor installations, but no distinct trend in that direction is evident. Most large hydroelectric stations are now of the so-called unit design in which each unit is actually a complete independent installation having its own turbine, governor, generator, exciter, auxiliaries, and step-up transformers.

Where hydroelectric generation with ample pondage is available, it is often economical to increase the installed capacity beyond that justified for producing kilowatt-hours only and to operate the hydroelectric plants for peak loads and as reserves. The increased installed capacity at such points can frequently be obtained at additional costs which are relatively small. The effectiveness of this practice depends on the shape of the load curve to be served, the load factor, and many other features. This practice has been in use for years, and developments of this kind are sometimes referred to as "peaking plants."

Summary

The foregoing brief résumé of the situation in the United States as related to water power will be recapitulated to give a condensed picture of this great industry:

1. Water power, the oldest form of mechanical force used by man, replenishes its energy practically continuously.

2. There is a large amount of potential water power in the country, but the two thirds in the Rocky Mountain and Pacific slope areas is not available to help carry the loads in the central and eastern areas, which must depend largely on fuel for energy. Even according to the most enthusiastic estimates, it will take many years for the growth in load to absorb the water-power energy reported in the Mountain and Pacific areas. Possibly load can be developed more rapidly than in the past to the vicinities of this water-power supply. Chemical, metallurgical, and atomic installations may be possibilities.

3. If the FPC predictions as to the amount of potential water power available

are used, the amounts in the nine geographic areas would provide for the increase in energy for each area for the following number of years:

Area	Years	Area	Years
New England	14	East South Central	13
Middle Atlantic	9	West South Central	7
East North Central	3	Mountain	125
West North Central	24	Pacific	50
South Atlantic	10		

If kilowatt-hours were the only feature to be considered, the results would be complete. However, in power work, particularly water power, vital requirements for firm power, load factor, and economics must be included. In effect, the number of years shown would have to be changed, and this could be serious in cases where the water power did not fit economically into the load curves and the other conditions to be met.

Should the potential water power actually available be less than the FPC predictions, the number of years shown would certainly be reduced.

4. Water power is one of the natural resources of the United States. Its use makes fuel reserves last longer. Experience proves that water power is a good, although not a perfect, resource. Like other natural resources, it should be developed where and when the application of sound principles—including private financing, which is known to be good—indicates that a given project should be built.

AMERICAN SOCIETY OF CIVIL ENGINEERS

Founded November 5, 1852

TRANSACTIONS

Paper No. 2604

HOW DAMS SERVE MAN'S VITAL NEEDS

By Gail A. Hathaway,[1] Past-President ASCE

Synopsis

Dams have always been valuable adjuncts to civilization. Like fire, water devastates mankind, or it can serve—through dams working against water ravages or for storage. Dams have been used for about 5,000 years, being found in the very cradles of civilization—India, Babylonia, Egypt, and the Roman Empire. In the United States, first they provided for sawmills and thus shelter and then for gristmills and sustenance. More modern needs, each briefly discussed, concern water supply, irrigation, power, navigation, and flood control. Looking ahead, it is certain that engineering for dams still has great potentialities—in technology, materials, and construction techniques. Engineers, through their dams, will continue to serve man's highest purposes.

Introduction

The dam was probably one of the first structures devised by the human race. In modern form it has become one of the most versatile and important of the structural servants of man. A child dams a small stream with mud and rocks, and modern engineering technology throttles the mighty Columbia River with the Grand Coulee Dam in Washington. These two extremes span the progress which has been made by the human race in utilizing such structures to constantly improve its standard of living.

It has been stated that "fire" is man's greatest friend and worst enemy, the difference lying in the degree of human control exercised. In a broader sense, the same statement may be applied to "water." Water is one of the essential requirements in sustaining life. Its various uses affect almost every phase of human existence. Commerce between continents still depends largely on ocean transport, and elaborate systems of inland waterways for navigation serve the interior areas of nations.

Forces inherent in moving water have been harnessed to provide power for industrial and domestic purposes, and large areas of barren lands have been made productive of food by means of irrigation. The ability of flowing water to carry

---

[1] Special Asst. to the Chf. of Engrs., Dept. of the Army, Washington, D. C.

solids in suspension provides the basis for modern sanitary sewerage systems. Without doubt, a large share of the enjoyment of life is associated with the recreational use of rivers, lakes, and reservoirs. In contrast, the devastation wrought by floods in many areas demonstrates that water can adversely affect the life of man, and that the very forces of nature which have brought about the formation of rich valley lands and delta areas over the ages can act also to destroy or nullify the advantages inherent in their use.

The examples just cited, and many others that could be given, reflect the importance of regulating or directing the forces of nature in moving water if the purposes of man are to be served most advantageously. The engineering, economic, and social problems involved in attaining such regulation are of extraordinary magnitude, but their solution is feasible and the necessity impelling. A "dam," defined by one lexicographer as "a barrier to prevent the flow of water * * * ," accomplishes that objective most effectively.

From a functional viewpoint, dams may be classified broadly under two major categories:

a. *Dams That Protect Against the Forces and Ravages of Moving Water.*— This category includes those that are constructed to store heavy flood runoff and those constructed to intercept and retain debris from mining operations and excessive erosion. Levees constructed along the banks of a river to prevent overflow are also actually dams.

b. *Dams That Store or Control Water for Man's Use.*—This broad category includes dams to increase depths for navigation and dams for storage or diversion of water for domestic or industrial use, for irrigation of agricultural lands, and for the development of water power. The multipurpose dam combines several of these functions in a single structure.

With respect to materials of construction, modern dams fall principally into four distinct classes: Earth fill, rock fill, masonry, and concrete, with combinations of materials being used in many cases. The design of dams and methods of construction have varied radically in recent years and are still undergoing progressive changes as advances are made in technical knowledge and equipment and as more rigid requirements are imposed. Recent technical progress has made feasible the construction of very large projects, including multiple-purpose reservoirs, that had long been known to be desirable but that hitherto had been considered hazardous or uneconomical.

The role that dams have played over the ages as man's vital servant for food, water, power, and protection from floods is referred to in many histories of ancient lands like India, Babylonia, Egypt, and the Roman Empire, to mention only a few. Since the dawn of civilization India has been primarily an agricultural country; and because of the uneven distribution of rainfall throughout each year, and from year to year, irrigation has been practiced for many centuries. Evidence still remains of the great Bhojpur Lake (circa 1100 A. D.) which had an area of 250 sq miles, created by the construction of two remarkable earth dams faced with immense blocks of stone. The spillway, 2 miles from the dams and cut through solid rock, still remains as proof of the practical ability of the Hindu engineers of that time. One of the dams was destroyed in order to cultivate the bed of the lake, which to this day grows the best wheat in all India(1).[2]

Well-preserved sections of masonry dams still remain in the Tigris Valley and the Aden protectorates of the Middle East (2). According to B. M. Hellstrom, M. ASCE (3), the well-preserved abutments of what may be the oldest dam in the world are situated in a dry river bed, Wadi Garawi, about 78 miles south of Cairo, Egypt. Archeological experts believe the dam was built during the third or fourth dynasty—that is, about 5,000 years ago. Evidence indicates that the central part was washed away by a flood shortly after completion. The existence of the abutments, a constant reminder of the failure, may have contributed somewhat to the 3,000-year period of inactivity of dam builders in ancient Egypt.

One other example of ancient dam building may be cited. Along the coast of Tripolitania a number of wadies which rise in the high Jebel Nefuza Mountains to the south carry large quantities of water and sediment to the Mediterranean each winter. It was near the mouth of these wadies that three great cities of Roman times, Leptis Magna, Oea, and Sabratha were situated. The Roman system of masonry dams in the wadies behind these towns was admirably adapted, not only to provide permanent water-supply reservoirs for the cities themselves but to counteract soil erosion.

During the dark ages, from the downfall of the Roman Empire in the fifth century until the beginning of the sixteenth century, the sciences were almost lost, being practiced only by the monks and other religious organizations. Late in the fourteenth century, the Spaniards began construction of dams in southern Spain of rubble masonry, faced with large cut stones, for irrigation purposes.

The type of construction of the early Spanish dams was similar to that used by the Romans in the fifth century; and, according to Robert A. Sutherland, M. ASCE (4), the initiative came from the Moors, who had preserved during the dark ages, among other things, the science of masonry dam construction. Similarly, the Spanish type of construction was brought to the United States via Mexico by the Jesuit padres who constructed the chain of Missions along the west coast of California. The Old Mission Dam (5) was erected in 1770 across the San Diego River to impound and divert water for irrigation and domestic use. It was antedated by a stone water-works dam at New Brunswick, N. J., built in 1743, which stood, with some strengthening in 1780, until it failed in 1888.

The first dams in what is now the United States were built to operate sawmills and gristmills, the sawmills to provide lumber for shelter for the early settlers and the gristmills to grind their grain for food (6). One of the earliest was constructed in 1623 to operate the first sawmill in America on the Piscataqua River at South Windham, Me. Another operated the first gristmill at Portsmouth, N. H. Tide dams, operating on the same principles as proposed for the Passamaquoddy Project, were built in many tidal inlets along New England's shores. A timber-crib dam constructed on the Schuylkill River in 1819 was used for slackwater navigation and as a source of water supply for the City of Philadelphia (Pa.) (Fig. 1).

Prior to 1850, the construction of many of the small dams was handled by

---

[2] Numerals in parentheses, thus: (1), refer to corresponding items in the Bibliography at the end of the paper.

skilled craftsmen, principally millwrights, who learned their trade as apprentices and imparted their knowledge to other apprentices by example and word of mouth. Being a busy and practical man, the old millwright had little time, inclination, or ability for putting his knowledge on record. He built his dam largely of wood, although later timber-crib construction filled with rock was used extensively. The dams were faced with oak planking which was plentiful at that time. Water diverted into a flume passed through an opening in the bottom of the flume on to a kind of paddle wheel. Later refinements were the overshot, the undershot, and the breast wheel types, which were used until replaced by the turbine around 1845.

Not only did the early dams play an important part in the economic life of the settlers in colonial days but they also laid the groundwork for the tremendous

FIG. 1.—DAM AND WATER WORKS AT FAIRMONT, PHILADELPHIA, PA., FROM AN OLD WOOD ENGRAVING, SHOWING COMBINED NAVIGATION (LEFT) AND WATER SUPPLY, POSSIBLY THE FIRST IN THE UNITED STATES FOR A MAJOR CITY; MORE THAN 1,000 FT LONG AND 30 FT HIGH

development of American water resources that has taken place during the past 100 years—in the form of projects for water supply, irrigation, power, navigation, flood control, and other uses.

WATER-SUPPLY DAMS

The welfare and growth of a community are intimately connected with its water supply. The early water works utilized springs and wells as sources, but, as the little communities grew into towns and the towns grew into cities, available springs and wells became inadequate. Moreover, these sources became highly polluted and offensive. Sanitary conditions were bad and severe epidemics of cholera, typhoid fever, and yellow fever were frequent. Most of the buildings were of wood, and the losses of life and property from fire were extensive. As the population of large cities increased with the constantly growing requirements of the population and industry for a pure and wholesome water supply, dams for surface storage began to play a large part in meeting the demand.

Probably the most notable of the early water-supply dams were the Old Croton, completed in 1842 on the Croton River for New York, N. Y.; Lake

Cochituate Dam completed in 1848 for Boston, Mass.; Mill River Dam completed in 1862 for New Haven, Conn; and the Druid Lake Dam completed in 1871 for Baltimore, Md.

Some of the larger cities have been able to develop storage close at hand while others carry their supplies great distances. Quabbin Reservoir, a part of the Boston metropolitan water system, 60 miles west of the city, has a capacity of 415,000,000 gal or 1,270,000 acre-ft. It is the largest city water-supply reservoir in the world and is created by two large earth dams. New York City has many dams in the Catskill and Delaware river basins which require that water be carried more than 100 miles by aqueducts.

The Hetch Hetchy and Lake Eleanor reservoirs, sources of supply for San Francisco, Calif., are 170 miles to the east in the high Sierra Nevada, and the City of Los Angeles, Calif., in 1913 completed an aqueduct that brought water from a dam in Owens Valley, a distance of 233 miles. The 250-mile tunnel and conduit system of the Metropolitan Water District of Southern California, bringing water from reservoirs on the Colorado River to the Los Angeles and San Diego metropolitan areas is probably the world's greatest water-supply undertaking.

Dams for Hydraulic Mining

No economic development in the history of the United States did more to promote the science of dam building than the discovery of gold at Sutter's Mill, California, in 1848. The initial use in 1852 of hydraulic placer mining techniques gave rise to many unique engineering problems which were boldly attacked and solved by California engineers (7). The evolution—from small volumes of water, low pressures, canvas pipe, and crude improvised nozzles to large volumes of water, high pressures, heavy double-riveted pipe of large diameter, the Pelton wheel, and the hydraulic monitor or giant—took place in a surprisingly brief period. Both placer and quartz mining techniques required the development of water supplies by construction of dams and reservoirs, ditches, flumes, and tunnels, and often under such unprecedented conditions that astonishing boldness of design and execution of construction resulted.

Water for hydraulic mining was first impounded by log cribs filled with loose stone. The next stage was an embankment consisting of rock dumped loosely except at the faces, which were laid carefully as a dry wall, with a surfacing of two or more thicknesses of plank to insure watertightness.

Construction of dams by the hydraulic-fill method—Fort Peck Dam on the Missouri River in Montana with 130,000,000 cu yd is the greatest example—evolved from hydraulic mining (5). The first small storage dams in and around the mines were built with the tailings from which placer gold had been washed.

Gold fields had another influence on dam building. The tremendous inundation of hydraulic mining detritus over the farming lands and river beds of the valleys eventually brought injunctions against such practice, which could be resumed only if dams were built to hold back the debris. Impounding dams of various kinds were tried for storing the detritus, but the resumption of hydraulic mining on the large scale formerly followed has never materialized.

In recent years two large concrete dams in California, the "North Fork" on the North Fork of the American River and "Upper Narrows" on the Yuba River have been constructed to impound debris from upstream placer mines. It is rather significant that high dams, which hydraulic mining played so important a part in developing, are being utilized to salvage in part what was at one time a great industry in the Sacramento and San Joaquin valleys.

In addition to debris dams for hydraulic mining wastes, others have been constructed to protect community facilities in places where exceptionally precipitous gradients of streams combine with unstable soil and rock conditions to bring debris down in hazardous quantities.

WATER-POWER DAMS

Dams were constructed to provide water power long before the advent of hydroelectric power. Water wheels designed to develop mechanical power by utilizing the force of falling water are of ancient origin and have played an important part in human progress. More important than the power actually produced by these relatively simple wheels was the knowledge and inspiration gained from their construction which greatly stimulated the rapid development of hydroelectric power in later years.

Around 1847, James B. Francis, Past-President and Hon. M. ASCE, a civil engineer, developed an efficient downward flow turbine which gradually replaced the wooden water wheel as a source of water power at low-head developments. About 1882, Lester A. Pelton, a millwright, developed an impulse turbine for high-head installations, mostly mining projects in the West (7). The original impulse wheel, of very simple design and called the "hurdy-gurdy," was introduced in California around 1860. Pelton, who lived where there were facilities for testing such wheels, bought and studied Francis' book on "Lowell Experiments" (8), constructed a Prony brake and a weir to measure the water used, and with these made continuous tests, until he arrived at the form of bucket and setting giving the highest efficiency.

During the latter half of the nineteenth century great advances were made in the development of the electric generator and transmission of electric energy. Although the first great water-power developments were built in the New England States followed by many large projects in California, principally in connection with the mining of gold, it appears that the Middle West first combined water power and the electric generator for the production of energy. The Minnesota Brush Electric Company built a plant operated by water power at St. Anthony Falls in Minneapolis, Minn. (Fig. 2(a)), that went into service in February, 1882 (9). A plant at Appleton, Wis. (Fig. 2 (b)), in which two Edison bipolar generators were connected to an hydraulic turbine, has been generally regarded as the first hydroelectric station. It went into service on September 30, 1882 (10). Undoubtedly the Appleton plant was the first in which an Edison generator was operated by water power and the St. Anthony Falls plant was the first in which arc machines were driven by hydraulic turbines.

Today there are about 1,850 dams in the United States involved in the development of hydroelectric power, representing about 22% of the electric power generated in the United States. Hydro-power projects have two distinct advan-

(a) Minnesota Brush Electric Company's Generating Station at St. Anthony Falls of the
Mississippi River at Minneapolis, Minn.

(b) Appleton, Wis., Plant on the Fox River: Cross-Sectional
Diagram—10-Ft Operating Head

FIG. 2.—EARLY AMERICAN HYDROELECTRIC DEVELOPMENTS

tages from a national viewpoint: They can be operated at peak load when requirements dictate, and can be shut down at other times, generally without loss of energy. Thus they can advantageously supplement fuel-power plants that must operate more or less continuously for maximum efficiency. The second major advantage lies in the fact that water is a renewable resource, whereas combustible fuels are not.

An astonishing comparison was made recently by a distinguished engineer from India that:

"* * * for ever man, woman, and child in the United States, electricity does the work of 11 servants, employed 40 hours per week; thus if every fourth inhabitant is employed in useful work, his productive capacity is augmented 44 times by the use of electricity."

Further investigation discloses that this analysis may be on the conservative side, and that electricity in the United States does the work of fifteen servants working 40 hours per week for every man, woman, and child in this country.

The total installation of hydroelectric power in the United States amounts to approximately 20,000,000 kw. In some areas, most of the more desirable sites have been developed; but in other regions there still remains a considerable amount of potential hydro power which can be economically put to use. A recent treaty with Canada will make it possible to increase the power installation at Niagara Falls between New York and Ontario, Canada; and the International Rapids section of the St. Lawrence River, also between New York and Ontario, offers one of the most attractive power possibilities in the world. The Columbia River Basin in the Northwest has the largest power potential in the United States, and this potential, by a continuing program of large dam construction and power installation, is being rapidly transformed into energy for the use of man.

IRRIGATION

Irrigation by Americans as distinguished from the small systems constructed around the Spanish Missions in Arizona, New Mexico, and California began when a company of Mormon pioneers entered the Great Salt Lake Valley in Utah and on July 24, 1847, diverted water from City Creek on the alkaline desert (11). Other western irrigation ventures followed shortly thereafter, many being associated with the food requirements of the thousands of gold miners who migrated westward following the discovery of gold in California in 1849.

By the turn of the twentieth century more than 9,000,000 acres of land had been brought under irrigation (7). In the two decades following the passage of the Reclamation Act of 1902, works of the United States Reclamation Service brought an additional 2,000,000 acres of land under cultivation. By 1920, 20,000,000 acres were irrigated, and the crops harvested were valued at about $760,000,000. Available data indicate that some 25,000,000 acres are now under irrigation with some 13,000,000 additional acres potentially susceptible to irrigation (12).

The construction of dams creating large storage reservoirs to fully develop the potentialities of western streams was in large part responsible for the remarkable development of irrigation. Concurrently, numerous cities and towns as well as roads, railroads, and all the other organizations of modern civilization have arisen on the reclaimed deserts of the west. It is significant that some of the outstanding dams of the modern era such as Hoover (on the Colorado River in Arizona-Nevada) and Grand Coulee are key features of these vast irrigation developments.

NAVIGATION DAMS

From the earliest colonial days until the present time, lakes, rivers, and canals have played an important and often controlling part in the development of the United States. These waterways provided the main pathways followed by the pioneers in conquering the continental wilderness, and these same waterways— improved, developed, and maintained by private and governmental effort—play

FIG. 3.—GALLIPOLIS DAM, ROLLER-GATE TYPE OF MODERN NAVIGATION STRUCTURE ON THE OHIO RIVER NEAR HUNTINGTON, W. VA.

a vital role in the country's present industrial activities. A controlling factor in the development of the inland waterways has been the construction of dams for the regulation of river and lake stages either to provide navigable depths for modern craft, or to store water during the flood seasons in order to increase river stages during low-flow seasons.

The series of main-stem locks and dams constructed on the Upper Mississippi River above St. Louis, Mo., the forty-six locks and dams on the Ohio River, and the system of reservoirs on the Tennessee River which provides a continuous slack-water navigation channel for a distance of more than 600 miles, in addition to the development of hydroelectric power, are notable examples of projects in which dams have been used to improve navigable features of major rivers. The Gallipolis Dam (Fig. 3) on the Ohio River near Huntington, W. Va., illustrates one type of structure used to provide present-day slack-water navigation.

Huge reservoirs formed by the existing Fort Peck Dam, and the Garrison (N. Dak.), Oahe (S. Dak.), and Fort Randall (S. Dak.) dams on the upper Missouri River, now under construction, will total more than 64,000,000 acre-ft in gross capacity. They will provide a high degree of stream-flow regulation to assure dependable open-river navigation on the Missouri River, while serving other multiple-purpose needs for flood control, irrigation, power, and recreation. Traffic on the inland and intracoastal waterways, exclusive of the Great Lakes, reached 40,000,000 ton-miles in 1948.

Dams for Control of Floods

Attempts to control floods in the United States began with the earliest settlers in the alluvial valley of the Mississippi River. Their work was followed by intermittent, uncoordinated, and largely ineffective efforts on the part of states and local governments. Federal interest in flood protection began with the Swamp Land Acts of 1849 and 1850 and took definite form with the establishment of the Mississippi River Commission by Congress in 1879. Successive acts of Congress have culminated in a nation-wide general flood-control program involving dams, not only for flood control, but for multipurpose uses such as domestic and industrial water supply, irrigation, recharge of ground water, navigation improvement, hydroelectric power, improvement in stream flow, pollution control, and recreation.

In spite of marked progress during recent years on the construction of flood-control projects, damages from floods still constitute a severe drain on the national economy. It is estimated that, with the degree of river-valley development prevailing in 1950, the total average annual flood damage in the United States would be more than $800,000,000 if no federal flood-control measures had been undertaken. However, flood-control works now in operation prevent flood losses aggregating more than $300,000,000 annually; the average flood damages actually experienced in the United States thus total some $500,000,000 annually.

The system of dams of the Miami Conservancy District in Ohio, constructed after the great Ohio River flood of 1913, is an outstanding example of effective flood control for an entire river basin made possible by local initiative. Federal basin-wide projects, utilizing multipurpose instead of detention dams, provide a high degree of protection from floods in the Tennessee, Muskingum (Ohio), and Willamette (Oregon) river basins, and also in the Ohio River Basin above Pittsburgh, Pa. There are many storage dams in the United States in which part or all of the storage capacity in the reservoirs is allocated to flood control.

Recent disastrous floods with the attending human suffering and property loss have again focused national attention on the problem of adequate flood control. The potentialities for floodwater storage dams in middle and lower river basins are great. There are extensive possibilities of flood retardation in the smaller upstream tributary valleys. Flood control is a national problem of first importance and the dam as a keystone structure in the program naturally assumes the number one position.

What of the Future?

Dams perform such an essential function in advancing civilization and higher standards of living that their continued improvement is one of the important problems of the future that faces the engineer.

Public demand for full and efficient utilization of water resources will require that many future dams be of the multipurpose type. Thus, they must be larger on the average than in the past, and probably individual ones will exceed in size any dams heretofore built. The 726-ft height of Hoover Dam is by no means the maximum to which concrete dams can be constructed, nor is the 390-ft height (above the stream bed) of Mud Mountain Dam, on the White River in Washington (Fig. 4), the maximum to which earth and rock-fill structures can be built.

FIG. 4.—MUD MOUNTAIN DAM ON THE WHITE RIVER IN WASHINGTON FROM UPSTREAM SIDE; ENTRANCE TO UNCONTROLLED FIXED-CREST SPILLWAY ON LEFT

It is certain that the dams of the future must frequently be more daring and original, since they will have to be built on many substandard sites. Most of the good locations for dams have been preempted. It cannot be assumed, however, that adequate safety factors can be sacrificed, as failure of such a major engineering structure would be disastrous.

Outstanding advancement in knowledge of dam construction during the past two decades, coupled with corresponding improvements in construction equipment, has paved the way for large multipurpose dams which can effectively meet the needs of flood control, navigation, hydro power, irrigation, domestic and industrial water supply, and other water uses with a minimum of conflict and in a vastly more economical manner than would be possible with projects designed for individual purposes.

Many future improvements in design and construction procedures for these multipurpose dams can be confidently expected. For example, low concrete-placing temperatures, low heat cement, and low cement factors, combined with the use of air entrained concrete and controlled aggregate grading, will minimize many difficulties that have plagued the dam designer and builder in past years. Increased emphasis on laboratory investigations has brought about the use of substitute materials such as special cements, and pozzolanic materials with portland cement.

Possibly the chemical industry, which has been developing so many new and unusual products, could bring forth a new cementitious agent that would provide durable concrete of desired strengths, would be inert to reactive aggregates, would not require curing, and would not produce heat with the resultant tendency toward cracking in massive structures. From the viewpoint of the dam designer, such a cementitious agent would be most desirable. Prestressed concrete will receive increasing attention and the massive head-buttress type of dam will replace some of the more conventional types now in use in the United States—because of an economy of some 40% under standard gravity design sections and freedom from uplift, shrinkage, and heating and cooling transformations.

Improvements in earth-moving equipment with attendant lower unit costs of embankments will place the large rolled-fill earth dam in a preferred position in many cases. Costs for earth dams may be appreciably reduced by the construction of concrete spillways over the main embankment or by raising the dam to store a large part of the spillway design flood, thus greatly reducing the size of the spillway.

In any event, it is safe to state, categorically, that modern engineering science will continue to provide dams that meet the needs of the day as it has during the past century.

Dams have served man well for many years. The dam of the future will become an even greater instrumentality to serve man's every vital need.

BIBLIOGRAPHY

(1) "Irrigation in India Through Ages," *Leaflet No. 7*, Central Board of Irrigation, Simla, India, January, 1951.

(2) "Middle East Science," by E. B. Worthington, His Majesty's Stationery Office, London, England, August, 1945.

(3) "The Oldest Dam in the World," by B. Hellstrom, *Bulletin No. 28*, Royal Inst. of Technology, Stockholm, Sweden.

(4) "Statistical Summary of Dam Construction," by Robert A. Sutherland (unpublished).

(5) "Reservoirs for Irrigation," by James D. Schuyler, 18th Annual Report, U. S. Geological Survey, U. S. Govt. Printing Office, Washington, D. C., 1897.

(6) "New England Dams and Our Water Resources," by Richard Martin (unpublished paper presented at Sixty-ninth Annual Convention, New England Water Works Assn., Poland Spring, Me., September, 1950).

(7) *Transactions*, ASCE, Vol. 1-116, 1872-1951.

(8) "Lowell Hydraulic Experiments," by James B. Francis, D. Van Nostrand Co., Inc., New York, N. Y., 4th Ed., 1883.

(9) "The Early Years of the Minnesota Section of the American Institute of Electrical Engineers," by Herbert W. Meyer, *The Minnesota Engineer*, May, 1952, p. 5.

(10) "Hydro-electric Power Stations," by David B. Rushmore and Eric A. Lof, John Wiley & Sons, Inc., New York, N. Y., 1917.

(11) "Irrigation in Utah," by Charles H. Brough, Johns Hopkins Press, Baltimore, Md., 1898.

(12) "The Reclamation Program 1948-54," Bureau of Reclamation, U. S. Department of Interior, Washington, D. C., 1947.

(13) "List of Dam Failures," rept. of Hydraulic Power Committee, National Electric Light Assn., New York, N. Y., 1929-1930.

(14) *Transactions*, 4th World Power Conference, London, England, 1950.

(15) "The Design and Construction of Dams," by Edward Wegmann, John Wiley & Sons, Inc., New York, N. Y., 8th Ed., 1927.

(16) "The Manual of American Water-Works," edited by M. N. Baker, The Eng. News Pub. Co., New York, N. Y., 1888.

AMERICAN SOCIETY OF CIVIL ENGINEERS

Founded November 5, 1852

TRANSACTIONS

Paper No. 2605

CONTINUOUS DEVELOPMENT OF DAMS SINCE 1850

By Julian Hinds,[1] M. ASCE

Synopsis

Within the limits of available space, this paper traces the development of dam design and construction. With selected examples, the various types of dam structures are described, and the factors affecting their design are analyzed. The following types are covered: Earth dams, masonry gravity dams, arched dams, buttressed dams, and rock-fill dams.

Introduction

The title of this paper is an invitation to an extensive discourse on the history of the design and construction of dams. However, time and space limit the actual discussion to a brief summary of the transition of the design of such structures from an art to a science. This discussion is drawn mostly from readily available American publications. Fortunately, Edward Wegmann, M. ASCE, in the period from 1888 to 1928, made an intensive study of the history of dams and left a concise statement of his findings in a classical volume (1).[2] With the permission of the publishers, this volume will be freely drawn on, as will be many other books and papers. The summary included in this paper must inevitably be incomplete. Examples are selected as they occur to the writer.

The reference to the transition from an art to a science is made purposely. Early dam building was purely an art, depending solely on experience. However, art is slowly giving way to science, the present tense again being used advisedly. Progress in dam building during the past 100 years is measured largely by the degree of this transition. Mathematics and physical research are being applied with ever-increasing effectiveness, making it possible to venture with safety beyond the limits of previous experience.

Earth Dams

The early history of dam construction is lost in antiquity. According to Wegmann (1), the remains of ancient works still existing in India and Ceylon

[1] General Mgr. and Chf. Engr., United Water Conservation Dist., Los Angeles, Calif.
[2] Numerals in parentheses, thus: (1), refer to corresponding items in the Bibliography at the end of the paper.

bear evidence that the construction of reservoirs for storing water dates from a very remote period of history. The ordinary manner of forming these basins, some of which were of vast extent, consisted of closing a valley by dams of earth, and not until comparatively recent times were walls of masonry employed for such purposes.

It is natural that the earliest dams should have been built of earth, the most abundant and easily handled material. Even today, many engineers consider a scientifically designed and constructed earth embankment, properly located and carefully maintained, the most enduring of man's structures. However, the ancient dam builders had no scientific knowledge of soil mechanics or flood flows, hence their dam building was haphazard and failures were frequent. Lacking even the conception of the possibility of improving the earthen structure, these men concluded that earth was inherently unsuited for dams. Earth dams fell into disrepute, a condition that continued into relatively recent times. In 1888 Wegmann, stated (1a) that

> "* * * where water having great depth is to be retained, it would be extremely hazardous to rely on earthen dams, as numerous failures of such works have been recorded, and walls of masonry are, therefore, employed."

Later, however, Wegmann recognized the earth dam as an adequate structure, but even in 1927, at the very threshold of the science of soil mechanics, he wrote (1b):

> "By the experience of centuries and the lessons taught by many catastrophes the proper dimensions of earthen dams and the precautions that should be observed in their construction have been fully established. The design of such works should not be based on mathematical calculations of equilibrium and safe pressure, as in the case of masonry dams, but upon results found by experience."

Obviously, Wegmann at this time still classified earth dam building as an art, and few if any practicing engineers disagreed with him. These two quotations point up rather dramatically the suddenness with which the science of earth dam design and construction has sprung into being.

Masonry Gravity Dams

Early History.—Just how or when the transition from the ancient earth fill to a supposedly more substantial masonry type occurred is not known to the writer. The first substitution might have been a pile of rock, stanched with earth or sod, or it might have been something else. In any event, the masonry wall eventually became the predominant type. The earliest masonry dams were just as unhampered by scientific considerations as were their predecessors, the earth fills, but being built of firmer materials they were more resistant to abuse (1c):

> "This method of construction seems to have been first adopted in the southern part of Spain where, about the sixteenth century, large reservoirs for irrigation were constructed. Much as these early masonry dams excite our admiration by their great dimensions and massiveness, their proportions

demonstrate that their designers had no correct conception of the forces to be resisted."

Three very old Spanish strucures are illustrated in Fig. 1 (taken from Wegmann). The Almanza Dam (Fig. 1(a)) is reported to be the oldest existing masonry dam, built perhaps in the early sixteenth century. The section has been standing for four centuries. It is built of cut stone facing with rubble masonry interior.

The Alicante Dam (Fig. 1(b)) is of more ample proportions. It was built in the late sixteenth century and, according to Wegmann, is the highest of the old Spanish dams. When constructed, it contained no spillway. One provided later was eventually closed, and the dam acts as an overflow structure with no serious evidence of damage in 300 years of operation. This dam also is faced with cut stone over a rubble masonry interior.

Interesting examples of old Spanish dams could be presented endlessly, alternating between those that are too thin and those that are too thick, but in the interest of brevity the series will be closed with the Puentes Dam (Fig. 1(c)), one that failed. This very pretentious structure was to have been founded on rock, but a deep earth-filled crevice in the center of the channel made such construction impracticable, hence the central part was founded on piles as shown. After 11 years of service, failure occurred by an underwash. The construction and failure of this dam are vividly described by Wegmann (1d).

Notwithstanding their lack of scientific knowledge, the early Spanish dam builders were far in advance of their contemporaries in other parts of the world. The wonder is that, with so little to do with, they accomplished so much. These early dam builders brought their art with them to the Spanish colonies in America. Hundreds of masonry dams were constructed in the semi-arid plateau regions of Mexico, again alternating between too thick and too thin structures, with the thin ones predominating.

Examples from the State of Aguascalientes (2) show the preponderant trend toward a buttressed type dam in this particular region. Dates of construction are difficult to ascertain, but the structures are believed to be early eighteenth century. All are built of rubble masonry known locally as "mamposteria." Some idea of the general appearance of the work can be gained from photographs. The stones are not cut although they are sometimes roughly squared by quarrying methods. The rock generally is rhyolitic in this particular region and the mortar is said to have been made with locally burned hydraulic lime.

The Pabellon Dam (Fig. 2(a)) intercepts the flow of the Pabellon River some 40 km north of the City of Aguascalientes. When this dam was built, a stop-log-controlled spillway was provided in the right abutment, but apparently the logs are never removed. Floods pass over the top of the dam. This operation has been going on for more than 200 years with negligible evidence of damage. The 200-year-old mortar is tightly bonded to the masonry and is harder than the rocks themselves. A close-up of the buttresses and of the masonry facing is shown in Fig. 2(b).

The dam consists of a masonry wall 580 ft long and 77 ft in maximum height. A typical cross section is shown in Fig. 3(a). An analysis of this structure, with

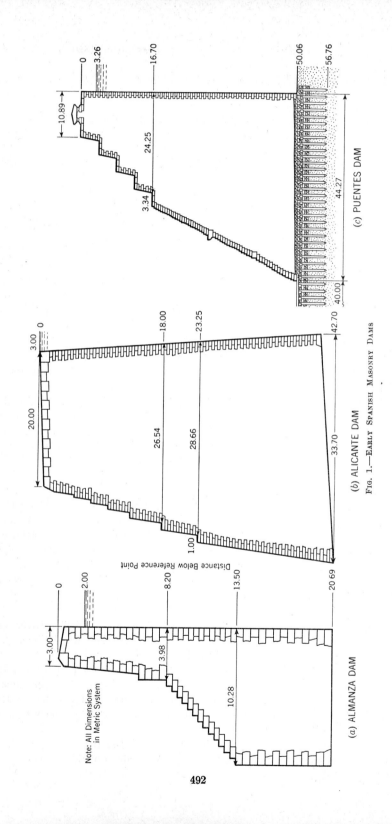

Note: All Dimensions in Metric System

Distance Below Reference Point

(a) ALMANZA DAM

(b) ALICANTE DAM

(c) PUENTES DAM

Fig. 1.—Early Spanish Masonry Dams

492

the buttress and adjacent body action as a T-section (the masonry being assumed to weigh 138 lb per cu ft with no uplift), gives a resultant falling well outside the kern; and yet the structure stands.

(a) GENERAL VIEW

(b) CLOSEUP OF MASONRY

FIG. 2.—PABELLON DAM

An equally interesting structure, known as Presa de los Arcos, is shown in Fig. 4. It has a length of 720 ft and a maximum height of 65 ft. The storage capacity is only a small fraction of the total stream flow, and floods pour directly over the dam. The section in this case is more nearly stable, as illustrated in Fig. 3(b).

A striking example of boldness is found in the San Jose de Guadalupe Dam (Fig. 5(a)). The body of this dam is so thin and the slender buttresses are so widely spaced as to simulate a buttressed wall with a reinforced face. However, the entire structure is of rubble masonry laid in hydraulic lime mortar. As illustrated in Fig. 3(c), the structure is theoretically stable against overturning. The

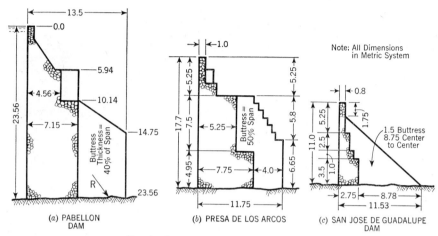

FIG. 3.—CROSS SECTIONS OF MEXICAN DAMS

FIG. 4.—PRESA DE LOS ARCOS

sliding factor is approximately unity. There obviously must be horizontal tension in the face slab. Again, there is a stop-log spillway that is never opened at floodtime. This remarkable structure has stood as an overflow dam for more than 100 years.

The ancient Mexican picture will be ended on a more conservative note with

(a) SAN JOSE DeGUADALUPE DAM

(b) SAUCILLO DAM

FIG. 5.—EARLY MEXICAN DAMS

a view (Fig. 5(b)) of the Saucillo Dam. Dimensions of this structure are not available, but it is obviously of ample proportions, and it has withstood centuries of overpouring waters without appreciable damage. These dams are presented in admiration for the outstanding accomplishments of their artisan builders.

The foregoing few examples are intended merely to show how the art of masonry dam construction started. Once begun, it continued to advance and spread. Both French and Spanish dams developed a regularity of form and a

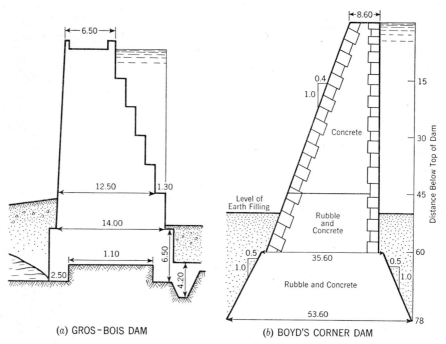

(a) GROS-BOIS DAM   (b) BOYD'S CORNER DAM

FIG. 6.—MASONRY DAM PROFILES

finished architectural appearance quite in contrast to the crude but picturesque early Mexican structures. However, until well into the nineteenth century there was no indication of any understanding of the underlying principles of the gravity dam. This fact is illustrated by the Gros-Bois Dam (Fig. 6(a)) built in France in 1830–1838, the Boyd's Corner Dam (Fig. 6(b)) built in New York State in 1866–1872, and the Folsom Dam (Fig. 7) built in California in 1886–1891.

However, French dams finally began to show an increasing trend toward economy of materials, and about the middle of the nineteenth century, French engineers began the investigation of rational approaches to dam design.

First Scientific Approach.—According to Wegmann (1c) "The first writer who investigated gravity dam design in a satisfactory manner was M. de Sazilly," whose initial paper appeared in 1853. Sazilly introduced the postulates that pressures must be held to safe limits and that there must be no possibility of sliding. He also introduced the idea that the pressures should be considered for reservoir empty as well as for reservoir full. Sazilly, as did many early writers, spent much effort seeking mathematical equations for his dam faces. In this endeavor he was not altogether successful and was forced into a step-by-step design that resulted in polygonal faces. He disliked the reentrant angles of the polygon and consequently recommended a stepped design. Why the step angles were less reentrant or less objectionable is not apparent. However, Sazilly's work marked the beginning of the scientific approach to gravity dam design. His stepped profile for a dam 50 m high is shown in Fig. 8.

The next scientific approach was made by Delocre (1e), another French engineer, who started with Sazilly's basic assumptions, but discarded the ob-

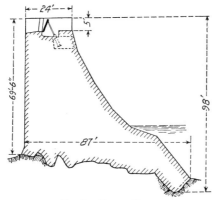

FIG. 7.—FOLSOM DAM

jections to a polygonal profile. He also aspired to mathematical faces and produced involved formulas for this purpose. His standard profile for a 50-m dam is shown in Fig. 9. This form bears considerable resemblance to modern sections. The pressures used were low (6.15 tons per sq ft), which accounts for the wide section.

Neither Sazilly nor Delocre recognized the "law of the middle third" or paid any attention to tension at either face. In addition, it was not recognized that the computed pressures on horizontal planes are smaller than the actual stresses normal to the face.

Attention was directed to these items (prior to 1881) by W. J. M. Rankine of England (1f). Rankine did not arrive at a mathematical relation between pressures on horizontal and normal planes, but proposed that this problem be solved by assuming different allowable unit pressures for the upstream and downstream faces. His recommendations in this respect were based on experience.

Although advocating a section capable of simple derivation, Rankine nevertheless joined the procession in the search for mathematical faces. He chose logarithmic curves, producing the section shown in Fig. 10. This section has less apparent conformity to modern forms than the sections of Figs. 8 and 9.

Accelerated Scientific Studies.—Following the work of the three last named writers, there appeared a rash of theoretical proposals for gravity dam design. Bouvier (1g) proposed to calculate pressures by applying the resultant to a joint laid normal to it, as illustrated in Fig. 11(a). Apparently Bouvier computed R from the forces above section m-n and assumed it to be applied to the part m-a of section m-b, drawn normal to the resultant. Pressures on a-b were

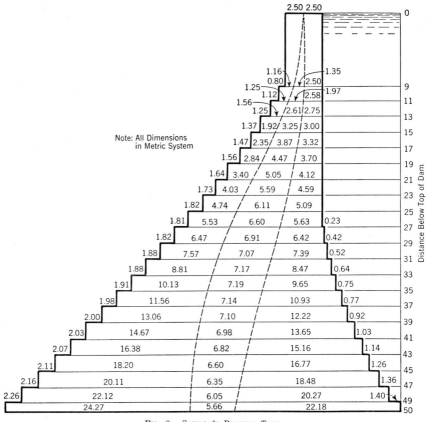

FIG. 8.—SAZILLY'S PROFILE TYPE

ignored. Presumably the pressure computed for a was assumed to apply at n. A device used to illustrate the "rationality" of this approach is shown in Fig. 11(b).

Guillemain suggested the use of inclined sections (1g), as shown in Fig. 12. He proposed that the pressure on section SM be based on the resultant of full water pressure to S and the weight of all the masonry above SM be applied to section SM. This procedure was presumed to give a greater pressure at M than that computed in the usual way for the horizontal joint NM. The inclination of the plane giving maximum pressure was found by trial sections.

Clavinad, around 1887, in an investigation of the failure of La Habra Dam in Algiers (1*h*) came to the conclusion that rupture resulted from shear on a downwardly inclined plane as shown in Fig. 13.

Results Assume Definite Form.—The virtue of the theories so far discussed lies in their influence on students of dam design rather than in inherent merit. They led men's minds toward the need for a scientific approach and laid the

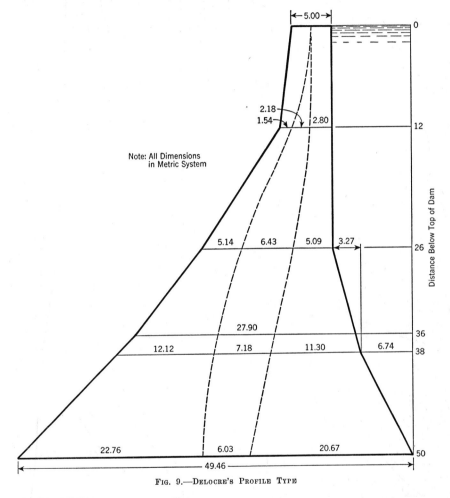

Fig. 9.—Delocre's Profile Type

foundation for the much improved although still imperfect procedures of the present day.

In 1904 L. W. Atcherly, inspired by the work of contemporary writers, suggested the possibility of tension across vertical or nearly vertical planes, particularly near the downstream toe. This theory led to an interesting series of experiments on stress distribution in dams by Atcherly, Pearson, Sir John Ottley, Arthur W. Brightmore, John S. Wilson, and William Gore early in the twentieth century (1*i*). This experimental work led to several interesting conclusions of lasting value (1*j*):

1. Tensile stresses, which may have large local magnitude, occur at the upstream toe.

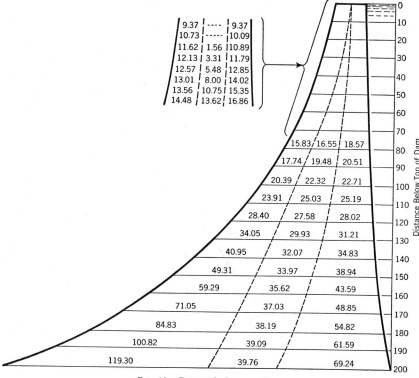

FIG. 10.—RANKINE'S PROFILE TYPE

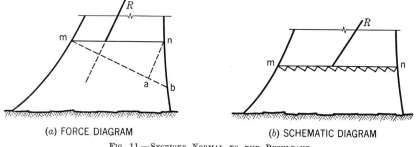

(*a*) FORCE DIAGRAM   (*b*) SCHEMATIC DIAGRAM

FIG. 11.—SECTIONS NORMAL TO THE RESULTANT

2. Tensile stresses occur in no other part of the dam.

3. Owing to the fixity of the base and the change of water pressure at the base, the stresses on the foundation are distributed almost uniformly.

4. For joints above the foundation the usual assumption of the linear distribu-

tion of normal stress on horizontal planes is approximately correct; it overestimates somewhat the maximum intensity of stress.

5. The maximum compressive stresses on the downstream face occur on planes normal to that face.

6. Near the base of the dam the maximum compressive stresses on horizontal planes do not exceed those calculated on the assumption of linear distribution of normal stress.

Although these conclusions were not complete and in some respects were not in full accord with later findings, they were a distinct step forward.

The Introduction of Uplift.—None of the theories heretofore mentioned recognized the possibility of water pressure within or under the dam. However, Morris Levy was contemporaneously working on the problem. About the beginning of the twentieth century he proposed that vertical pressures at all points along the upstream face, with reservoir full (computed without regard to uplift),

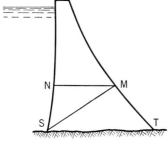

FIG. 12.—INCLINED SECTIONS

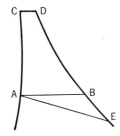

FIG. 13.—INCLINED SHEAR

exceed the hydrostatic pressure. The theory took care of the maximum possible effect of uplift on stresses and overturning, and, if fully carried through, on sliding also.

This proposal was not received with acclaim by most engineers, nor has it been fully accepted to this day. However, it launched an avalanche of discussion and some more or less successful attempts at experimentation. The existence of uplift is now generally admitted, but there continues to be diversity of opinion as to its magnitude.

Levy's principle, if applied to both the upstream face and the submerged part of the downstream face, gives an uplift intensity varying uniformly from headwater pressure at the heel to tailwater pressure, if any, at the toe, applied to the full area of the joint. Except where special control measures are adopted, this pressure intensity distribution has been generally accepted, but opinion differs as to the percentage of the cross-sectional area subject to pressure. There are strenuous advocates of the postulate that the dam "must have some solid support" and therefore the area subject to pressure must be less than the whole. A related theory is that actual molecular contact capable of excluding water under pressure must exist over a substantial part of any joint capable of sustaining tension.

Various attempts have been made by the advocates of these theories to determine the percentage of pressure area experimentally or by statistical methods. Masonry and rock are looked on by them as essentially solid materials permeated with small interconnected holes or pores. Barring faulty construction, uplift pressures are assumed to act only within these pores. Volumetric voids, determined by the absorption of water, run from 4% to 6% for concrete. Ingenious mathematical devices have been developed for computing the areas of these voids intersected by a joint. In an exhaustive study of this theory, D. C. Henny, M. ASCE (3), in 1934 concluded that the pressure area varies with the stress in the concrete and recommended values ranging from 25% to 40% of the total.

Many contemporary writers agreed with Henny, although the pressure areas in use were generally somewhat more liberal than 25% to 40%. The most common practice at the time was to assume pressure areas of from one third to two thirds of the total. Similar rules are still in use.

However, there is an opposite school of thought with many advocates. In discussing Henny's paper, Karl Terzaghi, Hon. M. ASCE, presented the results of carefully conducted experiments purporting to show a pressure area of at least 95% (3a). His experiments were thoroughly convincing to those who favored a full pressure area, but not to those who opposed such a theory. Other engineers have attempted experiments, generally with indifferent success. The problem is inherently difficult.

In 1949, L. F. Harza, M. ASCE, presented a theoretical discussion of the subject defending the theory of full pressure area (4). Again there was a mixture of agreement and dissent. The problem of creating a unified opinion on the subject remains unsolved, except that it seems generally agreed the full area is active in a defective joint.

Foundations of important dams are now provided with grout curtains near the upstream face to make this part of the foundation tighter than the average. Thus, there is a sudden drop in the uplift intensity gradient as the seepage enters the foundation. Further relief may be secured by drilling drainage holes into the foundation downstream from the grout curtain.

Maximum Stresses.—Although Rankine proposed that maximum pressures were on other than horizontal planes, and Wilson, Gore, et al., in conclusion 5 stated correctly that the maximum stress is on a plane normal to the face, none of them (as far as the writer knows) proposed a rule for finding such stresses. This seems to have been first done by William Cain, M. ASCE, who, in 1909, from a mechanics of materials principle, concluded that the stress on a plane normal to an unloaded dam face is equal to the corresponding stress on a horizontal plane times the square of the secant of the inclination of the face to the vertical (5). Subject to correction where the face sustains an external normal load (such as water pressure), this rule is still in general use. Cain also assumed trapezoidal distribution of normal pressure on horizontal planes (conclusions 3 and 4 previously mentioned). His conclusions have been investigated subsequently by many engineers and have been found inexact, but near enough to the truth for all ordinary structures.

Shear Distribution Across Horizontal Sections.—Cain also established rules for computing shear distribution across horizontal sections, thus making it possible to add shearing strength to friction as a resistance to horizontal displacement. Although discussed by previous writers, most designers still looked on shear strength as unreliable and continued to depend solely on friction. Because of allegedly improved methods of bonding construction joints, the practice of using a combined shear-friction factor rather than friction alone is now becoming widespread. Such a proposal made by Henny in 1934 (3) was enlarged on by Ivan E. Houk and Kenneth B. Keener, Members, ASCE, in 1941 (6).

Internal Stresses.—Cain's paper (5) also provided for the computation of principal stresses at points within the dam section. In gravity dams of ordinary dimensions such computations are not usually required, since as with the Cain assumptions maximum principal stresses occur at the faces.

Following Cain's paper, the subject of internal stresses in gravity dams lay dormant for a few years, but was revived about 1920 as a result of diagonal cracks observed in the buttresses of hollow dams. A further revival accompanied the analyses of Hoover (Arizona-Nevada), Shasta (California), and Grand Coulee (Washington) dams by the Bureau of Reclamation, United States Department of the Interior.

It was reasoned that, in concrete dams of great thickness upstream and downstream, cracks parallel to the axis and more or less vertical are caused by setting shrinkage. It was hoped that a knowledge of internal stresses would help in combating these cracks. Also, with higher dams and higher allowed stresses the intensity of special stresses at corners and elsewhere became important, leading to analysis and experimentation. An excellent paper on the subject was presented by J. H. A. Brahtz in 1936 (7).

The net result of all experimentation of this kind has not ruled out the simple theory of straight-line distribution for the practical design of structures of ordinary dimensions. However, it has been proved that rules are not exact, and very valuable data have been accumulated. Great pains are now being taken in the design of large dams to insure that vertical shrinkage cracks shall not occur on planes carrying appreciable shear.

Crest Shape, Overflow Dams.—Early builders gave little thought as to whether a dam was to be subject to overflow in determining its shape. Eventually some attention began to be paid to this item, and a rounded top was found to be preferable. At first the rounding was haphazard, but in 1929 W. P. Creager, Hon. M. ASCE (8), proposed fitting the crest to the lower nappe of the discharge from a sharp-crested weir, using H. Bazin's experimental nappe, as illustrated in Fig. 14. This proposal subsequently was tested by other experimenters and with a slight later revision by Creager is now accepted as standard.

Beam or Slab Action in Gravity Dams.—Gravity dams generally have been designed just as if each unit stood alone, like a cantilever. Actually, a straight gravity dam, as generally constructed, also possesses horizontal beam or slab strength. In a narrow canyon this action may be appreciable and not necessarily beneficial at all points. The interaction of horizontal, vertical, and inclined elements presents a complex analytical situation not too well understood as to method or necessity by the engineering profession generally. The subject has been thoroughly studied by engineers of the Bureau of Reclamation (9).

ARCHED DAMS

Although the arch was widely used by the ancients for other purposes, there is little evidence of its early use in dam construction. An isolated example is the Zola Dam built in France about 1843. Another is the Meer Allum Dam (a multiple arch structure) built in India about 1806. However, arch dams began to appear in number only near the end of the nineteenth century. Because of experience in the computation of arch stresses in other structures, arch dams approached a basis of partial rationality with reasonable rapidity.

Cylinder Theory.—Early arch dam stresses were computed on the theory that the arch ring is a part of a thin cylinder subject to a uniform normal load. This theory still is widely used for preliminary design purposes and occasionally for the final design of dams of restricted size, although its limitations

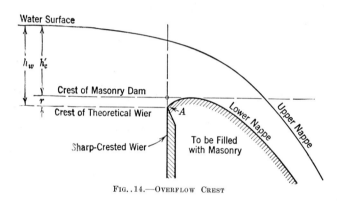

FIG. 14.—OVERFLOW CREST

are recognized. It makes no allowance for elastic effects produced by shortening under load, shortening caused by average temperature drop, deformation resulting from radial temperature variation, foundation deformations, and other factors.

Elastic Analysis.—Early attempts to compute more accurately the stresses in the arches of dams followed the procedures available for the continuous arches of bridges and other structures. These procedures were valid for dams, but usually involved nonintegrable factors requiring arithmetical integration, which is laborious.

In 1922 Cain presented a method of analysis for cylindrical arches under uniform normal loads (10) which eliminated most of the drudgery of arithmetical integration. Although incomplete as to theory, Cain's method was a distinct step forward.

As first presented, Cain's formulas made no allowance for shear deformation, a factor which is negligible in thin arches but important in thick ones. This omission was later corrected. Allowance was made for rib shortening caused by average temperature drop, but the effect of radial temperature variation was ignored. No allowance was made for foundation deformation. Nevertheless, the Cain equations are far superior to the thin cylinder theory and adequate for the design of most arch dams.

In 1927 B. F. Jakobsen somewhat expanded the Cain formulas, particularly for thick arches (11). He introduced shear deformations and equations for finding the true neutral axis, but did not include abutment deformation or radial temperature variation.

Although arch analysis by the Cain and Jakobsen formulas is infinitely easier than arithmetical integration, the use of these equations in the design of an arch dam is still time consuming. These formulas are for analyzing selected arches, not for finding them. Sections must be selected at various depths, tested, and revised until correct. To facilitate this procedure, much study has been devoted to the development of computation aids. Prominent among these are F. H. Fowler's (Past-President ASCE) curves (12) and a set of solution tables by R. S. Lieurance (13). These aids are useful tools at least in preliminary investigations, although they necessarily involve certain simplifying limitations.

Arches of Variable Thickness.—Unfortunately, a simple cylinder is not the ideal shape for the arch of a dam. Stresses in such an arch are appreciably greater at the abutments than at the crown, for which reason an arch of variable thickness is preferable. The best arch action and economy are promoted by thickening the third quarter of the arch next to the abutment, producing what may be called a fillet arch. The Cain and Jakobsen formulas are not applicable to such an arch. By combining a simple circle for the upstream face with a compound intrados, the extent of departure from the elastic cylinder analysis can be held to a minimum. However, such a section is not algebraically integrable, and resort must be made to at least partial arithmetical integration. A method of analyzing this special form was previously proposed by the writer (14a). By imposing certain restrictions, it would be possible to compute a set of integrals for fillet arches; but, because of the number of independent variables, such a table would be voluminous.

As a compromise between the fillet arch and a simple cylinder, several writers have proposed an arch gradually thickening all the way from crown to abutment. This design is intended to facilitate solution by tables or graphs. Two separate writers, A. L. Parme, A. M. ASCE (15), and W. A. Perkins, M. ASCE (16), have developed solution methods, diagrams, and tables for this purpose. These devices necessarily require certain compromises with best shapes and omit or simplify some theoretical factors. The results are adequate for preliminary design and in many cases for final design.

Control of Shrinkage and Temperature Stresses.—Concrete changes in volume with changing moisture content. However, loaded dams are generally moist and shrinkage stresses caused by drying out are not likely to be severe. Most net shrinkage is the result of the drop from high setting temperatures to ultimate normal values. In arch dams this is an important factor, introducing bending moments and secondary stresses that may far exceed the normal arch thrust. In all properly planned structures this factor is controlled. The dam is divided into blocks by radial vertical joints, closed at the faces by grout stops. The structure is left unloaded until it has reached its normal temperature, or it may be cooled artificially. The joints are then filled with neat cement grout under pressure. Setting shrinkage is thus nullified. For thick arches subsequent temperature changes are moderate.

Elimination of Tensile Areas from Computations.—One difficulty with the Cain-Jakobsen formulas and the computation aids previously mentioned is that the concrete arch is treated as if it were capable of sustaining tensile stresses. Most engineers doubt the dependability of the tensile strength of concrete although not all agree that serious error results from arch computations that include a tension factor. The most general method for eliminating the tensile strength effect is to make a trial solution on an assumed section, eliminate tension areas (for computation purposes), and repeat the analysis, continuing until a so-called net section, free from tension, is found. This procedure produces a more conservative estimate of stresses than if tension is assumed permissible, but

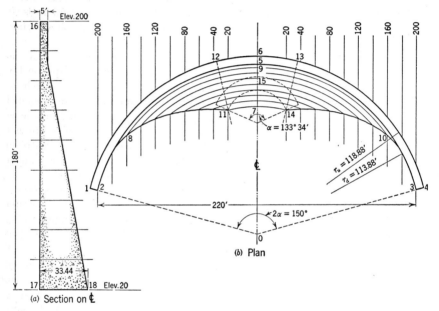

(a) Section on ℄

(b) Plan

FIG. 15.—CONSTANT-RADIUS ARCH DAM

involves many complications and uncertainties. It requires endless repetition of arithmetical integration. For important dams many designers, including the writer, prefer to make the final test on this basis.

Arch Dam Types.—Before the design of individual arches can be begun, the general form of the dam must be chosen. The simplest form is the single-centered or so-called constant-radius type (Fig. 15). This type is primarily suited to U-shaped canyons. For the usual V-shaped canyon, the radius should be reduced with depth. Ideally, each arch should be designed for its individual water load and span, and the separate slices stacked up to form the dam. This plan is impracticable for actual sites. A compromise is the variable-radius type dam (Fig. 16). The exact origin of this type is unknown to the author, but it was promoted by Lars Jorgensen, M. ASCE, in the early part of the present century (17). It can be noted from Fig. 16 that this dam avoids overhang except in the upstream abutment areas where rock can be left in place to support the over-hanging concrete.

There is considerable prejudice against overhang at the downstream crown, for construction and other reasons. However, dams with overhang are now being constructed (18), the center-line profile of an actual example being shown in Fig. 17. Appreciable economy may be effected by this method, but closure difficulties are increased.

Interaction of Horizontal and Vertical Elements.—The procedures so far discussed apply to separate arches, each considered to be independent of its neighbors. In a dam this is not actually true. The arches near the bottom of the canyon are restrained by the foundation. This restraint, in diminishing

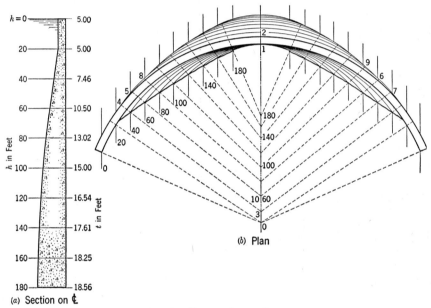

(a) Section on ℄

(b) Plan

FIG. 16.—VARIABLE-RADIUS DAM

amount, is passed upward to other arches. In high dams such as Hoover Dam (Fig. 18), in which the bottom arches are thick, the interaction becomes complex and important. If arch and secondary stresses are to be known with a reasonable degree of certainty, this interaction must be analyzed. An analysis is made by the trial-load method, in which the water load is divided between the horizontal and vertical elements of the dam. First a system of sample horizontal and vertical elements is chosen. A trial division of water load is made between them and the deflections of the elements are computed. If the resulting deflections of the horizontal and vertical systems are identical, the trial-load division is assumed correct; otherwise a new trial is made. This procedure is repeated until the requirements of continuity are satisfied. The origin of the trial-load idea is not known to the writer, but it was being urged by F. A. Noetzli, M. ASCE, about 1920. The idea was taken up by the writer and others in the Denver (Colo.) office of the Bureau of Reclamation. The first proposal contemplated the use of several

arch elements and a single cantilever at the crown. The number of elements
was increased as computation methods were developed.

About 1925 A. C. Jacquith of the Bureau of Reclamation supervised the

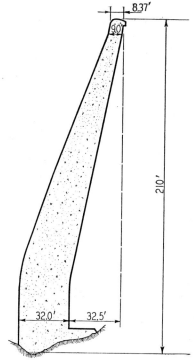

FIG. 17.—SWEETWATER FALLS DAM NEAR SAN DIEGO, CALIF.

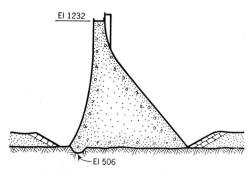

FIG. 18.—HOOVER DAM (ARIZONA-NEVADA) SECTION

design of a dam in Arizona on the basis of a limited trial-load theory. In 1927
the writer advanced the procedure a step further in preparing designs for the
Calles Dam (Fig. 19), in Aguascalientes, Mexico. In this design, an adequate
number of both horizontal and vertical elements was used, but only simple

radial deflections were considered. This procedure was adequate for the Calles Dam in which trial-load analysis was perhaps not essential, but later was found inadequate for Hoover Dam and other dams of great magnitude.

A searching study of trial-load needs and procedures has been made by engineers of the Bureau of Reclamation during the past 25 years. Many factors in addition to simple radial deflections have been found important, including tangential deflections, tangential shearing stresses between adjacent arches, and torsional forces resulting from the rotation of arch and cantilever elements.

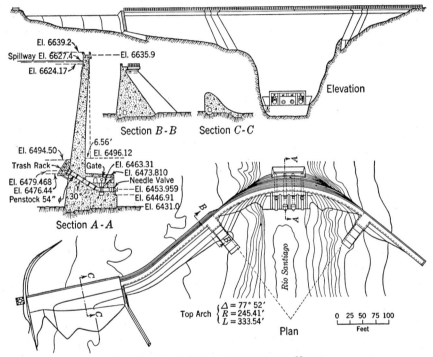

FIG. 19.—CALLES DAM IN AGUASCALIENTES, MEXICO

Many papers on the subject have been published by personnel of the Bureau of Reclamation, and detailed procedures are described in several official bulletins.

Some designers attempt to reduce or avoid cantilever action by providing a flexible joint between the lower part or base of the dam and the higher arches. Such a device has been used on several dams including the one illustrated in Fig 17.

Importance of Trial-Load Analysis.—There is perhaps a tendency among certain groups of engineers in the United States to overstress the importance of trial-load analysis. There is little, if any, doubt that such analysis is important if not essential for a structure such as Hoover Dam (Fig. 18). For the Calles Dam (Fig. 19) separate arch analysis would no doubt suffice. As a rule, large structures or those with complicated canyon profiles should be tested by trial load. Small or simple structures with relatively thin arches may be designed as simple separate arches.

A recent review of this question (19) shows a lack of sympathy for trial-load analysis in Europe. However, most of the arches illustrated in the review occupied such favorable sites that complicated computations were unnecessary.

Foundation Yielding.—The possible importance of foundation yielding on arch deflections and stresses was recognized early, but the problem is complex and its solution is progressing slowly. An important step leading to at least approximate solution was made by Frederik Vogt (20) with his equations for average deformation caused by a uniform load on a plane rectangular isotropic foundation of infinite extent. A method for applying these equations to arch dam design is available (14*b*).

BUTTRESSED DAMS

An important dam type that has been introduced during the present century consists of multiple units of concrete arches or flat slabs supported on buttresses. Two fundamental features of such dams are that their inclined faces utilize water pressure to give over-all stability and their restricted bases (when founded on rock) practically eliminate uplift. The slab-and-buttress dam (but not the multiple arch dam) is rated as well suited to the resistance of earthquake forces.

By properly choosing the face slope and buttress dimensions, both foundation and masonry stresses are readily controlled. The resultant can be (but seldom is) made to intersect the base at its center, thus producing at least theoretically a uniform foundation pressure.

Flat Slab Dams.—The flat slab type of buttress dam had its beginnning early in the present century along with the expanding use of reinforced concrete for other purposes. A small hollow dam of concrete and steel at Theresa, N. Y. (21), was the first constructed. The predecessors of the present Ambursen Hydraulic Construction Company recognized the importance of the idea and took up the design and construction of similar structures. Many such dams have been built since, continually increasing in size and importance. Details have been improved to keep pace with advances in other reinforced-concrete fields, but the original basic principle still prevails—a flat slab supported on buttresses. A typical example is shown in Fig. 20.

Multiple Arch Dams.—As the slab-and-buttress dam rose in popularity, proposals were made to substitute a series of arches for the flat face slabs. It was claimed that wider buttress spacing, thinner facing, and less reinforcing steel offered a favorable cost comparison. Many such dams were built during the first quarter of the present century. A typical example is shown in Fig. 21.

The arches of a multiple arch dam are analyzed just as are those for a simple arch dam, except that load intensity varies from crown to abutment. The thickness may or may not vary, and simple or multicentered arches can be used.

Design of Buttresses.—The slabs and arches of buttressed dams have given little trouble, but some of the larger early buttresses developed alarming shrinkage cracks. In later dams such cracking was controlled by reinforcing steel and by built-in cracks along lines of low shearing stresses.

Resistance to sidewise buckling is usually provided by flanges and by struts between buttresses. In 1924 Noetzli (22) proposed a hollow buttress that combined stability with a pleasing appearance. Transverse strength is perhaps more important for the buttresses of a multiple arch dam than for the flat slab type.

Buttressed Dams on Soft Foundations.—By using spread footings, a buttressed dam may be built on a foundation inadequate for other masonry types, but care

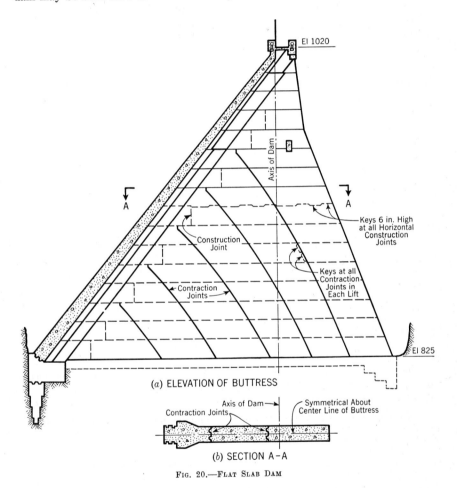

(*a*) ELEVATION OF BUTTRESS

(*b*) SECTION A–A

FIG. 20.—FLAT SLAB DAM

must be used to prevent underwash. In the case of sand and gravel or similar materials, the whole foundation may be covered with a reinforced slab on which the dam is constructed. Precautions against underflow must, of course, be taken.

ROCK-FILL DAMS

An important and not too generally understood dam is the dumped rock fill, a type that deserves far more space than can be given here (23). An extensive history of rock fills and other dam types was published by J. D. Schuyler, M. ASCE, in 1909 (24).

Rock-fill dams were first extensively developed in California about the time of the gold rush (1848) and were useful in remote locations where equipment and materials for other types of dam were expensive or nonexistent. Rock-fill dams were an outgrowth of the rock-filled timber crib, the timber being reduced and finally omitted with increasing size of structure.

The design of these dams has not been reduced to a scientific basis to the same extent as has that of concrete and earth dams. No mathematical rules for stresses and strains are available. However, at the present time such dams are not being constructed in the haphazard manner of the early masonry dams. They have been observed, studied, and tested by trained engineers, fully aware

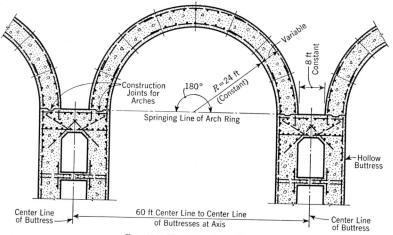

FIG. 21.—MULTIPLE ARCH DAM

of the general principles of dam design. Important details that make for success or failure have been carefully worked out. The building of rock-fill dams is still largely an art, but a fully rationalized one.

The cross-sectional form of the rock fill and the methods of construction have varied considerably during the development period. Typical sections are shown in Fig. 22 (23).

The four types shown indicate progress from cheap labor and poor machinery to high priced labor and good machinery from about 1900 to 1952. Many examples of these types exist. Each consists of a combination of loose rock fill and placed dry rubble facing and some kind of impervious upstream membrane.

Loose rock fills are subject to appreciable settlement, a situation which calls for heavy camber at the time of construction and careful design of the upstream impervious apron. Progressive experience has developed rules for alleviating the difficulties resulting from settlement and other factors, a few of which are:

a. Only strong sound rock of large size, clean and free from quarry muck or other fines should be used.

b. The foundation should be unyielding, preferably good rock.

c. The fill should be copiously sluiced during construction.

d. The dry rubble must be carefully built of large stones with stable rock to rock contact, using small rocks or spalls for chinking if required.

e. Both horizontal and vertical camber should be provided to allow for contemplated settlement.

f. The impervious membrane must be designed to withstand the expected settlement.

g. At steep abutments, differential settlement between fill and canyon wall requires special consideration to avoid rupture of impervious membrane.

The impervious membrane may be of concrete or timber or, rarely, of steel. Timber facing is likely to be lacking in watertightness and is used only where

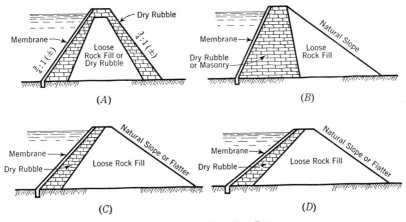

FIG. 22.—TYPICAL ROCK-FILL DAMS

moderate leakage is unimportant. It is sometimes used temporarily while the dam is settling. The timber usually is placed in multiple layers with calked joints, sometimes with a waterproofing material between layers.

Concrete membranes are reinforced and must possess flexibility to allow for settlement, particularly at the abutments.

The Salt Springs Dam (Fig. 23), on the Mokelumne River in central California, is a good example of a modern rock-fill dam. Constructed by the Pacific Gas and Electric Company in 1931, it is the highest (328 ft) and one of the largest rock-fill dams.

Composite Earth and Rock Dams.—Under suitable conditions, an excellent dam can be produced by combining a loose rock fill downstream and an earth upstream section. The earth part replaces the watertight membrane, and proper precautions against rupture of this section are essential.

The earth part may also be located within the rock fill as either a vertical or an inclined impervious core. Great caution is required in the construction of filter zones to prevent leaching of the core materials into the open rock fill.

MISCELLANEOUS MINOR TYPES

Several minor dam types that played important parts in early hydraulic history cannot be discussed here. Among these are steel, timber, and rock-crib dams. Although they were of considerable temporary and local importance, their contribution to progress in dam design was not great.

A recent type of some promise is the roundhead buttress dam, a buttress type in which the flat slab or arch is replaced by a bulbous head on each of the arches. The most important example to date is the Don Martin Dam constructed in Mexico in 1928. It possesses some of the virtues, and eliminates some of the difficulties, of the gravity dam, but so far has received little recognition.

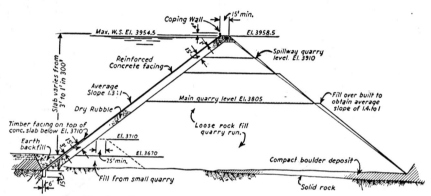

FIG. 23.—SALT SPRINGS DAM ON THE MOKELUMNE RIVER IN CALIFORNIA

MISCELLANEOUS INFLUENCES

Foundations.—To this point, discussion has been directed toward progress in the design of the dam structure itself. There are many subsidiary factors that also must be considered. An important one is the investigation of foundations. The ancients could rely on visual inspection for selection of dam sites because sites on exposed bedrock were available. This is no longer true. The engineer must be able to see underground if costly mistakes are to be avoided. A variety of procedures has been devised for accomplishing this: Core drilling, seismic testing, tunnels, test pits, and open cuts. The services of the geologist, the petrographer, the testing laboratory, and other scientific aids have been enlisted. Foundation testing has progressed markedly during the past half century.

Earthquake Forces.—Another newly recognized factor in the field of dam design is allowance for earthquake forces. As dam design moves toward a more scientific basis there is a tendency to hew ever closer to the limits of safety. This requires careful watch for possible neglected unfavorable influences. Earthquake action was not mentioned by early writers. Serious consideration of such forces in gravity dams began some 30 years ago.

The direct effect of an earthquake on any structure, including dams, is complex. However, fairly definite rules for simple cases are available. In the case of a dam an additional and even more complicated problem is introduced by the action of the water in the reservoir.

The subject of earthquake forces has been covered by many writers. A paper by H. M. Westergaard, M. ASCE (25), published in 1933, is comprehensive and is particularly useful to the dam designer.

Ice Pressures.—Allowance for the pressure exerted by an ice sheet on a dam is a comparatively modern innovation. Ice long has been known to expand and contract with changes in temperature. An expanding ice sheet can exert pressure on a dam, but little is known of the magnitude of such pressure. An absolute maximum pressure is the crushing strength of ice, which for a quickly applied load may be as high as 70 tons per sq ft. That actual pressures against dams never reach such a value is proved by the fact that many dams are standing today that otherwise would have failed. From experiments made at McGill University (Montreal, Que., Canada) in 1932 (26), it has been concluded that maximum field pressures are far below this level. The writer's analysis of the problem is available elsewhere (14c) and is too involved to be repeated here.

Spillway Capacity.—No element of dam design has been more discussed during the past 50 years than spillway capacity, nor is any other element in a more unsettled condition today. The reason is obvious. The operations of nature, at least in the matter of flood flows, are unpredictable and conform to no known mathematical formula.

Vast hydrographic data-gathering systems are in operation throughout the world, recording stream flows and collecting other information. In the United States, these records cover a relatively short period. New floods, greater than any ever known before, are continually appearing, and design spillway capacities go up. In terms of spillway costs the results are often frightening, but not as much as would be failure of a dam above a populous community. Great progress is being made in collection and analysis of data, and it is hoped that a safe and sane basis for spillway design will be available in the near future.

Reservoir Outlet Controls.—Water stored behind dams must be released to be useful for most purposes. Release is effected by a controlled opening through or around the dam. Early outlets were controlled by crude wooden devices. In fact the crudest wooden plug and pole devices are still in use on many very old dams. In some old structures, release was through a stop-log opening from the top to the bottom of the dam, the logs being removed one at a time to maintain flow.

As heights of dams and sizes of outlet passages increased, it became necessary to formalize outlet control devices. Wooden slide gates were developed followed by gate valve types of controls and steel and cast-iron slide gates. These devices were usually near the inlet end of the outlet opening. If the head was high, they gave trouble. If operated at part opening they were destroyed by vibration and cavitation. Iron castings were dissolved like sugar or were shattered by impact. Air introduced just below the control was found helpful. However, the old types could not cope with ever-increasing heads and discharges. They were made bigger and stronger, but still they failed.

Then, early in the present century, the needle valve appeared. It was hailed as a panacea but was soon found to have its faults. Early needle valves were placed at or near the conduit entrance. At part opening, large reductions in momentum occurred within the conduit, and destructive forces were developed.

A copious supply of air at the valve reduced this effect, but action was still imperfect. The needle valve was then moved to the outlet end of the conduit permitting energy destruction to occur harmlessly in open air. This was a great step forward.

However, the valves themselves were heavy and expensive. The larger ones were self-actuated—that is, opened and closed by pressure from the water flowing through them. With the passing of time, needle valves have been steadily improved. Present models are simpler, better, and, on a comparable price basis, cheaper. In the latest model the needle point has disappeared, resulting in the so-called hollow jet valve developed in recent years by the Bureau of Reclamation.

The fixed-dispersion cone type (Howell-Bunger) valve, a simple competitor of the hollow jet, delivers its flow in the form of an expanding cone. Many valves of this type have been installed and are operating successfully. The spreading discharge is objectionable where spray is troublesome, but it greatly simplifies the problem of stilling the flow.

In important installations it is necessary to provide a second line of defense so that the primary control valve may be repaired or replaced. This is accomplished by a second gate just upstream from the control valve or near the conduit inlet. The gates are too numerous to describe in detail here. Descriptions are available from many sources. Primary types are slide gates at the conduit inlet, gate valve type devices, butterfly gates, and cone valves. Guard gates are not designed for operation at part opening.

In concrete dams the outlet pipe or opening usually passes directly through the structure. For earth and rock-fill dams the outlet is preferably carried around the end of the structure in the tunnel.

Spillway Forms.—Spillway structures take many forms. The most popular is the gravity overflow directed squarely down the stream channel. This type is not always feasible or economical. An expensive but useful type is the side-channel spillway. There are also the morning glory type and endless other varieties. A popular spillway, particularly with earth and rock-fill dams, consists of a chute or overflow crest in a rock saddle completely removed from the dam.

Side-channel and other spillways close to the structure of a fill dam require concrete-lined channels all the way to the stream bed, and unless they discharge onto good rock may require stilling basins at their ends. Velocity-reducing facilities also are needed at the base of an overflow gravity section unless conditions are particularly favorable. The most popular stilling device is the hydraulic jump. If the tailwater depth is great, the jump may occur naturally, otherwise it must be induced by baffles, piers, walls, or other momentum-reducing devices. The value of the hydraulic jump as a stilling device was worked out by the engineers of the Miami Conservancy District of Ohio prior to 1920 (27).

Spillways of all types may be controlled or uncontrolled. Control may be accomplished by an endless variety of flashboards and automatic-tripping devices, as well as by the more formal drum and radial gates. The last two devices are growing in both size and popularity. Schematic drum-gate and radial-gate installations are illustrated in Fig. 24, sketched from actual designs. Radial gates may be hand or power operated, with or without counterweights, and control may or may not be automatic. Drum gates are operated by pressure of the reservoir water, manually or automatically controlled.

Arch dams are sometimes permitted to spill in a clear leap directly over the crest or through any type spillway around the end of the dam. Parker Dam

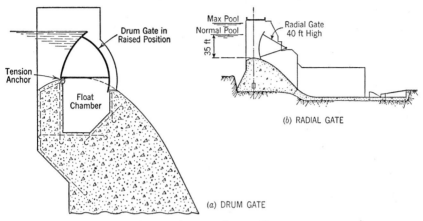

FIG. 24.—OVERFLOW CONTROL VALVES

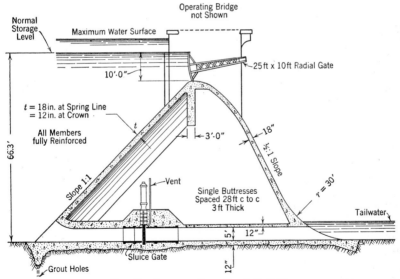

FIG. 25.—SPILLWAY OVER BUTTRESS DAM

(Arizona-California) is an outstanding example of an overpour arch. This spillway is controlled by five 50-ft by 50-ft vertical gates discharging into the stream below the dam. The action is made perfect by a more than 200-ft-deep pool.

Spillways for buttressed dams may be of any of the forms discussed. A controlled direct overflow over a buttressed dam is illustrated in Fig. 25.

Concrete Quality.—The quality of concrete is receiving much attention at the present time. Modern concrete, as used in the United States during the past 30 years is a far more speculative material than the stone masonry of the early dam builders. Although splendid results are being achieved generally, there are occasional unexplained failures. Much effort is being expended to find a solution to this problem, including the study of cements, aggregates, proportions, and admixtures. The troublesome interaction between cement alkalies and certain aggregate elements appears on the way to solution. The entrainment of air seems to be solving the problem of deterioration resulting from freezing and thawing. Other durability problems are being similarly dealt with.

Control of Cracking.—If there are no defects in design or masonry, cracking in gravity and massive arch dams results primarily from shrinkage at the time of setting, which in turn is largely the result of a temperature drop from high setting values to normal. The setting temperature is determined by the composition of the cement, the amount used, and the rate of placement. In ancient stone masonry dams cracking was not a problem. The lime mortar used probably had a low caloric value, its volume compared to the whole dam was relatively small, and placement was slow—offering maximum opportunity for heat dissipation before hardening.

In modern concrete dams, rapidly constructed, all elements are adverse to thorough cooling prior to full set. As a result, shrinkage cracks are likely to occur unless specially controlled. Special control methods in use include:

(1) Concrete is placed in thin layers with ample cooling time between successive lifts. This interferes with rapid placement and is being gradually abandoned.

(2) Aggregate grading is carefully controlled to insure a minimum cement content.

(3) Special low-heat cements are used.

(4) In hot weather, concrete aggregates can be precooled and ice can be added instead of mixing water to reduce potential setting temperatures.

(5) Cooling of the concrete may be hastened by circulating cold water or refrigerated brine through a grid of pipes cast into the structure for this purpose. Enormous refrigerating plants have been used for the cooling of Hoover, Shasta, and other recent dams.

(6) Large structures are built in sections, cooled, and united by grouting. Hoover Dam was constructed as a mass of very large interlocking columns, cooled, and joined by pressure grouting.

Progress in Construction Methods.—Very little has been mentioned in this paper about progress in dam construction procedures. It would be unfortunate if this omission were interpreted as implying that this subject is unimportant. In fact, much of the progress in the planning of dams has been made effective by improvements in construction practices. The transition from hand power and animal power to mechanical power has been spectacular and nearly complete, passing from manpower to horsepower, to steam, to internal combustion engines, and to electricity. Thousands of ingenious machines and devices have been brought to the aid of the builder, as well as materials in an abundance of varieties. These things are just as essential to the great dam projects of today as is technical knowledge of dam design. However, that is another story, the details of which cannot be told here.

BIBLIOGRAPHY

(1) "The Design and Construction of Dams," by Edward Wegmann, John Wiley & Sons, Inc., New York, N. Y., 1st Ed., 1888; 8th Ed., 1927. (*a*) 1st Ed., Preface. (*b*) 8th Ed., p. 221. (*c*) 8th Ed., p. 1. (*d*) 8th Ed., p. 57. (*e*) 8th Ed., p. 2. (*f*) 8th Ed., p. 3. (*g*) 8th Ed., p. 6. (*h*) 8th Ed., p. 7. (*i*) 8th Ed., p. 9. (*j*) 8th Ed., p. 10.

(2) "200-Year-Old Masonry Dams in Use in Mexico," by Julian Hinds, *Engineering News-Record*, September 1, 1932, p. 251.

(3) "Stability of Straight Concrete Gravity Dams," by D. C. Henny, *Transactions*, ASCE, Vol. 99, 1934, p. 1041. (*a*) p. 1107.

(4) "The Significance of Pore Pressure in Hydraulic Structures," by L. F. Harza, *ibid.*, Vol. 114, 1949, p. 193.

(5) "Stresses in Masonry Dams," by William Cain, *ibid.*, Vol. 64, 1909, p. 208.

(6) "Basic Design Assumptions," in "Masonry Dams: A Symposium," by Ivan E. Houk and Kenneth B. Keener, *ibid.*, Vol. 106, 1941, p. 1115.

(7) "The Stress Function and Photoelasticity Applied to Dams," by J. H. A. Brahtz, *ibid.*, Vol. 101, 1936, p. 1240.

(8) "Engineering for Masonry Dams," by William P. Creager, John Wiley & Sons, Inc., New York, N. Y., 1929, p. 106.

(9) "Reclamation Manual," Bureau of Reclamation, U. S. Dept. of the Interior, Washington, D. C., Vol. X, 1950.

(10) "The Circular Arch Under Normal Loads," by William Cain, *Transactions*, ASCE, Vol. 85, 1922, p. 233.

(11) "Stresses in Thick Arches of Dams," by B. F. Jakobsen, *ibid.*, Vol. 90, 1927, p. 475.

(12) "A Graphic Method for Determining Stresses in Circular Arches Under Normal Loads by the Cain Formulas," by Frederick Hall Fowler, *ibid.*, Vol. 92, 1928, p. 1512.

(13) "Design of Arch Dams," in "Masonry Dams: A Symposium," by R. S. Lieurance, *ibid.*, Vol. 106, 1941, p. 1131.

(14) "Engineering for Dams," by William P. Creager, Joel D. Justin, and Julian Hinds, John Wiley & Sons, Inc., New York, N. Y. 1945. (*a*) p. 492. (*b*) p. 440. (*c*) p. 270.

(15) "Arch Dams With Arches of Variable Thickness," by Alfred L. Parme, Reinforced Concrete, Portland Cement Assn., Chicago, Ill., No. 21.

(16) "Analysis of Arch Dams of Variable Thickness," by W. A. Perkins, *Transactions*, ASCE, Vol. 118, 1953, p. 75.

(17) "Memorandum on Arch Dam Developments," by Lars Jorgensen, *Journal*, Am. Concrete Inst., September, 1930, pp. 1–64.

(18) "Horizontal Joint Put in Arch Dam in Effort to Prevent Cracking," by George E. Goodall, *Engineering News-Record*, December 26, 1946, p. 76.

(19) "Modern Trend in Arch Dam Construction and Design," by Charles Jaeger, *English Electric Journal*, September, 1951.

(20) "Uber die Berechnug der Fundament-deformation," by Frederik Vogt, *Norske Videnskaps-Akad*, Oslo, 1925.

(21) "A Hollow Concrete-Steel Dam at Theresa, N. Y.," by Ambursen and Sayles, *Engineering News,* November 5, 1903, p. 403.

(22) "Improved Type of Multiple-Arch Dam," by Fred A. Noetzli, *Transactions,* ASCE, Vol. 87, 1924, p. 346.

(23) "Handbook of Applied Hydraulics," edited by Calvin Davis, McGraw-Hill Pub. Co., Inc., New York, N. Y., 1942, Section 8, p. 239.

(24) "Reservoirs for Irrigation, Water-Power and Domestic Water-Supply," by J. D. Schuyler, John Wiley & Sons, Inc., New York, N. Y., 2d Ed., 1908.

(25) "Water Pressures on Dams During Earthquakes," by H. M. Westergaard, *Transactions,* ASCE, Vol. 98, 1933, p. 418.

(26) "Ice Thrust in Connection with Hydroelectric Plant Design," by Earnest Brown and George C. Clarke, *Engineering Journal,* January, 1932, p. 18.

(27) *Technical Reports,* Miami (Ohio) Conservancy Dist., Dayton, Ohio.

AMERICAN SOCIETY OF CIVIL ENGINEERS

Founded November 5, 1852

TRANSACTIONS

Paper No. 2606

DAMS, THEN AND NOW

By K. B. Keener,[1] M. ASCE

Synopsis

Confining itself largely to the period since 1900, this paper considers the evolution of larger dams exclusively from the standpoint of a major builder, the Bureau of Reclamation, United States Department of the Interior. Designs of gravity, arch, and earth dams have progressed as a result of the dictates of experience in such items as compaction, riprap, aggregates, grouting, cutoffs, artificial cooling, cement economy, and air entrainment. In step with these advances, specifications have developed and improved, in accuracy and detail. The whole record of the Bureau comprises in effect a résumé of general trends in this important engineering field.

Much of the progress of the past century in the design of dams occurred during the latter half. Strangely enough, or coincidentally, that is the period during which reclamation, as sponsored by the Federal Government, has been in existence. The reclamation of vast arid and semi-arid regions in the West necessitated the construction of numerous storage reservoirs. As one learns largely by experience, there have been ample reasons for the numerous changes, generally improvements, in the design of dams since plans for the first ones to be constructed by the government were laid out on the drawing board. This paper can call attention only to a few of the many changes that have been made in both designs and specifications for dams prepared by Bureau engineers during the past 50 years. In addition, there has been much engineering progress during the same period in the designs of appurtenant structures, such as spillways and outlet works, but those important features will not be discussed here.

Early Dams

The first call for bids by the Reclamation Service, Department of the Interior, for construction of a dam was issued on April 30, 1904. It was No. 12 in the long series of plans and specifications drawn up by the Reclamation Service (later the Bureau of Reclamation). The advertisement announced that proposals

---

[1] Chf. Designing Engr., Bureau of Reclamation, Denver, Colo.

would be received for constructing and completing a dam, spillway, canal, and gates on the Snake River near Minidoka, Idaho.

Specifications Improved.—This dam (Fig. 1) was to be constructed for the triple purposes of diversion of water for irrigation, of storage, and of development of power to be used in pumping water for irrigation. The specifications covered the beginning of construction on the Minidoka project and involved earth, rock, and concrete work. The size of these specifications was significant—18 pages, 7 in. by 9 in., much smaller than current standard letter-size pages. They contained only five drawings. The schedule of work consisted of twenty-two bid items. Current specifications for identical work would, conservatively, be from five to ten times as long and would contain numerous drawings. For instance, the detail specifications for placing concrete consisted of two sentences, or a total of ninety words; whereas under the same subject in recent Bureau specifications for Palisades Dam and Power Plant (on the South Fork of the Snake River in Idaho) 1,070 words are employed. Of course there are more items of concrete in the latter specifications, but this accounts only in part for the greater verbosity in the latter.

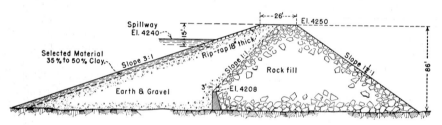

FIG. 1.—CROSS SECTION OF MINIDOKA DAM, ON THE SNAKE RIVER IN IDAHO

In regard to the quality of those early plans and specifications for the Minidoka project, today's engineers dare not be too critical for the structures are still in use. However, they might view with skepticism, if not with astonishment, certain of those early provisions were they included in present-day specifications. For example, there is the direction: "Concrete will be used 'wet' wherever practicable, and 'dry' only when the nature of the work renders such use unavoidable." In view of that provision, it is somewhat surprising that the word "laid" in addition to the word "placed" should be used in connection with concrete. For instance, there is the statement that: "No concrete shall be 'laid' in freezing weather," and the provision that: "Under no circumstances is concrete to be 'laid' in deep or moving water * * * and it must always be mixed and 'laid' in the presence of an inspector and to his satisfaction." The word "poured" came into use a little later.

Another example of deviation from modern practice is contained in the provision:

"The gravel and earth [embankment] shall be placed in layers of not more than one foot in thickness, and shall be thoroughly wet and compacted by rolling if so required by the engineer."

Under such a provision how urgent it must have been that bidders have a word with the engineer prior to the bidding date. Anyway, at some point between the early Minidoka and, say, the Boysen (on the Big Horn River in Wyoming (1952)) projects, 1-ft layers for compaction were reduced to 8 in. Also, it was decided to place the material on the dry side of the moisture content optimum for compaction and to roll with several passes of a sheepsfoot roller, regardless of the construction engineer's opinion.

Admittedly there is not much to either censure or commend in those early specifications—partly, may it be suggested, because of their brevity. What was lacking in definite instructions was probably balanced by the intelligence, authority, and responsibility of the engineer. Free use was made of expressions in-

FIG. 2.—MINIDOKA DAM, COMPLETED BY CONTRACT IN OCTOBER, 1906, SHOWING HAND-PLACED RIPRAP

dicating the ability of the engineer such as "fixed by, required by, and satisfactory to the engineer." Neither was the contractor neglected in those specifications, for frequently there appeared the phrase "at the contractor's expense."

Like two other dams constructed by the Reclamation Service in the early period prior to 1910, Minidoka Dam is a modified rock-fill or a composite type of earth dam (Fig. 1). It was the forerunner of the many earth and rock-fill dams that have been built since 1910, and in several respects it resembles many of the more recent ones. For instance, it has a crest width in keeping with many embankments constructed during the period from 10 to 25 years later; it has the quite common upstream slope of 3 : 1; it has a concrete cutoff wall; and its upstream slope is protected from wave action to a level below the minimum-reservoir operating surface by rock riprap (Fig. 2).

Although the old specifications provided that the gravel and earth embankment be compacted by rolling if so required, construction reports indicate that compaction was not accomplished by rolling. After initially excavating a diversion channel through the right abutment, the downstream rock and upstream earth and gravel embankments, 150 ft apart, were extended across the river, the materials being transported and deposited by two parallel cableways. After unwatering the space between those fills, which acted as cofferdams, the core wall was constructed. The procedure then in finishing the dam proper was to keep the earth fill some 15 ft or 20 ft lower than the rock fill and, by means of gates in the diversion channel, to maintain the water surface against the fill just below the top,

FIG. 3.—UPSTREAM SLOPE OF DEER CREEK DAM, ON THE PROVO RIVER IN UTAH, RIPRAP DUMPED IN PLACE

in order to puddle it for purposes of compaction. Most of the materials for the earth embankment were dumped from cars along a track laid on the upstream side of the rock fill. Thus the earth embankment was placed by the semihydraulic fill method.

Minidoka Methods.—Riprap on this early constructed dam, although only 18 in. thick, was hand placed (Fig. 2). General practice for the past two decades has been to protect the upstream slope with 3 ft of dumped rock riprap including larger pieces up to ½ cu yd in volume, as illustrated by Deer Creek Dam (on the Provo River in Utah (Fig. 3)). Experience indicates that the rough surface thus obtained dampens the action of the waves and prevents the riding-up effect so noticeable on smooth hand-placed riprap.

A cross section of the Minidoka Dam spillway (Fig. 4) would incite considerable attention among present-day designers. At the time the earlier section was planned, H. Bazin's experiments on overflow over sharp-crested weirs had not been

promulgated—those experiments being the first step leading to the current practice of designing the overflow crest profile to simulate the lower nappe of a sheet
of falling water. Such procedure results in greater discharges for the same
head than those obtained with broad-crested profiles, and therefore provides a
more economical design.

Before leaving the subject of the Minidoka Project, one precedent should be
mentioned which has been maintained to the present day—the right to make
changes in the specifications under a contract. Although construction of the power
plant was not included in the contract for the dam, part of the plans for the
dam depended on the location of the plant. At the time the contract was signed,

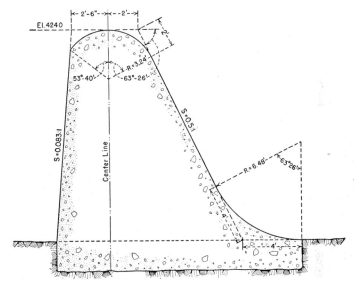

Fig. 4.—Cross Section of Minidoka Dam Spillway

the site of the powerhouse had been set about 2,000 ft downstream from the
right end of the dam and 900 ft back from the river channel. This would have
required a forebay channel or canal 67 ft wide, 10 ft deep, and 2,000 ft long.
However, on December 5, 1904, about 3 months after signing of the contract, a
radical change was made by a consulting board, the assembly of which, by the
way, was an early practice that has since continued.

As heretofore mentioned, plans provided for excavating a diversion channel
near the right end of the rock fill to control the river during construction. The
channel at its inlet end was to be closed by a concrete dam with five regulating
gates. The board proposed lengthening the concrete dam and constructing it as
a foundation and upstream wall for the powerhouse, also providing it with ten
penstock openings 10 ft in diameter, with two smaller ones for exciter units. The
revision in the plans, reducing the estimated cost of the project, was agreed to
by the contractor. In brief, this is the story of the inception of the Reclamation
Service's first power plant which was completed a few years later, the first main
unit being placed on the line on April 29, 1909.

Roosevelt Dam on the Salt River in Arizona.—The second specifications by
the Reclamation Service for the construction of a storage dam were issued on
November 23, 1904, and the contract was signed on April 8, 1905, practically 7
months after beginning of construction of Minidoka Dam. Like the specifications
for its predecessor, those for Roosevelt Dam were brief. There were only four
drawings and nine bid items—which may be hard to believe in view of both the
magnitude of the completed structure (Fig. 5) and the numerous drawings and
bid items accompanying the specifications for recent dams.

Fig. 5.—Roosevelt Dam, on Salt River in Arizona—an Historic Structure

Site Determines Details.—A maximum cross section of the dam (Fig. 6) reveals two unusual features as compared to modern structures. It may be noted
first that Roosevelt Dam was constructed of cyclopean masonry to a total volume
of 340,000 cu yd. Although that practice may have been somewhat common at
the time—the New Croton Dam (on the Croton River in New York) having been
constructed from 1892 to 1907 and the Wachusett Dam (on the South Fork of the
Nashua River in Massachusetts) from 1896 to 1906—precedents are not considered
to have been influential in determining the materials of construction for Roosevelt
Dam. Rather, it is thought that the design was strictly a matter of economy.
The site is in a desolate country on the Salt River 70 miles upstream from
Phoenix and 52 miles from the nearest railroad point at Mesa. Construction of
about 32 miles of winding mountain road was required. The inaccessibility, the
long haul by road, the high freight rates, and the availability of a tough fine-
grained sandstone in the vicinity with a specific gravity averaging 2.5 appear to
have been the principal factors in determining the materials of construction.

Roosevelt Dam was designed as a gravity structure so that the resultant force with the reservoir both full and empty would not fall outside the middle third. The curved plan on an axial radius of 410 ft, which added greatly to the stability, was not considered in the analysis as it undoubtedly would be at the present time. However, if the dam were to be constructed today, it is certain that, because of the high wage rates, the advances in construction machinery, and particularly the transverse profile of the site, it would be a thin concrete arch.

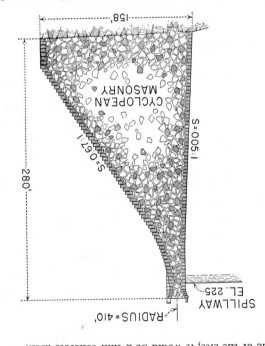

Fig. 6.—Roosevelt Dam, Maximum Cross Section of Main Arched Structure

A second unusual feature is covered by specifications for Roosevelt Dam providing that:

"A trench shall be cut in the solid rock of the foundation 15 feet from the heel of the dam, and parallel thereto, and shall be 10 feet wide and 6 feet deep below the bottom of the dam on the line of the trench. * * *."

as may be seen on the cross section. The practice of excavating a cutoff trench in good foundation rock near the heel of a masonry dam and then replacing it with other rock or concrete of questionable quality compared to that of the original foundation was discontinued early in the 1920's.

Although the earlier specifications for concrete at Minidoka Dam provided that the sand must be clean, sharp, and free from excessive clayey matter, the specifications for Roosevelt Dam went a step further in being more explicit. They provided that the sand should be free from organic matter and should contain not more than 10% of clay or other foreign mineral substance. In the interven-

ing years since then engineers have become more exacting in the quality requirements for sand. For instance, the specifications for Palisades Dam and Power
Plant issued on February 29, 1952, stipulate that the maximum percentage of
clay lumps in sand shall not exceed 1% by weight and that all deleterious substances shall not exceed 5% by weight. However, for those who might doubt the
integrity of the concrete between the quarried sandstone blocks in Roosevelt Dam,
it is comforting to record that natural sand was not used, but that sand was
manufactured by crushing the dolomite limestone found in the vicinity. Thus the
percentage of clay was negligible.

Another Feature Distinguished.—Of all the Bureau's dams, Roosevelt has the
distinction of being the only one where the portland cement was manufactured at
the site, the plant having been located 2,500 ft upstream. As in the case of
constructing the dam of quarried rock, economy dictated the manufacture of
cement—plenty of limestone and clay with the proper chemical composition being available in the vicinity, and the delivered price of cement at commercial
mills being unusually high.

Power for Construction.—The general construction contract reserved the
right to build a power plant without hindrance from the contractor, and this
was actually accomplished. Of more interest, however, was the means of furnishing electric energy promised to the contractor for construction purposes. On
February 8, 1905, bids were received for furnishing 100 cords of cottonwood and
500 cords of mesquite wood to the government power station at Roosevelt. The
small 150-hp, temporary steam plant using wood as fuel is believed to have been
the first power plant constructed by the Reclamation Service.

A 2,600-hp, two-unit hydroelectric plant was completed in the early spring
of 1906 before general construction had advanced very far. The hydraulic machinery was located downstream from the left abutment at the site of the future permanent plant. It was necessary to build a structure to divert the river
upstream from the dam site and a canal 19 miles long, with a capacity of 200
sec-ft. The discharge passed through the turbine wheels under a head of 220 ft.
The diversion served not only to develop power but also to keep the low water
flow from interfering with construction. Power was used for lighting, drilling,
rock handling, mixing mortar, crushing rock for use in concrete and mortar, and
for operating the cement mill.

PATHFINDER AND SHOSHONE DAMS IN WYOMING

Thus, the early work of the Reclamation Service started off auspiciously with
the construction of two major storage dams different in many respects from
those to follow (Fig. 7). The next two to be advertised for construction were
of the arch type. The contract for Pathfinder Dam (on the North Platte River)
was awarded on September 1, 1905; and that for Shoshone (later known as
Buffalo Bill) Dam (on the Shoshone River), on September 18, 1905.

In both the stresses were analyzed by what is termed the arch-and-crown
cantilever method—that is, distribution of the loads between arch and cantilever
elements by adjusting the deflections of the crown of each arch and the maximum cantilever section. The distribution thus found at those points was as-

sumed applicable to the entire structure, and the water loads were assumed uniform throughout the lengths of the horizontal arch elements. This method of stress analysis was a great advance over the cylinder formula theretofore commonly used, and resulted in great economy as compared with analysis by cantilever action only. The similarity of the resulting two cross sections is pronounced, although the maximum height for Pathfinder is 214 ft; and that for Shoshone, 325 ft.

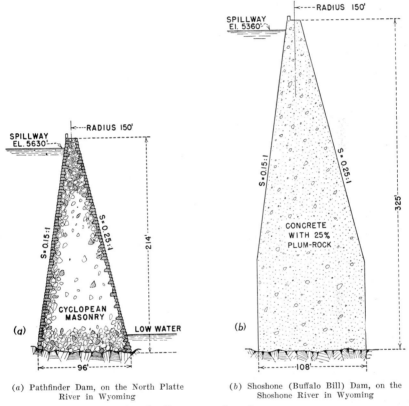

(a) Pathfinder Dam, on the North Platte   (b) Shoshone (Buffalo Bill) Dam, on the
River in Wyoming   Shoshone River in Wyoming

FIG. 7.—COMPARATIVE CROSS SECTIONS

Both dam sites were deep narrow gorges in granite, Pathfinder being about 90 ft wide at the bottom and 200 ft wide at the top with nearly vertical walls for the upper 75 ft. The sides of the Shoshone gorge were only 70 ft apart at the river level and 200 ft apart at a height of 250 ft. Thus both gorges were readily recognizable as excellent and economical sites for constructing masonry dams. Unlike conditions today when relocation is a usual problem, there were no highways or railroads through the sites. It is difficult to visualize that Pathfinder Dam, impounding 1,070,000 acre-ft of water for irrigation, was constructed for a cost of $1,795,000 or $1.68 per acre-ft of capacity. In 1922 a 5,600-kw power plant was constructed a few hundred feet downstream at Shoshone Dam.

Pathfinder was of cyclopean masonry, similar to Roosevelt Dam, whereas Shoshone was the Bureau's first concrete storage dam. However, concrete in the latter was distinctive from that currently placed in that it consisted of a large percentage of plum rock. The specifications provided that:

"In the freshly deposited concrete the contractor shall place by hand, sound and clean pieces of granite weighing between 25 and 200 pounds, which shall be rammed until well bedded. The proportion of such rocks shall be as nearly as practicable uniform throughout the dam, and shall form at least 25 percent of the total volume of the masonry."

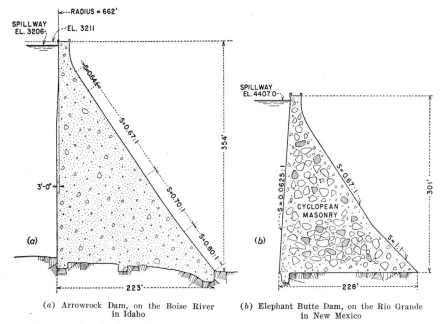

(a) Arrowrock Dam, on the Boise River in Idaho

(b) Elephant Butte Dam, on the Rio Grande in New Mexico

Fig. 8—Cross Sections of Two Similar Structures, About 1915

The arch at Pathfinder, with a crest length of 307 ft, abutted on two low reaches of straight concrete dam having a gravity section. The contraction joints at those points, the forerunners of many, more closely spaced, consisted merely of a formed tongue and groove.

Later Structures, Arrowrock and Elephant Butte

Because of certain similarities the next two major masonry dams, Arrowrock (on the Boise River in Idaho) and Elephant Butte (on the Rio Grande in New Mexico), may be fittingly discussed together. The former was completed in 1915 and the latter in 1916 (Fig. 8). Both are gravity dams, the sections shown in the specifications being nearly the same, although Arrowrock was curved in plan on a radius of 662 ft and Elephant Butte was straight. Of special interest is the deep cutoff in the heel of Elephant Butte and the double cutoff under Arrowrock.

Sand-cement was specified for both dams. In the case of Arrowrock Dam, portland cement was reground with granite in equal proportions by weight, whereas at Elephant Butte Dam, portland cement was reground with sandstone. Sand-cements were used in the mass concrete mixture in the same general proportions as unadulterated cement had theretofore been used, resulting in a lean concrete with a great reduction in the heat of setting and consequently with less cracking on cooling. The practice of embedding man-size plum rock, initiated at Shoshone Dam, was continued at Arrowrock Dam. Cyclopean masonry was used in the construction of Elephant Butte Dam, similar to that at Roosevelt and Pathfinder except that the exposed surfaces were concrete.

For the first time in the history of the Reclamation Service grout curtains and a closely adjacent row of downstream drainage holes were provided in the foundations at the heels of these large dams. Sand-cement grout was forced by compressed air into holes drilled into the foundation. Current practice requires use of straight cement grout. Both dams had regularly spaced contraction joints. Systems of drains were provided near the upstream face to intercept any water percolating into the concrete from the reservoir. At Elephant Butte Dam the upstream face was coated with a 1-in. thickness of 1 : 2 mixture, portland cement-sand mortar, applied with a cement gun, for the purpose of adding additional watertightness. This practice has not been continued by the Bureau.

New Methods Introduced

Thus ended in 1916 what might be termed the initial period of dam and power plant building by the Reclamation Service. At the expense of omitting some important events in the progressive growth of the science of designing dams but to keep this paper within reasonable limits, only the highlights of developments since the early period will be mentioned. First, Black Canyon Diversion Dam (on the Payette River in Idaho), a 183-ft-high concrete gravity dam completed in 1924, should be considered. The designs provided a concrete cutoff in the foundation at the heel, but this was eliminated during construction.

Although such a cutoff, which had become common practice in design, had been used on a few other dams in the twenties, it became completely obsolete by 1930. Black Canyon has keyed contraction joints at regular intervals, but no provisions were made for later grouting of those joints. The principal reason for mentioning Black Canyon is that this was the Bureau's first concrete dam on which the Abrams theory of low water-cement ratio concrete was applied. A low slump mixture has been used in all Bureau mass concrete since the construction of Black Canyon.

Gibson Dam (on the North Fork of the Sun River in Montana), a 196-ft-high concrete arch, completed in 1929, has the distinction of being the first designed by the trial-load method of analysis. It was also the first Bureau dam in which the contraction joints were grouted to make the structure monolithic. This was accomplished by installing grout stops at the upstream and downstream edges of the joints and pumping grout through a system of 1-in. and $\frac{1}{2}$-in. galvanized pipes embedded in the concrete and connected to electrical conduit boxes spaced on about 8-ft centers over the surface of the joints.

Furthermore, Gibson was the first concrete dam in which experimental equipment was embedded to determine the structural behavior, a procedure which has been practiced and has become much more highly developed on succeeding major concrete dams. There was no provision for plum rock in the specifications, but cobble rock up to 9 in. in diameter was permitted in the concrete mixture.

Owyhee Dam (on the Owyhee River in Oregon), a concrete arch-gravity structure 417 ft high, completed in 1932, was the last major structure to be undertaken prior to Hoover Dam (on the Colorado River in Arizona-Nevada). During the former's construction, the preparation of plans and specifications for the latter were in progress. Thus Owyhee naturally became a testing model for Hoover, and the experience gained was reflected in the specifications for the world's highest dam. The outstanding experiment was the artificial cooling of an integral 10,600 cu yd of the 537,500 cu yd of concrete in the dam, by circulating cold river water through 1-in. pipe, placed in parallel lines 4 ft $7\frac{1}{2}$ in. apart near the bottom of each 4-ft lift of concrete. Many important questions concerning temperature control of mass concrete were thereby answered.

Hoover Dam Sets Precedents.—Authorization in December, 1928, of the construction of Hoover Dam and Power Plant, both unprecedented in size at the time, created many new problems of design and construction. The final section of the dam, 726 ft in maximum height and curved on a radius of 500 ft was determined by the trial-load method of analysis. Hoover Dam was the first in which all the mass concrete was artificially cooled, and also the first designed with staggered circumferential contraction joints in addition to transverse joints, thus dividing it for purposes of construction into blocks roughly 50 ft by 50 ft square.

Those two features set the precedent for use in the later large concrete dams constructed by the Bureau. Artificial cooling has also been used in subsequent projects to reduce the heat of setting and consequently to eliminate the cracking in the mass of concrete around power plant scroll cases. The authorization of Hoover Dam also touched off a series of investigations of the composition of portland cement in order to reduce the heat of setting. Those investigations resulted in the use of a low heat cement in the mass concrete.

Marshall Ford Dam (on the Colorado River in Texas), a straight gravity structure completed in 1942, was provided with one continuous longitudinal contraction joint, largely because of a circumstance connected with appropriations of funds. When construction commenced in late 1936, sufficient funds were available only to construct a low dam. However, the upstream face was provided with horizontal shear keys to form the downstream part of a joint for use when funds were provided for increasing the height which occurred early in 1942. Although the maximum size of concrete aggregate had been increased to 9 in. at Hoover Dam, it was reduced again to 6 in. at Marshall Ford. The 6-in. size had been the maximum used in a few previously constructed dams and has since come into general use.

Grand Coulee Dam (on the Columbia River in Washington) was completed in 1942. It is the largest concrete dam in point of volume, 10,585,000 cu yd having been placed. A straight gravity structure, it was analyzed by the trial-load twist method of analysis—that is, account was taken of twist or beam action, five transverse twist-adjustment slots, 6 ft wide, being provided at various locations along the dam. Although the Hoover power plant generators, each of 82,500-kw capacity, were the largest hydroelectric units at the time of construction in point of output capacity, the 108,000-kw Grand Coulee units were the largest at the time of installation; and, for that matter, they still are.

Friant Dam (on the San Joaquin River in California) is a straight concrete gravity structure completed in 1942. It stands out as one in which the mass concrete contains only 0.8 bbl of portland cement per cu yd, as compared with the normal practice since the days of Arrowrock and Elephant Butte dams of using 1 bbl of cement per cu yd. Pumicite in the amount of 20% of the weight of the cement was added to the mixture.

Altus Dam (on the North Fork of the Red River in Oklahoma), completed in 1945, another concrete gravity dam, contains only 0.65 bbl of portland cement per cu yd, and pumicite in the amount of 35% of the weight of the cement.

On the subject of cement content, it is of interest to note that Canyon Ferry (on the Missouri River) and Hungry Horse (on the South Fork of the Flathead River) dams in Montana, the former a concrete straight gravity structure and the latter an arch, both under construction (1952) in Montana, utilize only 0.5 bbl of cement per cu yd in the interior mass concrete. In the former, pozzolan in the form of fly ash is added to the concrete mixture in the amount of 30% of the weight of the cement and in the latter, in the amount of 48%. Thus in the amount of cement per cubic yard of concrete, designers have returned to the days of Arrowrock Dam construction.

Angostura Dam (on the Cheyenne River in South Dakota) is a concrete straight gravity dam completed in 1949. It was the first in which air-entraining agents were used in the concrete mixture. Although the primary purpose of entrained air may be to increase durability, it adds to the workability of the mixture and in that sense permits a smaller cement content. Its use has become common practice by the Bureau.

Refined Compaction.—Specifications for the Bureau's first completed dam, the Minidoka earth and rock-fill embankment, provided that the embankment might be compacted by rolling; but actually much of it was placed in water. Since that early period (1904–1906), many earth dams have been constructed, and there has been a transition to greater compaction requirements. The earlier specifications stipulated compaction by smooth rollers such as those used in highway construction. In 1923 the specifications for McKay Dam (on the McKay Creek in Oregon) provided as follows:

> "It [the embankment material] shall be spread into horizontal layers not over 8 inches thick and thoroughly compacted by rolling. The rolling shall be done with traction engines weighing not less than 20 tons with at least 15 tons concentrated on two wheels having treads not over 24 inches in width. * * * The roller shall make not less than three trips over every portion of each 8-inch layer of the embankment."

As late as 1927 the specifications for Echo Dam (on the Weber River in Utah) contained similar provisions, although during construction the Rohl-type sheepsfoot roller was used.

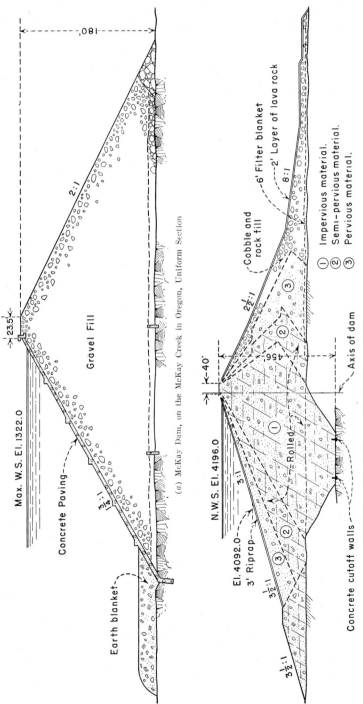

(a) McKay Dam, on the McKay Creek in Oregon, Uniform Section

(b) Anderson Ranch Dam, on the South Fork of the Boise River in Idaho, Zoned Design

Fig. 9.—Cross Sections of Earth Dams

Finally in 1931, the specifications for Cle Elum Dam (on the Cle Elum River in Washington) required compaction by the sheepsfoot type of roller. Not until August, 1934, in building Pine View Dam (on the Ogden River in Utah) was the specified number of passes of the roller increased from three to not less than five. For Rye Patch Dam (on the Humboldt River in Nevada) in October, 1934, the required minimum number of passes rose to six. By November, 1936, in the specifications for Bull Lake Dam (on the Bull Lake Creek in Wyoming), the number of passes was twelve, with provision for an adjustment in price to the contractor for a greater or lesser amount. Only on rare occasions has use been made of this provision.

In the early days it was a rather common opinion that compaction of impervious materials was enhanced by a liberal use of water. This idea gave way gradually to a requirement for lesser use and finally, through tests and a greater knowledge of soil mechanics—a science practically unknown for the first three decades of the Bureau's history—to the "optimum moisture content" for compaction. Currently, it is generally considered desirable to compact the material when it is 1% or 2% on the dry side of the optimum moisture content—to avoid setting up dangerous pore pressures in the fill.

Modern Tendencies

For some years it was the practice to design earth dams with high concrete core walls. Later this was considered objectionable because of the tendency of these walls to crack with movement of the dam. Current preference is for relatively impervious earth cores, with thicknesses dependent on such conditions as the height of dam, availability of suitable embankment materials, and the nature of the foundation.

Many dams, particularly in the early period, were designed for a uniform type of material and were thus classed as homogeneous. McKay Dam, completed in 1927, is an example of this type (Fig. 9 (a)). By far the most earth dams designed and constructed by the Bureau are of the zoned type of which Anderson Ranch Dam (on the South Fork of the Boise River in Idaho), completed in 1950, is typical (Fig. 9(b)). Early designs for the Bureau's earth dams were based on empirical knowledge, but such procedure has been supplanted in recent years by a combination of experience, knowledge of soil mechanics, and various methods of stability analysis. Much useful experience in the past 10 years has been obtained as the result of various embedded instruments which give a running record of pore pressure, settlement, and other movement in completed earth dams.

Structures mentioned in this paper illustrate the preponderant types designed and constructed by the Bureau. Attempt has been made to show by actual examples some of the changes and trends in the design of dams during the past half century. Obviously, the science of designing dams will not remain static during the next equal period of time. In fact, it is to be expected that progress will be even greater. However, it must remain a source of satisfaction to designers of dams in the past that much useful groundwork has been laid on which to base improvements in dams of the future.

AMERICAN SOCIETY OF CIVIL ENGINEERS

Founded November 5, 1852

TRANSACTIONS

Paper No. 2607

EVOLUTION OF THE MODERN HYDROELECTRIC POWER PLANT

By A. T. Larned [1] and M. G. Salzman,[2] Members, ASCE

Synopsis

The development of the modern hydroelectric plant has kept pace with the growth of industrial enterprise and the electric utility industry. It has been marked by a gradual transition from the small individual plant to the present-day plant which supplies a transmission network serving an extensive area. Hydroelectric units are now installed as component parts of power systems and are recognized as complementary to rather than competitive with thermal plants. Dissimilar natural conditions and diversified operation requirements result in various types of plant, and each plant is "custom made" to meet existing circumstances.

Outstanding advances in hydroelectric engineering occurred in first quarter of the twentieth century and included marked increases in unit capacity, attainment of high efficiencies, perfection of methods for supporting heavy revolving vertical loads, and effective means of controlling flow in long water columns. Subsequent less radical improvements—such as adoption of fixed and adjustable blade propeller-type turbines for low-head projects, development of an umbrella-type generator, refinements in governing and control equipment, increased flow line and draft tube efficiencies, standardization and use of improved materials in equipment, simplification of plant layout, and automatic control—have had a far-reaching effect in reduced costs and better performance.

Primary objectives in the design of modern hydroelectric plant are high-service reliability; low investment and operating costs; simplicity in physical arrangement, operation, and maintenance; and appearance in harmony with utilitarian purposes. More attention is being given to reducing operating costs by installing automatic operating features. Outdoor and semi-outdoor stations are gaining increased favor. The application of the pumped storage principle to hydroelectric development has been limited in the United States but may offer future possibilities. Construction costs have not favored the adoption of underground hydroelectric stations in this country although that type is being adopted elsewhere.

Hydroelectric plants may be expected to play a continuing important part in

[1] Chf. Civ. Engr., Ebasco Services Inc., New York, N. Y.
[2] Hydr. Engr., Ebasco Services, Inc., New York, N. Y.

the future expansion of the electric utility industry. Opportunities are present for additional improvements, and constant vigilance must be exercised by engineers to obtain all possible economies in design and operation.

INTRODUCTION

Since the techniques of alternating-current electric generation and long-distance transmission had not progressed to any great extent before the beginning of the twentieth century, the evolution of the central hydroelectric station has taken place principally during the past 50 years. Transition from the small individual plant of the early period serving an isolated industry or community to the modern hydroelectric plant feeding into a transmission network serving an extensive area has been gradual, and is largely an adaptation to the expanding requirements of industry and the consuming public.

The title of this paper suggests a very broad field about which many worthy textbooks and much descriptive material have been written. Some of these are referred to in the Bibliography. It is not intended here to cover the subject in its entirety or to go into specific details, but merely to point out some of the highlights of engineering achievement and the progressive technological development of the modern hydroelectric power plant as applied to American practice.

Examples are given to illustrate certain features, taken principally from those plants within the writers' own knowledge and experience. The omission of other notable projects does not in any way reflect on their importance or contribution to the development of the industry.

1. The Changing Role of Hydroelectric Plants in System Operation

In the early days of hydroelectric development, plants were considered as individual units competitive with alternative sources of power such as steam plants. With the growth of power supply areas and interconnection of generating sources, they are now installed as component parts of power systems and are recognized as being complementary to the thermal plants. On most systems a balance of steam and hydro plant capacity, with coordinated operation of all power producing facilities, results in a combination which reduces the over-all cost of energy. In the United States, and also in other countries, the extensive interconnection of plants and systems and the formation of "power pools" permit the most effective use of hydroelectric plants in the system load.

In the older plants it was necessary to provide duplicate equipment and install multiple units of small capacity for reliability of operation. Nowadays, however, the coordination of resources has made possible the development of plants with one or two large units, the reserve being supplied by other plants in the system.

There is considerable variation in types of hydro developments because of dissimilar natural conditions and diversified operating requirements. Each plant is "custom made" to fit the pattern of the prevailing load and must have flexibility to conform to changing conditions. Hydro plants with storage facilities and ample machine capacity are usually operated at a low-load factor to take care of peak-load generation. During times of surplus water, the secondary energy available may be used advantageously to replace fuel generation. Storage plants are elastic in meeting variable load requirements and are particularly adaptable for regulating tie-line loads. When not required for generation, hydro units may be used in interconnected systems for spinning reserve or for operation as synchronous condensers for voltage correction.

In general, the run-of-river hydro plants, which must utilize the water as it flows in the stream, are operated at higher load factors, on the base of the load. It is often possible to develop upstream storage projects advantageously on a river containing a number of downstream plants, the storage being used for generating at the upper plant and also for augmenting the output of the lower plant.

2. Engineering Achievements Stimulating Progress in Hydroelectric Development

The most revolutionary advances in the field of hydroelectric engineering took place in the early years of the twentieth century prior to 1925. That highly progressive era was marked by:

(1) A notable increase in the size and unit capacity of turbines and generators.

(2) The attainment of high efficiencies over a wide range of operation.

(3) The development of accurate methods of flow measurement in turbine efficiency tests.

(4) The perfection of methods of supporting revolving weights and hydraulic thrust loads to permit large-capacity vertical-shaft turbines.

(5) Effective control of the flow in long water columns.

Older types of hydraulic turbines (Fig. 1) with horizontal shafts and multirunners were relatively inefficient because of the variety of parts necessary to obtain reasonable generator speeds. They required considerable floor space, and the plants were already relatively large structures. Since about 1910 most of the turbines installed have been of the single-runner vertical-shaft type, which permitted the building of much larger units than would have been economically feasible with the horizontal type. The development of suitable thrust bearings to support large-thrust loads was an important contribution to the success of the vertical unit.

The hydraulic unit of the early 1920's was a highly efficient machine and practically reached the ultimate in prime mover efficiency. This is evident from the fact that the 55,000-hp turbine built for the Niagara Development of the Hydro-Electric Power Commission of Ontario (Canada) in 1921 attained a maximum efficiency of 93.8% and an efficiency of greater than 90% for 48% of the range in full capacity. The invention of the pressure-time method of water-flow measurement and the salt-velocity method enabled accurate determination of turbine efficiencies over a wide range of operating conditions.

Refinements in Design.—Development of dependable control valves for penstocks and pressure regulating equipment on flow lines and turbines also contributed much to modern design. Outstanding in this connection was the hydraulically-operated needle valve with balanced plunger for quick and reliable operation. The invention of the differential surge tank for controlling the pressure and speed regulation of the unit permitted the economical development of high-head installations with long conduits.

In the period subsequent to 1925 improvements took place that were less radical but that nevertheless had a far-reaching effect in reducing maintenance and operating costs. The most noteworthy were:

1. Adoption of fixed and adjustable-blade propeller-type turbine units for low-head developments, to permit higher-speed generators and improved efficiency range.

Fig. 1.—Horizontal-Type Hydroelectric Units in Early Plants—Interior View of Blewett Falls Station in North Carolina

2. The hydraulic design of turbines with increased casing-inlet velocity and higher specific speeds for reaction runners, to allow higher-head installations.

3. Progress in governing and control equipment.

4. Increased efficiency in draft tubes with modified design.

5. Cavitation research and advances toward the solution of the problems of pitting of turbine runners and proper setting of the units.

6. Better materials and construction techniques for gates, penstocks, turbines, and generators, including the use of: (a) Welded plate steel in place of riveted-plate and cast-steel casings; and (b) stainless steel on runners and on seal rings to resist pitting and corrosion.

7. The umbrella-type generator (Fig. 2) making possible the simplification of the mechanical plant layout and reduction of the powerhouse superstructure.

8. Simplified hydraulic design, with more efficient intakes and water passages to reduce head losses.

9. Improved thrust bearings, including the spherical and equalizing types;

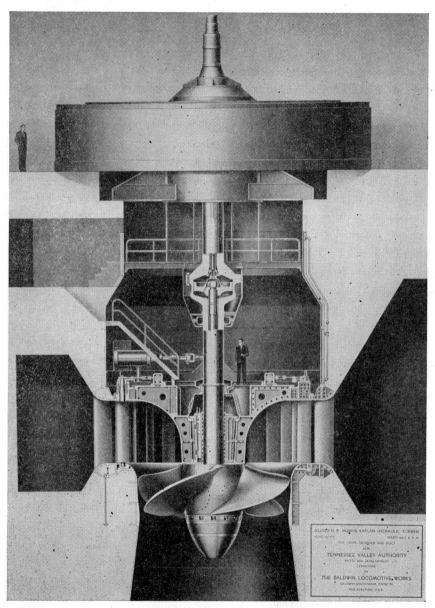

Fig. 2.—Example of Kaplan Adjustable-Blade Hydraulic Turbine in Modern Plant—Watts Bar Unit of Tennessee Valley Authority in Tennessee, 42,000 Hp Under Head of 52 Ft

and the adoption of: (*a*) Self-lubricating guide bearings, (*b*) automatic grease lubrication of turbine gate bearings, and (*c*) carbon seal rings to simplify operation and reduce field maintenance.

10. High-capacity generators for low-speed and high-speed operation with an enclosed cooling system, more durable winding and insulation, and a more effective mechanical arrangement of rotor and stator for increased stability.

11. More reliable and proficient electrical transformers and switchgear.

12. Automatic and supervisory control equipment to reduce operating personnel.

Kinds of Runners.—The type of hydraulic turbine used varies with the characteristics of the development and the loading conditions imposed on the station. Improvements in propeller-type runners have greatly expanded the range of heads to which these units are applicable and have made possible the utilization of low-head sites which were formerly undesirable. Units of this type operate under heads up to 100 ft.

Where there is not much variation in head and the unit will operate under fairly constant load, the fixed-blade propeller unit is the most economical, as high efficiency can be maintained and fewer mechanical parts are required. The Kaplan adjustable-blade propeller-type unit (Fig. 2) is employed where low pond or high tailwater during flood conditions necessitates curtailed gate operation. High efficiency is then maintained by automatically and simultaneously adjusting the angle of the runner blade with the guide vanes to suit any condition of load or head.

The largest size Kaplan turbines are those installed by the Corps of Engineers at the McNary Dam Project on the Columbia River in Oregon, which will be rated at 111,300 hp under a head of approximately 80 ft. At the Cabinet Gorge plant of the Washington Water Power Company on the Clark Fork River in Idaho (Fig. 3), recently completed, three fixed-blade propeller turbines and one adjustable-blade unit will be installed. The turbines develop 70,500 hp at 90-ft head and 82,500 hp at 105-ft head, and combine to provide an efficient and economical arrangement for variable head operation.

Reaction Versus Impulse Wheels.—For medium low heads and medium high heads the well-established Francis reaction-type runner predominates. In general, the improvements have been mainly in size of installation, simplification, and greater reliability of operation. Outstanding in this field are the vertical-shaft 115,000-hp Hoover Dam (on the Colorado River in Arizona-Nevada) units, operating under a rated head of 480 ft, and the Grand Coulee (on the Columbia River in Washington) units (Fig. 4), rated at 165,000 hp to operate under a head of 330 ft. The major problems involved in these large units were principally those of manufacturing and sectionalizing for transportation and of assembling in the field.

Extension of the application of the reaction turbine to higher heads has been significant because of the smaller physical size of the generator due to the increased speed and because of its higher efficiency and machine capability as compared with the conventional impulse wheel. The reaction turbine also requires less powerhouse space. In the United States the highest-head reaction-type unit is at the Nantahala Project (on the Nantahala River in North Carolina) of the

Aluminum Company of America, where a 60,000-hp turbine was installed to operate under a net head of 925 ft with a speed of 450 rpm.

The choice between the impulse and reaction turbines for higher-head developments is one involving economic and other considerations. At the Ixtapantongo Development (on the Rio Tilostoc) in Mexico, a 39,000-hp reaction-type water wheel has been installed for a net head of 1,028 ft and a speed of 600 rpm. Selection of this high speed and type of wheel resulted in a smaller and less expensive generator than that required with an impulse turbine.

Fig. 3.—Cabinet Gorge 200,000-Kw Development in Washington, During Construction, Showing Diversion, Contractor's Plant, Power Station, Penstocks, and Arch Dam

For development of heads higher than 1,200 ft, the double overhung, horizontal single-jet Pelton or impulse-type wheel prevails as the prime mover. The largest impulse units built in this country, in both power and physical dimensions, are the 63,027-hp wheels installed in 1928 at the Big Creek No. 2-A Development of the Southern California Edison Company (on the San Joaquin River in California). These units are of the two-runner, single-nozzle type and operate under a head of 2,200 ft at a speed of 250 rpm. An example of recent practice in this respect is the Electra Plant (on the Mokelumne River) of the Pacific Gas and Electric Company in California which went into operation in 1948; it has three units rated 37,500 hp at 1,223-ft net head, giving a total installed capacity of 112,500 hp.

To obtain increased efficiency over a wider range of loads and to reduce the powerhouse space requirements for large-capacity high-head units, the multi-jet vertical-type impulse wheel has been developed. A prominent example is the Bridge River Development (Fig. 5) of the British Columbia Electric Company in Vancouver, Canada, where three six-jet vertical impulse units are being used—each rated 62,000 hp at 1,118-ft net head and operating at a speed of 300 rpm. Efficiency tests on these units have indicated a maximum of approximately 92%, which approaches that of a Francis turbine.

Many Details Improved.—The hydraulic oil governor actuated by flyballs for controlling the speed of turbine units has been in use almost from the beginning

FIG. 4.—GRAND COULEE DAM ON THE COLUMBIA RIVER IN WASHINGTON, INTERIOR VIEW OF LEFT POWERHOUSE

of hydroelectric development. Sensitivity and quick response in hydraulic governors are necessary for close frequency control and accurate timing for electric clocks. Early designs with mechanical drive were sluggish and not conducive to close speed regulation. An important innovation in 1931 was the use of a permanent magnet generator for transmitting indications of turbine speed changes to the governor head. Since 1935 the cabinet-type actuator governor has been used extensively, as it consolidates the equipment in a steel cabinet which protects the working parts from dirt and damage. The operating controls are on the face of the cabinet on which also are many of the turbine and generator instruments. In the case of adjustable-blade propeller-type turbines the blade pitch controls are also mounted in the governor cabinet.

Interconnected system operation, with the tying together of considerable rotating machinery and transmission lines, has materially altered the speed regulation and governing requirements of hydroelectric units. Governors today are designed with provisions for speed "droop" and gate limit adjustment. In some cases, where the penstocks are not too long, the surge tank is omitted and the governors are slowed down to close the gates at such a rate that speed and pressure rise are not reduced excessively. The use of the automatic tie-line load and frequency control equipment and automatic balancing of load between units has resulted in better intersystem operation.

Three guide bearings, one on top of the turbine, one below, and one above

Fig. 5.—Complete Nozzle Assembly, Six Jets for 62,000-Hp Vertical Impulse Turbine, Bridge River Development, Vancouver, Canada

the generator rotor, with the thrust bearing located above the upper guide bearing and supported by brackets on the top of the generator stator frame, had become practically standard in this country by 1920. In 1923, a decided variation in this arrangement was introduced, which has been called the "umbrella" or "overhung" type of generator (Fig. 2). In this type of unit, the thrust bearing is placed under the generator rotor and is supported on brackets resting on the top of the concrete cylinder separating the turbine and the generator. The advantages of the umbrella-type generator are that it eliminates one of the guide bearings, materially shortens the span necessary for the bracket supporting the thrust bearing, and makes it possible to dismantle the generator for inspection and repairs without disturbing the thrust bearing, shaft, and turbine.

Important innovations in thrust bearing design were the spherical and equalizing types, which provide self-adjustment to compensate for settlement or inequalities of foundations. The spherical bearing combines the generator guide and thrust bearing and allows for lateral movement of the shaft. The equalizing bearing has the ability to readjust itself in case of misalinement caused by building settlement.

The generator is usually completely enclosed, with air circulating through it and through water cooling coils. The use of welded plate steel for fabricating the structural members facilitates sectionalizing and field assembly.

There has been a continuing tendency toward simplification in the provisions for exciting the generating units. Individual direct-connected exciters provide a reliable means of operation, independent of faults originating in other units. When a separate centralized system is employed, motor drives replace the water-wheel-driven exciters used in the earlier plants, where there was no reliable source of power supply for starting up the station.

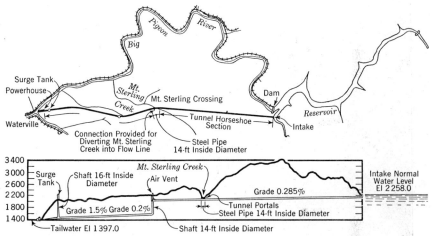

FIG. 6.—HIGH-HEAD TUNNEL DEVELOPMENT—PROFILE AND PLAN OF WALTERS (WATERVILLE) FLOW LINE IN NORTH CAROLINA

Plant Layouts.—High-voltage step-up transformers are usually placed outside the generating station building with the unit high-voltage circuits connected to high-voltage switches and buses either on the top of the generator station or in a switchyard at some distance from the station where a sufficiently large area of flat ground is available. The use of a single three-phase transformer in place of a bank of three single-phase transformers with one spare is becoming current practice.

The characteristics of the development influence to a considerable extent the plant layout, number of units, and the waterway arrangement. Low-head and medium-head developments are generally constructed with the power plant integral with the dam, whereas in the higher-head developments the power station may be some distance from the dam, with a long flow line or tunnels to conduct the water to the power station (Fig. 6).

Economic considerations and the nature of the terrain determine the type of waterway to be used. Tunnels, wood stave or steel pipe, open canals (Fig. 7) or flumes, and various combinations thereof are employed in modern stations. Improved methods have permitted larger diameters, and in some cases unlined tunnels have proved more economical than lined ones despite the increased head loss.

Other Factors.—High-pressure conditions require special precautions, and protective devices such as surge tanks and pressure regulators may be necessary. The trend towards larger-size units has necessitated large pipelines or tunnels, and in turn, larger valves to control the flow to the turbines. Of the various forms of valves available, the needle, butterfly, or pivot types are most common. Improvements have been made in the seals to insure greater watertightness. Recently a new type of rotary valve has been developed which offers less restriction to flow. The hydraulic design of these devices and the flow line calls for

Fig. 7.—Low-Head Canal Development—Exterior View of Upper Salmon Plants in Idaho

special engineering skill and study of surge and water-hammer conditions for successful performance.

Model tests and studies have resulted in the improved hydraulic design of bellmouth intakes and transitions, with low-head loss and reduced size of head gates. Particularly significant has been the application of structural steel gates weighted with concrete, for penstock closure on deep intakes. Fixed roller bearings are most common but in some cases caterpillar tractor rollers have been used. Recent designs employ welded plate steel in place of riveted sections and stainless steel or nonferrous wearing parts. Cathodic protection to mitigate corrosion is also utilized extensively on gate structures.

Steel flow lines, tanks, and penstocks are built by modern welding techniques instead of riveting. Sections of pipe are usually shop welded by automatic welding machines and shipped to the job on flat cars or by truck, for final assembly. This procedure simplifies fabrication of large-diameter pipe and results in considerable savings. Penstocks have been built in large sizes up to 30 ft in diameter and up to $2\frac{7}{8}$ in. in thickness. Special alloy steels have been developed which make possible the use of higher working stresses.

Efficiency of the turbine is allied with that of the draft tube. As manufacturers have striven for the maximum gain, complicated draft tubes of the hydraucone and spreading cone type have given way to the conventional elbow tube, which offers advantages in cost of construction. Deep settings of turbine units to resist cavitation require shortening of the vertical section and lengthening of the horizontal part with a draft-tube gate slot interposed at the end wall of the powerhouse.

In recent years there has been considerable standardization of powerhouse equipment and design. Substructure concrete has been minimized, in so far as consistent with safety and economy of construction. The function of the plant

Fig. 8.—Outdoor-Type Station Integral with Dam—Exterior View of Bliss Development in Idaho

superstructure is to afford protection for machines, instruments, and personnel. Esthetic considerations often lead to monumental structures with architectural embellishments which are "nonrevenue producing" and result in higher first cost. Simplicity and functional design should be in keeping with the utilitarian purpose of the structure and the component electrical equipment.

There are divergent opinions regarding the use of the outdoor and semi-outdoor types of power stations, to reduce the superstructure to the size necessary to enclose the generating units only. This arrangement, first used in the United States in 1912, has now been adopted for some of the largest power plants. Although it has been employed more readily in the south where milder climates prevail, the arrangement is also used extensively in the north where severe winter climates occur, such as at the Bliss Plant of the Idaho Power Company on the Snake River (Fig. 8) in Idaho. Under certain conditions, an indoor-type station might be preferable, as illustrated by the Kerr Development on the Flathead River in Montana (Fig. 9).

Plants for Low and High Heads.—Several typical plants built in the early 1930's will illustrate the "state of the art" at that time and some of the engineer-

ing developments which are preserved in modern design practice. The Morony
Plant of the Montana Power Company on the Missouri River in Montana is
an example of a low-head development having the power plant integral with the
dam. The semi-outdoor type of station has two 31,000-hp units installed, with
umbrella-type generators and overhead gantry cranes.

The layout is comparatively simple and efficient. The design of the water
passages with a straight penstock leading from the bellmouth intake to the
turbine casing reduced the head loss at the intake and through the penstock to
a minimum. Turbine efficiency in the field test was 93% and over-all hydraulic

Fig. 9.—Indoor-Type Station Remote from Dam—Exterior View of Kerr Development in Montana

efficiency from headwater to tailwater was 92.6%. In this type of development
no penstock valves are necessary, the water being controlled by the head gates.

The Merwin Plant of the Pacific Power and Light Company on the Lewis
River in Washington (Fig. 10) is an example of a medium-head installation em-
bodying the semi-outdoor type of construction. The plant has two 63,000-hp
units in operation under a head of 187 ft, with intake and penstock openings
provided for future installation of two additional units. The outdoor gantry
crane is of sufficient size to lift the rotor, shaft, and runner as a unit.

A thin arch dam 313 ft high is penetrated by relatively short straight penstock
sections to the powerhouse, resulting in a highly efficient hydraulic design. A
fish trap built directly over the elbow-type draft tube catches spawning salmon
on their return trek up the river; and by elevator hoist they are transferred to a
truck for delivery to a nearby hatchery.

One novel feature in the construction of this plant was the bridging of a deep ravine across the river channel by a reinforced-concrete arch on which the powerhouse substructure was placed. This resulted in the saving of considerable substructure concrete and excavation.

A high-head plant adopting the fully enclosed type of power station is the Walters plant of Carolina Power and Light Company on the Pigeon River in Waterville, N. C. Three 39,000-hp units operate under a static head of 826 ft (Fig. 6) with the water conducted through a 6-mile-long concrete-lined tunnel regulated by a differential surge tank on the hillside about 550 ft above the power station. The operating conditions and high pressure required the adoption of a special fast-closing Johnson plunger-type valve ahead of the turbine gates and a slower-closing butterfly valve to act as an additional safeguard and for maintenance.

FIG. 10.—MEDIUM-HEAD PENSTOCK DEVELOPMENT—SECTION THROUGH MERWIN (ARIEL) DAM AND POWERHOUSE IN WASHINGTON

3. MODERN HYDROELECTRIC STATIONS

Although most of the large hydroelectric installations now being built or contemplated in the United States are under government or state authority, there are many smaller storage and run-of-river developments under construction by private power companies. The urgency of the present demand for power necessitates those projects which can be economically and speedily built and readily adapted to system operation.

Small-capacity plants, involving minimum materials and a relatively short time for completion, are frequently looked on with more favor by private utilities than are large-scale projects requiring a longer construction period. Where plants can be built in successive stages as the load develops, economies in construction are evident. Extensions to existing plants, and the redevelopment of old or obsolete plants where the dam and major construction are already completed, are prominent among new capacity installations.

The primary objectives sought in the design of the modern power plant are:

a. High service reliability.

b. Low investment and operating costs.

c. Simplicity in physical arrangement, operation, and maintenance.

d. Pleasing appearance consistent with economy and utilitarian purposes.

An example of a simplified outdoor-type power station is the C. J. Strike Development of the Idaho Power Company on the Snake River in Idaho (Fig. 11), placed in operation early in 1952. It has a total installed capacity of 90,000 kva with three 38,000-hp fixed-blade propeller turbines operating under an 88-ft head. This development was built in 16 months and involved the construction of an earth-fill dam 3,222 ft long and a concrete spillway, with a power plant to house

FIG. 11.—OVER-ALL DEVELOPMENT VIEW—C. J. STRIKE PLANT, SNAKE RIVER, IDAHO

three 30,000-kva units. The power plant is of simplified design to reduce construction time and cost. It involves a minimum of concrete, with a downstream wall close to the turbines to provide a narrow structure.

Structural design of the generators (Fig. 12) is unique in that two important components—namely, the stator frame and lower thrust bearing bracket—are supported from an integrally built base ring and sole plate, so that there is a minimum possibility of distortion within the generator internal assembly. This arrangement also provides for easy correction should any distortion develop between generator and turbine as a result of concrete growth or foundation settlement. Switchboard and all auxiliary equipment are located on the operating floor of the powerhouse, which has no basement.

Another outstanding development now under construction in the northwest is the 200,000-kw Cabinet Gorge Installation of The Washington Water Power Company (Fig. 3). This project has a concrete arch dam 200 ft high built across a deep canyon of the Clark Fork River in Idaho.

Four vertical propeller-type turbines will be installed, to operate under a head of 90 ft to 105 ft, with individual 27-ft-diameter steel penstocks emerging from concrete-lined tunnels 560 ft long. By adjusting the governor closing time it was possible to eliminate a costly surge tank and obtain satisfactory system operation. The powerhouse, a semi-outdoor type, is located on the right bank of the river approximately 300 ft downstream from the dam. The design was based on construction expediency, and the downstream wall was built as a cantilever prior to the erection of the turbine, to protect against a seasonal 40-ft rise in tailwater

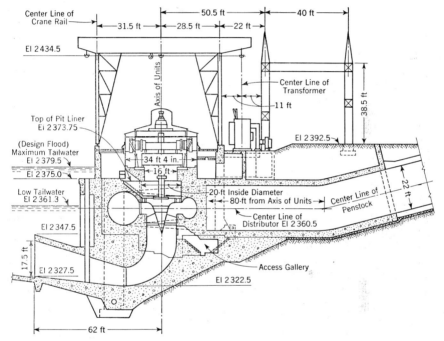

Fig. 12.—Modern Outdoor-Type Station—Cross Section of Powerhouse, C. J. Strike Development in Idaho

during flood stage. A 275-ton gantry crane spans the roof of the powerhouse, for assembly and dismantling of the units, and includes a 30-ton auxiliary hoist for handling the draft-tube gates.

The steepness of the sides and the depth of the gorge made the diversion of the river during construction a difficult problem. A rock-fill cofferdam was created by blasting with dynamite charges placed in holes in the left-hand wall of the gorge. Twin diversion tunnels of horseshoe section, 29 ft in equivalent diameter, were provided to handle a maximum of 30,000 cu ft per sec during low-water periods.

Automatic and Remote Control Operation.—To improve operation and reduce operating costs automatic control features are employed in the design of many of the newer plants. Automatic operation (pushbutton control) may involve starting and shutting down the machines and also headwater gate control, turbine gate control, turbine gate regulation, and various protective features on the units with remote supervisory control by other plants on the system. Only infrequent attendance is necessary for emergency and maintenance purposes by nonresident operators. Plants may also be designed for semiautomatic operation with a manual start but with automatic devices for load control and shutting down machines, which require only a "watchman" operator.

In a recent survey by the Hydraulic Power Committee of the Edison Electric Institute, it was reported that seventy-three hydro plants throughout the United States have various degrees of automatic control. The majority of these plants are conversions from originally manually-operated plants. All the companies indicated satisfaction with the economy of these partially attended and unattended plants. Most of the plants have a capacity of less than 20,000 kw.

The Owens River Gorge Project of the City of Los Angeles, Calif. (nearing completion), develops a total static head of 2,375 ft in a three-stage development with three powerhouses, each containing one 51,200-hp reaction turbine operating under an effective head of 743 ft. All powerhouses are of the outdoor type and identical design. The operation of the three plants is to be coordinated from a single control room in the lower plant, thus eliminating operators at the two upper plants.

Pumped Storage Plants.—A few pumped storage plants have been built in the United States to provide additional peak-load capacity where the water supply is limited. The Rocky River Project of the Connecticut Light and Power Company built in 1928 on the Housatonic River in Connecticut was one of the first in the United States. It consists of a 33,000-hp vertical-shaft turbine and a pumping plant with two 8,100-hp vertical-shaft centrifugal pumps. The power and pumping plant are connected by a single penstock with the reservoir located on a tributary stream. The inflow to the reservoir is supplemented by water pumped from the main river during off-peak hours. The application of this type of plant is limited, but it is again being considered and may prove advantageous in combination with other units on large systems.

An installation such as the Serra Hydro Electric Development of the São Paulo Tramway Light and Power Company, Limited, in Brazil is ideal for pumped storage. In this plant water is lifted by two pumping stations a distance of from 40 ft to 100 ft, then dropped a total of 2,300 ft to pass through impulse turbines having various ratings from 60,000 hp to 92,000 hp. In addition, both the pumping units are reversible and are used as turbine generators during peak-load periods.

Another pumped storage installation is a recent project at the Buchanan Dam on the Colorado River in Texas, where the stream flow is highly variable and off-peak steam energy can be purchased from neighboring utilities. Water used for hydro generation and passed into the downstream Inks Reservoir is pumped back into Buchanan Lake during off-peak hours. A common pipeline is used for both the turbine generator and the pumping unit.

Recently a turbine manufacturer made extensive tests to obtain a combined pump-turbine unit in which the efficiency of each part would be satisfactory.

A pumped storage type of installation with a reversible turbine for pump operation is being considered for the proposed Niagara Redevelopment Project. As one feature of this installation a storage reservoir is contemplated in which water can be pumped during periods of allowable maximum diversion from Niagara Falls and then withdrawn for generation during other periods when the diversion is reduced. A combination pump-turbine machine will be used, for which the maximum pumping head will be about 100 ft and the maximum generating head, about 96 ft.

With the more complete development of river systems and the need for additional peak-load capacity, it is probable that pumped storage units will receive more attention in future years. By pumping with low-cost system steam, or secondary hydro energy, more effective utilization of energy resources is obtained.

Underground Power Stations.—Considerable interest has recently been evidenced in underground hydro stations, which have been used extensively in Europe. Where site characteristics are favorable, this type of plant may have decided advantages. Future military considerations may also influence the adoption of underground plants. The only known example of such a station in the United States is at Snoqualmie Falls in the State of Washington. This plant has a capacity of 20,000 kw and contains a long tailrace discharge tunnel to the river. Several underground plants are being constructed in South America; and it is claimed that, because of lower tunneling costs, they are more economical than the conventional aboveground station, requiring steel penstocks with expensive anchorages and supports.

On several occasions in this country, comparative studies and cost analyses based on American labor and excavation prices have indicated no appreciable saving and some economic disadvantage from the use of underground power stations. Improved tunneling methods and prestressed concrete roof linings may in the future present a more favorable comparison.

4. FUTURE TREND OF HYDRO DEVELOPMENT

The hydroelectric station today stands as a tribute to the pioneer engineers whose inventive genius and resourcefulness have been so fruitful. As a result of the technological development of the first half of the twentieth century, the modern hydroelectric plant produces more power, at lower cost, than its predecessor could. It is a highly dependable source of energy in an industry which has materially improved the standard of living. Hydro plants have by no means reached a state of perfection, and continued technical progress and research will bring forth new ideas.

The electric utility industry is in a state of rapid expansion to meet unprecedented demands for power for defense and economic security. In the future program hydro plants will continue to play an important role in coordinated development. Higher-voltage transmission and greater areas of distribution will inevitably create new operating requirements and the development of the more remote sites. It is estimated that only about 18% of the potential water-power capacity in the United States has been developed, of which about 60% is located in the western mountain and Pacific regions.

To keep pace with the remarkable advances being made in thermal power plant design, new hydro developments must be carefully investigated and engineers should be constantly on the alert to reduce cost and make refinements in design. Additional economies appear possible by using more outdoor features. The barrel supporting the generator does not require housing and could very well be placed outdoors. Considerable mechanical equipment, such as governors, pumps, and motors, could also be adapted to outdoor operation by specifying suitable weatherproof enclosures.

The hydro plant of the future will undoubtedly be more "streamlined" and simplified, with larger capacity and more reliable operating units. Additional automatic features to control the functioning will characterize new capacity installations. Improved materials and construction procedure will result in reduced maintenance and better performance. The situation arising from present high labor and material costs challenges the resourcefulness and ingenuity of engineers and designers, to devise means of reducing production and over-all investment costs. Courage and vision will be the keys to further achievement.

BIBLIOGRAPHY

"Steam Power Gains on Hydro in California," by I. C. Steele, *Civil Engineering*, January, 1950, p. 17.

"Hydro-Electric Power—Design and Operation of Powerhouse and Equipment," by E. B. Strowger, *Transactions*, 4th World Power Conference, Percy Lund, Humphries & Co., Ltd., London, England, Vôl. IV, 1952, p. 2267.

"Trend in Hydroelectric Practice Favors Simplified Station and Automatic Operating Features," by W. S. Merrill and M. G. Salzman, *Civil Engineering*, June, 1949, p. 22.

"Economies in Design, Construction and Operation Control Rising Costs of Hydro Power," by M. G. Salzman, *ibid.*, April, 1948, p. 23.

"High Head Penstock, Ship Welded and Field Riveted," *Engineering News-Record*, October 28, 1948, p. 88

"Hydroelectric Power-Plant Design," by A. T. Larned, *Mechanical Engineering*, August, 1939, p. 575.

"Hydroelectric Practice in the United States," by A. C. Clogher, *Transactions*, A.S.M.E., Vol. 59, 1937, p. 65.

"Hydroelectric Practice in Canada," by T. H. Hogg, *ibid.*, p. 79.

"Ariel Hydro Development," by A. C. Clogher and W. S. Merrill, *Electric World*, March 5, 1932, p. 442.

"Umbrella Type Generators," by A. C. Clogher, *ibid.*, December 29, 1928, p. 1289.

"Hydro-Electric Plant Construction Simplified," by A. C. Clogher, *ibid.*, February 16, 1929, p. 344.

"Waterville Hydro Makes Possible Notable Interconnection," by A. C. Clogher, *ibid.*, August 30, 1930, p. 385.

"Pumped-storage Hydro Plant in Texas Proves Economical," by G. E. Schmitt, *Civil Engineering*, May, 1951, p. 21.

"Proposed Plan Would Triple Niagara's Generated Power," *Power*, March, 1950, p. 116.

"Hydroelectric Handbook," by W. P. Creager and J. D. Justin, John Wiley & Sons, Inc., New York, N. Y., 2d Ed., 1950.

"Water Power Engineering," by H. K. Barrows, McGraw-Hill Book Co., Inc., New York, N. Y., 2d Ed., 1934.

"Idaho Power Co. Combats Northwest 'Brown-out' with a Hydro Plant Built in 13 Months," *Western Construction News*, November, 1951, p. 61.

"Report of Subcommittee on Automatic Hydro Plants," Edison Electric Inst., Hydraulic Power Committee, New York, N. Y., 1951.

AMERICAN SOCIETY OF CIVIL ENGINEERS

Founded November 5, 1852

TRANSACTIONS

Paper No. 2608

PROGRESS IN SANITARY ENGINEERING IN THE UNITED STATES

By E. Sherman Chase,[1] M. ASCE

Synopsis

Sanitary engineering—a science dealing with water supply and purification, sewerage and sewage treatment, drainage, refuse collection and disposal, and insect and vermin control—has achieved a remarkable progress record in the 100 years since Louis Pasteur initiated his experiments in bacteriology. Insect-borne and water-borne diseases have been conquered through the persistent efforts of early practitioners of sanitary engineering. This paper reviews the development of sanitary engineering in the United States. Prominent milestones are listed and related to the pattern of growth of the science. Future prospects are briefly discussed.

Introduction

Sanitary engineering deals with those factors of environmental sanitation which profoundly affect man's well-being. The factors generally accepted as within the province of sanitary engineering are water supply, water purification, sewerage and sewage treatment, drainage, refuse collection and disposal, insect and vermin control, and, to a limited extent, the sanitation of foods.

In dealing with each of these factors the engineer must be guided not only by the laws of mechanics, hydraulics, and the other physical sciences, but by the laws of chemistry and biology. Until the so-called "germ theory of disease" was put forth, the civil engineer who designed works for the acquisition and distribution of water and the disposal of the by-products of man's activity was concerned mainly with physical laws. Furthermore, until the health hazards of intestinal organisms and the transmission of yellow fever, bubonic plague, and other infectious bacteria by insects were recognized, the application of engineering skills to environmental factors was without thought of benefit or harm to human health.

Historical Background

Development of Bacteriology.—Almost coincident with the founding of the American Society of Civil Engineers, a series of events was taking place in France

---

[1] Partner, Metcalf & Eddy, Boston, Mass.

which in subsequent years stimulated the development of that branch of civil engineering now called sanitary engineering. These events were the researches of Louis Pasteur, first in the diseases of wine and beer, then in the diseases of silkworms and of fowl, and finally in the diseases of man himself.

Many years were to pass before the discoveries of Pasteur, Robert Koch, Karl J. Eberth, and other scientists working in the embryonic field of bacteriology, were accepted by the medical profession or utilized by the engineer. Nevertheless, it is not too great an exaggeration to claim that the sanitary engineer's origin, albeit feeble, dates to the time of the founding of the ASCE and was coincident with the work of Pasteur and contemporary bacteriologists and chemists.

Conquest of Infectious Diseases.—Before proceeding with a review of the advance in sanitary engineering during the past 100 years, it is well to consider briefly the plagues which sanitary engineering has abolished, or nearly abolished, from western civilization. For example, cholera, local to India prior to 1817, spread throughout the world during the rest of the nineteenth century. Some 8,500 deaths in Hamburg, Germany, as recently as 1892, were attributable to this disease.

John Snow, in London, England, demonstrated in the famous Broad Street well case that cholera infection was carried by water polluted with excrement from an existing case of the disease. This demonstration had little effect on American practices inasmuch as the sanitary watchword of the period was "cleanse," and as late as 1885 the reduction of incidence of "filth diseases" was attributed to cleanliness. Eventually, of course, the method of transmission of cholera and the proper preventive measures were generally recognized, and the last reported death from this disease in the United States occurred in 1911.

Yellow fever, the dreaded Yellow Jack of Cuba, Panama, and the Gulf coast, swept up the Mississippi Valley from New Orleans, La., in the summer of 1870, with 100,000 victims and 20,000 fatalities in its wake. In *Harper's Weekly* of that year there appeared these words relating to those tragic days:

"This fragrant beauty seems the mark of Death,
The whispering south wind is his poisoned breath;
We weary for these warm bright days to end,
The summer lingers, at what fearful cost.
O, pitying God, in mercy to us send
The white gift of Thy frost!"

Those were the days before Walter Reed and his fellow workers demonstrated the role of the mosquito in the spread of yellow fever, but "the poisonous breath of the south wind" is an apt term for those infected insects. However, even close to the end of the nineteenth century, evil emanations and mysterious miasmas from the earth were accepted in many quarters as the causative factor for yellow fever, malaria, and even typhoid fever. The Johns Hopkins Hospital, in Baltimore, Md., which opened in 1889, had a basement insulated with a thick layer of asphalt, to check dangerous exhalations from the soil.

There were 1,282 deaths from yellow fever in Havana, Cuba, as late as 1896; but by 1902 this scourge was erased thanks to the labors of William C. Gorgas and his corps of doctors and engineers. Nevertheless, yellow fever appeared again in New Orleans as late as 1905. The construction of the Panama Canal was made possible by the eradication of the yellow-fever-bearing mosquito in the Canal Zone. In this connection, it has been stated that Ferdinand de Lesseps, during his abortive attempts to build the canal, lost one third of his white workers by yellow fever.

The history of the prevalence of that other mosquito-borne disease, malaria, and its control, more or less parallels that of yellow fever, although the eradication of malaria has not been nearly so complete. Proper drainage and the elimination of breeding places played an important part in the control of mosquitos and their spread of yellow fever and malaria.

It is to the elimination of typhoid fever that the sanitary engineer points with pride. George C. Whipple, M. ASCE, wrote in 1908 regarding typhoid:

> "The indications are that the disease is soon to become much less prevalent than it is today. In another generation the death rate ought not to be over one-third or one-fourth of what it now is, and who can say that the disease will not be all but obliterated just as smallpox has almost vanished from our midst."

These were prophetic words. In the United States, the typhoid fever death rate, which approximated 35 per 100,000 population in 1900, dropped to less than 1 per 100,000 in 1950.

Sanitary Engineering in the United States

The development of sanitary engineering in the United States since 1852 can be roughly divided into quarter-century periods from the middle of the nineteenth century to the middle of the twentieth century. In reviewing this development through each of the four periods, it is not amiss to refer to some of the more outstanding concurrent historical events.

Period from 1850 to 1875.—The acquisition of the present area of the continental United States by discovery, annexation, cession, and purchase (subsequent to the Louisiana Purchase of 1803) ended in 1867 with the purchase of Alaska from the Russians. The discovery of gold in California in the late 1840's stimulated the development of the west coast at the beginning of the period, and westward migration followed.

Although the Civil War retarded the normal progress of the country, particularly in the South, land grants to Union soldiers following the war and federal assistance to the railroads accelerated the westward flow of population. In the matter of sanitation, the death toll from diseases and wounds on the battlefield and in the prison camps led to well-intentioned but, in the light of modern knowledge, uninformed attempts to ameliorate the conditions causing the spread of infection. In other sections of the world, the dreadful conditions in war hospitals during the Crimean War of the middle 1850's aroused the pity and ire of Florence Nightingale. Similarly, the conditions during the Franco-Prussian War of 1870 evoked in Pasteur the concept of antiseptic treatment of wounds.

In 1850, Lemuel Shattuck prepared a forward-looking report to the Massachusetts Legislature on a plan for "Promotion of Public and Personal Health" in which occurred this significant recommendation:

"* * * that, in laying out new towns and villages, and in extending those already laid out, ample provision be made for a supply, in purity and abundance, of light, air, and water; for drainage and sewerage, for paving, and for cleanliness."

During this quarter century there developed the first glimmering of insight into the causes of those diseases now termed infectious, and the beginning of the recognition of the relationship of environmental conditions to the prevalence of those diseases. In the Second Annual Report of the Massachusetts State Board of Health, Dr. George Derby, its secretary, made the startling assertion that:

"It may be stated in round numbers that one person out of every thousand in Massachusetts, between the ages of 5 and 70, dies yearly from typhoid fever."

Nowhere in Derby's report on his inquiry into the causes of typhoid does he indicate that in his opinion the public water supplies of Massachusetts were in any way related to the prevalence of the disease. However, the English had begun to connect the occurrence of typhoid with the pollution of water supplies, and a few physicians in the United States suspected such a relationship.

According to George W. Fuller, M. ASCE, there were eighty-three public water supplies in the United States in 1850. By 1870 the number had increased to only two hundred forty-three. Generally, these supplies were confined to the larger cities and were derived from nearby rivers or ponds. Although an unsuccessful attempt at water filtration had been made at Richmond, Va., in 1832, not until 1872 was the first successful slow sand filter in the United States constructed at Poughkeepsie, N. Y., in accordance with the designs of James P. Kirkwood, Past-President ASCE. Construction of the filter at Poughkeepsie was followed 2 years later by a similar one at Hudson, N. Y. These two filter plants represent the only successful American attempts to filter public water supplies during the third quarter of the nineteenth century.

Prior to 1850, sewerage and drainage were installed in very few communities. In some cases, the discharge of fecal matter into drains was actually prohibited. This was true in Baltimore, even as late as 1910. Not until about 1850 did the water-carriage system for liquid wastes begin to be adopted. The first sewerage system in the United States designed on engineering principles was that of Brooklyn, N. Y. This installation was based on plans prepared in 1857 by Julius W. Adams, Past-President and Hon. M. ASCE. In 1858, E. S. Chesbrough, Past-President ASCE, presented his first report on a sewerage system for Chicago, Ill., and in 1874 J. Herbert Shedd, M. ASCE, prepared designs for the Providence, R. I., system. These three installations appear to be the only instances of the application of engineering principles to sewerage design in the period from 1850 to 1875.

The few sanitary engineering projects cited represent just about the entire development of that branch of engineering up to 75 years ago. The succeeding quarter century, however, is marked by the real beginning of modern sanitary engineering.

Period from 1875 to 1900.—The last quarter of the nineteenth century was free from wars of major intensity, although there were relatively minor conflicts, such as the Russian-Turkish War, the conquest of Egypt by the British, the Japanese War with China, the Spanish-American War, and the Boer War. Compared to the Civil War in the United States and the Franco-Prussian War of the previous quarter century, these wars were relatively insignificant in their effect on the rest of the world. The Spanish-American War, however, with its dreadful toll from typhoid fever in the army camps, aroused the United States to the necessity for preventive measures against the spread of the disease.

In these last years of the nineteenth century, rapid development in many fields of human activity resulted in the increasing concentration of population in cities, the exploitation of natural resources, the production of many materials and mechanical devices, and, above all, a tremendous expansion in the engineering arts and sciences. The development of agricultural lands and mines in the western part of the United States, the production of more and more wealth, and the increasing demand for improved living conditions turned men's thoughts more intensively to the means for betterment of those environmental factors relating to comfort and health. In this period also the bacterial origin of certain diseases became generally accepted, and epidemics were no longer attributed to acts of God. This was also the era of the American pioneers in sanitary engineering.

During the middle and latter years of this quarter century there appeared a group of pioneering chemists, biologists, and engineers, whose fundamental investigations at the Lawrence Experiment Station in Massachusetts prepared the way for the application of scientific principles to water purification and sewage treatment. These were the days in which a group of brilliant young men, under the leadership of Hiram F. Mills, Hon. M. ASCE, began careers which have meant so much to the practice of sanitary engineering in the United States. Their accomplishments, like the shot at the Concord Bridge (in Massachusetts in 1775), were "heard around the world." This group consisted of the chemists Allen Hazen, M. ASCE, and Fuller, and the biologist and outstanding teacher, William T. Sedgwick of the Massachusetts Institute of Technology (M.I.T.) at Cambridge. Coworkers and pupils of these men, and pupils of their pupils, probably constitute the bulk of sanitary engineers in the United States today, and their influence has been felt far beyond the confines of North America.

A partial list of early leaders in the profession would include the following men: Rudolph Hering, M. ASCE; W. R. Nichols and T. M. Drown of M.I.T.; Leonard P. Kinnicutt of Worcester Polytechnic Institute at Worcester, Mass.; George E. Waring, Jr.; Whipple; Harry W. Clark; Stephen deM. Gage; Frederic P. Stearns, Past-President ASCE; Harrison P. Eddy, Past-President ASCE; F. Herbert Snow, M. ASCE; Frank A. Barbour, M. ASCE; Leonard Metcalf, M. ASCE; and Emil Kuichling, M. ASCE.

The first, although short-lived, course in sanitary engineering, was established at Columbia University at New York, N. Y., in 1886. The second course, established at M.I.T. in 1889, has continued to this day, although it became a graduate course a few years ago.

Naturally, the investigations that received the greatest stress in this period were those relating to the purification of water supplies. The design of the early slow sand filters at Poughkeepsie and Hudson was based on Kirkwood's studies of European filters, but not until the middle 1890's were slow sand filters, based on scientific principles demonstated at the Experiment Station, installed at Lawrence (Fig. 1). The spectacular drop in the typhoid incidence at Lawrence following the installation of these filters demonstrated beyond question the role of polluted water in the spread of the disease, and served as an object lesson that has never been forgotten.

Although slow sand filters were proving their worth and practicability with the relatively clear waters of New York and New England, they had proved unsatisfactory for treating the muddy waters of the West and South. Even before the

FIG. 1.—INTERMITTENT SAND FILTER, LAWRENCE, MASS., 1906

work at Lawrence, the demand for clean water by the paper industry led investigators and promoters to devise filters that could be cleaned by mechanical means and hence used with muddy waters. These attempts were only partly successful, and only after thorough and painstaking experiments conducted at Louisville, Ky., under Fuller, from 1895 to 1897, were the fundamental requirements for the design of the so-called American or mechanical filter established. Heretofore these filters were operated with little or no period for presettling, and without coagulation or with half-hearted attempts at coagulation. In New Orleans one filter company constructed a large plant that failed most ignominiously and at great financial loss to the promoters. It was not until the results of research carried on by Robert Spurr Weston, M. ASCE, were available that the method by which muddy Mississippi waters could be purified was demonstrated.

Between 1875 and the end of the nineteenth century, engineering studies and reports were made on the sewerage and drainage of numerous individual cities and towns, and several systems were actually installed. Early sewers were of vitrified clay or cement pipe, in small sizes, and of brick in large sizes. The first large sewers of concrete were built in Washington, D. C., in 1885.

Prior to 1900 few sewage treatment plants existed in the United States; more than 90% of the nation's sewage was discharged without treatment to streams, lakes, or the oceans. Those treatment plants that were in operation were intermittent sand filters (Fig. 2) or contact beds in the smaller communities, or chemical precipitation plants, such as those at Worcester and Providence. The former plant was the largest in the United States, and served a population of about 118,000.

FIG. 2.—ORIGINAL OPEN SLOW SAND FILTERS AT LAWRENCE, MASS.

Period from 1900 to 1925.—The peaceful advent of the twentieth century was soon marred by the Japanese-Russian War, followed in due course by World War I. In spite of the retarding effect of war, the first quarter of the century marked the beginning of vast social, economic, and industrial changes in the United States, one of which—the widespread adoption of mass production—released men's physical and mental energies for the development of better and more healthful standards of living, in spite of continued concentration of population in great cities.

At the start of the period neither yellow fever nor typhoid fever had been conquered. Yellow fever was still a menace in the southern states, and typhoid was rampant in many northern and southern cities. Typhoid epidemics running to hundreds of cases were not uncommon.

As dark as the picture of water-supply sanitation was in general, Boston, Mass., New York, Providence, Rochester, N. Y., San Francisco, Calif., and other smaller cities, had sought out unpolluted upland supplies, thanks to the concept that "innocence is better than repentance." Unquestionably, however, these cities, and others with respectable water supplies, suffered from the sanitary sins of cities like Niagara Falls, N. Y., whose then unpurified water supply spread disease and death far and wide.

Strange, is it not, that a period at first free from the plague of war but afflicted with plagues of the flesh should before its end see the first great World War and the nearly complete eradication of many infectious diseases? Before the quarter century had ended, nearly every grossly polluted water supply in the United

FIG. 3.—EARLY CHLORINATION APPARATUS

States had been either purified or abandoned for a new and safe supply. By the end of the quarter century the great boon of chlorination had been demonstrated (Fig. 3) and applied to almost all surface sources, yellow fever had been eradicated, and malaria and other infectious diseases had been reduced. This progress was achieved partly as a result of better medical knowledge, but also in part as a result of the broad application of sanitary engineering to environmental factors. Credit for the reduction in deaths from infections is due to no single group, but should be shared by physicians, chemists, and biologists as well as by engineers.

In the field of sewage treatment shortly after the turn of the century the trickling filter was introduced from England—first at Reading, Pa. (in 1908) following experiments at Columbus, Ohio. The Imhoff tank, combining clarification and sludge digestion, came into favor about 1910, and soon became the most popular method of preparing sewage for secondary treatment processes. This popularity has continued to a lesser degree even to the present, particularly in the case of small installations. The disposal of sludge, still a problem, was usually accomplished by means of drying beds or sludge lagoons. Filter presses were used at chemical precipitation plants, and the vacuum filter was introduced at Milwaukee, Wis.

In this period the activated sludge process, inspired by research work at the Lawrence Experiment Station, but developed in England, began to receive serious attention in the United States. The first installation was at San Marcos, Tex. (in 1916), followed during the next 10 years by several others, that at Milwaukee (Fig. 4) being the most widely known. It was at Milwaukee that the pioneer development of a process for the manufacture of a salable product from the sludge was carried out.

Fig. 4.—Jones Island Activated Sludge Plant, Milwaukee, Wis.

Coincident with the increase of urbanization, there had developed problems incidental to the collection and disposal of solid wastes from towns and cities—such as garbage, rubbish, and street sweepings. During the period when certain diseases were attributed to the spontaneous generation of mysterious miasmas in decomposing organic matter and filth, efforts were made, more or less effectually—generally less—to cleanse cities of these solid wastes. Systematic private and public collections of the wastes began toward the end of the nineteenth century, and incinerators for rubbish and reduction plants for garbage were installed by a few cities before the beginning of the twentieth century.

During the first quarter of the twentieth century there was a time when the reduction of garbage became relatively popular, because of the recovery of grease and tankage. However, the introduction of mixed refuse incinerators by J. T. Fetherston, M. ASCE, at Staten Island, N. Y., was followed by the adoption of this method of refuse disposal by many other cities.

The demonstration of the part played by insects and rodents in the spread of disease led to greater efforts toward securing prompt removal and disposal of material serving to harbor the pests. The introduction of the motorcar and the gradual elimination of stables from urban areas did much to diminish the prevalence of the "filthy fly."

Sanitation of the production and handling of foods, particularly milk, was first given serious consideration early in the 1900's. Pasteurization of milk, a joint development of the chemist, the biologist, and the engineer, was recognized, before the end of the first quarter of the twentieth century as essential for the protection of milk quality. The decrease in the death rate among young children is undoubtedly due to a considerable degree to the widespread adoption of pasteurization.

This period marks the initial activity of the Cincinnati, Ohio, station of the United States Public Health Service, under the direction of Earle B. Phelps, in the study of stream pollution and water-supply quality requirements. There was also an increasing interest all over the United States in the prevention of stream pollution, although remedial measures were retarded by World War I.

During this same period the most spectacular victories were won by the sanitary engineer in the battle to stem the tides of death. In these years yellow fever was conquered, and the prophecy of Whipple regarding typhoid came to pass. There remained, however, many tasks related to general improvement of environmental conditions and to the refinement in techniques and skills. The pioneering period was over, and the day of consolidation of victories was at hand.

Period from 1925 to 1950.—The quarter century just ended has been a period of social and economic convulsions, first, the great economic depression, and then World War II and the atomic bomb. Nevertheless, progress in sanitary engineering and efforts to prevent the incidence and spread of disease have continued. As previously stated, however, the dramatic accomplishments of the sanitary engineer in the saving of life were consummated by about the middle 1920's and the period of refinement of design and particularly of the mechanization of sanitary works had begun.

During the second quarter of the twentieth century many modifications and variations of previously used water purification practices occurred. Among the developments of this period were: New methods of coagulation, changes in details of filter design, greater reliance on chlorination, new techniques in taste and odor control, and the greater use of filtration for improvement of chemical and physical qualities rather than for bacterial removal only.

In sewage treatment, however, there has been much more progress in the installation of treatment plants than had occurred in all preceding years. This resulted, first, from the adaptability of the activated sludge process for treatment of wastes in large cities and, second, from the development of high-rate modifications of both the activated sludge and the trickling filter methods of treatment. Other advances such as the digestion of sludge in separate treatment tanks, and the greater use of mechanical dewatering of digested sludge, were in the developmental stage barely a quarter of a century ago but have now become almost standard practice. All these advances have produced treatment plants of high mechanical complexity, but with far less space and labor requirements per unit capacity than the older plants.

During the second quarter of this century, more and more attention has been paid to the reduction of the pollution of waterways. Laws and regulations have been promulgated, enforcement agencies have expanded, public educational campaigns in behalf of clean waters have been waged, and hundreds of sewage treatment plants have been built. In spite of all these efforts, much remains to be done, particularly in regard to elimination of pollution by industrial wastes. This is the next broad field for the sanitary engineer to tackle, but he will need the help of the industrial engineer and the chemist as the problem is one of great complexity.

CONCLUSION

This brief discussion has necessarily omitted a multitude of interesting and significant details in order to present the progressive development and the glorious achievements of sanitary engineering during the past 100 years. Stress has been placed on the relation of sanitary engineering to the prevention of disease and to the promotion of health.

The Future.—What of the future? No man can say! The great days of conquest of disease in the United States by the sanitary engineer are in the past. From now on, he will hold the gains and press on to develop new and better techniques in his art. However, when the war drums no longer beat and the battle flags are furled, there are many other areas of the world where he can resume his struggle with those malignant environmental conditions that cause death and disease.

In the United States there will continue to be great demand for clean streams, lakes, and ocean shores. To restore waterways to the maximum degree of cleanliness consistent with economic limitations will require much research in the field of industrial wastes treatment and large expenditures on the part of industry in the application of such research.

In view of the need for conservation of natural resources it is not unlikely that in arid regions, reclamation of sewage and other liquid wastes may be realized. Much is to be done in this field. Salvage of the solid constituents in sewage and wastes will require more consideration, and in this connection research will undoubtedly provide answers to problems now unsolved. It is possible that, in the economical development of atomic energy, ways may be found to concentrate the soluble solids of waste liquors and thus permit their recovery or easy and cheap destruction. Atomic energy may also offer a method for economical distillation of fresh water from the ocean. In general, however, it is probable that the future, in so far as one can look ahead, will show more refinement in the basic techniques of sanitary engineering, the development of new techniques and continued research for better and cheaper methods in the purification of water, the treatment of sewage, the control of insects and vermin, the disposal of solid refuse, and the sanitation of foods.

Pasteur wrote many years ago, "It is within the power of man to cause all parasitic diseases to disappear from the world." Within his sphere and in the United States the sanitary engineer has almost reached this goal in less than 100 years of progress.

AMERICAN SOCIETY OF CIVIL ENGINEERS
Founded November 5, 1852
TRANSACTIONS

Paper No. 2609

WATER SUPPLY AND TREATMENT

By Harry E. Jordan,[1] Aff. ASCE

Synopsis

The history of water supply and treatment in the United States is an epic of constant progress and achievement. The paper reviews the development of water treatment from 1850, when there were only sixty-eight cities in the United States with planned water supplies, to 1952, when more than 15,500 urban supplies were in operation. Important phases in the rapid growth of water supply and treatment are described, and many early installations are mentioned. Among the treatment processes reviewed are filtration, sedimentation, chlorination, and fluoridation.

Introduction

Midway through the nineteenth century, sixty-eight cities in the United States and six in Canada had developed public water supply systems. Contrary to common assumption, the greatest number of these (thirty) was not in New England, but in the Middle Atlantic States. Although Boston, Mass., traditionally is credited with the first major public supply in the United States (1652), it was not until 1848 that the present system was started. New York, N. Y., began its first limited supply and distribution system in 1744, but not until 1835 was a substantial distribution system installed.

Historical Development

The first pumped supply in the United States was built in Bethlehem, Pa., in 1754:[2]

> "Water was taken from a spring issuing from magnesian limestone. It was conducted 350 ft through an underground conduit to a cistern, or well, whence it was raised by a 5-in. lignum vitæ pump, through bored hemlock logs, to a wooden tank in the village square, 70 ft above the pump. There being trouble from the bursting of the wooden pipes, 1¼-in. pipes of sheet lead were tried. They were soldered along the edges and bedded in a cement of pitch and brick dust, and laid in a gutter of brick. This expedient did not prove very successful."

---

[1] Secy., Amer. Water Works Assn., Inc., New York, N. Y.
[2] "The Manual of American Water-Works," edited by M. N. Baker, The Eng. News Pub. Co., New York, N. Y., 1888.

Among the older works of larger cities are those of Providence, R. I. (1772), Worcester, Mass. (1798), Philadelphia, Pa. (1801), Baltimore, Md. (1807), Albany, N. Y. (1813), Reading, Pa. (1819), Pittsburgh, Pa. (1820), Cincinnati, Ohio (1820), Richmond, Va. (1820), Detroit, Mich. (1827), St. Louis, Mo. (1830), and Chicago, Ill. (1840). Buffalo, N. Y., did not start its supply until 1852; Washington, D. C., until 1853; Cleveland, Ohio, until 1854; Denver, Colo., and Indianapolis, Ind., until 1871; Milwaukee, Wis., until 1872; and Kansas City, Mo., until 1873.

WATER TREATMENT

Springs and dug wells were the favorite sources of water supply exploited by the early engineers. Lakes or ponds were appropriated by fortunately located communities; but, as time went on and the cities grew, the need for more water led to the introduction of surface water from nearby streams.

Slow Sand Filtration.—Albert Stein built a sand filter for Richmond in 1832 that was hardly complete before its failure was obvious. At Elizabeth, N. J., when the works were built in 1854, a sand-and-charcoal filter was installed, which was still operating in 1889 when "The Manual of American Water-Works"[2] was compiled by M. N. Baker.

Because of the growing realization of the deficiencies in sanitary quality of supplies, in 1865 the Water Commissioners of the City of St. Louis employed James P. Kirkwood, Past-President ASCE, to travel in England and Europe and to recommend, on the basis of his studies, water treatment works for that city. His report, published in 1869, displayed great admiration for the works built by James Simpson and contemporary engineers in England, and recommended settling and slow sand filtration (on the British model) for installation at St. Louis. However, somewhat pathetically, Mr. Kirkwood observed in a note written in April, 1869, that "the public mind of St. Louis does not yet seem to consider filtration important."

A peculiar by-product of the St. Louis project was that Mr. Kirkwood's design of the settling basin and slow sand filters made for St. Louis was modified and used by him for the works at Poughkeepsie, N. Y., first operated in 1873. This system was initially developed in its complete form from the source (the Hudson River) through pumps, filters, distribution reservoir, and mains. The Poughkeepsie filtration system was the first one in the United States to follow accepted British designs and experience. Although substantial additions in structures and changes in methods have been made in the intervening 80 years, the filters still are operating and the water supply is acceptable. This supply, it should be noted, is taken from the Hudson River at a point below the location recommended in 1951 by the Engineering Panel (Thorndike Saville, W. W. Horner (Past-President ASCE), L. R. Howson, and Abel Wolman, all Members, ASCE) for diverting water for a rapid sand filtration plant to augment New York City's upland sources.

Rapid Sand Filtration.—Shortly after Mr. Kirkwood had completed the Poughkeepsie plant, J. W. Hyatt, I. S. Hyatt, and Patrick Clark developed units that were forerunners of the modern rapid sand filters. The first patents were granted in 1881, and by 1889 the Hyatt Company held fifty-nine separate patents for design, treatment materials, and methods. A dozen or more separate companies competed in designing and installing water treatment systems. The business was cruelly competitive. For example, one company advertised how many plants built by the Hyatts had failed and had been rebuilt by the advertiser. Although competition made for progress, one by one the various companies had financial difficulties and were liquidated or consolidated with others.

In 1895, Allen Hazen, M. ASCE, after a tour of European water works, wrote "The Filtration of Public Water-Supplies,[3] which was authoritative in content and was widely read by those who were then attempting to improve water supply quality in the United States. Hazen was one of that galaxy of great engineers— George W. Fuller, Paul Hansen, G. C. Whipple, and Robert S. Weston, all Members of ASCE—who were inspired by the brilliant leadership of William T. Sedgwick to strike out into the new fields of environmental sanitation. Few university professors have contributed as much as did Sedgwick through the work done by those whose genius he fostered.

Coagulation.—At the turn of the century, Fuller, Hazen, and Weston led the way in conducting experimental studies of the various filtration systems for cities where water treatment was needed. In 1895–1896 Mr. Fuller conducted objective and parallel tests of three competitive rapid sand filters for the Louisville (Ky.) Water Company (Fig. 1). These studies demonstrated the need for the settling of coagulated particles from the water before filtration. Neither the Hyatts' 1883 patent on the use of alum as a coagulant nor patents later issued to competitors had indicated knowledge of this important fact. In the modern rapid sand filtration plant, from 75% to 90% of the suspended material is removed from the water before it enters the filters. With predisinfection of the water, little bacterial removal is required of the filter layer.

The treatment plant built by local engineers of the Louisville Water Company (after Fuller had completed his studies and moved on to similar work at Cincinnati and with Weston at New Orleans, La.) embodied some of the recommended features, but failed to consider certain hydraulic requirements necessary for successful operation. However, at Little Falls, N. J., in 1902, the Fuller designs were built into operating structures. The round filter with the revolving rakes gave way to the rectangular unit with a higher wash-water flow rate.

The modern rapid sand filtration plant emerged. Today's great installations such as those at Chicago, Cleveland, Detroit, Milwaukee, and Toronto, Ont., Canada, are the descendants of the little wooden tubs built by Hyatt, Clark, Jewell, and others, welded into new form and efficiency by Fuller, Hazen, Weston, Joseph W. Ellms (M. ASCE), and their contemporaries.

Alum As a Coagulant.—About 1900, when several large cities were considering filtration of public supplies to reduce the typhoid death rate, the Engineer Corps of the United States Army assigned A. M. Miller, M. ASCE, to conduct experimental studies of filtration at Washington, D. C. (The supply works of that city were then and still are under the control of the Army Engineers.) Colonel Miller's report recommended that rapid sand filters be installed.

Objections were made by various persons, including representatives of the District of Columbia Medical Society. When the authorization for building the water treatment plant was before Congress, the Senate Committee on District

[3] "The Filtration of Public Water-Supplies," by Allen Hazen, John Wiley & Sons, Inc., New York, N. Y., 1895.

Affairs held hearings. The record of the hearings was published.[4] Testimony by Rudolph Hering, M. ASCE, and by Fuller, Weston, and others favored the installation of rapid sand filters, and the use of alum as a coagulant.

A report was made by a special committee of the Medical Society of the

(a) Exterior View

(b) Laboratory

FIG. 1.—LOUISVILLE, KY., EXPERIMENT STATION

District of Columbia which favored slow sand filters. Under the subheading, "Addition of Alum to Potomac Water Not Warranted," the committee stated (in part):

"An important consideration with reference to the use of mechanical [rapid sand] filters arises in connection with the effect of the chemical used as a coagulant on the health of the consumers of the filtered water.

---

[4] "Purification of the Washington Water Supply," Committee Hearings, U. S. Senate, U. S. Govt. Printing Office, Washington, D. C., 1903.

"Mr. Weston's statement that 'The almost unanimous conclusion is that, if the alkalinity of the raw water is sufficient to decompose completely the applied chemical, its use is in no way prejudicial to health' has certainly not been proved by the experience of the medical profession and [as stated by Mr. Weston, at least] is incorrect. Everything will depend upon the nature of the substances into which the 'applied chemical' is decomposed.

"The most that can be said is that it has *not yet been demonstrated* that the alum as used in mechanical filters is prejudicial to health. In the opinion of this Committee the people of this community should not be made use of to determine that question."

After the hearings were completed, the installation of slow sand filters was approved. The MacMillan filter plant was built and provided with a settling basin to preclarify the Potomac River water. However, in less than 5 years the operation of the settling basin and filters proved unsatisfactory. It was then decided to install a coagulating system (using alum) to assist the settling basin in preparing the water for the slow filters. The coagulant is still used; the filters still operate; the doctors who opposed alum as a coagulant have gone to their reward; and the residents of the District of Columbia as well as the many thousands in other cities who use water coagulated with alum before filtration have demonstrated no ill health attributable to the method of water treatment.

In fact, the reduction of water-borne typhoid and other intestinal disorders has been striking not only in Washington but also in all cities where modern water treatment is practiced. Other cities faced opposition from unorganized groups who confused alum used in baking powder (then being crusaded against) with alum used as a water-treatment chemical, but no documentation of opposing opinions equals that derived from the Senate hearings in the Washington case.

Chlorination Proved Beneficial.—After chlorination was first practiced in 1908 at the Chicago Stock Yards Plant and at the Boonton Reservoir (Fig. 2) of Jersey City, N. J., sanitary engineers and public health officials in the United States became greatly interested in the process as a means of reducing the bacterial content of public water supplies. Fortunately, the installation of chlorination equipment proceeded without much fanfare. The decision to chlorinate was often made by management, without public discussion, as a step in water-supply improvement. The annual death rate from typhoid and other water-borne diseases was still high in most cities, but it soon became evident that chlorination was producing highly beneficial results.

The most conspicuous opposition to chlorination developed in Massachusetts when one of the members of the State Department of Health firmly opposed chlorination of any impounded public supply under his jurisdiction. His theory was that the sources had not been polluted and that chlorination was not needed.

It should be remembered, however, that, before the work of E. B. Phelps, Ellms, S. J. Hauser, Wolman, Linn Enslow (A. M. ASCE), and others, chlorination proceeded on a rule-of-thumb basis depending on results of bacteriological examination of the water before and after treatment. The delays resulting from this method were often responsible for chlorinous tastes in the treated water and in turn for sporadic public complaint.

Of all the opposition to chlorination, the most serious in its possibilities was a communication addressed to the city officials of an Illinois city about 1910. The State Water Survey had recommended that the public supply be chlorinated and

a member of the city council had written to Harvey W. Wiley asking his opinion
of chlorination. As food chemist of the United States Department of Agriculture
during the "dawn" of food sanitation, Wiley had an international standing as an

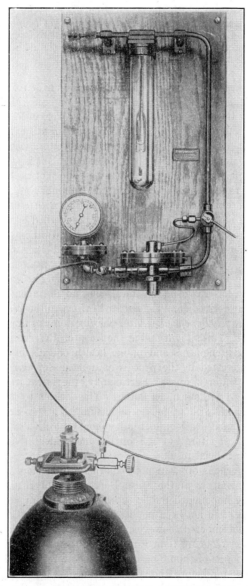

FIG. 2.—ORIGINAL CHLORINATOR INSTALLED AT BOONTON, N. J., IN 1913

opponent of food adulteration. He had vigorously combated the use of such
things as benzoate of soda in ketchup and formaldehyde in milk, and had built
up a great following. When the request for comment concerning chlorination

came to him, he did not take the time to examine the problem in detail, but replied that "chlorine is an adulterant chemical that should no more be used in water than formaldehyde in milk." Fortunately, the letter received little publicity. Dr. Wiley forgot about chlorination.

Liquid chlorine, instead of chlorinated lime, began to be used in the disinfection of water about 1912. Ellms and Hauser in Cincinnati and Wolman and Enslow in Maryland developed methods for the prompt evaluation of the adequacy of treatment with chlorine. Men in service in World War I came home with a firm belief in the protective value of chlorination. Coagulation, sedimentation, filtration, and disinfection had become the fabric of water purification.

SUMMARY

In the past 100 years the number of urban water supplies in the United States has increased from sixty-eight to more than 15,500. During the century, the water-served population has grown from less than a million to almost a hundred million. More striking than this simple growth, however, is the improved sanitary quality of public supplies. In 1900, large cities lost an average of more than 50 persons per 100,000 each year by death from typhoid fever alone. About that time, Hazen pointed out that improved water quality had already demonstrated that, for every death from typhoid fever prevented by improved water quality, at least two additional deaths from other related causes were prevented.

Water treatment as now practiced, with effective coagulation, sedimentation, filtration, and disinfection, reached a reasonably efficient state by 1920. (This statement should not be taken as disregarding the great improvements that took place during the ensuing 30 years.) Today less than 1 typhoid death occurs per 100,000 population. Therefore, it can be assumed that for the 30-year period, 50 typhoid deaths and 100 related deaths per 100,000 population have been prevented by water-quality control. During this period the average water-served population has averaged about 75,000,000 persons. Thus, the "life-saving" credit for improved water supply during the 30-year period ($750 \times 150 \times 30$) amounts to 112,500 persons per year, or a total of 3,375,000.

Fluoridation of water is now considered by all as a new and novel element in water-quality control. In 1945, communal fluoridation of public water supply was initiated at Grand Rapids, Mich., Newburgh, N. Y., Evanston, Ill., and Brantford, Ont., Canada; and by December, 1951, more than 200 cities had adopted the process.

Fluoridation, it should be understood, is not a protective treatment such as coagulation, filtration, or disinfection, nor is it a medication. It is an adjustment of the chemical make-up of the water intended to maintain sound teeth and thus indirectly improve the general health. In this way, growing children are provided with a dietary component known to exist in proper amount in many natural waters where dental caries is infrequent. Its introduction in any community water supply depends on support and advocacy by the dental and medical profession. The water-works industry cooperates in, but does not promote fluoridation. However, the practice is coming to be recognized as an important element in the service of public water supply.

AMERICAN SOCIETY OF CIVIL ENGINEERS

Founded November 5, 1852

TRANSACTIONS

Paper No. 2610

TESTING STATIONS FOR SANITARY ENGINEER-ING—AN OUTSTANDING ACHIEVEMENT

By Samuel A. Greeley,[1] Hon. M. ASCE

Synopsis

Sewage and water testing stations are recognized as one of the outstanding achievements in sanitary engineering. Data on these pioneer stations are given, with comments on the results of research and experimentation that they carried on so successfully.

Introduction

Sanitary engineering as a recognized, organized profession is 100 years old. It began to be practiced as a more or less exclusive occupation soon after 1850. From then on, for a generation, it grew in childlike fashion without knowing very much about itself. There were no courses of instruction to be taken until after 1890. As it left the adolescent age, a hunger and a thirst for knowledge and understanding possessed it, and sanitary engineering entered into the great era of testing stations. As a profession, it may be said to have come of age in 1923 with the creation of the Sanitary Engineering Division of the ASCE.

Testing Stations

The era of testing stations well deserves to be referred to as an outstanding achievement. It gave facts for the practice of a growing and indispensable profession. A testing station (Fig. 1) is a working model of a water or a sewage works. The tanks and other structures comprising a testing station are man-size and larger. Facilities for measurement, adjustment, and control were provided. Beginning with the testing station at Lawrence, Mass., in 1887, the era of testing stations continued actively until well after 1920. A third of a century may well be allotted to this achievement in sanitary engineering. During the period, more than thirty major testing stations for water and sewage works were built and operated. There is no definite time for the ending of the era, because the testing of new things and the application of old and new processes to special conditions is a continuing need.

---

[1] Partner, Greeley & Hansen, Chicago, Ill.

Early Work.—Most of these testing stations were built to investigate water and sewage problems separately. The one at Lawrence, generally recognized as the first, made "Experiments Upon the Purification of Both Sewage and Water." The State Board of Health of Massachusetts, under the leadership of Henry P. Walcott and Hiram F. Mills, Hon. M. ASCE, started the Lawrence Experiment Station in 1887.

H. W. Clark, chief chemist of the Massachusetts Department of Public Health was connected with the station from its beginning, and in 1895 became its director. In 1888 a chemical laboratory was installed, and in 1890 a laboratory

FIG. 1.—PRE-AERATION TESTING STATION—DECATUR, ILL.

for bacteriological and microscopical work was added. Besides these laboratories, the station was equipped with an hydraulic laboratory and with tanks, filters, and other apparatus for experimental work.

In 1893 a slow sand water filter, designed by Mills, was installed when an epidemic of typhoid fever swept down the Merrimack River. This filter showed conclusively that polluted water could be made safe for drinking.

Achievements.—Testing stations have produced many advances in the science of sanitary engineering, for example: Safe operating loads; special processes; details of operating facilities such as dosing equipment and nozzles for trickling filters; and determination of the effect of different raw water and raw sewage characteristics on processes and loads.

A few testing stations, like the one at the Massachusetts Institute of Technology at Cambridge, were used not only for the study of treatment processes, but also for teaching laboratories. At this station different materials for trickling filters were tested, such as stones, bricks, and wooden slats.

The writer, with Rudolph Hering, M. ASCE, visited the small testing station at Essen, Germany, in 1908 where the Imhoff, or two-story sewage sedimentation and sludge digestion tank, was developed. Karl Imhoff, M. ASCE, personally showed and explained the operation of the station. The experimental tank was of wood, about 15 ft long, 8 ft wide, and 20 or more ft deep. A new device was brought forth at this station that has been used successfully in many countries.

Location of Early Testing Stations.—Some of the major water testing stations and the dates of their establishment are as follows:

City	Date
Boston, Mass.	1890
Providence, R. I.	1893
Louisville, Ky.	1894
Pittsburgh, Pa.	1883 and 1896
Cincinnati, Ohio	1898
New Orleans, La.	1900
Philadelphia, Pa.	1901–1903
Harrisburg, Pa.	1903
Springfield, Mass.	1903
New York, N. Y., Jerome Park	1906–1907
Oakland, Calif.	1907–1908
Cleveland, Ohio	1913
Detroit, Mich.	1917
Benton Harbor, Mich.	1921
Princeton, Ill.	1923
Chicago, Ill.	1927

The first sewage testing stations were:

City	Date
Lawrence, Mass.	1887
Pawtucket, R. I.	1900
Worcester, Mass.	1904
Columbus, Ohio	1904
New York, N. Y.	1906
Massachusetts Institute of Technology at Cambridge	1906
Waterbury, Conn.	1907
Gloversville, N. Y.	1908
Chicago, Ill., Thirty-Ninth Street	1909
Chicago Stock Yards	1912
Philadelphia, Pa.	1909
Brooklyn, N. Y.	1910
Akron, Ohio	1912
Milwaukee, Wis.	1914
Cleveland, Ohio	1910
Decatur, Ill.	1914
Houston, Tex.	1916

City	Date
New Haven, Conn............................1917	
Decatur, Ind. 1917	
University of Illinois at Urbana..................1915	

RESEARCH AND PERSONNEL

The achievements of the testing stations were, of course, made by men and women. A discussion of this era is not complete without mention of the persons who designed and operated the stations and who envisioned and then solved the problems.

The early water testing stations at Cincinnati, Louisville, and New Orleans were remarkable not only for the development of rapid sand water filtration, but also for the engineers and chemists who operated them and later practiced sanitary engineering, much to the welfare of urban populations. Harrison P. Eddy, Past-President ASCE, was closely associated with the sewage testing stations at Worcester and Gloversville. The effect of industrial wastes on sewage treatment was studied—iron wastes at Worcester and leather wastes at Gloversville. The Gloversville report, written by Eddy, is a model of excellence. Other notable results came out of the stations in Columbus, New York City, Chicago (both sewage and water research), and Milwaukee.

Obviously, all the persons who brought great talents to this work cannot be mentioned in a brief paper. To understand the high quality of the accomplishments of the testing station era, however, it is necessary to give a few such references. The ability and later the personal leadership of many of those who operated important testing stations assured outstanding achievements.

Besides those already cited, the partial roster of men who have greatly contributed and have now passed from the scene, includes such names as: George W. Fuller, Allen Hazen, Joseph W. Ellms, Robert S. Weston, and George A. Johnson. All were Members of ASCE.

TESTING STATION DEVELOPMENTS

Just as there is no space to describe all the persons who worked at all the testing stations, so also there is none to discuss all the results. Reference to a few, however, will illustrate this outstanding achievement in sanitary engineering.

The water testing stations at Louisville and Cincinnati and later at New Orleans are considered to have developed and established rapid sand filtration for water. The sewage testing station at Columbus, together with others, brought out many things that resulted in the better design of trickling filters. The sewage testing station at New York City contributed notably to the understanding of oxygen balances with reference to the disposal of sewage effluents into the waters of oceans and tidal estuaries. The several sewage testing stations in Chicago added greatly to the knowledge required for the treatment of industrial wastes. They also further developed oxygen balance techniques. The sewage testing station at Milwaukee did much to establish the bases of design and the general usefulness of the activated sludge process.

Many of the more important investigations and advances of recent years are covered in the excellent reports made by Committees on Sewerage and Sewage Treatment[2,3,4] and on Water Supply Engineering[5,6,7] of the Sanitary Engineering Division.

In the century-long life of sanitary engineering as an essential profession, there have been many achievements. The era of the testing station marks the growth of the profession through the questing period. The high character and ability of the men and women who designed and operated these stations and the worth of the results constitute, as an event, an outstanding achievement in sanitary engineering.

---

[2] *Proceedings*, ASCE, November, 1942, p. 1559; April, 1944, p. 457; June, 1946, 799; and October, 1948, p. 1315.

[3] *Transactions*, ASCE, Vol. 115, 1950, p. 1261.

[4] *Proceedings-Separate No. 176*, March, 1953.

[5] *Proceedings*, March, 1943, p. 399; May, 1945, p. 673; April, 1947, p. 497; and September, 1949, p. 971.

[6] *Transactions*, ASCE, Vol. 105, 1940, p. 1740.

[7] *Proceedings-Separate No. 164*, January, 1953.

AMERICAN SOCIETY OF CIVIL ENGINEERS

Founded November 5, 1852

TRANSACTIONS

Paper No. 2611

CONTRIBUTIONS OF ENGINEERING TO HEALTH ADVANCEMENT

By Abel Wolman,[1] M. ASCE

Synopsis

The engineering profession has been instrumental in the successful fight against disease in the United States. Virtual elimination of the intestinal and insect-borne diseases proved the true value of engineering accomplishment. This paper reviews the unbelievable sanitary conditions that existed in former years and traces the work of the sanitary engineer in curbing the disease rate. Progress to date is evaluated, and a program for future development is suggested. The paper touches on many related problems that await solution by the sanitary engineer.

Introduction

Suppose the daily newpapers announced this morning that last year New York (N. Y.) had 95,000 cases of typhoid fever; Chicago (Ill.), 43,000; Philadelphia (Pa.), 24,000; Los Angeles (Calif.), 24,000; and Detroit (Mich.), 22,000. In 1952, this newspaper account would have somewhat the same effect as the dropping of an atomic bomb on the five largest cities in the United States. Times have changed. Nevertheless, that is exactly what would have happened to these five major cities if the 1850 death rates had prevailed.

The intestinal diseases were the chief concern of the public health officer 100 years ago. These were the diseases of fundamental importance in environmental sanitation, and were, therefore, those offering the engineer the opportunity to make his greatest contribution toward preserving the health of mankind.

Early Progress

The intestinal and the insect-borne diseases provided the great proving ground for engineering accomplishment. Geddes Smith has aptly described these opportunities in the following terms:

"The bacteria that survive a Rhine-journey down the water courses from one man's intestine to another's gullet—typhoid, bacillary dysentery, cholera—

---

[1] Prof., San. Eng., Johns Hopkins Univ., Baltimore, Md.

are vulnerable at any point of their extra-corporeal travel, but most accessible where they pass through the channels of a city water supply."[2]

Recall what kind of water the citizen used 100 years ago in the average American city. It was described by a professional in the following terms:

"The appearance and quality of the public water supply were such that the poor used it for soup, the middle class dyed their clothes in it, and the very rich used it for top-dressing their lawns. Those who drank it, filtered it through a ladder, disinfected it with chloride of lime, then lifted out the dangerous germs which survived and killed them with a club in the back yard."[3]

—an exaggeration perhaps, but those who remember the river water supplies on the Ohio as late as 1912 submit that the exaggeration is not too overdrawn. Where water was available, it was too frequently a carrier of silt and disease, rather than a safe potable liquid. Not until 1835 could even New York City pride itself on a substantial water distribution system, even though its first limited source and distribution system date back to 1744. The great city of Chicago did not have even the elements of a public water supply system until 1840. Buffalo (N. Y.), Washington (D. C.), Cleveland (Ohio), Denver (Colo.), Indianapolis (Ind.), Milwaukee (Wis.), and Kansas City (Mo.) only translated this public responsibility into a physical system between the 1850's and the 1870's.

Public sewerage systems came even later. Baltimore (Md.), has the unenviable distinction of having replaced the bulk of its individual cesspools by a comprehensive public sewerage system as late as the beginning of the twentieth century.

Not a city in the United States from 1850 to 1900 escaped the ravages of the intestinal diseases. Typhoid fever death rates ranged from 50 to 175 per 100,000 in the great cities of the New World. The death rates from cholera at times reached more than 300 per 100,000. The toll from environmental diseases of water-borne character was truly appalling.

From 1800 to about 1880 the insect-borne disease, yellow fever, visited the United States virtually every year. In the New Orleans (La.) epidemic more than 29,000 cases with 8,100 deaths occurred. In Memphis (Tenn.) a single epidemic accounted for 17,600 cases and 5,150 deaths.

Malaria covered almost every part of the United States, as far north as the Great Lakes and including the great state of Illinois. Insect-borne disease literally roamed the continent, and people either accepted the scourges or turned to quarantine, evacuation, and witchcraft to contain the epidemics.

New York City during the summer of 1798 was visited by one of the most virulent of yellow fever epidemics (Fig. 1). It treated the situation as its neighboring city Philadelphia and others had met it, by:

"* * * burning nitre in the streets, firing horse pistols at the bed-sides of sufferers and carrying garlic in their shoes and bags of camphor around their necks, and dousing themselves with Haarlem Oil, essence of aloes and Vinegar of the Four Thieves."[4]

---

[2] "Plague on Us," by Geddes Smith, Oxford Univ. Press, Oxford, England, 1941, p. 181.
[3] Ibid., p. 182.
[4] "Aaron Burr," by Samuel H. Wandell and Meade Minnegerode, G. H. Putnam's Sons, 1927, pp. 175-178.

In Philadelphia, the entire population:

"* * * had been driven into camps along the banks of the Schuylkill, Government had retired, entire streets had been barricaded, pest houses organized which surpassed all conceivable horrors."[4]

The elements of emergency civil organization were completely lacking. These events give perhaps a preview of the latter day community of 1953, struck by an enemy and ill equipped with a civil defense organization.

FIG. 1.—WALTER REED—YELLOW FEVER FIGHTER

These vivid examples of a country ridden with environmental disease could be multiplied indefinitely. Sanitary literature and public health literature are filled with detailed accounts of tragedies resulting from failures to interpose a barrier between the sick and the well. The record appears in dramatic detail in the papers of Stephen Smith, Lemuel Shattuck, Edwin Chadwick, C-E. A. Winslow, William T. Sedgwick, Gordon M. Fair, M. ASCE, M. P. Horwood, the writer, and others. The further repetition here of vital statistics and of lurid description would serve no useful purpose beyond that already achieved by the few examples noted. In the United States, in England, and in continental Europe, the sanitary conditions a century ago were the same. No country in the world then escaped the ravages of environmental disease. It was on this stage that the public health team of engineer, physician, and nurse created the miracles of the modern world in the control of these diseases.

The Scene Today

In the United States today typhoid fever, malaria, yellow fever, and cholera are vanishing or vanished diseases. The death rate from typhoid fever in the country as a whole is less than 0.1 per 100,000 population. Malaria is nonexistent in the greatest part of the nation and is rapidly declining even in those parts where it may still be found by the physician. Cholera has not been seen in the United States for more than a half century.

Each of these diseases remains a constant threat. Their disappearance for the most part is man made. The world has not been rid entirely of any single infection known to man. In the United States and in a handful of European countries, the elimination is largely the result of protective measures interposed by man between the diseased and the well. In practically no other nation in the world is it possible to drink water or milk with safety.

In England and in continental Europe, too, man has been well protected, but some phases of control still leave much to be desired. In the rest of the world, perhaps 75% of the total population of the globe, the intestinal diseases, the dysenteries, and the insect-borne diseases still demand the same toll of lives as prevailed on this continent 100 years ago. Typhoid death rates still run from 20 to 80 per 100,000; cholera epidemics periodically visit the unfortunate populations; malaria cases are measured in hundreds of millions per year; bubonic plague ravages unfortunate areas; and infant mortality in the first year of life at times rises to as much as 800 deaths per year out of every 1,000 births.

Disease Reduction Methods

Long before the specific organisms that cause many of the environmental diseases were identified, progress in their reduction began to take place on an empirical basis. The incentive in many instances was to make water supplies more palatable to the taste and more attractive to the eye. When the earliest filtration plants were built in England in the first third of the nineteenth century, they were demanded primarily to provide a physically more attractive liquid. Regardless of the empirical basis for these improvements, they brought immediate returns from the standpoint of reducing water-borne disease. Effective control of water supply, disposal of excreta, the control and pasteurization of milk, the elimination of insect breeding areas, the disposal of community refuse, the adoption of rodent-proof building techniques, and the institution of general practices of cleanliness were singularly effective in the reduction of disease.

Sanitary Engineering Leaders

It is always rash to assign credit for major accomplishments in any field. The invidious selection of the names of individuals or of professional groups to share this credit invariably causes controversy. In the subject matter of this paper, however, both individuals and professional groups may be singled out, on whom rests at least a major part of the responsibility for the successes achieved.

Nonprofessional Laymen.—A great contribution was made to the sanitary awakening of the nineteenth century by the nonprofessional layman, who, in the

United States and in England, played so significant a part in arousing the public to the deficiencies of individual and communal living. These laymen were pressed toward their task by the visible suffering of so large a part of the population surrounding them. Their contributions to sanitary accomplishments should be recorded time and again, if for no other reason than to awaken similar interest in the lay readers of today. Chadwick in England and Shattuck in the United States will go down in history forever as shining bearers of new light in the protection of people. They cried for solutions to environmental problems that the professional first ignored and was then permitted to develop.

FIG. 2.—GEORGE W. FULLER, M. ASCE, PIONEER SANITARY ENGINEER

The Sanitary Engineer.—In the United States, the engineer-medical officer-nurse combination (Fig. 2) carried the load. The peculiar contribution made by this nation, however, is in the development of that specialized individual, the sanitary engineer, who combined into a hybrid discipline and practice the fields of biology and engineering. To him may properly be attributed a major part of the success achieved in the virtual elimination of the intestinal and insect-borne diseases. He brought to the task an understanding of the biology of disease transmission and of the engineering techniques by which structures, devices, and physical adjustments in the environment could be provided so as to interrupt the hitherto successful link between the diseased and the healthy individual. Sanitary engineers, more than any other single professional group, provided the engineering tools with which to attack the physical environment so closely related to the transmission of the diseases of man. Sanitation programs have accomplished more to improve man's surroundings and reduce infectious disease than any other endeavor in the field of public health.[5]

Nowhere else in the world has this special discipline been developed to any high degree—not that accomplishments in environmental disease control are lacking in England and in continental Europe. In those countries engineers have to their credit similar accomplishments, but through more orthodox engineering channels. Some at least believe that these disciplines may in the course of time reach greater parallelisms with sanitary engineering functions in this country.

In the rest of the world these peculiar hybrid functions are virtually unknown. However, they are beginning to penetrate fairly rapidly into many areas, and they will gain force in numbers and in influence as the potentials for engineering accomplishment in public health are increasingly recognized.

What Remains to Be Done

One may never review the past with optimism only, although the long record of great accomplishments is certainly to its credit. Does this mean, however, that the engineer may rest on his laurels or does it mean that the past is only a prelude to the engineering necessities of the future? The work yet to be done is always as great as the work already completed.

The United States.—In the United States, a static situation would be almost an index of stagnation. Fortunately, the realities run contrary to this assumption. More than 5,000 communities in the United States still have no public water works systems. More than 79,000,000 people need important improvements or extensions in existing systems. These water needs represent a future expenditure of something more than $2,000,000,000.

In water quality much remains to be done. Investigative activities to disclose the impact of new contaminants of industrial or other origin offer only one index of many of the opportunities ahead. In sewerage, the next 10 years will demand an expenditure of about $3,000,000,000. The great metropolitan areas of the United States will require increasing attention. In many, modern sanitary facilities are virtually absent. Engineering skill, fiscal ingenuity, and administrative imagination all require detailed application and elaboration.

Pollution of surface waters will constitute a daily problem, involving domestic water supply, industrial water supply, recreational use, and agricultural necessities. Although more than 90,000,000 people are served by sewer systems, sewage from approximately one third of the population using such systems is discharged into streams without treatment.

The control of milk and other food products demands increasing perspective and development. In the past 20 years the United States has undergone a major revolution in food production, handling, processing, and distribution. In every phase of this development technology has played a significant part.

In insect and rodent control there is much to be done. Rocky Mountain spotted fever, murine typhus, encephalomyelitis in horses, and encephalitis in man

---

[5] "Health Resources in the United States," by George W. Bachman and Associates, The Brookings Institution, Washington, D. C., 1952, p. 199.

remain hazards of great human and economic significance in this country. The recent experience with encephalitis in the Central Valley of California was a dramatic reminder in death, economic loss, and community distress of how much still must be learned.

The World-Wide Picture.—In the rest of the world, it is easy to visualize the picture, at least for the next 25 or 50 years. Progress there can almost duplicate the phase of development that·the United States passed through from 1850 to 1930. Environmental deficiencies in the bulk of the population of the world are orthodox and simple in character. They revolve primarily around inadequate control of water, unsafe handling of human excreta, and almost complete absence of the control of milk and of other food products. Procedures for correction are elementary, and the promise of accomplishment by the simplest of expedients is tremendous. The new tools, such as insecticides, will certainly provide immediate reduction in insect-borne diseases, giving man time to undertake those major physical adjustments in the environment that would result in permanent eradication.

Rate of Progress.—Although these problems are the same as those of a century ago, their correction need not take as long. With the great body of information and tools now at hand, the engineer and the medical health officer should be able to telescope the rate of accomplishment in the rest of the world by many decades —but not by merely transferring the machines of the new world to the old. A wise adjustment of modern equipment to the needs of vast populations should, however, facilitate correction. The expanding horizon for the engineer in the protection of health offers one of the greatest opportunities the world has ever seen. Technical precedent is available and convincing. Scientific understanding is great and generally accepted. No one underestimates the fiscal, the cultural, the economic, and the political obstacles to such accomplishments, but there are no better traveling ambassadors than those alleviators of human suffering—the engineer and the doctor.

The Future

Environmental Control.—In the control of environment, the engineer has been perhaps least successful in the maximum adjustment of the air, the shelter, and the clothes of man to the vicissitudes of his surroundings. On a comparative basis, the successes in these fields are neither as obvious nor as great as in those with which this paper has so far been concerned.

The delays in accomplishment are probably caused by the fact that the effects of these features of the environment on man's health and well-being are more subtle, less susceptible to physiological measurement, and, of course, more difficult to adjust.

The engineer shares these deficiencies with other professional groups. The environmental physiologist has so far provided no sensitive measurements of the effect of the constituents of the air on physiological well-being.

The physiologist, the psychiatrist, and the sociologist have not provided the engineer with any accurate or comprehensive criteria of the effect of poor housing on man's physical and mental health. Scattered observations, many of them significant, in the field of housing are available, but are still meager in amount and scientific nature.

Advances, either in understanding of physiological reaction to climate or in the development of clothing best to meet such variations, have been significantly slow. Military pressures in recent years have forced science and art forward in important directions, but the field is still wide open for engineering scrutiny and contribution.

Atmospheric Pollution.—Perhaps one of the most unsatisfactory fields of the three mentioned is the control of atmosphere. The reaction of human organisms to the day-by-day exposures to varying physical, chemical, and biological contents of air has not been explored to the point at which these subtle influences, if any, may be evaluated. Only when extraordinary circumstances arise in the atmosphere such as in the Meuse Valley in Belgium and in Donora, Pa., does the significance of the atmosphere in the well-being of exposed individuals become apparent. It is disturbing to realize how little is known of the effect on the population of meteorological conditions, coupled with unusual concentrations of foreign materials in the air.

An interesting example of such potential atmospheric effects is the experience in Japan, with what has been designated locally as "Yokohama asthma." This disease has been reported by the American military forces since 1946. It ranges from mild bronchial irritation to severe respiratory distress, requiring emergency treatment, and differs markedly from any of the more familiar allergic types. The incidence is associated primarily with the Yokohama area, from September or October through March or April. Some of its aspects suggest that it stems from air pollution. The high industrialization of Yokohama and its location on a bay enclosed by hills and bluffs offer ideal conditions for the formation and retention of smog. The situation is being studied by the United States Army, with particular reference to meteorological phenomena. The weather data so far collected appear to provide supporting evidence, although indirect, implicating smog as a meteorological factor affecting the occurrence and density of Yokohama asthma.

As in the case of Los Angeles smog, a great deal more work needs to be carried out, jointly with critical examination of clinical data. The experience, however, is a reminder that there is a wide and unexplored field in the control of air, particularly in industrial regions.

Housing.—Little major modification has been made in dwellings over the past several centuries. Construction materials, house design, and housing orientation represent as fertile a field for engineering inquiry as they did in the 1850's. The cynical George Bernard Shaw once observed that: "* * * the house the peasant lives in has not altered as much in a thousand centuries as the fashion of a lady's bonnet in a score of weeks."[6]

Plumbing Deficiencies.—In Chicago it is not inappropriate to recall to engineers the continuing problem of controlling the hazards of plumbing deficiencies in buildings in which people live. Of the three epidemic outbreaks of amebiasis in the world, two occurred in Chicago; one in 1936, with 1,050 known cases and 70 deaths. The second in 1934, in the Union Stock Yards fire. The third, involving 118 cases, was among troops at El Paso, Tex., prior to 1933. Reference is made to these situations because there is a still more recent reminder of this ever-present danger in such orthodox items as plumbing.

---

[6] "Man and Superman," by George Bernard Shaw, Brentano's, Inc., New York, N. Y., August, 1915, Act III, p. 106.

During the early part of January, 1947, an amebic dysentery epidemic occurred in the Mantetsu Apartment Building in Tokyo, Japan.[7] This structure housed seventy-three family units of American occupation personnel. In all, one hundred sixty-one Americans and two hundred forty-eight Japanese employees were exposed to the threat of amebiasis. The protozoonal infection rate for the Americans was 62.9% for *endameba histolytica;* and for the Japanese employees, 22.2%. The exposures of the Japanese were fewer in the hotel, and their drinking customs were safer than those of the Americans. The epidemiological survey of the situation indicated that the epidemic was water-borne. The brief period of exposure, coupled with the extremely high rates of protozoonal infections, supported by physical investigation, showed a probable connection between the water system and the sewage from the apartment house.

Other Fields.—Only limited time prevents detailed comment on new areas of activity carrying challenges to the engineer. The development of aircraft and collateral ground operations lends new force to the necessity for exploring the health aspects of light glare, noise, odor, smoke, dust, insects, rodents, and land and water pollution.[8]

The rapidly evolving atomic energy operations disclose new vistas in the studies of gaseous, liquid, and solid wastes; in the use of radio-isotopes as research tools; and in the search for uses for waste radioactive products. The behavior of man and of materials under the impact of nuclear fission products provides an area for exploration that should inspire the most fertile mind.

One hesitates even to refer to another completely barren field of cooperative investigation, because engineers have so consistently shied away from it. Real opportunities for collaboration are in the physiologist's domain. Only feeble attempts have been made to apply engineering analysis to the orthopedist's problems, to the embryologist's problem of the "pumplike" behavior of the umbilical cord, to the physiologist's problem of the respiratory mechanism, and to the physician's problem of the filtration system of the kidney. The engineer's facility with the analysis of structures and of the dynamics of air and water flow must be applied to these collateral promises for the future. Not all the problems of hydraulics are in cast-iron pipe!

SUMMARY

The English sanitary engineer, A. J. Martin, once said:

"The poorest worker today is far better off than the wealthiest noble in the days of the Plantagenets or the Tudors. His home * * * is much healthier than the castle of a Norman baron."

The engineer in public health should be pleased with the progress in the past. He should be intrigued at the same time by the challenges of the future!

---

[7] "Epidemic Amoebiasis in Occupants of the Mantetsu Apartment Building, Tokyo, Japan," by Lawrence S. Ritchie and Cooper Davis, *The American Journal of Tropical Medicine,* November, 1948, p. 803.
[8] "Sanitary and Industrial Hygiene, Engineering Aspects of Master Planning," by Alvin F. Meyer, *The Military Surgeon,* July, 1952, p. 29.

AMERICAN SOCIETY OF CIVIL ENGINEERS

Founded November 5, 1852

TRANSACTIONS

Paper No. 2612

EXPANSION OF THE CHICAGO, ILL., WATER SUPPLY

By W. W. DeBerard,[1] Hon. M. ASCE

Synopsis

Chicago's water system has developed with the growth of the city from a privately-owned water system of one pump and 2 miles of wooden pipe in 1842 to the present system, consisting of six intake cribs, 63.6 miles of water tunnels, twelve pumping stations, approximately 4,000 miles of water mains, the world's largest filtration plant serving the south one third of the city, and a larger one planned to serve the remainder of the city.

In 1852, 100 years ago, the city took over the franchises of the private company and built the first municipally-owned pumping station on the lake shore, using cast-iron mains to distribute the water. To overcome the increasing pollution of the source, the city built its first water tunnel, 5 ft in inside diameter, to an intake crib, 2 miles offshore. It was a daring feat of engineering. The shore end was connected to a new pumping station, completed in 1869, the present-day Chicago Avenue Pumping Station with its famous water tower, built on the site of the original station. This new tunnel and station mark the beginning of the present Chicago water system.

Additional cribs, tunnels, and pumping stations were built to keep pace with the growth of the city. New pumping stations were equipped with the finest pumping machinery of the period. To safeguard the water entering the intake cribs from pollution, the direction of flow in the Chicago River was reversed when the Sanitary District of Chicago built the Drainage Canal, which was placed in service in 1900, and when all sewers were blocked off from emptying into the lake. To protect the bacterial quality of the water, chlorination of the water supply was started in 1912.

The largest of the pumping stations is the Western Avenue Station which was placed in service in 1927. In September, 1945, the South District Filtration Plant, the world's largest plant for filtration of water began operation. It serves only the south third of the city area.

Both the ASCE and the Chicago water supply celebrated a centenary in 1952. In the year 1852, 100 years ago, the small privately-owned water system serving

---

[1] Deputy Commr. for Water and Chf. Water Engr., Dept. of Water and Sewers, Bureau of Water, Chicago, Ill.

the city became a municipally-owned utility. It consisted of one 1.8-mgd steam pumping unit and 2 miles of wooden water mains. During the past 100 years, this has developed into the present vast 4,000-mile system.

When the first people settled at the mouth of the Chicago River, they went to the river for their water supply (Fig. 1). As the number of settlers increased, the river, "a sluggish stream," soon became contaminated and wells became a necessity. Chicago came into existence as a town in 1833, at which time the

FIG. 1.—In 1830, Primitive Water Supply Provided by Chicago River

population was 350 people. It was incorporated as a city on March 4, 1837, and its first officials were elected on May 2 of the same year.

The earliest effort of which there is any record to provide a public water supply for the citizens of Chicago was on November 10, 1834, when the Board of Trustees paid $95.50 for the digging of a well in Kinzie's Addition. This well was located at what later became the intersection of Cass Street and Michigan Street. However, Chicago was situated on a low and nearly level prairie, a few feet above the level of the lake, and the citizenry soon found wells im-

practicable since contaminated surface water could not be avoided. The lake
was the better source of water.

For some years private enterprise reaped a financial harvest in operating
water carts (Fig. 2) for the supply of lake water to the citizens. The peddler
came around two or three times a week and sold water to the inhabitants for

FIG. 2.—SCENE IN 1835—WATER PEDDLER GIVES IMPROVED SERVICE

5¢ to 25¢ per bbl, according to competition. However, there came a time when
water carts, tin cans, wooden pails, and barrels were deemed too crude.

In January, 1836, the Illinois State Legislature passed a law incorporating the
Chicago Hydraulic Company, a private organization, established with a capitaliza-
tion of $25,000. The charter was to continue in force for a period of 70 years.
The panic of 1837 interfered with the affairs of the concern so that operations
were not begun until 1840. The city then had a population of 4,500. The company
built Chicago's first pumping station and reservoir at the corner of Lake Street
and Michigan Avenue, with Lake Michigan as the source of supply.

This pumping station (Fig. 3) contained a 25-hp pump having a rated capacity of 25 bbl per min, or 1.8 mgd, taking water from an intake pipe extending about 150 ft into Lake Michigan. The reservoir, constructed of wood, was 25 ft square and 8 ft deep and was elevated about 80 ft above the ground

FIG. 3.—YEAR 1840—PRIVATE FIRM, CHICAGO HYDRAULIC COMPANY, BUILDS FIRST PUMPING STATION AT LAKE STREET AND MICHIGAN AVENUE

surface. Pressure from the reservoir was sufficient to force water to the second floor of buildings.

The distribution system consisted of about 2 miles of wooden mains. These were 10-ft cedar logs bored through the center with a hole 5 in. in diameter for the main distribution lines and 3 in. in diameter for the subordinate ones. The pipes were joined together by a special wooden fitting.

In 1840 the total area of the city was 10.7 sq miles. The water supply reached only a small part of the south and western divisions, or about one fifth of the city. The remaining four fifths still had to obtain its water for domestic or other purposes, from the river or by the water cart system.

Public Ownership.—The works of the Chicago Hydraulic Company were operated with varying success, until 1852, when the rights and franchises of the company were taken over by the city under the name of Chicago City Hydraulic Company. Three individuals were named to constitute the Board of Water Commissioners, with authority to borrow money and issue bonds up to the sum of $400,000. Thus a real start toward the present municipally-owned water system was made.

To keep up with the rapid growth of the city, which now had 45,000 people and an area of 17.93 sq miles, the Water Commissioners employed William J. McAlpine, Past-President and Hon. M. ASCE, to make the necessary surveys for

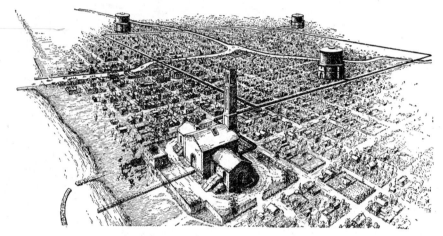

Fig. 4.—Chicago's Original Municipal System, 1858

a new and larger water supply. The plans that were followed provided for a pumping station on the lake shore at Chicago Avenue (Fig. 4). A timber crib 20 ft by 40 ft was to be sunk 600 ft from the then shore line, and from this crib a wooden inlet pipe with a 30-in. interior diameter was to be laid in a trench on the bottom of the lake to convey the water to the pump well in a new pumping station.

Several attempts were made to put the timber crib and the 30-in. wooden main in place in the lake, but rough water made the operation too difficult. This installation was finally abandoned, and the water was permitted to enter the pipe close to shore. Work on the intake, pumping station, distribution system, and reservoir was eventually completed, and the service of supplying water to the city began in February, 1854. By this time the population had increased to 65,000 people.

This, the first municipally-owned pumping station for Chicago, was at the site of the present Chicago Avenue Pumping Station. The original pumping engine, affectionately nicknamed "Old Sally," was installed under the direction of DeWitt C. Cregier, in 1853. This vertical condensing steam engine, with a single-acting pump of 8.0-mgd capacity, served Chicago faithfully for more than 50 years and outlived Cregier, who, during 41 years, held successive positions for the city as chief engineer, commissioner of public works, and finally mayor.

The water pumped was distributed through three reservoirs (Fig. 4), each holding 500,000 gal, which were located, respectively, at the intersections of LaSalle and Adams streets (built in 1853), Chicago Avenue and Sedgwick Street, and Morgan and Monroe streets (the latter two being built in 1858). It is interesting to note that in 1852 the first cast-iron distribution pipe, 4 in. in diameter, was laid in Clark Street and from then on, cast iron replaced wood for all mains.

The first full year of operation of the new water works was 1855. The report of the Board of Water Commissioners for that year indicated that the cost of the works totaled $650,000, and the daily pumpage averaged 2,170,000 gal. The water system was based on an estimate that by 1866 the population would be 100,000. As a matter of fact, in 1866 the population was more than double that amount.

To Avoid Contamination.—Problems confronting the water supply during the succeeding years involved not only meeting the requirements of a rapid increase in population, but getting away from the increasing pollution of the source of supply, along the shores of the lake.

During this period the sewage of the City of Chicago was discharged either directly into Lake Michigan or into the Chicago River which flowed into the lake. As the city increased in population, this sewage brought about a dangerous contamination of the water supply, and finally it became necessary that the intake be carried out beyond the line of shore contamination.

In 1867, Chicago's first water tunnel was completed. It was a daring feat of engineering and brought international fame to its designer, Ellis S. Chesbrough, Past-President, ASCE. The tunnel, 2 miles long, was dug through clay at a depth of 60 ft below lake level and lined to a finished diameter of 5 ft, with two shells of brick. It was designed to deliver 50 mgd.

A crib of timber construction, the original Two-Mile Crib, was placed 2 miles offshore at the lake end of the tunnel (Fig. 5), and the shore end was connected to a new pumping station, completed in 1869. The present-day Chicago Avenue Pumping Station, is on the same site as the original station, built in 1852. This new system marked the real beginning of the modern Chicago Water Works.

The old water tower erected in 1867 at the intersection of Michigan and Chicago avenues was part of the project. It has now outlived its usefulness as a water-works accessory but still stands (Fig. 6) as a monument to the vision and skill of the water-works engineers of a pioneering era.

Progressive Expansion.—Starting with a capacity of 8 mgd in 1869, by successive installation of additional and enlarged pumping equipment, the Chicago Avenue Pumping Station has increased its output until today it has a maximum pumping capacity of 210 mgd. The Great Chicago Fire of October 8 and 9, 1871, so damaged the machinery of the new station that it was out of service for 8 days. Although the new tunnel and pumping station had temporarily solved Chicago's water quality problem, the great conflagration seriously emphasized the need of a better balanced water system for fire protection. A break in a water main crossing the river, coupled with increasing demand for additional water service on the west side, resulted in a decision shortly after the Great Fire to build a new tunnel and pumping station to serve the west side of the city.

The second water pumping station, built at Twenty-Second Street and Ashland

FIG. 5.—PICTORIAL VIEW AS OF 1869—CHICAGO AVENUE PUMPING STATION, WATER TOWER, AND TWO-MILE CRIB

Avenue, was formerly known as the West Side Station (later the Twenty-Second Street Station). It was placed in operation in 1876 with two Corliss engines and single-acting pumps with a capacity of 15 mgd each. Two more pumping engines of the same type were installed 8 years later. They have since been replaced by four motor-driven centrifugal pumps—two of 20-mgd capacity in 1912, and two of 26-mgd capacity in 1919.

FIG. 6.—FAMOUS RELIC OF "THE FIRE"—CHICAGO AVENUE WATER TOWER, STILL A LANDMARK

A tunnel connecting this station to the Two-Mile Crib was completed in 1874. Known as the Crosstown Tunnel, it was built in clay, 7 ft in diameter, brick lined, and about 6 miles long. Because of interference with deep foundations and pilings for large buildings, the land section of this tunnel was abandoned in 1909, when the Blue Island Tunnel was put in service. This second tunnel, 8 ft in diameter under the city streets, was built under private contract and was Chicago's first long concrete-lined tunnel. In 1932, after 23 years, it was dewatered and found to be in good physical condition.

The Harrison Street Station (the third one) was built and placed in service in 1889. Supplied by a new branch tunnel extending from the Crosstown Tunnel, the station was equipped with two 17.5-mgd Allis-Chalmers triple-expansion engines, which were in operation until 1933 when the station was torn down and the Cermak Pumping Station (Fig. 7) was built on the same site.

By 1889, the sewage emptying into Lake Michigan was again contaminating the water supply to a dangerous extent. At this time the Chicago Sanitary District was formed. During the next 11 years, the entire sewer system of the city was redesigned. All sewers emptying into Lake Michigan were blocked off; the direction of flow in the Chicago River was reversed; and the Chicago Drainage Canal was constructed. The canal was placed in service in 1900, and since then all Chicago sewage or sewage works effluents have been carried away from the lake, down the Drainage Canal to the Des Plaines River. With the opening of the Drainage Canal the great change toward a clean lake began.

Through extensive annexations the city, in 1889, added several small inadequate water systems to its public properties. From then on it became necessary to provide more new cribs, tunnels, and pumping stations to meet the added demands for water. Some idea of this problem may be gleaned from the fact that in one day, July 15, 1889, the city area increased from 37 sq miles to 170 sq miles—through the annexations of the City of Lake View and the Town of Jefferson on the north and the towns of Hyde Park and Lake on the south—making the city's total population 1,170,000. The present expanded city and the enlarged main system with its pumping stations are shown on the sketch map, Fig. 8.

More Stations.—The Sixty-Eighth Street and Lake View pumping stations were obtained by the city through these annexations. Both stations have been considerably enlarged and improved in equipment in recent years.

Originally the Sixty-Eighth Street Station was served through a submerged lake intake; later by the Sixty-Eighth Street Crib built in 1894; and now by the Edward F. Dunne Crib built in 1911, from which the water passes through the South District Filtration Plant before it reaches the station. This station has six motor-driven centrifugal pumps with a total capacity of 240 mgd.

The Lake View Station is supplied through the Wilson Avenue Lake Tunnel by two branch tunnels, the old Lake View Tunnel and a branch tunnel from the Wilson Avenue shore shaft in Clarendon Avenue. It is equipped with four triple-expansion engines of 25 mgd each.

The sixth unit of the water system, the Fourteenth Street Pumping Station, was built and placed in service in 1892. It was equipped with three Allis-Chalmers triple-expansion engines (Fig. 9), each having a rated capacity of 15 mgd. These engines are still in service. In 1898 a large 30-mgd Lake Erie pumping engine was installed, but it has not been in operation in recent years.

The Four-Mile Tunnel and Crib Intake which provides water for the Fourteenth Street Station was placed in service in 1892. The crib, off Twelfth Street, is the second to be built for Chicago's water system. It is placed in 39 ft of water and consists of two concentric steel shells set on a wooden grillage. Connecting the crib and station is a tunnel, which was exceptionally difficult to build because of soft, swelling clay and quicksand. Compressed air, not known in those

FIG. 7.—INTERIOR OF CERMAK PUMPING STATION, BUILT IN 1936

days, would have made the work much easier. However, the tunnel was finally completed and is still in use after 60 years.

On the west side the Central Park Avenue and Springfield Avenue pumping stations were built as a part of the Northwest Land and Northeast Lake Tunnel Project, supplied from the Carter H. Harrison Crib (Fig. 10). Originally in 1900 and 1901 both stations were equipped with three Worthington vertical triple-expansion engines of 20-mgd capacity each. A larger unit of the same make and type, with a capacity of 40 mgd was added at both stations in 1906. In 1922–1926 these engines were replaced at each station with three steam-turbine-driven DeLaval 60-mgd centrifugal pumps, and later two 80-mgd pumps of the same type were added at each station. Both stations are now supplied from the Chicago Avenue Lake and Land Tunnel.

The Roseland Pumping Station was built when the Southwest Land Tunnel was put in operation in 1911. It serves the extreme south section of Chicago. At

first it was equipped with four vertical triple-expansion engines of 25-mgd capacity each. Two of them have been replaced with two 75-mgd steam-turbine-
driven DeLaval centrifugal pumps and the other two will also be replaced. This
is a two-pressure station, the higher pressure pumpage going to the west. To

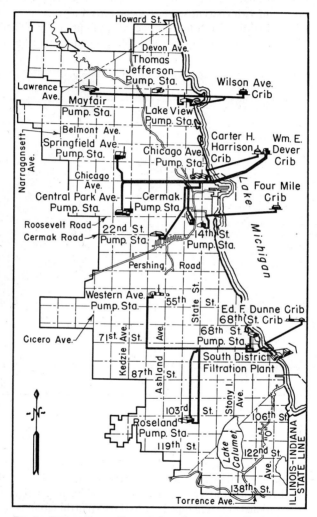

FIG. 8.—SKETCH MAP OF CHICAGO, ILL., SHOWING MAIN WATER WORKS

increase the water supply to this station the Stewart Avenue Tunnel, a branch
of the Southwest Land Tunnel, was completed in 1943. This station has been
supplied with filtered water from the South District Filtration Plant since 1947.

In the extreme northwest section of the city is the Mayfair Pumping Station,
placed in service with the Wilson Avenue Tunnel system in 1918. It has four
25-mgd Allis-Chalmers vertical triple-expansion engines and two high-pressure

FIG. 9.—VIEW INSIDE FOURTEENTH STREET STATION—TRIPLE-EXPANSION ENGINES, INSTALLED IN 1892 AND STILL IN USE IN 1952

FIG. 10.—CARTER H. HARRISON INTAKE CRIB, LAKE MICHIGAN, BUILT IN 1900

pumping engines of the same type, of 17.5-mgd capacity each. In 1932 two steam-turbine-driven DeLaval centrifugal pumps of 60-mgd capacity each were installed, and two more of this same make and capacity will soon replace two of the old 25-mgd vertical triple-expansion pumping engines.

The Western Avenue Pumping Station (Fig. 11) was put in service in August, 1927, when the Western Avenue extension of the Southwest Land Tunnel was completed. It is equipped with four compound steam-turbine-driven DeLaval centrifugal pumps of 75-mgd capacity each (Fig. 12). This station serves part of the south district of the city, including the Stock Yards and the Central Manufacturing District. It pumps more water than any other station and has been supplied with filtered water by the South District Filtration Plant since 1947.

Fig. 11.—Chicago's Largest—Western Avenue Station, Constructed in 1927, Pumps Most Water

Thomas Jefferson Pumping Station, built in less than a year, began operation in 1928. It is supplied from the Wilson Avenue Tunnel and serves the central part of the extreme north section of the city. Its pumping equipment consists of four motor-driven Fairbanks-Morse centrifugal units of 40-mgd capacity each.

Cermak Pumping Station (Fig. 7), built on the site of the old Harrison Street Pumping Station, was put in service in 1936. It is supplied from the Desplaines Street branch of the Chicago Avenue Lake and Land Tunnel. It serves the Loop and the south part of the central section of the city. Its equipment consists of six 50-mgd motor-driven Allis-Chalmers centrifugal pumps.

Experience Keeps Pace.—Water pumping practice in Chicago has followed developments in equipment for a century, beginning with "Old Sally" and the vertical single-acting condensating steam engine of 8-mgd capacity, installed in 1852. Since then the reciprocating type of pumping steam engines was evolved through the various stages of perfection and complication, only to be superseded by centrifugal pumps. The first centrifugal pump was installed by the City of Chicago after an exhaustive study of all pumping costs.

In 1920, two DeLaval 40-mgd electric-motor-driven centrifugal pumps replaced two triple-expansion pumping engines in the Chicago Avenue Station. Next a 60-mgd steam-turbine-driven centrifugal pump for the Central Park Pumping Station was installed.

In performance, economy, and flexibility, the turbine-driven units proved so satisfactory that additional installations followed in rapid succession. Today,

FIG. 12.—SCENE WITHIN THE WESTERN AVENUE PUMPING STATION—CENTRIFUGAL PUMPS WITH STEAM-TURBINE DRIVE

there are forty-two centrifugal pumps in ten pumping stations ranging in capacity from 25 mgd to 80 mgd. Two other stations, Lake View and Fourteenth Street (Fig. 9), still are entirely equipped with old triple-expansion engines.

Today the Chicago Water Works is a giant, but a carefully controlled, efficiently operated giant. Several additional intake tunnels have been built and some subsequently have been abandoned as they became obsolete. New pumping stations have been constructed as needed, all equipped with the finest machinery of the period. The original plan devised by Chesbrough has always been followed. John E. Ericson, M. ASCE, city engineer for many years, kept alive the tradition of public service by water-works officials and planned ahead to meet the city's constantly growing demands. He saw the potentialities of the centrifugal pump when it was first developed, and Chicago was among the first cities to use this equipment.

Filtration Also.—Ericson was among the first to realize the need of controlling purity and Chicago began in 1912 to chlorinate its water. An immediate decrease in typhoid and other water-borne diseases resulted. In 1926 he started a large experimental filtration plant where extensive research projects were carried out. Data collected there have formed the basis of the design of the new South District Filtration Plant (Fig. 13).

FIG. 13.—AERIAL VIEW OF SOUTH DISTRICT FILTRATION PLANT, WORLD'S LARGEST

Placed in operation on September 20, 1945, this is the world's largest plant for the filtration of water. It serves an area of 162 sq miles, with a population of nearly 1,500,000, and filters the water for three south-side pumping stations— Sixty-Eighth Street, Roseland, and Western Avenue. Its nominal capacity of 320 mgd can be greatly increased to meet any high demand, by stepping up filtration rates. There are a low-lift pumping station, three settling basins, eighty filters, two filtered water reservoirs, a chemical building, and allied structures, such as a laboratory, an administration building, and shops.

The South District Filtration Plant serves only the south area of the city. In addition a truly colossal plant with 1,000,000,000-gal per day capacity to supply the rest of the city is expected to be started shortly.

The City of Chicago has had a most remarkable growth, its population increasing from a few hundred souls in 1833 to 3,625,000 people in 1952. The water-supply system has always anticipated the rapid increase in population and industry, and has met every demand placed on it.

From its humble beginning in 1852, the system has grown until now it consists of six intake cribs; 63.6 miles of water tunnels in service, ranging in diameter from 5 ft to 16 ft; twelve pumping stations; the world's largest filtration plant; and approximately 4,000 miles of water pipe varying in diameter from 4 in. to 54 in. In the distribution system, there are more than 43,000 fire hydrants, more than 40,000 gate valves, and 121,834 water meters of various sizes.

The successful operation of the vast Chicago Water Works is due to the vision and skill of the city's officials and engineers. To them and their predecessors the city owes a great debt.

AMERICAN SOCIETY OF CIVIL ENGINEERS

Founded November 5, 1852

TRANSACTIONS

Paper No. 2613

PROBLEMS OF SUPPLYING LONDON, ENGLAND, WITH WATER

By H. F. Cronin [1]

Synopsis

The Metropolitan Water Board must solve eight major problems to assure London of an adequate water supply. After discussing rainfall and geologic conditions in south and southeast England as well as in London, this paper gives a detailed account of the operations and charges of the Board and the sources, character, and treatment of the water supply. Then each specific problem is considered and possible remedies are offered.

As the Society celebrates its first century of engineering accomplishments, with reviews of past activities and future promise in the United States, it is gratifying to find an interest in kindred problems of other lands. Among these, the water supply of London may well have a fitting place. The difficulties met and solved have a bearing on similar problems elsewhere. For convenience of reading and comparison by American engineers, all quantities in this paper are in United States gallons and all tons are in short tons, 2,000 lb. The conversion to dollars has been made at the rate of $2.78 to £1.

Introduction

In general, for sources of water supply, England and Wales may be regarded as one unit (Fig. 1), although the Welsh do not approve of the export of their water. Liverpool and Birmingham obtain their water from Wales, and someday London may have to do the same.

Rainfall.—The standard average annual rainfall (1881–1915) over the 58,343 sq miles of England and Wales is 35.2 in. It ranges from more than 150 in. in the west on Mount Snowdon in Wales and on the mountains in the Lake District to rather less than 20 in. in the east around the Thames Estuary. The value for London is 24.5 in.

Geology.—The older crystalline and other impermeable rocks outcrop in Wales and in the west and north of England, and the general dip is in an easterly direc-

---

[1] Chf. Engr., Metropolitan Water Board, London, England.

tion. In southeast England, the rocks are chalk and other limestones and sand-stones, together with thick beds of clay. Of these, the chalk (a soft fissured lime-stone) is the most important from the view of water supply. It is extremely permeable and probably has an outcrop of about 5,000 sq miles. In addition, an appreciable area of this formation is covered with permeable or semipermeable deposits. The amount of water pumped from the chalk for public water supplies

FIG. 1.—SKETCH MAP OF ENGLAND AND WALES

is estimated to be at least 450 mgd; and, in addition, considerable quantities are abstracted for industrial and private purposes.

The chalk and some of the limestone formations give rise to strong springs which maintain the flow of the rivers in this area, especially the Thames, during long dry periods.

The London Area.—London, which is difficult to define precisely, is in the center of what the planners call a "conurbation." In an area of 50 miles square (Fig. 2) with the City of London at the center, about 10,000,000 persons reside—the average density thus being 4,000 per sq mile. The public water supply to this area is in the charge of some sixty different authorities, both private companies and municipal undertakings. Among them they deliver on the average about 540 mgd, of which 370 mgd is obtained from rivers and 170 mgd from underground sources. In addition to this, appreciable quantities of water, mostly from underground sources, are used for industrial and private purposes.

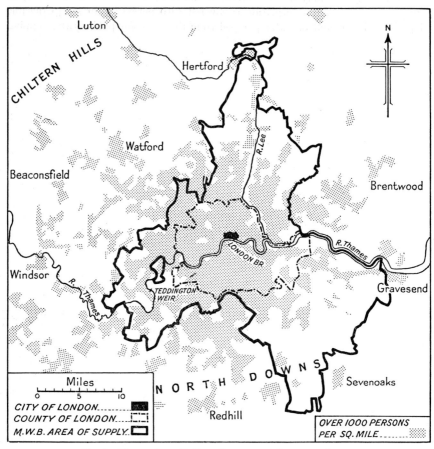

FIG. 2.—MAP OF AREA 50 MILES SQUARE WITH LONDON IN CENTER

THE METROPOLITAN WATER BOARD

The largest authority in Great Britain is the Metropolitan Water Board, whose irregular boundary of supply encloses about 540 sq miles. The Board is a public body composed of sixty-six members, elected by various local authorities within its area. It was established in 1903 and purchased the facilities of the eight separate private water companies which had hitherto supplied the metropolis. It makes no profit and adjusts its water rate and charges so that the yearly receipts balance the expenditure as nearly as possible.

The Board charges for water for domestic purposes—which is unmetered—based on the ratable (net annual) value of the premises supplied, the present rate being 10%. A garden hose and sprinkler cost additional. For industrial purposes water is furnished through a meter. There are about 1,344,000 domestic services and 31,000 supplies through meters, the relative quantities being 67% and 33%, respectively, of the total.

In the Board's area of supply the population is about 6,500,000; and these people and the industry they support, together with the daily influx of workers and shoppers, received during the year ending March 31, 1952, an average total daily supply of 379 million gal, divided into 124 mgd supplied by meter for trade purposes and 255 mgd for domestic use (which includes nearly all the leakage and waste). In addition, the Board sold in bulk to adjacent water companies an average quantity of 7 mgd, so that the present total demand is about 386 mgd. The average daily per capita consumption for all purposes is 58 gal.

Sources of Supply.—The Board obtains water from three sources, in the following approximate proportions:

Source	%
Underground	16
River Lee	16
River Thames	68
Total	100

These percentages vary, especially in drought years, when the River Lee is apt to fail.

System of Supply.—After abstraction, the water from the rivers is pumped to storage reservoirs where retention forms the first part of the purification process; it is then filtered, chlorinated, and pumped to supply (Fig. 3). In the case of the underground supply, 75% only is chlorinated and then pumped direct to the consumers, while the remaining 25% is passed through the filtration plant. On account of the low levels at which the water is obtained, the whole system of supply is dependent on continuous pumping.

CHARACTER OF WATER SUPPLIED BY THE BOARD

The water as abstracted from the Lee and the Thames rivers is polluted, the average coliform count of the raw water being about 3,500 per 100 ml, rising to maximum values of 60,000 per 100 ml. On the other hand, the water from most of the wells is very pure, except when subject to accidental pollution. It is the rule to obtain sterile plates from 10 ml of this water incubated in nutrient agar at body temperature.

All the water supplied by the Board is alkaline, the pH-value being between 7.2 and 8. The Board does not soften any of its supply, the hardness of which varies from about 250 ppm for Thames-derived water to about 350 ppm for that obtained from the Lee, and reaches 400 ppm in the case of some of the well supplies.

The color and turbidity of the river water as supplied to the consumers are 6 (Hazen scale) and 0.2, respectively, with but little variation. In the case of the well waters, both the color and the turbidity are zero.

About 90,000 samples are collected annually for analysis; and, in the year 1951–

1952, of the samples taken from the water as pumped to supply 99.84% contained no coliform bacteria in 100 ml. Of the samples collected at random in the distribution system 99.1% were free from coliform bacteria in 100 ml, indicating only a very slight deterioration in an extensive distribution system almost free from any residual chlorine.

All new mains and sections of main after repair are disinfected with chlorine before being returned to supply, and the jute yarn used for packing lead joints is sterilized by an organic mercurial compound (phenyl mercuric borate). During

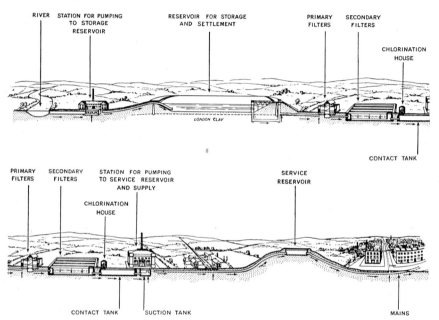

FIG. 3.—DIAGRAM SHOWING RIVER SUPPLY FROM SOURCE (UPPER LEFT) TO CONSUMER (LOWER RIGHT)

1951–1952 of the samples taken from new and repaired mains 99.5% contained no coliform bacteria in 100 ml.

CHLORINATION

The organization of the Board is such that the control of the chlorination of the water is not the responsibility of the engineer but of the Director of Water Examination, who is a chief officer of the Board with equal status, and who has charge of a fully equipped laboratory, centrally situated. The Director also undertakes all investigations into biological matters and advises on algal control.

All the river water is chlorinated after filtration, the average dose being 1 ppm. The standard practice is to allow 1 hour to 2 hours of contact time; but contact tanks have not yet been built at all the filtration stations and, where they are absent, prechlorination is usually carried out. Chlorination is effected by applying sufficient chlorine to produce a predetermined residual of free chlorine after a known period of contact. Conditions vary from one station to another, but it is found that the establishment of 0.2 ppm of free residual chlorine after a 10-min contact produces a satisfactory water from the bacteriological point of view.

Water derived from wells, pumped directly to supply, is of excellent chemical quality, and consequently doses of the order of 0.1 ppm would destroy any coliform bacteria in a matter of minutes. Many of the wells, however, are in urban areas, so that as a precautionary measure larger doses of chlorine, varying from 0.5 to 1.0 ppm, are applied. Dechlorination is then effected by sulfur dioxide after a minimum contact time of 20 min.

Major Problems—Metropolitan Water Board

Practical difficulties arise from the restriction on capital expenditure caused by the country's economic condition, which is holding up the construction of new works and the modernization of existing ones. Apart from this and from the constant vigilance necessary to transform the polluted waters of the Thames and Lee rivers into a safe and physically attractive supply, the major problems confronting the Board are:

1. To prepare reliable forecasts of the amounts of water required in the future.

2. To secure suitable and sufficient reservoir sites to enable the supply from the River Thames to be developed to the greatest possible extent.

3. To overcome the biological difficulties arising from the prolonged storage of River Thames water.

4. To provide an alternative for the supply from the River Lee in the event of failure of that source.

5. To devise equally (or more) efficient and reliable, but less expensive, methods of filtration.

6. To guard against the pollution of the underground sources.

7. To reduce the damage and expense caused by the external corrosion of mains in certain areas.

8. To prevent, detect, and stop all misuse, leakage, and waste of water.

These will be discussed briefly seriatim.

1. Future Demands.—It is generally agreed that London is too large and that the population in the metropolitan area should be reduced, but no one has yet been able to find a practicable method of doing this. At the present time general plans for the development of the area are being prepared; and, when these are available, they should form a guide for the future—provided always that they are carried out.

All the indications point to increasing demands as housing conditions improve. On account of the method of charging, the Board has no statistics on the numbers of premises in its area without baths or without a hot water supply. However, 5 years ago a survey was conducted with the help of the Medical Officers of Health, from which it appeared that, out of a total of more than 1,300,000 premises, at least 400,000 had no baths and 500,000 had no hot water supply systems. Since the close of World War II, great efforts have been made to provide modern housing accommodations for the working class, and blocks of flats—each flat equipped with six taps, a bath, and a hot water system—are everywhere appearing. Also many of the older, one-cold-tap houses are being demolished to provide sites for modern dwellings (Fig. 4).

This rebuilding is bound to result in an increased consumption of water, especially if and when fuel or power for heating water becomes cheaper and more plentiful. In addition to the domestic consumption, the demand for water for industry is steadily rising.

A usual method of estimating future demands is to attempt to predict both the future population and the per capita consumption; but, to try to eliminate

FIG. 4.—REBUILDING IN LONDON (WANDSWORTH, S. W.): FRONT, FITTINGS IN OLD HOUSES, ONE COLD TAP AND NO BATH; REAR, FITTINGS IN EACH NEW FLAT, THREE HOT AND THREE COLD TAPS AND BATH

these variable factors, a mathematical analysis of the rate of growth of the demands made on the Board for all purposes was undertaken in 1938, and again in 1952. The results indicted that from the year 1904 demand increased on the average at a rate of about 2.8 mgd per yr (diagonal line, Fig. 5). Because of a drive on waste the consumption at the moment is below the estimate; but, if this annual increment is accepted, it is possible that the average demand in 25 years may be 454 mgd. If that particular summer, 1977, should be hot and dry, the actual demand may well be 5% higher, say, 477 mgd. This forecast is hazarded with all due deference, and like many other predictions of future consumption, it may well prove to be inaccurate, especially considering the unsettled conditions now prevailing.

2. *Provision of Future Supplies.*—In common with many other undertakings, the Board has as its most important, expensive, and difficult problem the need

for more reservoirs. Of the three sources, the Thames alone is capable of expansion. However, before discussing how this can be effected and the extent to which it might be achieved, some relevant information should be given regarding this source from which about 280 million gal are now needed each day during the summer months.

The Thames supply (Fig. 6) may be described as a river supply assisted from time to time by water drawn from reservoirs. For several years on end the flow of the river is more than sufficient for the day-to-day abstraction, but from time to time a drought occurs during which there is insufficient water to meet the Board's and other requirements.

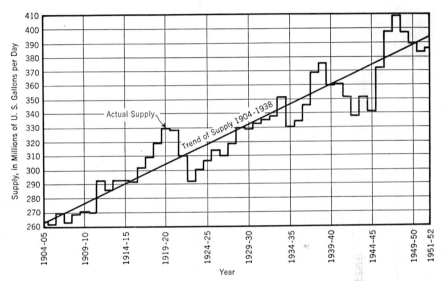

FIG. 5.—TREND OF SUPPLY, AS CALCULATED FROM RECORDS FOLLOWING 1904, SUPPLIES IN BULK INCLUDED

The flow of the river has been gaged since 1883 (Fig. 7) at the upper limit of the tidal part at Teddington Weir—a few miles downstream from the Board's intakes—so that the probable vagaries of the flow are more or less known. During that period there have been 5 years—namely, 1899, 1921, 1934, 1944, and 1949 —when the flow during the summer months was abnormally low; and for each of these years the natural flow at Teddington Weir (that is, the flow as it would have been had there been no abstraction), together with the standard average for comparison, is given in Table 1.

The relative severity of these droughts, measured by the amount of storage required to cope with each, and denoting 1921 by unity, is as follows:

1899 .... 0.69
1921 .... 1.00
1934 .... 0.99
1944 .... 0.91
1949 .... 0.69

FIG. 6.—RIVER THAMES, 400 FT WIDE AND 12 FT IN MAXIMUM DEPTH, LOOKING UPSTREAM FROM HAMPTON COURT BRIDGE (HAMPTON WORKS OF METROPOLITAN WATER BOARD, ABOUT 1 MILE UPSTREAM)

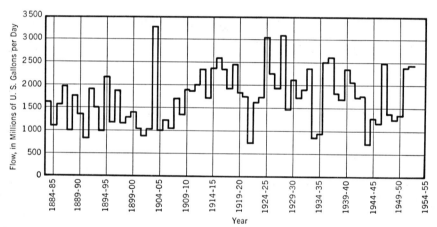

FIG. 7.—AVERAGE DAILY NATURAL FLOW OF RIVER THAMES SINCE 1883-1884

TABLE 1.—AVERAGE DAILY NATURAL FLOW OF RIVER THAMES IN DROUGHT YEARS, IN MILLION GALLONS PER DAY

Month	Standard average	1899	1921	1934	1944	1949
May	1,315	800	578	533	415	754
June	983	445	394	331	308	524
July	715	360	246	289	322	330
August	659	277	274	301	257	288
September	633	329	336	318	347	301
October	1,080	461	347	345	665	1,174
November	1,783	1,248	406	494	2,289	2,117

The amount of water which the Board may abstract is governed by Act of Parliament, by which certain conditions are imposed—the most important being that, to provide a flow of fresh water into the lower reaches of the Thames, the removal must be so regulated that the flow over Teddington Weir does not fall below 204 mgd. As will be seen from Table 1, this imposes a severe limitation on the available supply during the summer months of a drought; but, when these regulations were framed, it was recognized that it might not be possible to adhere to this particular requirement in a drought without endangering the water supply to London. In consequence, there is a provision in the Act whereby the "statutory flow," as it is termed, may be reduced in an emergency by an order drawn up by the Ministers of Transport and Local Government.

Incidentally, it should be added that the Board has never possessed enough storage and that this provision has been invoked in the droughts of 1934, 1944, and 1949. (The requirements providing for a statutory flow over Teddington Weir were not in force either in 1899 or in 1921.) Objections are always taken to this procedure by the Port of London Authority, the London County Council, and other organizations interested in the river. During and after every drought the Board is urged to construct more storage—but that is another story.

Assessing Needed Storage.—To compute the amount of storage which ought to be provided, the Board has decided as a matter of policy that its program is to be based on the assumptions that, during a period of low flows similar to those of 1944, a full supply will be afforded and that the conditions laid down for the abstraction of water and the flow over Teddington Weir will be observed. A 15% margin is also provided for contingencies. For the more severe droughts, like 1921 and 1934, the Board intends to rely on obtaining a relaxation of the minimum flow over Teddington Weir.

When these conditions are accepted and the combined supply from the River Lee and from wells is assessed at 131 mgd, it is a simple matter, after making allowance for the higher demands in the summer and the abstraction by the neighboring water companies, to prepare a chart from which the requisite amount of storage for any given total average daily demand can be read off. The data quoted hereafter have been obtained from such a chart.

It is now possible to review the existing position; and, in considering the future, the following facts emerge: First of all, at present the storage is inadequate. The Board now possesses reservoirs having a combined capacity of a little more than 21,000 million gal, but it is not possible to utilize the whole of this without a pumping-out plant, which is not yet installed. However, assuming that the whole 21,000 million gal is available, an average daily supply from all sources of 342 million gal would be afforded in a drought like that of 1944. Since the present demands are about 386 mgd, there is a deficiency of about 44 mgd which would have to be made up by the reduction of the statutory flow. In other words, the storage required to provide an average daily supply of 386 million gal is 30,000 million gal, so that the deficiency in storage is 9,000 million gal.

The Board has foreseen this and has obtained powers, as well as purchased the land necessary, to construct three additional reservoirs, which together will contain about 16,000 million gal. Because of economic conditions, permission has not yet been granted to undertake any construction on these reservoirs, and the Board has been informed by the Ministry of Local Government that for the time being it must rely on obtaining a reduction of the flow over Teddington Weir to make up the deficiencies and that facilities will be given to obtain the necessary order. However, if the Board had been able to carry out its program and if the three reservoirs were in operation, present storage would be 37,000 million gal, which would yield (with the other sources) a total of 420 mgd, and thus there would be a margin in hand of 34 mgd.

Second, the question arises, what storage would be necessary to meet a demand of 477 mgd which might be expected in 1977. From the chart this is 49,000 million gal, so that on the basis of this estimate, the Board should, in order to be solvent in 25 years, obtain powers and sites for, and construct, reservoirs to contain a further 12,000 million gal.

Obviously there is a limit beyond which it is uneconomical to develop the supply from the Thames, and the limit is governed by the amount of water available during a dry winter for refilling the reservoirs. From this point of view, the winter of 1943–1944 was the "worst" so far recorded; and it can be shown that, if the Board possessed 63,000 million gal of storage, it could just refill its reservoirs and afford a supply from the Thames alone of 413 mgd during such a drought—or the equivalent of a supply from all sources of 544 mgd.

More Reservoirs.—From the foregoing it will be evident that the future development of the Thames supply to the ultimate limit depends on the provision of reservoirs, beyond those authorized, capable of containing about 26,000 million gal. There is, however, great difficulty in finding sites for these.

The position of the existing reservoirs has been decided by two considerations—namely, (1) proximity to London to avoid expensive conduits, and (2) geological conditions. A third factor which will have an influence in the future is the desirability of finding reservoir sites in the lower part of the valley so as to obtain the maximum quantities of water for refilling in the winter. The Thames Valley, in the vicinity of London, is relatively flat and no sites exist for the construction of reservoirs by building a dam across a valley. Even if sites existed, impounding reservoirs could not be formed because of the limited gathering grounds and the low rainfall. In consequence, such reservoirs would have to be filled by pumping. As a result of the geography and geology of the district, a pond type of reservoir has been evolved, for which the geological formation for some 20 miles or so to the west of London is favorable.

The strata in this part of the Thames Valley consist of beds of ballast (flint and sand) about 20 ft thick in places and resting on solid London clay. The reservoirs have, therefore, been constructed with banks formed of the ballast and made watertight by a central core wall of puddled clay carried down and tied into the underlying solid London clay (Figs. 8 and 9). Unfortunately all the available sites for such reservoirs have now been either appropriated or built over or otherwise developed. The clay runs out in the neighborhood of Windsor, about 20 miles west of London, and upstream the formation in the vicinity of the Thames is the permeable chalk. Still further upstream at distances of 50 miles or more from London, the Oxford clay might provide some suitable sites but the cost of the conduits to convey the water to the works in the vicinity of London would be high.

It has been suggested that the water from such reservoirs might be discharged into the channel of the river and abstracted again at the existing intakes lower down. However, this proposal does not commend itself to the river authority—

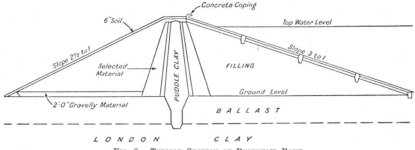

FIG. 8.—TYPICAL SECTION OF RESERVOIR BANK

the Thames Conservancy—on account of the algal growths which would occur in the reservoirs and which are not wanted in the river.

Question of Water Supply.—If the demand for water continues to increase and further reservoir sites cannot be found in the Thames Valley, there does not

FIG. 9.—AERIAL VIEW OF 5,400-MILLION GAL RESERVOIR UNDER CONSTRUCTION, WITH RIVER THAMES CUTTING ACROSS RIGHT-HAND TOP CORNER; NOTE EXISTING RESERVOIRS TO THE LEFT

appear to be any alternative but to obtain a supply from Wales. Unappropriated gathering grounds are still available in the southern section of mid-Wales, and it is estimated that an average daily supply of about 250 million gal could be obtained from these. No detailed surveys have recently been made of these sites; but, when they were suggested by the London County Council to a Royal Commission on the water supply of London at the end of the nineteenth century, it is understood that they were carefully investigated. At the same time estimates of cost were made. At present-day prices it would appear that, to provide for a first instalment of about 100 mgd from Wales, the cost might be in the neighborhood of $150,000,000, whereas the whole scheme, yielding 250 mgd, might cost as much as $300,000,000.

The Welsh supply to London would be an impounding reservoir scheme, the water being conveyed by gravity through an aqueduct of about 140 miles in length. The character of the water, of course, would be entirely different from that now supplied, being a soft upland water.

Difficulties of obtaining Parliamentary sanction for such a scheme would be great, as the opposition aroused would be extensive, powerful, and vocal, and it would have to be clearly demonstrated that no other practicable source existed for the augmentation of the supply to London. Further, a capital expenditure of about $150,000,000 on the first instalment would result in the water rate being raised by at least 3%. This problem is being actively studied. As is evident, however, its solution is not an easy one.

3. Biological Difficulties Arising from Storage.—The alkaline river waters containing large amounts of calcium carbonate give rise to prolific algal growths in the storage reservoirs, the count sometimes rising as high as 50,000,000 colonies per liter. Although the growths can be controlled by the judicious application of copper sulfate, this treatment is used with caution, as copper-resisting growths have on occasions been produced.

Until recently the Board possessed no reservoirs deeper than 42 ft, but during the past few years a new reservoir with a depth of 52 ft has been brought into use. From the economic point of view it is desirable to make the reservoirs as deep as soil conditions will permit, especially as reservoir sites are so scarce; but some apprehension is felt that with deeper reservoirs an appreciable proportion of their contents may become deoxygenated and unusable, because of decaying algae falling down into the lower and stagnant waters arising from thermal stratification. Some minor troubles have already been attributed to this cause, and research is actively proceeding. Nevertheless, experience in storing River Thames water in reservoirs, 60 ft and deeper, is most needed. The new 52-ft-deep reservoir has not as yet given any trouble, but probably it has not as yet matured.

A minor trouble arising from the storage of water is that caused by Chironomus flies. The eggs of this midge, laid on the water of the reservoirs, hatch out into red larvae of wormlike appearance, about ⅜ in. long. They live in the mud on the sides and particularly on the bottom of the reservoirs and eventually turn into a chrysalis from which the fly emerges at the surface.

Millions and millions of these flies hatch out about the end of May or in early June and, in performing their nuptial dance, form dense clouds over the reservoir banks and the vicinity. They are entirely harmless and unable to bite; but, since the reservoirs are situated in built-up areas, the nuisance caused, and the complaints raised, by these flies entering houses, hospitals, and other buildings, can well be imagined. At times they have been so numerous that traffic has been greatly impeded on adjacent roads. Considerable research has been undertaken to combat this nuisance; but so far, no cure has been found.

4. River Lee.—As its average daily flow of 132 million gal implies, the River Lee is a small river. It is some 60 miles in length, joining the Thames about 5 miles downstream from London Bridge. For more than 200 years it has been used for the water supply of the East End of London, a most important district, containing the Docks and a large industrial area, as well as housing more than 1,000,000 persons.

In recent years the valley of this river has become more and more developed for industrial and residential purposes, and its low flow in drought years has shown that it is an unsatisfactory source of supply. The development has resulted in numerous wells being sunk near the river and its tributaries; and, in addition to the exclusion of percolation into large areas, by reason of impervious surface structures, pumping from these wells has caused the drying up of many springs, so that the flow of pure water has been reduced. For this pure water there have been substituted large quantities of sewage effluent, thus making the water more difficult to treat.

In an attempt to maintain the supply from this source, several storage reservoirs having a total capacity of some 9,600 million gal have been built. Now, as a result the river is "over-reservoired."

There are four filtration works in the Lee Valley having a joint capacity of nearly 100 mgd, but in drought years the river and its reservoirs cannot now be relied on for more than 53 mgd. In addition to the filtration works several trunk mains lead from the pumping stations to the general distribution network.

In view of the capital sunk in these reservoirs, works, and trunk mains, it has been decided to supplement the abstraction from the Lee with raw water pumped across London from the Thames. The Board has therefore sanctioned the construction of a main 75 in. in diameter and about 21 miles in length for this purpose, at an estimated cost of $14,000,000. On account of the congestion below the surface of the roads leading into London and the streets in the metropolis (Fig. 10), this main is to be laid in tunnel through the London clay, possibly 100 ft below the surface. An experimental length of about 1,000 ft has already been constructed, lined with wedge-shaped concrete segments placed in position immediately after each push forward of the shield. A $\frac{1}{2}$-in.-thick steel pipe 77 in. in internal diameter and lined with 1 in. of concrete was then pulled into the tunnel and jointed by welding, after which the annular space tween the pipe and the tunnel was grouted up. As a result of the experience gained in the construction of the experimental length, the design of the main is proceeding, and investigations are being made to ascertain if it can be constructed by lining the concrete tunnel with cement mortar alone, thus obviating the use of steel pipe. The capacity of the main is to be 84 mgd with provision to increase it to 144 mgd by boosting.

5. Filtration.—On account of the high agal content and the almost complete absence of silt in the water derived from the storage reservoirs, is has not been found possible to devise a satisfactory and economical method of coagulation. Several attempts have been made and recently an experimental plant having a capacity of about 0.6 mgd has been erected, but the results thus far would not warrant a recommendation to embark on a large-scale plant of this type. In consequence, the Board is still using and constructing slow sand filters in spite of their high cost. To relieve these of some of their algal load and to speed up the rate of filtration, rapid gravity filters (usually referred to as primary filters)— cleaned by an air scour and an upwash of filtered water, but without the use of any coagulant—have been installed at most of the filtration plants. This method of dual filtration has been successful in providing a more flexible plant, in reducing labor costs, and in speeding up the rate on the slow sand beds from 4 in. to 8 in. per hr.

FIG. 10.—COMPOSITE PHOTOGRAPH AND DRAWING INDICATING SUBSURFACE CONGESTION UNDER A WEST LONDON STREET, SHOWING SIX WATER MAINS AND THREE GAS MAINS, AS WELL AS NUMEROUS SMALL MAINS, CABLES, AND TELEPHONE AND POSTAL DUCTS

Very little trouble is experienced in London from the freezing of the filter beds, all of which are uncovered. Such ice as does form is easily dealt with, and so is the freezing of the sand after the water has been drained down.

Apart from their capital cost and the area of land which they occupy, the principal disadvantages of the slow sand filters are the expense of cleaning and the difficulty of recruiting labor for this monotonous work. In consequence, mechanization is being introduced, but this process is handicapped by the layout of the older works where the aim of the designers frequently appears to have been—and often was successfully achieved—to crowd the maximum number of filters into the minimum area, frequently leaving no space for a road around or through the works (Fig. 11).

Before leaving the subject of filtration it may be of interest to refer to micro-straining. This process is performed by rotating drums which are now being constructed up to 10 ft in diameter and 10 ft in length, covered with a specially woven stainless steel gauze having some 72,000 apertures per square inch. The water passes from the inside to the outside, and the debris caught on the screen is carried around until it is above water level, where it is washed off, by jets of water playing on the top of the drum, into a hopper, and so to waste (Fig. 12).

FIG. 11.—HAMPTON WORKS WITH SLOW SAND FILTER BEDS IN FOREGROUND, RAPID FILTERS IN MIDDLE, AND ENGINE HOUSE BEHIND; NOTE LACK OF SPACE AROUND SLOW SAND FILTER BEDS

To an authority whose every gallon has to be pumped, the screening plant provides a great attraction, because the head loss through it is only about 6 in. as compared with 8 ft to 10 ft through a rapid filter. On the other hand, on the basis of the millions of gallons filtered per acre of the slow sand filters cleaned, the screens have not shown themselves as efficient as primary filters in preparing the water for the slow sand beds, and no chemical action takes place while the water is passing through them. Still, it is early to pronounce judgment, and a further advantage of the screens is that their cost for the same output is considerably less than half that of the primary filters.

The Board is at present (1952) installing two screening plants of 54-mgd and 108-mgd capacity, respectively, to operate in conjunction with slow sand filter beds.

6. Pollution of Underground Sources.—London is situated in an artesian basin or trough; but, because of excessive pumping, water will no longer overflow at the surface from boreholes sunk at the center of the basin. The chalk, which has a thickness of from 550 ft to 740 ft, outcrops between 10 miles and 30 miles to the north and south of London, and then dips under the center, where it is sandwiched between two beds of clay. The upper, the London clay, has a thickness varying from 300 ft to 450 ft, whereas the lower bed, known as the Gault, is from 130 ft to 300 ft thick.

Most of the Board's wells are situated on the outcrops where the chalk has only a thin covering of permeable material. The spread of urbanization has led to a considerable part of these areas being built over and sewered; and, since the chalk is highly fissured, rapid pollution of the water in it occurs if the sewers fracture or become defective. The workmanship in the laying of many sewers

Fig. 12.—Experimental Installation of Four Self-Cleaning Rotary Micro-Strainers at Kempton Park Works (Total Capacity, 6 Mgd to 8 Mgd), with Drums 7 Ft 6 In. by 7 Ft 6 In.; Raw Water Entering from Channel on the Right

often leaves much to be desired. Only by frequent sampling and inspection by a special staff employed by the Board can the pollution of the water entering the wells be detected and contermeasures be taken, such as the relaying of sewers in cast iron, to prevent the well becoming permanently contaminated. The well supply is of great importance, as more than 1,000,000 persons depend on it, especially in the relatively thinly populated areas in the southeast and north where no alternative sources of supply exist.

Another disturbing feature about the underground water on the east side of London is its pollution with estuarine water. This occurs about 20 miles downstream from London Bridge, where in years gone by springs from the chalk rose up in the bed of the Thames. Now, as a result of overpumping, the level of the water table has been reduced and the process is reversed, so that highly polluted brackish water from the Thames is finding its way back into the chalk. Whether or not recent legislation, which prevents further well sinking without a government permit, will check this unsatisfactory state of affairs remains to be seen.

Lastly, the water level in certain parts of London where large offices and blocks of flats have sunk their own wells (because they provide a cheaper supply than can be obtained from the Board) has fallen to such an extent, because of overpumping, that in many areas the top of the chalk, even at the lowest point of the artesian basin, is now dry. Before World War II, the water level under most of the built-up part of London was falling and under the City of London

FIG. 13.—CORRODED 16-IN. MAIN, REMOVED FROM LONDON'S WATER SUPPLY

itself, a small central area of about 1 sq mile, the rate of decline was more than 3 ft per yr. Since then, however, no records are available, but it is believed that this decline has been materially checked. In any event, in only one or two instances are the Board's wells affected as they are situated sufficiently far from the center of London.

7. *External Corrosion of Mains.*—Fortunately London water does not attack the interior of the mains, neither does it form any appreciable deposit in them. Some of the yellow clay, however, and the made-up ground especially near the river, cause graphitic corrosion of the exterior of cast-iron pipes (Fig. 13). The remedy is to protect new pipes with a $\frac{3}{8}$-in. coating of bitumen, always adopted where new mains are laid in corrosive soils; but there are many miles of old mains in the Board's area which have been laid without adequate protection and the renewal of these will be a costly matter.

The Board has more than 8,500 miles of main, nearly all cast iron, and about 2,000 bursts from various causes occur each year or, say, one for every 4¼ miles. The mains themselves are not affected by frost, but in very cold weather water at a temperature of about 36° F or less is pumped into the mains from the filtration plants. This causes contraction fractures, and numerous bursts are experienced, especially in the older pipes. A severe frost may cost the Board up to $200,000 in repairs from this cause alone. In contrast, during frosty weather,

FIG. 14.—WASTE WATER METER, WITH A CHART SHOWING THE REDUCTION OF THE NIGHT FLOW AS THE VARIOUS VALVES ARE SHUT DOWN AND INDICATING WASTAGE OR EXCESSIVE USE OF WATER IN ONE SECTION

the areas supplied with water from the walls, which is at a constant temperature of about 50° F, experience practically no breaks from this cause.

8. Detection and Prevention of Waste.—To detect waste the Board has always taken a great deal of trouble and employed a specially trained staff; and, now that capital expenditure is severely restricted, efforts in this direction have been redoubled. Also, it has adopted bylaws, enforceable by law, under which it can require internal plumbing to be installed in an approved manner. In addition, the Board can require all fittings to be stamped and tested before installation, but this is in abeyance because no buildings are available in which the work can be carried out.

Nearly all the service mains (4 in. and 6 in. in diameter) are so arranged that they can be isolated in lengths of $1\frac{1}{2}$ miles to 2 miles, and all the water passing into each length or section can be measured on a recording waste meter (Fig. 14) fixed on a bypass. These meters are operated at night once every 2 months as a matter of routine; and, if the "night line" shows an increase, a further test is carried out to locate the street or length of main from which the leakage or excessive use is taking place. For this purpose each street is shut off in succession between midnight and 2 a.m., and the drop in the flow on the chart soon reveals the street or the length of main in which the leakage is situated or from which there is an excessive waste.

In the case of a leak, its presence is discovered by sounding with a stethoscope or by the use of an electrical device, whereas misuse of water or defective internal fittings are detected by a daytime inspection. As a result of the drive on waste there has been a drop in the average daily consumption of 25 mgd since 1947; but, because of increased trade demands and the effect of new housing, the supply is again rising slightly.

This system is being extended as quickly as possible to cover the whole of the service mains, and only about 10% of these remains to be included. Tests for leakage are also made on the trunk mains but this process has not been very effective as yet. The equivalent of two hundred thirty-one in staff is employed solely on waste prevention and detection, at an annual cost of about $230,000. This expenditure is considered well worthwhile.

Conclusion

In conclusion, the writer is only too conscious of the many omissions and imperfections of this short paper. It is, however, with great pleasure that he acknowledges the valuable and kindly help which he has received from the Board's staff in its preparation, and expresses his thanks to his many friends who have assisted him with data and suggestions.

AMERICAN SOCIETY OF CIVIL ENGINEERS

Founded November 5, 1852

TRANSACTIONS

Paper No. 2614

THE SANITARY ENGINEER IN RELATION TO PUBLIC HEALTH

By Mark D. Hollis,[1] M. ASCE

Synopsis

With the expansion of human knowledge and the ever-increasing complexity of social management, the role of the sanitary engineer in public health has broadened to include all elements of the environment. Sanitary engineering and environmental control (in the interest of public health) are now synonymous terms.

In contrast to other engineers who are increasing their specialization, the sanitary engineer is obliged to diversify his knowledge. To his engineering training must be added an understanding of basic health practices, bacteriology, entomology, parasitology, chemistry, physics, administration, law, sociology, public relations, and education.

This paper discusses the importance of the work done by the sanitary engineer in relation to the over-all well-being of the nation. The problems facing the profession are presented, and suggested courses of future development are mapped out.

Introduction

The ASCE centennial celebration has found technological progress entering the steep incline of a huge S-curve. Many wonder but few dare predict where the trend will lead. The forces of engineering have tightened the network of human ties throughout the world. They have multiplied and concentrated the power of men at the control panel in human affairs. Nevertheless, as yet it is not known how to govern or tame the inevitable consequences or reactions.

Engineers have won high honors for contributing to productivity and to the instruments of social control. However, engineers cannot wear such honors proudly if they reject responsibility for certain consequences of their work, such as specific disruptive effects of technology on the environment and hence on public health. If the engineer is to live up to his popular reputation as the man who can work miracles, he must meet the challenge to do as much for public health as he has done for industry, commerce, communications, and defense.

[1] Asst. Surgeon Gen. and Chf. Engr., U. S. Public Health Service, Washington, D. C.

This paper concerns itself with only a small segment of the engineering profession—the sanitary engineers. For this group, the present moment is perhaps even more significant than for engineering as a whole. The profession is undergoing a transitional development. It faces a golden era. The extent to which health hazards in the environment are kept under control is likely to be the governing factor in the rate of advancement of the total technology.

As the physician practices a discipline that applies to the person of his patient, the sanitary engineer practices a discipline that applies to the whole of people's environment—air, water, food, and shelter. The sanitary engineer is distinguished from other engineers in that, as he works with these basic essentials, he is concerned primarily with their effect on the public health. In its original meaning, the term sanitary described a contribution to mass health. The common association of "sanitary" with pipes and drains resulted from the fact that water supply and the removal of human wastes were and are basic health needs of all people. Both the physician and the sanitary engineer have the same objective: Improvement of the health of the population—and this does not mean merely the absence of disease.

SANITARY SCIENCE

Evolution of Sanitary Engineering.—Sanitary measures were practiced from earliest times, long before the development of the knowledge necessary to explain them. Crude water purification procedures were used by the priests and physicians of India as early as 2000 B. C. The Mosaic law is an excellent example of how even the earliest civilizations recognized the interrelationship between environment and health. Frontinus prepared the first detailed descriptions of water works, and the aqueducts were an important factor in the high standard of living of Roman civilization. At the other extreme in history, the world is now on the threshold of the atomic age.

Present-Day Sanitary Engineering.—Modern sanitary engineering is a twentieth century product. This nation contributes to the profession an accumulated fund of knowledge dating from the origin of the Lawrence (Mass.) Experiment Station. Water treatment advances—rapid sand filtration, chlorination, fluoridation, and numerous other measures—have won for the United States world leadership in this field. The art of sewage treatment has substantially improved. High-rate trickling filtration and the activated-sludge process have transformed sewage treatment from the mere removal of settleable solids to the production of stabilized effluents. With industrial expansion, the science of waste treatment is becoming more and more complex. The industrial factor further complicates the pollution problem. Formulas relating to behavior and self-purification phenomena of streams are more involved with the increasing load and variety of organic and inorganic pollutants. Parallel to these developments is the ever-growing need for water to sustain the expanding technology. Greater demand as compared with fixed supply heightens the necessity for conservation. Water resources are more than ever a political issue. On the subject of water resources, certainly the sanitary engineer is at home. If he can balance his professional ability with public leadership, he will have the privilege and opportunity of resolving these issues sensibly and in the public interest.

Sanitary engineering has progressed along many other fronts. Milk and food sanitation is a major activity consuming half the time and effort of sanitation personnel in community health agencies. The multibillion-dollar food industry, with its continually changing methods of production, processing, and handling, presents the sanitary engineer many opportunities for public service. He has responded magnificently to the need for basic sanitation procedures. However, thus far, his services have applied largely to the food environment rather than to food itself. The primary objective has been to reduce danger of infection or poisoning. With

(a) Drainage of Stagnant Pools   (b) Spraying Pool Surface

Fig. 1.—Effective Mosquito Control

the development of a positive view toward health, the tendency is growing to think of food less as a commodity and more as an essential ingredient of life. Sound nutrition is a basic environmental requirement. The health of two thirds of an average group of American people suffers from conditions aggravated by poor nutritional habits.

With regard to insect vectors, employment of sanitary engineers in research, development, and application of control techniques has produced historic results. Plague and yellow fever are now virtually only of academic interest in the United States. Even malaria, dengue, and typhus have become of limited concern. Recent developments in insecticides overshadow earlier findings (Fig. 1). Techniques are being produced to permit an analytical approach to the study of insect behavior. Mosquito abatement programs have become a permanent part of health department operations. Even so, the recent epidemic of mosquito-borne encephalitis in California was a striking example of the continuing significance of insect vectors.

Closely allied to vector control is the field of refuse disposal. Except for improvements in the techniques of land fill, the sanitary engineer has neglected this subject. Admittedly, there has been lack of public support, but recently public attitudes have changed. Areas suitable for land fill are becoming scarce, and there is more need for reclaiming or salvaging the organic content and other valuable fractions contained in garbage and refuse. Composting, to produce a humus fertilizer, is, for the first time, attracting real interest in the United States. This same conservation awareness is evident in sewage treatment research. Studies are being directed toward reclaiming not only the water contained in sewage but also the fixed nitrogen. The time is approaching in the nation's history when less and less will be thrown away.

Other important fields of sanitary engineering include industrial hygiene, housing, air pollution, and the emerging field of radiological health. As to industrial hygiene, in addition to the obvious toxicological problems, the work in human engineering, noise control, and other factors must keep pace with industrial growth. All these fields offer vast potentialities.

Interest in housing, as indicated by the number of community health departments with organized activities, is only beginning to be explored. Because of its great effect on the total well-being of the individual, it seems certain that housing hygiene will command greater attention. It will be the job of the sanitary engineer, not simply to provide certain utility services for premises, but to master an understanding of the complex relationship between the home and the family's health. The importance of this relationship must not be underestimated. It may well govern future community organization.

Concern about air pollution parallels industrial expansion. The paucity of information on this subject has opened up a vast new field of endeavor. All sources of discharge to the atmosphere—industrial processes, municipal incinerators, automobiles, burning fuels and refuse, and the like—are being subjected to critical study and reevaluation in terms of chemical, physical, and biological effects. A closely related subject is that of air-borne pathogens. The problem of defense against biological warfare is bringing about a new and rigorous analytical approach to this subject. The results of this research will be of great value to peacetime public health programs. Precisely such data are needed to aid engineers in controlling the air much as they now control water.

With respect to radiological hazards, sanitary engineering activity is in its infancy. Even so, exposure to radiation today from medical diagnosis alone is at least ten times as great as was total lifetime exposure 50 years ago. Studies are under way on the treatment of radioactive wastes, the removal of radioactive materials from water supplies, and the behavior of radioactive substances in streams and in air. State health departments are adding to their staffs engineers trained in radiological health. This field imposes on sanitary engineers a complete new set of formulas, terms, dimensions, and concepts.

Present Scope of Sanitary Engineering

In its evolution, sanitary engineering has followed the pace of all technology. Early in the twentieth century, development of community water supplies and disposal of liquid and solid wastes were the paramount problems. The urgent need of the time was to suppress communicable diseases. In fact, in the public health movement, the past half century might be termed the era of germ disease control.

The environmental problems of the next half century promise to be much more complex. The chemical environment and the impact of the chemical age on the four fundamentals (air, water, food, and shelter) probably will become of major significance. The effect on health of the emerging atomic age and all its potential problems is yet to be diagnosed. Even in the realm of microorganisms, a full understanding of viruses as related to environmental facilities remains to be delineated.

Not to be ignored either are the rate, the pace, and the speed of the growing technology. Developments measured in the past half century by decades are now measured by years. The 700% increase in industrial production since 1900 is significant in that more than 350% occurred in the past 10 years. Chemical production today is three times as great as in 1936. Gone are the days when sanitary engineers could delay action on problems until public opinion crystallized. In the new age of rapid change, the sanitary engineer must influence public opinions and events in advance.

The new state of affairs brings concrete meaning to the concept of the sanitary engineer as he has seen himself. Even in the days when sanitary engineers were concerned only with the treatment of water and disposal of waste, the profession was identified with environmental control. Success with water fortified hopes for control of the other environmental factors. Today, the sanitary engineer is forced to face up to the problems of environment in all its phases and all its complexities. Many of these problems require not only engineering training but training in an extraordinary number of other disciplines. In practice, the modern sanitary engineer is a combination engineer-chemist-biologist-economist-sociologist. He must be a composite to an extent far greater than is demanded by any other branch of engineering. The requirements are becoming so severe that he needs to take stock of himself. Unless he lives up to the criteria that have been established, the present concept of the sanitary engineer will eventually disappear, and his role may once again be relegated to pipes and drains. The boldness with which the profession faces up to this issue will be the gage of its true stature.

Development of Research.—In the early development of sanitary engineering programs, basic research was bypassed in favor of applied research. Most of the work was conducted by the sanitary engineer himself. The funds available were so limited that only a few research scientists could be attracted to the field. Others found employment in such areas as petroleum research; and, of course, scientific advancement in these areas forged relatively far ahead. Meanwhile, the sanitary engineer was obliged to solve his own problems; and, in retrospect, he did so with surprising success. Further advances will require a much more fundamental, and far more expensive, approach. For example, consider the trickling filtration process used in sewage treatment. This has been improved to a high degree of engineering efficiency—but actually without basic knowledge as to the fundamental biochemical reactions. It is known that the filter teems with all sorts of organisms, but it is not yet known which organisms are doing the work. Theoretically, biological stabilization could be accomplished with greater efficiency through a more controlled process. Sewage materials would be acted on only by a selected organism or group of organisms reproducing in an ideal environment. The work of H. Humfeld in converting organic wastes to mushroom cells in a few minutes' time gives an idea of the sewage treatment plant of the future.

The problem of algae in water treatment is another instance where a dead end has been reached for lack of basic knowledge. Little additional knowledge can be gained from scattering copper sulfate in reservoirs until the symbiosis through which the algae produce tastes and odors is understood.

Although sanitary engineering research has been concerned primarily with practical applications, nevertheless, the sanitary engineer can claim credit for important basic developments, for example: (1) The flocculation process for removing suspended materials from water, an achievement in the field of colloidal physics and chemistry; (2) the broth-fermentation culture tube method for statistically evaluating bacterial concentrations in water, a fundamental advance in bacteriology; (3) residual spraying techniques for the control of disease-transmitting insects, an outstanding contribution in entomology; and (4) methods for minimizing scaling in the boiling sea water of vapor-compression distillation units, an advancement in inorganic chemistry.

PUBLIC HEALTH TOMORROW

The so-called wonder drugs are broadening the field of modern public health. Also contributing to the broadening process is an appreciation of the profound importance of the interrelation between man's health and his environment. The environmental factor is evident in the new public health programs in chronic disease control, nutrition, and problems of aging, as well as in the fields already mentioned. Environmental factors—the engineer's realm—bear an intimate relation to chronic diseases. A concept of "health maintenance" wherein personal medicine and preventive medicine are closely integrated is now approaching. If he has the capacity and competence, this movement will give the engineer increasing prominence on the public health team.

Challenge of the Future.—The foregoing survey of the past and present role of the sanitary engineer in public health has covered familiar ground. His potential role in world health, atmospheric conditioning, chemical environment, radiation, and energy engineering is also important. These problems place the sanitary engineer at the threshold of a new era. However, he needs a broader background in science, and in the humanities to help him to shoulder the new responsibilities.

World Health.—In 1952, in Chicago, Ill., the spokesmen of two major political parties emphasized the world-wide responsibilities of the United States government. In essence, they issued a stateman's challenge to the engineering profession in general, and to the sanitary engineer in particular. Engineers who have been associated with foreign programs in underdeveloped areas know that improvement of the environment to suppress health hazards is fundamental to economic advancement.

The concern of the sanitary engineer about international health will grow, too, as international travel grows in volume and in speed. Travel accelerated by jet turbines and rockets introduces a significant factor in health problems among the world's peoples.

Atmospheric Conditioning.—Investigations of the atmosphere have been limited for the most part to air pollution by dusts, fumes, mists, and pollens. Conditioning of the outdoor atmosphere may include control of precipitation as well as control of physical, chemical, and bacterial pollutants. A beginning toward complete atmospheric conditioning has already been accomplished within the

Fig. 2.—Measurement of Static Pressure for Calculation of Air Flow at Donora, Pa.

home. The status of this devlopment is comparable to that of central heating in 1900.

Smog or atmospheric pollution is at present generally thought to be confined to a few industrial centers such as Pittsburgh, Pa., Detroit, Mich., and Los Angeles, Calif., or to specific conditions as encountered in Trail, British Columbia, Canada, and Donora, Pa. The fact is that air pollution is significant in most industrial areas (Fig. 2).

The true effect of atmospheric pollution on the public health of a metropolitan area is virtually unknown. The evaluation of the relationship, if any, between pollutants such as coal tars and other hydrocarbons in the air and the increased incidence of chronic ailments such as lung cancer will require prolonged study.

The Chemical Environment.—As has been noted, the chemical industry has contributed heavily to the improvement of public health, especially in the fields of medication, nutrition, and vector control. At the same time, the growth of the industry is not without health hazards. Some of the new synthetics, when discharged into streams, produce serious tastes and odors even when measured in dilutions of a few parts per billion. Certain chemical reactions may also have serious consequences on aquatic life. Compounds in cosmetics and clothing create new and unevaluated environmental influences on the skin. Other compounds, incorporated into foods, introduce new elements into the diet. The problem of chemicals in the

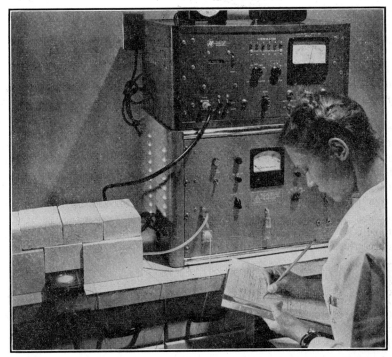

FIG. 3.—DETERMINING RADIOACTIVITY WITH GEIGER COUNTER

atmosphere has already been mentioned. The term "chemical environment" is coming into use to summarize the significance of the products and by-products of industrial chemistry. As yet unknown is the chronic effect of this increasing chemical exposure. From the toxicological point of view, the additive and synergistic effects compound the problem.

Radiation Wastes and Hazards.—No less ominous are the potential dangers associated with atomic energy, including nuclear power development. The advent of nuclear power will create problems that sanitary engineers must be prepared to meet. The keel of the first atomic-powered submarine has already been laid.

Nuclear reactors present two health hazards: Radiation from operation, and radiation from waste products. The operating crew and others nearby must be protected from excessive exposure, and the radioactive wastes must be safely handled (Fig. 3). The sanitary engineer must think of both hazards, but the disposition of the radioactive waste will be by far the more important and the more difficult. Informed scientists and engineers agree that radioactive wastes may be the limiting factor in industrial utilization of atomic power. One method of solving this problem would be to find some method of utilizing mixed fission products. This field is wide open for the application of sanitary engineering principles.

The epidemiology of radiation needs clarification. In general, some of the cumulative effects of radiation are known, and a great deal is known about measurement of external exposures. Not too clear, as yet, are techniques for evaluating the lifelong accountability of total exposure. Most important, a measure of dosage in living tissues that will make possible the prediction of specific changes has not yet been developed.

Energy Engineering.—There is a school of thought that looks beyond the atomic age to a new concept that eventually may have a great impact on the engineering profession. Those concerned about the wholesale application of atomic power as a prime energy source have watched with extreme interest the considerable study and stocktaking of the world's long-term energy resources. Atomic energy or nuclear fuels may at most be a stopgap or interim solution. Even before the supply of fossil fuels (coal, oil, and gasoline) nears exhaustion, nuclear fuels may give way to the direct use of solar energy. Solar energy may be concentrated through physical, chemical, or biological capture. Biological utilization through photosynthesis for the production of food or chemicals is especially promising. This field is already within the province of sanitary engineering. An example is the use of solar energy and sewage in the mass culturing of algae to produce a high-protein animal food supplement.

CHALLENGE TO THE SANITARY ENGINEERING PROFESSION

In the foregoing description of the manifold spheres of activity and responsibility of the sanitary engineer, the role of the sanitary engineer as a member of a team has been noted.

In early days, the sanitary engineer may have been the only man on the team or, at any rate, one of only a few. Today, however, the environmental team is composed of representatives of many scientific and professional disciplines. The sanitary engineer, as the name implies, is the engineer of the team. If he has the capacity, imagination, and perspective, he will continue to be the individual responsible for the coordination, guidance, and direction of the group activities.

It will not be easy for the sanitary engineer to grow up to his potential responsibilities and opportunities. What can he do to improve his capacities, to broaden his perspective, and to strengthen his influence? Several practical recommendations have been made within the profession. One suggestion is that education and training should be longer and more thorough. It has been proposed that experiment stations be set up at universities as a phase of extended education. Another suggestion is that sanitary engineers should have a strong professional society that would promote performance standards within the profession, act as a national spokesman for all sanitary engineers, and apply the influence of the profession more widely.

However, these measures will be of little avail unless more sanitary engineers, as individuals, demonstrate capacity for public leadership—leadership that at other stages of history gave prominence and prestige to the lawmaker, the scholar and teacher, the explorer, the merchant, and the doctor of medicine. At one or another period of history, these various groups gained respect because they satisfied demands of society. In this modern age, society needs the engineer's contribution. Society needs more than his technical services. Society needs educated engineering minds that can apply technical principles wisely. What has happened in the field of municipal planning is an example of the failure of the engineering profession to recognize trends of the times. Unfortunately the sanitary engineering discipline shows signs of similar deficiencies. Sanitary engineers must demonstrate to society the benefits that can be attained through environmental controls.

Conclusion

This paper may have given the impression that the sanitary engineer is indispensable in public health. Conceivably the reader may have inferred a portrayal of the future sanitary engineer as a rigorously trained and socially responsible leader, an executive, diplomat, and statesman. The impression that the discipline requires a competence and capacity not normally demanded of a single profession may also have been given. If that impression has been created, that is exactly what has been intended.

AMERICAN SOCIETY OF CIVIL ENGINEERS
Founded November 5, 1852
TRANSACTIONS

Paper No. 2615

STATUS OF INSECT AND RODENT CONTROL IN PUBLIC HEALTH

By J. A. Logan,[1] M. ASCE

Synopsis

Modern chemical compounds, which make possible the effective control of disease-carrying insects, have changed the course of man's effort to secure a more healthful environment. Effective residual spraying techniques are now widely used in public health work throughout the world.

This paper reviews the toll taken by insect-borne disease before the modes of transmission were fully recognized and control measures adopted. World history was often vitally affected by the course of insect-borne epidemics. The rise of sanitation is described, and the pioneers in this field are mentioned in connection with their accomplishments.

The effect of modern insecticides (DDT (dichloro-diphenyl-trichloroethane), BHC (benzene hexachloride), chlordane, and pyrethrum) on the control of such diseases as typhus, malaria, and sleeping sickness is briefly discussed. Field tests in insect eradication are described and evaluated. The need for further research on insecticides is emphasized.

Introduction

Today, such names as DDT, BHC, chlordane, and pyrethrum are household words. These compounds are among the modern developments which, together with preventive medicine and environmental sanitation, now make it possible for man to live and work in safety anywhere in the world. On the basis of the scientific discoveries of an international group of contributors—American, British, Brazilian, Indian, French, and Italian—doctors, engineers, and biologists are actively cooperating to make the present time a "golden era" in the field of insect control and are paving the way for a social and economic development of the backward areas of the world—which may well be the most significant phenomenon in the history of the twentieth century. Areas once considered as uninhabitable and as "white men's graveyards" are being made healthy; malaria, although probably

---

[1] Staff Member, Div. of Medicine and Public Health, The Rockefeller Foundation, London, England.

still the most important single disease afflicting mankind, is, in country after country, ceasing to be a public health problem. Yellow fever, once one of the great plagues of the world, has now been conquered; African sleeping sickness is no longer an important disease of man but is now essentially a veterinary problem; and typhus fever was stopped short in its one brief appearance in the western world during the last war and failed to become the major catastrophe that had usually accompanied the great wars of the past.

Nevertheless, it is difficult to express the full significance of these new developments. Perhaps it is because this is an age of miracles, when terms such as colossal, revolutionary, epoch making, and fantastic are commonplace; perhaps the public is now interested only in bigger and better miracles. In any event, each new development that comes along seems to dull the appreciation of its predecessors. Man has been characterized as a reasoning animal, with an inquisitive and adventurous spirit. However, he is also, unfortunately, forgetful, and it is this combination of inquisitiveness and forgetfulness that has brought about both the present state of scientific development and the lack of appreciation of this development in relation to the problems and conditions of the past. The remarkable and significant achievements that are now enjoyed tend, therefore, to be taken for granted, and the misery and suffering that the new discoveries have alleviated are forgotten. There is also a tendency to forget the scientists and technologists whose work has made these new advances possible.

It is the purpose of this paper to recall some of the important men and the important events that have contributed to the present position and to review briefly both this position and the possibilities for the future. Although it is still too early to say that "the future is here," and much remains to be done, the remarkable progress that has recently been made offers the potential power to banish much of the terror, the suffering, and the distress that still exist in many parts of the world because of insect-borne disease. Of equal importance, as P. A. Buxton recently said in London, the new insecticides "greatly increase the health, comfort and powers of the people who would be regarded as in normal health."

The Background

Insect-Borne Disease.—Although insects have been recognized as vectors of disease only in comparatively recent times, it is evident that they have been actively engaged in this role since the beginning of history. It was not, however, until about 1880 that the importance of insects in the transmission of disease began to be understood. Before acquiring this new knowledge, mankind, except for immunities and geographical barriers, was very much at the mercy of insects, and both individuals and nations lived a precarious existence. Malaria reigned supreme over large areas of the world; yellow fever dominated life within an important sphere of influence; sleeping sickness controlled large parts of Africa; and typhus and plague lay in an endemic state throughout most of the world, ready to blaze into epidemic form whenever war gave rise to the usual dislocation of populations and the resulting wandering, famine, and poverty.

Hans Zinsser deplored the lack of attention that insects have received from historians, for, as he states:

"Swords and lances, arrows, machine guns, and even high explosives, have had far less power over the fates of the nations than the typhus louse, the plague flea, and the yellow-fever mosquito. Civilizations have retreated from the plasmodium of malaria, and armies have crumbled into rabbles under the onslaught of cholera spirilla, or of dysentery and typhoid bacilli. Huge areas have been devastated by the trypanosome that travels on the wings of the tsetse fly, and generations have been harassed by the syphilis of a courtier. War and conquest and that herd existence which is an accompaniment of what we call civilization have merely set the stage for these more powerful agents of human tragedy."

Even in relatively recent times insect-borne disease has dominated certain periods of history. The Black Death (bubonic plague), in the latter half of the fourteenth century killed an estimated 25,000,000 people in Europe alone. In the

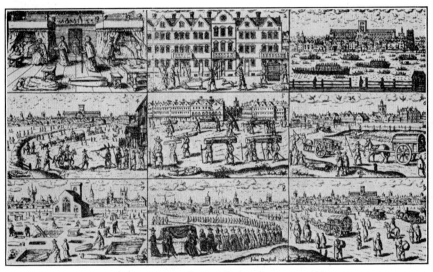

FIG. 1.—SCENES IN LONDON DURING PLAGUE OF 1665

year 1665 it ravished London, England, killing a third of the population (Fig. 1), and as late as 1700 it was still epidemic over a large part of Europe. Napoleon 100 years later was as effectively stopped in his Russian campaign by typhus as he was by the cold and enemy troops. Nearer the United States, the Haitian Republic owes its existence to the fact that more than three quarters of the French garrison of 30,000 picked troops died of yellow fever at a time when they should have been used to put down a revolution. In the more familiar field of engineering construction, two examples of the tragic failure of important projects toward the end of the nineteenth century may also serve as reminders of the power of insects.

Disease and Construction.—Following the successful completion of the Suez Canal in Egypt in 1869, Ferdinand de Lesseps turned his attention to Panama. Although the Suez Canal had been constructed with a remarkable freedom from disease, and was considered as a triumph of sanitation, the French attempt at the construction of the Panama Canal in 1880 was a different story. Panama proved to be a deadly locale. Neither Europeans nor natives were able to withstand the disease-ridden atmosphere and frequently not more than a fifth of the total force was able to turn out for work. More than 16,000 died in a brief period, the death rate being as high as 176 per thousand. The project was abandoned in a panic.

At about this same time, 2,000 miles above the City of Belem, Brazil, at the mouth of the Amazon, another tragic failure was being enacted. Here in the heart of the jungle on the Brazilian-Bolivian border, a 200-mile railway around a series of rapids and waterfalls on the Madeira River was designed to connect the 2,000 miles of navigable river in Brazil with 2,000 miles of channel in Bolivia and thus provide Bolivia with an outlet to the Atlantic. The line was surveyed in 1885 by an English company, and construction was started soon afterward. Various attempts were made, each defeated with great loss of life. Before 5 miles of railway were completed, 10,000 men had died, "a dead man for every railroad-tie in the line." The project was abandoned and seemingly forgotten. As with the Panama Canal, however, later developments in insect control created an entirely new situation and made the completion of both projects possible.

Comfort and Convenience.—The importance of insects from the point of view of comfort and convenience must also be considered. The mere presence of insects seems to annoy some people, and Sydney Smith's exaggerated defense of his statement that "insects are the curse of the tropics" represents a not uncommon point of view:

> "In a moment you are covered with ticks. Chigoes bury themselves in your flesh and hatch a large colony of young chigoes in a few hours. They will not live together; but every chigoe sets up a separate ulcer and has its own private portion of pus. Flies get entry into your mouth, your eyes, into your nose; you eat flies, drink flies and breathe flies. Lizards, cockroaches and snakes get into your bed; ants eat up your books, scorpions sting you in the feet. Everything bites, stings or bruises; every second of your life you are wounded by some piece of animal life. An insect with eleven legs is swimming in your teacup, a nondescript with nine wings is struggling in the small-beer, or a caterpillar with several dozen eyes in his belly is hastening over your bread and butter! All nature is alive and seems to be gathering all her entomological hosts to eat you up * * *."

THE RISE OF SANITATION

It is true, in general, that progress in the elimination of insect-borne disease had to await the knowledge of their etiology. Although most of the causes were not determined until the twentieth century, marked improvements were already in progress before this time. Many diseases, including both plague and malaria, were greatly reduced by improved sanitation. The importance of sanitation— including improvements in drainage, water supply, housing, and refuse disposal— therefore cannot be overlooked in any consideration of the present status of insect and rodent control. It is conversely true that with primitive conditions of sanitation both insects and rodents find an ideal environment, and no permanent progress can be made in their control until progress has first been made in environmental sanitation.

Historical Background.—Although a high standard of sanitation had been reached in many parts of the world long before the birth of Christ, the situation had greatly deteriorated during the Dark Ages. As late as 1760, in one of the most enlightened capitals of Europe, it was possible for E. Bascombe to write that:

> "Extraordinary as it may appear, there was not any such thing as a privy in Madrid; it was customary to throw refuse out of the windows at night, and it was removed by scavengers the next day. An ordinance having been issued by the King that every householder should build a privy, the people violently *opposed* as an arbitrary proceeding, and the *physicians* remonstrated against it, alleging that the filth absorbed the unwholesome particles of the air, which would otherwise be taken into the human body! His Majesty, however, persisted; but many of the citizens, in order to *keep their food wholesome*, erected their privies close to the kitchen fire-places."

However, the first signs of the new attitude toward sanitation were already in evidence. In England, in 1764, D. Munro wrote an excellent treatise on "Means of Preserving the Health of Soldiers," which discussed camp sanitation, privies, pit latrines, the purification of water, and precautionary measures against typhus fever. The belief that disease was conveyed by putrid air and the corrupted water of marshes led to the removal of excreta from around camps and dwellings, to the replacement of the rotting straw that was used to cover the floors in homes, and to an avoidance of swamps.

There followed, during the next 150 years, an increasing realization of the importance of the environment in the origin and spread of disease. Important milestones in the development of sanitation were the reports of Edwin Chadwick in England ("General Report on the Sanitary Condition of the Labouring Population of Great Britain, 1842") and of Lemuel Shattuck in the United States ("Report of the Sanitary Commission of Massachusetts, 1850"), both of which stressed the value of the engineering control of the environment.

Although environmental sanitation is one of the most important factors in the present standard of living, the situation in many parts of the world is, unfortunately, still similar to that of Europe in the 1700's. This condition is reflected to a greater or lesser extent in the presence of insect and rodent-borne disease in these areas.

Another significant factor that must be taken into consideration is the standard of living itself. Sir Malcolm Watson first stressed the importance of going deeper than merely finding the mode of transmission of disease; he maintained from the first and, rightly, that, if living standards could be raised, much of the disease throughout the world would automatically disappear as it had in Europe and the United States.

THE PIONEERS

The scientific discoveries of the last 20 years of the nineteenth century may be said to have set the stage for the present era of insect control. As a result, a degree of success has been obtained that would appear unbelievable to the scientists who made these discoveries.

Early Discoveries.—The year 1880 may well mark the initiation of this pioneer work. Before that time, insects had not been directly implicated in disease transmission, which was believed to be due to such things as miasmas, foul air, evil spirits, and decaying organic material. In 1880, however, Patrick Manson, a Scottish medical officer with the Chinese Imperial Maritime Customs Department in Formosa, published a paper in which he demonstrated conclusively that elephantiasis was carried by mosquitos, the parasite developing in the body of the insect. Shortly afterward, between 1889 and 1893, two Americans, Theobald Smith and F. L. Kilbourne, demonstrated that insects could transmit disease from one animal to another when they proved that cattle ticks were the intermediary host in the transmission of Texas cattle fever. In 1896, David Bruce, of the British Colonial Service in Zululand, demonstrated that tsetse flies could carry the trypanosome parasite from animal to animal. In 1897, Ronald Ross in India made one of the most important of medical discoveries when he found the parasites of malaria in anopheline mosquitos that had fed on a human being infected with malaria.

There followed in rapid succession a series of researches and investigations in all parts of the world that definitely established insects as important disease vectors. The most common of these and the diseases that they transmit may be summarized as follows:

Insect	Disease
Mosquitos	Filariasis, malaria, yellow fever, dengue
Sand flies	Papataci fever, kala-azar
Tsetse fly	African sleeping sickness
Fleas	Plague and common murine typhus
Lice	Relapsing fever, trench fever, typhus
Ticks	Rocky Mountain spotted fever
Mites	Tsutsugamushi fever

Verification of Insect Theory.—With the establishment of insects as vectors of disease, man had, for the first time, a rational objective to attack in the elimination of disease. In the early days there were, however, a great many skeptics to the Ross theory that diseases such as malaria could be controlled by a reduction in the number of insect vectors. The correctness of this theory was, however, brilliantly demonstrated by Gen. William Crawford Gorgas (Fig. 2) in Cuba in 1901. In 1881, Carlos J. Finlay had indicated that yellow fever was transmitted by mosquitos, and this theory was confirmed by the United States Army Yellow Fever Commission under Maj. Walter Reed in Havana, Cuba, in 1900. In February of the following year, General Gorgas, then chief sanitary officer for Havana, instituted measures to wipe out yellow fever through the use of vigorous antimosquito measures. By September, yellow fever had been completely eradicated and the incidence of malaria had fallen greatly. This success led to the selection of Gorgas by the United States Government as director of sanitation for the new Panama Canal Project. Gorgas appointed as his chief sanitary inspector, J. A. LePrince, a civil engineer. The success of these two men is legendary, and their work made it possible to complete the canal and constituted, as A. J. Warren of the Rockefeller Foundation has stated: "an epic in the history of sanitation and preventive medicine."

In Malaya, on the other side of the world, Watson was demonstrating in a less spectacular way the no less dramatic effect of anopheline control in the reduction of malaria. His work was instrumental in narrowing the "mosquito reduction theory" of Ross to "species sanitation," following the realization that only certain species of anophelines were responsible for malaria transmission.

Mosquito control was originally based on such measures as sanitation, screening, drainage, larviciding, and fumigation produced by the combustion of sub-

FIG. 2.—GEN. WILLIAM CRAWFORD GORGAS

stances like sulfur, pyrethrum, and tobacco stems. Spray insecticides were first used in 1928–1929 in controlling a yellow fever epidemic in Rio de Janeiro, Brazil. Later, pyrethrum was successfully used to control malaria in such widely separated countries as Zululand and India.

In Brazil, F. L. Soper, D. B. Wilson, and their coworkers, by a vigorous application of species sanitation measures against *Aedes aegypti*, realized the possibility not only of reducing this vector to a level that would break the yellow fever transmission chain, but also of eliminating the species entirely. The organization and techniques developed for this purpose were suddenly put to an even more rigorous test when they were utilized to eradicate the invading malaria vector *Anopheles gambiae* from northeast Brazil. The history of this invasion and its dramatic elimination now form a brilliant chapter in the saga of insect control. The value of the eradication technique thus developed was again demonstrated when an invasion of *gambiae* was stopped and eradicated from upper Egypt in 1945.

THE GOLDEN ERA

Development of DDT.—As the work of Manson, Ross, Gorgas, and Watson is remembered because of its importance in the development of a rational method of insect control, that of Paul Müller stands out as the pioneer of the modern "golden era." Working in Basle, Switzerland, in the years 1936–1937, he discovered the insecticidal properties of the synthetic chemical compound DDT, which was first prepared by O. Zeidler in Germany in 1874. In 1942, when R. Wiesmann in Switzerland noted that this material had a prolonged residual effect against houseflies, it was apparent that DDT had many of the properties of the ideal insecticide; it was stable so that it could be shipped and stored; it was highly lethal in small quantities against a number of insects; it was relatively safe to man; and its residual effect was a new and extremely desirable property in the field of insecticides. The possibilities inherent in this new material were immediately perceived by both the British and the United States armed forces and small quantities were obtained for test purposes. The initial tests indicated the potency of DDT against such insects as lice, houseflies, and bedbugs, and arrangements were made to put the compound into commercial production (Fig. 3).

Stimulated by the new possibilities offered by residual insecticides, researchers rapidly discovered other materials possessing properties similar to DDT in varying degrees, and new synthetic toxicants such as BHC, discovered in 1942, chlordane, dieldrin, aldrin, toxaphene, methoxychlor, and dilan have become available. All these compounds, like pyrethrum and rotenone, are both stomach and contact poisons, have varying degrees of residual effect, and can be used in a variety of ways.

General Effect of New Insecticides.—The advent of DDT and the other residual insecticides found malaria, plague, yellow fever, and the other insect-borne diseases disappearing in the more developed parts of the world because of improved sanitation, land reclamation, screening, and the use of household insecticides. However, as the situation in Italy during the war demonstrated, both malaria and typhus were ready to return in epidemic proportions when normal life was severely disrupted.

The first tests with DDT as a residual spray against adult mosquitos were, therefore, of particular significance. They were carried out early in 1943 in Orlando, Fla., as part of a plan to find a substitute for pyrethrum; and, as the results were promising, field tests were started in the same year in both Florida and Arkansas. By 1944 enough DDT was available for limited routine use by the allied forces, mostly in the form of an insect powder, and quantities for experimental use were also released. Late in 1945, DDT first became available for civilian use on a practical scale.

Typhus Control.—The results obtained since the first introduction of the new insecticide have been spectacular. Used as a routine prophylactic anti-insect measure by allied troops, DDT was an important factor in establishing the new standards of military health that were set. Its potentialities in the civilian field were first demonstrated in a dramatic way in Naples, Italy, when, late in 1943, an outbreak of typhus threatened to put this important allied port out of action. As an additional danger, the epidemic threatened to spread from Naples and menaced the entire Mediterranean area. On December 9, a Rocke-

FIG. 3.—MODERN RESIDUAL SPRAYING TECHNIQUE

feller Foundation Health Commission team, working in cooperation with the Allied Military Government and the United States Typhus Commission, began a systematic delousing of the Naples area using DDT insect powder. By the end of January, 1944, the trend of the epidemic was reversed, and by April it had been completely stopped. The outstanding success of this project aroused international interest.

Malaria Control.—By the end of 1945 it was evident, not only from military experience but from civilian investigations carried out in the United States, Venezuela, British Guiana, and Italy, that DDT could be instrumental in the development of new concepts and new standards in malaria control. By 1946 national programs were being initiated, not only in the aforementioned countries but also in Greece and Ceylon. The following year, control programs were started in India, Brazil, and Corsica, and each year since then has seen an increasing proportion of the malarious territory of the world under protection. C. B. Symes, of the British Colonial Insecticides Committee, has estimated that by 1952 more than 100,000,000 people were being directly protected by residual spraying. Malaria is ceasing to be a public health problem in an increasingly large part of the world.

Residual spraying for malaria control has also been responsible for a concomitant reduction in other household insects such as sand flies, houseflies, fleas, lice, bedbugs, and ticks; has had a direct effect on the comfort and convenience of the people concerned; and has greatly decreased the amount of disease caused by these vectors. Specific programs directed against such insects have also been highly successful, except in the case of houseflies where the problem of insecticide resistance has developed.

Sleeping Sickness.—In the case of African sleeping sickness, although planned resettlement of sleeping-sickness areas appears to have been the most effective method of eliminating the disease, both DDT and BHC have been extensively used. The yellow-fever vector, *Aedes aegypti*, has also proved vulnerable to residual spraying, and an active program for the eradication of this species is under way in the Americas under the sponsorship of the Pan American Sanitary Bureau.

It is evident, therefore, that in the use of residual sprays, man has developed a powerful new tool which, for the first time, gives him both a highly efficient and an economical method of controlling insect-borne disease anywhere in the world. In addition to residual spraying, other important methods of using the new insecticides have been demonstrated.

Eradication.—The possibility of eradicating the insect vectors of disease has always had a strong appeal because of its apparent finality. Two outstanding examples of this technique have been the eradication of *Anopheles gambiae* from northeast Brazil and from upper Egypt. In both cases, *gambiae* was an invading species and was attempting to establish itself in areas outside of its natural habitat. Many scientists believed that this factor made success possible, and that the eradication of an indigenous species would prove much more difficult. Within recent years, three major attempts at the eradication of indigenous malaria-vector species have been made—in Sardinia, in Cyprus, and in Mauritius. Whereas the program in Cyprus was based almost exclusively on larviciding and that in Mauritius on residual spraying, in Sardinia funds were available to use any method that it was believed would help in achieving success. Although malaria has been eliminated in each of the islands, in no case has eradication been achieved. In Cyprus, where the attempt included all anophelines, small pockets of some species are still being found. In Sardinia the attempt was confined to the malaria vector *Anopheles labranchiae*; and, although it has been reduced to exceedingly small numbers, a few still remain. In Mauritius, one species, *Anopheles funestus*, has apparently been eliminated, but the second important species, *gambiae*, has not been greatly reduced. It is apparently not, however, a malaria vector under Mauritian conditions. With the disappearance of malaria, the program in each of the countries has been modified to one of maintenance.

It is evident, however, that the eradication of an indigenous species is a difficult and expensive proposition (Fig. 4). The eradication technique may, nevertheless, offer some advantages under special conditions, particularly if incorporated in a general program of conservation and development where part of the cost of eradication can be charged to rehabilitation. Eradication should be based on an accurate knowledge of the biology of the vector involved, and recent experiments have emphasized the need for more basic information about insects and the action of insecticides.

FIG. 4.—SCOUTING FOR ANOPHELINE LARVAE IN SARDINIA

Larviciding.—The availability of DDT, BHC, and the other new insecticides, together with spreading agents, has made it possible to develop new and highly efficient larvicides, usually consisting of oil solutions of the toxicant. These can be used in relatively small amounts and are normally sprayed from airplanes, helicopters, or, more routinely, by newly designed hand and shoulder pumps (Fig. 5). Although a high percentage of kills of larvae can be obtained, it is extremely difficult to attain 100% success because of the difficulty in maintaining the larvicide film for the time required, and because of inefficiencies caused by a lack of basic knowledge of the insects concerned, the insecticide, and the oil carrier. Larviciding may, however, under certain circumstances, be the method of choice for mosquito control and is being widely used for the control of *Simulium.*

Rodent Control and Dusting.—Although the control of rodents has a special significance because of the tremendous damage that they do to crops and stored products, their chief interest from a health point of view is as carriers of fleas, lice, mites, and ticks. Highly successful techniques have been developed, mainly by the United States Public Health Service, in controlling rodents through

FIG. 5.—AIRCRAFT USED IN ANOPHELES ERADICATION PROGRAM IN SARDINIA

ratproofing, the use of land fill for the disposal of refuse, and rodent eradication. DDT dust has been widely used in controlling rat ectoparasites, and DDT and BHC dusts are also being used throughout the world in the control of lice, bedbugs, cockroaches, and so forth.

Resistance.—A not entirely unforeseen complication has arisen to confuse the almost unbroken series of successes enjoyed by the residual insecticides. This problem is resistance, the phenomenon of increasing tolerance on the part of certain insects to insecticides. First observed in houseflies in Sweden and Italy in 1947, it was for a time somewhat hopefully regarded as an exceptional and isolated occurrence, but housefly resistance was soon confirmed in Sardinia, Greece, Corsica, Egypt, and the United States. Resistance by insects other than flies has also appeared, that of culicine mosquitos being the most common, first reported from Italy by E. Mosna in 1948. Other insects that have shown varying degrees of resistance to the new insecticides include lice and bedbugs and, more recently reported from Panama, anopheline mosquitos, the latter to a relatively minor degree only. It has been observed that once resistance to one of the insecticides is established a rapidly increasing degree of resistivity to the others develops.

The resistance phenomenon, as such, has so far not affected the efficiency of the new insecticides in malaria control, although it has completely reversed the original hopes for widespread effective and efficient housefly control. Certain species of anophelines, however, notably *gambiae* in parts of Africa, appear to be sensitive to DDT, and residual spray programs using this insecticide have not been universally successful. Fortunately the insects do not appear to be sensitive to BHC and, by switching to this material instead of DDT, success has generally been achieved.

Insects, many of whose species preceded man as inhabitants of the earth by several thousand years, are proving, therefore, to be a difficult and versatile enemy. It has been found that not as much is known about their life and habits as had been imagined. Resistance itself is poorly understood. The urgency of war and the magnitude of the insect problem subject to immediate control by the known insecticides was the all-important factor in focusing most of the attention of chemists and biologists during the period 1942–1950 on the production of insecticides. As a result basic biological research was neglected. It is realized that this neglect has imperiled the benefits that have accrued, and much time and money are now being spent in an attempt to establish the mode of action of insecticides and the resistance phenomenon. There is every reason to believe that this work will be successful and that, in addition to maintaining present gains, even greater advances will be made.

Environmental Sanitation.—As previously pointed out, the development of modern environmental sanitation, together with an increasing standard of living, has been responsible for the elimination of insect-borne disease from large areas of the world and will continue to be an important factor in this regard. With modern machinery and equipment such as the crawler tractor, earth moving equipment, ditching dynamite, and modern transport, engineers have a wide variety of techniques for adaptation to any requirement.

Environmental sanitation is a primary necessity in many parts of the world and must form an integral part of any plan for community improvement. A primary requirement, however, is that such programs be economically justified, and this will necessitate in many instances a lowering of costs and the development of new and less expensive techniques, designed specifically for particular areas. It will also be necessary to evaluate the economic benefits to be derived from reclamation and to integrate sanitation with agricultural and water-use programs in order that the proper utilization can be made of potential new land and water resources.

THE FUTURE

In a review such as this paper, it has only been possible to touch briefly on the many phases of the history, development, and present status of insecticides. It is clearly evident, however, that engineers now have available a rich store of scientific data, powerful new toxicants, and highly efficient equipment and techniques that can be used in any part of the world in raising the standards of sanitation and in eliminating disease. It is also evident that, as the United States is taking a greater and greater interest in social, economic, and political development throughout the world, the use of these tools will be called on to an increasing extent. Although a great deal can and will be accomplished, two things stand out as being particularly important for the future:

(1) The need to encourage further research and development.
(2) The necessity of integrating insect control and health and sanitation with long-range social and economic planning.

The phenomenon of insect resistance is only one of the problems that have been called forcibly to public attention during recent years and that emphasize the meager knowledge of the physiology and ecology of insects. Although mosquitos, for example, are considered as one of the best known of all of the insects, knowledge of strains and subspecies and of their habits, dispersal, and physiology is definitely limited. Although engineers cannot effectively solve these problems, they can and should encourage any attempts to expand knowledge in this field.

The availability of techniques is of no significance if their use is prohibited by social and economic factors. To assure the success of their programs, it is of equal importance, therefore, that engineers pay particular attention to the necessity of obtaining public understanding and support and recognize the need for planning, from both an immediate and a long-range point of view. The World Health Organization has expressed one of the fundamental desires of the peoples of the world as the "physical, mental and social well-being" of man. Insect control can play a significant and increasingly important part in the attainment of this objective, and engineers must continue to take their share of responsibility to assure the success that is now possible.

BIBLIOGRAPHY

"Developments in the Use of the Newer Organic Insecticides of Public Health Importance," by J. M. Andrews and S. W. Simmons, *American Journal of Public Health*, Vol. 38, No. 5, 1948, pp. 613–631.

"Where Winter Never Comes," by Marston Bates, Charles Scribner's Sons, New York, N. Y., 1952.

"Symposium on Insecticides," by P. A. Buxton, *Transactions of the Royal Society of Tropical Medicine and Hygiene*, Vol. 46, No. 3, 1952, pp. 213–274.

"Rat-Borne Disease, Prevention and Control," Communicable Disease Center, Public Health Service, Federal Security Agency, Atlanta, Ga., 1949.

"Manson's Tropical Disease," by Philip H. Mason-Bahr, Cassell & Co., Ltd., London, England, 1950.

"Some Epidemiological Aspects of Malaria Control with Reference to DDT," by P. F. Russell, *Journal of the National Malaria Society,* Vol. 10, No. 3, 1951, pp. 257–265.

"Practical Malariology," by P. F. Russell, L. S. West, and R. D. Manwell, W. B. Saunders Co., Philadelphia, Pa., 1946.

"A History of Tropical Medicine," by H. H. Scott, Edward Arnold & Co., London, England, 1939.

"Anopheles Gambiae in Brazil, 1930 to 1940," by F. L. Soper and D. B. Wilson, The Rockefeller Foundation, New York, N. Y., 1943.

"Some Recent Progress in the Study of Insecticides and Their Application for the Control of Vectors of Disease," by C. B. Symes, *Proceedings,* Royal San. Inst. Health Cong., London, England, 1952, pp. 77–91.

"Yellow Fever," edited by G. K Strode, McGraw-Hill Book Co., Inc., New York, N. Y., 1951.

"Rats, Lice and History," by Hans Zinsser, George Routledge & Sons, Ltd., London, England, 1935.

"The Sardinian Project; An Experiment in the Eradication of Anopheles Labranchiae," edited by J. A. Logan, Johns Hopkins Press, Baltimore, Md. (in press).

AMERICAN SOCIETY OF CIVIL ENGINEERS
Founded November 5, 1852

TRANSACTIONS

Paper No. 2616

INFLUENCE OF WATER-BORNE SEWAGE

By A M Rawn,[1] M. ASCE

Synopsis

The advent of water-borne sewage systems is described as possibly the outstanding event in sewerage practice during the past century. The many problems created by the water-carriage system are more than balanced by the benefits therefrom. This paper traces the early history and development of water-borne sewage and the difficulties of early advocates of the system in making headway against public opinion.

Introduction

The great sewerage achievement in the latter part of the nineteenth century marked a new era in public health and ushered in innumerable problems in sanitation. This achievement became the inspiration for practically all modern sewerage practice.

It may be truly stated that today's methods of handling sewage found their inception in the outcome of a controversy that rocked civilized nations to their very privies; caused parliaments, congresses, and legislatures to enact summary laws; made fools of medical men; and set engineers at one another's professional throats in defense of outlandish sewerage schemes. However, when all the fuss had quieted down, the result was general acceptance of the water-carriage system of sewage collection, despite all the dangers then attendant on the mass concentration of large volumes of sewage and the consequent gross pollution of streams and other waters. Following acceptance of the principle of water-borne sewage, there began an intensive search for better sewage treatment methods, and the first half of the twentieth century has seen the establishment of the whole field of sewerage, as it is now known.

Since substantially all this development, from the old days of the "outhouse" to the present, has taken place during the lifetime of the writer, he feels qualified to select the water carriage of all sanitary sewage and industrial waste generated in urban communities as the most influential and impressive sewerage improvement in the past 100 years.

---

[1] Chf. Engr. and Genl. Mgr., Los Angeles County San. Dists., Los Angeles, Calif.

EARLY APPROACHES TO SEWAGE DISPOSAL

One has but to read the engineering discussion of the two or three decades after 1860 to recognize how little real knowledge of sewerage then existed and how limited was the comprehension of the informed citizen of that era about what the future held in the way of urban development.

An early article on water-borne sewage stated:[2]

"Although no system has yet been devised by which the liquid refuse of houses can be profitably and beneficially used, except it be by irrigation, it is clearly proved * * * that the solid part may be secured by a simple, inexpensive, and thoroughly effective plan, thereby yielding a large profit to the householder, and supplying agriculture with the most important food elements."

A Dutch engineer, Capt. Charles T. Liernur, had patented a process (to be installed at the Hague, Netherlands) that today would be looked on as an outlandish contrivance, but of which he was extremely proud and jealous. Arguing against the ocean disposal of water-borne sewage, Liernur stated in 1867:

"The effect of salt water upon putrid, organic substance is well known. It may be compared to a species of 'pickling' which delays the decomposition. * * * but even if salt water was a good purifier there are thus far no means found to make use of this property. Sewage discharged into the sea * * * is thrown back in a comminuted state by the return tides on the beaches. * * * It is this peculiarity which makes sea coast towns and harbors so frightfully unhealthy. * * * In the Medical Times * * * it is repeatedly stated and proved that more death and sickness occur along the lines of main sewers than elsewhere. * * *"

which he attributed to

"* * * letting the noxious gas out in the streets, conveniently to be inhaled by the citizens, both passing by and residing right and left; the bedroom chambers above generally getting the most of them."

The idea that sewer gases were accountable for sickness and death was advanced by eminent physicians of the day:[3]

"All London *knew*, and a very large portion of its inhabitants *smelt* the condition of the Thames when the sewage went into it and fermented in the hot weather. Now let it not be forgotten that all this sewage which poisoned the Thames is confined in some large brick tubes underground * * * the dirty water flows down hill, and the dirty gas up hill * * * and through every crack and crevice along this course out issues the poisonous fluit [gas] to the roads and houses above, filling the omnibuses and carriages as they pass. * * * It is everywhere. * * * Wherever there is a burrow in the earth, or a hollow space beneath the floors and above the ceilings, or in the partitions, there it lies in store, to issue forth whenever the fire burns brightly, to make us sicken and shudder."

Despite all efforts to the contrary Baldwin Latham, engineer of public works at Croydon, installed the water-carriage system of sewers for disposal (Fig. 1). Mr. Latham at that time was president of the Society of Engineers of England, and in describing the process enlarged on the method of final disposal as being

---

[2] *The Engineer* (London), May 24, 1867, p. 547.
[3] *Engineering* (London), January 12, 1866, p. 17.

Fig. 1.—Water-Borne Sewage System, Croydon, England, 1868

broad irrigation and field cultivation. In an estimate of the advantages of his sanitary scheme he stated that the death rate per thousand had dropped to such an extent that 2,439 deaths had not occurred, which under the old system of privy sewerage would have. To this benefit, he added £240,000—an amount covering funerals, illness costs, and the economic value of saving 6½ years of additional labor per individual.

Following publication of Latham's description, the ubiquitous Dutch engineer, Liernur bobbed up and commented caustically as follows:[4]

> "To Mr. Latham's estimate of savings on 2,439 citizens' lives might be added the following:

	£	s	d
"Value of labour done by individuals, who did not break their hearts by untimely deaths of beloved relatives, and thus continued their pursuits: 2 broken hearts for 2 days for 2,439 deaths at 2s each per day................................	975	12	0
"Value of labour done by disappointed greedy heirs, who, not getting the filthy lucre they hoped for, were compelled during an average of 5 years to continue working with perspiring countenances; £50 per annum per disappointed heir of 2,439 deaths.	609,750	0	0
"Value of labour done by people who did not idle away their time by gazing at the passing by of 2,439 funerals, 300 individuals for one hour, at 6d per hour	18,292	0	0
"Saving in wear and tear of hat-brims of people who keep to the old habit of taking off their 'tiles' when funerals pass by; 6 brims per funeral, at 1d per brim	61	0	0
"Three hundred children born of ladies who did not become widows by untimely deaths of husbands: value of labour done for one year in after life, at £100 per baby.........................	30,000	0	0

> "And so forth, until we really can get a couple of millions—at least, if we don't deduct the losses sustained by undertakers, doctors, hatters, etc., nor the value of the advantages gained by others."

And so the battle raged. In March, 1871, an engineer named W. H. Carfield stated, in part:

> "What the earth is in the case of the dry closet system so is water in that of the water closet, with some additional advantages in its favor.* * * In point of freedom from nuisance, and all offensive and injurious features, there is no system that for a moment can compare with it [the water carriage system].* * * One great and valuable feature attending the introduction of the water carriage system, is that the towns in which it has been even laterally [lately] employed have at once experienced a decrease in their death rate."

DEVELOPMENT OF SEWERAGE SYSTEMS

The water-carriage system of sewage collection had arrived. It would be most gratifying to be able to state that thus were all sewerage problems solved; but,

---

[4] *Engineering* (London), February 14, 1868, p. 140.

alas, nothing could be further from the truth, because with its arrival it brought a series of perplexing problems that still have not been solved despite the past 80 years of progress. However, in the very perplexities themselves were born and developed the greatest of modern sewerage engineering achievements.

It is not the intent of this short paper to attempt to trace chronologically and historically the development of separate sewers or the water-carriage system in the United States or elsewhere. The important fact is that, in the early 1900's, modern sewerage, as exemplified by the mechanical and biological process invoked today, was in about the same stage of development as was the airplane. Nevertheless, the method of waste-solids removal by the water-carriage system was so effective and economical that the engineering profession immediately set about finding ways and means to deal with the accumulated, contaminated water. To accomplish this end, the aid of the chemist, bacteriologist, and biochemist was invoked and the art and science of structural and mechanical engineering were called on for assistance. The monumental sewage treatment works of Chicago, Ill., New York, N. Y., Cleveland, Ohio, Detroit, Mich., and Milwaukee, Wis.—to name but a few—are testimony to the answer that the civil engineer supplied to the perplexing problems posed by the water-carriage system of sewage disposal.

A number of corollary benefits manifested themselves as soon as the water-carriage system was generally accepted: First, with increased medical knowledge, public health officials quite promptly surmised that fresh-water sources, deliberately polluted or contaminated with accumulations of water-borne sewage, were unfit for public consumption without as extensive treatment as was known in those days. As a result, there was an almost immediate decline in the mortality rates from water-borne disease. Second, more abundant water supplies were sought for urban use with consequent improvements in cleansing facilities in the growing cities.

The first of these two blessings is manifest in all public health reports dealing with such facts in the latter part of the nineteenth century, and the second (now well known) is ably emphasized in the "Report of the Committee on the Treatment and Utilisation of Sewage," appearing in 1871:[5]

> "* * * To limit a large population to a small supply of water, just as if they were living on board ship, would be a great injury to society and not a desirable arrangement. A large supply of water is wanted to keep a town healthy and pure, and as water must be supplied, it is the most convenient thing to carry off the excreta, so that this plan [the water carriage system] is the cheapest, easiest, and quickest."

Average daily contributions of sewage, as the term is understood today, to systems varying from 50 to 200 gal per capita, are mute testimony to the tremendous influence of the water-borne sewage practice on water supplies. The amount of sewage similarly testifies to the manner in which cleanliness has spread throughout the more enlightened nations of the world.

In the writer's opinion the institution of the water carriage of all household sewage, more lately including garbage, has been the greatest single event in the past 100 years of urban sewerage.

---

[5] *The Engineer* (London), August 25, 1871, p. 134.

AMERICAN SOCIETY OF CIVIL ENGINEERS

Founded November 5, 1852

TRANSACTIONS

Paper No. 2617

OUTSTANDING ACHIEVEMENTS IN TREATING INDUSTRIAL WASTES

By Don E. Bloodgood,[1] M. ASCE

Synopsis

Concern over the treatment of industrial wastes is a fairly recent development. However, a great amount of work has been done in this field, and this paper summarizes the more important achievements. Specific examples are given to show the remarkable progress in the utilization and disposal of industrial wastes.

Introduction

It would be quite impossible to establish the date when the first industrial waste problem presented itself. However, waste was probably produced by the first industry—whether or not it was a nuisance is quite impossible to determine at this late date. In Indiana, in 1886, a Mr. Mergentheim was indicted under the nuisance statute of Indiana "for discharging the water from his woolen mills into the canal at Peru, Indiana. * * *" It is unlikely that Indiana was the first state where the question of industrial waste nuisance was brought to the attention of the courts (even though courts like to claim early priority whenever possible.)

Langdon Pearse, M. ASCE, reports, in his history of the Chicago (Ill.) Sanitary District, that in 1909 it was concluded that dilution of Chicago wastes could no longer be considered a satisfactory method of disposal and that methods for treating packing-house wastes, stockyard drainage, tannery wastes, and corn products wastes must be found.

Milwaukee, Wis., undertook the elimination of sewage from rivers and harbors in 1914. Part of the problem was to find a method of sewage treatment that would remove the phenols from coke production wastes and would treat tannery wastes.

Interest in Industrial Wastes

These examples only indicate that industrial wastes have been under consideration for some time. A measurement of interest and activity in the treatment

---

[1] Prof., San. Eng., Purdue Univ., Lafayette, Ind.

of industrial wastes seems to be in order. Published information may show the developments. Any summary of the literature by years is bound to be inaccurate, but it may at least give an indication of what the trend has been.

The *Engineering Index* has been abstracting technical articles for more than a half century. Although it cannot be expected to cover all publications or positively to place in restricted categories all the material reviewed, a count of the published articles dealing with industrial wastes should be an indication of the interest and activity in the study of wastes and the methods for their disposal.

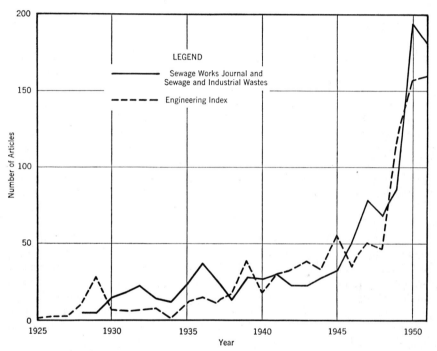

FIG. 1.—PUBLISHED ARTICLES ABOUT INDUSTRIAL WASTES

The *Sewage Works Journal*, which became *Sewage and Industrial Wastes* in 1950, has not been published for quite as long a time as has *Engineering Index*, but it was being circulated before interest in industrial wastes began to develop. Because of the scattered indexing of articles on industrial wastes between 1900 and 1925, it is not possible to give accurate data on the number of published articles, but it can be safely assumed that the average was not more than one per year.

A count of the indexed articles (including abstracts) in *Sewage Works Journal* and *Sewage and Industrial Wastes* has also been made. The data have been placed on the graph, shown as Fig. 1. It is apparent that the two sources did not give identical totals, but it seems reasonable to believe that the information gives a fair idea of the development of interest in industrial wastes. In the past years, up to 1944, articles on industrial wastes have been indexed in one of many ways in *Engineering Index*. In the old volumes they are listed under sewage disposal, the name of the industry, wastes, waste disposal, and many other classifications. Since 1944 *Engineering Index* has published a main heading, "Industrial Wastes," with a subclassification for each industry.

In 1950 *Sewage Works Journal* was changed to *Sewage and Industrial Wastes* because industrial wastes had become so important in the field of sanitation. The increased interest in industrial wastes as indicated by published material actually brought about action in the disposal of wastes.

PROGRESS IN WASTE TREATMENT

Within the past quarter century rather remarkable strides have been made in the utilization and disposal of industrial wastes. However, the industrial waste problems of the United States cannot be considered solved when one reads the cooperative reports of the United States Public Health Service and of the several state agencies. It is possible, however, to take some specific examples and show the advances that have been made.

Distillery Wastes.—The distilling industry has gone into the recovery of by-products and in places where stillage was formerly discharged directly into streams it is now screened, concentrated in triple-effect evaporators, centrifuged, and dried on drum driers and in rotary driers, thus producing stock food of appreciable value. The Hiram Walker plant in Peoria, Ill., is an example of one of the large distilleries that has made such a change in its methods of waste elimination. The problem of disposing of evaporator condensates still remains to be solved.

Food Canning Wastes.—The food canning industry developed by leaps and bounds during the first half of the twentieth century. Originally wastes were discharged without thought of mankind. The destruction of fish life in summer seasons was tremendous. To stop this, holding lagoons came into general use and in many instances, the odors from them were obnoxious. The malodorous lagoons are now usually kept under control with sodium nitrate. The most recent procedure in canning waste disposal has been the spraying of the wastes on to farm crop land. This newer method became possible with the development of light, quickly-connected piping. The Morgan Packing Company at Austin, Ind., has started the spray irrigation of more than 200 acres this year.

Even though there are comparatively few cases of gross pollution by canning industries, still unanswered questions remain on how to treat these wastes more effectively and economically. Among other problems, treatment of the odors and juices from pea vine stacks perplex the food packer of today.

Oil Refinery Wastes.—The oil refiner was almost overcome with his task when he came to realize that the exceedingly large volume of water from his plant had to be treated even though it might contain relatively small amounts of oil. The result was that organizations like the Sinclair Refining Company completely rebuilt the sewer system in their plant to separate the oil contaminated waters, the sanitary sewage, and the uncontaminated waters, so that the various liquids could be treated in the most effective manner possible. Notable developments in the treatment of the oil-contaminated wastes have been brought about through the design of the American Petroleum Institute separator, chemical coagulation, and biological treatment. A chemical treatment plant is shown in Fig. 2. Many of the peculiarities of emulsified oils are not yet thoroughly understood so there are still many unanswered questions on the complete treatment of oil wastes.

Milk Processing Wastes.—Wastes from the processing of milk have been particularly troublesome, primarily because of the high concentration of organic matter per unit volume. The elimination of wastage of raw milk by the installation of drip savers, spray rinsing, and other devices has done much toward reducing the so-called industrial wastes of this industry. The comparatively recent

Fig. 2.—Chemical Treatment Plant for Refinery Wastes, Daugherty Refinery, Petrolia, Pa.

utilization of whey in the production of milk sugar has been a development appreciated by those interested in stream pollution abatement. New methods for saving and using drip milk are needed. Because of the high concentration of organic material in milk wastes, it is essential that more economical designs of presently known biological treatment plants be made so that the industry can build and operate a waste treatment plant that does not cost more than the processing plant itself.

Paper Wastes.—Paper wastes have been objectionable because of their concentration and volume. Paper has been manufactured in large mills, and as a result the amounts of wastes discharged at any one location have been large. The paper industry organized the National Council for Stream Improvement (of the Pulp, Paper, and Paperboard Industries) in 1944. This grouping of the many companies shows a concerted effort on their part to do on a large scale what could not be undertaken by an individual. The accomplishments of the Council have been demonstrated by the many instances of marked reductions in the losses of usable pulp. Controlled lagooning of strawboard wastes has been a development which interested the writer. The growing of yeast on wood sugars has reached the stage of being undertaken as a full-scale operation. In some instances, magnesium cooks have come into use. This process is reportedly of great assistance in the reduction of the wastes discharged. The numerous reports published by the Council indicate activity in the elimination of paper manufacturing wastes and show, too, that not all the problems are as yet solved.

Oil Field Wastes.—Oil field brines discharged to streams have caused many complaints. The East Texas Salt Water Company, a nonprofit organization, has been carrying on recharging operations which have resulted in increased oil production from the affected fields.

FIG. 3.—TREATMENT PLANT FOR MEAT PACKING WASTES, RAYTOWN, MO.

Coal Mining Wastes.—In coal mining, the waste waters from the mines have acidified rivers and caused damage to structures. Studies have shown that oxygen and bacteria play important parts in the production of the acid. The mining states have taken steps to use this knowledge in controlling acid production and discharge.

Steel Mill Wastes.—The steel mills with their coke plants, as they have grown, have been contaminating the water supplies with phenol. Changes in processing have decreased the amounts of phenol discharged, and chlorination and biological treatment have been found effective in removing the remaining contamination before the water is reused.

Plating Wastes.—The rapid development of plating parts for many uses has brought about waste problems. The constituents of chromium and cyanide have aroused the greatest objection. Since chromium can be reduced and then precipitated, this method of treatment is used in some plants, and there are plant-scale installations of evaporators for concentrating the chromium solution. The quantity of chromium and other plating solutions lost into the rinse water has been decreased by taking steps to minimize the carry-out on each plated piece. Sprays of water or air and vibration are used in removing solutions from the plated parts, with return of the liquid to the solution tanks. The cyanide wastes can now be treated by chlorinating the alkalinized solution. The result of this treatment is the breaking down of the cyanide to carbon dioxide and nitrogen. The newly developed ion exchange resins show promise in the removal of plating constituents from waste waters and more concentrated solutions. The challenge spurring further study of this method is the promise of increased recovery of usable materials.

Meat Packing Wastes.—In the treatment of meat packing wastes (Fig. 3) it has been learned that it is important to eliminate paunch manure and offal from the sewers, and that the purchase of proper equipment for grease separation may even prove to be a profitable investment. The soluble materials in packing plant wastes are readily decomposed, but their concentration and large poundage necessitate the construction of extensive works. Studies must be made to determine the possibility of reducing equipment costs.

Conclusions

It would be possible to comment on each known industrial waste, stating the progress that has been made and indicating what yet must be done. However, there would hardly be a safe stopping place for fear of forgetting some particular industry that has made notable progress in decreasing the quantity of waste, developing a method of treatment, or devising some way to use the waste materials as by-products.

AMERICAN SOCIETY OF CIVIL ENGINEERS

Founded November 5, 1852

TRANSACTIONS

Paper No. 2618

EFFECTIVE UTILIZATION OF THE SANITARY ENGINEERING PROFESSION

REPORT OF THE COMMITTEE OF THE SANITARY ENGINEERING DIVISION ON ADVANCEMENT OF SANITARY ENGINEERING

Synopsis

In keeping with the general theme of the Centennial, this report first will present some of the factors that have contributed to the growth and development of sanitary engineering as a special activity in the field of civil engineering; second, will review some of the current problems that confront those who practice in this field; and, finally, will attempt to envision some of the situations that, as far as can presently be anticipated, may confront the profession in the not-too-distant future. If, through a review of the past, a better understanding of the present is obtained and if, through this understanding, engineers are better prepared to plan for the future, the purpose of this report will have been achieved.

Introduction

Engineers need to pause from time to time in their daily routine so that they may renew their strength in recapturing the spirit of service to mankind that stimulated the leadership of past generations. To do this, the engineer should restudy the philosophy of those pioneers of engineering thought whose deep sense of economic and social responsibility guided them in the application of available scientific principles to the development of the techniques that would give man a greater mastery over his environment. It should be realized that technological progress is not in itself an end. It is only a means to an end, and it has value only to the extent that it provides the better way to achieve engineering objectives.

Early Engineering

The Engineer's Function.—The early concept of civil engineering, as distinguished from military engineering, had as its professional objective the construction of the facilities needed by the civil population. This concept is suggested by the following quotation from a textbook on civil engineering[1] by John Millington, then a professor of chemistry, natural philosophy and civil engineering, in William and Mary College, at Williamsburg, Va.:

> "The term Civil Engineer that has been adopted by those whose profession it is to execute the internal improvements of the country in counter distinction to military engineers is of late origin and does not appear to have been known in England until about 1760."

and, further,[2]

> "The profession of the Civil Engineer has like all other pursuits flourished with the progression of society and intelligence. When first established in England, Civil Engineers were a self-created set of men whose profession owed its origin not to power or to influence, but to the best of all protection— the necessity for its existence and the encouragement of a great and powerful nation that needed their assistance."

Millington continued in his text to give his concept of the many duties of the civil engineer, as follows:[3]

> "In fact, the versatility of his occupations is such that it seldom happens that any one man can attend to them all; and thus it happens that the profession becomes divided into a number of branches and each man takes up that portion which is most congenial to his own views and abilities; and by this division of labor and talent greater perfection is insured to the public."

After listing the various functions of the engineer of interest to the civil public, he concluded:[3]

> "All these, however, are but parts of the general business of the Engineer and to be perfect in his profession he should possess a general knowledge of the whole of them, notwithstanding he may only practice a part. By judiciously selecting a part and pursuing it with steadfast zeal he cannot fail of arriving at perfection in that department; and the public readily find out those men that excel most in particular departments, and never fail to give them due encouragement."

These observations by an engineer, more than 110 years ago, are significant in that they envision the many and diverse services that would be required of those who would practice civil engineering in a young and rapidly growing nation.

The development of various branches of civil engineering during the past century, in response to public need and with an increasing knowledge of the sciences, laid the foundation required for technological growth. In the pioneering era of the United States this development was not concurrent in all branches. The westward migration from the Atlantic seaboard produced unprecedented demands on available modes of transportation, and the general pattern of early regional development reflected the great dependence placed on waterways in meeting this need. Cities grew and flourished first along the watercourses of the nation. Later,

---

[1] "Elements of Civil Engineering," by John Millington, J. Dobson, Philadelphia, Pa., and Smith and Palmer, Richmond, Va., 1839, p. 19.
[2] *Ibid.*, p. 21.
[3] *Ibid.*, p. 14.

the utilization of water to drive the wheels of industry gave rise to new communities at sites that were favorable for the development of water power. There was little appreciation, however, of the sanitation problems that were thereby created.

Transportation.—Because of the need for transportation in an inland empire, the main interest of the civil engineering profession has long been centered on the design and building of these facilities: First, through the construction of canals to supplement natural waterways; later, by the construction of a network of continental railroads; more recently, by a vast system of modern highways; and, most recently, by an ever-growing system of airports and flight lanes. The reduction of effective distance by the use of modern transportation assures the rapid distribution of food, goods, and people. Man is now protected from the threats of famine resulting from inadequate transport; he is provided with a variety of economic goods otherwise unattainable; and he is able to find in a short space of time the lands and hands necessary to solve the problems of locally inadequate resources and markets. The excellence of early transportation facilities made the development of large metropolitan areas both feasible and economically desirable. The excellence of modern transportation facilities makes possible a new kind of urbanization that may avoid the congestion and slum development that have too often marred the metropolitan centers of the past.

Power.—Concurrent developments in the field of mechanical power production and distribution not only increased man's capacity to produce economic goods, but also permitted him to utilize available concentrations of power and thus to create new industrial cities. The conversion of mechanical power into electrical energy has made man more independent of locally available sources of power. This factor, too, points toward a new kind of industrial development that may offer freedom from the evils of crowding.

Sanitation.—The sanitation problems that accompanied this rapid growth of cities created a need for a new type of engineering service and stimulated an appreciation of the essential importance of water supply and sewerage utilities. The civil engineer undertook this responsibility with such knowledge of its public health signficance as was evident at the time. The problems in this new field were approached in a manner in keeping with the fundamental concepts of engineering analysis, and applicable information in the field of the basic sciences was used in workable solutions.

Meanwhile, coincidental with the many advances that were being made in the fundamental sciences, and by applying the laboratory tools made available by these advances, research in the field of medical science was discovering many of the factors responsible for disease. For the first time a scientific concept of the causes of preventable disease was evolved—with all the implications of the possibility of controlling, by engineering means, the spread of many of these diseases.

SANITARY ENGINEERING

Beginnings.—It might be stated that sanitary engineering, as a special field of civil engineering, had its beginnings in a developing appreciation on the part of early designing engineers of the importance of water supply and water-carried waste disposal in the control of enteric disease. To the physical tests of the properties of construction materials, already well known to the civil engineer, it became necessary to add chemical and biological yardsticks to measure the functional efficiency of his designs.

The record of the many investigations and researches undertaken to obtain the basic data needed in the design of water purification plants and in the disposal of sewage is an inspiring one. An idea of the progress achieved may be obtained, for example, from the report of Samuel M. Gray, M. ASCE, city engineer of Providence, R. I., dated November 14, 1884, and prepared following a trip to Europe to study sewerage practices. His somber observations on American practice should be noted. Among other things, he states that:

"In this country very little progress has been made toward abating the sewage nuisance. With scarcely an exception, the prevailing practice has been to allow the crude sewage to flow into the nearest river or large body of water. The deplorable results produced by this method of disposal are too well known to require comment."

However, changes were soon to follow. By 1890 there was issued the classic report on water supply and sewerage of the Lawrence Experiment Station of the Massachusetts State Board of Health. Here, for the first time in the annals of American sanitary engineering research, the results of coordinated chemical and biological investigations of the basic principles of sewage treatment and water purification are recorded. Certain fundamental data destined to profoundly influence future sanitary engineering designs were established by this report.

Because of the high turbidities of midwestern streams, the City of Louisville, Ky., in 1895, undertook what was then described by the president of the water company as:

"* * * the first practical step taken toward solving the vexing question of filtration and purification of water supplies for large cities upon modern scientific principles."

Out of these studies came the report of George W. Fuller, M. ASCE, that established a sound basis for the design of rapid-filter water treatment facilities. These are but a few of the landmarks that guided the engineers' early progress in the field of sanitary engineering.

Regulating Bodies.—Because water supply and sewerage were early recognized as major public health necessities, it was logical that laws should be enacted delegating authority to state health departments for the supervision of the health aspects of these services. To this end, state health officials were authorized to review and approve basic engineering reports, plans, and specifications for public water supply and sewerage construction; and continuously to verify the quality of service rendered through periodic inspections, operator instruction, and laboratory investigation.

This public need for protection and technical guidance greatly stimulated the development of sanitary engineering services within state health departments during the 20-year period from 1905 to 1925. It also started a significant trend in American public health practice and introduced an important variation in the traditional pattern. For the first time, the technical qualifications of the engineer

gave him professional recognition and staff responsibility as the person best able
to provide a public health service in matters relating to man's physical environment. This was a period of rapid expansion of water and sewerage services, and
engineers with some knowledge of sanitary engineering design were in great
demand. Since staff positions in state sanitary engineering organizations afforded
excellent training opportunities, consulting engineers recruited freely from this
source. The exchange of sanitary engineering personnel was undoubtedly an important factor in insuring the close integration of public health objectives in the
design of water supply and sewerage systems—an easily recognized characteristic
of engineering practice in this field and one that has insured a high level of public
protection through the years. Although originally organized to provide a service
in matters relating only to water supply and sewerage, state sanitary engineering
departments soon were being requested to give advice on other engineering aspects
of public health work.

The engineer's foundation of general education in the sciences gave him, when
employed by a public health agency, a comprehension of the many problems of
environmental health and provided him with the ability to formulate workable
programs for the control of those nonpersonal conditions that might adversely
affect the public health. The health officer concerned with the more strictly personal medical aspects of public health readily recognized the value of the services
that could be rendered by the technically trained engineer and relegated to his
supervision an ever-increasing variety of duties.

Some of these duties required the application, in a varying degree, of the engineer's knowledge of chemical and biological as well as of physical sciences, thus
definitely widening the functional field of sanitary engineering. Other duties were
largely administrative in character and required in their execution attributes of
analysis and judgment frequently possessed by engineers, following but not inherently resulting from their professional training.

Summary

The engineer has come to the present with ever-broadening concepts of sanitary engineering. It is a field as diversified as are the needs of the public for
the technical service of men, who, with varied educational backgrounds, have a
common interest in the betterment of public health through the modification and
control of the many significant environmental factors. The field has indeed
become both diversified and specialized. However, as Millington indicated so
many years ago, the public is served best through specialization, provided only
that those who specialize have first a knowledge of the whole of the field and,
through this knowledge, an appreciation of their coordinate part.

In the preparation of this report, the committee has avoided any attempt to
define the boundaries of the field of sanitary engineering as presently envisioned.
Likewise, it has not attempted to outline completely the many problems that confront engineers in this field. These have been recorded with considerable detail
in previous committee reports, notably those made in 1942, 1946, and in 1949.
The committee has, however, recognized the importance of maintaining in some
way a basic coordination of the broad aims and objectives of sanitary engineer-

ing and to this end has recommended the organization of a now authorized Joint Committee under the sponsorship of ASCE to develop procedures for a unified approach to the many problems that confront not only those who work in the field of sanitary engineering, but, more important, the public, who look to this group for assistance and service.

Rich as is the heritage of the sanitary engineer who during the past century has made life more secure in these United States, his greatest opportunity and challenge lie before him as he extends his skill and knowledge to the peoples of the world. No service performed by any branch of engineering is in greater demand or has more direct application to the improvement of international good will than that which is within the realm of the sanitary engineer.

If sanitary engineers can achieve the opportunities that lie before them, if they can maintain the high ideals of service to humanity that motivated those who so many years ago planned a future that is now the present, then the engineering profession may have hope that, 100 years from now, posterity may find in what has been accomplished like reason to say "well done."

Respectfully submitted,

H. G. BAITY	L. M. FISHER
T. R. CAMP	W. A. HARDENBERGH
F. J. CLEARY	F. H. WARING
G. M. FAIR	A. H. WIETERS

EARNEST BOYCE, *Chairman*

Committee on the Advancement of Sanitary Engineering

AMERICAN SOCIETY OF CIVIL ENGINEERS

Founded November 5, 1852

TRANSACTIONS

Paper No. 2619

ORIGIN AND FUNCTIONS OF SOIL MECHANICS

By K. Terzaghi,[1] Hon. M. ASCE

Synopsis

Before applied mechanics came into existence, all major problems in civil engineering, such as the design of arches or domes, were solved intuitively or by trial and error, and the problems of foundation and earthwork engineering were no exception. Hence, every attempt to build a structure of unprecedented size or type involved serious hazards. This condition did not change until applied mechanics made it possible to predict the performance of structures of any kind solely on the basis of a knowledge of the mechanical properties of the materials involved. The branch of applied mechanics which serves this function in connection with earthwork engineering is now known as soil mechanics.

This paper gives an account of the influence of soil mechanics on some of the branches of earthwork and foundation engineering such as the design of retaining walls, building foundations, and earth dams. It concludes with a review of the present trends in soil mechanics research. These trends are chiefly determined by the practical difficulties involved in obtaining the basic data for theoretical solutions.

Introduction

In order to apply the laws of mechanics and hydraulics to the solution of a design problem of any kind, the mechanical properties of the materials involved must be known, at least in a general way. The designer of structures commonly deals with only two materials, steel and concrete, and the properties of these materials are known in advance because the materials are manufactured in accordance with standard specifications. By contrast, the designer in the field of earthwork engineering has to deal with an infinite variety of materials representing the results of natural processes which are beyond control, and in many instances structures have to be built on heterogeneous accumulations of such materials with erratic patterns of stratification.

Another radical difference lies in the mechanical properties of the materials themselves. In the early days of structural design it was taken for granted that the mechanical properties of both steel and concrete could adequately be de-

---

[1] Prof., Civ. Eng., Div. of Eng. Sciences, Harvard Univ., Cambridge, Mass.

scribed by two numerical values, the modulus of elasticity and the ultimate strength. In other words, the structures were designed as if the construction materials were perfectly elastic. The deviations from purely elastic behavior, such as elastic aftereffects and creep, and fatigue phenomena, were scarcely known; and, in connection with routine problems, they still do not receive any consideration because the resulting errors are commonly well within the customary margin of safety. By contrast, the differences between the mechanical properties of soil of any kind and those of ideal elastic or plastic materials are so important that they require consideration under almost any circumstances. This difference is illustrated by Fig. 1.

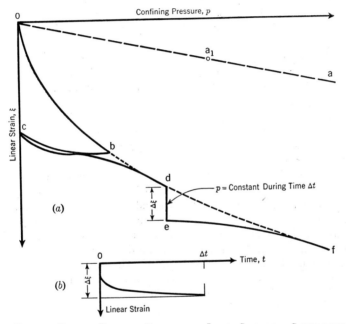

FIG. 1.—RELATION BETWEEN CONFINING PRESSURE AND LINEAR STRAIN FOR COHESIONLESS SAND

Fig. 1(a) represents the relation between unit pressure p per unit of area and corresponding linear strain ξ for a cube of steel (dashed line) and a cube of dry sand (solid lines) acted on by the same pressure in all three principal directions. For steel, within the range of stress to be considered in design, the relation between p and ξ is represented almost exactly by a straight line, Oa. If the pressure corresponding to state a_1 is reduced to zero and then again increased, point a_1 moves on Oa to zero and returns on the same line. For the cube made out of sand the curve Of is obtained. Every cycle of loading is represented by a hysteresis loop bcd. If the increase of the pressure is temporarily discontinued (state de) during a time Δt, the strain increases by $\Delta \xi$ at a decreasing rate as shown in Fig. 1(b).

For saturated, cohesive soils with a low permeability the relations between stress, strain, and time are still more complex than those for dry sand. Nevertheless, the strain effects of a confining pressure such as those represented by Fig. 1 are the simplest ones which have to be considered in connection with design problems involving soils. On account of the intricacy of the mechanical properties of soils, the successful application of the laws of mechanics to the problems of earthwork and foundation engineering lagged behind the scientific development of the other branches of structural engineering by more than a century. Another reason for the lag resides in the amount of time and labor required for determining the numerical values which appear in the equations of soil mechanics.

All the empirical data which are needed for the routine design of a steel bridge could be obtained by one experimenter in 1 hour, and the experimental procedures have been known for more than a century. By contrast the mere reconnaissance of the significant mechanical properties of soils required many years of strenuous experimentation. The reconnaissance was not even started until about 1915. It called for the development of new experimental techniques such as the consolidation test and the different varieties of shear and permeability tests. The account of the results of the reconnaissance filled a whole book (1).[2]

As the knowledge of the physical properties of soils increased, it became evident that the results of laboratory tests on subsoil samples could be very misleading unless the samples were practically undisturbed. The resulting demand for undisturbed samples had to be met by a radical modification of the methods of extracting samples from drill holes (2). On the other hand, the construction of artificial fills to be made out of natural soils, with very different characteristics and origins, created the demand for systems of soil classification which would permit the reliable identification of the principal types of soils on the basis of the results of a few rapid laboratory tests (3).

The amount of time and labor consumed by these developments was enormous and much still remains to be done. The successive steps are known to the readers of the ASCE *Transactions,* and a digest of the results can be found in various textbooks covering the field of soil mechanics. They constitute the prerequisite for the practical application of soil mechanics to design problems.

In every branch of civil engineering the practical application of theoretical principles calls for radical simplifications. The nature and importance of the resulting errors can be learned only by observation and measurement on full-sized structures. Knowledge of the order of magnitude of the inevitable errors forms the basis for the selection of the factor of safety to be used in connection with design.

In the realm of applied soil mechanics the differences between theory and reality are far more complex and important than in other branches of applied mechanics for two reasons: (*a*) The equations describing the mechanical properties of soils are less accurate than the corresponding equations for concrete or steel, although they are more complicated; and (*b*) all the computations in connection with earthwork design are evitably based on the assumption that the sub-

---

[2] Numerals in parentheses, thus: (1), refer to corresponding items in the Bibliography at the end of the paper.

soil consists of a few homogeneous strata whereas in reality its structural pattern may be very complex. Under extreme conditions the initial concept concerning the structural pattern of the subsoil represents no more than a crude working hypothesis, to be modified as the real nature of the subsoil is gradually disclosed by observation during construction.

In steel bridge design all the observational data which are required for detecting the differences between forecast and reality can be obtained with strain gages. By contrast, in the field of applied soil mechanics the task of securing adequate observational data requires a great variety of observations, such as the measurement of deflections with reference to base lines, settlement observations on points at and below the surface, the measurement of pore-water pressures, deflection observations in drill holes, and many others. The demand for observational data made it necessary to develop a great variety of entirely new techniques.

The preceding review has shown that the difficulties involved in the solution of design problems in earthwork and foundation engineering are infinitely greater than those encountered by designers of steel and concrete structures and that the limits which nature has set to the degree of accuracy of the forecasts are very much narrower. Nevertheless, within a few decades, soil mechanics has radically changed the mental attitude of the majority of engineers toward problems involving soils. It has disclosed the real causes of many of the failures which have occurred in the past. It has furnished conclusive information concerning the limits of validity of the different empirical rules which have been used, and it has replaced many of them by more reliable procedures.

In addition, soil mechanics has provided the engineer with the basic information required for avoiding the risk that essential features of the subsoil conditions may remain undetected on account of inadequate subsoil exploration, and under its influence both the quantity and the quality of available observational data have vastly increased. In the following sections these facts will be illustrated by a summary of the developments in some of the fields of earthwork and foundation engineering.

Origin of Soil Mechanics

An engineering problem cannot be satisfactorily solved unless the computation is based on a sound knowledge of the mechanical properties of the materials involved, and problems in earthwork engineering are no exceptions. Theories of earth pressure and bearing capacity have existed for more than a century, but their influence on engineering practice was almost nil. The reason is obvious—they were based on the assumption that the earth is either an ideally plastic or a perfectly elastic material and as a consequence they could account only for very few of the phenomena encountered in actual construction. Furthermore, practically all the difficulties encountered in earthwork and foundation engineering are due to the mechanical interaction between the solid soil particles and the water contained in or percolating through the voids of the soils. None of the theories which originated before the end of the nineteenth century made any provision for this interaction.

Several investigators with broad vision, such as A. Collin (4)(5), started to adapt the theories to the results of field observations and laboratory tests, but they did not succeed in establishing schools of thought and procedure, and their attempts were not followed up. However, some three decades ago, when the systematic investigation of the physical properties of soils became the concern of a large group of professional engineers and theories were modified in accordance with the findings, the contradictions between theory and reality disappeared, and theoretical methods for the solution of earthwork problems began to receive the attention which they deserve.

EARTH PRESSURE ON LATERAL SUPPORTS

Fundamental Principles.—Theoretical principles for the computation of the earth pressure on lateral supports were clearly formulated by C. A. Coulomb almost two centuries ago, and since then such theories have been a favorite topic for scientists and theoretically minded engineers alike. Therefore, the history of these theories is an exceptionally instructive example of the radical changes produced by the impact of soil mechanics on earthwork engineering.

Coulomb's theory is based on the simplifying assumptions that earth is incompressible, that its deformations prior to failure are negligible, and that it fails by shear along plane surfaces of sliding. It was also assumed that the shearing resistance of the earth per unit of area of the surface of sliding is equal to

$$s = c + p \tan \phi \dots \dots \dots (1)$$

in which c is the cohesion; p, the unit pressure on the surface of sliding; and ϕ, the angle of internal friction. For a cohesionless material such as dry, clean sand $c = 0$ and

$$s = p \tan \phi \dots \dots \dots (2)$$

Coulomb's theory was published in 1776 (6) in the *Memoires* of the French Academy of Sciences, at once attracted great attention, and has never ceased to preoccupy the minds of theoretically inclined engineers. Within the following century almost every theoretical aspect of the earth-pressure problem was investigated by analytical or by graphical methods on the basis of Eq. 1 or 2, and the bulk of earth-pressure literature steadily increased. However, the benefits derived by practicing engineers from these developments were almost nil as testified by the following passage in the classical paper (7a) on "The Actual Lateral Pressure of Earthwork," by Sir Benjamin Baker, Hon. M. ASCE, published in 1881:

"A knowledge, however imperfect, of The Actual Lateral Pressure of Earthwork, as distinguished from what may be termed the 'text-book' pressures which, with hardly an exception known to the Author, are based upon calculations that disregard the most vital elements existent in fact, is of the utmost importance to the engineer and contractor. * * * The vast divergence between fact and theory has perhaps impressed itself with peculiar force upon the Author, * * * because he has had the advantage of the experience gained in constructing about 9 miles of retaining walls, and * * * the still more valuable experience of 34 miles of deep-timbered trenches for retaining walls, sewers, covered ways and other structures. * * *"

The status of earth-pressure theories in engineering practice did not materially change, and the discrepancies between theory and reality did not decrease until a few decades ago, when the mechanical properties of soils became subject to systematic investigation. At that stage it soon became evident why Baker and his contemporaries failed to derive any tangible benefits from the extensive literature concerning the theoretical aspects of lateral earth pressure. Their failure was due to the fact that the computations were based on the assumption that the value ϕ in Eqs. 1 and 2 for any kind of soil is equal to the angle of repose of the soil.

In the English-speaking world the most influential proponent of the angle-of-repose concept was W. J. M. Rankine (8). The origin of the concept is not reliably known. Since Coulomb derived an equation for the critical height of vertical slopes on cohesive earth his name cannot be associated with it. Collin realized as early as 1846 (4)(5) that the maximum inclination of a slope on cohesive soil decreases with increasing height of the slope. In 1883 George Howard Darwin (9) demonstrated by small-scale earth-pressure tests that the angle of internal friction of a sand can be very much greater than the angle of repose of the same sand.

Nevertheless, none of these discoveries received more than casual attention and Rankine's authority continued to prevail. A possible explanation for it was given by a discusser of a paper by A. W. Skempton in 1946 (5a). This discusser, J. Wilton, pointed out "* * * that the long survival of Rankine's methods may have been due to their suitability as material for examination questions."

The fate of the Collin and the Darwin publications illustrates the fact, to be observed in all branches of pure and applied science, that a newly discovered phenomenon or relationship does not receive the attention it deserves unless and until it can be fitted into a coherent system which is useful and convincing enough to be accepted by the majority of those who are interested in the subject.

Soil mechanics represents such a system. As a consequence as soon as it became established it started to act as a catalyst. Discoveries and rediscoveries followed each other in rapid succession. As a matter of fact it was not realized until afterward how many of the vital phenomena and relationships had already been recognized, decades or even centuries earlier, but these discoveries failed to make any impression on contemporary engineers and, as a consequence, were forgotten.

As a result of soil mechanics research the fictitious angle-of-repose concept was replaced by the results of systematic experimental investigations concerning the relation between normal pressure and shearing resistance for soils. Starting about 1920 the investigations led first to the conclusion that p in Eqs. 1 and 2 must be replaced by $p-p_u$, in which p is the total unit pressure on the surface of sliding and p_u is the pore-water pressure (1). Therefore Eq. 1 was replaced by

$$s = c + (p-p_u)\tan\phi \dots\dots\dots\dots\dots\dots\dots(3)$$

Next it was found that the value p_u in Eq. 3 for saturated soils depends not only on the loading conditions but also on the rate at which the shearing stress is increased. This important discovery led to the distinction between "slow" and "quick" shear values (10). Finally it was realized that the cohesion c of saturated clays is a function of the water content w of the soil. This fact is expressed by the equation:

$$s = f(w) + (p - p_u) \tan \phi_t \dots \dots \dots \dots \dots (4)$$

in which ϕ_t is the true angle of internal friction (11).

On the basis of these findings the angle-of-repose concept has been discarded, and the limits of validity of Coulomb's Eq. 1 are now known to every competent soils engineer. Since the relationship between cohesion and water content, symbolized by $f(w)$ in Eq. 4, can be very complex, earth-pressure and stability computations are based on the results of shear or triaxial tests performed under conditions of loading and drainage equivalent to those which are anticipated under field conditions. The results of such tests can usually be represented without serious error by an equation with the form of Eq. 2. However, for any given soil, the values of c and ϕ in the empirical equation can have very different values, depending on the test conditions. Hence, in contrast to c and ϕ in the classical Coulomb equation, the values c and ϕ in the equation representing the results of tests on cohesive soils are parameters without well-defined physical meaning.

Design of Retaining Walls.—As long as angle ϕ in Eq. 1 was believed equal to the angle of repose of the backfill material, inexperienced retaining-wall designers proceeded under the illusion that the results of their computations were reliable whereas experienced engineers like Baker found that they could not be trusted and made decisions on the basis of their knowledge of precedents. There was no intermediate course. However, as soon as the fallacy involved in the angle-of-repose concept was generally recognized and the complexity of the relationship between c and p, Eq. 1, became known, the attitude of the engineering profession toward the problem of designing retaining walls underwent a radical change. It became obvious that the shearing resistance of a cohesive backfill cannot even be estimated in advance of construction unless a thorough borrow-pit survey has been carried out. Also the project must provide for placing and compacting the backfill in accordance with rigid specifications. On routine jobs none of these conditions is satisfied. Hence for the routine design of retaining walls simple semi-empirical rules have been developed which are based partly on Coulomb's theory and partly on what are now known to be lower limiting values for c and ϕ in Eq. 1 for the principal types of backfill materials. However, if a project calls for the design of an expensive retaining wall with a great height, soil mechanics provides the engineer with all the information required for preparing a safe and economical design, regardless of how unusual the design conditions may be. Since type and importance of the uncertainties in the evaluation of the basic data are known, they can be compensated by an adequate factor of safety and an appropriate selection of the backfill material.

EARTH PRESSURE ON TIMBERING IN CUTS

Coulomb's theory has also been used for computing the lateral earth pressure on the timbering in open cuts. According to this theory the earth pressure on the timbering in a cut in homogeneous ground increases like a hydrostatic pressure in simple proportion to depth as shown in Fig. 2(a). As early as 1908 (12), J. C. Meem, M. ASCE, an engineer with broad experience in subway construction, called attention to the fact that this theoretical conclusion was incompatible with his experiences and observations. However, the cause of the discrepancies remained unexplained and many municipal building authorities continued to insist on designing the lateral support in cuts in accordance with the classical earth-pressure theories, until the relations between stress and strain in soils were investigated.

On the basis of the findings it was realized that the application of Coulomb's theory to the computation of the distribution of the pressure on the timbering in cuts involves an unwarranted generalization. While an open cut is being excavated and the timbering installed, the lateral yield of the earth on both sides of the cut increases with increasing depth below the original ground surface.

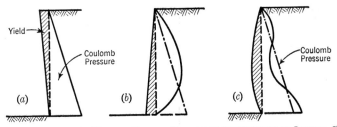

Fig. 2.—Effect of Type of Yield of Lateral Support on Distribution of Lateral Pressure

This type of yield is associated with a roughly parabolic pressure distribution, Fig. 2(b) (13).

This conclusion is in accordance with Meem's observations and it has subsequently been corroborated by the results of the measurement of the strut loads in many open cuts such as those illustrated by Fig. 3, a diagrammatic vertical section through an open cut in drained sand. The bracing system consists of soldier beams and timber struts. Before the excavation is made, every vertical section through the sand, such as ab, is acted upon by the earth pressure at rest, represented by the triangle abc. According to Coulomb's theory the excavation of the cut reduces the lateral pressure on ab to the values indicated by the width of the triangle abd. If the excavation operations caused the vertical section ab to move into the position a'b, this conclusion would be justified. However, in reality the installation of the first row of struts prevents an inward movement of the upper edge of the section as shown on the right-hand side of Fig. 3.

As excavation proceeds, the unbalanced load on horizontal sections through the bottom of the excavation increases and the loaded sand yields toward the cut. Thus an originally vertical section a_1b_1 moves into the position $a_1b'_1$. According to Fig. 2(b), this type of yield is associated with a roughly parabolic distribution of the lateral pressure on a_1b_1. The conclusion was confirmed by the results of the measurements of the strut loads performed by the Siemens Bau Union on seventeen sets of struts in the cut shown in Fig. 3 (14). The total horizontal pressure on the lateral support of the sides of the cut was approximately equal to the Coulomb pressure, but the distribution of the pressure was like that shown by the plain lines $a_1 d_1 b_1$ and $a_1 d_2 b_1$. The deviations of the measured strut pressures from the statistical average were due to variations in the force with which the wedges were driven and in other minor details of the construction operations. Since these deviations are inevitable, they must be considered in the design of bracing systems.

Anchored Bulkheads.—Along the waterfront the problem of providing artificial fills with a vertical lateral support is commonly solved by the construction of an anchored bulkhead. Although this method was already practiced in pre-Roman times, the empirical stage of bulkhead design prevailed until the end of the nine-

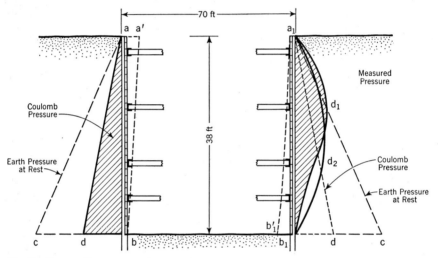

Fig. 3.—Coulomb Distribution and Measured Distribution of Lateral Pressure on Bracing in Open Cut in Moist Sand

teenth century. The first attempts to evaluate the forces which act on a bulkhead were based on Coulomb's theory, and they led to the following concept: If the sheet piles are not driven any deeper than necessary to provide adequate lateral support for the buried part of the sheet piles, they act like loaded beams with free end support. On the other hand, if they are driven to a considerably greater depth the piles perform like loaded beams with one fixed and one free support. The negative bending moment which develops at the fixed (lower) end reduces very considerably the maximum bending moment in the sheet piles (15).

The methods of bulkhead design based on this concept contain two assumptions which were inadequately substantiated: The first assumption is that the distribution of the active earth pressure on the inner face of the bulkhead is in accordance with classical earth-pressure theories. The second assumption is that the conditions of end support are independent of the degree of flexibility of the sheet piles.

The first assumption, involving the distribution of the earth pressure on the inner face, was contested on purely empirical grounds almost as soon as it appeared for the first time in print. During the following decades both experimental and theoretical evidence was produced to the effect that the distribution of the active earth pressure on a lateral support which deflects like a freely supported elastic beam has the characteristics illustrated by Fig. 2(c). However, the results of large-scale model tests performed in 1949 by Gregory P. Tschebotarioff, M. ASCE (16), under the auspices of the United States Bureau of Yards and Docks, showed that this pressure distribution develops only in the event that the open space on the outboard side of the bulkhead has been produced by dredging (dredge bulkhead). If the bulkhead has been backfilled (fill bulkhead), the error involved in assuming Coulomb's pressure distribution (Fig. 2(a)) is inconsequential. Subsequently in 1952 P. W. Rowe (17) demonstrated experimentally that the inevitable yield of the anchorage of a dredge bulkhead changes the pressure distribution shown in Fig. 2(c) into a distribution similar to the Coulomb distribution, Fig. 2(a). Thus, the first assumption was found to be fundamentally correct.

The second, equally important, assumption involves the influence of the flexibility of the sheet piles on the conditions of end support. This assumption remained unchallenged until serious objections were raised against it in 1934 by Paul Baumann, M. ASCE (18). However, conclusive information concerning the degree of validity of this vital assumption was not produced until 1952, when Rowe published the results of systematic experimental investigations concerning the influence of the flexural rigidity of the sheet piles on the maximum bending moment. According to his investigations, an increase of the degree of flexibility of the sheet piles at a given depth of sheet-pile penetration is associated with a gradual transition from free to fixed end support whereby the maximum bending moment in the piles may decrease by as much as 70%.

On the basis of these investigations the most serious discrepancies between bulkhead theory and reality have been eliminated. The uncertainties which remain are not due to inadequate knowledge of the fundamental principles involved but merely to the fact that the pattern of stratification of natural soil deposits, and sometimes even that of artificial fills, may be very complex, whereas the theories of bulkhead design inevitably presuppose that the bulkheads are in contact with homogeneous masses of soil. Therefore the center of gravity of the bulkhead problem has shifted from the domain of applied mechanics to that of subsoil exploration and field observation.

Ore Docks.—Ore docks are storage yards for the raw materials used in the metallurgical industry. The ore occupies a rectangular area with a width of several hundred feet and the ore piles may have a height up to 75 ft. The ore is commonly delivered in barges which are moored to anchored bulkheads or quay walls. In some docks, the ore pile is confined by ore retaining walls located parallel to the waterfront, as shown in Fig. 4. The transport of the ore from the barges to the ore pile and from the pile to the manufacturing plant requires an ore bridge. Its legs travel on rails resting on sills or else on the crest of the ore retaining walls, C and D in Fig. 4. The distance between these rails is equal to the width of the ore storage. An excessive lateral displacement of the ore retaining walls or the quay wall results in an equally important increase of the distance between the ore bridge rails, which may seriously interfere with the operation of the ore bridge.

Until recently the attention of designers of ore docks was concentrated exclusively on satisfying the conditions for the stability of the lateral supports such as quay wall A and the ore retaining walls C and D in Fig. 4. The effects of the ore load on the soil beneath the level of the base of the walls received no consideration. If the ore piles rested on sand or gravel, this attitude was justified because the weight of an ore pile of any height does not exceed a small fraction of the ultimate bearing capacity of sand or gravel—due to the fact that the bearing capacity of cohesionless soils increases in simple proportion to the width of the loaded area. However, if the subsoil contains a thick clay stratum, as shown in Fig. 4, even the weight of an ore pile with a moderate height may exceed the ultimate bearing capacity. Since this possibility has often escaped the attention of designers, many ore piles above clay strata have broken into the

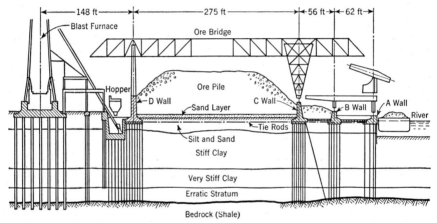

Fig. 4.—Diagrammatic Section Through an Ore Yard with Ore Retaining Walls

ground and the failures were associated with an outward movement of the quay wall or bulkhead, A in Fig. 4, over distances of tens of feet.

Since soil mechanics has developed reliable procedures for estimating the ultimate bearing capacity of subsoils containing thick clay strata on the basis of the results of unconfined compression tests on undisturbed samples of the clay, the most serious hazards involved in such design can now be avoided. Soil mechanics has also developed techniques for ascertaining the gradual increase of the strength of the loaded clay strata as a result of progressive consolidation under ore load, by pressure-gage observations.

If a metallurgical process requires the accumulation of ore supplies with a weight of more than about one half of the ultimate bearing capacity of the underlying clay strata, the load produces considerable horizontal movements in the clay associated with a lateral displacement of the supports of the legs of the ore bridge and of the quay wall. The relation between load and displacement is shown in Fig. 5 for the ore dock represented by Fig. 4. The estimated initial ultimate bearing capacity of the subsoil was 5 tons per sq ft. Fig. 5(a) represents the relation between time and average unit load on the ore yard. In Fig. 5(b) the horizontal displacement of the quay wall, A in Fig. 4, has been plotted against unit load. Although the factor of safety with respect to a failure of the subsoil of the ore pile never dropped below 1.5, the increase of the horizontal distance between the ore-retaining walls was important enough to stretch the tie rods interconnecting the walls far beyond the yield point of the steel; and at a constant load the quay wall moved out slowly (19).

The relation between the ore load and the corresponding horizontal deformation of a clay stratum beneath the loaded area cannot reliably be predicted on the basis of the results of laboratory tests. However, the lateral displacement of the ore bridge rails should not be important enough to interfere with the performance of the ore-handling equipment. Hence in the design stage the ratio between the allowable ore load and the failure load can only be guessed, and the estimated value is subject to subsequent correction on the basis of the results of

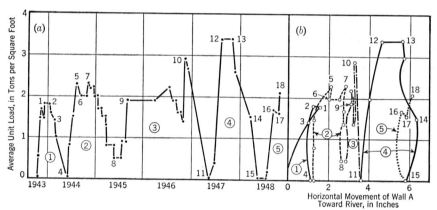

Fig. 5.—Behavior of Ore Dock, Fig. 4: (a) Seasonal Variations of Unit Load; and (b) Relation Between Unit Load on Ore Yard and Corresponding Horizontal Movement of Quay Wall A

deflection observations. The range of error involved in such estimates can be reduced, in the course of time, only by the accumulation and digest of displacement data obtained from observations and measurements on ore docks.

Earth Dams

Empirical Stage of Earth-Dam Design and Construction.—The construction of earth dams for the purpose of creating storage reservoirs has been practiced for at least two thousand years. It appears that until about 1500 A.D. the height of such dams was less than 70 ft. In 1500 A.D. the Mudduk Masur Dam with a height of 108 ft was built in the Province of Madras in India. For several hundred years this height was not exceeded. In the eighteenth century an attempt was made in Spain to construct an earth dam with the unprecedented height of 150 ft. However, the dam failed when the reservoir was filled for the first time, in 1802, and the failure discouraged experimentation along similar lines for almost half a century.

During the development of irrigation in the arid regions of the North American continent, which started about 1850, many earth dams with a height up to 125 ft were built, but the percentage of total and partial failures was alarmingly high. This fact can be learned from the contemporary records published in *Engineering News* and in *Engineering Record*. The failures were due to the absence of adequate rules for design and construction. Some engineers maintained that the upstream slope should be flatter than the downstream slope whereas others held the opposite view. According to one school of thought, the construction material should be placed in a completely saturated state. According to another one, the material should be moist but firm and in some instances, in the arid West, earth dams were made out of dust-dry desert soils. These examples show that the methods for the design and construction of earth dams were no sounder at the end of the nineteenth century than they were two thousand years earlier.

Improvements in the Methods of Construction.—The most important single item in the construction of an earth dam is the method of placing and compacting the fill material. In the early days of fill construction the earth was transported in baskets, and the compaction was produced unintentionally by the trampling of the feet of the basket bearers. In countries such as India and China, where labor is cheap, this method is still used. However, in industrialized countries basket transportation was superseded by more expedient procedures whereupon independent methods of soil compaction had to be developed.

In the eighteenth century compaction was accomplished in England chiefly by driving herds of sheep or cattle over the individual layers, whereas on the European continent smooth, heavy rollers were used. The European practice was introduced into California, about 1860, probably by émigré engineers. It led to the invention of the sheepsfoot roller in 1905 and various other mechanical improvements followed.

In spite of these developments it appears that the artificial compaction of earth dams was considered merely desirable but not essential. Until the beginning of the nineteenth century some major earth dams such as the Meurad Dam in Algeria, built in 1855 (20), were even placed in a single lift, by dumping from a trestle. Others, like some of the more recent earth dams in Colorado, were made out of uncompacted 4-ft layers (21). Artificial compaction did not become compulsory in connection with the construction of high earth dams until soil mechanics research conclusively demonstrated the beneficial effects of compaction combined with moisture content control on the shearing resistance of fill materials.

The most important step in this direction was made in 1933 by R. R. Proctor, M. ASCE, who showed that the degree of compaction produced by a given compacting effort depends to a large extent on the water content of the fill material subject to compaction. This relationship is illustrated by Fig. 6(a). The abscissas of the plain curve in Fig. 6(a) represent the water content of a fill material; and the ordinates, the corresponding dry density of the material after compaction. All the samples represented by points were compacted in the same manner. The procedure was so chosen that the resulting compaction is approximately equal to that produced by adequate compaction equipment in the field.

The water content at which the dry density of the compacted soil is a maximum is now known as the optimum moisture content. If the fill material is placed with a water content above the optimum, both its dry density and shearing resistance are lowered. If the water content is reduced to values below the optimum, the dry density decreases and the shearing resistance increases. However, subsequent saturation may reduce the shearing resistance to values which are far below the corresponding value at optimum water content. Since the time when Proctor published his findings, practically all the major earth dams in the United States have been built with rigorous moisture content control, combined with intense compaction. With increasing intensity of compaction the optimum moisture content decreases and the corresponding dry density increases as shown in Fig. 6(b) (22). In Fig. 6(b) the numerals, such as 10-50-40,

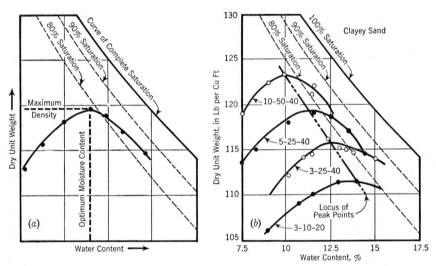

FIG. 6.—RELATION BETWEEN MOISTURE CONTENT AND DRY UNIT WEIGHT OF COMPACTED SOILS

attached to the curves have the following meaning: Ten layers, fifty 40-lb tamps per layer, in the miniature compaction test devised by S. D. Wilson, A. M. ASCE.

Discovery of the influence of the initial water content on the dry density of a compacted soil made it possible to construct earth fills having the maximum strength compatible with the nature of the available construction materials and to determine the significant physical properties of the fill in advance of construction. However, in order to design a dam, the information concerning the strength of the materials must be supplemented by a stability computation, involving an estimate of the factor of safety with respect to sliding.

Stability Computations.—The first attempt to investigate the conditions for the stability of an earth slope was probably made by Coulomb in 1773. He also derived an equation for the critical height of a vertical slope on the assumption that the shearing resistance of the soil is determined by Eq. 1. However, Coulomb and his immediate successors such as Français in 1820 (23) believed that the surface of sliding is at least approximately plane. Even Français, who for the first time derived an equation for the critical height of an inclined slope, was not yet aware of the serious error involved in this assumption. The fact that the failure of cohesive soils beneath inclined slopes occurs along curved surfaces of sliding was realized for the first time by Collin in 1846. This discovery represented the result of a painstaking investigation of about fifteen slope failures in open cuts and on earth dams (Fig. 7). Collin also determined the shearing resistance of cohesive soils with a primitive box shear apparatus, and he realized that the shearing resistance of clay in situ is practically independent of the normal pressure on the surface of sliding, p in Eq. 1. He also found that the strength of clay may gradually decrease on account of water absorption (5). However, the time for the recognition of the importance of the Collin findings had not yet come and, in contrast to Coulomb's classical paper on earth pressure, the Collin publication had no effect on the trend of contemporary research.

The fact that the failure of cohesive soils beneath inclined slopes takes place along curved surfaces did not receive the attention which it deserves until it

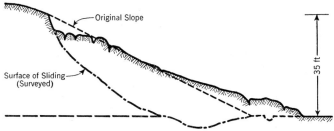

Fig. 7.—Failure of Downstream Slope of Cercey Earth Dam in France (After A. Collin, 1846), September, 1835

was rediscovered by K. E. Pettersson in 1916. He also found out that the real curve of sliding can be replaced, for the purpose of a stability analysis and without serious error, by an arc of a circle. This procedure was further developed by W. Fellenius in 1926 (24). It is now known as the Swedish method of slope analysis and forms the basis for modern methods of stability computations.

At the time when the Swedish method was invented, stability computations were based on Coulomb's Eq. 1, and the influence of the pore-water pressures on the shear strength was not yet suspected. Therefore the application of the Swedish circle method to the stability analysis of earth dams involved errors of unknown importance until the influence of the pore-water pressure p_u on the shearing resistance of soils was clearly perceived. This influence is determined by Eq. 3.

The pore-water pressure p_u at a given point in a given embankment, at the end of the period of construction, depends on the type of fill material, the initial water content, the intensity of compaction, and the rate at which the filling operations proceeded. This theoretical conclusion was subsequently confirmed by numerous field observations which were performed by the United States Bureau of Reclamation (25). Fig. 8 represents the results of the measurement of the hydrostatic pressures in the pore water in the Green Mountain Dam (Colorado) immediately after construction. The dam is 250 ft high and was built during the years 1940 to 1942. Construction periods were limited to about 6 months per year. The water content of the fill material was at or slightly above the optimum. Therefore part of the water contained in the fill had to drain out of it during and after construction, involving a process of progressive consolidation.

Immediately after a layer of cohesive soil has been placed and compacted at a given point, the pore pressure in the fill material is equal to zero; or it may even be slightly negative. As the height of the fill above that point is increased, part of the weight of the accumulated fill material, p per unit of area is carried by

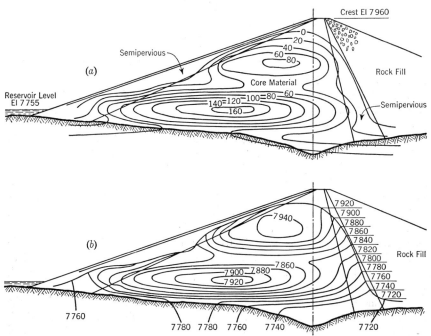

Fig. 8.—Distribution of Pressure in Pore Water of Green Mountain Dam in Colorado Immediately After Construction: (*a*) Curves of Equal Hydrostatic Head with Reference to Lower End of Piezometer Tubes, in Feet of Water; and (*b*) Curves of Equal Piezometric Elevation

the solid soil constituents and the balance by a hydrostatic pressure in the pore water, p_u in Eq. 3. Fig. 8(*a*) shows the curves of equal pore-water pressure, expressed in terms of feet of water. The pressure was measured at the time when construction was completed but the reservoir was still empty. During the middle of each construction season the water content of the borrow-pit material increased on account of irrigation of a hayfield above the borrow pit. In those parts of the dam placed during the irrigation season, hydrostatic heads developed with values up to 160 ft equivalent to values of p_u in Eq. 3 up to 10,000 lb per sq ft. As time goes on, the excess water will drain out of the dam and the pore-water pressure p_u will decrease.

Curves of equal piezometric elevation (Fig. 8(*b*)) were plotted on the basis of the data in Fig. 8(*a*). The flow takes place from the centers of high hydrostatic pressure in radial directions at right angles to the curves of equal piezometric elevation (Fig. 8(b)) toward the boundaries of the "impermeable" part of the dam. At the time when the pore-water pressures were measured, the fill was already partly consolidated.

Methods are being developed by the Bureau of Reclamation for estimating the pore-water pressures p_u in advance of construction on the basis of the results of laboratory tests. If the initial water content of the fill material is considerably lower than the optimum (Fig. 6(a)), the initial pore-water pressures are zero; but subsequent saturation of the embankment material during the first filling of the reservoir may increase the pore pressures to values higher than those that would develop if the fill material had been placed with a water content at or slightly above the optimum. Therefore, rigorous water-content control is one of the most important prerequisites for the successful construction of the impervious parts of high earth dams.

Present Status of Design and Construction.—The writer would be the last to claim that all the problems of earth-dam design have been solved. Present knowledge of the shearing resistance of cohesive soils is still incomplete, and techniques of earth-dam construction leave a wide margin for differences in opinion. Nevertheless it is scarcely an exaggeration to state that the progress made during the last three decades is ten times as important as that accomplished during the preceding 2,000 years. During these three decades the influence of pore-water pressure on the shearing resistance of cohesive soils was recognized; rational methods for evaluating the factor of safety of slopes with respect to sliding were developed; and the processes which led to the failure of dams due to piping were successfully investigated. As a consequence, it became possible to build without any risk earth dams with a height of more than 300 ft and to eliminate the hazards associated with the seepage through pervious strata beneath the base of earth dams without complete cutoff.

In connection with the design of earth dams having a moderate height, the designer faces the same situation as he does for an ordinary retaining wall. A reliable stability analysis can be made only if the embankment material has been adequately investigated and if the dam is to be built in accordance with rigid specifications concerning both water control and compaction.

Thorough compaction is generally considered compulsory for earth dams of any height, because the cost of compaction is very small compared to the resulting benefits. However, the enforcement of rigorous water-content control on small projects in remote districts may be impracticable. If economic or other considerations preclude rigorous water-content control, the designer is compelled to rely on semi-empirical rules. Such rules can be established only on the basis of the performance records of earth dams which were made of soils with a water content far above or far below the optimum and by correlating the findings with the index properties of the construction materials. Investigations along this line have been started (21).

FOOTING AND RAFT FOUNDATIONS

If the subsoil of a structure is firm enough, the load is transferred onto the soil by spread footings or a raft which covers the entire area occupied by the structure. Until the eighteenth century the design of footings was based only on guesswork. The quality of the subsoil was judged by its appearance on the bottom of shallow test pits. If it seemed satisfactory, the walls were made to rest on sills with a width equal to two or three times the thickness of the wall and the columns were established on the blocks of masonry. Hence if the soil strata at greater depth were weaker or more compressible than the top stratum exposed in the test pits, severe and detrimental differential settlements ensued. The consequences of the settlement of cathedrals such as Santa Sophia in Constantinople (sixth century), Ely and Winchester (eleventh century), Strasbourg (thirteenth century), and Saint Paul's in London (seventeenth century) are well-known examples.

The minimum requirement for reducing the danger of damage due to unequal settlement consists of adapting the pressure per unit of area of the base of the footing to the character of the supporting soil. The official recognition of this necessity led to the concept of the "allowable bearing values."

This concept probably originated about 1870 in Chicago, Ill. Since it appealed to common sense, it received world-wide attention within a short time; and it forms the basis for the tables of "allowable bearing values" which can still be found in the municipal building codes of almost every city. It served a useful purpose, but it diverted the attention of the designers from the fact that the settlement of a foundation depends on many factors other than the properties of the soil stratum on which the footing rests. Foremost among them is the size of the base of the footing and the soil profile.

Experience and intensified observation soon disclosed the shortcomings of footing design on the basis of allowable bearing values. Tests performed in 1888 on bearing blocks with different sizes showed that the settlement increases with increasing size of the loaded area, at equal unit pressure. William Sooy Smith, M. ASCE, in Chicago, realized before 1892 that the settlement of a footing on clay may increase in the course of time because of progressive consolidation of the loaded part of the clay.

In 1891 Francis Collingwood, M. ASCE, called attention to the hazards involved in the construction of footings on firm strata located above soft and compressible ones (26). Furthermore, as early as 1885 J. Boussinesq published a theory which made it possible to estimate the stresses in the soil beneath a loaded continuous footing. The theory also showed that the settlement due to a given unit load must increase with the size of the loaded area. However, the overwhelming majority of designers continued to adhere to the method of footing design on the basis of allowable bearing values and unsatisfactory results were accepted as "acts of God."

The reason for the conservative attitude of designers is obvious. The mere knowledge of the facts published by the earlier observers and of the Boussinesq theory did not enable them to draw any useful conclusions, because the estimate of settlement requires much more than the knowledge of general relationships—it calls for adequate subsoil exploration and experimental determination of the significant properties of the subsoil.

At the end of the nineteenth century the mechanical properties of soils were still unknown. Experimental methods for investigating soil properties such as compressibility did not yet exist and engineers did not even know about the serious effects of sample disturbance on the physical properties of soils. Therefore the traditional methods of footing design could not be changed until soil mechanics disclosed the fundamental relationships between load, subsoil conditions, and settlement, and developed the techniques for adequate subsoil exploration.

If a structure is very heavy or the bearing capacity of the subsoil is low, the weight of the structure is transferred onto the ground by a concrete mat or raft which covers the entire area occupied by the building. Until recent times many designers believed that a raft foundation would be satisfactory if the increase of the unit load on the soil due to the weight of the building did not exceed the "allowable soil pressure" specified in the building code of their district, because they were not aware of the influence of the size of the loaded area on the magnitude of settlement and of the fact that the settlement of a uniformly loaded area is nonuniform.

The consequences of this assumption are illustrated by the defects of the structure shown in Fig. 9. According to the local building code the allowable soil pressure for the fill beneath the base of the raft was 0.6 ton per sq ft. The structure was established on a 4-ft concrete mat, and the difference between the pressure due to the weight of the building and the weight of the soil removed during the excavation of the subbasement did not exceed 0.6 ton per sq ft. Nevertheless, the damage to the structure resulting from unequal settlement associated with distortion was very severe, and the differential settlement continued to increase.

In connection with the design of raft foundations, it is interesting to note the fluctuations in the attitude of designers toward the effect of the depth of subbasements on the settlement of structures supported by rafts, due to lack of well-defined mechanical concepts concerning the factors which determine the magnitude of settlement.

In the nineteenth century G. Hagen (27) pointed out that a raft-supported structure could safely be founded without piles on a subgrade of any kind, provided its total weight did not exceed the weight of the material which had been removed from the site by excavation. In other words, he realized that the settlement of a structure depended only on the increase of the unit load on the soil at the level of the base of the foundation and not on the unit load produced by the weight of the structure. Nevertheless, writers of textbooks on foundation engineering published during the first decades of the twentieth century consistently ignored this fundamental relationship. As a consequence the engineering profession lost sight of one of the most important means at its disposal for reducing or eliminating the settlement of structures located above highly compressible strata with great thickness.

This fact is illustrated by the following incident which occurred in 1926. A building with a subbasement had to be provided with a raft foundation because the floor of the subbasement was considerably below the water table. Although the weight of the soil and water displaced by the subbasement was almost exactly equal to the total weight of the building, the writer had great difficulties in persuading his clients, a well-known firm of consulting engineers, to refrain from supporting the raft on piles. Nowadays every engineer with adequate training in soil mechanics takes advantage of the benefits which can be derived from providing his structures with subbasements.

PILE FOUNDATIONS

The history of pile foundations goes back to the Stone Age. Wherever a structure had to be built offshore or on ground which was conspicuously too soft to sustain its weight, a pile foundation was established. Venice, Italy, founded on

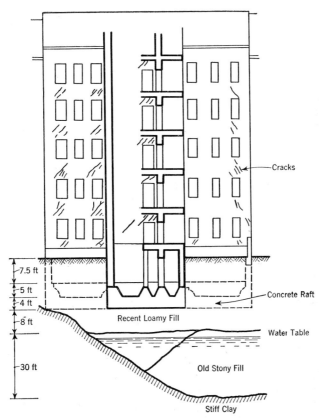

FIG. 9.—SHEAR CRACKS IN AN APARTMENT HOUSE, CAUSED BY UNEQUAL SETTLEMENT OF RAFT FOUNDATION

mud flats at the mouth of the Po River in the sixth or seventh century, is a well-known example of a pile-supported city of great age.

Until the beginning of the nineteenth century the rules for the design of pile foundations were as primitive as those for the design of footing foundations. In most instances, many more piles were driven than the weight of the structure called for. However, if the piles were too short or if they were driven into a firm stratum located above a soft and compressible one, excessive settlement took place.

At the beginning of the nineteenth century when structural engineering came under the influence of mechanics, an attempt was made to compute the ultimate bearing capacity of foundation piles on the basis of the relationship between the work performed by the falling hammer, the depth of penetration of the pile, and the resistance of the soil against pile penetration. The results of such computations are known as "pile formulas." Like Coulomb's theory of earth pressure, the theory which led to the first pile formula aroused widespread interest. Therefore the publication of the first pile formula, about 1820, was followed by that of many others, which were more refined. Research activities along these lines are still in progress, and the most popular formulas constitute a supplement to the table of "allowable bearing values" in many municipal building codes.

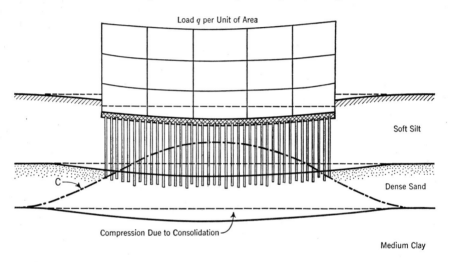

FIG. 10.—SETTLEMENT OF PILE FOUNDATION DUE TO CONSOLIDATION OF CLAY STRATUM BENEATH LEVEL OF POINTS OF PILES

It cannot be denied that pile formulas served a useful purpose, but they diverted the attention of designers from the fact that adequate bearing capacity of the individual piles does not preclude the possibility of excessive and detrimental settlement. Foremost among the causes of such settlement is the gradual consolidation of layers of clay beneath the level of the points of the piles, as illustrated in Fig. 10. The weight of the structure, q per unit of area, is transferred by point-bearing piles onto a stratum of dense sand which rests on a layer of clay. The load carried by the piles increases the initial vertical pressure on the clay stratum by the amounts represented by the ordinates of curve C. As a consequence a bowl-shaped settlement ensues.

The phenomenon illustrated by Fig. 10 was familiar to observant engineers such as Sooy Smith in Chicago before the end of the nineteenth century. Soil mechanics has supplemented such knowledge by developing procedures for determining in advance of construction the magnitude and distribution of the settlement due to the consolidation of the clay strata.

The soundness of the new procedures was demonstrated in 1929 by the satisfactory agreement between observed and computed settlement of a group of factory buildings on 70-ft piles with points driven into a sand stratum resting on a 30-ft clay stratum (28). Since that time rules for subsoil exploration at the site of pile foundations have been developed and a description of the methods for estimating the settlement due to the consolidation of clay strata can be found in several textbooks.

Nevertheless, many monumental structures, built after the publication of the first complete case record in 1929, were seriously damaged by the phenomenon described in the record and illustrated by Fig. 10. Some of the best known cases were the Palais de Justice in Cairo, Egypt (about 1935), Charity Hospital in New Orleans, La. (1938), and the Office Building of the Compania Paulista di Seguro, São Paulo, Brazil (1945).

The fate of these structures demonstrates that the importance of educational efforts can hardly be overemphasized. The observations of H. H. Howe, Sooy Smith, and other inquisitive engineers at the end of the nineteenth century were published but they had no influence on contemporary methods of designing pile foundations. Very few engineers read the publications and the contemporary writers of textbooks ignored them because the innovations did not fit into the existing systems. The situation did not materially change until about three decades ago, when soil mechanics revealed the physical significance of the existing observational data and furnished the key for their rational interpretation. Since soil mechanics is now taught at every reputable school of engineering, the younger generation is much better prepared to reap the benefits of growing experience than was the preceding one.

Protection of Dam Foundations Against Piping

Definitions.—In connection with water-retaining structures the term "piping" refers to the rapid removal of soil by a stream of water escaping from the reservoir through a tunnel-shaped channel. If the storage is retained by a concrete dam or a weir with a concrete foundation, the process starts with the formation of a spring at the downstream edge of the foundation and the subsurface erosion proceeds along the base of the foundation in an upstream direction. As soon as the intake end of the new channel arrives at the upstream edge of the base, the stored-up water rushes out of the reservoir. Within a few minutes the soil beneath the foundation is washed out to a depth of many feet, the structure breaks into the cavity, and the process terminates with complete destruction. Many failures due to piping have occurred without any warning, years after the reservoir was filled. Fig. 11 illustrates the consequences of such a failure. The concrete arch connecting the two sides of the valley is the remnant of the core wall of an earth dam. The core wall rested on a row of sheet piles. The failure occurred suddenly, many years after the reservoir was filled for the first time, and the resulting flood caused severe damage.

Bligh's Rule.—Until the beginning of the twentieth century the mechanics of piping were not clearly understood, in spite of the fact that piping failures were fairly common. The type of destruction left no doubt that the failures were caused by subsurface erosion. Common sense indicated that the danger of scour beneath the base of the dam could be reduced by driving sheet piles along the upstream and downstream edge of the base of the structure because the sheet piles form an obstacle to the flow of water. However, no rules were available for determining the depth to which the sheet piles should be driven.

Impetus to the establishment of such rules was given by the correct appraisal of the precarious condition of the Narora Weir on the Ganges River in India, prior to its failure, by Colonel Clibborn and Beresford (29). The forecast was based on the results of model tests. The failure occurred shortly afterward, in

FIG. 11.—REMNANTS OF AN EARTH DAM WITH CONCRETE CORE WALL AFTER FAILURE RESULTING FROM PIPING

1898, as a result of hydrostatic uplift on the apron. However, a definite rule for evaluating the degree of safety of dam foundations with respect to piping was not developed until 1910, independently and almost simultaneously by W. P. Bligh, W. M. Griffith, and W. Tefft. It is now known as Bligh's rule, and is based on two assumptions: (a) The vertical section through the surface of contact between substructure and subsoil is a flow line called the "line of creep"; and (b) the structure fails by piping as soon as the average hydraulic gradient along the line of creep exceeds a certain critical value of i_c which is independent of the shape of the line of creep. On the basis of these two assumptions the value of i_c was computed for a large number of dams which failed by piping, and it was found that i_c increases very conspicuously with increasing grain size.

Discrepancies Between Theory and Reality.—Bligh's rule provided the designer with a valuable tool; but, like the concept of allowable bearing values in the realm of footing design, it suffered from the defect that it considered only one of several equally important factors on which the degree of safety with respect to piping depends. The true complexity of piping phenomena did not become evident until a theory was established which permitted the computation of the critical head for dams resting on perfectly homogeneous and cohesionless sand (30).

In contrast to Bligh's assumption (b), both theory and experiment showed that the critical hydraulic gradient i_c for a homogeneous subsoil is independent of the grain size of the subsoil. They also showed that i_c for cohesionless and homogeneous sand depended to a large extent on the shape of the "line of creep" and that it could be many times greater than the critical gradients derived by Bligh from failure records. Furthermore, failure by piping through homogeneous sand takes place as soon as the hydraulic gradient assumes the critical value for the first time, whereas in practice many piping failures have occurred years after the reservoir has been first filled and at hydraulic heads which were even smaller than some of the preceding ones.

The only essential difference between laboratory and field conditions lies in the degree of homogeneity of the subsoil of the structure. The model dams rested on homogeneous sand whereas most of the full-scale dams are above regularly or erratically stratified sediments. Thus, it became evident that the value of i_c depends, not only on the average grain size of the subsoil or on any other average quantity, as Bligh assumed, but also on the details of the geological structure of the subsoil and on the shape of the line of creep. In 1935, E. W. Lane, M. ASCE (29), improved Bligh's rule by the "weighted creep" concept which takes the influence of the shape of the line of creep on the value of i_c into account. However, no definite relationship can possibly be established between the value of i_c for a sediment with a given average grain size and the geological structure of the sediment because it is impracticable to ascertain the essential details of the pattern by borings or other methods.

On account of the decisive influence of geological details on the value of i_c for dams on sediments the values of i_c assigned by Bligh and Lane to the different types of sediments, such as fine sand, represent only the smallest average hydraulic gradient at which piping in such sediments has occurred up to this time. If a sediment of the same category were perfectly homogeneous, its critical hydraulic gradient would be many times greater than i_c; but, under exceptionally unfavorable conditions, failure may occur in spite of foundation design on the basis of the i_c-value.

Design of Protective Measures.—According to theory and the results of model tests, the critical hydraulic gradients for dams on homogeneous soil are very high. Piping failures at very much lower hydraulic gradients, such as the Bligh and the Lane values of i_c, can be accounted for only by local flow concentrations along the boundaries between bodies of sediments with different permeabilities. The soil which is removed by the water veins leaves the ground at the exit of the veins. If the exit is covered with an inverted filter which retains the soil particles without interfering with the flow of the water, the critical hydraulic gradient assumes the value of i_c for homogeneous subsoils which can reliably be computed. Hence the problem of eliminating the danger of piping can be solved by locating the areas where the seepage water will come out of the ground and by covering these areas with an inverted filter.

Like many other facts in the field of applied soil mechanics the usefulness of inverted filters was anticipated many decades before the processes which lead to piping were clearly understood. However, the filters did not become a standard feature of the design of dams on sediments, and the prerequisites for the satisfactory performance of filters were not investigated until the mechanism of the piping failures was revealed by correlating field observations with theoretical reasoning and laboratory experiments.

PRESENT-DAY TRENDS

Determining Factors.—The significant physical properties of the principal types of soil are now fairly well known. The experimental procedures for soil investigations are satisfactory, and the majority of the theoretical problems concerning the performance of soils under stress have been solved. Therefore, it is scarcely an exaggeration to state that the engineer would already be in a position to solve most of the problems encountered in foundation and earthwork engineering provided he had to deal only with homogeneous bodies of soil or with layered systems composed of a small number of homegeneous strata. However, in practice this condition is seldom satisfied. Natural soil deposits and even artificial fills built of materials taken from borrow pits are likely to have a more or less erratic pattern of stratification.

To determine the significant properties of a natural sedimentary deposit with an erratic profile a great number of borings and soil tests is required. As a consequence, many foundations are still designed without adequate information about the subsoil conditions. The resulting design may be either wasteful or unsafe, depending on circumstances which the designer failed to determine in advance. This situation can only be remedied by educational efforts and by reducing the amount of time and money required for subsoil exploration.

One of the most important steps in this direction is the development of in situ tests, such as the static and dynamic penetration tests, and the vane test which aim to determine at least some of the significant soil properties by simple tests performed at the bottom of the drill hole. However, even under ideal conditions, if many borings, in situ tests, and laboratory investigations were made, the results of the subsoil exploration would still leave a wide margin for interpretation. In such instances, supplementary information must be secured from geological sources. The realization of this necessity has added a new link to the bonds between engineering and geology.

The first connection was established by William Smith (1780–1839), a canal engineer in Somerset, England, who made the first geological map, dated 1815, and who gave the impetus to the regional geological surveys which are still in progress. Since the middle of the nineteenth century, very few large tunnels have been built without the cooperation of a geologist. Beginning with the end of the nineteenth century the importance of geological information in connection with dam projects has also received increasing recognition. However, the intimate cooperation between engineer and geologist in all the other domains of civil engineering is a rather recent development and so far the results are very encouraging.

If geological conditions preclude the possibility of obtaining, prior to construction, all the information which is required for safe and economical design, observational procedures have to be used. The demand for suitable techniques had to be met by the invention of the required measuring instruments, such as pore pressure gages, strain gages, and deflectometers.

Application of Engineering Geology to Soil Mechanics Problems.—The significant mechanical properties of sedimentary deposits with an intricate structure, such as many fluvio-glacial deposits, can be ascertained only on the basis of field observations since they depend primarily on the pattern of stratification. To utilize the observational data in connection with the design of a structure at a new site, it is necessary to know the pattern of the sediments at the site. This pattern is not disclosed by the boring records unless it is very simple. However, experience has shown that there is a definite relationship between the pattern of stratification of a sediment and the process by which the sediment was formed. Hence, if the geologic origin of a sediment—for instance, deposition in a drowned valley or by meltwater on an outwash plain—is known, the general pattern of stratification of the sediment is also known.

On account of this relationship, the determination of the geological history of sediments has become an integral part of subsoil exploration. Since it is in many instances a prerequisite for the reliable interpretation of boring records, no engineer engaged in the practical application of soil mechanics can nowadays be considered competent unless he has at least a general knowledge of geology. On the other hand, the services which the geologist can render to the engineer are very limited unless the geologist is familiar with the fundamental principles of soil mechanics and their practical implications.

The accumulation of data concerning the relationship between the geological origin of sediments and the corresponding patterns of stratification is a laborious process. Few engineers have an opportunity to become personally familiar with the characteristics of more than one or two of the principal types. If they face a problem involving sediments in another category, they depend on second-hand information. Therefore, progress depends on the exchange of experiences across the borders of the different geological provinces by personal contact and printed word. This is now accomplished by the International Society on Soil Mechanics and Foundation Engineering which is scheduled to meet every 4 or 5 years. Within the borders of the United States, exchange of geological information of engineering importance will be organized by the Joint Committee on Engineering Geology.

Observational Procedures.—As a result of intensified field observations, it is now known that there are many cases in which an accurate forecast of the effects of construction operations is impracticable. If, for instance, a proposed dam is to be built on sediments with an erratic pattern, it cannot be known before construction where the water veins will emerge on the downstream side of the base of the dam. Also, if a slope above a nonhomogeneous sedimentary deposit is to be stabilized by drainage tunnels, it is usually impracticable to locate, in advance, the points where drainage will be most effective.

Under such conditions the designer is compelled to proceed on the basis of some working hypothesis compatible with what is known about the local subsoil conditions and to modify the design as the differences between assumption and reality are disclosed by observations during construction. The development of observational techniques is still in progress.

CONTRIBUTIONS OF SOIL MECHANICS TO OTHER SCIENCES

As the knowledge of the physical properties of soils increased, many facts and relationships were discovered which had escaped the attention of research workers in pure and applied science. For example, in the 1920's, when the writer began to investigate experimentally the relationship between pressure, time, and volume changes of saturated clay soils, he noticed that the observed facts were incompatible with the concepts of colloid chemists concerning the mechanics of swelling of gels. To clarify this issue he supplemented his investigations by swelling tests with pure gelatine and found that the observed swelling pressures were very much smaller than those computed on the basis of the theoretical relationship between swelling pressure and vapor pressure (31)(32).

In 1929 the writer was requested to contribute a section on the "Mechanics of Sediments and Gels" to the fourth volume of the edition of the German handbook on "Applied Physical and Technical Mechanics" ("Handbuch der Pysikalischen und Technischen Mechanik") edited by F. Auerback and W. Hort. The preceding editions did not contain such a section because at the time of their publication no adequate information concerning this subject was available. The numerical data furnished by soil mechanics research on the physical properties of soils gradually filled some of the gaps in the tables of physical constants. Among the latest contributions are data concerning the relationship between the porosity and the water and air content of frozen and unfrozen sediments and their thermal conductivity which were furnished by the permafrost studies of the United States Army Engineers (33).

A chance observation made about 1930 by L. Casagrande, M. ASCE, in connection with a laboratory test on clay led to the investigation of the electro-osmotic processes in soils and the subsequent practical applications of the results to the consolidation of soft sediments in the field (34). The physical causes of some of the observed phenomena are not yet satisfactorily explained.

Soon after the investigation of clay soils was started, it became evident that the physical properties of different clays containing equal percentages of particles of colloidal size can be extremely different. This observation led to intimate co-operation between soil mechanics, clay mineralogy, and colloid chemistry experts. Whereas the fields of clay mineralogy and colloid chemistry are concerned with the crystal structure of clay minerals and the molecular interaction between the minerals and interstitial liquids, soil mechanics furnishes a steadily increasing amount of information about the influence of the crystal structure of the minerals and of the adsorbed substances on the mechanical properties of the aggregates. Thus the two branches of soil science supplement each other.

Quite recently the demand for the improvement of the mechanical properties of soils by chemical admixtures led to the investigation of the interaction between solid soil particles and highly polymerized organic substances such as calcium acrylate (35). This research promises to make significant contributions toward better knowledge of the molecular mechanics of adhesion.

Physical geology, too, is continuously benefited by soil mechanics. Development of methods of undisturbed sample borings has opened up a new source of information concerning the pattern of the stratification of sedimentary deposits. The identification tests provide the geologist with an expedient method for distinguishing between different fine-grained sediments with similar grain-size characteristics. It was shown that the maximum overburden pressure caused by the weight of an ice sheet or of superimposed sediments which a clay stratum has carried in the course of its history can be estimated on the basis of the results of a consolidation test (36).

A rational explanation was found for the steep dip of the strata of fine-grained sediments which have been deposited along steep submerged rock slopes (37). Knowledge of the geological aspects of loess deposits has been supplemented by a large amount of information concerning the physical properties of loess (38). The causes of landslides have been explained on the basis of the laws of mechanics and hydraulics (19), and a rational basis for the study of permafrost phenomena has been established (39).

By these and similar contributions soil mechanics repaid part of the debt owed to the other sciences for the basic principles which they have furnished and on which the structure of soil mechanics rests.

Conclusions

1. The theories of earth pressure and bearing capacity which were established in the eighteenth and nineteenth centuries were based on the assumption that "earth" can be considered as either an ideally plastic or a perfectly elastic material. Since there are very few real soils with properties similar to the postulated ones, experienced engineers such as Baker rejected the theories summarily. As a consequence, the influence of the theories on engineering practice was almost nil. This condition did not change until the properties of real soils were as thoroughly investigated as those of manufactured construction materials.

2. At the end of the nineteenth and the beginning of the twentieth century, design in earthwork and foundation engineering was done almost exclusively on the basis of the angle-of-repose concept, tables of allowable bearing values, and pile formulas. Observant engineers in both the United States and abroad frequently emphasized the inconsistencies involved in these concepts and reported phenomena, such as the gradual consolidation of clay deposits under load or the difference between the settlement of piles and pile groups at equal load per pile, which were incompatible with prevalent concepts. Nevertheless, the publication of their observations had no influence on design practice as testified by the contemporary failure records and by the contents of textbooks which were published at the beginning of the twentieth century. Observational data were practically ignored until soil mechanics established a coherent system of which they form an integral part. As a result of the international recognition of the practical value of the system, instruction in soil mechanics is now compulsory in almost every reputable school of engineering.

3. On account of the variety of materials involved, the complexity of the mechanical properties of soils, and the heterogeneity of natural soil deposits, soil mechanics research and practice are much more difficult than the corresponding activities in structural engineering. In spite of this handicap, soil mechanics has established a splendid record in less than three decades, as testified by the review of five main subdivisions of applied soil mechanics contained in this paper.

4. The ASCE anticipated the need for the step from textbook theories to soil mechanics at an early stage. As a consequence it established in 1913 a committee to revise the data and concepts on which the design of foundations was based. In 1936 Harvard University organized the First International Conference on Soil Mechanics and Foundation Engineering at Cambridge, Mass., which was a spectacular success. When the members of this conference conferred upon soil mechanics the rank of an independent branch of applied science, the ASCE responded at once by the organization of the Soil Mechanics and Foundations Technical Division. During the following years this Division has never ceased to promote research activities in soil mechanics. It also kept the profession informed about the developments in this field by the organization of soil mechanics sessions, forming part of the regular ASCE conventions, and by the publication of the reports of committees engaged in the digest of the findings.

5. Soil mechanics research has disclosed many facts and relationships in physics, colloid chemistry, and physical geology which had escaped the attention of research workers engaged in these fields. Therefore the interchange of information between soil mechanics and related branches of pure science is in the interest of both.

BIBLIOGRAPHY

(1) "Erdbaumechanik," by K. Terzaghi, Franz Deuticke, Wien, 1925.
(2) "Subsurface Exploration and Sampling of Soil for Civil Engineering Purposes," by J. Hvorslev, Waterways Experiment Station, Vicksburg, Miss., November, 1948.
(3) "Classification and Identification of Soils," by A. Casagrande, *Transactions*, ASCE, Vol. 113, 1948, pp. 901–930.
(4) "Recherches Experimentales sur les Glissements Spontanés des Terres Argileux," by A. Collin, Carilian-Goeury et Dalmont, Paris, France, 1846.
(5) "Alexandre Collin (1808–1890), Pioneer in Soil Mechanics," by A. W. Skempton, *Transactions*, Newcomen Soc., Vol. XXV, 1946, pp. 91–104. (a) p. 104.
(6) "Essai sur une application des règles des maximis et minimis à quelque problèmes de statique relatifs à l'architecture," by C. A. Coulomb, *Memoires*, Académie Royale, Vol. VII, Paris, France, 1776.
(7) "The Actual Lateral Pressure of Earthwork," by Benjamin Baker, *Minutes of Proceedings*, Inst. C. E., Vol. LXV, 1881, pp. 140–186. (a) p. 142.
(8) "On the Stability of Loose Earth," by W. J. M. Rankine, *Philosophical Transactions*, Vol. 147, 1857, pp. 9–27.
(9) "On the Horizontal Thrust of a Mass of Sand," by George Howard Darwin, *Minutes of Proceedings*, Inst. C. E., Vol. LXXI, 1883, p. 350.

(10) Discussion by A. Casagrande of the paper by Leo Jürgenson on "**The Shearing Resistance of Soils**," entitled "**The Application of the Theory of Elasticity and Theory of Plasticity to Foundation Problems**," *Journal*, Boston Soc. of Civ. Engrs., Vol. 21, 1934, p. 276.

(11) "**Conditions for Failure of Remolded Cohesive Soils**," by J. Hvorslev, *Proceedings*, 1st International Conference on Soil Mechanics and Foundation Eng., Cambridge, Mass., Vol. III, 1936, pp. 91–92.

(12) "**The Bracing of Trenches and Tunnels with Practical Formulas for Earth Pressures**," by J. C Meem, *Transactions*, ASCE, Vol. 60, 1908, pp. 1–23.

(13) "**Distribution of the Earth Lateral Pressure on the Timbering of Open Cuts**," by K. Terzaghi, *Proceedings*, 1st International Conference on Soil Mechanics and Foundation Eng., Cambridge, Mass., Vol. I, 1936, pp. 211–215.

(14) "**General Wedge Theory of Earth Pressure**," by K. Terzaghi, *Transactions*, ASCE, Vol. 106, 1941, pp. 68–80.

(15) "**Design of Steel Sheet-Piling Bulkheads**," by R. P. Pennoyer, *Civil Engineering*, Vol. 3, 1933, pp. 615–619.

(16) "**Large-Scale Model Earth Pressure Tests on Flexible Bulkheads**," in the Symposium, "**Lateral Earth Pressures on Flexible Retaining Walls**," by Gregory P. Tschebotarioff, *Transactions*, ASCE, Vol. 114, 1949, pp. 415–454; discussion, pp. 507–538.

(17) "**Anchored Sheet-Pile Walls**," by P. W. Rowe, *Proceedings*, Inst. C. E., Vol. I, 1952, pp. 27–70.

(18) "**Analysis of Sheet-Pile Bulkheads**," by P. Baumann, *Transactions*, ASCE, Vol. 100, 1935, pp. 707–797.

(19) "**Mechanism of Landslides**," by K. Terzaghi, Geological Soc. of America, Eng. Geology (Berkey) Vol., 1950, pp. 83–123.

(20) "**Les Barrages en Terre**," by Ch. Mallet and J. Pacquant, Assn. pour la Diffusion de la Documentation Hydraulique, La Houille Blanche, Grenoble, France, 1950, p. 182.

(21) "**Influence of Soil Properties and Construction Methods on the Performance of Homgeneous Earth Dams**," thesis presented by J. L. Sherard to the Faculty of Arts and Sciences, Harvard Univ., Cambridge, Mass., in 1952, in partial fulfilment of the requirements for the degree of Doctor of Engineering Sciences.

(22) "**Effect of Compaction on Soil Properties**," by S. D. Wilson, *Proceedings*, M. I. T. Conference on Soil Stabilization, Cambridge, Mass., 1952.

(23) "**Recherches sur la Poussée des Terres, sur la Forme et les Dimension des Revêtements et sur les Talus des Excavations**," by Français, *Memoires de l' Officers du Génie*, No. 4, 1820, p. 157.

(24) "**Erdstatische Berechnungen**," by W. Fellenius, W. Ernst und Sohn, Berlin, 2d Ed., 1940.

(25) "**Ten Years of Pore Pressure Measurements**," by F. C. Walker and W. W. Daehn, *Proceedings*, 2d International Conference on Soil Mechanics and Foundation Eng., Rotterdam, Vol. III, 1948, pp. 245–250.

(26) "The Study of Earths—An American Tradition," by Francis M. Baron, *Civil Engineering*, Vol. 11, 1941, pp. 473–476; discussion by K. Terzaghi and A. E. Cummings, p. 614, and Hardy Cross, p. 733.

(27) "Handbuch der Wasserbaukunst," by G. Hagen, Ernst und Korn, Berlin, Vol. 2, 3d Ed., Pt. 1, 1870.

(28) "Settlement Analysis—the Backbone of Foundation Research," by K. Terzaghi, *Paper No. 337*, World Eng. Cong., Tokyo, 1929.

(29) "Security from Under-Seepage Masonry Dams on Earth Foundations," by E. W. Lane, *Transactions*, ASCE, Vol. 100, 1935, pp. 1235–1351.

(30) "Sicherung von Bauwerken gegen Grundbruch," by K. Terzaghi, *Wasserkraft*, München, 1922, p. 445.

(31) "The Mechanics of Adsorption and the Swelling of Gels," by K. Terzaghi, *Monograph*, 4th Natl. Colloid Symposium, New York, N. Y., 1926.

(32) "The Influence of Elasticity and Permeability on the Swelling of Two-Phase Systems," by K. Terzaghi, *Colloid Chemistry*, Chemical Catalogue Co., New York, N. Y., Vol. III, 1931.

(33) "Laboratory Research for the Thermal Properties of Soils," by M. S. Kersten, St. Paul Dist., Corps of Engrs., St. Paul, Minn., 1949.

(34) "Electro-Osmotic Stabilization of Soils," by L. Casagrande, *Journal*, Boston Soc. of Civ. Engrs., Vol. 39, 1952, pp. 51–83.

(35) "Stabilization of Soils with Calcium Acrylate," by T. W. Lambe, *ibid.*, Vol. 38, 1951, pp. 127–154.

(36) "The Structure of Clay and Its Importance in Foundation Engineering," by A. Casagrande, *ibid.*, Vol. 19, 1932, p. 168.

(37) "Compaction of Lime Mud As a Cause of Secondary Structure," by R. D. Terzaghi, *Journal of Sedimentary Petrography*, Vol. 10, 1940, pp. 78–90.

(38) "Der Löss," by A. Scheidig, Theodor Steinkopf, Dresden and Leipzig, 1934.

(39) "Permafrost," by K. Terzaghi, *Journal*, Boston Soc. of Civ. Engrs., Vol. 39, 1952, pp. 1–50.

(40) "The Sensitivity of Clays," by A. W. Skempton and R. D. Northey, *Geotechnique*, March, 1952.

AMERICAN SOCIETY OF CIVIL ENGINEERS

Founded November 5, 1852

TRANSACTIONS

Paper No. 2620

EARTH-DAM PRACTICE IN THE UNITED STATES

By T. A. Middlebrooks,[1] A. M. ASCE

Synopsis

This paper presents a brief history of earth and rock-fill dams, including a discussion of the types of failure to which such dams have been subject. General features of projects are covered including outlet conduits, spillways, riprap, and the earth embankment itself. Since, in many instances, adequacy of the appurtenant works determines the safety and economy of a project, these features are discussed. Best current practice in design and construction is described with detailed reference to slope stability, slope protection, cutoff and core walls, earthquakes, costs, maintenance, and grouting. Predictions of future advances are set forth, and helpful design criteria are outlined. An extensive Bibliography adds materially to the over-all value.

Earth dam design and construction constitute one of the oldest branches of civil engineering endeavor. This paper makes no attempt to explore the origin of this branch but instead is pointed toward the progress in this field in the United States since 1850.

The most rapid improvement in both design procedures and construction practices has been made since the introduction of soil mechanics. Rule-of-thumb methods have given way to procedures based on sound theoretical principles. It is now possible to design safe and economical dams and appurtenant structures on a wide variety of foundations with the embankments composed of almost any type of soil or rock or combination thereof, with full assurance that satisfactory performance will result. In Fig. 1 is shown the Youghiogheny Dam in Pennsylvania located above the City of Confluence in a highly developed valley. This dam is constructed of shales from spillway excavation in combination with overburden clay.

Design developments prior to the advent of soil mechanics, based on rule-of-thumb methods, were unsatisfactory since they attempted to apply cross-sectional dimensions of successful dams to the project being planned without adequate knowledge of the fundamental principles involved. Inadequacies that developed

---

[1] Engr., Corps of Engrs., Dept. of the Army, and Chf., Soil Mechanics, Geology & Geophysical Section, Washington, D. C.

in these early earth dams forced engineers to the conclusion that the design of embankments could not be based on a simple comparison of base-to-height ratio
similar to that employed for concrete gravity structures. Past experience confirms
the fact that an earth dam with its appurtenant structures must be "tailor-made"
to fit each individual location. Stereotyped plans invariably result in the construction of many inadequate as well as uneconomical projects.

The principal inadequacies that have developed in the performance of earth
dams during the past century often resulted in overtopping, detrimental seepage,
slides, and conduit failures. Although engineering knowledge during the past 25
years has developed sufficiently to provide safeguards against these inadequacies,

FIG. 1.—YOUGHIOGHENY DAM ON YOUGHIOGHENY RIVER IN SOUTHWESTERN PENNSYLVANIA; KEY PROJECT
IN FLOOD PROTECTION OF VALUABLE AREA

failures still occur. The major reasons engineers are still plagued with unsatisfactory performance of earth dams have been aptly summed up by Joel D. Justin,
M. ASCE (1)[2]:

> "Unfortunately there is a feeling among many people that the design and
> construction of earth dams are matters so simple that anyone can handle them.
> Men who employ experts to audit their books will sometimes entrust the
> design and construction of an earth dam, on the safety of which, perchance,
> their very lives and fortunes may depend, to anyone at all without inquiring
> into his competency."

The public must be brought to realize that an earth-dam project should not
be undertaken unless the design and construction are under the direction of engi-

---

[2] Numerals in parentheses, thus: (1), refer to corresponding items in the Bibliography at the
end of the paper.

neers experienced in this field. Small earth dams must not be eliminated from this stipulation, since the two failures that caused the greatest loss of life and property damage were of structures less than 50 ft high. Failure of the Mill River Dam in Massachusetts in 1874, which was only 43 ft high, is an outstanding example. Altogether, one hundred and forty-three lives were lost and property damage totaled more than $1,000,000 although the project cost only $34,000. No engineers were employed on its design and construction. William E. Worthen, Hon. M. ASCE (2), a member of the investigating committee, aptly concluded that "a man cannot make a dam by instinct or intuition."

A study has been made of inadequacies of earth dams in both design and construction, bringing up to date the studies made by Justin (1), the Pennsylvania Power Committee (3), and others. The list includes not only those dams usually classified as partial or complete failures, but also those which required remedial work that was not contemplated in the original construction.

The general term "failure," therefore, refers to the entire range from supplementary construction to total failure of the project. Table 1 lists dams giving unsatisfactory performance since 1914, Table 2 summarizes the results, and Tables 3 and 4 give various other phases of the study. Each category will now be examined to determine the causes for such occurrence and the progress made in design to eliminate these hazards.

Overtopping

There are two major reasons why the spillways of early dams were inadequate. First, data on rainfall and stream runoff were very meager. It was necessary that the engineer rely largely on limited observations of great floods in a few basins, without the benefit of analytical procedures that permit reliable adaptation of such information to projects in other basins. Second, engineers failed to recognize the risk involved in the possibility of an unprecedented flood.

Deficiencies in data still constitute a problem to be considered; however, they can hardly be an excuse for inadequate design today in the continental United States, since extensive hydrometeorological investigations have been made to determine the maximum rainfall and stream flow to be expected. Studies by the Corps of Engineers, United States Department of the Army, in cooperation with the United States Weather Bureau and the United States Geological Survey, have added greatly to the store of information available..

Experience has shown that underdesigned spillways present so great a hazard that engineers should design for nothing less than the maximum possible flood. Usually the potential loss of life and damage to property that would result from overtopping are so great that a "calculated risk" approach cannot be tolerated. For example, failure of the South Fork Dam (Johnstown, Pa., Flood) in 1889 resulted in the loss of two thousand two hundred and eighty lives and property damage of more than $3,000,000, although the dam cost only $167,000.

Gail A. Hathaway, Past-President ASCE, has pioneered the increase in knowledge and the development of better methods of computing spillway design floods. He has insisted on eliminating the "calculated risk" premises of design. If the methods for computing the maximum possible flood and the required freeboard

TABLE 1.—UNSATISFACTORY PERFORMANCE OF EARTH DAMS

Dam and location	DATE Built	DATE Failed	Reference [a]	Height	Type	Reason for unsatisfactory performance
Alexandrer, Hawaii	1932	1930	ENR, Vol. 104	140	Hydraulic	Core pressure slide before completion of dam
Anaconda, Mont.	1898±	1938	ENR, Vol. 121	72	Earth and concrete core	Seepage slide
Ansonia, Conn.	....	1894	{ER, Vol. 30 / EN, Vol. 47}	..	Earth, rolled	Piping along outlet
Apishapa, Colo.	1920	1923	ENR, Vol. 91	115	Earth, rolled	Piping through settlement cracks
Ashti, India	....	1883	ASCE Proc., Vol. 49	58	Earth, rolled	Seepage through foundation
Avalon (old dam), N. Mex.	1893	{1893 / 1904}	EN, Vol. 54	58	Earth and rock	Overtopped 1893, piping into rock 1904
Avoca, Pa.	....	1892	EN, Vol. 47	..	....	Overtopped
Baker City, Ore.	....	1896	EN, Vol. 47	..	....	Erosion from spillway
Balsam, N. H.	1927	1929	ENR, Vol. 54	60	Earth and concrete core	Seepage slide
Barton, Idaho	1910	1922	Sherard	40	Earth, rolled	Drawdown slide
Bear Gulch, Calif.	1896	1914	Sherard	63	Earth, rolled	Foundation leakage, repaired
Beaver Park, Colo.	1914	1914	ASCE Trans., Vol. 65	87	Rock	Drawdown slide, concrete slope paving failure
Belle Fourche, S. Dak.	1911	1933	ENR, Vol. 111	122	Earth, rolled	Piping along outlet
Blairtown, Wyo.	....	1888	EN, Vol. 47	..	Earth, rolled	Overtopped
Blue Water, N. Mex.	....	1909	EN, Vol. 62	35	Rock	Overtopped
Bolton, Conn.	1908	1938	....	..	Earth, rolled	Break in dam
Bonney Reservoir, Colo.	....	1903	EN, Vol. 47	34	Earth, rolled	Piping along outlet
Bradford, England	1901	1896	ASCE Proc., Vol. 49	90	Earth, rolled	Overtopped
Breakneck, Pa.	....	1902	EN, Vol. 47	..	Earth, rolled	Overtopped
Bridgeport, Conn.	1855	1905	ER, Vol. 52	..	Earth, rolled	Foundation seepage
Brooklyn, N. Y.	1893	1893	EN, Vol. 47	..	Earth, rolled	Conduit break
Brush Hollow, Colo.	1925	{1923 / 1928}	Sherard	..	Earth, rolled	Drawdown slide
Calaveras, Calif.	....	1918	ENR, Vol. 80	240	Hydraulic	Excessive core pressure
Castlewood, Colo.	1890	1933	ASCE Trans., Vol. 65	70	Rock	Spillway over dam failed
Cobden, Ont., Canada	....	1894	EN, Vol. 48	35	Earth, rolled	....
Cold Springs, Colo.	....	1912	ER, Vol. 66	50	Earth, rolled	Embankment seepage
Cold Springs, Ore.	....	1931	Corps of Engrs.	98	Earth, rolled	Riprap displaced by waves
Conshohocken Hill, Pa.	....	1873	{ASCE Proc., Vol. 49 / ENR, Vol. 18}	..	Earth, rolled	Piping
Costilia, N. Mex.	1920	{1924 / 1941}	ER, Vol. 75	125	Earth, rolled	{Embankment seepage / Sloughs}
Crane Creek, Idaho	1910	1928	Sherard	63	Earth and puddle core	Piping into tunnel outlet
Crane Valley, Calif.	....	....	Corps of Engrs.	..	Hydraulic	Riprap displaced by waves
Credit River, Ont., Canada	....	1910	EN, Vol. 63	50	Earth and concrete core	Overtopping
Dale Dyke, England	....	1864	Wegmann	95	Earth and puddle core	Probable piping along outlet
Dallas, Tex.	....	1891	EN, Vol. 47	29	Earth, rolled	Settlement
Dalton, N. Y.	....	1912	EN, Vol. 67	29	Earth and concrete core	Foundation piping
Davis Reservoir, Calif.	....	1914	EN, Vol. 72	39	Earth, rolled	Piping around outlet
Debris Barrier No. 1, Calif.	....	1904	{EN, Vol. 53 / EN, Vol. 58}	..	Hydraulic	Overtopped
Dells and Hatfield, Wis.	1910	1911	EN, Vol. 66	34	Earth and concrete core	Overtopped
Desabla Forebay, Calif.	1903	1932	Sherard	53	....	Piping through embankment
Dry Creek, Mont.	1938	1939	ENR, Vol. 122	46	Earth, rolled	Piping
East Liverpool, Ohio	1901	1901	ER, Vol. 44	..	Earth, rolled	Piping along outlet
Elk City, Okla.	1925	1936	ENR, Vol. 116	30	Earth, rolled	Overtopped

Name			Reference	Height	Type	Remarks
Ellington, Conn.	....	1890	EN, Vol. 47	..	Earth, rolled	Piping along outlet
Empire, Colo.	1906	1909	ASCE Proc., Vol. 49	30	Earth, rolled	Overtopped
English, Calif.	....	1883	Schuyler	..		Piping
Fairview, Mass.	....	1922	ENR, Vol. 89	30	Earth, rolled	Piping under spillway; drawdown slide
Forsythe, Utah	1920	1921	Sherard	65	Earth, rolled	
Fort Collins, Colo.	....	1902	EN, Vol. 57	250	Hydraulic	Foundation slide
Fort Peck, Mont.	....	1938	ENR, Vol. 121	25	Earth, rolled	Seepage slide
Frazier, Idaho	1915	1935	Sherard	12	Earth, rolled	Overtopped
Frazier Valley, B. C., Canada	....	1948	ENR, Vol. 140	..	Earth, rolled	Overtopped
Frenchmans Creek, Mont.	1951	1952	ENR, Vol. 118	36	Earth, rolled	Seepage slide
Fruit Growers Reservoir, Colo.	1898	1937	{ ENR, Vol. 94 / ENR, Vol. 100 }	80	Earth, rolled	Seepage slide
Garza, Tex.	1926	1926	ER, Vol. 66	115	Hydraulic	Core pressure slide
Gatun, Panama	....	1912	EN, Vol. 76	22	Hydraulic	Core pressure slide
Goose Creek, S. C.	1903	1916	ER, Vol. 42	25	Earth, rolled	Overtopping
Grand Rapids, Mich.	1874	1900	EN, Vol. 52	60	Earth, rolled	Overtopping
Greenlick, Pa.	1901	1904	{ EN, Vol. 100 / ENR, Vol. 103 }	140	Earth, rolled	Seepage
Greenville, S. C.	....	1927	EPG Journal, Vol. 44	20	......	Cast-iron pipe failed
Gunnison, Calif.	....	1890	ENR, Vol. 96	80	Earth, rolled	Piping along outlet
Half Moon Bay, Calif.	....	1926	{ Sherard / EN, Vol. 75 }	65	Earth, rolled	Overtopping
Hatchtown, Utah	1908	{ 1910 / 1911 }	EN, Vol. 66	24	Earth and concrete core	Seepage sloughs
Hatfield, Wis.	1908	1911	ER, Vol. 69	56	Earth, rolled	Complete failure due to seepage along conduit
Hebron, N. Mex.	1913	{ 1914 / 1942 }	ER, Vol. 69	65	Earth, rolled	Overtopping
Holmes Creek, Utah	1903	1924	Sherard	23	Earth and concrete core	Piping through dam
Hope Reservoir, R. I.	1882	1907	{ ER, Vol. 53 / ER, Vol. 56 }	..	Earth, rolled	Overtopped
Hornell, N. Y.	1912	1912	EN, Vol. 58	56	Earth and concrete core	Upstream slope slide, full pool
Horse Creek, Colo.	1911	1914	{ EN, Vol. 69 / ER, Vol. 71 }	34	Earth, rolled	Seepage
Horton, Kans.	1924	1925	ENR, Vol. 95	20	Earth, rolled	Seepage
Jeanette, Pa.	....	1903	EN, Vol. 48	47	Earth, rolled	Piping
Jefferson County, Colo.	1940	1897	EN, Vol. 47	70	Earth, rolled	Overtopped
Johnson, Nebr.	1852	1942–1945	Corps of Engrs., Vol. 24	70	Earth, rolled	Loss of filter through riprap
Johnstown, Pa.	1905	1889	ASCE Trans., Vol. 24	52	Earth, rolled	Overtopping
Julesburg (Jumbo), Colo.	1948	1907–1910	ER, Vol. 63	46	Earth, rolled	Serious leakage started in 1907, dam failed with 24-ft head in 1910
Kern, Ore.	....	1949	Sherard	18	Earth, rolled	Excessive settlement of fill
Kettering, England	1941	1905	ER, Vol. 52	170	Earth and concrete core	Slide
Killingsworth, Conn.	....	1938	ENR, Vol. 121	..	Hydraulic	Overtopping
Kingsley, Nebr.	....	1942	CE, Vol. 15	140	Earth, rolled	Loss of fill through concrete blocks, no filter
Knobrook, Pa.	1929	1894	EN, Vol. 32		Earth, rolled	Foundation seepage
Knoxville Reservoir, Tenn.	1930	1883	EN, Vol. 47	61	Earth, rolled	Foundation slide during construction
Lafayette, Calif.	....	1928	EN, Vol. 54		Earth, rolled	Foundation piping
La Fruta, Tex.	....	1930	{ ENR, Vol. 105 / ENR, Vol. 106 / ENR, Vol. 107 }	52	Earth and rock	Overtopped
Lake, N. Mex.	....	1893	{ EN, Vol. 23 / EN, Vols. 35 and 36 }	48	Earth, rolled	Overtopped
Lake Avalon, N. Mex.	....	1894	EN, Vol. 54			

TABLE 1.—(Continued)

Dam and location	Date Built	Failed	Reference [a]	Height	Type	Reason for unsatisfactory performance
Lake Avalon, N. Mex.	1894	1904	EN, Vol. 54	48	Earth, rolled	Seepage
Lake Coedty, Wales		1925	ENR, Vol. 96		Earth, rolled	......
Lake Dixie, Tex.		1940	ENR, Vol. 125		Earth, rolled	Overtopped
Lake Francis (old dam), Calif.	1899	1899	ASCE Trans., Vols. 58 and 59	50	Earth, rolled	Piping along outlet
Lake George, Colo.	1914	1914	Sherard		Earth, rolled	Piping
Lake Malloya, N. Mex.		1942	Sherard	50	Earth, rolled	Overtopped for 6 hours, did not fail
Lake Toxaway, N. C.	1902	1916	ENR, Vol. 94; ER, Vol. 74	62	Earth, rolled	Seepage
Lake Yosemite, Calif.	1884	1943	Sherard; Schuyler	53	Earth, rolled	......
Lancaster, Pa.		1894	ER, Vol. 30	21	Earth, rolled	Piping along outlet
Lebanon, Ohio		1882	EN, Vol. 9	30	Earth, rolled	Overtopping
Lebanon, Pa.		1893	ER, Vol. 27	40	Earth, rolled	Piping between fill and foundation
Leroux Creek, Colo.		1905	EN, Vol. 54	25	Earth, rolled	Overtopping
Lidderdale, Colo.		1909	ASCE Proc., Vol. 49	19	Earth, rolled	Overtopping
Lima, Mont.		1894	EN, Vol. 81; EN, Vol. 47	40	Earth, rolled	Erosion at spillway
Linville, N. C.	1919	1919	ASCE Trans., Vol. 84	160	Hydraulic	Core too flat
Lock Alpine, Mich.		1926	ENR, Vol. 96	25	Earth, rolled	Settlement on being saturated
Long Tom, Idaho	1906	1915	Sherard	50	Earth and puddle core	Piping into tunnel
Longwalds Pond, Mass.		1922	ENR, Vol. 89	30	Earth and concrete core	Piping
Lower Otay, Calif.	1897	1916	EN, Vol. 75	180	Rock and concrete core	Overtopping
Lyman, Ariz.	1913	1915	EN, Vol. 73	65	Earth, rolled	Piping
Lynde Brook, Mass.		1876	EPG Journal, Vol. 44	27	Earth, rolled	Piping along outlet
Magic, Idaho	1910	1911	Sherard; ER, Vol. 60; EN, Vol. 27	130	Earth, rolled	Piping through dam
Mahcnoy City, Pa.		1892	EN, Vol. 47; EN, Vol. 26; ER, Vol. 79		Earth, rolled	Piping
Mammoth, Utah	1912	1917	ER, Vol. 66	70	Earth and hydraulic	Overtopped during construction
Maquoketa, Iowa	1924	1927	ENR, Vol. 98	20	Earth, rolled	Piping at junction with concrete spillway
Marshall Creek, Kans.	1908	1937	ENR, Vol. 119	80	Earth, rolled	Foundation failure during construction
Marshall Lake, Colo.		1909	ER, Vol. 62	70	......	Seepage
Martin Davey Dam, Tex.	1950	1940	ENR, Vol. 125		Earth, rolled	Overtopped
Masterson, Ore.		1951	Sherard; Schuyler	60	Earth, rolled	Piping, dry fill
McMillan, N. Mex.	1894	1915, 1937	Sherard; Schuyler		Earth and hydraulic	Upstream earth piped into rock downstream
Meilville, Utah	1907	1909	ER, Vol. 36	36	Earth, rolled	Piping through foundation
Melzingah, N. Y.		1897	ER, Vol. 43	24	Earth, rolled	Overtopping
Middlefield, Mass.		1901		20	Earth, rolled	Overtopping
Mill River, Mass.	1865	1874	ASCE Trans., Vols. 3 and 4	43	Earth and concrete core	Seepage
Mission Lake, Kans.	1924	1925	ENR, Vol. 95	18	Earth, rolled	Settlement with overtopping
Mohawk, Ohio		1913	EN, Vol. 73	18	Earth, rolled	Overtopped and seepage
Montreal, Que., Canada		1915	EN, Vol. 73		Earth and rock	Settlement and seepage
Morena, Calif.	1912	1896	EN, Vol. 47; ASCE Trans., Vol. 65	167	Rock	Seepage; Overtopped, did not fail

Name and location	Year	Year	Reference	Height, ft	Type	Remarks
Mountain Creek, Tex.	1931	....	Corps of Engrs.	86	Earth, rolled	Loss of filter through riprap
Mount Lake State Park, Minn.	1937	1938	ENR, Vol. 120	....	....	Overtopped
Mount Pisgah, Colo.	1910	1928	Sherard	76	Earth, rolled	Upstream slope sloughed on drawdown, flattened to 1 on 3
Mud Pond, Mass.	1873	1886	ER, Vol. 13	15	Earth and rock	Piping
Narraguinep, Colo.	1908	1928–1951	Sherard	79	Earth, rolled	Continued sloughing of upstream slope and abutment leakage
Nebraska City, Nebr.	1890	1890	EN, Vol. 47	17	Earth and rock	Seepage
Necomah, Wis.	1866	1905	ER, Vol. 52	....	Earth and concrete core	Core settled
New Bedford, Mass.	1927	1868	ASCE Trans., Vols. 1 and 2	25	Earth, rolled	Piping along outlet conduit
New Bowman, Calif.	....	1928	ENR, Vol. 54	170	Rock	Break in outlet tunnel, repaired
Nezaxa, Mex.	1905	1909	EN, Vol. 62	190	Hydraulic	Slide in embankment during construction
North Dike, Wachusett, Mass.	....	1907	Merriman	82	Earth, rolled	Slide in upstream slope
North Scituate, R. I.	1892	1926	ENR, Vol. 96	6	Earth, rolled	Overtopped
Norwich, N. Y.	....	1905	EN, Vol. 54	34	Earth, rolled	Overtopped
Peapack Brook, N. J.	1903	1892	ENR, Vol. 100	32	Earth, rolled	Overtopped
Piedmont No. 1, Calif.	....	1903	Sherard	50	Earth and concrete core	Outlet pipe sheared off at core wall, replaced
Pleasant Valley, Utah	....	1905	ENR, Vol. 100	63	Earth and rock	Piping through settlement cracks
Point of Rocks, Colo.	1911	1928	Sherard	86	Earth, rolled	Concrete placed on 1½ upstream slope failed because of 5-ft waves, near failure in 1927 as a result of wave erosion
Portland, Me.	1889	1915	ER, Vol. 28	45	Earth, rolled	Concrete placed on 1½ upstream slope failed because of 5-ft waves, near failure in 1927 as a result of wave erosion
Portneuf, Idaho	1911	1893	Sherard	55	Earth, rolled	Piping along drain pipe
Prairie River, Wis.	1934	1950	EN, Vol. 68	....	Earth, rolled	Concrete conduit disintegrated, and was replaced in 1950
Pratts Fork, Ohio	1816	1912	OCE files	21	Earth, rolled	Overtopped
Providence, R. I.	....	1938	EN, Vol. 45	17	Earth and rock	Overtopped
Puddingstone, Calif.	....	1916	ENR, Vol. 96	....	Hydraulic	Overtopped during construction because of a clogged outlet
Rector, Calif.	1946	1926	Sherard	150	Earth, rolled	Overtopped during construction because of a clogged outlet
Rocky Ford, Utah	1914	1947	Sherard	70	Earth, rolled	Transverse cracking
Roxborough Reservoir, Pa.	1894	1915–1950	ER, Vol. 30	....	Earth, rolled	High saturated line, reservoir level limit in 1950
Saluda, S. C.	1930	1894	ENR, Vol. 104	208	Hydraulic	Piping
San Pablo, Calif.	1921	1930	Corps of Engrs.	220	Hydraulic	Core pool lost during construction
Santee Cooper, S. C.	1942	1942–1946	CE, Vol. 18	80	Earth and hydraulic	Fill loss, through riprap, no filter
Santo Amaro, Brazil	....	1907	Merriman	63	Hydraulic	Disintegration of porous concrete slope protection
Schenectady, N. Y.	1926	1916	EN, Vol. 76	30	Earth and rock	Failed during construction due to slide
Schofield, Utah	....	1927	ENR, Vol. 100	62	Earth, rolled	Overtopped
Scottdale, Pa.	....	1904	EN, Vol. 52	60	Earth and concrete core	Transverse cracking and piping into rock
Seefield, Utah	....	1925	ENR, Vol. 79	130	Earth, rolled	Piping
Sepulveda, Calif.	....	1914	ER, Vol. 74	65	Earth and rock	Overtopped
Sheffield, Calif.	1892	1925	ENR, Vol. 95	30	Earth, rolled	Earthquake slide
Shelton, Conn.	1916	1903	ER, Vol. 47	20	Earth, rolled	Piping
Sherburne, N. Y.	....	1905	EN, Vol. 54	34	Earth and rock	Overtopped
Sherburne Lake, Mont.	1910	....	Corps of Engrs.	....	Earth, rolled	Floating logs displaced hand-placed riprap
Short Creek, Ark.	....	1939	ENR, Vol. 122	57	Earth and rock	Overtopped during construction
Sinker Creek, Idaho	1893	1943	Sherard	70	Hydraulic and earth	Seepage slide
Six Mill Creek, N. Y.	....	1905	EN, Vol. 53	15	Earth, rolled	Overtopped
Snake Ravine, Calif.	....	1898	EN, Vol. 40	64	Hydraulic	Poor compaction
Spartanburg, Pa.	....	1892	EN, Vol. 27	10	Earth and rock	Overtopped

TABLE 1.—(Continued)

Dam and location	Date Built	Date Failed	Reference [a]	Height	Type	Reason for unsatisfactory performance
Spring Lake, R. I.	1887	1889	EN, Vol. 20	18	Earth and rock	Piping along outlet
Staffordville, Conn.		1887	EN, Vol. 4	20	Earth and rock	Piping along outlet
Standley Lake, Colo.	1911	1916	ENR, Vol. 78	113	Hydraulic	Core too large, slides during and after construction
Stockton Creek, Calif.	1950	1950	Sherard	80	Earth, rolled	Failed at abutment, probably along contact or crack
Sublette, Idaho	1915	1916	Sherard	40	Earth, rolled	Conduit cracked as a result of settlement
Summer Lake, Ore.		1914	ASCE Trans., Vol. 94	60	Earth, rolled	Foundation slide
Suputrida Canyon, Calif.	1867		SE, Vol. 3	65	Earth and concrete core	Overtopped
Swansen, Wales		1879	ENR, Vol. 100	80	Earth, rolled	Piping
Table Rock Cave, S. C.	1927	1928		140	Earth, rolled	Broken outlet pipe
Tappan, Ohio	1935	1934		52	Earth, rolled	Slide in foundation
Tecumseh, Ala.		1894	EN, Vol. 32	30	Earth and rock	Overtopping
Telluride, Colo.		1909	Colorado State Engr.	65	Earth, rolled	Overtopped, but did not fail
Throttle, N. Mex.	1912	1942	Sherard	35	Earth, rolled	Overtopped
Torranto, Ont., Canada		1912	ER, Vol. 65	25	Earth, rolled	Overtopped
Trout Lake, Colo.	1894	1909	ER, Vol. 60	18	Earth, rolled	Piping along outlet
Tupper Lake, N. Y.	1906	1906	ER, Vol. 57	22	Earth, rolled	Slide during construction
Turkey Creek, Colo		1910	Colorado State Engr.	56	Earth, rolled	Leakage around outlet
Turlock Irrigation, Calif.		1914	EN, Vol. 25	29	Earth, rolled	Foundation settlement
Turtle Creek, Tex.		1891	EN, Vol. 67	20	Earth and timber core	Overtopped
Union Bay, B. C., Canada	1874	1912	ER, Vol. 46	70	Earth, rolled	Insufficient compaction
Utica Reservoir, N. Y.		1902	ENR, Vol. 148	30	Earth, rolled	Settlement of spillway
Valentine, Nebr.	1911	1911	E & BR, Vol. 18		Earth, rolled	Overtopped
Val Marie Dam, Sask., Canada		1952	ER, Vol. 43	56	Earth, rolled	Slopes too steep
Valparaiso, Chile		1888	ENR, Vol. 103	25	Earth, rolled	Overtopped
Victor, Colo.		1901			Earth, rolled	Poor design and construction
Virgin River, Nev.		1929		120	Earth, rolled	
Wachusett (new dike), Mass.		1907	Schuyler		Earth, rolled	Upstream slope slide, water surface 40 ft below top
Wagner, Wash.	1918	1938	ENR, Vol. 120	50	Hydraulic	Spillway failure—erosion
Walnut Grove, Ariz.	1888	1890	Wegmann	110	Rock	Overtopped
Weisse, Czechoslovakia		1916		42	Earth, rolled	Piping along outlet
West Julesburg, Colo.	1905	1910	ER, Vol. 63	55	Earth, rolled	Piping
Wilmington, Del.	1864–1887	1900	ER, Vol. 42	12	Earth, rolled	Piping along outlet
Winston, N. C.	1902	1912	EN, Vol. 67	24	Earth, rolled	Overtopped
Wise River, Mont.		1927	ENR, Vol. 99		Earth, rolled	Overtopping
Wister, Okla.	1951			90	Earth, rolled	Piping
Worcester, Colo.	1912	1951	Sherard	68	Earth, rolled	Concentrated seepage
Worcester, Mass.	1871	1876	ASCE Trans., Vols. 5 and 6	41	Earth, rolled	Leakage in culvert
Yuba (old dam), Calif.		1907	EN, Vol. 58		Earth, rolled	Overtopped
Yuba (new dam), Calif.	1949	1951	Sherard	25	Earth, rolled	Seepage slide, downstream slope enlargement
Zuni, N. Mex.	1907	1909	EN, Vol. 62	70	Earth and rock	Piping through abutment

[a] ENR = Engineering News-Record; EN = Engineering News; ER = Engineering Record; ASCE Proc. = ASCE Proceedings; Sherard = "Influence of Soil Properties and Construction Methods on Performance of Homogeneous Earth Dams," by James L. Sherard, thesis presented to Harvard Univ., at Cambridge, Mass., in 1952, in partial fulfilment of the requirement for the degree of Doctor of Science, Civil Engineering; ASCE Trans. = ASCE Transactions; Corps of Engrs. = "Slope Protection for Earth Dams," Corps of Engrs. rept. (Waterways Experiment Station), March, 1949; Wegmann = "Design and Construction of Dams," by Edward Wegmann, Chapman and Hall, Ltd., London 8th Ed., 1927; Schuyler = "Reservoirs for Irrigation, Water-power, and Domestic Water-supply," by J. D. Schuyler, John Wiley & Sons, Inc. New York, N. Y., 2d Ed., 1908; EPG Journal = Journal of Electric Power and Gas; CE = Civil Engineering; Merriman = "American Civil Engineering Handbook," by Mansfield Merriman, Chapman & Hall, Ltd., London, 1930; OCE files = files of Office of Chief of Engineers, Department of the Army, Washington, D. C.; SE = Sanitary Engineer; Engr. = "Annual Report," Colorado State Engr., Denver, Colo., 1910; and E & BR = Engineering and Building Record.

as outlined by Hathaway and Albert L. Cochran, M. ASCE, in "Engineering for Dams" (4) are followed, a structure safe from overtopping is assured.

Failures due to overtopping, as noted by Tables 3 and 4, are reasonably well distributed. The grouping of failures between 10 years and 20 years after construction, as shown in Table 3, is probably due to the fact that designs were generally based on a storm having approximately this frequency of occurrence.

TABLE 2.—CAUSES OF INADEQUACIES OF EARTH DAMS SUMMARIZED

Cause of partial or complete failure	Percentage of total
1. Overtopping	30
2. Seepage	25
3. Slides	15
4. Conduit leakage	13
5. Slope paving	5
6. Miscellaneous	7
7. Unknown	5

TABLE 3.—RELATION OF FAILURE TO AGE OF STRUCTURE, IN PERCENTAGE OF TOTAL NUMBER OF STRUCTURES

No. of years after completion	CAUSE OF DIFFICULTY			
	Overtopping	Conduit leakage	Seepage	Slides
0– 1	9	23	16	29
1– 5	17	50	34	24
5– 10	9	9	13	12
10– 20	30	9	13	12
20– 30	13	5	12	12
30– 40	10	4	6	11
40– 50	9	0	6	0
50–100	3	0	0	0

TABLE 4.—CHRONOLOGICAL DISTRIBUTION OF FAILURES, IN PERCENTAGES

Calendar year	Overtopping	Seepage	Conduit leakage	Slides	Total[a]
1850–1860	0	0	0	0	0
1860–1870	0	0	7	0	1
1870–1880	0	6	7	3	3
1880–1890	6	4	11	3	5
1890–1900	12	11	21	3	13
1900–1910	23	19	18	16	17
1910–1920	22	25	18	23	21
1920–1930	14	13	18	26	16
1930–1940	11	8	0	23	10
1940–1950	9	6	0	3	8
1950	3	8	0	3	4

[a] Includes all inadequate dams even though cause of unsatisfactory performance was not determined.

SEEPAGE

The famous "creep" theory and the crude principle of "inclosing" the saturation (phreatic) line within the embankment have given way to sound soil mechanics principles of seepage control. Darcy's law, developed about 1850, forms the basis for all modern methods of seepage analysis. The flow-net method of analysis, pioneered in this country by Arthur Casagrande, M. ASCE (5), is now widely used. The first published attempt to rationalize seepage under dams was made by Arnold C. Koenig in 1911 (6). He attributed failure to buoyed-up particles at the seepage exit.

One of the earliest seepage model studies was made by J. B. T. Colman in

1916 (7). Shortly thereafter, James B. Hays, M. ASCE, presented a paper (8) on the use of seepage models in the design of dams.

Seepage through embankments is usually controlled by proper zoning of the available embankment materials. An ideal embankment section is one composed of a relatively narrow central impervious core (Fig. 2(a)) supported by well-graded, free-draining shells of pervious material. A properly compacted upstream section assures the safest and most economical slopes that can be designed to guard against drawdown forces. The pervious downstream section, with an adequate transition or filter zone, insures a low saturation line and full control of through seepage. Hydraulic fills and puddle core fills with sand and gravel shells were the earliest dams of this type in the United States.

Great progress has been made in designing earth dams on deep pervious foundations. Early structures were limited principally to sites where positive cutoffs to an impervious stratum could be obtained. Probably Gatun was the first

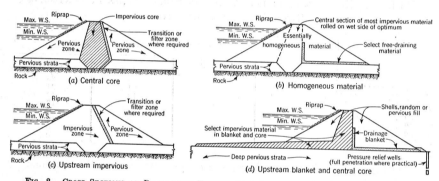

FIG. 2.—CROSS SECTIONS OF DAMS, WITH VARIOUS ARRANGEMENTS TO MEET CONDITIONS AND TO UTILIZE AVAILABLE MATERIALS

large dam to be constructed over a deep pervious foundation without a positive cutoff. The design was based on a long path of seepage and a downstream rock drainage toe. The principle now widely used—of designing an impervious upstream blanket and downstream drainage (Fig. 2(d))—was first proposed by Hays in 1917 (8).

Design methods based on theoretical seepage analyses are now available for determining the optimum width of impervious blankets (9) and provisions for downstream relief wells (10). In stratified pervious deposits, which include the bulk of natural formations, relief wells have been found to give most satisfactory results at a low cost.

Positive control of seepage through the embankment and foundation is an essential requirement in earth-dam design. Uncontrolled seepage, regardless of the amount, should not be tolerated. Seepage through the embankment is controlled by a pervious zone (Fig. 2) having the required gradation to form a stable filter. This zone may take the form of a pervious downstream section, a horizontal or inclined pervious drainage blanket, or a toe drain. Proper filtering characteristics of all the materials involved in foundation and embankment are essential to prevent piping and thereby to insure a safe structure. Karl Terzaghi, Hon. M. ASCE, in an unpublished report, and George E. Bertram (11) were the first to establish satisfactory filter criteria.

Foundation seepage is preferably controlled by a positive impervious cutoff to an impervious stratum with a drainage blanket or trench to collect whatever seepage may occur through the bedrock and the embankment. Where a positive cutoff cannot be obtained, careful design of a relief-well or a toe-drainage system together with an upstream impervious blanket is necessary. Steel sheet piling, used extensively in early earth-dam construction, cannot be depended on to reduce seepage appreciably. At Fort Peck Dam, on the Missouri River in Montana (12), although the steel sheet-pile cutoff was driven entirely through the pervious foundation, pressure from seepage through the cutoff developed a 40-ft hydrostatic head above the ground surface at the downstream toe, and relief wells had to be installed. At Denison Dam on the Red River in Texas, steel sheet piling was also ineffective in reducing seepage.

In addition to normal seepage through the soil mass, the pervious zone should be adequate to control seepage from a crack that might develop through the impervious zone. To provide greater protection against cracks, at least the center part of the impervious zone should be compacted on the wet side of the optimum placement moisture so that this mass will be plastic and will not consolidate further when completely saturated. Cracks through dams have long been recognized as a problem and have probably been the cause of many "piping" failures, but only recently has a complete study been made by James L. Sherard, A. M. ASCE (13), sponsored by the Bureau of Reclamation, on the performance of dams from this standpoint.

Permeability tests to determine the seepage characteristics of different soils were first conducted independently by the Massachusetts State Board of Health and D. C. Henny, M. ASCE (Oregon), in 1907. It was the earliest concept that the slope of the saturation (phreatic) line was governed by the material. As late as 1930, many dams and levees were designed on the basis of enclosing the saturation line. Progress in this field was rapid in the 1930's. It is believed that the piping phenomenon mentioned by Koenig in 1911 (6) was first comprehensively treated by L. F. Harza, M. ASCE, in 1936 (14).

Conduits

Unsatisfactory performance of conduits, due to deficiencies in design or construction, has been observed principally in the following ways:

a. Piping along conduit due to absence of seepage collars, or to poor compaction around it.

b. Failure of conduit due to unequal settlement where pipe was supported on piers or where foundation settlement was uneven.

c. Failure of conduit due to inadequate strength to resist earth pressure.

In current design all these deficiencies have been corrected. Seepage collars are provided on all conduits, and compaction of the surrounding fill is most carefully controlled. Anticipated settlement is closely estimated, and the conduit is designed accordingly. Wherever practical, conduits are placed on rock to reduce settlement to a minimum. Present structural design criteria are usually very conservative.

It is not expected that conduits will show unsatisfactory performance in the future. Past experience indicates that if trouble occurs it will be within the first few years after construction (see Table 3). New designs are sufficiently conservative to insure satisfactory performance. It should be noted (Table 4) that there have been no conduit failures in the past 20 years.

SLIDES

Rational methods for determining the stability of earth slopes were slow to develop because of the lack of adequate testing apparatus and procedure, and of adequate analytical methods.

A. L. Bell's paper (15) in 1914 and William Cain's (M. ASCE) paper (16), in 1916 are believed to be the first published works in the United States on tests made to determine the strength of soils. Then there was a gap of almost 20 years before shear testing was applied generally to earth-dam construction. The work of Harry H. Hatch (17) in 1934, Leo Jürgenson (18) in 1934, and Glennon Gilboy, A. M. ASCE (19), in 1936 probably indicated the earliest concerted efforts in the United States toward the soil strength determinations so essential for use in slope stability studies.

Outstanding progress has been made since this earlier work by practical testing on the job such as that at Muskingum (Ohio) and Fort Peck dams reported by R. R. Philippe, A. M. ASCE (20), and the writer (21), and by the extensive research work conducted in university and government laboratories. Probably the most comprehensive research was conducted at Harvard University in Cambridge, Mass., at Massachusetts Institute of Technology, also in Cambridge, and at the Waterways Experiment Station, Vicksburg, Miss., under the direction of the Corps of Engineers and reported by Philip Rutledge, M. ASCE (22). The best and most up-to-date treatment on soil testing can be found in publications by Casagrande and R. E. Fadum, M. ASCE (23), T. W. Lambe, Jun. M. ASCE (24), and the Bureau of Reclamation (25). Knowledge and techniques on soil testing are adequate for the satisfactory solution of all practical problems.

Terzaghi (26) in 1929 made the first attempt in the United States to outline a theoretical method of slope stability determination. Rapid development was made in the 1930's, reaching a climax about the time of the Second Congress on Large Dams held in Washington, D. C., in 1936, and the First International Conference on Soil Mechanics held in Boston, Mass., in the same year. Outstanding papers on stability, using the Swedish circular-arc method, were presented during this period by Gilboy (27), Casagrande (28), Terzaghi (29), and Donald W. Taylor, A. M. ASCE (30). Charts presented by Taylor are still widely used for preliminary examination of slope stability.

Also during the 1930's there was in process of development a new method of analysis based on the application of the theory of elasticity. The first papers presenting this method were by Jürgenson (31) in 1934, and by Theodore T. Knappen, M. ASCE, and Philippe (32) and the writer (33) in 1936. The general reaction at the time was one of astonishment that any engineer would seriously consider soil as being sufficiently elastic to apply this theory. All the research conducted since that time has added strength to the contention of the proponents of this method that, although soil is not perfectly elastic, its stress-strain characteristics are such that stresses computed by this theory are sufficiently accurate for most practical problems.

Liquefaction of cohesionless soil as a problem in the design of dams was first discussed in this country by Casagrande (28) in 1936. There was a tendency at that time to classify some normal shear failures as flow slides. A notable example was the Fort Peck slide (34) which occurred in 1938. The first reaction of some engineers was that it was a flow slide due to liquefaction of the hydraulic fill. After extensive investigation, the consulting board concluded that the slide was:

> "* * * due to the fact that the shearing resistance of the weathered shale and bentonite seams in the foundation was insufficient to withstand the shearing forces to which the foundation was subjected."

It is generally accepted at the present time that for a cohesionless soil to liquefy and cause a flow slide it must be very loose and uniform. Even with only a moderate degree of compaction of uniform sands, there is no danger of a flow slide, and there is no record of a slide being caused by liquefaction of the foundation sands under an earth dam. Nevertheless, as Casagrande pointed out in his 1950 paper (35), there is a great deal to be learned about the mechanics-of-flow failures, and further research in this field is needed.

TYPES OF CONSTRUCTION

Rolled Fills.—The compacted fill is the oldest type of earth-dam construction. Wagons and scrapers were the principal means of placing the material in the early dams. In most cases compaction was obtained during the normal hauling operations by spreading the material in thin layers. The South Fork Dam in Pennsylvania built in 1853 is a good example of the best construction practices at that time. Extracts from the specification for its construction are given in an ASCE committee report (36).

This is an excellent specification, considering that it was written 100 years ago. Some of the essential features of the South Fork specification were: Placement in layers and compaction with carts and wagons during normal hauling operations; prohibition of barrows, chutes, and railway equipment; scarifying of foundation and lifts; exclusion of stones more than 4 in. in diameter; downstream rock fill "of such nature as to resist the decomposing action of air, frost and water"; the use of a transition zone between rock and rolled earth; the earth to "be composed of best watertight material within ¼ miles of dam"; and puddling of the core if necessary to obtain an upstream impervious zone.

Compaction as an essential feature in earth-dam design and construction received only periodic acceptance before 1900. However, a pamphlet (37) published by *Engineering* in 1868 and a paper by W. J. McAlpine, Past-President and Hon. M. ASCE (38), in 1877, stressing the importance of compaction in layers, were major steps in developing an awareness of the need for special compaction equipment.

Use of special rollers for compaction has developed steadily since the first heavy smooth roller was used about 1860. About 1905, the sheepsfoot roller was introduced in the western states, and this started a gradual but general recognition of compaction as an essential feature of earth-dam construction. However, wide acceptance of compaction and moisture control was not realized until the early 1930's. In the course of improving compaction, the smooth roller was abandoned, and the weight of the sheepsfoot roller was increased from a total of 10,000 lb for a double-drum roller to approximately 42,000 lb. The heavy roller was first used by the Los Angeles (Calif.) Flood Control District, and shortly thereafter was adopted as standard equipment by the Bureau of Reclamation for the compaction of cohesive soils.

The latest trend in roller development is the medium weight (50,000-lb to 100,000-lb) four-wheel rubber-tired roller, the specifications for which were developed by the Corps of Engineers under the direction of Bertram. All earth construction contracts of the Corps of Engineers permit the contractor to use either a 42,000-lb double-drum sheepsfoot roller or a 100,000-lb (25,000 lb per wheel) rubber-tired roller for the compaction of cohesive soils. The rubber-tired type is specified for the compaction of cohesionless soils.

Specifications are usually written to allow layer thicknesses for rubber-tired rollers approximately twice those allowed for sheepsfoot rollers, and one-half the number of passes. Experience to date indicates that the rubber-tired roller generally gives somewhat greater density at a saving of 2¢ per cu yd to 5¢ per cu yd. Larger savings are realized in rocky soil where removal of oversize stones is an expensive operation. In these soils the use of the rubber-tired roller permits placement in 18-in. to 24-in. layers. It is predicted that the rubber-tired roller will gradually replace the sheepsfoot for compaction of all types of soil.

Moisture control, long recognized as an important feature in embankment construction, has only in recent years received the attention it deserves by reason of its importance in the stability of the structure. In the early years, puddling was the favored method for placing the core, the remainder of the dam being placed at the natural moisture content or with only a moderate degree of moisture control. Shortly after the turn of the century, Burr Bassell, M. ASCE (39), and J. D. Schuyler, M. ASCE (40), were active supporters of moisture control. The Proctor (41) test, first proposed in 1933, revolutionized the moisture and compaction control of embankments.

At present there are two schools of thought, one favoring compaction on the dry side of optimum moisture to eliminate high pore pressures, and the other favoring compaction on the wet side of optimum to prevent cracking, which might develop continuous seepage passages. Based on experience with earth dams and levees placed on the dry side of optimum, the Corps of Engineers favors embankments on the wet side of optimum and requires that the core or central part of the impervious section be placed at a moisture content and density that will not allow any additional consolidation on saturation. Use of this criterion generally results in the core material being placed well on the wet side of optimum moisture. Full consideration must be given in the stability analysis to the pore pressure that will be developed. J. W. Hilf, A. M. ASCE (42), in reporting on work of the Bureau of Reclamation, outlined a method of estimating these pressures.

Hydraulic Fills.—The hydraulic-fill method is exclusively an American development and was pioneered by Schuyler, J. M. Howells, and William Gerig, Members ASCE. The first hydraulic-fill methods were adapted from hydraulic mining processes. E. B. Dorsey, M. ASCE (43), in 1886 proposed the use of mining methods in excavation and placement of fills in the earliest published work in this field. It is believed that Lathan Anderson (44) in 1893 was the first to propose the use of a sluiced fill for a dam. Howells (45) in 1895 was probably the pioneer in building a hydraulic-fill dam. Schuyler (46)(47) probably was the first to propose construction methods based on actual experience.

After several failures due to excessive core pressures, there was a trend toward extremely flat slopes. Schuyler considered this trend unjustified and pointed out in his 1907 paper (47) "that in his experience there was no reason for building a dam of greater dimensions because the material was placed by hydraulic methods." Allen Hazen, M. ASCE, in his article (48) in 1919 stated:

"If core material can be fully drained and consolidated, there is no reason why a dam built by the hydraulic method on a section that is suitable for an earth dam built dry should not be safe."

J. A. Holmes (49) in 1921 was probably the leader in considering soil characteristics in design. Charles H. Paul's (M. ASCE) paper (50) in 1922 was the first comprehensive coverage of problems relating to the core. However, it was more than 10 years later before rational testing and analytical methods were proposed. Gilboy's papers (51)(52) in 1933 and 1934 clearly outlined the principles involved in hydraulic-fill dams and proposed a method of determining the stability of the shells that is still widely used. Hatch (17) proposed methods of tests for hydraulic-fill materials which were most useful at that time.

When designed and constructed in accordance with the latest soil mechanics practices, the hydraulic fill will give equally as satisfactory a performance as the rolled fill. Immediately after the Fort Peck slide in 1938 there was a tendency to discount the hydraulic fill, until investigation disclosed a weak foundation as the culprit. Nevertheless there have been no new hydraulic-fill dams constructed since Fort Peck, Sardis (in Mississippi), and Knightville (in Massachusetts) dams, which were completed by the Corps of Engineers prior to 1940. A number of potential hydraulic-fill dams have been investigated in recent years, but all have proved more costly than the rolled-fill type. The improvement in earth excavating, hauling, and compaction equipment has reduced the cost of rolled fills to such a degree that hydraulic fills cannot compete unless circumstances are exceptionally favorable.

Rock Fills.—The rock-fill dam has given the most satisfactory performance of all types. Records show no major rock-fill dam breaching from any cause other than overtopping. Only a few rock-fill dams appear in the compilation of failures in Table 1.

Rock-fill dams constructed with an impervious upstream earth section do not have as satisfactory a performance record as the plain rock fill with an impervious facing. Frequent piping of the earth fill into the rock fill has been due to inadequate transition zones. Modern dams having an upstream impervious earth section or a sloping or a "central core" have an excellent performance record since the transition zone is carefully designed and constructed.

Settlement of rock fills is slight, averaging less than 1.0% of the height. Under present construction practice these fills are sluiced with 1.0 to 2.0 cu yd of water per cubic yard of rock when dumped; or, where soft rock is used in construction, they are compacted with heavy rollers.

Core Walls and Cutoff Walls.—The earliest dams constructed in the United States followed the English practice of using a puddled clay core. Because of the low stability and the difficulty of placing the puddled core, it was replaced first by a masonry, and later by a concrete, core wall. Concrete core walls were never generally accepted. Experience showed that these walls invariably cracked and failed to provide the desired watertightness. Instead of following the practice of some foreign engineers—providing a puddled clay layer for watertightness upstream from the concrete core wall and a filter layer downstream to prevent loss of the puddled clay though the cracks—American engineers gradually changed to rolled earth cores. Apparently, the last concrete core wall was constructed in this country about 25 years ago. It is believed that there are no conditions that justify the use of a concrete core wall in a modern earth-fill or rock-fill dam.

Concrete cutoff walls, extending above the rock foundation from 5 ft to 50 ft into the earth core, are still used to a limited extent. These walls are merely carry-overs from the concrete core wall, and probably their use will soon be discontinued. Preferred modern practice is to place the core directly on the rock or impervious foundation, with a width at the contact usually equal to about 25% of the net head. Special care is taken in placement of material in the contact zone.

SLOPE PROTECTION

Riprap has been the material most generally used for upstream slope protection since the earliest dams. Other methods have been tried, but few have been as successful or as economical. On the Santee Cooper Dam (53) in South Carolina the porous concrete slope protection, which seemed to have much promise, deteriorated in a few years to such an extent that it had to be replaced with riprap in the active pool zone. The articulated concrete slabs used on the Kingsley Dam (54) in Nebraska failed during the first major storm, because the sand fill was sucked out from behind them. Possibly this articulated concrete slope protection would have been satisfactory had an adequate filter layer been placed under it. Continuously-reinforced-concrete slabs have been installed on some western dams (55), and their performance has been entirely satisfactory.

Until the mid-1940's very little progress had been made in establishing design requirements for riprap. It was fairly general practice to place dumped riprap 3 ft thick on all dams regardless of exposure, fetch, or slope, and to consider 18 in. of hand-placed riprap as equivalent to 3 ft of dumped riprap.

Since slope protection is a major item of construction cost, the Corps of Engineers instituted a performance survey in 1946 covering the bulk of the major earth dams in the United States and published a report (56) in 1949. The highlights of this report are: Riprap requirements as to thickness and size of stone are very conservative; hand-placed riprap is not as satisfactory as an equivalent thickness of dumped riprap; and a filter layer underneath all riprap is essential. The latest riprap requirements for embankments used by the Corps of Engineers vary from a 12-in. thickness (maximum 200-lb stone) where wave height is less than 2 ft, to a 30-in. thickness (maximum 2,500-lb stone) where the wave height is 8 ft.

These practices have resulted in substantial savings in earth-dam projects. The foregoing requirements apply to slopes steeper than 1 on 5. Additional work is needed to determine the necessary protection for slopes between 1 on 5 and beach slopes of 1 on 15 to 20. At the present time the riprap thickness, size, and quality are arbitrarily reduced when flatter slopes are involved.

None of the theories at present are adequate for computing riprap thickness and size. However, it is anticipated that more scientific approaches will become available in the near future.

EARTHQUAKES

Performance of earth dams during earthquakes has been more satisfactory than is generally assumed. In the 1906 San Francisco, Calif., shock no earth dam was seriously damaged although three water supply dams (57) were in the area of highest intensity—Temercal, Pilarcitos, and San Andreas. The San Andreas Dam was adjacent to the San Andreas fault; and, although a displacement in the abutment sheared the outlet conduit, the dam proper was not seriously disturbed. The steepest downstream slope on these dams was 1 on $2\frac{1}{2}$. All were on relatively strong foundation materials.

The only earth dam in this country on which there is a positive record of failure during an earthquake is the Sheffield Dam near Santa Barbara, Calif. It was thought by some that this was a typical foundation flow-slide failure due to liquefaction of fine sand or silt, set off by the earthquake. A special study of this dam was made by the Corps of Engineers, and a report (58) issued in 1949 concluded that: Failure was due to a weak zone in the foundation; and the factor of safety of the 1 on $2\frac{1}{2}$ downstream slope reduced to less than 1.0 when a horizontal earthquake force of 0.10 g (10% of gravity) was included in the stability analysis. The foundation was composed of clayey sand and sandy silt overlying sandstone. There had been no stripping of the foundation nor any drainage provided under the downstream slope.

It is the policy of the Corps of Engineers (59) to check the design of all earth dams in areas subject to earthquakes to be certain that the factor of safety is greater than 1.0 when earthquake forces are applied. In checking the stability, it is recommended that factors of 0.05 g be used for earth dams on rock foundations and of 0.10 g for those on weak soil foundations.

COSTS

Cost data have been reviewed, and the results (Fig. 3) show the general trend in the past century. Only the three major items—earth fill, rock fill, and masonry or concrete—have been included. In Fig. 3 individual projects are plotted, also certain average costs, marked as follows: (1) Fifteen western projects; (2) ninety contracts over the entire United States; and (3) twenty-one contracts over the entire United States. Earth-fill prices vary widely depending on the material, the job, and the location, and for that reason there is considerable scattering of the points. Nevertheless, it is evident (Fig. 3(a)) that since the middle of the nineteenth century earth-fill costs have remained constant or have shown a slight decrease, while, at the same time, the general price index (Fig. 3(c))

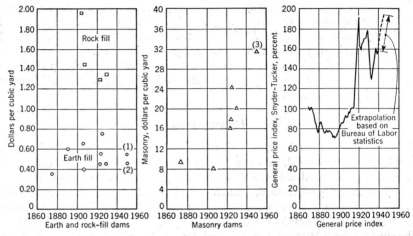

FIG. 3.—VARIATIONS OVER A CENTURY IN UNIT COSTS OF EARTH-FILL, ROCK-FILL, AND MASONRY DAMS AS COMPARED WITH PRICE INDEX

has increased from a low of about 70 in 1895 to a high of about 195 in 1952. This is a tribute to the equipment and the contracting industries for the improvement they have brought about in excavating, hauling, and compaction equipment and construction techniques.

Masonry prices (Fig. 3(b)) show a steady increase in the past 50 years, paralleling reasonably closely the increase in the price index, which has now reached about 2½ times the low of 1895.

MAINTENANCE

Earth dams, after their completion, are often left to the ravages of nature until serious troubles develop. Like other structures, they require periodic inspection and maintenance to assure continued satisfactory performance. It is not good engineering, nor even economically feasible, to design an earth dam so that no maintenance is required. Therefore, it is essential that provisions be made on all such projects for periodic inspections and for maintenance as required.

GROUTING

Extensive grouting of the rock under earth dams similar to that performed under concrete dams is not necessary. Seepage through the rock proper is usually not great enough to affect the safety and economy of the project. In highly fractured rock the contact with the core usually requires special treatment, to seal the cracks exposed to the core material, even though the rock has been grouted.

Grouting of pervious sands and gravels has not proved to be economically feasible in the United States. New chemical grouts that have been developed in recent years show promise, but they have not been fully tested in the field. Also, finely ground slag cement and clay grout, now being used by the French, may be found practicable in some cases where the high cost can be justified by the saving of water.

A Look Into the Future

Spillways.—Even in this modern age overtopping of some earth structures can be expected. Older structures not designed by the new concepts will eventually be hit by an unprecedented flood that will exceed the capacity of the spillway, and failure will occur. Also, new structures are still being built with underdesigned spillways, and based on the laws of probability some of these dams will be overtopped. The writer recommends most strongly that the spillway capacity and freeboard requirements of all old dams be reviewed in the light of modern theory and knowledge, and that the dams be raised or the spillways enlarged to accommodate the maximum possible flood without overtopping. The engineers responsible for such dams under both public and private ownership should not wait until these changes are forced by a public opinion aroused by failures. It is predicted that the underdesign of spillways will not be tolerated on any dams where loss of life and heavy property damage might result.

It is further predicted that, in the not too distant future, spillways will be safely and economically designed and constructed over earth dams. The foundation afforded by a modern compacted embankment is superior to many natural earth abutment foundations. Settlement can be eliminated as a problem by constructing the fill to a predetermined surcharge elevation and allowing time for consolidation before constructing the spillway.

In view of the high cost of reinforced-concrete structures and the demand for complete protection against overtopping, it is predicted that the use of formal concrete spillways will be reduced to a minimum. More and more dams will be designed to store a large part of the spillway design flood, and an emergency spillway, remote from the dam, consisting of an unpaved cut through rock, will prove satisfactory in view of its infrequent use.

The Corps of Engineers has many such dams planned or under construction. The Buford Dam on the Chattahoochee River in Georgia now being built is an outstanding example of this type of construction (Fig. 4). In this case it cost $5,000,000 less to raise the earth dam approximately 40 ft to take advantage of a favorable saddle in the abutment than to build a concrete ogee spillway in the river at a lower level. This project will provide 100% flood control, since only a small discharge passes over the spillway with the occurrence of the maximum possible flood.

The Kanopolis Dam on the Smoky Hill River in Kansas is a project typical of an unpaved spillway which will have more frequent operation (Fig. 5). Other dams of similar design are Blakely Mountain near Hot Springs, Ark., Cherry Creek Dam near Denver, Colo., Bayou Bodcau near Shreveport, La., Buffalo Bayou near Houston, Tex., several of the Muskingum group in Ohio, and the Merced group in California. The Bureau of Reclamation also has several dams with unpaved spillways. Many small dams are being constructed by the Soil Conservation Service with unpaved spillways in earth as well as in rock.

Seepage.—It is predicted that in designs made under the direction of experienced engineers, seepage will be eliminated as a source of possible trouble. Failures from this source will be rare since most old dams have been tested, and new dams will be designed to control all leakage through the dam as well as through the

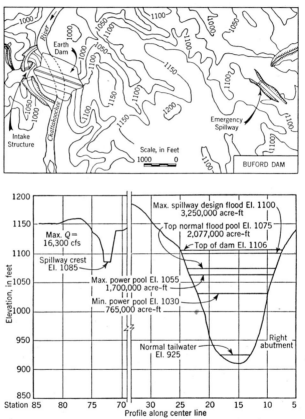

Fig. 4.—Buford Dam, Plan and Profile—Example of Economical Spillway Located Through Saddle at Some Distance from Chattahoochee River in Georgia

foundation and abutments. However, as indicated by Table 3, some failures can be expected in old dams that have not been subjected to the maximum reservoir level. Relief wells will be widely adopted for foundation seepage control because of their efficiency and economy. Proper zoning of available material, or use of thin drainage blankets, will be generally adopted as the most economical means of controlling seepage through dams.

Conduits.—Modern design and construction of conduits are sufficiently conservative that no new failures should occur from this source. Adequate wall thickness eliminates the danger of collapse. Rubber water stops and collars at all joints guard against leakage into or out of a conduit. Seepage collars and careful compaction of backfill insure that detrimental leakage will not occur along the conduit. Stilling basins are added where necessary to eliminate any troublesome scour.

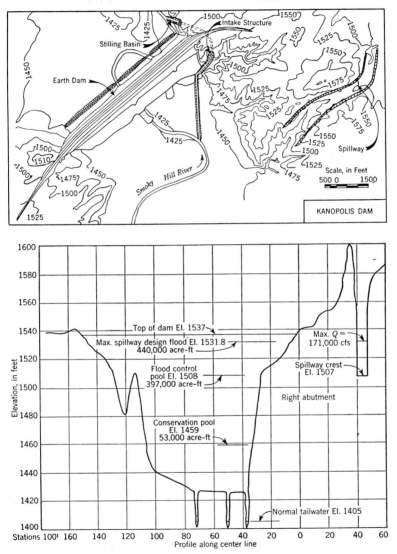

FIG. 5.—KANOPOLIS DAM ON SMOKY HILL RIVER IN KANSAS, PLAN AND PROFILE—AN INSTANCE WHERE UNPAVED SPILLWAY IS NEAR DAM ITSELF

However, conduits designed by present criteria are unnecessarily conservative, and in many cases add a burdensome cost to the project. It is predicted that the structural design of reinforced-concrete conduits will be drastically revised with the result that structures will be both more economical and safer. It is further predicted that on more and more dams, particularly the smaller projects, stilling basins will be omitted. The discharge end of the conduit will be so designed that scour will not cause excessive maintenance or serious erosion. There is no record of a dam failing, or of serious trouble developing, as a result of scour from this source. Considerable economy can be realized on earth-dam projects by giving careful consideration to avoiding these overly conservative design features.

Stability.—Present knowledge is such that inadequate design for stability should be eliminated as a cause of unsatisfactory performance on all new projects. Engineering knowledge is adequate to design for any known condition. It is therefore the duty of the engineer to obtain sufficient data on embankment and foundation conditions and then to apply present knowledge correctly. Some trouble from slides in old dams that have not been fully tested can be expected, as is evident from the percentages in Table 3.

Height.—The height of earth dams has increased along with knowledge of design and construction. In the past, some designers have ruled against this type of dam construction because they considered the height excessive. Knowledge today is adequate to design and construct a safe earth dam of any height which proves to be economically justified.

CRITERIA FOR DESIGN AND CONSTRUCTION

Based on past experience and present knowledge of design, the following criteria are considered essential for the construction of an earth dam which will be unquestionably safe:

1. Spillway capacity and freeboard should be sufficient to prevent overtopping when the maximum possible flood or floods occur.

2. Foundation and embankment should not be overstressed in shear.

3. Seepage through dams should be controlled by proper zoning of materials or by pervious drains. The use of pipe drains within the embankment section should be avoided.

4. Foundation seepage should be controlled by positive means such as an impervious cutoff to bedrock (not sheet piling), or relief wells, or a drainage trench at the downstream exit of the seepage.

5. Conduits should be conservatively designed to prevent collapse, leakage from or into the conduit, and seepage along the conduit.

6. Slope protection should be provided to the crest of the dam to protect against breaching of the embankment during a major storm.

7. At least the central part of the impervious section should be compacted to a density that will not produce settlement on saturation.

8. Careful design and construction must insure that no continuous seepage passages exist as a result of failure to bond and compact succeeding layers properly; that no zones or layers of pervious materials are allowed to extend through the embankment; that the embankment is properly bonded to the foundation; or that a tight contact is provided between the earth fill and the concrete structures.

9. Development of cracks in the embankment due to foundation or fill settlement should be avoided by proper consideration of slopes of abutments, river-

banks, and closure sections and by proper placement of fill material. Special attention should be given to the core or the central part of the impervious section to insure that the mass will be sufficiently plastic to deform without cracking.

Some dams may not meet all these criteria. Based on past experience their safety is questionable until they have been fully tested by time and high reservoir levels. However, any dam which does meet all these criteria will have an adequate margin of safety against unsatisfactory performance.

Each year an increasing percentage of the dams constructed in the United States are built of earth. This increase in the number of earth dams is due principally to three major factors: First, the science of soil mechanics has developed to the extent that as much confidence can be placed in the performance of earth dams as in other types. Second, the cost differential between earth and concrete construction favors earth and will undoubtedly continue to do so. Third, sites most adaptable to the construction of concrete dams have largely been exploited, leaving only those locations where great quantities of material must be used in construction. For these reasons, it can safely be predicted that 75% of future dam construction will be earth or rock fill.

Full realization of the potential advantages of earth dams is seriously handicapped by the lack of soil mechanics and general design engineers who are experienced in the design and layout of such projects. Engineering students and practicing civil engineers are urged to study soil mechanics and to seek experience that will add to their knowledge of earth-dam design and construction in order that the present shortage of experienced engineers in this field, as well as the anticipated demand in the future, can be met.

BIBLIOGRAPHY

(1) "Earth Dam Projects," by Joel D. Justin, John Wiley & Sons, Inc., New York, N. Y., 1932.

(2) Discussion of "The Failure of the Dam on Mill River," by William E. Worthen, *Transactions*, ASCE, 1875, p. 122.

(3) "List of Dam Failures," rept of Hydr. Power Committee, Natl. Electric Light Assn., New York, N. Y., 1929–1930.

(4) "Engineering for Dams," by W. P. Creager, Joel D. Justin, and Julian Hinds, John Wiley & Sons, Inc., New York, N. Y., Vol. I, 1945.

(5) "Seepage Through Dams," by Arthur Casagrande, *Journal*, New England Waterworks Assn., June, 1937, p. 131.

(6) "Dams on Sand Foundations: Some Principles Involved in Their Design, and the Law Governing the Depth of Penetration Required for Sheet-Piles," by Arnold C. Koenig, *Transactions*, ASCE, Vol. LXXIII, September, 1911, p. 175.

(7) "The Action of Water Under Dams," by J. B. T. Colman, *ibid.*, Vol. LXXX, 1916, p. 421.

(8) "Designing an Earth Dam Having a Gravel Foundation with Results Obtained from Model Tests," by James B. Hays, *ibid.*, Vol. LXXXI, 1917, p. 1.

(9) "The Effect of Blankets on Seepage Through Pervious Foundations," by Preston T. Bennett, *Transactions*, ASCE, Vol. 111, 1946, p. 215.

(10) "Relief Wells for Dams and Levees," by T. A. Middlebrooks and William H. Jervis, *ibid.*, Vol. 112, 1947, p. 1321.

(11) "An Experimental Investigation of Protective Fillers," by George E. Bertram, *Soil Mechanics Series No. 7*, Graduate School of Eng., Harvard Univ., Cambridge, Mass., January, 1940.

(12) "Seepage Control for Large Dams," by T. A. Middlebrooks, 3d Cong. on Large Dams, Stockholm, Sweden, 1948.

(13) "Influence of Soil Properties and Construction Methods on Performance of Homogeneous Earth Dams," by James L. Sherard, thesis presented to Harvard Univ., at Cambridge, Mass., in 1952, in partial fulfilment of the requirements for the degree of Doctor of Science, Civil Engineering.

(14) "The Best Means of Preventing Piping," by L. F. Harza, *Transactions*, 2d Cong. on Large Dams, Washington, D. C., 1936.

(15) "The Lateral Pressure and Resistance of Clay and the Supporting Power of Clay Foundations," by A. L. Bell, *Minutes of Proceedings*, Inst. C. E., Vol. CXCIX, 1914, p. 233.

(16) "Cohesion in Earth: the Need for Comprehensive Experimentation to Determine the Coefficients of Cohesion," by William Cain, *Transactions*, ASCE, Vol. LXXX, 1916, p. 1315.

(17) "Tests for Hydraulic-Fill Dams," by Harry H. Hatch, *ibid.*, Vol. 99, 1934, p. 206.

(18) "The Shearing Resistance of Soils," by Leo Jürgenson, *Journal*, Boston Soc. of Civ. Engrs., July, 1934, p. 242.

(19) "Improved Soil Testing Methods," by Glennon Gilboy, *Engineering News-Record*, May 21, 1936, p. 732.

(20) "Soil Mechanics Applied to Design of Dams," by R. R. Philippe, *Civil Engineering*, January, 1936, p. 25.

(21) "Exploring Foundations and Pits," by T. A. Middlebrooks, *Engineering News-Record*, August 29, 1935, p. 285.

(22) "Triaxial Shear Research," by Philip Rutledge, U. S. Waterways Experiment Station, Vicksburg, Miss., April, 1947.

(23) "Notes on Soil Testing for Engineering Purposes," by A. Casagrande and R. E. Fadum, *Bulletin No. 268*, Harvard Univ., Cambridge, Mass., January, 1940.

(24) "Soil Testing for Engineers," by T. W. Lambe, John Wiley & Sons, Inc., New York, N. Y., 1951.

(25) "Earth Manual," Bureau of Reclamation, U. S. Dept. of the Interior, Denver, Colo., 1951.

(26) "Mechanics of Shear Failures on Clay Slopes and Creep of Retaining Walls," by Charles Terzaghi, *Public Roads*, December, 1929, p. 177.

(27) "Stability of Embankment Foundation," by G. Gilboy, *Transactions*, 2d Cong. on Large Dams, Washington, D. C., 1936.

(28) "Characteristics of Cohesionless Soils Affecting the Stability of Slopes and Earth Fills," by Arthur Casagrande, *Journal*, Boston Soc. of Civ. Engrs., January, 1936, p. 13.

(29) **"Stability of Slopes of Natural Clay,"** by K. Terzaghi, *Proceedings,* 1st International Conference on Soil Mechanics and Foundation Eng., Cambridge, Mass., 1936.

(30) **"Stability of Earth Slopes,"** by Donald W. Taylor, *Journal,* Boston Soc. of Civ. Engrs., July, 1937, p. 197.

(31) **"The Application of Theories of Elasticity and Plasticity to Foundation Problems,"** by Leo Jürgenson, *ibid.,* July, 1934, p. 206.

(32) **"Practical Soil Mechanics at Muskingum. III,"** by Theodore T. Knappen and Robert R. Philippe, *Engineering News-Record,* April 23, 1936, p. 595.

(33) **"Foundation Investigation of Fort Peck Dam Closure Section,"** by T. A. Middlebrooks, *Proceedings,* 1st International Conference on Soil Mechanics and Foundation Eng., Cambridge, Mass., 1936.

(34) **"Fort Peck Slide,"** by T. A. Middlebrooks, *Transactions,* ASCE, Vol. 107, 1942, p. 723.

(35) **"Notes on the Design of Earth Dams,"** by Arthur Casagrande, *Journal,* Boston Soc. of Civ. Engrs., October, 1950, p. 405.

(36) **"Report of the Committee on the Cause of the Failure of the South Fork Dam,"** *Transactions,* ASCE, Vol. XXIV, January–June, 1891, p. 431.

(37) **"Earth Dam Construction,"** *Engineering,* January 10, 1868 (pamphlet).

(38) **"Dams and Reservoirs,"** by W. J. McAlpine, *Engineering Magazine,* (D. Van Nostrand), Vol. XVI, 1877.

(39) **"Earth Dams, a Study,"** by Burr Bassell, The Eng. News Pub. Co., New York, N. Y., 1904.

(40) **"Reservoirs for Irrigation, Water-power, and Domestic Water-supply,"** by J. D. Schuyler, John Wiley & Sons, Inc., New York, N. Y., 2d Ed., 1908.

(41) **"Fundamental Principles of Soil Compaction,"** by R. R. Proctor, *Engineering News-Record,* August 31, 1933, p. 245; September 7, 1933, p. 286; September 21, 1933, p. 348; and September 28, 1933, p. 372.

(42) **"Estimating Construction Pore Pressures in Rolled Earth Dams,"** by J. W. Hilf, *Proceedings,* 2d International Conference on Soil Mechanics and Foundation Eng., Rotterdam, Holland, Vol. III, 1948.

(43) **"Excavation and Embankment by Water Power,"** by E. B. Dorsey, *Transactions,* ASCE, Vol. XV, 1886, p. 348.

(44) **"A Proposed New Type of Dam,"** *Engineering News,* June 15, 1893, p. 554.

(45) **"Eighteenth Annual Report 1896–1897,"** U. S. Geological Survey, Washington, D. C., Vol. 18, Pt. 4, p. 649.

(46) **"Enormous Earth Dams,"** *Engineering Record,* July 29, 1905, p. 128.

(47) **"Recent Practice in Hydraulic-Fill Dam Construction,"** by J. D. Schuyler, *Transactions,* ASCE, Vol. LVIII, June, 1907, p. 196.

(48) **"Hydraulic Fill Dams,"** by Allen Hazen, *ibid.,* Vol. LXXXIII, 1919–1920, p. 1713.

(49) **"Some Investigations and Studies in Hydraulic-Fill Dam Construction,"** by J. Albert Holmes, *ibid.,* Vol. LXXXIV, 1921, p. 331.

(50) "Core Studies in the Hydraulic-Fill Dams of the Miami Conservancy District," by Charles H. Paul, *Transactions*, ASCE, Vol. LXXXV, 1922, p. 1181.

(51) "Hydraulic Fill Dams," by Glennon Gilboy, *Transactions*, 1st Cong. on Large Dams, Stockholm, Sweden, 1933.

(52) "Mechanics of Hydraulic-Fill Dams," by G. Gilboy, *Journal*, Boston Soc. of Civ. Engrs., July, 1934, p. 185.

(53) "Rock Riprap Replaces Porous Concrete Slope Protection at Santee-Cooper Project," by Henry H. Jewell, *Civil Engineering*, January, 1948, p. 14.

(54) "Protecting Upstream Slope of Kingsley Dam," by Henry H. Jewell, *ibid.*, November, 1945, p. 493.

(55) "Review of Slope Protection Methods: Report of the Subcommittee on Slope Protection of the Committee on Earth Dams of the Soil Mechanics and Foundations Division," *Proceedings*, ASCE, June, 1948, p. 845.

(56) "Slope Protection for Earth Dams," Corps of Engrs. rept. (Waterways Experiment Station), March, 1949.

(57) "The Effects of San Francisco Earthquake of April 18th, 1906, on Engineering Constructions," *Transactions*, ASCE, Vol. LIX, December, 1907, Appendix C, p. 245.

(58) "Investigation of Failure of Sheffield Dam—Santa Barbara, Calif.," Corps of Engrs. (Los Angeles Dist.), Los Angeles, Calif., June, 1949.

(59) "Summary of Regional Soil Mechanics Conference," Office of the Chf. of Engrs., Washington, D. C., November, 1950.

AMERICAN SOCIETY OF CIVIL ENGINEERS
Founded November 5, 1852

TRANSACTIONS

Paper No. 2621

EFFECT OF SCIENCE ON STRUCTURAL DESIGN

By L. E. Grinter,[1] M. ASCE

Synopsis

Engineering progress in the field of structural design from the earliest times until the present is discussed in this paper. The art of design has changed radically over the years until in some aspects it has now nearly become a science. Hundreds of projects are completed in a relatively short time today that each would have required a lifetime of work by a master builder of ancient times. The development of modern structural design techniques is traced through the ages. The influence of analysis on design is discussed, as well as the effect of experimentation. The place of standardization is explained, and the promise of the future is explored.

Introduction

This paper will attempt to survey engineering progress during the past century without taking an eye off the future. However, to look backward and forward at the same time would produce lack of focus so it is proposed, in sequence, to glance backward and then to look beyond the horizon of the future. This attempt will be gazing neither at the stars nor into a crystal ball, because the pattern of development in the field of engineering design has become rather clearly defined.

Design in the Ancient World

In glancing backward at structural design over the ages astonishment must be admitted at the physical achievements of ancient civilizations whose monuments are not a matter of legend but of observable reality. To build another Great Pyramid would probably cost as much in terms of human energy, if not ingenuity, today as would a mammoth skyscraper (Fig. 1), suspension bridge, or power dam. What it cost the Egyptians in 3700 B. C. is incalculable; but this was a simple problem in design. In the Temple of Amen at Karnak (completed about 980 B. C.) the Egyptian engineers faced and solved design and construction problems that strain the imagination. In mass, this 1,200-ft temple exceeds anything in the nature of shelter ever conceived by man. The great

---

[1] Dean, Graduate School and Director of Research, Univ. of Florida, Gainesville, Fla.

central stone columns are 66 ft high and 10 ft 7 in. in diameter. Here is a structure of such mass that it would shrug off the near blast of an atom bomb almost as readily as it has ignored the storms of thirty centuries. The designers intended it to last as long as their dynasties, and it did not fail them.

Fig. 1.—A Modern Skyscraper—LaSalle-Wacker Building in Chicago, Ill. Forty-Two Stories and 481 Ft High Above Wacker Drive

However, the ancient world went far beyond the Temple of Amen in complexity of design. The Colossus of Rhodes, the Pantheon at Rome, and the Church of Hagia Sophia at Constantinople presented design problems of much greater complexity. The masonry dome of the Pantheon is a hemisphere 114 ft in diameter, whereas the great nave of Hagia Sophia is 243 ft long by 107 ft wide covered by a central dome and two half domes at the ends partly supported on masonry arches. Where is the modern designer who would ask for the task of building these structures of stone without steel ties or cement mortar? Does this mean that design has deteriorated? No—only that times have changed. Each of these structures represented the undertaking of a kingdom for one or more generations. Costs were not considered, lives meant nothing, and sacrifices elsewhere were controlled by the king. The ancient world during three or four millennia produced a few hundred structures that kindle the imagination. On the other hand, today thousands of equally astonishing structures have been produced in a generation. The problems of the designer under the two situations are not to be compared.

Design in the ancient world must have been almost wholly art. Even the simple theory of the lever was unknown. At least, Aristotle failed to explain the action of the lever, and Archimedes got no further than an understanding of the ratio of arms to weights for the simplest case of the horizontal scale. Of course, the theory of the lever concerns analysis rather than design, but design for strength and economy cannot evolve in a scientific manner without the aid of analysis. Design in the ancient world was a matter of proportion, a matter of esthetics, and a matter of experience in terms of strength and stability—in short, a matter of the highest art.

Design in the Middle Ages

The argument that the pure art of design reached its height before present times receives further substantiation by study of the great cathedrals of the Middle Ages. A Canterbury or a Chartres cathedral cost its community a fantastic price in human sacrifice, but the result must have been a sublime satisfaction to the same peasantry whose sacrifice produced it. No higher art than that of the designers and artisans of these cathedrals has ever existed or ever will. As in the ancient world the cathedral art of the Middle Ages, although of structural form, differed markedly from the art of building as known today. Its objective was to produce feeling or even emotion, to provide an atmosphere or a setting without consideration for cost, time of construction, or safety of the workers.

It seems clear that design received very little help from science until the end of the Renaissance. Galileo took time to clarify the theory of the lever—thus indicating that it had not been well understood previously. He tried to explain the flexure of beams but placed the neutral axis incorrectly. Hence it is seen that the time of his death (1642) represents the very beginning of the influence of the science of analysis on structural design.

The Influence of Analysis on Design

From the time of Galileo, analysis began to creep, to walk, to run, and finally to fly ahead. Hooke devised the law of proportionality of stress and strain in 1678. Varignon conceived the equilibrium polygon. Bernoulli became interested in the elastic curve; but Euler, in 1757, derived the formula for determining the critical load at which a slender column will buckle.

Step by step, Galileo, Mariotte, Varignon, Bernoulli, Euler, and Coulomb brought the analysis of stresses in beams closer and closer to a design technique.

Coulomb's paper in 1776 should have settled the matter, but a half century had to pass before the ordinary M c/I-formula could be widely accepted and used to produce improved design of beams.

Credit must be given to the mathematicians, particularly the French, for their work in structural analysis. Navier, Poisson, Lagrange, Laplace, Cauchy, and later Saint Venant moved the mathematical theory of elasticity forward until it became a major field of mechanics. Lamé and Clapeyron, as engineers, added their contributions. By 1860 this development had resulted in many useful mathematical solutions to problems in continuous beams, slabs, arches, earth pressures, and torsion of shafts.

Rankine, professor at the University of Glasgow, Scotland, became one of the more successful interpreters of the mathematicians' works as well as an original contributor to structural mechanics. In Great Britain, in the field of mathematical elasticity Rankine followed Green and Stokes and was in turn followed by Maxwell and Lord Kelvin. To Maxwell goes credit for the first adequate theory of analysis of statically indeterminate structures, which ultimately led through a chain of original contributions and interpretations to the present simplified techniques of the design office.

The American tradition in analysis practically began in 1847 with the work of Squire Whipple, Hon. M. ASCE, on "Bridge Building." Whipple had succeeded at last in analyzing for the forces in the bars of a simple span truss.

By 1870 analysis had reached its unfolding and in about a decade Cullman developed graphical statics; Winkler explained the use of the influence line; Maxwell solved graphically the problem of truss analysis; Mohr and Greene devised the methods of area moments; Mohr and Land invented the circle of stress for determining principal stresses at a point; and Williot presented his diagram for determining deflections of trusses. Castigliano used least work as a tool for deflection computation. Müller-Breslau applied Maxwell's theorem of reciprocal deflections to show that the deflected load line of the structure may be made to represent an influence line for reaction or moment or stress. All these contributions came before the end of the nineteenth century.

During the past 50 years only two techniques in structural analysis of equivalent significance can be noted. The method of slope deflection, in part conceived by Manderla in 1878, was expressed and used by Wilbur M. Wilson, Hon. M. ASCE, and G. A. Maney, M. ASCE, in 1915; and, finally, the methods of distribution were initiated, as far as structural engineers are concerned, by Hardy Cross, Hon. M. ASCE, in 1930.

How have these developments of analysis influenced design? Design preceded analysis and would have progressed without analytical tools, but how far could it have gone? The concept of stress is not very helpful in design as long as it is merely qualified by the adjective high or low. However, when a stress of 20,000 lb per sq in. is mentioned, a design viewpoint is developed. Such a stress is beyond the capacity of timber or plain concrete. Therefore, it must refer to a structural metal—steel or aluminum alloy or titanium. Analysis further qualifies this stress of 20,000 lb per sq in. as tensile, compressive, or shear, and an axis or direction is specified. Stresses at 90° thereto are relevant and usually calculable. The change of the stress with time may be specified if fatigue or impact is significant. The derivative of the stress with respect to position or the stress gradient is a determinable factor of significance. These many scientific qualifications of unit stress, all of which influence the ability of stress to produce flow or fracture, indicate that analysis and design can no longer be clearly separated. They have grown together as the art of engineering has been changed by the age of science.

EXPERIMENTATION

Science has been brought to bear on the practical art of engineering design from another direction as well. The laboratory science of experimentation has

FIG. 2.—ARTHUR NEWELL TALBOT, 1857–1942, PAST-PRESIDENT AND HON. M. ASCE, WHOSE FAME IN RESEARCH IS PERPETUATED IN THE TALBOT LABORATORY, UNIVERSITY OF ILLINOIS AT URBANA

had an influence nearly equal to that of analysis. Many of the famous men already mentioned were also experimenters. If only one other man were to be cited, A. N. Talbot, Past-President and Hon. M. ASCE, whose contribution to the knowledge of reinforced concrete is of such magnitude as to make his name a symbol of thoughtful experimentation, would have to be chosen (Fig. 2).

The experimenters have given two approaches to improved design. Paramount in importance have been their studies of the physical properties of materials. Before the year 1900 a designer might have been reasonably certain of the tensile strength and possibly of the yield strength of the steel to be used in his structure. By comparison, today it would be felt that he had inadequate information as to even these two elementary properties and almost no information as to resistance to multiaxial stresses and impact. Ship failures occurred during and after World War II, and there are still great gaps in knowledge about the service life and fracture loading of fabricated structures. Current reports tell of ships that split in two, and this has happened while the vessels were floating beside the dock. Unhappily, it is known that bridges and buildings contain the same complexity of stresses, are built of the same materials, involve similar uncertainties of analysis and design, are exposed to the same temperature changes, and occasionally have failed in the same brittle fashion. Is the relatively small number of brittle fractures experienced in the structural field a matter of luck or will the same surprises that the naval architect has experienced face the structural engineer as the greater use of complete continuity by welding develops? Engineers who study the properties of materials and particularly how and why materials fail provide the foundation for design.

The other side of structural experimentation has been the testing of members, joints, and whole structures either as models or as field prototypes. The objective of such tests is invariably to extend the knowledge of the action and failure of materials in order to predict the action and failure of members, joints, and whole structures. This type of testing is much criticized by scientists as being unscientific because of the large number of variables encompassed in one model or its prototype. However, when faced with problems that cannot be solved by the approved techniques of scientific experimentation—that is, by isolation of variables or by tests planned for statistical analysis—the engineer turns to measurements of stress, deflection, or acceleration made on a structural model or on the prototype or on some isolated part or member. Such measurements have their greatest value as check points for testing the validity of a theory of structural action. When used in this manner the testing of large-scale models or prototypes becomes a scientific approach to the improvement of design.

The Purpose of Standards and Standardization

The great structures of the past were built by those who fully justified the title of master builder. Today hundreds of structures are built in a relatively short time to each of which a master builder of the past would have devoted months or years of his life. Plans are provided by offices staffed without genius and in many instances with only the lower levels of engineering competence. Standards like building codes and accepted or conventional tools of analysis, such as the transformed section of the concrete beam, provide controls for the safety of the end product that flows from the flume of American construction industry.

Engineers may grumble at the restrictions on their individuality as designers that codes and conventions produce, but there is no visible substitute therefor. The mere volume of construction in the United States, and its concentration into years of high activity, make standardization inevitable.

An influential consideration is the unbalanced system of education in which the great preponderance of attention is given to the mass production of young men who are trained to fill routine positions, with very limited attention paid to the special training of those who have the capacity to become master engineers or leaders of the profession. With the gradual change of structural engineering from an art to a science, the requirements for a master engineer in the future will differ considerably from the special abilities of those who have been named in the past.

In one respect, however, no change is possible. The unchanged characteristic must be vision—the quality of the planner, the thinker, the successful researcher, the inventor, the experimenter, and the real builder. The master engineer will have the vision and desire to search for solutions to man's need for better and less costly shelter and for new structural aids to transportation.

Science and Art in Design

At several places in this paper the gradual change from art to science and its influence on design have been noted. The effect of analysis on design has also been gradual, and the power of this influence is still increasing. In another century, with machines available to solve all equations, it seems likely that stress analysis of three-dimensional shapes and assemblages will be as common as the analysis of two-dimensional shapes or assemblages is today. Such information will be supplemented by extensive experimentation on the many important cases of three-dimensional stress to determine their influence on flow and on fracture.

To what extent then will design ultimately become a science rather than an art? As far as design for strength and design for resistance to vibration or shock are concerned, a dominating influence of science is to be expected. However, design has other facets that are not as subject to illumination by science. There are social and economic considerations in design. There are esthetic and functional aspects. There are time schedules and shortages and labor laws and codes and construction practices and even politics for the designer to weigh and consider. Structural design is the art of harmonizing all these influences with due consideration for strength and safety. Design will therefore always require the exercise of highly developed judgment, which is an application of art tempered and guided by scientific knowledge.

The Promise of the Future

After examining these thoughts about design, engineers have a right to wonder what the results of the envisioned developments should be after another century. Will structures be built more cheaply? They will—perhaps not in devalued dollars, but certainly in man-hours of labor. All considerations of the influence of science on design indicate that man's laborious placing of one small brick on another is a carryover from the Middle Ages. Except where esthetics may influence its use, hand labor is doomed to extinction. This principle goes far beyond a single application. Why has welding begun to replace riveting? Among other reasons, because it more nearly fulfils the proved superiority of a continuous operation over an intermittent one. When improvements in manufacture become available, research engineers eventually solve the new problems of stress and strain that they produce. Why have precast joists been so useful—because the precast joist most nearly fits the assembly-line technique that has cut the cost of every home gadget that can be mentioned.

In trying to picture the future direction of the development of the construction industry, highly centralized organizations such as the automotive industry and the oil refineries serve as a mirror. These examples clearly demonstrate that lower cost and greater service have come from a few great wholly American concepts that influence design: Continuous operations tend to replace intermittent operations; duplication of parts is essential to economic design; assembly-line techniques increase the productivity of labor; and machine operations continuously replace hand operations. Of course, certain standardizations in the design of the end product are essential to the effective use of the techniques mentioned, and these techniques require centralized organizations and volume production. However, no matter how designers may react to these trends, which clearly represent restrictions on individuality, it is evident that they produce lower costs in man-hours of labor and therefore will continue to raise the standard of living of mankind. These concepts represent the trend of the times. They will guide the mind of the designer as he guides the hands of the draftsmen of the future.

AMERICAN SOCIETY OF CIVIL ENGINEERS

Founded November 5, 1852

TRANSACTIONS

Paper No. 2622

WOOD FOR ENGINEERING USE

By L. J. Markwardt,[1] M. ASCE

Synopsis

Wood is among the oldest structural materials yet is still widely used in many capacities on construction and building projects. This paper emphasizes the relative importance of wood in construction and discusses the technical advances already achieved in the development and application of this versatile material. The subjects of grading and the establishment of working stresses are treated briefly in relation to their effect on the design of timber structures. The newer applications of wood are described, and a brief summary of necessary research is given.

Introduction

As a result of unprecedented engineering and related scientific progress during the past century, the engineer today has available a vast choice of materials that permit seemingly infinite variety in design and appearance. In fact, this period has embraced more technological advancement and development than occurred in the entire previous history of civilization—as if, over the centuries, the floodwaters of human achievement had been accumulating back of some huge dam, awaiting the magic of a twentieth century Aladdin's lamp to be released to perform miracles for the modern world.

However, this diversity of materials, together with the better technical information concerning them, has imposed on the engineer the serious problem and the challenge of keeping abreast of developments and of current literature. It has brought about the necessity of specialization—of knowing more and more about less and less—and of evolving means of integrating these specializations. In no field is this more true than in the technology of wood, which on the one hand has shared with other materials the significant progress that has broadened the horizons of use and, on the other hand, because of its orthotropic structure, has presented more complications from the standpoint of properties and design details.

Wood is among the oldest structural materials and has served man from time immemorial. It is not difficult to imagine that perhaps a fallen tree served as the first bridge across a stream. Later, fashioned by the skill of early craftsmen, wood

---

[1] Asst. Director, Forest Products Laboratory, Madison, Wis.

structural elements found their way into monumental structures, many of which are still in existence. It is a far cry from the empiricism of yesteryear to the efficient timber design of today.

The Importance of Wood.—In this industrial and mechanical age, with its guided missiles and pushbutton techniques, the question may well be asked:

> "What is the place of wood, one of our earliest and still one of our most abundant raw materials? Can wood and wood products compete with other materials in a mechanical age?"

On every hand, and in thousands of uses, there is abundant evidence of the utility of wood itself, as well as of the wood-base materials processed through mechanical and chemical conversion—railway ties, transmission line poles, piles, mine props, furniture, buildings, paper, rayon, photographic film, and smokeless powder, to mention but a few.

More specifically, there are nearly 2,000 miles of wood trestles and bridges on the first-class railroad lines of the United States. Thousands of large modern structures employing relatively new techniques and developments in the form of wood trusses and glued laminated arches have been constructed. Of the more than 1,000,000 homes a year built under the unprecedented postwar housing program, more than 75% are of wood-frame construction. The consumption of wood-fiber products has been materially increasing. The commodities today being made in unprecedented volume are largely packaged for shipment in wood or fiber containers, and the chemical products of wood are finding new and unpredictable uses and applications almost daily.

In addition to normal requirements, an ever-increasing quantity and greater variety of wood products are required for waging modern war. In naval use, for example, wood and steel rank as the two principal structural materials for building and maintaining the modern fleet. Approximately 9,000,000 tons of steel were needed by the United States Navy in a single typical war year. Wood requirements for a similar period were 3,000,000 tons, and wood was rated first in volume and second in tonnage of raw materials needed for all types of naval military construction, afloat and ashore. More than 2,000 vessels and 43,000 small boats made of wood were used during World War II.

Forest Products Industries.—Forest products industries collectively constitute big business, which is largely carried on by little businesses. There are some 25,000 to 50,000 small sawmills scattered over various sections of the United States. Together with a limited number of larger mills, the small units provide for the nation's lumber production. The wood products industries employ about 2,000,000 people, produce material valued at more than $10,000,000,000 annually, and in 1939 ranked fourth in number of wage earners and sixth in value of product.

Domestic Lumber.—In the United States alone the annual lumber production in recent years has been on the order of 35,000,000,000 board-ft to 40,000,000,000 board-ft. In a normal year, about 60% of this production is used for buildings and other construction. On a per capita basis, lumber consumption has, with some deviations, continued at the very high level of more than 200 board-ft per capita during the past century. The per capita use of 228 board-ft in 1949 compares closely with the 232 board-ft reported for 1849, a century ago. Greatly increased consumption for the two decades from 1890 to 1910 historically marked the logging of the great white pine forests of the Lake States and the pine forests of the South, concurrently with the building up of the Midwest at the time of its great industrial and agricultural expansion and development.

TECHNICAL PROGRESS

If the century of progress is reviewed in relation to the use of wood, it becomes clear that the most significant and extensive engineering developments took place during the latter half of this period.

Evaluation of Physical and Mechanical Properties.—The turn of the twentieth century found the United States with a splendid heritage of forest resources. Basic information about the strength properties of American species was, however, very scanty, inadequate, and unreliable for engineering purposes as regards all but a very few species of old growth. With the establishment of research facilities, the evaluation of physical and mechanical properties of wood was promptly recognized as one of the most important needs. Since test data are intimately related to test methods, it was first necessary to develop systematic standard test procedures. The procedures followed conform to ASTM Standard D143–52, "Standard Methods of Testing Small Clear Specimens of Timber."

With some progressive modifications, the basic test methods have continued to afford an accumulation of directly comparable data. Similar procedures have been used in other countries. In the evaluation of properties, it was wisely decided to select the test material in the forest. Thereby exact botanical identification was established and basic supplementary data obtained on origin, growth conditions, elevation, and like factors. Provision was made also for testing both green and dry material to afford data on the effect of moisture content.

During the past 50 years, extensive basic data have been obtained on the strength and related properties of some two hundred species of wood. These data are now being extended to cover second-growth timber, which often is found to have characteristics somewhat different from those of old-growth timber. Considering the many species of trees and their differences in growth characteristics, there will be a continuing need for further evaluation.

Factors Affecting Strength.—It has long been known that many factors affect the strength of wood, but continued research has greatly widened the available knowledge concerning them. Among these factors are moisture content, rate of loading, duration of stress, temperature, direction of grain, position of growth rings, and the influence of such growth and inherent variables as knots, cross grain, shakes, and checks. Through extensive studies on the effect of moisture content, for example, it has been shown that most strength properties increase with loss of moisture below the fiber-saturation point and that the relationship of strength to moisture can be expressed as an exponential curve (Fig. 1). The mechanics of moisture-strength adjustment has thus been established for wood in which the moisture is uniformly distributed so that there is no moisture gradient.

Likewise, related studies of structural members have shown the effect of knots with respect to size and position, and the effect of cross grain, shakes, and checks.

These data serve as a basis for establishing limitations on the natural characteristics that affect strength, for the purpose of assigning definite working stresses to structural timbers according to grade.

Structural Grading of Timber.—Individual pieces of lumber, as they come from the saw, represent a wide range in quality and appearance. There are varying degrees of freedom from knots, blemishes, defects, and other detrimental characteristics. Such random pieces, consequently, also represent a wide range in strength, utility, serviceability, and value. An obvious requirement for the orderly marketing of lumber, therefore, is the establishment of grades, the function of which is to provide utility classes that make it possible to segregate individual pieces generally similar in desired characteristics.

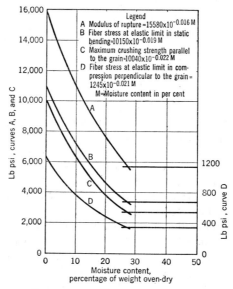

Fig. 1.—Relation Between Strength and Moisture Content of Small, Clear Specimens of Sitka Spruce

Many lumber grades are established on the basis of the appearance and physical characteristics of the individual piece, with certain uses in mind but without particular regard for strength. Other grades, called structural, are based on the classification of features relating to strength and strength uses. Marked improvement and unification in lumber grading resulted from the establishment of American Lumber Standards, and from the adoption by manufacturers of structural grades that permit the assignment of definite working stresses.

Economy of material is obtained when all structural units are used at a stress approaching the allowable maximum, and this can be effected only when the material is of relatively uniform quality. It is the function of an efficient grading specification to classify timber of any species into quality grades by properly and adequately limiting the permissible defects and strength factors to the end that definite minimum strength is assured and maximum efficiency of utilization is obtained. Structural grading is thus accomplished by visual examination of the timber, in which the location as well as the size of knots and other features appearing on the surfaces are evaluated.

Through the analysis and integration of available data, a comprehensive set of simple basic principles for grading structural timber has been established and has been adopted by the American Society for Testing Materials under the title, "Tentative Methods for Establishing Structural Grades of Timber," ASTM Designation D245–49T. The basic principles are applicable to all species of wood and permit the establishment of grades for different classes of lumber having any desired percentage of the strength of the clear wood. The important lumber-producing associations now provide lumber that conforms to the basic principles of structural grading and to which definite allowable working stresses can be assigned. This development is one of the most important from the standpoint of permitting efficient and economical timber engineering design.

WORKING STRESSES

Establishment of Allowable Stress.—Safe working stresses are an essential corollary of structural grading. Although tables of working stresses abound in engineering literature, many of the early recommendations were based on fragmentary and inadequate strength data, and on very incomplete information about the factors that affect strength. As a result, the recommendations often varied widely among themselves, were usually overconservative, and generally were not associated with particular structural grade requirements.

With the availability of technical research data on basic factors affecting strength and on properties of different species, a complete reanalysis of working stresses for structural timber was made. The principal factors entering into the establishment of the recommended working stresses for each species include the inherent strength of the wood, the reduction in strength from natural characteristics permitted in the grade, the effect of long-time loading, the variability of individual species, the possibility of some slight overloading, the characteristics of the species, the size of member and the related influence of seasoning, and the factor of safety.

The effect of these factors is to require a lower strength value for practical use conditions than the average value obtained from tests on small clear specimens. The combined effect may be embodied in a single factor, sometimes erroneously called a "factor of safety," that can be applied to averages from tests on small clear specimens to obtain safe working stresses. It is evident that the larger part of this factor is required to correlate laboratory test results with actual conditions of use, and that only a small part can be considered a true factor of safety.

The revised working stresses for the commonly available commercial species of lumber provide a means of economical and efficient design, particularly when used with structurally graded lumber. The working stresses have been widely accepted in general engineering design, and significantly are being incorporated in current revisions of engineering handbooks. They are the basis for the design recommendations presented in the National Design Specifications published by the National Lumber Manufacturers' Association.

Duration of Stress.—Wood is among the materials that are affected by rate of loading or duration of stress (Fig. 2). Studies have been under way to obtain more definite information on this factor as it affects design procedure. These studies have included rapid-loading tests, in which the maximum load may be reached in a few seconds or less, for use in aircraft design; and so-called dead-load tests, in which constant loads are applied for long periods or until failure occurs.

Studies on the effect of rapid loading have confirmed some less extensive earlier results, which show for Sitka spruce, at 12% moisture content, a 17% increase in modulus of rupture in bending for 3-sec loading over that for the 5-min loading in the standard static bending test.

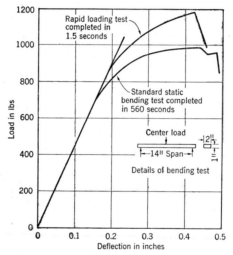

FIG. 2.—BENDING TESTS OF MATCHED SITKA SPRUCE SPECIMENS

Data have also been developed that provide a basis for modification of working stresses for loads of short duration, such as wind stresses and other conditions that involve engineering judgment. For example, a curve has been devised to express the relation between load in bending and duration of stress for small clear specimens of Douglas fir at a constant moisture content of 12%. Load is expressed as a percentage of normal strength, as in Fig. 3, and the duration appears on a logarithmic scale. The solid part of the curve indicates the limits of the test data in this study. Prolongation of the line in the direction of higher load is verified by other tests, whereas extrapolation in the direction of the lower load is yet unproved. These results are applicable to conditions of uniform moisture content.

Fatigue of Wood.—Another phase of research relates to the development of engineering data on fatigue. Fatigue tests of wood and glued wood constructions have indicated that failures due to repeated or reversed loads develop in much the same manner as they do for metals, except that, in fatigue of wood, the appearance of the failures produced by repeated loads is similar to that of the failures produced by a single loading.

The "S-N" (stress versus number of cycles to failure) curves obtained from tests of wood or wood-base materials are similar to those obtained for nonferrous metals—that is, the curves are concave downward for high levels of stress and

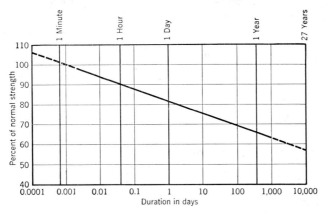

FIG. 3.—DURATION OF STRESS IN TRANSVERSE BENDING OF DOUGLAS FIR SPECIMEN

concave upward for the lower levels of stress, and the two curved sections are usually connected by an approximately straight line.

Comparisons of the results of tests on fatigue of wood with those on certain other materials suggest that, when other things such as conditions of loading are equal, wood ranks relatively high in fatigue resistance. For example, fatigue

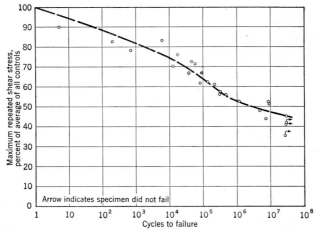

FIG. 4.—FATIGUE TESTS OF LAMINATED GLUED SHEAR SPECIMENS, DOUGLAS FIR

tests of wood in tension parallel to grain indicate that the level of stress at which the specimen can be expected to sustain many million cycles of stress without failing is a greater percentage of the static strength than that for some metals in tension. Data from these and similar studies, as shown in Fig. 4, are being published as they become available, and give reassurance regarding the ability of wood to withstand fatigue, and on the performance of glued construction as well.

Joints and Fastenings.—Because of the wide difference in the properties of wood along and across the grain, joints and fastenings are the Achilles heel of timber construction wherever they are employed. The older common forms of fasteners include nails, screws, bolts, lag screws, and drift pins. All these have advantages and also limitations.

One of the newer types of fastenings that have greatly widened the horizon of wood construction is the so-called metal connector. When this connector was introduced in the United States in 1930, its possibilities were quickly recognized. Strength tests established the most promising forms and furnished basic design

FIG. 5.—TIMBER TRUSSES FOR NAVY HANGARS

data for use under optimum conditions. Simultaneously, commercial development of certain improved types was undertaken.

The use by the construction industry of timber connectors in trusses and other heavy timber construction, on the basis of the technical design data developed, permitted the erection of large structures previously beyond the range of timber design (Fig. 5). In the decade after the introduction of timber connectors more than 100,000 structures were built in which modern connectors were used, employing about 5,000,000,000 ft of lumber valued at $165,000,000. The amount of lumber in these structures used directly with the connectors approximated 1,000,000,000 ft.

Connectors are devices used in conjunction with bolts to increase the efficiency of joints in wood members. The split-ring type fits into precut grooves; the alligator type is pressed into the wood between the members to be jointed; and other types fit into bored recesses. Whatever the type, they all serve to reinforce the joint by providing effective shear resistance between the members. Research has included evaluation of the strength of several of the types in a range of sizes, applied in various ways, when used with different species of wood.

Glued Laminated Construction.—Developments in adhesives and in gluing techniques—a result of cooperation among chemical industries, wood industries, and research laboratories—have made available adhesives to fit nearly any condition of service and have led to the establishment and expansion of the glued laminated construction industry. The products of this industry—structural members that are fabricated by gluing smaller pieces of wood, either straight or in curved form, with the grain of all laminations in the direction of the length of the member—have found wide acceptance because of their versatility and architectural possibilities.

A considerable amount of research has led to the development of much background data for the establishment of design procedures. Tests on arches, beams, and columns have covered such factors as knots, stress concentrations around butt joints, effectiveness of end joints of various types, result of bending laminations to a curved form prior to gluing, and the like.

In addition to laboratory tests, experimental installations to determine the practicability of large laminated timbers have been made on a number of railroads. The practicality of this type of construction for a variety of applications has been demonstrated over the past 20 years or so in the United States and for more than twice that long in Europe by the good service of existing structures.

Wood As an Orthotropic Material

The character, orientation, and arrangement of the fibers make wood an anisotropic material. For all practical purposes, however, it may be treated as orthotropic, with three principal axes of symmetry, the longitudinal, the radial, and the tangential. The assumption of three structural axes results in a variety and complexity of properties. These are: Three Young's moduli, varying from 150 to 1; three shear moduli, varying from 20 to 1; six Poisson's ratios, varying from 40 to 1; and nine strength properties, varying with grain direction (three in tension, three in compression, and three in shear). These widely different properties of wood along and across the grain involve a complicated mathematical treatment in special design problems. Through basic research, general formulas have been established for the solution of critical design problems for wood.

New Uses of Wood

Plywood.—Plywood is another wood product that is dependent on adhesives, and provides a dimensionally stable product of unique properties in large sheet form. In plywood, the orthotropic structure of wood is further diversified by a reorientation of the material. It consists of a combination of three or more sheets of veneer, with the grain of alternate plies usually at right angles.

Because plywood can be made with any desired number of plies from veneer of any desired thickness and from any species or combination of species, it has a versatility that affords almost unlimited choice in design for special purposes. Further diversification can be obtained by orienting the grain of adjacent plies not only at right angles but at various angles. By this means, material can be constructed to meet special design needs for aircraft and other uses. Dimensional stability results from the cross-banded construction, and freedom from warping and cupping is obtained by using balanced construction, which invariably consists of an odd number of plies.

In reorienting the direction of the grain of the veneer to make plywood, the strength of the wood in one direction is improved at the expense of that in the other direction. The greater the number of plies for a given thickness, the more nearly equal are the strength properties in the two directions of the panel, and the greater is the resistance to splitting.

"Stressed-Skin" Construction.—Another significant research development with various possible fields of application is "stressed-skin" construction, which has served as the basis for panel design in prefabricated house construction. The principle of the stressed skin is founded on the engineering concept that all material in a structure should contribute directly to its strength, as compared with conventional frame construction, in which a frame carries the interior and exterior wall covering largely as "parasite" material.

Stressed-skin construction is secured by gluing sheets of a rigid material, such as plywood, to either or both sides of an inner structural framework to form what is virtually a box girder. The stressed-skin principle of prefabricated construction thus gives opportunity to design more closely and with greater economy of material.

As an example of the strength and stiffness that can be obtained with smaller than conventional sizes, a 14-ft, stressed-skin floor panel about 6 in. thick has a maximum strength as a beam of about 300 lb per sq ft, with a deflection less than 1/360 of the span at design load. A 3-in.-thick wall panel has a transverse strength equivalent to 200 lb per sq ft.

Sandwich and Composite Construction.—There has been a growing interest in the possibilities, for many applications, of lightweight composite or sandwich construction. This development is based on the concept, not of using or favoring any one material, but rather of employing, as occasion requires, all available materials. It goes even further in that it sets up, for certain uses, desired requirements as to mechanical and physical properties that are not characteristic of any specific material. These objectives provide a target for further development. Another feature of the sandwich construction is the opportunity, through efficient structural design, of stressing each material to the practical limit of its possibilities.

While the concept of sandwich construction is not new, it is the combination of the relatively recent advances in adhesives and fabricating techniques, the development of a variety of facing and core materials, and particularly the need for more efficient lightweight structures in aircraft, that has brought about the sandwich era.

Special mention is made of sandwich construction because of the extensive use of wood and wood-base materials for facings and cores, and because the design criteria for plywood provided a logical and effective springboard for the development of design criteria for sandwich construction.

Present and potential uses for sandwich construction include radomes, airplane fuselages and wings, airplane flooring, doors, bulkheads, ailerons, and flaps; walls, ceilings, and partitions in railway cars; hatches, partitions, and bulkheads in boats; and doors, frames, wall panels, and floor panels in houses.

In this design, the physical properties of the plate are described by eight elastic properties: The flexural stiffness in the two plate directions; torsional rigidity in two directions; the two transverse moduli of elasticity in shear; and the Poisson's ratios in the direction of the two axes. The sandwich design procedure, perhaps oversimplified, may be considered to consist of: (1) Determining the thickness of the facings of a predetermined material necessary to carry the design load on the basis of the properties of the material; and (2) subsequently computing the thickness of the core required to permit the functioning of the facings while carrying the load.

Through the cooperation of the United States Navy Bureau of Aeronautics, the Wright Air Development Center, United States Air Force, and the Civil Aeronautics Administration, extensive design data for sandwich construction particularly applicable to aircraft design have been developed at the Forest Products Laboratory in Madison, Wis., but the methods generally apply to all sandwich design. The transportation industries have much to gain through lighter-weight constructions, and are exploring the possibilities that sandwich design offers. Thus, the already significant developments in sandwich construction in recent years presage ever-increasing applications to a wide variety of uses. Each type has its own requirements, its own range of possibilities, and its own problems to be solved.

A composite construction, in which a creosoted timber base is overlaid with a lightly reinforced-concrete mat intimately bonded to it in shear, has been extensively employed in bridge decks, piers, and other heavy-duty flooring systems. Special shear keys or other types of shear developers are employed to secure adequate bond between the two materials. A significant advantage of composite construction is its simplicity, in that joist-and-stringer systems are not required and the timber base serves in lieu of form material for supporting the concrete when poured. A considerable number of projects employing a composite design of wood and concrete are currently under construction.

Destructive Agencies and Their Control

There is of course no such thing as absolute permanence for any engineering material under all conditions of service and use. The engineer must be continually on the alert to improve properties to meet special serviceability requirements and to extend the useful life of the material. Hence, there is naturally much concern over destructive agencies and their control, and such terms as decay, rust, corrosion, electrolysis, embrittlement, spalling, decomposition, and aging are in everyday use.

Wood is no exception, and its preservation requires the control of a group of destructive agencies largely peculiar to itself. The principal causes of the deterioration of wood, in their general order of importance, are: Decay, fire, insects and marine borers, mechanical wear and breakage, weathering, and chemical decomposition. Damage or total destruction may result from any one of these causes alone, but it is more common where two or more of them are at work at the same time.

As a result of research and experience over a great many years, control and remedial measures are available to guard wood against most, if not all, of the destructive agencies to any desired extent. Economic considerations are also important in establishing a balance between cost of protective measures, when this cost is substantial in relation to the cost of replacement. In the problem of control, it is at once essential to know the nature of each destructive agent and the conditions under which it develops.

Decay in wood is produced by organisms known as fungi, which live on the wood substance. Wood-destroying fungi require favorable conditions' for their development with respect to moisture, temperature, and air; hence, if any one of these requirements is eliminated, the growth of fungi will be inhibited. Thus wood that is below a certain critical moisture content presents no decay hazard. Likewise, by maintaining wood at extremely high or low temperatures the development of fungi is prevented, just as it is where wood is immersed in water.

Under conditions favorable to decay, two effective methods of prevention may be employed: (1) Selection of species of high natural resistance to decay, or (2) use of a preservative treatment. A considerable variety of wood preservatives is available to meet different requirements.

Much study has been given to means for protecting wood from fire and for retarding or preventing the effects of exposure to fire. Fire-retardant coatings have been developed that are effective on interior finishing or structural wood products. Impregnation treatments with suitable chemicals may also be employed to impart fire resistance. It is generally recognized that large structural members of wood do not readily support combustion, and because of their low thermal conductivity maintain loads over considerable periods of fire exposure.

Length of Service.—Although wood, like other materials, is subject to attack by various destructive agents, methods are in general available to prolong its life when destructive agents are to be encountered. As far as is known, the lignin and cellulose which constitute the wood substance are not subject to chemical changes with time when kept dry, although the color of wood may be slightly changed by long-continued exposure to air. Consequently wood can be expected to last indefinitely when not subjected to deteriorating agencies.

Literally hundreds of well-designed bridges made entirely or partly of wood have served satisfactorily and with but little attention for long periods. Many that are more than a century old are still in service. Others, although still in satisfactory condition, have been altered or replaced to meet demands for greater width of roadway and higher load capacity than were called for when they were built.

In Europe, many wood structures or structural units that are centuries old are still in existence. Perhaps the most notable are the trusses in the Basilica of Saint Paul at Rome, Italy, part of which was constructed in 816, during the pontificate of Leo III. Certain such roof trusses are known to have given service for more than 1,000 years.

FUTURE RESEARCH

Significant as have been the achievements relating to the more efficient engineering uses of wood, it should not be overlooked that there are still many challenging possibilities. An important one is that of developing a system of preferred stresses so as greatly to reduce and simplify the number of design stresses to be used. Such a development would permit design at some selected stress level, with the assurance that suitable material to carry out the designs would be available from a choice of species, or at some future time. Another important contribution to timber design would be the simplification of design procedures, which admittedly are now more complicated than those for most other materials.

Much more research is also needed on joints and fastenings, to include the integration and unification of data for the various types of fastening mediums. More detailed and basic information is needed for the design of structures subjected to sudden or shock loading, such as that due to earthquakes, in order to insure safety and permit more economical design. These are but a few of the many problems awaiting extensive research to widen further the horizons of timber design and use, and to aid timber design in keeping pace with developments in other materials and with the requirements of the modern age.

Wood is unique in being a renewable resource. As long as the sun shines and the rains fall, there need be no shortage of wood in the world if the forests are managed well and man learns to use the tools of industry, the products of modern industrial civilization, for the more nearly complete employment of wood in meeting human needs. The forest resource is unique in that its proper harvesting is the best possible means of insuring a permanent timber supply.

AMERICAN SOCIETY OF CIVIL ENGINEERS

Founded November 5, 1852

TRANSACTIONS

Paper No. 2623

ACCOMPLISHMENTS IN TIMBER TECHNOLOGY

By Charles A. Chaney,[1] A. M. ASCE

Synopsis

The development of timber engineering has progressed rapidly since prehistoric man first utilized rough-hewn wood for weapons and crude shelters. This paper reviews the more important advances and the agents responsible for them. Mechanization and research are described in their relation to more efficient use of timber resources. A brief discussion of the need for conservation and reforestation is included.

Foreword

No more dramatic story can be told than that of man's use of wood for many of his vital needs, from primeval days up through the ages to the present. Wood was the first structural material and is still depended on for a multitude of uses.

Intensive research has been conducted for many years to determine the physical qualities of wood and its reaction under load. Educational institutions are keeping abreast of this research, and producing engineers trained by scientific methods to utilize wood economically and safely. This paper discusses the practical uses of wood developed in former years, and today's accepted practices that have resulted from greatly increased technical knowledge in the field of timber engineering.

Historical Development

As with all man's accomplishments, progress in developing proper treatment of forest products has been slow. To illustrate, early man used wood for his weapons and crude shelters. A little later he probably depended on wood as a fuel, and a hollowed-out log as his canoe. From this crude beginning he learned how to shape the wood and fit it together into more complicated structures, such as buildings, bridges, and ships. Structures built as late as 100 years ago followed practices developed mainly through experience. Very little was known at that time about stress grading and stress analysis, as these subjects are known and applied today. Also, at that time, machinery for milling was rather simple,

---

[1] Cons. Engr., Rockville, Md.; and Project Mgr., Graving Docks, Bureau of Yards and Docks, Washington, D. C.

limiting both the quantity and the quality of work that could be performed, thereby necessitating handwork for much of the milling, shaping, and fitting. As a result, artisans developed a skill that is still unsurpassed.

A brief review of man's assets in regard to timber construction a century ago is in order. There were virgin forests far in excess of his needs and therefore he undoubtedly passed by or simply destroyed many trees with stress grades used today. In fact, in some sections trees were a drug on the market and were removed indiscriminately to make room for much-needed tillable land and local improvements. Water-powered sawmills, with a capacity of only a few hundred board-feet of lumber per day were in vogue. This equipment was introduced in the early 1600's. The circular saw came into usage about 1820 and the first steam-powered mill was built in 1850, but water-powered mills continued for some years thereafter.

Several wood preservatives were available at that time, and as far as can be determined they were quite frequently used for dipping and brush treatments. Pressure treating plants had not been introduced prior to 1850, and much of the durability of the timber structures was derived from the selection of materials best suited for the intended purpose.

Mechanical and Other Limitations.—The driving of piles was based on a variety of rules, with resulting confusion as to supporting capacity. The equipment for the driving operation was equally as varied and ranged from the rapid-stroke hand-powered gang driver to outfits powered by hand winches, treadmills, and water-current devices. These devices were the forerunners to the drop hammer.

In early days people were considerably handicapped in the framing of timbers. They frequently used metal shoes and bearings for the seating of compression members but were forced to resort to large wood scabs, bolted in place, to develop timber tension members. More often, wrought-iron rods were introduced to carry the tension.

These and similar limitations placed on the construction of timber buildings, bridges, piers, bulkheads, and docking facilities tended to develop skill and ingenuity to a remarkable degree. Design and construction problems were solved as they were encountered. Warehouses and other buildings constructed in the middle years of the nineteenth century had sufficient structural capacity for their intended uses. Timber bridges, piers, and wharves planned a century ago were adequate for the vehicle and cargo loads prevailing at that time. In fact, a few of these structures were still functioning after 50 or more years of service under loads far heavier than originally contemplated. Bulkhead walls and quays built a century ago of timber, or combinations of timber with stone and concrete, were of equally sound design and construction. They seldom failed as a result of load conditions, but decay, termites, and marine borers took a heavy toll where conditions were favorable to such attacks and suitable protective measures were not taken. An example of old construction is shown in Fig. 1.

TECHNOLOGICAL IMPROVEMENTS

Design Standards.—As can readily be imagined, engineers, scientists, builders, and other progressive-minded citizens conceived many means by which the safety, life, and economy of timber structures might be improved. In some instances, in both the United States and abroad, development of these ideas had progressed to such an extent that beneficial changes were noticeable by the middle of the past century. However, the "century of progress" in the scientific use of timber has been the 100 years just gone by, with the greatest forward strides probably having been made in the past 40 years.

It was realized many years ago that economic and safe design was contingent on a thorough knowledge of the nature and strength characteristics of wood, its action when loaded, an accurate stress analysis, and a method of determining a reliable stress-grade classification. In this connection, the writer wishes to ex-

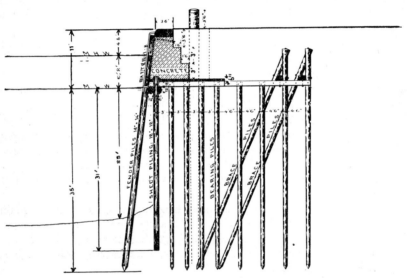

FIG. 1.—TRANSVERSE SECTION OF RELIEVING-PLATFORM-TYPE QUAY WALL, LEAGUE ISLAND NAVY YARD, PENNSYLVANIA, 1890—ALL WOOD EXCEPT CONCRETE MARGINAL WALL

press appreciation for the extensive research conducted for many years by the United States Forest Service (including the Forest Products Laboratory), the Department of the Navy, the National Lumber Manufacturers' Association, independent laboratories, and various universities. Their combined efforts have served to establish the basic principles which are in use today.

Concurrently, it was realized that companion steps must be taken in the more practical phases of timber application if the maximum value of timber was to be realized. As a result of other research—and studies of tests and structures under field conditions—tremendous gains have been made in manufacturing and assembling; selection of grades and species; discovery of causes of possible deteriorating influences; preservative treatments; and, probably most important, the conservation of forests. Progress achieved to date, of course, is in no small measure a result of the improvement in manufacturing machinery and construction equipment. A brief review of the development of a few of the more important of these features is worthy of consideration.

One illustration of major timber construction, built near the turn of the century is given in Fig. 2. Many timber structures have long service records because of research work. Two striking examples are: First, the Lake Ponchartrain (Louisiana) railroad trestle built of pressure-creosoted pine piles and timbers in 1883, which is still in use after 69 years; and, second, the fishing pier at Asbury Park, N. J., built on pressure-creosoted southern pine piles from 1885 to 1888. (When the Asbury Park structure was destroyed by a tidal wave in September, 1944, after 56 years of service, the piles still contained lots of creosote and were in excellent condition.)

FIG. 2.—SIMPSON-TYPE TIMBER GRAVING DRYDOCK NEW YORK (N. Y.) NAVY YARD; BUILT IN 1912 AND STILL IN SERVICE, 1953

Mechanization.—The development of the steam engine, and later the widespread use of electrical energy, revolutionized sawing and planing mills. Increased availability of power permitted the use of high-speed mechanisms; and semiautomatic controls, first introduced about 1880, eliminated many of the hazards and delays of hand operations. The year 1869 witnessed the initiation of the most important improvement in the sawmill: The band saw. This tool rapidly gained in popularity, particularly in the mills of the states on the Great Lakes, and during the next 20 years lumber production assumed great momentum. New inventions and more efficient techniques of operation rapidly brought lumber manufacturing to the forefront.

Most of the larger modern plants are now equipped with band saws of several types including single and double cutting saws, vertical and horizontal band resaws, and gang saws. Improved automatic conveyors, tables, and carriages now permit the log to enter the mill and fan out into manufactured timbers and lumber with a minimum amount of manual effort. The output of the mills in

1952 is many times that of the mills of a century ago. In addition, smaller mills often accommodate the cuttings from isolated areas and provide for local needs. The mills are now capable of meeting any national emergency requirement in a minimum of time.

The advent of heavy milling machinery, during the past 50 years, is another factor that has been of great benefit to timber engineering. Timbers that are dressed to uniform size facilitate fabrication and construction. Timber sheet piling, of the tongue-and-groove, or the ship-lapped, or the spline types, is now available for the construction of tight bulkheads to retain fine-grained fill materials. Of course, the beautifully finished millwork in homes and offices is tangible proof of the advantages of mechanization.

Timber Preservation.—The preservation of timber structures against attack by marine borers, termites, and fungus growths had been considered for many years as both desirable and necessary. Because of the usual impracticability of eliminating air or moisture, two of the necessities of these destructive agents, efforts were rightly centered on poisoning the timber that is the food supply for all three kinds of attack. However, a method of injecting the chemicals into the wood was lacking.

It is believed that early creosote, then known as heavy oil of coal tar, was first used by Franz Moll in 1836. However, the practical introduction of the process is credited to John Bethell of England, who in 1838 patented a process for impregnating wood in iron cylinders by vacuum and pressure. He also made recommendations concerning the uses for the various preservative oils and chemicals then obtainable. The first installation of such a plant in the United States is reported to have been in Vermont, in 1856, followed by one in Massachusetts in 1865. Neither of these remained in operation very long. Creosote manufactured by the distillation of coal tar was introduced in 1850. Many preservative salts, including zinc chloride, copper sulfate, and other chemical compounds in use today were discovered even before 1836.

The first successful pressure treating plant in the United States was installed by the Federal Government at the Charlestown Navy Yard in Massachusetts in 1872. In its early days the plant was used primarily for ship timbers. In 1875, the Bureau of Yards and Docks of the United States Navy, utilizing the facilities of this plant, made its first installation of pressure treated lumber and timbers in its program for the maintenance and improvement of that yard.

During this period many contributions were made to the science of wood preservation, but the one of major interest was the development of the Boulton process for treating timber by Samuel Bagster Boulton in 1879. Among other noteworthy achievements in this field were the studies of Octave Chanute, Past-President ASCE, at the end of the nineteenth century, and two important processes for pressure impregnation developed since 1900, the Rueping and Lowry empty-cell processes. Since that time the development of wood preservatives and pressure treating processes has been in equally capable hands, including several federal agencies, the American Wood Preservers' Association, and numerous industrial and private laboratories. Science and field tests have also definitely established the degree of serviceability of most preservatives for many and varied exposure conditions.

Today, most users of timber fully realize the economy of treated wood where conditions are conducive to decay or marine animal attack (Figs. 3 and 4). As a result, treating plants dot the United States and the bulk of timber subjected to destructive conditions has been previously treated according to recommended practice. Under severe destructive conditions, pressure treated wood is conservatively estimated to last from three to five times as long as the untreated wood used 100 years ago. Some 110,000,000,000 board-ft of lumber has been treated in the past 40 years. The greatly extended life of structures thus treated has been an important factor in timber conservation. Ex-

Fig. 3.—Pressure-Creosoted-Timber and Wood-Pile Relieving Platform Under Construction for Marina, Washington Channel, Washington, D. C., 1939

amples of creosoted structures that remained in usable condition after severe exposure for 40 to 50 years are too numerous and well known to mention.

Treatments.—The development of fire-resistive and fire-retardant chemicals for treatment of wood and the processes for this treatment have, in general, paralleled that of the materials used in resisting attacks by other destructive agencies. Although many have been known for several centuries and there were some isolated applications, no real progress was made until after 1900. The greatest increase in use of structural timbers treated to resist both fire and decay came during World War II. Several chemically treated timber structures of today have safely resisted fires that 100 years ago would have been disastrous. Authorities charged with the preservation of timber structures against destruction by fire are beginning to realize the value of fire-resistive treatments.

Timber Fabrication

In the mechanics of timber fabrication and construction, three developments—timber connectors, glued laminated members, and composite timber-concrete types of deck slab construction—have had a revolutionary effect. Timber has now replaced metal in many tension members. The economies effected in quantities of timber consumed and in the labor of fabrication and erection are high in comparison with earlier practices. Sticks of timber, of regulated quality, can now be fabricated in sizes otherwise difficult to procure.

A few years ago metal shoes, bearing plates, and metal gussets were usual in compression members of timber structures, but they served little purpose in the

FIG. 4.—COMPLETED MARINA IN WASHINGTON CHANNEL, WASHINGTON. D. C., 1939—AN ASSET TO PLEASURE CRAFT OWNERS

development of tension. Bolts were of small value in their bearing against wood. The advent of the timber connector served to increase the bearing value of timber per bolt to the extent that the use of timber in tension members is now definitely economical. These items are available in many types, for both interior and exterior uses. The construction of timber trusses, bridges, piers, and bulkheads is facilitated by timber connectors. The result is that timber structures are practicable under modern heavy load conditions, thereby retaining for timber uses a field that would otherwise have been limited to other materials. These small inexpensive items also permit economies in fabrication labor, and in the quantities of timber consumed. A type of large modern timber structure is shown in Fig. 5.

Modern equipment has made possible the manufacture of laminated timber members. Many of these are long-span arches and heavy-duty beams of such proportions as to render them unattainable in single sawed pieces. Waterproof glues are available for the lamination of pieces proposed for exterior use.

Not too many years ago, dredges had small capacities and did a commensurate amount of work. The dredge of today is a monster. Recently it was necessary to replace a large spud on one of these dredges. This spud, 85 ft long and weighing 8 tons without its point, was laminated from small pieces of timber. The spud was cured, surfaced, shipped, and installed within a few days. This procedure

FIG. 5.—FLOATING DRYDOCK OF TIMBER, BUILT DURING WORLD WAR II, 1943; 5,000-TON CAPACITY

FIG. 6.—COMPOSITE TIMBER-CONCRETE DECK CONSTRUCTION, SHOWING SHEAR DEVELOPERS

probably required less time than locating a suitable single piece on the market, granting that one could be found. Ribs, keels, and bow timbers containing up to seventy-six laminations, shaped to fit the hull contours, are now being constructed for ships with 30–ft beam and 160–ft length.

Another innovation of the present day is the timber-concrete composite deck for bridges and piers and for floors of commercial buildings (Fig. 6). In this type of slab construction, the concrete is utilized for compressive stresses whereas the timber is arranged to transmit tension, thereby releasing much of the critical reinforcement for other purposes.

These are only a few of the modern developments and improvements in timber construction during the past 100 years. There are, without doubt, many more, some of them of equal importance.

CONSERVATION

A brief discussion on the conservation of forests is appropriate at this point. During the early life of the United States, large tracts of land were heavily forested with virgin growth trees now estimated to have contained approximately 8,000,000,000,000 board-ft of timber. In view of this large reserve, the limited demands of the small population at that time were not conducive to thoughts of reforestation. The people's interests were concerned with survival and expansion. In those days little attention was paid to either forest conservation or reforestation. As population increased and people migrated westward, the abundant forest resources became a key factor in the phenomenal economic growth that followed. New natural forest growth was depended on to replace the old to a large extent. Later, it was realized that this was insufficient and about the turn of the century a new concept of forest conservation took form. Today, under the guidance of governmental agencies a well-planned, country-wide reforestation program is under way, that, combined with logical economies in consumption, promises to meet demands indefinitely. Through industry programs such as "Tree Farm," "Keep Green," and "Cash Crops," and federal and state activities, wise use of timber has become the established custom.

Developments in the use and conservation of timber have progressed as rapidly as those in similar fields. However, more progress is required. Research must be continued to achieve safer designs, better construction methods, more economies, less waste, and adequate reforestation.

AMERICAN SOCIETY OF CIVIL ENGINEERS

Founded November 5, 1852

TRANSACTIONS

Paper No. 2624

THE IMPORTANCE OF DYNAMIC LOADS IN STRUCTURAL DESIGN

By John B. Wilbur,[1] M. ASCE, and Robert J. Hansen,[2] A. M. ASCE

Synopsis

The purpose of this paper is to present a general review of the importance of dynamic loads in structural design rather than a long treatise on the mathematical intricacies of dynamic analyses. Accordingly, the paper is divided into three parts: (1) Dynamic loadings, (2) dynamic analyses, and (3) the effects of atomic bomb blasts on structural design.

1. Dynamic Loadings

Nature of Dynamic Loads.—Dynamic loads have been important in determining the behavior of construction ever since either fixed or moving structures have been built by man. Some of the forces of nature—such as those resulting from the action of wind and waves—are dynamic in character; and displacements—such as earthquakes—cause structures to be subjected to dynamic forces. Man-made forces, too—like those applied to structures by machinery and vehicles—are frequently dynamic in their action. The shock and blast waves from atomic bombs, currently uppermost in the minds of many structural engineers, are examples of a new and rather terrifying kind of dynamic loading. The importance of dynamic loads has not always been recognized, but with advances in techniques of analysis, and, more important—as a result of various dramatic failures of structures under the influence of dynamic forces—engineering attention has been directed increasingly toward problems of structural dynamics. Designers today are more and more cognizant of the effect of dynamic loadings.

Design Difficulties.—Both transient and oscillatory dynamic loads are important in structural design for three significant reasons:

1. Stresses induced by transient and oscillatory loads may be much greater than those caused by statically applied loads of equal magnitude. The magnification factor for transient loads depends on the rate of load build-up, duration of the load, and amount of damping; whereas, for oscillatory loads of proper

---

[1] Head, Dept. of Civ. and San. Eng., Mass. Inst. of Tech., Cambridge, Mass.
[2] Assoc. Prof. of Structural Eng., Dept. of Civ. and San. Eng., Mass. Inst. of Tech., Cambridge, Mass.

frequency and magnitude, stresses may increase to failure at loads which, if applied statically, would produce stresses well within the elastic limit.

2. Reversals of stress character, which result in the difficulties associated with the designing of structural elements to resist such reversals, may be induced by dynamic loads.

3. Fatigue failures are more likely if a structure is subjected to stresses of an oscillatory character.

Moreover, it is more difficult to design a structure to resist dynamic loads than static loads and, again, for three basic reasons:

a. The load-versus-time functions for dynamic loadings are usually poorly defined, and of such a variable character that it is extremely hard to establish reasonable design loadings.

b. Dynamic loads are, in some cases, in the "act of God" category. They may be applied only infrequently, yet they must be provided for in the basic design. The extent to which such provision should be made, however, calls for a high degree of engineering judgment.

c. The response of structural systems to dynamic loadings is, in many cases, so complex that the mathematical equations describing the motion of the structure versus time, and the derived equations of stress and strain versus time, are difficult to handle. In some cases, these relationships cannot be treated by the usual mathematical methods. Design procedures must be based on the fundamental equations that describe the motion of the structure. Nevertheless, the relationship of the design procedures to the basic equations is only approximate at best, and can result in either overdesign or, perhaps, catastrophic underdesign.

Design Procedures.—Dynamic loadings are experienced by nearly every type of structure in common use. In some cases, these loadings may require major consideration in the basic design. In the majority of instances, the designs need merely be checked for certain conditions of dynamic loading, and perhaps modified somewhat. In the remainder of the cases, no design or check need be made for the dynamic load.

The design procedures used in the many cases of dynamically loaded structures vary from very simple empirical methods, which depend on rather arbitrarily assigned static loadings, to very elaborate analytical procedures that require the approximate force-time loading functions and nearly exact mathematical expressions that relate response to forcing functions.

For three of the problems that confront the structural engineer in connection with transient dynamic loadings—namely, earthquakes, winds, and moving loads, as applied to stationary structures—standard empirical procedures have been evolved for the design problem. In all three cases, the procedures are definitely empirical in nature and, accordingly, approximate in results.

Earthquakes.—The problem of earthquakes has been serious in Japan and in regions of the United States. Much research has been carried out with respect to the nature of the earthquake and the responses of structures to a variety of types of such forcing functions. As a result of such studies and, in particular, as a result of observing damage to buildings in the many disastrous earthquakes that have plagued Japan and the western United States, special types of construction, certain recommended design details, and definite methods of design have been evolved. All the design procedures in common use involve the application of static lateral loads to each face of a structure, these lateral loads being a fixed or varying percentage of the weight of a part of the structure.

On the west coast of the United States, it has been general practice to consider as the design loads, static lateral loads amounting to 10% of the weight of relevant parts of the structure at each floor level. In Japan, higher seismic factors have been used. More recently, a modification of the fixed percentage has been introduced, and a sliding scale of percentages, related to height above ground, has been used. This refinement was made in accordance with the approximate dynamic behavior of structures, the foundations of which are subjected to translatory motion.

Wind Loads.—In the case of wind, the nature of the loading is again highly transitory, especially with respect to peak-gust intensities. Even for the case of a steady wind, the exact force distribution over the faces of a structure is complex. In spite of wind-tunnel tests on small models of various shapes, knowledge of such distribution is still limited. This condition, together with the unpredictability of the force-time relationship and other factors, has led to very approximate design procedures that ignore the dynamics of the situation. This practice has long been, and still is, usual in connection with the action of wind on stationary structures, although dynamic response considerations are now being investigated for a variety of special structures such as suspension bridges, which have demonstrated inherent aerodynamic instability in some cases (Fig. 1).

The basic problem involved in the use of static loads as the equivalents of the dynamic forces of wind is that of avoiding structures in which the dynamic response may be catastrophically different from the static response. In the past, as long as a structure conformed to certain general patterns of mass, stiffness, and aerodynamic shape, problems of magnification of stress resulting from wind loading were not serious. However, if the structure, as designed to meet all standard requirements, departs drastically from the previously safe structure in arrangements of mass, stiffness, and shape, problems of dynamic instability or serious dynamic magnification of stress are not inherently avoided. For structures that lie outside the range of proved satisfactory performance, dynamic responses must be considered. After such consideration, it is entirely possible that equivalent static analysis procedures can be devised; but they will have to be based, in essence, on dynamic considerations.

Moving Loads.—Impact from moving loads has caused no real difficulties in design, being handled on the basis of equivalent static loads. Nevertheless, it must be remembered that stresses caused by impact usually constitute a fairly small percentage of total stresses and that considerable latitude in the treatment of such impact stresses is tolerable, since neither the over-all cost of a structure nor its safety is, in general, likely to be affected to an important degree.

With respect to the effect of bomb-blast loads on structures, however, the situation is quite the opposite. Stresses caused by blast may well comprise such an overwhelmingly large percentage of total stresses that they predominate as a design consideration. The situation is further complicated by the fact that, in general, economic considerations dictate plastic design to resist the blast of bombs. The dynamic-plastic response of a structure to bomb blast is so inherently different from elastic action under static loads that it does not seem possible, in the present state of knowledge, to base such designs on equivalent static loads. Indeed, if it eventually becomes feasible to use such an approach, the procedure promises to be fairly complex, since it will have to be based on an interpretation of dynamic responses that involve so many parameters that the equivalent static loads will presumably vary rather widely under different circumstances. It is best, for the present at least, to think of this as essentially a dynamic problem.

FIG. 1.—FIRST TACOMA NARROWS BRIDGE, IN WASHINGTON JUST BEFORE BREAKUP, SEPTEMBER 7, 1940

Fixed structures are subjected to oscillating as well as transient dynamic loads, and these—like blast loads—must usually be treated on the basis of dynamic considerations. There have been many cases of severe vibration problems resulting from the improper installation of machinery in buildings that may have resulted from poor machinery design, not in itself a structural problem. However, the mounting of vibrating machinery imposes design requirements on the structure that must be met by suitable damping or spring-mounted systems, together with consideration of the dynamic response of the structure itself.

Moving Structures.—Moving structures—even more than structures that are fixed against motion as a rigid body—may have a variety of configurations, may be subjected to various types of dynamic loadings, and may, in addition, require the strictest economy in design. Aircraft, a prime example, is subjected to a variety of loading conditions. Actual design procedures for some aircraft include the use of some two thousand conditions of loading, a prodigious number under any circumstances. The primary dynamic loads to which aircraft may be subjected are: Wind gusts, landing impact, buffeting of tail surfaces, fluttering of wing and control surfaces, catapulting, and gunfire.

In the determination of inertia loads on an aircraft structure, it has generally been the practice to assume that the airplane is a rigid body. Thus, the externally applied dynamic forces, such as those imposed by air or ground, are put into equilibrium with the inertia forces that result from the acceleration of the plane as a rigid body. This procedure ignores the vibrations that may be induced in the airplane structure by the dynamic nature of the loading. Attempts to overcome the difficulties of dynamic overstress, which has produced failures in many cases, have featured the use of increased margins of safety or load factors. These methods have been found unsatisfactory in practice, and very active programs of research have been conducted in the United States and abroad to develop more rational design procedures.

Other moving structures are likewise subjected to dynamic loadings of a varied and equally unpredictable nature. Automobiles, trucks, railroad cars, and so on receive impacts of large magnitudes that must be absorbed in some manner without adverse effect on the basic structure. Procedures of dynamic shock absorption are used, based on analytical studies. Actual equipment is tested under service conditions, and revised to provide better performance. The vehicle structure itself is, however, often designed by empirical procedures that assure safe performance but not necessarily the most economical construction.

Safe and Unsafe Design.—Thus, in the majority of cases, present methods of design for dynamic loads rest on empirical or semi-empirical procedures that are adequate in the sense that they usually result in safe structures. However, when dynamic stresses constitute an appreciable part of total stresses, there are two major dangers: Overdesign or uneconomical design, and underdesign or unsafe design.

The extent of overdesign is unknown. It is undoubtedly substantial in many cases, resulting in uneconomical use of manpower and materials. Overdesign may not be entirely attributable to inaccurate prediction of loading functions. A good part of overdesign may result from the use of approximate methods of analysis. Tragic cases of underdesign are also evident from time to time. The relatively recent failure of the Tacoma Narrows Bridge in Washington furnished a spectacular example (Fig. 1). However, this collapse is no more significant than the total of many smaller failures occasioned by inadequate design, poor treatment of construction details, and, frequently, just lack of consideration of the dynamic factors that are present in a given situation.

2. DYNAMIC ANALYSES

Impulsive Load Analysis.—Consider an elastic system with one degree of freedom, as illustrated in Fig. 2(a), acted on by an impulsive load that varies with time as shown in Fig. 2(b). If load P were applied as a static load, the stress S in the spring would be $+P$. Since, however, the load is impulsive, the stress in the spring will vary with time, because of the effect of the mass M.

To obtain the maximum stress in the spring, there is a simple solution available, provided the duration of the impulsive load is small enough that the load has ceased acting before the displacement of the mass M is large enough to cause an appreciable stress in the spring. Under these conditions, the stress in the spring may be neglected while the load is acting, and the total impulse applied to mass M by load P is equated to the momentum of the mass at the instant load P ceases to act. This procedure permits computation of the velocity of the mass at the same instant and, consequently, the corresponding kinetic energy of the mass. The mass will continue to move in the direction of force P until its total kinetic energy has been converted into strain energy in the spring. The spring stress S corresponding to this strain energy is easily computed.

For the more general case, however, the duration of the impulsive load may be too great to permit the foregoing simple solution. If the relation between P and time t is known, a differential equation may be written, based on the relation

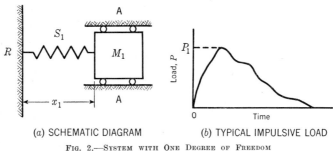

(a) SCHEMATIC DIAGRAM   (b) TYPICAL IMPULSIVE LOAD

FIG. 2.—SYSTEM WITH ONE DEGREE OF FREEDOM

that force equals mass times acceleration—thus connecting the displacement of the mass to time. If, for the case at hand, a rectangular loading pulse of intensity P_1 and duration t_1 is considered, it is found that, for $0 < t < t_1$,

$$S_t = P_1 \left[1 - \cos \frac{2\pi}{T} t \right] \dots\dots\dots\dots\dots\dots (1)$$

and that, for $t > t_1$,

$$S_t = P_1 \left[\cos \frac{2\pi}{T} (t - t_1) - \cos \frac{2\pi}{T} t \right] \dots\dots\dots\dots (2)$$

In Eqs. 1 and 2, T is the natural period of vibration of the system, and is defined by

$$T = 2\pi \sqrt{M/k} \dots\dots\dots\dots\dots\dots\dots (3)$$

in which k is the spring constant. The bracketed quantities by which P_1 is multiplied convert the impulsive load intensity into an equivalent static load for any given time t. For convenience, these bracketed quantities are called "dynamic load factors." For the rectangular pulse, values of the dynamic load factor D for varying pulse durations t_1 can be plotted against t (Fig. 3).

Of particular interest in stress analysis are the maximum positive and negative dynamic load factors. For the case under consideration, these values are determined by the ratio t_1/T, and are given in Fig. 4. For example, for

$t_1/T = \frac{1}{3}$, the maximum positive and negative dynamic load factors are $+ 1.73$ and $- 1.73$, respectively. Thus, the equivalent static loads that would cause maximum tension and compression in the spring are $+ 1.73\,P_1$ and $- 1.73\,P_1$, respectively, for this particular impulsive load. It is important, too, to note that, as the duration of the load (t_1/T) becomes very small, the dynamic load factors likewise become very small. This relation, in part, explains why very large loads,

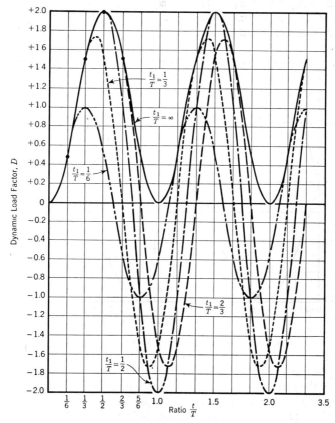

FIG. 3.—DYNAMIC LOAD FACTOR

applied for very short periods, may cause only nominal stresses in a structure. They may not act long enough to displace the masses and permit the structure to be subjected to large strains.

Indirect Solution for Dynamic Load Factors.—However, even for this simple structure, there are circumstances under which a direct mathematical solution for dynamic load factors becomes rather impractical. For example, the load-time relationship may be too complicated to lend itself to a simple mathematical treatment; or the spring may be stressed beyond the elastic limit and into the plastic range—in which case its stress-strain relationship is not only nonlinear but, for a given strain, dependent on the rate of strain. Therefore, in determining the motion of the mass, it is often convenient to utilize a step-by-step procedure, with consecutive investigations of the movement of the mass during succeeding short intervals of time.

If the condition of displacement and motion of the mass at the start of a given interval are known, the independent components of displacement and motion of the mass at the end of the interval may be investigated. This procedure permits the analyst to compute the corresponding average forces acting on the mass during the interval under consideration—including the force applied by the spring as well as the external load.

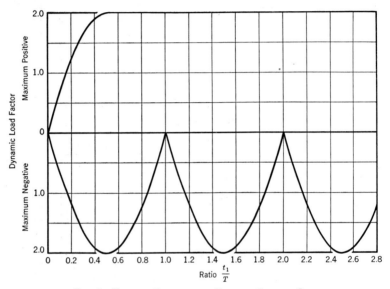

FIG. 4.—MAXIMUM POSITIVE AND NEGATIVE DYNAMIC LOAD

The condition of displacement and motion that the forces should have given the mass at the end of the interval can then be investigated. If these correspond to the original estimate, the motion of the mass for the interval has been defined. A step-by-step procedure, as just outlined, is in principle just as applicable to situations in which the movement of the mass is actuated by a displacement-time function applied to the "fixed" support of the spring, as it is to the case in which the movement of the mass is actuated by an impulsive external load. Therefore, this approach could be used for dynamic analyses of earthquakes as well as for determining the responses to dynamic loads.

Systems with Many Degrees of Freedom.—In most practical structures, however, the foregoing procedures, based on a system of one degree of freedom, are not directly helpful, inasmuch as masses are usually distributed in such a manner that an infinite number of degrees of freedom actually exists. However, to facilitate the analysis, it is convenient and usually possible to consider the mass of the structure as being concentrated at a number of points, these points being connected by massless springs, or by massless beams that act as springs.

Fig. 5 shows such a system with two degrees of freedom. In the more general case, however, there would be n discrete masses, hence n degrees of freedom.

The simplified analysis previously given, based on equating impulse and momentum and permissible when the load duration was extremely short, is not strictly applicable to this more complicated situation. Nevertheless, the method may still be used, under some conditions, to approximate maximum displacements. In a multistoried building under the action of blast load, for example, the structure might be treated as a system of one degree of freedom by assuming the relative displacements of the masses at each floor level to have certain values that remained constant throughout the motion.

However, a more accurate analysis must be based on the recognition that the actual motion of the structure is obtained by superimposing the movements corresponding to each of the n modes of vibration that can exist. A so-called

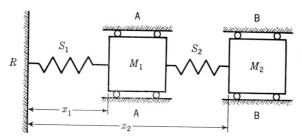

FIG. 5.—SYSTEM WITH TWO DEGREES OF FREEDOM

"exact" solution for this problem is available and is not too difficult, provided the number of degrees of freedom is not large.

Nevertheless, in view of complicated force-time functions and the possibility of plastic action, it is more likely that a step-by-step analysis, similar to the one previously described, will prove to be more attractive. Since there are now n masses for which the motion must be determined, the independent components of motion and displacement must be separately estimated for each of the n masses at the end of a given interval. When the average forces acting on each mass during the interval are computed, there is an interplay of spring forces, caused by the redundancy of the structure. This approach, although more complicated, is, however, basically the same as that described for the system with one degree of freedom; and, as was previously the case, it is applicable to earthquake analyses as well as to analyses for the action of dynamic loads.

There are various expedients for organizing and simplifying analyses of these types—tedious processes at best. Also there is certainly need for simplified methods of analysis wherever they can be demonstrated to be justified. However, it should be apparent that the dynamic problem is fundamentally different from the static problem. If stresses from dynamic loads are likely to control design, the use of equivalent static loads should be viewed with caution, unless such static loads constitute a simplified interpretation of a reasonably correct dynamic analysis.

3. EFFECTS OF ATOMIC BOMB BLAST ON STRUCTURES

Basic Problems Involved.—Protection of cities against atomic bombs involves not only technical complications of a very high order, but also social and economic aspects of the gravest importance. Indeed, solution is so difficult that some designers may well be tempted to belittle or evade the issue. "There may never be an atomic war," they may say to reassure themselves. "Even if there is," they may rationalize, "there is little that can be done in a year, or in 2 years, or even in 3 years, to make the buildings in cities very much less vulnerable to atomic attack."

It is acknowledged, and fervently hoped, that the United States may never feel the brunt of an atomic war; but, at the same time, it is impossible to deny that such a catastrophe is far more than a possibility. It is also known that, if atomic warfare comes in the relatively near future, there is little that can be done in the interim to make structures in the cities less vulnerable to attack.

However, this is scarcely the point at issue. If atomic war comes, no one knows when it will begin. It may not start within the next few years. There is always the hope that if it cannot be prevented, it may at least be delayed for a sufficient length of time to permit the engineering profession to make a significant contribution to the welfare of the United States. The situation presents such an opportunity for public service as has never before been offered. Perhaps before atomic warfare comes, there will be time to minimize significantly civilian and economic losses, and the reduction of industrial output as well. Indeed vulnerability to attack may be decreased to a point where it can become a positive factor in the prevention of war.

Such steps seem technically possible. Over a period of years, they may be economically and socially feasible. Of course, it is not known whether or not—in the wisdom of the people of the United States—it will be deemed proper to try to make the adjustments that would be necessary to implement such a program. Popular support is of utmost importance, for it goes almost without saying that any major steps taken to minimize the potential catastrophe of atomic warfare through changes in planning and new methods of building for the atomic age must, if they are to be carried out successfully, have a high degree of cooperation. Devising the tools and charting the program that will make protection possible will be difficult. However, it will certainly be even more difficult to arouse public support to a point where such a program, however excellent and justified it may be, can be translated into reality.

Philosophy of Design.—Although widespread action depends on popular support, professional people have a grave responsibility in the matter. The minimizing of the effects of atomic warfare demands the most effective planning and design, if it is desired to obtain the best results for the money. No one should think of the problem in terms of extreme measures.

As an analogy, it is not customary to make buildings completely fireproof, but all reasonable measures are taken to increase their resistance and to improve conditions for the safety of their occupants. Builders strive for the greatest protection to fire that can be afforded, considering all the factors involved. The same kind of thinking applies in connection with the atomic bombs. The problem

—to an important degree—is one of economics; and, because of this, extreme remedies must of necessity be set aside.

Therefore, it is necessary, for the most part, to think in terms of partial measures: Dispersal to a degree that will discourage, although in no sense prevent, the existence of attractive targets; shelters that will offer a reasonable degree of protection, although in no sense full protection, to the people who seek their haven; buildings with definite resistance to shock and blast load, even though very few structures will be erected that are actually bombproof.

There is a point involved in the foregoing statement that is, in the writer's opinion, quite worthy of emphasis: The difference between no provision for protection at all and some degree of provision, even though moderate, is the difference between darkness and daylight. However, the difference between some provision and more provision is only a matter of degree. It is well known that, if a structure has been designed to carry a certain type of load, it has some chance of standing up under that load, even though the exact character and magnitude of the load may differ rather widely from that assumed in design.

On the other hand, if a structure, or a part of a structure, is subjected to a type of loading for which no provision whatsoever has been made in design, the structure is, in effect (unless perchance prevented from so being by coincidence), in a condition approaching unstable equilibrium, and hence in readiness to collapse when such a loading is applied. Of course it is desirable, in designing structures to resist atomic bombs, to use accurate loadings and accurate methods of analysis, and to design against these loads to a degree consistent with over-all economic considerations. However, the point that should be emphasized is that even partial resistance, based on nominal loads and on methods of analysis that are frankly approximate, is insuperably better than is no resistance at all.

Assumed Loadings.—The matter of exactly what loading should be used in designing a given structure is indeed complex. Duration of loading as well as magnitude is involved. Among the variables that determine loading are the type and size of the bomb, the distance of the structure from assumed ground zero, the direction of the detonation from the structure, the height of the detonation above ground, and the depth of the detonation below ground.

Even if all these were known, uncertainties are introduced by atmospheric conditions, reflections from surrounding objects and from the building itself, and the behavior of the structure that is being designed. The actual loadings to be used must, of necessity, be determined rather arbitrarily, but only after exhaustive studies of the economics of the situation, in which size, importance, use, and location with respect to vulnerable target areas are important considerations. Again, it must be stressed that designing against any reasonable load is of far greater importance than estimating the exact blast to which a structure is likely to be subjected.

The design procedure is associated closely with the important matter of the degree of damage that is to be considered as permissible in a given design. In some cases, damage must be held to an absolute minimum—stresses for the most part are kept within the elastic limit. At the other extreme, conditions will be such that no provision whatsoever should be made for blast load. However, between the two extremes there are various intermediate stages. Sometimes a building should not be damaged beyond a point where it can be restored to usefulness within a reasonable length of time. For this result, the frame must not be seriously disturbed. Exterior walls and interior parts must be in such condition that a certain degree of protection, at least in vital areas, is afforded to the occupants and the contents of the building. It should also be remembered that machinery, electrical equipment, and water pipes may be as important as either the occupants or the structural frame.

Sometimes, large plastic deformations should be permitted, and the walls and roofs constructed of frangible materials so that only the plastically strained frames can be salvaged. Even more frequently, no special degree of bomb resistance should be built into a structure, but the design should nevertheless be carried out with this hazard in mind, and detailed so that whatever inherent resistance is present can be capitalized. The degree of protection that is desirable in a given instance is, to a certain extent, arbitrary. It must be determined on the basis of use, importance, and location, and is essentially an economic problem. Structurally, protection is related primarily to the maximum deformations, both transient and permanent, that can be tolerated.

Bomb-Resistant Construction.—For resisting the effect of atomic bombs, it is known that wall-bearing buildings are in general to be avoided but that reinforced-concrete buildings and steel-framed buildings are potentially capable, as types, of lending themselves to satisfactory designs. Underground structures, too, provide effective and sometimes economical protection. Buried structures are well suited for personnel shelters, and offer attractive possibilities for certain types of industrial plants and warehouses.

Nevertheless, quite aside from the basic type of construction selected, there are several considerations vital to good design. First and foremost among these is that the construction should be especially resistant to lateral loads. To produce this resistance, the connections of beams to columns should be moment resisting throughout. Columns should be fixed at their bases. The use of shear-wall construction, where feasible, is especially effective. Reinforcing rods should be welded at splices. Finally, in general, structural members should be reinforced for both positive and negative bending throughout, because under blast load they are subjected not only to either type of bending, but indeed to reversal of flexure.

The use of architectural devices such as copings, false ceilings, and heavy hung features should be avoided, since these all constitute unnecessary hazards in event of exposure to shock and blast loads. Glass windows present one of the greatest dangers. They break under relatively small blast loads, and their deadly fragments are hurled substantial distances. The elimination of windows in some modern industrial buildings is a step in the right direction in decreasing the hazard of bombs. The use of frangible walls and in some cases frangible roofs can, however, sometimes be incorporated to advantage in certain types of industrial buildings.

Provision should be made for minimum shelter areas, either suitably enclosed spaces such as stair wells on floors removed from the roof or basement areas enclosed with concrete walls and completely below ground. Of equal importance in structural and shelter considerations is the matter of fire resistance. The use of fire-resistant construction, a consideration of combustible contents, adequate sprinkler systems, and independent sources of water supply—all are needed to reduce the hazard of major conflagrations in event of atomic attack. The foregoing steps can be taken in new construction to improve the resistance of buildings to bombs, with only nominal increases in cost.

Dispersal.—Engineers are well on their way toward knowing how to design structures to resist atomic bombs, but lest the help that may come from this direction be overemphasized, it should be remembered that there is a second approach to the problem of protection. Space is an excellent defense against atomic weapons, and it should play an important part in the development of over-all protective plans. The first reason for this need arises in connection with the fire effects of atomic bombs. It is of special importance in the prevention of fire storms—the simultaneous action of hundreds of fires that set up a strong column of rising air that behaves like the central column of whirling and rising air that is present in a storm. This condition can occur in cities where the roof areas of combustible buildings constitute more than 20% of the ground area for a square mile or more, and can be prevented by spatial as well as by fire-resistant considerations.

Discussions have been held, in which the relative merits of dispersal versus structural protection were debated. However, it should be evident that both are vitally needed, and that each aids and abets the other in an effort to achieve protection. The intensive development of larger cities should be checked, since they are attractive as targets because of their industrial concentrations. Residential crowding should be reduced by urban redevelopments and slum clearances; the formation of new target areas should be prevented; new defense plants should be located at safe distances from large concentrations; and the entire operation should be planned on a comprehensive basis.

Dispersal, like protective construction, cannot be achieved at once. Cost, interim displacement, shortage of materials, and shortages of manpower all prohibit this. Nevertheless, the normal rate of replacement and change has been placed at $2\frac{1}{2}$% per year—a large enough factor to make a significant difference over a period of years. If the major part of new construction were carried out in accordance with sound principles of dispersal and designed with some consideration of its ability to withstand the effects of atomic bombs, the ability of the United States to meet an atomic attack in 30, or 20, or even 10 years hence could be significantly improved. It must be remembered that, if designers do not move in the direction of dispersal, cities will become even more attractive as targets as the years go by.

However, a balance must be struck between calculated risk, bomb-resistant construction, and dispersal. The matter is largely one of economics, although social values are involved, and is worthy of the most deliberate judgment. It is essential that whatever program may be followed be consistent with an honest endeavor to obtain the best protection for the money that may, considering all factors, be expended.

Over a period of years vast strides can be made toward protection against atomic bombs if only three minimum steps are carried out:

(1) New buildings in target areas should be designed for reasonable lateral

loads and fire resistance, and some attention should be paid to the correct structural details of bomb-resistant design.

(2) Provisions should be made for shelter areas even though they are far from perfect.

(3) Sound principles of dispersion should be followed for new construction, to reduce the attractiveness of target areas and the hazard of fire storms.

These steps will pay double dividends. They not only will help to protect the nation against atomic bombs if the need should ever arise, but will improve cities for peacetime living. With these measures in effect, the United States would be better prepared to meet the normal hazards of fire and earthquake, and would achieve some of the social benefits of decentralization that are recommended, irrespective of the danger of atomic bombs, by many city and regional planners. Without thinking in terms of extreme measures, a minimum program such as that just outlined appears to be worthy of careful consideration by the engineering profession.

Conclusions

In terms of either heavier new construction to resist atomic bombs, or more economical and daring structures to serve the more constructive needs of the future, it is evident that considerations of dynamic loadings are becoming increasingly important. On the one hand, dynamic loading constitutes the major factor that controls design. On the other, the nation appears to be working into an area of construction in which departures from the mass-spring relationships that have been in common use make it possible for dynamic loads to become critical in determining structural behavior.

Accordingly, if progress is to be made in the field of structural design, dynamic loading and analysis will require more concentrated study. This development will probably be in three forms:

(1) More exact determinations of the time-force character of all types of dynamic loads will be necessary.

(2) More exact analysis procedures will be developed, so that both simple and complex structures can be handled more accurately, at least for purposes of research.

(3) Perhaps of greatest importance will be the evolution of simplified design procedures that are straightforward and direct, that offer physical visualizations of the problems being solved, and that are, above all, firm in their foundation on a correct dynamic treatment of the actual phenomena involved.

AMERICAN SOCIETY OF CIVIL ENGINEERS

Founded November 5, 1852

TRANSACTIONS

Paper No. 2625

BRIDGES AND MAN'S INCREASED MOBILITY

By D. B. Steinman,[1] M. ASCE

Synopsis

The past century—the Society's first century—has seen the transformation of the United States, from a young pioneer settlement to a great and flourishing nation, taking its place in the leadership of the world. From forest and wilderness, mountain and desert, this country has been metamorphosed into a rich and dynamic land. First expanded and tied together with isolated wagon roads, canals, and railroads, it is now crisscrossed with magnificent systems of paved highways, boulevards, scenic parkways, throughways, and superhighways. From pack horse, oxcart, and prairie schooner, United States has been transmuted into a nation on wheels.

In this shrinking of distances and speeding of travel, bridges have played an indispensable role. The nation has become more closely knit together. Remoteness and isolation have been replaced by unity and mobility.

As late as 1923, speaking at a New York, N. Y., meeting of the ASCE, the writer advocated that the large municipal bridges of the future be planned for motor vehicle traffic and that rapid transit tracks be kept underground in subways and tunnels. A prominent older member dissented; he said it did not seem fair for the city to build bridges for the pleasure of the privileged few who happened to be wealthy enough to own automobiles.

The Engineer's Four Freedoms.—Today, 30 years later, the picture is transformed. There are now 50,000,000 motor vehicles rolling over paved roads, parkways, bridges, and express highways in the United States. The luxuries of yesterday have become the necessities of today. Almost every family nowadays demands, and somehow secures, at least one automobile, whereas such recent luxuries as telephones, electrical appliances, radios, and television sets in practically every home are now taken for granted.

How has this transformation been accomplished? The United States and its greatness have been built by the courage of the pioneer, the spirit of individual and concerted enterprise, and the grit and resourcefulness of the engineer.

Talk of the "Four Freedoms" is heard on all sides, but therein is the danger

---

[1] Cons. Engr., New York, N. Y.

of losing sight of the four freedoms on which this nation was founded and from which it achieved its greatness. They are:

> Freedom of Vision
> Freedom of Enterprise
> Freedom of Incentive
> Freedom of Achievement

These four freedoms spell the United States. They also explain much of its success in developing a transportation system that has involved the building of many of the world's greatest bridges.

For a New Transportation.—The early settlers were limited in mobility to footpath, pack trail, and local wagon road. Then, in succession, came the building of canals, railroads, and modern highways. Each of these in turn required bridges,

FIG. 1.—HELL GATE ARCH BRIDGE, COMPLETED IN 1917, WHICH CARRIES FOUR RAILROAD TRACKS OVER THE EAST RIVER, NEW YORK, N. Y.; SPAN, 977½ FT

and each depended on the bridge builder's art for feasibility and realization. The American spirit—at once daring and practical—is peculiarly adapted to excel in this development.

During the nineteenth century, the principal demand for bridge construction in the United States was in connection with the building and development of the railroads. At the turn of the century, many railroad bridges were being replaced or reconstructed to provide greater strength and clearance for the rapidly increasing size, weight, and clearance of locomotives and trains. Even thereafter, railroad extension involved the building of such monumental spans as the Hell Gate Arch (Fig. 1) in New York City and the Sciotoville continuous bridge (Fig. 2) across the Ohio River between Ohio and Kentucky.

Since about 1920, however, there has been no further extension of the rail systems, and the economic plight of the railroads has limited the improvement of existing construction. Instead, the phenomenal development of highway traffic has created a new phase of bridge building in which there are both the economic justification for bridges of unprecedented dimensions over crossings that previously had to be left unspanned and the need for myriads of smaller bridges and grade separation layouts.

There are more than 90,000 steel bridges on 240,000 miles of railroad in the United States, with an aggregate length of more than 1,500 miles; but the comparable number of highway bridges, both steel and concrete, probably exceeds 250,000 on the 3,000,000 miles of roads and highways. The aggregate investment in these highway bridges is more than $3,000,000,000.

FIG. 2.—SCIOTOVILLE TRUSS BRIDGE, COMPLETED IN 1917, ACROSS THE OHIO RIVER BETWEEN OHIO AND KENTUCKY; TWO CONTINUOUS SPANS OF 775 FT EACH CARRYING DOUBLE RAILROAD TRACKS

FIG. 3.—A FEW OF THE NUMEROUS BRIDGES CROSSING THE ALLEGHENY RIVER AT PITTSBURGH, PA.— THE THREE NEARER BEING SUSPENSION HIGHWAY BRIDGES BUILT AROUND 1927; BEYOND, A CAMEL-BACK RAILROAD TRUSS, DATED 1904

Bridges That Create Cities.—Cities located at junctions of rivers are particularly dependent on bridges for their development, and thereafter for the mobility of their population. The City of Pittsburgh, Pa. (Fig. 3), has sixteen

FIG. 4.—ONE CORNER OF MANHATTAN ISLAND, NEW YORK, N. Y., WHICH IS SERVED BY A DOZEN
IMPORTANT BRIDGES, MOSTLY OVER THE HARLEM RIVER (CENTER) INCLUDING, FROM
BOTTOM: TRIBOROUGH; FIRST, SECOND, THIRD, PARK, MADISON, AND
LENOX AVENUES; AND, AT TOP, GEORGE WASHINGTON 3,500-FT
SUSPENSION SPAN OVER THE HUDSON RIVER TO
NEW JERSEY AT 178TH STREET

highway bridges and seven railroad bridges spanning the Allegheny and Mononga-hela rivers. In New York City, in a single day, more than 750,000 automobiles and trucks cross the highway bridges entering Manhattan Island (Fig. 4)—450,000 on twelve free bridges (including 90,000 on the Queensborough Bridge (Fig. 5) and 80,000 on the Manhattan Bridge), and 300,000 on three toll bridges (George Washington, Triborough (Fig. 6), and Henry Hudson (Fig. 7))—besides more than 700,000 passengers daily on rapid transit trains and electric trolley cars.

Individual bridges have proved of tremendous importance as the key factors in the development of cities, regions, and the nation as a whole. The Eads Bridge

FIG. 5.—QUEENSBOROUGH BRIDGE, OVER THE EAST RIVER AT 59TH STREET, NEW YORK, N. Y., COMPLETED IN 1909—A CANTILEVER TYPE, SEMICONTINUOUS, WITH MAIN SPAN OF 1,182 FT

over the Mississippi River at St. Louis, Mo. (Fig. 8), completed in 1874, was the essential link in the development of the transcontinental railroad system, and its significance in "the winning of the West" has well been recognized. At the same time, the Eads Bridge was of prime importance in the development of St. Louis, establishing it as a focal railroad crossing and as one of the most important cities on the Mississippi.

This influence of the construction of a bridge on the transportation pattern of a region or of the nation, affecting its population, industry, and commerce, has been repeated time and again over the length and breadth of the land.

Probably no bridge has had more influence on the growth of a city than the Brooklyn Bridge, completed in 1883. The population of Brooklyn was soon doubled, and the erstwhile village became a thriving city and an integral part of the new-formed city of Greater New York. The three additional East River

Fig. 6.—Triborough Bridge, a Suspension Span of 1,380 Ft over the East River, New York, N. Y., Built in 1936

Fig. 7.—Henry Hudson Bridge Carrying Parkway over Spuyten Duyvil at Northernmost Point of Manhattan Island, New York, N. Y.—A Hingeless 800-Ft Arch with Two Decks, Second Added in 1937, Single-Way Traffic on Each Deck

bridges, which had to be built in quick succession, completed the transformation of Brooklyn into the largest borough of the enlarged metropolis and created the new great borough of Queens.

FIG. 8.—EADS BRIDGE OVER MISSISSIPPI RIVER AT ST. LOUIS, MO., A HISTORIC STRUCTURE, ERECTED 1869–1874, WITH THREE ARCH SPANS OF 502 FT, 520 FT, AND 502 FT, CARRYING RAILROAD ON LOWER DECK, HIGHWAY ON UPPER—NAMED FOR ITS BUILDER, CAPT. JAMES B. EADS, M. ASCE

The seven longest spans in the world are in the United States:

Bridge	Span (ft)
Golden Gate, across San Francisco Bay between San Francisco and Marin County, California	4,200
George Washington, across the Hudson River between New York City and Fort Lee, N. J	3,500
Tacoma Narrows, across an arm of Puget Sound in Washington.	2,800
Transbay, across San Francisco Bay between San Francisco and Oakland	2,310
Bronx-Whitestone, across the East River in New York City....	2,300
Delaware Memorial, across the Delaware River between southern New Jersey and Delaware	2,150
Detroit-Ambassador, across the Detroit River between Detroit, Mich., and Windsor, Ont., Canada	1,850

All these are of the suspension type, and all are highway toll bridges.

Span Lengths Measure Progress.—The largest bridge project in the world consummated to date is the Transbay Bridge between San Francisco and Oakland (Fig. 9), completed in 1936, costing more than $77,000,000. Its total length of 8 miles includes two joined suspension bridges of 2,310-ft main span each, a cantilever bridge of 1,400-ft main span, and other connecting spans.

Nearby is the world's longest span, the Golden Gate Bridge (Fig. 10), completed in 1937 at a cost of $35,000,000. The main span, 220 ft above the water, is 4,200 ft between towers 746 ft high. The two main cables are 36½ in. in diameter, the largest constructed to date.

FIG. 9.—SAN FRANCISCO-OAKLAND BAY BRIDGE IN CALIFORNIA, SUCCESSFUL TOLL STRUCTURE AND LARGEST SINGLE BRIDGE PROJECT; NOTABLE FOR TWO MAIN SUSPENSION SPANS OF 2,310 FT, A CANTILEVER SPAN OF 1,400 FT, AND DEEPEST SUBAQUEOUS FOUNDATION, 242 FT

The George Washington Bridge, spanning the Hudson River at New York (Fig. 4) with a main span of 3,500 ft, was opened in 1931 at an initial cost of $60,000,000. It has four main cables, each 36 in. in diameter. The present deck carries eight lanes of highway traffic and provision has been made for the future addition of a lower deck.

With wider and more numerous crossings required, the bridge builders of the United States and Canada have achieved and retained the world leadership in almost every modern type of bridge, including not only the unrivaled suspension bridges, but also the world's longest spans in cantilevers, steel arches, continuous trusses, simple trusses, timber spans, swing spans, vertical lift spans, bascule spans, and transporter bridges. American engineers have also pioneered in inventing or developing new bridge types including movable bridges, rigid frames, the Wichert truss, and prestressed concrete.

About the only types for which European engineers have established new records are concrete arches, prestressed concrete spans, and steel girder spans. These differences of emphasis and development are explained by differences in

FIG. 10.—GOLDEN GATE BRIDGE, SAN FRANCISCO TO MARIN COUNTY, CALIFORNIA, COMPLETED IN 1937, WITH WORLD'S RECORD SPAN OF 4,200 FT

tradition (the masonry arch), differences in economics (scarcity of steel), and differences in design preferences and fabrication customs.

Era of Toll Projects.—For spans of unusual magnitude and cost, also for interstate and international crossings, toll bridges have come to be the solution of the financing problem. Up to 1929, most of these toll spans were built under private ownership, but the more recent toll bridges in the United States have all been built by public commissions or "bridge authorities."

Toll bridges are financed, as a rule, by issuing revenue bonds which are secured only by the prospective earnings, so that the user pays for them until they become free, instead of adding them to the general tax burden. The motoring public has thus secured the benefit of many needed bridge crossings where such facilities would otherwise have remained unattainable. There are now more than one hundred and sixty-five toll bridges in the United States, representing a total investment of more than $500,000,000. Only about eighty, involving an investment of about $100,000,000, are privately owned, and this number is rapidly dwindling.

Bridges are an index of civilization. With the expanding needs of intercommunication and travel and with the advances in technical science and constructive skill, the development of bridges has been marked by a rapidly accelerated tempo of progress. The past century has encompassed more advance in the science and art of bridge building than all the preceding centuries, and the past generation has again more than doubled that record in the attainment of still greater and bolder spans.

Record Advances.—In recent years, new frontiers of unprecedented span lengths have been opened. The world's record span length for suspension bridges has been more than doubled, from 1,750 ft in the Philadelphia-Camden Bridge between New Jersey and Pennsylvania in 1926 and 1,850 ft in the Detroit-Ambassador Bridge in 1929, to startling new records of 3,500 ft in the George Washington Bridge in 1931 and 4,200 ft in the Golden Gate Bridge in 1937. The world's record for steel arches was increased from $977\frac{1}{2}$ ft in the Hell Gate Arch Bridge in 1917 (Fig. 1) to 1,650 ft in the Sydney Harbor Bridge in Australia in 1932, and to 1,652 ft in the Bayonne Bridge over Kill Van Kull between Staten Island, New York, and New Jersey in 1931. The world's record span length for concrete arches was increased from 450 ft at Annecy, France, in 1938 to 866 ft at Sando, Sweden, in 1943.

Never before in the history of bridge engineering have such amazing strides of progress been recorded. Length of span is one of the measures by which bridges are judged, since it provides a convenient over-all index of related advances in the art, including improvements in design, theory, economics, new materials, new bridge types, and methods of erection.

A generation ago, the cantilever type was dominant. The famous Quebec Bridge in Canada, completed in 1917 after two historic erection catastrophes, held the world's record span length of 1,800 ft. Since then, however, with improvements in the science and art of suspension-bridge construction, the cantilever bridge has dropped out of the race and has yielded its previously claimed supremacy to the suspension type. The world's seven longest spans are now suspension bridges.

Bridges of still greater span length and magnitude are already in the planning stage. The writer in fact has designed bridges for proposed locations over the Narrows in New York harbor and over the Strait of Messina between Italy and Sicily with spans of 4,620 ft and 5,000 ft, respectively. A generation ago, the feasibility of a span of 3,000 ft was seriously questioned. Now engineers can state with confidence that suspension bridge spans up to 10,000 ft are practicable and may be expected.

Conquest of Problems.—This statement is true despite the startling destruction in 1940 of the 2,800-ft span Tacoma Narrows Bridge by catastrophic amplification of aerodynamic oscillations. Similar failures with smaller spans had occurred a century earlier, and had remained a mystery; but since then better tools of research and analysis had become available for mastery of the problem. By combining three previously unrelated sciences—namely, the deflection theory of suspension bridges, the mathematical theory of vibration analysis, and the science of aerodynamics—a new science of suspension bridge aerodynamics has now been developed, permitting predictive control, solution, and cure of the problem.

Two directions of solution have been made available, one by scientific methods of increasing the stiffness of the structure to resist the action, and the other by scientific design of aerodynamically stable sections, thereby eliminating the cause of the action. Assured safety of future suspension bridges has thus been achieved, without sacrificing economy and graceful design, as exemplified by the new and finer Tacoma span (Fig. 11).

FIG. 11.—NEW TACOMA NARROWS BRIDGE, ACROSS ARM OF PUGET SOUND IN WASHINGTON, COMPLETED IN 1950, SPANNING 2,800 FT AND USING FOUNDATIONS OF ILL-FATED PRIOR STRUCTURE, DESTROYED IN 1940

As the result of progress in the science and art of foundation design and construction, new records have been achieved in the magnitude and depth of bridge foundations sunk under the most difficult conditions. For the Huey P. Long Bridge over the Mississippi River at New Orleans, La., a cantilever structure completed in 1935 (Fig. 12), a new record of 170 ft in foundation depth was reached, using the artificial sand-island method. For the Transbay Bridge, completed in 1936 (Fig. 9), a new foundation method was devised, using dome-capped caissons to regulate the sinking by controlling the release of air pressure. The piers were thus carried down to rock 242 ft below the water surface—the greatest foundation depth so far attained.

Thus, the bridge engineer, in addition to his knowledge of superstructure design, has to be an expert on geology, hydraulics, methods of subsurface exploration, foundation design, and underwater construction.

Adaptation of Materials, Also.—Development of longer spans has created an impelling need for improved bridge materials. This has taken two directions: One, the development of higher-strength steels; and the other, the development of lighter-weight metals for structural use. The economy of utilizing stronger or lighter metals obviously increases with the span length.

High-strength steels that have been successfully used in bridge construction include alloy steels (such as silicon steel, nickel steel, manganese steel, and chrome-nickel steel), heat-treated carbon steel, and cold-drawn high-carbon bridge wire. Materials with three or four times the safe working strength of ordinary steel have been developed.

FIG. 12.—HUEY P. LONG BRIDGE, JUST ABOVE NEW ORLEANS, LA., SOUTHERNMOST CROSSING OF THE MISSISSIPPI RIVER; A CANTILEVER TYPE, WITH A MAIN SPAN OF 790 FT, WHICH ACCOMMODATES BOTH RAILWAY AND HIGHWAY TRAFFIC; COMPLETED IN 1935

The principal lightweight material has been structural aluminum. Since 1932, aluminum has been applied in the construction of several notable bridges in the United States, England, and Canada, as well as to military bridges and pontons. New possibilities have thus been opened in the future attainment of longer spans.

Satisfaction of Arch and Suspension Forms.—During the past 25 years, new attention has been concentrated on the attainment of beauty in bridges. Annual Artistic Bridge Awards, inaugurated in the United States in 1928, have focused attention on the importance of making bridges beautiful. New goals of artistic bridge design have been achieved through beauty and harmony of composition, through beauty of line, form, and proportions, and through color and illumination.

To build their famous aqueducts, the ancient Romans used thousands of tons of masonry in massive piers and arches to carry a small conduit for water supply. Today graceful, airy spans, in seeming magic, carry thousands of tons of useful load. Ponderous proportions are no longer the visual expression of power.

The public has to live with the structures that engineers build. Their work becomes a part of the landscape, to mar or to grace. If the profession is to be true to its trust, each structure it raises and each span it builds must be a thing of uplift and inspiration. The rainbow spans of tomorrow will have simplicity of form, beauty of line, grace of proportion, harmony of color, and radiant illumination.

No one, unless he is completely without feeling, can remain unmoved at the sight of a beautiful bridge. In span after span, bridge designers have now demonstrated that beauty can be secured without sacrificing utility or economy. They are directing their efforts toward producing the most beautiful designs in the structural material itself, whether steel or concrete, by developing forms that express the spirit of the material—its strength, its power, and its grace.

The two bridge types that most naturally yield beauty of form, line, and

FIG. 13.—NEWEST OF LONG-SPAN SUSPENSION STRUCTURES, THE DELAWARE MEMORIAL BRIDGE, JUST BELOW WILMINGTON, DEL., OVER THE DELAWARE RIVER AT SOUTHERN END OF NEW JERSEY TURNPIKE, COMPLETED IN 1952, WITH A SPAN OF 2,150 FT

proportion are the arch and the suspension bridge. The arch contributes something dynamic—a feeling of a powerful thrust created in the span and carried down the curving arc to be resisted at the abutments.

To attain the most creative and inspiring beauty of composition in steel bridge design, the suspension type is ideal. The graceful curve of the cables is the most natural and therefore the most beautiful of all bridge outlines, and the vertical hangers, like the strings of a harp, are the most harmonious and satisfying form of filling members. The dominant pylons divide the crossing into three spans of artistic proportions. Between the pierced towers the arching roadway slowly inclines upward to meet the swift downward sweep of the cables. The ensemble is a natural composition of power and symmetry (Fig. 13).

The Engineer As an Artist.—The bridge designer of this era has to be an engineer and an artist combined. To a thorough understanding of structural design and function he must add a strong feeling, both innate and trained, for beauty of form, line, and proportion. Architects, before they can help the engineer, must learn to understand and appreciate the new material—steel—and not regard it merely as a skeleton to be concealed or clothed in some foreign raiment.

In addition to beauty of form and line, the graceful, arching spans of tomorrow, like their rainbow prototype, will have brightness and warmth of color to satisfy a color-minded people. Instead of a black or gray intrusion or disfiguration, the span of tomorrow will be a thrilling part of the colorful landscape.

Illumination is a comparatively new but vigorous contribution to the esthetic aspect of bridges. "Painting with light" will be an integral part of their design. With phosphorescent color and fluorescent radiance, unforgettable effects of luminous magic will be produced. At night the rainbow span will be an arc of radiant glow.

A bridge is the embodiment of the effort of human heads and hearts and hands. It is an expression of man's creative urge—of his conquest of the forces of nature. When viewed in the glow of sunset or the enchantment of moonlight, it is, indeed, "a poem stretched across a river."

In all the amazing evolution of spans—from primitive to modern, from simple to complex, from small to gigantic, and from commonplace to inspiring—there has been a unifying spirit dominating bridge builders from generation to generation. It has been a spirit of vision, of invention, of courage, of sacrifice, and of consecration.

Spirit of Accomplishment.—From the Brothers of the Bridge in the Middle Ages to the bridge builders of today, those who conceived and created spans for the race of man have done so in a spirit of dedication. They were building, not monuments for themselves, but enduring instruments of service for their fellow men. They blazed the trails, cleared away obstacles, broke down barriers, and spanned the rivers and chasms that halted the progress of humanity. They did this, not alone for their own generations, but for the generations of men to come.

In this review of the epic of bridge building through the centuries, there stands out one dominant impression. In every great bridge project there must be: First, the vision and, then, the compelling endeavor to bring that vision to reality.

Through the ages, the spirit of the bridge builder has been: "From dream to deed—from vision to accomplishment."

That has been the spirit of the engineering profession.

It has likewise been the spirit of the United States.

Bridge builders in previous days dreamed their dreams and wrought their dreams, giving health, strength, and even life itself as the price of achievement. This generation is profiting by the work of the pioneers and is tackling even greater tasks. Whatever today's engineers may accomplish will in turn be eclipsed by those who follow.

In large cities and over mighty rivers are great bridges, beautiful bridges—bridges that inspire, that stir the imagination. The souls of men have been poured into their creation.

Engineer's Monuments.—The spirit of dedication characterizes the bridge builder. In all that he does and all that he builds, beyond the steel and the stone, the timber and the concrete, there is one priceless ingredient—the spirit of consecration; and that includes the qualities of vision, devotion, inspiration, and integrity.

This spirit of the builders is eloquently expressed in the words of John Ruskin:

"Therefore when we build let us think that we build forever. Let it not be for present delight, nor for present use alone. Let it be such work as our descendants will thank us for; and let us think, as we lay stone upon stone, that a time is to come when those stones will be held sacred because our hands have touched them, and that men will say as they look upon the labor and wrought substance of them, 'See, this our fathers did for us.' "

A bridge is not only a steppingstone of civilization. It is also a symbol of unity, the embodiment of the aspirations of humanity.

AMERICAN SOCIETY OF CIVIL ENGINEERS

Founded November 5, 1852

TRANSACTIONS

Paper No. 2626

SURVEY OF TIMBER HIGHWAY BRIDGES

By Raymond Archibald,[1] M. ASCE

Synopsis

Timber is one of the oldest, and therefore longest used, materials for bridge building. At first it had an almost exclusive coverage of the field, including pins for connecting the members. Wood trusses were then introduced, and more than a century ago they were subject to logical mathematical treatment. Other structural materials successfully competed, especially for heavier loadings and longer spans. More recently, however, timber has again come into its own for bridge construction—through wider use of preservatives for extending its life; by the introduction of metal connectors, giving more efficient and rigid joints; and by the perfection of the gluing process, whereby laminated members can be built up and tailored to size and utility. Even the lower stress grades can be used economically.

According to historic records of the use of timber in highway bridges, the important part played by timber in the development of American highways began, not 100 years ago, but more than three centuries ago. Possibly the earliest bridges should not be classed as engineering feats, but they did require ingenious methods for their day.

The first wooden highway bridges connected with American history were probably three bridges constructed in the Bermuda Islands in 1620, or 332 years ago. The first bridge built in North America was a horse bridge over the Neponset River, near Neponset, Mass., in 1634. It was destroyed in 1655 and replaced with a cart bridge. In 1635, a footbridge was erected at Ipswich, Mass., which was later widened.

Colonial Practice.—Perhaps the first highway bridge of importance was constructed almost 200 years ago, in 1761, over the York River at York, Me., by Samuel Sewell, a civil engineer. This bridge is especially significant—as it is the first on record that was built from plans predicated on a survey of the site, and as the first pile trestle structure. It was 270 ft long, 25 ft wide, and was supported on 4-pile bents spaced approximately 19 ft on centers. The bents, assembled with caps and bracing, were driven as a unit, the length of the piles having been previously determined by probing the stream bed with an iron-shod pole.

---

[1] Chf., Western Headquarters, Bureau of Pub. Roads, San Francisco, Calif.

Driving of the pile bents was quite an achievement in itself. After the bents were hoisted in place, the butt ends of the heavy logs, the tips of which were attached to, and pivoted on, the previously driven bent, were raised and let fall with considerable force on the cap. The York River bridge contained a draw span to allow for the passage of sloops.

In 1785, another pile trestle bridge was constructed over the Charles River between what were then Boston and Charlestown, Mass., by methods similar to those used on the York River bridge. Its total length was 1,503 ft including the draw span, and it had a 42-ft roadway and a 6-ft sidewalk. The camber for the entire length was 2 ft. Forty lamps were installed for illumination. Here, built 167 years ago, was a bridge with a draw span, wide roadways, pedestrian walks, lighting, and camber.

FIG. 1.—OLD COVERED BRIDGE ACROSS ROCKY RIVER NEAR STOWE, VT., NOW REPLACED; COMBINATION OF WOODEN ARCH AND TRUSS, A TYPICAL FEATURE

The proprietors of this bridge were required to pay annually $666.66 "in consideration of the income loss from ferriage," to a ferry located nearby. Apparently toll ferries and bridges had their difficulties then, too.

Advances in the Bridge Art.—The development of the timber arch and truss spans widened the field, and marked the beginning of a period of bridge construction unprecedented in history. A composite structure, of combination arch and truss (Fig. 1), was later popular, although in those days distribution of load between the two integrated systems was evidently indeterminate mathematically.

Records of a bridge over the Shetucket River at Norwich, Conn., built 188 years ago, in 1764, indicate that a truss might have been used for the first time. The account reads:

> "It is 124 ft in length and 28 ft above the water. Nothing is placed between the abutments, but the bridge is supported by Geometry work above, and calculated to bear a weight of 500 tons. The work is by Mr. John Bliss, one of the most curious mechanics of the age."

Built in 1792, the Essex-Merrimac Bridge near Newburyport, Mass., had two 160-ft arched-truss spans. The Piscataqua Bridge near Portsmouth, N. H., contained a "stupendous arc," the chord of which was 244 ft, 6 in. long. The ribs were made up of curved timbers hewn from crooked logs and framed to produce firm abutting joints, which were staggered to secure rigidity and strength.

Laminated timber members were used 148 years ago, in 1804, in the Trenton Bridge over the Delaware River between New Jersey and Pennsylvania. The ribs were made of 4-in. by 12-in. planks on edges built up to form ribs 3 ft wide.

Fig. 2.—Interior of Covered Bridge Across Big Red Creek, Carroll County, Virginia; Multiple Latticing, with Tree-Nail Connections

Another engineering feat was accomplished in 1814 with the construction of the McCall's Ferry Bridge over the Susquehanna River at McCall, Pa. This timber-arch span 360 ft long was to be erected on scows to be floated into position. However, an ice jam prevented the use of this method, so the ribs were cut in half and skidded into place, resting on falsework supported by the ice.

In 1819, Ithiel Town developed a timber truss which was patented in 1820. It consisted of a top-and-bottom parallel chord with inclined members forming a latticework (Fig. 2), and with vertical posts at the piers. The truss members were usually built of 2-in. by 10-in. and 4-in. by 14-in. planks.

A patent was obtained by William Howe in 1840 on a parallel-chord truss which permitted a complete stress analysis by a mathematical practice then in use. Thus, it appears that, even 112 years ago, engineering principles were being applied to highway bridges of timber. Now what about the intervening 112 years?

Pressure Treatment Introduced.—Probably the most significant development affecting highway bridges has been the introduction of the pressure preservative treatment of timber. With the advent of steel and concrete, the useful life of the timber bridge had to be extended if it was to compete with these new materials. This useful life had been greatly lengthened in the covered bridge (Figs. 1, 2, and 3), in which the truss members were protected from the elements, but this was not entirely satisfactory.

Pressure treatment of piles was an important improvement because untreated piles deteriorate swiftly at the ground line and render the remainder of the structure useless. Stringers and caps were also given this treatment. The laminated timber deck appeared at first to solve the roadway flooring problem because it

FIG. 3.—COVERED BRIDGE NEAR ROSEBURG, ORE., SPANNING UMPQUA RIVER

was lightweight and rigid and had a good riding surface. However, replacement became a major task and it was difficult to protect it from the wear and tear of traffic. Use of this deck today is generally limited to bridges on secondary or lightly traveled roads. A modern structure using a laminated deck is shown in Fig. 4.

Structural Advances.—Probably the next important step was the introduction of the composite structure, in which timber and concrete are combined. By proper bonding of the timber stringers to the concrete roadway slab with shear keys, an economical T-beam design resulted which gave a satisfactory slab that did not have to be replaced during the life of the structure. Another type of composite design which has been used quite extensively is a solid, laminated, timber-slab span running parallel with the roadway. For a topping, a concrete slab is attached to the timber slab by shear keys to assure composite action.

The first timber joints and splices were made with wooden pegs (Fig. 2), and later ones with iron bolts and nails. Then the steel gusset plate, to which the members were attached with bolts, was introduced (Fig. 5). Steel shear blocks notched

FIG. 4.—PERMANENT TREATED-WOOD TRUSS BRIDGE, WITH LAMINATED DECK; ACROSS SIKANNI CHIEF
RIVER, NEAR FORT NELSON, NORTHERN BRITISH COLUMBIA, CANADA

FIG. 5.—DETAIL OF 160-FT DEZADEASH RIVER BRIDGE NEAR CHAMPAGNE, YUKON TERRITORY, CANADA;
STEEL USED FOR GUSSET PLATES AND FOR FLOOR BEAMS

into the member were used in tension splices, but this reduced the net section considerably.

With the development of the ring connector, timber fabrication for highway bridges took on new life. This type of joint eliminated most of the weaknesses of the other types of joints and is now generally accepted. Structures depicted in Figs. 4, 5, and 6 employ ring connectors.

Fabricated Members.—Perhaps the latest, and one of the most important, developments that directly affects the highway bridge is glued, laminated struc-

FIG. 6.—TAKHINI RIVER BRIDGE ON ALASKA HIGHWAY, YUKON TERRITORY, CANADA; MINERAL-SALT TREATED WOOD, USING RING CONNECTORS

tural lumber. The adhesive used to form the laminations into one piece resists exposure to weather and is not affected by pressure treatment. Curved chords and arch ribs are fabricated by bending relatively limber planks to shape, and gluing them into one piece while they are held in this position.

Glued, laminated timber has been a successful substitute for the now hard-to-get dense structural-grade timbers in the larger sizes and longer lengths. Also lumber of a lower stress grade can be inserted in that part of a member not subject to high stresses. The top and bottom laminations of a beam subject to high flexural stresses would be composed of a dense structural grade, whereas those near the center of the beam could be of a lower stress grade.

Thus timber has played an important role in the development of highway bridges and continues to do so by progressive improvements and developments in its manufacture, fabrication, and treatment. Engineers should not make the mistake of ignoring the great possibilities of timber highway bridges.

AMERICAN SOCIETY OF CIVIL ENGINEERS

Founded November 5, 1852

TRANSACTIONS

Paper No. 2627

COMMERCIAL LUMBER GRADES

By Frank J. Hanrahan,[1] M. ASCE

Synopsis

Standardized lumber production resulted primarily from necessity. When commercial timber was cut and used only locally, the problem was relatively simple; but, with depletion of nearby supplies, stocks had to be secured from many sources and localities. Different standards of manufacture met head on at the distribution centers and confusion ensued. The development of national standards took place after the organization of regional and national lumber manufacturers' associations some 50 years ago. Government bureaus, with their scientists, gave inestimable encouragement and help. Continuous and consistent improvements have meanwhile taken place, so that today there is excellence and uniformity of grading practice. Engineers can be assured of receiving quality material to meet specific needs.

The past century saw many great technical advances in the lumber industry—especially in the field of lumber grades and inspection. Although no one has tried to determine the saving in dollars resulting from standardization of commercial lumber, even in these days of astronomical sums of money, the amount would be amazing.

Local Consumption.—Wood products were exported to England from Jamestown, in the Colony of Virginia, in 1608. Early lumber practices varied widely with the different colonies and localities. The individual preferences of manufacturers and local purchasers prevailed. There was little or no lumber trade between the various communities and, consequently, no great need for lumber grades or standards. The purchaser and seller, being in intimate contact, both knew what was needed and understood the limitations of the timber available.

As lumber manufacturing moved away from the growing communities and manufacturing industries, a close personal relationship still continued between producers, merchants, and users. Customarily, buyers for retail and industrial establishments visited the sawmills annually to purchase their year's supply.

When the main production centers shifted hundreds of miles from the principal markets, this relationship was lost, and the need for standard grades became

---

[1] Exec. Vice Pres., Am. Inst. of Timber Constr., Washington, D. C.

more apparent. Obviously, lumber originating in widely separated communities could not be bought and sold intelligently without a common understanding by both buyer and seller as to quality, size, and other pertinent items.

Influence of Swedish Rules.—No one knows when the first grading rules were established, but the first set of which there is any authentic record was published in Stockholm, Sweden, in 1764. Four grades of lumber were recognized; the appearance of each piece was described; and lines of demarcation were drawn between grades on the basis of character and position of admissible characteristics.

Grading rules were used in the New England States early in the nineteenth century. In 1833 the State of Maine passed a law recognizing four official grades which were very similar to the Swedish grades. In the 1870's these rules had found their way to Michigan and became known to the trade as "Saginaw" inspection.

In the late 1880's lumber manufacturers' associations were organized in the widely separated regions of the Lake States, the Atlantic seaboard, and the South. Similar organizations soon followed in the western part of the United States. Their principal motive was to formulate and establish grading rules for the separation of their products into grades of nearly equal quality and to provide inspection service for their members. Although varied in detail, the earliest rules in each region were similar to those for the early Swedish and New England grades.

A Confused State.—This evolution of grading rules by various groups in the different regions resulted in multiple grades, sizes, and shipping practices—that is, in inconsistencies between regions or species. During this period, individuals and groups of distributors, as well as manufacturers, set up their own rules. There were variations in nomenclature, in finished thicknesses and widths of wood for the same nominal size, in inspection practices, and in other important respects. When all these regional softwood species met in common markets, confusion resulted among distributors, specifiers, and consumers.

For example, one single pine was known by twenty-nine different common names; there was more than one kind of board-foot; and 1-in. lumber was cut on the head saw as thick as 1⅛ in. in one species or territory and as thin as 31/32 in. in another. Patterns of worked lumber varied between species and regions, and differences occurred in inspection and shipping practices.

This unfortunate situation was the result of natural evolution. Eventually, the industry at large took measures to bring about simplification and standardization in the manufacturing, distribution, and use of its products. Other industries have had a similar history.

At the Fiftieth Anniversary Meeting of the National Lumber Manufacturers Association in 1952, it was stated that:

> "The production and distribution of lumber never could have been utilized to the extent that it has in the building of America had it not been for the consistent program of standardization that has been undertaken by various industry organizations."

The farsighted founders of the Association must have been thinking along similar lines when they listed lumber uniformity as one of the objectives of the organization.

In 1902, the industry had just emerged from the period when dealers had to take the product of the log run of the mills with culls out and then segregate the lumber into the different qualities and grades that were required by local trade. Not until the early 1880's was any attempt made by the lumber producer to grade his own product before shipping it to market. Then, for a while there were all kinds of specifications in use, some promulgated by the producer and some by distributors and other buying groups. Only when the manufacturers formed strong trade associations and established sound systems of inspection did grading standards begin to be applied on an industry-wide basis.

Organization, As a Remedy.—At the first annual meeting of the National Lumber Manufacturers Association in 1903, a committee was appointed to study lumber grading rules and to make suitable recommendations. Of course the national association as such has never issued grading rules.

No doubt even these early studies showed that the only effective approach was for the regional associations representing the manufacturers of each lumber species to issue grading rules, and then to police their application. It was recognized that, with lumber as with metals, it is impractical to write a single specification for all species and regions. Nevertheless, over all the years of its existence the Association, composed as it is of the principal regional lumber manufacturers' associations, has been a tremendously helpful influence in bringing about a close degree of uniformity between the grading rules and the inspection procedures of the different regions.

Although industry leaders recognized that something had to be done to dispel confusion and promote the sale of lumber, at first they had considerable doubt that a framework could be devised which would correlate and provide broad uniformity in the manufacture and grading for all types of softwood lumber of all domestic species. Furthermore, they doubted that, if devised, the various groups of manufacturers could and would bring their practices within such a framework. However, in time differences began to disappear. Standards took shape, and the industry began to accept and follow them.

At the time the first American Lumber Standards for softwoods were nearly completed, Herbert Hoover, Hon. M. ASCE, then the United States Secretary of Commerce, stated:

"This is indeed a most astonishing success. It is the outstanding thing that has been accomplished by an industry in bettering its own practices from the double standpoint of efficient service to the consumers of its products and the efficient use of its raw materials."

Efforts to Perfect Standards.—At the American Lumber Congress in Chicago, Ill., in 1919, softwood standardization was discussed for the first time in an industry-wide meeting. There, an organized program looking to simplification and uniformity of lumber grading, sizes, and other items was adopted. Another meeting was held in 1921.

During this period, the United States Forest Products Laboratory in Madison, Wis., made available scientific information on wood; and the Division of Simplified Practice was created by Hoover, who offered the services of the United States Department of Commerce to the lumber industry in the big job ahead. Hoover also called the First General Lumber Conference in Washington, D. C., in May, 1922, which was attended by one hundred and ten representatives of all interests, and he led the discussions during the daylong session. His keynote was that the lumber industry should develop conservation of timber resources; that the industry itself should formulate and implement standards and guarantees of lumber quantity and quality for the consuming public; and that, in carrying out these things, it should be self-governed. The industry accepted the challenge.

Then followed the formation of the Central Committee on Lumber Standards representing manufacturers, distributors, specifiers, and consumers to develop the basic standards on which the commercial grading rules could be based. After a large number of meetings and drafts, the first edition of what eventually became "Simplified Practice Recommendation No. 16—Lumber," better known as the "American Lumber Standards for Softwood Lumber," was published by the Department of Commerce in 1924.

Further revisions and refinements followed. Later, the Central Committee on Lumber Standards was replaced by the American Lumber Standards Committee which also represents similar interests. This latter committee is appointed by the United States Secretary of Commerce.

Regional manufacturers' associations began rewriting their grading rules to conform to the new American Lumber Standards as early as 1925. By 1930, practically every association had done so. By the mid-thirties the coverage was complete among manufacturers. Subsequently, changes in both the individual established grades and the basic standards were made only when technical advancements, wider use, greater economy, or some other worthwhile objective justified the change. The program was not limited to quality provisions, but included standardization and simplification in sizes, such as thicknesses, widths, and lengths. This progress in turn enabled the manufacturer to streamline production (Fig. 1). The consumer ultimately benefits from any such savings in costs.

General Adoption.—Also, by this time, distributors, large industrial consumers, more and more designers, and purchasers were specifying and ordering lumber on grading rules conforming to the American Lumber Standards. Many city and regional building codes and most master lumber specifications issued by different groups, publishers, and government agencies also called for commercial lumber conforming to the American Lumber Standards. The American Society for Testing Materials (ASTM), American Railway Engineering Association (AREA), ASCE, American Association of State Highway Officials (AASHO), and others incorporated in their specifications and recommendations provisions conforming to this standard.

Sound technical bases for stress grading of lumber and glued laminated lumber were developed. Then standard commercial grades of stress-graded lumber and glued laminated lumber were issued.

Most of these advances apply more specifically to softwoods than to hardwoods. However, there have been outstanding achievements in the field of lumber grades and standards which are applicable to hardwoods. The hardwood industry, which is spread from the upper reaches of northeastern Quebec, Canada, to the slopes of the Rio Grande in Texas, uses one set of hardwood grading rules to cover thirty-four different species. As is the case for softwoods, producers, dealers, and users have a hand in developing these grading rules. The National

Hardwood Lumber Association (NHLA) first issued grades for hardwood lumber in 1898 which since that time have been revised regularly and improved on. To-day hardwoods can be purchased by the simple expression, "NHLA rules to govern."

It is not the purpose of this paper to discuss the methods and details covered in the basic standards and commercial grades of the various kinds of lumber. Such published information is readily available from lumber manufacturers'

FIG. 1.—OPERATION OF MULTIPLE-SAW TRIMMER, WHICH CUTS LUMBER TO STANDARD LENGTHS

organizations, the Department of Commerce, the Forest Products Laboratory, and elsewhere.

Advantages Achieved.—The advancement made by the industry as a whole might be highlighted by mention of a few of the outstanding accomplishments. Today there is a high degree of uniformity in the grading rules for all the different softwood and hardwood species. Much of the confusion that previously existed has been eliminated. For example, thorough seasoning to assure satisfactory performance in service is a major requirement of some lumber grading rules. Thus a dependable method for accurately checking dryness (Fig. 2) is an important phase of the grading process, where seasoning to a certain moisture content is specified.

Nationally accepted commercial grading rules provide a wide range of quality classifications that are suitable for meeting the needs of practically any user.

Only occasionally, to meet highly specialized requirements, does it become necessary to add particular provisions to the grading standards or to write a new rule.

Today it is easy to take full advantage of the substantial economies and conservation of resources which result from the use of a standard rather than a made-to-order article. The development and standardization of lumber grades and inspection services have been based on many years of painstaking study and

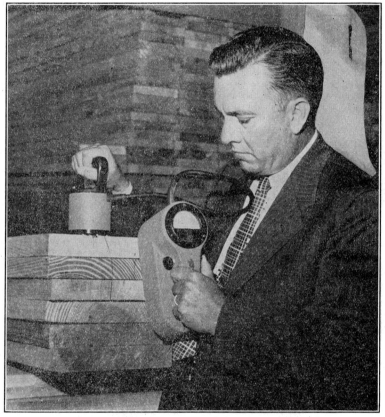

FIG. 2.—GRADING FOR MOISTURE CONTENT, AN ESSENTIAL STEP, SIMPLIFIED BY USING ELECTRICAL MOISTURE REGISTER, STANDARD EQUIPMENT OF INSPECTION BUREAUS

recognition of what the consumers need and what can be produced on a practical commercial scale from trees at hand with a minimum of waste. Modern stress grading and inspection have made lumber a true engineering material in every sense of the word.

Its structural and architectural versatility has been greatly increased by the introduction of glued laminated material which also is available in standardized commercial grades.

In all these developments in lumber grading and standardization, the industry's national and regional organizations and the American Lumber Standards Committee and its subcommittees have been assisted greatly by the wealth of technical data made available by the Forest Products Laboratory. Over the years the many able men comprising the laboratory staff have been most cooperative in working with industry on all its standardization projects, and have rendered outstanding service. This fine institution and its staff deserve a substantial share of the credit for many accomplishments.

Another important part in these activities has been played by Committee D-7 on Wood of the ASTM. It has served particularly in the field of standardizing

Fig. 3.—Grading Demonstration in the Deep South, for Members of Committee of American Railway Engineering Association; Half a Dozen Major Railroads Being Represented by Onlookers

the wood testing procedures used to obtain the reliable data necessary as a basis for establishing stress grades of lumber and for assigning stresses to these grades.

Engineering Benefits.—Now that commercial grades conforming to the American Lumber Standards are nationally established in the industry, the simple, practical, and economical procedure in buying lumber is to specify the desired established commercial grades, in accordance with the standard commercial rules. In recognition of this fact, the AASHO, ASTM, AREA, and other groups have substituted, or are in the process of substituting, standard commercial grading rules for the former special rules in their specifications. Such organizations also evidence more than casual interest in the maintenance and application of grading standards for lumber. Some of these groups have at times held committee meetings near points of lumber production, to secure first-hand experience (Fig. 3).

Today only the inexperienced write special grading rules (particularly in the stress-grading field) when lumber conforming to standard commercial grades will suffice. Trying to substitute special grades or rules for the standard ones, familiar to the trade, invites substantially higher costs—resulting from the special manufacturing, the special handling of the transaction by a considerable number of people between the manufacturer and purchaser, the possibility of errors, and the general breakdown of efficiency of operations when converting from a familiar mass-produced standardized article to an unfamiliar, custom-made article. Also delay ensues because nonstandard items are not stocked.

A few months ago an authority stated:

> "I'm sure that if the record of the industry were carefully examined it would be found that in every single year since 1902 there has been at least one progressive step in standardization by one or more branches of the industry."

Every type of engineer and technical man has had a hand directly or indirectly in the technical advances of the wood products industry. Mechanical equipment, steam and electrical power, communications, transportation, electronic devices, chemical processes, and practically everything else the industry uses are attributable to the past or present efforts of some engineer or scientist. With greater realization of their importance, leaders are encouraging greatly expanded technical activities and increased employment of engineers and other technical men in the industry.

The wood products industry is not resting on its laurels. It is constantly striving to increase the service of its products. The coming century will witness at least as great advances in the manufacture, marketing, and use of lumber as has the past century. Again, engineers and other technical men will be largely responsible for the progress made in the production and utilization of products from the nation's greatest renewable resource, its forests. Modern harvesting and conservation practices assure a perpetually available supply of material, which in turn assures a perpetual need for engineering talent.

AMERICAN SOCIETY OF CIVIL ENGINEERS

Founded November 5, 1852

TRANSACTIONS

Paper No. 2628

USE OF WOOD ON AMERICAN RAILROADS

By H. Austill,[1] M. ASCE

Synopsis

From their earliest days, railroads adopted timber for a myriad of purposes, such as roadways, cars, and bridges. It was plentiful and readily available; it possessed structural qualities both unique and serviceable. Many examples illustrate its wide and valuable use. When railway engineers learned the limitations of wood and adjusted designs to fit, the results were gratifying. In particular, creosote has been helpful in protecting against decay, as in the case of crossties. Some 1,750 miles of timber trestle, mostly treated, are still giving excellent results, although wood truss bridges, long utilized to great advantage for railroads, are now practically extinct. Such a plentiful and useful natural material deserves continued study and application, even today.

In 1829 Horatio Allen, later Past-President and Hon. M. ASCE, reported to the South Carolina Railway Company in favor of steam power instead of horse-power for that line. The basis of the report, he stated:

> "* * * was on the broad ground that in the future there was no reason to expect any material improvement in the breed of horses, while, in his judgment, the man was not living who knew what the breed of locomotives was to place at command."

According to available records, the first steam hauled train in the United States was on the South Carolina Railroad from Charleston to Hamburg, S. C., on November 2, 1830. In 1830, 23 miles of railroad were operated in the United States.

In 1852, 100 years ago, when this story begins, there were 12,908 miles of road. Economic conditions required that railroads be pushed through at the least possible cost and that the development of traffic with resulting revenue be depended on to improve the plant. The use of timber fitted into this situation admirably. Not until 1916 was the peak reached in miles of road operated with 254,036 miles; and not until 1930, in miles of track operated with 429,883 miles.

---

[1] Cons. Engr., Spring Hill, Ala.; formerly Chf. Engr., Terminal R. R. Assn., St. Louis, Mo.

Wooden Roadway and Cars.—Wood was utilized on early railroads for: Tracks, cars, bridges, buildings, fences, snowsheds, tunnel linings, docks, wharves, bulkheads, crossing planks, dams, and water pipes. Wood is still being used today on all such structures.

Except for a small amount of track, the rails of which were supported on stone blocks, the original roadway was almost wholly of wood. In 1944 a section of original track of the South Caroline Canal and Rail Road, about 35 ft long, was uncovered at Warrenville, S. C. It consisted of two longitudinal timbers or sleepers about 6 in. by 9 in. in section spaced at about 8-ft intervals; on top of these were placed cross timbers or crossties which were fastened at each end with wooden pegs or tree nails. A rail made of timber, about 6 in. by 10 in., was on top of the crossties and dapped into them, being held to gage by wedges. There was an iron strip on top of the wood rail. Along the center of the track beneath the crossties a wooden drain box was placed.

Early railways were not built or even conceived to have the high-speed, heavy-tonnage, carrying facilities that they do now. Rather their purpose was to transport bulk commodities from the point of production to the point of use. These railways generally used a wood plank or planks for rail. The next development was the application of an iron plate on top of the plank or runner, the latter being set in a dap in the crosstie and held to gage by wedges.

Freight cars were small and light, with a capacity of only 8 to 10 tons and, like passenger cars, were made almost entirely of wood. Then for years the trend was toward all-steel cars. As someone remarked: The engineers, having done all they could to reduce the number of wrecks, were now doing all they could to make them as comfortable as possible. At present the "Unicel" car, made mostly of wood, is the latest innovation, thus emphasizing the point that, instead of seeking substitutes, time might have been better spent on improved design.

The roadway is rather prosaic and unspectacular; yet it is fundamental—all operations depend on the track being there and being safe. Today there are few feet of track not supported by wood crossties. After just about exhausting all possibilities of finding a satisfactory substitute, much effort is now being directed toward protecting and extending tie life by use of larger tie plates, tie pads, anti-checking devices, and tie coverings, and by better drainage of the track. It is now not unusual to find ties that have served 30 years. The problem therefore is to make the resistance to mechanical wear equal to the extended life resulting from chemical treatment.

Development of glue that can be used to hold timber together, even during the creosote method of treatment, may make it possible to salvage the sound and un-rail-cut part of crossties by cutting that section out and gluing two or three such pieces together. The present high cost of crossties may make such an operation economically desirable. Glued laminated pieces of new wood are now being used experimentally for crossties.

A Unique Material.—Although timber has probably been used by man as long as any material of construction—certainly before he knew how to make iron, concrete, or steel—some of its more important characteristics are generally less understood than those of what might be called competitive materials. It is well, therefore, to consider some of the characteristics of this material which nature has provided so generously.

Timber, unfortunately, is subject to decay—a disintegration of wood substance due to the action of wood-destroying fungi. However, cypress and western red cedar or redwood resist decay almost completely. Air, moisture, and warmth are necessary for decay in timber. Eliminate any one of these and the life of timber will be greatly extended.

Since fungi, bacteria, and insects are the causes of decay, if the timber is impregnated with a substance poisonous to these, obviously its life will be dependent on its retention of the poisonous substance. The method of preserving timber by creosote treatment has been known for more than 100 years, but mankind was slow in adopting it.

Timber is essentially immune from deterioration caused by brine or locomotive fumes, both of which are quite destructive to steel and, to a lesser extent, to reinforced concrete. In fact, brine acts as a preservative for timber.

Timber, particularly when untreated, is also vulnerable to marine borers and termites.

The one form of destruction that has caused the greatest loss, not attributable to what might be called natural cause, is that great nemesis of wood—fire. However, in the 1925 report of the Committee on Wood Preservation of the American Railway Engineering Association (AREA), the following statement appears:

> "We have a few notable examples to prove that creosoted material when dry is not as susceptible to fire as untreated material and it is no harder to put out than untreated material. In most cases creosoted timber will stop burning after the excess oil has passed out of the wood, as it burns only as long as the heat converts the oil into gas, and when the excess oil is exhausted the fire goes out."

Moneywise, much more annual loss results from corrosion of metal than from burning of wood structures. It has been estimated that the annual loss to American railroads due to corrosion of metal is $268,000,000.00. There is increasing interest in fireproofing timber by impregnation of chemicals, with promise of much success by such treatment. Timber is a good insulating material against temperature.

It is admitted, of course, that, as is true of any material of construction, timber has its limitations. However, it also is ideally suited to many types of structures, and for these it should not be overlooked.

Reserve of Structural Resistance.—One characteristic of timber, quite peculiar to it as compared with other materials of construction, is its ability to support a much greater load for a short time than for a long time; and to support a greater load parallel to the grain than across the grain. As one supervisor used to remark: "It is surprising what a post will carry on its end and a rail on its edge."

In general, a beam will fail in several years under a load about 56% of what it will safely support for a few minutes. On the other hand, timber when green or wet is not as strong as when dry.

The most important factors which influence the strength of structural timber are the size, number, and location of defects and the extent of exposure to moisture during use. In computing the shear at the ends of a wood beam it is safe to ignore all concentrated loads between the support and a point three times the depth of the beam from the end support.

Although use of structural timber dates from prehistoric times, specifications are relatively of recent origin—not much more than half a century old—and they have been, unfortunately, somewhat a cause of conflict between engineers and lumber manufacturers. The latter take the position that trees grow by nature and incline to the theory or position that the engineer should find a way to utilize what nature provides—that is, that timber must be used as it is found in the forest. The engineer, on the other hand, argues that timber should be selected to meet the strength and life required by him. In fact, some engineers have considered the properties of wood too indefinite to make determination by analysis possible. Engineers of the United States Forest Products Laboratory at Madison, Wis., devote their entire study to wood, and recommend the working stresses to be used in designing wood structures.

Structural grades for timber offer criteria for selecting material for strength and for uniformity of strength, in order that appropriate working stresses may be assigned. Engineers need not know how to distinguish or identify the many different species of oak or of pine, but should be informed as to the effects that the principal defects—such as decay, knots, checks, and moisture content—as well as the duration of load, may have on safe working stresses.

Although the merits of treated timber as compared to untreated timber are well known, it is doubtful that the advantages of treated timber as compared to other materials of construction are so generally recognized. In 1909, 1912, and 1928, bending tests were made at Tulane University (New Orleans, La.) of treated stringers taken from the Lake Pontchartrain trestle on the Southern Railway, constructed in 1883. The lowest fiber stress at elastic limit occurred in two pieces tested in 1909; and the highest, in two pieces tested in 1928. The average stress in the outer fiber, at elastic limit, for fourteen tests in 1909 was 3,049 lb per sq in.; for ten tests in 1912, 3,760 lb per sq in.; and, for twelve tests in 1928, 3,940 lb per sq in. A similar structure in Louisiana is shown in Fig. 1.

Engineers are prone to lose sight of fundamentals and to grab at fads and specialties. They use quick setting or high early strength cement without a careful analysis to determine whether the increase in cost over standard portland cement is justified. They rushed to substitute other materials for timber without knowing how long a life would actually be required for the structure. In addition, they often overlooked the fact that a lesser life at a lesser cost is economical.

Early Timber Construction.—The origin of wooden bridge construction is not now possible to determine. Certainly it dates from prehistoric times. Although Americans think of the wood trestle and bridge as their own product, a wood pile trestle was built over the Tiber at Rome about 650 B. C., and one was built by Caesar across the Rhine in 55 B. C. Piles or posts driven partly into the ground by blows of a hammer are prehistoric in origin. Even the presumably later development of what are now termed foundation and sheet piles is too ancient to be a matter of record.

Some notable wood structures were built for American railroads, among which was one at Portage, N. Y., in 1852—some 800 ft long and 234 ft high. In more recent times a logging railroad constructed a trestle 203 ft high across Cedar River Canyon. A major existing structure is shown in Fig. 2.

Old bridge builders never used timber that had not seasoned as much as 2 years. They hand hewed and joined it by tree nails. When it was found that timber used as a rail would not stand up under wear, it was covered with an iron strip. However, when trestle caps failed because of splits from an excessive number of driftbolts or because of decay traceable to vertical holes which permitted retention of excessive moisture, little attention seems to have been given to improved design or to use of composite materials—instead the tendency was to condemn the timber as short lived.

Fig. 1.—Double-Track, Creosoted, Ballast-Deck Bridge, Illinois Central System, North of New Orleans, La.—2¼ Miles Long

In most cases of decay, such failures occurred at joints or in details where better design would have provided much longer life. Too many driftbolts through caps and vertical holes in stringers over caps were common instances of poor design.

Value of Preservatives.—A. F. Robinson, bridge engineer of the Atchison, Topeka and Santa Fe System, did a great deal to improve the design of the trestle. The extension of its useful life through proper design as well as through use of treated timber made it a truly engineered structure. One of the early attempts to extend the life of timber in trestles "took a tip" from the covered bridge and covered stringers and caps with metal sheets. As a result, the life of the untreated timber was extended more than 24 years.

A leading textbook states: "The only excuse for a timber bridge is that it is cheaper than some other form of construction. It is less durable than either steel or masonry." With the first sentence there can be no argument, but certainly the second is disputable. Untreated timber has served for more than a century in old covered bridges where it was protected from the weather. In other cases, treated timber has been found to be perfectly sound after half a century of service in the most exposed locations and in a territory with an annual rainfall of about 56 in. Nevertheless some engineers still claim that timber is temporary construction.

FIG. 2.—APPROACH TO McKINLEY BRIDGE, ILLINOIS TERMINAL RAILROAD COMPANY, ST. LOUIS, MO.— CREOSOTED TRESTLE 2½ MILES LONG

What might be permanent construction as applied to railroads is a most difficult matter to determine. Granting the permanence of the material of which a structure is to be built, what assurance is there that the structure itself will be needed for more than 50 years? Why should capital expenditures be increased to project the life of the structure beyond the time of foreseeable usefulness? Future changes in drainage, line, and grade and even abandonments might make unnecessary structures that are required today.

Timber is relatively easy to frame, repair, and reinforce. When preframed and treated, in most locations it will last longer without additional protection than would a steel structure that is not painted periodically.

The wood trestle (Figs. 1 and 2) is an economical and necessary part of a permanent railway. That it will last for the life of many railroads is witnessed by the AREA Committee on Wood Bridges and Trestles, which reported in 1951 that on seventy class I roads there were in service 9,267,381 track-ft or 1,755 miles of timber trestle work, of which: 2,128,668 ft were treated open deck; 2,678,427 ft were treated ballast deck; 2,992,095 ft were untreated open deck; and 838,104 ft were treated and had some type of protected deck. The remainder were some special combinations of forms. It is quite possible that the life of exposed timber might be extended by periodical spray treatment with a preservative.

Timber Trusses Developed.—The art of building wood truss bridges was developed by Theodore Burr, Lewis Wernwag (both Pennsylvania carpenters), and Timothy Palmer of Newburyport, Mass. They built combination arch and truss bridges in the early years of the nineteenth century, apparently with little appreciation of the stresses involved. Ithiel Town, S. H. Long, William Howe, and the Pratts (Caleb and Thomas) invented pure truss types soon afterward, but were unable to compute the stresses in various parts. Town, about 1820, added latticework to his truss.

The invention of the truss form permitted timber to be used to greater advantage than ever before and railroad bridges up to 250-ft spans were thus constructed. The truss combining wood and metal was soon developed; but little thought seems to have been devoted to the possibility of combining wood with some other material to extend its life.

In 1847 at Utica, N. Y., Squire Whipple, Hon. M. ASCE, published "Work on Bridge Building" which gave the analysis of stresses in trusses in a surprisingly complete manner, and Herman Haupt published an independent treatise in 1851. The Howe truss, patented in 1840, has the advantage of being adjustable so that timber shrinkage can be taken up. This type was in general use from 1840 to 1870. Wood stringers were also standard on metal bridges prior to 1870, about which time weights of locomotives and rolling stock began to increase rapidly.

A bridge built by Wernwag across the Delaware in 1803 was used as a highway bridge for 45 years and then reinforced and used as a railway bridge for 27 years. In regard to the Howe truss, Mansfield Merriman and H. S. Jacoby, Members, ASCE, state: [2]

> "The Howe truss bridge has been properly styled as preeminently the American wooden bridge. * * * No other type of truss was so extensively built during the thirty years following its introduction in 1840, and in various parts of the country where timber is plentiful, notably in the far west, it is still [1907] in use for both railroad and highway traffic."

The report of the AREA Committee VII in 1905 contains a bibliography of books and pamphlets dealing with wood bridges that is quite complete and of much interest.

Possibilities Old Yet New.—It took man hundreds of years to learn that he could put on a shirt without crawling through it, but since the advent of mechanical means of transport he has gone so far and so fast that it is almost impossible to visualize the conditions that existed a short 100 years ago when bridge building in the United States was just emerging from the status of a trade and entering the art of a learned profession.

It is certain that colleges have been inclined to give too little stress to the study of timber as a structural material and that much of the time and talent devoted to a search for a good substitute might have been better spent on working

[2] "Text-book on Roofs and Bridges," by M. Merriman and H. S. Jacoby, John Wiley & Sons, Inc., New York, N. Y., 6th Ed., Pt. I, 1907, p. 81.

out methods of preserving the material and improving the design of the older structures. Timber, being a replenishable, natural resource, will be available as a construction material indefinitely. It is therefore well to reconsider the conditions under which its use is advantageous.

AMERICAN SOCIETY OF CIVIL ENGINEERS

Founded November 5, 1852

TRANSACTIONS

Paper No. 2629

SCHOOLS ILLUSTRATE PROGRESS IN THE USE OF WOOD

By Harry W. Bolin,[1] M. ASCE

Synopsis

Historically, from the days of the "little red schoolhouse," wood has been the accepted material for such structures. With modern advances in adaptation, fittings, and design, timber has again asserted its dominance. Nowadays, the large multipurpose union school, also of wood, has supplanted a group of many local, single-room buildings. Usually it has a single story, with emphasis on lighting, security against earthquake shocks, and a multiplicity of uses. The transition, as illustrated by California's experience, has introduced many difficult problems that the structural engineer has been forced to meet—and to solve successfully.

Evolution of School Buildings

A century of engineering progress in the use of wood can well be illustrated by school buildings. During the "gay nineties" and, indeed, afterward until, say, the early 1930's, the symbol of education was the little red schoolhouse. As late as 1916 there were some 200,000 of these one-room, single-teacher institutions in the rural communities of the United States. Very likely, not many of them had received the benefit of architectural design; and, certainly, few if any were ever considered from the structural viewpoint. It is estimated that about 70,000 remain, but these are disappearing rapidly.

Not so well publicized as the rural school was its urban contemporary. As a rule, the city chool was also a standard type, consisting of a two-story or three-story masonry-wall building, with longitudinal central corridors flanked by instruction rooms on both sides. No doubt these schools were actually planned and designed by architects, but engineering services in connection with them seem to have been quite limited. Only the size of wood floor and roof joists and the design of footings required engineering knowledge; and, usually, the architect could determine these data.

Some of the criteria arbitrarily established for schools in the past still govern

---

[1] Prin. Structural Engr., Div. of Architecture, State Dept. of Public Works, Los Angeles, Calif.

or influence school design. It is true that the old rectangular classroom 24 ft by 40 ft in size has been changed to almost a square, 30 ft by 32 ft, but the area of an instruction room is, by and large, still 960 sq ft.

Public school construction was not of too great concern in the United States until 1817, when Michigan began its well-known program of instruction from kindergarten to and through the university. In the states along the Atlantic coast, European and English ideas prevailed—those financially able were educated in private schools and others received little or no formal education. In the newer communities farther to the west, there was little or no public instruction and what did exist was of the "little red schoolhouse" variety.

New Criteria.—Real progress in school construction has been concentrated in the period since about 1930. There are two principal reasons for new developments in the design of wood structures and buildings for schools: (1) The changing demands for school housing, and (2) the better quality of structural timber, together with increased efficiency of fastenings. Without considering, for the moment, the advances in the use of wood, improvement in fastenings, and changes in manufacture, such as gluing, some of the factors influencing or accelerating structural progress in the planning, design, and construction of school buildings are:

1. The automobile and the resulting good roads.
2. The California earthquake of 1933 (affecting California practice primarily).
3. New ideas as to the function of buildings, stressing—
    a. Uniformity of natural light;
    b. Change of shape of instruction rooms;
    c. Flexibility in size of rooms by avoiding permanent partitions;
    d. Multi-use; and
    e. Their utilization as community centers.

Factors 1 and 2 have brought structural engineers into the field of public school building design. Factor 3 is responsible for the creation of abnormal structural problems and for the necessity that the structural engineer exercise ingenuity, imagination, and judgment in the safe design of school buildings.

Certain school experts assert that structural engineers retard progress because they insist on safe and strong buildings for housing school children. On the contrary, the engineer has been responsible for the improvements demanded by the educators. If it were not for the ability and resourcefulness of the engineer, who designs structurally safe buildings, making use of new structural materials, new processes of assembly and fabrication, new types of fastenings, and better methods of structural analysis, the school experts could not obtain the types of buildings that are, to them, desirable. For example, Figs. 1 and 2 show framing evolved by the engineer to give adequate strength and at the same time to provide for certain light-reflecting surfaces.

EFFECTS OF THE MOTOR AGE

Good roads, promoted for the use of the automobile, are responsible for a complete change in educational ideas as far as housing is concerned. Single-room schools each for a small school district have given way to larger plants, fewer in number and spaced farther apart. Buses, in which school children are transported to and from schools, have enabled small districts to combine or unionize. The pooled resources have facilitated separate instruction for each age group and expansion of education far beyond the three "R's."

A modern school plant below the secondary or high school level (Fig. 3) may have one or more kindergartens, a number of buildings, usually similar and laid

FIG. 1.—WOODEN ROOF FRAMING—CURVED BEAMS, LAMINATED AND GLUED, SUPPORTING AUXILIARY FRAMING FOR LIGHT-REFLECTING CEILINGS

out in a finger pattern, housing rooms for instruction, gymnasium facilities, an administration unit, and a cafeteria. In some instances, a single building may have many purposes, serving as a cafeteria, assembly room, physical education room, and even as a community center. Such a building (Fig. 4) often takes a name which indicates its combined use. The exposed glued laminated timber arches give a pleasing appearance. A modern high school plant usually has a number of classroom buildings, shop buildings, an auditorium, a gymnasium (one each for boys and girls), shower and locker buildings, a swimming pool, a cafeteria,

FIG. 2.—CLASSROOM ROOF UNDER CONSTRUCTION, WHICH WILL SUPPORT SLOPED CEILINGS

FIG. 3.—UP-TO-DATE SCHOOL BUILDING FEATURING LOW OUTLINE WITH PLENTY OF LIGHT

and an administration unit. The campus and buildings for a junior college may rival those of colleges and universities.

Buildings for school plants are usually only one or two stories in height—in fact, predominantly one story. Wood is used extensively since it is adaptable to almost any size of building by proper utilization and assembly of structural parts. Likewise, it is not difficult to attain the proper degree of fire protection as required by use and occupancy.

FIG. 4.—"CAFETORIUM" FOR A NUMBER OF OBVIOUS USES

EFFECTS OF THE CALIFORNIA EARTHQUAKE OF 1933

Shortly after the destructive earthquake of March 10, 1933, in the Compton-Long Beach area of California, the state legislature passed, on April 10, 1933 as an emergency measure, the Field Act providing that public school buildings must be earthquake resistant. Because of their special qualifications, the structural engineers of California, since its enactment, have played a very prominent part in public school planning, design, and construction. The act had a further effect—it caused the elimination of heavy masonry ornamental features over exitways, of parapets, and of multistoried school buildings. Since unit masonry walls did not fare well in the earthquake, particularly in school buildings, they were discredited until relatively recently when improved methods of obtaining monolithic, integral reinforced masonry were evolved.

One-story school buildings appeared to be the answer to the earthquake problem and wood, as a structural material, was recognized to be suitable for such buildings. A structural assembly such as a wood stud and sheathed wall or a wood floor or roof is well adapted to act as a diaphragm. Since a diaphragm resists forces acting in or near its plane, it was natural for structural engineers to desire to use, as diaphragms, elements placed in buildings for other purposes such as walls, partitions, floors, and roofs—elements ordinarily designed for forces transverse to them. The need for more accurate data has been the spur for numerous tests on wood diaphragms to insure intelligent designs.

Earthquake-resistant construction requires that the structural engineer pay more attention to details. Wood has a great deal of give so that it can deflect and distort without injury; but the design must be such that failure cannot result from separation of structural parts. Thus it is imperative that forces propagated by earthquakes are resisted by structural elements acting as distributing agents, which transmit the forces to properly connected vertical elements and through them to the ground.

Although the value of the legislation regulating the construction of public school buildings had been tested in previous California earthquakes, such as those at Imperial on May 18, 1940, and in the Gardena-Torrance area on November 14, 1941 (in addition to five others of minor destructive effect), the number of buildings constructed under the act was small. Recently, however, two fairly intense and destructive tremors with strong aftershocks occurred in Kern County, California. The first was the Arvin-Tehachapi earthquake of July 21, 1952, resulting from an abrupt displacement along the White Wolf Fault (sometimes called the Bear Mountain Fault); the second was the Bakersfield earthquake of August 22, 1952.

Many school buildings of all types, employing all materials of construction—wood, masonry, reinforced concrete, and structural steel—were in the areas affected. A large number of masonry-wall schools constructed before passage of the Field Act were seriously damaged, and many collapsed in whole or in part. However, those erected subsequently were either undamaged or damaged to only a minor extent, with no collapses in whole or in part. Structural engineering design in compliance with the provisions of the earthquake law for schools proved adequate in furnishing earthquake-resistant, safe school buildings.

Effects of Functional-Use Change

Structural design of school buildings has been affected to a very large degree by new ideas as to the character of school housing. Changes began during the 1920's, but in the period since World War II they have made the former type of school building almost obsolete.

The first change was in regard to natural lighting. The aim today is to obtain uniform natural light over the entire instructional area with a minimum of shadows. This requirement has been accepted by architects as a challenge and their solutions are quite varied: Ceilings are sloped upward to exterior walls; one wall (north) is made practically all glass, and the opposite wall (south) above passage or arcade roofs is opened as much as possible, sometimes with suspended louvers or deflectors; or ceilings are partly omitted over classroom areas and baffles or reflectors are placed inside the rooms. Dependence on these devices results in the elimination of many of the building elements, such as walls and roofs, formerly utilized by structural engineers to obtain strength and rigidity. The engineer must resort to rigid or flexible frames or other devices to cope with the modern trend toward constructing exterior walls and roofs of glass.

The second change affecting the structural engineer was the development from the old standard rectangular classroom, 24 ft by 40 ft, to the almost square room, about 30 ft by 32 ft. For some time this innovation had an adverse effect on wood. The 2-in. by 14-in., or 3-in. by 12-in., roof rafters could easily span the older 24-ft width without serious sag or deflection; but, when the spans were increased to as much as 32 ft, the available commercial sizes of wood planks or joists were not suitable. For some time engineers employed structural steel or light gage steel in the form of joists or trusses to replace wood rafters. However, wood design has been reestablished by the use of frames spaced some distance apart (8 ft to 16 ft) supporting purlins or joists extending longitudinally, and also by the use of glued laminated members or trusses.

A third important change in modern classroom construction is the elimination of permanent partitions. Why this is considered important is difficult to understand since, indeed, rarely are partitions moved to increase or decrease size of rooms. This feature has been another source of difficulty for the structural engineer. It is convenient to design partitions as integral parts of a building doing their share toward providing strength and stiffness. Thus, again, the ingenuity of the engineer is taxed to make up for a deficiency. The rigid frame, often of glued-laminated construction, is one scheme employed to provide the necessary transverse structural elements for strength.

The fourth and fifth changes—multipurpose and community use—affect the engineer only in that building size is increased; and, accordingly, it is necessary to use frames, arches, or columns and trusses, all of which can be readily designed in wood.

Effects of the Material Itself

In addition to the effects of these outside developments, advance or progress in the design of wood structures has been influenced greatly by the material itself. In fact, the problems of structural design of modern school buildings could not have been solved if this were not so. For instance, Fig. 5 shows a roof supported by lamella framing. The lamellas and the roof sheathing not only furnish support for dead and live loads, but also serve as a diaphragm for distributing horizontal (earthquake) forces to resisting vertical elements and at the same time stay the walls laterally.

Structural lumber of all sizes is much more accurately graded than was the case years ago. Grade marking gives the engineer confidence in the material.

Another great improvement occurred in connection with timber fastenings. Although the nail is probably the most efficient connector considering its weight, it must be obvious that nail use is limited since the structural value of each nail as a connection is small. Besides nails, bolts and lag screws have been the most common fastening devices. All these are still valuable, but new types of connectors developed over three decades add to the variety of fastenings available. Timber connectors, such as split rings and shear plates, have had a tremendous influence in increasing the range or scope of structural design in wood. Recently another device, the triple-grip connector, has given the engineer opportunity to improve structural details. This type of fastening, virtually eliminates toenailing and many awkward connections formerly used for light loads can be avoided.

Perhaps structural design of wood has been most greatly influenced by the use of glue in fabricating large members from a number of smaller pieces. Glued laminated lumber permits the disposition of material so that poorer

FIG. 5.—LAMELLA-TYPE ROOF WHICH LENDS ITSELF TO A SPACIOUS HIGH SCHOOL GYMNASIUM

grades may be used in sections or parts of members with low or negligible stress, thus aiding conservation. It permits the engineer to obtain any structural shape necessary for his design, such as flat or sharply haunched arches, rigid frames and

(a) Glued Laminated Timber Arches in Place   (b) Detail of Hinge Support for Arches

FIG. 6.—CONSTRUCTION FOR HIGH SCHOOL GYMNASIUM

girders, and beams of different shapes including those which vary in depth throughout their length.

A good example of the use of glued laminated timber arch construction is shown in Fig. 6(a). The arch span is 103 ft 10½ in. center to center of pins with a rise at the crown of 42 ft.

Wood Solves School Problems

Modern housing demands plus the necessity for adequate strength and stiffness, together with the increased usefulness of wood, have resulted in a large percentage of modern schools being constructed of wood. Wood is a versatile material that can be used in all types of school buildings from the simple single-room portable unit to the most elaborate multipurpose building. After all, the little red wooden schoolhouse usually was merely a crude shelter, whereas the modern school built of wood provides not only shelter but also reasonable safety against earthquakes. At the same time it is esthetically and architecturally pleasing.

AMERICAN SOCIETY OF CIVIL ENGINEERS

Founded November 5, 1852

TRANSACTIONS

Paper No. 2630

VISIBLE EARTHQUAKE EFFECTS AND PRACTICAL CORRECTIVE MEASURES

By H. M. Engle,[1] M. ASCE

Synopsis

Experience has much to teach about designing for earthquake protection. Widespread shocks, which occurred as long as 140 years ago, are on record; but more recent ones, notably in California, are particularly instructive. They have led to eight criteria for design, most of which are generally accepted. However, renewed emphasis needs to be given to the advantages of structural reinforcing and to the dangers of poor foundations. Even more important is a generous allowance for lateral forces, using coefficients up to 8% g or 12% g. This necessity is proved by structural behavior, both good and bad, in recent shocks—in effect nature's shaking table for full-scale tests. Lacking better evidence, engineers are in duty bound to avail themselves of such practical warnings.

The west coast of the United States, and California in particular, is considered by many people to be preeminently the "Land of Earthquakes." Earthquake-resistant design is assumed as necessary and desirable only in that area. It should be borne in mind, however, that no part of the United States can be said to be immune. The seismic activity in the St. Lawrence Valley is well known. The strong tremor at Charleston, S. C., has not been wholly forgotten. The great shock centering near New Madrid, Mo., in 1811 and 1812, is now well authenticated. In fact, during the past year renewed seismic activity has occurred in this general area.

A school in northern Ohio erected about 40 years ago was damaged by an earthquake, according to the son of the contractor who built it. Some 20 years ago a masonry school at Anna, Ohio, was severely damaged in a shock. No area in the country should be too sure of immunity from earthquakes. The frequency of occurrence may be low but, when a shock does come, a major disaster may result.

Experience As a Teacher.—Earthquake-resistant design, heavy lateral force design, or whatever one may choose to call it, should be of value and interest in

---

[1] Civ. and Structural Engr., San Francisco, Calif.

any part of the United States. Experience has shown that earthquake-resistant design, involving proved principles and provision for heavy lateral forces, also can produce structures highly resistant to the effects of atom bombs and tornadoes. Therefore, ordinary common sense and foresight would dictate consideration of this type of design anywhere in the country.

General principles of earthquake-resistant design are recognized and accepted by most engineers. There have been sharp differences of opinion, however, on the detailed application of these principles. Some engineers assume and insist that too little is yet known to be positive on the subject. Some choose to consider the problem one of pure theoretical research, often largely ignoring the true nature of

FIG. 1.—WHAT HAPPENS TO BRICK BEARING-WALL BUILDINGS; SCENE AFTER IMPERIAL VALLEY SHOCK IN CALIFORNIA, MAY, 1940

earthquake motion, its chaotic character, sudden changes, and impacts. Some refuse to profit from building behavior in past disastrous shocks.

If engineers have not learned how to design and to build highly resistant structures from the experience of San Francisco, Calif., in 1906; of Tokyo, Japan, in 1923; of Santa Barbara, Calif., in 1925; of Long Beach, Calif., in 1933; of Helena, Mont., in 1935; of the Imperial Valley in 1927 and 1940 (Fig. 1); of Puget Sound in 1949; and now of the Tehachapi-Arvin-Bakersfield area in California in 1952— then the case is indeed hopeless. Actually, today engineers do know how to make any structure erected by man earthquake resistant to a high degree, and in most cases with little cost increase. Life can be positively safeguarded. Damage can be prevented in many cases, and at worst be held to rather moderate or minor proportions. It is a matter of wonder just how much convincing some members of the engineering profession require.

Basic Factors.—The principal requirements of earthquake-resistant design are:

1. Recognition of the fact that a careful and detailed lateral force design is necessary.

2. Use of the proper types and combinations of materials. Reinforced materials

having adequate tensile, compressive, and shearing strengths are necessary (Fig. 2). Sacrifice of any one of the three decreases or even nullifies the suitability of a material.

3. Analysis of the kind of soil on which a structure rests in order to evaluate the design details correctly. Structures on saturated, soft, alluvial soil, or on manmade fill are subjected to more severe earthquake motion that those on firm, natural, well-drained soil or rock. Foundation design on poor soils needs special and careful attention.

4. Understanding and acceptance of the concept of the building as a unit in the reaction to earth motion—not as a more or less unrelated assembly of parts. The frame cannot be considered without estimating the effect of walls, floors, partitions, and everything else that goes into the building. As the late Bailey Willis put it, the structure must be looked on as a unit or ship-built structure (Fig. 3).

FIG. 2.—REINFORCED-CONCRETE, RIGID TYPE SCHOOL BUILDING IN SOUTH GATE, CALIF., UNDAMAGED IN MARCH, 1933, LONG BEACH, CALIF., SHOCK

5. Realization that the lateral forces induced in the structure will automatically be first resisted by the most rigid elements in the building, usually the walls and partitions. The old concept of installing wind bracing in the frame alone, ignoring walls, partitions, and the other elements, is outmoded, obsolete, and unintelligent (Fig. 4).

6. The control of deflections to hold them to the minimum possible. To do this requires a heavily braced, stiff, rigid type of design (Fig. 5(a)). This feature will aid in avoiding excessive damage.

7. The knowledge that lateral forces are induced by the inertia of the structure as a whole or in part. The formula $F e \times M a$ holds good. Regardless of whether the designer is an ardent dynamics enthusiast or an advocate of the common static methods of design, he will have to compute lateral forces at any given level from the inertia of the whole building, or some part of it.

8. The adoption of heavy lateral force coefficients to give assured human safety and reasonable protection against damage. Coefficients as low as 2% of gravity (g), as presently sponsored by some engineers, are not enough, and never have been. The necessity for coefficients in the range of 8% g to 12% g in design of buildings has been amply proved.

Reinforcement Needed.—There has been considerable difference of opinion about requirements 2 and 3, and a very marked difference of opinion over requirement 8. On these three comment in detail is essential, in the light of the visible and demonstrable effects of many past shocks.

For assured earthquake safety, the need for use of reinforced materials has been brought out in every disastrous shock of modern times. In San Francisco on April 18, 1906, the behavior of the few reinforced-concrete wall buildings was outstanding. The museum at Stanford University at Stanford, Calif., and the Bekins

FIG. 3.—MANUFACTURING PLANT IN LONG BEACH, CALIF., AREA, DESIGNED FOR LATERAL FORCE OF 10% *g*; PRACTICALLY UNDAMAGED AFTER MARCH, 1933, SHOCK

Building in San Francisco were undamaged. In Tokyo in 1923, all the outstanding examples of successful earthquake-resistant design had reinforced-concrete walls.

In Long Beach on March 10, 1933, the behavior of reinforced-concrete walled buildings was in general markedly superior to that of similar buildings with unreinforced, unit masonry walls (Fig. 6). The reinforced-concrete Stanford Avenue School in South Gate (Fig. 2) stood like a beacon light, surrounded in the area by wrecked and shattered schools (Fig. 7) of unreinforced, unit masonry, bearing-wall design. In the 1952, Tehachapi (Bakersfield), shock, newpapers broadcast over the United States a picture of the more or less wrecked business area, with the caption "Tehachapi Flattened," yet in the background of the picture, looming like a lighthouse in the fog, was a two-story reinforced-concrete building practically undamaged. Reinforced concrete is mentioned on account of its proved merit, and also to denote a type. Brick and hollow masonry units are now being effectively reinforced, and can be considered dependable materials for use in earthquake-resistant designs.

Care in Foundations.—There are still people, including some engineers, who think that buildings on saturated, unfirm soils and on man-made fill receive a cushioning effect in earthquakes and that special design precautions in such loca-

(a) Outside—Trim Spalled   (b) Inside—Extensive Damage

Fig. 4.—Fire-Resistive, But Not Shock-Resistive Building; Evidence of Inadequate Strength and Rigidity, Following Long Beach, Calif., 1933 Shock

tions are not necessary. This strange idea or myth has no basis of fact at all. In every disaster on record, world-wide comment has been made by qualified geologists, seismologists, and engineers, to the effect that the severity of shaking in soft, saturated soils was much greater than that in well-drained firm soils or rock.

This theory was proved conclusively in the shocks at San Francisco in 1906; at Owens Valley, California, in 1872; at Fukui, Japan; at Puget Sound in 1949; at Tehachapi recently; and at many other places that could be mentioned. Buildings on loose, soft, saturated soils require special design attention.

Generous Provision for Lateral Forces.—The question of the magnitude of lateral force coefficients is still a subject of argument. In spite of ample evi-

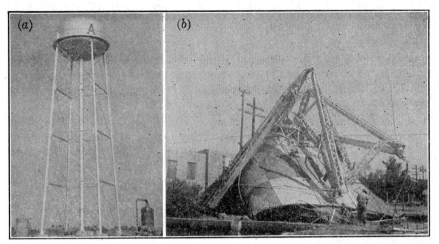

FIG. 5.—TALE OF TWO TANKS (a) 100,000-GAL WATER TANK, DESIGNED FOR 10% g, IN ACCORDANCE
WITH PACIFIC FIRE RATING BUREAU REGULATIONS; UNDAMAGED IN BAKERSFIELD, CALIF., 1952 SHOCK
(b) TANK AND TOWER BRACED FOR 30-LB WIND FORCE, COLLAPSED IN IMPERIAL VALLEY SHOCK
IN CALIFORNIA IN MAY, 1940

FIG. 6.—TWO BUILDINGS COMPARED FOR DAMAGE AND SAFETY, FOLLOWING LONG BEACH, CALIF., MARCH,
1933, SHOCK: LEFT, REINFORCED-CONCRETE WALL; AND, RIGHT, BRICK WALL

dence otherwise, there are advocates of the 2% g coefficient. Therefore it is necessary to examine this allowance in the light of the actual behavior of two specific types of structure: The tall steel tanks and towers so common around the United States, and the fire-resistive, limit height (150-ft) buildings in Los Angeles.

Tank Towers.—The behavior of these structures was poor in the Long Beach shock of 1933. Collapses occurred. The writer and others observed what happened to these towers, believed what they saw, and evolved a static method of design using lateral forces of 8% g to 12% g, or more. This design has been largely used or followed since that time. These engineers were strongly criticized—their required design was not dynamic, was not scientific, or was too severe. They were

FIG. 7.—JEFFERSON HIGH SCHOOL, NOT DESIGNED AGAINST EARTHQUAKES, AFTER LONG BEACH, CALIF., SHOCK OF MARCH, 1933; FOR COMPARISON WITH SCHOOL IN FIG. 2, SAME GENERAL AREA

told that nothing should be done until model tests were made. It was impossible to wait—something had to be done; so they went ahead, literally putting their necks on the block for a future earthquake to chop off.

The sequel is found in the 1952 Tehachapi shock. A conventional wind-braced 250,000-gal tank is good for a lateral force of about 1% g, the 150,000-gal size for a force of about $1\frac{1}{2}$% g, the 100,000-gal size for a force of about $2\frac{1}{2}$% g, and the 50,000-gal size for a force of about 4% g. In Bakersfield the 250,000-gal and 150,000-gal conventional designs collapsed; a 100,000-gal tank collapsed; and rods in the 50,000-gal tanks were stretched or broken. However, a 50,000-gal tank rebraced for a force of 8% g was undamaged, a new 8% g tank was undamaged, and two 10% g tanks were undamaged (Fig. 5(a)). The behavior of these towers is about in direct proportion to the degree of bracing.

In one of the 10% g towers the concrete piers under the column base plates were damaged somewhat, as the result of a defect in design for transmitting shear from column base to pier, and proper remedial steps will be taken for future designs. In the Imperial Valley shock of 1940 two wind-braced (2% g to 4% g) towers collapsed; one new 10% g tank and tower was undamaged; and one old tower rebraced for 10% g was undamaged. Other conventional towers had stretched and broken rods.

Los Angeles Buildings.—Consider now the limit height buildings in Los Angeles. Most of them were designed under a code which did not require earthquake-resistant design. They do not fall down and do not blow down, so they must have some bracing resistance. A check of dozens of them shows that they are good for lateral

FIG. 8.—SOUTHERN CALIFORNIA EDISON BUILDING IN LOS ANGELES, CALIF., WITH STEEL FRAME, CONCRETE WALLS; UNDAMAGED THROUGH NEARBY LONG BEACH 1933 AND BAKERSFIELD 1952 SHOCKS; DAMAGE SHOWN IN FIG. 4 ALSO IN THIS VICINITY

forces of from 1% g to $2\frac{1}{2}$% g. Many, perhaps the majority, should resist about 2% g. In the midst of this forest of older buildings is a rather unique building, the Southern California Edison Building (Fig. 8), designed as a limit height fire-resistive structure for a lateral force of 10% g.

What happened during the Long Beach shock in 1933 is significant. The 1% g to 2% g buildings were materially cracked up (Fig. 4); partitions were badly shattered; and exterior facings were cracked and spalled. Damage increased almost uniformly from negligible in the top story to a maximum in the first to the second or third stories. Large sums of money were spent to patch these buildings up for occupancy. How did the 10% g building fare? Nothing happened; it was not cracked or damaged at all.

After 19 years the Tehachapi shock occurred in 1952. It was centered about 100 miles from Los Angeles. What happened? The old 1% g to 2% g buildings were cracked up exactly as in 1933, although less severely. The 10% g Southern California Edison Building was undamaged. Other newer buildings designed for lateral forces in excess of 2% g were little affected, and the degree of cracking was about in direct proportion to the degree of bracing.

How can the engineering profession justify itself to the public if it allows building codes to use coefficients as low as 2% g, knowing that in every shock such structures will be loosened up and damaged? The public may get tired and irritated with such repeated destruction.

Summary

It must be made clear that there can be no objection to theoretical research or to dynamic studies and investigation—all these are essential. Any investigation which can help to refine and clear up difficulties in the problem of earthquake-resistant design is essential. There is still much to be done.

Things must not become unbalanced, however. Nature performs full-scale shaking-table experiments for the benefit of engineers. They must look closely, confirm their observations, and take immediate remedial steps where necessary. Time does not always permit putting off decisions to await the results of long-range scientific experiments.

AMERICAN SOCIETY OF CIVIL ENGINEERS

Founded November 5, 1852

TRANSACTIONS

Paper No. 2631

HOW NEW MATERIALS INCREASED MAN'S BUILDING ABILITY

By Walter C. Voss,[1] A. M. ASCE

Synopsis

The history of building is closely related to man's skill in the application of available materials. The progress made during any period depends on the co-ordinated use of knowledge, power, materials, and transport, and the economic ability of the people. This paper traces building history from the earliest times to the present. The various materials are discussed individually to show their effect on the cost and speed of construction. New erection methods are described.

Introduction

It would be impossible to speak of new materials without mentioning old materials. Likewise, it is equally as difficult to separate the consideration of materials from the methods of their use. Inasmuch as materials must be processed, the techniques of analysis and synthesis must be understood. This understanding must be based on scientific knowledge, research, and experiment. Economic factors also play an important part. Thus, this paper must discuss not only new materials, but also the developments leading to their discovery. These developments depend on available natural resources, present knowledge in the fields pertaining to them, the power resources available for their production, their distribution, and competitive economic advantages.

Early History

The progress that man has made during any period in any area of the world has depended to a large extent on the existence and coordinated use of available knowledge, power, materials, and transport, and the economic health of the peoples or civilizations involved. Throughout the ancient and medieval world the development of scientific principles, the adaptations of human, animal, and machine power, the development of transportation facilities, the means for the discovery and useful employment of local materials, and the increased opportunity

---

[1] Head, Dept. of Bldg. Eng. and Constr., Mass. Inst. Tech., Cambridge, Mass.; and Consultant on Architectural Constr. and Materials.

for economic advancement were slow, cumbersome, provincial, and poorly integrated.

Ancient Civilizations.—Thus, the Egyptians, knowing only the wheel and axle and the inclined plane, utilized the available stone to build pyramids, obelisks, and tombs, and their limited supply of bronze and wood to fashion sarcophagi and ornaments. They used the materials at hand, the buoyancy of water, and the endless supply of slave labor to fashion their monuments. The Assyrians, less competent technically, and having clay, some wood, and natural asphalt, pioneered in brick structures. The Persians, a warlike people who raided their neighbors, had large supplies of lumber and bronze. They augmented their choice of materials and available labor by military conquest. None of these ancient countries was afforded the interchange of knowledge, materials, or skills with other nations, that is so necessary to progress. Not until the Phoenicians, the sailing merchants of the ancient world, spread the activities of many nations abroad, did the interchange of materials and skills begin to stimulate advances in those nations to which they sailed their ships. Power was still furnished by man and later by beasts of burden. Power as it is known today was nonexistent.

Middle Ages.—This slow advance, although gaining some momentum, continued throughout the history of the medieval world. Rome, by conquest, marshaled the materials, means of transport, techniques, and wealth of the then known world. The results of coordinated and combined knowledge were emerging. Scientists began the tedious development of the fundamental natural sciences. Elementary knowledge of water power, heat, and steam was available. Craftsmen were given a more preferred status, mainly as a result of the egotism of rulers who wished glamorous buildings and public works. Atheism and polytheism were followed by the Hebrew, Christian, and other monotheistic faiths. These stimulated self-expression and a desire for edifices expressing creeds and honoring saints.

Still all buildings, aqueducts, bridges, and public works of that period were fabricated of stone, mortar, tile, and brick. Buildings and monuments were adorned with precious metals, bronzes, and jewels. The trabeated systems of construction of the ancients were supplanted by the arch, vault, and dome. Builders experimented in masonry to express the new scientific and technical concepts. The artistic elements of buildings progressed rapidly to meet the demands for sacred ornaments, paintings, and applied decoration. One could go on step by step through these eras only to find that progress in all of them was slow, difficult, and continually subject to frustration because of a lack of technical knowledge and the resultant lack of transport, power, and the financial prosperity that would have provided for more intensive study and development.

The Past Century.—One must not underrate the legacy that these more than forty centuries of effort, heartaches, and frustration had created at the opening of the nineteenth century. With the concepts, theories, and physical laws then in existence, there was no need to start "from scratch" in the use of the components of progress—knowledge, power, materials, transport, and economic health. All these factors had progressed to an unusually high degree of development as compared with any of the preceding ages of man's activity. However, something extremely revolutionary had happened in the meantime in the civilized world. Men were free, were afforded education, were given the right to profit in full from their ingenuity, had a multiplicity of materials, had machines and steam and electric power, and, in the United States, were subject to little or no dictatorial restrictions from government.

During the past century all these contributing factors were rapidly expanded. The manufacture of steel in quantity was made possible by the invention of the Bessemer process in 1856. The steam engine, developed continuously from Thomas Savery's effort in 1698 to the improvements of the steam turbine introduced by Gustav C. P. de Laval in 1889, multiplied the power potential. Electric power became a highly significant factor in the light of the improvements introduced in the dynamo by Charles Wheatstone, Antonio Paccinotti, and Zénobe T. Gramme from 1845 to 1870. Scientists and engineers, with the new tools that these and other inventions made possible, rapidly expanded their horizons. The knowledge of chemistry increased at an accelerated pace. Synthetics began to replace natural materials, and in turn, stimulated further efforts to solve newly discovered problems. The experimental urge to use the new techniques encouraged bold architectural concepts. Man's desire for comfort resulted in extensions of the available knowledge of heat exchanges and the utilization of solar energy. Today the tremendous possibilities of nuclear energy presage an era of surprising accomplishments that may override all other concepts of power. Notwithstanding the fact that the past century is only 2% to 3% of the known age of civilized man, the progress during this period exceeds by many times that which man had made in all the ages preceding it.

BUILDING MATERIALS

Brick.—When the history of clay products is reviewed, it is found that brick, discovered perhaps 12,000 years ago, has played the role of one of the most remarkable materials in the building industry. It is quite likely that the Tower of Babel and the walls of Babylon were built of brick. Similarly, glazed, burned clay products were used by ancient and medieval builders. Not until the middle of the nineteenth century was machinery introduced. Populations increased, more industries grew up, and greater freedom was being extended to the people. These all helped to increase the demand for brick and developments followed in quick succession.

In the United States, the old hand-made brick was rapidly replaced by the automatic wire-cut and mechanically molded varieties. Then followed the introduction of de-airing, the combination of various clays to produce colors and surface textures, and the production of cored brick and tile. Burning developed from the simple scove-waste kilns to the continuous kilns. Many shapes of brick and tile, both common structural and ornamental, were manufactured and have been important factors in architectural varieties of finish and plan arrangement (Fig. 1). All this development has taken place during the past 100 years and the cooperation between architects, engineers, and manufacturers has played no small part in the progress made in the production of these materials.

Mortar.—All brick and tilework was laid in a mortar, which varied from ordinary clay mud to the combinations of cement and lime in use today. Before the actual discovery of portland cement in 1824, mortars were generally prepared by combining lime or volcanic ash with sand and crushed stone particles. Quicklime made by calcining limestone had been used since ancient days, but not until the introduction of the modern rotary kiln and fuels, and improved methods of hydration, did hydrated lime become the reliable and adaptable material for mortars, plasters, concretes, and brick. All these uses, although reminiscent of early practice, have broadened the scope of activity of designers and builders.

Gypsum.—Gypsum, which in ancient days was almost exclusively utilized for plasterwork, has been adapted during the past 100 years to serve in many other ways. Besides its continued use for plaster, it forms the base for fireproof partition tile and plasterboard, and recently has been produced in such a hardened state that it can be employed by industry for shaping light-gage metal sheets.

FIG. 1.—ERECTION OF BRICK FOR RESIDENTIAL DWELLINGS

Cement.—Probably the most remarkable addition to the field of cementitious materials came in connection with the invention of portland cement. Although portland cement was employed only in small quantities from 1824 to 1850, its increased use was stimulated by the introduction of the rotary kiln and improved controls. These innovations have resulted in the modern high early strength cements and in a variety of types for particular uses. The cumulative effect of the industrial revolution increased the demands for the material, and research extended its horizons. The invention of the automatic block machine resulted in the extensive use of concrete masonry units. With the demand for lighter walls, various aggregates were developed and today Haydite, perlite, slag, vermiculite, and others are mentioned in addition to the original cinders. Because of the ease of producing many alternate shapes, concrete blocks have become a large factor in the reduction of weight and cost of modern buildings.

Probably the most general use of portland cement has been in cast concrete. In this field the development has been paced by technical advances in engineering design. Realizing the possibilities that concrete techniques afforded, engineers developed the theory of indeterminate structures and thereby made it possible to provide support for the many unusual structures that are so common in modern design. The knowledge of the design and control of concrete mixes, derived by tedious and continued research, added materially to the confidence that the engineer had in this highly adaptable material.

The recent application of prefabrication techniques to concrete has contributed to the economy of construction. Many structures are today erected by using prefabricated beams, slabs, walls, and arch bents (Fig. 2). The addition of pre-

FIG. 2.—PRECAST CONCRETE SLABS FOR MULTISTORY BUILDING

stressing to this technique is already adding greatly to its practicability. Long-span bridges are becoming more common. The basic elements of the frame and its envelope are now being made of smaller prefabricated units and this method will materially change techniques. Its great adaptability to a variety of shapes and contours has made architectural concrete popular. The architect can use this feature to eliminate the higher costs that are involved for natural or cast stone.

Stone.—Stone, like brick, has been utilized for structures since ancient days. The progressive effects of mechanization in the use of this material have been very marked during the past century. The modern carborundum cutting wheels, the large lathes, and automatic molders and cutters have greatly reduced the labor cost in fashioning stones. The manufacture of cast stone, when coupled with this mechanization, has reduced transport costs. Thus, great advances have been made in building in a variety of colors, finishes, and ornamentation.

Timber.—Wood, too, has been used since antiquity. It, also, was often an available natural resource that man soon adapted to many purposes. Through the ages, whenever a new technique, shape, or application seemed desirable, wood was put to the test and in many instances served a new and practical purpose. Here again, progress was slow until mechanical power and automatic machinery stepped in. Then there was rapid expansion.

The anticipated possibility that somehow the craftsman could do this or that prompted endless innovations. Although the principle of veneering was used for many centuries, it was primarily a method for the conservation of rare woods and grains. When the method of "peeling" logs was introduced in the 1880's, the use of veneers took an entirely new turn. Cross-veneering, with newly developed plastic adhesives, allowed not only dimensional stability control, but also simultaneous shaping.

This advance affected all the fittings of the modern building such as cases, cabinets, doors, and paneling, and served a multitude of other uses that have contributed so much to the progress experienced during the past 100 years. Plywood in its many forms has had a tremendous impact since the beginning of the twentieth century. It has introduced a new concept into the use of wood and has changed methods of construction. It has liberated the designer from rectangular joinery and its many difficulties and, at the same time, has brought into use heretofore more or less useless woods and wood qualities for cores, thus conserving the more desirable species for finished surfaces.

The limitations imposed by earlier adhesives, such as animal glues, were a challenge to the chemist. Intensive research, coupled with the recent rise in the technology of modern plastics, led to the development of adhesives that were resistant to moisture, that had promise of long life, and that could be compounded synthetically to bond wood to fabric, wood to metals, and metals to metals. These adhesives prompted the engineer to test their suitability as structural laminates. Thus were born the laminated arch, the laminated preformed truss, the preformed and laminated vault.

It became possible to span great distances with shapely timber structural units that eliminated all mechanical fastenings within themselves. These new adhesives, when used on assemblies of dimension lumber and plywood, have resulted in the present design of "skin-stress" panels that possess unusual strength and stiffness and light weight. The continual desire for lighter weight has become an objective of construction practice regardless of the basic materials used and has done much to absorb the economic impact of increasing labor costs by reducing the quantities of materials and by utilizing the ever-expanding development of automatic machinery. The increased standard of living so produced has played no small part in the progress that has only recently been noted in construction.

While all these innovations in composite assemblies as laminates were going on, the engineer and wood technologist—spurred on by the competition they were experiencing from specialists in other basic materials—sought to develop effective mechanical joints for structural elements to replace bolts and screws. This research resulted in the development of the timber connector, which has rendered the old techniques obsolete by making more effective use of the stress resistance of wood (Fig. 3). Then the more effective grading of timber became necessary and resulted in a much greater knowledge of timber characteristics.

METALS

Iron.—Although the earliest of the metals was probably a copper alloy such as bronze, the most important early developments were in the manufacture and use of iron. As the principal iron ores were oxides and carbonates, which yielded readily to smelting with carbon, all early varieties must have been iron-carbon compounds. Prior to 1870 the principal varieties were cast iron and wrought iron. One of the earliest uses of cast iron was for columns and beams, but the properties of this material placed many limitations on design and shape.

FIG. 3.—TIMBER ARCH WAREHOUSE CONSTRUCTION

Steel.—In 1856, Henry Bessemer, experimenting to improve the quality of metals for cannons, invented the Bessemer converter, which revolutionized the manufacture of iron products and produced steel in its early form. Not until later, however, did Alexander Holley develop a continuous process for producing ingots of steel, which was combined with further mechanization to produce shapes without extensive reheating. When the basic, open-hearth process was developed, it was found possible to roll large structural sections from single ingot without the previous difficulty of "hot short" cracking.

Thus came into being the wide-flange structural section that so familiar today and that has made possible the construction of the Ar an "skyscraper" (Fig. 4) and some of the more important bridges. All thi elopment was paralleled by similar progress in the fabrication of composite members in large shops. Welding replaced riveting for many shop joints and is now replacing riveting at the site. All these advances involved much trial and error, but the courage and ingenuity of the engineer and scientist were not to be denied.

The "know-how" developed in steel rolling was extended to the manufacture of plates, reinforcing steel, pipes, bolts, wires, and the like, and these products have played no small part in the parade of progress. These mechanical accomplishments were further employed in producing sheet metals which, because of

FIG. 4.—STEEL FRAME SKYSCRAPER

the ductile and malleable properties that research had made possible, resulted in the production of metal lath and preformed sheet metal products. With a variety of coatings, such as galvanizing, enameling, and surface immunization, to protect the metal from corrosion, these products have helped to reduce the weight of buildings, to provide a larger degree of prefabrication, and to reduce costs.

Aluminum.—Aluminum, now almost a byword to every American, was known to Antoine Lavoisier who, unable to smelt it, expressed the belief that alumina could not be reduced by carbon. In 1882, E. H. and A. H. Cowles heated alumina mixed with other metallic oxides by electricity and produced an impure aluminum. Not until 1907, however, did it become possible to win the pure metal by reduction of the ore by carbon. In the 1880's, Paul Heroult in France, and Charles M. Hall in the United States, utilized the electrical power made available by the newly developed dynamo to produce aluminum as it is known today. As soon as full scale production was commercially possible, all the available techniques of rolling, drawing, extruding, and casting were applied to the new metal, with the result that it is now possible to obtain almost any shape in a multitude of tempers for a multitude of uses (Fig. 5).

Magnesium.—Similarly, magnesium is the result of recently developed techniques in metallurgical reduction. The electric furnace method, developed just prior to World War II, produces the pure metal. Magnesium, like aluminum, is rolled, extruded, drawn, and cast. It has become an important element for lightweight structural shapes.

FIG. 5.—ALUMINUM SIDING FOR FACTORY BUILDING

GLASS

Glass has played no minor role in the record of accomplishment during the past 100 years. It, too, has been known and used for many purposes from antiquity. The United States has done very important work in the development of glassmaking. Wonderful automatic machinery has made possible the production, at low cost, of bottles, jars, electric light bulbs, tubing, rods, window plate, and glass block. Glass is now made in a laminated, nonshattering form, in double and triple insulating assemblies, with a variety of face patterns and degrees of transparency and translucency. The quality of glass has been improved so that there is now available bulletproof and nonshattering, relatively elastic glass. Glass is spun into fibers of amazing tensile strength and is used for heat insulation in the form of wool and unicellular blocks.

PLASTICS

Perhaps the most glamorous new materials have been the plastics. Although celluloids and rubber have been known during recent years, they were only the forerunners of the amazing variety of products now available. Being entirely synthetic in nature, plastics are made from elemental molecular compounds that are plentiful in nature. These basic compounds may come from vegetable bases, from oils, from sea water, or from the air. Plastics lend themselves readily to a myriad of combinations to produce materials with widely varying physical and chemical characteristics. Many of them can be made either thermoplastic or thermosetting and can be varied from thin, lacquerlike consistencies to rigid, strong, solid shapes. It would be impossible to enumerate the many types here because of space limitations.

The progress made in the technology of plastics has resulted in miraculous adhesives, protective coverings, and impregnating liquids for the manufacture of fabrics resistant to fire, acids, and alkalies, that possess many other characteristics to meet particular demands. Combinations of these applications have resulted in cored panels of great strength and light weight. Plastics serve in many products manufactured for insulating purposes. They have been the base for many new paints and finishes.

In the transparent form used as silicone lacquers, plastics produce a coating, which, when applied to masonry structures, allows the masonry to "breathe"—yet protects it from the entrance of water. The silicone compounds produce a calking material that is more effective than many older materials. In the varieties that are included in the synthetic rubber range, neoprenes and their related offshoots are used in valuable extruded shapes for gaskets, expansion joints, and fillers, without which the modern glass and metal building exterior would be impossible.

As adhesives, plastics become the vehicle for preformed laminates of wood, fabric, glass, and metal to serve in the production of panels, counters, furniture, and containers. Plastics may be said to be the latest example of progress resulting from scientific research in the pattern of development so characteristic of the past 100 years.

MATERIALS FOR COMFORT

The effects of heat and sound on building occupants have been the increasing concern of engineers and research scientists since the turn of the twentieth century. Although man always sought comfort to a greater or lesser degree, not until he was aware of the serious impairment of his health did he set about improving the conditions under which he lived. As intelligence grew among the masses, man became more sensitive to irritation. This, coupled with his improved economic status, made him covet the comforts theretofore known to only a few. Such demands made it profitable for manufacturers to risk the introduction of new products and to propose new methods. In such an economic atmosphere, linked with the expanded availability of materials that possessed the characteristics needed and of mechanical devices so necessary to mass production, experimentation in heat and sound insulation flourished.

Thermal Insulation.—Thus have come into being many successful combinations of materials to lessen the effects of differential heat variations and to control sound absorption, transmission, and reflection. Rock and glass wool, aluminum foil for reflective insulation, and surface treatments for controlled reflection and emissivity have made it possible to provide comfort in the face of high and low exterior temperatures. As a result, construction weights have been reduced, as has the cost of fuel or cooling apparatus, and an additional saving that might stimulate further building has been made possible. At the same time, comfort increased man's productivity by providing relief from the enervating and exhausting effects of toil under difficult atmospheric conditions.

Acoustic Insulation.—In the field of acoustics, new developments are even now gaining substantial headway. The phenomena of the transfer of energy due

FIG. 6.—ACOUSTIC TILE ON OFFICE CEILING

to sound are more clearly understood. Methods of combining sound absorbing materials and the arrangement of reflective areas so as to produce destructive interference and to reduce reverberation are producing extremely satisfactory results and materially changing many classic procedures of construction (Fig. 6). It is necessary only to scan the pages of leading popular, professional, and home magazines to become aware of the many materials offered.

Air Conditioning.—The field of air conditioning has moved from the archaic concept of heat exclusion by the use of heavy earthen or masonry walls to the provision of cooling air currents and controlled humidities. Refrigeration, first applied to food preservation using natural ice and later artificial ice, has advanced to the principle of cooling by evaporation of volatile liquids. Available electrical devices have steadily improved, and it is now commonplace to expect air-conditioned buildings.

STRUCTURAL DESIGN

The advance in the structural design applications has kept pace with the new materials and techniques. Foundations previously conceived only as spread bases to reduce unit concentration on the soil for low buildings, at first consisted of piles of wood and later of steel or concrete to afford a bearing for heavier loads. Caissons were constructed to bedrock where the rock was sufficiently close to the surface and were belled out where the compressible soil layer was too deep. The principle of pretest piling came later. From the old frames of masonry and wood for bearing walls and piers, present concepts of steel and concrete frames have developed during the past century.

Floor systems, ordinarily of wood, can now be built of concrete slabs (either solid or ribbed), of trussed steel joists, of all metal decking, and of prestressed concrete unit assemblages—to mention only some of the more usual types. The great development in the field of indeterminate structures has made it possible to reduce the amounts of materials necessary and to make materials work more closely to their capacity—because knowledge of the behavior of materials has become more exact as a result of the continual research conducted to control their quality.

ERECTION METHODS

All these developments in design, materials, equipment, and concepts have been a challenge to the constructer and the manufacturer of equipment for the erection of buildings. The old horse and plank scaffolds so common at the turn of the century have been replaced by suspended scaffolds; the ladder and hod, by the hoist, derrick, and crane; and the erection of small units one at a time, by composite areas prefabricated at ground level. Concrete, previously mixed by hand at the site, is now mixed in central plants, transported to the site in mixer trucks, hoisted to the pouring level and distributed at floor levels, or placed directly from bottom-dump buckets on cranes. The erection of structural steel has led the way in this improvement as the urge to utilize the properties of available steel fabrication grew apace. The most recent technique, using the advantages of prestressed concrete, now bids fair to provide the possibility of assembling and placing large wall, floor, and partition areas at one time.

OUTLOOK FOR THE FUTURE

It would almost seem that the peak of development in materials and methods for buildings has been reached. If the pattern of accelerated improvement is to be believed, however, this stage is only beginning. Although it is dangerous to risk predictions, certain possible advances seem sure to present themselves—in the fields of power, plastics, prestressed concrete, heating and air conditioning, and architectural design.

Although the development of conventional power will go on at an accelerated pace, atomic power will create the greatest revolution in methods and equipment for heating, motive power, and scientific research. The extension of present horizons in atomic physics will provide the tools to analyze the characteristics of materials more accurately, will suggest simpler methods in the field of production, will simplify equipment, and will greatly reduce the use of critical national resources. The impact of progress in this highly scientific area will stimulate greater activity in all the fields that heretofore have grown under the application of more conventional concepts.

It may well be true that the next 50 years will see plastics improved to such an extent that all panels, doors, much hardware, trim, floor and wall coverings, and many applied finishes will be greatly improved and reduced in price. The development in lightweight, cored units made of wood, fabric, and metals will be phenomenal. Prestressed concrete is used principally at present for bridges, and it is high priced. Low-cost blocks, assembled at ground level and prestressed to fabricate larger units, will be used more and more for walls, beams and slabs, and short-span bridge decks, thus utilizing the tremendous capacity that now exists in the concrete block industry and materially reducing the cost of fire-resistant buildings.

Prediction of progress in the fields of heating and air conditioning would be a dubious task. Nevertheless, the present cumbersome assemblage of pipes, fittings, ducts, and appurtenances may well be replaced by radiantly heated walls and floors. The exterior walls of buildings may become massive heating or cooling ducts, with the apparatus concentrated in the basement and roof areas. Hot or cooled air will provide the basic heating requirements and will afford comfort without the use of extensive pipelines. Structural frames will be quite different because of the need for vertical ventilating shafts at many points. The excessive weight of concrete fireproofing will be reduced by the use of fire-resistant prefabricated shields, which will also allow for ducts. Air-conditioning equipment, instead of being custom built for each building, will be provided by movable units fitted with strategically located wall shafts and will be used only when necessary. The tremendous amortization costs of seasonably useless equipment may well be eliminated.

Architectural details and planning will greatly affect the activity of manufacturers who will seek to provide materials and equipment to solve such challenges. Designs with movable partitions and for multiple usage will increase. Glass and metal skins will be used much more. This trend will be accelerated and gradually the new problems presented by this approach will be solved. Additions to the presently available materials will also be of great assistance. As architects realize that research, engineering, and manufacture can solve many vexing problems, they will be more bold and adventurous in their designs. This will stimulate still further advances.

Exhausted frontiers! Those who contend that the saturation point has been reached are mistaken. Present advantages in scientific knowledge, a broad and determined research program, the great advances in the development of power, the ever-expanding adaptation of present materials and the development of new synthetics, excellent communications, speedy transport, and a hoped-for high economic status—all can have only one effect, namely, continued progress. Unless the retarding forces of world troubles cause unhappy setbacks, and unless progress involves an extension of man's inhumanity to man, the next 100 years of industrial activity will make the present excellent status of the United States seem provincial in retrospect.

AMERICAN SOCIETY OF CIVIL ENGINEERS

Founded November 5, 1852

TRANSACTIONS

Paper No. 2632

A CENTURY OF TOPOGRAPHIC SURVEYING AND MAPPING

By R. H. Lyddan,[1] A. M. ASCE

Synopsis

The tremendous progress that has been made in providing adequate mapping coverage of the United States is a tribute to the men and organizations that prevailed against many obstacles. The earliest exploratory expeditions were more in the nature of reconnaissance trips than scientific mapping parties. This paper traces the development of the science of mapping, especially in the western section of the United States. The work of federal agencies is described, and the present status of mapping is examined.

Introduction

A map of the Great Salt Lake in Utah, published in 1852, depicts a large part of the area surveyed by Capt. Howard Stansbury, of the Corps of Topographical Engineers, during his explorations in 1849 and 1850. Stansbury's exploration was by no means the first of such expeditions. The expedition was a major contribution of surveying and mapping, but it is cited here, not so much because of its importance, but more because of its time relation to the Centennial of Engineering in 1952. Although surveying and mapping were both practiced many centuries ago, charting of the western two thirds of the United States did not begin in earnest until about the time of Stansbury's expedition.

Early Mapping

Explorations.—The initial attempts at exploration in a new nation are mostly concerned with location and extent. In 1803, the young republic of the United States purchased the Louisiana Territory from France for $15,000,000. In 1804, Meriwether Lewis and William Clark were sent out to ascertain just what had been obtained. Zebulon Pike started on a similar mission in 1806, and these expeditions were followed in rapid succession by many others.

In addition to the official expeditions there were then, as now, some arranged

---

[1] Chf., Plans and Coordination Branch, U. S. Geological Survey, Washington, D. C.

by private persons. Capt. B. L. E. Bonneville's explorations during the years 1832 to 1836 were of the latter type and were made in prosecution of the fur trade. Bonneville determined the existence of the Great Basin, of the Great Salt Lake, and of the Humboldt River in Nevada. In so doing he completely disproved the hypothesis of a great river, called Rio Buenaventura, that supposedly traversed the area and emptied into the Pacific Ocean.

In the years after Bonneville's expedition, I. N. Nicollet (1836 to 1840) explored the Upper Mississippi Basin. He came to this country from France for the express purpose of making a scientific tour, with a view toward contributing to the progressive increase of knowledge in the physical geography of North America. Nicollet was the first explorer to make extensive use of the barometer in obtaining elevations. As late as 1859, Lt. G. K. Warren said Nicollet's map of the Upper Mississippi was one of the all-time great contributions to American geography. Nicollet was very skilful in the use of the sextant and the telescope. These instruments, along with a pocket chronometer and an artificial horizon of mercury, constituted the major part of his surveying equipment. Lt. John C. Frémont worked with Nicollet during the last 3 years of the latter's explorations, and no doubt got some good pointers on surveying and mapping.

Frémont's major exploratory expedition started in 1843. He was equipped with a portable astronomical transit, sextants, chronometers, and barometers. He described the Great Basin and established four positions, among which were one for the camp at Great Salt Lake and another for the "Three Buttes" in the Sacramento Valley (California).

Maj. W. H. Emory, in 1846–1847, made a reconnaissance from Fort Leavenworth, Kans., to San Diego, Calif., which should be mentioned because his siphon barometer was the first mercurial barometer ever carried unbroken overland to the Pacific coast.

Road and Railroad Surveys.—As a result of discovery and exploration, the need for roads and railroads was well established. The earlier expeditions had, of course, procured valuable information along the routes they traveled, but collecting route information was not their main objective. Starting about 1850, surveys were made for roads and particularly for railroads. Stansbury's survey was of this nature. In fact, on September 12, 1849, he left Great Salt Lake City, as it was then called, to explore a route for a wagon road to Fort Hall, a frontier post established in Idaho in 1834.

The railroad surveys got under way in 1853 when an appropriation act authorized the Secretary of War to employ topographical engineers to ascertain the most practicable and economical route for a railroad from the Mississippi River to the Pacific Ocean. Odometers, compasses, and aneroid barometers were prominent items of equipment used in this work. In 1854, Lt. R. S. Williamson mentions two of the passes being surveyed in detail with chain and spirit level. A resolution by Congress in 1865 provided that all maps, profiles, and other drawings connected with the Pacific railroad be transferred to the Department of the Interior.

Boundary Surveys.—Extensive boundary surveys were made during the 1850's to establish both the Mexican and Canadian boundary lines. The instruments used by Lt. J. G. Parke in this work constitute an impressive list—astronomical transits, heliotropes, zenith telescopes, transits, theodolites, telescopes, sextants, chronometers, magnetic theodolites, dip circles, compasses, pocket levels, chains, tapes, barometers, hygrometers, and thermometers.

Surveys of several state boundaries were also made about this time. For example, on May 26, 1860, Congress authorized the President to appoint "a suitable person or persons" to run and mark the boundary line between California and the United States.

ACCURATE TOPOGRAPHIC MAPPING

A definite pattern had thus been established. First, the explorations were directed simply at determining what existed. Next, the more specific surveys for transportation routes and civil boundaries were undertaken. However, the third phase in the surveying and mapping of the United States is the one that will be stressed in this paper. This phase included the study, or at least the launching of the study, of the details of the nation's geographical features and the preparation of accurate topographic maps—maps depicting relief by elevations and contours rather than by the hachures used in the early surveys.

Surveys in the West.—Here again the Stansbury survey serves as an example. Although neither contours nor elevations were used (probably because the mercurial barometer with which Stansbury intended to determine elevations was broken before he even reached Great Salt Lake), the map he produced carried considerable detail and information. Stansbury was the first not only to make the trip around the Lake but also to survey its floor by taking soundings. It is interesting to note that 100 years later his data for depth are still used.

Warren began the reconnaissance of the Missouri and Yellowstone rivers in 1856, and his map of the territory west of the Mississippi, on a scale of 1: 3,000,-000, was used with revision up to 1867. F. V. Hayden accompanied Warren on these explorations as geologist for the party. Later he was to continue this work for the Interior Department.

The Interior Department entered the picture in 1856 when, by Act of Congress, funds were appropriated for the construction of the so-called "Western Wagon Roads." This work was carried on until the Civil War forced a halt, but was resumed after the war and apparently completed by 1873.

In 1857, Lt. J. C. Ives explored the navigation possibilities of the Colorado River to see if he could find a water route to Utah and New Mexico. An iron steamer was shipped in sections from the east to the mouth of the Colorado River by way of San Francisco, Calif. When they reached the head of navigation at Black Canyon, Ives and some of the party continued overland to Fort Defiance, Ariz. The party was well supplied with surveying instruments, including astronomical transits, sextants, chronometers, theodolites, transits, cistern barometers, prismatic clinometers, pocket compasses, chains, and tapes.

In 1859, Capt. H. J. Simpson led an expedition through Utah in an attempt to discover a shorter route to the west. He determined a more accurate longitude for Salt Lake City and actually shortened the route across the mountains by 200 miles. Simpson prepared a report of his investigations which was not published until 1876.

The Civil War put a stop to all major explorations and very little was accomplished until 1867, when Nebraska was made a state and an unexpended balance of $5,000 was used in financing a geological survey of the new state. Hayden was placed in charge of the survey, and the work was under the supervision of the General Land Office.

The next year, another $5,000 was appropriated for geological surveys in Wyoming. These surveys were also carried out under the General Land Office, but Hayden was with a party under Capt. W. F. Raynolds who was exploring the upper Missouri and the Yellowstone. Topography was sketched by means of a prismatic compass and odometer. Jim Bridger was guide for the expedition. He told Raynolds that he had seen "burning plains, immense lakes, and boiling springs" near the sources of the Yellowstone, and he also mentioned the existence of a "Two Ocean River" in the area.

In the meantime (1867), Alaska had been purchased from Russia for $7,200,-000, and in 1869, Capt. C. W. Raymond started on a reconnaissance of the Yukon River. The party sailed from San Francisco in the *Commodore,* carrying their small stern-wheel steamer, *Yukon,* under the deck. The small steamer was launched on July 1, and Fort Yukon was reached on July 31.

The King survey of the 40th parallel got under way in 1867 and was completed in 1872. The area included in this survey totaled about 86,390 sq miles. Contours were used in showing relief on some of the maps, and on others the hill work was represented by "brush shading with an oblique light" instead of hachures.

The year 1867 also saw the start of the Powell "Geological and Geographical Surveys of the Rocky Mountain Regions" that included the well-known trip down the Grand Canyon of the Colorado River.

The Wheeler surveys of the Southwest were commenced in 1869 to make a thorough reconnaissance of that section. The work was at first based on meander methods checked by astronomic observations, but later progressed into more elaborate surveys. The object of these surveys, as described in 1871, was "to obtain correct topographical knowledge of the country traversed and to prepare accurate maps of the region entered." In 1872, a plan for a systematic topographic survey of the territory of the United States west of the 100th meridian was prepared by Lt. G. M. Wheeler and was sanctioned by Act of Congress approved on June 10 of that year. This expansion of the original task led to the use of triangulation in 1873 and the establishment of a complete trigonmetric basis for the detailed topography that followed. Most of the work was completed in 1879, but Wheeler's massive report was not published until 1889. The area covered in the survey was 359,065 sq miles. For the most part, relief on the Wheeler maps is depicted by hachures, although contours appear on a few of them, especially those drawn to a larger scale.

Instruments used in the surveys include a combined meridian instrument for astronomic observations and, for topography, 3-in. transit theodolites, 4-in. gradienters, pivot levels, and compasses of various kinds. Steel and linen tapes, and odometers attached to vehicles, were used in determining distance. A "portable" plane table was utilized, to some extent, for the contour work.

Following the Nebraska and Wyoming surveys of 1867 and 1868, Congress, in 1869, appropriated $10,000 for a geological examination of Colorado and New Mexico. Hayden was in charge, and this time the work was placed directly under the Secretary of the Interior instead of remaining a function of the General Land Office. The over-all project was called the Geological and Geographical Survey of the Territories which continued the surveys until it was taken over by the new Geological Survey Bureau in 1879. Hayden remained in charge until that date and for this reason the project is commonly known as the Hayden survey. Most of the maps were contoured, and the topography was surprisingly good when consideration is given to the extent of the area covered each year and to the conditions prevailing at the time.

In 1873, an interesting item was recorded in connection with an expedition into the Ute country by Lt. E. H. Ruffner. A report on the survey states that the line was run by theodolite, the angles being referred to meridians determined nightly; the distance was ascertained by the use of a stadia. This is believed to be the first time the method was used in mountain work.

From the foregoing it can be seen that the job of exploring and mapping the United States has been attacked by many organizations. During the 1870's, systematic surveys were being made by four significant groups—two under the War Department, one under the Interior Department, and one under the Smithsonian Institution. Competition between these groups for the selection of areas and for congressional favors led to a recommendation by the National Academy of Sciences that such work be unified under one agency. As a result of that recommendation, a new bureau, the Geological Survey, was created in the Interior Department by an Act of Congress on March 3, 1879. Clarence King was the first director, followed after only 1 year by Maj. J. W. Powell.

WORK OF THE GEOLOGICAL SURVEY

Two questions faced the new bureau right at the beginning. One was whether the term "national domain," as used in the Organic Act, restricted the Survey's operation to public land; the other, whether geological mapping also implied topographic mapping as carried on by the previous surveys of Hayden and Powell. The first question was settled by the Appropriation Act of 1881, which made the funds available for "geological surveys in various portions of the United States." The second problem was ironed out in the hearings of 1883, when Powell convinced a skeptical Congress that a topographic map was essential as a base for subsequent investigations and development.

The first instruments used by the Survey were still rather crude. In 1882, one report describes a plane table as being made of pine slats $1\frac{1}{2}$ in. wide by 2 ft long, glued to heavy canvas so as to roll up to a diameter of 6 in. When in use, heavy wooden crosspieces were attached to the underside of the board by means of thumbscrews, and a light folding tripod was screwed into a plate on one of the crosspieces. An 18-in. open-sight alidade was utilized in determining direction. The gradienter was still used, as were mercurial and aneroid barometers. A season's assignment for one man might cover two "square degrees," about 7,800 sq miles. Solid plane-table boards were adopted soon thereafter, and about 1886 a telescope alidade and the Johnson tripod were designed. About this time vertical angles for elevations took the place of the mercurial barometer in determining elevation.

Early in the history of the Geological Survey a plan was formulated and adopted to map the entire country in a systematic manner. The area was divided into quadrangles bounded by parallels of latitude and meridians of longitude. At first a scale of 1: 250,000 was used in mapping quadrangles bounded by full degree lines. However, the public has always demanded larger and larger scales, so these "degree" sheets were soon supplanted by 30-min quadrangles on a scale of 1: 125,000. These in turn were replaced by the 15-min quadrangle on a scale of 1: 62,500, which is almost a mile to the inch. The 15-min quadrangles are still considered as the standard topographic atlas sheets; but, for urban communities and for areas of considerable economic importance, 7½-min quadrangles are now being published on a scale of 1: 24,000. It is anybody's guess what the standard scale will be a 100 years hence, but it is hoped that at least the 15-min coverage can be complete before this scale is abandoned in favor of still larger scales.

The transition from the four independent surveys of King, Powell, Wheeler, and Hayden to the Geological Survey is a graphic example of mapping progress. The "degree" map of Salt Lake City was published by the Geological Survey in 1885, but the field work was done before 1879 by two of the independent surveys —the north half by King and the south half by Powell. It is interesting to compare this map with the Fort Douglas (Utah) 30-min quadrangle, covering part of the same area, which was surveyed about 50 years later, and with the Fort Douglas 7½-min quadrangle, published in 1951.

Surveying Instruments.—An increase in map accuracy has naturally been induced by the change to larger scales, but increased accuracy has also been effected by improvements in instruments and techniques (Fig. 1). The telescopic alidade has already been mentioned. This instrument was later provided with a micrometer eyepiece having a movable stadia wire, which made it possible to determine distance without a graduated rod. The Beaman arc, which was invented later, enabled the topographer to compute differences of elevation by simple multiplication. Panoramic cameras were constructed with which an observer might in a few minutes obtain a "canned" record of the full horizon that could later be expanded, along with similar records from other stations, into a topographic map.

Aerial Mapping.—The one improvement that has had the most influence on mapping accuracy involves both instruments and techniques. This improvement is aerophotogrammetry and, to a large extent, it has made its great impact on the Geological Survey during the past 25 years. Topographers are still somewhat inclined, at times, to view this technique—this science, in fact—as another aid to mapping. Primary emphasis is on the hard work saved, on the advance planimetry available, and on the opportunity for a second look after field work has been completed. Actually, aerophotogrammetry is mapping itself; and one of its great contributions, perhaps its greatest contribution, is that it made practical the writing of standard specifications for topographic mapping. Only by aerial photography would it have been practical to attain, over an entire quadrangle, the consistency of results necessary to insure compliance with specific standards set high enough to be worthwhile. Among photogrammetry's many visible and tangible contributions to topographic mapping, this important one often is not recognized.

THE FUTURE OF MAPPING

It has already been shown that each phase of exploration merges into succeeding phases. This pattern becomes more noticeable as expansion and development accelerate, because the need for new phases appears long before previous needs

FIG. 1.—MODERN SURVEYING PARTY USES PRECISE THEODOLITE AND TWO-WAY RADIO COMMUNICATION

have been entirely satisfied. The first and second stages of exploration (determining extent and finding routes for travel) have long ago been completed. The third phase, exploratory reconnaissance and mapping, was completed only in part before the rapidly expanding economy enforced a demand for more detailed examinations. Reconnaissance maps are available for perhaps a little more than half of the area of the United States, yet that important phase has been discontinued in favor of the general-purpose map. Furthermore, the general-purpose map today carries a standard accuracy statement that largely relegates to inadequacy the maps that were made before such standards could be maintained.

Then, on top of all this, comes the increasing demand for still more detail in the form of what practically amounts to an engineering map. Right now, about half the nation has been topographically mapped in some fashion. Many of these maps, however, were made more than 50 years ago and are of little value, so that only about one fourth of the United States is covered with maps that are generally usable and only 15% with maps that can really be considered of good quality. The plan to cover the country with general-purpose maps on the scale of 1: 62,500 is still in view, and a project for converting larger-scale maps to this scale is in progress. No provision has been made by the Geological Survey for completing the reconnaissance mapping, but that government bureau is publishing and distributing the 1: 250,000-scale maps that are now being compiled by the Army Map Service. These maps will eventually provide reconnaissance coverage.

SUMMARY

This paper has, at some length but still superficially, covered the progress of surveying and mapping in the West during the past 100 years. In summarizing, it should be pointed out that the first organized body of any magnitude devoted to topographic mapping in this country was the Corps of Topographical Engineers, and that this group provided the leaders for most of the early mapping expeditions. Even the Frenchman, Nicollet, did part of his work as an employee of the Corps of Topographical Engineers, and Bonneville was on leave of absence from the Corps during his work for the fur trade.

Just before the outbreak of the Civil War, there were forty-five officers in the Corps of Topographical Engineers and forty-eight in the Corps of Engineers. During the war, these men performed various engineering tasks indiscriminately. In 1863, the two services were merged to form the present Corps of Engineers. Since that time, construction has gradually become the predominating activity of the Corps of Engineers, with the Army Map Service, a branch of the Corps, responsible for the preparation of maps for military use. Close cooperation with the Geological Survey permits each to publish the other's work—as a military edition for the one and a civilian edition for the other.

The Coast and Geodetic Survey has always done a certain amount of fringe mapping along the shore line, if topographic data were not already available, to supplement the hydrographic data on its navigation charts. The topographic mapping now being done for this purpose by the Coast and Geodetic Survey is, by interagency agreement, expanded to cover full quadrangles.

The Tennessee Valley Authority has nearly completed a 1: 24,000-scale mapping project for the entire Tennessee Valley. The Forest Service also, during recent years, has produced a considerable quantity of topographic maps to satisfy its needs in the National Forest Reserves. In line with the coordinated policies of the major map-making agencies, the topographic maps for all these agencies are produced according to specified standards.

The present practice in the Federal Government is for the Geological Survey to publish and distribute the topographic maps resulting from the activity of these other agencies. This provides for uniformity of treatment, and reduces to one the number of federal agencies with which the public has to deal to secure topographic maps. All the agencies involved subscribe to certain standards of accuracy and content. The map user is thus able for the first time to accept with confidence the maps now being published, and can expect them to be consistent in quality and completeness.

Although the effort that has been put into topographic mapping by the Federal Government during the past century has been considerable, the job has been tremendous, and is still a long way from being finished. The present rate of progress, fortunately, is much improved over the average for the past century, although in the eyes of some this work is still moving very slowly. At the rate at which new maps were published in 1952, between 30 years and 40 years will be required to complete the mapping of the United States for publication in either 15-min or 7½-min quadrangle units.

As for the future, the objectives can be seen rather clearly if it can be assumed that the requirements will remain the same—which they probably will not. Judging by the experiences in England and other older countries, future requirements will call for more accurate maps, published on larger scales. Looking about as far into the future as possible at this time, present belief is that about half the United States warrants mapping at a scale of 1: 24,000 with the remainder to be mapped at a scale of 1: 62,500. The demand for maps published at larger scales already exists, and undoubtedly will increase in the future. At this time, however, detailed surveys are limited in extent and directed toward providing the information required for specific projects. Such mapping is being done very successfully by commercial mapping organizations as an extension beyond the general map coverage provided at smaller scales by the Federal Government.

Although the future cannot be expected to offer the kind of romance that led the early map makers into unexplored areas, present mapping procedures should warm the heart of any engineer. Mapping is now a complicated production job involving an extensive combination of talent and machinery; and there is unlimited opportunity ahead for exploration—if not in new geographic areas, then in the techniques of mapping and in the application of many recent scientific developments to this worthy field.

AMERICAN SOCIETY OF CIVIL ENGINEERS
Founded November 5, 1852
TRANSACTIONS

Paper No. 2633

IMPROVEMENTS IN PHOTOGRAMMETRY THROUGH A CENTURY

By George D. Whitmore,[1] M. ASCE, and Morris M. Thompson [2]

Synopsis

There seems to be a rather widespread notion, even among some surveyors and mappers, that photogrammetry is newfangled, an infant prodigy that has yet to establish itself as a full-fledged science. It may therefore be a surprise in some quarters that this article can discuss 100 years of photogrammetry. However, it was in 1852, the year of the founding of the American Society of Civil Engineers, that a French army officer, Aimé Laussedat, produced the first maps ever made from photographs. As far back as 1888, Lt. Henry A. Reed, an instructor at the United States Military Academy (West Point, N. Y.), published a book entitled "Photography Applied to Surveying," [3] in which the first chapter was devoted to a history of photogrammetry. Since the time of Laussedat, the science of photogrammetry has developed continuously until it has now reached the status of a major engineering technique.

In looking back over a century of photogrammetry, the writers do not propose so much to delve into the historical details of bygone phases of photogrammetry (in itself an interesting subject), as to gain a new perspective. Although photogrammetry is used for many purposes, this paper will be confined to photogrammetry as applied to surveying and mapping.

What Is Photogrammetry?

As defined by the American Society of Photogrammetry, photogrammetry is the science or art of obtaining reliable measurements by photography. Terrestrial photogrammetry is photogrammetry using ground photographs, aerial photogrammetry is photogrammetry using aerial photographs, and stereophotogrammetry is photogrammetry using stereoscopic equipment and methods.

On reviewing a century of experience, it will be found that each of these three

[1] Chf., Technical Staff, Topographic Div., U. S. Geological Survey, Washington, D. C.; and President, Am. Soc. of Photogrammetry.
[2] Staff Engr., Photogrammetry, Topographic Div., U. S. Geological Survey, Washington, D. C.
[3] "Photography Applied to Surveying," by Henry A. Reed, John Wiley & Sons, Inc., New York, N. Y., 1888.

kinds of photogrammetry has a specific set of objectives and that each is also subject to a specific set of problems or limitations. The objectives and limitations are the constant factors from which specific developments of the past can be oriented and evaluated.

TERRESTRIAL PHOTOGRAMMETRY

In the first attempts at photographic surveying the plane table was, replaced by a measuring camera (Fig. 1). The camera was equipped with a leveling device for maintaining the photographic plate in a vertical (or horizontal) plane and a compass for reading the bearing of the optical axis of each exposure. Its purpose was identical with that of plane-table surveying—to locate objects on a map by the intersection of conjugate lines of sight from the ends of a known base. The

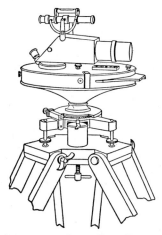

FIG. 1.—PHOTOGRAPHIC PLANE TABLE DESIGNED IN 1858

camera procedure had an advantage over plane-table methods in that the field work could be done quickly and that any desired point in the field of view could later be located on the map in the office, at the map maker's convenience. Laussedat, who pioneered the method in the 1850's, developed a mathematical analysis for converting overlapping perspective views into orthographic projections on any plane. This procedure permitted the determination of the elevation as well as the position of any point visible in two overlapping photographs.

There is nothing fundamentally wrong with the measuring camera procedure. Laussedat and others used it to produce serviceable maps a century ago, and it is still the basis of modern terrestrial photogrammetry. Today, however, the crude apparatus of the early days has given way to phototheodolites (Fig. 2) of the utmost precision. In one current application of terrestrial photogrammetry, the United States Geological Survey uses the phototheodolite in certain types of mountainous terrain to obtain fourth-order elevations for aerial photogrammetry.

Early plane-table photogrammetry and terrestrial photogrammetry in general also had limitations. Since the first lenses had a narrow field of view, a very large number of photographs was required, an item of great expense in those days and always a matter of inconvenience. In addition, photographic quality was poor. Pioneer efforts to solve the narrow field problem were centered chiefly on panoramic cameras, the first of which appeared as early as 1858. Their purpose was to give a continuous view by successive exposures on a strip of film. Some of these cameras were arranged to photograph only a part of the horizon, whereas others covered the entire 360°. The panoramic camera is still being used, notably by the United States Forest Service to photograph full horizons from lookout towers, in order to detect and locate forest fires.

FIG. 2.—A MODERN HIGH-PRECISION PHOTOTHEODOLITE

With modern wide-angle lenses, narrowness of field is no longer a serious problem. However, terrestrial photogrammetry still has certain inherent deficiencies of major importance. For mapping purposes, the field of view commanded by a ground station is much inferior to that commanded by an air station. The conversion from a terrestrial perspective to the map plane is, at best, a cumbersome process. Every ground station must be occupied by field surveying parties, just as when plane-table methods are used, and hence the saving in cost or time is not pronounced.

SUPERIORITY OF AIR STATIONS

The superiority of the aerial camera station over the ground camera station was recognized from the very beginning of photogrammetry. In 1858, Laussedat experimented with an aerial plate camera, first supporting it from a string of kites and later attaching it to a captive balloon. The results of these experiments were not satisfactory since it was difficult to take a sufficient number of photographs from one station to cover all the area visible from that position. In addition, the slow shutters of that day made it extremely difficult to obtain sharp photographs because of the oscillation of the balloon. Laussedat eventually abandoned the aerial method and returned to terrestrial photogrammetry.

Others experimented with aerial photography, using balloons (Fig. 3), kites, and even carrier pigeons, but it was not until the close of the nineteenth century that Theodor Scheimpflug, a captain in the Austrian army, provided a feasible solution for the problem that had baffled Laussedat. To obtain complete coverage

Fig. 3.—Camera Attached to Basket of Captive Balloon, 1884

of the visible area from a camera station, Scheimpflug used an eight-lens camera attached to the basket of a captive balloon. This camera (Fig. 4) consisted of seven lenses taking oblique photographs grouped around a central lens taking a vertical photograph. The eight exposures were transformed into an extremely wide-angle, single, composite photograph, by a universal transforming printer. Following Scheimpflug's work, there was a period of development of multiple-lens cameras, ranging from three to nine lenses, all with the single objective of obtaining wide photographic coverage from a given air station. The wide coverage of multiple-lens cameras is still considered very advantageous in some types of mapping. A nine-lens camera is used by the United States Coast and Geodetic Survey in this country and by at least one commercial organization in Europe.

Even with captive balloons, ground crews were still necessary to move the cumbersome apparatus across the countryside, a slow and costly operation. Free balloons, propelled by electric motors, were in use as early as 1884, but they were not used extensively for photography. Possibly the oscillations were so great that their use was impracticable.

Aeronautical developments changed the situation completely in the early part of the twentieth century. A German zeppelin captured in France in August, 1914, was found to be equipped with an aerial camera, as was an airplane shot down later in that year. This was a development of the utmost significance. The camera could now be carried to the desired aerial exposure station easily and rapidly without the necessity of placing a crew in the area to be photographed.

Conceding that there are a number of ways of utilizing aerial photography, the writers will confine themselves to problems connected with map making from single-lens vertical photographs using a plotting instrument. A vertical photograph is one taken with the optical axis of the camera nearly vertical or, in other words, with the plane of the photograph nearly parallel to the earth's surface. If the plane of the photograph were exactly parallel to the earth's surface at the time of exposure and if the surface of the earth were perfectly flat, the photo-

FIG. 4.—SCHEIMPFLUG'S EIGHT-LENS CAMERA, BOTTOM VIEW, 1904

graph would represent a true map. However, the airplane noses and rolls as it flies its course, so that the photograph is invariably tilted to some degree. As a result, the image of the earth's surface on the negative does not have a uniform scale. Furthermore, the relief of the terrain causes local displacements of the image. These are fundamental geometrical properties of the photograph arising from the orientation of the camera and the nature of the terrain. In addition, the image is distorted by the physical imperfections of the photography, such as lens aberrations, camera movement during exposure, film curvature, and film shrinkage. Because of these three factors—tilt, relief, and photographic imperfections—the task of converting aerial photographs into accurate topographic maps presents a formidable, but by no means insurmountable, problem. Some methods of solving this problem will now be examined.

STEREOPHOTOGRAMMETRY

When the problems of aerial photogrammetry or terrestrial photogrammetry are solved by the use of stereoscopic instruments, the procedure is referred to as stereophotogrammetry. It should be understood that stereoscopic plotting instruments do not offer the only solution to these problems. For example, the radial-line method of plotting, known as early as 1893, with its corollary, the slotted templet method, has a wide and useful application in photogrammetry. The positions of points in the radial-line method are plotted in their correct relative position to one another by a system of intersection and resection, using the radial center of each photograph as the origin of radials through the images of the points. There are also strong, although somewhat tedious, analytical methods of solution based on parallax measurements.

By far the greater part of photogrammetric mapping, however, is done with stereoscopic plotting instruments. The parlor stereoscope was a familiar instrument of the late nineteenth century, and photogrammetrists were quick to recognize the possibilities of three-dimensional viewing of photographs for surveying purposes. A stereoscopic plotting instrument (Fig. 5) for use with terrestrial photographs was devised about 1890 by E. Deville, Surveyor-General of Canada.

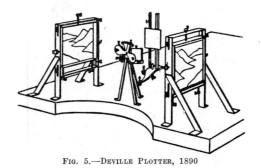

FIG. 5.—DEVILLE PLOTTER, 1890

This was probably the first such instrument to prove of practical value. At about the same time, the Italian Prof. I. Porro and the German Prof. C. Koppe developed the important Porro-Koppe principle of overcoming the effect of camera lens distortion by observing the photograph through a lens identical to the camera lens.

A fundamental problem in the utilization of stereoscopic principles was the necessity of devising a method of horizontal and vertical measurement in the stereoscopic model. In 1892, F. Stolze, of Germany, discovered the principle of the floating mark, and soon thereafter his compatriot C. Pulfrich developed a practicable method of measuring with floating marks. These advances opened the way for the development of modern stereoscopic plotting instruments.

The catalog of stereoplotting instruments is long and varied. They range from simple and inexpensive instruments of low accuracy to intricate and costly machines of the highest precision. Most of these instruments have a useful function for some specific purpose. If only form lines are required, there is no need to have a precision instrument. If high precision is required, it cannot be obtained with a low-cost instrument.

The problem of tilt and relief displacements is solved in the same general manner in most stereoplotting instruments, although there are wide differences in the mechanical details and in the degree of accuracy attained. A pair of overlapping photographs is oriented in the instrument to recover the relative orientation of the negatives at the instant of exposure. A stereoscopic viewing system is provided so that a miniature model of the terrain appears to be created. The model can be brought to the desired scale and oriented with respect to a datum, as represented by ground-survey control points. Measurements are made, and map detail is transferred to the manuscript sheet, by a floating mark. Since the space model is similar in every respect to the terrain in nature, the tilt and relief displacements are automatically solved. As the clarity and geometrical accuracy of the model and the precision of transferring detail to the map increase, the accuracy of the map produced increases and so, very likely, does the cost of the instrument.

FIG. 6.—STEREOCOMPARATOR, 1901

The mechanical and optical problems involved in the design of stereoplotting instruments are multitudinous, and often very complex. Beginning with the development of the Stereocomparator (Fig. 6) by Pulfrich in 1901, there has been a steady stream of plotting devices with many variations in mechanical and optical details. However, practically all have the fundamental objective of recovering the original relative orientation of the photographs as a step toward creating a space model. These devices may be roughly classified as follows, in ascending order of accuracy and cost:

1. Simple nonstereoscopic instruments for limited purposes, such as the Sketchmaster (Fig. 7), which do not provide a three-dimensional model.

2. Topographic mapping instruments utilizing paper contact prints, such as the KEK plotter (Fig. 8).

3. Topographic mapping instruments utilizing anaglyphic projection, such as the Multiplex (Fig. 9).

4. Topographic mapping instruments utilizing optical or mechanical-optical trains, such as the Autograph A-5 (Fig. 10).

The problem of imperfections in the original photography, common to all

FIG. 7.—SKETCHMASTER

FIG. 8.—KEK PLOTTER

plotting methods, has never been wholly solved. There are various methods for compensating the effects of camera lens distortion and film shrinkage, but the real solution is the elimination of these effects at the source. There has been some progress in this direction recently. New photogrammetric lenses, virtually distortion free, have become available and plans have been made for the installation of some of these in aerial cameras. One solution of the film shrinkage problem is the

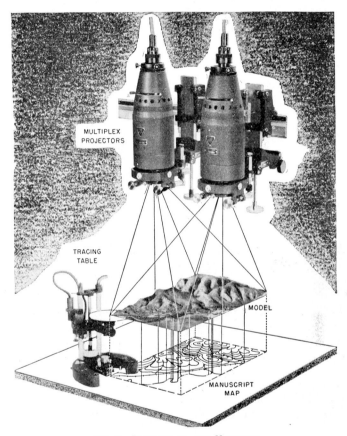

FIG. 9.—PRINCIPLE OF THE MULTIPLEX

use of glass plate negatives, but this is expensive and inconvenient. A new plastic-base film of very high dimensional stability has been announced, and may aid in eliminating the shrinkage problem.

ECONOMICS OF PHOTOGRAMMETRY

Only in the past decade or so has photogrammetry had a really profound influence on the economics of surveying and mapping. Until about 1935, photogrammetry had operated, relatively speaking, solely on the fringes of the broad field. However, when the full impact of a century of development was brought suddenly to bear, under the urgent necessities of World War II, the effect was revolutionary and permanent. Within the past 10 years photogrammetry instead of field work with the plane table has become the basic procedure for the making of topographic maps and for many other activities in the surveying field. This does not mean that field work is a thing of the past. Field engineers are still needed in considerable numbers for control surveys, for completion surveys, and for contouring flat terrain. Nevertheless, the undeniable fact is that, in major mapping enterprises, field operations are now supplementary to photogrammetric operations and must be tailored to fit the photogrammetric program.

FIG. 10.—AUTOGRAPH A-5

Such a revolution, which has affected governmental and commercial mapping organizations alike all over the world, would not have come about unless it paid in dollars and cents. Relative costs of field mapping versus photogrammetric mapping are not easy to evaluate for there is always the debatable question of how to amortize expensive plotting equipment and the additional service operations that are an inescapable part of photogrammetric procedures. However, photogrammetric procedures, if not always cheaper than field procedures, at least give better maps for the same money. Over and above the measurable cost per square mile of mapping, photogrammetry permits the completion of vast mapping projects within a time interval beyond the range of practicability for field methods. Considering that in many instances time is money, the economics of the situation consistently dictates the use of photogrammetric methods for extensive mapping projects.

The economics of photogrammetry has also brought a perennial mapping problem—the cost of ground-survey control—into sharper focus than ever. When topography was done by plane table, field parties had to be on the ground anyway, and it seemed quite natural that they devote part of their efforts to control surveys. However, now that the topography is determined from aerial photographs, the continuing need for even larger amounts of control to be done by surveying parties in the field makes everyone control-cost conscious. Indeed, the cost of control sometimes exceeds the cost of photogrammetric compilation. It is therefore only natural that intensive efforts are being made to eliminate, or at least reduce, the requirements for ground-survey control. Some progress has already been made in this direction for some classes of mapping, using air-borne radar and shoran techniques.

Mapping by photogrammetric methods has broadened the scope of skills and knowledge required. So many skills and varied scientific backgrounds are necessary that few can hope to master all of them. Thus, although the field of surveying and mapping has broadened immeasurably and has created a need for high-level scientific knowledge, paradoxically the participation of the individual in the construction of the map has narrowed. He now tends to become a specialist, participating in only one phase of the operations, whereas the old-time topographer knew the satisfaction of creating an entire map from beginning to end.

PHOTOGRAMMETRY INFLUENCES SOCIETY

Some might say, rather glibly, that the impact of photogrammetry on society is a rather farfetched conception, that photogrammetrists can scarcely make their weight felt. However, consider this conception further. What about the impact on society of aviation, of well-constructed highways, of the development of natural resources, of the conduct of wars? None would deny that all these have a far-reaching influence. Nevertheless each depends on maps, maps now made largely from photographs. Take away the pilot's aeronautical chart, the detailed strip map of the turnpike planner, the conservationist's topographic or resource map, the general's military map—and society has been deprived of vital tools indeed.

Without the speed of photogrammetry, the lack of maps would constitute a bottleneck in the development of other fields whose importance is more obvious. In this way, photogrammetry constitutes a very real, if indirect, force in the pattern of twentieth century civilization.

THE CRYSTAL BALL

It is good engineering practice to predict future developments by extrapolating the trends of the past. The trend, as can be seen in reviewing a century of experience, is toward the ever-increasing self-sufficiency of photogrammetric methods. Engineers can look forward then to new and improved instruments and techniques, to new methods of obtaining control without recourse to ground surveys, and to an ever-increasing demand for more and better maps. At the same time, since every new development has raised its new quota of problems, it can be expected that the photogrammetrist of the future, having solved the most baffling problems of today, will be vexed by questions beyond present-day conception.

Even if distortion-free lenses, mechanically perfect cameras, absolutely stable film, faultless developing techniques, and sharp-sighted, trouble-free plotting instruments could be produced, photogrammetry would still be confronted with difficult and interesting problems. In areas of heavy timber cover, the ground would still be invisible to the camera. Adequate ground control would still be difficult to obtain in remote or inaccessible areas. Personnel sufficiently skilled in both the science of photogrammetry and the art of topography to utilize the procedures to the best advantage would still be relatively rare.

Although photogrammetry has come a long way technically since 1852, it has still a long way to go.

AMERICAN SOCIETY OF CIVIL ENGINEERS

Founded November 5, 1852

TRANSACTIONS

Paper No. 2634

SURVEYING AND MAPPING IN CANADA, 1852–1952

By F. H. Peters,[1] M. ASCE

Synopsis

The picture of Canadian surveying efforts, on a national or Dominion-wide basis, starts with early explorer days. Later, the better populated areas, along both oceans and the southern border, accommodated themselves to standardized practice; but the central interior and mountain sections, less accessible and less hospitable, had to be attacked by new and sometimes pioneering methods, such as by camera and airplane. A brief history of Dominion surveying sets the stage, followed by comments on official survey organizations, their relationship and coverage. Special methods, perfected and widely used in these developments, include ground photosurveying, "shoran" trilateration, oblique air photography, and radar altimetry—all concisely described.

To describe the accomplishments of surveying and mapping in a country of such vast area as Canada, over so long a period as 100 years, is a monumental task. At the outset two points must be kept in mind. The first is that the Dominion of Canada had its birth in 1867 when the then existing provinces were confederated, and before that date most of the early explorer-mappers worked under the egis of the Hudson's Bay Company. The second point is that this paper deals particularly with the map surveyor and excludes the great work that has been done by the legal or cadastral surveyor in marking out the land for settlements and other landholdings.

Since the legal surveys, with the exception of those for the three prairie provinces, have always been a provincial responsibility, little will be said about them. As an exception to the rule the westernmost province, British Columbia, has also had a small but very efficient map survey organization for many years, which is still continuing. Generally speaking, however, the map survey and publication have been undertaken by the Dominion Government with the provinces confining themselves to the publication of special provincial maps.

[1] Retired, Aylmer East, Que., Canada ; formerly Chf., Surveys and Mapping Bureau, Dept. of Mines and Resources, Dominion of Canada, Ottawa, Ont., Canada.

PIONEERING DAYS

It seems fitting to commence this paper by paying tribute to the memory of those grand old men who, although more properly described as explorers rather than surveyors, really, with the maps they produced, paved the way for the accurate surveys that were to follow as better instruments and facilities for travel became available. Out of many only a few whose work was noteworthy can be mentioned without going too far beyond the century under review—always remembering that these rugged men accomplished their work under conditions of difficulty and physical hardship which seem almost unbelievable in these days when people have become softened by so much easy living.

Around 1770, Samuel Hearne, journeying with the Indians and sharing their mode of life, traveled the barren lands to the Arctic Ocean west of Hudson Bay. In 1789 Alexander Mackenzie followed the mighty river which now bears his name to the Arctic Ocean and a few years later forced his way across the Rocky Mountains to the Pacific Ocean. David Thompson, who by 1807 had explored the Saskatchewan River for 1,100 miles, went on and from 1808 to 1812 explored every foot of the great Columbia River, on the lower reaches of which, in the United States, recent years have seen such tremendous hydroelectric development.

Map of 1801.—A composite picture of what had been accomplished by the early explorers is shown on a reliable map prepared by J. Arrow-Smith, the cartographer of the Hudson's Bay Company, dated 1801. This map is quite good for eastern Canada except that nothing is shown of the interior of the northern part of the Province of Quebec. In regard to western Canada the map is much less complete, but it indicates the great north and south extent of the Rocky Mountains; and, thanks to the charting of Capt. George Vancouver and other mariners, the coast line of the Pacific Ocean is quite accurate. The interior of what is now British Columbia and Yukon is all a blank, and the coast line of the Arctic Ocean is entirely omitted except at two isolated points where Hearne and Mackenzie had penetrated. The map extends only to latitude 70°; and the Arctic islands, which have been so much in the public eye in recent years, are not shown at all. In the catalog of the maps of the Geographic Board of Canada, the earliest note of a map from actual survey refers to Thompson's map of "The North-West Territory of the Province of Canada," published in 1814.

Conditions in 1852.—So much for the earliest maps. As a starter for the 100-year period under review it may be well to picture briefly what Canada was like in 1852, principally to explain why surveys and maps were limited and rather disjointed in the first half of the nineteenth century. The country was of vast extent—about the same size as the United States—and it contained a population of about 2,000,000 people with a capacity for taxation too small to provide for anything more than the administration of the settled areas.

The populated areas were mainly in the Maritime Provinces on the Atlantic coast—Nova Scotia, Prince Edward Island, and New Brunswick—together with the land stretching up the St. Lawrence River in Lower Canada (later the Province of Quebec) past Quebec City and Montreal and along the north shore of lakes Ontario and Erie in Upper Canada (later the Province of Ontario) to Toronto and Windsor (across the St. Clair River from Detroit, Mich.). There were outposts on the north shores of lakes Huron and Superior at Sault Ste. Marie and Fort William.

Then came a 400-mile portage to what is now Winnipeg, Man. From there west to the Rocky Mountains there was 800 miles with nothing but small settlements in a territory still controlled by the great Hudson's Bay Company. The Rocky Mountains, growing higher and wider in these areas north of the 49th parallel, formed a giant barrier to the small Colony of Vancouver Island on the Pacific coast. In the Maritime Provinces and in Lower and Upper Canada,

FIG. 1.—SURVEYORS' AND MAP MAKERS' PROBLEM—AIR VIEW OF RATHER FORBIDDING COUNTRY IN CARCAJOU MOUNTAIN RANGE IN NORTHWEST TERRITORIES, CANADA

farmsteads had been surveyed, but practically no large areas had been accurately mapped in detail.

As regards the great bulk of Canada, the surveyor was starting from scratch. The areas waiting to be mapped were enormous, but the revenues of the country were quite inadequate to pay for the work. From the surveyor's point of view (Fig. 1), it is appropriate to quote from a poem by Robert W. Service: "There's a land where the mountains are nameless, and the rivers all run God knows where."

Railway Surveys.—Today, surveying and mapping considered together bring to mind the network of permanently marked control points established with great precision by the geodetic survey; and, within that network, the legal and engineering surveys executed with a high degree of accuracy and the mapping programs organized to produce topographic map sheets similar in design so they will all fit together with the same scales. However, in earlier years the situation was very different—to a large extent the best and usually the only connected surveys were those exploratory to, or for the construction of, new railways or canals.

Going back only 50 years, many a surveyor and engineer today remembers occasions when his survey was "tied in" to the railway line to check his location and perhaps particularly to get a "level reading" on the "base of rail" in order to verify his elevation. These old railway engineering surveys, although not made for the purpose of mapping, were of great help to the early mappers. Because of their importance a few of the railway surveys will be described briefly.

In 1824 the survey of the Rideau Canal, running a distance of 126 miles from Ottawa to Kingston in Upper Canada (later Ontario), was completed by a party of Royal Engineers sent over from England. From 1846 to 1848, again under the guidance of Royal Engineer officers, the survey for the Intercolonial Railway, following the long 1,158-mile route bordering the Gulf of St. Lawrence and River St. Lawrence, was completed from Halifax, Nova Scotia, to Quebec. In 1853 the Grand Trunk Railway constructed its first line which ran from tidewater at Portland, Me., to Montreal. Eventually this company operated a network of lines largely in the Province of Ontario. By 1880 their construction totaled about 950 miles in Canada and extended from Quebec City on the east, westward to Sarnia, Ont., northeast of Detroit. After the earlier surveys in 1833–1835, in 1887 the survey of the Trent Valley Canal was finally completed, following the short route of 197 miles from Trenton, Ont., on Lake Ontario to Georgian Bay on Lake Huron.

The construction of the Canadian Pacific Railway was provided for in the Confederation Act, to join British Columbia with eastern Canada. The original survey was started at Mattawa, Ont., on June 10, 1871, and was completed in 1877. Nineteen parties set out from various locations to cover a line from the Ottawa Valley to the Pacific coast, five of which surveyed various passes through the Rocky Mountains. The present rail distance from Montreal to Vancouver, B. C., is 2,881 miles; but during the original survey the length of lines surveyed and routes explored amounted to nearly 46,000 miles, of which nearly 11,500 miles were chained and leveled.

Geological Survey.—The Geological Survey of Canada, dating from 1842, has played a very important part in the exploration, survey, and mapping of the country. The Act of 1877, one decade after confederation, "to make better provision respecting the Geological Survey * * *" sets forth as its objectives:

"* * * to elucidate the geology and mineralogy of the Dominion and to make a full and scientific examination of the various strata, soils, ores, coals, oils and mineral waters so as to afford the mining, metallurgical and other interests of the country correct and full information as to its character and resources."

Obviously it is impossible to elucidate the geology of a country without first having some sort of base maps available, and a section of the Act provided for this deficiency. To understand properly the mapping by the geologists in the earlier days, it is important to realize that it was done only as a means to an end. The object of the Geological Survey was to indicate geology; maps were made where geological information was required; and the map was designed mainly to facilitate the understanding of geology.

In Canadian circles the memory is still green of geologist-explorers who did outstanding work in the period from 1870 to 1890 such as G. M. Dawson, A. P. Low, R. G. McConnell, and J. B. Tyrrell. In 1877 the Geological Survey published its first western map on which land forms were shown by hachuring. This map, published at a scale of 8 miles to 1 in., covered about 30,000 sq miles and was one of the first large contributions to the geographical knowledge of that part of Canada.

From 1894 to about 1902 regular sheet mapping on the scale of 1 mile to 1 in. was introduced. This innovation was the beginning of the change-over toward the production of modern topographic maps. These map sheets were controlled by transit triangulation; traverses were made by compass and measuring tape, or by measuring wheel or pacing; and land forms were drawn by vertical sketching based on transit readings on suitable points, both vertical and horizontal angles being recorded. In 1906 the plane table was added to surveying equipment. In 1908 a Topographical Division was organized and standards of work were established, with a regular system of mapping, based on the unit 1-mile sheet covering 30 min of longitude by 15 min of latitude. This event was notable because for the first time mapping was organized as a separate project and undertaken by a corps of men trained as map makers rather than as geologists.

Dominion Land Survey.—In 1870 the first large active survey was organized when the Dominion Land Survey was commenced near Winnipeg in western Canada. An idea of this type of work is given by Figs. 2 and 3. These legal or cadastral surveys were undertaken for the purpose of marking the boundaries of farmsteads for settlement under a system of township sections and quarter sections similar to that in the United States. However, they fit into the historic picture because later on they were used as the control for an extensive system of modern topographic maps. The eventual survey of about 8,000 townships covered the southerly half of the three prairie provinces, Manitoba, Saskatchewan, and Alberta, and a small part of the mountain province of British Columbia (Fig. 4).

The organized control by meridian and base line and by correction line was scientifically preplanned and the accuracy of the survey on the ground was far in advance of anything done before. Extending from the smooth bare prairie lands in the south to the forested lands in the north and on the west, through the rough foothills flanking the Rockies, the survey was laid down successfully over widely different types of country. Because the astronomic bearings were accurate throughout and all the control measurements were check chained, no serious discrepancies in any parts of the area subsequently penetrated have ever been discovered by the Geodetic Survey.

Sectional Map Series.—In 1891 there began an office compilation of these latter surveys for the production of the so-called "Sectional Map Series" at the rather odd scale of 3 miles to the inch. Lacking contours (because no leveling was done in connection with the legal survey), these sheets scarcely met the requirements of a true topographical map. They did however serve a most useful purpose in the earlier days of development because all the roads and the farmers' homesteads were accurately shown.

In the west it was common practice (and still is) to describe all locations by section, township, and range and so with these lines all shown on the maps it was

Fig. 2.—Early Survey on Canadian Western Prairies, in 1880; with Tepee and Red River Carts

Fig. 3.—Manpower Required to Pull Survey Barges Upstream in Swift Current, About 1900

easy to find any given site. Furthermore, as the western prairies are ordinarily smooth and the topographical features generally scarce, the lack of contours showing the elevations was not as serious a matter as it would be in rough or hilly areas.

Later on, in 1919, in keeping with the development of Canada, these sectional maps were improved by the inauguration of field mapping surveys for drawing contours and obtaining other information to produce complete topographical maps. In this operation a distinctly new technique, utilizing batteries of aneroid barometers for obtaining elevations between spirit level controls, was employed. Through cooperation with a British instrument maker an accurate yet robust type of instrument was developed, and a standardized technique for its use in the field

Fig. 4.—Type of Topography in Rugged British Columbia, Canada—Channel Between Maitland and Hawkesbury Islands

produced a reliable and consistent accuracy never before attained by aneroids. Before they were discontinued some years ago, one hundred and thirty-three of these maps were issued covering in all about 536,000 sq miles.

Ground Phototopographic Survey.—The sequence of events leads next to what was a distinctly Canadian enterprise—the ground phototopographic survey commenced in the Rocky Mountains in 1886. When an attempt was made to extend the Dominion land surveys westward into the Cordilleras of western Canada, one of the great mountain systems of the world (Fig. 1), it was found that the methods which had been employed over the flatter areas were inadequate. In the mountains the difficulties of survey transport were at a maximum; up to a certain elevational limit, vision was impeded by the heavy forest growth; and above timber line the rocky surface was frequently so rugged and precipitous that measurement of distance by ordinary methods was nearly impossible. However, the peaks of the mountains did provide points of commanding vision, and it was realized that if this natural advantage was capitalized by setting up survey cameras (Fig. 5) on them it might overcome or balance the other problems.

The idea of ground phototopography originated in France but was never used there. However, it was employed to some extent in Italy for mapping the Alps. E. Deville, the then Surveyor-General, developed the idea and applied it in practice to mapping the high mountainous areas of Canada. The earlier work covered many of Canada's national parks including Banff and Jasper, Alta. Work scales of 1 mile and 4 miles to 1 in., are still being continued by the Dominion Topo-

FIG. 5.—SURVEY CAMERA DEVELOPED IN CANADA: CAMERA, LEFT, REPLACING ALIDADE, RIGHT, ON TRANSIT HEAD

graphical Survey, and to date the area covered is about 400,000 sq miles (not all as yet published).

The ground phototopography survey and map are noteworthy because nowhere else in the world have they been carried on so extensively or successfully. The same principles are still being employed by the Province of British Columbia and the Dominion in conjunction with vertical air photographs. Furthermore the undertaking of this work was the reason that, later on, there were in Canada a number of map surveyors well versed in the science and practice of photographic surveying. This fortunate circumstance paved the way after 1918 for an early realization of the possibilities of mapping with the air survey camera and for practical solution of the many new technical problems which were involved.

Chief Geographer's Maps.—In regard to topographical maps, inferring a reasonably large scale, office-compiled maps are always suspect because they lack the reliable check on details which results from having trained topographers actually go over the ground. The Chief Geographer's maps were nevertheless important because they covered most of the better developed parts of eastern Canada and for a period of perhaps 25 years were the best ones available.

In 1894 a Geographer was appointed at Ottawa. In addition to producing small-scale maps of Canada as a whole, his duties were to gather together the information resulting from the many land surveys which had been made and to compile it into maps coordinated into a series of standard design. The first sheet was published in 1903. The maps were known as the Chief Geographer's Series. No attempt was made to show contours, but spot elevations were indicated at railroad stations. Fifty-six of these maps were issued. The scales of publication were 3.97 and 7.89 miles to 1 in. These peculiar scales—1: 250,000 and 1: 500,000—apparently were chosen in keeping with the decimal system and because they come quite close to the conventional English scales of 4 and 8 miles to 1 in.

Army Survey Establishment.—Although military map work had been undertaken previously, what is now known as the Army Survey Establishment, Department of National Defence, goes back to 1904 when the section was organized to produce standard topographical maps at the scale of 1 mile to 1 in., covering the southern parts of Ontario and Quebec. It was at first hoped that the existing township surveys of Ontario would supply the necessary horizontal control and that the railroads and other public works would provide the necessary elevations thus leaving the topographers, equipped with plane tables, with the task of filling in the contours and other essential details. However the necessity for better control both horizontal and vertical soon became apparent and within a year special control parties were sent into the field.

The Army Survey Establishment is a self-contained unit with all the facilities for printing its own maps. The work of this military organization has been an important factor in the mapping of Canada; but, because of the special functions which it inherits from the department to which it belongs, its methods and fields of action have been more versatile than its opposite numbers in the civil departments. In addition to a continuing program of regular mapping work, the Survey has maintained a connection with civilian work, has executed the mapping of special areas at special scales, and has kept itself up to date and practiced the particular techniques which it might be called on to exercise in times of emergency.

SURVEY INSTRUMENTS

The preceding sections have brought this history up to about the date 1900, and to some account of the instruments which the surveyors had used in their work. Until about 1850 the survey compass was the main direction-finding instrument, its great weakness being the deviation of the magnetic needle from true north in an uncontrollable and variable manner. Probably by 1867 the field transit theodolite was widely used. With its telescope and carefully divided plate read by vernier, angles could be read with accuracy on signal marks at long distances; at the same time the old chain, made up of long links of steel wire, was available and gave good results in measuring if carefully treated.

There is no record as to when the first engineer's level was made; but, at the time the first large engineering works were undertaken in Canada, such an instrument was available with quite good telescopes and level bubble vials. Generally, over a long period survey instruments were not basically changed but only improved so that the measurements were more accurate and the instruments handier and lighter. Today the old link chain has been replaced by steel measuring tapes which are still lighter and can be made much longer. Perhaps the most radical and important change was the new type of optical transit designed by Henry Wild and introduced in Canada about 1925.

GEODETIC SURVEY

Thus far the accomplishments of surveying and mapping have been presented through a historical statement about the organizations engaged directly in such work. The Hydrographic Survey was omitted because its assignment, a notable and most important one, is to chart the navigable waters of Canada rather than the land. However, it would not be correct to fail to mention the Geodetic Survey because, although it does not produce any maps, its work is really the basic foundation of all large-scale accurate mapping and, wherever available, provides the highly precise framework on which the mapping control surveys are hung. The Geodetic Survey of Canada performs all geodetic work undertaken in the Dominion, together with all precise leveling.

Commencing in 1907 it has to date completed about 11,000 miles, axial length, of first-order triangulation; about 2,500 miles of secondary triangulation; and about 500 miles of precise traverse. The primary triangulation net when marked on a map of Canada looks like an immense capital letter U. The bottom leg extends from the Atlantic to the Pacific oceans through the southerly settled areas; the left leg extends north from the 49th parallel and, with combinations of United States Coast and Geodetic Survey and International Boundary triangulation, control is available up to and along the 141st meridian (Alaska boundary) to the Arctic coast; and the right leg extends north from the Gulf of St. Lawrence to Ungava Bay of Hudson Strait.

However, there is still an immense area in the northern interior without any geodetic control, and efforts to overcome this deficiency will be discussed subsequently under "Shoran Trilateration." The lines of precise leveling have been extended from ocean to ocean and in general cover all the main railway lines and some northern highways. As of 1952 there have been completed approximately 33,000 miles of precise leveling and in addition 17,000 miles of secondary leveling; about 16,000 bench marks have been established in a network connected to six tidal stations, which establish the mean sea level datum.

The triangulation work of the Geodetic Survey is based on the 1927 North American Datum which is in common use by the United States, Canada, and Mexico. The order of accuracy of the work is in keeping with the best modern practice.

SHORAN TRILATERATION

The latest accomplishment has been the use, by the Geodetic Survey, of shoran trilateration. This recent electronic device, with its clever application of many new gadgets is much too intricate for description here. Shoran emits electromagnetic pulses from an airplane in flight which are received at ground stations, amplified, and returned, the elapsed time between dispatch from and reception at the plane being measured very accurately. Since the speed of the electronic waves is known, the distance is computed from the time interval.

In the immense northern interior areas, having only control points fixed by astronomic observation, shoran trilateration was started in 1949 for the purpose of providing better control so that more accurate maps at larger scales could be produced from the air photos. The advantage of shoran is that great distances and areas can be covered much more quickly than by the old orthodox method of triangulation based on the precise measurement of angles. Shoran trilateration has sides, 200 miles in average length, as compared to 10 miles or 20 miles in triangulation, and points are fixed with an accuracy of, say, 25 ft, as compared to an accuracy of, say, 400 ft with astronomic observations.

AIR PHOTOGRAPHY

During World War I, over and above the great clash of arms, there was great concentration on, and important progress made in, the development of what might be called, for want of clearer term, auxiliary instruments of war. Significant strides were made in improving the airplane; and, from the airplane, cameras were used to take photographs for reconnaissance of enemy positions and maneuvers. Very shortly after the war this procedure led to developments which revolutionized and accelerated the whole business of producing accurate topographic maps. It also radically changed the basic process because the plotting of all the details of topography which previously had been the work of the surveyor in the field was now done in the office from the air photo. Extensive literature is now available on all technical phases of the taking and the use of the air photo, together with descriptions of the many clever, and sometimes very complicated, machines employed for plotting the photographs in the office. Hence only a very brief history will be given of the work in Canada.

This new development was taken up in 1920 by the Topographical Survey Branch; but much credit is due the old Air Board of Canada for fostering the work in the early stages. Up to the outbreak of World War II in 1939 the actual flying and photographing was done by the Royal Canadian Air Force.

In accordance with European practice, first air photos were taken vertically; and, although these were found quite satisfactory, they were expensive because each photo covered only a small area and could be plotted only where numerous and accurate control lines were available in the settled areas. At this time however there was a pressing need for reasonably accurate maps of the great interior northlands where, since the control points were far apart, a different type of photo was necessary, one suitable for projection over much longer distances.

For solving the problems which had to be faced, a new type of oblique air photography was evolved. The photos were taken from an airplane flying at an elevation of about 5,000 ft above the ground, with the camera depressed so as to show the horizon line at the top of the picture (Figs. 1 and 6). The method was practicable because much of the northern area lay within the Laurentian Shield where the rocky surface is rough in a small way, but there are few high hills.

Also, the many lakes with irregular but well-defined rocky shores provided plenty of points which could be recognized on the photos.

The airplane is today a common sight and travel by air is no longer a novelty; to any surveyor or engineer the use of air photos is taken for granted. However, anyone who has "been through the mill" will recall the many difficulties which had to be overcome in the early days. The first cameras were fairly crude military models which needed adapting for mapping purposes, and the early photographic film was beset by static electricity which would discharge every now and again and ruin a picture by covering it with a tracery of lines representing an oversize

FIG. 6.—OBLIQUE AIR PHOTOGRAPH, WITH HORIZON SHOWING; SCENE OVER CARCAJOU RANGE, NORTHWEST TERRITORIES, CANADA, EMPHASIZING MAP PROBLEMS POSED BY RUGGED TERRAIN AND SHORT SEASON

lightning storm. The early oblique photos were taken from slow flying boats with a maximum range of 500 miles. To guard against the danger of failure of the single propeller, the plane was supposed to always keep within 1 mile of a lake where it could make a safe landing (Fig. 7). In the forward open cockpit there was a single camera which the photographer had to stand up and operate, exposed to the full force of the wind.

Oblique air photography was a distinctly Canadian development, but contemporaneously vertical photographs were being taken and used in the southerly districts where they were suitable. As of the year 1930 when oblique photography was at its peak, it may be said that as regards the actual application of the new methods, with maps produced from air photography, Canadian surveyors had accomplished far more than those of any other country.

The first maps of the north from air photos printed about 1926, covered an area of which formerly nothing was depicted except the main water routes and the very large lakes. To advertise the improvements of the new methods, one sheet including 5,500 sq miles was carefully examined and was found to show a total of 5,486 lakes and 6,144 islands. Today about 3,000,000 air photos have been taken covering about 90% of the land area of Canada.

RADAR ALTIMETRY

In addition to the very recent development of shoran trilateration to provide horizontal control in the undeveloped northern areas, another new method has been produced which is still in process of further trial and improvement. In the north, what is generally designated by surveyors as vertical control, or altitude

FIG. 7.—EARLY USE OF FLYING BOAT (1924) FOR SUPPLYING SURVEY PARTY IN NORTHERN CANADA

of the ground, is even scarcer than horizontal control. In an endeavor to produce vertical control economically over wide areas, the airplane is again employed in radar altimeter surveys, or "radar altimetry." The apparatus used is, like shoran, very complicated. Briefly, it works like this: The plane flying at relatively low altitude is equipped with an air camera and from the photos its course can be charted; it also carries a sensitive altimeter which plots the elevation profile of the plane suitably related to the photographs. The radar apparatus sends out micro waves and records the time interval required for them to bounce back from the land or water directly under the plane. Thus the distance from the plane to the earth is calculated, and subtracting this from the elevation of the plane gives the elevation of the ground (Fig. 8).

Up to the beginning of 1952, 33,000 miles of profile have been surveyed, and although it is of course not as yet accurate enough for large-scale topographic maps, the work has served for contouring 370,000 sq miles on a map scale of 8 miles to 1 in. with a vertical interval of 500 ft.

Long Surveyed Straight Lines

Surveyors and other scientists have always been interested in very long surveyed straight lines. The survey of the 4th meridian (longitude 110°), as one of the governing lines of the Dominion Lands Survey, was begun in 1878 and completed as the boundary between the provinces of Saskatchewan and Alberta in 1938. Throughout its length of 761 miles (11° of latitude), it has been actually surveyed, prolonged by continuous measurement, and monumented at frequent intervals. Surveyors, chainmen, rodmen, woodsmen, and packers have actually walked to and fro many times along its course. There are 1,350 survey monuments established at ½-mile intervals.

Fig. 8.—Procedure in Radar Altimetry, to Obtain Ground Profile from Airplane Elevation by Radar Sounding

Another long straight line boundary is the 141st meridian which was surveyed jointly by Canada and the United States as the boundary between Yukon and Alaska. Perhaps the longest straight line boundary in the world is the easterly boundary of the State of Western Australia, about 1,160 miles long; but probably very little of this length has actually been surveyed and marked on the ground.

Canadian Board on Geographical Names

In a paper on surveys and maps it always seems fitting to give credit to the office workers, particularly to the draftsmen. They solve many problems in their own field and perform much exacting labor in processing the surveyors' work and producing the ultimate plans and map sheets for general use.

The mention of office work leads appropriately to the Canadian Board on Geographical Names which was originally created by an order in council in 1897 as the Geographic Board of Canada. The general public has no idea of the tremendous amount of work involved in searching for and establishing the correct names to be used on the published map sheets, not only when they are being printed for the first time but also when they come up for revision. The Board, clothed with final authority as regards the publications of all government agencies at Ottawa has done outstanding work and shortly the old published lists of decisions will be replaced by a "Gazetteer of Canada" to be published in several volumes.

In the matter of place names special effort has always been made to cooperate with the Provinces, all of which are represented on the Board except Quebec and Newfoundland, which have their own provincial boards with which an intimate liaison is always maintained. The Ottawa members of the Board represent the principal mapping and charting agencies, together with the Post Office and the Public Archives departments.

Economic and Human Significance

To indicate the economic and human significance of what has been accomplished in the field of surveying and mapping in Canada, the following is quoted from an old report issued, strangely enough, by the Royal Survey Department of Siam perhaps 30 years ago:

"Not only is science in general benefited, but every branch of the industrial and commercial development of a country is advanced, if good topographical maps of the area of operations are available. The general administration in all its branches, the location of railways and highways, the planning of schemes for water supply, for irrigation and drainage projects, the installation of electric transmission lines, even the location of the boundaries of reservations and holdings, are all dependent on the supply of good topographical maps. Therefore, in order to mobilize all the available resources of this country and to enable them to be exploited to the best advantage, it is expedient that all the territory within its borders should be topographically surveyed at the earliest possible date."

Summary

A short résumé of the mapping done in Canada to 1952 is indicated by the following data:

Area mapped to:	Square miles	
1-mile accuracy	226,848	(5.9%)
2-mile accuracy	181,131	(4.7%)
4-mile accuracy	832,966	(21.6%)
8-mile accuracy	1,933,893	(50.3%)
Total	3,174,838	(82.5%)

The total area of Canada, mapped and unmapped, is 3,845,144 sq miles (100%).

Considered in cold terms, this work adds up to a mighty accomplishment, in itself a tribute to a host of hardy, conscientious, and capable workers. The engineering profession has every right to be proud of them.

AMERICAN SOCIETY OF CIVIL ENGINEERS

Founded November 5, 1852

TRANSACTIONS

Paper No. 2635

GEODETIC SURVEYING MOVES FORWARD

By H. W. Hemple,[1] M. ASCE

SYNOPSIS

Development and perfection of geodetic surveying techniques in this country are best illustrated by the activities of the United States Coast and Geodetic Survey. Starting with imported instruments and establishment of base lines in the North Atlantic States, the system has grown to cover the nation and finally also Mexico, Canada, and Alaska. Major arcs are tied in with state plane-coordinate systems, so that geodesy has come to have local as well as national significance. Over the years theodolites have been improved in performance while made smaller in size; invar tapes have become standard for base measurements; portable steel towers and automobile transport have increased speed of operation; and mechanical computation has transformed office methods. Throughout, high standards and practical objectives have been combined by the engineers of the Survey to secure results at the same time scientific and useful.

The history of geodetic surveying in the United States begins with the survey of the Atlantic coast originally proposed as a function of the Federal Government during the administration of President Thomas Jefferson in 1807. F. R. Hassler, an eminent Swiss scientist who had emigrated to the United States, submitted a plan which was accepted for the charting of the coast line, whereby the location of points along the shore would be determined accurately by triangulation. These points would be used to fix the positions of the vessels engaged in sounding the depths of the channels entering the principal ports along the Atlantic coast. Mr. Hassler was appointed the first superintendent of the United States Coast Survey. His immediate concern was to obtain precise survey instruments from Europe; this took several years and not until 1832 were actual field surveys undertaken.

Original Base Line.—For the early base measurements the unit of length was an iron bar 1 m long—one of fifteen similar bars standardized by an International Committee on Weights and Measures at Paris, France. It was brought to this country by Hassler in 1805 and presented to the American Philosophical Society

---

[1] Chf., Div. of Geodesy (Retired), U. S. Coast and Geodetic Survey, Washington, D. C.

of Philadelphia, Pa. When the Coast Survey was established, it was placed in the custody of that organization. This unit, known as the "Committee Meter," was the standard of length until 1889 when the platinum-iridium prototype meter bars, standardized by the International Bureau of Weights and Measures in Paris, were brought over. These prototype bars, now in the custody of the National Bureau of Standards, have been the standard of length in the United States since that time. The comparison between the Committee Meter and the prototype meter made in 1889 showed a difference of only 1 micron.

The first base line, $8\frac{3}{4}$ miles long, was measured by Hassler in 1834 at Fire Island, Long Island, New York. From this base triangulation was extended in both directions. Surveys between 1833 and 1844 from central Long Island to the headwaters of Chesapeake Bay, united the detached surveys of New York, N. Y., and Philadelphia, and of New York Harbor, Delaware Bay, and Chesapeake Bay. In 1844 a base line 5.4 miles in length was measured at Kent Island, Chesapeake Bay, Maryland, and another base line, $10\frac{3}{4}$ miles in length was measured in Massachusetts, northeast of Providence, R. I.

These three bases were measured with four rectangular iron bars 2 m long placed together lengthwise and alined in a wooden trough. The iron bars were compared with the Committee Meter. A microscope on an independent stand held the end position while the bars were moved. Three to six thermometers were used for the purpose of obtaining temperature corrections. It required about 6 weeks to prepare and measure a base. For the Massachusetts base, three measurements were made: One in the fall, one in the winter, and one in the summer. The probable error in measurements of these bases ranged from 1/240,700 for the Kent Island base to 1/439,000 for the Massachusetts base.

Early Triangulation.—The original theodolite (Fig. 1) used by Hassler in extending the triangulation from the Fire Island base was manufactured by a Mr. Troughton of England, whose firm is now known as Cooke, Troughton and Simms. It had a graduated circle 2 ft in diameter. Either the direction method or the method of repetitions was used for the theodolite observations. Pointings were made either on heliotropes or on signals consisting of triangular, equilateral pyramids from 10 ft to 30 ft in height surmounted by a pole projecting from the apex with a globe $1\frac{1}{2}$ ft to 2 ft in diameter symmetrically placed on top. Observers spent several weeks at a station, working under different atmospheric conditions. An average of twenty-four sets (direct and reverse) were observed at each station between Fire Island and Kent Island.

In the arc from the Kent Island base to the Massachusetts base the average closing error of the triangles was 0.85 sec. The length as carried through the triangulation from the Fire Island base checked the Kent Island base measurement by 1/90,000, and the Fire Island base measurement checked that of the Massachusetts base by 1/165,000.

When Mr. Hassler died, in 1843, he was succeeded by Alexander Dallas Bache, Hon. M. ASCE. Between 1844 and 1859 the primary arc was extended from Rhode Island to Calais, Me., uniting the detached surveys of Boston, Mass., Portland, Me., and intervening harbors. Bache measured the Epping base in Maine in 1857, using the Bache-Wurdemann contact-level compensating apparatus consisting of two 6-m bars, one of brass and one of iron, placed parallel to each other.

The length of the base was 5.42 miles; and the probable error of measurement, 1/551,650. The theodolite used between the Epping base and the Massachusetts base had a 30-in. graduated circle, and the average closing error of the triangles was 0.92 sec. The length as carried through the triangulation from the Epping base checked the Massachusetts base measurement by 1/76,000.

Astronomic Observations.—Astronomic instruments used in early triangulation

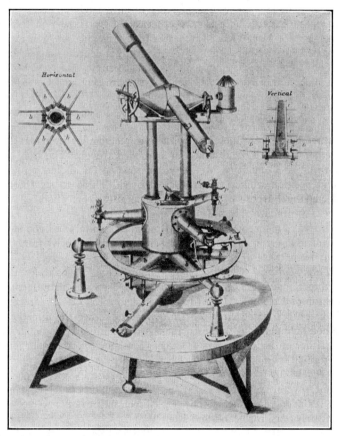

FIG. 1.—THE 24-IN. THEODOLITE INTRODUCED BY F. R. HASSLER

for determining latitude, longitude, and azimuth were large, cumbersome, and very heavy. The zenith telescope for latitude observations was 45 in. long with a $3\frac{1}{2}$-in. aperture and an axis 24 in. high. The Talcott method of observing was followed, determining the differences of zenith distances of stars in the meridian on opposite sides of the zenith.

The transit instrument, used for early longitude observations, had a 46-in. telescope. The first longitude observations were made by comparison of chronometers transported between Liverpool, England, and Cambridge, Mass., on the expeditions of 1849, 1850, 1851, and 1855. A longitude comparison by cable was obtained in 1876. Telegraphic longitude comparisons have been used on land since 1851. Later, since the advent of wireless communication, radio comparisons of time have been in constant use.

Present-day observations of astronomic latitude and longitude are made with the Bamberg broken telescope transit. It has a focal length of 26 in. and an aperture of 2¾ in. An ocular micrometer electrically records the time of transit of the stars.

Azimuths were first observed on Polaris using the same theodolite as for the triangulation observations. Until about 1904 these azimuth determinations were made by the astronomic parties; thereafter, they were taken during the course of observations by the triangulation party.

Establishment of Major Arcs.—Shortly after the Civil War the transcontinental arc of triangulation along the 39th latitude from Cape May, N. J., to San Francisco, Calif., was started, to relate the charts of the Pacific coast properly with those of the Atlantic. Surveys were initiated at several different places along the arc. The general plan was to have as long lines as possible so as to span the continent with the least number of stations. The average length for this arc is 50 miles. However, in the Rocky Mountains, many lines are longer than 100 miles.

Theodolites varied from 30 in. to 14 in. in diameter; most of them having 3 micrometers. They were heavy and cumbersome. Heliotropes were the targets almost without exception. Parties consisted of two units, each with an observer, a recorder, and a handy man, and with four lightkeepers who handled the heliotropes. From sixteen to twenty-four sets of observations were taken on each target, each set consisting of a direct and reverse reading. The number of stations observed per party per season ranged from six to eight. The arc extending from Cape May to San Francisco was completed in 1895. It measures 2,500 miles and is one of the longest continental arcs of triangulation.

Primary triangulation was also continued in the eastern states southward from Chesapeake Bay, connecting the detached coastal schemes. By 1877 it had reached Atlanta, Ga., and in 1889 it extended to Mobile, Ala. This main arc, following the trend of the Appalachian Mountains, is 1,632 miles long and traverses sixteen states. It was the first major arc of triangulation whose axis is oblique to the meridian—one result of which was the decision to adopt, as the reference ellipsoid, the Clarke Spheroid of 1866 as better adapted to this continent than the previously used Bessel. The change was made in 1880.

Angle and Distance Measurements.—The arc along the 98th meridian was begun in 1898 and completed in 1907. In 1900 nine bases were measured, using four steel tapes (two, 50 m long, and two, 100 m long) and the duplex base bars. A portion of each base, about 1 km, was measured with all five sets of apparatus. The remainder in each case was measured partly with the steel tapes and partly with the duplex bars. The criteria specified that measurements of sections must agree within $20 \text{ mm}\sqrt{K}$, in which K is the length of the section, in kilometers.

All tape measurements were made at night. Each tape was compared with the 100-m ice-bar comparator. The steel bar in the comparator was compared directly with the Prototype Meter No. 21 before the field season started. The average probable error of these base measurements was 1/1,200,000.

Theodolites with graduated circles 12 in. and 14 in. in diameter (Fig. 2) read with 3 micrometers to single seconds, were used for the arc along the 98th meridian, with sixteen to twenty-four positions measured on each target. Observations were made on tall signal poles or on heliotropes. In 1902, night observations were taken, sighting on acetylene signals—modified bicycle lamps which required recharging several times a night. Because of their success, some form of signal lamp has continued to be used from that time on. The electric signal lamp, powered by dry batteries, was first used in 1916.

Fig. 2.—The 12-In. Theodolite Used by the United States Coast and Geodetic Survey

In 1906, invar tapes were adopted for base measurements in the United States. Three base lines were determined at Port Isabel, Tex.; Stephens, Minn.; and Brown's Valley, Minn., respectively. They were measured twice in the daytime with three invar tapes and twice at night with three steel tapes. Each tape was used to measure two thirds of the length of every line, to provide an intercomparison of the tapes.

With steel tapes, all measurements must be made at night on account of the difficulty of obtaining the temperature of the tape with sufficient accuracy in daylight. It is necessary, also, to standardize the tapes in the field with the ice-bar comparator. With invar, an error of 2.8° F in the temperature reading is necessary to produce as large an error in measures as would one of 0.1° F with the steel tape. The cost of base measurement was reduced 25% by using invar tapes because it was not necessary to use the ice-bar comparator. The average probable error of measurement for these three bases was 1/2,760,000. Results with the invar tapes were uniformly better than those with steel tapes. Since 1906 the United States Coast and Geodetic Survey has measured all base lines with invar tapes.

The 12-in. theodolite, reading with 3 micrometers to single seconds, was used until the early 1920's. About 1924, 9-in. theodolites were introduced, and in 1927 the Parkhurst 9-in. instrument was perfected (Fig. 3). This theodolite can be

FIG. 3.—THE PARKHURST 9-IN. THEODOLITE, DEVELOPED IN THE UNITED STATES COAST AND GEODETIC SURVEY INSTRUMENT SHOP

read to a single second of arc by means of the two drum-type microscopes which are placed 180° apart to eliminate the error due to the eccentricity of the horizontal graduated circular plate. The graduations on these 9-in. theodolites were more accurate and superior to those on the larger instruments. In 1927, the Coast and Geodetic Survey first used the optical-reading type of theodolite, such as the Wild T3 (Fig. 4), with a 5½ in. horizontal circle.

A number of 9-in. theodolites are giving good service and will be used for years. They are comparatively simple in construction and easy to clean in the field. The Survey also has some of the optical-reading type, used principally in Alaska, where transportation is by plane and helicopter and weight must be kept to a minimum.

Survey Observation Towers.—In triangulation surveys, it is necessary to elevate the instrument and observer so as to obtain a clear line of sight above the trees and buildings and to overcome curvature of the earth. Wooden towers rising to heights from 15 ft to 90 ft were used for a number of years. In a week, a crew of four men can erect a 90-ft wooden tower for triangulation observations, consisting of two structures. In 1927, the Coast and Geodetic Survey first adopted the portable steel tower; one 90 ft high can be erected by a crew of five men in a day.

Although the initial cost of the steel tower is greater than that of a wooden one, the steel tower can be used time and time again, which is not true of the

FIG. 4.—LEFT FACE OF THE WILD T3, A FIRST-ORDER THEODOLITE

wooden one. The introduction of steel construction made it possible to undertake triangulation surveys in flat country where the cost of building high wooden towers would have been excessive. With the steel tower, the criteria for first-order triangulation were changed in that, instead of having lines from 50 to 100 miles long, an average of from 8 to 10 miles is specified.

Automobile trucks were introduced into geodetic survey operations in 1915. Triangulation parties before the use of the steel tower usually consisted of a building foreman assisted by three hands, and an observing unit with one observer, one recorder, a foreman, and five lightkeepers—a total of twelve men. A double observing party would require fifteen men. With the steel tower the Survey employs a party of thirty-eight men consisting of three or four observing units, two building units, and one teardown unit. There are about twenty trucks and one or two office trailers on a large triangulation party. With the wooden towers, six stations were observed per month on an average. With the steel towers, from thirty to forty-five stations may be covered per month.

Computation Helps.—Development of methods for processing survey data has of necessity kept pace with improvement of instruments and techniques used in the field. The early computations for triangulation were made with logarithmic functions, and geographic positions were computed with the Bessel Ellipsoid. Not until 1880 were the functions for the Clarke Spheroid introduced into the computational procedures. The first least squares adjustment of triangulation undertaken by personnel of the Bureau was completed in 1851. This involved a small network in the eastern part of the United States. The development of several computing machines, about 1900, simplified the processes.

About 30 years ago desk calculators became available, and it was not long before a machine was made available to every computer. The ease with which computations could be made and the speed at which they could be completed brought a gradual change from the use of logarithmic functions to that of natural functions for all types of geodetic computations. The latter method was introduced in the early 1940's. Its basic principles have now been adopted by many geodetic organizations in other countries.

In 1948, the Coast and Geodetic Survey installed a unit of automatic punched-card computing equipment. The complexity of the surveys and the requirements for extensive area networks increased the computational phase of the work to a point where this modern equipment was feasible. At present this unit processes large adjustments for triangulation and leveling networks and assists in the reduction of geomagnetic, tidal, and current data.

Standard Datums.—When the transcontinental arc of triangulation along the 39th parallel of latitude was completed, the previously separate pieces of triangulation were united into one scheme. Examples of such detached portions were the early triangulation in New England and along the Atlantic coast; a separate part of the transcontinental work near St. Louis, Mo.; another part in the Rocky Mountain region; and three separate parts in California near San Francisco, Santa Barbara, and San Diego. As surveys expanded, these separate datums touched or overlapped. Since the transcontinental arc joined all the detached portions mentioned and made one continuous arc, the logical step was to substitute one datum for the several previously used.

On March 13, 1901, the United States Standard Datum was adopted and the positions of all triangulation stations were reduced to that basis. It was the one formerly used in New England, and therefore no changes were necessary in the positions used for geographic purposes in that locality, along the Atlantic coast to North Carolina, and in the states of New York, Pennsylvania, New Jersey, and Delaware. Sections along the transcontinental arc and the oblique arc were adjusted to this datum.

In 1913 the governments of Mexico and Canada adopted the United States Standard Datum for their horizontal surveys and the name was changed to the North American Datum. Connections to the geodetic triangulation of Mexico have been made at the 98th, 101st, and 106th meridians of longitude and on the Pacific coast. The Mexico-United States boundary line is a part of the triangulation network of the United States. Likewise, the United States-Dominion of Canada boundary line is connected to the network of triangulation in both countries.

Readjustments.—As the triangulation coverage developed, additional arcs were observed and adjusted to the previously computed nets. When any loop of triangulation was completed, the total discrepancy in closure was adjusted into the last arc that closed the loop. This quite frequently imposed unfavorable conditions on the last arc, resulting in distortions of the observations that were not justified by the general agreement of the recorded field data. It was necessary to follow this procedure for otherwise the whole system of triangulation would have to be readjusted each time a new loop was closed.

The main network was completed in 1926, and at that time it was decided that a readjustment of the entire net would be made. In the earlier computations no true geodetic azimuths derived by applying the Laplace correction to observed astronomic azimuths were held in the adjustments—principally because the experience of the Survey had not shown that an arc of triangulation tends to swerve in azimuth unless it is controlled by observed astronomic azimuths corrected for the deflection of the vertical. In the readjustment, the Laplace correction was applied to the astronomic azimuths and these were held fixed. The readjustment resulted in the triangulation data being expressed on the North American Datum of 1927. This datum applies at present to all of North America from the southern end of Mexico, throughout that country, the United States, Canada, Newfoundland, Yukon Territory, Alaska, and the Aleutian Islands.

State Plane-Coordinate Systems.—To promote a greater use of geodetic data by local surveyors, the Coast and Geodetic Survey in 1932 initiated a program of expressing geodetic coordinates of latitude and longitude on a plane-coordinate base; that is, in terms of x and y—the x-expression referring to the distances east and west and the y-expression giving the distances in a north and south direction. A system was developed for each state, by which all points in the adjusted triangulation are converted to plane-coordinate values.

The engineer can connect his local survey to stations of the federal net expressed in the state plane-coordinate system and compute his records by the mathematical means with which he is familiar. Any inaccuracies in his own work are immediately evident by failure to check on the plane-coordinate values of the stations to which connections are made. The introduction of the state plane-coordinate systems has brought about a more general use of geodetic control by engineers and surveyors throughout the United States, and this use is increasing as more practitioners become aware of the ease with which geodetic data can be used.

At the present time there are more than 125,000 miles of first-order and second-order triangulation arcs throughout the United States; more than 150,000 points for which accurately located positions have been determined; and about 400 base lines measured accurately with an average probable error of 1/1,200,000. The average check on base lines as carried through the triangulation is about 1/75,000.

The policy of the Coast and Geodetic Survey now is to place at least one triangulation or traverse station in each $7\frac{1}{2}$-min mapping quadrangle. Marked triangulation stations are also established along the principal highways at about a 4-mile spacing. In urban areas the stations are established at about 2-mile intervals.

Techniques for Leveling.—Precise leveling in the United States started in 1875. Its purpose was to provide elevations above mean sea level for the transcontinental arc of triangulation along the 39th parallel of latitude, so that the observed horizontal directions could be reduced to sea level. During this leveling, bench marks were established at most of the important towns, and it soon became evident that these marks were of importance to engineers and surveyors who could base their own surveys on the elevations provided.

In the early leveling surveys, the lines were run simultaneously. Target rods were used, and a stride level was placed on the telescope. The rods were of wood with a brass strip along the face on which the readings were made. A thermometer attached to the rod gave the temperature. Later, readings were made on brass plugs 5 mm in diameter inserted in the face of the rod at 2-cm intervals. The

FIG. 5.—THE FISCHER PRECISE LEVEL

original criterion was a check on two runnings within 5 mm$\sqrt{K}$ —in which K represents the distance, in kilometers.

In 1899 the direct reading rod was developed. The telescope diaphragm had three horizontal wires, and readings were made to the nearest millimeter. Criteria were established to the effect that the maximum sight would be 150 m; that no backsight should differ from the corresponding foresight by more than 10 m; and that the continuous sum of the backsights should not vary by more than 20 m from the continuous sum of the foresights between successive bench marks. Forward and backward measurements were made under different conditions; the forward running was made in the morning and the backward running in the afternoon. The check for first-order leveling was specified at 4 mm$\sqrt{K}$.

At that time the level net comprised twenty-five circuits and included only the eastern half of the United States. An adjustment of this network was made, to include surveys of the United States Geological Survey, the United States Engineers, and the Pennsylvania Railroad.

The Fischer Precise Level (Fig. 5) was introduced in 1900 and with slight modifications has remained the standard instrument for precise leveling since then. European manufactured levels such as the Wild N3 (Fig. 6) are equally adaptable to precise survey operations.

Introduction of the Fischer level speeded up progress, and the network of leveling was extended more and more rapidly. In 1903 a second adjustment of the leveling net was made, to take care of the increased field work accomplished since the 1900 adjustment.

Level Network Expanded.—Progress in leveling continued at an accelerated pace, and by 1907 the spirit-level connection had been completed across the continent. At that time there were nine tide stations on the Atlantic and Gulf coasts and one tide station on the Pacific coast connected to the level net. The additional leveling and the connection to sea level on the Pacific coast made it desirable to readjust the net in order to take advantage of these new increments. After the rigid adjustment was completed, certain areas showed such small changes from

Fig. 6.—The Wild N3, a European Manufactured Level

the previous adjustment that no changes in elevations were made for a considerable part of the net.

By 1912 a number of additional level lines had been provided, particularly in the western states, and a connection to tide level had been made at San Diego. In the 1912 adjustment the policy was again followed of not changing the elevations of bench marks in sections of the network where variations were slight.

Up to 1929 additions included connections to many more tide stations and to a number of bench marks in Canada. The net consisted of approximately 45,000 miles of leveling in the United States and 20,000 miles in Canada. In that year a general adjustment was made combining the first-order level nets of Canada and the United States in one unit. The General Adjustment of 1929 gives the best available elevations of all bench marks and is the standard at the present time.

Rapid progress in the expansion of the level net was made from 1934 to 1936 because of the availability of emergency funds for the relief of unemployment during the depression years. At present there are about 147,000 miles of first-order leveling and 238,000 miles of second-order leveling, or a total of 385,000 miles.

The program of leveling of the Coast and Geodetic Survey comprises fundamental first-order lines at approximately 100-mile intervals (Fig. 7) and the subdivision of these lines with second-order levels into approximately 25-mile intervals. Additional development is now being carried out by using second-order levels to subdivide the smaller areas with lines about 6 miles apart.

Availability of Data.—Final adjusted values for the horizontal and vertical control points are reproduced by photolithography for distribution to federal agencies, state organizations, and local engineers. Pamphlets containing the descriptions of these points are printed and made available to the public. Diagrams showing the configuration of the triangulation networks and the location of lines of leveling are printed and are also available on request.

Accomplishments Realized.—The main objectives to be attained by geodetic surveying operations in the United States are: First, the control of navigational and aeronautical charts published by the Coast and Geodetic Survey and the control of mapping accomplished by the Geological Survey, the United States Forest Service, and other federal agencies; and second, the furnishing of geographic positions (latitudes and longitudes), distances and azimuths, state plane coordinates of triangulation and traverse stations, and elevations of bench marks above mean sea level to engineers and surveyors not only in the Federal Government but in states, counties, and cities as well as in commerce, industry, and private practice.

To attain these objectives, it is necessary that the reference spheroid and the adopted datum give such a close approximation to the truth that any correction which may hereafter be derived from observations shall not greatly exceed the probable errors. If the geodetic survey is to be a coordinating medium for all surveys, it is essential that one spheroid and one geodetic datum be used throughout the entire United States. The Clarke Spheroid of 1866 and the North American Datum of 1927 for horizontal control surveys, and the General Adjustment of 1929 for vertical control, conform to these standards.

From the very beginning of geodetic surveying in the United States there have been criteria providing for a strong rigid network of triangulation and leveling. The average triangle closure for first-order work of 1 sec, with a maximum of 3 sec, has been in effect since the earliest field operations. The length check on bases as carried through the triangulation averages 1/75,000, with a minimum of 1/25,000 specified. The check for early leveling surveys, 5 mm$\sqrt{K}$ later became 4 mm$\sqrt{K}$, which is specified for first-order leveling at the present time. People in the United States are fortunate in that their forefathers had the foresight to adopt plans and programs for geodetic surveys that have been followed meticulously throughout the nation's history. The geodetic surveys are a rigidly adjusted network of precisely located points and bench marks. Engineers may accept the data concerning them with complete confidence that the positions and elevations are accurately determined.

FIG. 7.—PRECISE LEVELING

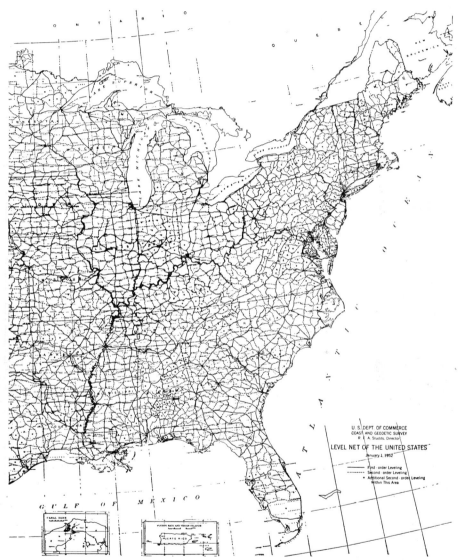

U. S. DEPT. OF COMMERCE
COAST AND GEODETIC SURVEY
R. A. Studds, Director
LEVEL NET OF THE UNITED STATES
January 1, 1952

First - order Leveling
Second - order Leveling
• Additional Second - order Leveling
  Within This Area

NET OF THE UNITED STATES

AMERICAN SOCIETY OF CIVIL ENGINEERS
Founded November 5, 1852
TRANSACTIONS

Paper No. 2636

ADVANCES IN CARTOGRAPHY

By Helmuth Bay [1]

Synopsis

To appreciate fully the recent advances in the science of cartography it will be necessary to go back about 100 years and to describe briefly the map-making processes of that period. In the 1850's the western states were being opened up. Settlers were flocking to the rich prairie states, railroads and roads were being built, promoters were carrying on what is now referred to as a "land-office" business, and the demand for maps was unprecedented in the history of the country. Since then great strides have been made in the art of cartography.

The problem before the map maker was twofold. Maps had to be drawn more quickly than by the old stone and copper engraving processes; and, because of the rapid development of communications and the settlement, it was also important that the maps be corrected faster and more cheaply.

Cartographers and engravers who made maps in these early days were masters at their art, having had to work and practice at their craft for years before attaining top professional skill. Their hand-lettering ability was remarkable and their linework was perfection itself. Each finished drawing as well as each engraved plate or stone, was a masterpiece of the cartographic art; but the work took too much time. It is interesting to note that about the only progress made in speeding up this type of map making lay in the construction of engraving machines. Some specimens of these are still reposing (and fondly regarded) in a few map-making establishments. A modern mechanical device for use in engraving is shown in Fig. 1.

New Processes Found.—When Rand McNally and Company went into the map-making business in the middle 1860's, it was decided not to employ the slow and costly methods of stone engraving. Instead the wax-engraving process was utilized. The first step in this method was to make a compilation drawing as accurately as possible, but with no regard for carefully lettered names. This drawing was then photographed and the positive image superimposed on a sensitized copper plate covered with a very thin coating of wax. The linework was

---

then cut through the wax to the copper. Next the names were set in type, placed in a holder, and also stamped through the wax to the copper. The remaining wax was then built up with more wax to give depth to the printing plate, after which this wax-covered positive was placed in an electrolytic bath where a thin copper-shell negative was formed. The shell was then backed up with lead, fastened to a wooden block, and made ready for the press. For many years, it may be noted, the line engravings in the ASCE *Transactions* were prepared by this same process.

FIG. 1.—ENGRAVING SOUNDING FIGURES ON A GLASS NEGATIVE OF A NAUTICAL CHART

Color drawings were produced in the same way, tint values being attained by parallel or cross-hatched fine lines. Corrections were easily made by engraving patches which were inserted in the printing plate by soldering. Naturally, the wax process completely eliminated the necessity of fine hand lettering, so that today there is not one cartographer in a hundred who can do it satisfactorily.

Later on when photoengraving became economically profitable, finished drawings were made and the names inked in by stamping with type, after which a zinc plate was manufactured, mounted on blocks, and used for printing. This method has now been adopted for ASCE publications.

Advantages by Using Offset.—These were the two most commonly used processes for map making until the advent of offset lithography. Offset printing is a much more flexible method of reproduction than letterpress or flat-bed-press printing. The only requirement is a finished drawing. Color separations on separate negatives are possible by eliminating selected features on one plate and retaining them alone on another. Corrections can be made on the negative and, if not too extensive, on the printing plate itself. Color tints or combinations can be photographed directly by the camera through the use of screen, dot, or line as the case may require. "Make-ready" to print is less expensive and the printing cost is lowered through the greater speed of the presses. All in all, offset is an almost ideal form of printing.

In keeping up with the flexibility and advantages of offset printing, the cartographer has, in a sense, had far greater opportunity than ever before to exercise his ingenuity and inventiveness in preparing the drawings of the maps that are to be run. The compilation and drawing of a map are extremely costly propositions at best, without considering the time consumption which often runs to thousands of hours for a single map sheet.

With the advent of World War II and with this country sadly lacking in blueprints on which to wage it, the cartographers did a remarkable job. They developed methods and processes which made it possible not only to produce more maps during a given time but also to employ a large number of untrained but able people and teach them to become adept and expert in drawing linework, pasting up names, editing, compiling, and taking the other necessary steps to produce a map. The specialization in cartography can be said to have begun during World War II; it has continued to increase ever since. It is only fair to mention that the activities of the chemical industry have been largely responsible for many of the cartographer's forward strides.

Other Improvements Now Available.—To enumerate briefly some of the recent advances in the cartographic art which are being intensely studied and perfected:

1. Most important is the development of stable plastic sheets as substitutes for, or adjuncts to, the paper on which the map is drawn. They are known by several names, but basically they are all a form of vinylite. Some map-making organizations use practically no drawing paper any more, making both compilation and finished drawings on a plastic medium. The stability qualities of the plastics are regarded by most experts as greatly superior to those of paper. Fiber-glass sheets are even more stable than vinylite but are more difficult to work on.

2. The abrasive effects of a plastic sheet or a fiber-glass sheet on drawing instruments force the draftsman to sharpen them more frequently. One instrument maker, after considerable study of the problem, now manufactures more durable and highly tempered instruments. In general, however, there has been great improvement in drafting instruments during recent years and many new timesaving devices are available.

3. Experimental work on new types of drawing inks, to make them more suitable for drafting on plastic sheets, has been conducted by ink manufacturers as well as by government agencies. Many satisfactory kinds are obtainable.

4. Practically all map makers employ the so-called stick-up method of inserting place names, titles, and notes on maps. In this technique the names are printed on paper or plastic sheets, cut out, and pasted in place.

5. Photolettering machines, substituting a photographic mechanism in place of the conventional typesetting machines, are being produced by a half dozen organizations. They enable the setting of place names for maps without the use of hot metal and at a faster rate.

6. Several manufacturers of typewriters are developing new type styles for

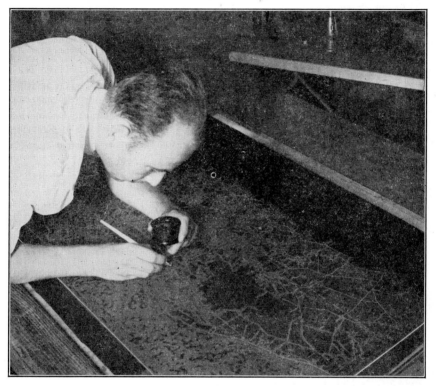

FIG. 2.—ENGRAVING A NEGATIVE ON GLASS

their machines to resemble more closely the conventional faces now available only through the use of monotype and linotype.

7. A machine capable of ruling curved or straight parallel lines has been invented, greatly simplifying the task of laying out projections and grids.

8. A thin base film which can be slightly stretched is available, permitting to some degree the changing of a map from one projection to another by mosaic methods, thus saving considerable drafting time.

9. The shaded relief method of showing the physical variations of terrain on maps is now employed extensively by map makers. The drawings are prepared by airbrush or crayon and in some cases by using actual relief maps for photographic negatives, from which press plates are then made.

10. Presensitized lithographic plates, with which the press plate of the map can be obtained from a drawing in a matter of minutes, can be purchased from several companies.

11. Glass engraving (Figs. 1 and 2), a method employed extensively by some mapping organizations, consists of coating the glass negative of a compilation drawing and cutting the linework with fine pointed gravers. The result, a finished negative from which press plates can be made, is obtained without the finished drawing and photograph. The technique can also be used on plastic, and there are already several precoated sheets on the market.

12. The cost of making compilation drawings of maps has also been greatly reduced, largely because of the almost unbelievable developments in photogrammetry. Recent improvements in plotting devices as well as in lenses, camera shutters, and film have made possible the faster production of exceedingly accurate maps from aerial photographs.

Cartography is the final stage of surveying and mapping—the stage in which the facts and data gathered by surveyors and engineers are put together. The result is a printed map. In speaking for the cartographers it is to be sincerely hoped that they can hold up their end with ingenuity, inventiveness, and development; but it must be admitted that the engineers' electronics, photogrammetry, and new instruments and methods are providing real competition.

AMERICAN SOCIETY OF CIVIL ENGINEERS

Founded November 5, 1852

TRANSACTIONS

Paper No. 2637

ROLE OF RAILROADS IN UNITED STATES HISTORY

By Fred G. Gurley [1]

Synopsis

Since the first colonists landed in North America, development of an adequate transportation system has played an important role. The railroads, in large measure, are responsible for the remarkable growth of the United States to its present preeminent status.

This paper traces the history of the nation, and the coincidental development of a transportation network. Early roads and canals soon proved inadequate to serve the growing country. The railroad filled the need for rapid, economical mass transportation. Factors contributing to the growth of the railroads are listed. Development of improved motive power is noted, as well as new machinery that increases the speed of right-of-way construction. The outstanding characteristics that have advanced the efficiency of rail transport are discussed. The possibilities for future progress are explained in the light of current conditions.

Introduction

Although it is always difficult to determine with a high degree of accuracy the so-called first about anything, it is generally agreed that the first railroad—in the sense in which the word is used today—was the Stockton and Darlington Railway in England, which was completed in 1825. The idea caught on, and within a relatively short time a substantial number of steam railways were in operation on the continent of Europe, in Great Britain, and in the United States.

The important role of the railroads in the development of the United States can be more fully appreciated when it is recalled that the future of the new nation depended on making a success of an experiment in government. In turn, that great accomplishment depended in no small part on good communication and transportation. Although it may not have been immediately apparent, surely the problem required a better answer than could be provided by the historic use of roads and waterways.

---

[1] Pres., Santa Fe System Lines, Chicago, Ill.

HISTORICAL BACKGROUND

Opening the Northwest Territory.—With the peace treaty of 1783, a new nation with a relatively small population living along the Atlantic seaboard held title to a territory extending to the Mississippi River, some 1,000 miles to the west (Fig. 1). There were only rough trails across the mountain ranges to the vast area that became known as the Northwest Territory under the famous Ordinance of 1787, passed by the Continental Congress prior to the adoption of the Constitution.

The Northwest Territory comprised the lands lying north and west of the Ohio River, south of the Great Lakes and east of the Mississippi. Ohio, admitted

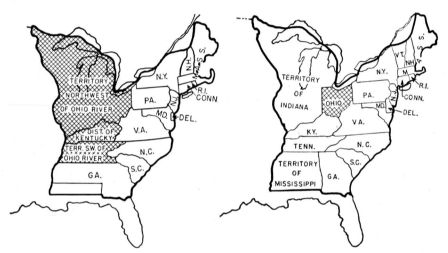

FIG. 1.—AREA FROM ATLANTIC TO MISSISSIPPI RIVER TO WHICH THE UNITED STATES HELD TITLE AFTER PEACE TREATY WITH GREAT BRITAIN IN 1783

FIG. 2.—IN 1803, OHIO, FIRST OF FIVE STATES CREATED OUT OF NORTHWEST TERRITORY, ADMITTED TO UNION

to the Union in 1803 (Fig. 2), was the first of the five states that were created out of this region.

Transportation to and from this vast area was provided in large part by vessels on the Ohio and Mississippi rivers. Movement via Natchez, Miss., and New Orleans, La., was through territory controlled by a foreign power. The whole valley of the Ohio was dependent on the permission of a foreign power for an outlet to the Gulf of Mexico. Trade restrictions and impositions on river traffic became unbearable. Confiscation of vessels, of cargoes, and imprisonment of crews were usual occurrences.

Louisiana Purchase.—In response to a feeling of general indignation, President Thomas Jefferson sent James Monroe to France with instructions to negotiate for the purchase of territory that controlled movement on the Mississippi River. As it turned out, Monroe purchased the entire area controlled by France throughout the length of the Mississippi and which, in the central and northern sections, extended to the Continental Divide (Fig. 3).

This historical development is interesting because it indicates that the need to control an important artery of transportation necessitated the Louisiana Purchase. Without this territory subsequent expansion to the Pacific coast, including the acquisition of the Republic of Texas, would not have been possible.

Westward to the Pacific.—The first step in the expansion beyond the western limits of the Louisiana Purchase to the Pacific coast was accomplished by an arrangement with Great Britain in 1818 for the joint control of Oregon. By 1848, California and New Mexico had been acquired, as had the State of Florida. Texas had been annexed and the United States had complete control of Oregon. The nation extended some 3,200 miles from the Atlantic to the Pacific.

FIG. 3.—LOUISIANA PURCHASE, NEGOTIATED BY JAMES MONROE IN 1803, WHICH INCLUDED ALL TERRITORY CONTROLLED BY FRANCE, EXTENDING WESTWARD FROM MISSISSIPPI RIVER

DEVELOPMENT OF COMMUNICATIONS

Early Roads.—The necessity for the best possible communication and transportation became manifest quite early in the history of the United States. One of the first problems encountered was transportation between the eastern seaboard and the Ohio Valley.

In 1806 President Jefferson signed a bill authorizing the National Road, to extend from Cumberland, Md., to Wheeling, Va. (later W. Va.). This road (Fig. 4) greatly facilitated the movement of commerce and aided in the development of the Ohio Valley although its rate of construction was slow. In fact, by the time it reached the Indiana-Illinois state line (about 1850) railroads were being built in many places and meeting with public favor. They then totaled more than 9,000 miles, chiefly in states bordering the Atlantic Ocean (Fig. 5).

Canals.—Oddly enough, probably the greatest stimulant toward railroad building was the Erie Canal. Construction of the canal began in 1817 and was completed by the State of New York in 1825—thus making it possible to move by barge from Lake Erie to the Hudson River. The canal provided the City of New

York (N. Y.) with improved access to the area previously identified as the North-west Territory, out of which the states of Ohio, Indiana, and Illinois had emerged by the time the project was in operation.

The transportation facilities provided by the Hudson River and the Erie Canal gave an advantage to New York City which was quite disturbing to the rival cities of Baltimore, Md., and Philadelphia, Pa. By what process could they better their position? The National Road was of some help to Baltimore, but there was need for better facilities. From the competitive standpoint, Philadelphia was in third place and a poor third place at that.

Committees representing the commercial interests of both the City of Balti-more and the City of Philadelphia, working independently of each other, began

FIG. 4.—THE NATIONAL ROAD, CUMBERLAND, MD., ON THE POTOMAC RIVER TO WHEELING, VA. (LATER W. VA.), ON THE OHIO RIVER, CONSTRUCTED FROM 1811 TO 1818

investigations as to what ought to be done. Both groups first embarked on plans for the construction of canals, but each decided that, although a canal might do fairly well during warm weather in the relatively flat country through which the Erie Canal had been constructed, it would be highly impracticable in the moun-tainous area lying to the west of Philadelphia and Baltimore.

The First Railroads.—Finally, the people of Baltimore decided to build a rail-road, and in 1827 the Baltimore and Ohio Railroad was incorporated. In the writer's opinion, there is ample justification for the claim that the Baltimore and Ohio was the first of the railroads in the United States for the public transport of passengers and goods. Other railroads, including the Pennsylvania (which served the City of Philadelphia) were placed in operation not long thereafter.

The modest beginning of the present New York Central System was inspired by a desire to expedite traffic between the Hudson River and Schenectady, N. Y., a relatively short distance over which the slow movement via the canal had been particularly bothersome. In addition, people who originally had been content with canal transport, which was possible only during warm weather, soon became dissatisfied when ice closed the canal in cold weather. Thus, although New York had secured the earliest outlet to the west, it soon proved inferior to rail service.

Present Status.—Other communities found that the railroads were the answer to their problem, and construction, in the light of all circumstances, was relatively

FIG. 5.—RAILROADS OF 1850, MOSTLY SHORT LINES, BUT MANY CONNECTED TO
FORM THROUGH ROUTES

rapid. By 1852, the year the ASCE was founded, the railroads extended as far west as Illinois. Today, the rail system of the United States totals some 225,000 miles, approximately one third of the world railroad mileage. Thus it is fair to state that the country and the railroads grew together. Territorial expansion, utilization of vast natural resources, and development of sound and diversified industry would all have been impossible without the efficient mass transportation provided by the railroads.

Growth Factors

Improved Engineering.—It is a matter of grave importance today and will be in the future to remember that the railroad and the nation grew together because the United States is a nation of free men dedicated to a belief in free private enterprise as the only economic system under which the full capabilities of men and industry can be realized. The United States could not have attained its present position of preeminence had it not been for a constantly expanding railway system that helped open new frontiers and develop commerce. Neither could the railway plant have become the greatest in the world had the economic system not offered incentives to efficiency and high productivity. Even in connection with the engineering aspect of railroading, it must not be forgotten that transportation service is an economic product and that here, as elsewhere in industry, a high level of efficient productivity is the key to success.

The engineering history of railroading down to the present day has been almost wholly a search for methods and means of attaining higher productivity. In one sense, the goal of railroad management has been the adaptation of techniques that would put service on a nation-wide mass production basis.

Standardization.—Looking back over the past century, it can be seen that one of the most important advances was the standardization of the track gage, which made possible the interchange of cars and the operation of through routes. Before that development, rail transportation was somewhat localized and the transfer of freight from one line to another was cumbersome. By standardizing track gage and equipment the railroads made continuity of movement simple and expeditious and thereby placed a nation-wide transportation system at the service of every shipper. In fact, the free movement of standard-gage cars extends to Canada and Mexico.

Interchangeability of equipment and unrestricted movement over multiple lines are commonplace today, but in any review of rail transportation those innovations must be noted as major steps toward greater and more efficient utilization of the railways. It must not be forgotten either that, although maintenance of through routes and interchange of equipment are now provided for by law, it was private management, acting voluntarily under the incentives of a free enterprise system, which conceived and engineered those developments.

Standardization of tracks and equipment seems prosaic when compared with the marvels of engineering in other industrial fields during the past century; and, as a matter of fact, the engineering history of the railroads has not been marked by the spectacular types of inventions and discoveries that are so amazing in other fields.

However, engineering marvels are not lacking in the railroad industry. Anyone who contemplates the feats that were performed in crossing mountain ranges, in bridging rivers and gorges (Fig. 6), or in spanning wastelands—mostly before the days of instant communication and complete mechanization—will have deep respect for the courage and ability of early railroad engineers. Nevertheless, in the field of operations, the record is rather one of constant research and steady improvement, an unending quest for more efficient devices and methods by which to produce more and more units of service at less and less cost.

Motive Power

Steam to Diesel.—Perhaps nowhere can this striving for increased productivity be more clearly traced over the years than in connection with motive power. With the opening of the west after the Civil War, increased emphasis was placed on improvements in the steam locomotive, which at that time was capable of producing considerably less, on the average, than 20,000 lb of tractive effort per unit. By 1893 freight locomotives had been developed with a tractive effort in excess of 35,000 lb; and by 1905 the Santa Fe-type compound locomotive was able to develop more than 62,000 lb of tractive effort.

These progressive increases in power were accomplished principally by improvements in boiler efficiency and by utilization of the advantages of higher pressures. However, the resulting product was still merely a better steam engine (Fig.

Fig. 6.—Canyon Diablo Bridge Near Winslow, Ariz., Santa Fe Railway

7). The effort to find still more efficient sources of power continued; and at the turn of the century the electric locomotive was developed. This type gradually increased in rather limited use until a maximum ownership of about 870 units was reached in 1943. Finally, in the 1930's, the efficiencies of the diesel engine were applied to rail motive power; and, if any discovery in the art of railroading in the past century may be called revolutionary, the advent of the diesel deserves that description.

A diesel-electric locomotive was first used to propel a streamlined train in 1934. The first diesel-electric freight locomotive was placed in service in 1940. Although the diesel-switching locomotive was introduced somewhat earlier, it was not perfected for general use until abut the middle of the 1930's.

Thus, during a relatively short period, the diesel locomotive has become the dominant source of motive power for the railroad industry. In May, 1952, 66% of the road freight business and 68% of the road passenger business on all class I railroads in the United States were handled by diesel locomotives. Diesel power performed 76% of the yard work.

With the advent of the diesel-electric, less attention was focused on the straight electric locomotive, and recent years have seen little expansion of electrification systems. Some 2% of the road freight business, 6% of the road passenger business, and 1% of yard work for the class I railroads is now handled by electric locomotives.

Right-of-Way Construction

In an entirely different field of engineering and railroading the search for efficiency and improved productivity led to changes that were nearly as important as the development of motive power, if somewhat less dramatic. As the traveler speeds along by rail, in this age of almost complete mechanization, through deep cuts and over long high fills, it is difficult for him to comprehend the fact that, when railways first pushed west across the Alleghenies and later across the Continental Divide, earth-moving methods almost as old as recorded history were in use.

FIG. 7.—HEAVY-DUTY FREIGHT LOCOMOTIVE, SANTA FE RAILWAY—ITS TENDER CARRYING 20,000 GAL OF WATER AND 23 TONS OF COAL

The early roadbeds were literally hand-made, for the construction tools were picks, shovels, and wheelbarrows, and the most modern labor-saving device during many of the years of great railway expansion was the horse-drawn dump cart. It would make a fascinating story in itself to trace the development of earth-moving machinery and track-maintenance devices down to this day of giant diesel-powered bulldozers, scrapers, draglines, multiple tampers, and mechanical ballast cleaners (Fig. 8). This story would tell of the great contribution by engineers and manufacturers to the development of the transportation system.

Technological Advances

It is possible to go on almost endlessly in recounting engineering advances during the past century. The old method of applying car brakes by hand, for example, was inefficient and unsafe and seriously limited the length and speed of trains.

Braking Devices.—The air brake, first developed in 1867 and now greatly improved, solved the problem and made a great contribution to safety, efficiency, and economy. With the electric locomotive, regenerating braking was helpful on descending grades in mountainous territory. This braking is accomplished by utilizing the traction motors as electric generators while descending grades. The electric current so generated is turned back into the power transmission lines.

When the diesel was first used in freight service, it was recognized that a brake similar in principle to the electric regenerative brake would be desirable. The first "dynamic brake" was applied to Santa Fe freight diesel locomotive No. 100 in January, 1942. With the diesel locomotive, which does not require the use of a power transmission line, the energy coming from the traction motors used as generators is dissipated through air-cooled grids. The dynamic brake has proved to be of substantial assistance on descending grades since it will retard the movement of a train to a degree that greatly reduces dependence on the customary air

Fig. 8.—Ballast Cleaner in Operation: Stone in Shoulders Is Removed, Elevated, Cleaned, and Redeposited, Correcting Improper Drainage That Causes Soft and Uneven Track

brake. It is primarily a retarding or holding brake, however, as distinguished from a stopping brake. Its use as a holding brake has eliminated much of the damage to wheels and brake shoes resulting from overheating, which has plagued freight-train operations in mountainous territory.

Signaling Systems.—The automatic signaling system, made possible by electric energy, has provided scores of devices and techniques for improved safety, high speeds, and greater utilization of tracks. One of the latest developments in signaling is centralized traffic control, which, by taking advantage of advancements in electronics, permits safe operation of trains under a system where train movements are authorized entirely by signal indication.

The greater efficiency of the centralized traffic control system enables a single line of railroad virtually to do the work of a double track. The contribution to higher productivity and lower cost is manifest.

Equipment.—Private management's constant striving for the rewards of enterprise and efficiency is also evident in regard to freight and passenger equipment.

The results are significant in two aspects. From the standpoint of engineering design, freight cars have steadily increased in carrying capacity, in availability for service, and in durability. In the field of passenger equipment the twin developments of lightweight streamlining and air conditioning were perhaps the chief engineering and service advances.

The other aspect of engineering progress in the field of equipment relates to diversification and the adaptation of rail facilities to the needs of commerce. Nowhere are the results of that progress more striking than in the fresh fruit and vegetable industries.

In New York and cities similarly situated, it is commonplace to buy oranges, grapes, and apples from such distant states as Florida, California, and Washington. Fresh meat and other perishable food products are available everywhere. Without the mass transportation service of a vast refrigerator car fleet this sort of trade would be impossible. Moreover, the tremendous and far-flung agricultural industry that lies in the hinterlands could never have come into existence without the marketing outlets afforded by this specialized form of transportation.

CHARACTERISTICS OF RAIL TRANSPORT

Today the United States has a railway system totaling about 225,000 miles of line over which moves about 60% of the nation's domestic freight commerce. In relation to other forms of transportation, the three outstanding characteristics of this rail system are its extensive coverage of the nation, its ability to handle anything movable at any time for any destination, and its almost unlimited reserve capacity.

Expansibility.—The unique ability of railroads to expand as volume carriers and as instruments of mass transportation was strikingly demonstated during World War II. The increase in railroad passengers from 1940 to 1944 was greater than the total growth in that traffic during the entire 110 years of American railroad history from 1830 to 1940. The increase in railroad freight traffic from 1940 to 1944 was greater than the total growth in that traffic during the first 85 years of railroad service, or from 1830 to 1915.

Expressed in percentage relation to other agencies of transportation, the railroads moved a little more than 62% of commercial intercity freight traffic in the prewar year of 1940, whereas in the peak war years of 1943 and 1944 they handled more than 72% of all freight and more than 90% of the war traffic. It is staggering to consider that the total amounted to approximately 1,500,000,000 tons of freight a year, or 50% more than the railroads had hauled in prewar years.

Adaptability.—This accomplishment reflected most of the fundamental characteristics of the rail method of transportation as it has been developed under private management in the United States. All other forms of transportation are limited in the territory served, or in the seasons and weathers in which they can operate, or in the nature of what they can haul, or in their ability to expand capacity readily and economically. No one of them, nor all of them together, could take the place of the railroads as the true common carrier of the nation's commerce.

Efficiency.—The engineering developments and advances that have been only briefly noted are yielding measurable returns today. By any standard of operating efficiency, the railroads are a vital and progressive industry. During the period from 1921 to 1951 the average freight-train load increased 100%, and these larger loads were hauled farther and faster per day and per hour. In that same period, freight-car miles per serviceable car day increased from 26 in 1921 to 45 in 1951.

When comparative transportation service is expressed in terms of net ton-miles per freight-train hour—a revealing measure of performance—it is found that service increased from 7,500 in 1921 to nearly 22,000 in 1951. In other words, in comparison with 1921, a freight car moved three-fourths more cargo in 1951. The

FIG. 9.—WITH DIESEL POWER, SANTA FE'S "SUPER CHIEF" ASCENDING GRADE AT WOOTON, COLO.

average freight train handled double the amount of freight at almost half again as much speed, and consequently the net ton-miles per freight-train hour, which reflect the combined effect of both increased load and greater speed, were nearly three times as great.

The diesel-electric, when used in a combination of four units (to make up a powerful locomotive in keeping with common practice in heavy over-the-road service) will outperform the best of the steam engines. Largely through the use of the diesel (Fig. 9) the railroads, in 1950, were able to increase by 50% the output of tons per train, and to double the output of tons per train hour as compared with that in 1929. The year 1929 was the last year of high-level economy prior to the tragic depression of the 1930's.

IMPORTANCE OF THE RAILROADS

These improvements in efficiency are not so apparent on the surface as are the changes in some other fields of transportation. To the offhand glance, a railroad today looks much the same as the railroad of 1900. However, improvements in motive power, particularly dieselization and almost complete mechanization in construction and maintenance departments, have wrought a revolutionary change in operations, largely in the past generation. Also the improved efficiency revealed by the performance statistics that have just been cited has benefited the public in two ways.

Low-Cost Transportation.—First, this greater efficiency has brought better service at lower cost. The average revenue per ton-mile received by the railroads is a direct reflection of what shippers pay for rail service. In 1950 the railroads received an average revenue per ton-mile of 1.329¢ as compared with 1.275¢ in 1921 —an increase of slightly more than 4% in actual dollars. However, if the results are equated to a dollar of constant value, it is found that there was a decrease of 37% in net ton-mile revenue over the 30-year period. Thus, shippers are today receiving considerably better rail service at substantially less real cost.

In the second place, improved efficiency and higher productivity have enabled the railroads to survive the subsidized competition that they have been forced to meet in the past quarter century. Rail expenses per ton-mile amounted to 1.078¢ in 1921 and 9.05 mills in 1950, or a reduction of 16%. In terms of constant-value dollars, the record is even better. Thus railroad management not only preserved the position of the railroads as the lowest-cost form of transportation, but also enabled the industry to withstand the constantly increasing wage and material costs and taxes and the diversion of traffic to competitive agencies that enjoy the benefits of extensive promotional programs and direct aid from federal, state, and local governments.

The full impact of governmental policies in fostering competitive transportation agencies would have fallen even more heavily than it has on the public had it not been for the high level of traffic that the economy has produced in the past two decades, and for the steady drive toward lower rail cost. Although the railroads' share of the nation's traffic has declined relatively, the absolute volume has continued to grow. The problem does not lie in any deterioration or obsolescence in the railroad plant. There is still vital need for the sort of mass transportation service that only the railroads can give. The problem lies at the doorstep of governmental subsidy, which seems to have extended far beyond the limits of fairness and economic justification. Already, there are signs that the people are growing tired of footing the bills implicit in subsidized transportation, and the writer confidently looks for a change in governmental policy in this area.

Current Performance.—Rapid improvement in railroad efficiency has also been brought about by the constant investment in new facilities and the development and adoption of new operating methods. The industry can indeed be proud of its record at the close of this 100 years. Age has not slowed the railroads' pace in improved service. In the 10-year period between 1939 and 1949, the productivity of the railroads increased more than 30%, or at an average rate of 3% per year.

In comparison the manufacturing industry of the United States is universally regarded as having made outstanding technological progress in recent years, and certainly some segments of the manufacturing industry are enjoying youthful vigor. However, in the period from 1939 to 1949, the increase in the rate of manufacturing productivity was only one half that of the railroads.

OUTLOOK FOR THE FUTURE

The nation and its industries, including the railroads, reached their present position because they came into being and were able to develop under a system of free private enterprise.

The keystone of that system is a product, whether it be goods or services, of continuously improved quality at the lowest possible cost. The health of the system depends on the level of productivity that business is able to attain. Whatever reduces productivity weakens the economic structure—whether it be technical problems that engineering might solve, whether it be management's ineptitude or labor's inefficiency, or whether it be ill-considered governmental policies that deaden initiative and incentive. Initiative and incentive must be stimulated rather than discouraged. Competition under a free economic system is a great stimulant. It has been stated that, although competition may be the restless pillow of management, it is the motive power of progress.

No matter how great or how small the engineering problems of tomorrow may be, the highest level of productivity will be attained only if the spur of a free competitive market exists. The vital spark of imagination and the indispensable will to achieve have not survived elsewhere and would not here survive the deadening influence of state ownership. Neither can their best results be achieved under the stifling influence of unfair and burdensome regulation.

However, if the future offers a healthy climate for continued improvement, the United States can be assured of rail transportation that will remain unequaled in the world. The past century of engineering is an indication that what the future holds in the way of technological advancement is not forseeable or predictable. It is quite amusing today to read that in 1830 there were men who worried about the displacement of horses and their drivers by the coal-burning steam engine, and there were men who worried about the grave situation with which America would be confronted when the last pound of coal had been placed in the firebox.

Who knows what tomorrow may produce in the field of motive power? Who knows the full potential of the newest source of power—atomic energy? It may ultimately open sources of power so vast as to be incredible by today's standards. In the field of equipment, present developments have only scratched the surface as far as reduction of friction and deadweight are concerned. Today the cost of metals that reduce deadweight imposes a limitation on their wider use, but the day will come when lightweight streamlined freight trains will be as common as are their counterparts in the passenger field.

AMERICAN SOCIETY OF CIVIL ENGINEERS

Founded November 5, 1852

TRANSACTIONS

Paper No. 2638

SOLVING HIGHWAY TRAFFIC PROBLEMS

By D. Grant Mickle,[1] M. ASCE

Synopsis

Among the liabilities of the automobile era is what appears to be a continuous traffic emergency—how to accommodate 50,000,000 cars with existing thoroughfares, particularly city streets and parking facilities. Money and accident losses are staggering. In planning to conquer the problem, all sorts of traffic facts and habits have to be determined through research by government, state, and city, with particular emphasis of course on the accident nightmare. One great help has been the trained traffic engineer, finding his most fruitful field in the cities. Experience shows many examples of how the problem is being intelligently attacked, and gives confidence that advanced engineering can evolve the best solution.

Introduction

Demands of modern automotive traffic have, in effect, revolutionized the mission of highway engineering, as traditionally accepted since the days of antiquity. In the current philosophy, the highway is not merely a structure to permit movement; it is a productive facility, whose output in transportation is measurable in both quantity and quality. The basic objective is no longer to create roads, or even mobility, but the safest, fastest, and most economical transportation possible.

Through the centuries, and into the early developmental period of the automobile, the engineering approach to the highway problem was almost exclusively structural. Strength of surface and subgrade was the main consideration. Questions relating to actual movement on the facility, except as to the impact of live loads on the pavement, were considered beyond the engineer's purview. Except for maintenance chores, his responsibilities ended when the road was completed.

The advent of the high-powered motorcar changed all that—as it did the contours of cities, the patterns of land use, the tempo of daily living, and the very nature of the national economy. In the field of highway engineering, the functional requirements of the new type of traffic swiftly came to the fore. There

---

[1] Director, Traffic Eng. Div., Automotive Safety Foundation, Washington, D. C.

began a progressive shift in emphasis from the static aspects of road design to the dynamic factors that bear on free-flowing movement. Opportunities to apply engineering skills broadened to an undreamed-of degree with this reorientation toward mobility and safety—especially since the volume, speed, and composition of motor traffic generated a welter of complicated new problems, as illustrated in Fig. 1.

Old Handicaps Still Hamper.—Because the major part of present key systems of roads and streets was built to design standards prevailing under the old philosophy, it is not surprising that a perpetual traffic crisis seems to be impending. This is no reflection on the technical competence or the practical achievements of the men who engineered the basic road plant. In little more than three decades, they accomplished the almost superhuman feat of extending the surfaced system from a few thousand to more than a million and a half miles. Without this engineering conquest of sheer distances, the spectacular growth of automobile use in the United States could never have occurred.

These roads made possible the expansion of cities, the development of suburban communities, the launching of new industrial and agricultural enterprises, and a steady rise in standards of living.

Back in 1920, when the large-scale road program got under way and when the number of motor vehicles in the United States was only about 9,000,000, no one could have foreseen that by 1952 the total would skyrocket to 52,000,000. There was no indication that the truck, a comparative novelty in the early 1920's, would become such a vital factor in the transportation system that it would multiply to today's 9,000,000 trucks. Between 1940 and 1951 alone, truck travel increased 165%; and, of this movement, fully 75% was accounted for by combinations of the truck-trailer type, and only 25% by single units. The road and street network was never designed to accommodate the 500,000,000,000 or so miles per year that motor vehicles roll up, or to cope with the extremely diversified and complex traffic patterns embraced in this astronomical travel mileage.

Critical lack of capacity on rural trunk lines and urban arterials lies at the root of much of the present highway dilemma. This is apparent from the fact that 86% of all highway travel occurs on less than one fourth of the rural road mileage. Half of the total annual travel is concentrated on city streets, which comprise only one tenth of the road network. The latter fact, of course, explains why virtually every one of the one hundred sixty-eight metropolitan areas in the nation has become a chronic traffic bottleneck.

Financial Problems, Too.—Structurally, most of the older roads and streets are still fairly sound. Capacity-wise, many of them were already obsolete before World War II. A huge backlog of needs was piled up during 15 years of depression and war, when the facilities were not properly maintained, rebuilt, or expanded. Now, with scarcely a breather, all highway agencies are faced with inflated costs and shortage of materials in carrying forward a program commensurate with civilian and defense transportation requirements.

In the cities, the street capacity problem is usually aggravated by a more or less acute shortage of off-street parking space; in rural areas, it is compounded by a wide variety of design deficiencies. Steep grades, excessive curves, narrow

(a) In 1900

(b) In 1938

Fig. 1.—A Significant Comparison of City Traffic; "Easter Parade" on Fifth Avenue, New York, N. Y.

shoulders, inadequate sight distances, and other shortcomings drastically limit the service and safety of many roads.

The growing inadequacy of the street and highway plant exacts heavy penalties in blood and dollars. The 1951 accident toll was 37,500 killed and 1,250,000 injured. The economic waste entailed in these mishaps was estimated at $3,500,000,000.

It is believed that over-all money losses from congestion and parking shortage (Fig. 2) even exceed those from traffic accidents. These losses are reflected in rising vehicle-operating costs, urban blight, depressed realty values, decreased city tax revenues, and decline of downtown business centers. For example, the

FIG. 2.—TRAFFIC AND PARKING CONGESTION; VIEW NEAR INDUSTRIAL PLANT IN SEATTLE, WASH.

Regional Plan Association of New York (N. Y.) declared that traffic delays in the late 1940's were costing the city's businessmen more than $300,000,000 annually. Before World War II, Detroit, Mich., computed its congestion losses at $10,000,000 per year. St. Louis, Mo., set its losses from congestion and accidents at $125,000 per day. Boston, Mass., was said to be losing $40,000,000 per year in trucking business because of traffic conditions. In terms of today's dollars and unprecedented travel volumes, current losses are doubtless even more staggering.

NEW PLANNING

The intolerable waste and inconvenience caused by traffic inefficiencies have served to focus increasing attention on the operational aspects—both in the design of new facilities and in the utilization of existing roads and streets. It has become clear that highway planning, design, and operation are integral parts of the total engineering problem, and that functional principles cannot be ignored without grave jeopardy of the public interest.

To Be Scientific.—Hence the modern engineering approach strives to keep in perspective the relation of geometric details to the amount, behavior, and speeds of the traffic the road must carry. It is realized now that the fullest possible understanding of the desires and abilities of drivers, the characteristics of their vehicles—and the definite limitations of both—is prerequisite to sound construction and operation. Giving due weight to these factors offers the best assurance that the roads now being built will retain planned capacity and safety potentials throughout their service life.

Translation of this new thinking into operational procedures applicable to specific traffic requirements obviously called for engineering study and technical supervision. It was necessary to embark on intensive fact-finding in areas that, from the standpoint of research, were almost virgin territory. Such advances as were effected in design practices in the early days of the automobile were rarely based on traffic performance and need, as interpreted from facts obtained in the field. There was no fund of accumulated knowledge such as existed in the developed sciences of structural strength of materials and maintenance.

Thus new frontiers of scientific fact-gathering were opened up, and new techniques for the collection and analysis of traffic data were created. The broad base of investigation now includes facts on road use, traffic volumes, origin and destination, vehicle sizes and weights, time and delay, accidents, and parking. Related inquiry in the area of highway dynamics delved into such matters as speed zoning, establishment of no-passing zones, and design and application of traffic control devices.

With the quantitative and qualitative information developed through these new methods, it became possible to determine not only where the traffic goes, but where it wants to go and where it will probably go in the future. This type of data has become the core of long-range highway planning.

Traffic Defined by Tests.—The origin and destination study, in particular (Fig. 3), has proved invaluable for determining present traffic patterns and future trends. It reveals the termini of individual trips, their purpose, and their frequency. Resultant facts are used successfully in attacking the problems of congestion and parking, as well as for location and design of urban expressways and for improvement of other arterials and distribution routes.

Volume studies turn the spotlight on the size and composition of the traffic stream, the types of vehicles and vehicle loadings, the numbers of pedestrians, and the periods of minimum and maximum flow. These investigations help to establish the relative efficiency and utility of specific roads and streets and to disclose elements that require corrective treatment. By the same token, they show what facilities have reached their saturation point and, in cases where major physical improvements are indicated, aid in selection of appropriate design standards. Naturally, too, traffic volume data serve to determine priority of needs.

As a result of studies, it became clear that accidents are symptoms of inefficient transportation, and not the inevitable toll of motor vehicle use. By establishing the locations, times, circumstances, conditions, and actions that contribute to mishaps, the findings assist in getting at the root causes. A factual basis is provided for eliminating physical hazards on existing roads, and for developing and incorporating protective features in new facilities. Similarly, time and delay studies probe into the factors that contribute to traffic disorders and interruptions, which not only fray the nerves of the motoring public but hit its pocketbook through time losses and increased vehicle-operating costs.

Parking studies measure the demand for storage space both on and off the street, and the availability of parking areas in relation to the principal destination points of vehicle trips. Other phases may be concerned with appraising the influence of parking shortage on congestion, accidents, urban decentralization, and diversion of downtown travel and trade. This factual investigation is used to determine immediate parking needs and to forecast the requirements that will be created as a result of any extensive street or building construction. Research in

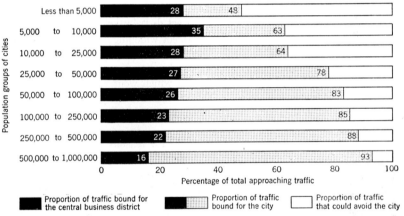

FIG. 3.—STUDY OF ORIGIN AND DESTINATION—AS APPLIED TO TRAFFIC IN CITIES OF VARIOUS SIZES

recent years has also developed new parking equipment and structures including meters and mechanical garages.

Public, and Governmental, Interest.—One important result of this diversified fact-finding is that gradually the public is being brought to understand the dollars-and-cents implications of bad traffic conditions. The availability of facts makes it possible for the taxpayer intelligently to weigh measured needs against anticipated benefits. It enables him to judge what engineering steps are economically justified to raise the level of highway transportation. Therefore, in addition to their other values, traffic studies have become a vital means of securing public support for essential improvements.

The era of comprehensive traffic research was ushered in when progressive highway administrators decided that the trial-and-error methods and expedients of the past would never provide solutions for the complex problems of motorized movement. In the early 1920's a few states, notably Ohio, and several large cities, including Chicago, Ill., Pittsburgh, Pa., and Seattle, Wash., began to assign engineers to the collection and analysis of traffic facts on a full-time basis. The United States Public Roads Administration (later the Bureau of Public Roads) initiated a series of fundamental traffic studies about the same time, and several universities undertook similar research. In 1936 the state planning surveys, conducted jointly by the states and the Public Roads Administration on a continuing basis, began building up a vast reservoir of valuable transportation knowledge.

New information produced by the quickening of research spurred the general improvement of functional design and control. The technical studies brought to the surface many of the underlying weaknesses in the highway transportation system, formerly either overlooked or misinterpreted.

City Traffic Studied.—For instance, it had been commonly believed that the great bulk of traffic approaching on main rural roads wanted to avoid cities. Origin and destination surveys emphatically disproved this (Fig. 3) and showed that attempts to relieve urban street congestion by routing traffic around medium-sized and large-sized cities were by no means the complete answer. It had been assumed, also, that most of the traffic that enters cities was headed for the central business district. Studies revealed that up to 50% of the downtown volumes are merely passing through, for lack of more direct distribution routes.

Formerly municipal officials looked on street widening as a sort of cure-all for street congestion. Research indicated that the real bottleneck is the intersection, and that merely broadening a thoroughfare did not correct the basic cause of jamming. Moreover, it was indicated that cities which went to substantial expenditure in widening major streets could have obtained the same or even better results by eliminating the space waste and traffic disorders due to indiscriminate parking at the curb.

Accidents, a Major Problem.—In searching for reasons for the preponderance of night-time accidents, it became apparent that many street lighting systems had been designed with too much emphasis on beautification and too little on safety. Most of the illumination, instead of being directed onto the pavement, was being thrown into the air, with small benefit to motorists and pedestrians.

New findings revised old theories about the relation of speed to accidents. Setting arbitrary limits, usually without engineering determination, was having no perceptible effect on the accident curve. Speed in keeping with conditions, rather than a general slowdown of motor vehicles, became a more realistic objective of control—especially since in the public mind the velocity of the automobile is one of its prime assets.

Similarly it became clear that misuse of traffic control devices and other regulatory measures not only was widespread, but was adding materially to traffic confusion. It began to be recognized that a badly-timed signal light or a poorly-placed traffic sign (Fig. 4) could do more harm than good; or, for instance, that because of unsound routing the place where transit vehicles must make a turn could become the focal point of a perennial traffic snarl. In short, the cardinal lesson taught by the factual studies was that efficient traffic operations are impossible without the guidance of tested engineering principles.

INTEREST IN TRAFFIC ENGINEERING

Before the traffic problem was attacked scientifically, the handling of such operational tasks as were then being performed was regarded as a phase of enforcement. Historically the job had been delegated to the police as just another chore in connection with keeping order on the streets. When the swelling tide of motor vehicles began to swamp police efforts to improve chaotic traffic conditions, it be-

(a) The Traveling Motorist in Need of Sympathy Here

(b) Easy Choice Made Possible by Simplicity and Visibility

FIG. 4.—DIRECTION SIGNS, A HELP OR A HINDRANCE?

came obvious that regulatory measures were not enough. In the past it had been believed that the only alternative was to resort to capital improvements like street widening or other major construction. Since cities particularly are as a rule hard pressed for highway funds, the prospect for early traffic relief was none too encouraging.

The activities of the small group of men who were pioneering in the application of engineering techniques to traffic problems in different parts of the United States drew public attention to a new alternative. Through careful technical analysis of specific traffic difficulties, followed by scientific treatment embracing a variety of traffic aids, these individuals demonstrated that a simple and economical remedy could often serve almost as well as an extensive redesign job or a new roadway (Fig. 5).

Gradually it came to be realized that practical solutions must come largely through the positive resources of engineering rather than through the restrictive methods of enforcement. The next logical step was to give formal recognition to the fact that traffic operation is properly one of the important technical functions of state and municipal government.

State and City Staffs.—To insure continuity for an effective program of research and operation, some state highway departments initiated special units within their organizational structure. In certain cases traffic engineering functions were integrated with the maintenance division, in others with the planning survey. The units which proved most successful, however, were those set up as an independent division having both study and operational responsibilities. Progressive cities, too, began to adjust their street management structure to give full scope and continuity to traffic engineering activities.

By 1946, most of the states had established traffic engineering divisions. A survey conducted by the Eno Foundation at Saugatuck, Conn., showed that in only four states were these functions still handled by the highway police, and in only four others by maintenance engineers.

The sampling of cities revealed that all those with a population of more than 500,000 and 67% of those in the 100,000–500,000 group had traffic engineering units. The ratio in the smaller cities was 48% in the 100,000–200,000 group and only 32% in the 50,000–100,000 group. In most of the communities which reported no traffic engineering agency, the functions were under police jurisdiction, or shared with the engineering division or electrical bureau. In a few instances, the responsibilities were handled by the department of public works or safety.

Professional Training.—Emergence of traffic engineering as a specialized field of highway engineering created a growing need for trained technicians to give full time to operational aspects and related problems of planning and design. In 1926, with financial aid provided by leaders of the automotive industry, a national center for traffic engineering research and training was established at Harvard University, in Cambridge, Mass. In 1938 the program was transferred to the Yale Bureau of Highway Traffic, in New Haven, Conn., with the expanded support of industry groups channeled through the Automotive Safety Foundation. To date, nearly 300 engineers have received graduate training under this program, and hundreds of others have received short-course instruction at numerous other universities. Today, the paramount need is for more rapid integration of basic operational principles into the highway engineering courses given at all engineering schools.

Just as 100 years ago civil engineers found it desirable to form the American Society of Civil Engineers, for the interchange of information and the advancement of their professional field, so did the practitioners in the fledgling field of

(a) Traffic Lanes Evenly Divided, Unevenly Used

(b) Five Lanes Conveniencing Preponderance of Traffic and Relieving Congestion

FIG. 5.—IMPROVEMENT WITHOUT MAJOR STREET CHANGE, SHERIDAN ROAD, CHICAGO, ILL.

traffic engineering find it advantageous to band together as the Institute of Traffic Engineers in 1930. This comparatively new technical society, with headquarters at Yale University, functions as a central agency for correlating and disseminating factual information and techniques developed by members of the profession and for improving operational and administrative standards.

The duties of the traffic engineer have been vastly enlarged during the past quarter century. In the early days his job began only after the planners and the builders had finished their work, and then he devoted virtually all his research to traffic control and accident reduction. Operationally, most of his efforts were devoted to putting up traffic signs and stop lights and installing pavement markings where accidents and congestion indicated some physical deficiency.

State Highway Efforts.—In the state highway department, responsibilities of a division of traffic engineering now include the gathering of essential traffic facts, including: Accident analysis, the review of highway design to insure proper geometric detail, installation of warning and directional signs and route markers, installation of signals at high-volume intersections, and the marking of center lines and no-passing zones. Also within the scope of the state traffic engineer are the determination of speed zones and the control of roadside exits.

In addition, the state traffic engineering division frequently provides consulting service to cities and counties within the state, and conducts urban origin and destination surveys and studies of parking demand. Traffic engineers have played a prominent part in state-wide engineering studies of highway need in some twenty-five states since the war.

City Streets, a Challenge.—However, the most fruitful vineyard for the traffic engineer's labors is in the cities. Three out of five Americans lived in rural areas 50 years ago; today the situation is reversed, with three fifths of the population now located in urban communities. More than 80% of the nation's population gain in the past decade occurred in metropolitan areas. This growing concentration of people, and their increasing dependence on the motorcar in their daily pursuits, is one obvious reason for the worsening traffic plight of American cities.

There are also other reasons. The bulk of urban traffic, comprising approximately half of the total highway travel of the United States, is crammed into a limited number of arterials serving major destination points. Generally speaking, little attempt has been made to modernize principal thoroughfares for expanding traffic; and the mileage of new express-type facilities constructed within cities or metropolitan areas is still infinitesimal.

It has been stated—without too much exaggeration—that cities have been trying to make eighteenth century streets serve twentieth century traffic. The gridiron street pattern common to most communities, with its characteristic frequency of intersections, was never ideal even for horse-drawn traffic, let alone today's tremendous volumes of high-powered motor vehicles. Add to this fundamental handicap the acute shortage of off-street parking and truck-loading space, and it is easy to see why unsnarling the city's traffic jam is a monumental challenge. Pedestrian conflicts, cross traffic and turning movements, curb-parking maneuvers, and the mixing of private, commercial, and transit vehicles make congestion and accidents almost inevitable.

In this situation, it becomes imperative to make a realistic appraisal of the existing street plant to determine whether or not it is being used to maximum advantage and, if not, how the full service potential of the facilities can be obtained. In cases where main urban arteries are taxed beyond their absolute capacity, the only solution is expressway construction or other capital improvements. Nevertheless, it is realized that, by and large, the present street system will have to continue to serve for a long time to come. Thus, there is no alternative but to find ways and means of reducing physical hazards and of utilizing available riding surface to the utmost (Fig. 6).

Expedients Developed.—The recognized procedures of traffic engineering can be used to correct an amazing number of weaknesses in the street plant. Not only are these measures, for the most part, relatively inexpensive, but many of them

Fig. 6.—Approach to Holland Tunnel, Jersey City, N. J., with Adjustable Overhead Traffic Lights; Roadway Apportioned Quickly to Meet Greatest Traffic Need

result in benefits which are both immediate and lasting. Some of the techniques have been newly developed; others are adaptations or refinements of practices that predate the automobile, and in some instances go back to ancient times.

For instance, safety islands for pedestrians (Fig. 7) were already common on the streets of London, England, and Paris, France, in the 1860's. Road markers were used abroad for many centuries, and in America since colonial days. Frontiersmen blazed trees or bent saplings to mark their trails, and ancient peoples often piled up stones as trail markers. At the time the "horseless carriage" first became popular in the United States, state route numbers were often painted on convenient barns, bridge railings, and telephone poles.

EXPERIENCES OLD AND NEW

Because the streets of imperial Rome were narrow and congested, the Caesars established the first one-way movement in recorded history. Parking restrictions go back almost as far, as evidenced by a law in old Pompeii which forbade chariots to stop on the road for loading. In England, regulations of 1660 vintage prohibited the parking of hackney coaches on the king's highway. Albany, N. Y., passed an ordinance in 1697 to limit the speed of horse-drawn vehicles and horseback riders. Although the first traffic survey in this country—a study made in New York City to determine customary curb-parking distances of motor vehicles —was conducted as early as 1910, the origin and destination study is a relatively recent development.

At any rate, numerous cities have substantially increased their street capacity, opened up critical bottlenecks, eliminated recurrent traffic disorders, and reduced their accident rate by carrying forward an intelligent and up-to-date program of operational measures.

FIG. 7.—SAFETY ISLANDS IN WASHINGTON, D. C., TO AID BUSES, AUTOMOBILES, AND PARTICULARLY PEDESTRIANS

Both Big and Small Cities.—Chicago offers a classic example of beneficial traffic engineering treatment. As early as the 1920's congestion reached intolerable proportions on State Street, in the Loop district. A threefold program was put in operation: Curb parking was banned; left turns were prohibited; and signal lights were coordinated to keep traffic moving. The combination of these steps brought prompt relief; but, more than this, the street has remained comparatively uncongested ever since, despite heavy increases in traffic.

Grand River Boulevard, in Detroit, one of the nation's busiest streets, carrying upward of 60,000 vehicles daily, formerly suffered from perennial clogging and an inordinately high accident rate. Frequency of left turns rendered the two inner lanes of the six-lane pavement virtually useless as carriers of arterial traffic to and from the city. Prohibition of left turns throughout the 14-mile length of the thoroughfare, off-center lane usage during peak periods, a modern progressive signal control system, and banning of curb parking between certain hours have served to achieve maximum capacity. Running time has been cut by nearly 12 min, and accidents have been materially reduced. Making certain streets one way only has also been beneficial in Detroit (Fig. 8).

In Hagerstown, Md., heavy traffic funneled into the heart of the city by several major state highways created an unceasing nightmare, until a system of one-way streets extending all the way through the city was developed. As a result, through traffic has been immeasurably eased, with comparable relief for local users.

FIG. 8.—ONE-WAY TRAFFIC SOMETIMES THE ONLY SOLUTION, AS DEMONSTRATED BY THIS VIEW IN DETROIT, MICH.

Extensive use of the principle of unbalanced lane flow has made it possible for Los Angeles, Calif., to carry fantastic volumes of traffic into and out of the central business area on existing streets. Currently, with the completion of the freeway system into the downtown section, a one-way plan is being worked out so that the anticipated high-density traffic can be collected and distributed with ease and dispatch.

Realization of Finances.—Failure to make more use of operational techniques in many cities is ascribable to official reluctance to understand the importance of street transportation or the magnitude of the losses engendered by bad traffic conditions. Most cities spend only a fraction as much on traffic accident prevention as on fire protection. However, in monetary terms—as well as in total lives lost annually—traffic accidents are a vastly greater menace.

About 1938 Toledo, Ohio, released a report which indicated that one year's traffic accident losses amounted to $1,022,325, as compared with fire losses totaling $311,802—a ratio of three to one. Nevertheless during that same year, according to the report, for each dollar of traffic accident loss, only 34¢ was expended for traffic control and betterment services, whereas $2 was allotted to the fire department for each dollar of actual fire loss.

Centralized Control Needed.—Another factor which militates against an effective attack on the traffic problem in many cities is weakness in administration. Manifestly, relief of strangling communities through freer circulation—in the face of antiquated streets and record-breaking travel volumes—poses a supreme test of sound management. In the majority of cases, however, the organizational structure for administering the facilities is as seriously deficient as the street plant itself. Scattered responsibilities, split authority, and scrambled organization seem to be the earmarks of this vital phase of public administration.

In the case of the older municipal services, such as water supply, welfare, and public works, unity of the managerial structure and centralized authority are provided for in the city charter. Few cities have given charter recognition to street and traffic administration as a major municipal function, with the attention and stature accorded to the long-established departments. Instead, responsibilities in this area have been parceled out, as occasion arose, among existing city agencies. Usually the new duties relating to street development or operations have been assigned to departments having superficially similar functions. The instance of the assignment of traffic engineering to the police is typical.

Such diffusion naturally results in divided powers, duplicated effort, conflicts, and other inefficiencies. Desirable physical improvements, even those of a minor character, may be hung up indefinitely as the proposed project is shuttled back and forth from one municipal agency to another. Moreover, proper correlation of physical improvements and traffic operations becomes a virtual impossibility.

Over-all City Plans.—An all-too-common result of this glaring administrative weakness is the failure to make a specific agency responsible for the development, design, and programming of a master street plan. Without a master plan—and the authority to carry it forward—it is hard to budget expenditures prudently for even individual projects, not to mention a comprehensive street program.

Traffic is a decisive factor with respect to locations and mutual relations of the various community activities. The master plan, therefore, can exert a powerful influence in defining neighborhoods, stabilizing land values, integrating the different modes of transportation, controlling abnormal decentralization, and rectifying the jumbled land uses which have generated so many of the headaches of the average city.

Lack of a centralized street and traffic agency also makes it difficult for the city to carry on effective liaison in highway matters with other jurisdictions. This consideration is important, since modernization of arterial routes often demands the cooperation of other levels of government—county, state, and federal. The present setup of most municipal street agencies provides no focal point for effective intergovernmental relations, which of course are essential not only in planning of facilities, but in joint financing, acquisition of rights of way, and contract letting.

The rapid growth of suburban sections in recent years emphasizes the necessity of the area-wide approach in municipal thinking and planning, whether the objective be improved transportation or some other sphere of civic interest. To preserve the economic health of parent cities and to foster sound development of fringe communities will require the utmost in harmonious adjustment of transportation, land use, zoning, traffic laws and controls, and administration.

An encouraging sign is the recent action taken by a few larger cities, notably Detroit and Philadelphia, Pa., in consolidating some of the basic functions of street and traffic management. Because of its vital importance to every city's economy, street transportation deserves major attention, and this can best be achieved through integration in a single department of those functions pertaining to the planning, construction, maintenance, and operation of the street system. It appears certain that in the future more and more cities will assign these functions to one agency and insure continuity by giving it charter status.

A Better Day in Prospect.—Looking ahead, the spacious modern motorways that have begun to make their appearance in a few leading cities will some day be part of expressway networks that will lace broad metropolitan areas. By the same token, it may be expected that the sheer volumes of motor traffic will give impetus to an accelerated effort in making better use of existing facilities.

Such progress will involve more productive methods of lane usage and reversal of the direction of traffic during peak periods by signal control. Instead of lane efficiencies of only 20% and 30%, as now developed on many urban arteries, service approaching a high efficiency ratio on expressway lanes will be sought and probably obtained.

Surface arterial streets will be converted to semilimited access facilities by closing minor cross streets and controlling turns at major intersections. Progressive signal timing, giving preferential treatment to the direction of principal traffic flow at different times of the day, will also be employed to a far greater extent than at present.

Modern signal control methods will be a "must," and electronic devices may be utilized to change signal cycles several times during the day to accommodate shifting patterns of traffic movement. Even radar or modified television may be adapted for use at strategic points to advise a central dispatching office of unusual traffic tie-ups, so that emergency measures can be promptly taken.

Parking on the street will disappear, and off-street parking structures will sprout plentifully in the downtown sections. Mechanical garages will be commonplace. Devices for parking vehicles will become just as much a part of business facilities as the elevator and the escalator. In rural areas, spot treatment will provide extra lanes on steep grades for commercial vehicles. Roadside controls will be much more extensive, and road signs will be modernized to provide greater visibility and convenience.

A Vital Decision.—The United States is, without question, on the threshold of a transportation era when automotive travel will exceed anything previously visualized. Present (1952) traffic volumes have already outrun the volumes predicted for 1960. In terms of number of motor vehicles, progress is 10 years ahead of estimates; in terms of roads and streets, at least 10 years behind. To lose sight of this fact would be tragic, since the highway system is the backbone of both civilian economy and national defense. The traffic problem is a great challenge to all citizens. To the engineer, it is both a challenge and a tremendous opportunity. For to serve the nation adequately in the critical years ahead, highway transportation must be made safer and more efficient than ever before; and the only way to do that is to put highway transportation on a sound engineering basis.

AMERICAN SOCIETY OF CIVIL ENGINEERS

Founded November 5, 1852

TRANSACTIONS

Paper No. 2639

REVIEW OF AMERICAN HIGHWAY MAINTENANCE

By Rex M. Whitton,[1] M. ASCE

Synopsis

Because 1952 is the centennial year of the ASCE, this paper traces the history of road maintenance during the past 100 years, with primary emphasis on developments in the United States. In so doing the years before 1900 are marked off as of "little consequence," those between 1900 and 1920 are labeled as "educative and preparatory," and the past quarter of a century is cited as a period of awakening and actual progress. Many examples illustrate these trends.

Highway maintenance has approached an acceptable efficiency only during the final quarter of the century of service that is being celebrated by the ASCE centennial. This improvement in upkeep has been achieved largely through mechanization, by the training of highway maintenance personnel, and through the awakening of engineers to a realization that highway maintenance means far more than just mending or smoothing a rough or broken roadway.

Although great strides forward have been made in maintenance efficiency, engineers should be the first to admit that the ultimate has not yet been reached—nor should they be satisfied until it is achieved. The future holds far greater service that may be rendered to the motoring public, and to communities, states, and nations. By further mechanizing activities, by adopting new and improving existing methods and materials, and by giving more and more attention to personnel training programs, a higher level of maintenance efficiency should be attained at an absolute minimum of cost.

Just what is highway maintenance? It is the preserving and keeping of each type of roadway, roadside structure, and facility as nearly as possible in its original condition as constructed or as subsequently improved. It means patching holes, filling ruts, cutting corrugations, pouring cracks, cleaning ditches and culverts, removing snow, spreading cinders, fighting floods, mowing weeds, erecting proper traffic controls and warning signs, and innumerable other operations which contribute to keeping a highway smooth, safe, efficient, and attractive. The

---

[1] Chf. Engr., Missouri State Highway Comm., Jefferson City, Mo.

end result of adequate highway maintenance is smooth and safe roadways, clear waterways, and clean rights of way.

Early Care, A Localized Responsibility.—Prior to the 1900's the United States trailed Europe both in highway development and in maintenance progress. The main reason was that just when it appeared this country was headed for extensive highway development in the 1830's the steam locomotive was introduced. Having such long distances to conquer, the United States turned to the railroad as the answer to its transportation needs, leaving highways to serve little more than community purposes. Feeder roads were built to transport farm products to railroad shipping points, but general interest in highway improvement was not aroused until the coming of the motor vehicle.

Fig. 1.—Hand Labor, the Basis of Maintenance, Even As Late As the Twentieth Century

Therefore, up to the early 1900's, with but few exceptions, maintenance was a local responsibility, charged to either townships or counties. Usually the county was divided into local districts, and virtually all authority was delegated to untrained men appointed or elected to care for the roads. When and if any actual work was carried out, it was largely by persons working out the highway taxes levied by the individual communities.

During this "dark age" of the nation's roads the town plow, the axe, the hoe, the pick, and the shovel (Fig. 1) were the principal tools for making repairs. A summary of the procedure, actually followed in Massachusetts in 1866, provides a typical picture of maintenance as it existed until about 1890. This story comes from an 1888 history of transportation compiled by J. L. Ringwalt, early editor of *Railway World.*

"Surveyors," elected at town meetings and having no particular skill, were charged with directing the work. Labor was performed by persons, old and young, rich and poor, working out a "highway tax." The "surveyors" were farmers who took turns at the job, often seeking it so that they might repair their own roads.

Repairs seldom were made at the time most needed, but rather when it was convenient for brother farmers to work—after planting or harvesting was done. Citizens in town meeting would fix the prices to be paid for the labor of men and animals, with the rate set at the highest level that the best men and teams could command because each voter had a direct interest in that price.

Slipshod Methods Prevailed.—Then came the actual day for repairing the road. Ringwalt recounts it thus, as taken from an 1866 *Agriculture Report:*

"A motley assemblage gathers, of decrepit old men, each with a garden hoe; of pale, thin mechanics from their shoe shops, armed with worn-out shovels; half grown boys, sent by their mothers who, perhaps, are widows; with, perhaps, the doctor, the lawyer, and even the minister, all of whom understand that working on the road does not mean hard labor, even for the soft hands.

"Farmers bring their steers * * * the old mare in the lead, with a cart. A new citizen drives up, with rickety cart and mortal remains of a railroad horse * * *. The only effective force consists of two or three yokes of oxen and a half dozen men hired by the surveyor with money paid by non-residents and men whose time is of too much value to waste on the roads.

"Cattle are put to the big town plow * * * boys ride the beams, drivers put on the lash. Gutters, half filled with sand and soil and leaves of a half dozen seasons are ploughed up. * * * Teams then stand idle and this mixture, more fit for the compost heap, is thrown upon the road by the old men with their hoes and shovels. The occasion is regarded more as a frolic than as serious labor."

The report drew this conclusion on the procedure:

"No one who has once witnessed the process of 'mending the roads' in a small New England town needs any argument to convince him that a system more ingeniously devised to accomplish nothing was never invented."

Reviewing the maintenance progress that has since been achieved, one conspicuous result can be noted—the era was not a total loss. Some people, at least, were thinking about roads, and about methods needed for improving or maintaining them. Such thoughts were good, because they were bound to bear fruit.

Nevertheless, Some Material Advances.—The period prior to 1900 did, in fact, bring some developments that were to have an important influence on advancement of modern methods. For example, Jerome Tresaguet, the great French road engineer of the late 1700's, not only advanced the idea of lighter pavements and crowned subgrades, but also stressed the necessity for continuous, organized maintenance, instead of intermittent repair, to keep roads in condition at all seasons of the year.

Tresaguet organized the "cantonnier" system of maintenance which, manned at first by untrained laborers, soon developed into a specialized organization paid for and supervised by the French Government. Also, he initiated the idea that rapidity of wear is in direct proportion to bad road condition. Therefore, to insure the longest possible life, it becomes mandatory to preserve the integrity of the surface by prompt and incessant maintenance.

An early English authority on roads, Thomas Aitken, in a book entitled "Road Making and Maintenance," makes this philosophical statement: "The good condition in which roads are maintained is a fair indication of the progress or prosperity of any age or peoples." Another authority put in this way:

> "Roads are the physical symbol by which to measure the progress of any age or people. If the community is stagnant, the condition of the road will indicate the fact; if they have no roads, they are savages."

Again, Thomas Telford, a famous road builder of the 1800's made an observation in 1820 that is just as important and true today as it was when spoken: "It ought never be forgotten that in order to have the surface of a road perfect, it must be kept completely dry,* * *" and:

> "* * * a certain number of laborers ought always have the care of the surface of the road, and never quit it for a single day to do anything else; they will always have sufficient to do in spreading materials in ruts and hollows, in scraping the road, in cleaning out the side channels and keeping open the water courses, and generally in maintaining the road in a clean and sound state. A few men constantly so employed will do a great deal toward preservation of the road."

Effects of Materials, Machinery, and Vehicles.—Other advancements were also made in the period from 1850 to 1890 that are now known to have been important in bringing about present methods. In Missouri, the plank road craze began about 1849. Nearly fifty companies were chartered to establish toll highways using plank as the surface layer. In other parts of the United States, at an earlier period, the so-called corduroy roads were built consisting of logs laid side by side as the supporting element of the wagon load. These plank roads gave way to macadam within a few years because of the fast wearing and warping of the plank. In fact, in some places, warping of the plank was controlled by placing creek gravel on the plank ends. This resulted in the discovery that creek gravel made an excellent surfacing material, and its use on low traffic roads has continued to this day.

Numerous other developments in the latter half of the nineteenth century have contributed to present-day methods: Du Pont's new blasting powder in 1856; Blake's introduction of a jaw rock crusher in 1857, and a gyratory crusher in 1881; the birth of the petroleum industry in 1859, when the first oil well was sunk at Oil Creek, Pa.; the discovery of the internal combustion principle in 1859, with the first vehicle propelled by an internal combustion engine being built early in the 1860's; and a steam roller imported in 1869, when the Commissioners of Central Park, New York City, N. Y., purchased a 15-ton machine manufactured in England.

The bicycle, which was to plant an early seed of desire for better roads, appeared in sizable numbers in 1877. In that same year the steam mortar mixer was introduced. William H. Diedrick of Fresno County, California, perfected an improved earth scraper that was to become the parent of the one so widely used for many years, before the advent of the wheeled scraper in 1884. The first portland-cement concrete pavement in this country was laid in Bellefontaine,

Ohio, in 1893. In that same year Stephen Duryea first successfully operated an automobile in this country and Henry Ford built his first car.

Era of Split-Log Drag.—From the beginning of the highway development program, the need for special equipment to perform work became evident. Possibly one of the first devices for road maintenance was the split-log drag for crowning and smoothing the earth road surface. Its initial use is lost in antiquity but it probably was introduced in this country by the earliest settlers. In the writer's home state of Missouri, D. Ward King exploited the split-log drag in the 1890's, and spread its virtues by visiting some twenty-three states, from Maine to Texas and from Maryland to the Dakotas, to promote it as a cheap way to obtain good roads.

The King drag was made of a log, 7 to 9 ft long, split in half lengthwise. The halves were set horizontally flat sides to front, and fastened about 30 in. apart. There was a platform on top on which the driver could stand. In 1908, a pamphlet prepared by Missouri's first state highway engineer, Curtis J. Hill, M. ASCE, asserted, "the best and most economic implement with which to maintain an earth road is the drag". He estimated the cost at not more than 30¢ per mile. The self-propelled power grader of today, an evolution of the split-log drag, is one of the most useful machines for road maintenance.

King, although he gained no special recognition for it, along with promotion of the drag also pressed for adoption of another idea that to this day remains of utmost importance in any maintenance program. That was the need to control weeds, not only on the road shoulder but on the roadway itself. He noted, of course, that weeds and grass held moisture and prevented the road surface from drying out rapidly. Today the weed control program has been expanded to embrace the entire right of way.

State and Federal Recognition.—The 1890's brought also a development important not in the mechanics of maintenance, but in its organizational legal phase—one that has played an important part in paving the way for the progress since achieved. In 1891, New Jersey began contributing state aid for road improvements. Massachusetts adopted the plan in 1893, Connecticut in 1895, Rhode Island in 1896, Vermont in 1898, and so on until all states had adopted this program by 1917.

Still another development that must not be overlooked, because of its great bearing on maintenance progress attained in this century, was the establishment by Congress on March 3, 1893, of the United States Office of Road Inquiry, with an appropriation of $10,000 to carry on research and educational work in connection with road management and construction. This agency grew into the Office of Public Roads and finally into the Bureau of Public Roads, which throughout its life has contributed much, not only toward making construction of adequate roads possible, but also toward providing for their proper maintenance.

The New York Enabling Act of 1898 was designed not only to aid financially in the maintenance of the network of earth roads that then existed, but also to encourage the abandonment of the antiquated system of working out the road tax. The Federal Aid Act of 1916 provided, among many things, that states must maintain highways on which federal aid was received for construction.

In the early 1900's the nation's expanding economic needs and the increase in the number of automobiles combined to create both a desire and a need for more and better roads. With that demand came the building of new types of roads and, with them, the need to revise, improve, and expand maintenance practices.

The steam roller and the rock crusher still were the only power tools in general use. Horse-drawn vehicles (Fig. 2) and hand tools were the rule, and they were becoming far from adequate. Likewise, the long-established principle of local maintenance was proving more and more inadequate and unsatisfactory. Soon after the New York State Commission of Highways was set up in 1909, it

Fig. 2.—Blade Grader, 2 Hp, Long Standard Equipment on Earth and Gravel Roads

was decided to establish a patrol system to insure constant care and attention to the roads.

To keep up with the changing picture, by 1917 every state in the Union had adopted some form of state participation in highways. Actual building and maintenance still were carried out at the local level in many states, but even this procedure was changing form. Trained engineers were taking over supervisory work, and expert advice was becoming more readily available and more often sought, as state highway departments were set up and became active agencies.

This same period also brought, in 1914, organization of one of the oldest agencies in the United States whose prime goal is better highways—the American Association of State Highway Officials. The AASHO was formed, primarily, to bring together highway officials so that they might discuss and compare their problems, exchange ideas, and promote research. This pooling of ideas and "know-how" has made invaluable contributions down through the years.

Various Bases of Maintenance.—Patrol systems, long used in Europe to care for roads, were introduced, with special gangs designated to repair hard-surfaced roads of brick, concrete, or block. Often a contract system was practiced, by which maintenance responsibility would be charged to some individual or company. Also, in several states, such as New York, the plan of permanently employing men to work the roads began to take form—patterned after the systems in France, Germany, and other European nations.

The idea of state-controlled road programs took hold quickly and grew. By 1920 several states had adopted it, most of them even going as far as to establish a special maintenance department or bureau to meet mounting needs. In Missouri, for example, the State Highway Department was created in March, 1917, and that year the first move was made to aid in maintenance. State aid began when the new board established a policy of paying $1.25 per mile per month for dragging roads connecting county seats of adjoining counties. By 1923 the commission found it expedient to set up a maintenance bureau in the State Highway Department.

With the organization of maintenance divisions or bureaus came a broadening in ideas and understanding of just what maintenance actually meant. Not only did it mean mending roads, but it began to embrace the marking of them so travelers could find their way about more readily. Experimentation with new surfaces to provide not only a smoother road, but also a more serviceable one was also started. The trimming of hedges, as well as the cutting of roadside brush and weeds was begun, to permit the sun to reach the roadway and keep it dry.

The year 1920 was notable for the creation of the Highway Research Board of the National Research Council, the accomplishments of which any highway engineer quickly recognizes. That same year brought also a rising cry to lift the nation out of the mud, with many fund campaigns carried out in Missouri among other places.

Then Mechanical Power for Roadwork.—Wars, destructive as they are to human life and property, always have contributed some later recognized benefit toward the advancement of civilization. Highway maintenance may well be said to have benefited by World War I in that this period brought about the beginning of motorization and mechanization of maintenance departments, by making available surplus army trucks and tractors. Although the old solid-tired trucks were far from ideal for country roads in wet seasons, they proved their value in the over-all picture by speeding up many other activities.

However, even with those trucks and their hard rubber tires, or the iron-wheeled and lugged tractor, pulling drags and light graders, the most effective maintenance patrol still was composed of the four-up light team, light patrol graders, wagons, slips, and shovels in the hands of husky and willing men. The blade and team smoothed the surface; the slip built up and drained the low spots; and the wagon hauled stone, gravel, and cinders to fill soft places, or bridge lumber and culvert pipe as needed.

Manpower was extremely short during the postwar period of the early 1920's too, because jobs were plentiful and the pay was high in that era of "prosperity." This condition served to emphasize the value of equipment in supplementing men and thus helped to speed up maintenance mechanization.

The one-man power grader (Fig. 3) might well be considered the child of the manpower shortage. The need for this piece of equipment developed during the early 1920's and by 1926 a few appeared on the market. Those first units are remembered as not too successful since their operator usually was so busy keeping the machine between the fences and out of side ditches that he had little time to devote to the real task at hand—smoothing the road surface. By 1926, however, several fairly good motor graders were available, although still equipped with spade lugs, or solid rubber tires.

Another Step—Pneumatic Tires.—The inadequacy of lugs and solid tires, and recognition of that inadequacy, was to be the springboard for another de-

FIG. 3.—THE MOTOR GRADER, WITH SOLID TIRES, WHICH ADDED MOBILITY, SPEED, AND PRODUCTION

velopment that has contributed heavily toward making today's maintenance equipment what it is—the introduction of the pneumatic tires on road machinery.

Again, the State of Missouri can claim some credit for promoting this forward step. A grader salesman convinced a division engineer and his maintenance chief that putting pneumatic tires on a motor grader would be a good idea. They spent some time in conveying to their superior the merits of such a plan, but eventually the experiment was undertaken. This was the first such test by the manufacturer, and one of the first, if not the very first, in the nation.

The new type tires were put on 10–20 graders. The company assigned a mechanic to stay on the spot and work out the "bugs," of which there were plenty. However, by the end of the year the innovation had proved success-ful—more than doubling mileages of work that could be performed by the old iron-wheeled and solid tired machines. Within the year practically all equipment concerns had adopted the idea which now can be recognized as a giant stride toward road maintenance in its more efficient and economical form.

Traffic Signs and Counts.—During the 1920's marking and erecting signs on highways also came into prominence as a maintenance duty. Wisconsin was one of the first states to engage extensively in such an activity, widely publicizing the claim then that "it is harder to get lost in Wisconsin than in any other state." Ohio and Indiana also gave much early attention to marking, and it was one of the first assignments of Missouri's maintenance bureau in 1923 and 1924. Although the practice of marking roads dates back at least to 1739 on the North American continent, with the axe as the means, its efficient development came first because it was a convenience to motorists, and then because it was a necessity.

The popularity and need for highway markings and signs became so important, and actual results were so varied in the different states, that highway leaders soon accepted the urgency of promoting uniformity. This led to action by the AASHO which, in cooperation with the Bureau of Public Roads, decided to design and adopt standard markers and signs for use on United States routes.

Even now studies and experiments are constantly carried on, seeking to perfect the system. The Missouri maintenance bureau has erected special blank signboards, to pick up wet weather splashing patterns, at various points throughout the state. These are being used to determine at what height above pavement level, and what distance out from the pavement edge, signs should be erected to prevent them from being made illegible by mud splashing from passing vehicles. Although the experiments are not yet completed, there is a strong indication that signs erected 8 ft out (to the center of the sign), and 4 ft up (to the bottom of the sign) will escape 80% to 90% of the mud carrying splash. Most of these signs, in the past, have been erected from 6 ft to 10 ft out, with the bottom of the sign approximately 2 ft 6 in. above the pavement. It is felt that the results of this experiment will help to avoid much of the maintenance expense of sign cleaning.

Taking traffic counts and making traffic flow maps, to provide information needed in developing better maintenance practices as well as better roadways, were other contributions of the 1920's, carried out as part of expanding maintenance activities. Consideration of the effect on highways of the weights of vehicles using them was begun, as were center striping and the issuing of detour and road condition maps as a public convenience.

Although not necessarily a part of the maintenance undertaking, the addition of cost and control accounting systems has made a definite contribution to maintenance work—particularly because such computations have provided data from which the most economical methods could be determined while the results achieved were observed. Such a system was put into operation in Missouri in 1924 and 1925.

Upkeep of Surfaces and Roadsides.—The late 1920's brought extensive experiments in bituminous road surfaces, many of them done in the maintenance bureau. These experiments resulted from the demand of increasing traffic for elimination of dust on loose aggregate surfaced roads. Limited funds for this work dictated the need for a low-cost dustless surface. Although the Missouri Highway Department had a service truck as early as 1917 (Fig. 4), it was in 1928 the state purchased its first distributor, rollers, heaters, and necessary crane and trucks for such a program. Retread, oil mat, and other experimental bituminous surfaces were built. Many rock asphalts and patented bituminous mixes were tried, and various grades of tars, cutbacks, and emulsions were used. This period might well be listed as the era of development of low-cost bituminous surfaces, not only in Missouri but elsewhere. With the development and widespread use of bituminous pavements and surfaces came the necessity of devising new maintenance methods to care for such roadways.

Roadside beautification also began at this time. It evolved into a maintenance operation largely because civic, patriotic, and commercial organizations and prominent individuals became interested in making roadsides more attractive.

Fig. 4.—An Innovation, About 1917, Although Still Solid Tired—The Highway Maintenance Truck

At first such work was limited largely to the planting of trees and shrubs at city and town entrances. Many of the plantings later were wiped out as the cities expanded and as traffic increased to make widening of the entrance roads mandatory. In truth, however, the hue and cry for beautification eventually became the "spark plug" which resulted in obtaining wider rights of way, stabilizing slopes and planting them to grasses to control erosion and improve appearance, and building roadside parks. The latter today are looked on as an essential part of a highway, not only to preserve natural and scenic beauty of the land, but also to promote safe driving and comfort for travelers.

Progress in the 1930's.—The depression years forced a slight retardation of maintenance effectiveness, with the demand that manpower replace machines to provide work for the jobless. In a nation like the United States, however, such a condition could not prevail for long because the people have too much initiative, vision, and determination to be held back. In fact, despite depression handicaps, the decade that followed was notable for outstanding contributions toward perfection of maintenance methods and activities.

For example, in 1929 Missouri developed and built a truck-mounted road magnet and operated it over all state gravel roads to remove metallic articles capable of puncturing tires. During 1930 this machine covered 7,212 miles of roads and picked up 27,033 lb of nails, screws, bolts, and so forth. The device prevented many a tire puncture and gained much favorable publicity throughout the state and nation. Even today such magnets are in demand and are operated over rural roads.

During this decade more attention was paid to controls on vehicle weights, vast expansion in bituminous road surfacing, and maintenance of secondary or farm-to-market roads. Traffic safety became an important maintenance responsibility. The problem developed because motor vehicles were already increasing faster than were the facilities to care for them. With this problem came the necessity for even more extensive studies of signs and traffic control, and for consideration of the element of speeds and traffic movements at heavily used intersections.

Mud-jacking of pavement slabs was introduced early in the 1930's. In its initial phase, the practice was to pump a soil-cement and water mixture under pavements to raise sunken areas, and thus restore the smooth riding surface. Now the mud-jack is used primarily to fill voids under concrete pavements which have been developed by "slab pumping."

By 1939 a new war period was approaching. National defense preparations brought increasingly heavy defense traffic, not only in numbers but in added weights of the vehicles themselves and of the loads they carried. These factors were responsible for two outstanding maintenance developments of the 1940's—the perfection of undersealing to control slab pumping and the realization by highway engineers that maintenance was a big time job.

"Slab pumping" first was noted and recognized several years earlier, but not until 1939 and 1940 did soaring traffic loads begin to take their terrific toll on highways so that this particular difficulty became a major maintenance problem. As the condition developed, particularly affecting the older pavements, it took only a short time to prove that mud-jacking and concrete replacement would not suffice.

Development by Trial and Error.—Again experimentation began. About 1942, Ohio began to experiment with the pumping of a low-penetration asphalt under the pavement instead of the soil-cement slurry to control slab pumping. The practice was further developed in other states and is now known as "undersealing." It is considered a highly successful method for controlling slab pumping.

Another operation, largely perfected in the early 1940's, was the upper decking of existing cold-mix bituminous surfaces. Previously, when a thin bituminous surface was to be renewed, it usually was scarified, and the old surface remixed and relaid. About 1939, however, a system of windrowing new materials on top of the existing surface, mixing them with bitumen, and spreading the mixture as an upper deck, was adopted—thus adding to the thickness and strength of the surface as well as retaining the compaction of the original road. This procedure has proved worthwhile and still is practiced in road-mix resurfacing.

Emphasis on reconstruction also increased during this period. Many of the older pavements broke down at a speed too fast for repairs by undersealing and full depth patching, and to such an extent that mere repair was not economical. Since lack of funds made wholesale replacement impossible, hot mixes were widely used to resurface old concrete pavements, with such work being done primarily on a contract basis with most satisfactory results.

It might well be noted that maintenance activities have fathered several highway operations which have since grown to such an extent that they are now conducted through individual bureaus or departments. Chief among these are equipment, safety, traffic control, roadside improvement, and highway planning—planning having started in most maintenance departments as a traffic

Fig. 5.—Compact But Widely Useful, This 1½-Ton Truck Essential for Road Maintenance in the Mechanized Era

count. Not to be overlooked, too, is the fact that workmen's compensation, now in force generally, had its beginning in highway departments as a benefit to maintenance men.

Today's Equipment.—The truck (Fig. 5), which is utilized for transporting men and materials, for pushing snow plows, and for pulling underbody blades, drags, light blade graders, pull mowers, and other maintenance units, is the most commonly used piece of maintenance equipment today. The forerunner of the truck was, of course, the team and wagon. An early instruction to maintenance men was to the effect that they would have to shoe their horses on their own time.

The next most popular unit is probably the motor grader, which is used for blading surfaces, cleaning ditches, trimming back slopes, mixing and laying bituminous patches and surfaces, and many other vital maintenance operations. Next in line of evolution after the split-log drag was the small-wheeled blade grader pulled by horses or oxen; then came the larger-wheeled grader pulled by tractors; and finally the modern self-propelled motor grader, a most efficient machine in the hands of a skilled operator (Fig. 6). Many, many other pieces of equipment, and small tools, far too numerous to mention, have been developed and are being used in the maintenance of today's highways.

Combination of Essentials.—Thus far attention has been given primarily to the part money, machinery, materials and methods have played in the history of highway maintenance during the past century. To end the story there would leave it just as incomplete as if a highway were built without bridges and culverts, or bridges and culverts were built without the highway.

Not to be overlooked is the all-important fact that highway maintenance

Fig. 6.—The Modern Method—a Fleet of Graders with Pneumatic Tires—Greatly Increasing Output and Economy

involves the proper blending of five factors, not four. In addition to money, machinery, materials, and methods, there must be men. To be more exact, it would be preferable to state there must be well-trained men, who enjoy their work.

During World War II, it was found necessary to substitute for critical materials. Likewise, one piece of machinery had to take the place of another that was not obtainable. That period of substitution proved the adage, as most highway engineers will agree, that: "There is no substitution that can be made for the knowledge and ability of a trained highway maintenance man."

Today a maintenance man must have a wide knowledge of the use of many materials such as asphalt, tar, portland cement, aggregates, and chlorides. He must have personal skill in the operation of many pieces of equipment such as the truck, motor grader, concrete mixer, bituminous distributor, power mowers, power shovels, and many other units. Last, but certainly not least, he must be able to manage men and meet the public.

The maintenance man, by the very nature of his work, comes in very close contact with the public. How well he does his job determines to a very great extent the attitude of the road user toward the entire highway program. Thus, despite the highly competent character of most maintenance organizations today, the greatest opportunity to advance further the effectiveness and efficiency of maintenance operations lies in the attention given to the human element.

Maintenance materials are, in general, selected in accordance with meticulously prepared specifications, tested for adequacy and compliance, and carefully placed on a road in their finished form. The same attention is given the selection, improvement, and operation of machinery.

World War I called limited attention to the value of men in maintaining highways, but that fact was overshadowed then, to a considerable extent at least, by the introduction of equipment that would actually replace some men. Further emphasis on the human element also was noted during the 1930's, but not until during and after World War II did the public begin to realize in full the true value of the men who maintain highways.

Human Attributes and Their Just Rewards.—Most highway organizations already have turned to the practice of selecting maintenance men on a basis of ability, both mentally and physically, and willingness to do their job. Furthermore, these men must be given proper on-the-job training, and good men must be retained on their jobs by establishing incentives that will encourage them to stay.

It must ever be remembered that the primary goal of highway maintenance is to provide smooth, safe roads at the most economical level possible. The future undoubtedly will bring machinery that will outdo that now available and materials undreamed of today. Also, no doubt methods far superior to those in use today will be devised. Proper blending of money, machinery, materials, methods, and men should bring about perfection in maintenance operations; nevertheless, it should always be remembered that new construction is the only cure for highway obsolescence.

Nevertheless, one thing is certain—the man who is doing the maintenance job today is identically the same, in physique, as the one who will do it tomorrow. Thus, the challenge to all who are charged in any way with maintaining the highways of tomorrow clearly lies in molding that man into a workman who is both capable and willing to do the job at hand. The potential for human development and improvement is unlimited.

The man first, of course, will want a fair day's pay for a fair day's work, comparable to that of his friend who is engaged in skilled labor elsewhere. He will want his job to be a steady one, not seasonal, with acceptable protection against physical injury and from the elements. Also he will want economic security—protection from unjust and indiscriminate discharge, along with provisions for retirement with some degree of security for his old age. The encouragement of individual initiative is a highly important item at all levels of operation in a maintenance organization. All personnel should have a thorough understanding of the assigned task and be busy doing that task. The entire organization of the maintenance operation, from the worker to the state maintenance engineer, should be composed of skilled and trained men.

Paper No. 2640

PRINCIPLES OF AMERICAN HIGHWAY DESIGN

By Dewitt C. Greer,[1] M. ASCE

Synopsis

As part of the celebration of a century of progress in engineering, it would seem most proper to evaluate the advances made in the design of highways and roads and then to examine the present status of the science, as well as to look ahead in an effort to project future trends. This review of the past, the present, and the future should yield a complete inventory of highway design as it appears to the highway engineers of today.

In attempting to review and comment on the characteristics of highway design for the past 100 years, much time can be saved by canceling out approximately the first 50 years. Since in this era roads provided only for the pedestrian and the horse-drawn vehicle, highway designers were few and far between and had no need to cope with traffic problems like those encountered in the past 50 years.

It would be interesting indeed to revert back to those early years of the century in order to reflect a bit on what engineers then did about problems of designing and building roads. Such a review, however, would only be for purposes of curiosity. It might cause a detour into the zone of ridicule of those pioneers who were, with a very few dollars, really trying to open trails for pedestrian and horse-drawn traffic.

Advent of the Automobile.—Actually, public attention was turned toward the necessity for more and better roads a short time before the development of the automobile. In 1895 there were only four registered motor vehicles in the United States, but in the early 1890's the country was in the midst of its first "good roads" movement. Bicyclists had organized to urge rural road improvement. The free delivery of rural mail created a further demand for better highways. During this period sand clay surfacing, concrete pavement, and brick rural roads were introduced. These pavements were built at the time the first automobile was being operated successfully in the United States.

Automobile registrations jumped to 8,000 in 1900, and to nearly 500,000 in

---

[1] State Highway Engr., Texas Highway Dept., Austin, Tex.

1910. During this period of the growing popularity of the horseless carriage, oil was first used as a dust palliative, and experimental bituminous concrete rural roads were built. By 1914 motor trucks with solid tires were damaging the thin macadam roads built for wagons and light automobiles. The question naturally arose: What to do to save the roads from destruction—a question which today has a familiar ring.

The construction of roads in the United States by technical engineering processes appears to have begun in 1912 with the first post road construction appropriation, followed by the 1916 Federal Aid Road Act, the "kickoff" legislation for the current method of federal aid. At first, roads were built within existing rights of way, using alinements and grades developed for the original horse-drawn vehicles. This procedure resulted in sharp curves, steep grades, and improvements within as little as 30 ft of right of way. A 15-ft metal surfaced road with narrow or no shoulders and deep ditches was not uncommon and was accepted design. By 1920 pavements generally were 16 ft wide; and, as the need for greater widths became apparent, the average slowly increased to 18 ft in 1925 and to 20 ft by 1930.

Quarter Century of Advancement.—The United States then entered the era of the past 25 years during which the greatest progress in highway design has occurred. The country became conscious of the geometrics of highway design— namely, alinement, curvature, both horizontal and vertical, width of right of way, sight distance, and other basic factors that it was realized were becoming out-moded even before the road was completed.

Engineers saw the crown width expand, and surfaced shoulders appear on the horizon. Then, probably most important of all, they began to realize the need of structural strength in roadway surfaces. Also, during the middle of this past era constructive thinkers in highway design started the pioneering movement of modern times toward the controlled access or freeway type of facility (Fig. 1). During the past 10 years highway design progress has moved ahead by great strides in a commendable effort to keep pace with traffic demands.

Basis of Detail Design.—For a moment the present status of progress in highway design should be considered carefully. In the first place, the highway designer of 1952 finds himself involved in everything from the lowly yet important farm-to-market or secondary road to the multimillion dollar, controlled access expressway. Certain basic characteristics are applicable to both of these extremes. Volume and speed, size, and weight of traffic must determine the fundamental design regardless of the designation that may be applied to the type of facility to be constructed. Names are for public consumption and identification but should in no way affect the designer. After weighing carefully the type of traffic to be served, both present and future, he usually develops his designs somewhat according to the following general plan:

A design year in the future is selected, the year usually depending on the permanency of the location in question. From the volume and characteristics of the traffic ("characteristics" meaning the type of vehicle, percentage of trucks, and speeds), the designer evolves horizontal geometrics, design speed, and con-trolling horizontal and vertical curvature. For highways in excess of 4,000 vehicles per day a divided four lane highway is indicated.

In working with traffic volumes, the thirtieth highest hour during the year is normally used as the appropriate criterion, since traffic then usually amounts to about 10% to 15% of the daily volume. Assuming that the design hour for

Fig. 1.—A Modern Highway for Modern Times—The Gulf Freeway Serving Heavy Traffic for 50 Miles Between Houston and Galveston, Tex.

the design year shows 500 vehicles, the designer would conclude that a four lane highway was necessary, with two 24-ft divided pavements, 4-ft shoulders on the inside, and 8-ft to 10-ft shoulders on the outside. The outside shoulder width would depend on the height of fill and the steepness of side slopes—the steeper the slopes the wider the shoulders and vice versa. Such a road would require a right of way wide enough to accommodate a frontage road for property service and partial or full control of access, these facilities to be built at once or in the future as the need demands.

Assuming further that a 60-mile per hr design speed had been selected, the designer would use a desirable maximum horizontal curvature of about 2° with an absolute maximum in mountainous terrain of 6°. Desirable and absolute maximum gradients would be about 5% and 6%, respectively, but possibly about 7% on short tangents in mountainous or rough country. Nonpassing sight distance—defined as the distance from the driver's eye to an object 4 in. high when first sighted on the pavement—would not be less than 475 ft. Had this been a two lane road, passing sight distance would have had to be considered; and in view of the 60-mile per hr design speed it would have been not less than about 2,300 ft.

The Pavement Itself.—The determination of structural design is not quite so simple, but the development and improvement of rational procedures have been the objectives of continuing world-wide research for several years. In modern flexible pavement design, the structure frequently consists of at least four layers: Subgrade (or foundation soil), subbase, base, and bituminous surface, with strengths increasing in that order. A sample of each of these components is subjected to rigid testing, after which each layer is assigned a thickness that will be sufficient to protect the weaker layers below from the greatest of the anticipated wheel loads.

In the case of rigid pavements, it is important that the materials immediately under the slab be of the granular type which, when saturated, will resist ejection, or "pumping," through the joints or at the edges of the pavement. The thickness of the slab itself is determined from the anticipated wheel loads and the bearing value of the underlying material, as well as from the strength and elasticity of the concrete.

Modern Trends for Bridges.—Bridge design in 1952, a specialized branch of highway design, generally follows trends that lead to the following typical characteristics:

The designer's aim is to eliminate, or to minimize in so far as practicable, any sense of confinement or constriction in the free movement of traffic approaching and crossing a bridge and to blend the bridge structure into the road so skilfully that traffic will proceed at the same uniform, undiminished speed across bridges as on other sections of the highway. Overhead bracing and truss members which extend above the roadway level are avoided by placing the supporting members below the bridge floor on all structures except those with such great span length and underclearance restrictions that this treatment is impossible or prohibitively expensive. In other words, through truss spans, which give a definite impression of restriction, are eliminated from consideration for the average highway bridge, and I-beam spans, deck girder spans, deck truss spans, or spans of the rigid frame type are used instead.

On short bridges the full roadway width, shoulder line to shoulder line, is carried across the structure. This treatment, although desirable for all bridges, becomes prohibitively expensive on bridges more than 100 ft to 200 ft long. On these longer structures the full, effective travel width is maintained by setting the bridge curb back 2 ft or more beyond the edge of the pavement of the roadway approach and by using curbs of sufficient width to place the bridge rail well back from the edge of the travel lane. Railings are built at lower heights than in the old horse-and-buggy days, which makes for better visibility and further elimination of constrictive effect.

The separate simple span units of yesterday have largely been replaced by multiple span continuous units. The advantages of continuous unit construction are greater economy, increased rigidity, and smoother riding surfaces resulting from the reduction in the number of floor joints.

The trend in architectural treatment is to streamline the bridge structure by emphasizing the horizontal lines of supporting members and the railing and by eliminating complicated detail. Extraneous treatments and adornments of the gingerbread type are avoided and pleasing appearance is achieved through symmetry, simplicity of outline, and proper proportioning of the component parts of the structure. In short, the good bridge designer does not conceal the true structural outline of the bridge by covering it with bric-à-brac, but attains true beauty through emphasizing the structural outline in a symmetrical and harmonious manner.

Looking to the Future.—To visualize just what the future holds in the way of highway design involves a gaze into the crystal ball. The highway engineer most enjoys discussing, designing, and building roads and structures of the greatest magnitude, almost bordering on the monumental in appearance and utility; nevertheless, it is now and always will be his duty to remain adaptable enough to take the funds available and the traffic to be served and, with these limitations, to design a road or structure commensurate with the need. Thus, his duties will include work on both the simple secondary road and the monumental "skyway" of 1972.

It is not difficult to imagine the strides that highway design will make within the next few years in the elimination of all possible friction between opposing lanes of traffic. The motor vehicle accident toll must be held to a minimum; the public is going to demand it. In turn, highway designers are going to be called on to bear their burden of responsibility, and they will not fail. However, all motor vehicle accidents will never be eliminated as long as a human being is under the steering wheel.

The trend of present and future highway design toward the separation of opposing directional traffic will, to a large extent, free the driver from fear of the careless and thoughtless acts of other drivers and concentrate responsibility and authority on one driver and one motor vehicle, thus bringing the responsibility for accidents home to the driver himself and effecting material reductions in present and future accident trends. This elimination of traffic friction is going to be expensive, but it can be done. The divided highway is almost a number one "must" in highway design.

In the near future research men and chemical engineers will be needed in highway design to assist the designer with the complicated molecular chemical and physical characteristics of the soils. The next 25 years will produce a method for taking the soils as found and, through atomic or chemical treatment, changing them into an entirely different type of material which can readily be adapted to the building of good roadways that will render reasonable and substantial service to the wheels of future traffic.

Expanded Ideas of Design.—Likewise, the next 25 years will see substantial progress made on the completion of the heavy-duty interstate system of highways throughout the United States, as well as on highways in many other parts of the world. Some reasonably positive design factors for loads should result. Thus, highway designers will be given badly needed relief from the feeling that their designs might not have reasonable longevity. When a heavy-duty highway system for automobile transportation is completed connecting the metropolitan areas of this country, it will be possible for roads to be divided into groups with carefully calculated load characteristics for each and every group. This classification should be conducive to rather spectacular advances in highway design and a much needed remodeling of the economy of public road construction.

Bridge designers in the future will bring to automotive transportation the answers to the psychological width restriction of the hand rail and to the rapidly approaching thrombosis of the bascule, or lift bridge, operation. At the same time they will produce the ultimate in esthetics in that most graceful and spectacular part of highway design, the bridge.

The challenge to highway design in the future is wide open. Its possibilities are unlimited. The young engineer of today is on the threshold of the greatest era of progress in highway design yet experienced by mankind. The gray hair of the highway design engineer of 1952, backed by his half century of contribution to his fellow man, should be recognized with a crown of glory bearing the inscription of a job well done.

AMERICAN SOCIETY OF CIVIL ENGINEERS

Founded November 5, 1852

TRANSACTIONS

Paper No. 2641

THE GROWTH AND STATUS OF HIGHWAY TRANSPORT

By B. B. Bachman [1]

Synopsis

The advent of motor vehicles emancipated the individual from his dependence on mass transportation. Similarly, motor trucks have supported this independence by making possible the rapid, sure delivery of the necessities. This paper discusses the various aspects of the trucking industry and its influence on the American way of life. The development of the truck and its integral components are discussed in detail.

Introduction

Transportation is a service that is vitally necessary; and, of all the common forms of transportation, the type that moves over the highways is the most important and serves the nation most intimately.

The accuracy of the famous statement that, if a man makes a better mousetrap, a path will be made to his door although he lives in the forest, may be debated. There are instances in which merit has not been recognized or rewarded; but it is certain that, if the reward is to come, the path must first be made. An essential element in getting supplies to and from any home and many—probably most—business establishments is highway and street transportation.

In the primitive state, man can satisfy, or at least provide for, the basic necessities of life with materials that he can carry or drag overland and by water. As he advances in the scale of civilization and his standard of living rises, man reaches out to other villages, nations, and continents to obtain the materials and products required to support that higher scale. To accomplish this goal, an adequate transportation system for delivery of the commodities that will provide the better scale of living must be available.

Mechanical Transport

Early Travel.—Until early in the nineteenth century, the winds on the water and the beast of burden on land were the sole aids to man's own muscles in getting

---

[1] Vice Pres. of Eng., The Autocar Co., Ardmore, Pa.

from place to place. Then, after the Napoleonic wars ended at Waterloo, the steam engine was harnessed to ships and vehicles. The result was a strange paradox. Here on the North American continent, and particularly in the United States, the railroad made it possible to move out of the coastal areas, into and across the plains, and finally to span the continent. This accomplishment represented a great expansive movement, not only dispersing the people of the United States but also attracting immigration from abroad.

On the other hand, rail transportation was a powerful factor in promoting large centers of population and industry. This was so because industry had to be located near siding facilities to bring materials in and take finished products away. At the same time, the workmen had to live sufficiently near the shop so they could get there by horsecars or on foot, within a reasonable amount of time.

The elevated railroad, electric cars, and subways, in turn, made it increasingly possible to extend the distance between the home and the shop or office. The first move toward individual transportation, the bicycle, used the muscles of the passenger for propulsion. Nevertheless, it was relatively cheap and extended the limits of travel materially.

Appearance of the Automobile.—Then, just at the turn of the century, the internal combustion engine reached a stage of development that made its use in the automobile possible. At this point the emancipation of the individual from dependence on mass transportation became possible. Instead of having to live on or near a railroad or a car line, the individual is kept in touch with all the world by a street wide enough to permit the passage of a car. The resulting freedom of movement has exploded the big cities into the suburbs.

This movement could not have been sustained nor could it have grown to its present proportions unless the passenger car, which started it, had not soon been followed by the introduction of the delivery car and truck. The materials for building new homes, fuel, food, furniture, and all the necessities of modern life are transported by the truck. Without it, many of these communities could not have come into being or, if they had, could not have flourished or survived.

Although the first automobiles were passenger vehicles, and as a matter of fact were looked on as strictly for pleasure or sport, their practical implications gradually became evident. To this end, the Ford model T undoubtedly contributed in no small measure. However, from the earliest days many of the pioneers of the automotive industry thought of the possibilities of the delivery car or truck. Alexander Winton is credited with a delivery wagon in 1898; an Autocar delivery truck was built by L. S. Clarke in 1899; and the first White truck was produced in 1900 (Fig. 1). The White truck, a light vehicle powered by a steam engine, was delivered to the Denver Dry Goods Company of Denver, Colo., in 1901. The Mack Brothers began experimenting with motor trucks and buses, and in 1900 delivered the first Mack to Harris and Maguire, bus concessionaires in Prospect Park, Brooklyn, N. Y.

The first automobiles were literally horseless carriages. In like manner, the first trucks were horseless wagons. Although the Mack, which was built in 1900, had a power plant located under a hood, in general the Rapid, White, Reliance, International Harvester, and Autocar followed the practice of locating the engine under the seat thus preserving the general appearance of the wagons of that day, minus the horse (Fig. 2).

FIG. 1.—EARLY DELIVERY TRUCK (1899)

FIG. 2.—ENGINE-UNDER-THE-SEAT TRUCK (1910)

Truck Types.—The 1911 Diamond T is an appropriate example of an early departure toward conventional automobile lines. This trend has continued through the years with development roughly parallel to that of the passenger car (Fig. 3). The enclosing of the driver's compartment to provide shelter from inclement weather soon followed, after which lines were refined and proportions modified. Eventually the truck became, if not a thing of beauty, at least less ungainly.

In the truck field, there were definite reasons for the existence of the type that

Fig. 3.—Early Conventional Design (1911)

has come to be known as the "engine-under-the-seat" or the "cab-over-engine" model. For a given length of body, the wheelbase of a cab-over-engine truck can be made up to 54 in. shorter than the conventional type. As the turning circle is approximately four times the wheelbase, this reduction in wheelbase results in a turning circle about 18 ft smaller than a conventional type having the same body length. In city traffic, this feature is desirable.

It is also possible to obtain a larger proportion of the body and pay-load weight on the front axle without an objectionably long wheelbase. With single tires on the front axle and dual tires on the rear axle (all the same size), the desirable weight distribution is one third on the front axle and two thirds on the rear axle. Such a distribution is possible with the cab-over-engine type, but in a conventional truck about 28% is the maximum load that can be obtained on the front axle while still maintaining reasonable length. For these reasons there has been, over the past 20 years, a return to the earlier form of construction, using more modern styling (Fig. 4).

After the reappearance of this vehicle, many people in the industry thought that it would replace the conventional vehicle entirely. Although this prediction has not been fulfilled, there are many cab-over-engine trucks in all sizes.

Purely as a personal opinion, it is the writer's feeling that this vehicle has its principal field of usefulness wherever trucks are required in relatively short haul work involving considerable operation in congested areas. There are many factors, such as regulations governing over-all length, which create pressure for the use of this type to the sacrifice of the more desirable characteristics offered by the longer conventional vehicle. This opinion may be violently rejected by other competent authorities.

INFLUENCES ON TRUCK TRANSPORTATION

Adequate Roads.—The degree to which a car or truck can function is limited only by the dependability of the vehicle and the extent and character of the roads. The advent of the bicycle in the latter part of the nineteenth century awakened

FIG. 4.—MODERN CAB-OVER-ENGINE TRUCK (1952)

the need for better roads. When the automobile was introduced, the desire to go places and see things pushed the idea of good roads along.

Events such as the Glidden tours provided publicity that helped to make the need for more and better roads known to the nation. During the early years of the twentieth century, as the industry grew and the number of cars multiplied, road building was started as a local movement and rapidly grew to a national program. Until World War I, it was impossible to use trucks except in and around towns and cities. The inadequate roads, the solid tires used on all trucks, and the limitations of the capacity and ability of the vehicles combined to make intercity highway transport impossible. During World War I, the need for assistance to the railroads became painfully evident. As a result, when the war ended, an attempt was made at once to place roads on a national scale.

The Lincoln Highway became a symbol around which the people rallied. In

1913, a motor caravan traveled from Indianapolis, Ind., to San Francisco, Calif. In 1919, the Army sent a motor convoy from the initial milestone of the federal road system to San Francisco.

These early developments served to make it known that except for a comparatively limited area in the northeastern section of the country comprising parts of New England, New York, Pennsylvania, New Jersey, Delaware, and Maryland, there were no highways adequate for either passenger or freight haulage. Then a miracle happened. Almost as though Aladdin had rubbed his lamp, road building started all over the nation, until today it is almost impossible to find the kind of roads the people were happy to ride on 30 years ago.

The thousands of miles of modern highway that have resulted from this program have pulled the nation out of the mud, but have not solved all problems. Great as the building program was, it was interrupted by World War II. The enforced limitation of labor and material and increased costs have prevented resumption of the prewar tempo, and have adversely affected maintenance operations. These factors, coupled with the tremendous increase in the number of all types of vehicles, have overloaded the highway system to such a degree that in many sections of the country the situation is critical.

The highest type of highway constructed to date is typified by the Pennsylvania and New Jersey turnpikes. That these two roads have filled a need is evident by their great use, not only by passenger cars, but also by trucks. There is a divided opinion as to the soundness of the policy of building toll roads, but this paper will not discuss the merits of the differing points of view. They have served the purpose of demonstrating the benefits that can be derived from such features as wide traffic lanes, divided lanes, limited grades, large radii of curvature, long sight distances, and limited access.

Tires.—The rubber tire was a prerequisite to a successful road vehicle. The first tires used on trucks were solid bands of rubber vulcanized onto a steel rim. This rim, in turn, was pressed onto a wheel made of wood with a steel felloe band shrunk on to hold the spoke and felloe assembly in place. The wheel assembly was provided with a cast malleable iron or steel hub. For the first 15 years, various types and sizes of solid and cushion tires were developed and used.

The first type of tire had a trapezoidal cross section and a perfectly plain tread. Modifications to this basic type were made by increasing the height of the section and by providing a tread pattern designed to improve traction and to allow the rubber to flow so as to give better cushioning against road shocks. The ultimate in this development was to core out the section, thus providing further shock absorption. At best, these tires provided inadequate protection against road shock and poor traction and life. There was, moreover, a very definite limit to the speed at which they could be operated.

These tires were made in a variety of sizes. One list[2] shows a range from 32×3, rated at 1,000-lb capacity, up to 40×14, rated at 12,000-lb capacity. The first number of the size designated (32×3) in this instance is the nominal outside diameter of the tire, and the second number is the nominal width of the cross section. The largest size reported[3] is 44×16, and the rating would probably have

---

[2] "Handbook," S. A. E., New York, N. Y., 1921.
[3] "Notes on the Development of the Truck Tire," by Earle C. Zimmerman, Firestone Tire and Rubber Co., Akron, Ohio, July 2, 1952.

been 14,000 lb. In many cases, preference was shown for mounting two tires—
40×7 instead of a single 40×14. Although the rating of the two tires was not
equal to that of the single tires, many users felt that better service was obtained.

Sometime around 1910, pneumatic tires were introduced. The initial units
were used on vehicles of 3,000-lb to 4,000-lb pay-load capacity and gross weights
of less than 10,000 lb. The size used was 36×6 or 38×6. The latter size
was developed in 1908[3] for use on fire trucks. Early delivery trucks were equipped
with single tires on all wheels. For the limited mileage of those days and on small
vehicles in delivery service, these tires furnished an acceptable improvement over
solid tires. Serious work on pneumatic tires for trucks began in 1914–1916.[3,4] The
introduction of cord fabric and its demonstrated superiority to the older square
woven fabric was a start.

During World War I, dual wheels for pneumatic tires were produced by the
Michelin Company in France and used on trucks in the French Army. A set of
the dual wheels was applied to a Locomobile used by Gen. John J. Pershing as a
staff car. The Budd Company acquired rights to the Michelin dual disk wheel in
1920, and gives credit to the White Motor Company as having been its first customer in 1921. This marked the beginning of the practical use of pneumatic tires
on heavy vehicles.

The tire sizes that were available at this time ranged from 34×5, rated
at 1,700 lb with 80-lb inflation pressure, to 48×12, rated at 8,500 lb at 140-lb
inflation pressure. It will be noted that the diameter of the tire seat was 24 in.

For several years, the merits of the large single tire as compared to those of
dual tires were considered. This evaluation resulted in the universal adoption of
dual tires for highway vehicles. Although the movement in this direction was
started by the introduction of the disk wheel, the cast-type wheel, suitable for
the application of demountable rims, was not far behind. The next development
was the low-pressure or balloon-type tire, around 1925. These tires are designated
by the nominal cross section and the tire seat diameter, as 6.00-20. The range of
sizes available starts at 6.00-17, with a rated capacity of 1,250 lb at 50-lb inflation
pressure, up to 14.00-24, rated at 8,525 lb when inflated to 80-lb pressure. Legal
provision for a maximum vehicle width of 96 in., which is prevalent in a large
number of states, limits the largest tire in common use to the 11.00 size.

There are three tire seat diameters in use—20 in., 22 in., and 24 in. It is
difficult to understand why this condition developed and still more difficult to explain why it persists.

In recent years, a trend in favor of the 22-in. diameter has developed; but, because of the cost of changing existing equipment and the desire for interchangeability between tractor and trailer, it does not seem probable that the 20-in. and
24-in. sizes will soon be entirely replaced.

The service life of pneumatic tires has increased almost continuously since they
were first introduced (Fig. 5). Between 1915 and 1935, there was a rapid and continuous improvement in the service life of tires, made possible by the use of new
cord fabric, changes in the compounding of the rubber, the adoption of lower inflation pressures, and also better roads. In recent years, the adoption of rayon

    [4] "Development and Use of Pneumatic Tires for Trucks," by W. E. Shively, Goodyear Tire and
Rubber Co., Akron, Ohio, 1950.

cords has brought about further improvement. First adopted in 1937, rayon cords came into extensive use during World War II, and now are utilized for practically all truck tires. Nylon cord has been tried but apparently its higher cost is prohibitive. Wire cords have also been used, having been introduced by the Michelin Company in Europe. There seems to be considerable difference in opinion as to the merits of this type, particularly on the highway.

Accurate data on current mileage are not available. It can be seen that in 1935 the curve was showing a tendency to gain less rapidly than it had 10 years earlier. The dotted line that has been added in an attempt to extrapolate the curve is frankly a guess, based on the known inclination for curves of this charac-

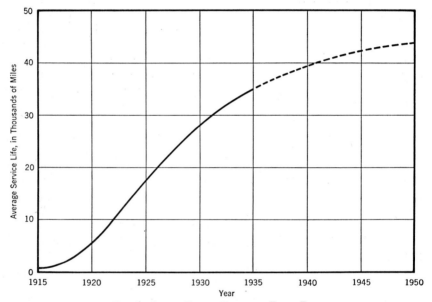

FIG. 5.—SERVICE LIFE OF PNEUMATIC TRUCK TIRES

ter to become asymptotic. The value of 44,000 miles is probably not far wrong for present-day experience where the best operating practice is followed.

The statement has been made that the number of tires sold in 1949 was about the same as in 1941.[4] In Fig. 6, it is shown that the total number of vehicles in 1949 was 8,000,000; and in 1941, 5,000,000, or an increase of 60%. There is no doubt that the total annual mileage has increased, at least as great an amount. Thus, it could be estimated that tire life had increased by 60%. Undoubtedy, this is not correct because many other factors make such a method of estimating inaccurate. Among other things, the scarcity of new tires during the war served to produce greatly improved methods of recapping, and this practice is being more generally followed than before. However, the data are significant in showing that improvements in tires are still continuing.

DEVELOPMENT OF HIGHWAY TRANSPORT

With roads coming into existence that would permit high-speed, long-distance operation, and tires available that could cushion the shock for both the vehicle and the road, the era of modern highway transport began. The earliest trucks were essentially horseless wagons. Later, the truck followed the passenger car in locating the engine under a hood. However, the single vehicle was the predominant type. As with many innovations, the use of a third axle was first adopted on the west coast. This area has been a leader in providing relatively liberal regulations for highway users. Of course the incentive for using trucks was great. The railroads either ran east and west or hugged the coast line—leaving the large valley

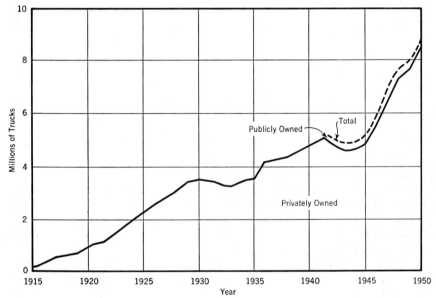

FIG. 6.—TOTAL NUMBER OF TRUCKS IN THE UNITED STATES

between the Coast Range and the Sierras dependent on highways—and the great amount of agricultural products that rewarded irrigation had to be brought to the markets. At the same time, fabulous stores of petroleum were discovered. All these factors, together with the native energy of the people of that region, resulted in the trial of many things. Here the six-cylinder engine was first used. The initial trials were made by converting passenger cars into buses to carry sightseers into the great scenic areas. Dual pneumatic tires and then dual axles were tried. At first, the extra axle was little more than an appendage that had slight practical value, but the idea was sound and soon developed into practical construction that spread into the East.

Multiple Unit Vehicles.—During this period, which witnessed many beginnings, tractors and semitrailers made their appearance. The Columbia Terminals Company of St. Louis, Mo., started experimenting with this combination in 1919, and by 1924 had converted from horse-drawn to mechanical transport. The possibility of keeping a separable power unit busy while the load-carrying unit was being loaded and unloaded provided evident and profitable economies.

The trailer manufacturers who began to develop this market had an erroneous idea of the basic value of their product. A slogan, stating that a vehicle could pull more than it could carry and citing the ability of the horse in this respect, was obviously one of those half truths that so often cloud the real facts. Although it was true that some excess horsepower and torque were provided to meet the demands of grade and road conditions, it was also true that the capabilities of the engines of that period were inadequate to provide the power for the most efficient operation of even a single vehicle.

The big and impelling reasons that promoted the development and use of the tractor-semitrailers were: (1) The flexibility in operation made possible by the separable power and load-carrying units; and (2) the ability to use longer and more capacious bodies than could be mounted on a single vehicle.

Advantage (1) is so obvious that it is scarcely necessary to elaborate: To move a truck around in terminal areas with what amounts to the equivalent of a shifting engine, to service the power unit without the space requirement for a big body mounted on it, and to send a spare tractor to pick up a box on the road when a failure occurs in the original power unit—all can be readily understood and appreciated.

Advantage (2) is equally important. The articulation provided by the fifth wheel reduces the space needed to maneuver the vehicle and makes it practicable to turn around and to turn corners in city streets and in traffic that would be impossible for a single vehicle with a body only a fraction of the length of the combination. The longest bodies mounted on a single vehicle rarely exceed 20 ft, whereas many trailers are 33 ft and 35 ft long.

Another very important factor is the ability to provide additional axles. In a single vehicle, three axles have been the maximum number generally used. It is true that four-axle designs have been built and found useful in military and off-road operations, and several designs have been produced in England and Europe, principally for export to colonial areas. These have been relatively few in number; and the mechanical complications in providing for the equalization of loading and the articulation in the front bogie, together with the need for provision for steering four wheels, are difficult and complicated, even though not insoluble.

On the other hand, a two-axle or even a three-axle tractor to which a two-axle semitrailer is attached provides four or five axles in a two-unit combination that is relatively easy to construct with designs that are, by comparison, much simpler. Therefore, it is not difficult to see why, for long-distance highway hauling, the tractor-semitrailer combination has become the accepted unit for all but a very few special cases.

Relative Growth.—With all these developments sprouting up, the middle of the second decade of the twentieth century witnessed the start of highway transport on a large scale and over long distances. It began with perishable and valuable commodities and has continued until the current statistics are almost fantastic.

Truck sales to the domestic and export markets and the totals are shown in

Fig. 7.[5] Here, the rise from 1921 to the depression years is plain. The drop from 1929 to 1932 was followed by an equally steep climb to 1937. The real jump came when civilian production was restored in 1945.

The cumulative effect of these sales on total vehicles in service is shown in Fig. 6.[5] In 1919, at the close of World War I, there were about 900,000 trucks in use. In 1951, there were 8,775,000 with 375,000 publicly-owned vehicles in addition—or a total of 9,150,000, more than half the trucks in the world.

According to the latest data, the population of the United States is 151,132,000, and that of the world is 2,400,000,000. This country has an abundant supply of highway transport as well as of many other services. The largest number of

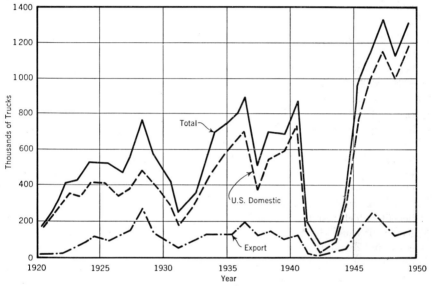

FIG. 7.—ANNUAL TRUCK SALES

trucks[5] (2,300,000) are owned and operated by farmers. They serve in the production and distribution of food and other farm products. In ten out of sixty-three major markets, all livestock is delivered by truck. More than half of this number receives 90% or more of all shipments by truck, and the average for all sixty-three is 75%.[5] Half of the vegetables and fruits shipped out of Florida is hauled by truck.[5] There are 1,000,000 trucks operated by for-hire carriers; 360,000 are used by industrial establishments; 425,000 serve the needs of wholesale stores; and 625,000 are used in retail delivery.[5]

Out of 11,100,000,000 tons of freight hauled in 1949, 75% was carried in trucks. Total ton-miles amounted to 1,146,000,000,000, or an average haul of 100 miles. The truck share of this was 122,000,000,000 ton-miles, an average of 15 miles.[5] The number of people specifically employed to drive these vehicles is 5,137,000. When the production and sales and service personnel are added, the total is more than 5,500,000.[5]

---

[5] "Motor Truck Facts," Automobile Mfrs. Assn., Inc., Detroit, Mich., 1951.

Although these data are stupendous, they are, like all statistics, dry and un-interesting. To arrive at an understanding of the real meaning of highway trans-portation, it is necessary to exercise the imagination and visualize the myriad points of origin and of destination between which these vehicles are traveling every minute of every day. When this is done, some comprehension can be ob-tained of the degree of individual service that is provided by highway transport.

Before mechanical highway transport became available, anyone who was lo-cated more than a very few miles from a seaport, navigable stream, or railroad was isolated and dependent on his own resources for everything not obtainable in a very circumscribed area. Today, the highway and the truck have made it possi-ble to burst out of these limitations, and have integrated every place in which it is desirable to live into one community.

The number of trucks in use is 17% of the total of all motor vehicles in the United States. In 1950, the total of special motor vehicle taxes was \$4,354,-033,000.00, and of the sum \$1,201,532,000.00, or 27.6% was paid by this 17%. A large part was for gasoline taxes which amounted to \$1,667,229,000.00, and of this \$435,000,000.00, or 26% was paid by trucks.[6]

All other forms of transportation thus far have been limited to travel be-tween fixed terminals. Therefore, in order to get the articles of commerce to the loading point and from the unloading point to the ultimate destination, auxiliary transport must be provided. The time consumed in transfer from one form to another comprises such a large part of the total movement time that the elimina-tion of this delay results in a great saving. The benefits of this saving are most evident in small-size shipments.

A most important aspect of the flexibility of truck transport is shown by the benefits which result from the increase in turnover of inventory that can be ef-fected. Because shipments can be scheduled and completed with such great fa-cility and certainty, banks of material needed to insure against interruption of operations can be reduced from weeks to days.

THE ENGINE

Development.—The internal combustion engine has been the nucleus around which the automobile and truck have evolved. There were two other essentials to making a successful machine that fortunately became available at the same time: A liquid fuel having the properties of being relatively easily vaporized and of containing a large amount of energy, and a material that could be used in a pneumatic tire. When crude oil was discovered in Pennsylvania and a refining in-dustry was created to produce a better illuminant than the candle, the way was opened for the production of gasoline and fuel oil to power cars, trucks, buses, locomotives, farm equipment, and many other vehicles. Likewise, when Charles Goodyear in England discovered the process of vulcanizing rubber, a start had been made toward manufacturing tires that would cushion road shocks and pro-vide a material having a high natural adhesion on the road.

The way in which processes for producing fuel of various and desirable char-acteristics have developed and the work of Charles F. Kettering, Hon. M. ASCE,

---

[6] "Automobile Facts and Figures," Automobile Mfrs. Assn., Inc., Detroit, Mich., 31st Ed., 1951.

and Thomas Midgley, Jr., in learning about the causes and nature of detonation are stories of immense interest and importance. The same is true with regard to the development of the tire. However, these subjects, important as they are, do not properly come within the scope of this paper.

The truck engine, however, even though it is basically similar to the passenger car engine, has required sufficiently different design to meet the intended service that a study of its characteristics is desirable. The earliest engines had two or four cylinders. The speed was limited to 1,400 rpm, or 1,800 rpm at the most. Compression ratios were around 4 to 1, and the power output was low, as was the fuel efficiency.

Even up to 1917, when a group of specialists was recruited by the Society of Automotive Engineers and worked under the control of the Quartermaster Corps and later the Motor Transport Corps, slow speed and moderate performance were characteristics of the engine developed for the class B military truck. After World War I, the advent of pneumatic tires and the road improvement, already commented on, stirred the idea of intercity hauling and the need for more power and better performance became apparent. It soon became evident that the inherent limitations of the four-cylinder engine, in both displacement and speed, made it necessary to take a new look. At about this time, in the passenger car field, engines with six, eight, twelve, and even sixteen cylinders were being produced. This trend gave added impetus to the development of new engines. Not long after 1920, some old six-cylinder passenger car engines were modified and put into trucks, but their use principally showed up weaknesses that had to be corrected to provide a desirable truck engine.

In 1925, Mack produced a six-cylinder truck engine, and by the early 1930's the move to six cylinders was in full swing. This type has been used almost to the exclusion of any other for the past 20 years. Ford, with its eight-cylinder V-type engine, has been almost, if not entirely, alone in the use of anything other than a six-cylinder engine. The Le Roi Company has produced an eight-cylinder V-type engine of 540-cu in. displacement for the Autocar Company, and vehicles with this engine have been offered just recently.

The six-cylinder engines which were built at first had about a 500-cu in. displacement, and at that time would produce about 100 hp at a speed of 2,000 rpm. Since then, engines as large as 1,000 cu in. have been built, developing up to 300 hp at about 2,200 rpm.

However, in the middle 1930's, these larger engines were not available; and, if they had been, there would have been considerable resistance to their use because of the cost of fuel. There was an insistent demand for more power, particularly on the west coast where gross combination weights of 72,000 lb were permitted. Also, in this area, many long and severe grades were encountered. The demand was met by the Cummins Engine Company with a six-cylinder diesel engine of 677-cu in. displacement that developed 150 hp at 1,800 rpm. Several things occurred at about the same time to make the introduction of this engine auspicious. First, there was the demand for more power to provide better performance. Second, there was available a large supply of fuel oil of adequate quality at a very low price compared to gasoline. Third, the lower specific fuel consumption of the engine gave added economy.

The first installations were effected as a field change by replacing the gasoline engines with which the vehicles were equipped. Soon vehicles with these engines were offered by several companies, and for some years this type was used almost to the exclusion of anything else on the west coast. Naturally, these exceptionally favorable conditions did not last. The demand created for fuel oil in trucks, together with the industrial development and railroad use combined to raise prices. Also, it was inevitable that the absence of a tax on fuel oil for highway use would soon be noted and changed.

Curves of horsepower (Fig. 8), of indicated mean effective pressure (Fig. 9), and of specific fuel consumption (Fig. 10) give graphic illustrations of engine improvements. With diesel engines which, as has been stated, were first put into trucks around 1930, the story has been much the same. The improvements in

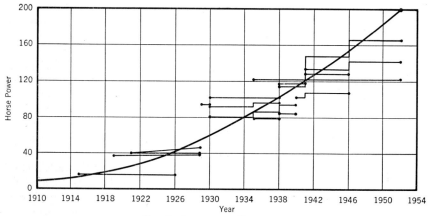

FIG. 8.—INCREASE IN HORSEPOWER

materials have played an equally important role in developing the performance and dependability of this type. Starting with an advantage over the gasoline engine, in that the fuel consumption was lower, the diesel was handicapped somewhat in the greater weight and cost of the original engines.

Power-to-Weight Ratio.—One of the big problems of the industry is the amount of power required. In the early days, when single units were the predominant type, with the limitations of solid tires and poor roads, even the low horsepower of the engines then available still produced an acceptable performance as measured against the standard of that day. When roads were improved, pneumatic tires arrived, and long-distance hauling was started, the question of how much power should be provided became very important.

Beginning in the middle 1920's and coincident with the introduction of six-cylinder engines, the trend to more power developed and seemed to be here to stay. The depression of 1929 and the early 1930's brought a change. With the introduction of tractor-semitrailer combinations, there began a period during which light tractors with moderate powered engines came into use. These tractors were originally modifications of the smaller trucks made in large volume and, consequently, were relatively low in price. Naturally, the builders of these vehicles

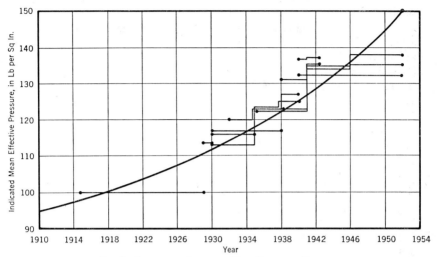

FIG. 9.—INCREASE IN INDICATED MEAN EFFECTIVE PRESSURE

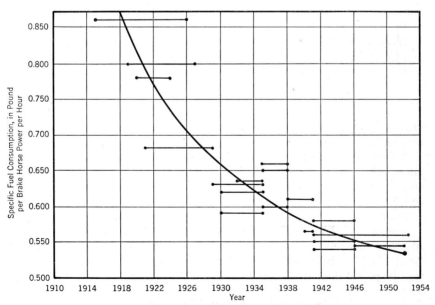

FIG. 10.—DECREASE IN SPECIFIC FUEL CONSUMPTION

exploited the new market. Although the trials showed that there was an area in which the tractors were successful and practical, they also served to point out the desirable features inherent in better performance potentials.

As a result, around 1940, a trend toward larger and more powerful tractors started and is still continuing. Fig. 11 shows the general trend[5] quite clearly. Prior to 1946, the classification was different from that for the period between 1946 and 1951, but there is enough similarity to make a reasonably good comparison. Vehicles up to and including 14,000 lb in gross weight are probably all single units used in retail delivery, on farms, and for similar services. Consider-

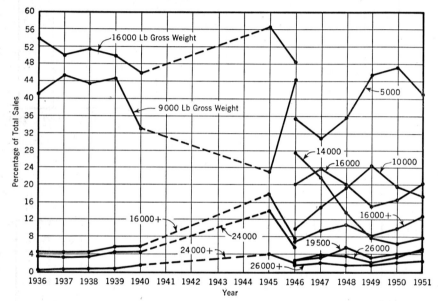

FIG. 11.—TRUCK SALES

able numbers of trucks from 16,000 lb in gross weight and more are used as tractors, and the proportion increases as the gross weight goes up.

This trend toward larger vehicles is a natural reflection of the lower cost per ton or other unit that can be obtained from more capacity and better performance. Unfortunately, there is not too much information readily available especially in a form that can be used to provide quantitative data to support this statement.

Pennsylvania Pilot Study.—The Highway Research Board, several years ago, adopted a program and formed committees to develop the basic relations between the size and weight of vehicles and the type and construction of the roads that must be provided for them. The first part of the program was designed to determine the effect on fuel consumption and travel time of a large range of vehicle sizes and weight-to-power ratios over two different types of roads.

The roads used were a section of the Pennsylvania Turnpike and a parallel route over state and county roads. The vehicles selected were seven, ranging from a single vehicle weighing 20,000 lb to a combination tractor-semitrailer and trailer weighing 140,000 lb.

The results contained in "Research Report No. 9A" of the Highway Research Board are believed to be the only material of the kind available. It seems that the differences in performance and fuel consumption shown must be taken into consideration in planning roads for the future. The fact that vehicles can be built that can capitalize on the characteristics of these high-type roads is encouraging in that it shows great areas of opportunity still to be exploited in highway transport.

MECHANICAL FEATURES

There are, of course, other components of the truck that are important, even though the contribution they have made is not so spectacular. The clutch is essential because the internal combustion engine cannot be started under load. The clutch performs the function of coupling the engine to the driving mechanism in a manner which makes it possible to effect the connection at will.

The cone clutch was the earliest type to be used. Although it was simple and effective after engagement, it was difficult to construct in a manner which would permit smooth engagement. Various other types of clutches have been used, such as multiple disks, both dry and in oil, but the plate clutch has become the surviving type in general use. The single-plate type has proved to be adequate for engines of 500-lb-ft torque; beyond this limit two-plate types are used most generally. The distinction is made by the number of driven plates. Although the plate type provides easy and smooth engagement and produces a powerful drive after engagement, it is far from being ideal. Since the clutch is a friction device, the time of the engaging is limited; otherwise, the heat generated by slipping will destroy it. Although the fluid coupling has many desirable features, the comparative cost and susceptibility to misuse have prevented the use of this device.

The transmission operates in conjunction with the clutch to provide for the limited torque range of the engine. Within the range of speed that the engine will run satisfactorily, the torque developed is essentially constant. Therefore, to meet widely varying requirements, some means must be provided to multiply this torque. The device that was originated, the clash gear, is still in use, albeit with some improvements. There probably is no similar example of such an unsuitable device surviving for as long a time anywhere. The original transmissions had three speeds and were of the "progressive" type. Succeeding improvements have provided dog or toothed clutches for engagement instead of the driving gear teeth, and the application of clutch brakes or synchronizers has facilitated making the required changes with less skill, effort, noise, and destruction.

In the effort to provide more flexibility, the five-speed transmission was produced, also of the "selective" type, and this has become predominant except in the smaller vehicles. The five-speed boxes have also been developed into overdrive and direct-drive types.

As the size of vehicles increased and the range of operation was extended, the need for more gear steps was provided by dual-range transmissions that had ten speeds, or auxiliary transmissions which provided fifteen speeds. This trend is a recognition of the fact that the ideal would be a device which would provide an infinite range of speeds without definite steps. Many attempts have been made to produce such a device, but none has yet been successful because of size, weight, cost, or low efficiency. To a very large degree, the continuing use of the friction clutch and shiftable gear transmission, despite the degree of service given, is a result of the skill exhibited by truck drivers.

The final drive for automobiles has generally been through the rear wheels. None of the designs of front wheel drive have survived. In trucks, four-wheel drives were produced early and have continued to be used largely for special purposes. Most trucks are two-axle types with the drive in the rear axle.

The value of dual-speed axles and auxiliary transmissions, together with the desirable steps between ratios, has been and still is being vigorously debated. No attempt will be made here to add to this discussion beyond the observation that, where they are applied intelligently, each will give a helpful improvement in flexibility, and thus will permit a given vehicle to cope with a wider range of load and road conditions. On the other hand, gear ratios are mechanical means for relating torque and speed, and are unable to change horsepower. As horsepower is a function of the engine, it should be obvious that gear ratio changes are useless as a means of increasing maximum speed, either on the level or on grades.

There probably are many instances where the use of a slow ratio when loaded and a faster ratio for a return empty is an economy feature that is worthwhile. With the more powerful engines and higher road speeds of today, the need for slow gear ratios is reduced; and single reduction axles, using spiral bevel or hypoid gears, have come into increasing use. For equal capacity and serviceability, there is little difference between any of these types as far as size, weight, and cost are concerned.

The fact that gear sets have been developed of such relatively small size, weight, and cost is little less than a miracle. If the classical concepts of gear design had been followed, there never would have been such a device built. By breaking away from rules, through many trials and errors, failures were studied and weaknesses corrected. This process has resulted in a triumph that has been accorded little recognition or even understanding.

CONTROLS

Direction.—Control of the speed and direction of a highway vehicle is obviously of paramount importance. Steering, the control of direction, has until comparatively recently been accomplished by the muscular effort of the driver through a steering gear and a system of links connecting the steering gear to wheels pivoted on the front axle. By providing a satisfactory mechanical reduction in the steering gear and linkage and by conforming to simple geometric requirements in arranging the links, the effort necessary for steering was kept within the limits set by the driver's strength, and stable directional control was obtained.

A number of designs calculated to improve steering have been proposed and have been used with reasonable success. Francis Davis, some 20 years ago, started to design a hydraulically assisted type that has resulted in a design recently incorporated in steering gears for passenger cars. The impetus thus provided will probably produce similar equipment suitable for truck use. Units of this type are now available, and it remains to determine how to apply them in the most practical manner.

Speed.—With regard to speed control, there are two requirements—acceleration and deceleration. For facility in meeting emergencies, both are equally important. Acceleration is limited by the reserve drawbar pull available; and deceleration, by the adhesion between the tire and the road surface. Indeed, this adhesion also restricts acceleration. However, it is not so easy to obtain the engine power to reach this limit on heavy vehicles as it is to provide braking sufficient to slide the wheels. There is one catch to sliding the wheels with the brakes. When they are sliding, the wheels have no effective directional control.

The first brakes were located on the rear wheels only and were generally external band or shoe types operated by manual effort. After front wheel brakes were put on passenger cars, they soon were installed on trucks. Extensive work was done in developing servo mechanisms of various types in the endeavor to lessen the manual effort required, but none of these was adequate. The introduction of a hydraulic system to replace rods and levers simplified the installation of controls and made them more efficient, but they were still inadequate for the larger, heavier vehicles and the higher speeds required.

The vacuum booster produced by Bendix was the first practical application of auxiliary power to assist the driver. At about the same time, a full power system was produced by Westinghouse. Both systems have been intensively developed and are used on all but the lightest trucks. Although all the power needed to operate the brakes with minimum manual effort on the part of the driver has been provided, there is some inevitable and, so far, irreducible loss of application time. When it is recognized that at 60 miles per hr each 0.1 sec represents a distance traveled of 8.8 ft, and when it also is recognized that the maximum rate of deceleration cannot generally exceed 15 ft per sec, the importance of reducing this lag in application time to the minimum can be realized. With apparatus presently available, application time of the order of 0.5 sec can be obtained and retained with careful inspection and maintenance.

REGULATION

There can be no rational disagreement about the need for regulations to control the characteristics and performance of the vehicles that use the highways. Ideally, such regulation should be uniform throughout the whole nation. It is also desirable that such greatly different objectives as license fees and size and weight regulation should not be confused. Neither should there be anything which tends to influence design in a manner that produces undesirable and inefficient and unsafe vehicles.

When the regulations of the different states are compared for uniformity, it can be seen that there is a great deal that remains to be done. It is practically impossible to take a vehicle meeting the regulations of a specific state into a neighboring state.

Conclusion

Mechanical highway freight transport crossed its fiftieth birthday during the Centennial of Engineering. Its contribution to the American mode and scale of living is that it has brought to everyone's doorstep the means of sending and receiving the necessities which are beyond the individual's capacity to produce for himself. In modern life, urban, suburban, and rural, this convenience is most important.

In this paper, an effort has been made to outline in a broad way rather than in detail the need for and the place of trucks and highways in the nation's transport system, and also to trace the development of the vehicle.

AMERICAN SOCIETY OF CIVIL ENGINEERS
Founded November 5, 1852

TRANSACTIONS

Paper No. 2642

BELT CONVEYOR TRANSPORTATION

By William L. Hartley [1]

Synopsis

Belt conveyors have proved extremely valuable in expediting the transportation of bulk materials. Although they have only recently come into widespread use, conveyors have already established their efficiency and economy. This paper illustrates the effectiveness of belt conveyor transportation in several large industries, including construction. A brief discussion of design factors is included. Many examples of successful installations are described, and typical belt speeds and capacities are given.

Introduction

Belt conveyors occupy a unique position in the field of transportation. They are particularly suited to the transportation of bulk materials—such as coal, stone, and ore—and they are capable of handling tonnages of these materials in excess of any current requirement. Belt conveyors work continuously, without loading and unloading delays or loss of time for empty return trips. They can operate up or down grades as steep as 32%. Their relatively light and compact structures are adaptable for service in mountainous country, over soft marshy ground, above city streets, across rivers, or through small tunnels. They are extremely versatile.

Although belt conveyors are a comparatively recent development in the field of long-distance transportation, they boast a long record of experience in handling vast quantities of materials in industrial plants. As early as 1795, conveyors were used to handle grain in flour mills. They have been in general commercial use about 60 years; but only in the past 25 years have they attained their present dominant position in the bulk-handling field.

Until World War I, there was little need for high-capacity materials-handling systems. Few power plants required coal-handling equipment rated at more than 150 tons per hr. Under these circumstances, a compact bucket elevator or skip hoist, augmented by distributing conveyors, served the purpose. Output from coal and metal mines at that time was well within the capacity of traditional cars and hoists, and the economy of such methods remained virtually unchallenged.

---

[1] Engr., Link-Belt Co., Chicago, Ill.

The construction industry had yet to find a job where its transportation problems could not be solved through the use of cars or trucks, or by sluicing. Only in by-product coke plants, a few large stone plants, and an occasional aggregates plant were belt conveyors given much consideration other than as just another type of conveyor.

However, as tonnage requirements throughout all industry reached higher levels in the 1920's and 1930's, other types of conveying equipment proved inadequate for the major tasks—or at least uneconomical in comparison to belt conveyors. Today, it is difficult to imagine any other practical method of handling coal at a rate of 1,500 to 2,000 tons per hr—a normal requirement at several of the new central power stations. Conveyors also transport from 6,000 to 8,000 tons of ore per hr in large-scale mining or dock operations. The magnitude of this quantity is evident, as 6,000 tons per hr is equivalent to 100 tons every minute.

This paper will not go into the technical science and art of belt conveyor design, since up-to-date authentic data are available in the catalogs of manufacturers of conveying machinery and rubber belts. Instead, a short review of a number of installations that illustrate the reasons why belt conveyors have gained their current stature in the field of transportation will be presented.

MINING AND QUARRYING

Stripping Overburden.—Nowhere have belt conveyors fulfilled a current need more effectively than in the mining, quarrying, and other extractive industries. In all mining and quarrying plants the greatest single item of operating cost is materials handling, of which transportation in one form or another is a major factor. Such transportation is required in stripping and disposing of overburden; in conveying excavated material from the face of the mine to the processing plant; in intraplant handling between crushing, grinding, screening, washing, concentrating, and loading operations; and, finally, in transporting refuse to the spoil pile.

A typical belt conveyor, such as the one shown in Fig. 1, is made up of only five essential elements—the belt, the carrying idler rolls, the head and foot pulleys that tension and drive the belt, the drive that powers the pulleys, and the supporting structure.

This conveyor is part of an extensive system of 36-in.-wide belts that transports overburden from a stripping operation on the Mesabi Iron Range in Minnesota. The system is capable of handling more than 1,100 tons per hr, continuously night and day. There is no fatigue factor in belt conveyors.

In a typical modern stripping operation at an open-pit iron ore mine in Minnesota, it is often necessary to remove a layer of overburden up to 150 ft thick to expose the marketable ore. From a 10-cu yd stripping dragline, the overburden is transported by belt conveyors directly from the mine and up steep inclines, thus saving miles of costly roadways. Some 25,000 tons (50,000,000 lb) of overburden are handled on this 10-min trip out of the pit every day.

Finally, more than a mile from the dragline, the overburden is discharged to the pile by the self-propelled stacker conveyor with a 100-ft radius boom, which is illustrated in Fig. 2. This apparatus, too, is a form of belt conveyor, especially designed for flexibility in stock-piling operations. These machines can be either crawler-mounted or track-mounted.

Where the overburden is spoiled only a short distance from the excavation,

FIG. 1.—TYPICAL TROUGHED BELT CONVEYOR

FIG. 2.—STACKER CONVEYOR

one conveyor may be sufficient, with crawler-mounted receiving hopper and feeder. Thus, as shown in Fig. 3, a 54-in.-wide stacker belt is mounted on a structural boom with an over-all length of 250 ft. It has handled the output of a 6-cu yd shovel in a Pennsylvania limestone quarry dependably and economically for more than 13 years, much of the time working two shifts. Based on the performance of this machine, a second unit was recently placed in service to meet increased production schedules.

Transportation from Mine.—Transportation of the marketable products from mines and quarries involves some very interesting applications of belt conveyors. For long belt haulage, the real pioneer installation was that in the Colonial Mines of the United States Steel Company, in western Pennsylvania (1924). The system of twenty belt conveyor flights, with a total length of about 4½ miles, is still in operation, transporting up to 15,000 tons of coal per day, through a mountain to barges on the Monongahela River. Operating records of this conveyor system provide some astonishing data on belt conveyor performance for a number of years. The total tonnage carried over this 48-in.-wide belt system by late 1952

FIG. 3.—BOOM-MOUNTED STACKER BELT

was 85,000,000 tons. Between 1931 and 1943 the system operated 27,000 hours, carrying 40,000,000 tons of coal—with a total lost time record of only 26 hours and 46 min. The longest down-time period was 5 hours and 48 min, reportedly as a result of power failure due to lightning. Some of the belts were in service long enough to carry from 25,000,000 tons to 30,000,000 tons—almost double the original estimated belt life. The safety record achieved in this operation has been considered phenomenal.

The longest single belt conveyor in operation to date carries washed coal from a preparation plant to a river loading station, in the coal fields of West Virginia. The conveyor enters a 10,900-ft-long rock tunnel through a mountain. After an elapsed time of 36 min—at a speed of 300 ft per min—the conveyor emerges on the other side of the mountain on the banks of the Monongahela River, where it discharges 250 tons of coal per hr into barges. As the conveyor line drops 135 ft in total length, only a 150-hp drive is required. With a high ratio of live weight to tare weight and the ability to actually generate power on downgrades, belt conveyors have lower power requirements than many other forms of transport.

Fig. 4 shows this conveyor as it enters the tunnel through the mountain. The tunnel measures 7 ft high by 13 ft wide, and is of unlined rock drift construction, with a track alongside for a service car. In the planning stage of this installation, rail, trucks, aerial tram—and, in fact, all methods of transportation—were considered. However, this continuous 2-mile-long belt conveyor offered the lowest cost per ton—and actual performance has surpassed the engineers' estimates.

The highest lift in a single belt conveyor flight is achieved by a 42-in.-wide steel cord belt installed at a coal mine near Waltonville, in southern Illinois. Climbing nearly a 29% grade, the conveyor handles 1,200 tons of coal per hr, lifting it 862 ft—nearly twice as high as the Tribune Tower in Chicago, Ill.—in a length of 3,167 ft, on pulley centers. This conveyor is equipped with the largest

FIG. 4.—SECTION OF WORLD'S LONGEST SINGLE BELT CONVEYOR

single pulley drive yet developed—a 1,500-hp unit, direct-connected to a motor through an enclosed gear reduction unit and dynamatic clutch. These two installations are records at the present time, but the imagination and ingenuity of engineers and improvements in technology will probably soon result in the construction of conveyors that will far surpass these achievements.

In a typical heavy-duty installation, iron ore is transferred from the crushing station at the pit bottom to the concentrating plant by five belt conveyors, as illustrated in Fig. 5. When installed several years ago, they combined lowest cost transportation with dependability—but an expensive cleanup problem was created when transferring sticky ore from one conveyor to the next.

Belt manufacturers met this challenge with a variety of high-strength belts. In one installation a single 30-in.-wide belt conveyor, 1,700 ft on centers, performs the same function as the five units in Fig. 5, without transfers and their cleanup problems. Just consider this continuous belt running straight up a hill of 30% grade with its heavy load. Then contrast this conveyor with a winding truck road of 10% maximum grade to the same destination, or a railroad that normally climbs no more than 3% grade.

DESIGN FACTORS

Objectionable transfers can now be eliminated by textile and steel cord belts that are four to ten times stronger than their predecessors since the job can be done in one single flight. These stronger belts have opened up entirely new fields of usefulness for belt conveyors as a means of "main-line" transportation.

Modern, high-strength belts cost substantially more than those of standard construction. To justify this higher first cost, they must be operated at their maximum safe loads. Also, because of the extremely severe service in the mining industry, great care must be taken to eliminate excessive wear and damage.

The design of mechanical and electrical components to meet these conditions

FIG. 5.—CONVEYORS ON 30% GRADE

is far more difficult than that for ordinary belt conveyors, particularly with regard to:

1. Overloads and the accelerating load of motor which must be kept within the limits of recommended maximum belt stress. Selection of drive motor and its control require careful consideration.

2. Slippage of the belt on the drive pulley which must be eliminated by conservative application of tension ratios and the use of properly grooved pulley lagging.

3. A low friction factor, for carrying idlers—important in obtaining maximum centers, especially on horizontal conveyors where friction forces predominate. However, before applying optimum friction factors in horsepower calculations, it must be remembered that the basic design is predicated on utilizing the full strength of the belt. For this reason, the factor must reflect a careful study of the conditions which affect it, such as temperatures, alinement, maintenance methods, and other operating conditions.

4. Taking up slack in the belt, a problem that increases with its length. Long horizontal belts require a weighted gravity take-up adjacent to the drive pulley

to provide constant pressure between belt and drive pulley. Where the slope of conveyors and the weight of the empty belt provide enough pressure, gravity take-ups may be located more conveniently.

Take-up travel must be sufficient for the full stretch of the belt, including that developed by starting stresses. Under certain conditions an allowance should be made for shrinkage. On exceedingly long conveyors it may be advisable to use a steel cord belt to reduce take-up travel to practical limits.

5. Protection of belts against excessive wear and damage at all loading and transfer points. Closely spaced rubber-tread idlers effectively cushion the impact of loading large lumps. Long and expensive belts can be protected from both impact and scuffing action of abrasive materials by the use of short belt-transfer conveyors. The drop to the main belt is reduced to a minimum over the small head pulley of the transfer conveyor. The scuffing of main belt is reduced, since the material flows from the transfer conveyor at the same speed and in the same direction as the main belt.

Other typical protective units include electrical devices to detect and remove tramp iron and backstop brakes. Regardless of the location of the conveyors in the flow sheet, all become more important as the size, strength, and cost of the belt increase.

Typical Installations

The extensive use of belt conveyors in the mining industry is illustrated by the modern coal preparation plant shown in Fig. 6. Here, belts are used in transporting both coal and mine rock from the dump house down the slope to the washing plant, to the crushing station, to and from the blending bin, and between many of the process operations. Finally, they convey the mine and washer refuse up a mountainside to a bin, from which the waste is trucked to the spoil bank.

At this mine, coal is taken down a mountain from the dump house to the preparation plant at the rate of 750 tons per hr. Mine refuse travels over an adjacent belt in the same structure. This is conveyor transportation at its best, with the equipment accessible and well enclosed for protection from wind and weather. Fig. 7(a) shows the enclosure gallery for the conveyors. The belt conveyor structure gracefully follows rolling terrain in an "air-flight" path.

At another coal mine, the final slope belt to the preparation plant is 60 in. wide, and can convey up to 3,000 tons per hr—or as much as sixty 50-ton-capacity railroad cars. The continuous stream of material travels along at a speed of 700 ft per min.

In coal mines alone, of all underground mining operations, it is estimated there are almost 6,000,000 ft—more than 1,000 miles—of belt conveyors; yet, the general use of belts in coal mines dates back only slightly more than 20 years, to 1928–1929.

The suspension bridge (Fig. 7(b)) is known as the Kentucky version of the Golden Gate Bridge. A 36-in.-wide belt conveyor transports 400 tons of coal per hr from the mine preparation plant, crossing the picturesque Cumberland River on a cable suspension bridge of about 870-ft span, to deliver its load directly to a power plant. It started operation in the spring of 1949 and has since carried

FIG. 6.—COAL PREPARATION PLANT

(a) STEEL BENTS   (b) SUSPENSION BRIDGE

FIG. 7.—TYPICAL CONVEYOR-SUPPORT STRUCTURES

millions of tons of coal to produce power for Kentucky homes and industries. Prior to the installation of this direct system from mine to powerhouse, it was necessary to haul the coal over a long roundabout route.

POWER PLANTS

Modern steam-generating plants require extremely high-capacity systems for transportation and storage of coal. In 1952, the installed capacity of public utilities reached 82,000,000 kw, or almost seven times the 12,000,000-kw capacity of 1920, and more than double the 1940 capacity.

As a result of the proportionate increase in the size of individual power-generating stations, belt conveyors provide the only practical means of handling and storing the high tonnages of coal, and they are doing it most dependably and economically. At one Great Lakes plant, coal is unloaded from self-unloader

FIG. 8.—TRAVELING TRIPPER AND STACKER UNIT

ore boats at the rate of 1,800 tons per hr, and is handled by belt conveyors to and from storage. En route, these conveyors also perform such other functions as feeding, weighing, sampling, and finally distributing to the bunkers.

In Fig. 8 are shown a traveling tripper and a stacker belt on rails over a main-line belt delivering coal into initial storage piles. The main-line conveyor is 1,230 ft long, with a rated capacity of 1,200 tons per hr to 1,800 tons per hr. This is a good example of the versatility of belt conveyor construction in serving large generating plants that require up to 1,000,000-ton reserve-storage piles of coal.

Coal is automatically delivered into bunkers by a motor-propelled belt tripper that travels back and forth along the belt over the length of the bunkers. To control dust, this tripper has a special discharge chute that slides between rubber sealing strips at floor level.

DOCKS AND TERMINALS

Belt conveyors are now an indispensable tool for speeding the flow of materials through docks, piers, terminals, and other bulk transfer stations, and from railroad cars to ships or barges; or, in reverse, for rapidly unloading bulk cargo from ships. Terminals must provide minimum loading and unloading time for the common carriers they serve. For such operations, the ability of belt conveyors to supplement other transport media is well demonstrated. At one Virginia seaport, 100 railroad carloads of coal (totaling 6,000 tons) can be transferred from cars to ships every hour. Cars are switched from railroad storage yards to a weighing station and then are pushed by electric "mule" up an incline to rotary car dumpers, near the inshore end of the pier, which empty the cars by turning them upside down. From each of the four dumpers a belt conveyor transports the coal toward the offshore end of the pier to its own traveling ship loading

FIG. 9.—TRAVELING SHIP LOADER

tower (Fig. 9). Thus, it is possible to load, simultaneously, four ships with four different grades of coal. The towers move easily from hatch to hatch, so that the ships are moored only once—a saving in dockage time and expense to the shipowner.

The adaptability of belt conveyor systems is illustrated by their use on self-unloading boats that sail the Great Lakes with cargoes of coal and limestone. Belt conveyors built into the bottom of the hold withdraw the cargo. It is then transported to the dock over another belt mounted on a swiveling boom. Some of these boats can unload stone at the rate of more than 4,000 tons per hr, or coal at 2,000 tons per hr.

Some terminals must provide for rather extensive storage of materials in addition to their primary function of transferring material from one carrier to another. At a Canadian dock coal is distributed to storage by a belt conveyor, whose range of operation is extended by a track-mounted traveling tripper with a conveyor-type stacker boom which distributes coal to either side of the main-belt conveyor.

For long, narrow storage areas or for materials that cannot be stored in a deep pile, traveling stackers are built with booms of any reasonable length. The stacker in Fig. 10 has a 100-ft radius and handles iron-ore concentrates.

Conveyors in Construction

Probably no greater contrasts are found between primitive and modern bulk-handling methods than in the field of public works—the building of dams, levees,

Fig. 10.—Traveling Stacker with 100-Ft Radius

and other large-scale construction projects. These jobs always require the transportation of great quantities of excavated materials and aggregates.

Dams.—When the Anderson Ranch Dam was built on the South Fork of the Boise River in Idaho a few years ago, the earth-moving problems of logistics and economy were solved with the belt conveyor system shown in Fig. 11(a). It transported impervious core material a distance of about 2 miles from borrow pits to the dam site over terrain that was better suited to mountain goats than to conventional methods of transportation.

At Shasta Dam on the Sacramento River in California (Fig. 11(b)), a series of 36-in.-wide belt conveyors was used to carry 10,000,000 tons of gravel a distance of 9.6 miles at the rate of 1,100 tons per hr. Not only was the job done for three quarters of the cost per ton compared with other methods, but the contractor recovered a substantial part of the first cost by selling many of the components of this system after the dam was completed. This installation has been termed "The Push-Button-Operated Rubber Railroad."

At Hungry Horse Dam on the South Fork of the Flathead River in Montana, a 36-in.-wide belt carried 900 tons per hr of blended sand and sized aggregates up a steep canyon wall to a concrete mixing tower. It traversed with ease terrain that would have been formidable and costly for ordinary roads (Fig. 11(c)). It achieved practically air-flight direction with a minimum of "cuts" and "fills." Belt conveyors have also aided in the construction of many other dams, including Grand Coulee on the Columbia River in Washington and Bull Shoals on the White River in Arkansas-Missouri. Each of these projects had to be engineered and "tailor-made" to suit unusual conditions and requirements.

Grading.—In the field of public works, one of the very early belt conveyor transport systems was the Denny Hill Project in Seattle, Wash., undertaken in 1928 and 1929. This job involved the removal of a massive hill from the heart of the business district of Seattle. More than 6,000,000 cu yd of earth and rock were loaded into barges for dumping into Puget Sound.

(a) Anderson Ranch Dam on the South Fork of the Boise River in Idaho (b) Shasta Dam on the Sacramento River in California (c) Hungry Horse Dam on the South Fork of the Flathead River in Montana

FIG. 11.—TYPICAL CONSTRUCTION CONVEYORS

The material was transported over city streets to the water's edge without interference with traffic or damage to street paving (Fig. 12). There were three main conveyors of about 3,000 ft on total centers—not very long conveyors, but impressive for pioneering a new method of transportation.

Aggregate Plants.—In addition to the problems of materials transportation, public works projects require extensive plants for the production of concrete aggregates. Although temporary, such installations must provide for handling, storing, and reclaiming the various sizes and grades of sand and stone in large quantities. Belt conveyor systems have long been preferred for performing these functions. Sometimes they become quite complex, like the one at Hungry Horse Dam (Fig. 13). Contractors rely more and more on belt conveyors to keep down handling costs, at an ultimate saving to the taxpayer.

Other Applications.—Thus far this paper has discussed only spectacular and high-tonnage bulk-handling installations. However, practically every major industry has transportation problems that can be solved by the use of belt conveyors, resulting in lower handling costs and increased production.

FIG. 12.—DENNY HILL PROJECT, SEATTLE, WASH.

FIG. 13.—AGGREGATE PLANT AT HUNGRY HORSE DAM ON THE SOUTH FORK OF THE FLATHEAD RIVER IN MONTANA

For example, in the paper industry in Canada, a 1,450-ft-long belt conveyor is used in storing and reclaiming pulpwood logs. A shuttle belt, 490 ft long and nearly 100 ft above the ground, is utilized to store wet phosphate rock. The latter installation is in Florida, where large deposits of this valuable raw material are found. For gypsum rock transported by ships from Canada to Baltimore, Md., a 30-in.-wide belt conveyor with a traveling tripper, enclosed in a long gallery, delivers the raw material to the storage pile or direct to the processing plant. In by-product coke plants, belt conveyors are standard equipment for carrying the coal through various steps of preparation to the charging bins ahead of the ovens, and they take quenched coke from the wharf through its processing to cars or blast-furnace storage bins.

The extensive and varied use of belt conveyors for assembly lines and package handling should not be overlooked. In factories, warehouses, department stores, mail order houses, and even restaurants they perform countless tasks in the mass movement of materials. In some of the major post offices and transportation terminals, great reductions in time and costs have been realized through the use of belt conveyors in handling and dispatching thousands of tons of mail daily.

Nevertheless, in this field, like many others, a great deal more remains to be accomplished. Engineers in the conveyor industry feel there are endless opportunities for increasing production and reducing costs, thus contributing to the expansion of the national economy.

Future Developments

In the future one of the outstanding conveyor installations may be the proposed "Riverlake" belt conveyor line from Lorain, Ohio, on Lake Erie, 103 miles across country to East Liverpool, Ohio on the Ohio River. This system, which is mechanically and technically sound, has been developed by a group of engineers to handle the transfer of up to 30,000,000 tons of iron ore annually from Lake Erie ports to barges on the Ohio River, for eventual delivery to the furnaces of the steel mills in the Youngstown (Ohio) and Pittsburgh (Pa.) areas. It is also planned to carry millions of tons of coal back to the lake ports from river barges loaded from the great coal mines of Kentucky, Virginia, West Virginia, and Pennsylvania. This project was brought before the Ohio Legislature in order to seek the right of eminent domain which would assist the proponents in acquiring the necessary right of way.

The ultimate dream of the engineer is to be able to run belts in one long continuous flight—the length of the Mississippi River if desired. At present, the maximum length of one continuous belt conveyor flight is limited to the permissible tension of the rubber belt itself. Longer flights will be possible and the development of intermediate drives to be installed at various points along the conveyor line, which will transmit power to the belt and thus eliminate the necessity of undesirable transfer points. Only engineering and research will bring this about.

Belt conveyors are now "knocking at the door" of passenger transportation. This new field of application offers far-reaching possibilities. One design being developed is similar to a moving sidewalk complete with safe entrances and exits. Another is equipped with cars that are carried along through various speed zones on a series of belt conveyors. Just visualize a smooth ride on a continuously moving rubber belt for the thousands of people making the daily trip from Grand Central Station to Times Square in New York, N. Y.

In American industry there is an increasing need for conveyor systems to transport the million of tons of ore, coal, stone, and the other bulk materials consumed each year. The people of the United States have an insatiable appetite for these raw materials which are the foundation of the nation's economy and way of life. Economic and social development have reached the stage where the primitive transportation methods of many other countries are completely outdated. They are not only inadequate for modern plant flow sheets, but are inconsistent with objectives of safety and the elimination of drudgery from the industrial scene.

Belt conveyors have contributed greatly to the solution of transportation problems during the past century. As American industry moves forward toward the production of more goods for more people, transportation will present many new challenges for engineers.

The prosperity and industrial might of a nation can rise only in proportion to the development of its transportation, both indoors and outdoors, whether it be for thousands of miles, or for but a few feet.

AMERICAN SOCIETY OF CIVIL ENGINEERS

Founded November 5, 1852

TRANSACTIONS

Paper No. 2643

WATERWAY GROWTH IN THE UNITED STATES

By C. H. Chorpening,[1] M. ASCE

Synopsis

Interest and activity in development of the waterways of the United States began during the colonial period, and exercised a strong influence on the establishment of this nation. Federal activity in improving waterways dates from the first sessions of the Congress; and since 1824 this work has been assigned to the Corps of Engineers of the United States Army. The first half of the nineteenth century, which may be designated as the era of state and private canal construction, witnessed important contributions to the waterways of the country and to waterway engineering.

These early projects laid a solid foundation politically and technically for the major waterway improvements which have taken place during the past 100 years and which have provided the present waterway system of the United States. Similarly the important developments of the past century in engineering, in construction equipment and methods, and in use and management of waterways, as well as the dynamic growth of this country, point the way to sound waterway progress in the years to come. Details of the history, development, status, and potentialities of the nation's water transportation system are summarized in this paper, from the midcentury vantage point.

The story of the development of waterways in the United States is in many respects the story of the development of this country. From the earliest colonial days until the present time, harbors, lakes, rivers, and canals have played an important and often controlling role in shaping the destinies of this nation in peace and in war. Waterways provided the main pathways which were followed in conquering the continental wilderness; and these same waterways, improved, developed, and maintained by private and governmental effort have provided the basic framework on which has risen this great industrial nation.

Although the major part of modern waterway development has taken place during the past century, this growth, and the influence of waterways on the very formation of the Union, began at a much earlier date. It is necessary therefore to

---

[1] Brig. Gen., Corps of Engrs., Dept. of the Army ; Asst. Chf. of Engrs. for Civ. Works, Washington, D. C.

review briefly the events and factors in earlier years which led to this development, in order to present the story fully and with understanding.

In this paper the term "waterways" is used in its broadest sense to embrace harbors and coastal channels as well as rivers and canals. These are all integral parts of the over-all water transportation structure. Their development has proceeded in coordination; and waterway engineering practices and developments involve all these components.

Routes of Exploration and Settlement

It is pertinent and interesting to examine a relief map of the western hemisphere and to note the physical advantages which were available to the explorers and colonists of North America as compared with the difficulties and barriers which confronted the men of Spain and Portugal who attempted the exploration and conquest of lands south of the Rio Grande. Access to the interior of Central and South America was barred by high mountains extending down to narrow coastal plains; high plateaus and dense jungle were broken only by a few great streams, the Orinoco, Amazon, and the Plata-Uruguay system in the far south. Once the interior was reached it was usually jungle or arid mountain land.

North America, on the other hand, presented a different picture, which was largely responsible for the fact that it soon outstripped its southern neighbors in development even though its full exploration and settlement began many years later. The Atlantic coast of North America, where the first permanent European colonies were established, was broken by numerous large rivers—the St. Lawrence, Hudson, Delaware, James, Savannah, and St. Johns. These and many others with long tidal reaches provided relatively easy access for miles into the interior, and permitted a measure of navigation generally to the fall line, the beginning of the rolling lands of the Appalachian plateau.

Waterways Serve Explorers.—Perhaps of even greater importance, however, in so far as access to the continental interior is concerned, were two great natural waterway systems. The St. Lawrence River and Great Lakes on the north provided a route by which explorers and traders passed into the Ohio Valley, to the headwaters of the Mississippi, and on to the great Missouri Basin. From the Gulf of Mexico on the south the "Father of Waters" with its great eastern tributary, the Ohio, provided a waterway opening up the vast territory lying just west of the Appalachians.

Western tributaries of the Mississippi such as the Red, Arkansas, and Missouri led across the western plains toward the distant Rocky Mountains and the Pacific coast. Finally when this nation had expanded overland from coast to coast the need for expeditious movement of its maritime commerce between Atlantic and Pacific ports, and its growing interest in the Pacific area, led to construction of a ship canal across the Isthmus of Panama, completing the age-old search for a direct westward water route from Europe to the Orient.

The availability and location of these natural bays, estuaries, lakes, and rivers flowing from the interior governed to a large extent the exploration and subsequent settlement of North America. On the Florida peninsula, the site of the earliest Spanish settlements along the Atlantic coast line, the St. Johns River provided access in the sixteenth century to Spaniards in search of gold and the fabulous "fountain of youth." Hernando De Soto used Tampa Bay as a base for his subsequent overland journey to the Mississippi. Sir Walter Raleigh established his ill-fated colony along the sounds of North Carolina; and, although its disappearance remains one of the unsolved mysteries of history, it may well be assumed that those desperate colonists used the Roanoke River and other streams in their explorations and trade with the Indians.

Early Colonization from the Atlantic.—Further north the broad waters of Chesapeake Bay, and the numerous rivers tributary to it, offered a more secure haven to the ships of the London Company which established at Jamestown, Va., in 1607, the first permanent English colony in the New World. These colonists, while unwise in the selection of a site for their first settlement, were fortunate in the natural facilities for inland and maritime navigation which were available.

The rugged New England coast presented a more difficult and forbidding aspect to the hardy seekers for religious freedom who first came to those shores in 1620; but not many years elapsed before Boston, Plymouth, and other coastal towns in Massachusetts had become centers of commerce. Trade with the Indians and French to the north began via the Connecticut River; and vessels were rounding Cape Cod in commerce with the Dutch at New Amsterdam (New York, N. Y.) and in the Hudson Valley.

The Dutch explorations and settlements in North America were frankly commercial in character and were concentrated rapidly on two of the most strategic waterways along the Atlantic coast—the Delaware and Hudson rivers. The latter stream afforded contact with the French in Canada via Lake Champlain, and its tributary, the Mohawk, provided the most practicable route to the Great Lakes and the Ohio River Valley.

The French, however, first grasped the two great water routes which flanked the seaboard colonies and led most deeply into the interior of the continent. To the Frenchman Jean de Bienville went the honor of first sailing up the Mississippi River and of founding the City of New Orleans, La., in 1717, thereby establishing the sway of France over the outlet of the greatest inland waterway system in North America. At an earlier date, in 1534, the French had also entered the Gulf of St. Lawrence. A century later they had gone on by portage to the Great Lakes (Fig. 1), and by canoe and bateaux had traversed those waters to pass on to the Upper Mississippi River, to establish a claim to an empire surpassing in scope their wildest dreams—but beyond their power to colonize and hold.

BEGINNINGS OF DEVELOPMENT—COLONIAL PERIOD

The history of the original British Colonies, which joined to form the United States, spans a period roughly equal in length to the life of the country as an independent nation. During this colonial period and for some years after independence, or for a total of about 200 years, the waterways of North America were used largely in their natural state. There was little effort to improve or extend these facilities, as by and large such improvements, although recognized as desirable by farseeing individuals, were beyond the physical and financial abilities of the time. Nevertheless waterway development in the United States began during the colonial period; not only in the vision and planning of statesmen, traders, and men of scientific turn of mind, but in actual small works by individuals, companies, and governments. Its purposes were to remove obstructions, bypass rapids, extend piers to deeper channels, and generally in small ways make the natural bays and rivers more usable.

No Easy Navigation.—Although the broad tidal reaches of the rivers of colonial America provided fairly adequate drafts for the sailing vessels of the time, navigation of the rivers far into the interior even by canoe and bateau was most difficult. The pleasant picture often drawn of canoes gliding swiftly over the mirrorlike surfaces of rivers winding through the virgin forests of the New World can scarcely be squared with the available facts on the condition of the streams. Riverbanks and streambanks were lined with aged trees whose predecessors had

FIG. 1.—INDIANS HELPING IN PORTAGE FROM ST. LAWRENCE TO GREAT LAKES

fallen into the streams which they choked with trunks and branches. The difficulty of removing, or even passing, such obstructions was enormous; and every windstorm might add to the problem. Rapids necessitated the portage of boats and cargo; and shifting sandbars and submerged rocks were constant hazards. The Mohawk, Susquehanna, and Ohio in their natural state presented difficulties of this kind.

From the very first years of the settlement of tidewater Virginia the men of that colony used the many rivers and creeks tributary to Chesapeake Bay as highways to widely scattered plantations. Ocean-going vessels of that day were able to sail for considerable distances up the James, York, Rappahannock, and Potomac rivers to discharge and load cargoes at the wharves of individual plantation owners (Fig. 2). While a considerable amount of legislation in the House of Burgesses of colonial Virginia was directed at the improvement of navigation on those and other streams, little was accomplished as the rivers provided generally satisfactory navigation to the fall line. In fact, the improvements accomplished were generally limited to marking channels and establishing wharves and piers at plantations and settlements. Eventually the need for transference of cargo from water to overland transport led to settlements at the fall lines of these rivers which grew to become the cities of Petersburg on the Appomattox, Richmond on the James, Fredericksburg on the Rappahannock, and Georgetown and Alexandria on the Potomac.

Access to the Ohio Valley.—The idea of a water route to the Ohio River appears to have originated with Governor Alexander Spotswood of Virginia in 1716. The first organized effort, however, to open a transportation route between the English tidewater settlements and the country west of the Alleghenies was the establishment in 1748 of the Ohio Company of Virginia, which was probably the strongest of the prerevolutionary trading corporations. Shares in that company

FIG. 2.—COLONIAL TOBACCO AND OTHER PRODUCE OF CHESAPEAKE BAY LOADED FROM PLANTATION
WHARVES TO OCEAN-GOING SHIPS BEFORE REVOLUTIONARY WAR

were held by prominent individuals and firms both in America and in London. The organization contemplated operations as far down the Ohio River as the "falls" at the present site of Louisville, Ky. Routes from tidewater to the Ohio were explored with the assistance of friendly Indians as guides, storehouses and trading posts were established, and the Potomac and Monongahela rivers were used for movement of supplies.

The immediate success of this combination land and water route to the Ohio Valley brought repercussions both domestic and foreign. The traders of New York and Pennsylvania disapproved of the Virginia monopoly of this trade, were antagonistic, and began planning and promoting routes of their own. The French to the north viewed with concern this invasion of a domain which they claimed the sole right to exploit; and sent armed forces into the Upper Ohio Basin in 1753. In spite of warnings carried by George Washington to the French camp on the Allegheny, their forces succeeded in destroying some of the depots of the Ohio Company. There followed the considerable period when the frontier was harrassed by what is known as the "French and Indian War," which eventually resulted in the loss of the French empire in America.

Potomac Improvement Difficult.—Both Washington and his militia and Maj.-Gen. Edward Braddock and his ill-fated regular British expedition followed the route of the Ohio Company. During those campaigns, boats heavily laden with supplies passed up the Potomac River. Braddock's Commissary General after inspection of the Potomac in 1755 reported that, although artillery could not be carried by water, the route was practicable for movement of all other supplies. The practical strategic and military value of an American waterway was thus recognized, and the Potomac was so used almost 200 years ago.

Proposals for improving the navigation of the Potomac were put forward in the decade following the war on the frontier, as evidenced by correspondence in 1770 between Washington and Thomas Johnson of Maryland. These men contemplated clearing the river and providing locks for passage around rapids, and considered the interest and participation of the states of Virginia and Maryland in the project. Early in 1772 Washington, then a member of the Virginia House of Burgesses, secured passage of an act for opening the Potomac to navigation from tidewater to Fort Cumberland, Maryland. This act empowered the raising of money by subscriptions and lottery. A similar act failed in the Maryland Assembly because of opposition by commercial interests of Baltimore, who did not favor the channeling of western trade to the Potomac River towns of Georgetown, Md. (later D. C.), and Alexandria, Va.

Later, in 1773, a private citizen, John Ballendine, the proprietor of certain iron works near Richmond, became intensely interested in improvement of both the James and Potomac rivers, and proposed canalization past the rapids by means of locks with a 4-ft minimum depth of water over the sills. He was able to interest many leading men of the colony in his scheme, as well as carry his proposal to Great Britain and arouse considerable interest there.

From all sources over £10,000 appears to have been subscribed; trustees were appointed; plans were approved; and work was started toward construction on a lock at the "lower Falls" on the Maryland side of the Potomac. In 1774 Ballendine was authorized by the trustees to employ fifty slaves on this work. The Maryland Assembly remained antagonistic, however, and Ballendine transferred his operations to the beginning of similar work on the James, where his activities would not be complicated by intercolony rivalry. The records indicate that he advertised for hire of one hundred slaves for canal work along the James, agreeing to "assist with the best part of their winter clothing, if not otherwise provided." The approach of the War for Independence effectively stopped these early attempts at waterway improvement, although the same interest and activity were to revive even more strongly after that war.

Further to the south an act of the Assembly of South Carolina in 1734 directed the clearing of certain streams for navigation. Some minor work was accomplished under this law by commissioners appointed for each section of a river who were authorized to make assessments of labor or money against persons living within a certain distance of the streams, or persons benefited by the improvement.

Work on Other Middle Atlantic Rivers.—At the head of Chesapeake Bay the Susquehanna provided a water route northward into Pennsylvania, difficult and little used because of rapids and shoals; and its improvement in colonial times seems to have had few proponents. The Delaware River to the north, however, provided satisfactory navigable depths for ocean-going sailing ships up to the falls at the present site of Trenton, N. J. The river was a heavily used commercial artery during the colonial period; became a center of shipbuilding, earning the name of "The American Clyde;" and enabled Philadelphia, Pa., to take its place as one of the major colonial ports.

The Hudson River, first navigated by the Dutch in 1609, offered adequate channels up to the present site of Albany, N. Y., and excellent harbor facilities which led to the establishment of New Amsterdam and its development into the great modern port of New York. About a year before Henry Hudson's voyage up the river that now bears his name, the Frenchman Samuel de Champlain had sailed up the St. Lawrence and founded Quebec, Canada. In 1615 Champlain in company with allied Indians of the Algonquin nation explored the St. Lawrence and penetrated to what is now Lake Champlain and then to the Great Lakes themselves. The Dutch allied with the Iroquois nation were pushing up the Hudson during the same period, and the natural watercourses between these two colonies became routes of both trade and war.

Use of these waterways continued after the Hudson Valley colony came under British rule, to become the Colony of New York; and with increasing knowledge of the geography of the country came a greater appreciation of the strategic and commercial values of the water routes. As early as 1724 Cadwallader Colden, Surveyor-General of the Colony, made a comprehensive and accurate study of the rivers of New York, particularly the watercourses and carrying places between Albany and Montreal, Canada, and between Albany and Lake Ontario. Colden appears to have been one of the first to appreciate the value of these streams as commercial highways, and in his report even envisioned a line of communication from the Hudson to the Great Lakes and thence to the Mississippi River and the Gulf of Mexico. That this was no impracticable dream is shown by the fact that before the Revolutionary War six hundred bateaux passed annually over the carrying place between Wood Creek and the Mohawk River—the route to Lake Ontario.

This same Colden, who later became Lieutenant Governor of the Colony appears to have maintained his interest in waterways and was responsible for construction in 1750 of a short canal in Orange County, New York, which was probably the first canal constructed within the territory which became the United States. (The first canal in North America, however, antedated this by some 50 years, being a French attempt at Lachine on the St. Lawrence River.)

In New York as in Virginia the restrictive measures imposed by Great Britain, and the lack of financial and technical resources in the colonies, were not conducive to public improvements; but in 1768 Governor Sir Henry Moore of New York in a message to the General Assembly commended to the serious consideration of that body the improvement of navigability of the Mohawk River. The Assembly was, however, in a hostile mood over recent actions of the British Parliament and this resulted in its dissolution by the Governor before the project for improving the Mohawk could be acted on. The War for Independence interrupted further activity.

The broad vision of Washington, whose stature as a statesman and engineer grows with time, was not limited to the waterway possibilities of his native state. Even before peace with Great Britain was declared, he made a journey through northern New York and in 1783 wrote to his friend Chevalier François Jean de Chastellux concerning that journey and described the possibilities of water transportation in that area. He concluded:

"I could not help taking a more contemplative and extensive view of the vast inland navigation of these United States * * *. Would to God we may have wisdom to improve them."

In New England, Limited Waterways.—The New England Colonies did not have the wealth of tidewater bays and rivers which were available farther south along the Atlantic coast and, except for the Connecticut, lacked navigable streams leading far into the interior. Consequently at an early date this section became a center of shipbuilding and was preeminent in maritime commerce with the other coastal colonies, England, and the West Indies. The first town wharf at Boston was erected in the 1630's, a little more than a decade after the first settlement on New England shores.

The hazards of navigation around Cape Cod, which had to be risked if the New Englanders were to trade with the Dutch at New Amsterdam, attracted early attention to the possibility of cutting a canal across that cape to provide a safer sheltered route. Agitation to accomplish this was apparently started in 1676 by the small town of Sandwich, Mass. The project was surveyed by direction of the General Court of Massachusetts in 1697, and again in 1776 when an engineer named Thomas Machin was engaged to make a survey of the proposal. This survey however was interrupted by the war and General Washington's call to Machin to serve with the Continental Army. This is probably the first of many subsequent instances where American engineers engaged on waterway improvements have been called to serve in the armed forces on military engineering during the various wars.

The Connecticut River appears to have been first explored about 1610, by the Dutchman Adriaen Block, who sailed up the river as far as the rapids at present Enfield, Conn. For almost 200 years thereafter the Connecticut provided the most important transportation route in New England. During the colonial period flatboats and canoes carrying furs from trading posts and the produce of the interior moved between the falls on the river, transferred cargoes over the various falls until they finally reached Hartford, Conn. There lumber, produce, and furs were placed on sailing craft bound for Boston, New York, and the West Indies. A considerable shipbuilding industry grew up at Middletown and Wethersfield, Conn. Thus by the end of the colonial period a substantial, but rather difficult, system of water transportation had developed on the Connecticut from Wells River Junction in Vermont to the sea.

This development was based on use of the natural river; and there was little effort at improvement. Vessels could sail only a short distance above Hartford, and in this reach navigation was complicated by sandbars between Hartford and Middletown, as evidenced by the fact that as early as 1764 Hartford merchants had petitioned the Connecticut Legislature to incorporate a company to deepen that part of the river channel. Above Hartford, Enfield Rapids constituted the main obstacle to shallow draft navigation for more than 200 miles to the foot of Fifteen Mile Falls between Vermont and New Hampshire.

Down and Up the Mississippi.—Exploration and first use of the Mississippi River were closely related to explorations on the Great Lakes—one has only to recall the names of Louis Joliet, Jacques Marquette, and René Robert Cavelier, Sieur de La Salle, all of whom under orders from the French governor at Quebec undertook to pass from the Great Lakes and follow the Mississippi River to its mouth. Accomplishment of this task fell to the intrepid La Salle who began his journey through Lake Michigan in August, 1678, to reach the mouth of the Mississippi almost 4 years later in April, 1682.

Another Frenchman, Pierre Lemoine, Sieur d'Iberville, and his lieutenant Bienville, sailed up the Mississippi from its mouth in about 1699; and history records the first navigation improvement on the Mississippi when Bienville on that voyage removed a "drift wrack" to secure upstream passage of his boat. The same Bienville chose the location of New Orleans and established that city, which subsequently was made the capital of the region known as Louisiana. From the very beginning, levees and wharves were constructed along the river to protect New Orleans from overflow and to handle the growing river traffic.

The next improvement work was that of the French Government in 1726, when in order to deepen the mouth of the Mississippi River an iron harrow was dragged across the sea bar to loosen silt desposits so that they might be carried by the current to deeper water. Later in the eighteenth century the Spanish Government did some work opening the entrances of bayous Manchac and Lafourche. The methods used are not specified. No purely navigation improvement work was recorded on the river above New Orleans in the eighteenth century.

In this river traffic during the colonial period, under the French and after Louisiana was ceded to Spain in 1764, the Indian canoe was displaced by the flatboat and this in turn gave way to the more reliable keelboat. The first cargo carried on the Mississippi was a shipment of bear and deer hides in 1705 which was floated and paddled down from the Wabash and Ohio rivers to reach Biloxi, Miss., eventually for shipment to France. During the entire colonial period and up until the advent of the steamboat in 1811 practically all cargo movement was downriver.

Thus not only France and Spain but the colonists of the Atlantic seaboard, who were pushing across the Appalachians into the Ohio Valley, recognized the importance of the Mississippi; and disposition of the Lower Mississippi Valley was one of the most difficult problems during the negotiations of the American treaty of independence in Paris. The success of the American commissioners in gaining for the United States control of the east bank of the Mississippi from its source to a short distance from the Gulf of Mexico was a diplomatic victory for the new nation.

Although waterway improvements and canal building are human activities of great antiquity, which antedate the Christian era by thousands of years, it is interesting to note the indispensable canal lock came into definite use in Europe, in Italy and Holland, during the latter part of the fifteenth century; that the period 1605 to 1681 was the great time of canal building in France; and that large-scale activity in canal building in England came in the latter part of the eighteenth century, spanning the end of the colonial period in North America. Thus, in spite of the meager technical and financial resources available to them, and in spite of the lack of interest by an absentee government in Great Britain, the Americans of the colonial period were not far behind their European contemporaries in their interest in waterway development.

INFLUENCE ON ESTABLISHMENT OF THE UNION

Commerce and transportation were among the basic reasons for separation of the North American seaboard colonies from Great Britain. These same factors on the one hand pulled toward more complete union of the states after independence had been gained, and on the other hand tended toward discord and interstate rivalry.

Having grown up along the Atlantic seaboard commercially dependent upon Europe, the colonies and subsequently the thirteen original states were actually closer commercially to Europe than to each other. Furthermore, as recognized by the ablest men of the time, the allegiance of the settlers and communities developing in the vast area west of the Alleghenies would naturally follow their commercial interests. The fact that "the flanks and rear of the United States are possessed by other Powers" (Spain and Britain) was recognized by Washington in 1784 as a threat to the continued unity of the transmountain settlements and an urgent argument for routes of transportation connecting the Ohio Valley and the eastern seaboard.

Interstate Rivalries Emerge.—The convention in Philadelphia which drew up the Constitution of the United States in 1787 actually stemmed from an earlier meeting in 1785 at Mount Vernon in Virginia where representatives of two states, Maryland and Virginia, met under the guidance of Washington to settle their differences regarding navigation of the Potomac River. For almost 200 years the navigation of that stream had been a source of constant bickering between the governments and people of the two colonies. The river itself was in Maryland but the entrance to Chesapeake Bay was in the hands of Virginia and that Commonwealth had built and maintained lighthouses, and had provided buoys and other aids to navigation in both the bay and river which were essential to use of the waterway by both states.

Measures restrictive on navigation had been imposed and considered by Virginia and Maryland. Thomas Jefferson and James Madison therefore proposed in 1783 that both states appoint commissions to consider and settle this problem. The selected representatives met at Mount Vernon to draft what has become known as "the Mount Vernon Compact"—one of the most important documents in American history, as it contains on a two-state basis many of the principles which were ultimately incorporated into the Constitution.

It became apparent immediately, however, that Pennsylvania had an interest in any compact affecting Chesapeake Bay because of the Susquehanna River, and that Delaware was interested because of its desire for a water connection between the Delaware and Susquehanna rivers. This additional interest resulted in the Annapolis Convention of 1786, which, through the vision of Madison, was expanded by extension of the invitation to all states. The Annapolis gathering led in turn to the calling of the Constitutional Convention in Philadelphia in 1787. Thus waterways and the necessity for regulating commerce were major elements leading to development of the Constitution, and the "Mount Vernon Compact" foreshadowed the commerce clause of the Constitution, which remains today the basic law under which waterway improvements are undertaken by the Federal Government.

Compact Proves Unifying Force.—Furthermore this interstate compact of 1785, under which Maryland agreed to admit Virginia freely to navigation on the Potomac, and Virginia agreed to allow Maryland shipping past the capes of Chesapeake Bay without payment of duties, antedated by almost half a century the interpretation of the "commerce clause" of the Constitution by the Supreme Court in the historic case of Gibbon versus Ogden. That case established firmly the right of citizens of one state to pass freely over the rivers and waterways of another; asserted the federal control over interstate commerce that exists today; and showed that the right of the Federal Government to control included the right to improve. The historian A. J. Beveridge stated that John Marshall's decision in that case "has done more to knit the American people into an indivisible nation than any force in history except only war."

BEGINNING OF FEDERAL ACTIVITY

From the beginning of the history of the United States as an independent nation, waterways, their development and use, have been a matter of national concern. The Treaty of Independence from Great Britain, for example, contained a provision assuring that the Mississippi River "shall forever remain free and open" to the citizens of the United States and the subjects of Great Britain. Similarly the Northwest Ordinance adopted during the first session of the first Congress, in 1789, delared that:

> "The navigable waters leading into the Mississippi and St. Lawrence, and the carrying places between the same, shall be common highways, and forever free * * *."

The Constitution itself expressly delegated to Congress the power "to regulate commerce with foreign nations, and among the several states, and with the Indian tribes."

Legislative action on waterways and waterway developments was begun by the Congress in 1790; the first acts gave the consent of Congress to certain state legislation which imposed duties on cargo at ports, and provided for construction and maintenance of piers. These early acts, however, also gave congressional sanction to improvements under state law, such as

> An act of the State of Georgia * * * for the purpose of clearing the river Savannah, and removing the wrecks and other obstruction therein—approved 1790.
> An act of the general assembly of Virginia for improving the navigation of the James River—approved 1804.

The first congressional act making federal appropriations for improvements related to waterways was that of April 6, 1802, which provided for an appropriation of not more than $30,000 for repairing and erecting public piers in the Delaware River.

Farsighted Gallatin Report.—So great was the interest at this time in internal improvements such as waterways, canals, and roads that in March, 1807, the Senate passed a resolution directing the Secretary of the Treasury to investigate and report on this broad subject. Under this authority Albert Gallatin submitted a report on April 4, 1808, which was an admirable summary of the various improvements that had been proposed and a farsighted guide to future development. In that report Gallatin outlined and advocated a complete system of inland water routes which would bind together the seaboard states; and projected a system of communication between the Atlantic and the interior. His proposals were grouped as follows:

a. Canals along the seacoast, uniting New England and the South: Mainly canals cut across the necks of land which separated the major rivers and bays of the North Atlantic coast.

b. Communications between the Atlantic and the "western waters." A canal uniting the Santee and Cooper rivers in South Carolina; improvement of the Roanoke River; canalization of the James and of the Potomac; a canal around falls on the Susquehanna; and a canal connecting the Tombigbee and Tennessee rivers to connect with the port of Mobile, Ala.

c. Connections between Atlantic and Great Lakes: Canals connecting the Hudson River and Lake Champlain, between the Mohawk River and Lake Ontario, and around Niagara Falls.

d. Interior roads and canals: A fairly long list of smaller canals many of which were subsequently built by the states.

Included with Gallatin's report was a letter from Robert Fulton dated December 8, 1807, in which that noted man wrote that a balanced transportation system should include both canals and roads—canals for "the long carriage of the whole materials of agriculture and manufacture" and roads "for traveling and the more numerous communications of the country." This recommendation was a concise and accurate prediction of the present relation between waterway and overland movements. Fulton also envisioned the important principle of multiple-purpose waterway development by pointing out the possibilities of using water from the canals for irrigation. In addition, he proposed storage reservoirs for water supply for lockages and maintenance of water levels.

The Gallatin report was at once a farsighted document pointing the way to planned waterway development and a shrewd bid for political support by all the states for internal improvements of this kind. The Inland Waterways Commission appointed by President Theodore Roosevelt stated, in its preliminary report of February, 1908, that in so far as waterway development was concerned the Gallatin report was second in importance only to the "Mount Vernon Compact," and that "Gallatin's work, in conjunction with that of George Washington, may be said to have inaugurated the waterway policy of the United States."

This indication of federal interest was followed in 1809 by an act of Congress authorizing $25,000 for extension to the Mississippi River of the Carondelet Canal, leading from Lake Pontchartrain to the City of New Orleans, and its enlargement "to admit an easy and safe passage of gunboats"—one of the earliest federal recognitions of the military value of these improvements.

Early Mississippi River Legislation.—In the years following there were a number of acts in which Congress appropriated "for the military service of the United States" funds for surveying the watercourses tributary to the Mississippi—including an investigation of methods for improving the navigation of certain of those rivers and appropriations for harbor investigations on the Atlantic Ocean and Great Lakes. The Act of March 3, 1823, for example authorized $150 for examination and survey of the harbor of Presque Isle on Lake Erie in Pennsylvania and specified that it be,

> "* * * examined and surveyed by one of the Topographical Engineers of the United States, whose duty it shall be to make a probable estimate of the expense of removing the obstructions, and report on the best manner of removing them, and the effect of such removal on the channel in the future."

This act appears to be the first definite legislative assignment to the Corps of Engineers of the United States Army of a survey of a navigation improvement. It is interesting to note that this brief legislative directive contained three of the basic elements of a present-day study for an improvement of this kind: (1) Preparation of a plan of improvement, (2) an estimate of cost, and (3) an appraisal of the future effect of the work.

Two congressional acts of 1824, however, are of particular significance as they definitely mark the real beginning of the federal effort to improve the waterways of the country, and the assignment of this work to the Corps of Engineers. By Act of April 30, 1824, the President of the United States (James Monroe) was authorized to cause the necessary surveys, plans, and estimates to be made of "the routes of such roads and canals as he may deem of national importance, in a commercial or military point of view * * *." That act further authorized the President, in order to carry out the work, to employ "two or more skilful civil engineers, and such officers of the Corps of Engineers, or who may be detailed to do duty with that Corps, as he may think proper * * *." The original authority to employ civil engineers was later repealed by act of July 5, 1838; but service of the Army Engineers on this work continued without interruption.

The other act, that of May 24, 1824, authorized actual improvement of navigation on the Ohio and Mississippi rivers, appropriated $75,000 for this work, and authorized the President to employ "any of the engineers in the public service which he may deem proper." This act also specified particular sandbars in the Ohio where an effort should be made to improve the channel and provided that experimental work would be undertaken at two bars, to prove the possibility of accomplishing the work, before proceeding with the full improvement. The act also specified methods of improvement for the Ohio and Mississippi rivers (Fig. 3) to include removal of trees and snags, and the procurement of the watercraft, machinery, and equipment necessary to accomplish this purpose. This work was initiated immediately by the Army Engineers. At the same time the federal government undertook to assist in waterway development in a less direct manner by canal and navigation land grants to various states and by cash subscriptions to the stock of canal companies.

Use of "Navigation Grants."—In 1824, a special canal act for Indiana was passed by Congress but was not utilized. The first effective act making land grants to states for the specific purpose of building canals was that of March 2, 1827, which originally granted more than 500,000 acres to the states of Indiana and Illinois. Similar legislation enacted over the years through 1866 resulted in

FIG. 3.—AFTER 1811 FLATBOATS AND KEELBOATS REPLACED BY STEAMBOATS ON MISSISSIPPI RIVER AND TRIBUTARIES

TABLE 1.—LAND GRANTS TO STATES FOR BUILDING CANALS, 1827–1866

State	Canals	Acres granted
Indiana	Wabash and Erie Canal	1,457,366
Ohio	Wabash and Erie Canal	266,535
	Miami and Dayton Canal	333,826
	General canal purposes	500,000
Illinois	Illinois River to Lake Michigan	290,915
Wisconsin	Milwaukee and Rock River	125,431
	Breakwater and Harbor Ship Canal	200,000
Michigan	St. Marys Ship Canal	750,000
	Portage Lake-Lake Superior Ship Canal	400,000
	Lac LaBelle Ship Canal	100,000
Total		4,424,073

land grants of more than 4,000,000 acres to five states of the old Northwest Territory, as shown in Table 1.

Although not always productive of immediate results, the grants were basic elements in a substantial canal development in this area, particularly in Ohio. There were additional "navigation grants" of land to the Territory of Iowa for improving the navigation of the Des Moines River, and to Wisconsin, on its admission into the Union, for improvement of the Fox and Wisconsin rivers, and construction of a canal to connect them.

Beginning in 1825 and continuing through 1866 Congress by various acts authorized the Federal Government to subscribe to or purchase stock of private canal companies or to loan them money. The canals involved and the amounts involved in purchase of shares or loan were:

Canal	Amount
Chesapeake and Delaware Canal	$450,000
Louisville and Portland Canal	235,000
Dismal Swamp Canal	200,000
Chesapeake and Ohio Canal	400,000

These land grants and monetary contributions by the Federal Government gave impetus to the state and private waterway development which took place during the first half of the eighteenth century and which will be described subsequently.

Other Federal Efforts Helpful.—The earliest harbor improvements undertaken by the Federal Government were on the Great Lakes. Works at Erie, Pa., and at Cleveland and Fairport, Ohio, all on Lake Erie, were begun in 1824 and 1825. This initial harbor work carried out by the Corps of Engineers involved construction of breakwaters, jetties, and piers and the deepening of channels. From that time on and through 1850 harbor improvements were made by the Corps of Engineers with federal appropriations along the Atlantic and Gulf coasts and included work from Portland, Me., to the Head of the Passes of the Mississippi River in Louisiana. Rivers in Florida were cleared for movement of military supplies during the Seminole War; and work was started to remove the 92-mile-long "raft" of sunken logs and stumps which blocked the Red River near the present site of Shreveport, La.

Surveys were made in the Ohio River in 1821 by officers of the Corps of Engineers and the first dike construction for improvement of the Ohio River channel was started in 1825 at Henderson, Ky. The dangerous state of navigation on the Ohio River, expressed in a memorial of the citizens of Cincinnati, Ohio, to Congress, is shown by the record of one hundred and thirty-eight steamboats wrecked in the years from 1839 to 1842. Work on the Cumberland River below Nashville, Tenn., began about 1832; and work on the Missouri River, in 1838.

After appropriation of funds in 1824 for removal of snags from the Mississippi and Ohio rivers the War Department selected Capt. Henry M. Shreve to superintend this work. He designed and supervised construction of the special snagboats necessary to remove dangerous obstructions. By 1830 snagging of the main Mississippi River channel was essentially complete; and thereafter it became a matter of routine maintenance. Shreve had the first artificial cutoff constructed on the Mississippi River near Angola, La., and was also the engineer who attempted to remove the Red River raft.

Prior to 1850 there was a considerable commerce on the western rivers; and steamboats ascended the Missouri to near Independence, Mo., the eastern terminus of the Santa Fe Trail (Fig. 4), and upstream to Fort Benton, Mont. Water transportation on the difficult Colorado River began in 1851, to supply the military post at Yuma, Ariz.

American interest in waterway improvements on the Pacific coast appears to have begun shortly after the Mexican War, when California became a part of the national territory. The shipping to California, and other activity, arising from the 1849 "Gold Rush," developed more interest in the western coastal harbors. Federal harbor improvements on the Pacific coast began at San Diego, Calif., in 1852.

Most of the improvements undertaken by the Federal Government before 1852 were relatively small by present-day standards, although important in their time; and, in spite of the broad geographic distribution of the activity, the federal appropriations from 1787 through 1850 for river and harbor work totaled only about $13,000,000. The early federal improvements prior to 1852,

FIG. 4.—WESTWARD ADVANCE—FROM STEAMBOAT ON MISSOURI RIVER TO WAGONS ON SANTA FE TRAIL AT INDEPENDENCE, MO.

however, laid the groundwork for the major waterway developments which were to take place in the next century.

ERA OF STATE AND PRIVATE CANALS

Concurrently with the beginnings of federal waterway development there was a large amount of state and private activity in waterway improvements—particularly canals. This activity reached its height during the first half of the nineteenth century, was slowed down by the financial depression of 1837, and finally was terminated by the growth and ascendency of the railroads. Most of these canals were not successful financially, but in their time they represented an important phase of waterway development in the United States.

New England.—As early as 1795 a canal had been built in Maine along the line of the Stevens River connecting the Kennebec River and Casco Bay. Canal construction in Maine also included the work of the Cumberland and Oxford Canal Company which completed in 1829 a waterway 40 miles long connecting Sebago Pond and Portland harbor with 20 miles of artificial canalization.

In New Hampshire waterway improvements involved chiefly the Merrimack and Connecticut rivers. Three canals, Bellows Falls, Water Quechee, and White River, were constructed around falls to improve the navigability of the Connecticut; and the Merrimack was made navigable by various methods. The Amoskeag Canal, the most important Merrimack River improvement, was first built chiefly of wood within the natural banks of the river but was not successful and was replaced by a canal in the banks around falls. It was a mile in length and had three locks, of white oak timber and pine planks, to overcome a total fall of about 45 ft. The locks are reported to have been 100 ft long and 10 ft wide.

Western Vermont was more accessible for trade with Montreal and Quebec via Lake Champlain and the St. Lawrence than with the seaboard ports of New England. Plans were made for a canal from Rutland to Windsor on the Connecticut; but nothing came of this scheme, or of later surveys undertaken jointly in 1825 by commissioners appointed by Vermont and by engineers of the Federal Government.

The most important early waterway developments in New England were those of Massachusetts. Construction was begun in 1793 on a canal connecting with the Merrimack, leading around Pawtucket Falls, and by 1821 this project was 90 ft wide and 4 ft deep. The South Hadley Canal, begun in 1792 to pass a fall of 50 ft in the Connecticut, was 2 miles long, with five locks which replaced an inclined plane first used for raising and lowering boats. A feature of this canal was a cut more than 40 ft deep and 300 ft long through rock—a difficult construction task for that day.

The most important and ambitious early waterway improvement in Massachusetts was the Middlesex Canal which was begun by a company incorporated during the period 1789–1793. The original project contemplated an extensive navigation system extending to the lakes of New Hampshire. By 1804 the project was partly accomplished and provided a canal 27 miles long from the Merrimack to the vicinity of the Charles River near Boston. The canal with a bottom width of 20 ft was intended to carry boats of 25 tons, drawing 3 ft of water. It was carried over seven rivers and streams by an aqueduct and was fed by the Concord River. The Gallatin report states that this canal included nineteen locks to overcome a total fall of 107 ft. The cost of the canal up to 1804 was reported to be about $914,000. It was successful in providing a route for trade from New Hampshire to Boston.

Subsequently, the opening of the Erie Canal in New York and the growing importance of the port of New York began to draw New England trade down the Connecticut to Hartford and to New York. As a result there was considerable agitation and planning for a waterway from Boston to the Connecticut and on westward to the Hudson. Loammi Baldwin, an engineer employed by the Massachusetts Canal Commissioners, estimated the cost of such a canal at more than $6,000,000 and pointed out the almost insurmountable difficulties west of the Connecticut River. This project was not undertaken as it depended largely on state aid which was not forthcoming; and the proposal was superseded in 1829 by interest in railroads.

Navigation improvements in Connecticut largely involved the Connecticut River. Traffic reached its height early in the nineteenth century, and by 1810 it was possible to go as far north as the foot of Fifteen Mile Falls, 220 miles above Hartford, with only Enfield Rapids as an obstruction. The Connecticut

River Company was chartered by the State in 1824 to develop the Connecticut, operate shipping, and dig a canal around Enfield Rapids. This company was later authorized to attempt to interest the Federal Government in improvement of the Connecticut; and in 1825 an Army Engineer is reported to have arrived to direct surveys of the proposals. In 1829 the digging of the Enfield Canal was finished by the hand labor of Irish immigrants, and by 1833 water power was being used at the Enfield site to turn millwheels.

The Blackstone Canal constructed in 1826-1828, with a total length of 45 miles, permitted navigation between Worcester, Mass., and Providence, R. I.

State and private canals built in New England aggregated about 200 miles

FIG. 5.—ERIE CANAL, OPENED IN 1825, WHICH ENCOURAGED BUILDING OF MANY CANALS BY STATES AND PRIVATE COMPANIES

in length. They were abandoned after construction of the railroads in the period from 1848 to 1875.

New York.—The rivers and topography of New York presented unique opportunities for water routes to the western country via the Mohawk Valley and northward via the Hudson and Lake Champlain.

The Hudson-Mohawk route, used in colonial times, continued to hold the interest of those concerned with communication with the Great Lakes and Ohio Valley. Much has been written of the early development and subsequent enlargements of the Erie Canal, but this development (Fig. 5) is particularly noteworthy in any chronicle of American waterway development because of the immediate and lasting success of the enterprise in providing a water route to the west, and because the same canal enlarged by the Federal Government and the State of New York is in use today—the only one of the early major state canals which has large commercial usage at the present time.

The Mohawk route to the west was urged in early colonial times. Successive acts of the New York State Legislature from 1787 to 1792, when the Western and Northern Inland Lock Navigation Company was incorporated to open navigation from the Hudson to the Great Lakes and to the St. Lawrence, laid the groundwork for actual construction. Christopher Colles who has been designated as the "first projector of inland navigation in America" had promoted a canal via the Mohawk route as early as 1773; and De Witt Clinton was a subsequent proponent. Many difficulties were encountered, however, particularly those stemming from claimants for rival routes, including the question as to whether the western terminus should be in Lake Erie or Lake Ontario; and not until 1817 was excavation of the canal begun across the divide to Wood Creek near the present site of Rome, N. Y.

The work involved great difficulties including the excavation and removal of buried tree trunks, and was accomplished by mule-drawn scrapers, an innovation greatly superior to the pick-and-shovel methods previously employed. As originally constructed the canal was 40 ft wide at the top, 28 ft wide at the bottom, and 4 ft deep. In October, 1825, the first boat passed through from Lake Erie to the Hudson River, and a month later the completion of the canal was celebrated in New York City.

The importance of opening the Erie Canal route was summarized in *Executive Document No. 136, Thirty-Second Congress*:

> "It is difficult to estimate the influence this canal has exerted upon the commerce, growth and prosperity of the whole country. But for this work the West would have held few inducements to the settler, the East would have been without elements of growth."

Although this appraisal now appears somewhat exaggerated, it was an accurate portrayal of the thought of the time regarding this outstanding development.

After the opening of the Erie Canal there was great interest in canals in New York (which was reflected in other parts of the United States). During the period from 1825 into the 1870's more than 1,000 miles of canals were constructed in New York alone, including the canal to Lake Champlain. Depths of the canals varied usually from 4 ft to 7 ft. Many carried substantial traffic and more than 600 miles of New York canals were still in operation in 1907—almost a century later.

Middle Atlantic States.—Waterway development in New Jersey during this period resulted in construction of two canals:

a. The Delaware and Raritan Canal, connecting the Delaware and Raritan rivers, was built by a company incorporated in 1830 and completed about 1838. This canal, with an extension to Trenton, had a total length of about 66 miles, with depths of about 8 ft, and numerous locks. Used by self-propelled craft and by barges pulled by animal power along a towpath, it carried considerable traffic but was finally taken over by the Pennsylvania Railroad in 1871.

b. The Morris Canal from the Delaware River opposite Easton, Pa., to the Hudson River at Jersey City, N. J., was constructed by the Morris Canal and Banking Company, a private corporation chartered by the State of New Jersey in 1824, and completed to the Hudson in 1836. It was about 102 miles long; provided depths of 5 ft and included twenty-three locks and an equal number of inclined planes for raising and lowering boats. The canal is reported to have crossed an elevation of 914 ft above tidewater; and its major purpose was shipment of coal. It was successful only during the War Between the States when heavy tonnages of coal were moved along this route. It could not compete with rail transportation, however, and came under control of the Lehigh Valley Railroad Company in 1871.

In Pennsylvania, as in the other seaboard states there was strong interest in communications and trade with the country west of the Alleghenies. Rivalry for this trade was particularly keen between Philadelphia, Baltimore, and New York. As early as 1791 a society headed by Robert Morris was influential in promoting inland navigation in Pennsylvania; and a canal from Philadelphia to Pittsburgh, Pa., was projected. This ambitious plan was never completed, although parts of a canal along this route were placed in operation.

Many of the waterway improvements in Pennsylvania during this period have been characterized as the "anthracite" canals, because they were, like the Morris Canal, built primarily to haul coal. In fact many of the early corporations engaged in mining coal in Pennsylvania were designated as "coal and navigation" companies. About 1,100 miles of these canals were constructed in Pennsylvania between 1821 and 1844—including canals connecting the Delaware and Hudson and a canal connecting the upper Delaware and the Hudson rivers at Kingston, N. Y. Navigation of the Schuylkill was bettered by canalization and open-channel work, and improvements were made along the Lehigh and Susquehanna rivers.

Navigation developments in connection with coal mining along the Lehigh River are of particular interest as the early coal-carrying canals connecting with the Hudson were built largely to supplement the Lehigh improvements. At first coal is said to have been floated down the Lehigh in wooden arks by means of "artificial freshets," the arks being broken up for lumber on arrival in Philadelphia. Coal-carrying canalboats were used after completion of the Lehigh waterway in 1820.

The Susquehanna River and its tributaries largely provided the basis for the waterways of Pennsylvania. By 1790 there was a considerable traffic on the Susquehanna as far downstream as Middletown, Pa. Below that point and on to tidewater at Havre de Grace, Md., navigation of the natural river was difficult and dangerous. In 1811 certain earlier canal companies were reorganized as the Union Canal Company; and by 1827 the 77-mile-long Union Canal had been completed joining the Susquehanna at Middletown with Reading, Pa., on the Schuylkill to provide a water route via the latter stream to Philadelphia. This canal was too small to accomplish its purpose of diverting Susquehanna River trade to Philadelphia.

At this time Pennsylvania permitted the building of dams on the Susquehanna below Wrights Ferry which interfered with navigation and stirred up protest on the part of Maryland interests, who benefited from trade down the Susquehanna. With completion of the Chesapeake and Delaware Canal in 1830, navigation on the lower Susquehanna assumed greater importance, both to Philadelphia and Baltimore, and the Susquehanna and Tide-water Canal was constructed in 1837–1840. This canal continued in operation with considerable success until 1895. By 1907 more than 900 miles of the Pennsylvania canals had been abandoned, generally because of railroad competition for handling coal.

In Delaware and Maryland, the waterway interest centered largely on a canal connecting the Delaware River and Chesapeake Bay. This project was conceived in 1799 but was not completed until 1830 by a reorganized company to which the states of Delaware, Pennsylvania, and Maryland and the Federal Government subscribed. As constructed the canal had a bottom width of 42 ft and a depth of 10 ft. It was subsequently adopted as a federal project and enlarged by the Federal Government. As originally constructed the canal proved to be an important element in trade of the interior with both Philadelphia and Baltimore.

Southern States.—State and private interests in waterways in Virginia were concentrated on the routes to the Ohio Valley which had been given much attention during the colonial period: The Potomac River-Youghiogheny-Monongahela route through Pennsylvania; and the James River-Kanawha route through Virginia (later West Virginia).

In 1786 the Potomac Canal Company was organized with Washington as president, to undertake improvement of the Potomac channel to Cumberland, Md. This company completed a canal by 1802 with large masonry locks, one cut in solid rock, on the Virginia side of the river, bypassing the Great and Little Falls of the Potomac. The company also built other short reaches of canal bypassing falls above and below Harpers Ferry, Va. (later W. Va.), and deepened and improved the river channel. Although accomplishment of this work was a noteworthy engineering achievement in its time, the cost was great, about $7,000,000, and the company became bankrupt in 1819. However, interest in the route continued and the Corps of Engineers prepared a report in 1826 which proposed a canal on the Maryland side of the river from Georgetown to Cumberland. This was accomplished by the Chesapeake and Ohio Canal Company (Fig. 6), incorporated originally by the Virginia Legislature in 1823, and by 1830 some 20 miles were open to navigation above Little Falls. The canal was completed up to Cumberland with depths of 6 ft to 7 ft at a cost of about $11,600,000. The Federal Government took part in this canal work by appropriation of funds for surveys in 1824 and later by purchase of stock in the company.

The earliest improvement of the Potomac at Washington, D. C., appears to have been the cutting, in 1804 and years immediately thereafter, of a channel through shoals in the river. A "mud machine" was used to do this work.

The James River Canal (Fig. 7), on which work was begun prior to the Revolutionary War, was one of the last of the major canals constructed during the era of state and private waterway activity. It was built in the period 1825–1856. Although the original purpose was a water connection with the Kanawha and the first division to Lynchburg, Va., was completed in 1840 with a depth of 5 ft, work was discontinued after 15 miles of the division beyond Buchanan, Va., had been put under contract. The cost of the work was more than $10,400,000. The James River Company did some canal work in the Blue Ridge and made some improvements on the Kanawha River from Charleston, Va. (later W. Va.), to its mouth by means of wing dams and sluices, but no through waterway was ever completed.

Another waterway improvement of interest was the Dismal Swamp Canal,

FIG. 6.—OLD CANAL LOCK CONSTRUCTED IN EARLY NINETEENTH CENTURY ON CHESAPEAKE AND OHIO
CANAL IN GEORGETOWN, MD. (LATER D. C.)

FIG. 7.—SCENE NEAR MOUTH OF NORTH RIVER, JAMES RIVER CANAL, ONE OF LAST VENTURES BY
STATES AND PRIVATE COMPANIES—WHICH NEVER REACHED ITS DESTINATION, THE OHIO VALLEY

one of the oldest artificial waterways in the United States, which was begun in 1787 and completed in 1794. This canal with a length of about 22 miles extended from Deep Creek, Va., to South Mills, N. C. It was originally constructed to pass, during the dry season, vessels drawing 3 ft of water, and was also the initial step toward drainage of lands of the Dismal Swamp. The project was built by a private company incorporated by the general assemblies of Virginia and North Carolina, and under its original charter was empowered to receive subscriptions in "Spanish" milled dollars. The Federal Government bought shares in the company in 1829. It was taken over and used by the Union Army during the War Between the States, and eventually became a federal project as a part of the present Intracoastal Waterway.

In North Carolina there was interest in improvement of the Roanoke, Yadkin, Catawba, Tar, Neuse, and Cape Fear rivers, and in coastal waterways to channel commerce to ports in the state. Charters were granted by the state legislature in 1819; but the only construction appears to have been a 12-mile canal built in 1829 around the falls of the Roanoke near Weldon.

Farther south in South Carolina and Georgia the unimproved, or slightly improved, natural rivers furnished the best means of transportation to the interior of the Piedmont country. It was reported that as late as 1818 two thirds of the market crops of the southern Piedmont were raised within 5 miles of some river. The Santee, Savannah, and Altamaha provided routes to the Piedmont; and further South in Florida the St. Johns was utilized. The usual rivalry for trade with the interior sprang up between the ports of Charleston, S. C., and Savannah, Ga.

South Carolina inaugurated a large program of internal waterways between 1819 and 1828; and by 1825 locks, sluices, and open-channel work on the Saluda, Congaree, and Santee rivers and the Santee Canal made it possible for boats laden with forty bales of cotton to descend from near Abbeville to Charleston. Improvements were also made on the Wateree and Great Pee Dee rivers. These projects appear to have been accomplished by companies or by individuals working as groups. As a general rule both South Carolina and Georgia accomplished their own river improvements through local boards and state appropriations. This policy continued as late as 1829.

The Middle West.—Interest in waterway improvements in the region west of the Appalachians appears to have begun with the first settlement of the territory; and it was given powerful impetus by the success of the Erie Canal in New York. The falls of the Ohio at Louisville, obstructing open-river navigation on that important stream turned the minds of the early settlers to canals.

There was considerable competition between the people of Indiana and Kentucky as to which side of the river should be the site of a canal around the Louisville Falls. Not until 1828, some 40 years after settlement in the area, was the Louisville and Portland Canal constructed, with federal aid, and Ohio River navigation was improved greatly.

Meawhile, during the first half of the nineteenth century, Ohio, Indiana, and Illinois became the scenes of a large amount of canal construction. Ohio was a leader in this work. As early as 1812 a private individual was empowered by the Ohio Legislature to build a dam on the Muskingum which was constructed to improve navigation and to produce water power. In 1825 Ohio began its two major canals:

  a. The Ohio and Erie Canal (generally called the Ohio Canal) extended from Cleveland on Lake Erie to Portsmouth on the Ohio River, a distance of 309 miles. This canal followed the valleys of the Scioto and Muskingum rivers. It was completed in 1833, and involved lockages totaling 1,218 ft.

  b. The Miami and Erie Canal connected Toledo on Lake Erie with Cincinnati on the Ohio, a distance of 244 miles, passing by Dayton in the valley of the Great Miami River.

The Muskingum River was canalized from Dresden to Marietta on the Ohio, a distance of 91 miles, and numerous feeder canals were constructed connecting with these two major routes. By 1846 Ohio had more than 800 miles of canals and canalized rivers.

Kentucky undertook the canalization of the Green and Barren rivers about 1835. Although the work was never fully completed by the state, it was opened to navigation in 1841.

In Indiana a network of 900 miles of canals was projected, but was accomplished only to the extent of building the Wabash and Erie Canal in 1832–1851 for a length of 379 miles from Evansville to the Ohio state line.

Early waterway improvement in Illinois largely involved the completion by 1848 of the Illinois and Michigan Canal connecting Lake Michigan at Chicago with the Illinois River—the initial step toward the present Great Lakes to Gulf waterway. Abraham Lincoln began in that area the active interest in waterway improvements which continued throughout his public life. The State of Michigan, concerned largely with traffic on the Great Lakes, began construction of the St. Marys Falls Canal between lakes Superior and Huron in 1853, to inaugurate the development at the "Soo"' (Sault St. Marie).

Louisiana was also the site of considerable state and private activity in canal construction during the early part of the nineteenth century. The canal fever also spread to the Pacific coast at a later date when the canal and locks at Oregon City, Ore., were built in 1870–1872.

  Canals Important, Despite Limitations.—The period of intense state and private activity in waterway development, particularly canal construction, largely came to an end at about the middle of the nineteenth century. A considerable part of the work was ill advised and influenced to a large degree by the success of the Erie Canal in New York—without full realization of the physical and economic factors favoring that project. The railroads provided faster and more flexible transportation with which the small private and state canals could not compete; and most of them were abandoned.

The most complete résumé of the state and private canals constructed during this period is that contained in the 1908 preliminary report of the Inland Waterways Commission. The data given in that report are admittedly incomplete but indicate completion of more than 4,400 miles of canals at a cost approaching $300,-000,000. At the time of the report more than 2,400 miles of these canals had been abandoned. At the present time the Erie Canal—in the form of its successor, the New York State Barge Canal—is the only one remaining in substantial commercial use, except for those, such as the Chesapeake and Delaware Canal, which have been incorporated into modern federal projects. Numerous reaches of the old canals, however, remain open for local and recreational use; and in some instances they provide water supplies and water for development of power.

There has been a tendency to deprecate the importance of this phase of waterway development in the United States; but as a matter of fact the period of state and private activity and the works resulting therefrom represented a significant stage in the development of the United States. Heavy traffic moved over the better located and managed canals; and towns, cities, and industry grew rapidly along their banks.

The canals were equally important to the rise and development of the engineering profession and construction industry in the United States. At the close of the Revolutionary War there were few engineers in this country; but engineering talent was found and developed to build the thousands of miles of state and private waterways which were placed in operation during the following half century. Army engineers were detailed by the Federal Government, or employed as private individuals, on many of these projects.

The works themselves with canal locks of wood and masonry which superseded inclined planes for raising and lowering ships, open-channel structures such as wing dams and wooden flumes; aqueducts whereby canals were carried across streams; reservoirs to supply water to summit levels hundreds of feet above tidewater; surveys of routes of available water supply; and estimates of cost—all represented pioneer advances in engineering theory and practice. Methods of construction advanced from the use of the pick and shovel, by slave labor in some cases, to the use of animal-drawn scrapers, dredges, and the crude beginnings of other construction machinery. Companies were organized and contractors were found who were willing to undertake the work.

WATERWAY DEVELOPMENT, 1852–1952

The 100 years just passed have witnessed both a decline and resurgence of inland waterway development in the United States. The revival of water-borne commerce and the development of waterways to their present status have in fact mostly come about in the past 40 years.

1. Résumé of Over-All Program

Although the engineering advances and technical improvements which have been a basic element of this development have been continuous, and have stemmed from earlier noteworthy achievements, their pace has greatly accelerated since the beginning of the twentieth century.

Federal Appropriations.—While the federal interest in waterway development began at a much earlier date, after 1850 the improvement of waterways in the United States has been carried on essentially as a federal activity. Consequently federal authorizations and appropriations for this work are an indication of the rate of progress and represent a measure of the scope and status of the program that has developed. These federal appropriations, by decades, including those made in recent years for flood control, have been as follows:

Decade	Appropriations
1824–1830	$ 3,900,000
1831–1840	7,800,000
1841–1850	1,400,000
1851–1860	3,300,000
1861–1870	17,300,000
1871–1880	60,400,000
1881–1890	108,500,000
1891–1900	166,700,000
1901–1910	254,700,000
1911–1920	347,200,000
1921–1930	674,800,000
1931–1940	1,904,000,000
1941–1950	3,126,900,000
1951	619,000,000
1952	581,200,000
Total	$7,877,100,000

Of the total amount appropriated through fiscal year 1952, $4,144,000,000 was for navigation improvements—about 90% since 1910. Allocation of the total appropriation for federal river and harbor activities through fiscal year 1952 is given in Table 2. Fig. 8 illustrates the snagging and clearing of channels.

TABLE 2.—FEDERAL FUNDS FOR RIVERS AND HARBORS, INCLUDING FISCAL YEAR 1952, IN MILLIONS OF DOLLARS

Item	New work construction	Maintenance, operation, and care	Total
Seacoast harbors	807.9	547.7	1,355.6
Great Lakes harbors and channels	228.3	159.8	388.1
Inland and intracoastal waterways	1,159.2	564.5	1,723.7
Total	2,195.4	1,272.0	3,467.4
Old work superseded and prior to current program			410.0
Snagging and clearing channels, and other general authorities			266.6
Total			4,144.0

The appropriations in Table 2 have been made to carry out "river and harbor" work under the jurisdiction of the Corps of Engineers. In addition, a substantial part of the project for flood control and navigation in the alluvial valley of the Mississippi River is chargeable to navigation; part of the appropriations for the Tennessee Valley Authority have been expended for navigation on the Tennessee River; and parts of the cost of certain projects undertaken by the Bureau of Reclamation have been allocated to navigation.

Present Status Summarized.—The federal appropriations have been utilized to carry out navigation improvements authorized specifically by Congress over the years in river and harbor legislation, and to maintain and operate the works on completion. The magnitude and status of the waterway program which has resulted is given in Table 3.

2. Procedure for Investigation and Authorization

The current waterway program is the result of a procedure for authorization and investigation which has developed as a result of practical experience and

Fig. 8.—Removing Snags from Navigation Channel of Mississippi River

TABLE 3.—Federal Authorizations, Status of Works for Navigation

Status	No. of authorizations	Estimated federal cost[a] (1951)	Funds[a] appropriated through 1952[b]	Funds required to complete[a]
Completed	1,721	914.7	859.2	55.5
Under construction:				
In operation	155	1,367.8	1,052.9	314.9
Not yet in operation.....	34	1,171.4	271.1	900.3
Authorized; not started...	369	3,174.1	12.2	3,161.9
Total	2,279	6,628.0	2,195.4	4,432.6

[a] New work, in millions of dollars.   [b] Fiscal year.

congressional legislation almost entirely during the past 100 years. It consists of two major steps:

   a. Authorization of specific investigations and reports; and

   b. Authorization of specific projects and plans of improvement.

This authorization procedure covers the life history of a project from the time its investigation is initiated by local interests acting through their representatives in Congress until, if it is found to meet the standards prescribed by law, it is authorized by Congress for construction by the Federal Government. As a general rule both investigations and projects must be specifically authorized by Congress. The authority for independent action delegated by Congress to the Chief of Engineers is limited to necessary project modifications, and that delegated to miscellaneous general and continuing authorities is limited to work of an emergency nature or to operations that are required annually.

The first step toward authorization of a given waterway improvement is taken when local individuals and organizations express to their representatives in Congress their interest in and desire for the project. The Representatives or Senators concerned then obtain an authorization for an investigation and a report by the Corps of Engineers, either by legislative authority in a River and Harbor Act or, in appropriate cases, by a resolution of one of the committees on public works.

Methods of Authorizing Investigations.—Thus a study and report may be authorized by Congress in either of two ways:

a. If no previous study and report has been authorized, an item directing the study must be incorporated in a river and harbor bill. Enactment of that bill into law authorizes the investigation and report.

b. If a previous study and a report have been made, the Public Works Committee of the Senate or House may by resolution request that the Board of Engineers for Rivers and Harbors or the Chief of Engineers review such prior report or reports, with a view to determining if circumstances have so changed as to justify modification of the previous conclusions and recommendations. Congress has limited the scope of such review reports.

As of January, 1952, the authorized program of three hundred and fourteen navigation investigations and reports assigned to the Corps of Engineers—exclusive of reports which had been completed by the field offices and were before the Board of Engineers for Rivers and Harbors or with the affected states or other federal agencies for review and comments—can be broken down as follows:

Cost	Dollars
Total estimated cost.......................	12,600,000
Appropriated to June 30, 1951..............	6,200,000
Required to complete......................	6,400,000

At the rate of appropriations for examinations and surveys which prevailed during the 5-year period prior to fiscal year 1952, completion of the current survey program would require from 5 to 6 years. Despite the magnitude of the navigation program already reported on and authorized, there remain many problems and potentialities that have not been passed on.

Survey Procedures.—After authorization of an investigation the next step in the authorization procedure is the study and report by the Corps of Engineers. The engineering and economic soundness of waterway improvements depends largely on the adequacy of the investigation and planning procedures utilized by the Corps of Engineers which are a basis for its recommendations. These policies and procedures which have resulted in the current Civil Works Program have been improved and modified as the federal interest in water resource development has expanded, on the basis of experience gained over the years. They have passed through definite stages from studies of individual situations and projects to planning for harbors and rivers, and to comprehensive investigations for entire river basins.

In brief, the current investigating and planning procedures of the Corps require that full consideration be given to all water resource potentialities and problems, with a view to development of sound and comprehensive plans for river basin improvement. It is possible to incorporate a vast amount of technical and scientific experience which has been made available largely during the past 20 years. This advance in engineering studies has been paralleled by a more exhaustive economic evaluation of proposed improvements, and by greater coordination with federal, state, and local interests.

The policies followed by the Corps in investigating and planning civil works stem from the commerce clause of the Constitution, and from the various acts of Congress which form the body of the river and harbor and flood-control legislation. These legislative bases have been expanded from requirements pertaining solely to navigation to the many related aspects of river basin improvement, such as hydroelectric power, preservation of fish and wildlife, and others which have been incorporated into civil works legislation during the past decade. Accordingly, it has been necessary for the Corps of Engineers to develop administrative policies and procedures to keep pace with the expanding federal interest expressed by legislative enactments.

Prior to 1900 most investigation and planning by the Corps of Engineers were for navigation, except for the work of the Mississippi River Commission which began in 1879. Since 1900, advances have included establishment of the Board of Engineers for Rivers and Harbors in 1902, provisions for consideration of hydroelectric power in reports in 1909; and provision for consideration of flood control and other water problems and uses in studies by act of 1917. The River and Harbor Act of 1920 first defined the local cooperation to be required in navigation improvements.

Investigations, Followed by Reports.—In 1925 and 1927, authorization by Congress of the "308" surveys broadened the basis for investigation by the Corps of Engineers and resulted for the first time in a comprehensive effort to assess the problems and potentialities of practically all the major river basins of the United States. These studies covering some 200 rivers considered navigation, flood control, power development, irrigation, and other water uses and problems; and were the first application of multiple-use water resource planning on a nation-wide basis. The "308" surveys were largely completed in the decade following 1927.

Authorization of the major project for navigation and flood control of the alluvial valley of the Mississippi River in 1928 placed with the Corps of Engineers the responsibility for planning and executing that most important improvement. Establishment of the Beach Erosion Board in 1930 recognized the importance and necessity for coastal engineering and federal assistance in planning coastal improvements. The first general flood-control act of 1936 established federal interest in nation-wide flood control and initiated a chain of legislative actions which necessitated rapid expansion of planning procedures that are applicable to many navigation improvements, including:

> More detailed coordination with other federal agencies,
> Acknowledgment of rights and interests of affected states,

Provision for hydroelectric power development,
Consideration of consumptive uses of water,
Recognition of major drainage as an element of flood control,
Provision for recreational facilities and public use of reservoir areas,
Preservation of fish and wildlife resources,
Disposal of hydroelectric power and allocation of costs,
Distribution of water for domestic and industrial use,
Regulation of flood storage in reservoirs, and
Study of need for highway crossings over dams.

These provisions were embodied in the law in the various acts up to and including that of May, 1950, and the Corps of Engineers has implemented them by administrative procedures.

The actual work of investigation and planning, including surveys and preparation of reports, is done by the staffs of the division and district offices of the Corps of Engineers. In this paper, it need be stated only that the studies fall into two general groups:

a. The preliminary examination, prepared at small cost, on the basis of reconnaissance and readily available data, to determine whether the proposed improvement has sufficient apparent merit to warrant a detailed survey.

b. The survey, based on more detailed field surveys and on engineering and economic studies, to develop the best plan of improvement, to estimate its approximate cost, and to determine its economic value.

All reports resulting from these investigations are reviewed by the Board of Engineers for Rivers and Harbors. Unfavorable preliminary examination reports are submitted to Congress, and no further investigations are made. Favorable preliminary examinations result in surveys and survey-type reports. These are also transmitted to Congress after review by the Board of Engineers for Rivers and Harbors, by affected states, by other federal agencies concerned, and by the Bureau of the Budget. A favorable report does not constitute authority for construction; any improvement recommended therein must be authorized by Congress before it can be undertaken.

During the 21-year period, 1930 through 1950, the Board of Engineers for Rivers and Harbors has acted on 3,177 reports, with the following results:

Unfavorable preliminary examinations............   926 (29.1%)
Unfavorable survey reports......................   827 (26.1%)
Favorable survey reports........................ 1,424 (44.8%)

Total 3,177 (100%)

Those proposals having little possibility of justification are turned down at the preliminary examination stage; surveys are recommended when preliminaries show possibilities of developing feasible and economical projects. It is to be expected, therefore, that a higher proportion of favorable recommendations occur in survey reports. In the 21-year period, 37% of 2,251 survey reports was unfavorable, and 63% was favorable.

Action by Congress.—The reports and recommendations prepared by the Corps of Engineers are transmitted to Congress; and on the basis of favorable recommendations projects are authorized individually, usually as an item in a river and harbor bill prepared by the House Committee on Public Works, then sent to the corresponding comittee of the Senate for its action. Both committees hold extensive public hearings in connection with the bill, at which representatives of the Corps of Engineers, of other interested federal agencies, and of state and local interests may and do appear to voice their views on the proposed improvements. On enactment of the bill, the improvements become authorized for construction by the United States, and eligible for appropriation of federal funds. The authorized project is always specific and limited, either in the report of the Corps or as specified in the act; the authorized plan may not be materially modified without additional authorization by Congress.

Summary of Basic Features.—The procedure for authorization and investigation of waterway improvements which has developed on the basis of federal legislation, largely during the past half century, has been considered by some as cumbersome and time consuming. However, it insures that a project recommended to and authorized by Congress is the result of careful investigation and review and should be sound from engineering and economic standpoints. The procedure includes the following essentials:

a. Positive control by Congress over the authorization process.

b. Full consideration of local and state views and interests through local public hearings during preparation of the report, public hearings before the Board of Engineers for Rivers and Harbors, and final review by the affected states.

c. Coordination with other federal agencies to avoid conflicts and insure consideration of all water uses and problems.

d. Critical review at successive levels of the organization of the Corps of Engineers—by districts, divisions, the Board of Engineers for Rivers and Harbors, and the Office, Chief of Engineers.

e. Review by the Bureau of the Budget for conformance with the programs and policies of the administration.

f. Review and consideration by the Public Works Committee of Congress, involving public hearings where all interests may appear to express their views regarding authorization of an improvement.

3. Continuing and General Authorizations

In addition to the individual authorizations of specific navigation projects and plans previously discussed, Congress has made available to the Chief of Engineers certain continuing and general authorizations, under which he may perform certain recurring works of waterway development.

Survey of Northern and Northwestern Lakes.—In 1841, Congress authorized the charting of 9,500 sq miles of the Great Lakes system, with an initial appropriation of $15,000, and assigned this work to the Corps of Engineers. The survey was for the dual purposes of furnishing charts to lake navigators and of determining improvements necessary to maintaining the rapidly growing lake commerce. In 1911 the scope of this lake survey was extended to include the lakes and other navigable waters of the New York State canals; in 1913, to include Lake Champlain; and, in 1914, to include the boundary waters between Lake of the Woods and Lake Superior.

The lake survey has necessarily been a continuing work in which enormous engineering difficulties have arisen in the precise charting of these large bodies of water. In carrying out this work, the survey has made numerous contributions in the field of engineering. It devised and projected the "wire sweep" that today is the accepted method of locating underwater obstructions; it designed and built the first metal tower for use in triangulation and the first electric-recording current meter; it was the first agency to print navigation charts in color; and it provides the basic information needed for maintenance of adequate channels in one of the most important waterways in the world.

Replacement of Obsolete Navigation Structures.—Under the River and Harbor Act of July 5, 1884, as amended by the Act of March 3, 1909, the Secretary of the Army is charged with preserving and continuing the use and navigation of canals and other public works. Whenever, in his judgment, the condition of any federal navigation work is such that its entire reconstruction is essential to its efficient and economical maintenance and operation, the Secretary may authorize reconstruction to include modifications in plan and location necessary to provide for existing navigation.

The only instance in which the Corps of Engineers has exercised this general authority was for the Morgantown lock and dam on the Monongahela River, which was constructed to replace two obsolete lock-and-dam structures that were more than 45 years old. Many of the older navigation locks and dams are now becoming obsolete, however, and a major lock and dam replacement program is imminent. The Corps of Engineers has begun plans for such a program on the Ohio River.

Supervision of New York Harbor.—The New York Harbor Act approved June 29, 1888, forbids discharging, or depositing debris, other than that flowing from streets and sewers in a liquid state, in the tidal waters of the harbor of New York, or in its adjacent or tributary waters, or in those of Long Island Sound, within limits to be prescribed by the Supervisor of the Harbor. The "adjacent" waters include the sea approaches to New York harbor. The tributary waters include the Hudson River to Troy, N. Y.

The office of Supervisor of New York Harbor was established pursuant to the act and was placed under the direction of the Secretary of War and under the supervision of the Chief of Engineers. Subsequently, the Supervisor has been charged with enforcing in that area the Oil Pollution Act of 1924. Under the original law the Supervisor of New York Harbor was required to be a naval officer, but a recent act of Congress in 1952 assigned this duty to an officer of the Corps of Engineers of the Army.

The Supervisor designates dumping grounds for stone, ashes, mud, cellar dirt, sewage, sludge, and other refuse. He also issues permits for removing material from the harbor. Since 1890, more than 1,368,000,000 cu yd of material have been disposed of under his supervision; in 1950 alone he issued 2,867 permits for removing more than 26,000,000 cu yd of material from the harbor.

Provision of Fishways.—Under the Act of August 11, 1888, the Secretary of the Army is empowered by Congress, in his discretion, to provide "practical and sufficient fishways" whenever federal improvements are found to obstruct the passage of fish.

Future Power Development.—In 1912, to preserve the possibilities of future power development, Congress delegated discretionary power to the Secretary of War to provide in the permanent parts of any authorized navigation dam "such foundations, sluices and other works, as may be considered desirable for the future development of its water power."

Control of Mining Debris.—Control of mining debris in the Sacramento-San Joaquin River Basin in California has been a continuing responsibility of the Corps of Engineers since 1893, when, because of the impairment of navigation and the serious flood problems caused by uncontrolled and unregulated disposal of debris from hydraulic mining activities, Congress created the California Debris Commission, consisting of three officers of the Corps of Engineers appointed by the President with the consent of the Senate. Its duties as prescribed in the creating act are: (1) To regulate hydraulic mining so as to permit its resumption and continuance under restrictions to prevent debris from being carried into navigable waters or otherwise causing damage; and (2) to study and report on general hydraulic and hydraulic mining conditions and to make surveys and plans for improving the navigability of the rivers and for affording relief from flood damages.

TABLE 4.—ACCOMPLISHMENTS OF CORPS OF ENGINEERS IN WRECK REMOVAL

Item	1946	1947	1948	1949	1950	1951
No. of wrecks investigated or removed	118	65	106	95	71	121
Funds allotted	$195,911	$574,755	$670,521	$921,657	$397,579	$989,000

The act creating the Commission did not empower it to carry out plans adopted by it. Congress, however, has from time to time adopted certain plans formulated by the Commission and has charged it with their execution under the direction of the Secretary of the Army and the supervision of the Chief of Engineers.

Removal of Wrecks.—The River and Harbor Act of March 3, 1899, provides authority for the Secretary of the Army to remove sunken vessels obstructing or endangering navigation. Operations under this authority during recent years are given in Table 4.

Removal of Aquatic Plants.—The River and Harbor Act of March 3, 1899, as subsequently amended, provides for the destruction or removal of the water hyacinth in the navigable waters of Florida, Alabama, Mississippi, Louisiana, and Texas, so far as the plant constitutes an obstruction to commerce, using any mechanical, chemical, or other means whatsoever, except that in Florida the Act of 1905 prohibits the use of chemicals injurious to cattle. The law also provides for constructing and operating boats equipped with machinery suitable for such destruction or removal, and for using booms to prevent the plants from drifting from one stream to another.

In addition to the continuing authorization for hyacinth removal, the Committee on Rivers and Harbors of the House of Representatives, on February 6, 1945, authorized the Corps of Engineers, in cooperation with the Fish and Wildlife Service, the Department of Agriculture, and the United States Public Health Serv-

ice, to make a study with the view of determining the cost of permanently eliminating the hyacinth and other marine vegetable growths, and much study and experimental work are being carried on under this authority.

Drift Removal.—The river and harbor acts of 1930, 1948, and 1950 authorized the Secretary of the Army to make direct allotments from appropriations
for maintenance and improvement of existing river and harbor works or other
available appropriations "for the collection and removal of drift" in New York
harbor and its tributaries, Baltimore harbor and tributaries, and Hampton Roads
and the harbors of Norfolk and Newport News, Va., and their tributaries, respectively. During the fiscal year ending on June 30, 1950, more than 2,400 cords of
driftwood, ranging from small blocks to large timbers, and including piles and
parts of wreckage, were removed from New York harbor and 765 cords of driftwood were removed from Baltimore harbor. Operations have not yet started at
Hampton Roads and the harbors of Norfolk and Newport News.

Maintenance of Harbor Channels.—Each appropriation action since 1936 has
carried a provision empowering the Secretary of the Army, in his discretion and
on recommendation of the Chief of Engineers, based on recommendation by the
Board of Engineers for Rivers and Harbors in review of reports authorized by
law, to expend sums necessary "for the maintenance of harbor channels provided
by a State, municipality, or other public agency, outside of harbor lines and serving essential needs of general commerce and navigation." That authority has been
used in only a few cases. The most recent case was during World War II, when
a channel provided by the Defense Plant Corporation of Cleveland, Ohio, was
maintained pending specific authorization of that project by Congress in the River
and Harbor Act approved March 2, 1945.

Snagging and Clearing of Channels.—The River and Harbor Act of 1945 permits the Secretary of the Army to allot not to exceed $300,000 from appropria-
tions made for any one fiscal year for improving rivers and harbors by:

"* * * removing accumulated snags and other debris, and for protecting,
clearing, and straightening channels in navigable harbors and navigable
streams and tributaries thereof, when in the opinion of the Chief of Engineers
such work is advisable in the interests of navigation or flood control."

An example of such work on the Mississippi River is shown in Fig. 8.

Minor work permitted under this general authority is needed and fully justified
at many localities and communities throughout the United States. Without such
continuing authority, minor improvements could be undertaken only after individual authorization of many small projects by Congress. In most instances
the cost of the necessary formal survey reports would approach, and in many
cases exceed, the actual cost of the desired improvement. Another advantage of
the general authority is that almost immediate action may be taken in emergency
cases. The total allotments for work under this authority in recent years have
been as follows:

Year	Allotment	Year	Allotment
1946	$124,600	1949	$113,500
1947	185,500	1950	228,400
1948	244,100	1951	193,800

Summary of General and Recurrent Activities.—Although the annual cost of these continuing operations adds up to a considerable sum, it amounts to a very small part of the total cost of the Civil Works Program—less than 4% in the fiscal years 1948 and 1949. The continuing authorizations permit accomplishment of routine and recurring operations at a great saving in time and cost over that required if each individual instance of such work were to be subject to specific authorization by Congress.

4. Engineering and Construction

Engineering is the basic element which ties together all the varied activities of the Corps of Engineers in carrying out the federal navigation program. It is ultimately involved in the planning procedures described in this paper, in the estimating of costs, in the determining of requirements for lands and relocations, and in the maintenance and operation of improvements.

From the purely technical and professional standpoint, modern navigation improvements involve the use of all the major branches of engineering—civil, mechanical, chemical, and electrical—as well as their specialized subdivisions. In addition, this work requires the services of scientists qualified in fields such as geology, biology, and economics, as well as those of experts specialized through long experience in land appraisals, statistical analysis, and transportation and conservation activities. The professional quality of the engineering performed by the Corps of Engineers is fundamental to obtaining sound plans, accurate estimates of cost, and structures which over the years will accomplish the purposes for which they are authorized and built.

All Types of Engineering Personnel.—The engineering organization of the Corps includes both Army officers and civilians. The officers are graduates of the United States Military Academy at West Point, N. Y., or of civilian colleges and universities, and many of them have during their period of career training taken postgraduate work in engineering at the major technical schools of the United States. The civilian engineers who comprise the bulk of the engineering organization have a similar educational background and training, and carry out the details of management, planning, and operation as well as the technical engineering requirements. Officers of the Corps are rotated between civil and military assignments, and continuity is maintained by the civilian staffs at the various levels of the organization.

Every effort has been made throughout the years to insure that the engineering positions in the organization of the Corps are staffed by the most highly trained and best qualified engineers obtainable, both officer and civilian. The fact that many of them are recognized by the engineering profession in this country and abroad as leading authorities in their respective fields may be taken as an indication of the success of this policy. The composite abilities of the individual engineers of the organization contribute largely to the preparation of sound and economical plans of development and to orderly and effective construction.

Engineers of the Corps serve on many technical committees; many are members of professional engineering societies and organizations; and several have been elected or appointed to responsible offices in such organizations. One has recently completed his term of office as President of the ASCE; another is a member of the International Joint Commission which handles American-Canadian boundary water problems; others have served as engineering consultants to foreign governments under the sponsorship of the State Department. During World War II, representatives of the Corps constituted the organization that handled the hydrological problems of the Rhine River in aid of the Army crossings, and many civilian employees were commissioned into the Army to meet its expanding engineering needs.

With the increasing scope and complexity of the navigation projects planned and provided by the Corps, the branches of engineering involved have correspondingly multiplied. In the early years of the Corps, the engineering required for the simple navigation improvements undertaken was correspondingly simple. In these days of basin-wide development and multimillion-dollar multipurpose structures, experts in hydrology, hydraulics, soil mechanics, geology, structural design and materials, hydroelectric construction and operation, coastal engineering, and other branches are required; and the best qualified men obtainable have been recruited to fill these needs. These men not only are informed as to the best current theory and practice of their respective branches, but are placed in a position to require an intimate knowledge of the physical and economic characteristics of the basins and regions with which they must deal. This training and experience should eminently qualify them to formulate sound and effective plans for the comprehensive development of the national waterways in the integrated interests of all water uses, and to establish criteria and techniques of construction that will provide safe and economical structures.

Although engineering personnel of the Corps of Engineers has used the best engineering procedures current at any given time, it has not been content to accept them as the ultimate ideals in planning and construction. Engineers of the Corps have played a leading part in improving old methods and techniques and in developing new ones. Many of the practices now generally accepted and used by the engineering profession and construction industry were originated or improved by the Corps of Engineers in its constant effort to better its operations.

Hydrology.—In improving its hydrological studies and data, which are essential to navigation as well as to flood-control work, the Corps has investigated or is investigating some 1,500 major storms of record, compiling basic precipitation data and accumulative rainfall curves for areas ranging from 10 sq miles to 100,000 sq miles or more. In 1938, the Corps initiated and entered into a cooperative agreement with the United States Weather Bureau for the establishment in the Bureau of a "Hydrometeorological Section," financed by transfer of funds from the Corps of Engineers. That section has prepared comprehensive studies on maximum possible rainfall on twenty-six river basins and special estimates for about seventy-five reservoirs, and also has contributed valuable technical assistance to the personnel of the Corps in analyzing wind and hurricane data.

A cooperative agreement with the United States Geological Survey and the Weather Bureau provides for accumulating stream-flow and stage data at more than 7,000 stream-gaging stations and 4,600 rainfall stations; a cooperative flood-forecasting service is also maintained that has proved very valuable in flood-fighting and rescue operations. The effect of snow melt on floods is being studied, as are the conditions contributing to sedimentation in reservoirs and stream channels. Studies on wave and wind-tide heights under various wind velocities have led to important savings in the formerly prescribed freeboards and slopes of levees and dams and in the amount of riprap required on exposed slopes.

Hydraulics.—Hydraulic engineers of the Corps have developed a number of new methods and techniques to replace the "rule-of-thumb" practices in use up to only a few years ago. Less than 10 years ago, the Corps developed a technique of superelevating and spiral-transitioning high-velocity channels that saves about 15% of their cost and insures nearly perfect flow. The use of vertical-face baffle blocks and an end sill in stilling basins was developed by the Corps and reduces required stilling-basin lengths by as much as 40% and depths by 10%, with a

FIG. 9.—WORK OF WATERWAYS EXPERIMENT STATION—MISSISSIPPI BASIN MODEL

50% saving in costs. The Corps developed the use of the "flip-bucket" energy dissipator, instead of the more costly equivalent stilling basin. Improvements devised by personnel in the shape of spillway crests, outlet gates, entrance curves, and gate slots have greatly improved their performance and reduced the cost of provision and maintenance.

To solve many of the hydraulic problems involved, the Corps has established the United States Waterways Experiment Station at Vicksburg, Miss. (Fig. 9), and subsidiary laboratories at Los Angeles, Calif., Portland, Ore., and St. Paul, Minn. This system of laboratories, not seriously rivaled by other similar institutions in the world, not only solves the problems of the Corps of Engineers but is an important element in international advancement of hydraulic engineering. It is conservatively estimated that model studies at these laboratories have saved the United States at least $90,000,000—about $10 for each dollar spent on the studies.

Soil Mechanics.—The Corps of Engineers pioneered the development of theoretical and applied soil mechanics in the United States. At nine soil mechanics laboratories scattered strategically over the United States, the Corps determines the characteristics of soils as foundation or construction materials. These investigations have made possible steeper embankment slopes and more widespread use of locally available materials, reduced riprap protection, and lowered underseepage pressures at dams by providing relief wells at the toe of the dam. They have yielded a greater knowledge and use of soil as a structural material, which have resulted in construction of the largest earth dams in the world. One accomplishment of the Corps has been the introduction of heavy rubber-tired rollers for compacting suitable materials in rolled earth-fill dams, now in general use by contractors.

Geology.—Many of the achievements of the Corps have resulted in large part from the work of the staff of eighty outstanding engineering geologists trained during the past 20 years. Improvements have been devised by them in geophysical surveys, soil drilling and sampling, core drilling, borehole photography, hydraulic pressure testing, and grouting.

Structures.—Many instances might be cited of the ingenuity displayed by the Corps of Engineers in originating or improving construction practices. Probably the earliest such instance was the design and construction, in 1824, of a revolutionary snagboat employing steam power to pull large water-soaked trees out of the Mississippi River mud. Two experimental suction dredges were also designed and built at that time. Completion of the Panama Canal in 6 years was an outstanding engineering accomplishment.

Canalization of the Ohio and Upper Mississippi rivers required the construction of locks larger than anything theretofore built, and entailed design by the Corps of lock gates, dam control gates, and other features not previously undertaken. The Corps has participated in developing radar-controlled and radio-controlled aids to navigation, new paints for protecting steel in contact with water, steel sheet-pile cofferdams in water of great depth and velocity, and other improved construction methods and practices.

Concrete.—Perhaps in no other aspect of its work has the Corps produced more beneficial innovations in practice than in the designing and placing of the millions of cubic yards of concrete that have gone into the structures it has built. The use of special cements, of local cementitious materials, and of air-entraining mixtures has been largely pioneered by the Corps and has become general practice. The design of concrete buckets, aggregate-producing plants, and batching plants has been vastly improved. Better methods of temperature control in curing concrete have been developed. The testing laboratories of the Corps have attained a position of leadership in devising improved methods and materials.

Hydroelectric Generation.—Among the improvements in hydroelectric generation originated by the Corps, the use of fewer and larger adjustable-blade generating units is outstanding. On the Columbia River between Washington and Oregon, the first two turbines at Bonneville Dam, constructed for navigation and power, were rated at 57,500 hp at 40-ft head, mated with 43,200-kw generators. The remaining eight generators were increased to 54,000 kw each—at that time the largest of their type (Kaplan) ever manufactured. As a result of experience at Bonneville and of further studies, the fourteen turbines for the McNary Dam have been planned for a rating of 111,300 hp with a range in net head of 62 ft to 92 ft—the largest Kaplan turbine built today. As a result of further study, the Dalles Project is being planned for the initial installation of fourteen 123,000-hp turbines rated at an 82-ft head.

Coastal Engineering.—The Corps has pioneered in much of the technical development in the field of coastal engineering, and is widely recognized as an authority in that field. The Beach Erosion Board is the principal technical agency of the Corps on this work.

Dredging.—Dredging is an important feature of waterway construction and constitutes a large part of the work of the Corps of Engineers under the navigation program. It is an ancient art which has become within the past 100 years one of the most powerful tools of the engineer—particularly in the field of waterway development and maintenance. Waterway improvement and development of

FIG. 10.—HOPPER DREDGE *Goethals* IN NEW YORK HARBOR, N. Y.

dredges in the United States have been complementary. The Corps of Engineers, in carrying out the waterway program, has been intimately concerned with dredges and dredging techniques. The hydraulic dredge, both the sea-going hopper type (Fig. 10) and the cutterhead pipeline type normally used on inland waterways, has become the most important of these tools, although various other types of dredging and excavating machinery are widely used on waterways.

Modern development began when the principle of hydraulic dredging with a centrifugal pump was first conceived. There is some disagreement among historians as to originator, but it has been claimed that the French hydraulic engineer, H. Bazin, first suggested the principle in 1867 in connection with excavation of the Suez Canal. However, in 1855 at Charleston, S. C., the Corps of Engineers experimented with an old freight steamer by placing a bin in its hold and adding a centrifugal pump and suction pipe. This vessel, named *The General Moultrie* was successful only when the sea was quiet, but the principle was sound and the honor of first using a hydraulic hopper dredge thus went to the United States. Since that time development of dredges of this kind has proceeded rapidly, culminating in completion of the *Essayons* in 1950, the largest sea-going hopper dredge in the world, 525 ft long, drawing nearly 30 ft, with a capacity of 8,000 cu yd.

It is interesting that much of the impetus in development of dredges and dredging came from the Pacific coast, beginning with Alexis Von Schmidt's outstanding work in building a cutterhead suction dredge in 1876. Dredging gained prominence in that area in connection with mining and irrigation as well as with navigation improvements.

Dredging on waterways under the jurisdiction of the Corps of Engineers is divided between river and seacoast work—the latter constituting about 75% of the total annual dredging. River dredging, largely new work on channels and maintenance of existing canals and waterways, is accomplished largely by cutterhead hydraulic dredges, although clamshell, dipper, and dustpan dredges are used in restricted areas, at lock approaches, and in maintenance of channels across bars.

During recent peacetime years, before World War II, the total earth movement by dredging approximated 430,000,000 cu yd, of which 60% was by contract and the remainder by government plant. During World War II some government dredges normally employed on harbors and waterways were taken overseas and used in both European and Pacific theatres of operations.

Cost Estimating and Cost Experience.—Accurate cost estimates were difficult for engineers to make 100 years ago and still are. The Corps of Engineers recognizes that one of its most important functions, in administering the waterway program, is the preparation of cost estimates. These are the basis for determining the economic value of proposals; they form the basis for authorization by Congress and for appropriation of federal funds; and they serve as a basis for judging the reasonableness of contractors' bids. Thus at every stage they must be as complete and accurate as possible, and adequate for the purposes intended.

The basic procedures used by the Corps of Engineers in preparing cost estimates are those in general use by the engineering profession and construction industry. The experience of the Corps, like that of private industry, indicates a record of rising costs. The increases have varied in magnitude from project to project. For the entire civil works program under its jurisdiction, however, the record is as follows:

a. For the current program of civil works now under construction, including navigation, flood-control, and multiple-use projects, the increase of current (1951 level) costs estimates over original estimates used as a basis for authorization by Congress has been 126%. Although this increase has been due to a number of factors, it is generally in line with the trend of indexes affecting private and public construction and industrial costs, which during the period 1937–1951 have risen generally from 100% to 171%.

b. About three fourths of the rise in costs of civil works projects has been a result of increasing construction costs (indexes) plus project extensions authorized by Congress. These are two factors, economic and legislative, over which the Corps has no control.

c. The remainder of the cost increase stems largely from estimates prepared before 1939, and used by Congress for authorization of improvements because they were the best estimates available and because it was necessary to start the work. These earlier estimates, however, are not representative of present design and estimating procedures.

d. Estimates prepared since 1939 have shown progressive improvement, and in the more recent projects, engineering inadequacies, unforeseen conditions, and structural and engineering modifications account for less than 10% of the increase over original estimates.

The Corps of Engineers does not claim that its estimating procedures have been perfect. It does maintain, however, that its estimates have provided Congress with a sound basis for legislative action on waterway improvements, and that on the whole they have been a credit to the engineering profession.

Economic Analysis.—The procedures for economic analysis of the navigation improvements used by the Corps of Engineers are of fundamental importance to the soundness of the waterway program. Only those projects whose estimated benefits equal or exceed their costs are recommended. In general, the benefit of a waterway project which is compared with its cost in determining economic justification is:

Cost to shippers of transportation by the cheapest available alternative

less

Cost to shippers of transportation by waterway (which includes cost of bargeline service and terminal and transfer costs but not the cost of the waterway)

Economic analyses are made by the engineers and economists on the staffs of division and district offices, assisted by transportation experts and economists from the Board of Engineers for Rivers and Harbors. This work involves careful study of the traffic that will probably use an improved waterway and of the savings which will result from such use.

5. Maintenance and Operation

After construction, the effectiveness of federal civil works improvements depends primarily on the manner in which they are maintained and operated. If they are allowed to deteriorate, their effectiveness is impaired or lost, and the return to the nation on the federal investment, in the form of public benefits, is minimized or destroyed.

Through the fiscal year 1952, the total of appropriations to the Corps of Engineers for maintaining and operating the current civil works installations has been as follows:

Rivers and harbors (navigation).......... $1,272,000,000 (85%)
Flood control 212,500,000 (15%)

Total .... $1,484,500,000(100%)

This tabulation accounts for about 20% of all appropriations for civil works. Maintenance and operation of improvements therefore constitute substantial parts of the civil works activity of the Corps.

The upkeep of navigation facilities entails dredging river and harbor channels to preserve authorized navigable depths, repairing jetties (Fig. 11) and other navigation structures, and maintaining and operating locks and dams. It includes 85% of all civil works maintenance and operation by the Corps.

In general, dredging of harbors susceptible of advertisement is performed by contract. However, maintenance of channels and turning basins in exposed water and removal of bars in the open ocean at harbor entrances are hazardous; they require the use of sea-going hopper dredges which are not available as contractors' equipment. As of January, 1952, the Corps of Engineers owned nineteen sea-going hopper dredges of various sizes, ranging from the *Pacific*, 180 ft long and drawing less than 10 ft, with a capacity load of 500 cu yd, to the *Essayons*, the largest sea-going hopper dredge in the world.

For administrative and operating purposes, these dredges are assigned to various district offices along the coasts and on the Great Lakes in accordance with the work loads in various sections of the United States. In order to minimize the cost of providing in each district office the specialized organizations required for hopper dredge operations on coastal and Great Lakes waters, the dredges, except

FIG. 11.—STONE AND CONCRETE JETTY, ARANSAS PASS, TEXAS

in special cases, work out of strategically located district offices, but serve a general area without regard to district boundaries.

Other dredging not susceptible of advertisement includes emergency removal of fast forming bars in rivers and other channels and work which is not attractive to contractors because of its location, the small amount of material involved, or other reasons. Forty-four government-owned dredges are available for this type of work. Of these, ten are dustpan-type pipeline dredges especially adapted to use on rivers for removing fast-forming bars. The remainder consists of twenty-five cutterhead pipeline dredges and nine bucket-type and dipper-type dredges of various sizes. This equipment and its attendant plant are mostly located on inland and intracoastal waterways, principally on the Mississippi, Missouri, and Ohio, and are transferred from one district to another in accordance with the need for any particular item of dredging.

The government-owned cutterhead pipeline, dipper, and bucket dredges are, in general, of the same types and capacities as those in contractors' equipment, and might compete with contractors for work in which contractors are interested. In practice, however, such dredging is advertised for contract; an estimate of its cost if performed by appropriate government dredge is submitted with the contractors' bids. If the contractor's bid does not exceed the government estimate by more than 25%, a contract is awarded. If all contractors' bids are more than 25% higher than the government estimate, the work may be done by government plant or may be readvertised. This government plant, therefore, serves the additional purpose of providing a yardstick to determine the reasonableness of contractors' bid prices and has been effective in holding federal dredging costs on both new work and maintenance to a minimum.

During fiscal year 1951 the Corps of Engineers maintained and operated three hundred and twelve locks and two hundred and nineteen navigation dams in the

Fig. 12.—Ore Boats Passing Through "Soo" Locks, St. Marys Falls Canal, Michigan

interest of water-borne commerce. The sizes and types of these structures vary, according to the requirements of commerce and local river conditions, from structures such as that at Moss Bluff, Florida, 30 ft wide and 125 ft long, to those on the Ohio River, most of which are 110 ft wide and 600 ft long, and to the "Soo" Locks 1,350 ft long and 80 ft wide (Fig. 12). These factors, together with the age of the structure and its location, largely determine the method and cost of maintenance and operation.

Some waterways are closed by ice during the winter, so locks and dams are operated on a seasonal basis. Other waterways, such as the Ohio River, are subject to seasonal rises which permit open-river navigation at high stages. The volume of commerce in some areas requires use of the locks 24 hours a day on either a year-round or a seasonal basis. Elsewhere, locks are operated on a part-day basis; at a few locations they are operated only by appointment. The personnel stationed at any single location varies from one to one hundred eighty depending on the volume of traffic and the type of structure.

Ordinary maintenance of locks and dams, consisting of minor painting and repairs and general upkeep of the grounds, is done by the regular crew. Major maintenance may be accomplished by regular forces, by a traveling crew, by contract, or by a combination of those methods. In districts in which a system of several locks and dams is in use, and particularly when wicket-type dams are involved, a traveling crew is usually employed. Other individual installations are generally maintained by contract or by the regular crew.

Unfortunately during recent years congressional appropriations for maintenance operation and care of waterways have not kept pace with the need for such work, and it has not been possible to maintain all these facilities properly. It must be recognized that the return on the substantial public investment in waterways, and the safeguarding of that investment, depends in large degree upon adequate maintenance after completion of the work.

6. Coastal Harbors

The present excellence of the seacoast and Gulf harbors of the United States, although based on favorable natural facilities, is a result of their continuous development by the Federal Government and private initiative, to meet the requirements of an expanding maritime commerce and the larger ships needed to handle that commerce. In their natural state there were few bays and tidal estuaries along the Atlantic, Gulf, and Pacific coasts of the United States with natural depths as great as 20 to 30 ft. Bars with relatively shallow water over them blocked the entrances to most major rivers. This situation still prevailed to a large extent 100 years ago, even though works for improvement were well under way.

Although natural facilities were transversable with difficulty by sailing vessels, the advent of steam navigation increased the demand for their improvement. In its original condition the Delaware River was obstructed by a number of shoals over which the usable depths at mean low water varied between 17 ft and 22 ft. In 1876 ships sailing upchannel to Philadelphia required 4 days, in some cases caused by waiting for high water to pass the shoals. In the same year the maximum available depth in parts of Norfolk harbor was 20 ft. Prior to improvement by the United States the maximum depth over the bar at Charleston, S. C., was 12 ft; in 1879 there was 6 ft of water over the bar at the mouth of the St. Johns River, the entrance to Jacksonville harbor, in Florida; and the depth over the bar at Mobile was 8 ft.

On the Pacific coast depths at the mouth of the Columbia varied from 15 ft to 18 ft, occasionally increasing to more than 20 ft. Oakland harbor in California had only a 2-ft depth at its entrance at mean lower low water; and San Diego offered better facilities with depths of 21 ft.

The improvement of these harbors over the past 100 years has been a progressive development, to meet first the needs of sailing ships, then the greater drafts required by developing steam navigation, and finally the requirements of both the ocean liners of today and the larger modern tankers often loaded to drafts of 33 ft or more. As a result channel depths of 35 ft prevail at harbors on the Atlantic seaboard and Gulf coast, and range up to the 45-ft depth in New York harbor

(Table 5). Depths of 21 ft are controlling generally for Great Lakes harbors and connecting channels; and on the west coast harbor and channel depths ranging from 30 ft to 40 ft are generally available.

In all, two hundred and eighty-six commercial coastal harbors, along the coast lines of the continental United States and its overseas territories, have been improved by the Federal Government. Estimates vary depending on how improvements in harbor area are counted. In addition, the program has included the development of fishing harbors and harbors of refuge for small commercial

TABLE 5.—DEPTHS AT PRINCIPAL AMERICAN HARBORS, IN FEET

Harbor	Controlling depth	Authorized project depth
Boston, Mass.	35 and 40	35 and 40
New York, N. Y.	Up to 45	Up to 45
Baltimore, Md.	37.4	39
Norfolk, Va.	40	40
Mobile, Ala.	32–35	32–36
New Orleans, La.	35–36*a*	35–40*a*
Detroit, Mich.	21–25	20–27
Chicago, Ill.	20	21
Great Lakes channels	21–25*b*	21–25*b*
Los Angeles, Calif.	40	40
San Francisco, Calif.	33–44	40–50
Portland, Ore.	30–35	30–35
Seattle, Wash.	30–34	30–34

a Southwest Pass of Mississippi River.   *b* For downward-bound ore boats

and recreational craft. These harbor improvements have been provided with the following federal appropriations:

Construction ....$ 807,900,000
Maintenance and operation................ 547,700,000

Total $1,355,600,000

Local Benefits and Support.—In addition to federal expenditures for waterway improvements, states and other local interests have spent considerable sums for that purpose. The law prescribes that every navigation report submitted to Congress shall contain a statement of the respective general and local benefits and of the amount of local cooperation that should properly be required. Such cooperation includes: Furnishing, without cost to the United States, all lands, easements, and rights of way; holding and saving the United States free from all claims of damages; providing and maintaining at local expense adequate public terminal and transfer facilities open to all on equal terms; accomplishing, without expense to the United States, alterations and maintenance of sewer, water supply, drainage, and other utilities; making necessary changes in highways and highway bridges and approaches and assuming their subsequent operation; and contributing sufficient cash toward the first cost of the project when deemed warranted and appropriate. The amount of local cooperation required varies from project to project, and it has not been practicable to obtain an over-all estimate of the local expenditures that have been involved, although it appears that such expenditures would exceed $100,000,000.

In addition to the local cooperation required by law, local interests spend large amounts on providing private terminals, access thereto by rail and highway, and other adjuncts to a complete waterway facility. In 1939, the Federal Coordinator of Transportation estimated the total of such local expenditures for terminal facilities at $1,100,000,000, and the outlay up to the present would probably far exceed that sum.

The Atlantic coast of the United States has been developed to provide some of the greatest harbors in the world. This development, which began in colonial times has been continuous during the past 100 years. The ports of Boston, New York, Philadelphia, and Hampton Roads, and the smaller southeastern ports of Wilmington, N. C., Charleston, Savannah, and Jacksonville have been improved progressively. They have been able to handle tremendous tonnages of cargo and to serve as wartime ports of embarkation.

Important Gulf Ports Developed.—On the Gulf coast the improved port of New Orleans has become a gateway for commerce with South and Central America; and Mobile is rising in importance because of ore shipments from South America. Along the Texas Gulf coast the development of harbors has proceeded with the increasingly heavy movement of petroleum products, and channel depths have been provided to meet the need of deep draft tankers. Petroleum and petroleum products represent by far the largest water-borne commerce movement in that area.

The Houston Ship Channel in Texas may be cited to illustrate an important coastal harbor development. It was investigated by local people in 1846 and begun as a private enterprise in 1869. The first stage involved a ship canal through Morgan Point, which permitted the passage of steamships of 10-ft draft to Clinton, about 8 miles from Houston. The existing project provides for a channel 36 ft deep at mean low tide from deep water in Galveston Bay to and including the Houston turning basin, with widths varying from 400 ft to 300 ft. The total length of the improved channel is 57 miles—50 miles from deep water in Galveston Bay to the turning basin, and then a 7-mile channel for light-draft navigation to Houston. Federal costs of the existing project to June 30, 1950, were $26,572,000. The total local cash contribution has been more than $2,700,000; and local interests have also cooperated by providing terminal facilities at the turning basin, a belt-line railway, and other features. Many important industries have been established above and below the turning basin.

The principal commodity considered in the original transportation-saving estimate for Houston, and one which was carried during the early days, was cotton barged to Galveston, where it was transferred to sea-going ships. In recent years petroleum and its products have dominated the channel traffic. In the calendar year 1910 a total of 1,371,650 tons was moved; in 1950 the port of Houston transported a total of 40,825,048 tons. The vision of the various business and industrial associations in Houston, plus the federal participation planned by the Corps of Engineers, has provided the southwestern area with one of the great ports of the country.

Pacific Coast and Ocean Work.—Harbor improvements on the Pacific coast came rapidly as a result of the increasing use of west coast harbors after the California gold rush in 1849, the development of lumbering in the Pacific Northwest, and the growth of the fishing industry and trade with the Orient. Harbors and channels in Alaska, and across the Pacific in Hawaii and the Philippines, were lineal descendants of this work on the Pacific coast of the United States.

San Diego appears to have been the site of the first federal work on the Pacific coast when shortly after 1852 an embankment was built across the mouth of San Diego River in an effort to change its course. San Francisco harbor, with its broad and deep entrance and extensive areas of deep water, was made hazardous by submerged rocks. The most dangerous of these, Blossom Rock right in the main ship channel east of Alcatraz Island, was only 5 ft below the surface at low tide. It was removed dramatically in 1870 by one of the first efforts at submarine blasting by Colonel Von Schmidt under contract to the Corps of Engineers.

Dredging through bars blocking the mouth of the Columbia River began as a result of congressional appropriations in 1866; but these measures gave only temporary relief until the original project for improvement was begun in 1878. Work in the Puget Sound area began in the 1890's.

In 1901 shortly after the Spanish-American War, the United States decided to develop Manila harbor in the Philippines. This work, accomplished by a subsidiary of the Atlantic, Gulf and Pacific Company, included rebuilding and extending the Spanish-built jetties, dredging a large anchorage basin to a depth of 30 ft, and other work. It was the first overseas job of this kind ever tackled by Americans.

There is no accurate record of the traffic using coastal harbors in 1852, but it was undoubtedly quite small as compared with that of the present day. In 1929 the cargo handled through all coastal ports amounted to 306,600,000 short tons; in 1950 this commerce had increased to 430,600,000 short tons. These totals are net after eliminating duplications involved in computation by ports. Commerce handled at major ports in 1950 was:

Harbor	Tons
Atlantic:	
Boston	14,400,000
New York	144,800,000
Delaware River	68,800,000
Baltimore	35,600,000
Hampton Roads	25,000,000
Gulf:	
New Orleans	35,100,000
Beaumont (Tex.)	21,400,000
Houston	40,800,000
Pacific:	
San Francisco	30,600,000
Portland	12,000,000
Seattle (Wash.)	11,900,000

It is not practicable to place a monetary evaluation on these harbors or on their contribution to the welfare of the nation, as they are essential facilities both for maintenance of maritime commerce in peace, and for use in time of war as ports of embarkation and as locations for naval bases and shipyards. It is safe to state that, if their returns to the nation could be expressed in monetary terms, they would be worth many times the relatively small amount that the Federal Government has expended.

7. Inland and Intracoastal Waterways

Steamboat navigation on the Mississippi River and its tributaries, which now comprise the great central inland waterway system, reached its peak in the decade 1850–1860 (Fig. 13). The records show that in 1859 more than 1,000 steamboats were in operation on the Mississippi River alone. This navigation development was halted by the Civil War but revived afterward, and until the early 1880's the Mississippi and its tributaries still provided the major route for movement of

FIG. 13.—STEAMBOAT TRAFFIC ON MISSISSIPPI AT ITS HEIGHT JUST PRECEDING THE WAR BETWEEN THE STATES

freight in the Mississippi Valley. Steamboats carried the greater part of the traffic, but barge navigation began in 1860.

This period also saw the beginning of the accumulation of engineering data on American rivers, particularly the Mississippi. The most noteworthy achievement was the comprehensive investigation and report of Maj.-Gen. A. A. Humphreys, Hon. M. ASCE, and Henry L. Abbot of the Corps of Engineers, entitled "Report on the Physics and Hydraulics of the Mississippi River." This study still stands as a monumental contribution to the engineering of river improvements.

A Changing Economy.—By the end of the decade 1870–1880 the difficulties of river transportation and the increasing competition of railroads began to take their toll, and river traffic declined on the Mississippi and on other waterways. The result was graphically described in a paper published in 1908 by Senator

Newlands of Nevada, vice-chairman of the Inland Waterways Commission, in which he reviewed the possibility of restoring transportation on the waterways:

"I must confess that when I went down the Mississippi last summer, and traveled for miles without seeing a single boat, I was inclined to doubt it also. There were a few tow-boats, but the river towns were neglected, the wharves rotting, and the river fronts largely occupied by the tracks of railroads, whose trains of cars, running at frequent intervals along the banks, showed how thoroughly they had absorbed the commerce of the region."

A most important step in waterway development and in asserting the growing federal interest in inland waterways was the establishment by Congress in 1879 of the Mississippi River Commission. According to the law, the Commission is composed of three officers of the Corps of Engineers, a representative of the Coast and Geodetic Survey, and three civilians, two of whom must be engineers. The law designates that its president shall be an officer of the Corps. Improvement of the Lower Mississippi River is still carried out under the jurisdiction of that commission.

The Commission as originally organized included such distinguished engineers as James B. Eads, M. ASCE, and Col. Cyrus Comstock. It set to work immediately on improvement of the river both for navigation and flood control, as it soon became apparent that these two matters were inseparable on the Lower Mississippi. By 1907 the Commission was able to assure river traffic of a dependable channel with 9-ft depths. This work was of basic importance to the further development of the central inland waterway system and the ultimate revival of water-borne commerce.

Numerous other important inland waterway improvements were undertaken during the latter part of the nineteenth century. Prior to that period improvement of the Ohio, except for the locks bypassing the falls at Louisville, had been done by open-channel methods. Its canalization was proposed however by Milner Roberts, a civil engineer, in 1870; and, after study by a board of engineers, Maj. W. E. Merrill, M. ASCE, of the Corps of Engineers recommended in 1874 canalization between Pittsburgh and Wheeling by construction of thirteen locks and movable dams with "Chanoine" wickets. A year later Major Merrill proposed extension of canalization to the entire river above Louisville.

In 1875 Congress appropriated funds for construction of a movable dam as a test of the best method of improving the Ohio, and this dam was built at Davis Island. From that time, improvement of the Ohio by both open-channel methods and lock-and-dam construction (Fig. 14) was continuous, and twelve such structures were completed between 1885 and 1912, to provide 6-ft navigable depths generally. The present project for complete canalization of the Ohio to provide 9-ft depths was adopted by Congress in 1910. This action has often been cited as the beginning of modern inland waterway development, as about 90% of present waterway improvements have been accomplished since that date.

Decline of commerce on the rivers of the United States (Fig. 15) was the natural result of the development of the railroads, a faster and more flexible medium of transportation, with which the steamboats and early barge lines with limited carrying capacity operating on unimproved or partly improved rivers, could not compete. The ruthless competitive tactics of the railroads speeded this trend, which by the end of the nineteenth century had almost eliminated traffic from the canals and rivers.

FIG. 14.—STERN-WHEELER TOWBOAT WITH BARGES OF COAL PASSING THROUGH LOCKS OF CANALIZED OHIO RIVER

FIG. 15.—ECONOMICAL STEAMBOAT TRANSPORTATION ON MISSISSIPPI PRACTICALLY ELIMINATED BY LATTER PART OF NINETEENTH CENTURY

Prosperity Returns to Waterways.—The revival of water-borne commerce on inland and intracoastal waterways (Fig. 16) has been the equally natural result of the pressure of a growing population and of the rapid industrialization of the nation. These major factors created the demand for movement of large quantities of bulk commodities such as grain, lumber, fertilizers, coal, ore, petroleum, and manufactured articles for which rapid transit was not necessary, and such shipments in many cases overburdened the railroads. Thus the important role of the water carrier in the economical transportation of bulk commodities gained recognition. More intensive improvements of waterways by the Federal Government encouraged the development of powerful and efficient floating equipment. The net result has been a strong resurgence of water-borne commerce until the cargo movement now far surpasses that of the best days of steamboat navigation on the Mississippi. In this way, waterways have regained

FIG. 16.—OCEAN-GOING TANKER IN LOCK FROM GULF INTRACOASTAL WATERWAY TO MISSISSIPPI RIVER

their proper place, along with the rails, highways, pipelines, and airways, as an integral part of the transportation structure of the nation.

Federal appropriations for the current inland and intracoastal waterway program under the jurisdiction of the Corps of Engineers have totaled $1,723,-700,000 through the fiscal year 1952, broken down as follows:

Construction $1,159,200,000
Maintenance   564,500,000
    Total $1,723,700,000

Additional expenditures for navigation cover appropriations to the Tennessee Valley Authority, and to the project for flood control and navigation on the Lower Mississippi River.

Under the federal program more than 28,000 miles of inland and intracoastal waterways are authorized for improvement, and some 23,170 miles of waterways have been completed, according to the latest mileage computations (Table 6). Channels with depths of 9 to 12 ft, totaling some 6,132 miles, comprise the bulk of the inland waterway system and include canalization projects such as the Ohio, Upper Mississippi (Fig. 17), and Illinois rivers (Fig. 18). Channels with

TABLE 6.—CLASSIFICATION OF IMPROVED WATERWAYS, BY LOCALITY, DEPTH, AND LENGTH

Location	LENGTH OF WATERWAYS, IN MILES					
	Under 6 ft	6 to 9 ft	9 to 12 ft	12 to 14 ft	Over 14 ft	Total
Atlantic coast rivers...	1,502	1,241	584	938	1,202	5,467
Intracoastal Waterways:						
Atlantic	0	65	65	1,104	0	1,234
Gulf	0	0	.0	1,073	0	1,073
Others	0	0	108	0	0	108
Gulf coast rivers......	2,055	654	813	80	385	3,987
Mississippi system ...	2,484	1,003	4,325	780	268	8,860
Great Lakes[a]	45	89	0	8	348	490[a]
Pacific coast	730	498	237	26	460	1,951
Total	6,816	3,550	6,132	4,009	2,663	23,170

[a] Includes rivers flowing into Great Lakes and the connecting channels, discussed under the heading, "Great Lakes Harbors and Connecting Channels."

FIG. 17.—UPPER MISSISSIPPI RIVER CANALIZATION—TOWBOAT AND BARGES PASSING THROUGH DOCK No. 11

depths less than 9 ft include more than 6,800 miles of river channels, providing depths of less than 6 ft which are kept open at small cost by minor snagging and clearing operations.

The Mississippi River system, the largest and perhaps the most important element of the inland waterway program, consists of more than 5,000 miles of waterways with depths of 9 ft or more, including the main Mississippi River trunk line from Minneapolis, Minn., to the Gulf of Mexico—a distance of more than 1,800 miles. The Illinois Waterway (Fig. 18) with a length of 327 miles provides a link between the Mississippi River and Lake Michigan at Chicago—a Great Lakes-to-Gulf waterway with 9-ft depths. The canalized Ohio extending 981 miles from the Mississippi at Cairo, Ill., to Pittsburgh receives the commerce of tributary improved streams such as the Tennessee, Kanawha, and Monongahela. The Missouri River is navigable from the Mississippi, 15 miles above St. Louis, for about 760 miles to Sioux City, Iowa, although the latter part of the project is not yet complete. Many other tributaries of the Mississippi serve as feeder waterways with depths generally less than 9 ft.

FIG. 18.—ILLINOIS WATERWAY—AERIAL VIEW OF LOCKPORT (ILL.) LOCK

On the Pacific coast the outstanding waterway improvement is the canalization of the Columbia River, a part of the comprehensive plan of development on that river basin for navigation, flood control, and hydroelectric power. Bonneville lock and dam has been completed and similar multiple-use structures are being provided at McNary Dam and the Dalles. With completion of the remaining structures on the Columbia and Snake rivers, 9-ft slack-water navigation will be provided from the ocean for 465 miles to Lewiston, Idaho.

Kinds of Waterways and Improvements.—Waterways fall into four categories in so far as development and use are concerned:

a. Waterways, such as the Lower Mississippi, Ohio, Monongahela, and Illinois which have been completed long enough to have passed through their developmental stage and which now carry a heavy and increasing volume of traffic.

b. Waterways opened to traffic within the past 25 years, where traffic has been developing, but is not fully developed. The Upper Mississippi canalization project is an example.

c. Waterways which are not yet fully completed or are still in an early stage of development as a part of a program for river basin development, on which only a limited amount of commerce has developed. The Columbia and Missouri river projects are examples of this category.

d. Waterways which because of changing economic conditions and other factors have failed to develop and maintain water-borne commerce. They represent less than 10% of the cost of the inland waterway program. Only nominal amounts are expended annually on these waterways for caretaking and maintenance, and the Corps of Engineers is abandoning these projects, with congressional approval, where appropriate.

Engineering and construction methods by which the waterways have been improved include:

    (1) Removal of obstructions—largely by snagging and clearing (Fig. 8).
    (2) Dredging to increase the depths and widths of natural river channels.
    (3) Canalization by construction of locks and dams.
    (4) Construction of jetties, revetments, and training works to protect banks and hold channels at proper alinement and depth.
    (5) Construction of artificial connective canals.
    (6) Realinement of channels by cutting across natural bends of rivers.

Although there is nothing particularly novel about these methods, their usage is the result of many years of engineering experience with rivers in the United States and foreign countries; and their application to major American rivers involves hydraulic and other detailed engineering problems of great complexity.

Floating Equipment and Cities Develop.—Improvement of the inland and intracoastal waterways has been paralleled by a tremendous advance in the development of floating equipment for use in movement of bulk commodities. In 1948 more than 4,000 towboats and some 11,700 barges (9,800 for dry cargo and 1,900 tankers) with an aggregate capacity of more than 8,700,000 net tons were in use on these waterways. Powerful towboats, with both diesel and steam engines, rated at more than 3,000 hp, have been put in service. In some cases these push more than twenty loaded barges in one tow. The floating equipment which carries the waterway freight is operated by common carrier barge lines, contract carriers, and private carriers operating as a part of some business or industry.

The steel barge has been a basic improvement which has been developed in a number of specialized forms including: Hopper barges, acid carriers, tankers for oil and asphalt, and dry cargo barges decked and open. Capacities of these barges vary from 500 to 3,000 net tons for dry cargo and from 9,000 to 25,000 bbl for tank barges. Specially designed self-propelled automobile carriers have been put in service. The American Waterway Operators, Incorporated, has estimated that in the two years 1948 and 1949 the inland waterway transportation industry expended a total of $109,000,000 on new vessels. This continuing development of floating equipment has been a basic element in the revival of water-borne commerce.

The rise of cities and towns, terminals, and industry along improved rivers and other waterways has been an important aspect of waterway development during the past 100 years. It is no accident that, of thirty-six cities in the nation with populations of 300,000 or more, thirty are on navigable waters and that, of one hundred and six cities of 100,000 or more, seventy-three are on federally improved waterways. Water transportation, when available, is the cheapest method of moving bulk raw materials and heavy low-value commodities. This fact has led to the location of large and diversified industries, vital to the commerce and defense of the nation, on improved harbors and inland waterways.

Development of terminals for the handling and transshipment of cargo has proceeded rapidly in recent years. In 1926 there were only forty-nine water terminals on the Mississippi River and its tributaries for handling petroleum products; in 1949 there were three hundred and thirty-two, with an aggregate capacity of more than 78,000,000 bbl.

Record of Usefulness.—Traffic on the inland and intracoastal waterways has risen sharply from about 8,600,000,000 ton-miles in 1929 to 51,700,000,000 ton-miles in 1950—an increase of 500% in the 22-year period. About 80% of this traffic is carried on fifteen major waterways and about 80% of the federal expenditures for waterway improvement have been made on that group. This commerce comprises various bulk cargoes, based on 1948 statistics:

Commodity	%
Petroleum and petroleum products	34
Coal and cokes	19
Iron and steel	17
All other bulk commodities, including grain, sulfur, fertilizers, and automobiles	20
Package freight, such as canned goods, sugar, soap, nails, and beverages	10
Total	100

It is interesting that many federal waterways are being more extensively used and proving to be better investments of federal funds than was anticipated when they were recommended by Corps of Engineers and authorized by Congress (Table 7).

The heavy traffic carried on the inland and intracoastal waterways represents a large saving to industry and to the public in transportation costs. There have been considerable controversy and disagreement about waterways between proponents and opponents, particularly the railroads, regarding the economics of improvements and the savings effected by water-borne transportation. In this connection, however, the President's Water Resources Policy Commission of 1950 has pointed out in its report:

"The contention of the railroads that the benefits of transporting these commodities on the inland waterways are absorbed by a few shippers and not passed along to the public is similarly contradicted by facts. * * * It is no more possible for shippers on the rivers to retain the benefits of low water rates for themselves than it is for lake and ocean shippers to retain the benefits of low water rates."

The Corps of Engineers has estimated on a conservative basis, in a study covering fifteen major waterways, that savings have ranged from 4.6 mills per ton-mile on coal carried over the Illinois Waterway to 19.5 mills per ton-mile for petroleum products on the Sacramento River. The average saving appears to be about 6 mills per ton-mile. This unit saving applied to the 51,700,000,000 ton-mile cargo movement of 1950 would indicate a total saving for that year of $310,-200,000—more than three times the cost of the inland and intracoastal waterway program expressed in average annual terms.

A Basic Transportation Service.—During World War II, the inland and intracoastal waterways proved their value to the national defense and justified their provision in several ways. They relieved the already overburdened railroads of the necessity of transporting many bulk commodities; they provided a medium protected from submarine attack and carried petroleum and petroleum products alone equivalent to 7,000,000 tank-car loads; and they permitted a widespread geographical distribution of manufacture and industry that would otherwise have been forced into already congested coastal areas. Also 4,031 landing craft and

TABLE 7.—COMPARISON OF ACTUAL AND ANTICIPATED ANNUAL TONNAGES

Project	BASIS FOR AUTHORIZATION		Actual traffic in 1950 (1,000 tons)
	Original date	Estimate (1,000 tons)	
Upper Mississippi	1930	9,000	11,025
Gulf Intracoastal	1945	7,028	18,971[a]
Illinois	1933	8,330	16,421
Kanawha	1931	2,300	6,388
Ohio	1908	9,000	48,598
Cape Cod Canal	1934	7,000	13,624

[a] West of New Orleans, La., only in 1949.

small ships of various types were built along the Mississippi River system and floated to sea via the federally improved channels. In another such emergency it is probable that the inland waterways will be even more extensively used, because hundreds of industrial plants have been established along the waterways since the war.

The intent of Congress that the inherent advantages of each mode of transportation be recognized and preserved is stated clearly in the declaration of policy in the Transportation Act of 1940, with a view to providing—

" * * * for fair and impartial regulation of all modes of transportation * * * all to the end of developing, coordinating and preserving a national transportation system by water, highway and rail, as well as other means, adequate to meet the needs of the commerce of the United States, of the postal service, and of the National Defense."

More recently the Water Resources Policy Commission of 1950, which was composed of engineers, economists, and other professional men drawn from all parts of the United States, recognized in its report: "That there are certain parts of the transportation job which waterways can perform better and cheaper than any of the other transport forms," and that commission included among its recommendations that:

"The Nation should continue the improvement of its inland and intracoastal waterways to standard depths as an important objective of comprehensive multiple-purpose basin programs."

8. Great Lakes Harbors and Connecting Channels

Water transportation on the St. Lawrence and Great Lakes gave the French a head start over other colonizing nations in penetrating the vast interior of North America. This early navigation, however, was only by canoes and bateaux. In their natural state the lakes themselves afforded easy and unobstructed navigation, except during periods of closure by ice; but in so far as modern navigation is concerned they did not provide a usable waterway, as connecting channels either did not exist or were adequate only for very small craft. There were almost no natural harbors so located on the American shores of the lakes as to be of commercial value. In their natural state the mouths of most rivers and creeks entering the lakes were blocked by bars over which there was as little as 2 ft to 4 ft of water.

Lake Superior stands about 22 ft higher than lakes Huron and Michigan. Under natural conditions navigation between Lake Superior and the remainder of the lake system was blocked by St. Marys Falls (Sault Ste. Marie) in the St. Marys River. The Straits of Mackinac provided access between lakes Michigan and Huron which are essentially at the same level. Lakes Huron and Erie are connected by the channels of the St. Clair River, Lake St. Clair, and the Detroit River, with a total fall of about 8 ft between the lakes. These channels were obstructed originally by a shoal at the entrance of the Detroit River and bars at the mouths of the St. Clair. The usable depth in the Detroit River was limited to 12.5 ft. Navigation between lakes Erie and Ontario was of course completely blocked by Niagara Falls.

Actual waterway improvements on the Great Lakes appear to have begun in 1797 when the British "Northwest Fur Company" built the first lock and canal around St. Marys Falls between lakes Superior and Huron to eliminate the portage. This lock was 38 ft long, 8 ft 9 in. wide, and had a lift of 9 ft. It was built on the Canadian side of St. Marys River, where a towpath along the shore permitted oxen to haul canoes and bateaux through the canal and lock.

A Great Natural Waterway Made Better.—Work on the harbors of the Great Lakes by the United States began in 1824 with the improvement of Erie harbor; and the first Welland Canal, bypassing Niagara Falls and connecting lakes Erie and Ontario, was constructed by the Canadians in 1829. It had a depth of 8 ft. The charting of the Great Lakes was begun as the result of congressional authorization in 1841. The development of the Great Lakes harbors and channels has been accomplished, however, almost entirely within the past 100 years.

The beginning of this modern improvement may be said to date from 1853–1855 when the State of Michigan completed a canal 11.5 ft deep around St. Marys Falls, again, opening through navigation to Lake Superior. The development by both the United States and Canada has been continuous, and consists of two elements—improvement of connecting channels and improvement of harbors.

Improvement of the connecting channels, begun at St. Marys Falls in 1855, was continued by completion of the Weitzel Lock in 1881 and by deepening St. Marys River to 16 ft. The canal on the Canadian side of the falls, built by the Dominion Government during the years 1888–1895, has a lock 900 ft long and

60 ft wide, and a controlling depth of 17 ft. In 1943, the United States replaced the old Weitzel Lock with the present MacArthur Lock to complete the present "Soo" installation (see Table 8 and Fig. 12).

The connecting channels of the Great Lakes are maintained by dredging to provide as nearly as possible 25-ft depths for downbound ore boats and 21-ft depths for upbound shipping. At average lake levels these depths accommodate ore boats loaded to 23 ft of draft, and the same boats returning with other cargo to a somewhat shallower draft. Maintaining these channels is an exacting and continuous activity of the Corps of Engineers, because, with the navigation season on the upper lakes limited to about 8 months of the year, shippers desire to load their boats as heavily as possible, and small variations in channel depth are matters of great concern to them. This activity is complicated by the fact that the mean annual lake levels fluctuate from year to year—sometimes as much as several feet.

TABLE 8.—DATA ON LOCKS BUILT BY THE UNITED STATES, SAULT ST. MARIE, MICH.

Lock	Completed	Length	Width	Minimum depth over sills
Poe	1896	704	95	16.6
Davis	1914	1,350	80	23.1
Sabin	1919	1,350	80	23.1
MacArthur	1943	800	80	31.0

Harbors, the second element of the Great Lakes waterway system, have been improved continuously since 1824. Up to the present time many commercial harbors (eighty to one hundred thirty-one depending on how certain harbor areas are counted) and numerous small harbors of refuge have been improved by the Federal Government. Channel depths vary considerably, according to the primary purpose for which they were constructed. Harbors which have large ore docks (Fig. 19) are provided with depths of at least 26 ft. There are five harbors in the Chicago area, each with a different depth, ranging from 18 ft to 28 ft.

Harbor work on the Great Lakes is generally similar in character to seacoast artificial harbor construction. Breakwaters, however, may be of somewhat lighter section because of less severe wave attack. Furthermore, the absence of the marine borer (teredo), and a former abundance of timber around the Great Lakes, have led to a much wider use of timber crib and timber pile construction than is usual in salt water.

Federal navigation improvements of the Great Lakes waterway system, excluding lighthouses and aids to navigation, have been accomplished with appropriations through fiscal year 1952 of about $388,100,000 (construction $228,-300,000 and maintenance and operation $159,800,000). This relatively small outlay of federal funds, which has provided the basic improvements that make the Great Lakes system one of the most important waterways in the world, has been followed and paralleled by vastly greater expenditures by states, communities, industry, and shipping interests to supply terminals, cargo-handling facilities, rail and highway connections, utilities, and vessels.

Ships Handle Immense Volume.—Development of shipping to carry the traffic on the Great Lakes has been an important feature in the progress of this waterway and has, in fact, exercised a controlling influence on it. Until 1887 there were more sailing craft on the lakes than steamers; but the opening of the Mesabi Range in Minnesota in 1892 and the traffic in iron ore created a demand for fast movement of bulk cargo. Now, more than two thirds of the ships on the Lakes are more than 450 ft long, with a beam of 60 ft and a draft of 23 ft. The larger boats carry about 17,000 or more tons of ore at maximum draft; and the trend toward larger and faster boats appears to be continuing.

The water-borne commerce of the Great Lakes is of vital importance to the United States, consisting as it does largely (about 80%) of iron ore, coal, lime-

FIG. 19.—DULUTH-SUPERIOR HARBOR (MINNESOTA)—SHOWING BREAKWATERS AND GREAT NORTHERN AND NORTHERN PACIFIC IRON ORE DOCKS

stone, and grain. In 1855 freight passing through the St. Marys Falls Canal amounted to only 14,000 tons. Since then the record has been as follows:

Year	Tons
1870	+ 500,000
1876	+ 1,000,000
1929	+ 92,000,000
1948	+ 115,400,000
1950	+ 106,100,000

In 1950 the cargo tonnage passing through this canal exceeded the combined cargo tonnages passing through the Panama and Suez ship canals. The "Soo" canal is operated only about 8 months of the year, whereas Panama and Suez operate on a 12-month basis. The total traffic on the Great Lakes system has been as follows in recent years:

Year	Ton-miles
1929	97,000,000,000
1932	25,000,000,000
1948	119,000,000,000
1950	112,000,000,000

The peak year was 1948, and traffic was lowest during the depression year of 1932.

The improved Great Lakes harbors and channels are connected with the central inland waterway system at Chicago via the Illinois Waterway and the Mississippi River, providing a 9-ft-deep water route from the Great Lakes to the Gulf of Mexico. At the eastern extremity of the system, the Great Lakes-Hudson River waterway, extending from Buffalo, N. Y., on Lake Erie and Oswego, N. Y., on Lake Ontario to Waterford, N. Y., on the Hudson River, provides a 14-ft-deep waterway connection with the Hudson and via the Hudson to New York.

Potentialities of St. Lawrence Waterway.—In addition, The Great Lakes waterway system is also connected with the St. Lawrence River via Lake Ontario by way of present Welland Canal, constructed by the Dominion of Canada during the years 1913–1933, to bypass Niagara Falls. This canal now provides for passage of ships some 700 ft long and 75 ft wide, with a draft of 23.5 ft. The present controlling channel depth is 25 ft, but lock sills are set at 30 ft. Although the St. Lawrence was improved in 1929–1933 by the United States and Canada in its upper 68-mile section by removal of shoals to provide a depth of 27 ft downstream to Ogdensburg, N. Y., and Prescott, Ont., Canada, through navigation to Montreal, involving an additional 114 miles, is limited to a depth of about 14 ft in the lateral canals built by Canada a half century ago. The full potentialities of the Great Lakes waterway system will not be realized, however, until the proposed St. Lawrence Seaway is constructed to give access to ocean-going shipping, and to extend the arm of the Great Lakes fleet to the Gulf of St. Lawrence. This great project, involving open-channel improvements, locks, and power developments, has been under active consideration for a number of years.

On June 18, 1952, the United States Senate by a close vote of 43 to 40 recommitted a bill which would have authorized construction of the project jointly by the two countries. Shortly thereafter the two governments filed corresponding applications with the International Joint Commission for a permit for the construction of the power phase development in the International Rapids Section, to be built by entities to be later designated. With such power phase construction assured, Canada will concurrently build a seaway, Montreal to Lake Erie, having a controlling depth of 27 ft, with locks at least equal to those now on the Welland Canal—namely, 800 ft by 80 ft by 30 ft. Such a seaway will accommodate virtually the entire Great Lakes fleet, and the Maritime Administrator has testified that it will handle 75% of the sea-going merchant fleet of the United States laden to 75% to 100% of capacity—which means with profitable pay loads. The commercial and military value of this seaway extension of the Great Lakes system would be enormous.

At the present time a period of unusually high levels on the Great Lakes, although not seriously affecting navigation itself, is causing damage to shore properties and difficulties in harbors and at terminals. The Corps of Engineers recently prepared a preliminary examination report on this problem, and has been authorized by Congress to conduct a detailed survey of the Great Lakes to determine whether regulation of fluctuating levels would be feasible and justified in the interests of navigation, power development, protection of shore properties, and related purposes. In addition, the governments of the United

States and Canada have requested the International Joint Commission to study and make recommendations on the problem in order that any appropriate international action may be considered.

The great natural facility of the Great Lakes themselves, as improved by the Federal Government, with the terminals and shipping provided by nonfederal interests, provides the basic transportation structure for the industrial midwest. There is no alternative for this system, and it is not practicable to set a dollar value on, or to compute by ordinary methods of economic analysis, the returns to the nation which have resulted from the federal improvements which have made possible this essential national development.

9. The Panama Canal

No résumé of waterway development in the United States would be complete without mention of the Panama Canal, constructed by the United States across the Republic of Panama to connect the Atlantic and Pacific oceans. This lock canal originally cost about $380,000,000 and was opened to traffic in August, 1914.

Since the Panama Canal, the engineering problems involved in its construction, and the construction methods used have been described exhaustively in various publications of ASCE, they need not be repeated here. In 1947 the canal was reported to have a minimum depth of 37 ft (salt water) in Balboa harbor at low tide, and a minimum depth of 42 ft (fresh water) in Gaillard Cut through the divide. The minimum channel width is 300 ft in Gaillard Cut (Fig. 20), and the lock chambers are 110 ft wide and 1,000 ft long. The Canal is about 50 miles long. As a waterway it has been changed little since it was placed in operation, except for the addition of the Madden Dam in 1935 to provide storage of additional water for lockages, flood control, and power generation.

Because of the restrictive effect of the relatively small locks on naval construction, Congress in 1939 directed the construction of a third set of locks 140 ft wide and 1,200 ft long, which it was then believed would be adequate for all future needs. Plans were prepared and construction was started in 1940. Excavation for two of the locks was substantially completed, when the work was suspended early in 1942, as it became apparent that the new locks could not be completed before the probable end of the war and because of conflicting wartime demands for men and materials. This work remains uncompleted up to the present.

By Act of December, 1945, Congress authorized an investigation of means of increasing the capacity and security of the canal, directing the Governor of the Panama Canal to make the study and report to Congress through the Secretary of War and the President, not later than December, 1947. An exhaustive study was made under the direction of Brig.-Gen. James H. Stratton, M. ASCE, Corps of Engineers, which utilized the services of many federal agencies and experts on commerce and transportation, as well as the most distinguished engineers in the United States in consultation and review. The report was completed on schedule.

It considered a minimum improvement of the existing lock canal to adapt it to meet the needs of commerce for the remainder of the twentieth century at an estimated cost of $130,000,000; and an essentially new lock canal to meet the needs of future commerce, with the maximum security measures feasible for a lock canal, at an estimated cost of $2,308,000,000. The report, however, recommended conversion to a sea-level canal at an estimated cost of $2,483,000,000.

Some major engineering problems and difficulties to be encountered in achieving the sea-level conversion were pointed out. Part of the wet excavation, for example, would require the use of special dredges working to a depth of 145 ft. There was also a considerable difference of opinion regarding the need for a tidal

FIG. 20.—EXCAVATION OF CULEBRA (NOW GAILLARD) CUT, PANAMA CANAL, IN 1909

lock and navigable pass to regulate currents due to differences between tide levels on the Atlantic and Pacific sides. Although it was found that navigation of a sea-level canal would be practicable even if tidal currents were not regulated, a tidal lock and navigable pass were incorporated in the sea-level plan proposed.

This report was presented to Congress after its completion, but no further action has been taken toward increasing the capacity and security of the canal. As it stands, however, the Panama Canal represents the most important waterway development of the past century, and one of the greatest engineering achievements of all time.

10. Summary of a Century of Work

The interest in waterways of the United States and in their improvement which began in early colonial times, and which had an important influence on the formation and development of this nation, has, during the past 100 years, developed into a definite national policy and program.

Improvement of waterways, including harbors, rivers, and canals, has become essentially a function of the federal government; and through fiscal year 1952 more than $4,000,000,000 of federal appropriations has been utilized on this work. It is not possible to estimate with any degree of accuracy the complementary expenditures which have been made by states, municipalities, port authorities, and private enterprise in providing the necessary terminals, rail connections, floating equipment and utilities to complete this program. These nonfederal expenditures, however, would undoubtedly far exceed the amount of federal participation. Thus the waterway program that has developed in the past 100 years is truly national in scope and is the result of the joint effort of governmental and private enterprise.

This development has been made possible by, and has required, important developments in engineering and in construction methods. River systems, lakes, and harbors in the United States have been surveyed; hydraulic and other engineering studies of major rivers have indicated applicable methods of improvement; and engineering structures of great magnitude and complexity have been built. Construction equipment has advanced from the man-powered wheelbarrow and mule-drawn scraper to the heavy earth movers of today; and dredging has advanced from crude beginnings to become the most powerful tool of the waterway engineer and builder.

Waterway developments have given the United States an unequaled array of coastal harbors which have been indispensable facilities in peace and war. Inland and intracoastal waterways now provide thousands of miles of improved channels over which moves an ever-increasing tonnage of basic heavy produce of factory, field, forest, and mine. Finally, the Great Lakes with their improved harbors and connecting channels have become the world's most heavily used waterway system, and the basis for much of the industrial expansion of this country. The engineering profession may well take pride in its basic contribution to this development and look forward to future improvements of equal magnitude and importance.

WATERWAYS IN THE YEARS TO COME

In 1952 the ASCE celebrated its centennial. The century that has been the life span of the Society has encompassed vast social, political, and technological changes. It has witnessed the growth of the United States from a thinly settled agricultural nation to the strongest industrial power in the world; the transition from steam and mechanical motive power to the age of electricity; and the inauguration of atomic energy as a source of power, for both peace and war, with full potentialities as yet little known.

This paper has traced the development of waterways in the United States up to the present and has shown the great strides which have been made, largely during the past century, in this important field of engineering activity. An engineer would be rash indeed to try to predict with any certainty the waterway developments which will come to pass in the years to come—having in mind the rush of startling changes which have so recently taken place, and which will in all probability continue. There are, however, certain indications as to what may be anticipated in this field in the future.

In 1850 the population of the United States was 23,200,000; today it exceeds 150,000,000. How the population will continue to grow in the years to come is problematical; but grow it will. The President's Water Resources Policy Commission of 1950 explored this matter, during its studies of water resource development, and indicated that a population of 190,000,000 appeared probable by as early as 1975. With continued growth, greater industrialization, more agricultural requirements and production, and greater needs for raw materials may be anticipated. In addition, it seems likely that the overseas commitments and responsibilities of this nation will increase rather than diminish. All this means more transportation, and waterways are an important and necessary element of the transportation structure. Accordingly, it seems most probable that the years to come will bring a continuation of the present upward trend in water-borne commerce, both inland and maritime, and in consequence a continuation of sound waterway improvements.

In the future, progress may well be along the following lines:

a. Waterway development will and must proceed as a part of comprehensive and coordinated plans for river basins and water resources. Improvement of rivers and waterways for multiple purposes, including control of destructive floodwaters, development of hydroelectric power, irrigation, and other uses, as well as navigation, will become of the utmost importance.

b. Even deeper and broader harbor channels than are now available will be required to meet the needs of maritime commerce. As this nation depletes its resources of ores and other basic materials, larger importations will follow. Seagoing ore-carrying vessels are increasing in size and draft, just as tankers have increased in recent years, and American ports must be made able to handle this traffic.

c. The position of inland waterways and modern barge lines as efficient and economical movers of bulk cargoes has been amply demonstrated. Further recognition and use of this transportation medium will influence the location of future industrial and urban development. In turn, it will be necessary to deepen existing waterways, to replace locks, as they grow obsolete, by structures able to handle the commerce of the day, and to extend waterways.

d. The St. Lawrence Seaway which has been, and is now a matter of lively engineering and international interest, is a specific project which may be consummated in the near future.

e. The Panama Canal connecting the Atlantic and Pacific oceans remains a most important strategic and commercial asset to the United States. With the increasing sizes of both naval and commercial craft its locks become more obsolete. They are vulnerable to enemy attack, particularly attack by atomic bombs. Consequently the conversion of the Panama Canal to provide a sea-level route, more adequate for commercial shipping and more secure against attack, may again become a live issue.

f. The provision of 12-ft navigable depths in the Mississippi, now authorized by Congress, will be completed as rapidly as possible, and it seems probable that similar depths will be extended to certain other waterways, such as the Ohio, when required by water-borne commerce and by larger and more powerful floating equipment.

This continued waterway development which may be partly envisioned for the years to come will be accomplished more expeditiously and with a more economical expenditure of effort and materials than in the past, because of increasing engineering and scientific knowledge, and because of improvements in construction methods and equipment. Continuing hydrological and meteorological studies, for example, and the accumulation of long-term records of precipitation and stream flow will furnish increasingly sound bases for computation of water supplies for navigation and other river improvements. These data will also permit better planning for meeting the consumptive uses of water, which will become more critical with further population growth and industrial development. More accurate records and studies of this kind should assist in obviating or reducing conflicts between water uses.

Improvement in structural materials, methods of construction, dredges, and other construction machinery should result in more efficient construction, saving of critical materials, increased productivity per man-hour of labor, and thus perhaps in lower cost measured by effort, materials, and time. The cost in dollars will apparently continue to increase until the present inflationary trend is arrested.

Above all, future waterway development in the United States will be guided and influenced to a marked degree by the vast store of engineering, economic, construction, and administrative experience with waterway improvements that has been accumulated during the past 100 years.

BIBLIOGRAPHY

"The Statutes at Large," by W. W. Henning, Richmond, Va., 1810-1823.

Virginia Gazette, Williamsburg, Va., October 25, 1775.

"Historic Highways of America," by A. B. Hulbert, A. H. Clark Co., Cleveland, Ohio, 1902-1909.

"History of the Canal System of the State of New York," by N. E. Whitford, Brandow Printing Co., Albany, N. Y., 1906.

"Early Chapters in the Development of the Potomac Route to the West," by Corra Bacon-Foster, Columbia Historical Soc., Washington, D. C., 1912.

"The Navigation of the Connecticut River," by W. Del. Love, *Proceedings,* Am. Antiquarian Soc., Worcester, Mass., 1904.

"The Improvement of the Lower Mississippi River for Flood Control and Navigation," by D. O. Elliot, Mississippi River Comm., St. Louis, Mo., 1932.

"Improvement of the Mississippi River and Aids to Navigation," by Austin B. Smith, Mississippi River Comm., Vicksburg, Miss., 1950.

"History of Transportation in the United States Before 1860," by B. H. Meyer, Carnegie Institution of Washington, Washington, D. C., 1917.

"Bulwark of the Republic," by B. J. Hendrick, Little, Brown and Co., Boston, Mass., 1937.

"Report of the Secretary of the Treasury, April 4, 1808," *American State Papers,* Class X, Gales and Seaton, Washington, D. C., Vol. I, 1834.

"American Waterways," *The Annals,* Am. Academy of Political and Social Science, Vol. XXXI, No. 1, January, 1908.

"Preliminary Report of the Inland Waterways Commission," *Senate Document No. 325,* 60th Cong., 1st Session, U. S. Govt. Printing Office, Washington, D. C., 1908.

"Public Aids to Transportation," Federal Coordinator of Transportation, U. S. Govt. Printing Office, Washington, D. C., Vol. III, 1939.

"Great Lakes Transportation," by M. C. Tyler, *Transactions,* ASCE, Vol. 105, 1940, p. 167.

"Waterway Traffic on the Great Lakes," by John R. Hardin, *ibid.,* Vol. 117, 1952, p. 351.

"Panama Canal—The Sea-Level Project: A Symposium," *ibid.,* Vol. 114, 1949, p. 607.

"Pioneering in Hydraulic Dredging," by C. N. C. Wilson, 1950 (unpublished).

"A Water Policy for the American People," rept., President's Water Resources Policy Comm., U. S. Govt. Printing Office, Washington, D. C., Vol. I, 1950.

"Water Resources Law," rept., President's Water Resources Policy Comm., U. S. Govt. Printing Office, Washington, D. C., Vol. III, 1950.

Annual Reports, Chf. of Engrs., U. S. Army, U. S. Govt. Printing Office, Washington, D. C.

"Columbia River and Tributaries, Northwestern United States," rept., Chf. of Engrs., *House Document No. 531,* 81st Cong., 2d Session, U. S. Govt. Printing Office, Washington, D. C., Vol. I, 1950.

"Report on the Federal Civil Works Program, As Administered by the Corps of Engineers," *Annual Report,* 1951, Chf. of Engrs., U. S. Govt. Printing Office, Washington, D. C., Vol. III, Pt. I, 1952.

AMERICAN SOCIETY OF CIVIL ENGINEERS
Founded November 5, 1852
TRANSACTIONS

Paper No. 2644

HISTORY AND FUTURE OF FLOOD CONTROL

By George R. Schneider,[1] M. ASCE

SYNOPSIS

The flood-control program in the United States developed as the country grew. At first, individuals struggled with the flood problem; then, as population increased and more people occupied the flood plains, flood losses became greater and local governmental units worked with the problem. Larger units assumed the work until finally the Federal Government accepted much of the responsibility. The development of this federal interest as it emerged from the national interest in commerce is described chronologically.

Subsequently, local efforts at flood control and how they merged with federal efforts are traced for five areas: The Sacramento-San Joaquin and the Los Angeles basins in California; New Orleans, La.; the Miami Valley in Ohio; and the land around Lake Okeechobee in Florida. These were selected because they illustrate the nation-wide character of the problem and also the complicated interrelationships between flood control, use of water, and growth in population. Problems in these areas, in addition to floods, include debris control; water supply for irrigation, industrial, and municipal use; salt-water repulsion; navigation; protection from hurricane tides; and swamp drainage.

Finally, the federal program for flood control as developed by the Corps of Engineers and the work of other agencies whose related duties bring them into the field are outlined. The program is now less than half completed but has prevented much loss. Recent floods show the value of the existing work and emphasize the need for finishing the current program. When it is completed, flood losses will be reduced and water will be conserved for beneficial use. However, as population increases, flood control will have to be extended to places where it is not now justified and in other places a higher degree of protection will be necessary because of more intensive development.

HISTORICAL DEVELOPMENT OF FEDERAL PROGRAM

Floods made the United States. Long before the mound builder found a way to live in a valley subject to floods, floodwaters had been bringing rich sediment

---

[1] Chf., Eng. Div., Corps of Engrs., Little Rock, Ark.

from the highland to build the fertile lowland. Floods built the banks high next to the regular channel of the river, and on these high banks men settled. Thus the settlers were near the fertile, flat plains where part of their food was grown and near the natural waterway which brought them trade.

Flood-control work began in the United States about 1718, soon after the site of New Orleans was selected, when the settlers were ordered to build levees to protect themselves and their neighbors from future floods. The work has been going on ever since. Until 1917 individuals and local and state governments provided the funds for flood-control work although the Federal Government provided some funds for levees along the Mississippi River in the interest of navigation. The 1917 act authorized the construction of levees with federal funds for flood-control purposes, contingent on local cooperation.

After the 1927 flood disaster in the Mississippi Valley and a similar flood in the Sacramento Valley in February, 1928, Congress passed, in May, 1928, the first comprehensive legislation for control of floods in the Mississippi and Sacramento river valleys. That date marks the real beginning of the federal flood-control program. Then in June, 1936, Congress declared:

> " * * * that flood control on navigable waters or their tributaries is a proper activity of the Federal Government in cooperation with States, their political subdivisions, and localities thereof."

This decision may well be said to mark the culmination of efforts that began when the first group of pioneers settled in a river valley. It marked a general recognition of the need for unity and teamwork—recognition that followed growth in understanding and appreciation of the problem. The history of the federal interest in flood control is part of the history of the United States, as will be shown in the following sections.

1543–1802.—Hernando De Soto's expedition encountered a flood on the Mississippi River in 1543. The contemporary account is especially significant in that it describes a large flood, how the Indians built on high ground or constructed mounds that would be above floods, and how they reported that such great floods do not occur every year but at 14-year intervals, especially when heavy winter snows in the sources of the streams are followed by spring rains.

René Robert Cavelier, Sieur de La Salle, found the Mississippi River out of its banks in 1684. A flood occurred on the Delaware River at Trenton, N. J., in 1692 which, if repeated today, would be disastrous. Records of the French settlement at Kaskaskia, Ill., refer to a flood in 1724 which caused severe losses to agriculture. Trouble from floodwaters began in New Orleans the year after the city was established. Later it was inundated by a flood that began in December, 1734, and lasted until June, 1735. In 1763 the "Point" at Pittsburgh, Pa., was submerged by a large flood. The Mississippi and Los Angeles rivers produced great floods in 1770, and in 1771 the rivers of Virginia east of the Allegheny Mountains went on a rampage that was described recently as:

> " * * * probably the most devastating act of God which has been experienced in Virginia during the three and one-half centuries since the English planted their colony at Jamestown."

In 1782 the Mississippi River rose to greater heights than ever before in the memory of old inhabitants, and 1785 was long remembered as the year of "great waters." During this year the Connecticut River in Massachusetts and the Androscoggin and Kennebec rivers in Maine demonstrated that nature is not partial in the distribution of floodwater.

The first steamboat experiment was made in 1785 by John Fitch who demonstrated a boat with mechanical oars and who was given river rights by New Jersey, Pennsylvania, Delaware, Virginia, and New York. In 1787 the State of New York granted Fitch the sole and exclusive right to make and use every kind of boat or vessel impelled by steam in all creeks, rivers, bays, and waters within the territory and jurisdiction of New York.

Also in 1787 the Northwest Ordinance applying to the territory north of the Ohio River and west of New York State was adopted. It provided that:

> "The navigable waters leading into the Mississippi and St. Lawrence, and the carrying places between the same shall be common highways, and forever free * * *."

The United States Constitution, framed the same year, did not change this. John Jay was negotiating with Spain to obtain for the United States the right to free use of the Mississippi River. The flatboatmen were tough fellows who paid little attention to the rights of Spain. The frontiers were moving westward. In Ohio, Marietta was a backwoods seaport where ships were built for foreign trade, and Cincinnati was an Army post with 300 families. The population of the country was about 5,000,000. Many of the floods and other events of the early years 1800–1850 are located graphically in Fig. 1.

1802–1824.—Congress established the United States Military Academy at West Point, N. Y., and placed it in charge of the Corps of Engineers in 1802. Secretary of War James McHenry urged the enabling legislation on Congress, stating:

> "We must not conclude * * * that the service of the engineers is limited to * * * fortifications. * * * Their utility extends to almost every department of war * * * besides embracing whatever respects public buildings, roads, bridges, canals, and all such works of a civil nature."

President Thomas Jefferson went "beyond the Constitution" and bought the Louisiana Territory from France in 1803 for about 4¢ per acre. He was supported by the public who recognized the purchase as a bargain even though flood problems came with it.

With Louisiana the United States acquired an area whose legal principles of servitude of the shores of navigable rivers trace back to "Las Siete Partidas" compiled and adopted by Spain in the thirteenth century. Both France and Spain, while in possession of the territory, reserved all rights to the shores of all navigable streams to keep them "free for the common use of man." The influence of this reservation is found in the Louisiana Civil Code:

> "Servitudes imposed for the public or common utility, relate to the space which is to be left for the public use by the adjacent proprietors on the shores of navigable rivers and for making and repairing of levees, roads, and other public or common work."

Thus the right to use property for levees is vested in the State of Louisiana as a sovereign, and payments for lands used for levees are made to riparian owners to relieve them of the burden imposed by the "ancient" law, and are "in the nature of gratuities." This is in contrast with the legal principles based on English law that the banks of public rivers are private property of the adjacent owners as fully as their other land. The public has no right to use the banks, and when it does so under the right of eminent domain it must compensate the owner.

In 1809 a flood in the Lower Mississippi Valley was so disastrous that many thought the Great Lakes had found a channel to the Gulf of Mexico by way of

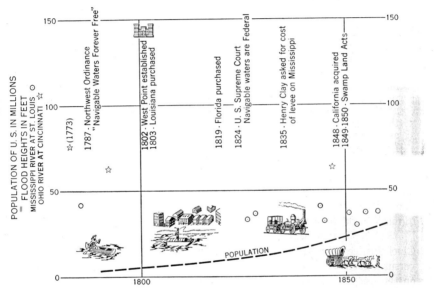

FIG. 1.—FLOODS AND OTHER EVENTS OF EARLY AMERICAN HISTORY, 1800-1850

the Mississippi River. In 1810 Robert R. Livingston and Robert Fulton secured Fitch's monopoly rights to use steamboats on inland waters. Fulton interested Capt. Nikolas Roosevelt in supervising construction of the *New Orleans*, the first steamboat on western water. Captain Roosevelt piloted the *New Orleans* from Pittsburgh, Pa., to its namesake city in 1811. In the same year the Legislature of the Territory of Orleans granted to Livingston and Fulton the "sole privilege of using steamboats * * * in the territory." In 1814 Capt. Henry Shreve took the steamboat *Enterprise* loaded with ordnance and ammunition from Pittsburgh to New Orleans in 14 days. Gen. Andrew Jackson commandeered the boat before it could be seized for violating the Livingston-Fulton monopoly, and Shreve took part in the Battle of New Orleans. In 1816 Shreve built the *George Washington* at Wheeling, Va. (later W. Va.), and piloted it to New Orleans where he was arrested and his steamboat confiscated for venturing into waters controlled by the Livingston-Fulton monopoly. This trip by Shreve marked the beginning of the steamboat era. The river was much more hazardous for the fast-moving steamers which took 3 weeks to go from Cincinnati to New Orleans and back, than for the sail and oar-propelled barges which required 17 weeks to make the journey.

The trip by Shreve was preceded a year earlier by a flood in which all the major tributaries of the Mississippi River north of the Arkansas River combined to produce a stage at Cairo, Ill., near the mouth of the Ohio River that remained a record for 67 years. In 1819 Florida with its flood problems was purchased from Spain. As a consideration, the United States agreed to pay some $5,000,000 in claims held against Spain by citizens of the United States. That year the State of Mississippi passed its first legislation authorizing construction of a levee in Warren County and providing for collection of levee taxes.

John James Audubon wrote the following vivid description of some of the floods in 1820:

> "To give you some idea of a BOOMING FLOOD * * * When it happens that, during a severe winter, the Allegheny Mountains have been covered with snow to the depth of several feet, and the accumulated mass has re- mained unmelted for a length of time, the materials of a flood are thus prepared. * * * On such occasions, the Ohio itself presents a splendid, and at the same time an appalling spectacle; but when its waters mingle with those of the Mississippi then is the time to view an American flood in all its astonishing magnificence."

Congress in 1820 appropriated $5,000 for the Corps of Engineers to make a survey and prepare maps and charts of the Ohio and Mississippi rivers in the interest of navigation. In 1822 two engineer officers made a report on an inspec- tion of the Ohio and Mississippi rivers which gave considerable attention to the formation and removal of snags.

1824–1849.—On March 2, 1824, the Supreme Court of the United States, Chief Justice John Marshall presiding, rendered a decision in the case of Gibbon versus Ogden which denied the right of New York State to grant a monopoly on the use of steamboats on its waterways and affirmed the power of Congress over navigation within the limits of every state in the Union. Congress by an act approved May 24, 1824, appropriated $75,000 for the removal of sandbars from the Ohio River and of snags from the Mississippi. This was the first distinct act of Congress for the improvement of a river. Losses of steamboats and their cargo on the Ohio and Mississippi rivers by snags alone were amounting to an average of $250,000 per year.

By 1828 there were 12,000,000 people in the United States; and, according to the records, some of them believed that deforestation was causing the floods. That year the flood on the Rio Grande was a memorable one in New Mexico and at El Paso, Tex. The one on the Mississippi River was the first great flood for which reliable stage records are available throughout the lower river. After the waters receded, Indian mounds in the Yazoo River Basin were found covered with the remains of wild animals which had perished from starvation. During this year Abraham Lincoln made a trip from Troy, Ind., to New Orleans down the Ohio and Mississippi rivers on a flatboat.

In 1835 Henry Clay introduced a resolution in Congress that an estimate be made "of the probable cost of constructing a levee on the public land on the western bank of the Mississippi and the southern bank of the Red River."

The winter of 1843–1844 was not unusually severe but an extremely heavy snow blanket covered the headwaters of the Missouri and Arkansas rivers. The Mississippi River at St. Louis, Mo., rose early in May and began to recede, then rose again and receded until on June 7 it was within banks; but the flood from the Missouri was yet to come. From June 3 to 10, inclusive, there was a succession of heavy rainstorms which were general throughout the northwest. Very great floods occurred on the Missouri River and its tributaries. At St. Louis the Mississippi River was almost as high as it was during the great flood 59 years earlier and nearly 4 ft higher than it has been at any time since then. Great destruction resulted throughout the Mississippi Valley.

In 1845 at Memphis, Tenn., John C. Calhoun presided over a convention which was attended by more than 500 delegates from twelve states. One resolution presented was as follows:

> "Resolved That millions of acres of public domain lying on the Mississippi River and its tributaries, now worthless * * * might be reclaimed by throwing up embankments * * *, and that this convention recommend such measures as may be deemed expedient to accomplish that object by grant of said lands or an appropriation of money."

The resolutions passed at the meeting were presented to Congress in the form of a memorial. The following year Calhoun introduced a bill in Congress for the general improvement of the Mississippi River.

In 1847 a combination of floods on the Ohio and Arkansas rivers produced higher stages between the mouth of the Arkansas River and Natchez, Miss., than had the great flood 3 years earlier. As a result of continuous agitation throughout the Mississippi River Valley, a national convention was held in Chicago, Ill., to consider the subject of commerce and navigation in that valley.

Lincoln argued in the House of Representatives in 1848 that the Mississippi River should be improved even though the improvement would benefit certain individuals along its banks. In that year Mexico ceded its rights in California and other parts of the West to the United States on the payment of $15,000,000 and the assumption of $3,000,000 in American claims. Again the United States acquired some flood problems in its acquisition of new territory.

The war with Mexico as well as the Indian wars had helped to acquaint many people with the fertile lands and climate of the southern part of the country. Gen. Zachary Taylor, who was elected President in 1848, was one of these. He had fought the Seminole Indians in the Florida Everglades; and for a time, before he became famous in the Mexican War, he had lived on a plantation in the Mississippi Valley near Baton Rouge, La. He knew the value of the soil as well as the problem created by recurring floods.

1849–1879.—Congress passed the first of the "Swamp Land Acts" on March 2, 1849. This act gave to Louisiana those federally-owned swamp and overflowed lands within her borders on condition that they be reclaimed and made available for settlement. According to one historian, the people of Louisiana had at that time constructed 1,400 miles of levees at a cost of at least $20,000,000. The levees protected more than 3,000,000 acres of public land which had been sold and the proceeds deposited in the United States Treasury. The next year President

Taylor with thousands of others from the Mississippi Valley was stricken with typhus and died.

Also in that year, Congress passed the second Swamp Act which gave the State of Arkansas and other states the unsold swamp and overflowed lands to reclaim. Louisiana and Arkansas organized state agencies to administer their responsibilities under the Swamp Land Acts but Mississippi held to the plan of county administration. There were no provisions in the acts which conditioned the transfer of title from the United States to the state on the actual improvements. The Swamp Land Acts were the first provisions made by Congress for flood control.

A summer flood in 1850 apparently originating west of the Mississippi River between the Red and Missouri rivers caused crevasses at Bonnet Carre upstream from New Orleans and at seven other places downstream from the mouth of the Red River. In September, Congress appropriated $50,000:

> " * * * for a topographical and hydrographical survey of the Delta of the Mississippi, with such investigations as may lead to determine the most practicable plan for securing it from inundation, and the best mode of so deepening the passes at the mouth of the river as to allow ships of 20 feet draft to enter the same * * *."

A report by Charles Ellet, Jr., a pioneer in flood-control engineering in the United States, was submitted to Congress in 1851. At the same time an extensive and thorough investigation was initiated, the result of which has become a classic in river hydraulics—namely, the Humphreys and Abbot report on the delta survey. The report, which assembled historic data on the Mississippi River, was submitted after 10 years of exhaustive surveys and investigations including study of the rivers of Europe. This important step, and other significant events including floods for the five decades, 1850 to 1900, are portrayed in proper relationship in Fig. 2.

After a flood occurred in 1851 on the Mississippi River, in 1852 Congress appropriated an additional $50,000 for the delta survey. In 1858 heavy rains over the Ohio, Upper Mississippi, and Missouri river valleys, added to the water from melting snow in the Rocky Mountains, produced a flood on the Mississippi River in June that crevassed many levees upstream from the mouth of the Red River. This flood provided Maj.-Gen. A. A. Humphreys, Hon. M. ASCE, and Henry L. Abbot with a profile on which to base levee grades. It also created sufficient public demand in Mississippi that the State Legislature ordered liquidation of the county levee boards and placed the work in the Yazoo-Mississippi area under one board responsible to the Legislature.

The War Between the States caused a suspension of work on Mississippi River levees, and abandonment of the delta began. Planters had gone to war; their slaves went to federal camps as fugitives. The neglect brought about by the war would have been serious enough, but to make matters worse opposing armies destroyed important parts of the levee system in the name of military necessity. The Mississippi River flood of 1862 exceeded practically all previously recorded stages south from Cairo. Another flood in 1865 caved miles of bank into the river, crevassed some the remaining levees, and left floodwaters standing over the lowland for months. Homecoming for the Confederate soldier meant wading through miles of destroyed and overflowed country. It was a dismal time but the spirit of the people seems to have been expressed by the Board of Levee Commissioners of Louisiana in a memorial to Congress. After reciting the importance of the products of the delta to the country and the reasons why the Federal Government should help restore its economy, the Board summed up as follows:

"The State, crippled as she is in her resources, is still making herculean efforts to protect her citizens; but the impoverished condition of her treasury,

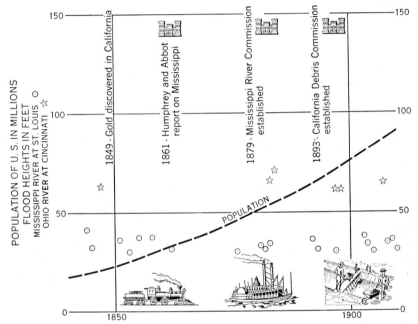

FIG. 2.—POPULATION RISES AND FLOODS CONTINUE, AS GRAPHICALLY SHOWN, WITH SIGNIFICANT HAPPENINGS, 1850–1900

the low state of her credit [brought about by the overthrow of her system of labor], and the loss of revenue from the overflowed lands, have operated greatly to her detriment in the sale of bonds issued for levee purposes; and although we deem the levee system of sufficient importance to be placed under the charge of the General Government, yet we only ask for such assistance as will build up and maintain our levees until such time as our industry can restore the finances of the State to their former condition, and our alluvial lands become the homes of an energetic and thrifty population."

In December, 1865, the Chief of Engineers, General Humphreys, was directed to make an estimate of the cost of repairing the levees along the Mississippi River. He estimated that 9,750,000 cu yd of earthwork would be required at a cost of $3,900,000. Humphreys also stated that:

"The proper establishment and maintenance of the first order of levees requires some authority entirely beyond the influence of local interests."

In 1866 Congress added to the burden of the Mississippi Valley people by placing a tax of 3¢ per lb on cotton. Levee construction was dependent on profits from cotton growing and more than one half of the land in the rich Yazoo River Basin in Mississippi had been forfeited for taxes. Farm lands in Arkansas, Louisiana, and Mississippi were valued at one fourth of their value 10 years earlier.

In 1870 Congress directed the Secretary of War William W. Belknap to provide for making meteorological observations and giving notice to mariners of the approach and force of storms. Reports relative to river stages were authorized in the appropriation bill of the following year, and the next year provision was made for reports that were necessary for agricultural and commercial interests. Congress relieved the War Department of this activity 20 years later and established the Weather Bureau.

The year 1871 was another flood year, during which the State of Louisiana granted a charter to the Louisiana Levee Company and then contracted with that company to build the levees. The law provided that all levees would be located by a commission of three engineers: One to be selected by the State, one to be detailed by the President of the United States from the Corps of Engineers, and the third to be an employee of the levee company. This apparently was the first official participation by a representative of the Federal Government in the actual planning and construction of flood-control works.

A flood in 1874 caused widespread suffering and produced levee crevasses totaling 143 miles in length along the Mississippi River. Appeals to Congress following this flood resulted in the appropriation of $90,000 for the relief of flood sufferers, apparently the first on record. The sum of $25,000 was appropriated for a commission composed of three officers of the Corps of Engineers and two civil engineers eminent in their profession to report on the best system for the permanent reclamation of the alluvial basin of the River. The commission reported five principal causes of the defects in the levee system: Vicious levee organization, insufficient levee height, injudicious cross section and construction, inadequate inspection and guarding, and faulty location. It added:

> "It is a common and apt figure of speech to personify the Mississippi and to speak of the conflict waged to protect the country against the inroads of a terrible enemy; and yet the army of defense has always been content to remain a simple aggregation of independent companies with here and there a battalion under command of a board of officers."

In addition to a plan for protecting the alluvial region from overflow, the commission recommended a permanent over-all organization for levee administration throughout the valley. Whether this organization should be constituted by the Federal Government or by mutual compact between the states, how the money should be raised, and how the work should be done—all were considered matters for legislative action and beyond the scope of the plan which the commission was instructed to submit. The commission pointed out that all existing levees were so low they would certainly be overflowed in any great flood and that, owing to the impoverished condition of the country, little could be done either by the states or landed proprietors without aid from the Federal Government.

Capt. James B. Eads, M. ASCE—of Eads Bridge (St. Louis) fame—was a nationally known civil engineer at that time. His statement before congressional committees that he believed it entirely feasible and practical for the Federal Government to improve the Mississippi and to control its floods at reasonable cost added prestige to the movement for federal participation in flood control.

The California Legislature in its 1877–1878 session created the office of state engineer and made river investigations part of his work. Congress had made its first appropriation for removal of snags on the Sacramento River 3 years earlier, and the Corps of Engineers was engaged in making a survey with a view to improving navigation. The Corps of Engineers officer in charge of the navigation work and the state engineer agreed that best results could be obtained at minimum cost by cooperating in the survey. This action was taken and marks the early cooperation between the Federal Government and the State of California in river basin planning.

A board of engineer officers was appointed in 1878 to report on improvement of low-water navigation on the Mississippi and Missouri rivers. The board was later instructed to consider the effect of a permanent levee system on the Lower Mississippi for both navigation and flood control. The report was submitted in January, 1879. It concluded that a complete levee system would be an aid to high-water navigation but would have little or no influence on navigation at low stages. The board also concluded that the levee system, if undertaken, should be developed and matured in connection with the navigation improvement.

1879–1917.—The law creating the Mississippi River Commission was approved on June 28, 1879. The duty of the Commission was to mature and submit plans to Congress, together with estimates, that would permanently locate and deepen the channel and protect the banks, improve navigation, and prevent destructive floods.

The Mississippi River Commission submitted its preliminary report in 1880 recommending the appropriation of $4,000,000 for initial work on channel contraction and bank protection and for closing gaps in levees. Congress appropriated $1,000,000 in the River and Harbor Bill of March 3, 1881, for improvement of the Mississippi River in accordance with the recommended plan; with the proviso:

> " * * * that no portion of the sum * * * be used in the repair or construction of levees for the purpose of preventing injury to lands by overflow, or for any purpose whatever except as a means of deepening or improving the channel of said river."

The year 1882 was one of the worst flood years in the Mississippi Valley. A flood started with heavy rains on the Ohio and Upper Mississippi rivers, followed by severe rainfall in the Lower Mississippi Valley. Congress appropriated $100,000 on February 25 to be:

> " * * * used by the Secretary of War in the purchase and distribution of subsistence stores to aid in the relief of destitute persons in the district overflowed by the Mississippi River and its tributaries."

The sum of $150,000 was appropriated on March 21 and another $100,000 on

April 1 for the same purpose. President Chester A. Arthur sent a message to Congress urging:

> "* * * the propriety of not only making an appropriation to close the gaps in the levees occasioned by the recent floods but that Congress should inaugurate measures for the permanent improvement of the navigation of the river and security of the valley.* * *
>
> "It may not be inopportune to mention that this Government has imposed and collected some seventy millions of dollars by a tax on cotton, in the production of which the population of the Lower Mississippi is largely engaged."

Mark Twain made a trip on the Mississippi River during this flood and wrote about it in his book entitled "Life on the Mississippi River." The next year another flood on the Mississippi River, which also started in the Ohio River Basin, was of about the same magnitude as the flood of 1882. As if the two successive superfloods were not enough to upset frequency calculations, 1884 produced a flood which exceeded even the two preceding ones at some places.

This succession of floods so aroused the people of the upper part of Mississippi in the Yazoo-Mississippi Delta that they finally united to form an efficient levee organization. Following the War Between the States some of the large landowners felt that they could build private levees sufficient for themselves and thus avoid a tax burden. Then a district was formed, bonds sold, and the money dissipated in waste and inefficiency. Many planters forfeited their lands for taxes and at one time 90% of the taxable lands in Sunflower County were owned by the levee board.

Formation of the Mississippi River Commission marked the beginning of systematic organized cooperative effort by the Federal Government and local interests. The Commission established standard levee grades which were accepted and followed by the levee boards. Jurisdiction during flood times became centralized with the Commission, and the assistance of the Federal Government throughout the valley minimized the fears that people from one area would cut the levees in another to save their own. The states of Louisiana, Mississippi, and Arkansas provided levee boards that were legally authorized to cooperate with the Federal Government acting through the Commission.

Although appropriation bills by Congress included money for work on the Mississippi River, they prohibited its use for levees on, or for reclamation of, lands subject to overflow. However, the levee boards with the advice of the Commission and such financial help as Congress gave them continued to close gaps in the levees, reinforce them, and build them higher in so far as their resources permitted.

In 1889 there was the great man-made disaster at Johnstown, Pa., where failure of a privately-owned dam destroyed 2,200 lives and $10,000,000 worth of property. Echoes of this disaster are heard today in the rumors during floods that "a dam burst." In 1890 heavy rains and severe floods on the Ohio, Middle Mississippi, and White rivers caused a total of fifty-three crevasses with a combined length of 6.8 miles along the Mississippi River. Congressional hearings threshed over the whole problem of flood control and the levee system. The net result was appropriation of $3,200,000:

" * * * for the general improvement of the [Mississippi] river, for the building of levees, in such manner as * * * shall best promote the interest of commerce and navigation."

A board of engineers reporting on the Sacramento River in 1891 stated:

"The United States is concerned that the levee system shall be properly aligned and be adequate to the duty required of it, namely, to compel the flood waters to follow the course of the river channel and thereby scour an improved waterway.* * * It is estimated that on the banks of the Sacramento and Feather Rivers about $7,000,000 have been expended in isolated and uncombined efforts of separate districts, each aiming to give local protection without concern for the general interest. In these operations the State has not undertaken to exercise engineering control."

The year 1892 was a year of floods in California. For several days the City of Stockton on the San Joaquin River was under water, and there were numerous breaks in the levees along the Sacramento River which caused heavy loss to farmers. Floods on the Mississippi that year made forty breaches in the levees with a combined length of 2.3 miles. The appropriation act provided $2,000,000 for levees, surveys, and general improvements and also provided that:

" * * * additional contracts may be entered into * * * as may be necessary to carry on continuously the plans of the Mississippi River Commission, * * * not exceeding in the aggregate two million six hundred and sixty five thousand dollars per annum for three years, commencing July first, 1893."

Work would be paid for through future appropriations. Thus, the Commission and levee board could plan their work more effectively than the year-to-year appropriation had permitted. Congress passed a bill in 1893 creating the California Debris Commission.

The 1897 flood on the Mississippi River broke all records at the mouth of the White River and was 1.7 ft higher than any previously recorded at the Carrollton gage near New Orleans. Congress authorized the Commerce Committee to examine and report on the entire situation, which it did in a volume of 518 pages. It reported: "The burden of completing the levee system is too great for local and State authority." Appropriations by Congress in 1897 combined with an appropriation of the preceding year made nearly $5,000,000 available. Local people made greater contributions than ever, the breaches were closed, and for 5 years the Mississippi River levees successfully held back floods.

Another half century and its accomplishments are shown visually in Fig. 3 for the years 1900 to 1950. Frequency of catastrophic floods on the Ohio River at Cincinnati and on the Mississippi at St. Louis show up vividly.

Passage of the Reclamation Act marked the year 1902. Floods occurred rather generally over the United States in 1903. In the vicinity of Kansas City, Mo., sixteen bridges were destroyed and all but one was still in the stream channel when the flood of the following year occurred. The 1904 flood on the Sacramento River was the most destructive known up to that time. Floods in Colorado, Kansas, the Dakotas, and Pennsylvania were also very harmful. The United States Geological Survey published a paper on "Destructive Floods," and pointed out that:

> "The value of property along the streams is rapidly increasing and data on the flood flow of streams and means of preventing overflow are of increasing interest and value."

In 1907 Pittsburgh suffered from a great flood. Sacramento, Calif., also had a disastrous flood. President Theodore Roosevelt appointed the Inland Water-

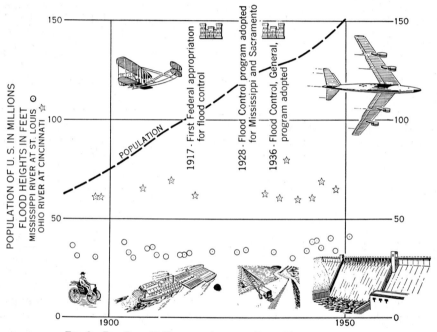

FIG. 3.—THE PAST 50 YEARS OF AMERICAN FLOOD HISTORY, 1900–1950

ways Commission which in its preliminary report a year later recommended that "* * * hereafter plans for the improvement of navigation in inland water-ways * * * shall take account of * * * the control of floods." Congress created the National Waterways Commission in 1909. Its preliminary report pointed out that:

> "The time has already come, especially in the more thickly settled river valleys, when a stream must be considered with a view both to minimizing harmful influences and to securing the maximum benefit from all its uses."

The California Debris Commission presented a plan for flood control on the Sacramento River and tributaries in 1910. The Mississippi River was having a long respite from severe floods, and local levee boards guided by the Mississippi River Commission and aided by federal funds were industriously building their levees to a grade and section above any previous high water. This work was progressing so well that the boards began to devote their attention to revetments to protect the banks. Levee heights and volume were increasing so that it became more important to keep the levees from caving into the river. Apparently it was decided that little further assistance would be needed to build levees along the Mississippi River, because in 1911 only $130,000 out of the $2,000,000 appropriated was allotted for that purpose.

Then in 1912 the Ohio and Upper Mississippi river basins each produced great floods which on the Lower Mississippi exceeded all previous flood stages downstream from Cairo except at Vicksburg, Miss. The Weather Bureau reported that its forecasts enabled prevention of loss of property valued at more than $16,000,000. A flood commission was appointed which investigated forty-three reservoirs above Pittsburgh. The commission said that, if the reservoirs had been in operation in 1907, the flood stage at Wheeling would have been reduced 14.5 ft.

This flood was followed by a double-header the following year. The first came from the Ohio Basin in January and the second from the Missouri, Upper Mississippi, and Ohio basins. The United States Geological Survey report on the Ohio floods of March-April, 1913, pointed out that problems connected with the improvement, regulation, and use of the Ohio River and its tributaries had been considered for more than a century. However, it stated, none of the numerous philosophic and scientific reports that discussed these problems contained any consecutive records of discharge; and, largely because of this lack of basic data, the problems seemed little nearer solution than they were 50 years earlier. The Weather Bureau ventured a prediction of the probable maximum flood at Pittsburgh based on the 1913 flood and several earlier floods. The people of Dayton, Ohio, and other inhabitants of the Miami River Valley became so aroused that they immediately built an effective system of reservoirs and channel improvements. The Connecticut Valley and Vermont felt the effects of these storms in floods that caused record stages and suspension of operations of many manufacturing plants, and in the Mississippi Valley 272,000 people, made homeless by floods, were furnished food and shelter.

There were more reports and more discussion. The entire subject of flood control on the Mississippi was studied by Congress, the ASCE, and the public. Levees versus reservoirs versus outlets, food versus forests, the Nile versus the Mississippi—all were reviewed again, and outstanding engineers pointed out that each was all right in its place and there were places for each, but the most urgent need on the Mississippi River was for higher levees. At that time the levees contained 243,000,000 cu yd, and the President of the Mississippi River Commission stated that an additional 200,000,000 cu yd would make them safe against any flood which had occurred. He pointed out that, although 13 miles had failed, 1,525 miles had held. The River and Harbor Act of March 4, 1915, directed the Commission to report to Congress the amounts spent by local interests for levee construction. The report showed expenditures of more than $91,000,000 by local interests and the value of area protected at $994,000,000.

Southern California streams became torrents in January, 1916, and destroyed the work of generations. For nearly a month San Diego County was practically cut off from the rest of the state. Twenty-two persons were drowned by the flood wave following the failure of nearby Lower Otay Reservoir. Six lives were lost in other parts of the area, and damage was estimated at $10,000,000. The Mississippi River flood that year came from the Arkansas and White rivers. Although it was the greatest of record between the mouth of the Arkansas and Vicksburg, there was only one crevasse.

Discussion continued. The ASCE received a "Final Report of the Special Committee on Floods and Flood Prevention" at its annual meeting. The committee urged uniform methods of investigation; systematic rainfall, runoff, and flood observations; and flood control, not subordinated to navigation or power development.

1917–1928.—Congress responded on March 1, 1917, with "An Act to provide for the control of the floods of the Mississippi River and the Sacramento River, California." At last federal funds were permitted to be spent for levees for flood control. The sum of $45,000,000 was appropriated to be spent under the direction of the Mississippi River Commission at the rate of not more than $10,000,000 annually. Local interests were required to provide rights of way, contribute not less than one half of the cost of the work, and maintain the levee after completion. The sum of $5,600,000 was appropriated for the control of floods, removal of debris, and the general improvement of the Sacramento River in accordance with the recommendations of the California Debris Commission. It was stipulated that funds be spent at a rate not exceeding $1,000,000 per yr on condition that an equal amount would be spent by the State for construction. The State also would provide rights of way and maintain the works after completion.

Congress declared war 5 weeks later against the Imperial German Government and directed President Woodrow Wilson to employ the entire resources of the government to bring it to a successful termination. Wars take priority over flood control, but for a time there was a respite from disastrous floods. The Mississippi River Commission raised the standard levee grade. It was also widening and strengthening the levees. T. G. Dabney, who had been chief engineer of the Upper Yazoo-Mississippi Levee District for many years, was subjected to considerable public criticism because of his efforts to complete the levee line of his district to the new standards. In 1920 a flood was caused by abnormally high winter temperatures which rapidly melted the accumulated snow in the Upper Mississippi and Ohio river valleys. There were only two crevasses with a total length of 475 ft in the Lower Mississippi Valley. That year the Federal Power Commission was created by Congress.

The year 1921 was marked by a "cloudburst" flood which caused the loss of about 150 lives and property damage of about $20,000,000 in the vicinity of Pueblo, Colo. In September floods occurred in south central Texas with resultant loss of 224 lives and property damage of $10,000,000. The United States Geological Survey commented in its report that:

> "* * * over 30 million acre-feet of water annually passes unutilized from the streams of Texas to the Gulf of Mexico, much of it in floods that cause great destruction. Good business sense demands that the floods of Texas be controlled and that the flood water be stored so far as practicable for the many uses for which it is needed."

The flood of 1922 in the Mississippi Valley broke records for stages downstream from the Arkansas River. The levees of the Upper Yazoo District in Mississippi held secure, and the criticism of engineer Dabney changed to praise for his efforts to build the levees in his district to full line and cross section. It was the first time as far as history and tradition show that the main stream and all its tributaries were at high stages or in flood about the same time. Stages were everywhere below the provisional grade established by the Mississippi River Commission 8 years earlier. The Weather Bureau was commended by the newspapers for the accuracy and timeliness of its flood predictions. Even while this flood was in progress the ASCE was holding a symposium on flood problems. It and the discussion which followed gave a thorough review of the flood problems of the United States at that time.

Congress responded by passing an act in March, 1923, "to continue the improvement of the Mississippi River and for the control of its floods" and authorized appropriation of $10,000,000 per yr for 6 years beginning July 1, 1924. In 1925 Congress directed the Corps of Engineers and the Federal Power Commission to submit an estimate of the cost of investigating navigable streams and their tributaries whereon power development appeared feasible and practicable, with a view to forming plans for improvement for navigation in combination with development of water power, control of floods, and the needs of irrigation. The Colorado River was excluded. The report of the two agencies was submitted to Congress in April, 1926. It was published as *House Document No. 308,* Sixty-Ninth Congress, First Session, and was enacted into law the following January. The so-called "308 reports" on the river systems of the United States followed this law. While the stage was being set in the fall of 1926 for the great disaster to follow in the Mississippi Valley, tropical hurricanes killed nearly 400 people in Florida and the Gulf States and destroyed 5,000 homes.

The floods in the spring of 1927 in the Mississippi River Basin were so disastrous and received so much publicity that a detailed recital is unnecessary. The Weather Bureau reported:

"This flood because of its magnitude, protracted duration, far-reaching extent, and economic destructiveness, eventually assumed such vast proportions that it became a national calamity * * * whose depressing effects will be felt for years to come."

It was estimated that one half of the wild animals in the inundated area perished. Herbert Hoover, Hon. M. ASCE, then Secretary of Commerce and Chairman of the Mississippi Flood Committee, stated:

"One bright ray which comes out of the situation confronting the Mississippi Valley is the realization that the 125 million people of the United States have been awakened to the fact that this valley must be protected from future catastrophe."

The *Cleveland* (Ohio) *Plain Dealer* concluded that the flood had spoken louder than a 5-ft shelf of engineer's reports and resolutions by organizations in calling attention to facts about floods. A question which had been debated at length was whether works should be built to protect against the great floods that occur at infrequent intervals or only against ordinary floods that occur frequently. After the 1927 flood there were few who did not agree that it was necessary to provide protection against the greatest flood.

The ASCE held a symposium in October, 1927, at which the Chief of Engineers and many other noted engineers presented facts and expressed opinions on the problems of the Mississippi and Sacramento rivers, on reservoirs, drainage, reforestation, sediment, and other phases of the flood problem. The presentations and discussions of some forty engineers filled 312 pages of the 1928 *Transactions*. The discussion among the engineers centered on engineering aspects of the problem but discussions in Congress centered on economics—how much money should be provided and whether any local contributions should be required. Many hearings were held and six special reports were submitted in accordance with the instructions of Congress. Out of these came the first comprehensive flood-control legislation.

1928–1936.—The Flood Control Act approved May 15, 1928, authorized the project for flood control in the alluvial valley of the Mississippi River in accordance with the plan recommended by the Chief of Engineers. It declared that the principle of local contribution toward the cost of flood-control work is sound and, in view of the $292,000,000 spent by local interests, the legislation did not require local contribution toward construction on the Mississippi River. It provided that local interests should maintain the projects after completion and provide rights of way with the exception that the United States would provide flowage rights for the additional destructive floodwaters that would pass by reason of diversion from the main channel of the Mississippi River.

The greatest recorded flood had occurred 3 months earlier on the Feather River, the main tributary of the Sacramento River. Congress recognized this situation by including in the 1928 act a modification of the previously approved project for "alleviation of debris conditions in the Sacramento and Feather rivers to increase the total cost to the United States from $5,600,000 to $17,600,000." The state or other local interests were required to contribute one half of the cost of construction of the project levees. This act also authorized establishment of the Hydraulic Laboratory later known as the United States Waterways Experiment Station at Vicksburg as recommended by the Chief of Engineers.

In September, 1928, 4 months later, another hurricane and flood caused the death of some 2,000 people in Florida, and on December 21, 1928, the same Congress passed the "Boulder Canyon Project Act" which provided for the construction of what was later known as the Hoover Dam on the Colorado River in Arizona-Nevada. The law provided:

> "* * * that the dam and reservoir * * * shall be used, First, for river regulation, improvement of navigation, and flood control; second, for irrigation and domestic uses and satisfaction of present perfected rights * * * of [the] Colorado River compact; and third, for power."

It also specified that "reclamation law shall govern the construction, operation, and management of the works."

The River and Harbor Act of July 3, 1930, modified existing projects for improvement of navigation in the Lake Okeechobee region to include flood-control works for prevention of disasters such as those which had occurred 2 and 4 years earlier. The State of Florida or other local interests were to contribute $2,000,000 toward the cost of the project, provide lands, and maintain works and channels within the Everglades Drainage District.

Nature went from extreme flood conditions in the late 1920's to extreme drought conditions in the early 1930's. At the same time the United States was afflicted by a great financial depression. Congress resolved the debate which had been going on for many years about the disposition of the project on the Tennessee River at Muscle Shoals, Ala., by creation of the Tennessee Valley Authority in an act approved on May 18, 1933.

Broad powers were given President Franklin D. Roosevelt to relieve unemployment, and many important projects for flood control were started with funds provided by Congress for unemployment relief. Among these was the Muskingum (Ohio) Watershed Conservancy District Project for flood control and conservation. The district was created under the laws of Ohio on June 3, 1933; in December, 1933, an allocation of $22,090,000 was made to the Corps of Engineers by the Public Works Administration; and in March, 1934, an agreement with the District was signed and work on design of the project was commenced by the Corps of Engineers.

Under the original agreement the Federal Government acting through the Corps of Engineers was responsible for construction of the project including relocation of railroads and other public utilities; and the State of Ohio through the conservancy district was to provide all lands and rights of way and through its highway department, all necessary road relocations. Other projects initiated under similar authority during this period were the Fort Peck, Mont., Reservoir Project for navigation and flood control; the Conchas Reservoir Project in New Mexico for flood control and irrigation; and the Tygart Reservoir Project on the Monongahela River in West Virginia for flood control, navigation, and water supply.

On April 27, 1935, Congress declared a policy of preventing soil erosion for the preservation of natural resources, control of floods, and related purposes. The most sudden and destructive flood that had ever occurred in the Upper Susquehanna River Basin in New York State came in July, 1935. "Cloudbursts" over the basin produced torrents of rain becoming sheets of water that destroyed buildings, made highways and railroads impassable, and covered farm lands with boulders. Forty-three people were reported killed.

On August 20, 1935, Congress authorized Parker Dam on the Colorado River in Arizona-California and Grand Coulee Dam on the Columbia River in Washington:

> "* * * for the purpose of controlling floods, improving navigation, regulating the flow of the streams of the United States, providing for storage and for the delivery of the stored waters thereof, for the reclamation of public lands, and Indian reservations, and other beneficial uses, and for the generation of electric energy as a means of financially aiding and assisting such undertakings."

1936–1952.—March, 1936, brought the most destructive flood known at Pittsburgh and nearby on the Allegheny, Monongahela, and Ohio rivers. The stage at Pittsburgh was 7 ft higher than it had been in the flood 29 years earlier. It was even 5 ft higher than the prediction made 23 years earlier by a venturesome Weather Bureau meteorologist of the probable maximum flood stage at Pittsburgh. Thus it was 5 ft higher than the highest previously known flood which had occurred 173 years earlier.

Congress modified the Lower Mississippi River Project on June 15, 1936, by abandoning a floodway that did not please the local people and authorizing protective works on the St. Francis and Yazoo rivers in the Lower Mississippi Valley. Then, in an act approved on June 22, 1936, Congress summed up the interest of the Federal Government in flood control in a comprehensive "Declaration of Policy" stating that flood control is a federal responsibility.

The act authorized some 211 flood-control projects, at an estimated construction cost of about $300,000,000, in thirty-one states which would affect nearly every state in the Union. No appropriations were made for construction but funds were provided for surveys, foundation investigations, and detailed plans. The act authorized examinations and surveys for flood control on 222 rivers and established procedures for surveys and studies. It made improvement of rivers for flood control and allied purposes the responsibility of the Chief of Engineers under the direction of the Secretary of War and placed water-flow retardation and soil-erosion prevention under the direction of the Secretary of Agriculture.

Nature's reply to this declaration of Congress was delivered in January and February, 1937. Unprecedented rains fell over a zone extending from central Arkansas northeastward to south central Ohio almost parallel to the Ohio and Lower Mississippi rivers. Southern Missouri and Illinois were covered with ice early in January. Rain persisted for several days at a time without moving far from the axis of the zone. The resulting flood exceeded previous stages at Cincinnati by nearly 9 ft; at Louisville, Ky., by more than 10 ft; and on the Mississippi River at Memphis, by nearly 4 ft. It was the largest flood of record on the Mississippi River above the mouth of the Arkansas River, and below that it was only a little smaller than the disastrous flood 10 years earlier would have been if it had been confined by levees. Most gratifying was the fact that the works previously provided on the Lower Mississippi River successfully held the water within bounds except in the backwater areas of the tributaries. Under the direction of the Mississippi River Commission the levees had been raised and strengthened, the Mississippi channel between the Arkansas and Red rivers had been shortened by cutoffs, and the Bonnet Carre spillway above New Orleans had been built. All these operated effectively, and the flood was carried to the sea without the horror and disaster that had accompanied so many earlier floods.

In April, 1937, Congress amended the Flood Control Act of the previous year to include a system of reservoirs for the protection of Pittsburgh, and in August another act appropriated nearly $25,000,000 for the construction of levees, flood walls, and drainage structures. It also provided that, if a city or town, by reason of its financial condition, was unable to comply with the established requirements of local cooperation, the President might waive such requirements, not to exceed 50% of the estimated cost of the lands, easements, and rights of way.

December, 1937, marked the first time a great flood was known to occur during that month in the Sacramento River Basin. Stages in the river system were the highest since the beginning of the Weather Bureau records 33 years earlier and apparently exceeded the high water of 75 years before in the upper valley. In late February and early March, 1938, Southern California suffered from excessive rainfall. Moisture-laden warm air forced upward by the San Gabriel and San Bernardino mountains precipitated the heaviest known rainfall for the region. One station reported 10.89 in. of rainfall in 8 hours, another 17.55 in. in 24 hours, and 32.2 in. during the 6 days of the storm. Seventy-nine deaths and $25,000,000 worth of damage resulted, not including the value of millions of tons of soil and subsoil removed from the mountains and deposited in the lowlands and even in the ocean.

A large appropriation for the "Flood Control, General, Program" as it is known was made in June, 1938. Later in the same month an act authorized and directed the Secretary of War:

> "* * * to acquire in the name of the United States title to all lands, easements, and rights-of-way necessary for any dam and reservoir project or channel improvement or channel rectification project for flood control"

and provided that local agencies be reimbursed for expenditures made by them for such a purpose. It also provided that, where construction cost could be substantially reduced by the evacuation of an area, the Chief of Engineers might arrange for the evacuation and pay the cost from project funds.

The United States Supreme Court entered the picture again in a decision made in the New River (West Virginia) case, on December 16, 1940, when it stated that: "* * * flood protection, watershed development, recovery of the cost of improvement through utilization of power, are parts of commerce control." Another significant decision was made by the Supreme Court 6 months later in the Red River (Texas and Oklahoma) case, on June 2, 1941, which stated in effect that federal authority extended upstream to all the headwaters of any river system above its navigable reach.

The Act approved on December 22, 1944, declared it:

> "* * * to be the policy of Congress to recognize the interests of the States in determining the development of the watersheds within their borders and likewise their interests and rights in water utilization and control, * * *."

and set up procedures for obtaining the views of the states; and, in the case of waters arising west of the ninety-seventh meridian, the views of the Secretary of the Interior. This act stated that the words "flood control" shall be construed to include channel and major drainage improvements. It also provided for the sale by the Secretary of the Interior of electric power generated at reservoir projects under control of the War Department and established preferences in sale. Recreational features in reservoir areas were authorized by the 1944 act.

After World War II appropriations were made by Congress for continuing the program. Although interrupted by an Executive Moratorium in August, 1946, work was resumed on a limited scale and has proceeded in accordance with the funds provided.

In 1947 central and southern Florida suffered from hurricanes and floods. The Columbia and other rivers in the Pacific Northwest made national headlines because of floods in 1948. The Sacramento-San Joaquin Basin in California experienced a severe flood in 1950. In 1951 a series of storms which began in May and continued into July culminated in a flood which broke all previous records on the Kansas River and on the Missouri River at and below Kansas City. In the spring of 1952 rapid melting of snow and ice in the upper reaches of the Missouri River caused a flood which was nearly 6 ft higher than the previous record at Omaha, Nebr. Council Bluffs, Iowa, and Omaha were saved from inundation and from $50,000,000 to $100,000,000 losses by a valiant and successful flood fight. This flood was remarkable in that there was no loss of life directly attributable to the flood.

As this condensed review indicates, floods continue to occur even as they did in 1543. However, a major step toward their control was taken when the Federal Government assumed responsibility for the task.

SACRAMENTO-SAN JOAQUIN VALLEY

The Sacramento-San Joaquin Valley (Fig. 4), also known as the Great or Central Valley of California, covers one third of that state. It is enclosed by the Sierra Nevada on the east and the Coast Range on the west; it extends almost to Oregon on the north and nearly to Los Angeles on the south. Near the center of the Coast Range at San Francisco is a notch which admits moisture-bearing air from the ocean and which permits the runoff from the basin to return to the sea through Golden Gate. The Sacramento River rises in the northern part of the valley where Mount Shasta towers more than 14,000 ft above sea level. Precipitation in the northern part of the basin averages about 70 in. annually, much of it falling as snow. The San Joaquin River drains the southern part of the basin where the average annual precipitation on the valley floor is as low as 10 in. although it amounts to as much as 60 in. in the high Sierra Nevada to the east. The extreme southern end of the valley is the Tulare Lake Basin, which has no outlet to the sea except a branch of the Kings River which flows northward and joins the San Joaquin.

Gold was discovered in the Sacramento Valley in 1849, and it is estimated that more than $1,000,000,000 worth has been taken from the gravel of the stream channels. The Sacramento River was the chief means of transportation for miners and traders when the population of the new state was less than 100,000. Hydraulic mining started about 1852 when a canvas hose and wooden nozzle were used to wash a gravel bank. That the debris problem might be serious for the lower valleys seems to have been first demonstrated by the floods of 1861 and 1862 which brought large amounts of placer mining and natural debris down the channels to the foothills where much of it filled the river bed and spread out over the adjoining land.

By 1870 the population of California was more than 500,000, and the hydraulic giant, comparable to present-day machines, had been developed. Old gold-bearing river channels higher than present-day river channels had been opened up, and it was a simple matter for the hydraulic giants to sluice large masses of gravel from them to the present channels. The debris continued to flow out of the mountains, so valley dwellers formed an Anti-Debris Association. Levees were built to protect the towns and brush dams were constructed to retain the debris, but they were inadequate. Nearly all the swamp lands, about 1,000,000 acres, granted to the State by the Federal Government in 1850 had passed to private ownership by 1871. Landowners found leveeing their own lands unsatisfactory and began to form districts for building more substantial levees. Each district leveed for its own protection without regard for others, and flood heights were increased by elimination of storage areas and confinement of the flow.

In 1873 Congress authorized a study of irrigation in the valley, and the Corps of Engineers a year later submitted the first plan for using and controlling the water resources. The California Legislature in its 1877–1878 session created the

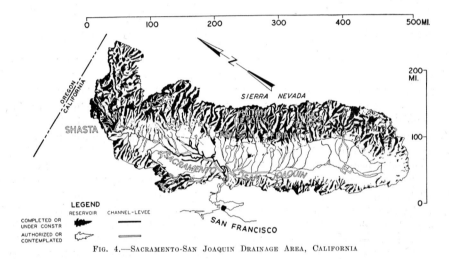

FIG. 4.—SACRAMENTO-SAN JOAQUIN DRAINAGE AREA, CALIFORNIA

office of state engineer. Another act authorized survey of a canal to tap the Sacramento River upstream from Sacramento and enable part of the floodwaters to bypass the city. The river bed at Sacramento had built up 7 ft during the preceding 30 years. After a long, bitter court fight, a federal court injunction known as the "Sawyer" decision finally stopped hydraulic mining in the basin in 1884.

By 1890 California had a population of 1,250,000. In 1893 Congress passed the "Caminetti" act to "create the California Debris Commission and regulate hydraulic mining in the State of California." The act required a commission composed of three officers of the Corps of Engineers to make plans for the improvement of navigable rivers affected by hydraulic mining or other debris and to permit hydraulic mining if it could be done without injury to the navigability of the rivers or to adjacent lands. California provided at once for appointment of a competent "civil engineer" as debris commissioner and appropriated $25,000 for joint construction of debris barriers.

The work continued with California and the Federal Government cooperating until a series of disastrous floods in the Sacramento Valley in 1904, 1907, and 1909 caused renewed demands for flood control. Losses from these floods were approximately $10,000,000. Timely Weather Bureau warnings were credited with preventing a $2,000,000 additional loss. By that time the population of California was nearly 2,500,000.

A plan for "Sacramento River Flood Control" was submitted to Congress by the Debris Commission in 1910. Part of the plan was adopted in the River and Harbor Act of 1910, and $400,000 was appropriated contingent on the State of California appropriating a like sum. It resulted in dredging about 25,000,000 cu yd of material from the river during the next 7 years.

The Sacramento River flood-control project adopted by Congress on March 1, 1917, provided that the United States would do only certain items of work such as construction of weirs and cutoffs in the river. State and local interests were to do the remainder of the work and maintain the works after completion. The population of Sacramento at that time was a little more than 50,000. The plan was expanded in the Act of May 15, 1928, by which time the population of Sacramento had increased to nearly 100,000 and that of California to more than 5,500,000. San Francisco looked to Hetch Hetchy (Fig. 4) for water.

The State of California, working with the federal agencies, was developing its own plan for control and use of water in the valley, and in 1933 the plan was approved by the voters and a bond issue authorized. However, because of economic conditions at the time, the bonds could not be sold and help was sought from the Federal Government. In 1935 President Roosevelt authorized the start of construction of Shasta Dam, one unit of the Central Valley project, for operation in accordance with the reclamation law. Congress confirmed this authorization and it became a federal reclamation project.

The initial features, which are now largely completed and in operation, include two major storage dams—Shasta and Friant—power plants, pumping plants, and water distribution canals. The total cost as presented in *House Document No. 146*, Eightieth Congress, First Session, is more than $384,000,000, of which $31,500,000 was allocated to flood control. Other uses of the project include navigation, irrigation, salinity repulsion, power generation, and municipal water supply.

Operation of Shasta and Friant reservoirs illustrates the use of storage in multiple-purpose reservoirs in regions having a fairly well-defined flood season. Shasta Reservoir, which is in the northeastern part of the basin where precipitation is heavy, has a total capacity of 4,500,000 acre-ft. For dead or minimum storage 500,000 acre-ft is allotted; 2,700,000 acre-ft of capacity is used to increase the supply of water for irrigation, navigation, and power; and 1,300,000 acre-ft is used seasonally for flood control, power, and irrigation—that is, it is filled gradually as the end of the season of large floods approaches. The Friant Project is in the southeastern part of the basin where precipitation is light. Of its 520,000 acre-ft, 130,000 is allotted to dead storage and 390,000 to joint use for flood control and irrigation.

The Flood Control Act of 1936 authorized complete reexamination of the flood-control situation in the valley. Additional work was authorized in 1941 and 1944 and numerous flood-control and multiple-purpose reservoirs, levees, and channel improvements have been constructed. Several projects are under construction, notably Pine Flat and Folsom dams scheduled for completion in 1953 and 1955, respectively. Pine Flat Dam is being built by the Corps of Engineers primarily for flood control although it will provide water for irrigation and is expected to be used for power generation and for reregulation of water from upstream power development. At Folsom, the dam is being constructed by the Corps of Engineers; and the power plant, by the Bureau of Reclamation in accordance with congressional action. In addition to flood control and power generation, Folsom Dam will provide storage for irrigation and municipal water supply.

The flood-control works of the valley were tested late in 1950 when a series of intense storms during November and December produced record-breaking floods throughout the basin. Practically all the streams except those draining the mountains on the north and west and the Sacramento River itself overflowed their banks at least once. Some areas were inundated as many as three and four times by successive flood peaks. The total area flooded was estimated to be about 700,000 acres. Approximately 25,000 persons were evacuated, and the American Red Cross reported giving assistance to about 15,000 flood victims. Shasta and Friant reservoirs each regulated all the floodwater originating upstream from them, and all the works completed by the Corps of Engineers operated satisfactorily and prevented damages of about $75,000,000; but, even so, the loss was estimated as from $30,000,000 to $35,000,000. Folsom and Pine Flat dams would have prevented considerable losses had they been in operation; but, as it was, construction operations at Pine Flat were delayed and losses resulted from the work being flooded.

Nowadays the economy of the Sacramento-San Joaquin Basin is based on agriculture rather than gold. Large areas of deep, fertile, alluvial soils make it one of the world's choice agricultural regions. The population of the metropolitan area of Sacramento was about 275,000 in 1950 and that of the Central Valley about 2,000,000. The San Francisco Bay area, which is dependent on the Sacramento-San Joaquin basin for water, had a population of 2,500,000; and the population of California, which ranks second among the states of the nation, was 10,600,000 and still growing.

The problems of water control and use in the Sacramento-San Joaquin Valley are about as complex as those found anywhere. They became complicated when the population of California was less than 500,000. As the population increased, the complexity of the problems increased. However, even as the engineers cooperated in 1878 on a survey of the Sacramento River, they have continued to cooperate in planning the best use of all the resources of the valley.

Los Angeles

Los Angeles and its satellites (Fig. 5), which include Burbank, Glendale, Pasadena, Long Beach, and Santa Monica, are blessed with a climate which has attracted more than 4,000,000 people. The almost rainless summers are 8 months long with an average temperature during the warmest month of 71° F. What rainfall does occur, usually about 15 in., is concentrated in one or two of the remaining months. The average temperature of the coldest month is 55° F, and the relative humidity averages from 50% to 55%.

A map of the area resembles a flower pot decorated with fluted ruffles at the

top where it is 60 miles wide. The bottom of the pot, 20 miles wide, is San Pedro
Bay and the Pacific Ocean. The height is 45 miles in a north-south direction. The
fluted ruffles are the San Gabriel Mountains which make up about 40% of the
area. The mountains rise from an elevation of about 750 ft, 30 miles inland from
the ocean, to 10,080 ft at the crest of Old Baldy in the northeastern corner of the
basin, 50 miles from San Pedro Bay.

Moisture-bearing air from the ocean is deflected upward by the mountain
range so the seasonal rainfall of 10 in. along the coast increases to about 45 in.

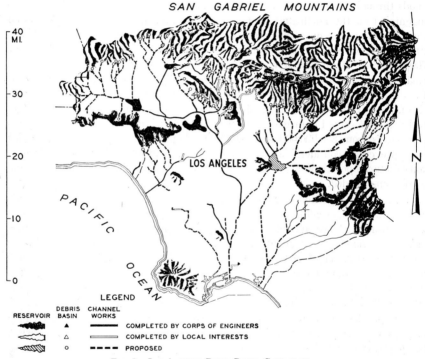

FIG. 5.—LOS ANGELES RIVER BASIN, CALIFORNIA

along the mountain crest. Tributary streams converge so that the intense rain
falling in the mountains produces floods of high peak discharge. Because of the
steep slopes—many denuded by fire—great quantities of silt, rock, and other debris are carried to the canyon mouths where most of them are deposited in what
are called debris cones. Farther down the flow spreads out and alluvial fans have
been formed. The foothills, the alluvial fans, and the valley areas are occupied
by homes, apartments, and industry so that impervious areas of roofs and streets
have been substituted for the natural pervious surface over much of the area,
further intensifying floods and flood losses. This combination of physical features
and high concentration of population and property values creates conditions that
do not exist elsewhere.

The area involved is the part of Los Angeles County south of the mountains which drains into the Pacific Ocean. It totals 1,717 sq miles, of which 620 sq miles are mountains, 640 sq miles are foothills and alluvial fans, and 457 sq miles are valley and coastal plains. More than 500 sq miles are subject to overflow.

Works built and those planned by the Los Angeles County Flood Control District and the Corps of Engineers representing the Federal Government are among the largest and most varied engineering projects in the country. They include storage reservoirs using dams of earth, rock fill, gravel fill, and gravity concrete as well as arch dams of all types; dams designed to be watertight and to resist earthquakes; debris basins to induce deposit of outwash from the mountains (which may include boulders up to 40 tons each and, in a single storm, amount to anywhere from 1,500 cu yd per sq mile from a well-forested area to 100,000 cu yd per sq mile from a recently denuded area); spreading grounds to conserve as ground water as much as possible of flood flows, thus serving for water supply and irrigation, and to repel salt water from the ocean; and rectified channels paved with a variety of materials, to carry flood flows at velocities up to 70 ft per sec with streamlined bridge piers and superelevated curves carefully designed in hydraulic laboratories to operate at high efficiency. The work is further complicated by the high value of water rights and by 5-ft subsidence of the harbor at the Los Angeles River outlet, thereby reducing the channel capacity.

The present situation is a far cry from a century ago when the population of the county was 3,530. The population more than doubled during each decade of the next 50 years until in 1900 it reached 170,300. Flood information is meager. In 1815 the Los Angeles River changed its course; in 1825 it changed back again. A flood in the winter of 1861–1862 seems to have been greater than any known before or since. Newspapers reported flood damages of $1,000,000 in 1884 and of $400,000 in 1889. Growth was limited by the water supply until 1913 when the Owens Valley Aqueduct with an ultimate capacity of 450 cu ft per sec reached the Los Angeles area bringing water from the Sierra Nevada some 250 miles to the north.

In 1914 the county population was estimated at 790,000 and land and improvements were assessed at about $850,000,000. There were two floods that year. Many lives were lost; thousands were made homeless; thirty-five bridges were destroyed; and for 6 days the area was isolated. Losses from the two floods were estimated at $10,000,000. These floods shoaled the harbor, which was being improved, so that large vessels could unload at the port. Commerce had increased 126% during the preceding 11 years. In 1915 the Los Angeles County Flood Control District was initiated by an act of the State Legislature. Reports and a plan to protect the harbor from silt at a cost of $1,080,000 subject to certain specified cooperation by local interests were submitted to Congress. Another flood in January, 1916, depositing more than 2,000,000 cu yd of silt, added impetus to the work. In July the Federal Government appropriated $500,000 conditioned on local cooperation for diversion of the Los Angeles River to protect the harbor from silt.

A flood-control district was formed which included practically the entire county south of the mountains. A bond issue of $4,500,000 was voted to carry out a plan which provided for dams in the mountains, bank protection, channel rectification, spreading and storing of flows underground for conservation, and protection of the harbor. By 1922, the sum of $5,000,000 had been spent on the project.

The authorized river diversion to protect the harbor was completed in 1923. Along with an unprecedented dry period following 1916, the great increase in population focused attention on conservation of water, and in 1924 a bond issue of $35,000,000 was voted—to be used for construction of storage dams in the mountains. Some of the smaller dams were built, but the prospect of an ample supply of water from the Colorado River caused interest in conservation of the local supply to wane. Home sites were sold in the foothills; and, in addition to crowding former channel and ponding areas, which generally were not well defined, about 55 sq miles of paved and built-up areas reduced infiltration and increased runoff.

By 1931 the county population had increased to about 2,200,000, the assessed valuation was $4,500,000,000, and commerce amounting to more than 25,000,000 tons with a value of $1,000,000,000 used the harbors each year. Twelve regulating reservoirs had been built along with numerous unrelated channel improvements. The flood-control district officials realized that the program was barely keeping pace with the increase in storm runoff because of the growth in population and issued a comprehensive plan report in 1931, drawing attention to the menaced areas and outlining needed protective works. However, interest waned since less than 8% of the people living in the area had experienced the 1914 flood or were aware of the hazard. Furthermore, the activities of the legal organization of the district were included in the general county administration, so that the district lacked centralized control as well as authority to publicize the danger. Nevertheless, the partly completed works safeguarded lives and prevented much destruction of property by such floods as did occur.

Then on New Year's Day 1934, a flood in a relatively small localized area caused the loss of forty-one lives and property damage of $6,000,000. An extensive construction program was inaugurated at once, and in 1935 the County Flood Control District requested and was given allotments under the Federal Emergency Relief Act. The allotments were made on condition that the County Flood Control District would contribute $3,500,000, furnish rights of way, and assume liability for all damages; that 90% of the labor would come from relief rolls; and that the work would be prosecuted by the War Department under the Chief of Engineers. The Federal Flood Control Act of 1936 placed flood-control work under regular civil appropriations of the Corps of Engineers with an authorization for the Los Angeles Project at an estimated construction cost of $70,000,000.

A 4-day storm which reached a climax on March 2, 1938, produced the greatest flood of record in the Los Angeles area. Forty-nine lives were lost and $40,000,000 worth of damage was incurred within a few hours. At the time of this flood nearly 220 miles of channel had some kind of protection. About half of it consisted of wire fence supported on piling; about 30 miles was dumped riprap and derrick stone; 35 miles was paved with concrete; 15 miles was hand-placed rock paving; and similar amounts were wire and rock mattress and gunite slope paving. Generally, the protective works functioned properly with the exception of the wire fence and gunite which did not do so well on the outside of bends or wherever the direct attack of the current caused the water to get behind it.

Debris flows resulting from the 1934 New Year's Day flood had hastened construction of debris basins, and sixteen were in operation and functioned as expected within the limits of their capacity. Fires in 1933, 1934, and 1935 had denuded most of the areas; and basin capacities were insufficient for the great mass of debris that flowed down the canyons. Ten flood-control dams were in operation or partly in operation. Most of them were too small to effect a material reduction in the 1938 flood peak, but the partly completed San Gabriel Dam No. 1 with a drainage area of 202 sq miles reduced the peak from 90,000 cu ft per sec to 52,600 cu ft per sec. Losses in storage capacity due to debris ranged from 9% to 82%.

Transportation of Colorado River water to the area in 1939 through a 300-mile conduit with an ultimate capacity of 1,500 cu ft per sec again raised the ceiling which water supply put on the population. By 1940 the county, city, and other agencies had spent more than $110,000,000 on flood-control and storm-drainage works and had constructed 200 miles of channel improvement, fifteen dams, several debris basins, and numerous small check dams. Federal expenditures amounted to more than $90,000,000. The population at this time was 2,500,000.

A report was submitted to Congress in 1940 with a general plan of improvement which included all existing works and extensions that could be justified. The plan included five flood-control basins, thirty-three debris basins, 97 miles of channel improvements on the main streams and 181 miles on tributary streams, sixty-three main-stream bridges, and two hundred sixty-five tributary stream bridges. The estimated cost of work to be done was $268,000,000, $55,000,000 of which would be borne by local interests. Average annual benefits were estimated at more than $20,000,000. This work was approved in the Flood Control Act of 1941.

Another flood struck the area in January, 1943. The rainfall over a 66-hour period was about 50% greater than any previously recorded. At one mountain station an automatic gage recorded 25.82 in. of rain in 24 hours, and several stations recorded more than 20 in. in 24 hours. However, because less than 3 in. of rain had fallen since the previous April, the runoff volume and peak flows were only 40% of those that occurred during the flood of March 2, 1938. A flow of 19,000 cu ft per sec was reduced to 1,800 cu ft per sec by the Hansen Flood Control Basin, completed in 1941 as part of the federal project. Practically no damage occurred in the area below it, which had sustained heavy losses in the 1938 flood.

The Los Angeles flood-control project is now less than one third complete, yet damages in the amount of $20,000,000 have been prevented. When finished, the fabulous storybook land in and around Los Angeles, famous for movies, airplane factories, oil wells, and sunshine, will have one of the largest and most comprehensive flood-control projects in the world so that the millions who live there can be safe and secure from floods.

New Orleans

The story of flood control at New Orleans is unique in many respects. It is the only city where floods have been fought continuously for more than two and a quarter centuries; the only city of its size in this country having important areas below Gulf and sea level; and the only city so dependent on levees to protect 500,000 people that a single local failure would be disastrous. In addition, New Orleans is a most important seaport. In one direction it is the gateway to the great agricultural and industrial heart of the United States, the Mississippi Basin; in the other direction, to Latin-American neighbors and the rest of the world.

The story is unique because, as the key city of the Mississippi Valley, New Orleans was a leader in presenting to Congress the case for federal flood control. Nevertheless, when Congress finally adopted the Mississippi River flood-control project in 1928, the people of the Orleans Levee District, which is New Orleans, did not desire any levee work done by the United States in their district. With its own funds New Orleans provided levees on its riverfront with a crown so wide and slopes so flat that they were safe against failure except by overtopping or by bank caving. Not until 1950 did the levee district desire to be included within the purview of the 1928 Flood Control Act, and it was then so included by Congress.

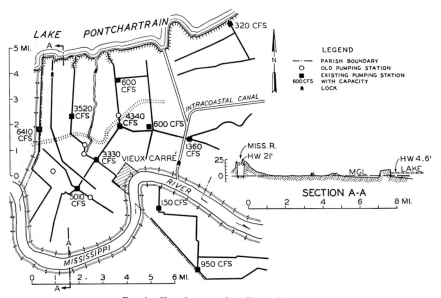

FIG. 6.—NEW ORLEANS, LA., FLOOD CONTROL

New Orleans (Fig. 6) is on both banks of the Mississippi River about 115 miles from the Gulf of Mexico—at a crescent-shaped bend in the river where the distance between the river and Lake Pontchartrain is from 4½ to 7 miles. New Orleans proper is on this narrow neck between the lake and the left bank of the river. Lake Borgne, which connects with the Gulf of Mexico through Mississippi Sound, is about 12 miles east of the city.

In times long past the Mississippi River broke through to Lake Pontchartrain west from New Orleans so that the site of New Orleans is often referred to in old writings as the "island." These connections have long since been closed by the Mississippi levees and now it is only through the Bonnet Carre spillway, a controlled outlet upstream from New Orleans, that the floodwaters of the Mississippi can enter Lake Pontchartrain.

The Intracoastal Waterway along the Gulf coast crosses the Mississippi River at New Orleans, emphasizing the importance of the city in today's navigation system and pointing up its former still greater importance in communications when the water road was the most practicable way of travel.

One of the old bayous or connections between the Mississippi River and Lake Pontchartrain is about midway between the river and the lake at the widest place. Part of the river flowed this way for many years, forming a channel about 100 yd wide. Banks of silt were deposited alongside the channel as is usual on alluvial streams. These banks finally were built up to about 4 ft above Gulf level and until less than a half century ago were the only footway eastward through the swamps. This bayou was diverted north into Lake Pontchartain through Bayou St. John apparently in recent geologic time because there is little silt deposit on the banks of Bayou St. John.

The natural riverbank within the crescent varies from about 5 ft to 15 ft above Gulf level. North toward the lake about halfway to the ridges left by the old bayou the street curbs are now about 2 ft below Gulf level, and between the ridges and Lake Pontchartrain the established curb grade is 4.5 ft below Gulf level. The levees along the left bank of the river are 13 miles long generally with a top width of 50 ft, a riverside slope of 1 on 3, a landside slope of 1 on 10, and the top about 23 ft above Gulf level.

About 80 miles of levee and sea wall built to 9.5 ft above Gulf level protect the city from hurricane tides in Lake Pontchartrain and Lake Borgne. The river levees on the right bank are nearly 14 miles long, and the rear levees are about 10 miles long. Pumps with a combined capacity of 25,500 cu ft per sec in ten pumping stations keep nearly 50,000 acres unwatered. The river is from 1,800 ft to 3,400 ft wide and as deep as 200 ft at high water. The average velocity during floods approaches 8 ft per sec at the smallest cross section. The highest stage, reached in both the 1922 and 1927 floods, was about 21 ft above Gulf level. Since then the Bonnet Carre Floodway has been built and operated so that a stage of 20 ft has not been exceeded.

The Morganza control structure (including rail and highway crossing facilities) is under construction about 185 miles upstream from New Orleans on the west bank of the river, near the head of the Morganza Floodway. The necessary highway and railway crossings are also being built across the West Atchafalaya Floodway which comes into action through operation of the "fuse plug" levee at its head as the final means of controlling the design flood. Entrance to this floodway from the Mississippi is through Old River, 20 miles upstream from Morganza. Although not completed, both these floodways can be operated if the nature of a flood so requires, and the Mississippi River in front of New Orleans would have to carry only 1,250,000 cu ft per sec during a design flood as compared with 1,358,000 cu ft per sec in the 1922 flood.

New Orleans was settled by the French about 1717. Naturally the first area occupied was on the high ground adjoining the river above small floods and close to the docks. This is the "Vieux Carre" or "old square" which has been glamorized by many able writers. Drainage ditches or canals divided the area into squares 100 meters on a side, known as "islets." Sidewalks, or "banquettes," were built up adjoining the houses. Sewage went into the ditches, thence into Bayou St. John.

Levee construction began in 1718. By 1727 the levee was 5,400 ft long, 3 ft high, and 18 ft wide on top. By 1735 it had been extended from about 30 miles above to 12 miles below New Orleans. A large flood that year caused crevasses and the city was flooded. In 1743 the government passed an ordinance requiring landowners to complete their levees by January 1, 1744, or forfeit their lands.

France lost the "Seven Years' War" (1756–1763) and with it lost Canada, the Ohio Valley, and her possessions east of the Mississippi except the "Isle of Orleans," which the King of France had given with Louisiana to the King of Spain by secret treaty in 1762. Spain took actual possession in 1769. The French were not happy with the change in rulers, especially when a Spaniard by the name of O'Reilly, who came over to take charge of the colony, insisted that things be done his way. Among other innovations the laws and ordinances of Spain relating to lands were made applicable to the land grants in Louisiana. Regulations imposed by O'Reilly provided for land grants with narrow fronts along the river and required levees to exclude the river and ditches to remove the water. Front owners were given a prior right to claim land in the rear of their own grant.

New Orleans was neutral in the Revolutionary War. However, the British had interfered with its trade, and the Americans looked like good customers so the British in West Florida were given little encouragement. At the end of the war Britain ceded her claims to the Floridas to Spain. John Jay was sent to Spain to negotiate the boundary between the United States and Spain and to secure unlimited freedom of navigation and a free port.

In 1788 a fire destroyed New Orleans, by this time a congested city of wooden houses. Five thousand people had lived in the burned-out area and the province had a population of more than 42,000. The city was flooded in 1791, and Baron Francisco Luis Héctor de Carondelet, the governor, issued a levee ordinance in 1792 emphasizing the importance of levee maintenance and specifying a fine for those who disobeyed. In 1794 Governor Carondelet had a canal dug to one of the branches of the Bayou St. John to provide better access to Lake Pontchartrain. There was a yellow fever epidemic in 1799. One official pointed out the fact that the overflowing water and filth did not help the situation.

A visitor to New Orleans in the summer of 1802 tells of coastwise vessels from Mobile, Ala., and Pensacola, Fla., coming up the canal into the town. The canal also received all the water from the town drains, the levee preventing any communication with the river. River water was delivered in carts throughout the city. When kept in jars and filtered, it was cool, clear, and pleasant, but many used it as it came from the river.

By a secret treaty Spain traded Louisiana to France who in turn sold it to the United States. The formal transfer from Spain to France was effected on November 30, 1803. The French flag was replaced by the American flag 21 days later. The population of New Orleans was about 8,000. In 1805 a charter was granted by the territorial legislature and confirmed by Congress to the New Orleans Canal and Navigation Company to clear the canal and bayou chiefly for navigation. Americans moved in rapidly, and by 1810 New Orleans had a population of more than 17,000. In late 1814 and early 1815 preparation for the Battle of New Orleans and the battle itself were the chief interest.

The city was flooded in 1816 and again in 1823. In 1830 the population of

Louisiana was more than 215,000. In 1831 the state chartered the New Orleans Canal and Banking Company to dig a new canal from the city to Lake Pontchartrain. This canal was dug with spades and the 500,000 cu yd of dirt were moved by wheelbarrows on trestles to the bank. Water was pumped from the trench with Archimedes-type pumps. Yellow fever and cholera broke out, and there were more than 8,000 deaths, but the canal was completed in 1838 at a cost of a little more than $1,000,000.

A similar "improvement bank" began construction of the St. Charles Hotel in 1835, and in the same year the state granted a charter to the New Orleans Drainage Company which undertook to drain a large area east of the new canal. The area was to be divided into sections and the completed sections were to be turned over to the city to be maintained. Two sections were transferred in 1846 and another in 1850. The inhabitants of each section paid the company for the drainage. By that time the population of Louisiana was 517,000. The sections were consolidated in 1852, and drainage became the duty of the city as a whole. That was the year Paul Hebert, who had been state engineer, introduced a measure in the State Constitutional Convention to have English as well as French admitted as the official language of the government. The leading French paper of New Orleans never forgave him for retiring his native language, and his action was used against him politically.

Louisiana was scourged again by a yellow fever epidemic in 1853. A joint committee of the Legislature recommended for New Orleans a system of quarantine, street repair, drainage of swamp lands, better homes for the poor, and enough "water works to throw a constant stream of water down every gutter." In 1858 the Legislature created three districts, each with a board of commissioners, to reclaim the swamp lands. The work was to be done by 1871 and not more than $350,000 was to be spent in each district.

In 1868 the city surveyor made a report to the City Council pointing out that the system of having work done by the commissioners and then the city taking over the maintenance was inadequate; that assessments for drainage should be based on the value of the property rather than on the area, as the swamp lands were not worth the amount assessed; and that much more work would be necessary before the land would be habitable. He recommended that the city be responsible for the work.

One board of commissioners replied by admitting that additional works would be needed from time to time by the extension of improvements toward the swamp and the increase of building, roofing, and paving in the older section of the city. The board also pointed out that the preceding 8 years had been years of misfortune and embarrassment; that only about one half of the assessments had been paid; and that the board, recognizing the financial embarrassment of the people, felt it should not compel payment by law. The board concluded by saying that the one thing which could have advanced operations more rapidly was money and that this was not obtainable.

In 1871 the Legislature abolished the three boards and transferred their duties to the administrators of the City of New Orleans. The same act created the Fourth Drainage District and authorized the Mexican Gulf Ship Canal Company to dig canals within various districts and to build levees. This company dug many new canals, cleared all the existing canals, built the protection levee above the city from the river to the lake, and spent altogether nearly $2,300,000. In 1878, as the jetties built by Captain Eads to provide deep-water navigation to New Orleans were nearing completion, the city suffered another epidemic.

The State Legislature established the Orleans Levee Board in 1890 and since then it has been responsible for protection of the city from Mississippi River floods and from hurricane tides on Lake Pontchartrain. By 1893 Louisiana had a population of nearly 1,250,000 including 250,000 people in New Orleans. That year the City Council decided with appropriate "whereas-es" that the drainage of the city was in an extraordinarily disastrous condition. No general plan had been adopted for drainage, and there were no topographic maps or other data on which to base a plan. The city engineer was directed to prepare maps and obtain the necessary data, and an advisory board of engineers was appointed.

Public meetings were held before and after a plan was prepared. The report was submitted 2 years later. It reviewed the history of the work and pointed out that little had been done since the Mexican Gulf Ship Canal Company finished its work 22 years earlier. The existing canals and drainage system had a maximum capacity of handling $\frac{1}{8}$ in. of runoff per hour. There were four drainage machines having a combined pumping capacity of 1,170 cu ft per sec and one centrifugal pump with a capacity of 44 cu ft per sec. The draining machinery had been in service more than 40 years and was primitive and uneconomical. There was no drainage system across the river in Algiers, La.

Establishing a comprehensive system of drainage for the city was a unique and intricate problem for which no precedent existed in either this country or Europe. In fact, the reason so many plans had been proposed and abandoned was the lack of information to determine their hydraulic features. As the city continued to grow, it was expected that means would become available to improve public service including drainage. Also, it was pointed out that the improvements should be based on plans to take care of future contingencies to the extent they could be estimated.

A sanitary system was being planned at the time which involved pumping the sanitary sewage into the Mississippi River, so this problem did not have to be met. Since it was considered that drainage should be excluded from the two navigation canals which served the city, the plan proposed a main outfall to Lake Borgne with pump capacity of 38 cu ft per sec for dry-weather flow. The estimate of total probable runoff was nearly 13,000 cu ft per sec; and the estimated probable cost for the completed system, about $8,000,000. The estimated cost of the works recommended for early construction, which was considered to be within the financial ability of the city, was $1,300,000.

In 1897 and 1898 the people of the city were again forcibly reminded of the need for better drainage and sanitation by an epidemic, mild compared to previous ones, but serious enough to stir the inhabitants to a frenzy which culminated in a definite program for obtaining adequate funds and for removing that work from political control. A drainage commission was organized to carry out the plans of the advisory board. The commission was absorbed in 1903 by the Sewerage and Water Board of New Orleans which was created in 1899 by an act of the Legislature. This board is now responsible for the water supply, sewerage, and drainage of the city with its more than 570,000 people—a population twice that when the board came into being, and which represents almost one-fourth the population of Louisiana.

The last inundation of New Orleans by Mississippi River floodwater was more than a century ago, but that does not mean the battle has been won. The banks and bed of the river in the lower reaches are relatively stable as compared with those farther upstream. However, the attack goes on unceasingly. The bends in the river at New Orleans are very sharp, and the docks along the waterfront are not only very valuable to their owners but essential to the business of the city and the great area it serves. Hence even a slow erosion is of serious concern.

Many miles of bank revetment, below the water surface and known to few of its people, are actually the first line of defense of New Orleans. The great depth of the river in the bends adds to the problem. Maintenance of the upper banks against waves and maintenance of revetments, particularly during floods, require constant vigilance. In 1882 the river was above flood stage at New Orleans 91 days, and in 1884 that record was exceeded by 16 days. In the flood of 1897 nearly a mile of the protection of the city against inundation consisted of a box levee 8 ft wide placed directly against highly improved property, and the riverbank had caved so that the mud boxes were on the brink of the river.

The floods of 1912 and 1922 went above 21 ft on the Carrollton (New Orleans) gage, more than 1.5 ft higher than any flood of record before 1912. A crevasse at Poydras, La., about 13 miles downstream, relieved the situation in the 1922 flood. The people of New Orleans had never been very happy with the closure by levees of the old outlets to the swamps, the lakes, and the Gulf. They felt that the river in flood needed more capacity than the channel could provide and that increased levee heights with consequent increase in bank caving and subsidence troubles was not an adequate answer to their problem. As a result they organized a "Safe River Committee of 100" to make their wants and fears known.

In 1926 approval was obtained to create a relief outlet by removing a stretch of levee 60 miles downstream from New Orleans at a cost to the State of Louisiana of $1,000,000. Authorization for survey and study of a spillway was secured. These studies and the work of the committee had much to do with obtaining authority during the 1927 flood for the artificial crevasse at Caernarvon, near Poydras. The stage at New Orleans in the 1927 flood just reached 21 ft. The Flood Control Act of May 15, 1928, provided for the controlled outlet at Bonnet Carre, 32 miles upstream from New Orleans.

The control of floods at New Orleans is not complete. It will require constant watchfulness and additional works from time to time, but it has advanced far since the first levees of 234 years ago.

MIAMI VALLEY

The Great Miami River is so named to distinguish it from the Little Miami; both are tributary to the Ohio, the Little Miami entering just east of Cincinnati and the Great Miami entering just west of Cincinnati almost at the Indiana-Ohio State line. The Great Miami River drains 5,433 sq miles in southwest Ohio.

Its valley is a large industrial area which includes Dayton, Hamilton, and several other important cities.

The valley (Fig. 7) was the site of important Indian villages when the first white man saw it. The land was rich, level, and abounded in game and fruit. Its ownership, like that of much of the country, was disputed by Spanish, French,

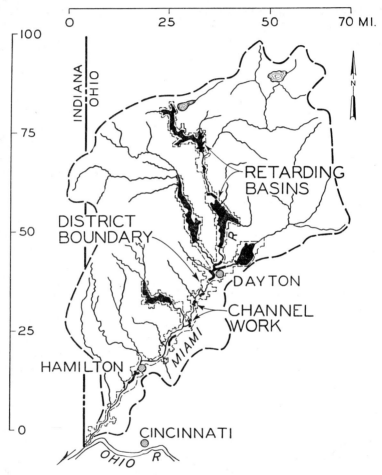

FIG. 7.—MIAMI VALLEY, OHIO

British, Indians, and Americans. A treaty with the Indians was signed the same year Dayton was laid out—1795. By 1810 the population of Dayton was 383. Contact with the outside world was largely by the "water road," the river. Brush dams and fish baskets interfered with navigation and there were conflicts between fishermen and boatmen, but in 1826 about thirty boats went down the Miami to the Ohio thence to the Mississippi and New Orleans. The last boat left Dayton for this journey in 1828.

Completion of the Miami Canal from Dayton to Cincinnati in 1829 relieved the river of this task. The canal north to Lake Erie was completed in 1845, and for 25 years it contributed greatly to the development of the valley. Then the railroads supplanted the canal; and at Dayton in 1903 the Wright Brothers, Orville and Wilbur, developed a flying machine, which is in turn supplanting the railroads for fast transportation. Today the population of Dayton and its environs is nearly 500,000, and it is an important part of a great industrial area.

The first major flood after the town was settled was in 1805 when water was about 8 ft deep in Main Street. Many inhabitants wanted to abandon the site and move to the plain on the second rise above the river. The "unyielding opposition of some of the citizens" defeated the move, and levees were built to protect the town from the annual floods. The levees were broken by floods in 1814 and 1828, and in 1832 the middle pier of the bridge was washed out.

Effects of another flood in 1847 were so exaggerated by some reports that at least 150 people were drowned and that the damage was $1,500,000 that another writer was constrained "to do an act of justice by stating the extent of the flood." He said that "not one-fifth of the whole town plat was overflowed and the loss sustained by private individuals in Dayton could not have exceeded $5,000." He added, "A levee was soon after constructed which will completely secure the lower parts of town from any such catastrophe for the future."

This levee gave way in 1866 and all rail communication was cut off. There was another flood in 1883 which was increased by ice in the stream, but the levees held. In 1886 another large flood occurred, but the principal loss apparently was from interior drainage or runoff from within the leveed area. In 1897 and 1898 there were major floods with losses largely from interior runoff and backwater through ineffective gates. The latter flood reached the top of the existing levee in many places and during the next year the levee was raised about 3 ft.

The winter of 1912–1913 did not differ greatly from other winters in the valley, but on Sunday, March 23, 1913, it started raining. On that day the precipitation amounted to only ½ in. to 2 in. Monday it rained harder—from 2 in. to 5 in. Tuesday was a little worse than Monday, the range being from 3 in. to 5 in., the 5-in. depth occurring across a wide part of the valley 25 miles north of Dayton. Wednesday the rainfall tapered off, being from 1 in. to 2 in. in depth, and Thursday was the last day of the storm with a maximum of 1 in. Eventually, 90% of the rainfall ran off. The flood hit Piqua and Troy, 30 miles and 20 miles, respectively, upstream from Dayton on Monday night. The people of Dayton and Hamilton, 35 miles farther downstream, slept unaware of the impending disaster. Early the next morning the levees at Dayton began to break with the river channel carrying 100,000 cu ft per sec or about 40% of the flow at the peak. The water at Dayton rose rapidly until noon on Tuesday; but, from then until midnight, when the crest was reached, the rise was slow.

Rescue work which was started during the flood continued as relief work, and the American Red Cross did not complete its task until the following winter. Known loss of life was 361. Property losses in cities and losses to utilities in the valley were estimated as more than $66,000,000 excluding depreciation which was estimated by real estate men as more than $10,000,000 in Hamilton and $30,-000,000 in Dayton. Losses to valley farms, many of which had the topsoil completely eroded or covered with gravel, were not estimated.

Less than 2 weeks after the flood, committees of citizens of the Miami Valley were seeking security from future floods. Each community started out to solve its problem independently, but it soon became evident that it would be impossible for the smaller communities to obtain complete relief through local improvements. Hamilton, the lowermost city in the valley with 3,672 sq miles of drainage area upstream, allied itself with Dayton, where the drainage area is 2,698 sq miles, in a movement for a comprehensive plan. On May 15 representatives of neighboring cities met to discuss the possibilities of cooperative action, and on May 25 the Miami Valley Flood Prevention Association was organized by delegates from the flood-relief committees of each of the nine affected counties. Dayton alone raised more than $2,000,000 in 10 days by subscription from 23,000 individuals. These funds were used for engineering and legal work and real estate appraisals.

In 1913 Ohio had no law to enable formation of a cooperative enterprise such as that needed, so a bill known as The Conservancy Act of Ohio was prepared. It was passed by the Legislature on February 16, 1914, and approved by the Governor the next day. It provided for establishment of a district by a court consisting of representatives of the Common Pleas Court of each county in the proposed district. This Conservancy Court appoints a board of directors consisting of three landowners who are residents of the district. The work of the district is directed by this board which is empowered to appoint a chief engineer and necessary staff. The Court also approves the official plan and appoints a board of appraisers to determine benefits and damages.

A petition for formation of the Miami Conservancy District was filed the day after the Governor approved the legislation. Every effort had been made during the preceding months to keep the public informed of the work. The general features of the proposed plan, which included five retarding basins, were announced 6 months after the flood. Violent opposition developed, chiefly in towns upstream from Dayton and downstream from the proposed basins. A virulent campaign was carried on in newspapers, arousing the people who lived upstream from the cities against those in the cities. Efforts were made to add crippling amendments to the conservancy law in the Legislature. The constitutionality of the law was questioned, and the county judges who would form the district were divided and every possible legal obstruction used to delay and prevent action. It was June, 1915, before the State Supreme Court finally sustained the Conservancy Act in its entirety.

Planning the work was not delayed by the legal activities as it was being carried out with funds raised by popular subscription. A board of noted engineers had been assembled and alternate plans for protection of the valley were developed. Essentially, these were resolved into three plans: One providing for protection of the valley by channel improvements, another for protection by numerous small retarding basins, and the adopted plan, which provided for five large retarding basins with channel improvements in critical places, balanced between reservoir storage capacity and channel flow capacity so as to secure the desired protection at least cost.

It was found that protection of only the cities by channel improvement would cost much more than the combined plan and that protection of the entire valley by channel work would cost more than twice as much as protection of only the cities.

The channel improvements would protect only against a flood as large as that of 1913, but the balanced system would protect against a flood 40% larger. The advantages of the small reservoirs over the large ones were recognized. A system of forty-five small retarding basins was studied thoroughly; and it was found not only that it would cost considerably more than the adopted plan but that it would be impossible to provide the same degree of protection. The official plan was filed with the district in May, 1916. The report describing the plan was widely distributed. Newspaper articles informed the public and leading engineering publications drew out the criticism and comment of engineers.

Opponents of the work objected to the plan, and hearings lasted 7 weeks. They presented an engineering report alleging that the estimated cost was low, that the dams might not be safe, and that channel improvement was preferable. The district presented an imposing array of noted engineers who gave the proposed plan their unqualified approval. A former Chief of Engineers, United States Army, testified that the plan had been worked out with more care and thoroughness than any engineering project—even the Panama Canal—of which he had knowledge. The Court approved the plan on November 24, 1916, and the way was open for appraisal of benefits and damages.

Some 60,000 pieces of property were appraised for benefits and 5,000 for damages. They belonged to 40,000 owners and the tax duplicate value of the properties assessed for benefits was $1,200,000,000. Property was zoned and benefit factors assigned depending on the depth of past flooding and the degree of protection provided. Agreements were reached with owners in special cases such as the railroads. Exceptions by owners to the appraisals were heard by the Conservancy Court, and unsettled cases which went to the court of the county in which the land was situated amounted to less than 2% of the total benefited. As appraised the total benefits amounted to more than $77,000,000. The total cost was estimated at $27,800,000 so each property was assessed 36% of its appraised benefit. World War I was in progress and the Secretary of the Treasury William G. McAdoo was consulted about sale of the bonds. He offered no objection because of the industrial importance of the area; and so the bond issue, amounting to nearly $25,000,000, to be retired in 30 years and bearing 5½% interest, was sold.

The greater part of the proposed work was advertised for bids in September, 1917; but, owing to war conditions, nearly all the bids were unsatisfactory so the district formed a construction organization. The total cost of construction of the flood-control works was $30,800,000 including the cost of land and relocation of highways, railroads, and utilities. The district purchased 30,000 acres of land outright and acquired flood easements on 25,000 acres in the retarding basins. Now only about 3,500 acres of the purchased land is held by the district, the remainder having been resold to private owners, with the district retaining a flood easement. The bonds were fully paid in December, 1949, and delinquencies in payment amounted to less than 0.4%. Annual maintenance assessments are about 1.4% of the original total cost.

The system was first tested by flood in April, 1922, and every part worked according to plan. Other notable floods followed in 1924, 1929, 1933, 1937, and 1943, the greatest being in 1937 when the total rainfall upstream from Dayton was more than 9 in., almost as much as that in 1913 although less intense. The controlled stage at Dayton for this flood was 14.5 ft which compares with a danger stage of 18 ft and a 1913 river stage of more than 27 ft.

A new generation has grown up since the works were completed. About four times as many people live in and around Dayton as did in 1913, when the city was devastated by flood. The Miami project is a prominent and handsome mark in the history of flood control.

LAKE OKEECHOBEE

The Lake Okeechobee and Everglades area of central and southern Florida (Fig. 8) illustrate the complex relationship between navigation, flood control, drainage, water supply, soil conservation, wildlife, agriculture, finance, economics, legislation, and the growth of the country. The comprehensive plan developed for flood control and other purposes, to include Lake Okeechobee and the Everglades, will provide flood protection and water control for an area of about 15,000 sq miles, more than one fourth of the total area of the State of Florida. The heart of the plan is Lake Okeechobee, one of the largest fresh-water lakes in the United States. In its natural condition it is said to have averaged $20\frac{1}{2}$ ft above sea and Gulf level. The maximum stage of record, which occurred in 1912, is 20.1 ft. The surface has been lowered by drainage until it is normally 14.6 ft above sea level. Water flows into the lake from a 5,000-sq mile area to the north where the maximum elevation is less than 200 ft above sea level. It flows out to the east through the St. Lucie Canal, south into the Everglades, and west into the Gulf of Mexico through the Caloosahatchee River. The amount of rainfall varies throughout the area as well as from year to year. The range at Miami, Fla., during the 50-year period from 1902 to 1951 was from 28.7 in. to 85.4 in. with an average of 56.6 in.

The white man's interest in the Everglades for food production began with the Seminole Indian wars from 1835 to 1842, when the soldiers saw the islands on which the Indians grew melons, beans, tobacco, sugar cane, corn, and bananas. By the Swamp Land Act of 1850 Congress gave this land to the State of Florida, and the Legislature passed an act in 1851 to secure it for the state. The total population of the State of Florida at that time was about 88,000. Lands were sold and efforts made to drain the Everglades, but returns were not enough to pay interest on the bonds that had been issued. In 1881 some 49,000,000 acres were sold on the condition that drainage works would be constructed. Sugar production was undertaken, and a record of 5,000 lb of pure granulated sugar per acre was established before 1890.

By 1891 the population of Florida had grown to nearly 400,000. The annual report of the Secretary of Agriculture for that year stated:

> "There is practically no other body of land in the world which presents such remarkable possibilities of development as the muck lands bordering the southern shores of Lake Okeechobee."

The report pointed out that there was ample fall to tidewater to drain the area if a drainage canal were dug large enough. It also pointed out that the soils were organic and deficient in mineral constituents and that if the organic matter decayed there would be a marked shrinkage in the soils. More work was done, but it was unproductive because the undrained land could not be sold for enough money to pay for draining it. By 1899 the value of the best land in the Everglades was reported as 40¢ per acre to 50¢ per acre.

The State Legislature created a Board of Drainage Commissioners in 1905

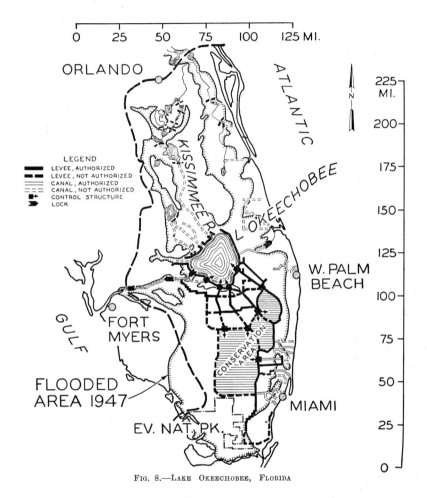

FIG. 8.—LAKE OKEECHOBEE, FLORIDA

and empowered it to levy a tax of 10¢ an acre to drain and reclaim the swamp lands. Work was started, but in 1907 the law was declared unconstitutional so a new act was passed which limited the tax to 5¢ an acre. Dredging the canals progressed and land sales increased. In 1909 a tract of 25,000 acres was sold for $2 an acre; another tract of 80,000 acres brought $1.25, an acre; and still another of 500,000 acres was purchased for $1 an acre. A committee of the Florida Legislature visited the work in 1909 and approved it. The drainage board contracted for 184 miles of canals. The publicity apparently attracted land buyers, and there were reports that thousands of 10-acre and 20-acre tracts were sold for from $20 to $50 an acre to buyers in distant places.

The State Legislature of 1911 sent a joint committee to inspect the work. Its opinion was that no land was completely drained and that the canals then being dug would not suffice to drain all the Everglades. Criticism of the project was followed by a panic among the land buyers who let payments lapse, and soon there were no funds for construction.

One land company employed a group of engineers composed of D. W. Mead, Hon. M. and Past-President, ASCE, and Leonard Metcalf and Allen Hazen, Members, ASCE, to examine the situation. They recommended that the area be developed in large tracts for production of sugar cane, fruit, or similar crops. They pointed out that processing plants and facilities which go with population growth would be necessary in connection with such development, and that progress would be slow. They warned of overdrainage, muck fires, and shrinkage of the soil. Following this the Board of Drainage Commissioners employed a Board of Engineers, who recommended the construction of the St. Lucie Canal to dispose of floodwater from Lake Okeechobee, provide a 12-ft navigable channel, and generate power. In 1913 the State Legislature authorized the sale of bonds and work was resumed.

In spite of all the activity there were few settlers in the area in 1914. In 1917 a settlement called Moore Haven was started on the western shore of Lake Okeechobee, and by 1921 there were about sixteen settlements on or near the lake with an estimated total population of 2,000. By that time Miami had grown to nearly 30,000, and the population of Florida was approaching 1,000,000. The year 1922 was a wet year and several of the towns around the lake were underwater. Nevertheless, the population of the area increased, truck crops were produced in increasing amounts, and another land boom was under way.

Dry years followed, and by 1926 there were unprecedented muck fires. The site of Moore Haven had subsided below lake level, and muck levees were built around it. Then in September, 1926, a tropical hurricane drove the lake water to that side, the muck levees melted, and more than 350 people were drowned. The land boom collapsed, the Board of Drainage Commissioners employed an engineering board of review, and Congress directed the Chief of Engineers to submit a report with a view to control of floods. By that time navigation across Florida was possible by way of the Caloosahatchee River (on which two sets of locks had been constructed by the State to control the level of Lake Okeechobee), thence through the lake and the St. Lucie Canal which had also been dug by the State.

In September, 1928, another hurricane swept the lake leaving 2,000 or more dead. The Chief of Engineers reviewed the previous reports and recommended improvement of channels, construction of levees, and other works at a total cost of about $13,500,000, of which $3,800,000 would be furnished by local interests in addition to necessary lands and other work. The River and Harbor Act of July 3, 1930, authorized this work provided local interests would contribute $2,000,000.

Collapse of the land boom, the two hurricanes, and the economic depression of that time led to default of payments on the bonds of the drainage district.

All construction and practically all maintenance work ceased. In the spring of 1932 the water level in Lake Okeechobee fell to 10.7 ft, the minimum stage of record. Muck fires which started in the fall of 1931 continued to burn until rain extinguished them in June, 1932.

In 1935 Congress reduced the contribution required of local interests to $500,000 and assumed responsibility for maintaining the works which were nearing completion. These works permitted control of the level of the lake between 12.5 ft and 15.5 ft above sea level and prevented lake waters from getting out of control and flooding the surrounding country. In 1937 a new lock and spillway were authorized on the St. Lucie Canal. The lock was completed in August, 1941; and the main spillway, in March, 1944—providing 8-ft navigation between the Atlantic Ocean and the Gulf. A dry period during 1938–1939 impressed on agricultural interests and the growing cities on the east coast the fact that conservation of water was highly important to preserve the organic soils and to replace ground water. Salt water began to encroach on the cities' supplies. In 1939 the United States Geological Survey began an intensive investigation of the water resources of the area, and Congress appropriated $75,000 to be used by the Soil Conservation Service to determine land-use capabilities.

In 1940 the population of Miami, not including the surrounding towns, was 172,000. The population of Florida had increased to nearly 2,000,000. By that time the owners of district bonds were suing to force payment. They had obtained a tax levy of $15,000,000, but most landowners refused to pay. Taxes were delinquent to the extent of $25,000,000 and practically every landholder's title had been forfeited. In 1941 the Legislature authorized the district to refinance its obligations. This was done, and landowners were permitted to regain current status of their taxes by payment of 1 year or 2 years of the delinquent taxes; and the annual tax burden was reduced from $2,000,000 to $600,000. By 1943 most landowners had regained title to their lands. The years 1943 through 1946 were dry. Cattle died in the pastures for lack of water, smoke from burning muck lands darkened the sky, and salt water crept in from the sea as the supplies of ground water were exhausted in the cities.

However, 1947 was one of the wettest years of record. Between the first of May and last of November, rainfall in the Lake Okeechobee area was about 57 in. Two hurricanes swept the area that fall and many places recorded double the average rainfall for the year. Water stood on the flat lands for months. Urban areas, crops, and pasture lands were submerged; and losses were estimated at $60,000,000. The high levee along the southern edge of the lake and the control gates of the project, completed 10 years earlier by the Corps of Engineers, operated effectively although Lake Okeechobee went to 18.8 ft, more than 3 ft above the preferred maximum elevation.

The district engineer of the Corps of Engineers submitted a report in December, 1947, recommending modification of the existing project to provide protection against a storm equal to that of 1947, to improve drainage outlets, to conserve water and control salinity, to regulate water levels for agriculture, to improve navigation, and to aid in the preservation of fish and wildlife. Other federal agencies and local agencies which had been working on the problems of the area for many years participated in preparing the plan. The total cost was estimated as $208,000,000, of which local interests would bear about $29,000,000. Annual benefits were estimated as $24,500,000 and annual costs were less than half that much.

Congress modified and expanded the existing project to include the first phase of the recommended plan in the Flood Control Act approved on June 30, 1948. In 1949 the State Legislature of Florida passed legislation enabling cooperation of State agencies and providing funds. Since construction began in January, 1950, enough work has been done to provide a reasonable amount of flood protection for the east coast cities.

The plan includes:

a. Rapid removal of floodwaters. If there is not enough fall to do this by gravity, pumps are contemplated.

b. Control works to prevent overdrainage. Otherwise the enlarged channels would drain the water too low.

c. Salt-water barriers. These will be control structures where drainage channels enter salt water.

d. Salt-water levee. This will prevent wind-driven seas from inundating the rich agricultural land south of Miami.

e. Water storage. To prevent drought damage, water must be stored:

    (1) By extending the existing hurricane levees at Lake Okeechobee all around the lake and raising them so the top will be from 37 ft to 40 ft above sea level.

    (2) By constructing three large conservation areas (Fig. 8) totaling 1,344 sq miles between the fertile land south and east of Lake Okeechobee and the highly developed area along the coast. Floodwater will be stored in these areas for release during drought. Spillways on the south will provide water for maintaining suitable conditions for wildlife in the Everglades National Park even in times of severe drought.

f. Levees, pumps, and control works to protect rural and urban areas that are now developed or suitable for development.

g. Last, but by no means least, continuing study of the plan as the work progresses. In order that the needs and desires of local people may be learned well in advance of construction, an active program is under way to educate the general public and obtain from each county its concept of the objectives of the program. This is being done through county committees composed of people representing both private and governmental interests. These committees are assisted by technically qualified persons, usually engineers and agricultural experts.

It appears that now—some 100 years after people began to look longingly at the rich soil of the Everglades—a genuinely comprehensive program for its development is under way which with the help of the Federal Government will be accomplished. The population of Florida is 2,750,000, an increase of nearly 1,000,000 in the past decade and three times what it was 30 years ago. The program for central and southern Florida will help insure safer and better living for many more people.

The Present Program

Much floodwater has flowed down the rivers of the United States since 1543, and various successful projects show what can be done to combat flood dangers. Out of this have come definite programs, both regional and national. The plans of eight important agencies are discussed in the following sections:

Corps of Engineers.—The present program for flood control is largely the federal program as planned and being constructed under the direction of the Corps of Engineers. Other agencies have important assignments relating to conservation of water resources, and their work in connection with flood control

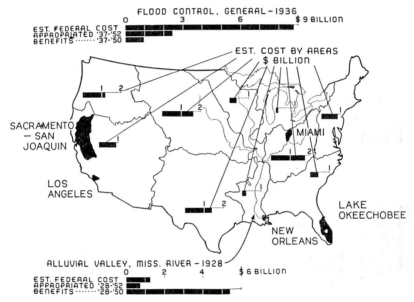

Fig. 9.—Present Flood-Control Program for the United States As Developed by the Corps of Engineers

is incidental to the beneficial use of water. Fig. 9 shows graphically the estimated cost of the program, the amounts that have been appropriated, and the benefits to 1950 of the works that are in operation. The map also shows the distribution of the program by areas.

When Secretary McHenry recommended establishment of a Military Academy under the Corps of Engineers for the training of engineers to serve the country and when he pointed out that their usefulness was not limited to fortifications, he knew whereof he spoke. However, he could have had little idea of the scope of that usefulness a century and a half later. The history of the development of the federal interest in flood control shows that the Corps of Engineers has been intimately connected with improvement of the rivers of the country since 1820. It not only explored, mapped, and reported on projects that might be needed, but also did the work for which Congress provided funds. Soon after improvement work was started, an invention by Captain Shreve, then a civilian of the Corps, simplified the problem of removing snags so as to make the rivers less dangerous to steamboats. Not many years later Humphreys and Abbot made the study that defined the size and scope of the problems on the Mississippi River.

In the 1880's the Corps of Engineers planned and built reservoirs at the headwaters of the Mississippi River. It undertook bank-stabilization works and built dredges to help control the shallow places in the rivers. Many years of experience with hydraulic dredges for river and harbor improvements were applied in designing, building, and operating the dredges that built the mammoth Fort Peck Dam. This dam formed one of the first large multiple-purpose reservoirs in the country. On the military side, Corps dredges went overseas for harbor work in World War II. Floating emergency electric power plants that were used in this country and overseas were designed and built in a manner similar to that used for the dredge power plants. The knowledge of floods gained in flood-control work was used against the enemy in Europe and Korea. Likewise flood fighters from the Mississippi River districts formed the first amphibian units in World War II.

The "308 reports" made by the Corps of Engineers were the first complete survey and inventory of the resources and problems of water use and control for all the important river basins of the country except the Colorado. The reports presented broad, comprehensive multiple-purpose plans for improving the rivers for navigation, irrigation, power generation, flood control, and other beneficial uses. They have been and still are the basis for congressional authorizations and the planning of work by the Corps and other agencies. The development of the Tennessee River, for example, follows the plan set forth in the "308 report" on that river.

Research has come into use more and more in recent years. The Waterways Experiment Station, authorized by Congress in the 1928 Flood Control Act as recommended by the Chief of Engineers, has pioneered not only in river and harbor and structural hydraulics, both civil and military, but also in soil mechanics for levee and dam construction and for military airfields. Extensive research has been undertaken and is continuing in the field of concrete construction to improve structures and reduce costs. The 500-acre Mississippi River Basin Model at Clinton, Miss., which is part of the Waterways Experiment Station, was kept in operation 24 hours a day for 2 weeks during the 1952 flood on the Missouri River. Stage predictions made with its help assisted in determining critical points and made it possible to concentrate flood-fighting activities successfully.

Sediment studies and research, bank-stabilization planning and construction, and investigations of the hydrology of floods have all been part of the work of the Corps of Engineers for many years. Hydrometeorological research on floods was initiated by the Corps and has been conducted cooperatively with the Weather Bureau for some 15 years. Research on snow and its effects on runoff have been under investigation for a similar length of time. The Weather Bureau has cooperated in this work since 1915; and the Geological Survey, the Bureau of Reclamation, and the Forest Service also assist.

Operation of multiple-purpose reservoirs so as to make the most effective use of the available storage capacity is a complex problem that has been intensively studied. The methods of economic evaluation now used by the Corps are in line with policies which were developed for navigation studies and which were favorably considered by Congress. As the problems of water control and use became more and more complex, the Corps assisted in organizing what is now the Federal Inter-Agency Committee to insure proper coordination among the agencies concerned. Thus the engineering of the federal program for flood control began much more than a century ago.

The presently approved federal program for flood control is estimated to cost, on a 1951 basis, about $10,000,000,000 for construction. Local or other interests will have to spend about $500,000,000 to meet the requirements of the Federal Government. Appropriations to June 30, 1952, amount to about $3,750,-000,000, and the benefits to June 30, 1950, amount to well over $6,000,000,000. The authorized work includes 996 projects, of which 330 or about one third are in operation, 86 more are under construction but not in operation, and 580 await appropriation of construction funds.

The largest and oldest project in the program is that for the alluvial valley of the Mississippi River which was begun in 1928 and which now protects some 2,377,000 people who live on 202,000 farm units and in 108 urban centers. The total area benefited in the alluvial valley is more than 20,300,000 acres. To date, the total cost, federal and local, is nearly $1,000,000,000; and the estimated flood damages prevented amount to five times that sum. About 60% of the project now authorized is completed and a high degree of protection is provided for the people who live in the area.

The Flood Control, General, Program adopted in 1936 now protects some 2,228,000 people living on 39,000 farm units and in 753 cities and towns. When all authorized projects are completed, they will afford protection to an area which as of 1950 included 154,000 farm units, 1,814 communities, and 7,471,000 people. The average annual benefits, including damages prevented, those resulting from higher use of land, and other benefits such as sale of hydroelectric power, amount to $121,000,000 for the projects now in operation and, on the basis of 1950 conditions, would be about $560,000,000 for all authorized projects. The estimated benefit to cost ratio, based on a 50-year economic life, for all authorized projects is 1.25 to 1. The projects now in operation prevent more than 15% of the total estimated potential flood damages; and, when the authorized program is completed, they will prevent about 53% of the total potential damage. It should be noted that this estimate of damages averted applies only to the areas affected by the authorized projects and is not applicable to the entire United States.

As of 1950, the area of rural land afforded protection by the Flood Control, General, projects in operation in 1950 amounted to 5,700,000 acres, which added to the 20,300,000 acres in the Mississippi River alluvial valley program, makes a total of 26,000,000 acres receiving benefits. The entire authorized general program will protect about 23,200,000 acres, so that a total of 43,500,000 acres will be benefited on completion of both programs. This is an area about equal in size to the State of Oklahoma. It includes 356,000 farm units which average about 122 acres each.

According to a report by the Department of the Interior dated December,

1947, the federal reclamation program which began in 1902 had provided a full supply of irrigation water for about 2,500,000 acres and a supplemental supply for another 2,500,000 acres. Thus, the area of land already benefited by irrigation and flood protection is about 31,000,000 acres—more than 1.6% of the total 1,905,000,000 acres of land in the United States and nearly 3% of the 1,142,000,000 acres which were in farms as of 1945. The area of land improved by provision of water and protection therefrom is about 0.2 acre per person.

The rather startling returns from some of the individual projects indicate that the investment in the Flood Control, General, Program will be repaid much sooner than expected. The six-reservoir system which protects Pittsburgh cost about $51,000,000 including new work and maintenance. It has been in operation about 11 years and has returned more than $67,000,000 in benefits through preventing flood damages. The local protection works at Mandan, N. Dak., which cost $697,000, returned benefits in the amount of $2,650,000 in 2 years. The Cottage Grove, Ore., local project cost $2,542,000 and produced benefits totaling $3,433,000 in 10 years. During the same period the Knightville, Mass., Project returned $3,577,000 on a total cost of $3,324,000. The City of Augusta, Ga., built flood-protection works 34 years ago. The works were enlarged and improved in cooperation with the Federal Government so that the total cost was $4,062,000, of which the local people spent $2,510,000 or about 62%. Benefits to date amount to $13,404,000, or more than three times the cost.

Appropriations for the Flood Control, General, Program to June 30, 1952, total $2,461,400,000; and, to June 30, 1950, local interests spent $159,000,000 to meet the requirements of local cooperation, making a total of $2,620,400,000. Many of the projects have been in operation only a short time and some 86 projects are still under construction but not in operation; yet the benefits to June 30, 1950, total $957,400,000 of which flood damages prevented amount to $731,100,000.

The Flood Control, General, Program reaches into all parts of the United States as is shown in Table 1.

Until only recently as the life of the nation goes, flood control was left almost entirely to local interests. Congress has now accepted a considerable part of the responsibility. However, it has repeatedly emphasized the principle of local contribution where project benefits are largely local. It is estimated that the local share of the annual charges for projects which are local in scope is about 30% of the economic cost. Reservoirs which include uses other than flood control are generally constructed and operated entirely at federal cost. These works constitute about three fourths of the Flood Control, General, Program. Benefits from the hydroelectric power features of these projects are about one third of the benefits of the entire program; and, although revenues from the sale of power cannot be determined at this time, they will return to the United States Treasury a large part of the cost of these projects. It appears that power revenues plus the local share of charges will cover about 60% of the economic cost of the program.

Department of Agriculture.—The responsibilities of the Department of Agriculture in runoff and water-flow retardation and in prevention of soil erosion under the flood-control laws are assigned to two of its agencies—namely, the

Forest Service and the Soil Conservation Service. In addition the Extension Service, Bureau of Agricultural Economics, and Production and Marketing Administration provide consulting service in developing the departmental program. The program is described briefly as follows:

1. It consists of land treatment measures—conservation of crop and range land, reforestation, and fire protection—plus water-flow retardation and sediment-control measures—construction of water-flow retardation structures, diversions, minor waterways, and floodways; major gully stabilization; and stream channel improvement.

2. It is aimed primarily at prevention of floodwater and sediment damages to agricultural lands in tributary valleys as well as protection of downstream dams, rivers, and harbors against silting damage.

TABLE 1.—Cost and Benefits, Flood Control, General, Program—in Millions of Dollars

| Region | Estimated federal cost of program | Estimated Benefits to June 30, 1950 | |
		Flood damage prevented	Total
New England and North Atlantic...	832.3	104.0	106.8
South Atlantic	422.3	68.8	114.0
Lower Mississippi Valley..........	183.1	27.1	35.1
Upper Mississippi Valley..........	366.1	175.0	175.3
Ohio River Basin.................	1,776.3	152.9	176.2
Great Lakes Basin................	105.2	2.9	2.9
Missouri River Basin.............	1,621.4	42.4	51.9
Gulf Southwest	1,386.5	41.6	63.9
Pacific Northwest	919.5	54.3	136.9
Pacific Southwest	1,176.7	68.1	94.4
Total	8,789.4[a]	737.1	957.4

[a] Excludes alluvial valley of Lower Mississippi Valley project (1,243.7) and territories (2.8).

3. It is most effective in preventing or minimizing damage from small to moderate floods of the kind that occur more frequently than once in 10 years but that cause 75% to 95% of agricultural losses in most tributary valleys.

4. It has comparatively small effect on large floods which occur in main river valleys at infrequent intervals but will reduce the sediment carried by the rivers and thereby maintain the usefulness of the main-stream improvements that are designed to control such floods.

5. It is carried out through soil conservation districts, in cooperation with other state and local organizations such as flood-control districts, counties, and highway departments.

The program involves:

a. Preparation of work plans for small watersheds and designs and specifications for water-flow retardation dams and related structural measures.

b. Successive treatment of small watersheds by landowners and technical, financial, and other forms of federal assistance after planning (as rapidly as funds are made available), based on priority of needs as determined in cooperation with soil conservation districts and other local interests.

c. Provision of more technical assistance and other aids in small watersheds under treatment to help landowners apply conservation measures on their own lands in accordance with the work plan.

d. Installation, mainly by government contract with cost sharing by local people, of the water-flow retardation and sediment control measures needed to complete the work plan.

Land treatment work such as contour plowing, terracing, cover crops, and woodland management are primarily the responsibility of the landowners and the greater part of the work and cost is borne by them. Advice and assistance in planning and layout are furnished by the Soil Conservation Service. Research work is under way at experiment stations in various parts of the United States which will permit appraisal of the effect on runoff and soil erosion of land treatment programs under many different conditions.

Watershed reports to Congress are based on sample subwatershed plans because: (*a*) The cooperation of many individual farm operators is involved and working plans should not be prepared much in advance of actual work; and (*b*) many of the programs are recommended to be carried out over a period of time (10 to 30 years) and changes in ownership or use may require changes in plans.

At the end of December, 1951, Congress had authorized watershed programs under flood-control legislation in eleven watersheds with an area of more than 30,000,000 acres. Work plans had been prepared for more than one third of the area authorized. These plans cover more than 55,000 farms and will cost a total of nearly $175,000,000, of which about $100,000,000 will be paid by the Federal Government. About 20% of all the planned work has been completed.

The Soil Conservation Service estimated agricultural losses from the storm and flood of July, 1951, in Kansas and Missouri at many millions of dollars. These included loss of crops on upland farms, loss of topsoil removed by floodwater, and losses by inundation and sedimentation in small stream valleys upstream from proposed specific flood-control measures.

It is estimated that more than 5% of the total agricultural land in the United States is in the flood plains of small streams. Reduction of flood damage in these valleys is a large potential source of increased food production. The land treatment program of the Department of Agriculture will conserve and improve the uplands and the valleys of the small streams and will supplement other measures for flood control.

Bureau of Reclamation.—The federal reclamation program began in 1902 with the passage of the Reclamation Act by Congress on June 17 of that year. The act provided that money received from the sale of public lands in sixteen western states (later also applied to Texas) should:

> "* * * be used in the examination and survey for and the construction and maintenance of irrigation works for the storage, diversion and development of waters for the reclamation of arid and semiarid lands in those states."

Construction costs were to be repaid by users of water from the project over a period of not more than 40 years, and water users were also responsible for maintenance and operation.

To some extent flood control is inherent in storage of water for release when needed for irrigation. For example, the Elephant Butte Reservoir on the Rio Grande in New Mexico, completed in 1916, has such a large storage capacity that water is seldom wasted. Sometimes flood-control works are constructed to offset changes in river conditions brought about by operation of Bureau of Reclamation reservoirs. Among such works are extensive dredging and levees on the Lower Colorado River; channel improvement on the Middle Rio Grande to conserve water and control aggradation which interferes with drainage of irrigated lands; and extensive levees, channels, and diversion works on the Klamath Project in Oregon to prevent flooding of reclaimed land. These benefits and works are incidental to irrigation.

The Boulder Canyon Project Act of December 21, 1928, provided for construction of what is now known as Hoover Dam for the purpose, among other things, of controlling floods on the Colorado River. Since that time Parker and Davis dams, lower down the river, also have been completed, and the three projects remove the threat of floods from the Colorado and the Imperial valleys.

In the Reclamation Project Act of 1939 Congress included a general provision for the allocation of part of the construction costs of Bureau projects for flood control or navigation as nonreimbursable costs. Flood damages have been prevented on many western rivers through the projects built under the act of 1939 or operated for flood control in accordance with such allocation. Operation of reservoirs for flood control is based on schedules agreed on by the Bureau and the Corps of Engineers. The Flood Control Act of December 22, 1944, provided for coordination of Bureau of Reclamation investigations and reports with the states and the Secretary of War. This act also approved the plan of the Bureau of Reclamation and the Corps of Engineers for control and use of the waters of the Missouri River Basin. Several completed projects in the Missouri River Basin functioned effectively in the flood of 1951.

Flood-control operation in Bureau projects is largely dependent on the way the reservoir storage is allocated. In single-purpose reservoirs, flood control is incidental to the primary purpose of conserving water for irrigation. Where provision is made for joint use of storage for irrigation and flood control, the joint storage pool is maintained at a level based on snow surveys and rainfall forecasts until the flood season is well advanced. Near the end of the flood season the joint-use storage capacity is gradually filled to insure an adequate supply of water for irrigation.

When storage capacity is specifically allocated to flood control, this space is maintained inviolate, except when it is needed to regulate flood flows. In such a case Congress has provided that regulations for use of the flood storage shall be prescribed by the Secretary of the Army. The benefits, cost allocations, and methods of operation for flood control are determined in consultation with the Corps of Engineers.

Studies are being made of some of the older Bureau projects with a view to allocating specific amounts of storage capacity for flood-control purposes. The reallocation of storage may improve the effectiveness of the project for flood control, and irrigation may benefit by the reallocation of costs. A restudy of the Grand Coulee Project now under way indicates that a large volume of storage space may be made available at low cost to aid in controlling Columbia River floods.

Tennessee Valley Authority.—The Tennessee Valley Authority was created by an Act of Congress approved May 18, 1933,

> "* * * for the purpose of maintaining and operating the properties now owned by the United States in the vicinity of Muscle Shoals, Alabama, in the interest of the national defense and for agricultural and industrial develop- ment, and to improve navigation in the Tennessee River and to control the destructive flood waters in the Tennessee River and Mississippi River Basins."

The corporation was given broad powers. In addition to river control and develop- ment, its responsibilities include production of chemicals, soil conservation, re- forestation, steam generation of electric power, and other activities. Its total fixed assets, including construction in progress and investigations for future proj- ects, totaled more than $1,100,000,000 as of June 30, 1951. Of this amount, $688,000,000 is in multiple-use water projects, and $178,000,000, or about 17%, is charged to flood control. Construction of the reservoir system began with Norris Dam on the Clinch River near Knoxville, Tenn., which was closed in March, 1936, and the system was practically completed with the closure of Ken- tucky Dam near the mouth of the Tennessee River in Kentucky in 1945.

Flood damages prevented in the valley to June 30, 1951, amounted to more than $50,000,000. About 90% of these losses would have occurred at Chattanooga, Tenn., which is the principal flood damage center in the basin. It is estimated that, if the largest flood of record at Chattanooga, which occurred in 1867, had recurred in 1948 without upstream reservoir control, the resulting flood losses would have been about $103,000,000. Of this total, losses amounting to about $90,000,000 would be prevented by the reservoirs. Most of the remaining loss would be averted by a levee system which has been authorized by Congress for construc- tion as part of the Flood Control, General, Program when the local interests fulfil requirements for cooperation.

There are nine tributary reservoir projects upstream which control runoff from 13,421 sq miles, or 63% of the drainage area above Chattanooga. Storage capacity in individual reservoirs reserved for flood control varies from 8.87 in. in depth over the drainage area above Norris Dam to 4.21 in. above Douglas Dam on the French Broad River. Three main-stem reservoirs provide flood stor- age capacity of 1.3 in. to 2.46 in. for net intervening areas so that the total flood storage available on January 1 each year is 6,750,100 acre-ft, which is equivalent to 5.92 in. over the 21,400 sq miles upstream from Chattanooga. It is estimated that this flood storage would enable lowering the stage of a flood like that of 1867 at Chattanooga from 58 ft to 44 ft.

Four other main-stem reservoirs between Chattanooga and the mouth provide additional flood storage so that the total amount allotted to flood control on January 1 each year is 11,689,700 acre-ft, which is equivalent to 5.45 in. on the 40,200-sq mile drainage area. Of this capacity, 4,010,800 acre-ft is in the Ken- tucky Reservoir. The Kentucky Dam is 25 miles from the junction of the Ten- nessee and Ohio rivers and 50 miles from Cairo, at the junction of the Ohio and Mississippi rivers. This enables close regulation of the flow for benefits on the

Mississippi River at Cairo and downstream therefrom. The flood crests in January and February, 1950, were reduced 2 ft and 1.2 ft, respectively, at Cairo. It is estimated that the Tennessee River system may, in some cases, effect as much as a 4-ft reduction at Cairo.

The Corps of Engineers estimates that the Tennessee River system will reduce the Mississippi River project flood of 2,450,000 cu ft per sec at Cairo about 150,000 cu ft per sec corresponding to a stage reduction of 1.5 ft. The average reduction of Mississippi River floods by the Tennessee Valley Authority reservoirs is estimated at 100,000 cu ft per sec. The annual value of these reductions in terms of avoiding the cost of raising levees, reducing flood damage, and avoiding flood fighting is estimated at $240,000 for the Ohio River and $3,600,000 for the Mississippi River. Total losses prevented annually will average about $9,000,000 based on 1948 conditions and prices.

American Red Cross.—The American National Red Cross is a flood-control agency in the sense that it reduces the loss and suffering that accompany and follow a flood disaster. Its program consists of providing emergency relief in the form of food, clothing, shelter, and medical care to sufferers immediately and then helping to rehabilitate those who are unable to take care of themselves.

During the 70-year period from 1881 to 1951, the Red Cross took part in 1,021 flood-relief operations and gave relief to more than 1,000,000 families or about 5,000,000 flood sufferers at a total cost of more than $93,000,000. Records of the Red Cross show that since 1925 it has helped in 932 flood operations wherein 33,300 homes were destroyed, 475,000 homes were damaged, 88,000 other buildings were destroyed, and 350,000 other buildings were damaged. Loss of life in these operations totaled 1,700 persons exclusive of the deaths at and near Lake Okeechobee in 1926 and 1928.

The results of flood-control projects are very apparent to the Red Cross. Communities that were seriously damaged by floods 10 or 15 years ago often report little or no damage today even though flood crests are sometimes higher than those which caused serious damage a few years earlier. One example is the Miami River Valley in Ohio which incurred severe loss in 1913 but was unaffected by the great floods of 1936 and 1937 because of the work done by the Miami Conservancy District. Another example is the Lower Mississippi Valley where one of the major disasters of all time occurred in 1927 but which passed a flood almost equally great in 1937 without serious loss.

United States Weather Bureau.—The United States Weather Bureau was organized by Act of Congress on October 1, 1890, and on the following July 1 the Weather Service of the Signal Corps was transferred to it. The Bureau began issuing forecasts of river and flood stages in 1892. Since then its work in climatology and meteorology has grown with the country, and its accuracy in forecasting has constantly improved.

Modern forecasting techniques require networks of precipitation and temperature stations. As the data gathered are of interest to both the project operator and the forecaster, the Weather Bureau cooperates with the Corps of Engineers, the Bureau of Reclamation, and the Tennessee Valley Authority in establishing and maintaining a network of reporting stations. Data are now being collected from approximately 10,000 reporting substations—in addition to a network covering the North American continent, which makes detailed surface and upper air observations. The observations are assembled at twelve weather forecasting centers at 1-hour, 3-hour, and 6-hour intervals, and predictions are made of the amounts of precipitation to be expected.

These forecasts prevent much flood damage. For example, a great deal of the land in the Upper Sacramento Basin subject to overflow is used for winter pasture. Flood warnings permit removal of livestock with no loss except the cost of removal. Another typical instance occurred in Cincinnati during the April, 1948, flood. Warnings of high stages a day and a half in advance enabled the produce dealers in the low-rent flood zone of downtown Cincinnati to move out their stocks and dispose of them in an orderly manner.

More than 15 years ago the Weather Bureau and the Corps of Engineers entered into a cooperative arrangement for determining the maximum possible precipitation over areas upstream from large reservoir projects. The data thus provided help to insure the safety of the structures by insuring that spillway capacities are adequate. Later the Weather Bureau undertook similar studies for the Bureau of Reclamation.

The Weather Bureau has continued to improve the accuracy of its flood forecasts so that now the losses on uncontrolled streams are held to a minimum. The cooperation between the Weather Bureau and other agencies engaged in the control and use of water better insures adequate information for proper design and operation of projects.

United States Geological Survey.—The United States Geological Survey began publishing stream flow records in 1884. It recognized the need for records of floods and for publicizing that information, and its reports of a half century ago furnish some of the most valuable data now available concerning large floods. It is the official federal agency for topographic and geologic mapping. In addition to this work it participates in the flood-control program by cooperating with all agencies requiring data on stream flow and ground water and in obtaining and publishing such data. Reliable stream flow records are essential to adequate planning of flood-control projects.

Federal Inter-Agency Committee.—The first formal steps were taken in 1939 toward coordination of studies among the federal agencies for water control and use, when representatives of the Corps of Engineers, Department of Agriculture, and Department of the Interior entered into an agreement on cooperative procedures in matters of mutual interest. The Federal Power Commission joined in the agreement in 1943. Later the Department of Commerce and the Public Health Service assented to the agreement. The quadripartite agreement led to the formation in 1943 of the Federal Inter-Agency River Basin Committee, a voluntary association of agencies interested in basin-wide integrated development of water resources. The Committee holds regular monthly meetings. It works through subcommittees and task committees in developing uniformity of practice. It also promotes and coordinates agency cooperation at state and local levels.

One of the most significant results of inter-agency cooperation was the completion in May, 1950, of a report on "Proposed Practices for Economic Analysis of River Basin Projects" by the Subcommittee on Benefits and Costs. The report proposes criteria which should be met by each project or segment of a project before it would be recommended for authorization.

It also proposes that the assumed interest rate for federal investments be 2½%, that nonfederal public investments be not less than 2½%, and that private investments be not less than 4%. It proposes that the period covered by the economic analysis be taken as the expected economic life of the project, but not more than 100 years. An effort is being made to base analyses on average prices expected to prevail during the life of the project rather than on current or past average prices. The practices finally adopted for economic analysis of river basin projects will have an important effect on national policy for the control and the use of water.

There are four inter-agency committees operating on a regional level under the guidance of the Federal Inter-Agency Committee. Two of these are the Columbia Basin Inter-Agency Committee and the Missouri Basin Inter-Agency Committee which are responsible for coordinating over-all basin plans, already approved by Congress which are under construction or in partial operation. The other two are the Arkansas-White-Red Basins Inter-Agency Committee and the New England-New York Inter-Agency Committee. These committees include the governors of the affected states as well as a representative of each of the federal departments concerned. They work through subcommittees and task committees in the same manner as the Federal Inter-Agency Committee, except that the basin committees make use of educational institutions, research organizations, and state and local agencies to a greater extent. The chairmanship of the first two committees rotates in the manner of the federal committee.

In effect, the two latter committees are task committees appointed by the President which operate under the chairmanship of the Corps of Engineers. They will make investigations and prepare comprehensive and integrated plans for developing water and related land resources in their respective basins. Six federal departments—Agriculture, Army, Commerce, Interior, the Federal Security Agency, and the Federal Power Commission—and eight governors in the case of Arkansas-White-Red, seven in the case of New England-New York, compose the committees. These two committees are making the broadest studies of river-basin water resources development that Congress has yet authorized, and the plans they submit will be the first in which such thorough coordination among all levels of use and interest has been effected.

THE FUTURE

This review of floods and the history of their control show that the floods themselves are not the result of man's activities. There were great floods in the United States before ever a tree was cut or a furrow plowed. Moreover, although some of man's activities tend to aggravate the problems that floods create, great floods have been followed by still greater ones. Within the period of recorded history there are few if any localities that have experienced the greatest flood that nature can produce. It seems clear from the experience on the Lower Mississippi, the Miami Valley, and many other places that floods can be controlled and that works should be based on controlling the great flood that occurs at rare intervals.

When some security is provided, development is encouraged and a higher degree of protection is necessary. However, progress is being made as shown when a flood like that of April, 1952, on the Missouri River flows throughout the length of the river without loss of life and when local works like those at Omaha and Council Bluffs hold against it even though the planned protective works are less than half complete. The description of this recent flood fight is suggestive of those on the Lower Mississippi River of 40 years ago.

History shows the need for educating the public and the difficulty of inducing it to realize the necessity of adequate control works. General Humphreys was amazed at the lack of understanding of floods when he investigated the cost of repairing the levees along the Lower Mississippi River after the Civil War. He recommended to Congress that a large number of copies of the report made by him and Colonel Abbot be printed and distributed in the Mississippi Valley. Even when the need for control is made obvious by a flood disaster, there seem to be always those who will oppose and obstruct even as did the opposition to the Miami Valley Project. In New Orleans only the fear of an epidemic compelled action. In Los Angeles and Sacramento and Florida it took disasters to force the realization of the need on the public. The Los Angeles people forgot or were completely unaware of the flood hazard after a few years during which there were no floods.

Conflicts between control and use and between different users of water become more and more pronounced as population increases. Boatmen and fishermen fought about water in the Maimi Valley a century and a quarter ago. Gold miners and farmers fought about water in California in the Sacramento Valley three quarters of a century ago. Today the interests concerned in control and use of water are almost too numerous to mention. The more people there are, the more their interests are likely to conflict.

Electric power production more than doubled in the decade from 1940 to 1950 and may double again by 1960. The population of California increased from less than 7,000,000 in 1940 to more than 10,500,000 in 1950 and continues to increase. The national population has increased an average of 1,500,000 a year for the past half century and is increasing more rapidly now. Growth means more and more multiple-use projects, more need to protect and to conserve as well as greater capability to do so.

An essential part of constitutional government in the United States is what Calhoun defined as the "negative power," the power whereby a minority can protect itself against the "tyranny of the majority." The requirement of Congress that local people cooperate with the Federal Government gives them this "negative power" so that conflicting interests among local people must be reconciled in order that work may progress. The spirit of cooperation so necessary to successful flood fighting, which is brought out most strongly in a fight against a common enemy, has helped in resolving the conflicts. Engineers have pioneered in working out equitable and practical solutions for such problems from the time they got together on the navigation and flood-control survey three quarters of a century ago to the inter-agency committees of today.

Much technical progress has been made that enables more effective planning, construction, and operation of flood-control projects. The hydrometeorological research of the Corps of Engineers and the Weather Bureau shows the probable limits of storm rainfall that can be expected, and methods of synthesizing flood flows enable estimates to be made of floods that might occur under such conditions. The model of the Mississippi Basin at Clinton, even though incomplete, has demonstrated its usefulness in predicting flood stages.

Data on storms that may produce floods, and data on snow and ice and the probable effect they might have in producing floods, are collected and carefully evaluated. The possibility of the April, 1952, Missouri River flood was recognized a month in advance on the basis of snow and ice surveys. Some progress has been made in estimating rainfall and runoff in advance of the rainfall but much more remains to be done. This field is important in future progress toward more efficient reservoir operation.

Floods are the best salesmen for flood control. The people of the Miami Valley spent more than $30,000,000 to secure protection from floods on the 5,400-sq mile area of the Great Miami River after suffering losses of more than twice as much as the protective works cost. A multiple-purpose program in the 40,200-sq mile basin of the Tennessee River cost to June 30, 1951, a total of $1,100,000,000, of which $668,000,000 was for water projects.

As the New Orleans board explained nearly a century ago, the principal item needed to secure flood control is money. The $10,000,000,000 federal program is applicable to practically the entire 3,000,000-sq mile area of the United States. If the federal program were complete, the situation would probably be as well in hand on a national scale as it is in New Orleans, the Miami Valley, the Muskingum Valley, at Pittsburgh, and in many other localities where a high degree of protection has been provided.

The sum that has been appropriated to date for the federal program is large. It is more than the total expenditures of the Federal Government from its inception through the year 1905. On the other hand, it is about 60% of the amount appropriated for direct foreign aid for the fiscal year 1953. It is about one twentieth of the total budget of the Federal Government for 1953 and is a little more than 1% of the current estimated annual national income.

At the rate of recent appropriations for new flood-control work the present program will require almost 20 years for completion. Long before that time the growth of the United States will have made more works necessary. However, flood control is an example of action and reaction. A great flood occurs and much talk follows; then another great flood, followed by more talk and perhaps a study; and then another great flood, more talk, more study, and maybe some action. In view of the nation-wide series of record-breaking flood disasters of the past few years, it seems probable that funds will be made available so that flood-control work can proceed more rapidly.

The past century has seen great progress in the control of floods and the conservation of water. The public can be assured that engineers are ready for even greater progress in the future.

COOPERATION

Much of this story is about the work of the writer's colleagues and without their help in obtaining data it could not have been written. To list all of them would take much space so acknowledgment is made to them as a group—the civilians and officers of the Corps of Engineers.

Responsibility for accuracy of statements and for opinions rests with the writer. Artistry on charts and maps is the work of Joseph H. Buehrle.

BIBLIOGRAPHY

General.—

Annual Reports, Chf. of Engrs., and other Corps of Engineers reports, Dept. of the Army, U. S. Govt. Printing Office, Washington, D. C.

Congressional Record, and other congressional documents, U. S. Govt. Printing Office, Washington, D. C.

Engineering News-Record.

"The Ohio River Handbook and Picture Album," by Benjamin and Eleanor Klein, Young and Klein, Inc., Cincinnati, Ohio, 1950.

"Ten Rivers in America's Future," President's Water Resources Policy Comm., U. S. Govt. Printing Office, Washington, D. C., 1950.

Reclamation Era, U.S.B.R., U. S. Govt. Printing Office, Washington, D. C.

Reports, SCS, U.S.D.A., U. S. Govt. Printing Office, Washington, D. C.

Transactions, ASCE.

Water-Supply Papers, U. S. Geological Survey, U. S. Govt. Printing Office, Washington, D. C.

U. S. Weather Bureau Bulletins, U. S. Govt. Printing Office, Washington, D. C.

Monthly Weather Review, U. S. Govt. Printing Office, Washington, D. C.

Virginia Cavalcade, History Div., Virginia State Library, Richmond, Va., Vol. 1, No. 2, autumn, 1951.

Lower Mississippi River System.—

Annual Report, Board of Levee Commissioners, to the Legislature of the State of Louisiana, January, 1867, session, State Printer, New Orleans, La., 1867.

"The Improvement of the Lower Mississippi River for Flood Control and Navigation," by D. O. Elliott, U. S. Waterways Experiment Station, Vicksburg, Miss., May 1, 1932.

"The Development of the Federal Program of Flood Control on the Mississippi River," by Arthur DeWitt Frank, Columbia Univ. Press, New York, N. Y., 1930.

"Levee Districts and Levee Building in Mississippi," by Robert W. Harrison, Delta Council, Stoneville, Miss., October, 1951.

Biennial Reports, Louisiana Dept. of Public Works, Baton Rouge, La., 1942–1943, 1946–1947.

Louisiana Historical Quarterly, Louisiana Historical Soc., New Orleans, La.

"Report on the Drainage of the City of New Orleans," New Orleans, La., 1895.

"Report of Surveyor and Comment of Commissioners of Second Drainage District," New Orleans, La., October 5, 1868.

"Riparian Lands of the Mississippi River," by Frank H. Tompkins, New Orleans, La., 1901.

Miami River System.—

"History of the Miami Flood Control Project," by C. A. Bock, *Technical Reports*, Miami Conservancy Dist., Dayton, Ohio, Pt. II, 1918.

"Local Group Action," by A. F. Griffin, a proceedings report on a forum held at Kansas State College, Manhattan, Kans., November 27–28, 1951.

"The Miami Valley and the 1913 Flood," by Arthur E. Morgan, *Technical Reports*, Miami Conservancy Dist., Dayton, Ohio, Pt. I, 1917.

Lake Okeechobee, Florida.—

"A Brief History of the Florida Everglades," by J. E. Dovell, *Proceedings*, Soil Science Soc. of Florida, West Palm Beach, Fla., April, 1942.

"Central and South Florida Flood Control Project," *Water Survey and Research Paper No. 4*, State Board of Conservation, Div. of Water Survey and Research, Tallahassee, Fla., August, 1950.

"Soils Geology and Water Control in the Everglades Region," *Bulletin No. 442*, Univ. of Florida Agri. Experiment Station in cooperation with SCS, U. S. D. A., Gainesville, Fla., March, 1948.

Tennessee Valley Authority.—

Annual Reports, TVA, Knoxville, Tenn.

"Engineering Data," *Technical Monograph No. 55*, TVA projects, Knoxville, Tenn., March, 1948.

AMERICAN SOCIETY OF CIVIL ENGINEERS

Founded November 5, 1852

TRANSACTIONS

Paper No. 2645

ONE HUNDRED YEARS OF IMPROVEMENT ON LOWER MISSISSIPPI RIVER

By P. A. Feringa,[1] M. ASCE and Charles W. Schweizer [2]

Synopsis

Historic accounts of the Mississippi Valley and its river problems date back to the time of Hernando De Soto. Floods during the past century were disastrous, particularly because remedial measures were too difficult and expensive to secure support. Formation of the Mississippi River Commission was an important step, but the flood catastrophe of 1927 was the crowning influence—it caused adoption of a comprehensive flood-control plan. Under this, vast construction works have been effected—reservoirs, levees, cutoffs, revetments, floodways, and outlets. The story of the improvement and development of the Mississippi River for navigation and flood control during the past century is a significant chapter of achievement in the engineering history of the United States.

Drainage Area

The main streams within the drainage area of the basin above Cairo, Ill., are the Missouri and Upper Mississippi, the Ohio, the Tennessee, and the Cumberland. These rivers, together with their tributaries, draining an area of 921,400 sq miles, may be compared to the upper branches of a large tree whose trunk is the Lower Mississippi River.

Below Cairo (Fig. 1), additional tributaries, the St. Francis, White, Arkansas, Yazoo, Red, and some smaller streams, together with the Mississippi River main channel below Red River Landing, increase the drainage area to 1,243,700 sq miles at the Head of Passes in Louisiana. There the river enters the Gulf of Mexico by three main distributaries—Southwest Pass, South Pass, and Pass a Loutre.

The drainage basin extends from longitude 78° to longitude 114° and from latitude 29° to latitude 50°—or approximately 1,900 miles in longitude and 1,400 miles in latitude. Its extremities are, respectively, in western New York, western Montana, southern Louisiana, and western Canada, 70 miles north of the northern

---

[1] Brig. Gen., U. S. Army (Retired), New Orleans, La.; formerly Pres., Mississippi River Comm., Vicksburg, Miss.

[2] Special Eng. Asst., Mississippi River Comm., Vicksburg, Miss.

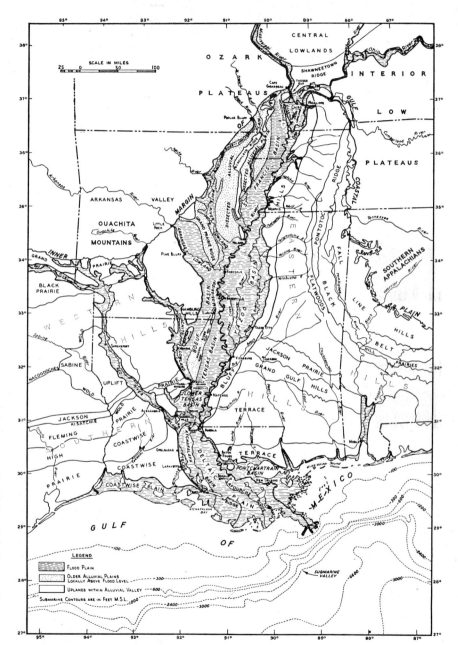

FIG. 1.—PHYSIOGRAPHIC MAP OF CENTRAL GULF COASTAL PLAIN

boundary of Montana. The basin includes all or parts of thirty-one states and about 13,000 sq miles of Canada. Over the area, the average precipitation totals about 90,000,000,000,000 cu ft of water per year.

EARLY EXPLORATIONS

De Soto and his expedition explored the Mississippi River in the vicinity of Memphis, Tenn., and descended the river from about the mouth of the Arkansas to the Gulf of Mexico. Their historian described the first known Mississippi River flood as severe, beginning about March 10, 1543, and reaching its peak about 40 days later. The depth of water over the riverbank was described as about belly-deep on the horses when the maximum stage occurred.

This group of explorers also provided the earliest map of the junction of the Mississippi, Red, and Atchafalaya rivers, drawn in 1576 in Madrid, Spain, by Monk Ptolemy who accompanied the expedition. Ptolemy's map is said to show conclusively that the Atchafalaya then, as now, served as an outlet for the Mississippi River. This expedition was composed of many well-to-do men, and was provided with all necessary equipment, including horses and cattle. Only a few survived the trip, and these eventually arrived at Tampico on the Gulf of Mexico.

Louis Joliet and Jacques Marquette, in 1673, and René Robert Cavelier, Sieur de La Salle, in 1682, using Indian canoes for transportation, also explored this part of the Lower Mississippi River. Early maps of the river were made by Lieutenant Ross (1765) and by Capt. Phillip Pitman (1768), both British officers, and by Gen. Victor Collot (1796), a French officer.

THE LOWER ALLUVIAL VALLEY

From Cairo southward, the Lower Mississippi River flows through a flood plain 25 to 80 miles wide, and averaging about 40 miles in width. This plain, known as the Lower Alluvial Valley, is of low relief, except where an occasional Pleistocene remnant escaped the process of erosion and rises above the general level as a ridge or an island.

Borings were made to determine the character of the river-bed strata and to ascertain the depth of the blue clay formation. Data from these borings, together with studies and investigations, established the fact that, for the whole length of the river from Cairo to the Gulf of Mexico, the depth of the alluvium was ample to permit the lowering of the bed of the river to any extent required in the improvement of the channel for normal navigation purposes.

In point of origin, the alluvial valley is a compound feature, a "valley within valley," formed during the final cycle of world-wide glaciation. During the last glacial stage, when sea level was several hundred feet lower than at present, the Mississippi River Valley system became deeply incised within the coastal plain sediments. Slow aggradation, during and subsequent to the period of rising sea level when glacial ice masses were melting, incompletely filled this entrenched valley system and gave rise to the present surface, the alluvial plain. The topography buried under the alluvium is rugged, and in many places the bottoms of the trenches extend farther below the plain than the exposed valley walls rise above it.

The alluvial plain of the Mississippi Valley merges with the alluvial plains of the tributary valleys that extend into the marginal uplands. These plains also overlie deep trenches and are bordered by steep valley walls. Inasmuch as the over-all pattern is similar to that exhibited by coast lines embayed by estuaries, the expressive term "alluvial drowning" has been used to point out that the valleys of the Lower Mississippi River system are drowned by a deep and wide filling of alluvium in much the same fashion as the embayed coast line of the northeast United States is drowned by the sea.

The plain includes both the flood plain subject to seasonal flooding and dissected alluvial plains not completely covered by floodwaters. The river, in times of flood, goes out of its banks, dropping its load of sediment as it goes. For this reason, the banks are generally from 10 to 15 ft above the lowlands away from the river with the steepest slope usually in the first mile from the riverbank. The slopes of these bank lines conform generally to the elevation of the mean high water.

Early Navigation

Since the early settlement of the continent, the Mississippi River has been an important artery of commerce. It was a vital factor in the westward population expansion, as it furnished the most comfortable and fastest avenue of transportation available at that time. Down its broad waters, craft carried the commerce of a vast inland empire to the sea.

Early navigation, however, was hazardous and only the hardiest of the pioneers in the western country braved the Mississippi's dangerous currents and defied the hostile Indians along its banks. Men built rafts which they maneuvered downstream to New Orleans, La., where they were sold or abandoned after the discharge of their cargo. However, since it offered the best, and in many cases the only, means of transportation, the river was vital to the prosperity of the new country, as an outlet to the rest of the world.

In 1820 the United States Government authorized a survey to be made in connection with navigation on the Mississippi and Ohio rivers. This was the first federal work on the Lower Mississippi River and was followed by enactment of legislation in 1824 for the removal of snags, "sawyers," and so forth, from the channels of these rivers.

Capt. Henry Shreve, an employee of the Corps of Engineers, United States Army, and father of the Mississippi River steamboat, was intimately connected with the original design of snagboats and the removal of snags and log rafts in the Atchafalaya and Red rivers. To improve navigation in the Mississippi River near the mouth of the Red River, he proposed and made an artificial cutoff in 1831 which still bears his name.

Invention of the steamboat brought about a great change, as it made the river an avenue for two-way commerce, upstream as well as downstream. The vessels carried cotton, staples, and other products, and offered comfortable passenger accommodations over waterways that were unimproved and had shallow channel depths.

In 1834 there were about 230 packetboats in the trade; and by 1849, about 1,000, approximating 250,000 tons. Although the packetboat era reached its peak in the decade preceding the Civil War, the packet continued to be the principal method of transportation in the Lower Mississippi Valley until the latter part of the nineteenth century, when more and more of the traffic was diverted to the expanding railroads.

Reports and Surveys Prior to 1879

Nature has provided a physiographic pattern in the Mississippi Valley which facilitates protection from high water by earth embankments, as the land slopes downward from the riverbank so that surface drainage is away from the structure instead of toward it. Aside from the tributaries that enter the river there are no features to interrupt the continuity of the embankments, and for this reason it is possible to protect a maximum area of land with a minimum of expense.

The first settlers in the alluvial valley recognized the need for protection from floods. Efforts on the Lower Mississippi River began with the French government in 1717, when Chevalier Leblond de la Tour, at the direction of Jean de Bienville, established the first levee line at New Orleans and constructed a riverside embankment to protect the city in 1727. This structure was 3 ft high, 5,400 ft long, and 18 ft wide at the top.

Extension of the system kept pace with the growth of the settlements along the Mississippi River, and by 1735 the embankments on both sides of the river extended from about 30 miles above New Orleans to a point 12 miles below the city. The expense of the construction was borne solely by the riparian landowners. However, the levees were of insufficient strength and were crevassed at many localities by any unusual high water.

The system was gradually extended and about 1858, prior to the Civil War period, attained its greatest length as a discontinuous line reaching northward as far as Memphis, Tenn. Lack of coordination between states and levee districts prevented the construction of effective structures, but the levees constituted a necessary beginning of efforts to control the river by this method. Embankments constructed during this period had a top width of about 4½ ft, a base of about 10 to 14 ft, and a height of 4½ ft.

Beginning with the year 1840, and after the widespread damage from the 1849 and 1850 floods, the view was advanced that flood protection was a national problem. In 1851, Charles Ellet, a civil engineer, working under the direction of Secretary of War Charles M. Conrad, made his report on the Mississippi and Ohio rivers to the Thirty-Second Congress. His proposals for flood protection included the prevention of cutoffs, the enlargement of natural river outlets, the creation of an artificial outlet, the construction of reservoirs, and the strengthening of the levee system. Since he believed that any levee system which could be constructed would be inadequate for the protection of the valley, he proposed, in addition, reservoirs in the upper reaches of the streams composing the Mississippi River system.

At about the same time, in 1851, the Delta Survey was undertaken. After exhaustive studies and investigations the report, generally known as the Humphreys and Abbot report, was published in 1866. Reservoirs and the areas necessary to store the estimated rainfall were considered. The report stated that the advantages of a reservoir system on certain western rivers were not questioned and that low-water navigation might be improved by their operation, but that the idea that the Mississippi delta could be economically secured against inundation by the construction of dams had been conclusively proved by the operations of the survey to be in the highest degree chimerical.

In its natural state, the Mississippi River had numerous distributary outlets along its lower reaches. Above New Orleans, these natural outlets have all been closed off by the construction of levees or by navigation locks, except the one at Old River.

During these formative years, the various administrations considered themselves without authority to initiate or recommend plans for flood control as such. As local interests continued their efforts, increasingly confining the river, flood heights rose higher and higher. Development of the valley progressed as the feeble works were extended, with the result that each succeeding flood became more devastating to property and life than the previous one.

In 1874, Col. Charles R. Suter, M. ASCE, Corps of Engineers, was designated to make a survey of the river between Cairo and New Orleans, and the semi-accurate results were published on a scale of 1 in. to 1 mile. About this time the United States Coast and Geodetic Survey undertook survey operations on the Lower Mississippi River, and by 1879 had accurately mapped the river from its mouths to Donaldsonville, La. Also, the United States Lake Survey was surveying the river at the upper end of the valley, and by 1879 had completed accurate maps of a part near Cairo and another near Memphis.

With the various agencies making surveys of sections of the river, with the local levee districts building structures without any coordination or reference to an accepted flow line or cross section, and with no provision for navigation or stabilization of the Mississippi, it was generally recognized that the establishment of some central planning organization was necessary, to coordinate all the planning and engineering operations and also to be responsible to Congress for the expenditure of federal funds during construction.

MISSISSIPPI RIVER COMMISSION CREATED

A bill was introduced in Congress in 1879 providing for the creation of the Mississippi River Commission and, after hearings, was enacted on 28 June 1879. The Commission consists of seven members, appointed by the President of the United States, with the consent of the United States Senate. Three are selected from the Corps of Engineers; one from the Coast and Geodetic Survey; and three from civil life, two of whom are civil engineers.

The Commission was charged with the preparation of surveys, examinations, and the preparation and consideration of plans to improve the river channel, protect and stabilize the riverbanks, aid navigation, prevent destructive floods, and promote and facilitate commerce and the Postal Service. A proviso in the law required the Commission especially to consider the practicability of the various plans known as the jetty system, the levee system, and the outlet system, as well as such other plans as might be deemed necessary.

As organized, the Mississippi River Commission was an executive body reporting to the Secretary of War. For administrative purposes, the Commission now has three districts with offices at Memphis, Vicksburg, Miss., and New Orleans, respectively. Area offices under the districts carry on the local construction and flood-fighting operations.

Under date of 17 February, 1880, the Commission submitted its first or preliminary report which was confined to general methods, principles, and plans for the river from Cairo to the Head of Passes. Various groups interested at the time in river improvement held divergent views as to the best method of treating the river, but in general terms four plans were advocated: (*a*) Reservoirs, (*b*) outlets, (*c*) cutoffs, and (*d*) levees. Navigation was considered essential by everyone connected with the river, so it was not under discussion.

With specific reference to the proposed reservoir system for the improvement of navigation, the Commission in its report held that reservoirs alone would not prove adequate. It felt also that the cost of construction was too great and the time required to place them in operation was too remote to offer any sizable relief from overflow.

The outlet system was rejected, as it was feared that flood levels would be raised as a result of silt deposit in the main stream. In addition, the diversion of water overland would flood the area adjacent to the outlet, and it would be very difficult to select an area where the adjacent property owners would be willing to have their land damaged by diverted floodwaters. The proposal to open an outlet below New Orleans into Lake Borgne was not approved.

As to cutoffs, no attempt was to be made to straighten the river or to shorten it.

The repair and maintenance of the existing levee lines would hasten channel improvement; and, as this was an operation that would furnish immediate protection and could be performed by the states and local levee interests, the levee plan was utilized. The report also recommended navigation improvement by the regulation of the river channel and by the protection of the banks. Dredging might be necessary as an auxiliary to the general plan.

Recommendations by the Commission met with approval of Congress, and $1,000,000 was appropriated in March, 1881, for actual operation. Although the organic act required the Commission to prepare plans to prevent destructive floods, earlier appropriations restricted levee construction and repair to such work, as a part of navigation improvement plans.

Plans and Development of the River

Surveys were made and the entire river was mapped. Discharges were determined for the various stages at stations on the Mississippi River and its principal tributaries, and the physical characteristics of the river ascertained with regard to its length, widths, depths, slopes, types of material composing the banks, sediment movement, and general alinement, all of which were necessary for proper planning.

The control of a river about 1,000 miles long, carrying a discharge of 2,000,000 to 3,000,000 cu ft per sec demands extensive planning by experienced engineers. It is a man-sized operation.

After the planning stage, the actual development and stabilization of a river require large sums of money for construction and maintenance. These funds are obtained through appropriations made by Congress and are designated for specific purposes. The expenditure of these allotments must be made according to law and at the localities specified.

The levee and navigation work progressed as more funds became available, but the navigable depths over the channel crossings did not develop as anticipated. Commercial interests demanded better transportation on the river. So in 1896 a project for a 9-ft channel depth, with a width of 250 ft at low water, was inaugurated and, when necessary, maintained by dredging between Cairo and the Head of Passes.

Confining the river in a restricted area created better flow conditions in the main stream but also raised flood heights. These in turn caused the structures confining the flow to be overtopped or crevassed.

During the 1882 high water, 284 crevasses, aggregating 56 miles in length, occurred; but, as levee embankments were consistently raised and strengthened, the number of crevasses decreased materially. In 1927, during the greatest flood of record, 13 crevasses occurred. Since then earth levees built to Commission grade and cross section have held all floods without any breaks. A levee breach that occurred at Free Nigger Point (mile 234) in March, 1949, was due to an unusual caving bank and was not a normal levee crevasse caused by flood stresses.

After the disastrous flood of 1927, Congress recognized flood control of the Mississippi River as a national obligation and passed the Flood Control Act of 15 May, 1928.

FLOOD-CONTROL PLAN FOR PROJECT FLOOD

Under the plan in the adopted project, protection against the maximum flood predicted as probable is to be afforded the alluvial valley of the Mississippi River. This includes the St. Francis, the Yazoo, the Tensas, and the Atchafalaya basins, and also alluvial lands near the mouth of the Arkansas and Red rivers and around Lake Pontchartrain, in Louisiana (Fig. 2).

The project flood (a hypothetical condition used as a basis for designing flood-control works) is the maximum or superflood which meteorologists believe possible (Fig. 3). It premises a flow which on reaching Cairo would amount to 2,450,000 cu ft per sec.

At the latitude of Old River the maximum probable flood has been determined under the project as 3,000,000 cu ft per sec. This flood flow is to be routed to the sea by passing 900,000 cu ft per sec from the Red River backwater area into the Atchafalaya Basin at the latitude of Simmesport, La. Of the latter amount, a discharge of 650,000 cu ft per sec is to enter the Atchafalaya Basin through the main channel of the Atchafalaya River, and 250,000 cu ft per sec is to pass down the West Atchafalaya Floodway. A discharge of 2,100,000 cu ft per sec is to be carried down the Mississippi River to the head of Morganza Floodway, where 600,000 cu ft per sec is to be diverted through the Morganza control structure into the Atchafalaya Basin.

The Mississippi River below the Morganza control structure is to carry a

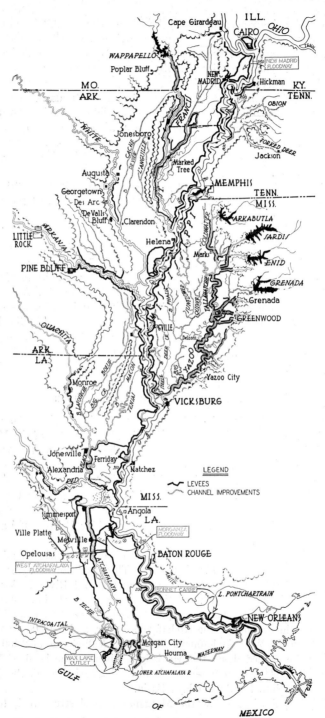

Fig. 2.—Flood Control on Lower Mississippi River and Tributaries

discharge of 1,500,000 cu ft per sec to the head of the Bonnet Carre Floodway, where a discharge of 250,000 cu ft per sec is to be diverted into Lake Pontchartrain. The remaining water, 1,250,000 cu ft per sec, is to be carried down the Mississippi River into the Gulf of Mexico (Fig. 3).

To provide for a flood of such magnitude it is necessary to use every practicable means of flood protection, especially (1) reservoirs, (2) levees, (3) cutoffs, (4) revetments, and (5) floodways.

(1) *Reservoirs.*—Reservoirs afford one method of protection, not only those utilized in the valley itself, but those constructed on the Ohio, the Tennessee (Tennessee Valley Authority), the Cumberland, the Missouri, the Upper Mississippi, the Arkansas, the White, and the Red rivers. They are needed to control the tremendous volume of water that falls on this 41% of the United States and that must find its way down the Mississippi Valley. However, reservoirs alone cannot control the floods.

In *House Document No. 308*, Sixty-Ninth Congress, First Session, a report was presented by the Chief of Engineers, United States Army, and the secretary of the Federal Power Commission, showing all navigable streams on which power development appeared to be feasible and an estimate of the cost of the examination. Under this authority, investigations, commonly called 308 surveys, were made of all reservoir sites in the United States, with the view of ascertaining where combined power and navigation projects appeared feasible.

A comprehensive report on reservoirs in the Mississippi River Basin was submitted and ordered printed 2 August, 1935, as *House Document No. 239*, Seventy-Fourth Congress, First Session. This report covered 151 reservoirs, of which 81 were in the Ohio Basin; 14 in the Upper Mississippi; 7 on the Missouri; 4 on other tributaries above Cairo; 26 in the Arkansas and White basins; 7 on the Yazoo; and 12 on the Red and Ouachita. The Mississippi River Commission recommended that the Federal Government adopt a policy encouraging and participating in the construction of feasible tributary reservoir systems which would fit into an ultimate general system for the control of Lower Mississippi River floods. Various reservoirs have been or will be constructed in the Mississippi drainage basin with this purpose in view.

Within the alluvial valley, five reservoirs (Fig. 2) form part of the flood-control project: In Missouri the Wappapello Reservoir on the St. Francis River is completed and operating; in Mississippi the Arkabutla Reservoir on the Coldwater River, the Sardis Reservoir on the Little Tallahatchie River, and the Enid Reservoir on the Yocona River are completed and working; and also in Mississippi the Grenada Reservoir on the Yalobusha and Skuna rivers will be completed in 1953. The last four reservoirs are within the Yazoo Basin drainage area. This part of the project is well on its way to success. Incidentally, public use of reservoir areas for recreational purposes has developed far beyond expectations at Wappapello and Sardis reservoirs.

(2) *Levees.*—Levees are also needed as part of the project. A general misconception by those who have not seen the Mississippi River Valley is that the levee sits right on the bank of the river. However, that it not a fact, as the levees may be back as far as 5 miles from the main river so that they will not

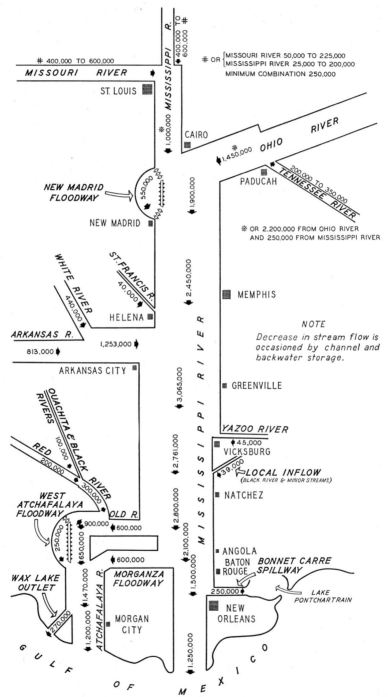

FIG. 3.—DISTRIBUTION OF PROJECT FLOOD, IN CUBIC FEET PER SECOND

encroach unduly on the flood plain. When the river is at a low stage, it has a normal scouring action and does not fill up as an over-all condition. When the river reaches a high stage, the large flood plain forms an automatic relief valve as the water goes over the banks and is retained by the project levees. Part of the flood plain is leveed, and not the river itself. As the river goes back within the channel, it automatically scours out the area to take care of its discharge.

A levee system is the backbone of any method used to solve the major flood-control problem in the Lower Mississippi Basin. A levee may be defined as an earthen embankment extending generally parallel to, but removed from, the river channel and designed to protect the area in back of it from overflow by floodwaters. To accomplish this purpose, the levee must be high enough to be secure against overtopping by flood stages, broad enough to be secure against destruction by seepage or piping, and far enough from the riverbank to prevent undue encroachment on the flood plain.

In passing, reference should be made to the uninformed view that the Lower Mississippi River is forever building up its bed to higher levels and that levees built for protection against the project flood of 3,000,000 cu ft per sec will have to be raised indefinitely because the river will lift itself above its flood plain. Emphatically, that is not so! The Lower Mississippi River became adjusted when sea level reached its present elevation and has remained relatively stable since that time. The river is now "poised," since it shows no apparent natural tendency to either degrade or aggrade its bed as an over-all feature.

Surveys indicate changes in depth in the river bends and on the crossings, some fill, and some scour, but the bed of the stream as an average does not have an over-all raising or lowering tendency. Comparison of cross-section elements of the river below Cairo shows there has been no general elevation of the river bed since the accurate surveys made in 1880.

At present the bed of the Mississippi River just above the bridge at Vicksburg, 451 miles above the mouth of Southwest Pass and the Gulf of Mexico, is 66 ft below mean sea level, or 112 ft below the low-water stage of the river at that point. The top of the adjacent alluvial riverbank is 90 ft above mean sea level, or 44 ft above the low-water stage.

At Algiers Point (New Orleans), 114 miles from the Gulf of Mexico, the bed of the river is 208 ft below mean sea level and the top of the alluvial riverbank is 14 ft above mean sea level, making a total depth of 222 ft from the top of the bank to the bed of the river. At Cairo on the Ohio River, 986 miles from the Gulf, the bed of the river in 1937 was 236 ft above mean sea level at the Cairo gage and 237 ft above mean sea level at the highway bridge. At present the elevations of the river bed at these localities are 235 ft and 237 ft above mean sea level, respectively.

Levees are not a panacea for the alleviation of flood evils, but their use is generally successful to the extent that scientific methods and intelligent planning are employed in their location and construction. Levees were built at first by hand labor, filling up the low places that permitted overflow. These were replaced later by levees of larger cross section (Fig. 4), built by labor (sometimes convicts), using wheelbarrows. Mules and small scrapers were then used as equipment for levee building, until the cross section and yardage became too large. As the levee section increased, mechanical methods were developed to move large volumes of earth at reasonable prices. Dragline machines and levee tower machines were introduced in levee work under contracts, and this type of equipment, together with various types of wagons with engines and tractors, is now in use. Where justified, large dredges are also used on levee construction.

Local interests and the states provided funds for levee building until about 1912. After the 1912 flood the United States took over some of the construction work, with the local interests paying not less than one third of the expenditures. The levees were built to a grade line that was dictated by the financial standing of the valley and was usually 3 ft above the highest water.

After 1928 the United States took over practically all the main-line levee construction and built the levees to a grade line in accordance with the project

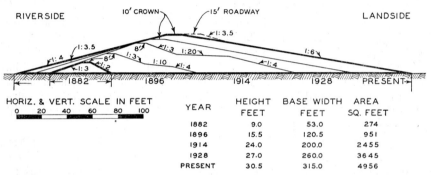

YEAR	HEIGHT FEET	BASE WIDTH FEET	AREA SQ. FEET
1882	9.0	53.0	274
1896	15.5	120.5	951
1914	24.0	200.0	2455
1928	27.0	260.0	3645
PRESENT	30.5	315.0	4956

FIG. 4.—CHANGE IN STANDARD LEVEE CROSS SECTIONS, LOWER MISSISSIPPI RIVER, 1882 TO THE PRESENT

flow, with a section large enough to keep the seepage line well within the inside toe of the levee. Progressive development of levee cross sections is shown in Fig. 4. It should be noted that local interests must provide the rights of way for the construction and maintain the levees when completed.

At the present time there are 138 local levee and drainage districts in the Mississippi River Valley. The Commission makes at least two trips per year by steamboat over the river below Cairo, and holds hearings at various towns along the river. At the hearings any representative of these districts, or any one else, can and does present his views and the needs for levee work, pumping plants, floodgates, protection from caving banks, and flood fighting, together with any special improvement, such as harbor facilities.

In the Memphis District the levees along the Mississippi River, all of which have been placed in the past 100 years, extend for 630 miles. These levees are in excellent condition to withstand high water. In addition, there are 395 miles of completed levees in the St. Francis Basin and 89 miles of miscellaneous levees at various localities in the District. In the Vicksburg District there are 459 miles of Mississippi River levees, 154 miles of Arkansas River levees, 680 miles of the Yazoo Basin levees, and about 110 miles of miscellaneous levees. In the New Orleans District there are 510 miles of Mississippi River levees (Fig. 5), 448 miles of Atchafalaya Basin floodway levees, 63 miles of Red River levees, and 16 miles of Lake Pontchartrain levees.

Along the main stem below Cairo, there are 1,599 miles of levees. In addition to the main-line levees there are 1,507 miles of levees on the tributaries, not including the 448 miles in the Atchafalaya Basin. The total length of these levees is 3,554 miles, practically all of which have been constructed since 1850. The levees now contain about 1,325,500,000 cu yd of material; but, when entirely completed, should have a volume of 1,530,500,000 cu yd and afford protection to about 29,000 sq miles in the basin. They have been instrumental in the development

FIG. 5.—MISSISSIPPI RIVER LEVEE PROTECTING RESIDENTIAL AND INDUSTRIAL AREAS OF NEW ORLEANS, LA., FROM HIGH WATER

of a great alluvial valley from an annually flooded wilderness to a rich agricultural area, well adapted to the needs of a stable and prosperous civilization.

(3) *Cutoffs.*—Cutoffs are used as another phase of the over-all program to control floods. Natural cutoffs have always occurred in the Mississippi River below Cairo. In fact, from the available records (1722 to 1928) 22 such natural cutoffs have occurred, creating a reduction of 249 miles. However, the over-all river distance between Cairo and the Head of the Passes has remained practically the same. Under the project, 16 cutoffs were utilized, 15 of which were made artificially between 1933 and 1942 and one of which occurred naturally in 1929. They were made in order to shorten the path of the river to the sea, to speed up the velocity of the flow, to increase the discharge, and to make room for more water. The river, being a meandering stream, has many bends in its course, and the cutoff is a short cut across the narrowest neck in the bend.

The river has hundreds of thousands of horsepower working every day, moving water, wearing away banks, shifting channels through sand bars, or merely wasting energy in boils and eddies. By cutting across necks and dredging in critical locations, it has been possible to transfer a part of this vast force from abandoned bends to the work of developing a better navigation and flood channel.

On the basis of discharge measured at key points along the river, both before and since the cutoff program was undertaken, the flow line of major floods has been lowered about 12 ft at Arkansas City, Ark., and about 7 ft at Vicksburg. The effect of the cutoffs in reducing stages runs out at about Memphis on the upper end of the work, and at about the mouth of Old River on the lower end.

All the cutoffs now form part of the main stream; and, as the length of the river from Cairo to the Head of Passes has been practically constant since early geological periods, the Lower Mississippi River will, if left alone, meander until it regains most of the 152 miles removed by the cutoff program. The only method of retaining the benefits derived from the cutoffs is to systematically stabilize the river below Cairo to a planned alinement.

(4) *Revetments.*—Revetments are also needed to prevent meandering and to stabilize the river along the alinement planned under the project. The river valley is extremely rich, and people are using every bit of the land. Because there are so many people living in the valley, it is no longer economical to allow the river to meander and force its bends downstream year in and year out, taking the land with it and destroying industries, farms, and communities close to the levees. To stop this loss of valuable property and stabilize the river, a revetment program has been developed which, in effect, constitutes paving along the banks of the stream at selected locations.

Bank protection work on the Lower Mississippi River below Cairo and on its principal tributaries, the Arkansas and Red rivers, includes structures such as revetments, permeable pile dikes, and groins installed for the purpose of defending the riverbanks against attack by the current, with an alinement suitable for complete stabilization of the river and consequently the protection of levees and flood-control structures located landward from the riverbanks. On the Lower Mississippi the problem is a difficult one because of the magnitude of the work involved in any one river bend. Over a large part of the river, the banks extend from 30 to 40 ft above the low-water plane, and the depth of the river at the sites of caving banks varies from about 40 ft to more than 120 ft below the low-water datum. In the vicinity of New Orleans the banks are about 14 ft above low water; and the depth of the river is 208 ft below low water. Thus, the vertical height of erodible bank varies from 70 to 222 ft. Current velocities of 8 to 10 ft per sec are common in the river during high-water flows and the rate of bank recession ranges from a few feet annually to as much as 1,500 ft in the course of one high-water cycle.

A properly-designed bank protection work fulfils two requirements: First, it affords protection against subaqueous scour and upper bank erosion; and, second, the structure and the bank are made reasonably permanent. Many types of protective works have been used, including screens of wire or light timber, abatis built of poles and brush, permeable cribs or retards, submerged spur dikes, and sunken groins—all of which have, in general, proved inadequate.

Up to the present time, the revetment is the only satisfactory type of bank protection yet developed for use on the Lower Mississippi River. The standard revetment now in use is a flexible, continuous pavement laid along the bank below the water surface, together with paving on the upper bank, all of which extends from the top of the bank to the thalweg of the stream.

Early efforts to provide protection by the use of light noncontinuous structures were all failures, and experience has indicated that revetment must be heavy and substantial to be successful on the lower river. Constructing and sinking the mattresses in connection with placing the revetments are highly specialized operations, requiring advance planning and a large outlay of special boats and equipment (Fig. 6).

FIG. 6.—BANK PROTECTION, ON MISSISSIPPI RIVER, NEAR ARKANSAS CITY, ARK.—SINKING UNIT LAUNCHING ARTICULATED CONCRETE MATTRESS

At present there are about 1,301,500 lin ft of revetment in effective use, located at ninety-seven strategic points on the Mississippi River below Cairo, that have been constructed since 1880. Each of these structures is stabilizing the river in a planned location and with a suitable alinement.

The existing project was modified in 1944 and the stabilization of the river by revetment from Cairo to Baton Rouge, La., as recommended in a special report, was authorized by Congress. The Mississippi River is roughly 1,000 miles long from Cairo to the Gulf, or 2,000 miles along both banks, and it is planned that about 450 miles will be revetted when the program is complete.

South Pass and Southwest Pass at the mouth of the river have been stabilized by special protective jetties at their junction with the Gulf of Mexico, thus providing the deep channel required for ocean-going vessels to reach New Orleans. James B. Eads, M. ASCE, an outstanding engineer and at one time a member of the Mississippi River Commission, undertook the construction of jetties in South Pass in 1875. He overcame tremendous natural, financial, and legal obstacles, and with willow mats, rock, and piling, confined the flow through South Pass and solved the navigation problem at the river's mouth for that period. The Eads jetties were eminently successful and, with certain modifications, have effectively solved the problem of maintaining deep-water navigation at the mouth.

Southwest Pass was later improved by jetties, the work being done by the Corps of Engineers. These works suffice, with moderate assistance by dredging, to keep the ports of New Orleans and Baton Rouge open to sea-going navigation.

Stabilization of the Lower Mississippi River below Cairo by bank protection must not be confused with controlling a river by contraction works. Under the bank protection plan the river may create the cross-sectional area required to carry its discharge, as only one riverbank is maintained in a bend to create a suitable alinement.

(5) *Floodways.*—Floodways constitute an additional method of securing flood protection. All the water must go down the Mississippi River and, to do so safely, all the methods enumerated are needed. Finally, additional means are required to pass the water into the Gulf of Mexico. This is accomplished by building controlled overbank floodways.

Under the project, overbank floodways to reduce flood heights were suggested at various locations on the river below Cairo. Eventually three localities were selected for controlled floodways to release water at high stages of the river.

The New Madrid Floodway was built on the west bank of the river between Cairo and New Madrid, Mo., to remove a bottleneck in flow conditions at Cairo and to reduce high-water stages in this area. The construction of this floodway is complete, and it was operated once.

The Bonnet Carre Floodway (Fig. 7) was built on the east bank of the river above New Orleans, to maintain a project flood stage of 20 ft in the river at that locality. Although the river at New Orleans is at one place 222 ft deep, it can carry only 1,250,000 cu ft per sec between the levees when the gage reads 20 ft. The project flow below Morganza Floodway is 1,500,000 cu ft per sec, so the project gage height at New Orleans is maintained by releasing up to 250,000 cu ft per sec of this discharge through Bonnet Carre Floodway into Lake Pontchartrain and the Gulf of Mexico. This floodway is complete and has been operated satisfactorily three times.

The Morganza control structure is on the west bank of the river just above Morganza, La. This structure controls the diversion of 600,000 cu ft per sec from the Mississippi River into the Atchafalaya Basin, as provided under the project plan. It is necessary because, if the levee were opened up in time of flood, it would be impossible to close off the flow of water until the river again dropped below bankfull stage, which might not occur for 3 to 7 months after the flood. In addition, the control structure will be used for a railroad and a highway elevated crossing when floodwater is actually diverted. This structure (Fig. 8) was made operative in December, 1952.

Between the guide levees the Atchafalaya Basin will be used as a floodway to pass excess floodwater from the Mississippi and the Red rivers into the Gulf of Mexico. The West Atchafalaya Floodway, between the Atchafalaya River levee and the west guide levee, will also be used to divert floodwater up to 250,000 cu ft per sec, if necessary. These floodways are practically complete.

FIG. 7.—BONNET CARRE SPILLWAY, MISSISSIPPI RIVER, IN OPERATION DURING HIGH WATER IN 1950 TO PROTECT THE CITY OF NEW ORLEANS, LA.

FIG. 8.—MORGANZA CONTROL STRUCTURE, WITH ADJACENT CONTROLLING LEVEES

OLD RIVER OUTLET

Old River (Fig. 8), which provides a connection between the Mississippi River and the Red-Atchafalaya Basin, diverts water at all times into the Atchafalaya River and forms part of the flood-control project. In times of flood, a probable 600,000 cu ft per sec can be passed through this outlet into the Atchafalaya Basin. However, Old River and the Atchafalaya River are actively enlarging their channel area and consequently taking more and more water from the Mississippi River. In recent years the increase has been so marked that active consideration has been given to the possibility that the Atchafalaya River might capture the Mississippi River via Old River and then become the main stream to the Gulf.

With other ancient diversions as criteria, geological studies indicate that the present status of the Atchafalaya and Mississippi rivers at Old River may be a stage in such course diversion. Studies of sediment diversion indicate the Atchafalaya River may capture the Mississippi River. Therefore artificially-controlled water regulation in the vicinity of Old River that will retain the benefits of sediment diversion and flood-control flow, as now authorized on both major streams, may become necessary.

To determine the conditions of flow, special geological and engineering studies have been made of the Atchafalaya Basin. The geological report shows that the Atchafalaya River has now cut down into the sand strata for some distance below its head, with the river cross section rapidly enlarging. The engineering report finds that the Atchafalaya River and Old River have enlarged their channel capacities so that from 50,000 to 110,000 cu ft per sec in excess of the project requirements for these streams can be discharged when project flood elevations occur at Simmesport.

WATERWAYS EXPERIMENT STATION LABORATORY

Under the flood-control project for the Lower Mississippi Valley, which was actually the first real authorization for over-all protection, it was essential that grade lines be established to provide for the proposed discharges in the main river and through the floodways. Computations were made for the various conditions of flow, but in addition a laboratory was established under the 15 May, 1928, Flood Control Act to make all types of experiments for flood-control works.

In this laboratory at Vicksburg (Fig. 9), models of all types are made to selected scales. Models were made covering all the features in the adopted project, and flow conditions were checked by tests to verify the computations. The Mississippi River model is constructed of concrete to a horizontal scale of 1: 2,000 and a vertical scale of 1: 100. It is about 1,055 ft long, about 168 ft wide at its widest part, and covers an area of 2½ acres.

A new and more comprehensive model covering the entire Mississippi watershed, 1,243,700 sq miles, on scales of 1: 2,000 horizontal and 1: 100 vertical, is under construction some miles east at Clinton, Miss. On completion it will be about 3,900 ft in a north-south direction, 4,500 ft in an east-west direction, and will cover an area of 200 acres. This model includes all tributary streams and all the reservoirs, and when entirely constructed can simulate any flood condition by its testing operations.

Transportation Facilities

The need for the development of transportation facilities and the safeguarding of navigation on the river, open to all on equal terms and free of monopoly, has been one of the firm convictions of the American people since the birth of this nation. At the beginning of the nineteenth century the self-propelling steamboat made its appearance and replaced earlier floating types of craft. In time, however, the steamboat gave way to powerful towboats and barges. The Federal Barge Line was established after World War I to demonstrate that cargo barges could carry freight profitably on the interior rivers. With the issuance of a joint

Fig. 9.—The Waterways Experiment Station at Vicksburg, Miss.

river and rail rate, cargoes could be shipped on one through bill of lading from the point of origin to the ultimate destination.

Canalization of the Ohio, the Upper Mississippi, and Illinois rivers, the completion of the Gulf Intracoastal Waterway all along the Gulf Coast (with connecting locks to the main waterways where required), and improvements on the Lower Mississippi River—all combine to produce a great inland waterway system having 9-ft to 12-ft depths, except when blocked with ice north of St. Louis. On the Lower Mississippi River the present requirements for barge and deep-draft navigation are met by maintaining a 9-ft by 300-ft channel above Baton Rouge and a 35-ft by 500-ft channel below Baton Rouge. These depths permit ocean-going vessels to navigate the Mississippi River from its mouth to just above Baton Rouge, some 250 miles, during the entire year.

Remarkable improvements in the design, power, and efficiency of towboats, and in design and capacity of barges, have been made in recent years. After the

Federal Barge Line blazed the trail, private capital invested in barge line equipment, for both contract and private carrier service. As a result, a large number of well-equipped barge lines are now operating, giving service between ports on the Gulf coast and industrial areas in the Ohio Valley, at the foot of Lake Michigan, at St. Louis, and at Minneapolis-St. Paul, Minn. Modern tows are illustrated in Fig. 10.

During World War II the Mississippi River and its tributaries were used in the movement to the sea of about 1,000 new government-owned vessels from the Great Lakes and upriver shipyards where they were built and from which they could not reach the ocean by any other route or method of transportation. Fleet

FIG. 10.—WATERBORNE TRAFFIC ON MISSISSIPPI RIVER—INTEGRATED TOW WITH 44,000 BBL OF PETROLEUM AND REGULAR TOW WITH 8,000 TONS OF PIPE

submarines, destroyer escorts, tank landing ships, freighters, tankers, and ocean-going tugs were the outstanding classes of vessels in this transport movement.

Existing river terminals for transfer of freight between barge and rail or truck, and between barge and oil tank storage, are available to serve the commerce now carried by the river. New Orleans has excellent harbor facilities for all purposes, and Baton Rouge has wharfage to meet present needs, although a new development is under way to create additional harbor facilities. A complete harbor on and adjacent to President's Island is being constructed at Memphis. Vicksburg has a new harbor project under consideration. There are also excellent harbors at Greenville, Miss., and Helena, Ark.

There are no locks or dams in the main river south of Cairo so the capacity of the river to carry commerce is practically unlimited. The Coast Guard maintains adequate shore lights for navigation between Cairo and the Gulf. The Mississippi River Commission, through the Memphis, Vicksburg, and New Orleans districts, marks the navigation channel between Cairo and Baton Rouge during low-water season with buoys supplied by the Coast Guard. Channel information is furnished by radio during each channel inspection trip, and reports are issued and distributed weekly for the information and guidance of navigators. The shore lights, channel buoyage, and channel reports have made night navigation safe.

Standard barges, used by commercial towing companies, carry about 1,000 tons, although later type barges, 280 by 48 by 11 ft, carry 2,000 tons. Large towboats (Fig. 10) generally move from 10,000 to 15,000 tons in one operation. The most modern towboat is propelled by about 5,000 hp. It pushes a tow containing as much as 200,000 bbl of oil, which is equivalent to two modern ocean-going tanker loads of oil.

Accurate commercial statistics have been collected annually, and the internal tonnage carried on the Mississippi River between New Orleans and the ports of Minneapolis and St. Paul, exclusive of any traffic on the Ohio, Missouri, and Illinois rivers, is shown in Fig. 11 for the 10-year period, 1941 to 1950.

The tonnage on the Mississippi River from the Gulf of Mexico to Minneapolis and St. Paul for the calendar year 1950 amounted to slightly less than 67,000,000 tons, which includes both deep-sea and barge (internal) traffic. Tonnage data for 1951 should reach about 72,000,000 tons for the same stretch of river.

COMPARISON OF CONDITIONS, 1852 AND 1952

Since 1852, all types of structures and many methods have been used to control and improve the Mississippi River below Cairo for both navigation and flood control.

Reservoirs.—None was in existence in the early period, but now many large reservoirs are operated for navigation, power, and flood control, on practically all the Mississippi River tributaries.

Levees.—In 1852 these structures were a disconnected line of earth embankments that were overtopped by any normal flood. Now an excellent line of levees, built under flood-control laws, extends from below Cape Girardeau, Mo., to the lower limits of the Mississippi River. Since 1929 these levees have contained all floods, affording protection to adjacent alluvial valley areas in accordance with the flood-control project plan. Large floods, formerly disastrous, are now held under control when passing through the Lower Mississippi River reach, where an anticipated flood of 3,000,000 cu ft per sec was used as a criterion for building the levees up to the proper heights.

Cutoffs.—During the century, cutoffs have been made artificially in the river at selected localities below Cairo.

Revetments.—Unknown 100 years ago, revetments have been and are now being built, of concrete, asphalt, and willows, at strategic locations, to stabilize the river, maintain a suitable alinement, protect adjacent property, preserve the levee locations, and create a river channel for efficient use as a transportation route for the interior markets of the nation. Dikes and retards have been used as necessary to aid the revetment structures.

Floodways.—Previously nonexistent, floodways have been constructed near New Madrid on the Mississippi River, in the East and West Atchafalaya river

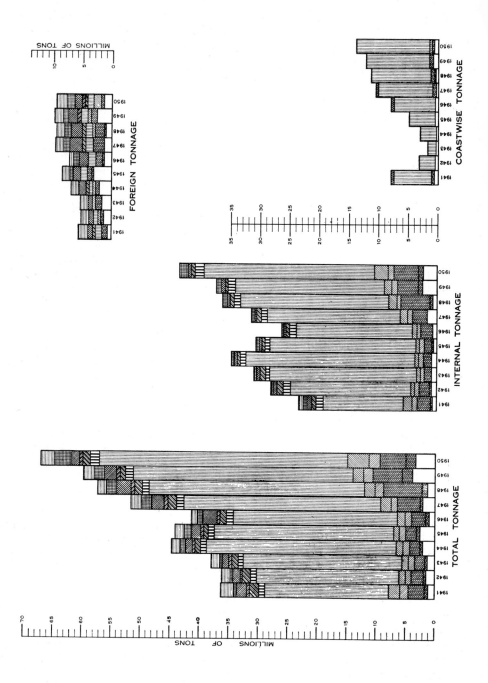

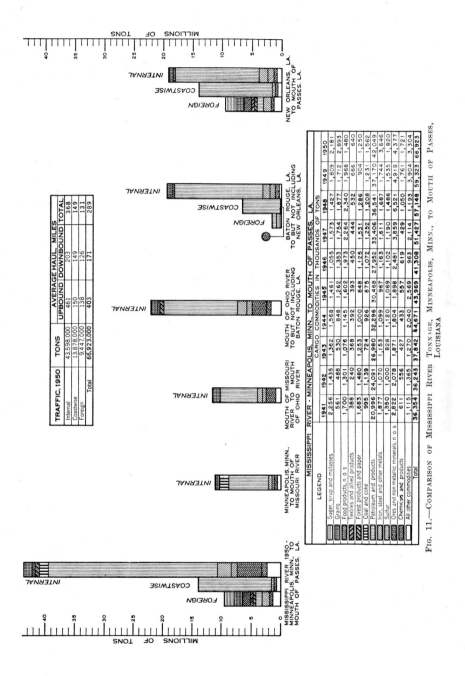

TRAFFIC, 1950	TONS	AVERAGE HAUL, MILES		
		UPBOUND	DOWNBOUND	TOTAL
Internal	43,598,000	461	203	368
Coastwise	13,878,000	150	149	149
Foreign	9,447,000	138	126	131
Total	66,923,000	403	171	289

MISSISSIPPI RIVER - MINNEAPOLIS, MINN. TO MOUTH OF PASSES, LA.
CARGO COMMODITIES IN THOUSANDS OF TONS

LEGEND	1941	1942	1943	1944	1945	1946	1947	1948	1949	1950
Sugar, sirup and molasses	2,256	1,435	1,362	1,568	1,461	1,055	1,573	1,427	1,809	2,181
Grains	561	488	530	848	1,262	1,353	1,754	1,877	1,712	2,893
Food products, n o s	1,700	1,301	1,076	1,145	1,602	1,973	2,264	2,340	1,668	1,480
Textiles and allied products	388	240	368	392	393	450	444	2,532	666	640
Forest products and paper	1,683	1,480	1,253	1,000	848	1,125	1,531	1,286	904	1,250
Coal and coke	995	1,139	724	926	875	1,072	1,252	1,208	1,231	1,562
Petroleum and products	20,996	24,091	26,980	32,296	30,468	27,952	33,406	36,541	37,170	42,049
Iron, steel and other metals	1,877	1,070	1,153	1,099	967	1,163	1,611	1,687	1,744	3,646
Sulfur	1,350	1,000	828	1,120	1,069	1,103	1,190	1,486	1,535	1,820
Ores and non metallic minerals, n. o s.	2,822	2,078	1,871	1,804	1,898	2,481	3,859	6,521	4,919	4,377
Chemicals and products	611	556	427	433	557	619	429	1,050	1,761	1,721
All other commodities	1,115	1,365	1,270	2,040	2,569	963	2,114	1,193	3,904	3,304
Total	36,354	36,243	37,842	44,671	43,969	41,308	51,427	57,148	59,323	66,923

FIG. 11.—COMPARISON OF MISSISSIPPI RIVER TONNAGE, MINNEAPOLIS, MINN., TO MOUTH OF PASSES, LOUISIANA

basins below Simmesport, and at Wax Lake Outlet to the Gulf of Mexico, just west of Morgan City, La. Spillways at Bonnet Carre and at Morganza now form part of the flood-control project on the Lower Mississippi River.

Outlets.—Above New Orleans there were many outlets on the Mississippi River in former years, but these have all been closed off except Old River, which is an important diversion into the Atchafalaya Basin at its head.

FLOOD CONTROL ACCOMPLISHED

All these methods were combined to secure the best possible results in controlling floods on the Lower Mississippi River, its tributaries, and the Atchafalaya River outlet. To date planning and foresight have created a flood-control project that actually regulates and controls the flow of floodwaters in this area. This flood-control and navigation project within the Lower Mississippi Valley is a great accomplishment. It is an actuality—not merely an idea in the planning stage.

The growth of the nation can be attributed in part to the efficient and effective flood protection and to the improvements in the inland waterway routes that have been made in the Lower Mississippi Basin in the past century.

AMERICAN SOCIETY OF CIVIL ENGINEERS

Founded November 5, 1852

TRANSACTIONS

Paper No. 2646

MULTIPURPOSE RIVER DEVELOPMENTS

By James S. Bowman,[1] M. ASCE

Synopsis

The trend toward multipurpose projects is traced through the historical development of various uses, by reason of both technological advancement and statutory influence. No attempt is made to establish firsts among multipurpose projects. This would impose a burden which in the end would not be useful. The task may better be left to statisticians. Rather, projects are cited which are representative of the trend of the times in various phases of the development—projects which are widely known and which, for their time, were of major importance.

A multipurpose development may be considered as a water-control project, or as a system of projects, serving two or more primary purposes, one of which is the production of power. A purpose may be thought of as primary only when it is one for which the project was authorized or constructed, or otherwise has become a substantial paying partner in the enterprise. Incidental benefits arising solely from the operation of a project for other objectives are not deemed to rate as multipurpose. Although these limitations may appear arbitrary, some rules must be established to keep the subject within bounds that can be readily treated.

Hydraulic Development Along Canals.—From this standpoint the first significant multipurpose developments were the early canals which antedated the railroads. These waterways furnished water for power development as well as for navigation. Head was created at the dams built along the streams for diverting feed water, at the lock sites, and at points where water could be returned from the canal to the stream with considerable fall. These power sites were in great demand by the early manufacturers on the frontier and were the nucleus of many of today's large industrial centers.

As an early example, Arthur T. Safford, M. ASCE, stated that:

> "The Proprietors of Locks and Canals on the Merrimack River were incorporated in 1792 for the purpose of making the stream navigable from tidewater to the New Hampshire line. The development of the water power available at Pawtucket Falls, in Lowell, Massachusetts, was commenced by the Proprietors in 1821 * * *."

[1] Chf., Water Control Planning Engr., TVA, Knoxville, Tenn.

With the movement away from the Atlantic seaboard, many of the new states built canals to supplement the rivers as a more stable means of transportation to the interior. Power leases at strategic points along these canals proved an important source of revenue to the growing commonwealths. During the two decades from 1825 to 1845, prosperous manufacturing communities sprang up around these sites. Isolated sections of the old canals can still be found, supplying water for the power rights, almost a century after the last canalboat disappeared.

It is interesting to note that much of the early development of hydraulic turbines in the United States was contemporary with the development of power sites along these old canals. Many early inventors did their work on turbines along the Merrimack River or along other waterways near the seaboard. Farther west in Ohio, small iron works along the early canals, licensed under the patents of the eastern inventors, built turbines to supply the local need. A number of these became important in the field of hydraulic turbine design and manufacture.

Domestic Supply and Irrigation Adopted.—For almost a century after the beginning of the canals, there seem to have been no other multipurpose developments that those for navigation and power; but with the passage of the Reclamation Act in 1902 irrigation became a primary purpose and projects of considerable magnitude were soon constructed. These projects were dams and reservoirs for the storage of irrigation water with appurtenant hydroelectric plants to develop power from the water released during the irrigation season. This power was used for lifting the same water into high-level canal systems and for other project purposes.

Roosevelt Dam on the Salt River in Arizona and Shoshone Dam on the Shoshone River in Wyoming, built between 1906 and 1911, are prominent examples of this type. During this period and in later years, many multipurpose irrigation and power projects were completed by the United States Reclamation Service and its successor, the Bureau of Reclamation, United States Department of the Interior.

During the early years of this same period, the City of Los Angeles, Calif., built the aqueduct from Owens Valley primarily for domestic water supply but also to provide water for municipal power generation and minor irrigation. Later, in 1914, the City of San Francisco, Calif., began the Hetch Hetchy Project to supply water and industrial power to the San Francisco area. The initial phases of this project were substantially completed by 1924. Both of these projects were paid for almost entirely by municipal bond issues.

Responsibility for Building Locks.—Contemporary with the construction of the early projects of the Reclamation Service for the combined purposes of irrigation and power, several projects for navigation and power were built on navigable streams by power companies under special legislation by Congress and under the supervision of the War Department. However, in these instances, the power companies were required to build not only the dams and the power facilities but also the major part of the locks at their own expense, in return for long-time leases of the power rights. The Hales Bar Project on the Tennessee River (1905–1913) and the Keokuk Project on the Mississippi River at Des Moines Rapids (1910–1913) are examples of this procedure.

After 20 years, the procedure changed to the extent that the Corps of Engineers, United States Army, constructed the locks and dams on navigable streams, and the utilities provided the power facilities at the dams under license from the Federal Power Commission. A license fee for use of the power privilege was also fixed by the Commission. This practice was followed at the Winfield, Marmet, and London dams on the Kanawha River in West Virginia, completed between 1934 and 1937. The principle involved was in fact a reversion to that in use when the states built the early navigation canals.

Increasing Government Interest.—Thereafter the influence of national legislation became more and more evident in establishing the broad basis for multipurpose development. Apparently, the first definite move in this direction was in the authorization by Congress of the so-called "308 reports." Section 3 of the River and Harbor Act, approved March 3, 1925, provided that the Corps of Engineers and the Federal Power Commission jointly should prepare and submit reports on navigable streams (except the Colorado), indicating possibilities of improvement for navigation, power, flood control, and irrigation.

On April 12, 1926, the Secretary of War, Dwight F. Davis, submitted *House Document No. 308* to Congress. This report presented an estimate of cost of examinations and surveys of about 200 rivers. Section 1 of the River and Harbor Act, approved on January 21, 1927, authorized the survey of the streams recommended, as well as several others. It should be noted that none of these acts authorized construction of projects on these streams; but the multipurpose idea stands forth very clearly.

Following the great flood of 1927 in the Lower Mississippi Basin, the various flood control acts of 1928 recognized the responsibility of the Federal Government for protection of communities from damage by floods. Ultimately they opened the way for construction, by the Federal Government, of great flood-control works with multipurpose features.

Experience on Boulder Canyon Project.—The signing of the Boulder Canyon Project Act on December 15, 1928, authorized the first of the great federal multipurpose projects. This project on the Colorado River was for the purpose of river regulation, navigation, flood control, and irrigation. It is believed that this was the first project in which federal legislation recognized flood control as a definite purpose of a reservoir. In the original authorization, no allocation of cost was made to flood control—the entire cost of the project was to be amortized, with interest, out of the revenues from the sale of water and power.

However, in 1940, Congress allocated the sum of $25,000,000 to flood control, repayable after 1987, following the amortization of the cost of the power and irrigation features. This allocation was accompanied by a reduction in the rates for water sold for power generation. It is worthy of note that at the time of construction of Hoover Dam on the Colorado River in Arizona-Nevada, the size of the project was so unprecedented that the combined resources of six of the largest contracting firms in the United States were required to handle the work.

The principle embodied in the Boulder Canyon Project Act—that the Federal Government be reimbursed for flood control, as well as for other purposes—prevailed for a number of years on projects where flood control was involved. Then the statute was changed so that the Federal Government would build the structures, provided that local interests furnished the reservoir lands and land rights and made the necessary relocations. In 1938 the law was again liberalized by Congress so that thereafter the Federal Government bore the entire cost of reservoir projects, with no reimbursement for the cost allocated to flood control.

Power Added to Flood Control.—In Section 4 of the Flood Control Act, approved on June 28, 1938, certain flood-control and river and harbor projects were authorized to be prosecuted under the direction of the Secretary of War and the supervision of the Chief of Engineers. This act, and practically all such acts since that time, further provided:

> "That penstocks and similar facilities adapted to possible future use in the development of hydroelectric power shall be installed in any dam herein authorized when approved by the Secretary of War upon recommendation of the Chief of Engineers and of the Federal Power Commission."

This statute gave great impetus to the inclusion of flood control in multipurpose projects; and, since the government had also assumed responsibility for the entire cost of flood-control reservoirs, the many projects of the Corps of Engineers in which flood control and power are combined originated with the Flood Control Act of 1938. The first recommendation to this effect by the Federal Power Commission was for the installation of a penstock in the proposed Knightville Dam on the Westfield River in Massachusetts, on December 3, 1938. Since that time the Commission has recommended the installation of penstocks in some sixty dams.

To Embrace a River Basin.—The Tennessee Valley Authority Act, approved in May, 1933, actually applied for the first time, as far as is known, the multipurpose concept to the development and utilization of the water resources of an entire river basin. The multipurpose feature is implicit in the Act which gives the power to:

> "* * * construct such dams and reservoirs, in the Tennessee River and its tributaries, as * * * will provide a nine-foot channel in said river and maintain a water supply for the same, from Knoxville to its mouth, and will best serve to promote navigation on the Tennessee River and its tributaries and control destructive flood waters in the Tennessee and Mississippi River drainage basins; and * * * acquire and construct powerhouses, power structures, transmission lines, navigation projects, and incidental works in the Tennessee River and its tributaries. * * * The directors of the Authority are hereby directed to report to Congress their recommendations not later than April 1, 1936, for the unified development of the Tennessee River system."

Norris Dam, on the Clinch River in Tennessee, the first built by the Tennessee Valley Authority (TVA), was authorized in the original act as a multipurpose structure. Since then seven multipurpose dams on the Tennessee River have been constructed, as illustrated by Fort Loudoun Dam in Tennessee (Fig. 1); and the 9-ft channel from the mouth to Knoxville, Tenn., has been completed. Nine multipurpose dams on the tributaries have been completed and are in operation as, for example, Douglas Dam on the French Broad River in Tennessee (Fig. 2). Most of these projects were referred to in the Unified Development Report of 1936. Because of World War II, some of the projects were built much sooner than had been anticipated.

FIG. 1.—FORT LOUDOUN DAM ON THE TENNESSEE RIVER BELOW KNOXVILLE, TENN.; ON NEAR SIDE, SWITCHYARD, POWERHOUSE, DAM, AND SPILLWAY—ALL FOR MULTIPURPOSE USE

FIG. 2.—DOUGLAS DAM ON FRENCH BROAD RIVER ABOVE KNOXVILLE, TENN.—A MAJOR MULTIPURPOSE STRUCTURE OF THE TENNESSEE VALLEY AUTHORITY; POWER AND FLOOD-CONTROL FACILITIES CLEARLY INDICATED

Multipurpose Idea Accepted.—For more than 25 years, beginning with the authorization of the 308 reports, Congress appears to have adopted the multipurpose project as a desirable means of developing and conserving the water resources of the United States. This fact is not concerned with the controversial issues that have grown up in connection with projects. Meantime, the methods of operating such projects, and extent of reimbursement of the Federal Government, and the distribution of the benefits have become subjects of acrimonious debate. However, these arguments have not obscured the fact that a nation faced with a serious water shortage in many of its regions can ill afford to conserve water for one purpose and at the same time neglect its utilization for other purposes where economical means are available for such use.

The construction and operation of major navigation, flood-control, and irrigation projects seem to be no longer questioned as a legitimate function of the Federal Government. Such objections as have been made to specific projects for any or all of these three purposes appear to stem from the idea that if such projects are not built there will be no opportunity for including power facilities. The objection to generation of hydroelectric power seems to center mainly about the arguments over transmission and distribution of the output.

Evolution of Practice.—Discussion of these questions may throw light on their effect on the future trend in multipurpose development. It is probably true that some federal multipurpose projects have been built, which because of meager data or overenthusiasm were undertaken when they should not have been. On the other hand, it is not necessary to burn the barn to get rid of the rats. Although changes in policies may be expected from time to time, the intent of Congress with respect to water conservation is too clear to encourage the belief that it can be persuaded to stifle meritorious projects by enacting legislation to impose far more rigid tests of economic justification, for instance, than those applied customarily to either public or private work.

Farm ponds and improved land-use practices are very good in themselves, but recent attempts to substitute these for major flood-control reservoirs, thus eliminating the opportunity for multipurpose projects, can only lead to disillusionment and disaster in downstream areas when flood-producing storms occur. One example of this should be sufficient to sustain faith in the large reservoir as the only dependable means of reducing flood stages in many areas.

The present practices of federal agencies with respect to authorization, justification, reimbursement, allocation, and other phases of multipurpose projects are extremely diverse. Congress has authorized projects without much thought of uniformity of policy and, in fact, has drifted away from uniformity by frequent amendment of the basic acts to conform to the demands of local groups. The appointment of the President's National Water Resources Policy Commission was recognition of the confusion that exists, but the chances for remedial legislation in the near future do not seem to be hopeful. The recommendations of the Water Resources Committee in the mid-1930's merited much attention but received little. Nevertheless the enactment of a sound, fair, and consistent national water policy should eliminate much of the suspicion and misunderstanding that now exist as to the importance of the multipurpose development in conservation of the water resources of the United States.

Current and Prospective Activities.—The trend of multipurpose projects in recent years should afford some indication of future trends. Accordingly, the data given in Table 1 have been prepared to show the multipurpose projects completed between 1921 and 1950, inclusive, by 5-year periods, classified as to the agency that financed the construction.

TABLE 1.—MULTIPURPOSE PROJECTS INVOLVING HYDROELECTRIC POWER COMPLETED BETWEEN 1921 AND 1950, INCLUSIVE

Period	Total projects	MEANS OF FINANCING		
		Federal	Loan-grant	Private
1921–1925	6	3	...	3
1926–1930	7	1	...	6
1931–1935	4	2	...	2
1936–1940	15	13	1	1
1941–1945	18	14	3	1
1946–1950	19	19	...	...
Total	69	52	4	13

It will be observed that in these three decades sixty-nine major multipurpose projects have been completed. In the first half of this period there were seventeen; in the last half, fifty-two. In the first half six were built wholly with federal funds, except for power plants at two dams; and eleven were built by municipalities, irrigation districts, and other local bodies. In the second half forty-six were built wholly with federal funds, except for the power station at one dam; four others were jointly financed by the Federal Government and by local agencies; and only two were built entirely by local financing.

A comparison of the number of federal multipurpse projects involving electric power and financed by federal funds since 1933 shows that in 1946 there were thirty-three such projects completed and in service. In 1952 there were fifty-two projects in service, an increase of nineteen in 6 years. In 1946, twenty-eight projects were under construction whereas in 1952 there were thirty-four. The approved and authorized federal multipurpose projects on which no work has been started total ninety-five.

Stabilizing Policies.—These data seem to indicate that the multipurpose water-control project has been rather widely accepted and will probably continue to be the appropriate means of developing water resources where this type of project is needed and is economically justified. The number of such projects now in operation should afford opportunity for careful examination of the engineering soundness based on facts rather than on speculation.

The proposition of whether the Federal Government should continue to dominate such projects will undoubtedly undergo some changes as time goes on. The number of those authorized for federal construction is almost twice the number of those completed in the past 20 years and more than the total of those now in service and under construction. Hence, it is probably safe to predict that present trends will persist for some time to come.

AMERICAN SOCIETY OF CIVIL ENGINEERS

Founded November 5, 1852

TRANSACTIONS

Paper No. 2647

DEVELOPMENT OF THE TENNESSEE RIVER WATERWAY

By C. E. Blee,[1] M. ASCE

Synopsis

The Tennessee River as it exists today, with 630 miles of continuous slack-water navigation channel, 11,500,000 acre-ft of storage space reserved for flood control, and hydroelectric plants having a total installed capacity of 2,600,000 kw, is one of the most highly developed river systems in the world. This coordinated and almost complete system has been made possible by the application of the multiple-purpose principle of development. For more than a century money and effort were expended on the Tennessee River to develop navigation as a single-purpose objective, but little was accomplished beyond some isolated local improvements. It was the multiple use of structures for navigation, flood control, and power production which made economically feasible the high degree of coordinated development that exists today.

The river has been closely interwoven with the history of the United States, both before and after the formation of the nation. A review of this early history —as it relates to the Tennessee waterway—is of interest as a background for the engineering works which followed.

The river has been used extensively as a trade route for centuries: First, by the aboriginal inhabitants of the region; next by the Spanish, French, and English explorers and traders; followed by the early settlers from the American colonies; and, finally, by the people of the United States engaged in what has recently become a highly developed commerce. The first recorded history of an expedition to the Tennessee by white men was that of Hernando De Soto and his company of Spanish soldiers. Traveling west from Florida they followed down the course of the Hiwassee River and reached the Tennessee near the location of Chattanooga, Tenn., in 1540. They then proceeded down the river for about 150 miles to the vicinity of Guntersville, Ala. (Fig. 1).

---

[1] Chf. Engr., TVA, Knoxville, Tenn.

Indians, French, and British Vie for Control

For nearly two centuries after De Soto's expedition the Cherokee Indians were left in undisturbed possession of the Tennessee Valley area. They made extensive use of the river for transportation within the Cherokee nation. All the larger Cherokee towns were on the banks of the river and its tributaries or on the islands in these streams.

French traders used the river in the 1690's as part of their trade route between the Mississippi Valley and Charleston, S. C. By 1714 they had built trading posts along the Tennessee for some distance above its mouth.

The territory around the Tennessee River was involved in the conflict between the French and the English, wherein each sought supremacy to control trade with

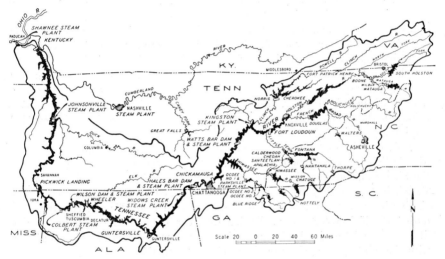

Fig. 1.—Map of the Tennessee River System

the Indians. In 1756 the British built Fort Loudoun on the Little Tennessee River in the heart of the Cherokee country; 4 years later the Cherokees turned on the British and captured Fort Loudoun. The trouble between the French and English culminated in the French and Indian War which left the British dominant.

Increasing Use of the River Highway

The early settlers from the American colonies along the Atlantic coast came into the Tennessee Valley largely from Virginia, following down the Holston River, or from North Carolina, by proceeding up the Yadkin River with pack horses, crossing the divide, and following down the course of the Watauga and Nolichucky rivers. The early settlements and towns in Tennessee were all located along the streams. Kingsport was established at the junction of the north and south forks of the Holston in 1770. Dandridge on the French Broad River was founded some time prior to 1785. Knoxville became the capital of The Territory South of the Ohio in 1791. Ross' Landing, the original site of Chattanooga, was an Indian trading post from very early days but was not incorporated as the City of Chattanooga until after the removal of the Cherokee Indians in 1838.

Substantial use was made of the river system for transportation throughout this entire period of intensive settlement. Rafts, flatboats, and keelboats were built upstream, loaded with the local produce—mostly cotton and corn whisky—and floated down the Tennessee into the Ohio and Mississippi and so on down to New Orleans, La., where the cargo was disposed of and the rafts and boats were broken up and sold as timber. There was no upstream traffic, and the boatmen had to walk back to their homes over the long and dangerous trail known as the Natchez Trace.

An epic in American history was the trip during this period by a party under the leadership of Col. John Donelson, which set out from Fort Patrick Henry near Kingsport on the Holston in December, 1779, with men, women, children, and their household goods in a flotilla of flatboats and pirogues. They floated down the Holston and Tennessee to the Ohio, then poled upstream on the Ohio and Cumberland to a place called French Licks where they founded the City of Nashville. The trip consumed a year's time, and was full of hardships and danger. In addition to the navigation hazards in the narrows below Chattanooga and to running the rapids at Muscle Shoals, in Alabama, the party was attacked a number of times by Indians. The attacks were particularly severe in the section below Chattanooga where the narrow river with high bluffs on either side enabled the Indians to shoot down on the people in the boats.

It is thought that the first steamboat to venture up the Tennessee as far as Muscle Shoals reached there in March, 1821. The passage of a steamboat over the Shoals and up the Tennessee to the confluence of the Holston and French Broad, just above Knoxville, was first accomplished by the *Atlas* in 1828. Beginning in 1835 steamboats plied regularly between Knoxville and Decatur, Ala., during the high-water season. During the War Between the States there was little commercial navigation but extensive use was made of the river in connection with the military campaigns of the armies on both sides.

BENEFITS FROM FEDERAL INTEREST

For a number of years after the adoption of the Federal Constitution, the power to appropriate funds for internal improvements was neither claimed nor exercised by Congress. The very early attempts to improve navigation conditions on the Tennessee were sporadic efforts by chartered companies and by local communities. A change in the attitude of the Federal Government toward internal improvements came in March, 1818, when the House of Representatives passed a resolution declaring that Congress had the power to appropriate money for building roads and canals and for improving natural watercourses. A bill, enacted into law in April, 1824, authorized President James Monroe to have the necessary plans, surveys, and estimates made of routes for such roads and canals as he might deem of national importance and as necessary to the transportation of the public mails.

The enactment of this law had direct influence on the matter of improving the navigability of the Tennessee River. John C. Calhoun, then Secretary of War, appointed a Board of Engineers to make the nation-wide surveys as ordered. In his report to the President, Calhoun designated the Muscle Shoals section of the Tennessee River as one of the improvement projects of most importance. This official listing of Muscle Shoals as one of the most serious obstacles in the transportation routes of the nation was highly significant as it marked the first recognition by the Federal Government of the Tennessee navigation problem.

Attempts were made by Congress to secure the improvement of the Tennessee River through grants of large amounts of land and small amounts of money to the states. Following the approval of plans by President Andrew Jackson in 1831, the State of Alabama constructed a lateral canal around that part of Muscle Shoals called the Big Shoals at a total cost of about $650,000. Because of the inadequacy of the structures, however, the canal was not a success and was abandoned in 1837, one year after completion of construction.

Money and Improvements Follow

The year 1852, as well as being the year which marked the beginning of the century which the ASCE is commemorating, was a significant one in the attempts to improve the Tennessee River for navigation. At that time $50,000 was allotted to the Tennessee River by Congress. The project called for a minimum navigable depth of 2 ft downstream from Knoxville to Kelly's Ferry, 22 miles below Chattanooga. The stretch of the river below Chattanooga presented some of the most dangerous waters which boatmen had to face—hazardous passages with such picturesque names as the Suck, the Skillet, and the Boiling Pot.

Under the Act of 1852 some work was done in this mountain gorge section, but nothing permanent was accomplished until April 26, 1904, when Congress granted a 99-year franchise for the construction by private interests at Scott's Point, 17 miles below Chattanooga, of a hydroelectric dam, with navigation locks to be provided by the Federal Government. On January 7, 1905, the concession was slightly modified, allowing the location of the dam to be changed to Hales Bar, 33 miles below Chattanooga. Great difficulties were experienced in overcoming foundation troubles, and the dam and lock were not completed until 1913, after a construction period of 8 years. This dual-purpose structure provided a minimum 6-ft navigation depth from Hales Bar to Chattanooga and produced 51,000 kw of power through fourteen small hydroelectric units.

The Federal Government in 1871 again became officially interested in building a canal around Muscle Shoals. An appropriation was made by Congress in that year; construction work was started in 1875 and completed in 1890. The project comprised one canal 3.5 miles long with two locks, built on the left bank around the troublesome Elk River Shoals; and another canal a few miles farther downstream along the right bank, 14.5 miles long with nine locks providing a new channel around Big Muscle Shoals. Both canals provided a minimum 5-ft depth.

War Work Becomes Predominant

During the ensuing years there were a number of attempts to enact legislation providing for power development at Muscle Shoals. With the coming of

World War I the question of national defense emerged to take its place beside navigation and power in any development which might take place at the Shoals. This triple interest crystallized in the passage of the National Defense Act of 1916 which led to the building of Wilson Dam, just above Florence, Ala.

With the completion of this dam in 1925, a stretch of river extending 15.5 miles upstream from the dam was converted into a slack-water pool with a navigable depth of 7 ft or greater. Some century-old navigation problems were thereby solved.

The Wilson Dam and Power Plant were built by the Army Engineers in accordance with the plans and design of Hugh L. Cooper, M. ASCE. Although the initial power installation consisted of only four 20,000-kw units, with commendable foresight stalls were provided in the powerhouse building for an ultimate installation of eighteen main units with a total capacity of 436,000 kw. The eighteenth unit was installed and placed in service by Tennessee Valley Authority (TVA) 2 years ago.

Navigation Develops Slowly

In the period from about 1868 to 1925 many other projects for the improvement of navigation on the Tennessee River and its tributaries (Fig. 1) were authorized by Congress. The permanent improvement resulting from these was quite limited. However, the construction did result in a navigable depth of about 4 ft being ordinarily assured on the lower river between Muscle Shoals and the mouth.

An extensive survey of the Tennessee River system with regard to possible navigation developments of a comprehensive nature was begun under the direction of Secretary of War John W. Weeks, through the Corps of Engineers, United States Army, by an appropriation approved September 22, 1922. Later the scope of the survey was widened to include, along with navigation, matters relating to flood control and power development. The final report on the survey was published in 1930 as *House Document No. 328,* Seventy-First Congress, Second Session. A comprehensive plan for the development of the Tennessee River, to be executed in progressive steps over a long period of years, was envisioned. The document was of great value in the planning undertaken shortly thereafter by the TVA for the development of the river system.

The report concluded that the traffic potentialities justified the adoption of a project for the development of the river as a waterway with a controlling depth of 9 ft throughout its entire length from Paducah, Ky., to Knoxville (Figs. 1 and 2). It was stated that this could be accomplished by the construction on the main stream of thirty-two low dams or, alternatively, seven high dams. It was recommended that work be initiated at once by the Federal Government on the low dams with the provision that a high dam might be built by private interests, states, or municipalities, and substituted for any two or more low dams.

A review of the situation as of 1930 indicates that the then-existing navigation improvement works comprised four rather widely separated lateral canals with locks, one low navigation dam (Widow's Bar Dam), two navigation-power dams (Wilson Dam and Hales Bar Dam), and numerous lateral dikes and dredged cuts. The results were disappointing in terms of physically improved navigation or economic benefits, as the projects were necessarily disconnected, isolated attempts to improve navigation. In fact by 1933, more than a century of effort had resulted in dependable channel depths of only 4 ft from the Ohio River to Florence, 257 miles; 2 ft to Chattanooga, an additional 207 miles; and 1½ ft to Knoxville, another 184 miles.

COMPREHENSIVE PROGRAM ENVISIONED

The Tennessee Valley Authority Act, passed by Congress in May, 1933, recognized the wisdom of combining navigation, flood control, and hydroelectric

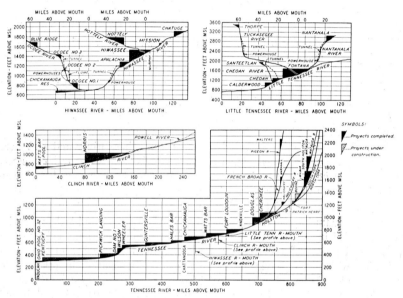

FIG. 2.—PROFILES OF THE TENNESSEE RIVER SYSTEM

power production in a series of multiple-purpose dams and reservoirs on the Tennessee River and its tributaries. Section 4(j) of the Act provided that TVA:

"* * * shall have power to construct such dams and reservoirs, in the Tennessee River and its tributaries, as * * * will provide a 9-ft channel in the said river and maintain a water supply for the same from Knoxville to its mouth, and will best serve to promote navigation on the Tennessee River and its tributaries and control destructive flood waters in the Tennessee and Mississippi River drainage basins; and shall have power to acquire or construct powerhouses, power structures, transmission lines, navigation projects, and incidental works in the Tennessee River and its tributaries, and to unite the various power installations into one or more systems by transmission lines."

Section 9(a) of the Act further provides for the regulation of the stream flow primarily for the purposes of promoting navigation and controlling floods and, in so far as may be consistent with such purposes, for the generation of electric energy.

Thus by defining the objectives of navigation, flood control, and power production, the foundation was laid for the full development of a great river system in an economical manner through the use of multiple-purpose structures assembled into a planned and integrated whole.

MULTIPLE-PURPOSE SYSTEM UNDER TVA

Early in its history, TVA prepared a comprehensive plan for the development of the river system. The plan was embodied in a report issued under date of March, 1936, and filed with Congress. It provided for the development of the main river (Figs. 1 and 2) by the construction of seven dams which with the two existing dams would give nine "high" dams, converting the river into a continuous series of slack-water pools from the mouth of the river to Knoxville—a sailing line distance of 630 miles. Each dam included a navigation lock, power-generating equipment, and flood-control facilities. Certain of the principal proposed storage dams on the tributaries were definitely designated and others were included in the report by reference. All have since been constructed. A pictorial representation of the system is given in Fig. 3.

At the time of the formation of the TVA in 1933, the United States was in the midst of a depression, and it was desirable to get work under way as soon as possible. The construction of Norris Dam on the Clinch River and of Wheeler Dam on the main river was started at once. Norris Dam with its large storage capacity was a key structure in the system. Wheeler Dam extended slack-water navigation over the upper part of Muscle Shoals, added considerable power capacity, and contributed to flood control.

The three-dam improvement formed by Norris, Wheeler and Wilson provided a well-rounded interim system, adapted to integrated operation. This first step in the development of the river as a whole furnished 92 miles of slack-water navigation with a 9-ft navigable depth, improved navigation in other critical stretches by low-water releases, provided 2,000,000 acre-ft of flood-control storage space, and gave an installed power-generating capacity of 350,000 kw. It is interesting to note that the primary power capability was increased fourfold, from 39,000 kw for the Wilson plant operating alone to 155,000 kw for the three-plant system.

EXPANSION FROM INTERIM SYSTEM

The next dam to be started on the main river was Pickwick, the first site downstream from Wilson and some 206 miles from the mouth of the river. At first thought it would appear more logical to begin at the mouth of the river and develop progressively upstream, to obtain the maximum benefit from navigation, but in this case the lower stretch of the river afforded fairly good navigation depths under the conditions of low-water release then existing, whereas there were several bad shoals between the Pickwick site and Wilson Dam. Moreover, it was known that Kentucky Dam at the mouth of the Tennessee would be difficult to build, requiring extensive exploration and a long construction period.

During 1939, in connection with the acquisition by purchase of the properties of the Tennessee Electric Power Company, five major hydroelectric plants and

FIG. 3.—SCHEMATIC DIAGRAM OF TVA WATER-CONTROL SYSTEM (FOR PROFILES, SEE FIG. 2)

several steam plants were added to the TVA system. The acquired plants had been designed and operated as single-purpose power plants and continued to be regarded as such with the exception of the Hales Bar Dam on the main river which was treated as a multiple-purpose project. One of the dams, Great Falls (Fig. 1), was located on a tributary of the Cumberland River. The power capability added by the acquired plants totaled 244,000 kw of installed capacity and about 180,000 kw of primary power when operated as an integral part of the TVA system. Such operation substantially increased the usefulness of the former Tennessee Electric Company plants compared with their operation as a separate system.

Following Pickwick Dam and in accordance with the normal program envisioned by the 1936 report, the construction of Chickamauga, Guntersville, Kentucky, Watts Bar, and Fort Loudoun dams had gone forward in an orderly manner. Likewise Hiwassee Dam with its large storage reservoir and its generating station had been built on the Hiwassee River, affording control of the second of the five major tributaries of the Tennessee above Chattanooga.

Defense Dictates Emergency Advances

Then in 1940 and ensuing years there was felt the impact of the demand for power—first for the preparatory defense program and then for World War II. On July 31, 1940, came the first emergency authorization under the National Defense Program. This included Cherokee Dam on the Holston River and Watts Bar Steam Plant, followed on July 16, 1941, by the second emergency authorization which included four additional dams in the Hiwassee watershed. Two of these, Nottely and Chatuge, were multiple-purpose dams but initially without power-generating equipment at the site; the other two, Ocoee No. 3 and Apalachia, were single-purpose power developments involving long tunnels. Cherokee Dam formed a large storage reservoir, thus contributing to the control of the third of the main tributaries of the Upper Tennessee.

Douglas Dam on the French Broad River and Fontana on the Little Tennessee were also constructed as part of the defense program. With the completion of these two dams, storage was provided for the control of each of the five main tributaries of the Tennessee. It is significant that, notwithstanding the emergency nature of the work, planning and investigations were ready so that design and construction could be started at once.

The completion of Kentucky Dam, or Gilbertsville as it was first called, near the mouth of the river and the filling of its reservoir stretching 184 miles to Pickwick, marked the fulfilment of the 9-ft waterway from Paducah to Knoxville. Just after Pearl Harbor, Fontana Dam—at that time fourth highest in the world—was begun under the third emergency authorization. All these projects and their relation to the general system are shown, with others, in Figs. 1, 2, and 3.

The years just prior to the war and running through the war period were years of intense construction activity. The accelerated schedules to produce power for war production called for twelve major projects to be under way at one time, and for one of these projects, Douglas Dam, to be in operation 13 months after starting work.

After World War II the further development of the Tennessee River went forward at a more normal pace for a time. The Watauga Dam, a 320-ft multiple-purpose structure on a tributary of the Holston River, was begun in 1946 and completed in 1949. Also the South Holston Dam, a similar structure on another tributary of the Holston, was constructed a year later. Two more dams, Boone and Fort Patrick Henry, are under construction farther down-stream on the Holston River.

A number of dam sites are available for future development on the Tennessee River although these are relatively small in comparison with the earlier projects.

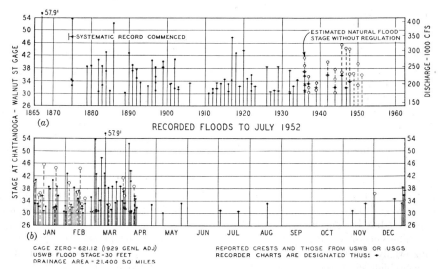

Fig. 4.—Distribution of Floods at Chattanooga, Tenn.: (a) Chronological Plotting of Recorded Floods Since 1865; and (b) Same Floods Plotted in Accordance with Their Time of Occurrence Within the Year

An Encouraging Over-All Picture

Conditions in the Tennessee River Basin are particularly favorable to the design and operation of a water-control system founded on the principle of making use of the structures for the multiple purposes of navigation, flood control, and power development. A basic characteristic of the Tennessee River system is that with respect to most of the reservoirs the same space in a reservoir is utilized for flood control during the flood season and for other purposes during the remainder of the year. The principal factor required for such a method of multiple-purpose operation, and one which is present to a high degree in the Tennessee Valley, is that major floods are consistently confined to a definite flood season.

Stream flow records on the Tennessee are available (Fig. 4) for the past 87 years and historical records extend present knowledge to cover a period of more than 100 years. The records show that no major flood has occurred in the period from about the first of April to the middle of December. This established climatic condition has been used to advantage in the design of the water-control system on the Tennessee by making multiple use of the same storage space in many of the reservoirs.

To summarize the development of the Tennessee River as it exists today, there are nine dams on the main river and nineteen on the tributaries, all operated as a single integrated system under one centralized control; 630 miles of continuous slack-water navigation channel with a minimum navigable depth of 9 ft, formed by a series of nine dams each with a navigation lock; 14,669,000 acre-ft of storage for low-water release, of which 11,500,000 acre-ft of storage space is reserved for flood control as of January first of each year; and hydroelectric plants having a total installed capacity of 2,600,000 kw.

Recently in order to meet the power demands of rapidly growing loads, it has been necessary to build a number of very large steam-electric plants along the shores of the reservoirs. The development of the Tennessee waterway made possible the construction of these steam plants by furnishing the large amounts of water required for condensing and by supplying an economical means of bringing coal for fuel to the plants.

Navigation Benefits Materially

During the earlier stages of the development of the Tennessee River, and in fact until the completion of Kentucky Dam, the water-control operating requirements for navigation under conditions of open-channel navigation were quite exacting. With the completion of the main-river dams giving slack-water navigation to Knoxville, the maintaining of full navigable depths in the main channel has become a relatively simple matter.

The control of floods and the release of water in the periods of low flow materially benefit navigation by stabilizing the pools. Also maintaining a relatively high discharge from the Tennessee into the Ohio during the low-water periods is of definite assistance to navigation on the Lower Ohio and Mississippi rivers.

At the time of the very low flows on the Ohio during 1947 about two thirds of the total flow in the Ohio at Paducah and about one fifth of the total flow of the Mississippi at Cairo came from the Tennessee. Without the regulation afforded by the TVA reservoir system over the 6-week low-flow period between September 21 and November 1, 1947, the discharge of the Tennessee at that time would have averaged about 15,000 cu ft per sec instead of 27,000 cu ft per sec and the flow in the Ohio at Paducah would have been reduced by about 12,000 cu ft per sec. Likewise, the flow in the Mississippi at Cairo would have been reduced by the same amount. Such reductions at this critical time would have materially affected the navigation depths on these rivers, eventually lowering the reach of the Mississippi River just below Cairo by about 1 ft.

The depth of 9 ft for the Tennessee waterway was specified in the TVA Act, but this was the result of long, practical experience on the river and of findings by the Corps of Engineers. It was entirely consistent with the pattern of waterway design at that time. When it came to interpreting the meaning of "9-foot channel," there seemed to be an unusual opportunity to provide for 9-ft draft by obtaining some overdepth at no great additional cost. A gross channel depth of 11 ft at minimum pool levels was therefore adopted. A minimum channel width of 300 ft in dredged cuts with some widening at bends was considered adequate with the thought that this could be increased if found desirable.

DESIGN OF LOCKS BECOMES COMPLEX

The question of lock sizes was not so readily solved. There was no well-defined pattern to serve as a guide. The existing locks at Wilson Dam were 60 ft by approximately 300 ft; the lock at Hales Bar Dam was 60 ft by 265 ft. There was a lock chamber under construction at what was to become Wheeler Dam which was 60 ft by 360 ft. The Corps of Engineers recommended that single-lift locks providing clear dimensions 110 ft wide and 600 ft long be constructed in the two dams to be built downstream from Wilson Dam and that single-lift locks 60 ft wide and 360 ft long be constructed in each new dam upstream from Wilson Dam.

This recommendation was coupled with the further provision that space be reserved for the future addition of a small lock (60 ft by 360 ft) at each dam below Wilson and of a large lock (110 ft by 600 ft) at Wilson Dam and at each new dam above, so that ultimately there would be one large and one small lock in parallel at each dam. This proposition was thoroughly reviewed by TVA and adopted for construction.

Traffic has now developed to a point where the locks at Wilson Dam are becoming a rather serious bottleneck. Those at the main dam consist of two locks in series. Downstream about 2½ miles at the end of a canal is a low-lift lock (known as Lock and Dam No. 1). Planning is actively under way for a 110-ft by 600-ft lock to parallel the existing locks.

One proposal being studied is to eliminate Lock and Dam No. 1, dredge the navigation channel up to the entrance of the new lock, and provide an auxiliary lock for entrance to the existing lock. This would result in the new lock having a lift of close to 100 ft. An alternative scheme would be to rebuild Lock and Dam No. 1 thus providing navigation into the new lock as well as the existing one. Under this plan the new lock would have a lift of about 90 ft. One of the high-lift locks already built, at Fort Loudoun Dam, is shown in Fig. 5. When constructed this was the highest single-lift lock (80 ft) ever built.

TRAFFIC GROWTH MEASURES IMPROVEMENTS

A century ago no record was kept of the traffic on the Tennessee River, but in terms of tons of freight it must have been very small. Furthermore, the movements of freight were mostly local so the ton-miles for the year 1852 must have been exceedingly small indeed. In fact, through the next 86 years there was very little growth in the traffic on the river.

Then in 1938 following the completion of the Wheeler Reservoir immediately upstream from Wilson Dam and of the Pickwick Reservoir immediately downstream, and with the improvement in depth of the stretch of the river below Pickwick due to upstream releases of water, a navigable waterway with a 6-ft depth became available from Paducah to Guntersville—a distance of nearly 350 miles. The opening of this waterway marked the beginning of a continuing growth of traffic. Again in 1944 the filling of Kentucky Reservoir completed the canalization of the river and from that date the curve representing the freight traffic by years (Fig. 6) swings sharply upward.

FIG. 5.—VIEW OF LOCK AT FORT LOUDOUN DAM FROM DOWNSTREAM

In the calendar year 1951, approximately 1,800,000 tons of commodities exclusive of sand, gravel, and stone moved on the Tennessee River—representing about 630,000,000 ton-miles of traffic, an increase of nearly 15% over the previous year. The estimates of navigation benefits on which the project was founded were based on the assumption that a matured traffic of 1,500,000,000 ton-miles per year would be realized by the year 1960. The present trend indicates that this assumption will be met quite readily.

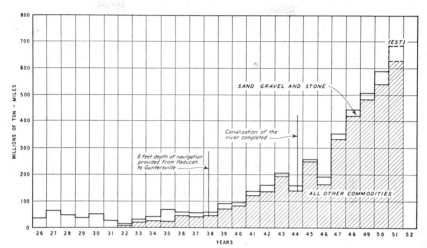

FIG. 6.—TENNESSEE RIVER FREIGHT TRAFFIC, IN TON-MILES

FIG. 7.—AUTOMOBILE CARRIER ON THE TENNESSEE WATERWAY—NORMALLY CONSISTING OF THREE UNITS, WITH A CAPACITY OF ABOUT 600 NEW AUTOMOBILES

In recent years there have been sharp increases registered in the volume of higher value commodities shipped on the waterway—petroleum products, grain, iron and steel, chemicals and chemical products, sulfur, and new automobiles (Fig. 7).

Changes and progress in waterway design are being made, although these are necessarily slow because of the very large investment in permanent structures. At any time these structures could be rendered obsolete by increased depth requirements or by changes in lock dimensions. However, the shippers and transportation companies continue to use larger barges, faster and more powerful towboats, and longer and wider tows, until the waterway structures become the limiting factor in determining the development of the towing equipment.

At the present time the coal haulage equipment used on the Tennessee River is in the midst of a transition period resulting from the large increase in the amount of coal to be shipped by water to supply the new steam plants along the river. The 500-ton coal barges are being replaced by 1,000-ton and 1,500-ton barges. Consideration is being given to building integrated coal barges, locked together with a single molded prow and stern, similar to the latest oil barges. The oil companies seem inclined to build their barges just as large as the dimensions of the controlling lock will permit.

Change and progress are bound to come. The Tennessee River waterway may see as great changes during the century ahead as it has during the past century

AMERICAN SOCIETY OF CIVIL ENGINEERS

Founded November 5, 1852

TRANSACTIONS

Paper No. 2648

THE PASSES OF THE MISSISSIPPI RIVER

By W. C. Cobb,[1] A. M. ASCE

Synopsis

Large sea-borne commerce on the Lower Mississippi is entirely dependent on free access from the Gulf through a number of channels or passes. In the old days, sandbars at each mouth limited the navigable depth to about 9 ft. For more than 100 years, maintenance of a deep channel has engaged the best efforts of noted engineers. Capt. James B. Eads, M. ASCE, contracted to develop a 26-ft depth; his final successful jetties at South Pass were historic, and a model for later continuous construction and maintenance at Southwest Pass. The development of methods, modifications, and repairs—by Eads and latterly by the Corps of Engineers—is described to show how a standardized and successful status with a 35-ft ruling depth has been achieved.

General Description of River and Passes

During 1950, the latest year of published records, the total inbound and outbound, coastwise and foreign, commerce which moved through the passes of the Mississippi River consisted of some 8,500 vessels transporting more than 23,000,000 tons of cargo. The facts that this great quantity of goods could move and that New Orleans, La., is the major port and metropolis which it is today are due to the perseverance of its early leaders who insisted that there be "a ship channel of sufficient capacity to accommodate the wants of commerce." No less credit should go to those pioneers who set out to make such a channel a reality.

The Mississippi River is a silt-bearing and delta-forming stream. For the lower several hundred miles it flows through deep beds of its own deposits. As it nears the Gulf of Mexico, it naturally tends to throw off branches from the main stem. Then the branches subdivide into smaller branches, and these still further subdivide (Fig. 1) until the individual outlets to the Gulf are of small capacity when compared to the main river.

There is evidence that this tendency has existed for centuries. The Atchafalaya River, 322 miles above the mouth of the Mississippi and for centuries a major outlet, is still in existence; and, in conjunction with the Atchafalaya Floodway

---

[1] Chf., Operations Div., New Orleans Dist., Corps of Engrs., New Orleans. La.

during a superflood, it may carry as much as 40% of the flow of the Mississippi
at the latitude of Old River. Other waterways, such as bayous Plaquemine,
Lafourche, Manchac, St. John, and Bienvenue, which at one time were major
outlets, are, with the exception of Bayou Plaquemine, no longer connected to the
parent stream because of the construction of main-line Mississippi River levees.

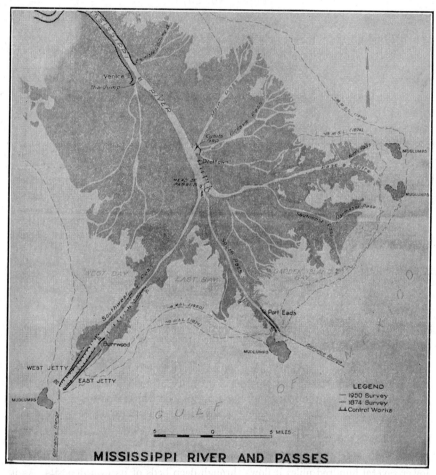

MISSISSIPPI RIVER AND PASSES

FIG. 1.—MISSISSIPPI DELTA AREA, SHOWING LOCATION OF PRINCIPAL WORKS FOR
NAVIGATION IMPROVEMENTS

At the head of Bayou Plaquemine a navigation lock provides passage between the
Bayou and the Mississippi.

Below Old River the Mississippi is relatively stable. During times of flood
it is confined largely to its natural bed as the levees closely parallel the river
as far downstream as Venice, the end of the levee system, 84 miles below New
Orleans and 11 miles above the Head of Passes in Louisiana (Fig. 1).

New Orleans, A Strategic Port.—The site for the future city of New Orleans was selected by the French about 1718. This location on the Mississippi was chosen because of its closeness to Lake Pontchartrain and the presence of Bayou St. John which flowed from the river and emptied into Lake Pontchartrain. At that time commerce and travel were largely upstream and downstream on the Mississippi above New Orleans and east through Lake Pontchartrain and along the Gulf coastal waters to Mobile, Ala., and Pensacola, Fla.

New Orleans today, with its 16 miles of general cargo wharves located at the intersection of the Mississippi River and the Intracoastal Waterway, is the second port of the United States in dollar value of foreign commerce handled. Through its harbor and to the Head of Passes 95 miles downstream, the Mississippi provides a natural navigable channel at low water 40 ft or more deep and not less than 1,800 ft wide.

River Discharge Through Passes.—Below New Orleans the river flows into the Gulf of Mexico through six natural outlets (Fig. 1). The upper two, Baptiste Collette and the Jump, are relatively small and together handle less than 5% of the total floodwaters which pass the city. The other four in order of size are Cubits Gap which at a mean flood stage carries about 13% of the total flow of the Mississippi; South Pass, 14%; Southwest Pass, 32%; and Pass a Loutre, 36%.

Major works of improvement have been confined to South and Southwest passes, and these alone are navigable for ocean-going shipping. Some of the other passes, however, are used by small fishing craft and vessels engaged in petroleum operations. In its original condition neither South Pass nor Southwest Pass was suitable for deep draft navigation. South Pass was obstructed by bars at the head and foot, the maximum depth of water being about 9 ft. In the pass itself the waterway was not less than 19 ft deep and from 500 to 1,000 ft wide. The length of the pass before prolongation by the jetties was 11.3 miles.

Southwest Pass was also obstructed by bars at the head and foot which provided about 9 ft of water, the same as at South Pass. In Southwest Pass proper, depths varied from 19 ft to more than 100 ft; and the width, from 1,200 ft to in excess of 1 mile. Before construction of the jetties the pass was 15 miles long.

Delta Characteristics.—During periods of flood the banks of the passes are subject to overflow to a depth of from a few inches to possibly a foot. The entire land area in this vicinity is constantly settling, but sediment is generally deposited on the banks during flood periods in quantities sufficient to maintain uniform heights of bank and at a rate approximately equal to the general subsidence.

The banks of both South and Southwest passes are kept intact, care being taken to maintain at all times sufficient strength of bank to prevent break-through or crevasses. A number of small unregulated outlets 50 to 100 ft wide and from 2 to 6 ft deep are maintained through the banks for the purpose of supplying the adjacent bay areas with silt transported by the river water during times of flood.

Below the Head of Passes few trees exist but the land is generally covered with marsh grass and, except for the grazing of a few scrub cattle, is worthless from an agricultural standpoint. In this area oil production operations are proceeding on an increasing scale. Recently also, a large sulfur dome has been discovered, and plans are under way for its development.

Early Attempts Toward Better Navigation

The first attempt to improve the passes for navigation was made in 1836 and 1837. The federal appropriations for those years, totaling $285,000, were expended in an attempt to secure a satisfactory navigable channel through Southwest Pass bar by using an ordinary bucket drag. No permanent improvement was effected, as a single storm destroyed all trace of the work that had been done.

No further effort was exerted until 1852 when an appropriation of $75,000 was made "to open a ship channel of sufficient capacity to accommodate the wants of commerce." A contract was entered into and an attempt made to secure a channel across the bar, 18 ft deep and 300 ft wide. The harrowing and dragging process proved successful and an 18-ft-deep channel was maintained for a year.

Engineering Boards Are Utilized.—Although this method did prove successful, no additional funds were provided until 1856 when $330,000 was appropriated and a board of engineers was appointed. This board recommended the stirring of the bottom, the construction of jetties in Southwest Pass and Pass a Loutre, and the closure of other outlets. Work was commenced at the lower end of Southwest Pass by building a jetty along the east side 1 mile long. This jetty was a sheet-pile structure of light construction; and shortly after being started it was seriously damaged by a storm, so the plan was abandoned. Dragging and stirring of the bottom were again attempted and an 18-ft channel was secured and maintained as long as the operation was in progress. Intermittent stirring was continued until the War Between the States stopped all further work.

In 1871 a board of engineers reported as feasible the construction of a ship canal, with lock, from the Mississippi River near Fort St. Phillip, 77 miles below New Orleans, to the Gulf of Mexico. A minority report recommended jetties. However, no work along either line was performed.

Up to 1875 the channel across the Southwest Pass bar had been inadequate for the needs of the port of New Orleans so in that year Congress appointed another board which recommended the construction of jetties at South and Southwest passes at estimated costs of $5,342,000 and $8,253,000, respectively.

Substitute Cure Offered.—After considerable controversy as to the best means of securing a satisfactory channel from the river to the Gulf—that is, a jetty system versus a canal and lock—Congress in 1875 accepted the proposition of Captain Eads of St. Louis, Mo., wherein he was

> "* * * to secure by the construction of jetties and auxiliary works and maintain for 20 years a channel 26 feet by 200 feet having through it a central depth of 30 feet without regard to width * * *."

—all for the sum of $8,000,000.

Eads' original proposal had been to improve Southwest Pass (Fig. 1) as he believed that that pass offered the better possibilities and would provide a more satisfactory channel. Congress, however, insisted on improving South Pass so the Captain had his choice of either working on the latter outlet or missing the opportunity altogether.

In the light of later events it is probably just as well that the jetty experiment was first attempted in South Pass. Since that pass was the smaller, less work and expense were required to obtain the desired channel dimensions. Also, South Pass served as a model when some 25 years later it was found desirable to provide a still larger and deeper route through Southwest Pass.

EADS' PRACTICAL SOLUTION

Why was Eads so confident that he could secure and maintain for 20 years a 26-ft channel from deep water in the South Pass to deep water in the Gulf? He had studied the jetty systems of Europe and there had found both successes and failures. At no place, however, had he seen works of the magnitude that would be required at the passes. In spite of this Eads believed in his reasoning and plan so strongly that he was willing to make a "no cure, no pay" contract with the United States Government. In his pamphlet entitled "Jetty System Explained," published in July, 1874, he advanced his arguments on "Why the bar will not advance if jetties are constructed."

Basis of Jetty Idea.—Eads contended that, in the course of nature, levees, jetties, or natural banks, were formed on each side of the passes; that these natural banks and the bar itself advance seaward at the same rate; and that the bar moves out not as the cause, but as the effect, of the bank or jetty building of the river. By comparing two surveys of Southwest Pass made some 40 years apart he noted that in both cases there was a distance of $7\frac{1}{3}$ miles between a point where the banks were well established and the crest of the bar. He wrote: "* * * since the white man has known the river this distance between the bar and the narrow and completed banks of the Pass above has been the same, viz: $7\frac{1}{3}$ miles."

It was evident to Eads that, as the natural banks or jetties advanced, the upstream face of the bar eroded and this material was deposited further out in the Gulf. He believed that the volume and current which passed out between the finished banks were so great that the bar could not form any nearer than $7\frac{1}{3}$ miles distant and that, if by artificial means the natural banks were suddenly extended $7\frac{1}{3}$ miles to the crest of the bar, the velocity at the outer end of the jetties would be nearly as great as it had been back in the narrow section of the pass where the banks were well formed and as much as 60 ft of water existed in the channel.

Eads estimated that, at the rate the completed banks and bar had been advancing, it would require 178 years for the river to extend its banks from their present location out to the crest of the bar. He was certain that, if man should do in 3 or 4 years what would require the river 178 years to do, centuries would pass before the bar would reappear because it would have to be located at least 7 miles beyond the artificial jetties, where the water is several hundred feet deep.

Conflict of Theories.—The then Chief of Engineers, Maj. Gen. A. A. Humphreys, Hon. M. ASCE, was a foe of the jetty system. He believed that the bar would form directly in front of the jetties.

Although Eads' theory was wrong and General Humphreys was right, the work of Eads proved a success. This apparent contradiction was due to the fact that neither of these engineers gave sufficient consideration to the littoral current which generally flows from east to west, roughly normal to the mouth of the passes.

Eads started construction of the east and west jetties, South Pass, in 1875. As built they were parallel, 1,000 ft apart and curved slightly to the west to intersect the littoral current at right angles. Originally the jetties were to extend to the −30-ft contour in the Gulf, but as actually built they stopped in about 15 ft of water.

Operations Affected by Experience.—The jetties were constructed of willow-brush mattresses and stone. The mats were built in sections from 100 to 150 ft long, towed into place, anchored, and then ballasted with sufficient riprap to cause them to sink. They were approximately $2\frac{1}{2}$ ft thick and varied in width from 20 ft to 80 ft. The wider mats were generally sunk first, the smaller sections being placed so as to form tiers thereon. The top mats had an elevation of approximately 2 ft above mean Gulf level.

Then the structure was topped with a layer of riprap several feet thick. This stone was brought down the Ohio and Mississippi rivers by barges from Indiana. Later, ships from many foreign ports discharged their ballast in the form of gravel and riprap at Port Eads, and this material was incorporated into the works.

During the first 2 years several severe storms seriously damaged the jetties, especially the outer ends. Larger stones up to 3 tons in weight were then used, but these too did not prove satisfactory; so Eads switched to concrete as ballast and also used it to form the top course, or cap, of the jetty. This cap was constructed by casting in place concrete blocks which weighed from 12 to 268 tons. The blocks, constructed end to end, formed a continuous wall which proved effective against displacement by waves. The top elevation ranged from 5 ft to 9 ft above mean low water.

It was soon apparent that the 1,000-ft width between jetties was too great. To obtain additional contraction and at the same time protect the jetties against the scouring action of the river, submerged groins or spur dikes were constructed on the riverside of, and normal to, the jetties. These groins spaced 500 ft to 800 ft apart were composed of layers of brush mats similar to those used in the jetties. They reduced the channel width to about 650 ft and greatly increased the scouring action of the river.

In obtaining the channel across the bar approximately 7,600,000 cu yd of material was removed by scour and dredging, the latter however accounting for only about 1% of the total. By July, 1879, 4 years after work was started, a channel of project width and depth was obtained and the 20-year period of maintenance commenced.

Modifications Insure Final Success.—Although Eads had reached his first objective, his troubles by no means were over. He was experiencing difficulty in maintaining project dimensions in the pass proper. At the head of South Pass there were two channels, neither of which was of sufficient size. It was necessary to close one of these and enlarge the other. Several wide and shoal reaches in the pass had to be contracted by spur dikes; and Grand Bayou, a large side outlet taking 25% of the flow of South Pass, had to be closed. In an attempt to prevent Southwest Pass and Pass a Loutre from enlarging at the expense of South Pass, Eads constructed submerged-brush mattress sills across the head of those passes, but they had no appreciable effect on the flow.

At the lower end of South Pass he built inner jetties which connected the ends of the spur groins built during the first years of his operations. Today only these inner works are maintained; the outer jetties and groins have long since subsided beneath the surface of the water and are completely covered with silt and mud.

A still further serious difficulty arose in 1891 when a major crevasse occurred in Pass a Loutre (Fig. 1). This reduced the discharge through South Pass to the lowest point on record. Several attempts were made to close the opening but without success. Finally it partly closed of its own accord, and by 1907 the flow through South Pass was back to its original volume.

As time went on Eads also had trouble maintaining depths across the bar which persisted in forming just seaward off the end of the jetties, and not 7 miles out as he had predicted. During the latter half of the Eads maintenance period the axis of the bar channel was inclined 36° 30′ eastward (Fig. 1)—which made the jetty system at South Pass a complete success. The littoral current moving from east to west kept this channel in the Gulf free from the silt brought down by the river and permitted the bar to form only partly in front and to the west of the axis of the jetty channel.

The maintenance period of 20 years was extended by 572 days, the total number of days that project dimensions did not prevail during the period. The deficiencies were: In South Pass proper, 198 days; jetty channel, 330 days; and bar channel, 44 days. The Eads contract ended in January, 1901, and since that time South Pass has been maintained by the Corps of Engineers.

IMPROVEMENTS IN SOUTHWEST PASS SINCE 1900

As a result of the success at South Pass, ocean commerce to the port of New Orleans increased at a rapid rate, creating the need for a deeper channel to meet the growing demands of navigation. A board of engineers in 1898 recommended the expenditure of $13,000,000 for building two parallel jetties at the foot of Southwest Pass, raising the natural banks of the pass with levees to prevent any water from flowing overbank, placing a sill across the head of Pass a Loutre, and constructing two dredges.

The only action Congress took on this recommendation was to appoint another board. The new board in 1899 recommended a project to secure a 35-ft by 1,000-ft channel through Southwest Pass and across the bar by dredging, by constructing sills across all nonnavigable outlets, and by purchasing a large dredge—all at an estimated cost of $6,000,000 with annual maintenance of $150,000. These recommendations were adopted in 1902, the act further providing that the details of the work might be modified at the discretion of the Secretary of War.

Again, Jetties and Dikes.—Jetty construction was started in 1904 and completed in 1908, the lengths of east and west jetties being 21,000 ft and 15,000 ft, respectively, with the outer ends spaced 3,600 ft apart, stopping in 10 ft to 12 ft of water. The construction was practically the same as that used at South Pass, brush mats ballasted with stone and topped with a concrete cap. As a result of the jetties and annual dredging, the depth over the bar increased from 9 ft to 20 ft, an amount far short of that expected.

During the period from 1908 to 1912 the bar advanced 2,400 ft and the jetties were extended approximately 3,200 ft. This work did not result in attainment of project dimensions, but depths across the bar did increase slightly.

In addition to extending the jetties, spur dikes were constructed (Fig. 2) in the lower 7 miles of the pass contracting the width to about 3,000 ft. The objective was to secure higher velocities and thereby greater scouring action. Anticipated results, however, did not follow largely because the flow through the pass was decreasing during the period.

Between 1917 and 1921 parallel inner bulkheads consisting of sheet piles, brush, and rock were constructed (Fig. 3) in the lower 5 miles of the pass reducing the width to about 2,400 ft. The jetties were also extended about 1,000 ft.

The lesson learned at South Pass had not been heeded and from the beginning of construction at Southwest Pass all dredging on the bar had been directed toward securing a channel on the prolongation of the jetty channel. Finally, in 1921 it was decided to incline the axis of the bar channel 35° to the eastward (Fig. 1). As in the case of South Pass 25 years earlier, this decision was the determining factor in the ultimate success of the Southwest Pass Project.

FIG. 2.—TYPICAL CREOSOTED-PILE SPUR DIKE, BUILT TO REDUCE WIDTH OF CHANNEL BETWEEN SOUTHWEST PASS JETTIES

Dredging Also Helps.—Even after the reduction in width of the lower jetty channel to 2,400 ft, conditions were not entirely satisfactory, and in 1923 the lower 8 miles of the pass was further reduced in width to 1,750 ft. This last contraction, combined with 7,000,000 cu yd of dredging, resulted in a 35-ft channel at the foot of the pass and across the bar. In the pass proper between 1926 and 1935 there was generally a 1,000-ft-wide 35-ft-deep channel with central depths of 42 ft to 60 ft. In the hope of still greater improvement on the bar the lower 2 miles of the pass in 1934 was further reduced in width to 1,420 ft but no material improvement resulted.

The surface width of 1,420 ft was determined by using South Pass, which was largely self-maintained, as a model. This width was also the average for the upper half of Southwest Pass where excellent channel conditions existed. In 1939 the reach between mile 10, the halfway point in the pass, and mile 18 was contracted by spur-pile dikes to this theoretically correct width. Thus a uniform width now prevails from just below the head to the foot of the jetty channel.

From time to time when contraction works were placed in the pass some channel dredging was also performed to compensate for the loss in cross-sectional area caused by the contraction works. Without dredging the discharge through the pass might have been materially reduced. In 1940 and 1941, 13,600,000 cu yd was dredged from the channel between mile 10 and the Gulf. This cut was dredged to −50 ft over a bottom width of 400 ft, the dredged material being placed between the dikes and over bank.

Attendant Work at Head of Passes.—During the time that operations were in progress at the lower end of Southwest Pass, other work was being done in the Head of Passes area (Fig. 4). One of the problems has been the continuous struggle to keep the proper distribution of flow through the major outlets. This has been more difficult because the main stem of the Mississippi branches three ways

FIG. 3.—SOUTHWEST PASS ON RIGHT LOOKING DOWNSTREAM; EAST JETTY, INNER BULKHEAD, AND SPUR DIKES SHOWN

simultaneously. It is not subject to theoretical analysis and has been to a large extent solved by cut-and-try methods.

From time to time sills have been placed across the head of all passes to help regulate the flow. The sills across the head of South and Southwest passes were later removed. Apparently it made little difference whether they were in or out, as channel conditions through the passes themselves have been the controlling factor in determining the discharge of each outlet.

Model studies have indicated that the sill across the head of Pass a Loutre has prevented that pass from taking its share of the heavy bed load and also that the discharge would not increase if the sill were removed. Two major breaks occurred in this sill between 1950 and 1952, and subsequent surveys indicated that heavy shoaling resulted just below the sills. Since 1948 the percentage of flow through the pass has declined slightly, South Pass apparently gaining the water lost by Pass a Loutre.

In 1918 spur dikes were built along the left bank of the main stem between Pass a Loutre and Cubits Gap. These structures were intended to deflect water from Pass a Loutre into Southwest Pass. In 1923 and 1935 they were extended several hundred feet, and additional dikes were built at the lower end of the system. These works possibly were effective to a small degree.

West Headland, a timber pile, brush, and rock-filled structure, was constructed in 1924 in an effort to deflect a part of the South Pass flow into Southwest Pass. However, no special changes followed this construction.

Fig. 4.—Aerial View Looking Down South Pass from Head of Passes, Showing Typical Delta Formation—Southwest Pass on Right and Pass a Loutre on Left

Further Deepening in View.—A board of engineers in 1939 recommended a 40-ft project from New Orleans to the Gulf of Mexico. Since an excellent channel exists between the Head of Passes and New Orleans, all the work necessary will be concentrated at the Head of Passes, in Southwest Pass proper, and in Southwest Pass jetty and bar channel (Fig. 5).

This project was authorized in 1945, but construction funds have not yet been made available (1952). In general, the work will probably consist of one or two small dike systems in the pass proper and some 16,000,000 or more yards of dredging at different locations between Pilottown and the 40-ft contour in the Gulf of Mexico. When funds are made available, the work can be completed in approximately 12 to 18 months.

In addition to the initial dredging, it will probably be necessary to perform heavy maintenance dredging in the pass proper for a period of several years. This work should insure that the desired project dimensions are well established.

MAINTENANCE

Channel dredging constitutes one of the major items of maintenance. A sea-going hopper dredge generally works from 4 to 6 months annually, its operations being confined largely to the lower half mile of the jetty channel and

FIG. 5.—AERIAL VIEW LOOKING UP SOUTHWEST PASS DURING FLOOD STAGE, WHICH ACCOUNTS FOR VARYING DEGREES OF DISCOLORATION OF GULF WATER

the bar channel. A few weeks' dredging is done in the entrance to Southwest Pass and at the Head of Passes; and, during recent years, the South Pass bar channel has required about 10 days of dredging annually.

The sea-going hopper dredge *Langfitt* which is owned and operated by the New Orleans District has two 30-in. centrifugal pumps and 3,100-cu yd hopper capacity. Average daily production varies from 50,000 cu yd to 80,000 cu yd depending on material encountered and the method of operation. When operating in the lower jetty channel and on the bar during medium and high river stages, the dredge agitates—that is, the material is pumped up and discharged into the hoppers and allowed to flow back into the river or Gulf, where the currents are sufficient to carry most of it in suspension until it clears the channel.

It is desirable to commence dredging when the Carrollton gage reaches 10 ft or 12 ft on a rising stage. The operation continues until about the same stage on a falling river.

Permanence of Jetties Secured.—Jetty maintenance represents a major item of cost. Because of the nature of the bottom material the jetties are constantly subsiding, necessitating a major restoration program every 6 to 10 years. Average subsidence has varied from 2 in. to 6 in. annually, depending on location along the jetty.

FIG. 6.—EAST JETTY, SOUTHWEST PASS, LOOKING UPSTREAM, WITH DERRICK PLACING JETTY STONE

Storm waves play no appreciable part in jetty deterioration; however, some consideration is given to wave attack in that the East Jetty of Southwest Pass which is subject to greater attack is maintained on the whole as a more substantial structure than is the West Jetty (Fig. 1). The East Jetty is maintained by adding 3-ton to 10-ton stones to the sides and top (Fig. 6). Subsidence of the structure has lowered the concrete cap to where it is now generally below the water surface. Until recently the cap served as a core or seal to prevent loss of river water through the structure. Some consideration has been given to placing hot asphalt mix on top of the submerged concrete cap and in the voids between the top jetty stones. This should prove effective as a seal and more economical than concrete.

With the exception of the outer end, the West Jetty is maintained by grout bonding 4-ton to 20-ton precast concrete blocks to the existing concrete cap.

The outer 1,700 ft, where greater wave attack might be expected, has been brought up to grade by construction similar to that used on the East Jetty.

The pile-dike contraction works (Fig. 2) require some maintenance. Teredo offers no problem with creosoted piling, but the salt air affects hardware used in the structures. Ships and other craft cause some damage, and subsidence of the general area and structures have recently made it necessary to raise a number of dikes by driving new piling or by splicing extension piles to the original structure.

Since 1922 approximately 440,000,000 tons of cargo has moved through the passes while the cost of maintenance for this period has been $21,756,000, or about $0.05 per ton of cargo moved.

HYDRAULICS OF THE PASSES

South and Southwest passes as extended by jetties are 15 and 20 miles, respectively, in length (Fig. 1). These lengths have been in existence since 1879 (72 years) in the case of South Pass and since 1921 (31 years) in the case of Southwest Pass. At present there are no recognizable indications that jetty extensions will be required in the near future.

Discharge Distribution.—The discharge through the main outlets is measured at frequent intervals during periods of high water. Since 1925 the percentage of discharge through South Pass has been relatively uniform, varying only by some 3.8% of the total water passing Pilottown.

In Southwest Pass and Pass a Loutre the variation has been approximately twice that of South Pass. The larger variation in these two passes has no doubt been caused by the operations which have been carried on in Southwest Pass. With the exception of the flood periods of 1945 and 1946, Southwest Pass during the last high water carried the smallest percentage of flow in its history, whereas South Pass carried the largest percentage on record.

At the crest of the 1951 high water, average cross-sectional velocities at the foot of South and Southwest passes were 6.3 ft per sec and 4.7 ft per sec, respectively.

Sediment.—During flood periods the Mississippi transports a vast sediment load. Some authorities have estimated that material in suspension in Southwest Pass during a considerable number of days of an average annual flood will exceed 2,000,000 tons. In addition to the suspended matter it has been estimated that roughly 50,000 cu yd of heavier material moves downstream along the bottom of the pass. Much of this latter material stops when it reaches salt water which during flood periods forms a very effective barrier just outside the ends of the jetties. Bottom samples taken at several locations in the New Orleans District during the major flood of 1937 indicated that more than 98% would pass a 48-mesh sieve and that 23% to 36% would pass the 200-mesh sieve.

Material in suspension has little direct effect on channel conditions. It is transported and deposited to the west of the entrance channels at the foot of both South and Southwest passes.

Bed-load material, which fortunately is a small fraction of the total material in transport, is deposited at the Head of Passes and in the lower jetty and bar channels of Southwest Pass. In South Pass, where velocities are greater, it is largely discharged onto the bar and from there moved westerly by river and salt-water currents.

The velocity of fresh-water currents at the foot of Southwest Pass is not sufficient to carry any appreciable quantity of the bed load past the ends of the jetty to where salt-water currents could continue its movement to the west. Therefore, it is necessary to dredge annually at the foot of Southwest Pass.

Problem of Sludge.—In addition to the bed-load material another cause of shoaling is the presence of what is locally known as "sludge" or "slush." This material occurs just after the river starts to rise and also as it approaches low water on a falling stage. Formation of slush takes place when the salt water in the pass comes in contact with the fine clays carried in suspension by the outflowing fresh water.

This material, before too much settlement and consolidation has taken place, weighs about 65 lb to 70 lb to the cubic foot. Generally it lies in a relatively level layer along the bottom of the channel. However, at times it might build up to within 10 ft or 15 ft of the surface. It is very effective in causing ships to slow down and has even been known to cause vessels to stop completely, much to the confusion of the crew who, on heaving the lead line, may find 40 ft of water, yet their vessel drawing 25 ft is unable to proceed.

Suspended matter placed in a container may require 20 to 30 days before showing signs of settling. Eventually this material consolidates into a stiff blue, so-called marine, clay.

Occasional low-water shoaling may follow infrequent storms from the west, when waves move material from the bar into the bar channel. In such cases dredging is not required as shoaling is generally not severe and salt-water currents, assisted by the scouring action of ships' propellers, soon restore satisfactory channel depths.

Salt-Water Intrusion.—Investigations of salinity conditions in the Lower Mississippi River reveal that, below certain fresh-water discharges from the upper river, there is intrusion of dense salt water from the Gulf of Mexico through South and Southwest passes. The intrusion is in the form of a wedge with a fairly well-defined interface which moves upstream under the outward fresh-water flow.

At stages of 10 ft to 12 ft or greater at Carrollton (corresponding to a flow of 800,000 cu ft per sec), the Gulf water is held just outside the outer end of the jetty channel by the strong river current. At mean low water, about 3 ft above mean sea level on the Carrollton gage (a discharge of 300,000 cu ft per sec), the salt-water interface is normally located at the Head of Passes. At lower stages the salt water proceeds upstream, the extent of its progress depending on the duration and amount of low-water river discharge. In October, 1936, the upper end of the salt-water wedge was about 22 miles above New Orleans, or about 145 miles from the Gulf, at a depth of approximately 120 ft below the water surface.

In locating the wedge, it is observed that the salinity content changes from fairly fresh water, several hundred parts per million of chlorine, to dense Gulf water, 10,000 ppm to 15,000 ppm of chlorine, within a depth of a few feet. The line of demarcation between fresh and salt water, referred to as the "interface," is arbitrarily taken as the point at which a chlorine content of 5,000 ppm is observed.

Observations show that the entrance of salt water into the river is generally confined to South and Southwest passes, and that under normal wind and tide conditions no intrusion occurs through Cubits Gap, Pass a Loutre, or any of the other shallow outlets. This upstream flow may at times occupy one third or more of the lower cross section of a pass and may move at a velocity of 1 ft per sec or more. Discharge observations are seldom taken in the passes during low water; and, when they are made, care must be taken to distinguish between upstream and downstream flow.

Littoral Current.—Today, before any major coastal project is planned, more or less extensive investigations and studies are made to determine the existence and the effect of the littoral currents and other ocean conditions on the proposed works. In the early days at the passes few such observations were made. Some of those interested in the matter spoke of coastal currents whereas others either denied that such a thing existed or belittled its effect. Eads was aware of, but apparently did not realize the extreme importance of, this westerly current.

After work was started in Southwest Pass, current observations were made from time to time. These have indicated that generally there is an east to west current of from 1 mile per hr to $1\frac{1}{2}$ miles per hr, which largely prevents river water from flowing in the navigation channels to the east of the bars at the feet of both South and Southwest passes. During times of flood the river water may spread out in a fan-shaped lens over the surface of this area (Fig. 5) but will seldom be found along the bottom of the bar channel.

THE BAR

Before jetty construction was started in Southwest Pass, there was a maximum depth of about 9 ft over the crest of the bar. The crest was some 5.5 miles seaward of the −35-ft contour in the pass; the forward face of the bar had a much steeper slope, the −35-ft contour in the Gulf being only 2,000 ft seaward of the crest. Between 1905 and 1909, or about the time of the first jetty construction in Southwest Pass, the −35-ft contour in the Gulf advanced 2,300 ft, or at a rate of 580 ft per yr. Between 1909 and 1921, the year the last jetty extension was made, the advance was from 300 ft per yr to 650 ft per yr.

Since 1922, the year after the last jetty extension and the year the lateral entrance channel was opened, the maximum advance has been 200 ft annually, the average being about 130 ft. In recent years the bar has had no well-defined crest, the minimum depth across it varying from 9 ft to 12 ft over a distance of approximately 1.5 miles.

As Gen. Max C. Tyler, M. ASCE, in 1932 pointed out in his report on Southwest Pass:

"* * * the crest of the bar will continue to advance into the Gulf, most rapidly at a point to the west of the axis of the jettied channel, less rapidly to the east of that axis. A time will come when the loss of head over the bar, or, what is the same thing, the superelevation of the outgoing fresh water above the Gulf level, will be sufficient to overbalance all salt water in the channel. The salt water currents in and across the channel will then be obliterated and the channel will discharge fresh water for its full depth. It will then shoal, probably very rapidly."

This change will probably not take place suddenly. It is expected that the routine surveys and observations carried on at the passes will give the necessary indications, and possibly sufficient warning, to permit extending the jetties or taking some other remedial action.

Personnel.—The passes of the Mississippi River are a part of the Rivers and Harbors Project, Mississippi River, Baton Rouge, La., to the Gulf of Mexico. All operations were under the general supervision of the Chief of Engineers, Washington, D. C., and the division engineer, Lower Mississippi Valley Division, Vicksburg, Miss. The district engineer, New Orleans District, has direct supervision of the project. The writer, as chief of the Operations Division, New Orleans District, is responsible for the maintenance of the navigation channels and structures at the passes.

AMERICAN SOCIETY OF CIVIL ENGINEERS
Founded November 5, 1852

TRANSACTIONS

Paper No. 2649

RIVER TRANSPORTATION DEVELOPMENT

By Alex. W. Dann,[1] A. M. ASCE, and Carl B. Jansen,[2] M. ASCE

Synopsis

For present purposes, the scope of this paper is restricted to the transportation of people and commodities on the Ohio and Mississippi rivers and the tributaries thereof, and to the era beginning with the discovery of these rivers by the Caucasian race. This period of time, which people today call the "civilized" era, may be considered to fall into three general, although heavily overlapping, periods, which may be termed the eras of muscle power, steam power, and diesel power.

Era of Muscle Power

The first of the "muscle power" craft was the flatboat, essentially a box, sometimes provided with a rake fore and aft, but always difficult to steer. Its first use on record was in 1765. It drew little water and was small in size, usually around 40 tons to 50 tons in capacity. Some records indicate, however, that experiments were made with lengths up to 150 ft and loads up to 1,400 tons requiring more than 8-ft draft. This was a "one-way" craft—at the downstream end of its journey it was usually dismantled and the materials were used for housing.

Disturbed by lack of maneuverability and the economic waste of no upstream return, coupled with an increased demand for upstream transportation, enterprising men were stimulated to devise the keelboat (Fig. 1). It steered better because of its shaped ends and was not as subject to disaster under stress of storm and grounding. Keelboats varied between 15 tons and 50 tons in cargo capacity, averaging less than 30 tons. Downstream commerce still exceeded upstream commerce. The keelboat was laboriously poled upriver by hand, aided at swift places by cordelling—the use of ropes attached to convenient bank or bar. Hand-over-hand pulling on the rope gave way to crude hand-made winches, which, in turn, were supplanted by a well-designed hand capstan which could be "dogged off" (held on a ratchet) to give the men a rest. Towpaths appeared along some sections of the river, used by men, horses, or mules pulling

---

[1] Exec. Vice-Pres., Dravo Corp., Pittsburgh, Pa.
[2] Pres., Dravo Corp., Pittsburgh, Pa.

on a rope attached in the middle third of the keelboat, rather than at the bow, to facilitate steering.

ERA OF STEAM POWER

The first steam craft to navigate any interior stream was the *New Orleans,* built in Pittsburgh, Pa., in 1811 by Robert Fulton. A replica, constructed in 1911 to celebrate the centennial of steamboating, shows her with side wheels (Fig. 2). There is still considerable difference of opinion, however, as to whether she was a side-wheeler or a stern-wheeler.

A new and vitally important development in engineering achievement on the rivers was marked by the *Washington,* built by Henry Shreve in 1816. Instead

FIG. 1.—RIVER SCENE, SHOWING FLATBOAT AND TWO KEELBOATS, ONE USING A SAIL FOR AUXILIARY POWER

of modeling the hull after Hudson River craft, he gave it a sharply curved bow and shallow draft to assure flotation on rather than in the water. Captain Shreve upset tradition further by installing machinery on deck and building another deck over it. Thus the first two-decker was born.

The machinery was equally revolutionary. Boilers were placed horizontally for the first time, delivering steam to horizontal high-pressure engines with oscillating pitmans. The weight of machinery and boilers was but 20% and fuel consumption, about 60% that of the *New Orleans.*

In the spring of 1817, the *Washington* made a round trip between Louisville, Ky., and New Orleans, La., in 41 days. This trip was the debut of general steam navigation in the Mississippi Valley. Shreve's designing ability marked the start of an era of riverboat engineering achievements which outpaced ocean steamship development for many years. In general, the river vessels used steam pressure up to three and four times that of contemporary coastwise and ocean-going ships and actually developed speeds superior to their salt-water kin.

Packets.—The "packetboat," carrying both passengers and freight on a self-propelled hull, held its leading position in the powerboat field until after the Civil War. Early engineering achievements were those famous packets, the *Natchez,* the *Robert E. Lee,* and the *J. M. White,* all of which made the upstream voyage from New Orleans to St. Louis, Mo., in less than 4 days. The *J. M. White* recorded the 2,300-mile round trip between St. Louis and New Orleans in 7 days, 15 hours, 9 min.

Packetboats were constantly growing in size, with more elaborate facilities to appeal to and attract passengers. However, channel limitations precluded greater draft, so the owners cast about for methods which would carry more

Fig. 2.—The *New Orleans,* First Steam Craft to Navigate Any Stream of Interior United States (This Replica Built in 1911 to Celebrate the Centennial of Steamboating)

freight with the same power. Several acquired unused power-driven boat hulls. Disastrous attempts were made to tow such hulls aft of packetboats. About 1865 some operators equipped the packets with a form of "knee" for pushing ahead, but usually the extra hull was taken "under the wing" or alongside—a method of accommodating added cargo dating back to the inception of steamboating.

Towboats.—"Towing," as the term is used on the inland rivers—combining barges into a compact mass and pushing from behind with a "towboat," originated in the Ohio River coal traffic in the 1840's. The first towboats had no towing knees. Indeed these were not used until about 1865. Many so-called "poolboats" towing coal on the Monongahela River in Pennsylvania even as late as 1875 to 1880 were not equipped with knees and operated "duck-pond style," with a barge lashed along each side of the propelling unit and the main tow forward of the two barges.

Development of the power unit for push towing, to which the name "towboat" was permanently applied, came slowly. The *Juniata*, 21 tons gross registered, built in Pittsburgh in 1841, is believed to be one of the first such vessels built exclusively for the towing of coal. The *Walter Forward* made a successful trip from Pittsburgh to Cincinnati, Ohio, in June, 1845.

The nineteenth century was a period of daring cut and try, marked by many failures and successes. Often, plans for a vessel existed only in the mind of the builder, although he might reduce them to paper after completion of the boat so that data would be available for future reference. Vessel depth was limited by the shallow channel, with the length and width restricted accordingly. Common ratios were length equal to 17 times the depth and 6 times the width. Through development of the hog rod with Sampson posts, a kind of truss construction, builders were able to increase this length-to-depth ratio to 35 to 1. Early hulls were provided with keels, later abandoned in favor of plain flat bottoms to cope with shallow channels and crossings. At the end of this initial period, about the time of the Civil War, there was little essential change in wooden-hull design. Shallow longitudinal bulkheads, acting as trusses to add to the stiffness of the hull, had already been developed. Much thought had been given also to the distribution of weights occasioned by concentrated loads of machinery, boilers, and fuel.

Improved Boilers.—Designers of equipment for the production of steam were confronted with the problems of weight on one hand and of steam-making capacity on the other. Many early boilers were upright and, whether upright or horizontal, were plain cylinders without internal flues. These were very short lived. The preferred fuel was usually bituminous coal, although certain of the early craft burned wood exclusively whereas others resorted to it in emergencies when the coal supply was exhausted. Single-flue boilers came into use before 1820, and double flues shortly thereafter.

Increased steam consumption on larger boats, and a limitation on the size of any boiler, necessitated the use of multiple boilers. By 1820 there was introduced what became known as the "western rivers" type of boiler, horizontal in construction, with two to five large flues. Forced draft in the stacks was used prior to 1850, but natural draft was preferred, because this resulted in less deterioration of stacks and boilers. In search of natural draft, stacks were built higher and higher until some of them wound up 90 ft above water level. Little change was observed until around 1890, when some steamboats were equipped with Scotch marine boilers, which had varying degrees of success. Steam gages were first added about 1840 and were made a federal regulation requirement in 1852. An old record indicates that in 1837, three fifths of the steam power available in the United States was on steamboats, and such engines possessed an average power rating $3\frac{1}{2}$ times larger than that for engines used in industry and on the railroads.

Side-Wheelers.—Until the end of the nineteenth century, power-driven boats on the rivers were usually equipped with steam engines using high-pressure steam. The early models were worked full stroke. However, Shreve's development of the cutoff demonstrated the economies associated therewith, and full stroking became restricted to emergencies only. The first side-wheeler had two wheels, one port and one starboard, both driven by a common steam engine. This arrangement did not work well, so each wheel was equipped with an independent engine. The first such side-wheeler on the Mississippi was the *United States*, built in 1819 at Jeffersonville, Ind., but equipped with foreign-built machinery. The first fully successful application of the principle took place on the side-wheeler *George Washington* at Cincinnati in 1825—again Shreve's idea (Fig. 3).

Stern Wheels Replace Side Wheels.—Some use was made in the 1860's of a split stern wheel, each wheel being driven by two engines, in the belief that better maneuverability would result. This idea gained little acceptance and was confined to a few low-water boats built with exceptionally wide hulls for shallow draft. The stern-wheel "delegation of power" was ultimately standardized through motivation by an engine on each side with cranks set at various angles to avoid dead center. Engine sizes grew to such a point that the packet *Eclipse*, built in 1852, had cylinders 36 in. in diameter with an 11-ft stroke.

FIG. 3.—FIRST SUCCESSFUL APPLICATION OF INDEPENDENT ENGINES FOR EACH WHEEL ON SIDE-WHEELER *GEORGE WASHINGTON*, BUILT IN 1825 BY HENRY SHREVE

A record is found of the installation of a double expansion, or compound engine, 16 in. by 32 in. with a 6-ft stroke on the steamboat *Clipper* built at Shousetown (now Glenwillard), Pa., in 1843. The first independent pair of compound engines appeared on the *Clipper No. 2*, built at Shousetown in 1846—two sets of 16-in. by 32-in. cylinders with a 7-ft stroke. Both of these ships, of course, were packets. The compound idea developed slowly. The *Great Republic*, built at Shousetown in 1867, had 28-in. by 56-in. cylinders with a 10-ft stroke. The first towboat with compound engines was the *John A. Wood*, built at Pittsburgh in 1870. Excessive weight held back universal adoption of the condensing equipment, although condensers date back to the 1830's. Compound-condensing towboats flourished only when shallow water ceased to be a problem.

By 1880 stern-wheel-driven power craft outnumbered side-wheelers on the Ohio River by 3 to 1. The largest of any era, and the most powerful in her day, was the *Sprague*, constructed in 1902. She was 276 ft long and 61 ft wide (Fig. 4), with a depth of 7.4 ft and registered horsepower of 1,600. The stern wheel had a diameter of 40 ft and a width of 40 ft, and in normal operations turned 8 rpm. This vessel moved fleets as large as fifty-six barges carrying 54,000 tons of cargo—downstream. The *Sprague* represented an outstanding example of engineering as to both size and strength. "Big Mamma," as the *Sprague* was affectionately known, continued in operation until 1949, when she was retired and presented to the City of Vicksburg, Miss., for use as a river museum. Her duties were taken over by the modern twin-screw, diesel-driven towboat *Esso Tennessee* (Fig. 5).

Screws Versus Side Wheels.—Screw propulsion was first introduced about 1850, but met with only nominal acceptance until about 80 years later. This was due, in part, to inertia and the limited understanding of this method of propulsion, with consequent inadequate steering ability when engines were in reverse. Of even greater importance, however, is the currently recognized fact that the propeller was not feasible in shallow water and probably never will be. On the other

FIG. 4.—AFFECTIONATELY KNOWN THROUGHOUT WATERWAYS AS "BIG MAMMA," RETIRED STERN-WHEELER *SPRAGUE* NOW RIVER MUSEUM AT VICKSBURG, MISS.

hand, the stern wheel was ideal for the shoals and sand bars characteristic of the precanalization era. The propeller developed rapidly as slack water became an accomplished fact—finally achieved through the series of navigation dams, concurrent channel dredging, and improvement on the Lower Mississippi River, with the resulting dependable depths of channel.

Today few towboats are built equipped with other than screw propulsion, in some cases augmented by the Kort nozzle, contraguide rudders, and improved design of both rudders and hull. These ships now maneuver and steer both ahead and astern with control far superior to that of any stern-wheeler. They have the additional advantage that the ratio of power astern to power ahead (for a twin-screw Kort nozzle-equipped towboat) is about 60% to 75% compared to 40% to 55% for the stern-wheeler.

Basically, the Kort nozzle (Fig. 6) is a steel ring, of airfoil section, encircling the propeller to guide the water to, through, and away from the propeller. It is so designed as to offer increased towing push in the order of 18% to 22% at normal towing speeds. Maneuverability is obtained by an arrangement of three rudders, with one aft of the nozzle for steering ahead and two forward for backing. In somewhat different fashion, the contraguide rudder increases the

FIG. 5.—*ESSO TENNESSEE*, TWIN SCREW, DIESEL POWERED, KORT NOZZLE EQUIPPED, WHICH TOOK
OVER DUTIES OF *SPRAGUE* IN FLEET OF ESSO STANDARD COMPANY

FIG. 6.—KORT NOZZLES, STEEL RINGS OF AIRFOIL SECTION, WHICH ENCIRCLE THE PROPELLERS OF MOST
MODERN RIVER TOWBOATS

performance of propellers by utilizing the normally wasted rotational energy of the discharged water. It does this by twisting the rudder blades into corkscrew-like airfoil sections opposing the rotation of the propeller.

ERA OF DIESEL POWER

When at the beginning of the twentieth century the principle of internal combustion was adopted for furnishing power, engines utilizing gasoline as fuel were soon widely accepted for towboat propulsion. Diesel development for this same purpose began in the 1920's; but, as this type of power was especially adaptable to propeller drive, progress was restricted until technical advances provided the successful application of screw propulsion. An era of sharply rising costs literally forced its acceptance. Savings in operating cost of diesel-powered towboats over steam-driven towboats, combined with research and development on hull shape and rudder design and location, have led to construction of boats with power far in excess of that formerly developed by steam. ·

Better channels in the Ohio River have allowed ready acceptance of draft up to 8½ ft, permitting the use of shallower tunnels and considerably more efficient application of power. The unprecedented demand for upstream towing before and during World War II gave the final impetus to the change-over—the stern-wheeler having been designed primarily for downstream loads.

Until about 1945 diesel engines were of the generally low-speed, reversible type and, having less than 300 rpm, were direct-connected to the propellers. An occasional and relatively costly variation of this method has been the diesel-electric drive. Over the past 10 years there has been a marked tendency to use nonreversing engines with speeds as high as 750 rpm, equipping them with reverse and reduction gears. Several of the newer boats may be rated up to 4,800 hp.

Some towboats have been built with one engine and propeller, but such construction has not gained momentum because of problems of maneuverability. Most of them use two engines and propellers, and some success has been achieved with triple-screw vessels, requiring a hull of greater width—which is necessary to provide space between the wheels so that one does not rob others of water.

As competitive transportation facilities, first railroads and then highways, began to take over passenger and express freight business, river transportation gradually was converted toward bulk freight movements. In 1916 Herbert C. Sadler published excellent studies highlighting advantages available to operators through better barge forms. His report was prepared for the United States Army, and a few barges were constructed with spoon-shaped ends as a result of these experiments. Unfortunately, the series was incomplete and received scant attention from commercial operators.

BARGE DEVELOPMENT FOLLOWS

At first river fleets were an accumulation of hastily constructed wooden barges, with little acknowledgment of resistance to motion through water. Design and construction of barges used on inland waterways paralleled the development of powerboat hulls. The problem of length-to-depth ratio was a limiting factor, especially since wood was the sole material of construction. Open-type barges were from 120 ft to 175 ft long and were quite limber when loaded. Additional stiffness achieved through full-deck or half-deck construction occasionally supplemented by hog rods or chains, increased this maximum length by 25 ft.

Scant attention was paid to rakes on these early timber barges primarily because loaded barges were customarily towed only downstream at speeds slightly faster than the river current. However, those barges designed of wood to carry upstream tonnage were given model bows, and their shape was carefully engineered. They were known as "model barges" and served as vehicles for transportation of iron ore from St. Louis to the early Pittsburgh steel mills. Similar problems were also mastered ingeniously.

In the late 1800's introduction of first iron and shortly afterward steel as building materials for hull construction simplified the problems somewhat. There was little variation from accepted length, depth, and breadth ratios until full-stream canalization became a reality, thus permitting greater draft and deeper hulls.

Metal Replaces Wood in Hulls.—The first American steamboat to use native iron for the hull was the packet *Valley Forge*, built in Pittsburgh in 1839. She was a failure commercially. The first iron-hull towboat on inland waterways was named the *Alex Swift*, built in 1873 near Cincinnati. Originally 151.3 ft in length, the hull was later extended to 178 ft. This vessel achieved success through the years and ran until April, 1912, when she burned at Cairo, Ill. Her iron hull served as a barge for many years after the fire. James Rees and Sons Company was responsible for the general introduction of steel-hull towboats, building the *Vesta* at Pittsburgh in 1902 for Jones and Laughlin, at cost price to demonstrate the worth of such construction. Previously Rees had built a number of steel hulls for the foreign rivers, as well as many steel-hull packets for domestic trade.

The switch from wood to metal in hulls was slow, caused, no doubt, by several economic factors including lower cost of wood, dwindling profits in river trade, and extreme buoyancy of timber construction. Steel did not gain important momentum until World War I. Riveted construction prevailed until the mid-1930's, after which welding became almost universal.

Barge Design Slow to Develop.—During these early years, slow progress was made in design of barges as compared with the improvement in motive power. However, when canalization of the Ohio River was completed in 1929—a milestone event which opened the Pittsburgh to New Orleans run to commercial development—it was soon realized that barge size, form, and fleeting formations represented important factors in ton-mile costs. The speed gain due solely to regrouping of the same five-barge fleet (Fig. 7) amounts to approximately ¾ mile per hr. This information was obtained during one of the early attempts at the 4,000-mile round trip between Pittsburgh and New Orleans. It served two useful purposes: (1) To demonstrate the feasibility of the run, and (2) to re-emphasize the necessity of further engineering development for efficient push towing.

Barge Fleets Formed.—The next step involved further model basin studies, continuing beyond the Sadler tests. These led to important changes in rake forms and barge groupings, the latest of which have been semi-integrated and integrated fleets. The former consists of barges having one square and one rake end, assembled in pairs, whereas the latter comprehends towing assemblies in which all but the leading and trailing units have two square ends and may be made up into a single unit of barge fleet formation, or into a single unit including both the barges and the towboat. These new arrangements have been favorably received by river operators. It is interesting to note that the earliest recorded

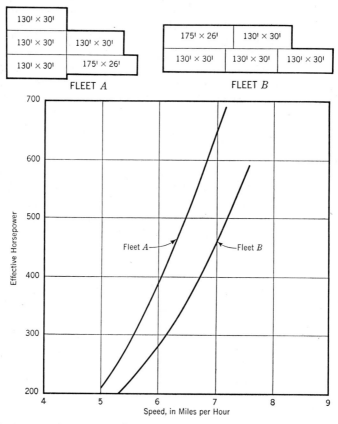

FIG. 7.—ECONOMIES IN ARRANGEMENT, COMPARING SAME FIVE BARGES IN TWO DIFFERENT TOWING FORMATIONS

use of integration appears to have been about 2,500 years ago, when the Chinese utilized this principle.

Greater permissible draft resulting from a better channel, with availability of increased power to push and maneuver, has led to the acceptance of barges with increased capacity. Some now in service can carry more than 3,000 tons of cargo.

Full integration, the current ultimate in engineering refinement, represents an accumulation of improvements in both fleet and propulsion units. A typical example is the Federal Barge Line's integrated tow, *Harry S. Truman,* which assembles into a 1,200-ft-long flotilla. It develops upstream speeds of about 8 miles per hr and downstream speeds of a maximum of 13 miles per hr.

Advantages of Integrated Fleets.—Interesting comparisons have been made (Fig. 8) of relative cargo-carrying efficiencies for eight diverse types of modern river fleets, based on information furnished by the barge line operators, and supplemented by certain dynamometer tests. Fleets I and II are involved in

Fleet No.	Fleet Assembly	Cargo in Short Tons	Cargo Ton-Miles per Shaft Horsepower
I	Fleet — 670' × 52' 0" Non-Integrated	5400	31.92
II	Fleet — 670' × 78' 0" Non-Integrated	8100	40.13
III	Fleet — 920' × 105' 0" Non-Integrated	14962	20.84
IV	Fleet — 920' × 105' 0" Part Non-Integrated — Part Semi-Integrated	15825	28.48
V	Fleet — 1120' × 105' 0" Semi-Integrated	22000	48.13
VI	Fleet — 1006' × 50' 0" Fully Integrated	9600	53.33
VII	Fleet — 1170' × 100' 0" Fully Integrated	25000	46.88
VIII	Fleet — 1200' × 54' 0" Entire Fleet Fully Integrated	12000	44.00

Symbol ⌀ Indicates Square End Rakes

FIG. 8.—FLEET MAKEUPS AND MODIFICATIONS, AS AFFECTING TRANSPORT ECONOMIES

coal towing in the Pittsburgh area. Fleet I is the standard Monongahela River fleet. Fleet II is a regrouping at Pittsburgh making two Ohio River fleets out of three Monongahela River fleets. All these coal barges are nonintegrated with relatively short rakes. The cargo ton-miles per shaft horsepower for the Monongahela River section of the run is 31.92 (fleet I). Regrouping at Pittsburgh to nine-barge fleets increases the cargo ton-miles to 40.13.

Fleets III and IV show the advantage returned by integrating the leading six barges only in a twelve-barge coal fleet of "jumbo" barges (195 by 35 by 11 ft) as used by the coal trade in Chicago, Ill. Fleet III, using all double-raked barges, returns a cargo ton-mile per shaft horsepower of 20.84 whereas fleet IV with the leading six barges integrated developed a cargo ton-mile per shaft horsepower of 28.48, an increase of 36%. The towboat used by fleets III and IV is not equipped with Kort nozzles, resulting in these relatively low values.

Fleet V is a fleet of fifteen "jumbo" barges integrated in locking units; that is, the first nine barges go through first, then the last six barges together with the towboat pass through on the second locking. This fleet demonstrates the value of size, power, integration, and modern rake ends, showing values for cargo ton-miles per shaft horsepower up to 48.13. The last three fleets are outstanding examples of integration and high-speed fleet designs.

Fleet VI, while the smallest, shows the highest value of cargo ton-miles per shaft horsepower—namely, 53.33—largely because it is a single-width fleet. A simi-

Fig. 9.—Modern, High-Speed, Two-Barge Integrated Petroleum Fleet with Capacity of 50,000 Bbl

lar but smaller formation is shown in Fig. 9. A bow-steering arrangement on the lead unit enables this fleet regularly to run the wild Atchafalaya River in either direction at full speed. It also has negotiated the restricted Illinois Waterway at full speed.

Fleet VII is probably the largest of the fully integrated fleets. It delivers cargo of up to 25,000 short tons and develops a cargo ton-mile per shaft horsepower of 46.88.

Fleet VIII is an outstanding example of full integration of both barges and towboat. In considering its very creditable performance of 44 cargo ton-miles per shaft horsepower it is well to bear in mind that, in the mixed freight trade, some water ballasting is required to bring all units to an even draft. No credit for this ballast is allowed in the performance data. If the fleet were used in bulk cargo trades, then the returned cargo ton-miles per shaft horsepower value would naturally be higher.

This comparison does not include a mixed barge fleet since such arrangements are seldom duplicated for barge size, barge arrangement, or other factors, and barges having wide variation in rake ends, many of inefficient design, must be accepted. It is probable that such a fleet will show a net return in the order of, or somewhat less than, fleet III.

It should be recognized that these data show highly specialized fleets using controlled barges in favorable fleeting arrangements and, with the single exception of fleet VIII, arranged for bulk cargoes in specific trades. They indicate the trend toward greater power and higher speed and also give an evaluation of the possible returns. The selected unit of cargo ton-miles per shaft horsepower offers an excellent measure of the engineering development that has been characteristic of design of craft for inland waterways.

It must be remembered that the values for cargo ton-miles per shaft horsepower recognize only operating returns of full load under free running service conditions. This survey is purely an engineering study and under no circumstances should the values be assigned to cost differences. The cost aspects of commercial towing are affected by many other elements, such as returning "light"; locking losses; loading and unloading time; navigational hazards including fog, bad weather, or "double tripping"; unusual channel conditions encountered during floods, low water, or ice; mechanical delays; length of voyage; loads with or against the current; and so forth. All these substantially reduce the net value of cargo ton-miles per round trip in varying degrees, depending on the trade. A range of from 20% to 40% of the engineering values would more closely approach average over-all operating returns, with 60% representing probable maximum under ideal return-load conditions.

Propelling Units Improved.—Paralleling developments in barge form and fleeting, important and progressive steps were taken toward increasing the efficiency of the propelling units. As a specific illustration, the towboat *Tri-State* was changed first from a naturally aspirated to a supercharged engine, without alteration of the propeller. Second, the propeller was changed to obtain the best results from the vessel as an open-screw ship. Finally, Kort nozzles were installed complete with new propellers so that in the over-all analysis the net productive push returnable at 7 miles per hr was changed from 20,000 lb to 40,000 lb, an increase of 100% in output for the same towboat. Similar progressive engineering alterations on the towboat *Peace* increased the 7-mile per hr productive push from 11,500 lb to 26,500 lb, a value 2.3 times the original. Gains of this character involve corrections to stern lines, repowering, and the addition of Kort nozzles.

MODERN RIVER TRANSPORTATION EQUIPMENT

Advances made in design, engineering, and construction of river transportation equipment demonstrate the ingenuity of this vigorous industry in its perpetual search for improved performance and lower costs. The modern diesel-powered towboat is a precision machine, carefully tailored to its specific job, and fitted with many innovations contributing to its dependability and safety. Kort nozzles with proper rudder arrangements (Fig. 6) give it increased pushing power and better maneuverability; pilot-house engine control eliminates the old telegraph system between pilot and engine room; ship-to-shore telephone improves traffic control; and radar helps to maintain around-the-clock schedules regardless of weather conditions.

In addition to the larger vessels of 2,000, 3,000, and even greater horsepower which operate throughout the inland waterways system, many smaller towboats perform vital tasks exactly suited to their capabilities. In the Ohio River coal trade, for instance, around-the-clock service is maintained to insure an uninterrupted flow of fuel for steel mills, utilities, and other industries.

FIG. 10.—LAUNCHING OF ONE OF FIRST HOPPER BARGES TO UTILIZE THE PRINCIPLE OF INTEGRATION, FOR HAULING COAL ON THE ILLINOIS RIVER

Keeping pace with towboat progress, naval architects and marine engineers have so refined barge design and application that each year finds a larger and wider use of water transportation throughout the entire industrial field. Petroleum continues to be a major cargo on the rivers, most of it moving in specially designed barges of great capacity. The oil industry, with large volume movements between refineries and distribution points, has become a leader in the use of the high-speed, integrated tow. A typical two-barge fleet is composed of twin 290-ft-long barges with a total cargo capacity of 50,000 bbl (Fig. 9).

The hopper barge, perennial work horse of the rivers (Fig. 10), maintains its numerical leadership principally because of the large tonnages of coal it feeds to the American industrial machine. In addition, it is called on to transport many other commodities and, when fitted with weather-tight covers, adds another function in moving dry and perishable cargo such as grain, sugar, and finished steel products. Streamlining has caught up with the hopper barge, as it has with many other things, and an integrated model was recently introduced which immediately demonstrated its advantages by appreciably improving towing efficiency.

Although not exactly a newcomer, the chemical industry is rapidly expanding and widening its use of barges in delivery of both raw materials and finished

Fig. 11.—One of a Fleet of Barges Specially Designed and Constructed to Transport Liquid Chlorine

products. Many notable design and engineering achievements have been recorded in specialized barges to transport such products as liquid chlorine (Fig. 11), hydrochloric acid, ammonia, and sulfuric acid. Indications are that the rivers will play an increasingly important role in solving the gigantic transportation problem of this growing industry.

In Retrospect, A Great Achievement

It is difficult to estimate the place which the inland rivers have occupied, since discovery of the Ohio by the English in 1671, in the lives of the people near their banks and in colonization and development—not alone of adjacent territory, but of the central and western country and the Pacific coastal area.

Some measure of the mass movement of families with all their possessions, floating down the Ohio River in flatboats and keelboats seeking adventure and a better life, is indicated by the fact that in 1807 more than 2,000 such craft reached New Orleans. Probably many more people used these rivers annually as great numbers of passengers stopped off to engage in farming, hunting, or trapping. For a long time, these streams were the only means of relatively safe transportation for the movement of people and freight throughout this midwestern country.

The flatboat, the keelboat, the packetboat, and the heavy transportation of coal southward each succeeded the other, and all of them, except a handful of packetboats, have disappeared from the river. Each disappearance is more or less natural when viewed in retrospect; but it is reasonable to state, particularly with respect to packetboats and long-distance coal transportation, that insufficiency of channel, together with large financial losses due to irregularity of movement and wrecks, may have been the primary cause.

One of the golden eras of the packetboat was between the year 1830 (when the Louisville and Portland Canal was opened) and 1855. Then came a succession of low-water years from which the packetboats never recovered. There was a partial redevelopment after the close of the Civil War; but, again, a gradual reduction in this activity continued until the first decade of the present century when few packets continued to exist. The competition provided by railroads and towboats with barges served to accelerate the decline of this picturesque period of marine activity. The record shows that the Ohio River carried out about 1,500,000 passengers and 2,500,000 tons of freight per yr in the early 1870's, whereas in 1950 Ohio River transportation of freight had reached about 42,800,000 tons.

The Ohio River was not available for unobstructed year-round navigation until 1929—two and one-half centuries after it was discovered by white men. The owners of private capital invested in river equipment have constantly sought methods of reducing costs, freely and successfully experimenting with every worthy development. In this towboat and freight-carrying era, river operators have been quick to build towboats of sufficient size and power to push flotillas of barges in sizes up to the capacity of available channels and locks.

Since completion of the 9-ft channel project on the Ohio River, progress in design and construction of bulk cargo carriers has been rapid. It is reasonable to anticipate equal or greater improvement in the next 25 years, concurrently with construction of high-lift dams, larger locks, and development of a contemplated 12-ft channel. Any normal transportation problems can be met by either standard or special equipment, as both builders and operators are constantly alert to the needs of shippers and the opportunities afforded by these waterways.

It may be stated that some equipment built for Lower Mississippi River service, particularly towboats, is too big for the Ohio River under present circumstances. Recognition of this situation is indicated by current studies of the Corps of Engineers, Department of the Army, with respect to increasing the project depth of the Ohio River from 9 ft to 12 ft.

Ever since the Ohio River was available for year-round dependable transportation, there has been a marked and increasing tendency, on the part of large receivers of bulk raw materials (Fig. 12), and large shippers of finished goods, to locate new plants along the banks of the rivers, obviously to take advantage of low-cost river transportation. The fighting of World War II or any other conflict does not lend itself to economic study. Nevertheless, it can be generally stated that the contributions made by the Ohio and Mississippi rivers and adjoining streams to the winning of World War II repaid the citizens of the United States for all the money invested in providing open-channel or slack-water navigation.

FIG. 12.—ELEVEN-BARGE TOW CONTAINING APPROXIMATELY 6,000 TONS OF SAND AND GRAVEL, ONE OF GREAT RIVER INDUSTRIES

Some support may be found for this statement in that 4,031 combat and supply vessels were built by inland shipbuilding yards for use at sea, a feat in support of overburdened coastwise shipyards which could not have been accomplished had the river improvement money not been spent. This performance was supplemented by movement of large tonnages of essential materials on these streams during the war period.

Equipment may depart further and further from the picturesque. However, in so doing, efficiency of operation and economy in the interests of the public will provide a satisfactory and modern substitute for the spectacular performances of the *Natchez* and the *Robert E. Lee*.

AMERICAN SOCIETY OF CIVIL ENGINEERS

Founded November 5, 1852

TRANSACTIONS

Paper No. 2650

AMERICAN HYDRAULIC DREDGES

By Carl H. Giroux [1]

Synopsis

Dredging is required on all sorts of waterways, each with individual types of machines suited to its peculiar needs. The dustpan type is used on inland waterways for maximum efficiency in excavating material that is redeposited by natural stream action in more suitable areas. Then there is the sea-going hopper dredge, operating in harbors and deep channels to dig material, deposit it in the vessel itself, and convey it to deep water for dumping. A third main type is the cutter-head pipeline dredge, designed primarily for construction of original channels or hydraulic fills; as its name implies, it also cuts and economically transports immense volumes by pumping. All these types were developed by experience over many years, as regards general principles and perfection of detail. Examples of modern units evidence major American engineering achievements—in design, construction, and operation.

Earth moving from one place to another is one of the oldest engineering tasks. Methods of accomplishing this have taken various forms, of which only one is to be considered here—hydraulic dredging. Probably the first reference to such a procedure is found in Greek mythology, describing how the Augean Stables were cleaned by diversion of the Alpheus and Peneus rivers. The equipment used for the Herculean feat is not disclosed, but it is a safe conclusion that, with a modern dredge, the project could have been completed even more speedily than mythology records.

This paper, however, does not deal with mythology or ancient history, but rather with early efforts in underwater dredging as it is now known, and particularly with accomplishments in developing modern tools for this purpose in the United States.

The early history largely revolves around the activities of the Corps of Engineers, which since 1824 has been concerned with the improvement of rivers and harbors for navigation. This work involves three major classifications of conditions each presenting its own problems, with a decided effect on the types of equipment that can be used. These three will be discussed separately.

---

[1] Special Asst., Office of Chf. of Engrs., Dept. of the Army, Washington, D. C.

Equipment for Harbor Work

The first classification is the initial dredging and maintenance of deep-water channels in harbors abutting on the open sea. Here the problems are those of continuous operation, avoiding serious interference with traffic, and overcoming adverse weather conditions. Obviously any piece of equipment anchored in the channel is a menace to navigation, and in case of high seas is difficult to operate. Then there is the problem of disposing of the dredged material; pumping the spoil ashore requires further obstruction of the navigable waters and, again, the use of barges and tugs adds to the confusion.

As early as 1855 the idea of a self-propelled and self-contained dredge was born. After a number of experimental vessels had been tried, with varying degrees of success, the Corps of Engineers in 1891 built the *Charleston*, the first specially designed sea-going hopper dredge. Although it had a capacity of only about 300 cu yd, it incorporated most of the essential elements still in use. It was self-propelled; it could dredge while under way; and it had integral hoppers with bottom-dump doors.

Then, and for many years thereafter, efficiency was of secondary consideration, the main idea being to find a device that could physically remove and dispose of the material. Low costs of construction, cheap labor, and proximity of disposal areas—all tended to minimize the importance of output and cost of operation. At that time, the low-pressure reciprocating steam engine was the only prime mover available; it was used for propelling the vessel, for driving the pumps and winches, and for all auxiliary purposes. Coal was the fuel.

Mechanical Advances.—As time went on there were improvements not only in the type of equipment available, but also in the conditions of operation. The first significant change in motive power was the introduction of the diesel engine, which for moderate power showed a marked improvement in weight, space, and fuel economy. Coupled with this, electrical equipment became more and more popular for marine service. Consequently, in 1922, the Corps of Engineers decided to use diesel-electric drive on four 1,250-cu yd dredges originally designed for steam-reciprocating machinery. Their performance has been outstanding; two are still in service and the others were outmoded only by the change in dredging conditions.

As deeper and more extensive channels were demanded for major harbors with greater distances to disposal areas, the relative effectiveness of the small, slow, and somewhat inefficient dredges decreased. Obviously, if the work was to be done quickly and at a reasonable cost, new equipment had to be provided. During the steam-engine era a number of dredges were built having hopper capacities of approximately 3,000 cu yd and one as high as 4,000 cu yd, but the running speed was low and fuel consumption high.

As these vessels neared the end of their economic life, the Corps initiated a program for replacement, utilizing its experience of many years and taking advantage of the latest improvements in motive power. This program culminated in the design and construction of the *Essayons*, which reflects the latest thinking in large sea-going hopper dredges. Of course, there still remains a field for small dredges of this same type, with light draft for use in minor harbors. Those constructed in recent years and those contemplated for the future have or will have many of the basic features of the *Essayons*.

Efficiency, Self-Contained.—The vessel has an over-all length of 525 ft, a beam of 72 ft, a light draft of 20 ft, a fully loaded draft of 29 ft, and a hopper capacity of 8,000 cu yd. It has a speed of 17 miles per hr light, and 16 miles per hr fully loaded. The propulsion power is 4,000 hp on each of the two screws, and the dredging power is 1,850 hp on each of the two pumps.

Maneuverability is paramount in a sea-going hopper dredge even when running at slow speed during dredging, and therefore twin screws are essential. Furthermore, each screw must run independently throughout its complete range of speed from full ahead to full astern in order to keep the vessel on its course

Fig. 1.—An Example of the Highest Development in Sea-Going Hopper Dredges—the *Essayons* of the Corps of Engineers

and to turn it sharply. For this purpose, an electric drive controlled from the pilot house has proved to be the best solution and is used on the *Essayons*.

Early dredges of this type were equipped with a single drag arm suspended from the stern; others had it located about amidships in a well on the fore-and-aft center line. These designs had the disadvantages of not permitting dredging close to a bank and of using valuable space within the ship's structure. The scheme of using two drag arms, one pivoted from each outboard side of the dredge (Fig. 1), has been found to be the best arrangement for most conditions. It does introduce, however, appendages which are vulnerable when docking or in case of collision and which offer considerable resistance with the ship running full speed and loaded. To overcome these disadvantages, the arms are pivoted from sliding trunnion plates and can be raised clear of the side of the vessel when not dredging.

Handling Excavation.—One of the most difficult problems in connection with this type of hydraulic dredging is the retention of solids in the hoppers, particularly when the material is light and slow to settle. Many experiments with different arrangements of hoppers, discharge pipes, overflows, and baffles have been tried. No one scheme has been found ideal for different sizes of hoppers and for the various kinds of material to be handled. The objective is to dissipate the energy in the discharge from the pump as quickly as possible, to eliminate turbulence, and to provide as long a path as feasible to the overflow weirs so that the solids will have an opportunity to settle out of the mixture and to fill the hoppers, permitting water only to pass overboard. The arrangement gives good results, but there is still room for improvement.

Allied to this problem is that of continuously dredging a mixture of high solid content and keeping the surplus water to a minimum. This is not so serious when dredging sand, which settles readily, but with silt or soft mud there is great difficulty in preventing the suction from choking if the drag is too deeply submerged. When choking does occur it is necessary to raise the drag and pump water only until the pipe is cleared, an operation which tends to wash overboard some of the material already in the hoppers. For this reason, modern drags have been equipped with auxiliary openings on the upper side which can be adjusted for the specific conditions so as to give the greatest practicable percentage of solids without choking the pump. This arrangement works fairly well but does not completely overcome the difficulty.

Observation and study disclosed that it was not always the fault of deep submersion of the drag or of too dense a mixture; but that the entrained gas had some effect. Such gas was liberated under the vacuum created by the dredging pump and the pump would become air or gas bound.

Acting on this theory, ejectors were installed on the suction side of one of the dredging pumps whereby any accumulation of gas was immediately removed. The results were at once apparent, and it was found that a much more concentrated mixture could be maintained than formerly. As a consequence, all modern hopper dredges of the Corps of Engineers which are called on to handle mud with entrained gases are equipped with gas ejectors or pumps, and the output under these conditions has been remarkably improved. Such a system is also applicable to any other suction dredges handling material containing gas.

A word should be said here about a very important adjunct of the sea-going hopper dredge—the suction drag. All sorts of devices have been tried with the view of increasing the percentage of material entering the suction pipe. These have included drags of various sizes, shapes, and weights, some plain and some with teeth, ridges, disks, and other types of scarifiers. The most satisfactory drag for general conditions is a shoe type, articulated so as to be self-adjusting to the depth and contour of the bottom and having an abrasion-resisting grid on the underside. Special drags are used for dredging coral and for banks with steep side slopes and other unusual characteristics.

Many improvements have been made in dredging pumps since the first ones, designed primarily for water, were used. Particularly the shape of the vanes to prevent clogging, and the design and types of material used for various parts to resist abrasion, have been given a great deal of study.

Comfort, Safety, and Improved Performance.—As the costs of construction, operation, and maintenance of sea-going hopper dredges have risen, it has become imperative to increase the hours of operation per year in order to keep net costs at a reasonable amount. Therefore, provision is now being made to quarter and feed a crew for continuous operation and to provide recreational facilities, comfortable accommodations, and conveniences for maintaining high morale. Also navigational aids such as radio-telephone, radar, radio direction finders, gyro compass, and fathometers have become standard equipment so as to permit continued operation during adverse weather conditions.

The matter of safety also has not been overlooked. Since these vessels must work in congested waterways, collisions are bound to occur, with danger of complete loss of the dredge and sometimes loss of life. To minimize these hazards, the safety requirements of the United States Coast Guard and the American Bureau of Shipping are observed, and the hulls are so designed that any two compartments may be flooded without sinking of the dredge, even when fully loaded.

As an indication of the improvement in performance that has been gained by increasing the hopper capacity and the speed of travel, it should be mentioned that the *Essayons* has attained a monthly output of more than 500,000 cu yd when discharging to a disposal area 25 miles distant, and an output as high as 1,500,000 cu yd per month with a haul of 3 miles. In comparison, one of the older dredges, with a hopper capacity of 2,500 cu yd, had an output of less than 100,000 cu yd and 250,000 cu yd, respectively, under the same conditions.

INLAND, MISSISSIPPI RIVER, OPERATIONS

The second classification of conditions suitable for hydraulic dredging is that pertaining to inland waterways, particularly the Mississippi and its tributaries. Here the problem is to maintain a channel of sufficient depth and width to accommodate packet and barge traffic. On these streams the integrity of the channel is continually jeopardized by deposits of silt and sand wherever slack water occurs. This is particularly true during subsidence from a period of high water, when sandbars form very rapidly, many of them of considerable proportions.

Much improvement has been made in the original channel conditions by building contraction works to confine and speed up the flow, by cutoffs in the bends to increase the hydraulic gradient, and by bank revetment to keep the channels in proper alinement and reduce the amount of entrained material. Despite these efforts, large quantities of sediment continue to be deposited and must be removed by hydraulic dredges.

Special Devices for Particular Uses.—In streams of this character, where the quantity of dredged material is small compared to the amount carried by the river, it is not considered necessary to remove material permanently from the river bed, but merely to put it back into the water, where it will be carried away and dropped at some unobjectionable point. This method has given rise to the trial of many kinds of agitators which merely stir up the deposits in the hope that they will be carried away without further help. Although some of these experiments have met with a small measure of success, a type of hydraulic dredge developed particularly for this use has proved to be the most efficient. This is known as the dustpan dredge.

As a result of earlier experiments with hydraulic dredging, the Mississippi

River Commission in 1893 built the *Alpha,* which incorporated most of the features of the present dustpan dredge. A complete description and plan of this dredge appeared in the ASCE *Transactions.*[2] A few of the salient features will be described.

The hull was of wood about 140 ft long with a draft of 4 ft. Two types of dredging machinery were installed, one at each end of the vessel. One had a suction pipe with water jet agitator, and the other had no agitator but was constructed in the form of a scraper. Subsequently the scraper was discarded and the suction with the jet agitator retained. This principle has been found to be simple and effective, and is used universally on dredges of this type today.

Another feature developed in early experiments and still in use is the means for disposing of the dredged material. It was found that discharge directly at the dredge did not suffice but that, if the material could be deposited only a short distance away, most of it would be either carried off or redeposited where it would do no harm to the channel. A short floating pipeline was devised for this purpose, with joints flanged and articulated at the dredge. Under hydraulic operation, such a line tends to straighten out, but it must be controlled so as to discharge at the most advantageous point. To accomplish this, an adjustable baffle plate is placed at the end of the discharge pipe. The water, impinging on this baffle, creates a reaction sufficient to move the pipeline even against the current, and thereby permits spotting of the discharge point quite accurately. When the pump is stopped, the pipeline floats with the current and lies parallel to the dredge, out of the way of traffic, permitting easy movement of the dredge.

The first dustpan dredges had to be towed to and from the site. Eventually propelling machinery was added so that the dredges were independent of attendant plant. Stern or side paddle wheels were used where extremely shallow draft was required, and tunnel screws where more draft was permissible.

Dustpan Type for Mississippi Work.—In the earlier dredges the suction heads were of various forms, some being equipped with mechanical devices for loosening the material. Such devices were discarded rather quickly, however, as it was found that high-pressure water jets did the job effectively and the equipment was less costly to manufacture and maintain. On adoption of the water-jet principle of agitation, the tendency was to flatten and widen the suction head so that it truly resembled a dustpan and gave rise to the name by which this type of dredge is now known.

About 1930 the Mississippi fleet of dredges had nearly reached the end of its economic life, and increasing traffic on the lower river and on the Missouri necessitated the construction of more and larger dredges. Experience gained over a long period clearly indicated that the dustpan type was the most suitable. Between 1932 and 1934, nine dredges of this type were built with pumping power ranging from 1,000 hp to 2,100 hp. All are self-propelled; one has a stern paddle wheel; four have side paddle wheels; and four have tunnel screws. Those with paddle wheels, designed to operate in the Upper Mississippi and Missouri rivers, have a draft of less than 5 ft, while those with tunnel screws, designed for the Lower Mississippi River, have a draft of more than 6 ft.

[2] "Dredges and Dredging on the Mississippi River," by J. A. Ockerson, *Transactions,* ASCE, Vol. XL, December, 1898, p. 215.

Representative of the largest and most modern of existing dustpan dredges is the *Jadwin* (Fig. 2). It is 250 ft long, has a beam of 52 ft, and a draft in working condition of about $6\frac{1}{2}$ ft. The suction head is 32 ft wide and has thirty-four nozzles for agitation, passing 11,000 gal of water per min. The dredging pump has a runner 80 in. in diameter, and a suction pipe and discharge pipe 34 in. and 32 in. in diameter, respectively. It is driven through reduction gears by a 2,100-hp steam turbine. The vessel is propelled by two triple-expansion steam engines, each of about 1,000 hp, driving twin screw propellers. The free-running speed of the vessel is approximately $9\frac{1}{2}$ miles per hr.

When dredging at a depth of 20 ft to 30 ft below the water surface, and with about 800 ft of floating pipeline, this dredge will excavate at least 3,000 cu yd

FIG. 2.—A LARGE DUSTPAN DREDGE USED ON INLAND WATERWAYS—THE *JADWIN*

per hr. With a 12-ft bank of sand ahead, its rate of advance is approximately 3 ft per min. The velocity in the pipeline is about 20 ft per sec. This may be compared to the *Alpha,* which had a pumping power of about 300 hp and excavated less than 500 cu yd per hr under similar conditions.

EXCAVATION FOR NEW CONSTRUCTION

Third, hydraulic dredges are suitable for the dredging of new channels, the deepening of old ones, and the placing of hydraulic fill for the construction of dams or the reclamation of land contiguous to waterways. For this work a type of plant known generally as the cutterhead pipeline dredge has been developed.

Such a dredge consists essentially of a barge-type hull, a ladder hinged at the forward end carrying the suction pipe and revolving cutter, a centrifugal pump discharging to a floating pipeline, two spuds for swinging and advancing the dredge, and necessary machinery. These dredges are usually not self-propelled.

Special Type Developed.—The early use of cutterhead dredges seems to be centered around San Francisco Bay in California. There in about 1875 the need for a machine to build levees and reclaim land, using material lying beneath the water surface, resulted in the development of dredges having some modern characteristics. The history of this development is long and involved; it is sufficient to state that progress in improving performance has been continuous and has kept pace with modern trends in motive power and machinery. Here, as with hopper dredges, the reciprocating steam engine has given way to the diesel engine, the steam turbine, and the widespread use of electrical apparatus.

As an illustration, the dredge *Mindi*, built by the Ellicott Machine Corporation for the Panama Canal (Fig. 3), is representative of modern self-contained high-powered dredges of this type. Oil-fired boilers operating at 400 lb per sq in. are used to furnish steam for the main machinery. The dredge pump, which has a 32-in. suction and a 28-in. discharge, is driven through reduction gears by a steam

FIG. 3.—THE *MINDI*, A MODERN CUTTERHEAD PIPELINE DREDGE; SPUDS AT LEFT (DISCHARGE) END

turbine rated at 5,000 hp but capable of producing 5,500 hp under favorable conditions. A separate turbine-driven generating set furnishes power for the cutter motor, the hauling and hoisting winch motor, and other auxiliaries—all using direct current.

The cutter motor is rated at 600 hp, is waterproof, forced ventilated, and drives the cutter through a self-contained speed reducer, all mounted directly on the ladder. The motor for the hauling and hoisting winch is rated at 200 hp and is also forced ventilated. The speed of both these motors is adjustable over a wide range by variable voltage control.

The *Mindi* is capable of dredging to a depth of 72 ft, and for this purpose has a ladder and spuds which are approximately 100 ft long. The output of such a dredge is of course dependent on many conditions such as the nature of the material, the length of the pipeline, the dredging depth, and operational interruptions. It has dredged as much as 1,500,000 cu yd in 22 days, and its peak output was 83,500 cu yd in 21 hours. This was in sand, silt, and clay with 8,000 ft of pipeline.

Benefit of Electric Power.—Where a specific project is of sufficient magnitude to warrant the construction of a special dredge and where electric power can be obtained readily at a low rate, it is sometimes advantageous to replace the prime mover with commercial power. In such cases alternating current at a fairly high voltage is usually carried aboard by means of insulated portable cable. Commonly, the dredge pump is direct-connected to a variable-speed, wound-rotor, induction motor designed for the voltage of the supply. Power for the cutter motor and other auxiliaries may be merely transformed to a lower voltage or may be converted to direct current by motor-generator sets in order to obtain more economical or wider speed variation, as conditions may demand.

An outstanding example of the use of electric dredges was the construction of the Fort Peck Dam on the Missouri River in Montana under the direction of the Corps of Engineers during the years 1934 to 1939, inclusive. For this purpose, four dredging units were constructed on the site, each consisting of one cutterhead hydraulic dredge, one floating booster unit, and one booster unit mounted on railway trucks, all driven by commercial electric power generated nearly 300 miles away. Each dredge and each floating booster were equipped with two 28-in. pumps driven by 2,500-hp, 257-rpm, 6,600-v induction motors; each railway unit had one such pump. The cutter motors were rated at 700 hp, 720 rpm, 6,600 v.

Both the dredge pump motors and the cutter motors were of the wound-rotor induction type, and the speed was controlled by liquid slip regulators connected in the secondary windings. Other auxiliaries were driven by alternating-current motors of lower voltage. Power was brought to the floating units by flexible, rubber-insulated, rubber-jacketed cable, supported on floating pontoons and connected at the shore end to overhead distribution lines which were moved from time to time to keep within reasonable distance of the dredges.

As the work progressed, the booster units were shifted as required to maintain optimum velocities and pressures in the pipelines. The peak was reached in August, 1939, when the dredge *Jefferson* by means of its own two pumps and eight additional ones, pumped through 36,420 ft of pipeline with a static lift of 110 ft. Under this condition a velocity of approximately 21 ft per sec was maintained, transporting 16% solids with an output averaging 2,000 cu yd per pumping hour. The energy consumed during this period was 8 kw-hr per cu yd as compared with an average of about 4 kw-hr for the entire job. A typical view of these dredges at work is shown in Fig. 4.

The period during which the Fort Peck dredges were in operation afforded an excellent opportunity to study the effect of varying pipeline velocities, cutter speeds, and other operational factors, and much valuable information was obtained. The nature of the material (sharp sand and gravel) caused rapid erosion of the pump impellers and casings, the pipelines, cutters, and other exposed parts.

Innumerable experiments were made using various abrasion-resisting materials and renewable pump liners, and changing the shape of affected parts. These experiments resulted in greatly reducing the cost of maintenance and lost time consumed in changing equipment.

A new electric cutterhead pipeline dredge for the Beauharnois Light, Heat and Power Company, an agency of the Quebec Hydro-Electric Commission, far exceeds in power and capacity any previous plant. This dredge is to deepen and widen the forebay channel leading to the Beauharnois Power House, through cemented boulder clay which is extremely hard to remove. It receives power through a flexible cable at 13,000 v, alternating current.

The pump is driven by an 8,000-hp, 275-rpm, wound-rotor, induction motor with an adjustable speed of 200 rpm minimum. Power for the cutter and hauling and hoisting machinery is converted from alternating current to direct current so as to utilize variable voltage control through a wide speed range. The cutter motor, of 1,000 hp, is mounted directly on the ladder. The pump has a discharge diameter of 36 in. and is designed to pass boulders up to 28 in. in diameter.

Developments in Small and Large Units.—It must not be inferred that all the recent advancement in cutterhead dredges has been in the matter of increasing their size and capacity. Similar development on medium and small-capacity plant ranging in discharge size from 6 in. to 20 in. has made it more efficient, lower in cost, and adaptable to a variety of work which would not justify the use of a large dredge.

FIG. 4.—ELECTRIC CUTTERHEAD PIPELINE DREDGES AND BOOSTERS AT WORK IN BORROW PIT, FORT PECK DAM ON THE MISSOURI RIVER IN MONTANA

Diesel engines are almost universally used for such applications. In most cases the dredge pump is directly connected to a diesel engine of proper speed and power, although in some instances an electric drive is employed to obtain the additional flexibility and reliability of multiple engine drive. Electric auxiliaries, alternating current, direct current, or a combination of both, are almost universally employed. The wide range in speed and economy of variable voltage control usually dictates direct current for the cutter and hauling machinery. Recently an 8-in. dredge of simple design, with diesel-driven machinery, which can be dismantled and transported by railway or trailer truck, has been put on the market.

In 1946, when the means of excavating a sea-level canal across Panama [3] was being studied, the use of cutterhead hydraulic dredges was considered for part of the work. The problem here was not only to remove an extremely large volume of material but to dredge to a depth of 135 ft below the water surface—far deeper than any similar project to date. Although the dredges were never built, the design was carried to a point which indicated their feasibility. Aside from the unprecedented size and power of the dredging machinery, the most novel feature

---

[3] "Panama Canal—The Sea-level Project: A Symposium," *Transactions,* ASCE, Vol. 114, 1949, p. 607.

was a booster pump, part way down the ladder, to aid the main pump in over-coming the suction losses. So great would be these losses because of the long suction line that otherwise there would be little head available for lifting the material.

EVOLUTION IN ESSENTIAL FEATURES

Progress in any field is dependent on the continued improvement of the individual components, and this has been true in the field of hydraulic dredging. In many of the early dredges, the failure of one part to do its duty often penalized the whole operation. Rectification of the trouble would then transfer the strain to the next weakest link. The history of the development of the hydraulic dredge to its present state of high perfection is a recital of the struggle to overcome a succession of such difficulties. A few of them deserve further discussion.

Better Spuds.—The spud, for instance, is a very necessary adjunct to a modern cutterhead dredge (Fig. 3). It is a kind of mooring pile, a part of the dredge itself. At first, dredges were merely moored with lines and moved forward with winches; this is still the way the dustpan type operates. Then some ingenious soul discovered the principle of the walking spud, which is one of the basic elements of the present cutterhead dredge.

Until the past 20 years or so, the spuds were of wood; but, as the size, weight, and power of the dredges increased, spud casualties became heavy. Then riveted steel spuds were substituted, but when installed in the wells provided for the wooden ones they were difficult to remove if they became bent, as sometimes happened. This led to the gated well at the extreme stern of the dredge—the present practice. Next came the cast steel spud, which offered much more rigidity and permitted an increase in length for deep dredging. With the perfection of electric welding, spuds fabricated from steel plate came into vogue, offering sufficient strength combined with lighter weight and lower cost.

Improved Cutterheads.—The cutter is another part which has been the source of many trials and tribulations since the invention of hydraulic dredges. No matter how perfect the operation of all other components, the cutter or agitator must be able to move the dredged material to the suction or the results are negative. The development of this device has run the gamut of jets, plows, knives, teeth, blades, and various other contraptions.

After many years of experimentation, the spiral cutter with inward delivery, and with the suction pipe within the periphery, has emerged as the most successful solution. The form is varied, using blades of different sizes and shapes or equipped with teeth, depending on the material excavated. Full advantage has been taken of modern methods of fabrication, and of new discoveries in metallurgy, to decrease the cost and increase the life of this very vital part.

Sleeve Connections.—Some seemingly simple elements such as pipe connections have given dredge operators much concern and have been responsible for many delays. For connections between the suction pipe and the dredge, between the discharge pipe and the floating line, and between sections of the latter, a degree of flexibility combined with strength to resist pressure and bending is required. From the first, rubber sleeves have well served this purpose. Fortunately, in the earlier days, pipe sizes were small and pressures low, so that the available materials sufficed after a fashion.

As the pipe sizes increased and the pressures rose, the duty became much more severe so that the procurement of a sleeve that would have a reasonable life became a real problem. However, the automobile-tire industry was faced with the same problem on a much larger scale, and the art of making better rubber compounds and better reinforcing did much for dredging sleeves. Such sleeves, brought to a high degree of perfection, are used in large quantities on modern dredges and pipelines. The rubber sleeve, however, is not the final answer for the larger sizes of pipe and high pressures. For such work the steel ball joint and swivel joint have been developed and, although much more costly to manufacture, are in most cases fully justified because of their longer life and freedom from failure.

Pump Development.—It is obvious that the pump used to pick up and dispose of the excavated material is one of the most important elements of a hydraulic dredge of any type and warrants very careful consideration so that it can meet the varied and severe conditions imposed upon it. The first dredges utilized the only types available—the screw pump or the centrifugal pump designed for handling water. The centrifugal variety soon demonstrated its superiority and became the basis on which the modern dredge pump has been developed.

One of the weaknesses of the ordinary centrifugal pump is its tendency to clog when handling entrained material of appreciable size. This difficulty was largely solved rather early in its development by increasing the size and improving the shape of the water passages to conform to those of the so-called "trash pumps" used for drainage work. From that point on, however, the gradual perfection of the dredge pump has been an art of its own, developed to meet the unparalleled conditions imposed.

Wear has been a major problem with dredge pumps because the inherent nature of the substances handled causes rapid erosion of parts. The first major improvement was the use of removable liners for areas most affected. Although this did not reduce the wear, it permitted replacement of parts, rather than of the entire pump. Gradually liners came to be made of materials that were much more resistant, so that their useful life has been increased as much as 400%. The use of rubber-faced liners has become prevalent where the nature of the dredged material is such that they will not suffer physical damage due to impact. The art of vulcanizing rubber directly to steel, so as to avoid exposed fastenings, has made such liners much more successful.

Although the large clearances required on dredge pumps make high efficiency impossible, there has been appreciable improvement in this respect due to more scientific and careful design. There are several other features which make the modern dredge pump much superior to those of a few years ago, and it may be safely stated that this element has kept pace with the general improvement in the art of hydraulic dredging.

This limited picture of what has taken place during nearly a century of development of hydraulic dredges in the United States is necessarily sketchy. However, it should give to those who have not been intimately connected with this fascinating industry some conception of the problems encountered; and it should show the achievements of engineers who have devoted their time and energy to a work which has proved so beneficial to American waterborne commerce.

AMERICAN SOCIETY OF CIVIL ENGINEERS

Founded November 5, 1852

TRANSACTIONS

Paper No. 2651

NAVAL DRYDOCK CONSTRUCTION

By J. R. Ayers,[1] M. ASCE

Synopsis

The increase in width and depth of graving docks, to keep pace with the ever-increasing size of ships to be served, has introduced many difficulties in drydock construction. Three stone docks, small by today's standards, provided for naval needs until almost 1890. Then for 30 years expansion took place, and twenty-four larger structures were added. These were built of timber, then of concrete backing with stone interior lining, and finally of concrete throughout. Today's drydocks are usually built of concrete although a few have walls made of earth-filled steel sheet-pile cells. Ground conditions dictate construction methods, allowing for full or partial hydrostatic uplift, as required. Recent improvements permit construction in the dry with the help of well points, as well as construction without unwatering, using tremie-placed concrete. These advances made possible phenomenal increases—thirty major naval drydocks, mostly built during World War II.

The cleaning and repair of ships have always been difficult problems. Three types of ship repair facilities are in current use: The marine railway, the floating drydock, and the conventional drydock constructed in the foreshore of a harbor area, often called a graving dock. The latter facility and its evolution over the past 100 years will be treated in this paper.

The drydock is of surprisingly recent origin when compared to the antiquity of ship construction. For centuries the average ship seldom exceeded a 100-ton displacement and could be beached with comparative ease. The war galleys of the Romans, with their tiers of rowers, were less than 100 ft long and were hauled from the water on slideways for graving or repairs. The size of ships increased so slowly that not until near the end of the fifteenth century was the first permanent drydock, with primitive closure gates, built in England. Only a few docks were constructed in the next 300 years, and it was 1833 before the first naval drydock was completed in the United States.

The four principal structural materials used in naval drydock construction, in the order of their appearance, are stone, timber, concrete, and steel. Each of these may be identified with a particular period.

---

[1] Consultant, Waterfront Structures, Bureau of Yards and Docks, Navy Dept., Washington, D. C.

EARLY STONE DRYDOCKS, 1827–1851

The United States Navy's first graving docks were built of stone. Three of them have completed more than 100 years of continuous service.

Gosport (Norfolk, Va.) and Charlestown (Mass.) Drydocks.—For more than 30 years after the establishment of the first navy yards in 1801, the only method of examining and repairing the underwater hulls of heavy ships was that of careening or heaving down—while cables held the floating ship tilted at a sharp angle, so that first one underwater side and then the other were exposed for inspection and maintenance work. This process was so slow and unsatisfactory that Secretary of the Navy Samuel L. Southard in 1825 strongly urged the

FIG. 1.—SKETCH OF *U. S. S. DELAWARE* BEING ADMITTED TO GOSPORT DRYDOCK, NORFOLK, VA., JUNE 17, 1833

construction of at least two drydocks for the Navy, one to be built at the Gosport Navy Yard and the other at the Boston Navy Yard in Charlestown.

Accordingly in 1827, Congress appropriated funds to start construction on the first two drydocks in the United States from identical plans made by Col. Loammi Baldwin. Both docks were built of cut stone with rough stone backing, that at Gosport being completed in 1833, when on June 17 the *U. S. S. Delaware* was admitted to the drydock. An artist's conception of this event is shown in Fig. 1. Only 1 week later, the drydock at Boston received its first ship when the *Constitution* was docked. These two structures were the only drydocks available to ships of the Navy prior to 1851.

First New York (N. Y.) Drydock.—On August 30, 1851, the first drydock at New York was completed, an event which might be said to mark the beginning of the historic century under review. This dock, built of stone, was regarded as one of the outstanding achievements of the engineering profession 100 years ago—

rightly so, because no comparable structure whose building presented so many difficulties had previously been constructed in the United States. A section through it is shown in Fig. 2. The masonry foundation was 400 ft long and 120 ft wide. The height of the dock wall was 36 ft. The floor was constructed as an inverted stone arch varying from 4 ft to 6 ft in depth.

These three stone docks had turning gates for closing the entrance during normal docking operations, and in addition had a floating gate or caisson made to fit into grooves in the masonry. The floating gate was used to permit repair of the turning gates or to relieve the water load on them by allowing the water in the intervening space to stand at some intermediate elevation. The total length of dock chamber from caisson to head of dock was 350 ft. The main chamber

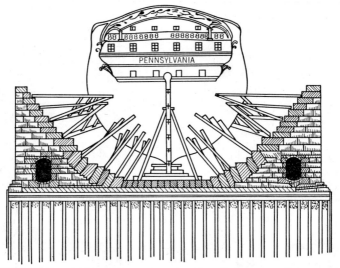

Fig. 2.—Cross Section of First New York, N. Y., Drydock, Completed August 30, 1851

within the turning gates would permit the docking of any ship of the line, whereas the largest steamers afloat could be docked by using the floating gate.

After taking borings in several places to a depth of more than 80 ft, engineers realized from the start that the construction of a dock at New York would be considerably more difficult than at either Norfolk or Boston. The work required 10 years during which time five chief engineers succeeded each other in charge of the project. It was attended by many difficulties, including three major failures of the cofferdam and continual delays when bottom springs carried both water and sand in such quantities as to wash out large cavities below the foundation timbers. These cavities were filled by driving timber piles and with rock so that the flow could be forced to other locations, where it would be admitted through pipes into the excavation, and removed by pumping.

Before construction started, it was intended to space the piles at about 3-ft centers in each direction; but, after opening the pit, it was decided to drive as many piles as could be forced into the earth. These were driven to refusal with a

2,000-lb drop hammer falling 35 ft. More than 8,000 bearing piles were used in the foundation. Courses of the stonework were generally 24 in. to 27 in. thick and the individual stones averaged about 6,000 lb in weight. Many of the large ones used in the coping exceeded 15,000 lb each. The total cost of the dock complete was approximately $2,000,000 at the prices which prevailed 100 years ago.

TIMBER DRYDOCKS, 1885–1900

The first three stone docks were designed to resist full hydrostatic pressure, their weight being enough to offset the total maximum external buoyancy with the dock empty. Soon after 1850, another type of dock was developed commer-

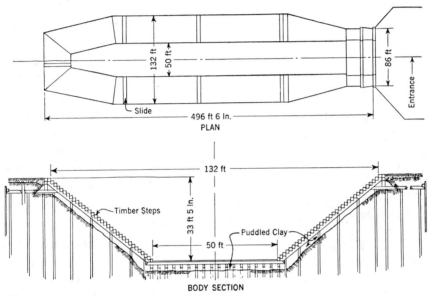

FIG. 3.—SIMPSON TIMBER DRYDOCK, NORFOLK, VA., 1887

cially which was to play an important part in naval drydock construction. This was a "relieved" dock, whereby admission of water from the subsoil into the dock chamber reduced the hydrostatic pressure on the floor and side walls to a minimum value. The docks first utilizing this principle were built of timber and were known as "Simpson's Improved Dry Docks" (Fig. 3).

The sides and inshore end were built on a slope to minimize the lateral earth thrust. Several rows of piles were driven beneath these slopes for support of the inclined heavy cap timbers to which the altars or steps were secured, thus forming a broad stairway around the entire dock periphery. As the sloping sides were built up, the space behind the altars was carefully filled in with clay which was well compacted by ramming. To reduce the quantity of percolation, two lines of tongue-and-groove sheet piling were driven around the site.

Provision was made for open drains suitably spaced beneath the floor timbers and leading to the pump well in order to remove any water entering the dock through the substratum. The slope of the sides was increased for a short distance near the dock entrance, to provide a narrower and a more favorably shaped cross section for gate closing. The Simpson docks had the advantages of rapid construction and low first cost—about one third of that of a stone drydock. Several Simpson docks, as repaired and rebuilt, have come down to the present day.

DRYDOCKS OF STONE WITH CONCRETE BACKING

As the sizes of ships increased, the difficulties of building docks to receive them multiplied many times. By 1895, the width and depth required were beginning to exceed safe limits for timber structures at many locations, while maintenance costs for existing timber docks were mounting. There was urgent need

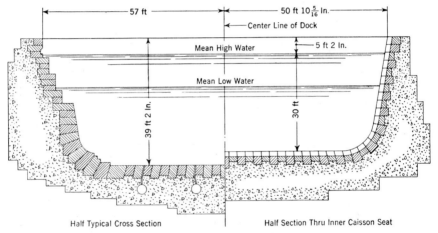

FIG. 4.—FIRST GRANITE-LINED CONCRETE DRYDOCK, BOSTON, MASS., 1899

for a building material which possessed the strength and durability of stone but which could be obtained for a fractional part of the cost. Although the casting of concrete was becoming popular, the art had not advanced sufficiently to warrant the use of this material alone in so large a structure.

As would naturally be expected, the next development was a compromise between two materials—concrete for the backing and cut stone for the exposed interior lining of the basin. In this development, economic considerations played an important part. In 1898 a congressional limitation of $825,000 was placed on the construction of each of four docks, this being the estimated cost of timber structures. On the strong recommendation of the Chief of the Bureau of Yards and Docks in favor of masonry, Congress authorized the Secretary of the Navy to build one of them of masonry at a cost not to exceed $1,025,000.

Accordingly, Drydock No. 2 at Boston became the first granite-lined concrete drydock. A cross section is shown in Fig. 4. The dock is 750 ft long, supported directly on the soil. After 40 years, it was necessary to reconstruct the entrance section because of settlements which affected the alinement of the caisson seats.

CONCRETE DRYDOCKS OF VARIOUS DESIGNS

The construction of a graving dock requires the placing of large quantities of heavy and durable material at a minimum cost. For this reason, concrete was destined to occupy an important place as soon as the processes of cement manufacture and proportioning of mixtures had progressed sufficiently to yield a product of reasonably consistent quality and durability.

Full Hydrostatic Uplift Design.—The first dock (Fig. 5) built of concrete throughout was Drydock No. 2, Philadelphia (Pa.), designed to resist full hydro-

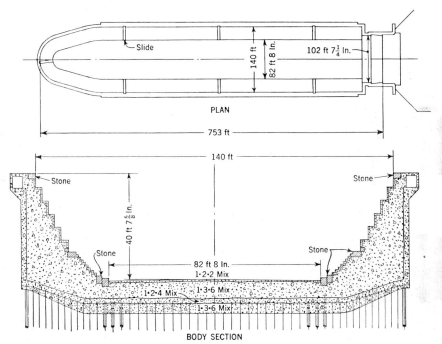

PLAN

753 ft

140 ft

BODY SECTION

FIG. 5.—FIRST CONCRETE DRYDOCK, PHILADELPHIA, PA., 1903

static pressure. Stone was used only on low and intermediate altars and at the dock coping. It is of interest that the concrete of the dock floor was cast in several horizontal layers of different mixes. Two different qualities were used in the side walls also. Although modern practice does not permit horizontal construction joints in floors, this dock has required very little maintenance.

Full Hydrostatic Relief Design.—At the site of the San Francisco (Calif.) Naval Shipyard, an outcropping of serpentine rock is found which presents a very favorable geological formation for building docks of the full hydrostatic relief type. Here drydocks may be built by lining the excavated basin with a thin slab of concrete. The dock constructed in 1901 for the Union Iron Works Company and later purchased by the Navy is illustrated in Fig. 6.

Theoretically if there were no seams or fissures in the rock formation, no provision for relief of hydrostatic pressure beneath the floor would be necessary.

For practical reasons however, it is customary to include means whereby any water collecting behind the walls and beneath the floor is allowed to enter the dock through a system of relief openings.

Full Hydrostatic Relief of Floor Only.—Occasionally a site is found where the top of sound bearing rock occurs at about the required elevation for the dock floor. In such a case it is possible to construct the floor by applying a relatively thin lining over the rock and building the side walls to carry full hydrostatic pressure.

The first dock of this type was built in connection with the Panama Canal project at Balboa during the period from 1913 to 1916. Gravity walls built of concrete resist the overturning effect of full water pressure throughout the height of the wall, whereas the thin floor is relieved of water pressure by suitable openings and construction joints.

Partial Hydrostatic Relief Design.—At the site of the Puget Sound Naval

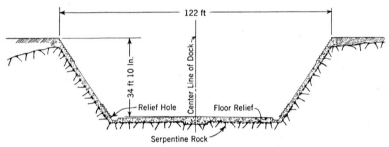

FIG. 6.—HYDROSTATIC RELIEF OF SIDE WALLS AND FLOOR—DRYDOCK AT HUNTER'S POINT, CALIFORNIA, 1901

Shipyard (Bremerton, Wash.) the geological formation is favorable for the building of docks of the partially relieved type (Fig. 7). The soil is a relatively impervious mixture of clay, sand, and gravel. By providing a suitably porous backfill behind the walls, the hydrostatic pressure is reduced by admission of the seepage water into the dock basin and its removal by drainage pumps.

Design for this structure was based on lowering the water level behind the walls to the elevation of the horizontal open-jointed drain extending around the dock periphery. The dock body has a weight sufficient to balance about two thirds of the full hydrostatic uplift, rather than the full uplift as would be required for a nonrelieved dock. The design assumes appropriate reductions in lateral load in accordance with the reduced hydrostatic head against the side walls.

There are two basic requirements for a dock of this type: First, that the quantity of seepage water can be removed within practical limits of pumping; and, second, that the total cost, or first cost plus maintenance charges over the life of the structure, must be less than the corresponding amount for a full hydrostatic dock of much heavier cross section but which requires little or no maintenance for continual seepage pumping. Considerable economy can be realized by using the partially relieved design at sites where natural conditions are favorable.

Drydocks Having Sheet-Pile Side Walls.—Sheet piles have been used to advantage to form the side walls of shipbuilding drydocks of the relieved floor type. As structural members in bending, sheet piles are limited to drydocks of shallow and intermediate depth because the lateral pressures encountered in deep graving docks are too large for piling of practical and commercially available sizes.

Straight-web steel sheet piles, driven to form cells enclosing large masses of earth fill, have high lateral stability. During World War II, such cells were employed successfully in several instances for the side walls of shipbuilding docks at economical cost. One at Newport News, Va., has 43 ft of water over the dock floor.

Developments in Construction Methods

Construction methods have an important bearing on the safe and economical building of drydocks. An examination of the construction records of individual

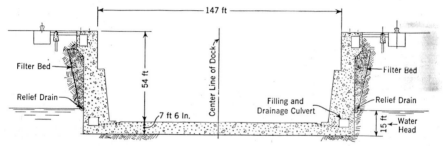

Fig. 7.—Partial Hydrostatic Relief—Example of Drydock at Puget Sound Yard, Bremerton, Wash., Built 1938–1940

docks reveals a long list of major problems. Some of these were serious enough to delay completion of work for several years. Many cofferdam failures and bankruptcies of contractors have occurred. In some cases, foundation conditions encountered after starting the work have necessitated a change in the type of design for the entire structure. Today, the risk of foundation uncertainties has been largely eliminated by knowledge of soil mechanics, whereas improvements in all types of heavy construction equipment have greatly simplified operations and made the rapid building of the largest docks possible.

Construction in the Dry

The principal difficulty in dry construction is hydrostatic pressure, which becomes increasingly severe as the width and depth of drydocks increase. The development of steel sheet piling has helped to overcome this difficulty by providing an effective means for preventing or reducing the entry of water into such deep excavations. A further advance in methods of reducing hydrostatic pressure has been the use of a combined system of deep wells and surface well points.

For example, Fig. 8 illustrates the method used to construct Drydock No. 1 at the Long Beach (Calif.) Naval Shipyard in a large open excavation. The drydock is so located in the foreshore that two thirds of the structure lies beyond the original shore line. A cofferdam was built around the outer periphery of the site, consisting of a rock sea wall for wave protection and an inner earthen dike with a steel sheet-pile cutoff wall. The site was underlain by a blanket of silty loam and clay at about the level of the dock floor beneath which was a 50-ft stratum of fine to coarse sand. Next lower was a 10-ft to 20-ft thickness of silty loam and clay, beneath which was a thick stratum of coarse sand.

Around the periphery thirty-six deep wells were installed, each provided with a pump of 2,000-gal per min capacity. All the casings penetrated the upper sand stratum and some extended well into the lower sand. Pumping from these wells lowered the hydraulic gradient throughout the entire site to such an extent that there was no difficulty from sand "boiling" or "piping" at the bottom of the excavation during the entire construction process. Control of seepage on the slopes of the excavation was maintained by three rows of well points. Without

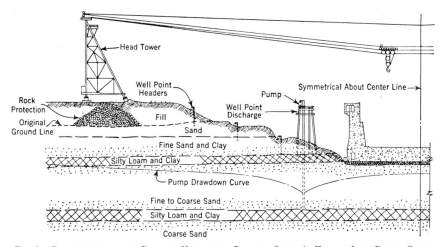

Fig. 8.—Construction in the Dry, for Moderately Pervious Soils, As Used at Long Beach, Calif.

relief of pressure in the pervious sand strata, construction would have involved many serious difficulties, entailing extensive changes in construction procedure.

UNDERWATER CONSTRUCTION

Natural conditions prevailing at certain sites often preclude, or seriously endanger, success in building graving docks in the dry. In such cases, underwater methods, developed in recent years, permit construction without entailing the risks and hazards involved in maintaining an open excavation.

Application to Drydock Floor Only.—The first large-scale tremie concreting operation for building a naval drydock occurred at Pearl Harbor, Hawaii, in 1939. Concrete for the entire floor of Drydock No. 2 was cast underwater. All formwork used to retain the tremie concrete was made of steel and incorporated in the completed drydock. Special slots were formed in the top perimeter of the floor concrete for insertion of the steel sheet piling used to enclose a series of internally braced side-wall cofferdam units. The side-wall concrete was cast in the dry after unwatering of individual units.

Left-in-Place Forms for Floor and Side Walls.—The first applications of tremie concrete to both floor and side walls were at Philadelphia and New York in 1942. Forms for casting the floor were long narrow boxes open at top and bottom with cross bulkheads at the inner faces of the side walls. The side-wall forms were supported on the outer ends of the floor forms. All forms were fabricated of structural steel shapes and covered with sheet metal having deep corrugations. The individual floor form units were so spaced with respect to the length of the

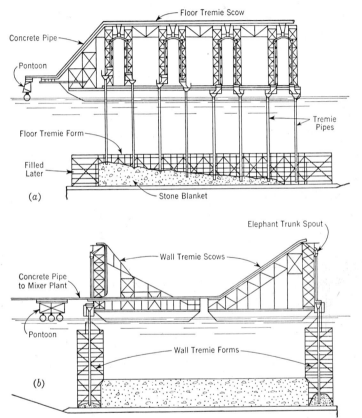

Fig. 9.—Arrangements for Concreting Drydock by Tremie—Forms to Be Left in Place: (a) First Stage of Floor Tremie Pour; and (b) Floor Pour Completed; Beginning of Wall Tremie Pour

dock that the distance between two adjacent units was about the same as the width of the unit. In the tremie concreting operations, material was deposited first within the floor form units (Fig. 9(a)). After several adjacent forms had been filled and the concrete had set, concrete was deposited in the spaces between the individual form units. Sections of side wall were cast in one continuous operation (Fig. 9(b)) from the bottom of the dock to the top of the wall forms without horizontal joints. Several thousand tons of form steel were embedded in the concrete of these first tremie docks as the forms were not designed for recovery and repeated use.

Development of Removable Forms.—After concrete for several docks had been successfully placed underwater, a design was developed by the Bureau of Yards and Docks for removable forms. Floor forms extend between the inner faces of the side walls, whereas the wall forms are made in three sections—the lower part or side base form, which remains in place, is equal in height to the floor thickness; the intermediate part or lower side-wall form is removable and extends from the top of the floor to the level of the single altar; and the upper

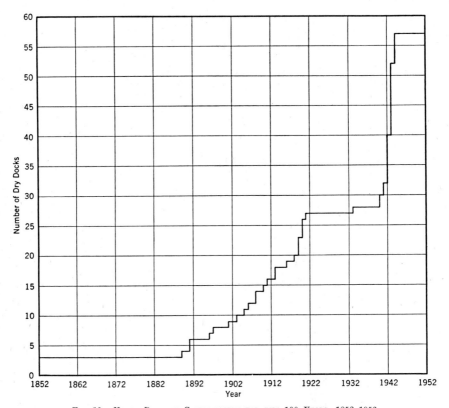

Fig. 10.—Naval Drydock Construction for the 100 Years, 1852–1952

side-wall form is also removable and extends from the altar level to a level above low water.

The two sides of the removable floor forms were sheathed with timber and separated by pipe struts to which all reinforcing steel was rigidly fastened by spot welding. The sides were secured to the ends of the spacer struts by specially designed bolts which could be loosened by divers to permit stripping of the forms from the concrete after setting. The lower and upper wall forms were removed similarly. Removable forms were used with marked success in constructing Drydock No. 4 at Pearl Harbor in record time and with a large saving in steel.

CONSTRUCTION RECORD FOR 100 YEARS

The Navy had just three small drydocks 100 years ago. The number has increased until today fifty-seven graving docks are actually in service (Fig. 10). Rapid construction in connection with World War II practically doubled the number of drydocks built since 1940. The magnitude of this recent program is even more impressive when the size of a modern dock is compared with that of the first docks.

This great expansion is shown in Fig. 11. Although the length ratio is only about 3 to 1, the hydrostatic uplift ratio is nearly 12 to 1. The difference in

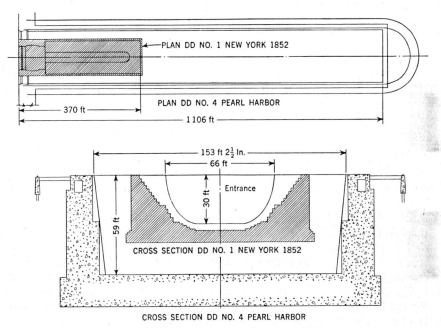

FIG. 11.—INCREASE IN DRYDOCK SIZES SINCE 1852

volumes of these docks is reflected in the respective pumping capacities required— 38,000 gal per min and 600,000 gal per min. Another comparison is possible for the caisson closure gates (Fig. 12). The total water load against the small caisson is 675 tons as compared to 6,000 tons on the large one.

THE FUTURE OF GRAVING DOCKS

There is a wide difference in the life span of graving docks as compared to that of their ship contemporaries. Whereas naval vessels are doomed to obsolescence in only a few years, drydocks continue to serve the fleet through many decades. As ships increase in size, new docks must be built to repair and maintain them, but the wide diversity in sizes of naval vessels assures a future service position for every existing drydock. Emphasis therefore must be on permanency.

Durability will continue to be the primary criterion for evaluating construction materials. Research will concentrate on methods of preventing deterioration and increasing longevity. The steady improvements in concrete offer promise of docks requiring less and less maintenance. As steel sheet piles of larger bending strength become available, these will no doubt be used, with protective cover and appropriate anchorages, for the side walls of many relieved-type drydocks.

Graving docks of the future will be subject to both stabilizing and changing influences. Radical changes in the general types of design are not expected as these are determined by natural conditions of the site. On the other hand, the application of atomic energy to ship propulsion may bring about revolutionary changes in ships and their repair facilities. Present general methods of drydock

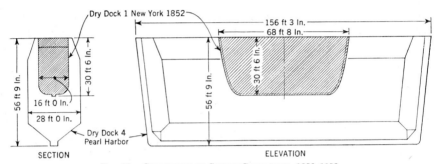

Fig. 12.—Comparison of Caisson Dimensions, 1852–1952

construction should remain, but improvements in performing the various operations should be anticipated.

Increased economy in design is expected from several sources. More intensive studies of the soil properties for a given site will be made to determine the relative economy of a relieved type of dock as compared to one designed for resisting full uplift. A combination of the two types may be feasible at certain sites, whereby the outshore part would be designed for full uplift and the inshore part would be of the relieved type. A wider use of impervious cutoff walls should extend the field of the relieved dock. Finally there is the possibility of economy which must await better methods of evaluating the forces acting between the structure and the earth which surrounds and supports it. As more knowledge becomes available in this field, greater economy in design is bound to result.

In the years to come, the construction of new naval drydocks will keep abreast of all advances in engineering, and will continue to attract the profession's highest type of ingenuity and resourcefulness.

AMERICAN SOCIETY OF CIVIL ENGINEERS
Founded November 5, 1852
TRANSACTIONS

Paper No. 2652

SYSTEM OF WATERWAYS AT CHICAGO, ILL.

By Ralph L. Bloor,[1] M. ASCE

Synopsis

Waterways gave the first impetus to budding Chicago, but they in turn have been crowded almost out by the giant they themselves created. Both commercial and health needs combined to stimulate waterway activity. The construction of the Sanitary and Ship Canal and its smaller predecessor actually reversed the flow in the Chicago River, from Lake Michigan to the Mississippi Valley. Nearby industrial growth a few miles south on the Lake brought about the building of the Calumet-Sag Channel which, like its neighbor, connects with the Illinois Waterway; but it never was an adequate navigation channel. City growth and cross-highway traffic are obstacles to improvement of the earlier canal, whereas, on the newer waterway, clearances both horizontal and vertical throttle traffic. Although there is still the opportunity to meet it, this problem should not be further ignored.

As related to the year 1952 and its celebration of the Centennial of Engineering at Chicago, it seems especially appropriate to consider the nearby waterways. They have had an important influence on the history of this great but young city, now 120 years old; its first major waterway engineering work was completed 104 years ago, and in this sphere the future is just as challenging today as it ever has been in the short but intensely energetic history of the city.

Attention will be confined principally to the inland waterways as distinguished from those of the open lake—not that the inland waterways are more important, but they impose more interesting engineering problems than the lake waterways which have been so completely endowed by nature. The two are related, of course, and together account for the fact that Chicago has reached the position of the second lake port and the third port of the United States, with water-borne annual tonnages of more than 60,000,000.

Transition—Village to Metropolis.—Among the first white men at Chicago were Jacques Marquette and Louis Joliet in 1673. The priest and explorer had paddled up the Illinois and Des Plaines rivers, portaged to the South Branch of the Chicago River under the direction of the Indians, and entered Lake Michi-

---

[1] Chf., Structures Branch, Office, Chf. of Engrs., U. S. Army, Washington, D. C.

gan. Joliet reported then that the mouth of the Chicago River offered a convenient harbor and that a canal cutting through half a league of prairie was all that
was necessary to permit boat passage from the Great Lakes to the Gulf of
Mexico. This idea, so early established, has intrigued the minds of men ever
since. However, perhaps the greater wonder, and certainly a more important
fact today, nearly 300 years later, is that a navigator wishing to operate commercially over this route of wonderful possibilities must push his barges through
a ditch 60 ft wide or under a multitude of bridges which, when opened for passage,

FIG. 1.—SIMULTANEOUS INTERRUPTION OF TRAFFIC OVER FOUR IMPORTANT ROADWAYS—VESSEL ON
CHICAGO RIVER IN DOWNTOWN PART OF CHICAGO, ILL.

will have an almost calamitous effect on the street traffic in the very center of
the city (Fig. 1).

Chicago was almost certainly founded by reason of its position on the principal
portage route between the Great Lakes and the Mississippi River. It was from
the Indian designation for the river that Chicago received its name—the phonetic
descendant of the Indian words which referred either to the strongly odored wild
onions abounding along the stream, or to the well-known characteristic of the
skunk. The stockyards on the South Branch and the sewage in the drainage
canal across the old portage perpetuated the meaning for many years, but constant
efforts of engineers are reducing this connotation to only a memory.

It is not certain that the French established a post on the Chicago River,
but it is certain that they used the route in their fur trade. The United States

established Fort Dearborn at the mouth of the Chicago River in 1803, and the known permanent settlement dates from that time. The purpose of the fort was to control the traffic route; and it gave rise to a city that formed the gateway, the market place, and the supply center for the whole northwest territory.

Perhaps it would be interesting for engineers to note in passing that the site possessed little other local advantage. The ground was low and flat and very difficult to drain. Grades had to be raised as much as 10 ft over large areas by city ordinance to get the streets out of the mud. A world-renowned work of sanitary engineering, the Chicago Sanitary and Ship Canal, had to be built to carry the sewage away from the water supply in Lake Michigan.

Foundation conditions were bad, with rock as much as 80 ft below the surface and soft blue clay very near the surface. This condition made Chicago a full-scale foundation laboratory for two or three decades following the great fire of 1871 when heavy building construction boomed and deep foundations were not yet acceptable as the practicable and sure solution.

Waterways Serve Growing City.—A brief résumé will show what was done with Chicago's waterways commencing in 1833, when the town was incorporated on the basis of twelve voters in favor as compared to one voter against. Fort Dearborn had been burned by the Indians in 1812 and rebuilt. The Chicago River flowed around it in a semicircle—that is, the South Branch flowed northward on the west side and the main stem flowed eastward on the north side, in about the same positions as these segments now occupy. However, at that time the main stem turned southward for a distance corresponding to several blocks before entering Lake Michigan. The sandbar lakeward of this southward bend made entrance to the river very difficult in stormy weather. The first improvement alleviated this condition when the Federal Government between 1833 and 1840 dredged a cut straight eastward from the upper section of the main stem and constructed jetties along the sides of the cut.

By 1836, Chicago had 4,000 people, hosts of land speculators, and a strong urge to grow. An Indian treaty 20 years before had reserved a strip of land from Chicago to Ottawa, Ill., on the Illinois River for the express purpose of providing a site for a canal connecting the Great Lakes with the Mississippi River system. The old portage, about 7 miles long, extending from just west of where Damen Avenue crosses the South Fork of the Chicago River to near Summit on the Des Plaines River (Fig. 2), had served the fur traders. During high water, large canoes could be floated across; during dry seasons, the canoes could be carried over the baked mud of the dried swamp; and there were in-between times when nothing but dogged determination and heartbreaking toil did much good. However, the new city needed something better.

The Federal Government considered the military need for a heavy traffic route to newly opened country and authorized a canal. To encompass the anticipated canal and the Chicago River entrance to Lake Michigan, the northern boundary of the State of Illinois had been relocated. Engineers computed the costs; and, as droughts struck the Des Plaines River which had been planned as the water supply, the cost estimates went up. Railroads were considered in lieu of the canal, but at that time Chicago was not a railroad town—it had grown up with the canal idea. Finally the State of Illinois authorized a loan of $500,000, and in 1836 contracts were let for the Summit Section of a canal having a bottom 36 ft wide and 6 ft deep.

Vicissitudes of the Ship Canal.—During the 12 years required for building the canal, the population of Chicago multiplied itself by five, to reach 20,000; and during the first year of canal operation, 1848, Chicago's imports and exports increased more than four times over those in the previous year, to somewhere near $10,000,000 worth each. Tolls collected on the canal the first year amounted to less than $100,000, and such earnings could not have been an impressive return on the investment. Nevertheless, it would have been extremely difficult to convince

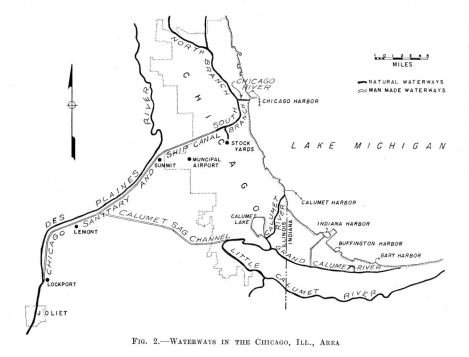

FIG. 2.—WATERWAYS IN THE CHICAGO, ILL., AREA

a Chicagoan that the canal was not an outstanding success. Despite the fact that the canal was fighting a losing battle with the railroads after the 1860's, it would require temerity to brand it a failure. Rather, the issue is that engineers have not yet learned to estimate all the benefits which may be set up against costs on projects of this character.

The original canal had a lock and a pump station at the Chicago end. Boats were raised a few feet from the Chicago River to the canal level by pumping from the river. The pump station was an engineering wonder of its day attracting a visit from the Prince of Wales (later Edward VII of England). However, boatmen complained that the canal was not big enough, and by 1865 the Chicago sewage problem demanded attention. As a result the bed of the canal was lowered at Summit; and in 1871 water flowed westward by gravity, so that the mouth of the Chicago River became the source of the canal.

Calumet Development.—By 1870, the traffic in the Chicago River harbor was getting in the way of other elements of the growing city. The population was more than 300,000; slips and wharves lined miles of the shore line of the main stem and the north and south branches; and the bridge problem was becoming acute. To alleviate this condition, the Federal Government began improvement of Calumet harbor at the mouth of the Calumet River 12 miles south (Fig. 2).

Chicago River harbor traffic grew to 11,000,000 tons in 1889 and since then has declined to 1,500,000—that is, the harbor was overgrown by the city it had produced. Calumet harbor, however, had advantages of its own which were recognized as early as 1833 by Lt. Jefferson Davis of the Army Engineering Corps. The Calumet River with its eastward and westward branches more or less paralleled the lake shore, and low-lying land extended westward toward the Des Plaines River. It offered the possibilities of an artificial channel between Lake Michigan and the Mississippi River watershed without traversing the Chicago Loop.

Thus, the Calumet region (Indian for pipe of peace) entered the Chicago waterway story, together with its extension westward through a swamp with an unpronounceable Indian name, which white folks in a hurry have termed the Sag—the briefest possible description of the topography. Railroads began crossing the Calumet soon after 1850. Work started on a steel plant there in 1880, and now the Calumet region is a steel center that ranks close to Pittsburgh, Pa. Railway and highway congestion is becoming severe, and perhaps engineers should speculate on how much time remains before this second waterway route to the Mississippi develops itself out of practicable existence as the Chicago River has done.

Drainage for Pollution Abatement.—One more major waterway development must be mentioned. Diversion of sewage through the old canal did not suffice for long. The canal flow was too small and contamination of the river and lake became intolerable. Extension of water intakes several miles into Lake Michigan did not solve the pollution problem. In 1900, a new canal, the Sanitary and Ship Canal (Fig. 2), was completed approximately parallel to the older canal; but it was 160 ft wide, 22 ft deep, and 34 miles long. It cost $70,000,000 and could carry a flow of 10,000 cu ft per sec.

A branch from the Calumet region through the Sag, joining the main canal at Lemont, was begun in 1910 to relieve Lake Michigan of pollution from the communities rapidly developing along the south shore near the Indiana-Illinois state line. These canals admittedly were built to do more than carry pollution. Even at that time, dilution as the solution for pollution was not completely accepted by thoughtful engineers. Lawsuits threatened from the outset and these materialized to the extent of a Supreme Court decision in 1930 reducing the ultimate diversion flow to 1,500 cu ft per sec plus local pumpage, a total of about 3,100 cu ft per sec as of 1952. As a result, sewage treatment on a large scale is necessary despite these channels. However, the channels did point a way toward the Mississippi River for waterway traffic, and they maintained a tradition far older than Chicago, by holding open a waterway route until at long last in 1933 the canalization improvement of the Illinois and Des Plaines rivers joined with the western end of these channels—built at least in part on a vision.

Status of Canals and Shipping.—After touching on the origins of the waterways at Chicago, it is in order to sum up briefly just what the situation is today. Chicago harbor proper, at the mouth of Chicago River, is formed of breakwaters enclosing an inner harbor of 224 acres and an outer harbor of 970 acres. Depths vary from 12 ft to 24 ft, and the depth maintained by the Federal Government for entrance and turning is 21 ft. There are two slips and three wharves for commercial navigation, and the Navy pier. Anchorage areas are available for commercial and pleasure craft. Traffic amounted to 290,000 tons and nearly 60,000 passengers in 1951.

The channel of the main stem of the Chicago River (less than a mile) is 21 ft deep for a width of 200 ft or more, and the same depth is maintained up the North Branch for a little more than 2 miles. For about 3 additional miles, a 9-ft depth is maintained. Main river frontage along Wacker Drive (Fig. 1) is public property, and there are numerous private terminals in excess of the needs of 1951 commerce, which amounted to about 1,600,000 tons.

The South Branch of the Chicago River, as extended by the Chicago Sanitary and Ship Canal, is 34.5 miles long from the junction of the branches in downtown Chicago to Lockport on the Des Plaines River. The depth is 21 ft, and the width is 160 ft. Bridges over the waterway are important features on this section. There are twenty-four movable bridges in $4\frac{1}{2}$ miles in downtown Chicago, and they have a major effect on both water and land traffic (as noted in Fig. 1). In 1951, in the Chicago port area, the traffic was about 2,100,000 tons, of which about 1,900,000 tons was through traffic. There is much private wharfage, and the State of Illinois has a barge terminal and elevator at Damen Avenue.

Beyond Lockport and down the Illinois River (Fig. 3) to the Mississippi River are locks 110 ft wide by 600 ft long, and channels with minimum dimensions 9 ft deep and 300 ft wide. Calumet harbor is about 12 miles south of Chicago harbor proper and is within the Chicago city limits. The outer harbor is formed by 12,500 ft of breakwaters built in the open lake, an entrance channel 28 ft deep, and an anchorage area 26 ft deep. In the Calumet River, a channel of 21 ft to 25 ft deep and 200 ft wide, with turning basins, is maintained for a distance of about 6 miles. There are extensive private slips, drydocks, and wharves, and a terminal is available to the public in Calumet Lake. Traffic was about 23,500,000 tons in 1951.

The Calumet-Sag Channel, a part of the Little Calumet, and the Calumet River, is a waterway about 24 miles long, extending from Calumet harbor to a point on the Chicago Sanitary and Ship Canal about 12 miles northeastward of Lockport on the Des Plaines River. Controlling channel dimensions are 9 ft deep and 60 ft wide in the Sag Channel which also contains a lock 50 ft wide at Blue Island. There are three passing places in the 16-mile length of this narrow waterway. The channel in Little Calumet and Calumet rivers is 9 ft deep by 300 ft wide. Exercising at least as much restrictive effect as the small channel widths are some forty bridges with horizontal clearances no greater than the channel and vertical clearances of as little as 15 ft (Fig. 4). In 1949, the traffic on this waterway was nearly 3,000,000 tons, and in 1950 and 1951 it was somewhat more than this amount.

In addition to these connected waterways, there are three harbors for lake

FIG. 3.—BRANDON ROAD LOCK AND DAM ON THE ILLINOIS WATERWAY

FIG. 4.—RESTRICTED CLEARANCES ON THE SAG CHANNEL—TOWBOAT AND BARGES AT WESTERN AVENUE
BRIDGE, JOLIET (ILL.) AREA

vessels within the 12 miles of lake shore to the southeast of Calumet harbor: Indiana harbor, Buffington harbor, and Gary harbor (Fig. 2). The latter two are private harbors, but all are susceptible of connection to the Chicago inland waterway system and the Mississippi River by way of the Grand Calumet River. They accommodated 26,500,000 tons of lake traffic in 1951.

The 9-ft depth project was completed on the Illinois River and up to Lockport on the Des Plaines River in 1933, thus permitting normal inland waterway traffic from the Mississippi up through Chicago to Chicago harbor. The deficiency was that the South Fork of the Chicago River contained so many bridges, and the dense urbanization precluded industrial expansion within the city and quite effectively cut off any developments westward thereof from the lake harbor. The

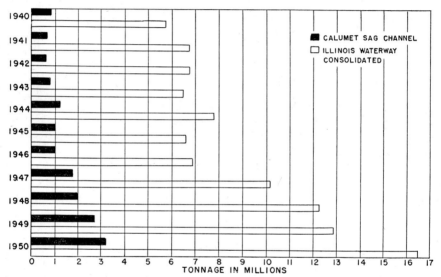

FIG. 5.—COMPARISON OF GROWTH IN COMMERCIAL TRAFFIC ON ILLINOIS WATERWAY AND CALUMET-SAG CHANNEL, 1940–1950

Calumet-Sag Channel, really a narrow drainage ditch, was improved with passing places, and the Little Calumet and Calumet rivers between the Sag and Calumet harbor were widened and deepened, all in 1939. No important progress has been made since that time.

Even with all their deficiencies, the Chicago waterways have exceeded expectations. The Illinois Waterway was estimated to be justified by traffic of 10,000,000 tons. It achieved that volume in 15 years and carries more than 17,000,000 tons now. Through traffic on the Chicago Sanitary and Ship Canal route was 1,900,000 tons in 1951, but the traffic through Calumet-Sag Channel has exceeded 3,000,000 in spite of the 60-ft channel with many obstructive bridges (Fig. 5). This canal was once estimated to have an efficient capacity of little in excess of 1,000,000 tons.

Deficiencies and How to Meet Them.—The impetus behind this traffic development in spite of serious obstacles is not difficult to understand. Unquestionably the Great Lakes furnish the lowest cost transportation in the United

States. The Calumet area has developed into one of the largest steel centers of the world, and it has better promise for future development than do some other areas. Only 35 miles from the Chicago lake ports is a free and easy inland waterway channel that reaches to the Gulf of Mexico; to the Pennsylvania and West Virginia coal fields, as well as many others with somewhat lower grade coal; to the oil fields of Louisiana and Texas; and to the wheat fields of the Missouri and Upper Mississippi river basins. Just as the old Chicago portage was accepted as one of nature's blessings by the fur traders, so the present waterways across this 35 miles are used heavily in spite of serious obstacles that would render less favorably situated waterways practically valueless.

The Corps of Engineers has a plan authorized by Congress for improving this situation—the Calumet-Sag Channel is to be enlarged to 225 ft in width;

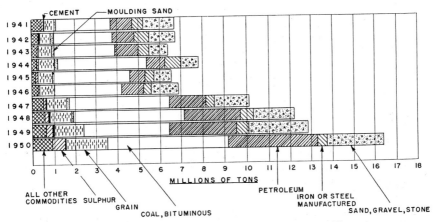

FIG. 6.—TOTAL TRAFFIC AND PRINCIPAL COMMODITIES ON ILLINOIS WATERWAY,
BY CALENDAR YEARS, 1941–1950

bridges are to have clearances of at least this width and are to be 25 ft above the water surface; Indiana harbor is to be connected with the Sag Channel by way of the Grand Calumet River; and locks to avoid contamination of Lake Michigan are to be built. The plan is estimated to cost $144,500,000, and benefits are estimated to exceed twice the cost. However, if experience with other estimates made on the same basis holds true, the benefits will greatly exceed even this favorable ratio.

An examination of the commodities being carried on the Illinois Waterway shows that there are important and increasing quantities of coal, oil products, and grain moving to Chicago (Fig. 6). These are items which are far from having reached a saturation point in such a vast market, and the quantities are clearly limited by the nature of the waterway. The manufactured iron and steel moving away from Chicago have increased many times, but the amount still is small compared with the output of the Chicago district.

By comparison, the Ohio River below Pittsburgh, which city has little more steel production capacity than Chicago, carries approximately 1,800,000 tons of steel products, or three times the Chicago output placed on inland waterways leading to the same or similar markets. The total traffic on the Ohio bears almost exactly the same ratio to the total traffic on the Illinois. Here again the limitation imposed by an inadequate waterway is evident.

A special use for the waterway occurred during World War II. Many sea-going ships were built along the inland waterways and floated to the sea in various stages of completion as limited draft permitted. The purpose of this method, of course, was to use to the fullest extent a strained industrial capacity. Of nearly 4,000 ships so built, almost 1,000 passed through Chicago and down the Illinois Waterway on the way to the sea. The presence of the Great Lakes lent impetus to this operation, and with an adequate connection to the inland waterway system they should serve also to augment more normal traffic.

Waterways in the Traffic Picture.—It probably can be stated without argument that the future prosperity and safety of the United States depend on an expanding industrial capacity and that one of its essential elements is a much more commodious transportation system. Available statistics show that railroads, waterways, and highways have all carried increasing volumes of traffic since the depression years of the early 1930's. Waterway traffic receded during the war years, whereas railroad traffic increased during those years and receded later. Truck traffic on highways has increased at a phenomenal rate since the war (from 50,000,000,000 ton-miles to more than 120,000,000,000 ton-miles in the 6 years ending in 1950). One steel company at Chicago has revealed that 43% of its output is placed on trucks. At the same time, there is a general lament regarding the inadequacy of the American highway system; and, of course, one important element in this inadequacy is the astounding increase in heavy truck hauling.

In the face of such a situation, it seems unwise, to say the least, to permit a 35-mile bottleneck between the Great Lakes and the major part of the inland waterway system in the United States to remain for long. The problem is especially significant when it is realized that this inland waterway system can carry at least four times the present amounts of traffic with almost no major improvements. However, all concerned should reflect that Chicago overgrew its first harbor, once the greatest on the Great Lakes by far. The present industrial section to the south is growing, and the greater it grows, the more difficult it will be to build an adequate waterway through it.

Perhaps it should be emphasized also that Chicago has been engaged in building waterways almost from the first days of its existence, but all except the very first were built for drainage, with navigation included only as an idea. Before it is too late, Chicago waterways should be viewed critically, as arteries of transportation which seem to offer the promise of filling so perfectly some of the important future needs of the United States.

AMERICAN SOCIETY OF CIVIL ENGINEERS
Founded November 5, 1852
TRANSACTIONS

Paper No. 2653

METALS IN THE AMERICAN ECONOMY

By Zay Jeffries [1]

Synopsis

Metals have had a profound influence on the course of civilization from the earliest times. In the conduct of military campaigns, the use of metals has often decided the outcome of crucial struggles. This paper traces the history of the development and utilization of metals, and the relation of these materials to the world's economic structure. Particular attention is paid to the growth of metallurgy in the United States, and the men responsible for the increase in knowledge. Each of the broad classes of metals—ferrous, nonferrous, and radioactive—is discussed and evaluated. The paper includes a brief résumé of the possible future trend in the application of metals.

Introduction

One does not need to be an engineer, nor does one have to be connected in any direct manner with the metal industry, to realize how impossible it would be to have the present industrial civilization without metals in large quantity and almost infinite variety. The industrial revolution is only about 200 years old. Even a superficial knowledge of history and archeology indicates that, for tens of thousands of years after the origin of man, metallic ore remained practically untouched in the earth's crust. It is clear that man's intelligence and social organization had to evolve to a certain point before metals could be useful to him. Then a period of thousands of years followed during which knowledge was gained in the refining of metals that could be separated from their ores by simple processes, such as gold from placer deposits. Man next learned to reduce iron, copper, lead, and tin in a charcoal fire. Perhaps there was also some utilization of a few iron-alloy meteorites.

There can be little doubt that social and intellectual evolution went hand in hand with the whole procedure of production, fabrication, and utilization of these early metals. Thus, the metal industry could not have been developed without man, but the civilizations that eventually rose to prominence could not have done so without metals. This partnership is not ended nor is any end in sight.

---

[1] Vice Pres. (Retired), Gen. Elec. Co., Pittsfield, Mass.

INFLUENCE OF METALS

The use of metals must not be looked on as an end in itself but as a means toward the achievement of man's goals as he may comprehend them from time to time. Furthermore, it is but one of many factors constituting an intricate mesh of interdependent human activities. True, it is an important and even a necessary factor, but so are others. Among these, the development and maintenance of an ordered society in which individuals can live in peace should have first place. A money system, transportation, communication, the electrical industries, mechanical power, machines, instruments, devices for comfort, convenience, and recreation, housing, clothing, food, education, publications, and an elaborate system of distribution are also important. To these and still others must be added the military.

Military.—How many times and with what small margins military superiority has changed the course of history can never be known. That it has been a dominant factor in the existing order of things is certain. There have been a few instances in which possession of metals definitely seemed to be a deciding factor. For example, at the battle of Marathon in 490 B. C. the Athenians were outnumbered by the Persians, but won a decisive victory, leaving 6,400 of the enemy dead on the battlefield, although their own losses came to only 192 soldiers, each of whom carried 57 lb of armor. Apparently the Koreans produced the first metal armored fighting boat, the *Tortoise,* in the sixteenth century, enabling them to win a naval engagement against the Japanese.

However, it is also certain that the early use of metal by the military was not always controlling. Genghis Khan developed great military power with very little metal. Many horses, large numbers of men, and expertness with bow and arrow provided a combination which, for a considerable period, was unbeatable.

Gradually, however, the advantages of metal began to tell. In the long struggle for existence, for coexistence, and for a place in the sun, it is recognized that metals became more and more a controlling factor. The designations, "Bronze Age" and "Iron Age," are the historians' recognition of the importance of metals in the economy.

SEARCH FOR FREEDOM

Ancient Struggles.—These early people had little idea what the outcome of their activities would be. Their first objective was to live, to live well if possible, and in any event to live with as much peace and security as practical. It appears that in early times it was just as natural to enslave other peoples as to domesticate animals. Although there is some truth in Thomas Carlyle's statement that "It is not to taste sweet things but to do noble and true things that even the poorest son of Adam dimly longs," probably the early urge to free slaves came from the experience of slave owners that their own lives were not secure when the slave population was large.

Personal Freedom.—Regardless of the motives, the idea grew that individual freedom was important. The principle did not occupy a prominent place in the practices of many early "rulers," so the people strove for a greater voice in their own government. As progress was made, larger horizons came into view. Ideals were envisioned in which government by the consent of the governed seemed practical. Checks and balances were devised. Government by law instead of by men became an objective. Freedom of the individual called for refinements such as freedom of religion, freedom of speech, freedom of the press, free markets, and freedom of enterprise. Man acquired the right to own property and to use his ability and energy, within the law, to better his own condition. For a service well rendered to society there was the incentive of personal gain and a favorable recognition by one's fellow men. The profit incentive stimulated the use of risk capital. Profits also provided a measure of the contribution to society. By encouraging competition, only the "fittest" groups could survive, so a system that automatically insured high efficiency came into being.

METALS IN AMERICA

These forces were evolving when America was discovered a few hundred years ago. There developed here an opportunity to take advantage of the successes as well as the mistakes of the ages and literally make a new world. That process continues in full force today.

The people of the United States were eventually able to enjoy the benefits of a large area of land with vast natural resources and to work in harmony with their neighbors who had generally similar ideals and were similarly blessed with natural wealth. To the favorable political atmosphere and vast natural resources must be added the necessary ingredient of a people endowed with intelligence, industry, character, and vision, capable of cooperative effort in the achievement of worthwhile goals, willing to sacrifice for the common good, and so imbued with the idea of personal freedom and all that goes with it that they were willing to risk their lives to preserve it. It is against this background that the economic importance of metals should be viewed.

Status a Century Ago.—Although the use of metals had been slowly but surely developing for thousands of years, it was relatively slight a century ago. The total annual production of all metals at that time was on the order of 6,000,000 tons. Although ferrous production consisted almost entirely of pig iron, some of which was converted into wrought iron and crucible and cemented steel, iron was then, as now, the dominating factor in the metal industry.

Among the nonferrous metals, copper, lead, zinc, tin, and mercury were in common use; gold and silver production was important; and platinum was used in small quantities. Several of the other metals had been isolated and some, like nickel and antimony, were present in certain alloys. Among the nonferrous alloys, brass, bronze, type metal, and pewter were common, and the noble metals, gold and silver, were usually alloyed for both coinage and other purposes.

It would be easy to underrate the importance of the metal industry prior to the middle of the nineteenth century. The art developed from nonexistence to flourishing activity. Railroad equipment was fabricated from cast and wrought iron, and crucible steel. Engines and cars ran on wrought-iron rails, and wrought iron was used in many structures such as bridges. Steamboats were utilizing metal. A great variety of tools of all kinds were made from crucible and cemented steel.

Military weapons of various sorts were fashioned from the metals then available by processes which, in many instances, showed great ingenuity. Damascus steel swords, for example, were not only beautiful but effective as well. Agricultural equipment was revolutionized by the judicious use of metals. The printing industry was immeasurably expanded mainly by utilization of type metal and metal presses. Some historians give the textile industry credit for ushering in the modern industrial revolution. It could not have been developed to such an advanced state without the proper use of metals. One could go on almost indefinitely, citing the profound changes in many arts that would have been well nigh impossible without metals.

Processes.—Hardening by cold work and softening by annealing are very old techniques. Rolling, pressing, forging, wire drawing, extruding, founding, surface coating, machining, welding, alloying, and heat treating also have been known for a long time. Even powder metallurgy was practiced. Aside from work in powdered iron, Wollaston made wrought platinum products by consolidating the metal powder at a high temperature without melting. The art of founding was early developed to an advanced state. Even the lost wax method had been discovered. Some of the early cast objects of art are among the best the world has so far produced.

Thus, in considering the role of metals during the past century, credit should be given to those thousands of people who, during a period of thousands of years, laid such a solid foundation.

Present Situation.—There is great contrast between conditions 100 years ago and those today. The annual world production of new metal is now in excess of 150,000,000 tons. Although the records pertaining to world population were not accurate 100 years ago, the best estimate for 1845 is slightly in excess of 1,000,000,000 people. Thus the population has approximately doubled during the past century, whereas metal production has increased about twenty-five times.

Impressive as these volume data are, they do not begin to tell the whole story. The richness in the variety of available metals and alloys, in multiform shapes and sizes, incorporated in ingenious devices and mechanisms, makes the quality factor paramount. Unfortunately, there is only space enough in this paper to touch on a few high spots of this fascinating picture.

Iron and steel represent more than 90% of the total tonnage of new metal. If manganese and chromium are considered part of the ferrous industry, then copper, zinc, lead, and aluminum constitute more than 90% of nonferrous metal production. Collectively accounting for less than 1% of the total metal tonnage is a large group of metals including antimony, arsenic, barium, beryllium, bismuth, boron, cadmium, calcium, cerium and other rare earth metals, cesium, cobalt, columbium, gallium, germanium, gold, indium, iridium, lithium, magnesium, mercury, molybdenum, nickel, osmium, palladium, platinum, potassium, rhodium, ruthenium, selenium, silver, sodium, strontium, tantalum, tellurium, thorium, tin, titanium, tungsten, uranium, vanadium, and zirconium. Some of these will be recognized as common metals, others are rare but are used in significant amounts, and still others may be considered as laboratory metals. In addition to the metallic elements listed previously, certain nonmetallic elements, such as hydrogen, oxygen, sulfur, nitrogen, and phosphorus, and some near metals, such as carbon and silicon, intimately combine with some metals to form metallic end products.

Uses of Metals

Alloys.—The elemental substances are combined chemically to form a great variety of alloys having a wide range of properties. Useful alloys of significantly different chemical composition now run into the thousands. Many of these also vary in properties by virtue of differences in method of production, differences in working, and differences in heat treatment or other treatments, so that scores of thousands of specifications are required for modern utilization.

With all this richness, engineers should be able to find any combination of properties they desire for their various structures. This is far from true. They are continually calling for new combinations. Sometimes need stimulates the development of new alloys, but often new alloys are developed and engineers adopt them to improve old devices or to make new ones. There are no dull moments in the quest for new and better alloys, and no end is in sight.

Physical Combinations.—While metallurgists are busy increasing the number and nature of alloys, inventors and engineers make an endless variety of physical combinations of these metals and alloys with other materials in special arrangements and in cooperation one with another—to insure continuing progress in the industrial revolution. Metallic products are essential in all the major industrial developments of the age.

Ferrous Metals.—There was a great improvement in steelmaking about 90 years ago. Henry Bessemer, by blowing air through molten pig iron, and William Siemens, with the open-hearth process, made steel available in abundance with a variety of properties. The cost was also substantially reduced. The railroad industry expanded rapidly as steel replaced wrought and cast iron. Steel ships became common; structural steel was used in large tonnages for buildings, bridges, and the like; and many devices could be produced and sold in quantity for the first time. As new activities such as the electrical and automotive industries were born, cheap steel gave them a good start.

However, the iron and steel industry was not content to rest its future on volume alone. Great strides were made in quality and in variety of ferrous products. In due course electric furnace steel, many different alloy steels, and significant improvements in sizes and shapes of ferrous products kept pace with, or at times led, industrial advances. It seems remarkable that one metal, like iron, can serve so many of man's needs. This phenomenon is not due solely to its cheapness but quite as much to the sweeping range of properties obtainable. Iron alloys can be made very soft or very hard, ductile or brittle, magnetic or nonmagnetic, stainless if necessary, with high or low coefficients of thermal expansion, easily machinable, and capable of use at very low as well as at elevated temperatures. Ferrous products can be processed in many ways—by casting, rolling, pressing, forging, extruding, wire drawing, welding, powder metallurgy, and a great variety of heat treatments. Wrought products from heavy forgings to fine wire and thin sheets are currently available. Single pieces range from more than 100 tons to a small fraction of an ounce.

It is not surprising that, when John R. Dunning asked the editors of thirty-two trade and business publications the question—"What is the most significant engineering development in the past century?"—a majority answered "* * * developments in the production and use of steel."

Nonferrous Metals.—Accomplishments in the nonferrous metal field have been on a smaller scale, but they are no less spectacular. No ready market awaited the availability of aluminum in the 1880's when the Hall process was invented. At times the metal seemed to be a "drug on the market," and many people interested in other materials regarded it as an intruder. However, with continued research, reduction in cost, improvement in alloys, and the increasing importance of rapid ground and air transportation, the aluminum industry has enjoyed a most rapid growth so far in the twentieth century.

On a later timetable, magnesium is going through much the same type of cycle. The magnesium business is already large, and it is growing at a fast rate.

Titanium, having a density about midway between steel and the strong aluminum alloys, good corrosion resistance, and a strength comparable to many grades of steel, is a most attractive metal. However, it is a metallurgical "toughy." It wants to combine with hydrogen, nitrogen, oxygen, and carbon, and reacts at high temperatures with all crucible materials thus far tried. At present, therefore, it is expensive. Nevertheless, the military advantages are so great that a substantial expansion program is now under way which will make the metal available in the near future in thousands of tons per year.

These four metals, iron, aluminum, magnesium, and titanium, have special significance for the long future because of the relative abundance of the ores. Since magnesium can now be recovered economically from sea water, its production will be geographically universal, and its cost should become relatively more favorable with time.

Steady progress has been made in the older metals, copper, zinc, and lead. Not only has volume multipled many times during the past century, but uses of these metals have been diversified and many new alloys have been developed. The electrical industry gave a big boost to copper and at the same time accounted for an increase in the consumption of iron and steel as well as that of the nonferrous metals.

Many minor metals play an important economic role. Bismuth, cadmium, mercury, antimony, and a few others have special uses for which replacements would be difficult to find.

The noble metals, gold, silver, and the platinum group, have an economic importance so great that any attempt to arrive at a definite evaluation would be difficult. This group, aside from its use in jewelry and in the creation of objects of art, has great industrial value. Even at relatively high prices, they are more economical for many purposes than any other material.

Silver is most important, partly because of its use in flatware and allied applications, partly because of its photochemical properties for photography, partly because of other industrial uses, and partly because of its use as money.

Gold is in a class by itself. Its value to the economy of the world cannot be measured. For hundreds of years it has been the standard of exchange for practically the whole earth. Although its status as a money base is now somewhat in a shadow, it is well to contemplate that even now every official quotation of the exchange rates of the currencies of the various countries is in terms of gold. It is by no means certain that the world can go on indefinitely with the present loose treatment of gold as a money base. Perhaps gold will be rediscovered sometime in the future and will serve as a fixed instead of as a movable base.

Tin occupies a special place. The world can use more than 200,000 tons of this metal a year at current prices. This is a measure of its usefulness. On the other hand, when and if necessary, it is possible to get along with a small fraction of the desired amount.

Nickel is a most valuable economic asset. As nearly pure nickel and as nickel base alloys, its field of utility is large. It is one of the most important ingredients in alloy steels. Recently its value as a component in high-temperature alloys for jet engines and similar uses has been brought into the limelight. More nickel could be used to advantage if it were available.

In addition to nickel, the metals most needed for the high-temperature parts of jet engines are chromium, cobalt, molybdenum, tungsten, and columbium. Although only a few million pounds of cobalt a year are available, this metal is necessary in small quantities for such a variety of products that a short supply would cause a serious economic dislocation. It is especially useful in high-temperature alloys, in permanent magnet alloys, and as a binder for cemented carbides.

Columbium is valuable in minimizing intergranular corrosion in chromium-nickel stainless steel. It also improves stainless steel weldability and the high-temperature properties of some jet engine alloys.

Molybdenum, which is available in the tens of millions of pounds per year, is rapidly becoming a key metal in alloy steel. It is utilized in small quantities in wrought form in the lamp, electronics, and electric-furnace industries. Failure to provide a substantial tonnage of molybdenum would be devastating to the nation's economy whether in peace or war.

As was indicated previously the quality factor in the metal industry should be given a high economic rating. Although the production of tungsten amounts to only a few million pounds per year, this metal has made possible three major industrial advances during the past 50 years. Early in the century, high-speed steel was introduced. A prominent mechanical engineer estimated that high-speed steel has already made possible the production in 5 days of what would otherwise have required 6 days. In the first decade of the twentieth century the tungsten incandescent lamp filament was developed as a replacement for the carbon, tantalum, and osmium filaments. Within 20 years the savings in light production in the United States alone were about $3,000,000,000 a year. The fluorescent lamp requires more tungsten per lumen output than the incandescent lamp; and, in addition, tungsten has become indispensable in the rapidly growing electronics industry.

In the 1920's cemented tungsten carbide made its appearance. It is used mainly for cutting tools, wire drawing, and forming dies and wear-resistant parts. Tungsten carbide has entered the mining field and is in demand for armor-piercing projectiles. It has greatly stepped up production. There seems little doubt that tungsten carbide will make possible the production in 5 days of what would take 6 days with high-speed steel.

One reason for giving special consideration to the economic advantages of tungsten is the implied hope that other minor metals may be responsible for similar future major economic advances.

Although it would be interesting to consider some of the other metals, such as sodium (which is produced in relatively large tonnages and used in the chemical industry), calcium, beryllium, tantalum, gallium, and indium, such discussion is not within the scope of this paper.

It is anticipated that germanium will be required in amounts of thousands of pounds per year, but a little of this metal goes a long way. When formed into single crystals, the metal has advantageous electronic properties that make possible the construction of devices such as rectifiers and amplifiers that are very compact and highly efficient when compared to "hot wire" electronic tubes. This development looks like the beginning of a revolution. Of special interest is the purity of the germanium. If germanium is to perform satisfactorily as a "transistor," certain trace elements should be controlled to around one part in a hundred million or to even one part per billion.

Radioactive Metals.—Perhaps it is impossible to estimate the economic role of uranium 235 and plutonium at present; but, when World War II was at its peak, the cost of conducting the conflict was around $500,000,000 a day. Certainly shortening the war was an economic plus; and, if Winston Churchill is correct in his conclusion that the free nations' stock pile of fissionable materials has so far dissuaded Russia from starting World War III, the economic benefits are incalculably large. However, peacetime benefits are now appearing. Many isotopes not found in nature have been made available at relatively low cost for experimentation. Radioactive iodine and radioactive cobalt are already articles of commerce. Radioactive strontium is now automatically controlling certain industrial operations. Nucleonic research tools and experimental techniques are constantly being developed. The use of "beams" of nucleons and heavier nuclear elements is part of the daily routine of several laboratories. Nucleonic science is advancing rapidly, so new applications should not be long delayed.

METAL PRODUCTION

Scrap.—The 150,000,000 tons a year production mentioned previously includes new metal only. The metal industry is much larger than this because of the recovery of scrap. Around 200,000,000 tons a year of steel is produced. Much of the "feed" for this steel is scrap recovered from previous use, such as material from borings, turnings, and punchings unavoidably accumulated in current fabricating processes; and perhaps upward of 25% is current captive steel mill scrap from croppings, chippings, scale, rejects, and the like. There is also a large "secondary" metal business in the nonferrous field. The scrap business becomes larger as the total metal industry expands, and it also becomes more complicated. In addition to conserving ore resources, many industrial products can be made at less cost because of scrap recovery. The economic advantages are very substantial.

Total Output.—Although the carbon and the graphite that are used in electrodes, furnace linings, and so forth, should not be considered part of the metal industry, when pig iron is produced in the iron blast furnace, a small percentage of carbon is captured as part of the iron alloy. If the pig iron carbon is considered to be part of the metal industry, the tonnage produced each year much exceeds that of any one of the nonferrous metals.

Considering manganese, chromium, silicon, and carbon as part of the new iron production, the total is now around 145,000,000 tons per year. Only four nonferrous metals have reached more than 1,000,000 tons per year: Copper, aluminum, zinc, and lead. No one of these has exceeded 3,000,000 tons a year. Tin, magnesium, and nickel have been produced in amounts per year exceeding 100,000 tons. The others range from less than 100,000 tons per year to laboratory quantities.

Metallurgy.—During the past century the science of metals has developed in pace with other sciences. The technical schools and universities have done a great job not only in educating and training metallurgists but in advancing the scientific frontiers. Much of the newer metal industry has been created by science, and the old techniques have had such a face lifting that they are sometimes difficult to recognize. Inventors and engineers have, of course, made excellent use of the advances in metal science, and captains of industry have made them an integral part of their activities. Metal technologists must have a knowledge of each of the intricate uses of the metals. A metallurgist dealing with electronics, for example, must know a lot about electronics theories, electronics devices, and the economics of the electronics industry. The same can be said with reference to all industries, even including the very new field of nucleonics.

Until very recently it was thought that ninety-two elements were the maximum possible, with the probability that a few would never be discovered. Now, since the nucleus of the atom has been probed and the nature of the atom is better understood, it is believed that the maximum number of elements with significantly different chemical properties, including a few transuranium synthetic elements, is actually much more than ninety-two. However, with the many isotopes so far isolated and those yet to be discovered, there must be about a thousand kinds of atoms differing from one another in certain physical properties. If things were complex a generation ago, they must now be considered supercomplex.

Bessemer, Siemens, and Charles M. Hall have been mentioned as inventors in the metal industry. No one will question the importance of their contributions. The metal industry was spoken of previously in this paper, however, as only a means to an end rather than an end in itself. Alexander Graham Bell, who invented the telephone, Thomas A. Edison, the father of the modern electrical industry, and Charles F. Kettering, Hon. M. ASCE, who has made significant contributions to the automotive industry, to mention three of thousands, created a great demand for metals in large volume and high quality. Andrew Carnegie, Elbert H. Gary, and Charles M. Schwab, three of thousands of captains of industry, were also a necessary part of the team. No one of these groups could have functioned without the others. The whole front had to move forward together or no part could advance significantly.

FUTURE PROSPECTS

This paper closes with an attempted look into the future economical role of metals. First, however, some general observations should be considered.

Aspects of Industrialization.—In the industrial revolution, certain patterns can be recognized. The early stage was the substitution of mechanical energy for human effort, followed by a tremendous amplification of that energy. At present, so much mechanical energy is utilized that all the human beings on earth could not supply it even if quantity were the only factor involved. Quantity, however, is not the only factor. The nature of the energy and the devices in which it is used would make it impossible for human beings to accomplish the things now done by mechanical energy. How, for example, could human energy be applied to propel modern aircraft? This phase of the industrial revolution is by no means concluded.

Another phase has advanced a long way and is now growing faster than the first phase. It is the use of mechanisms as substitutes for human skills, to do things more cheaply, with greater precision or with greater uniformity than is possible by "hand operation." Among these devices are the so-called servo-mechanisms, a great variety of automatic machines, business machines, controls, inspection and safety devices, and the like. This phase has already importantly affected the nation's economy, and it is destined to profoundly modify the future.

A third phase is just off to a good start. This involves the application of the most advanced scientific methods, including higher mathematics and computing machines, to solve problems either more quickly or at less cost than would otherwise be possible, or to solve problems beyond the capabilities of former generations. One activity in this phase is called Operations Research or just "OR." This scientific research relates to a study of the operations of a going organization carried out for the guidance of and in cooperation with the administrators of the organization. It is not clear where this phase will lead but the implications are indeed exciting.

These three phases are now proceeding simultaneously and each has an impact on the others. Most people's opinions of what all these things can do in the future are more likely to be underestimates than overestimates.

In passing, it should be noted that no one of these phases would be possible without a healthy metal industry. Conversely, new developments play a dominating role in making the metal business healthy. The element of interdependability is indispensable.

Obviously, all these advances make the world ever more complex. Knowledge is increasing at a rapid rate while mechanisms, governments, finances, services, and professions are becoming more complicated as the industrial revolution marches on. At the same time the ability of the human individual is changing very slowly. The problem now is to carry on indefinitely without becoming casualties of the growing complexity.

Outlook for the Future.—Fortunately, in the midst of this complexity, there are concurrent movements toward simplification. Although transportation devices, such as automobiles, aircraft, and ships are becoming more complicated, transportation itself has been greatly simplified. Although ordinary people understand little about the internal workings of many commercial devices, the same people find these devices relatively easy to operate. Simplifications in science and technology are constantly being made by developing working theories, by standardizing, by specializing, by codifying, and by abstracting. Progress can go on indefinitely if the simplification processes keep in step with the complications. Directly or indirectly, most industrial complexity stems from science and its applications. When imbalances become apparent, they can be corrected by consciously devoting extra scientific and technologic effort toward simplification.

There seems to be little doubt that the system which has served so well in the past can lead to a more abundant life, and incidentally, to an expanded and richer metal industry. Assuming a favorable political climate, a continuing predominance of iron and steel is in prospect for the indefinite future. Aluminum is surely destined to be the second metal. It is now second in cubic inches produced per year, but in, say, a few decades it will be second also in weight. Magnesium production should increase rapidly, too. Copper, zinc, and lead will continue to be big metal business. Prices may vary from time to time to reflect scarcity or cost changes, but there will be no end to the great utility of these metals.

Nickel is so valuable in both peace and war that a search for better deposits must be made, and all available scientific and engineering ingenuity must be used in extracting the metal from marginal ores and in conserving it for the most important uses.

The titanium industry will be large some day, its rate of expansion depending on military evaluation and technological improvements in production and fabrication.

Some of the metals now regarded as rare will surely gain in economic stature. Germanium can definitely be put in this category.

No one can foresee the full possibilities of nucleonics. Certainly the production of uranium 235 and plutonium is on a large scale. Although the production data are not available, it should be kept in mind in making forecasts that however small the output may be, it is larger than that of man-made iron at some early date in history. From this statement it is not to be inferred, in regard to quantity, that the production of fissionable materials will be more than a minute fraction of that of iron. However, some day the nucleonics industry will be bigger than the iron and steel industry even in peacetime. No one can now foresee the advances in the nucleonics art, and no one can say what economic value the future may put on one or more nucleonic products. Suffice it to state that the future of nucleonics cannot be forecast by chapter and verse. There are so many attractive unexplored avenues, including power production, that some must have a high statistical probability of being opened for heavy traffic. An important and large uranium industry is assured because natural uranium is the source of uranium 235 on which the nucleonics industry now mainly depends.

A steady march of progress is predicted in the science of metals. In addition to the metallurgical laboratories in educational institutions, there are hundreds connected with industrial corporations and the federal and state governments. In these laboratories balanced teams of scientists are available, who can solve problems that no individual can. Such teams are even available to companies too small to support teams of their own. Some of these teams are connected with educational institutions and others are in independent laboratories willing to do sponsored research and development. It is interesting to note that not only the small companies but also the large companies and the government sponsor research and development in these laboratories.

Thus, in contemplating the future, it is certain that all the essential ingredients for growth are present in so far as industry, science, and technology are concerned. There is no lack of confidence among captains of industry, scientists, or technologists. Only an unfavorable political atmosphere can arrest or reverse industrial progress.

AMERICAN SOCIETY OF CIVIL ENGINEERS

Founded November 5, 1852

TRANSACTIONS

Paper No. 2654

SYNERGISM BETWEEN ENGINEERING AND PETROLEUM

By Robert E. Wilson[1]

Synopsis

Engineering has helped the petroleum industry, and oil products have helped engineering. Working together as a team, petroleum and engineering have accomplished far more than they could have separately—an example of synergism. Petroleum is often located in distant places and is usually deep in the earth. It became available only because engineers have helped in manifold ways to find it, obtain it from the ground, transport it, and refine it.

Petroleum reciprocated by providing the engineers with large amounts of cheap, mobile energy in forms tailored to meet a variety of needs. Fuels derived from oil made possible whole new branches of technology, such as automotive and aeronautical engineering. Severe lubrication requirements often limit the operating conditions of machines, and petroleum met these ever-more-severe requirements. Oil has also supplied new materials for construction, of which a wide variety of asphalts is particularly important; and by-product gases from cracking became the raw materials of a great new petrochemical industry.

Petroleum and engineering mutually stimulated each other to the greater use of technology. New techniques useful in the chemical and other industries have resulted. As they work on future problems, engineers should recognize that there is such a thing as overengineering, especially on gadgetry, as is particularly apparent in certain military equipment.

Introduction

The dictionary defines synergism as "cooperative action of discrete agencies such that the total effect is greater than the sum of the two effects taken independently, as in the action of the mixtures of certain drugs." In other words, this cooperative action cannot be the mere adding together of two effects, like the hitching up of two horses to form a team. One or both of the agencies must have a stimulating effect on the other.

[1] Chairman of the Board, Standard Oil Co. (Indiana), Chicago, Ill.

Synergism is of course nothing new. When two small boys get together, they think up far more devilment than if they were kept separate. The increase in devilment seems to arise from competition between the boys to see which one can think up the worst things to do. The real synergistic influence is the mutual stimulation. The same effect can be observed in other—and more constructive—fields of human activity.

BRIEF HISTORY OF THE OIL INDUSTRY

To continue the illustration, engineering and the petroleum industry were small boys at about the same time. If organized professional engineering was born with the American Society of Civil Engineers in 1852, it was 7 years old when the petroleum industry was born with the Drake well in Titusville, Pa., in 1859. Unfortunately, these two youngsters did not immediately get together and start goading each other to greater and greater achievements. Only after they did get together, years later, did both the oil industry and engineering begin their rapid rate of progress, which has contributed so much to the modern world.

The oil business was slow to recognize its need for engineering, primarily because the first oil fields, in Pennsylvania, had certain advantages not possessed by the fields discovered later. For one thing, the oil in Pennsylvania was near the surface. The Drake well was only $69\frac{1}{2}$ ft deep, about $1\frac{1}{2}\%$ as deep as the average well today. Also, the crude product so readily obtainable in the Pennsylvania field was present in quantities more than adequate for existing needs. It was therefore a low-priced raw material, which did not justify expensive engineering in either production or refining. As still another factor, the Pennsylvania crude was easy to refine, mainly by simple distillation, to yield both burning and lubricating oils that were better, as well as cheaper, than such competing products as whale oil.

Although the early oil industry had these advantages, which tended to make it technologically lazy, petroleum also had certain characteristics that were eventually to require the extensive utilization of engineering and that were to stimulate greatly the development of engineering itself:

(1) Petroleum is widely in demand. Oil products were to find so many and such varied uses, that more and more engineering assistance was inevitable.

(2) Petroleum proved somewhat contrary in its geographical location. It tends to occur in areas remote from the principal markets (Fig. 1), and so has presented many transportation problems.

(3) Petroleum occurs over a wide range of depths and kinds of strata in the earth's crust, thus necessitating the development of radically new techniques for exploration, drilling, and production.

(4) Petroleum is a complex mixture, containing thousands of different hydrocarbons, along with numerous impurities. Improved separation and purification methods were necessary, particularly for crudes other than Pennsylvania crude, to yield fractions that would give superior performance in different jobs.

(5) The hydrocarbons making up the bulk of petroleum are relatively, although not wholly, unreactive. When research chemists finally learned how to use petroleum as the raw material for dozens of chemical conversions, the conditions required were severe. This was a great stimulus to engineering, as will be illustrated later with a specific example.

(6) Oil products were eventually to be used in several different types of internal combustion engines. This use has been so important to civilization that it merits separate consideration. Internal combustion engines were themselves in their engineering infancy. As they gradually improved through the application of their own branch of engineering, they provided more and more opportunities for other engineers. As an outstanding example, these engines were light enough for flying and so made possible the airplane industry, which otherwise could not have come into existence.

Fig. 1.—Oil Exploration, Frequently at Inaccessible Localities

Any one of these six characteristics of petroleum would have called forth engineering developments. Taken in combination, they have made the oil industry one of the chief users, and stimulators, of engineering advances.

Exploration

Although exploration was not the petroleum activity that first made use of engineering, exploration should be discussed first in any logical story of the industry.

Early exploration consisted largely of hunting for oil seepages—places where oil was oozing out of the ground. Next came surface geology. The step after that, and the one that is by far the most important today, was the mapping of underground structures by means of various types of instruments located at the surface of the earth. Development of these instruments required great engineering skill—particularly on the part of electrical engineers. The devices must be sufficiently sensitive to measure unbelievably small motions, or variations in magnetic or gravity fields, but they must also be rapid in operation and rugged enough for use in rough terrain (Fig. 2).

The Principal Instruments.—One such geophysical instrument is the magnetometer. The earth's magnetic field is affected by the character of the underground rocks. It is possible to locate places where folds in the nonmagnetic

Fig. 2.—A Seismograph Crew Exploring for Petroleum in Southern Louisiana Swamps—
Typical of Difficult Territory Sometimes Encountered

sedimentary rock have been caused by upwardly projecting masses of relatively magnetic igneous rock. The information obtained by measuring the magnetic differences does not give very exact picture, but it tells which areas are worth investigation by more exact methods. One form of magnetometer can be flown over a wide area, making continuous records.

Another useful instrument is the gravity meter (Fig. 3). It measures the minute changes in the earth's gravity arising from the fact that some underground rock layers are more dense than others. The variations measured may be as small as 1/100,000 of 1%, or one part in 10,000,000. Like the magnetometer, the gravity meter is utilized chiefly to find areas worth exploring by more accurate means.

By far the most widely used geophysical instrument is the seismograph. Charges of dynamite are exploded at or near the earth's surface. The shock waves reflected from underground strata are picked up and accurately timed by recording devices strung out over distances of as much as a half mile. Movement of the surface as small as 0.000001 in. and times as short as 0.001 sec are recorded. Engineers have devised ingenious patterns for placing their detection devices. In particular, it is necessary to overcome various effects of surface soils and subsoils, which otherwise would mask reflections from the deeper layers of real interest.

FIG. 3.—A GRAVITY METER IN OPERATION IN LOUISIANA

When exploration of the offshore lands in the Gulf of Mexico was undertaken, the operation of seismographs presented many problems. The engineers finally solved them and worked out novel techniques for getting reliable information from dynamite shots fired just below the surface of the water (Fig. 4). A boat moves along steadily, dragging the listening devices behind and setting off a charge every so often. Radio ranging devices make a simultaneous record of the ship's exact location.

These three instruments have greatly increased the efficiency of exploration. When so-called "rank wildcat" wells are drilled without the assistance of technical information supplied by geology and geophysics, only one in twenty-five strikes oil. With such information, one in eight strikes oil—an improved performance that has meant much to the oil supply of the United States—and to the solvency of the oil companies.

PRODUCTION

The production of oil required engineering of a simple type right from the start. Even the Drake well had to have a derrick and drilling tools although the drill used was of a rather crude percussion type.

Engineering Problems in Drilling.—Modern wells (Fig. 5) present far more serious engineering problems. A fundamental engineering problem is that of finding steels strong enough to stand drilling service. When a well is 2 miles or 3 miles deep, the string of pipe is under very great stress from its own weight,

FIG. 4.—EXPLORATION IN THE GULF OF MEXICO—UNDERWATER SHOT, WITH SEISMOGRAPH READINGS FROM GEOPHONES TOWED BEHIND BOAT

and it must in addition stand severe twisting. A long string may take as many as eight complete turns before the torsion builds up enough to rotate the drill bit at the desired rate.

Drilling muds alone have required much technical study. These muds, circulated by special pumps, bring up the cuttings, prevent blowouts by raising bottom hole pressures, and help in sealing the sides of the well bore. They must be carefully selected to suit the needs of the various types of rock encountered.

An ingenious and useful engineering development is directional drilling. It enables drillers to go around broken drill strings after "fishing" had failed to recover them. Its really spectacular use, however, is for drilling from the shore under rivers or lakes or on the edge of the ocean—in short, where it would be difficult to locate derricks directly above the point to be reached. Directional drilling is also used to tap the holes of runaway wells that may have caught fire.

Another engineering job is the fracturing of rock structures, to increase the flow of oil into the well. The early procedure used one of the engineer's favorite tools—explosives, which are still employed. However, more effective means are now available. The latest is the "Hydrafrac" process (Fig. 6). This fractures the rocks by a very high-pressure injection of jellied kerosene. The jellied kerosene contains coarse sand to hold open the fractures after the hydraulic pressure is released.

In the oil fields it is always important to know the nature of the formations through which the drill is going. Electric logging now provides information about

FIG. 5.—CIVIL ENGINEERING KNOW-HOW APPLIED TO OFFSHORE DRILLING PLATFORM IN 30 FT OF GULF WATER, DEVISING CONSTRUCTION FOR MAN TO WORK AND LIVE SAFELY

thickness and porosity of the reservoir beds and indicates whether they contain oil, gas, or water. Electric logging also enables drillers to locate points of water entry, where sealing-off operations should be used.

Actual Problems.—After drilling has been successfully completed, engineers control and operate the producing well. In many people's minds a good oil well still comes in with a fountain of oil spouting twice as high as the derrick. This is no longer true. Modern drillers are ashamed of themselves if they let a well "run away" as a gusher, with its resulting waste of oil.

Many wells do not flow at all, and so must be pumped. The pumping of liquids from 2 miles or 3 miles down in the earth is itself an engineering feat.

A whole new field of engineering practice is the one known as reservoir engineering. Since what is called a producing "sand" may actually have about the porosity and permeability of a concrete sidewalk, reservoir engineering is indeed a special science. It involves study of the rates of flow under high pressure, in systems complicated by the presence of water and gas. The problem is further complicated by the phenomenon known as "retrograde condensation"—the strange tendency of certain highly compressed gases to absorb liquid as pressure is increased and to release it when pressure is reduced under conditions near their critical points. This is of course just the opposite of what happens at moderate pressures.

FIG. 6.—PREPARING TO SPLIT UNDERGROUND OIL-BEARING ROCK BY HIGH-PRESSURE PUMPING OF JELLIED KEROSENE—BEING MIXED IN TANK AT CENTER

Oil field engineers must also determine the most efficient rate of production. Each field presents a different problem of how to recover the economic maximum amount of oil from the formation.

Secondary Recovery.—A major engineering accomplishment in the oil fields has been the development of secondary methods of recovery. Free flow and ordinary pumping will get out of the average well only about one third of the oil present. For every barrel obtained, two are left in the ground. Those two barrels are tempting, and engineers have been working for years on methods of getting more of this oil. The commonest procedures have been water drives and gas drives (Fig. 7), but still more effective methods are beginning to be developed.

Although any type of secondary recovery is expensive, these methods will be used more and more as the cost of finding and producing new oil increases. It is not too much to hope that secondary methods will yield a total of two thirds of the oil, and so leave only one barrel in the ground out of every three. Even that one remaining barrel will call forth a great deal of engineering ingenuity in attempts to obtain it.

TRANSPORTATION

Once the oil is above ground, it must be transported. The preferred method is by pipeline—the greatest contribution the oil industry has made to commodity

FIG. 7.—RECYCLING PLANTS LIKE THIS LARGE STATION IN TEXAS INCREASE OIL RECOVERY BY PUMPING NATURAL GAS BACK INTO WELLS

transportation. The pipeline turns the liquid nature of oil into an advantage instead of the handicap it once represented. In spite of the existence of water pipes, human imagination was so small that for a long time crude oil and products were transported by wrapping steel around them and shipping this package, with all the attendant disadvantages. Most of the containers, such as tank cars, tank trucks, or tankers weigh about as much as the liquid hauled, and there is always a back haul on the empty container. Pipelines avoid all this; but tankers, tank cars, and trucks still have an important place in the over-all transportation picture.

Today gasoline and other oil products are delivered everywhere in the United States at an average over-all transportation cost from well to consumer of about 3¢ per gal. In other words, 7 lb of oil is transported 1,000 miles and delivered to the consumer at lower cost than that for a 1-ounce letter over a shorter average distance.

Pipelines are feasible partly because oil has become a large-scale business, and partly because engineers have shown much ingenuity in building them. The necessary ditches are now dug by mechanical ditch-digging machines. Wrapping

FIG. 8.—MANIFOLD IN MISSOURI RECEIVING CRUDE FROM WYOMING, TEXAS, OKLAHOMA, AND KANSAS AND DISTRIBUTING MORE THAN 300,000 BBL DAILY TOWARD CHICAGO, ILL., ST. LOUIS, MO., OR SUGAR CREEK REFINERY IN MISSOURI

machines cover the pipeline with layers of asphalt-impregnated heavy paper. Ways have been found to prevent corrosion by the liquids inside the pipeline and by water, soil, or stray electric currents outside the pipelines. Means have also been devised for scraping out wax and other deposits. The shipping of different types of product is now simplified (Fig. 8) by selectors that automatically switch each batch into the proper receiving tank when it reaches them.

Thus, engineers have contributed greatly to oil transportation. At the same time the country-wide availability of low-cost liquid fuel has been of tremendous value to the engineers—and to the public. Petroleum owes much to engineers but engineers owe much to petroleum.

REFINING

In the field of refining, the engineering was rather simple for the first 50 years of the oil industry. Because kerosene costing in the neighborhood of 20¢ a gallon was a better burning oil than whale oil at $2 a gallon, refineries were not compelled by economic considerations to make the best possible use of their raw materials. The early stills were little more than teakettles. When refiners wished to increase refinery capacity, they built more teakettles. Even in the early years of the twentieth century, refinery engineers simply got out the old blueprints and built more of the same.

The Advent of Cracking.—The factor that changed all this, and accelerated the need for engineers, was the advent of oil cracking. In 1909 William M. Burton of the Standard Oil Company (Indiana) decided that the 18% or so of gasoline obtainable from typical crude oil by fractionation would not be adequate to supply the rapidly growing number of automobiles. With the real spirit of the entrepreneur, and with the thought of making some money for his company, he decided that the whole Whiting, Ind., research staff should be put to work on the problem of cracking heavy petroleum oils into gasoline. Although this staff was probably the best and largest in the industry, it actually consisted of only two chemists!

The research was successful, and resulted in the first commercially feasible process for oil cracking. The process doubled the amount of gasoline obtainable from a barrel of crude oil and so insured a low-cost fuel for American automobiles.

The Burton process, however, involved heating oil up to high temperatures at pressures much higher than had previously been used. In addition to these severe and troublesome conditions, refinery engineers also had to wrestle with the problem of coke. The tendency to form coke in cracking is practically inescapable, because the percentage of carbon in the heavy oils to be cracked is higher than it is in the gas and gasoline produced. The high-carbon material left behind deposited on the heating surfaces of the early cracking units (Fig. 9), where it obstructed heat transfer and caused local hot spots and other troubles.

There was little knowledge available with which to solve the many practical difficulties. Almost nothing was known about the strength of metals at high temperatures. Only the crudest estimates could be made of heat transmission rates or of the friction developed by liquid flow in pipes. A decade was to elapse before creep, the gradual distortion of metals at elevated temperatures, began to be understood. Modern alloys had not been invented, and very few other developments in metallurgy had been made. Even for plain carbon steel, only the simplest equipment, such as tubing, pipe, and plates, was available.

Refinery engineering had its real beginning through consideration of all these problems and of various troubles that arose in connection with operating the units. Welded construction gradually replaced the leaky riveted construction. Improved alloys were developed. More accurate knowledge about the strength of materials was obtained. The original Burton stills were designed with a factor of safety of 5, based on the handbook data for the strength of steel at ordinary temperatures. When engineers finally got around to measuring the strength of the metal at temperatures prevailing in the direct-fired still bottoms, they found the actual factor of safety was only from about $1\frac{1}{2}$ to 1.

Several new types of pumps were developed for handling hot oil—in itself no minor problem. All these various engineering advances tended to complement each other, as so often happens in the engineering field.

The old practice of simply building more batteries of small units gradually faded out as labor costs rose, and also as basic knowledge about the physical properties of hydrocarbon mixtures was obtained. The new knowledge put engineers in a position to design giant combination cracking and crude running units charging not 300 bbl of gas oil per day, but 50,000 bbl of total crude oil per day.

Large-Scale Operation Led to More Engineering.—The new, large-scale operations required larger quantities of fuel, which, together with rising fuel costs, made

FIG. 9.—EARLY BURTON CRACKING STILLS—BY COMPARISON, CAPACITY OF ONE MODERN CATALYTIC
CRACKING UNIT, TWO HUNDRED TIMES AS GREAT

it worthwhile to undertake careful engineering studies of such items as heat transfer and heat exchange. The oil industry has appreciated engineers, and has used them widely. One reason is that raw material costs about 0.9¢ per lb, and the average gross realization on finished products at the refinery gates is only 1.2¢ per lb. All the complicated processing plus the refining profit must come out of 0.3¢ per lb. The economies that engineers made possible have therefore been essential. Engineers have been a major factor in keeping the price of gasoline at the low levels that the oil industry's customers have enjoyed.

Other Stimulating Effects of Cracking.—Cracking not only drove engineers to many specifically needed achievements, but also had indirect stimulating effects on technology. For one thing, the profits from the cracking operation encouraged every progressive oil company to undertake research; and research always leads to new and improved products, usually at lower costs.

As able chemists and engineers were drawn into the oil industry and demonstrated their value, more and more of them entered the operating and management sides of the business. This trend has done much to keep the industry progressive and to speed up the application of science and engineering.

Even the by-product gases from cracking turned out to be highly important (Fig. 10). The composition of these gases was largely unknown 30 years ago. Companies that collected them as a safety measure and burned them under the stills were considered to be quite progressive. Research eventually showed that the cracked gases contained large amounts of unsaturated hydrocarbons, not present in crude oil or natural gas. These reactive hydrocarbons became starting materials for the synthesis of hundreds of important chemicals. For example, ethylene, made by one or another type of cracking operation, is today used to make ethylene glycol, the popular permanent antifreeze. It likewise supplies most of the coun-

FIG. 10.—VAPOR RECOVERY UNITS, TO COLLECT AND FRACTIONATE VALUABLE LIGHT ENDS FROM CATALYTIC CRACKING UNITS

try's ethyl alcohol and acetic acid, as well as polyethylene and other plastics. Also present in these cracked gases are propylene, butylene, and isobutane, which are largely converted into high-quality gasoline by polymerization or alkylation. Butylene is also the principal raw material used in making synthetic rubber.

As a striking illustration of the magnitude of cracking operations today, the relatively small by-product of cracked gases contains more than 3,000,000 tons a year of propylene and butylene alone! It is as if the industry has uncovered veritable chemical mines in its own back yard.

The Catalytic Revolution.—Thus cracking presented engineers with many new problems and opportunities. Perhaps the next biggest big batch of new problems came with the catalytic revolution, which has brought about major changes in petroleum refining during the past 15 years.

Cracking itself was not the first refining process to make use of catalysts, but it is now the most important. It had been known for some time that solid catalysts could be used to crack gas oils. Since the gasoline obtained was higher in octane number than that produced by thermal cracking, the possibility of a catalytic process created considerable interest. The stumbling block was the old enemy coke, which deposited on the catalyst and destroyed its activity in a few minutes of operation. Eugene Houdry finally solved this problem by building multiple reactors. After a short period of reaction service, the oil was switched to another reactor, and the catalyst was regenerated by burning off the coke with compressed air.

Use of multiple reactors is cumbersome and involves rapid changes in vessel temperatures; efforts were therefore made to improve the process. One procedure was to use mechanical elevators, which moved the catalyst continuously from the reaction to regeneration zone and back again.

Fluidized Solids Technique.—A more popular new engineering technique is the use of fluidized solids (Fig. 11). The powdered catalyst of carefully chosen range

FIG. 11.—UNITS FOR FLUIDIZED SOLIDS TECHNIQUE, ELIMINATING PRESSURE PROBLEM IN CRACKING

of particle size can be maintained in "fluidized" beds, can be kept turbulent by the upwardly bubbled gas or vapors, and can be moved about through lines in much the same way that liquids are moved. The spent catalyst is continuously withdrawn from the reactor and is sent by means of an air lift to a regenerator, where the coke is burned off. The coke—once so troublesome—is now used to supply most of the process heat. One such modern unit circulates the catalyst at the rate of 25,000 tons per day without any internal moving parts.

The fluidized solids technique is useful in other processes besides cracking. It permits continuous operation with catalysts requiring frequent regeneration. It is well adapted to adjustment of activity by addition of a fresh catalyst. However, the greatest advantage is the essentially isothermal operation it makes possible even for reactions that are highly exothermic or endothermic—thus permitting the use of ideal operating temperatures and so minimizing undesirable side reactions.

The technique of handling fluid catalysts has required much engineering study, not only on the fundamentals of controlling the process but also on the prevention of erosion in pipes, slide valves, and other equipment by the rapidly moving streams of solid catalyst particles.

Other Catalytic Processes.—Among the other processes that helped bring about the catalytic revolution in the oil industry are polymerization and alkylation. Like most new processes, they brought new engineering problems. Alkylation with sulfuric acid involved a corrosion and a dehydration problem. In alkylation with hydrogen fluoride, both these problems are even more serious. Severe corrosion difficulties have also been encountered in the isomerization process by which normal butane is converted to isobutane for alkylation. (By variations of the same process, low-octane pentanes and hexanes can be converted to the high-octane branched isomers.)

Another important catalytic process is hydroforming, which turns certain low-octane components of virgin naphthas into high-octane aromatics. If desired, the aromatics can be separated for use as pure chemicals. This was done during World War II to make toluene for TNT. It is being done today to make the additional benzene needed so badly for chemicals, drugs, and synthetic rubber.

Improvements in Refining.—Although the most spectacular improvements have been in the catalytic field, the older petroleum refining processes have also experienced engineering advances. Better design of bubble towers and packed columns has improved the close fractionation necessary for so many petroleum processes.

Azeotropic distillation, extractive distillation, and selective adsorption are helping to sort the many different hydrocarbon molecules into separate bins, where simple fractionation will not do the job. Dewaxing, deasphalting, solvent extraction, acid treating, sweetening—all have become more efficient through engineering study, with the result that the customer receives better lubricants (Fig. 12), waxes, asphalts, heater oils, and many other products.

By-Products.—It is a somewhat intriguing fact that the petroleum industry can improve a remarkably large number of oil products by adding to them some of its own by-products. In the search for a better lubricating oil or cutting oil, it often turns out that the necessary ingredient is something also made from oil.

By-product sulfonates are placed in cutting and grinding oils and in agricultural sprays. Additives made from oil products go into modern heavy-duty lubricating oils, and into the highly critical fluids used in such complicated new devices as automatic transmissions. The petroleum industry apparently has a synergistic effect on itself.

The Principal Contribution of Petrolem to Engineering

Thus far, discussion has mostly concerned the petroleum industry's benefits from engineering. Now, what has petroleum done for engineering?

In passing, a few of the important ways have been mentioned in which the oil industry has stimulated engineering developments. However, probably the chief contribution has been to make available large amounts of cheap, convenient mobile energy in forms tailored to meet a variety of needs. One of the primary jobs of engineers is to utilize energy—to rescue the human race from doing all its work with muscle power, wind power, and water power.

The enormous expansion since 1918 in the use of power in the United States has been almost entirely due to oil and gas. Coal, once the principal source of energy, has actually slipped backward. More than half the British thermal units consumed are now supplied by petroleum and natural gas, as against about 14% in 1918.

An important additional fact is that the increase in useful work has been far greater than the increase in British thermal units consumed. This result has been

FIG. 12.—SOLVENT EXTRACTION UNIT, FOR MANUFACTURING HIGH-GRADE LUBRICATING OILS REQUIRED BY MODERN ENGINES

possible because oil-burning equipment is relatively much more efficient. A diesel locomotive does about five times as much work per British thermal unit as does a steam locomotive—one principal reason why diesels using relatively expensive diesel fuel are more economical than steam locomotives using comparatively cheap coal or residual oil as fuel. The gasoline engine is also efficient, with amazingly high output per pound of weight.

Largely because technology combined with business initiative enabled the American oil industry to make available a convenient form of energy, the number of internal combustion power plants has grown enormously. Today the combined horsepower of the Otto cycle and diesel engines in the United States is about eighty times that of the central power plants using steam! Of course, most of the internal combustion engines are operating only part of the time, but some of them —such as diesel locomotives and the diesels used in central power plants—have rather high operating factors.

Internal Combustion Engines.—The internal combustion engine has led to an entirely new branch of engineering—automotive engineering. This branch has taken its present form largely because of petroleum and the technological advances of the oil industry. Without the invention of cracking, family automobiles might be steamers or electrics, and automotive engineering would be essentially a branch of steam or electrical engineering.

The relation of cheap, high-quality liquid fuels to the automobile is an outstanding example of synergism—a beneficent rather than a vicious technological circle. The automobiles needed more gasoline, and cracking increased both the quantity and the quality. Thus, more cars were built, which required still more gasoline, and refiners built larger-scale and hence more economical refinery units— and so the process continued. It should be remembered, incidentally, that only the existence of many different centers of initiative in a free country is likely to produce such a result.

When companies—or industries—use technology to try to stay ahead of their competitors, the public benefits from a sort of technological bonus. Technology is like nature—nature seldom just barely solves a problem. For example it equips fish with enough egg-laying capacity to provide a new crop of fish and also to supply shad roe for lunches.

Technology likewise solves its problems with something to spare, and this little something extra always stimulates other technologists. The race between automobile compression ratios and octane numbers has led to 1952 gasoline that can do 50% more useful work than could the gasoline of 1925—and it incidentally led to the air superiority that helped win a war in the meantime. All this progress, of course, does not count the enormous technological bonuses obtained from totally unexpected applications of any new advance in technical knowledge.

The engineer specializing in economics often enters the picture, and should not be forgotten. For example, he helps decide what increases in compression ratio are economically justified at a given time. There comes a point where the decrease in fuel consumption is more than offset by the cost of the fancy high-octane ingredients needed.

Lubrication.—There has also been a race in the field of lubrication. People designing automotive and similar equipment are constantly inventing new devices, which the old oils will not lubricate. The ability of lubricating oils to stand up under high temperatures and pressures is often the limit on the performance of a given engine or machine. Fortunately, better and better oils have constantly raised those limits. For example, extreme-pressure lubricants now make the use of hypoid gears in automobiles possible.

A tougher problem has been complicated automatic transmissions. They must operate in hot weather and under subzero starting conditions, without change of oil. Oils have been developed that meet these seemingly impossible requirements.

Airplanes.—In the air, the piston-engine airplane has had many of the same engineering headaches as the automobile, plus many of its own arising from the need for combined lightness and power. To realize what has happened the power output of the aviation engines of the two world wars should be compared. The Liberty engine of World War I generated about 400 hp. The American version of the Rolls Royce-Merlin, used in World War II, had the same cylinder volume, but could generate 2,000 hp—almost five times as much as the Liberty engine. To stand the compression pressures and do the supercharging required to attain this high output, the Rolls Royce engine had to be about twice as heavy as the Liberty; but, since the horsepower was so much greater, the power output per

Fig. 13.—Units to Produce Alkylate, the Backbone of the World War II Aviation Gasoline Program

pound of engine was still more than doubled. The Liberty had to operate on gasoline of only about 55 octane number, but the World War II engines had gasoline of 100 octane number or better (Fig. 13), and improved lubricants as well. Better fuels and lubricants do much to enable the modern military piston engines to deliver about 1 hp per pound of engine weight and per cubic inch of piston displacement—about two thousand times as much as the horse which, for engineering purposes, will soon survive only in the name "horsepower"!

The airplane has itself created several entirely new forms of engineering. There is not only the engineering connected with structural design of airfoils and air frames, but also the whole new field of aerodynamics—recently extended to supersonic flight. Nowadays news releases refer to an American plane that can travel at twice the speed of sound! Only yesterday people were wondering whether planes could penetrate the sonic barrier at all.

The jet airplane, which made this supersonic flight possible, has brought terrific engineering problems of its own. At first it was thought that the jet was going to be a simple device, just as was optimistically thought about the diesel, which was originally supposed to burn anything. Actually, high-output diesels are now quite critical of their diets, and so are jets. They will probably become even more critical as they strive for maximum performance.

Materials of Construction.—In the construction field, the petroleum industry has demanded that engineers find new materials for building refinery equipment.

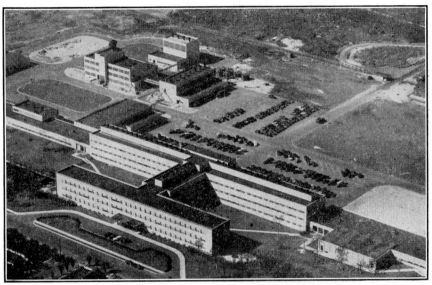

Fig. 14.—Whiting, Ind., Research Laboratory of the Standard Oil Company (Indiana),
Illustrative of Large-Scale Research in the Petroleum Industry

The petroleum industry has also contributed to the construction field materials of its own—particularly to the roads on which automobiles and trucks travel. A recent major contribution to the highway engineers has been the development of asphalts containing additives that permit effective mixing with wet aggregate and so enable roads to be laid in damp weather. Perhaps at this point a synergistic moral effect, as well as an economic effect, might be claimed for petroleum research. Since the new additives permit road building in wet weather, rain no longer drives the road gangs into taverns and other places where they can get into trouble.

Estimating roughly the dollar value to the public of the synergistic effects of petroleum and engineering is well nigh impossible. Who, for example, can gage the value to the public of research (Fig. 14), of more than doubling the gasoline supply by cracking, of increasing octane numbers of motor gasoline from 50 to 90, or of increasing aviation gasoline octane numbers from 55 to more than 100—all the latter accomplished was to win the Battle of Britain, and in large measure to win the war. Toluene and synthetic rubber from petroleum also played a major part in that victory.

Then there is the fourfold increase in farm tractors in the past 15 years, which has nearly doubled the farm output per worker and has at the same time reduced the farm population of horses and mules by about 10,000,000. This latter fact means that about 40,000,000 more people can be fed from the same farm acreage. Consider also the value of the dozens of new chemicals, plastics, and fibers made largely from petroleum, and one begins to realize how inadequate even billion-dollar units are to measure public benefits.

Future Developments

So much for the past and present. A more elusive question is: Where is the United States going from here?

Oil Fuels Will Be Available and Needed.—The most important question for the future is whether energy from liquid fuel will continue to be available. The world certainly will continue to prefer this form of energy for most uses, especially in the field of transportation. Although atomic energy may be used for very large central power installations and perhaps for ships, hydrocarbon liquids will long continue to be the preferred fuels for most mobile equipment.

In the report issued recently by the President's Materials Policy Committee, headed by William S. Paley, it is estimated that the domestic demand for petroleum products will more than double again in the next 25 years. Obviously such a huge demand will put a tremendous load on the oil industry, and will increase the need for engineers and scientists of all kinds, particularly for those concerned with finding and producing petroleum.

If there is no unwise political tampering with the incentives that cause men and companies to risk their money in the search for oil, it may be confidently expected that petroleum will continue to be the principal raw material of the liquid fuels industry during the coming 25 years. Although it sounds unduly alarmist to state that total underground reserves of crude oil are dwindling, it is an inescapable fact that each barrel of oil taken out of the ground means one less still to be found. Exploration and production will require even more highly expert engineering attention, and at least a continuation of the incentives that have made these activities so successful in the past.

Liquid fuels will come from petroleum for many years and later will be manufactured from other raw materials, probably oil shale and later coal. In examining these possible future replacements for petroleum, most of the problems are found to be engineering ones. For example, coal might be used as the starting point for Fischer-Tropsch synthesis of gasoline. Here the chemical reactions have been well worked out; highly efficient catalysts have been developed; and the chief problems are economic. Improving process economics is a job on which engineers are especially useful.

Oil Shale.—If oil shale instead of coal is used for future gasoline—and it does today appear closer to being able to compete— a still different set of engineering problems arises. The Bureau of Mines at its small demonstration mine in Rifle, Colo., has made considerable progress toward solving the problem of mining the shale at low cost. Because the shale occurs in thick beds—unlike coal—mechanical shovels can be taken inside the mountain. They scoop down the shale at the rate of 100 tons per man-day.

Both the Bureau and the oil industry have worked on the problem of retorting the shale. Here one of the serious engineering problems is cooling. In an area where water is scarce, much of the cooling is effected by taking off the hot oil vapors countercurrent to the incoming shale itself. Another job for engineers is to perfect the best possible means of handling the 85% to 90% of spent rock after the oil is recovered.

FIG. 15.—ANALYSIS OF REFINERY BY-PRODUCT GASES—ITSELF AN OPERATION REQUIRING HIGHLY SPECIALIZED AUTOMATIC EQUIPMENT

Shale reserves are large—enough to last for more than 100 years. Coal reserves are even larger. Therefore a future supply of liquid fuels is assured, for use in the flexible and efficient machines that such fuels make possible. Although research and pilot plant work on such processes should continue, the building of commercial size units at this time would be wasteful and premature, and require large operating subsidies by the government. When these processes can stand on their own feet, industry will be glad to build them with its own money.

The Danger of Overengineering.—Machines themselves seem to have ahead of them a future of increasing mechanical complications. The objective of the complications will be to obtain either operating ease or increased performance (Fig. 15).

At this point a warning is needed against the tendency of a few engineers to be hypnotized by the beauty of their own complications, and to lose sight of the main objective. There is such a thing as overengineering. The question always arises, as to whether a new complication is worthwhile, particularly at a time when engineering complications cost rapidly increasing amounts of money. The painfully slow-acting pushbutton mechanism for raising and lowering the toilet bowls in Pullman bedrooms is a case in point!

The United States is an outstanding nation of gadgeteers. As users, Americans are fascinated with gadgets; and, to some engineers, the chance to devise one more gadget, either to replace a manual operation or to perform a completely new operation, is almost too intriguing to resist. There are many evidences that too much emphasis is being placed on gadgetry and automaticity. The cockpit of an air liner is a frightening thing to behold. Automatic window-raising devices for automobiles are convenient, provided there is time to keep the children from playing with them and running down the battery—but how helpless is the driver when they get out of order! Even the modern home is dangerously close to the place where the merits of automatic gadgets may be offset by increasing frequency of failure to operate.

True engineering does not necessarily mean increased complexity. The highest achievement would consist in eliminating the difficulties or situations requiring gadgets, rather than in inventing new gadgets to handle the trouble. The most satisfactory solution to the problem of the leaky fountain pen is not the introduction of rubber gloves.

True needs must be met. However, one of the toughest exercises in engineering judgment is that of determining whether an apparent problem should be wrestled with through the avenue of additional equipment and complexity, or whether it can be eliminated by simplification. This question recalls a clever definition of a good engineer—one who can draw sound conclusions from insufficient data!

Without question most of the automatic equipment devised by engineers is highly worthwhile—for example, in the places where it eliminates the possibilities of human error. The giant refinery units of the oil industry are operated largely by automatic control devices. To give a rough idea of the extent to which instruments are used, one medium-sized refinery went from 15 process instruments in 1922 to 11,000 instruments in 1952 (Fig. 16).

The Third Synergist

In any discussion of synergism between petroleum and engineering, particularly in looking at the future, mention must be made of the third of the synergists that have been responsible for progress. That third synergist is the hope of profit. Profits are truly a synergist, because they act as a stimulant to creative thinking and to risk taking, and so produce benefits worth many times more than the amount of the profits themselves. They also finance the tools of progress.

Economic rewards are tricky things. For a definite, measurable job, like a lawn to be mowed, someone can be hired to do it at a specific rate. If the job is not measurable, and requires a great deal of initiative, a prize or reward can be offered. The hope of large gain is a wonderful incentive. It will stimulate people to spend their time and invest their money, even where the hope of making anything net is so small as to be almost nonexistent; otherwise, people would not play slot machines and bet on horse races.

When there is a real chance for major gain, intelligent people will put forth large efforts. So there are explorers, prospectors, and inventors—and companies that hire explorers, prospectors, and inventors. Their efforts determine material progress.

FIG. 16.—CONTROL ROOM OF THE FLUID HYDROFORMER, DESTREHAN, LA., REFINERY, WITH AUTOMATIC INSTRUMENTS TO SIMPLIFY RUNNING COMPLICATED UNITS

The reward for getting ahead of the other fellow has sparked the search for cracking, for improved engines, for improved refinery processes, and for the other technological advances that have contributed so largely to American prosperity. In addition, many of these advances have been encouraged by the sound American patent system.

Engineers who understand these matters have a peculiar responsibility to help make certain that no political nostrums and no unsound theories, such as socialism —whether overt or covert—prevent the continued operation of the highly beneficial synergism between the petroleum industry and the engineering profession.

Paper No. 2655

IRON AND STEEL PRODUCTION, 1851–1951

By Walther Mathesius[1]

Synopsis

The true value of industrial production is its contribution to the economic welfare and strength of the United States.

It is the proud achievement of American iron and steel to have won during the past 100 years, and to hold unchallenged today, the enviable position among all manufacturing industries as the foremost agent in building the present national economy. Zeal and inventive capacity led from the Bessemer process to the open hearth and the electric furnace; from the beehive oven to the by-product coke plant, with all its ramifications; and from hand-operated sheet-plate and tin-plate rolls to multimachine continuous hot-rolled and cold-rolled wide strip mills, handling half of today's steel production. This glorious record can be projected into the future, but only through a sane appreciation of, and adequate provision for safeguarding, the American free economy.

With iron and steel entering now, directly or indirectly, into practically every phase of business and personal activities, it is fitting on this centennial occasion to review the backgrounds and events that have made iron and steel the prime industry of the United States. It is well also to pause and pay tribute to the ingenuity, foresight, and enterprise of the great men in steel—to give thanks to a kind fate which granted them the privilege to build and to produce in a free country, under a government of laws, based on the Constitution.

Pioneers in Steel

The American Age of Steel was born during the decade from 1850 to 1860 when steel—previously to be had only by the pound as the product of either the ancient cementation process or of the crucible melting process, rediscovered by Benjamin Huntsman of England in 1742—became available in thousands of tons through the development of the Bessemer and the open-hearth processes. Historically, credit for the invention of the former is shared by Henry Bessemer of England, whose English and American patents were issued in 1856, and by William Kelly, of

---

[1] Consultant, Eng. and Constr. Eng. Div., Koppers Co., Inc., Chicago, Ill.

Eddyville, Lyon County, Ky., whose American patent was granted on July 23, 1857, on the basis of prior use of his "pneumatic process" dating back to 1847 (Fig. 1).

However, Bessemer and Kelly could not advance beyond the experimental stage of their proposals, until they were able to avail themselves of another invention by a Scottish metallurgist, Robert Mushet, whose American patent was

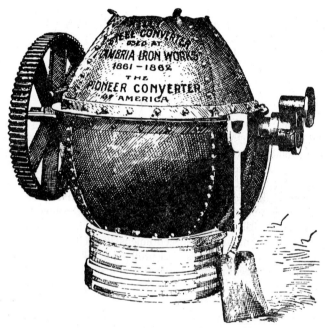

FIG. 1.—THE KELLY CONVERTER, AMERICAN COUNTERPART OF A HISTORIC UNIT BY HENRY BESSEMER IN ENGLAND

granted on May 26, 1857. To Mushet belongs the honor of having made possible the controlled production of liquid steel, through, according to his patent claim,

> "* * * the addition of a triple compound or material of, or containing iron, carbon and manganese, to cast iron which has been purified and decarbonized by the action of air, whilst in the molten state."

Preceded by some years of successful "Bessemer" steel production in England, the first commercial steel production in the United States was achieved by the Kelly Pneumatic Process Company at Wyandotte, Mich., during September, 1864, and the first American "Bessemer" steel rails were rolled from "Kelly" steel made at Wyandotte, by the North Chicago Rolling Mill on November 24, 1865. They were installed in the tracks of the Chicago and Northwestern Railroad, where their successful service spearheaded the stupendous rise of American steel production and American railroad building during the next 30 years. In turn, the railroads developed the West, linked together the North and South, gave new opportunities for gainful employment and a rising standard of living to millions of Americans, natives and immigrants alike, and built the foundation for the country's economic strength of today.

Open-Hearth Process.—Perhaps because its appearance on the American scene came later and its establishment here was more gradual, without the dramatic suddenness which marked the advent of "Bessemer" steel, the birth of the open-hearth process has heretofore received relatively less attention despite the fact that it outranks today by a wide margin all other steelmaking processes in production as well as in economic importance.

By a strange coincidence the "regenerative principle of heating" was invented by the German-born brothers, Frederic and William Siemens in London, England, just a few houses away from Henry Bessemer's residence. Their original English patent was issued on December 2, 1856, and their early attempts to apply its teachings to the melting of steel were made at a crucible steel shop in Sheffield, England. Steel was successfully produced in a furnace of their design after their collaboration with Emil Martin and his son, Pierre, at Sireuil in southern France, where the first heat of open-hearth steel was produced on April 8, 1864, using Martin's pig-iron and steel scrap process. This was followed in 1868 by William Siemens' successful demonstration of his "pig and ore" process for making open-hearth steel.

In the United States, the first open-hearth furnace was built at Trenton, N. J., in 1868. It was followed by other installations: At Boston, Mass., in 1870; Nashua, N. H., and Pittsburgh, Pa., in 1871; and Cleveland, Ohio, where eight furnaces were built by the Otis Iron and Steel Company between 1874 and 1887. All these furnaces had acid linings, using sand bottoms for the hearth.

Commercial production of basic open-hearth steel, permitting the use of higher phosphorus iron and thereby enabling the smelting of vast iron ore resources of non-Bessemer grade, was achieved in this country first at the Homestead (Pa.) Works of Carnegie, Phipps and Company on March 28, 1888. It is interesting to note that this accomplishment, which has outdistanced greatly in economic importance all those previously mentioned, has never been credited to an inventor, nor has it been covered by patent protection, being antedated by a report, published in a Russian periodical in 1879, of experiments conducted at Alexandrowsky near St. Petersburg (Leningrad), Russia.

This brief account of inventions which made possible the birth of the Age of Steel would be incomplete without paying tribute to the thousands of men who contributed to progress in the making, shaping, and treating of steel and who worked side by side and often ahead of the engineers, operators, managers, and owners in the steel industry, to produce more and better steels, at lower cost, for a constantly widening market. Man's burdens were eased and his living standard was raised to unheard-of heights in the United States and abroad. Regretfully, it must be admitted that a large share of this monumental accomplishment of inventive genius, of constructive and productive effort, has been directed to and absorbed by the manufacture of huge quantities of more powerful and more destructive instruments of war.

FANTASTIC GROWTH

Available records of American steel production show clearly that the underlying technical reason for the remarkable progress made in the 25 years following the close of the Civil War in 1865 was the introduction of the Bessemer process (Fig. 2). In 1870 American production of steel totaled 77,000 net tons, while 1,445,920 tons of wrought iron were made. By 1890 steel production had risen to 4,790,320 tons, exceeding the wrought-iron tonnage by more than 1,500,000 tons. Nearly 30,000,000 tons of steel were produced in 1910 against less than 2,000,000 tons of wrought iron—and on went the march of steel to more than 63,000,000 tons in 1929, nearly 90,000,000 tons in 1944, more than 105,000,000 tons in 1951, and a capacity of 120,000,000 tons projected for 1954.

FIG. 2.—BESSEMER CONVERTERS IN OPERATION AT UNITED STATES STEEL PLANT, IN LORAIN, OHIO

The annual production of open-hearth steel exceeded that of Bessemer steel for the first time in 1907 and has continued its progress to this day, when fully 87% of the yearly American steel tonnage comes from open-hearth furnaces, with the remaining 13% divided between Bessemer and electric furnace output. Clearly, the basic open-hearth process has become firmly established as the preferred source of large tonnages of quality steel (Fig. 3).

Impressive as these data are in highlighting the history of a most remarkable industrial growth, they assume a still greater significance, when viewed with respect to their importance in the national economy and in enabling the United States to attain a high position of leadership in world affairs.

National Significance.—Although the basic value of agriculture continues undiminished, the uprecedented industrial development of the past century with its amazing advances in engineering, management, and productivity created new prosperity and strength in the United States and made it great among the nations of the world. Truly, no better measure may be found for the country's industrial strength than the record of its growth in steel production during the past 100 years.

It is to be remembered that as late as 1860 manufacturing in the United States was largely carried on in relatively small units located in the areas adjacent to the northern Atlantic coast. It served mainly nearby market demands, unable to

FIG. 3.—MODERN OPEN-HEARTH STEEL FURNACES, POURING SIDE, WITH LADLES AND HOT-TOPPED INGOT MOLDS (LEFT) AT POURING PLATFORM

reach more distant customers because of limited, slow, and costly transportation. Industries were owned principally by individuals and partners, who managed their factories themselves and kept in close touch with their employees.

By 1880 manufacture and transportation had made rapid strides, thanks to the availability of steel from the growing number of Bessemer converters which had come into production following the epoch-making success of Kelly's pneumatic process. Corporations were formed to assume financial and managerial responsibilities as they grew beyond the capacity of individual owners, and small corporations gave way to larger aggregations of capital and of productive capacity. Owner-managers became employees and the distance grew between top management and labor. With success came new wealth and better earnings, making capital less tolerant and respectful of the interests of others and giving labor a new sense of importance and independence, with neither capital nor labor paying due heed to the power of public opinion.

Social Implications.—Conditions in the steel industry were typical of this period of youthfully exuberant growth. Too often management of the "free enterprises" was lacking in appreciation of the fact that power must be guided by responsibility and by constant regard for common good. Company heads were apt to judge the performance of their organizations by the profits they made, giving scant attention to the at-times dubious methods employed. The interests of the public were often disregarded, monopoly was not yet outside the law, labor was sometimes exploited, and competition was frequently destructive—in short, business ethics too often did not measure up to the golden rule.

Contemplation of those lusty days through the perspective of more than half a century emphasizes that their evils—although they have been corrected long ago under the compulsion of antitrust laws, plus the power of public opinion and the teachings of enlightened self-interest—linger on in memories. Thus even now, politicians find popular appeal in anti-big-business campaigns, whereas those who would have the United States forsake its system of "free enterprise" continue to condemn it with arguments which they deem justified because of the selfish violations committed by a relatively few in the distant past.

It is a credit to the common sense of the American people that in spite of these early aberrations they have continued to have faith in and to support a free economy, so that enlightened corporation management, aware of its responsibility fairly to represent the interests of the public as well as those of the employees and the stockholder-owners, could build and expand production through an ever-widening application of engineering knowledge and of skill in construction and operation. Thus, "free enterprise" has made its contributions to the march of progress, leading the United States to its present stature of economic greatness. By no other development are these truths more clearly exemplified than by the growth of iron and steel production, including on the one hand the anterior operations of winning and assembling the raw materials and, on the other, the distribution and manufacture of its products into the myriads of structures and articles of commerce, whose utility is enjoyed today in the "Age of Steel."

Economic Sufficiency.—Nevertheless, the mere growth in producing capacity and in output, the employment of more and more people, and the addition of their individual efforts have not brought these results. The crowning achievement of the engineering profession in this development is the continued construction of better tools and of facilities enabling greater output per unit of manpower, so that employee wages could, as they have done, rise from decade to decade substantially above the level of a constant living standard; and so that at the same time prices could be maintained which have to this day assured for steel its position of advantage in competition with the nonferrous metals and the many nonmetallic materials which have come to claim their share of the consuming market.

Steel welcomes the new strength of aluminum, magnesium and titanium, the plastics, and many other materials which render further service to the common good. Steel has no reason to fear their competition, as long as steel engineers remain true to their tried principles of planning and building for greater productivity per unit of manpower and, in consequence, for relatively lower production costs.

The achievements in steel through engineering progress during the past 100 years accentuate the confidence placed in engineers—that they will reach the right solution of the problems that lie ahead. A few examples will be cited.

Historic Accomplishments

At the beginning of the century whose progress is being honored, the industry concentrated on the eastern seaboard relied exclusively on local sources for the iron ore requirements of its furnaces. Although rich iron ore deposits had just been discovered in Michigan, their utilization seemed to be a matter of interest only in the far-distant future.

Ore Supply.—However, in 1852 the first shipment of these western ores, comprising 6 bbl, was made. By 1860 the westward trek of pig-iron smelting was under way and by 1870 Pittsburgh was well established as the new center of the industry. Coke made from Connellsville (Pa.) coals had become the accepted blast furnace fuel, in place of the charcoal and anthracite, which had supplied the eastern furnaces; and the apparent handicap of great distances from the Lake Superior ore mines to the Pittsburgh furnaces was overcome through the development of low-cost water transportation on the Great Lakes.

By 1880 new and larger steel plants were being built at the mouth of the Calumet River, in Chicago, Ill., where along the southwestern shore of Lake Michigan steel production today rivals that of the Pittsburgh district. In 1892 the Merritt brothers made their first iron ore shipment from the Mesabi Range in Minnesota, whose importance as the major source of metallics for the country's blast furnaces has continued to grow to the present day. However, plans are beginning to ripen into action to provide other sources of metallics as the Mesabi reserves decline.

Engineering progress is on the march toward two major objectives in this field, the beneficiation of the Mesabi's vast reserves of low-grade "Taconite" rock and the development of foreign ore deposits, in Labrador, Liberia, Venezuela, and Brazil. The latter also requires transportation facilities to deliver these high-grade foreign ores to American blast furnaces in adequate quantities and at reasonable costs.

Perfecting the Blast Furnace.—It is interesting that the most recent improvement in the principles of blast furnace operation for the smelting of iron ores was the application of heated air, or "hot blast," by J. B. Neilson in Scotland, in 1828. Nevertheless, no phase of the steel industry is more typical of its remarkable progress than is the evolution of the modern American blast furnace—the acknowledged standard of the world today—a tribute indeed to engineering progress in the United States.

In retrospect, as recently as 100 years ago, American blast furnaces were very crude affairs, when judged by present standards (Fig. 4). Production per furnace per day ranged from 1 ton to 6 tons. Charcoal was the principal smelting fuel, until displaced by anthracite coal in 1855, which in turn was overtaken in 1875 by beehive coke made from bituminous coal. Coke had been used successfully as blast furnace fuel for the first time in the United States in 1859 by the Clinton furnace in Pittsburgh.

Engineering progress assumed a faster pace with the building of the Isabella and Lucy furnaces, which went into production on the banks of the Allegheny River near Pittsburgh in the early summer of 1872, each starting out by making about 55 net tons of iron a day, which represented a fair average for that time.

FIG. 4.—OLD-TIMERS—ELIZA BLAST FURNACES OF JONES AND LAUGHLIN, AT PITTSBURGH, PA., 100 YEARS AGO, WITH BEEHIVE COKE OVENS, LOWER LEFT; SIX MODERN FURNACES AT THIS SITE TODAY

However, in the spirit of rivalry these free competitors outperformed each other year after year, until in March, 1880, Lucy produced 1,050 net tons in a single week, only to be outdistanced by Isabella, which turned out a weekly production of more than 1,100 net tons during February, 1881.

Thus began an era of engineering developments, of improvements in facilities, of labor savings through mechanization, and of process understanding and process control, which produced the modern American blast furnaces (Fig. 5). Their sustained production records have risen to more than 1,500 tons per furnace day, with a coke consumption rate of less than 1,800 lb per net ton of iron—equal to the lowest attained anywhere when smelting comparable raw materials. In total production the blast furnace industry during the past century has likewise evidenced sturdy growth as may be seen from Table 1.

Beehive to By-Product Coke.—Table 1 illustrates also the direct relationship

FIG. 5.—THREE BLAST FURNACES OF LATE DESIGN, AT GENEVA, UTAH, BUILT IN 1943

TABLE 1.—TOTAL BLAST FURNACE OUTPUT IN THE UNITED STATES DURING REPRESENTATIVE YEARS, ACCORDING TO FUEL

Fuel used	PRODUCTION OF PIG IRON, NET TONS				
	1875	1890	1916	1944	1951
Anthracite and coke mixed.....	908,046	2,448,781	243,922	......	......
Coke from bituminous coal.....	947,545	7,154,725	43,505,950	60,947,973	70,274,278
Charcoal	410,990	703,522	417,100	59,466	......
Total	2,266,581	10,307,028	44,166,972	61,007,439	70,274,278

between the growth of pig-iron output and that of coke production. Following its initial technically and commercially successful use, production of beehive coke for iron smelting rose rapidly, with the Connellsville region in Pennsylvania leading in output as well as in quality. By 1871 about 30% of the iron then produced was made with coke as fuel; and about 42%, in 1875. Beehive coke remained king for nearly another 20 years, since the by-product coke oven, although it had operated in Europe for a number of years with reasonable success, was not used in the United States prior to 1893, when the Solvay Process Company put into operation twelve Semet-Solvay ovens at Syracuse, N. Y.

Not until 1895 was by-product coke produced for blast furnace use, beginning with the installation of sixty Otto-Hoffman ovens by the Cambria Steel Company at Johnstown, Pa. (Fig. 6). More installations of the Semet-Solvay and the Otto-Hoffman type, as well as some others, were made during the next few years. However, not until the introduction of the cross-regenerator type of oven by Heinrich Koppers, and the installation, in 1908, of four batteries of this type at

FIG. 6.—FIRST AMERICAN BY-PRODUCT COKE PLANT, JOHNSTOWN, PA., BUILT IN 1895

the Joliet (Ill.) plant of the Illinois Steel Company, was this development launched on its phenomenal rise.

By 1919, by-product coke ovens produced 57% of the total fuel consumed by American blast furnaces and the use of beehive coke continued to decline until 1938, when it accounted for only 2.6% of the total United States production. However, the extraordinary demands occasioned by World War II brought large numbers of these old ovens back into life, with beehive coke production reaching a secondary peak of 8,275,000 net tons, or 11.7% of total coke output during 1942. Tonnages of coke produced in the United States since 1880 are shown in Fig. 7, which illustrates the importance of the coke industry and its growth in response to the rising demands for blast furnace fuel.

Several factors prompted the adoption of the by-product coking process in the United States. No doubt the most important was that initially in spite of its far greater requirements for investment of capital, as compared to beehive ovens, it gave promise of lower coke costs through increased yield of coke from coal and through the recovery and use of the gas, tar, and other by-products. Subsequently, however, two other factors have been recognized as having at least equal importance in the national economy.

Because of the foresight of the steel industry's engineers, the American by-product coke plants generally were located at or near the points of coke consumption rather than adjacent to the coal mines as had been the prevailing

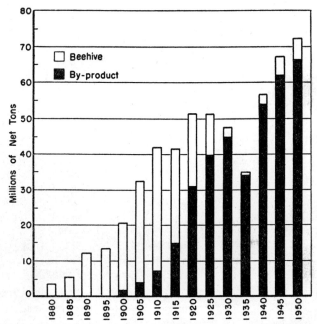

FIG. 7.—GROWTH OF COKE PRODUCTION IN THE UNITED STATES, 1880 TO 1950

practice in Europe. Thus it became a readily possible and soon a widely adopted practice to blend coals of different grades, thereby not only achieving improvements in coke quality which could not have been attained while coking only a single type of coal, but, what is still more important, making available to the coke industry vast additional reserves of coal, which were not suitable for coking, by themselves, in beehive ovens.

The second claim to nation-wide economic prominence is based on the fact that the by-product coke industry, after initially having disposed of most of its gas and tar production for fuel purposes, recognized the greater potential values of these and other by-products as raw materials for an entirely different manufacturing field. This field has since grown into the important coal-chemical industry, and is busily engaged in turning out a long and steadily growing list of chemical and pharmaceutical products. Many of these are entirely new and of great value, and have found myriads of useful applications in nearly every phase of economic and personal life. That crowning achievement entitles the by-product coke industry (Fig. 8) to a high rank as a contributor to the engineering accomplishments of this country. By-product coke and its coal chemicals, having grown to mature stature on the fertile soil of the free enterprise system, have created new earning opportunities, new economic values, and new benefits for all the people in this country.

Two Typical Accomplishments

From the vast array of important developments in the iron and steel industry only two typical examples of engineering progress will be discussed. The first

Fig. 8.—Today's Model of By-Product Coke Ovens, Weirton Steel Company, Weirton, W. Va.

is the utilization of electric energy; the second, the development of the modern wide hot rolling mills and cold rolling mills for the production of flat-rolled products.

Expansion in Electricity Use.—It is of interest to recall that the total electric power generating capacity installed in the American steel industry has grown from 160,000 kw in 1905 to more than 50,000,000 kw in 1945, the latter supplying however only about two fifths of the 19,400,000,000 kw-hr consumed by the industry during 1946. On a comparative basis the iron and steel industry became the second largest user of electric energy among all manufacturing industries, exceeded only by the chemical industry. Electric motors, previously used only on hoists, cranes, and auxiliary machinery, were first applied to main rolling mill drives in 1903 on the light rail mill of the Edgar Thompson Works in Braddock,

Pa., followed in the same year by the first reversing drive and the Ward-Leonard motor generator set on the 36-in. universal plate mill of the South Works in Chicago. By 1920 electric main mill drives had been installed with a total capacity of nearly 1,000,000 hp; and by 1946 this amount had grown to nearly 5,000,000 hp, aided in no small measure by the concurrent development of numerous precision control circuits and devices, a prerequisite for the exacting requirements of power and speed regulation in modern rolling mill practice.

The first heat of electric steel made in the United States was produced at Syracuse by the Halcomb Steel Company on April 5, 1906, employing the arc-type furnace invented by Heroult and first installed at La Praz, France, in 1899. Originally this furnace was considered primarily as an improvement over the

FIG. 9.—RECENT INSTALLATION OF ELECTRIC FURNACES, BUILT BY KOPPERS COMPANY

crucible process for the manufacture of a limited range of high-cost, high-quality steels of special composition, such as steels for tools, dies, watch springs, and cutlery. The electric furnace process has since greatly expanded its economic utility, becoming a major factor in the development and use of the structural alloy steels and commanding almost entirely the field of stainless and heat-resisting steels. As experience was gained and costs decreased, larger furnaces (Fig. 9) supplied by relatively low-cost electric energy have still further widened their scope, until today typical units of 70 tons to 90 tons in heat capacity are producing in many localities a wide range of tonnage steels, competing successfully in quality and cost with open-hearth steel production.

In 1930, electric steel production in the United States amounted to 686,111 net tons, or 1.5% of the total steel ingots and castings produced; but in 1948 the output had grown to more than 5,000,000 tons, or 5.7% of all steel production. For the year 1950, the country's installed capacity is reported to have risen to 6,039,008 tons, and further sturdy growth continues, proving the worth of this modern engineering development as a healthy contributor to the economic well-being and strength of the nation.

Old and New Rolled Plate.—Until approximately 1920 all the light-gage flat-rolled products comprising the sheet, tin-plate, and tin-mill black-plate classi-

FIG. 10.—ROLLING SHEET IRON, INVOLVING MUCH HAND LABOR, IN THE LATE NINETEENTH CENTURY

fications were produced from sheet bars by rolling, singly and in packs, in two-high "hand" mills. These operations, compared to those in other rolling mills of that day and in spite of the installation of many ingenious mechanical devices, were noted for their arduous labor (Fig. 10) requirements, a rather low product yield, and a quality which in physical properties and in constancy of dimensional precision left much to be desired from the standpoint of the cold-forming, cold-drawing, stamping, spinning, and other manufacturing industries. Hence they were handicapped in their competitive strength and economic usefulness by the prevailing quality standards.

Also, until 1920, the term "hot-rolled strip" was commonly applied only to light-gage flat-rolled products narrower in width than the usual pack mill sheets. No hot-rolled strip was more than 24 in. wide nor did it have a ratio of width to thickness greater than 250.

In 1923, 10 years of diligent and ingenious experimentation by John B. Titus led to the successful operation of the first continuous wide-strip mill at the Ashland, Ky., plant of the American Rolling Mill Company and to the production of strip, 36 in. wide, in 30-ft lengths. To Titus, the engineer, belongs the credit for having disproved through factual determination numerous then generally accepted theories and ideas. He established that the factors essential for the successful continuous rolling of wide, thin steel strip were:

(1) The shape or contour of the mill rolls;
(2) The temperature of the rolls;
(3) The deflection occurring in the rolls;
(4) The spacing of the rolls (screw-down adjustment); and
(5) The shape, composition, and temperature of the steel prior to and during the strip rolling process.

A parallel development by A. J. Townsend and H. M. Naugle was based on the performance of a mill they had designed and built in Massillon, Ohio, during 1916 for the National Pressed Steel Company to produce strip up to 24 in. in width. In 1926, hot-rolled strip was successfully manufactured in widths up to 36 in. on a mill of their own design and construction in the plant of the Columbia Steel Company at Butler, Pa. This mill was the first installation to combine in successful use:

(a) Four-high roll stands in the continuous finishing group;
(b) Roller bearings on hot mill roll necks;
(c) Control of the direction of travel of the steel through the pass line of the tandem finishing mills by progressively decreasing the crown of the rolls and of the product in successive passes; and
(d) Hot coiling equipment to receive the finished product.

Importance of Rolled Strip.—It is fitting to salute these men today. Their inventive talent and engineering skill blazed the trail for a revolution in the art of making flat-rolled steel products which has not only replaced the pack mills almost entirely in the United States, but has carried the fame and the products of American engineering progress to the far corners of the world.

From 1923 to 1948, thirty wide, continuous, hot-strip mills (Fig. 11) were built in the United States alone. As a group these mills have raised the ratio of width to thickness in flat hot-rolled steel strip from 250 to 1,000, delivering strip from 24 in. to 96 in. wide, 0.04 in. to 1.25 in. thick in lengths of 2,000 ft and more at delivery speeds up to 2,300 ft per min. Their combined nominal annual capacity rating exceeds 25,000,000 net tons of product, and individual monthly mill output records of more than 200,000 net tons are being made with increasing frequency. All this adds up to another proud achievement in the progress of American engineering.

The result has been the turning out of a superior product which has conquered an ever-widening market through its competitive merits and its excellent behavior in fabrication and in service. Today, the output of American wide strip mills—which reaches the fabricating trade as hot-rolled strip, plates, and sheets, or which is further converted by cold rolling (Fig. 12) and includes substantial tonnages protectively coated with zinc (galvanized sheets), tin, and many other metallic, nonmetallic, and organic materials—accounts for a fair one half of the

FIG. 11.—CONTINUOUS HOT-STRIP MILL, WITH ROUGHING STANDS IN DISTANCE; SIX FOUR-HIGH FINISHING STANDS, CENTER; FLYING SHEAR, LEFT; AND FINISHED STRIP ON WAY TO COILERS

FIG. 12.—THREE-STAND TANDEM, COLD REDUCTION MILL, ROLLING WIDE STRIP; SHOWING AUTOMATIC UNCOILER AND STRIP FEEDER

country's entire annual steel production. It supplies a vast market with durable, semidurable, and consumer goods and in this way represents the largest share of the contributions, which in this generation have been made by the iron and steel industry to the American standard of living, the envy of the world.

POLITICAL AND SOCIAL JUSTIFICATION

These contributions have made possible extensive transportation systems, public utilities, skyscrapers and homes, the automobile and appliance industries, and the endless number of articles that are considered necessary for daily life, but that were rare luxuries only a generation ago, if they existed at all. This is the proud record of the American iron and steel industry in this century of engineering progress, to which should be added the duties which the industry discharged with dispatch and credit during two world wars.

Public Understanding.—Despite these achievements some people are busily engaged in holding up to scorn the iron and steel industry, time and again, as a greedy monster, deviously striving to enrich itself at the expense of the country's general welfare. To them it is the prototype of all that a large section of the un-informed public still believes to be bad in all "big business," a horrible product of the "free enterprise" system, which must be chained and restricted, controlled and taxed, lest it wreck the United States economy.

Admittedly, the iron and steel industry delayed too long the task of laying bare the facts of its financial and other affairs, for all to see who were willing to look. The interests of the industry have not been served well by those who hoped through silence to erase from the public mind the memories of the gambling spirit, at times bordering on financial recklessness, which characterized the early growth of iron and steel works. Many more years went by, after the industry, now grown to full stature, had developed high excellence in management and operations as well as high ethical standards of business conduct, before it was recognized that good public relations required from industry not only a good job of production and selling conscientiously done, but also a diligent and constant effort to let the people know of it and to make them understand it.

Had this effort been made earlier, it would have furthered a general under-standing of facts which can be proved beyond the slightest doubt through public records and government statistics. The truth is that over the long term the distribution of the iron and steel industry's gross earnings has distinctly benefited the employees and the public in general; but that the invested capital of the owners or shareholders has not fared so well, receiving only a modest return indeed for providing the tools of production through which an outstanding service has been rendered to American steel consumers.

Economic Taboos.—That lack of understanding by the general public for the need of a fair return to capital as a condition for survival by any industry in a free economy is the underlying cause why the iron and steel industry together with other "big business" is still confronted—and to an increasing degree in recent years—with governmental policies demanding more curbs and restrictions and more taxes. Likewise, this public ignorance makes it seem good strategy for all politicians to include anti-big-business planks in their campaign platforms every 4 years and to sound warnings at every occasion against the "concentration of economic power" by the "economic royalists."

Last, but not least, this same uniformed public lends its sympathy, if not its support, to the growing demands of organized labor, with governmental backing more often than not, for an ever-greater share of industry's gross earnings. Thus, the iron and the steel industry having helped to make the United States strong and great, and still theoretically "free" under this system of private enterprise, finds itself today approaching the position of the proverbial goose that laid the golden eggs. It faces the alternative of socialistic nationalization or of pricing itself out of the market through obsolescence because of lack of depreciation reserves and of capital to renew and expand its facilities, or through cost increases resulting from higher wage rates without correspondingly increased productivity.

It should be clear by now, that in either case capital and labor, as well as industry's third partner of more recent date, the government's tax collector, would lose. Of still greater importance, however, would be the availability of fewer goods, at higher prices only, to all the people throughout the land, in which industry has raised the living standards to their present-day level—as David E. Lilienthal has stated, "with fewer very poor and fewer very rich than in any comparably large community since the dawn of history."

A Glimpse Ahead.—Probably another century of American iron and steel will see continued progress through the proved ability of research, engineering skill, and management talent to cope with the problems of raw materials, production, and sale. Also if this industrial giant is to continue its performance in the service of the nation effectively and with healthy growth, iron and steel must be given the opportunity to work in a healthy and helpful economic and political climate which can be created and maintained only through public understanding for, and endorsement of, the industry's needs, performance, and principles.

To spread this gospel has become an important added duty for the members of the engineering profession pleading not in their own behalf or for the industry in which they work, but speaking and acting as American citizens concerned with the welfare of the nation. Pledged to support the Constitution of the United States and armed with the privileges of free speech and the ballot box, they must join and lead in the fight to defend the endowment granted through the Declaration of Independence, with the unalienable rights of "Life, Liberty and the pursuit of Happiness."

By preserving what is left and by recapturing what has been lost of the personal, political, and economic freedoms willed by the founders of the nation, today's engineers can lay the foundation for another century of engineering progress.

ACKNOWLEDGMENTS

In general, authors or their organizations have furnished all the data, including illustrations for their papers. The Society and the profession are greatly indebted to them. Where special courtesies need mention, the required acknowledgments are here listed, in consecutive order for each of those papers concerned.

FINCH, J. K. (Paper No. 2576).—The view of the Brooklyn Bridge (Fig. 11), by Philip Gendreau was made available by the American Institute of Steel Construction. Fig. 15 is from a lithograph by Joseph Pennell, supplied through the courtesy of the Metropolitan Museum of Art. Fig. 19 is from a photograph by the Reclamation Service (now the Bureau of Reclamation) of the United States Department of the Interior.

HUBER, WALTER L. (Paper No. 2577).—Figs. 1 to 3 are used through the courtesy of the California Historical Society.

MAVIS, FREDERIC T. (Paper No. 2580).—The writer is indebted to T. F. Hickerson, M. ASCE, for information about Hinton James; to Col. W. J. Morton, librarian, United States Military Academy, West Point, N. Y., for supplying Fig. 3; and to H. H. Jordan, M. ASCE, associate dean, University of Illinois at Urbana, for supplying Fig. 4.

LEWIS, HAROLD M. (Paper No. 2584).—Fig. 2 is used through the courtesy of the Department of Public Information of the United Nations; Fig. 4, through the courtesy of the Port of New York Authority; and Fig. 5, through the courtesy of the Metropolitan Life Insurance Company.

CHEVALIER, WILLARD T. (Paper No. 2587).—Fig. 3 is used through the courtesy of *California Highways and Public Works;* and Fig. 4, through the courtesy of the Bureau of Reclamation.

HARDIN, JOHN R. (Paper No. 2589).—Fig. 5 is an official Corps of Engineers photograph.

ROGERS, LESTER C. (Paper No. 2590).—Photographs were supplied by United Steel Corporation and Caterpillar Tractor Company.

CARTER, A. N. (Paper No. 2592).—In the preparation of this paper many sources were used for background data. These include *Engineering News-Record, The Constructor, The Virginia Road Builder, Excavating Engineer, Roads and Streets, Civil Engineering,* and other publications. Numerous texts were also reviewed, and "Tools of the Earthmover—Yesterday and Today," by J. L. Allhands, Sam Houston College Press, Huntsville, Tex., 1951, proved especially helpful. Also much assistance was secured from the Bureau of Public Roads. Figs. 1, 2, 3, 4, and 6 are used through the courtesy of the Bureau of Public Roads.

DIXON, J. W. (Paper No. 2596).—The illustrations in this paper are used through the courtesy of the Bureau of Reclamation.

HILL, J. ERNEST (Paper No. 2599).—The writer wishes to acknowledge with gratitude the help given by the following men in the preparation of this paper: N. L. Terteling, president, J. A. Terteling and Sons, Incorporated; J. W. Terteling, vice-president, J. A. Terteling and Sons, Incorporated;

W. C. Foss, vice-president and general manager, J. A. Terteling and Sons, Incorporated; D. S. Walter, regional engineer, Region 1, Bureau of Reclamation; and Hubert Blonk, Public Relations, Region 1, Bureau of Reclamation. The photographs in this paper are used by the courtesy of the Bureau of Reclamation.

McClellan, L. N. (Paper No. 2600).—The illustrations in this paper are official Bureau of Reclamation photographs.

Nalder, W. H. (Paper No. 2601).—The illustrations are from the files of the Bureau of Reclamation. Fig. 6 was drawn by John MacGilchrist.

Hathaway, Gail A. (Paper No. 2604).—Fig. 2(a) is used through the courtesy of the *Minnesota Engineer*.

Hollis, Mark D. (Paper No. 2614).—The illustrations in this paper are used through the courtesy of the United States Public Health Service.

Logan, J. A. (Paper No. 2615).—Fig. 1 is used through the courtesy of John Lane, The Bodley Head, Limited; and Fig. 2, through the courtesy of the Wellcome Historical Medical Museum in London, England. Figs. 3 to 5 are photographs by W. Suschitzky.

Terzaghi, K. (Paper No. 2619).—Fig. 8 is used through the courtesy of the Bureau of Reclamation.

Archibald, Raymond (Paper No. 2626).—The writer wishes to give credit for the information on early bridges to his friend and fellow highway bridge engineer, Llewellyn N. Edwards, M. ASCE, recently deceased. Figs. 2 to 6 are used through the courtesy of the Bureau of Public Roads.

Hanrahan, Frank J. (Paper No. 2627).—For help in preparation of this paper the writer is deeply indebted to Arthur Upson and Lawrence W. Smith, former secretaries of the Central Committee on Lumber Standards, and to William Murray and T. M. Millett, who have been closely associated with the establishment of lumber grades and standards for many years. In some instances, their writings have been used directly in this paper.

Austill, H. (Paper No. 2628).—It will be recognized that the publications of the ASCE and the American Railway Engineering Association have been drawn on in preparing this paper. For this, full credit is hereby recorded.

Engle, H. M. (Paper No. 2630).—Fig. 8 is used through the courtesy of Art Streib Studio, Los Angeles, Calif.

Whitmore, George D. and Thompson, Morris M. (Paper No. 2633).— Figs. 1 and 3 are from "Photography Applied to Surveying," by Lt. Henry A. Reed, John Wiley and Sons, New York, N. Y., copyright 1888, reproduced by permission. Figs. 4, 5, and 6 are from "Photogrammetry," by O. von Gruber, American Photographic Publishing Company, New York, N. Y., 1942, also reproduced by permission. All other illustrations are United States Geological Survey photographs.

Bay, Helmuth (Paper No. 2636).—The photographs in this paper are used by courtesy of the United States Coast and Geodetic Survey.

Gurley, Fred G. (Paper No. 2637).—Figs. 6 to 9 are used through the courtesy of the Santa Fe Railway.

Mickle, D. Grant (Paper No. 2638).—Figs. 1 and 4 are used by the courtesy of the Bureau of Public Roads; and Fig. 6, by the courtesy of the Port of New York Authority.

GREER, DEWITT C. (Paper No. 2640).—Fig. 1 is used in this paper by the courtesy of the Texas Highway Department.

CHORPENING, C. H. (Paper No. 2643).—Figs. 1, 2, 4, and 5 are used in this paper through the courtesy of the Bureau of Public Roads; and Figs. 3, 6, 7, 13, and 15, through the courtesy of the Library of Congress. Fig. 20 is a United States Army photograph. All other photographs were supplied by the Corps of Engineers.

SCHNEIDER, GEORGE R. (Paper No. 2644).—Appreciation is expressed to the following for assistance in assembling and reviewing material for this history: Alexander Allison, Jr., designing engineer, Sewerage and Water Board of New Orleans, La.; Bernhard Dornblatt, M. ASCE, consulting engineer of New Orleans; H. C. Gee, M. ASCE, consulting engineer of West Palm Beach, Fla.; Edward Hyatt, M. ASCE, consulting engineer of Sacramento, Calif.; Gerald H. Jones, M. ASCE, principal hydraulic engineer, State Department of Public Works, Sacramento; Gerard H. Matthes, Hon. M. ASCE, consulting engineer of New York, N. Y.; F. W. Reichelderfer, chief, Weather Bureau, Washington, D. C.; Robert M. Salter, chief, Soil Conservation Service, Washington, D. C.; and Michael W. Straus, recently commissioner, Bureau of Reclamation, Washington, D. C. Artistry on charts and maps is the work of Joseph H. Buehrle.

COBB, W. C. (Paper No. 2648).—Illustrations are used by the courtesy of the New Orleans (La.) District, Corps of Engineers.

DANN, ALEX. W. AND JANSEN, CARL B. (Paper No. 2649).—Fig. 1 is used through the courtesy of the University of Pittsburgh Press in Pittsburgh, Pa.

MATHESIUS, WALTHER (Paper No. 2655).—Fig. 1 is from "William Kelly—A True History of the So-Called Bessemer Process," by John Newton Boucher, J. J. Little and Ives Company, New York, N. Y., 1924, page 80.

TRANSACTIONS

OF THE

AMERICAN SOCIETY OF CIVIL ENGINEERS

INDEX

VOLUME CT

1953

Titles of papers are in quotation marks when given with the author's name.

CENTENNIAL TRANSACTIONS

VOL. CT
SUBJECT INDEX

AIR SANITATION
Atmospheric conditioning outdoors and indoors, 630.
Inadequacy of pollution control, 586.

ALLOYS
"Metals in the American Economy," Zay Jeffries, 1215.

ALUMINUM
History and usage, 830.

AMERICAN SOCIETY OF CIVIL ENGINEERS (General)
First national association of American engineers, 122.

Addresses
1953—Address at the Annual Convention, San Francisco, Calif., March 4, 1953,
Walter L. Huber, 97.

Committee Reports—Engineers and Engineering
"Effective Utilization of the Sanitary Engineering Profession": Report of the
Committee of the Sanitary Engineering Division on Advancement of Sanitary Engineering, H. G. Baity, T. R. Camp, F. J. Cleary, G. M. Fair, L. M.
Fisher, W. A. Hardenbergh, F. H. Waring, A. H. Wieters and Earnest
Boyce, 660.

ANALYSIS, DESIGN
See under relative subject, e.g., STRUCTURES

APPARATUS
See under relative subject

AQUEDUCTS
Early Roman aqueducts, 8.

ARCH BRIDGES
See BRIDGES, ARCH

ARCH DAMS
See DAMS, ARCH

ASPHALT
"Synergism between Engineering and Petroleum," Robert E. Wilson, 1226.

ASSOCIATIONS
See SOCIETIES, TECHNICAL

ATMOSPHERIC POLLUTION
See AIR SANITATION

ATOMIC ENERGY
See also RADIOACTIVITY
Atomic bomb action and structural design, 753, 755, 762, 764.

AUTHORITIES
See MUNICIPAL AUTHORITIES; RIVER VALLEY AUTHORITIES

AUTOMOBILE PARKING
"Solving Highway Traffic Problems," D. Grant Mickle, 904.

BRICK
History and usage, 825.

BRIDGES (General)
See also COSTS, BRIDGE; FAILURES, BRIDGE
Attainment of beauty, 778, 779.
"Bridges and Man's Increased Mobility," D. B. Steinman, 767.
Data on more important U. S. bridges, 767.
Ead's Mississippi River (St. Louis, Mo.) arch bridge, 43.
18th century bridges, 16.
Longest spans in the world, 773.
Modern trends in bridge design, 938, 940.
Railroads' progress from wooden to iron bridges in the U. S., 21.
Types and factors influencing design, 81.

BRIDGES, ARCH
Early American bridges and their builders, 43, 86.

BRIDGES, CANTILEVER
History of the Quebec cantilever railroad bridge, 82.
Record spans; early bridges and their builders, 40.

BRIDGES, SUSPENSION
As feature of 20th century, 84.
Early American and European bridges and their builders, 44.

BRIDGES, TIMBER
See BRIDGES, WOODEN

BRIDGES, TRUSS
Early American bridges and their builders, 33, 38.
"Use of Wood on American Railroads," H. Austill, 797.

BRIDGES, WOODEN
Early American bridges and their builders, 32, 38.
"Survey of Timber Highway Bridges," Raymond Archibald, 782.

BUILDING (process)
See CONSTRUCTION

BUILDING LAW
California schools to be earthquake resistant, 809.

BUILDING MATERIALS
See MATERIALS OF CONSTRUCTION

BUILDINGS
See also FOUNDATIONS; STRUCTURES
Early construction methods, 238.
"Schools Illustrate Progress in the Use of Wood," Harry W. Bolin, 805.
"Visible Earthquake Effects and Practical Corrective Measures," H. M. Engle, 814.

BULKHEADS
Early bulkhead problems and design, 674.

BUSES
See MOTOR BUSES (cross reference thereunder)

CABLE RAILWAYS
See RAILROADS, CABLE

CAISSONS
Early pneumatic caisson for deep bridge foundations, 69.

CANALS (General)
See also COSTS, CANAL
Hydraulic developments along canals, 1125.

CANALS (Geographical)
Chicago, Ill.
"System of Waterways at Chicago, Ill.," Ralph L. Bloor, 1205.

Erie Canal
Opening of Erie Canal and its effects, 992, 993, 994, 999.

Illinois Waterway
See WATERWAYS (Geographical)—Illinois Waterway

Louisiana
"The Passes of the Mississippi River," W. C. Cobb, 1147.

Panama Canal
Development and conversion improvements, 1036, 1037, 1039.
Early history of Panama Canal, 72.

United States
Early canals, 184, 235.
Early land grants to states for specific canals, 989.
Early state and private development, 991.

CANALS, IRRIGATION
See IRRIGATION CANALS

CANTILEVER BRIDGES
See BRIDGES, CANTILEVER

CARRIERS
See CONVEYORS AND CONVEYANCE; MOTOR . . .; RAILROADS; TRANSPORTATION

CARTOGRAPHY
See MAPS AND MAPPING

CEMENT
History and usage, 826.
Natural cement by Romans, 10.

CENTRIFUGAL PUMPS
See PUMPS AND PUMPING, CENTRIFUGAL

CHANNELS (waterways)
See also RIVERS; WATER DIVERSION; WATER, FLOW OF, IN OPEN CHANNELS
Calumet Sag Channel development in Chicago, Illinois area, 1205.
Development of hydraulic dredges for excavating and deepening channels, 1186.
Federal channel maintenance authority, 1009, 1017.
"The Passes of the Mississippi River," W. C. Cobb, 1147.

CHARTS
See GRAPHICAL CHARTS

CHLORINATORS AND CHLORINATION
Chlorination developed for water supplies, 571, 572.

CITIES
See also CITY PLANNING; ELECTRIC POWER; ENGINEERS AND ENGI-
NEERING—Government Relationships; GAS AND GASWORKS; MUNICI-
PAL . . .; SEWAGE . . .; SEWERS; SUBWAYS; TRAFFIC, STREET
(and other relative traffic headings); WATER SUPPLY; *see also* geographical
subheadings under relative subject, e.g., WATERWAYS
Absorption of suburbs, 214.
"America's Costliest Bedrooms: The Suburbs," Richard G. Baumhoff, 206.
Characteristics of Los Angeles, California, 1065.
Decentralization affects suburban trends, 206, 209, 214.
Development of Chicago, Illinois, 1205.
"Engineers' Contribution in Developing American Cities," Harold M. Lewis, 182.
Importance of bridges in the development of cities, 769.
Industrial decentralization in Missouri, 208.
Industrial decentralization in the U. S., 195, 198.
Needs of metropolitan cities, 216.
Suburbs outgrow metropolitan cities, 207.
"Today's Engineer and Tomorrow's Metropolitan Problems," L. P. Cookingham,
194.

CITY PLANNING (General)
Early city planning, 183.
Over-all city plans as related to traffic, 918.

CITY PLANNING (Geographical)
United States
"Engineers' Contribution in Developing American Cities," Harold M. Lewis,
182.
"Today's Engineer and Tomorrow's Metropolitan Problems," L. P. Cookingham, 194.

CIVIL ENGINEERS AND ENGINEERING
See AMERICAN SOCIETY OF CIVIL ENGINEERS; ENGINEERS AND
ENGINEERING

COAGULANTS AND COAGULATION
See SEWAGE SLUDGE; WATER TREATMENT

COAL
Problems involving coal supply, 165.

COAL HANDLING MACHINERY
See also COSTS, COAL HANDLING
"Belt Conveyor Transportation," William L. Hartley, 961.

COATINGS, PROTECTIVE
See CORROSION AND PROTECTION OF . . .; FIREPROOFING

COKE
Development of U. S. coke industry, 1257, 1259.

COKE PLANTS
"Iron and Steel Production, 1851-1951," Walther Mathesius, 1249.

COLLEGES AND SCHOOLS, ENGINEERING
See EDUCATION

COMMERCE
See CANALS; CITIES; DOCKS AND WHARVES; FREIGHT; RAILROADS; RIVERS; TRANSPORTATION; WATERWAYS

COMMITTEE REPORTS
See AMERICAN SOCIETY OF CIVIL ENGINEERS—Committee Reports; *see also* under subject of report

COMMUNICATION
See TRANSPORTATION

CONCRETE (General)
See also COSTS, CONCRETE CONSTRUCTION; PAVEMENT AND PAVING, CONCRETE; *also* under special structure or structural part, e.g., DAMS, MASONRY AND CONCRETE
Types of concrete production plants, 254.

Construction
"Lowering Concrete Costs by Improved Techniques," John R. Hardin, 247.

Cracking
"Lowering Concrete Costs by Improved Techniques," John R. Hardin, 247.

Placing. *See also* TREMIES
"Lowering Concrete Costs by Improved Techniques," John R. Hardin, 247.

CONCRETE DAMS
See DAMS, MASONRY AND CONCRETE

CONDUITS
See also FAILURES, CONDUIT
"Structures for Irrigation Diversion and Distribution," J. Ernest Hill, 412.
Summary of unsatisfactory performance, 707, 716.

CONNECTORS AND CONNECTIONS
Benefit of timber connectors on construction, 738.

CONSERVATION
See FISH INDUSTRY (cross reference thereunder); FORESTS AND FORESTATION; GROUND WATER; PRESERVATION . . .; WATER CONSERVATION; WILDLIFE (cross reference thereunder)

CONSTRUCTION
See also COSTS, CONSTRUCTION; MATERIALS OF CONSTRUCTION; *see also* under type of construction, e.g., DRY-DOCKS; RAILROADS
"Accomplishments in Timber Technology," Charles A. Chaney, 744.
Accomplishments of the construction industry, 241, 242, 244.
Advances through knowledge of behavior of materials, 834.
Ancient construction wonders, 303.
Bomb resistant construction, 764.
Construction as an industry, 223, 224, 225.
"The Contract Method for American Construction," H. E. Foreman, 231.
Development of American equipment, 305, 306.

DIVERSION
See WATER DIVERSION

DIVERSION DAMS
See DAMS

DOCKS AND WHARVES
"Belt Conveyor Transportation," William L. Hartley, 961.

DRAGLINES
See CRANES, DERRICKS AND POWER SHOVELS

DRAINAGE
See MULTIPLE PURPOSE PROJECTS

DRAWINGS
See also under relative subject
"Advances in Cartography," Helmuth Bay, 886.

DREDGES AND DREDGING
"American Hydraulic Dredges," Carl H. Giroux, 1180.
American types for specified uses, 1180.
Channel dredging on Mississippi River passes, 1154, 1156, 1157.
Development of dredges, 282.
"Waterway Growth in the United States," C. H. Chorpening, 976.

DRILLS AND DRILLING
Development of drill types, 284.
"Synergism between Engineering and Petroleum," Robert E. Wilson, 1226.

DROUGHTS
See RAINFALL

DRY-DOCKS
Development and details of American naval dry-dock types, 1192.
Future methods of constructing graving docks, 1203.
"Naval Drydock Construction," J. R. Ayers, 1192.
Tremie concreting for dry-dock floor and walls, 1200, 1201.
Underwater methods of construction, 1200, 1201.
Use of various types of side walls, 1199, 1201.

DYNAMICS OF GASES
See AERODYNAMICS

DYNAMICS, STRUCTURAL
See STRUCTURAL DYNAMICS

EARTH DAMS
See DAMS, EARTH

EARTH PRESSURE
Coulomb's and other theories, 670, 672.
Earth pressure on lateral supports, 670.
"Origin and Functions of Soil Mechanics," K. Terzaghi, 666.

EARTHQUAKES
Effects of earthquakes on earth dams, 713.
Effects on California school buildings, 806, 809.
"The Importance of Dynamic Loads in Structural Design," John B. Wilbur and Robert J. Hansen, 753.

Bibliography
Development of modern hydroelectric power, 554.

ELECTRIC POWER (Geographical)
United States
"Evolution of the Modern Hydroelectric Power Plant," A. T. Larned and M. G. Salzman, 536.

Future trends of hydroelectric power development, 553.

Principal interconnected transmission lines, 470.

Production statistics for public and private utilities, 1920-1950, 465.

Statistics for generating capacity, 1890-1950, 463, 464.

Usage in U. S. steel industry, 1260.

ELECTRIC TRANSMISSION
See ELECTRIC POWER

EMBANKMENTS
See also DAMS, EARTH

Irrigation canal structures, 414.

ENERGY
See ATOMIC ENERGY; ELECTRIC POWER; POWER; STEAM POWER; STRUCTURAL DYNAMICS; THERMAL POWER (cross reference thereunder); WATER POWER

ENGINEERING
See ENGINEERS AND ENGINEERING

ENGINEERING COLLEGES AND SCHOOLS
See EDUCATION

ENGINEERING EDUCATION
See EDUCATION

ENGINEERING HISTORY
See ENGINEERS AND ENGINEERING—History; *also* under relative subject

ENGINEERING SOCIETIES
See AMERICAN SOCIETY OF CIVIL ENGINEERS; SOCIETIES, TECHNICAL

ENGINEERS AND ENGINEERING (General)
Danger of "overengineering," 1246.

Development of automotive engineering, 1242.

Early concepts of civil engineering, 660.

"Effect of Science on Structural Design," L. E. Grinter, 723.

Energy engineering as a new concept, 632.

"Engineers' Contribution in Developing American Cities," Harold M. Lewis, 182.

Essential characteristics of an engineer, 142.

Esteem shown builders of Egyptian pyramids, 113.

Evaluation by leading thinkers, 123, 124.

First usage of engine and engineer, 117.

Forerunners of modern engineering, 138.

French pioneers in engineering, 118, 119.

The Greek *architekton* and Roman *architectus* compared, 114.

Importance of art in bridge design, 778, 779.

Influence of Smeaton, 18th century British engineer, 121, 122.

Inter promotion of engineering and oil industry, 1226.
Research activities of U. S. Corps of Engineers in flood control, 1086.
Revolutionary advances in hydroelectric engineering, 538.
The rise of the specialist, 219.
Social considerations in future projects, 129, 132.
Total number of engineers in U. S. in 1852, 1880 and 1952, 148.
U. S. Corps of Engineers in dredging work, 1180.
Visualization of improvements in sanitary engineering, 127, 129.
Work of U. S. Corps of Engineers, 976, 1010.
Work of U. S. Corps of Engineers in flood control, 1042, 1085.

Bibliography

Historical bibliography, 27.

Government Relationships

Problems develop the "municipal" engineer, 189.

History

American pioneers in sanitation, 560.
"Backgrounds of Engineering Education," Frederic T. Mavis, 133.
"Civil Engineering through the Ages," Charles J. Merdinger, 1.
"Contributions of Engineering to Health Advancement," Abel Wolman, 579.
Development of timber engineering, 744.
"Effective Utilization of the Sanitary Engineering Profession": Report of the
    Committee of the Sanitary Engineering Division on Advancement of Sani-
    tary Engineering, H. G. Baity, T. R. Camp, F. J. Cleary, G. M. Fair, L. M.
    Fisher, W. A. Hardenbergh, F. H. Waring, A. H. Wieters and Earnest
    Boyce, 660.
"The Engineering Profession in Evolution," J. K. Finch, 112.
Genesis of engineering, 133, 135.
"A Hundred Years of American Civil Engineering, 1852-1952," J. K. Finch, 28.
John Smeaton (1724-1792) first "civil" engineer, 2, 17.
"Origin and Functions of Soil Mechanics," K. Terzaghi, 666.
The past 50 years in review, 57.
"Progress in Sanitary Engineering in the United States," E. Sherman Chase,
    556.
Resume of sanitary engineering as a profession, 574.
U. S. sanitary engineering since 1850, 558.

Philosophy

Engineer's Four Freedoms, 768.

Present and Future Trends

"Effective Utilization of the Sanitary Engineering Profession": Report of the
    Committee of the Sanitary Engineering Division on Advancement of Sani-
    tary Engineering, H. G. Baity, T. R. Camp, F. J. Cleary, G. M. Fair,
    L. M. Fisher, W. A. Hardenbergh, F. H. Waring, A. H. Wieters, Earnest
    Boyce, 660.
Emphasis on specialization, 95.
A free economic system and engineering problems, 903.
"Future Possibilities in Civil Engineering," John B. Wilbur, 125.
Irrigation engineering advancement, 388, 389.
"Origin and Functions of Soil Mechanics," K. Terzaghi, 666.
"Progress in Sanitary Engineering in the United States," E. Sherman Chase,
    556.
"Prospects and Programs—Engineering Education," S. C. Hollister, 163.
"The Sanitary Engineer in Relation to Public Health," Mark D. Hollis, 624.
Summary of sanitary engineering work needed, 584, 585.

Professional Relationships

"Achievements in Engineering Education," Thorndike Saville, 147.
The devolpment of a separate city planning profession, 191.
Different branches contribute in. developing cities, 190.
Early U. S. sanitary engineering leaders, laymen and cooperating physicians, 581, 582.
"The Engineering Profession in Evolution," J. K. Finch, 112.
Opportunities in urban redevelopment, 192, 193.

War and Peace

Early use of metal by the military, 1216, 1218.
Effects of atomic blasts on structural design, 753, 755, 762, 764.
Work in the Renaissance and 18th century, 14, 18.

ENGINES

American development of diesel marine engine, 1170.
Development of U. S. motor vehicle engines (1910-1950), 952, 954.
Introduction of the diesel engine, 897, 901.
Oil industry contribution to better performance, 1242.
Oil products and internal combustion engines, 1228, 1241, 1242.
Usage of diesel engines in pipeline dredges, 1189, 1190.

EROSION, LAND

Work of U. S. Department of Agriculture, 1088.

ESTHETICS

See under relative technical subject, e.g., BRIDGES

ETHICS

See also ENGINEERS AND ENGINEERING—Professional Relationships
Standards for early American workmen, 262.

EXCAVATION (General)

See also COSTS, EXCAVATION
"The Mechanization of Construction Work," Francis Donaldson, 272.

EXCAVATION, HYDRAULIC

"American Hydraulic Dredges," Carl H. Giroux, 1180.

EXCAVATORS (machinery)

See CRANES, DERRICKS AND POWER SHOVELS; EXCAVATION

EXPERIMENTS AND EXPERIMENTATION

See HYDRAULIC LABORATORIES; LABORATORIES; MODELS . . .;
TESTS AND TESTING (cross references thereunder); *also* under material, structure or structural part tested

EXPLOSIVES

Development of explosives and their use, 285.

FABRICATION

See under relative subject; *see also* CONSTRUCTION

FAILURES, BRIDGE

Early suspension bridge failures, 46.
Tacoma Narrows disaster, 773, 776.

FORESTS AND FORESTATION
Conservation of U. S. forests, 752.

FORMULAS
See relative subject, e.g., PILES AND PILE DRIVING

FOUNDATIONS (General)
Deepest foundations and method of excavation, 70.
Early American and foreign foundation records, 43, 49.
Early foundation methods and American and foreign pioneers, 68.
"The Mechanization of Construction Work," Francis Donaldson, 272.
"Origin and Functions of Soil Mechanics," K. Terzaghi, 666.
The pneumatic process influencing foundation engineering, 49, 69, 70 .
"Visible Earthquake Effects and Practical Corrective Measures," H. M. Engle, 814.

FOUNDATIONS, BUILDING
Early footing and raft designs, 682.

FOUNDATIONS, DAM
"Earth-Dam Practice in the United States," T. A. Middlebrooks, 697.
Protection against piping, 687.

FOUNDATIONS, PILE
See PILES AND PILE DRIVING

FOUNDATIONS, RAFT
See FOUNDATIONS, BUILDING

FREE ENTERPRISE
See PRIVATE ENTERPRISE

FREIGHT
See also MOTOR TRUCKS
American freight traffic summary, 900.
Tonnages for Chicago waterways, 1205.
Volume on Mississippi River by kind, commodity and river section (1941-1950), 1121, 1122, 1123.
Volume on the Tennessee River, 1143, 1145.

FUEL
See also COAL; COKE . . .; GAS AND GASWORKS; OIL (cross reference thereunder)
Fuel consumption of motor vehicle engines, 952, 955.

FURNACES, BLAST
See BLAST FURNACES

GAS AND GASWORKS
Depletion of natural gas, 165.

GAS ENGINES
See ENGINES

GENERATORS
See ELECTRIC GENERATORS

GEODESY

"Geodetic Surveying Moves Forward," H. W. Hemple, 872.

GEODETIC SURVEYS AND SURVEYING

See SURVEYS AND SURVEYING, GEODETIC

GEOGRAPHY

See relative technical subject, e.g., MAPS AND MAPPING . . .

GEOLOGY

"A Century of Topographic Surveying and Mapping," R. H. Lyddan, 836.
Relation to soil mechanic problems, 691.

GEOMETRY

See MATHEMATICS

GLASS

History and usage, 831.

GOVERNMENT

See also ENGINEERS AND ENGINEERING—Government Relationships;
PRIVATE ENTERPRISE; PUBLIC . . .; TAXATION; also LAW subject
heading under related topic, e.g., WATER LAW
Activities of Canadian government land surveys, 860, 866.
Benefit of federal interest in Tennessee River navigation, 1134, 1135, 1136.
"Dams, Then and Now," K. B. Keener, 521.
Early interstate and federal action relating to waterways, 985, 986.
Federal work in Mississippi River flood control, 1100.
Helping construction toward a sound economy, 227.
History of federal interest in flood control, 1042.
Railroad problem as related to other transportation subsidies, 902.
Urban redevelopment and federal aid, 202, 204.
Water law as related to U. S. government, 343, 344, 348, 354.
Work of U. S. Bureau of Reclamation in flood control, 1090.
Work of U. S. Department of Agriculture in flood control and soil erosion, 1088.
Work of U. S. Geological Survey and other agencies, 836, 840, 843.

GRADING

See EARTHWORK

GRAPHICAL CHARTS

"Advances in Cartography," Helmuth Bay, 886.

GRAPHIC STATICS

Developers of graphic statics, 726.

GRAVING DOCKS

See DRY-DOCKS

GRAVITY DAMS

See DAMS, MASONRY AND CONCRETE

GRINDING MACHINERY

See under specific type of machine, e.g., ROD MILLS (cross reference thereunder)

GROUND WATER

"United States Water Law," S. T. Harding, 343.

HIGHWAYS AND ROADS (Geographical)
United States
Better roads movement, 945.
Machinery, vehicles and materials in road maintenance, 921.
"Principles of American Highway Design," Dewitt C. Greer, 935.
"Review of American Highway Maintenance," Rex M. Whitton, 921.
"World's Best Highways through Modern Equipment," A. N. Carter, 293.

HIGHWAY TRANSPORTATION
"The Growth and Status of Highway Transport," B. B. Bachman, 941.

HISTORY, ENGINEERING
See ENGINEERS AND ENGINEERING—History; *also* under relative subject

HOUSING
Problems to be solved in buildings and plumbing, 586.
Stressed-skin construction, 740.

HYDRAULIC EXCAVATION
See EXCAVATION, HYDRAULIC

HYDRAULIC-FILL DAMS
See DAMS, EARTH

HYDRAULIC LABORATORIES
U. S. Waterways Experiment Station at Vicksburg, Mississippi, 1118.

HYDRAULIC MINING
See MINES AND MINING

HYDRAULIC MODELS
See MODELS, HYDRAULIC

HYDRAULICS
Future possibilities, 127, 129.
Historic aspects of hydraulic engineering in California, 97, 109.

HYDRAULIC TURBINES
See TURBINES, WATER

HYDROELECTRIC PLANTS
See POWER PLANTS

HYDROELECTRIC POWER
See WATER POWER

HYDROSTATIC UPLIFT
See WATER PRESSURE

IMHOFF TANKS
See TANKS, SEPTIC

IMPACT
Influences of dynamic forces in structural design, 753.

INDUSTRIAL PLANTS
See also under general types of plants, e.g., MILLS; *also* under specific type of
plant, e.g., POWER PLANTS
American companies with waste treatment systems, 656.

Lake Okeechobee, Fla.

Flood control plan for region, 1080.

LAND . . .

See also EARTH . . .; EROSION, LAND; GROUND . . .; MAPS AND MAP-PING, LAND; SOIL . . .; SURVEYS AND SURVEYING . . .; VALUA-TION

LAND MAPS AND MAPPING

See MAPS AND MAPPING, LAND

LAND RECLAMATION

See also COSTS, LAND RECLAMATION

Accomplishments of U. S. Bureau of Reclamation, 331, 338.

"Dams, Then and Now," K. B. Keener, 521.

"Economy Dictates Reclamation Design," L. N. McClellan, 428.

"Forward Steps in Irrigation Engineering," L. N. McClellan, 388.

Growth of U. S. reclamation, 332, 339.

"Planning an Irrigation Project Today," J. W. Dixon, 357.

"Structures for Irrigation Diversion and Distribution," J. Ernest Hill, 412.

Usage of available materials, 428, 429.

LAND RECLAMATION LAW

Influence of 1902 act, 330, 333.

LANDSLIDES

Development of methods to prevent slides, 708, 718.

LAW

See LAW subject heading under related topic, e.g., WATER LAW

LEGISLATION

See under relative subject (under the subject law heading, e.g., IRRIGATION LAW)

LEVEES

See also FAILURES, LEVEE

Crevasses produced by Mississippi flood of 1874, 1050.

Importance of levees at New Orleans, Louisiana, 1069.

"One Hundred Years of Improvement on Lower Mississippi River," P. A. Feringa and Charles W. Schweizer, 1100.

LEVELING

See SURVEYS AND SURVEYING

LEVELS

See SURVEYING INSTRUMENTS

LININGS

See under relative topic, e.g., IRRIGATION CANALS

LITIGATION

See under relative subject (under the subject law heading, e.g., WATER LAW)

LOAD

See BEARING CAPACITY; FAILURES; IMPACT; STRESS AND STRAIN; VIBRATION; WIND PRESSURE; *also* under structure, structural member or part

LOAD, SUSPENDED
See SILT AND SILTING

LOCKS
"Development of the Tennessee River Waterway," C. E. Blee, 1132.

LOCOMOTIVES
Development of braking devices, 898.
Steam to diesel motive power, 897.

LUBRICANTS AND LUBRICATION
Brief history of the oil industry, 1227, 1242.
"Synergism between Engineering and Petroleum," Robert E. Wilson, 1226.

LUMBER AND LUMBERING
See TIMBER AND TIMBERING

MACHINERY
See under general types of machinery, e.g., CONSTRUCTION MACHINERY; *also* under specific type of machine, e.g., CRANES, DERRICKS AND POWER SHOVELS; *also* under usage, e.g., HIGHWAYS AND ROADS; LUBRICANTS AND LUBRICATION

MAGNESIUM
History and usage, 831.

MANAGEMENT
See CONSTRUCTION MANAGEMENT

MAPPING INSTRUMENTS
See SURVEYING INSTRUMENTS

MAPS AND MAPPING (General)
"Advances in Cartography," Helmuth Bay, 886.
Brief enumeration of improvements in cartography, 888.
Resume of Canadian mapping to 1952, 871.
"Surveying and Mapping in Canada, 1852-1952," F. H. Peters, 857.
Wax engraving process techniques, 886.
Work of Canadian Board on Geographic Names, 870.

MAPS AND MAPPING, AERIAL
"A Century of Topographic Surveying and Mapping," R. H. Lyddan, 836.
"Improvements in Photogrammetry through a Century," George D. Whitmore and Morris M. Thompson, 845.

MAPS AND MAPPING, LAND
"A Century of Topographic Surveying and Mapping," R. H. Lyddan, 836.
Development of terrestrial photogrammetry and stereophotogrammetry, 846, 849.

MASONRY
See FOUNDATIONS

MASONRY DAMS
See DAMS, MASONRY AND CONCRETE

MATERIALS, CONVEYANCE OF
See CONVEYORS AND CONVEYANCE

MATERIALS OF CONSTRUCTION

See also ALUMINUM; BRICK; CEMENT; CONCRETE; CORROSION AND PROTECTION OF . . .; COSTS, MATERIAL; EARTHWORK; FIRE-PROOFING; GLASS; GYPSUM; IRON; MAGNESIUM; METALS; MORTAR; PERMEABILITY OF MATERIALS (cross reference thereunder); PLYWOOD; QUARRIES AND QUARRYING; SAND; SEEPAGE; SOILS; STEEL; STONE; STRESS AND STRAIN . . .; TIMBER AND TIMBERING; WOOD; *also* under types of materials, e.g., PLASTIC MATERIALS; *also* under usage, e.g., INSULATORS AND INSULATION; LAND RECLAMATION

Forecasts in field of construction materials, 834.
History and use of specific materials, 825.
"How New Materials Increased Man's Building Ability," Walter C. Voss, 823.
Improvement through oil industry, 1244.
Steel and concrete revolutionize construction, 291.
Thermal, acoustic and air conditioning materials, 832, 833.
Usage of local materials in olden times, 823, 824.
Wood as an anisotropic material, 739.

MATHEMATICS

Development of mathematical theory for structural design, 726.
Pioneers in geometry, 6.

MECHANICS, SOIL

See SOILS

MECHANIZATION

See CONSTRUCTION

METALLURGY

"Metals in the American Economy," Zay Jeffries, 1215.

METAL PROTECTION

See CORROSION AND PROTECTION OF METALS

METALS

See also under specific metal or its alloy, e.g., ALUMINUM; IRON; MAGNESIUM
Future prospects in economics and usage, 1223.
"Metals in the American Economy," Zay Jeffries, 1215.
Uses of specific metals, 1219.

METERS AND METERING

Meters used in petroleum industry, 1229.

MILITARY ENGINEERS AND ENGINEERING

See ENGINEERS AND ENGINEERING—War and Peace; NATIONAL DEFENSE

MILLS

See also under specific type of mill, e.g. SAWMILLS; STEEL MILLS (cross reference thereunder)
"Belt Conveyor Transportation," William L. Hartley, 961.

MINES AND MINING

"Belt Conveyor Transportation," William L. Hartley, 961.
Dams for hydraulic mining, 480.

MODELS, HYDRAULIC
Mississippi River models, 1118.

MODELS, STRUCTURAL
Influence of testing on design, 728.

MOISTURE
See SOILS

MORTAR
History and usage, 825.

MOSQUITOES
See PUBLIC HEALTH

MOTIVE POWER
See ELECTRIC POWER; STEAM POWER; WATER POWER

MOTOR BUSES
See TRAFFIC . . .

MOTOR CARS
See AUTOMOBILE . . .; MOTOR VEHICLES

MOTOR TRUCKS
Early truck and tire types in the U. S., 941.
Highway maintenance motor trucks in U. S., 929, 932.
Mechanical features, controls and regulations, 957.
Number and uses of trucks in U. S., 948, 950, 951, 952, 956.
Types and service of U. S. truck tires, 947, 948.

MOTOR VEHICLE LAW
Type of regulation desirable, 959.

MOTOR VEHICLES
"The Growth and Status of Highway Transport," B. B. Bachman, 941.
Number of vehicles, 1920 and 1952, 905.
Pennsylvania pilot study (Research Report No. 9A) on performance relative to roadway type, 956.

MOTORWAYS
See HIGHWAYS AND ROADS

MOVABLE SIDEWALKS
See SIDEWALKS, MOVABLE

MULTIPLE PURPOSE PROJECTS (RIVER PROJECTS)
See also RIVER VALLEY AUTHORITIES
"Multipurpose River Developments," James S. Bowman, 1125.
Origin of multiple purpose concept in river basin development, 1128, 1130.
Planning and benefits of multiple purpose projects, 376, 381.

MUNICIPAL AUTHORITIES
Creation of authorities to combat economic stagnation, 201, 202, 204.

MUNICIPAL ENGINEERS AND ENGINEERING
See CITIES; ENGINEERS AND ENGINEERING

NATIONAL DEFENSE

Army surveys, Department of National Defence of Canada, 865.
World War II and emergency work on Tennessee River, 1140.

NAVIGATION

See DAMS; MULTIPLE PURPOSE PROJECTS; RIVERS; WATERWAYS

NUISANCES, ABATEMENT OF

See INDUSTRIAL WASTE; INSECT CONTROL (cross reference thereunder);
RODENT CONTROL (cross reference thereunder)

OBSOLESCENCE

See VALUATION

OIL

See LUBRICANTS AND LUBRICATION

OIL CRACKING AND CRACKING STILLS

See OIL REFINERIES

OIL REFINERIES

Catalytic processes, 1238, 1239, 1240.
Oil cracking, its problems and benefits, 1226.
"Synergism between Engineering and Petroleum," Robert E. Wilson, 1226.

ORGANIZATIONS

See SOCIETIES, TECHNICAL

OSCILLATION

See VIBRATION

PARKING REGULATIONS

See AUTOMOBILE PARKING

PASSES

See CHANNELS (waterways)

PAVEMENT AND PAVING (General)

Modern pavement design, 938.
"Review of American Highway Maintenance," Rex M. Whitton, 921.

PAVEMENT AND PAVING, CONCRETE

Equipment and procedures effect economies, 259.

PERMEABILITY OF MATERIALS

See CORROSION AND PROTECTION OF . . .; SEEPAGE; STRENGTH OF
MATERIALS (cross reference thereunder); *also* under type of material, e.g.,
SOILS

PETROLEUM

See OIL (cross reference thereunder)

PHOTOGRAMMETRY

See MAPS AND MAPPING, AERIAL; SURVEYS AND SURVEYING,
AERIAL

POWER (Geographical)

Tennessee

"Development of the Tennessee River Waterway," C. E. Blee, 1132.

Tennessee River

"Development of the Tennessee River Waterway," C. E. Blee, 1132.

United States

Power production in central stations and industrial plants, 1900-1950, 457.

POWERHOUSES

See POWER PLANTS

POWER PLANTS (General)

See also COSTS, POWER PLANT
"Belt Conveyor Transportation," William L. Hartley, 961.
Design objectives for modern plants, 550.
Underground hydroelectric stations, 553.

Bibliography

Development of the modern hydroelectric plant, 554.

POWER PLANTS (Geographical)

United States

Capacity and output by public and private utilities in 1950, 458.
"Evolution of the Modern Hydroelectric Power Plant," A. T. Larned and
M. G. Salzman, 536.
Future trends of hydroelectric plants, 553.
Improvement in station equipment and design, 536, 547.
Power plants as adjuncts to reclamation, 397.
Public developments under U. S. Department of the Interior, 1952, 460.

PRECIPITATION

See RAINFALL

PREFABRICATION

See CONSTRUCTION

PRESERVATION OF TIMBER

See TIMBER, PRESERVATION OF

PRESIDENTIAL ADDRESSES (American Society of Civil Engineers)

See AMERICAN SOCIETY OF CIVIL ENGINEERS—Addresses

PRESSURE

See EARTH PRESSURE; PUMPS AND PUMPING; STRESS AND STRAIN;
WATER PRESSURE; WIND PRESSURE

PRINTING

Advantages of offset printing in cartography, 887.

PRIVATE ENTERPRISE

Evolution of the competitive system, 1216.
Free enterprise system in the American steel business, 1254, 1265.
Plea for free enterprise as related to engineering, 903.

PROFESSIONAL STANDARDS

See ENGINEERS AND ENGINEERING—Professional Relationships; ETHICS

REFRIGERATION
See AIR CONDITIONING

REPORTS OF COMMITTEES
See AMERICAN SOCIETY OF CIVIL ENGINEERS—Committee Reports; *see also* under subject of report

RESEARCH
See also LABORATORIES; MODELS . . .; STRUCTURES, THEORY OF; *also* under relative subject, e.g., PUBLIC HEALTH; SOILS
Activities of U. S. Bureau of Reclamation, 380, 381.
Contributions to science in engineering colleges, 153.
Needs of insect control, 634.
Value in oil industry, 1244.

RESERVOIRS, FLOOD CONTROL
"History and Future of Flood Control," George R. Schneider, 1042.
"One Hundred Years of Improvement on Lower Mississippi River," P. A. Feringa and Charles W. Schweizer, 1100.

RESERVOIRS, WATER STORAGE
"Problems of Supplying London, England with Water," H. F. Cronin, 604.

RETAINING WALLS
"Origin and Functions of Soil Mechanics," K. Terzaghi, 666.

REVETMENT
"One Hundred Years of Improvement on Lower Mississippi River," P. A. Feringa and Charles W. Schweizer, 1100.

RIGHTS OF WAY (land strips)
Early U. S. railroad construction, 898.

RIGHTS, RIPARIAN
See RIPARIAN RIGHTS

RIGHTS, WATER
See WATER RIGHTS

RIPARIAN RIGHTS
"Parallel Irrigation Development—United States and Australia," Lewis R. East, 400.
"United States Water Law," S. T. Harding, 343.

RIPRAP (stone protection layer)
See DAMS, EARTH

RIVER BANKS AND BANK PROTECTION
See FLOODS; LEVEES; REVETMENT

RIVER BASINS
See RIVER VALLEY AUTHORITIES; VALLEYS

RIVER CHANNELS
See CHANNELS

River Murray, Australia
Irrigation development to harness waters, 400, 405.

Tennessee River
"Development of the Tennessee River Waterway," C. E. Blee, 1132.
Final report (1930) by U. S. Corps of Engineers, 1136.
Summary of structures as of 1952, 1142.
The Tennessee River system (TVA), 1133, 1137, 1139.

Thames River
Flow data since 1884, with drought details, 612.

United States
"Multipurpose River Developments," James S. Bowman, 1125.
"Waterway Growth in the United States," C. H. Chorpening, 976.

RIVER TRAFFIC
See TRAFFIC, RIVER

RIVER TRANSPORTATION
See WATER TRANSPORTATION

RIVER VALLEY AUTHORITIES
"Development of the Tennessee River Waterway," C. E. Blee, 1132.
Development of "valley authority," 354.
Early development of TVA, 1128.
Objectives, accomplishments and structures of TVA, 1092.
Work of Federal Inter-Agency River Basin Committee, 1095.

RIVER VALLEY AUTHORITY LAW
The Tennessee Valley Authority Act (1933), 1128, 1137.

RIVER VALLEYS
See VALLEYS

ROADS
See HIGHWAYS AND ROADS

ROCK
"The Mechanization of Construction Work," Francis Donaldson, 272.

ROCK-FILL DAMS
See DAMS, ROCK-FILL

RODENT CONTROL
See PUBLIC HEALTH

ROD MILLS
See under usage, e.g., SAND

ROLLED-FILL DAMS
See DAMS, EARTH

ROOFS AND ROOFING
"Schools Illustrate Progress in the Use of Wood," Harry W. Bolin, 805.

RUNOFF (Geographical)
United States
Work of U. S. Department of Agriculture, 1088.

SAFETY (General)

See EARTHQUAKES; HIGHWAYS AND ROADS—Safety; STREETS—Safety; WATERWAYS—Safety

SALT WATER INVASION

See WATER, FLOW OF, IN OPEN CHANNELS

SAND

Elastic behavior of confined sand, 667.
Rod mill for manufacturing sand, 253.

SAND BARS

See BARS (alluvia)

SANITARY ENGINEERS AND ENGINEERING

See ENGINEERS AND ENGINEERING; SANITATION

SANITATION

See also AIR SANITATION; ENGINEERS AND ENGINEERING; FILTERS AND FILTRATION; INDUSTRIAL WASTE; PUBLIC HEALTH; SEWAGE DISPOSAL; SEWAGE SLUDGE; SEWERS; WATER . . .
"Contributions of Engineering to Health Advancement," Abel Wolman, 579.
Environmental sanitation as a modern technique, 638, 646.
"Progress in Sanitary Engineering in the United States," E. Sherman Chase, 556.
"Status of Insect and Rodent Control in Public Health," J. A. Logan, 634.

SAWMILLS

Types of early sawmills, 745, 747.

SCHOOL BUILDINGS

See BUILDINGS

SCHOOLS AND COLLEGES, ENGINEERING

See EDUCATION

SCIENCE

The basic sciences and research as affecting civil engineering, 130, 131, 132.
Contributions of soil mechanics to other sciences, 692.
"Effect of Science on Structural Design," L. E. Grinter, 723.
Experimental science of the 17th century, 14.
Interrelation of science and engineering, 58, 59.

SCIENTIFIC SOCIETIES

See AMERICAN SOCIETY OF CIVIL ENGINEERS; SOCIETIES, TECHNICAL

SEAWAYS

See WATERWAYS

SEDIMENT AND SEDIMENTATION

Sediment conditions in the Mississippi River during flood periods, 1147, 1159.

SEEPAGE

"Earth-Dam Practice in the United States," T. A. Middlebrooks, 697.

SETTLEMENT OF STRUCTURES

See BEARING CAPACITY; EARTH PRESSURE; FOUNDATIONS . . .; SOIL . . .

SEWAGE DISPOSAL (General)
See also INDUSTRIAL WASTE; WATER POLLUTION—Sewage Pollution
Benefits of water carriage for sewage, 649, 653.
"Effective Utilization of the Sanitary Engineering Profession": Report of the Committee of the Sanitary Engineering Division on Advancement of Sanitary Engineering, H. G. Baity, T. R. Camp, F. J. Cleary, G. M. Fair, L. M. Fisher, W. A. Hardenbergh, F. H. Waring, A. H. Wieters and Earnest Boyce, 660.
"Influence of Water-Borne Sewage," A M Rawn, 649.
20th century sewage problems, 94.

SEWAGE DISPOSAL (Geographical)
United States
Accomplishments of early testing stations, 577.
Early sewage treatment processes, 563.
List and dates of early testing stations, 576.
Summary of achievements of American testing stations, 575.
"Testing Stations for Sanitary Engineering—An Outstanding Achievement," Samuel A. Greeley, 574.

SEWAGE SLUDGE
U. S. development of sludge treatment processes, 564.

SEWAGE TREATMENT
See SEWAGE DISPOSAL

SEWERAGE
See SEWERS

SEWERS (Geographical)
Europe
Early history of European sewage systems, 53.

United States
Early history of American sewage systems, 53.

SHAFTS
European and American shaft construction compared, 286.

SHALE
Future development of oil shale, 1245.

SHEAR
"Origin and Functions of Soil Mechanics," K. Terzaghi, 666.

SHIP CANALS
See CANALS

SHIPS AND SHIPPING
See WATER TRANSPORTATION

SHOCK
See ATOMIC ENERGY; EARTHQUAKES; IMPACT

SHORAN
See under usage, e.g., TRIANGULATION

SIDEWALKS, MOVABLE
Passenger transport by conveyors, 974.

SIGNALS AND SIGNALING
See TRAFFIC, HIGHWAY AND ROAD; TRAFFIC, RAILROAD

SIGNS
See HIGHWAYS AND ROADS—Safety

SILT AND SILTING (General)
Problems in irrigation works, 439.

SIPHONS
"Structures for Irrigation Diversion and Distribution," J. Ernest Hill, 412.

SLIDES
See LANDSLIDES

SLOPE PROTECTION
See DAMS, EARTH

SLOPES, EARTH
See DAMS, EARTH; EARTHWORK

SLUDGE, SEWAGE
See SEWAGE SLUDGE

SOCIAL PROBLEMS AND ENGINEERING
See ENGINEERS AND ENGINEERING; *also* under relative technical subject,
e.g., FLOODS

SOCIETIES, TECHNICAL
"Achievements in Engineering Education," Thorndike Saville, 147.
American groups further economical highway construction, 297, 300.
Earliest civil engineering societies, 18, 25.
Emergence of engineering societies, 122.
Organization of lumber associations, 790, 791, 792, 794.

SOIL MECHANICS
See SOILS

SOIL PRESSURE
See EARTH PRESSURE

SOILS (General)
See also BEARING CAPACITY; DRAINAGE (cross reference thereunder);
EARTH PRESSURE; FOUNDATIONS . . .; LAND . . .; PAVEMENT
AND PAVING . . .; SAND; SEEPAGE; SILT AND SILTING; *also* under
name of soil structure, e.g., DAMS, EARTH
Adaptation to site, 128, 129.
"Origin and Functions of Soil Mechanics," K. Terzaghi, 666.
Value of soil research to other sciences, 692, 693, 694.

Bibliography
Development of soil mechanics, 694.

Compaction. See BEARING CAPACITY

Tests and Testing
First U. S. soil permeability tests, 707.

SPECIFICATIONS
Improvement in dam specifications for U. S., 521, 522.
Lowering irrigation costs, 426.
Reduction of reclamation cost, 435.

SPILLWAYS
Future problems in design and construction, 715.
Overbank floodways on Mississippi River, 1116.
Types of spillways used, 516.

STANDARDS AND STANDARDIZATION
Benefits in lumber industries, 789, 795.
Importance of standardization of railroad tracks and equipment, 896.
The purpose of standards and standardization, 728.

STATIONS
See under type of station; *see also* under relative subject, e.g., SEWAGE DIS-
POSAL; WATER TREATMENT; WATERWAYS

STATISTICS
See relative subject

STEAM POWER
Early water and steam power competition, 454, 456.
Era of American steam power on rivers, 1164.
Steam supplements water power in the U. S., 462, 466.
Thermal and water power capacity, 1900-1950, 457, 458.

STEAM SHOVELS
See CRANES, DERRICKS AND POWER SHOVELS

STEEL
Development in the usage of steel, 1219, 1221.
High-strength steel for bridges, 778.
History and usage, 829.
"Iron and Steel Production, 1851-1951," Walther Mathesius, 1249.
Pioneers in steel, 1249.

STEEL MILLS
See STEEL PLANTS

STEEL PLANTS
"Iron and Steel Production, 1851-1951," Walther Mathesius, 1249.

STEEL TAPES
See SURVEYING INSTRUMENTS

STEREOSCOPIC INSTRUMENTS
See SURVEYING INSTRUMENTS

STONE
History and usage, 827.

STORAGE
See RESERVOIRS . . .; WATER STORAGE

STORAGE YARDS
Foundation problems of ore retaining walls, 675, 676.

STREETS

See also TRAFFIC, STREET

Planning and Design

"Solving Highway Traffic Problems," D. Grant Mickle, 904.

Safety

"Solving Highway Traffic Problems," D. Grant Mickle, 904.

STREET TRAFFIC

See TRAFFIC, STREET

STRENGTH OF MATERIALS

See under specific material (*see* list of materials under MATERIALS of CON-STRUCTION)

STRESS AND STRAIN (General)

"The Importance of Dynamic Loads in Structural Design," John B. Wilbur and Robert J. Hansen, 753.
Pioneers in theories, 725, 726.

Dams, Masonry and Concrete

Stresses in early masonry gravity dams, 490.

Wood

Accepted working stresses in design, 735.

STRUCTURAL ANALYSIS

See STRUCTURES, THEORY OF

STRUCTURAL DYNAMICS

"The Importance of Dynamic Loads in Structural Design," John B. Wilbur and Robert J. Hansen, 753.

STRUCTURAL MATERIALS

See MATERIALS OF CONSTRUCTION

STRUCTURAL MEMBERS

See STRUCTURES, THEORY OF; *also* under name of material, e.g., WOOD

STRUCTURAL MODELS

See MODELS, STRUCTURAL

STRUCTURES (General)

Design in olden times, 723, 725.
Dynamic analyses in relation to structural design, 757.
"Effect of Science on Structural Design," L. E. Grinter, 723.
Future trends expected, 127, 129.
"The Importance of Dynamic Loads in Structural Design," John B. Wilbur and Robert J. Hansen, 753.
Moving structures and dynamic loads in structural design, 756.
"Visible Earthquake Effects and Practical Corrective Measures," H. M. Engle, 814.

STRUCTURES, SETTLEMENT OF

See BEARING CAPACITY; EARTH PRESSURE; FOUNDATIONS . . .; SOIL . . .

TANKS, IMHOFF
See TANKS, SEPTIC

TANKS, SEPTIC
Development of the Imhoff tank in Germany, 576.

TAXATION
City-suburb commercial and industrial competition, 198, 202, 204, 205.
Motor vehicle taxes in 1950, 952.

TECHNICAL SCHOOLS
See EDUCATION

TECHNICAL SOCIETIES
See AMERICAN SOCIETY OF CIVIL ENGINEERS; SOCIETIES, TECH-NICAL

TENNESSEE VALLEY AUTHORITY
See RIVER VALLEY AUTHORITIES

TERMINALS (structures and localities)
"Belt Conveyor Transportation," William L. Hartley, 961.

TERMINOLOGY (Arranged hereunder by specific or comprehensive subject word when possible)

City. (Concept of word), 182.
Civil engineer. (Early ideas regarding profession), 660, 661.
Construction defined sociologically, 218.
Education. (Total education in relation to the student), 178.
Education versus training, 170.
Engineer and civil engineering. (Early usage), 2, 3.
Engineer defined, 182.
Engineering defined, 272.
Highway maintenance defined, 921.
Photogrammetry and allied terms, 845.
Piping in reference to earth dam failure, 687.
Sanitary engineering defined, 556.
Synergism as applied to technology, 1226.

TESTING STATIONS
See under relative subject, e.g., SEWAGE DISPOSAL; WATER TREATMENT

TESTS AND TESTING
See FAILURES . . .; LABORATORIES; MODELS . . .; SHEAR; STRESS AND STRAIN; STRUCTURES, THEORY OF; *also* under material, structure or structural part tested, e.g., WOOD

THEODOLITES
See SURVEYING INSTRUMENTS

THEORIES
See cross reference hereunder; *see also* under relative subject or its relative science

THEORY OF STRUCTURES
See STRUCTURES, THEORY OF

THERMAL POWER
See STEAM POWER

TIMBER AND TIMBERING
See also WOOD
"Accomplishments in Timber Technology," Charles A. Chaney, 744.
"Commercial Lumber Grades," Frank J. Hanrahan, 789.
Earth pressure on timbering in cuts, 672.
History and usage, 828.
Long-service structures, 747.
Lumber production statistics for the U. S., 732.
Oldest bridge material, 782.
Research accomplishments, 744, 746.
Technological improvements, 745.
Timber resources problem, 165.
"Wood for Engineering Use," L. J. Markwardt, 731.

TIMBER BRIDGES
See BRIDGES, WOODEN

TIMBER, PRESERVATION OF
Destructive agents and their control, 741.
Destructive agents and treatment methods, 799, 800, 801.
Earlier preservatives and methods, 748.
Introduction of pressure treatment, 785.

TIMBER STRUCTURES
See STRUCTURES, TIMBER

TIRES
See AUTOMOBILES; MOTOR TRUCKS

TOLL CROSSINGS
Era of toll bridge projects, 775.

TOOLS
Early tools, 272.

TOPOGRAPHIC SURVEYS AND SURVEYING
See SURVEYS AND SURVEYING, TOPOGRAPHIC

TOWBOATS AND TOWING
See WATER TRANSPORTATION; *see also* BARGES

TOWERS
See also SURVEY OBSERVATION TOWERS
"Visible Earthquake Effects and Practical Corrective Measures," E. M. Engle, 814.

TRACKS
See under type of track, e.g., RAILROAD TRACKS

TRACTORS AND TRAILERS
Introduction of trailers in U. S., 949, 954, 956.

TRAFFIC (General)
Waterways in relation to U. S. traffic, 1214.

TRAFFIC ACCIDENTS
See HIGHWAYS AND ROADS—Safety; STREETS—Safety

TRAFFIC, BUS
See TRAFFIC, HIGHWAY AND ROAD; TRAFFIC, STREET

TRAFFIC, HARBOR
See TRAFFIC, WATERWAY

TRAFFIC, HIGHWAY AND ROAD
"Solving Highway Traffic Problems," D. Grant Mickle, 904.
Suburban commuting creates city problems, 196.

TRAFFIC, LAKE
Volume on Great Lakes waterways, 1034.

TRAFFIC, RAILROAD
Development of signaling systems, 899.

TRAFFIC, RIVER
"One Hundred Years of Improvement on Lower Mississippi River," P. A. Feringa
  and Charles W. Schweizer, 1100.
Traffic growth on Tennessee River, 1143, 1145.

TRAFFIC, STREET
Research surveys by various agencies, 904, 908, 909, 910, 912.
"Solving Highway Traffic Problems," D. Grant Mickle, 904.

TRAFFIC, WATERWAY
Commercial traffic on Illinois Waterway and Calumet Sag Channel, 1940-1950,
  1212, 1213.
Inland and intracoastal volumes, 1929 and 1950, 1030, 1031.
Volume in more important U. S. seaports in 1852, 1929, 1950, 1022.

TRAILERS
See TRACTORS AND TRAILERS; *see also* AUTOMOBILE . . .

TRANSPORTATION
See also CANALS; CONVEYORS AND CONVEYANCE; COSTS, TRANS-
  PORTATION; HIGHWAY TRANSPORTATION; PIPE LINES; RAIL-
  ROADS; RAIL TRANSPORTATION; RIVERS; SUBWAYS; TRAFFIC;
  WATER TRANSPORTATION; WATERWAYS
Basic trends, 126, 129.
Belt conveyors in cross country transportation, 961, 974.
"Bridges and Man's Increased Mobility," D. B. Steinman, 767.
Development of U. S. roads, canals and railroads, 893.
History of 20th century problems and improvements, 71.

TREMIES
Use in concrete dry-dock construction, 1200, 1201.

TRESTLES
"Use of Wood on American Railroads," H. Austill, 797.

TRIANGULATION
"Geodetic Surveying Moves Forward," H. W. Hemple, 872.
Radar altimeter surveys in Canada, 869.
"Surveying and Mapping in Canada, 1852-1952," F. H. Peters, 857.
Usage of shoran trilateration in Canada, 866.

TRIANGULATION STATIONS
See TRIANGULATION

Ohio Valley

Early access to the Ohio Valley, 980.

Sacramento-San Joaquin Valley

History and future of flood control, 1062.

Tennessee River Valley. *See also* RIVER VALLEY AUTHORITIES

"Development of the Tennessee River Waterway," C. E. Blee, 1132.

VALUATION

Obsolescence in American cities, 210.

VALVES

Hydraulic valve types, 515, 516, 517.
Progress in design of hydraulic valves, 391.

VEHICLES

See under general types of vehicles, e.g., MOTOR VEHICLES; *also* under specific type of vehicle, e.g., AUTOMOBILE . . .
Evolution of excavating methods, 276, 280.

VENTILATION

See AIR CONDITIONING

VIBRATION

Design difficulties in oscillatory loads, 753, 756, 757, 761.

WALLS

See under relative structure or type of wall, e.g., DRY-DOCKS; RETAINING WALLS; *see also* EARTHQUAKES

WAR AND ENGINEERING

See ENGINEERS AND ENGINEERING—War and Peace; NATIONAL DEFENSE

WATER CONSERVATION

"Multipurpose River Developments," James S. Bowman, 1125.
"Planning an Irrigation Project Today," J. W. Dixon, 357.

WATER DISTRIBUTION

See IRRIGATION

WATER DIVERSION

"Diversion Structures and Distribution Systems for Irrigation," W. H. Nalder, 437.
"Irrigation in the United States," George D. Clyde, 311.
"Structures for Irrigation Diversion and Distribution," J. Ernest Hill, 412.

WATER FILTERS AND FILTRATION

See FILTERS AND FILTRATION, WATER

WATER, FLOW OF (General)

"Structures for Irrigation Diversion and Distribution," J. Ernest Hill, 412.

WATER, FLOW OF, IN OPEN CHANNELS

Intrusion of ocean water in Mississippi River passes, 1160, 1162.
"The Passes of the Mississippi River," W. C. Cobb, 1147.

WATER TREATMENT

See also BACTERIA; CHLORINATORS AND CHLORINATION; FILTERS AND FILTRATION, WATER

"Contributions of Engineering to Health Advancement," Abel Wolman, 579.
Early American usage of alum as a coagulant, 569.
Filtration of London water with high agal and low silt content, 617.
Fluoridation to improve water quality and dental health, 573.
List and dates of early American testing stations, 576.
"Problems of Supplying London,. England, with Water," H. F. Cronin, 604.
Summary of achievements of American testing stations, 575.
"Testing Stations for Sanitary Engineering—An Outstanding Achievement," Samuel A. Greeley, 574.
"Water Supply and Treatment," Harry E. Jordan, 567.

WATER TUNNELS

See TUNNELS, WATER

WATER TURBINES

See TURBINES, WATER

WATERWAY LAW

Acts relating to early Mississippi River and canal improvements, 988, 990.
Early U. S. interstate and federal legislation, 985, 986, 987, 988, 1000.
Investigation and Congressional action for river and harbor development, 1002, 1003, 1005, 1006.
"Waterway Growth in the United States," C. H. Chorpening, 976.

WATERWAYS (General)

See also CANALS; CHANNELS; COSTS, WATERWAY; HARBORS; LAKES; RIVERS; TRAFFIC, WATERWAY; WATER TRANSPORTATION
U. S. Waterways Experiment Station at Vicksburg, Mississippi, 1118.

Bibliography

Waterway growth in the U. S., 1040.

Safety

Safety requirements for sea going hopper dredges, 1183, 1184.

WATERWAYS (Geographical)
Chicago, Ill.

"System of Waterways at Chicago, Ill.," Ralph L. Bloor, 1205.

Eastern United States

The Gallatin report (1808) advocating inland waterways improvements, 987.

Illinois Waterway

"System of Waterways at Chicago, Ill.," Ralph L. Bloor, 1205.

New England

Development in Colonial period, 983.

St. Lawrence Waterway

Potential advantages of seaway, 1035, 1039.

United States

Development of hydraulic dredges for inland waterways, 1184.
Future of existing and new developments, 1038.

Inland and intracoastal development, 1023.
"Waterway Growth in the United States," C. H. Chorpening, 976.
Work of U. S. Corps of Engineers, 976, 1010.

WATERWAY TRAFFIC
See TRAFFIC, WATERWAY

WATER WHEELS
Development of Pelton wheel, 100.

WATERWORKS (General)
"How Dams Serve Man's Vital Needs," Gail A. Hathaway, 476.

WATERWORKS (Geographical)
Chicago, Ill.
Early Chicago system, 591, 592, 593.
Location of main units, 598.

United States
Early waterworks listed, 568.
Status and needs in 1952, 584.

Victoria, Australia
19th century waterworks trusts, 403.

WEIRS
See IRRIGATION

WELLS
"Synergism between Engineering and Petroleum," Robert E. Wilson, 1226.

WHARVES
See DOCKS AND WHARVES

WHEELS
See WATER WHEELS

WILDLIFE
See under relative technical subject, e.g., MULTIPLE PURPOSE PROJECTS

WIND PRESSURE
"The Importance of Dynamic Loads in Structural Design," John B. Wilbur and
Robert J. Hansen, 753.

WOOD
See also PILES AND PILE DRIVING; PLYWOOD; STRESS AND STRAIN—
Wood; TIMBER AND TIMBERING
"Accomplishments in Timber Technology," Charles A. Chaney, 744.
Decay and its treatment, 741, 742.
Destructive agencies and their control, 741.
Fatigue tests of wood and glued wood, 736.
History and usage, 828.
Many factors affecting strength, 733, 738.
Needed future research, 742.
"Schools Illustrate Progress in the Use of Wood," Harry W. Bolin, 805.
"Use of Wood on American Railroads," H. Austill, 797.
"Wood for Engineering Use," L. J. Markwardt, 731.

WOODEN BRIDGES
See BRIDGES, WOODEN

WOOD, PRESERVATION OF
See TIMBER, PRESERVATION OF

WORLD WAR II (1941-1945)
See under relative technical subject, e.g., NATIONAL DEFENSE

YARDS
See type of yard, e.g., STORAGE YARDS

AUTHOR INDEX

ARCHIBALD, RAYMOND
"Survey of Timber Highway Bridges," 782.

AUSTILL, H.
"Use of Wood on American Railroads," 797.

AYERS, J. R.
"Naval Drydock Construction," 1192.

BACHMAN, B. B.
"The Growth and Status of Highway Transport," 941.

BAITY, H. G.
"Effective Utilization of the Sanitary Engineering Profession": Report of the Committee of the Sanitary Engineering Division on Advancement of Sanitary Engineering, 660.

BAUMHOFF, RICHARD G.
"America's Costliest Bedrooms: The Suburbs," 206.

BAY, HELMUTH
"Advances in Cartography," 886.

BLEE, C. E.
"Development of the Tennessee River Waterway," 1132.

BLOODGOOD, DON E.
"Outstanding Achievements in Treating Industrial Wastes," 654.

BLOOR, RALPH L.
"System of Waterways at Chicago, Ill.," 1205.

BOELTER, L. M. K.
"Looking Ahead in Engineering Education," 169.

BOLIN, HARRY W.
"Schools Illustrate Progress in the Use of Wood," 805.

BOWMAN, JAMES S.
"Multipurpose River Developments," 1125.

BOYCE, EARNEST
"Effective Utilization of the Sanitary Engineering Profession": Report of the Committee of the Sanitary Engineering Division on Advancement of Sanitary Engineering, 660.

CAMP, T. R.
"Effective Utilization of the Sanitary Engineering Profession": Report of the Committee of the Sanitary Engineering Division on Advancement of Sanitary Engineering, 660.